כל הנשמה

Kol Haneshamah

מחזור לימים נוראים

Prayerbook for the Days of Awe

The Reconstructionist Press
Wyncote, Pennsylvania
2014

Library of Congress Number: 98-68728

International Standard Book Number: 0-935457-48-8

Art by Betsy Platkin Teutsch

Book Design by Alvin Schultzberg

Composition by El Ot Pre Press & Computing Ltd. (Tel Aviv)

Printed in the United States of America

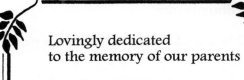

Lovingly dedicated
to the memory of our parents

Rachel Becker
Naphtali Becker
Rose Zeitlin Goldstein
Nathan Lee Goldstein

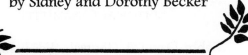

by Sidney and Dorothy Becker

PRAYERBOOK COMMISSION

Adina Abramowitz
Rabbi Devora Bartnoff ז״ל
Milton Bienenfeld
Rabbi Carl Choper
Rabbi Dan Ehrenkrantz

Lillian S. Kaplan
Marlene J. Kunin
Leroy C. Shuster
Rabbi Reena Spicehandler

Rabbi David A. Teutsch, Chairperson

Ex-Officio

Rabbi Lee Friedlander
Rabbi Mordechai Liebling
Dr. Joel Rosenberg

Rabbi Michael Strassfeld
Jane Susswein

EDITORIAL COMMITTEE

Rabbi David A. Teutsch, *Editor-In-Chief*

Micah Becker-Klein, *Editorial Assistant*
Rabbi Judith Gary Brown, *Editorial Assistant*
Rabbi Jeremy A. Schwartz, *Editorial Assistant*
Rabbi Reena Spicehandler, *Editorial Assistant*

Rabbi Michael Strassfeld, *Hebrew Text*
Dr. Joel Rosenberg, *Translation*
Rabbi Lee Friedlander, *Readings*
Betsy Platkin Teutsch, *Art*

Rabbi Mordechai Liebling, *Publisher's Representative*
Lani B. Moss, *Publisher's Representative*

iv

TABLE OF CONTENTS

TABLE OF CONTENTS / vi

Commentators

At the end of each section in the commentary, the authors' initials appear. Their full names are:

Rachel Adler
Ronald S. Aigen
Micah Becker-Klein
Devora Bartnoff
Leila Gal Berner
Caryn Broitman
Martin Buber
Dan Ehrenkrantz
Lee Friedlander
Everett Gendler
Arthur Green
Edward L. Greenstein
Abraham Joshua Heschel
Richard Hirsh
Mordecai M. Kaplan
Levi Weiman Kelman
Marlene J. Kunin

Herbert Levine
Mordechai Liebling
Hershel Matt
Eric Mendelsohn
Marcia Prager
Seth D. Riemer
Joel Rosenberg
Steven Sager
Sandy Eisenberg Sasso
Zalman Schachter-Shalomi
Jeremy A. Schwartz
Mel Scult
Rami M. Shapiro
Reena Spicehandler
Betsy Platkin Teutsch
David A. Teutsch
Sheila Peltz Weinberg

See also SOURCES, pages 1248-1268, for citations of previously published materials.

ix

PREFACE

With the publication of this volume, the *Kol Haneshamah* series is complete. A few of those involved in the project began work on the theoretical underpinnings of the series in 1981. Many joined in 1987 when work began in earnest on the then experimental Friday evening volume. Over the course of the eighteen years that have passed in the editing of this full set of prayerbooks, many Prayerbook Commission members, assistant editors, editors and administrative assistants have come and gone. Each has lovingly labored on this sacred task. They join the stream of those who have given heart and soul to the task of linking heaven and earth, of making manifest the divine aspect in the human soul. All who find solace, insight, or meaning in these pages are in their debt.

Michael Strassfeld in editing the Hebrew text added his own compositions and emendations in ways that have substantially enriched this book. Joel Rosenberg was the translator of all liturgical, scriptual, and medieval poetic texts in this volume, as well as selections from rabbinic literature and modern Hebrew poetry, except where credited to another translator. He has brought clarity and elegance to this translation. Lee Friedlander's impeccable taste has brought depth and refinement to the readings. Betsy Platkin Teutsch has again vastly enhanced the book with her art. Jeremy Schwartz, who acted as editorial assistant during the early years of this project, brought fine skills as a linguist and researcher. Micah Becker-Klein, his successor, has labored diligently for several years to see this project through to publication. David Golomb and Adina Newberg provided invaluable consultation in matters of Hebrew grammar and style. Sarra Levine, Reena Spicehandler and Ezra Spicehandler did very helpful research. Mordechai Liebling has ably handled the publication arrangements for the book. Alvin Schultzberg of Townhouse Press has again overseen the design, typesetting and

production of this volume. Special thanks are due our proofreaders, David Dunn Bauer, Micah Becker-Klein, Judith Gary Brown, Tamar Kamionkowski, Lillian Kaplan, Nina Mandel, Reena Spicehandler and David Sulomm Stein.

Others who have contributed to this volume include: Rachel Becker-Klein, Dee Einhorn, Wendy Gabay, Nilli Gold, Susan Gonen, Leah Mundell, Jennifer Petersohn, Diane Schwartz, Elaine Snyder, Elliott Tepperman, Elie Wise, and Phyllis Zeeman.

PUBLISHER'S NOTE

This book is published by the Reconstructionist Press, which is sponsored by the Jewish Reconstructionist Federation. The JRF also publishes *Reconstructionism Today*. Founded in 1955, the JRF is the congregational arm of the Reconstructionist movement. The JRF does outreach, provides a variety of services to its congregations and havurot, and does regional and movement-wide programming.

To order copies of this book, or to obtain book lists or other information, please contact:

JEWISH RECONSTRUCTIONIST FEDERATION
Beit Devora
101 Greenwood Avenue, Suite 430
Jenkintown, PA 19046

Phone: 1-215-885-5601   Fax: 1-215-885-5603
Email: press@jrf.org
Website: www.jrf.org

ACKNOWLEDGMENTS

We wish to express our thanks to authors, translators, adaptors, and other copyright holders for permission to include or quote from works indicated below. Every effort has been made to identify copyright holders and obtain permission from them. Works are listed by title in alphabetical order. For additional information, see SOURCES, pages 1248-1268.

Abyss of Despair: The Famous Seventeenth Century Chronicle Depicting Jewish Life in Russia and Poland During the Chmielnick Massacres of 1648-1649, by Nathan Nata Hanover, translated by Abraham J. Mesch. Reprinted by permission of Transaction Publishers.

"All the Vows on Our Lips..." by Ze'ev Falk. Used with the kind permission of the author.

"And I Have Felt a Presence..." by James Agee. Houghton Mifflin Publishers.

"Autumn" by Yevgeny Yevtushenko from *Bratsk Station and Other New Poems*, translated by Tina Tupikina Glaessner, Geoffrey Dutton and Igor Mezakoff-Koriakin. Doubleday & Co., Inc. Copyright © 1967.

"Babi Yar" by Carole Glasser from *Midstream Magazine – A Monthly Jewish Review*. Used with permission of the publisher.

Berahah formulation by Marcia Lee Falk, from *The Book of Blessings: New Jewish Prayers for Daily Life, the Sabbath, and the New Moon Festival*, Harper, San Francisco, 1996. Used by permission of the author.

"Coming Upon September" by Marge Piercy from *Eight Chambers of the Heart*. London Penguin Copyright © 1995.

"Connections Are Made Slowly..." by Marge Piercy from *Circles on the Water*. Copyright © 1982 by Marge Piercy. Reprinted by permission of Alfred A. Knopf, Inc. NY.

"The Death of a Parent" by Linda Pastan from *A Fraction of Darkness*. Copyright © 1985 by Linda Pastan. Reprinted by permission of W. W. Norton & Company, Inc.

"The Death of Rabbi Hannina ben Tradyon" by Danny Siegel. United Synagogue, New York. Copyright © 1976. Used with permission of the publisher.

"Each Year Should Be the Best Year I Have Yet Lived" by Kenneth L. Patton. Used with the kind permission of the author's daughter, Claris Patton.

"The Existence of Love" by Marjorie Pizer from *To You, the Living: Poems of Bereavement and Loss*. Published by Second Back Row Press, Australia.

The Fate of the Earth, by Jonathan Schell. Copyright © 1982. Published by Alfred A. Knopf, Inc. Used by permission of the publisher.

"The Five Stages of Grief" by Linda Pastan from *The Five Stages of Grief*. Copyright © 1978 by Linda Pastan. Reprinted by permission of W. W. Norton & Company Inc.

Forms of Prayer for Jewish Worship, Vol. iii Days of Awe prayerbook. Reform Synagogue of Great Britain, London 1977.

"Fresh and Pervasive Is the Weeping of Our Lost Communities..." by Yaakov Glatshtein; translation by Max Rosenfeld. Used with the kind permission of the Estate of Max Rosenfeld.

"God Created Man in His Intellectual Image..." by Nehama Leibowitz in *Studies in Bereshit: In the Context of Ancient and Modern Jewish Bible*. Published by the Publishing Department of the Jewish Agency at Alpha Press, Jerusalem. Used with permission of the publisher.

"God of Mercy" by Kadya Molodowsky, translated by Irving Howe from *The Penguin Book of Modern Yiddish Verse* by Irving Howe, Ruth R. Wisse and Khone Shmeruk. Copyright © 1987 by Irving Howe, Ruth Wisse, and Khone Shmeruk. Introduction and Notes Copyright © 1987 by Irving Howe. Used by permission of Viking Penguin, a division of Penguin Putnam Inc., New York.

Hannah Senesh: Her Life and Diary by Hannah Senesh, translated by Marta Cohn. English Translation copyright ©1971 by Nigel Marsh. Reprinted by permission of Schocken Books, distributed by Pantheon Books, a division of Random House, Inc.

Harvest: Collected Poems and Prayers by Ruth Firestone Brin. The Reconstructionist Press, copyright © 1986 by Ruth Firestone Brin.

Hasidic Tales of the Holocaust, by Yaffa Eliach. Copyright © 1982 by Yaffa Eliach. Reprinted by permission of the Miriam Altshuler Literary Agency on behalf of Yaffa Eliach.

"I Will Never Be Able to Stop My Tears" by Su Tung P'o. Translated by Kenneth Rexroth from *One Hundred Poems From the Chinese*. Copyright © 1971 by Kenneth Rexroth. Reprinted by permission of New Directions Publishing Corp.

"In Praise of the Living" by Rabbi Harvey J. Fields, Senior Rabbi, Wilshire Boulevard Temple. Used with kind permission of the author.

"In the City of Warsaw Such a Long Time Ago..." by Si Kahn. Used with permission of the author.

"In the Hour When the Temple was Destroyed" by Gil Nativ. Used with the kind permission of the author.

"In the rising of the sun..." by Jack Reimer and Sylvan D Kamens from *New Prayers for the High Holy Days*. Reprinted by permission of Media Judaica Inc.

"Inheritance" by Haim Guri from Holocaust Poetry. Copyright © 1995. Published by Harper Collins Publishers, Inc.

"Isaac Arama Sees the Three Shofar Notes..." by Herman Kieval from *The High Holy Days: A Commentary on the Prayerbook of Rosh Hashanah and Yom Kippur – Book One: Rosh Hashanah*. Copyright © 1959 by The Burning Bush Press, New York.

"It Is Not You Alone Who Pray" by Michael Joseph Berdyczewski; English translation by Rabbi Ivan Caine, Society Hill Synagogue, Philadelphia Pennsylvania. Used with the kind permission of Rabbi Ivan Caine.

The Jewish Holidays, edited by Michael Strassfeld. Copyright © 1985 Harper & Row.

A Jew Today by Elie Wiesel. Copyright © 1978 Vintage Books, Random House. Permission granted by publisher.

"Journey to a Nightmare: The South African Connection" by Jacob Neusner from *Israel to America*. Beacon Press, Boston, 1985. (Edited). Used with the kind permission of the author.

"Kaddish" by Charles Reznikoff from *Poems 1918-1975: The Complete Poems of Charles Reznikoff*. Copyright © 1977 by Marie Syrkin Reznikoff and reprinted with the permission of Black Sparrow Press.

"Kaddish for Marilyn" by Hannah Kahn from *CCAR Journal*, Autumn 1972.

"Kadish D'rabanan/And You Shall Be A Blessing" by Debbie Friedman. Copyright © 1988 by Deborah Lynn Friedman (ASCAP), Sounds Write Productions, Inc. Used with permission of the publisher.

"Kol Nidre in Auschwitz" by Yoysef Vaynberg from *From A Ruined Garden: The Memorial Books of Polish Jewry*, edited by Jack Kugelmass & Jonathan Boyarin. Indiana University Press, Bloomington, 1998. Used with permission of the editors.

A Leak in the Heart by Faye Moskowitz. David R. Godine Publishing. Copyright © 1985 by Faye Moskowitz. Reprinted by permission of the author and Russell & Volkening as agents for the author.

Legends of Jerusalem by Zev Vilnay. Jewish Publication Society, Philadelphia, PA. Copyright © 1973. Used by permission of the Jewish Publication Society.

"Lehol Ish Yesh Shem/Each of Us Has A Name" by Zelda Mishkowsky. Translation copyright © 1993 by Marcia Lee Falk. From *The Book of Blessings: New Jewish Prayers for Daily Life, the Sabbath, and the New Moon Festival*, Harper, San Francisco, 1996. Used by permission of the translator. Hebrew original used by permission of ACUM, Israel.

"Let us ask ourselves hard questions..." by Jack Riemer from *New Prayers for the High Holy Days*. Reprinted by permission of Media Judaica Inc.

"Little Cosmic Dust Poem" by John Haines from *Songs from Unsung Worlds*, edited by Bonnie Bileu Gordon. Reprinted by permission of Springer-Verlag Publishers, New York, NY.

"A man went from village to village..." by Jeffrey Newman from *Forms of Prayer for Jewish Worship, Volume III Days of Awe prayer book*. Copyright © 1977. Used by permission Reform Synagogues of Great Britain, London.

"Memory" by Rainer Maria Rilke from *The Book of Images*, translated by Edward Snow. Translation copyright © 1991 by Edward Snow. Reprinted by permission of North Point Press, a division of Farrar, Straus & Giroux, Inc.

"Merger" by Judy Chicago from *The Dinner Party*. Copyright © 1979 by Judy Chicago. Reprinted with permission of Through the Flower, New Mexico.

"*Mibeyt Imi*/From My Mother's House" by Lea Goldberg. Translation copyright ©1996 by Marcia Lee Falk. From *The Book of Blessings: New Jewish Prayers for Daily Life, the Sabbath, and the New Moon Festival*, Harper, San Francisco, 1996. Used by permission of the translator.

"My Approach to Life" by Sheva Weiss. Published in *The Jerusalem Post*. Used with the kind permission of the author.

"My Grandfather Was a Farmer..." by Dana Shuster. Used with kind permission of the author.

"On the Pulse of Morning" by Maya Angelou. Copyright © 1993. Random House Publishers, Inc.

On Wings of Awe: A Machzor for Rosh Hashanah and Yom Kippur. Used with permission of B'nai B'rith Hillel Foundation. Copyright ©1985.

"Our Rabbis taught..." English translation of Tractate Berakhot, 61B from the Soncino Talmud, I. Epstein editor. Used with the permission of The Judaica Press, Inc., New York.

"Out of the Strong, Sweetness" by Charles Reznikoff from *Voices Within the Ark*. Schwartz & Rudolf, editors. Copyright © 1980, Avon Books, New York.

"Pilgrim at Tinker Creek" by Annie Dillard. Copyright © 1974 by Annie Dillard. Reprinted by permission of HarperCollins Publishers, Inc.

"A Prayer for Children" by Ina J. Hughes from *A Prayer for Children* published by Simon & Schuster. Used with the kind permission of the Children's Defense Fund.

"Prayers I and II" by Kadya Molodowsky; translation copyright © by Kathryn Hellerstein. *Paper Bridges: Selected Poems of Kadya Molodowsky*, Wayne State University Press, 1999.

"Raised in a Distinguished, Acculturated Jewish Family in Hungary..." from *Four Centuries of Jewish Women's Spirituality: A Sourcebook*. Ellen M. Umansky and Dianne Ashton, editors. Beacon Press, Boston Copyright © 1992. Used with permission of the editor.

"A Rebbe's Proverb" by Danny Siegel from *And God Braided Eve's Hair*. United Synagogue, New York. Copyright © 1976. Used with permission of the publisher.

"Sanhedrin 98a" by Francine Klagsbrun from *Voices of Wisdom*. Copyright © 1980 by Francine Klagsbrun. Reprinted by permission of the author.

Seek My Face, Speak My Name, by Arthur Green. Jason Aronson Inc., Copyright © 1992. Used with permission of the author.

"Sort of Apocalypse" by Yehuda Amichai from *The Selected Poetry of Yehuda Amichai*, translated/edited by Chana Bloch and Stephen Mitchell. Copyright © 1996. Permission granted by the Regents of the University of California and the University of California.

The Strife of the Spirit, by Adin Steinsaltz. Used with permission of The Aleph Society.

"The Sun" by Mary Oliver from *New and Selected Poems*. Beacon Press, Boston, Mass.

"Tattered Kaddish" by Adrienne Rich from *An Atlas of the Difficult World: Poems 1988-1991*. Copyright © 1991 by Adrienne Rich. Reprinted by permission of the author and W. W. Norton & Company, Inc.

"This Night as the New Year Begins..." by Sidney Greenberg from *Maḥzor Ḥadash*. Reprinted by permission of Media Judaica Inc.

This People Israel: The Meaning of Existence, by Leo Baeck. Used with permission of the Jewish Publication Society. Copyright © 1965.

"The Thread" by Denise Levertov from *Denise Levertov Poems 1960-1967*. New Directions Publishing Corp.

"The Time of Your Life" by William Saroyan. Originally written in 1939. Used by permission of the Trustees of Leland Stanford Junior University.

"This people had..." by Leo Baeck from *The Essence of Judaism*. Copyright © 1961. Reprinted by permission of Schocken Books, distributed by Pantheon Books, a division of Random House, Inc.

"To Touch Hands in Peace" by Nahum Waldman. Prayerbook Press © Used by permission of the publisher.

The Way of Man: According to The Teaching of Hasidism, by Martin Buber. Copyright © 1966, 1994 by The Citadel Press. Published by arrangement with Carol Publishing Group.

ACKNOWLEDGMENTS / xvi

"To everything there is a season..." adapted from Jack Riemer from *New Prayers for the High Holy Days*. Reprinted by permission of Media Judaica Inc.

"When We Really Begin a New Year..." by Rabbi Stanley Rabinowitz, adapted by Rabbi Shamai Kanter & Rabbi Jack Riemer. Used with the permission of the authors.

"Where is the dwelling of God?" by Martin Buber from *The Tales of the Hasidim: The Later Masters*. Copyright © 1948 by Schocken Books, Inc. Permission granted by Random House.

"*Zot Tefilati*/This Is My Prayer" by Hillel Bavli, from *Mahzor for Rosh Hashanah and Yom Kippur*, edited by Rabbi Jules Harlow. Copyright © 1972 by The Rabbinical Assembly. Reprinted with permission of The Rabbinical Assembly.

ACUM, Ltd. has granted permission for use of the following Hebrew poems by Amir Gilboa. "*Ani mitpalel mitoh halev sidur*," "*Adam be'emet eyno tzarih*," and "Yitzhak."

Yehuda Amichai has graciously granted permission to use his poems: "Sort of An Apocalypse," "The Real Hero of the Sacrifice of Isaac," "*Me'aharay kol zeh*," All the Generations That Preceded Me," and "*Rut haketaneh*/Little Ruth."

The Central Conference of American Rabbis (CCAR) has kindly granted permission to use the following pieces from *The Gates of Repentance* mahzor: "This Rosh Hashanah Each of Us Enters This Sanctuary,..." "Al Het/We Sin Against You," and "Welcoming the Newborn (on Rosh Hashanah)."

Sylvia Heschel gave permission for use of works by Abraham Joshua Heschel.

Koren Publishers in Jerusalem has kindly granted permission to use their biblical passages in Hebrew from The Jerusalem Bible.

The Jewish Publication Society has kindly granted permission to use the following pieces by David G. Roskies: "A Tale Is Told that Rabbi Akiba Was Once Walking Through the Graveyard," "When Akiva Was Being Tortured for Teaching...," "An Old Jew Was Running Down the Street...," "I Heard from Aged Exiles of Spain" and the translation of *kaddish de rabbanan*, all from *The Literature of Destruction*. Copyright © 1988.

Jack Riemer has kindly granted permission to use the following pieces of his work. "Let Us Ask Ourselves Hard Questions...," "We Remember Them in the Rising of the Sun...," (with Sylvia Kamens) and "To Everything There Is a Season, And There Is an Appointed Time" (adapted).

INTRODUCTION AND GUIDE TO
SERVICE LEADING

More Jews attend more services for more hours during the High Holy Days than at any other time of the year. Much of the liturgy that developed in response to this reality came into existence later than the Shabbat or weekday liturgy. Therefore more freedom in selecting among the myriad of High Holy Day liturgical choices exists for liturgists. This *maḥzor* has retained *piyutim* (Hebrew liturgical poems) that are easily sung, those whose meaning is clear and thematically helpful to the worshippers who will use this book, and those to which many people have strong emotional attachments. In eliminating the least accessible *piyutim*, we have made space for contemporary and classical Hebrew poetry, new liturgical compositions, meditations and commentary.

This High Holy Day *maḥzor* reflects the same theology and aspirations as the other volumes in the *Kol Haneshamah* series. The Introduction in *Kol Haneshamah: Shabbat Veḥagim* provides an explanation of its underlying principles, theology and history. Also in that introduction are explanations regarding the nature of the Hebrew text, commentary, transliteration, translations and overall design. For the sake of brevity, those explanations will not be repeated here.

While this volume is in many ways similar to its predecessors in the *Kol Haneshamah* series, it is organized somewhat differently. Readings and songs are interspersed throughout the book rather than grouped in the back because easy access to them is critical in a book that is only used a few days each year. Where possible, repeated printings of the same prayers (such as the silent Amidah) have been avoided, and rubrics indicate when the service leader may choose to include sections found elsewhere in the prayerbook. Several alternatives for the same section often exist side by side to provide variety from year to year and to

accommodate the differences in taste and traditions that exist among different communities. These differences include the length of services, balance between Hebrew and English, choice of Torah readings and English readings, and degree of formality. Thus, this *mahzor* was intentionally designed to be used in a variety of ways. Service leaders should therefore be aware that substantially more material exists between the covers of this volume than can be covered effectively in services of any reasonable length. That is especially the case in those communities that choose to read some of the commentary aloud.

The liturgy in this book spans over three thousand years of Jewish creativity. It includes poetry and prose, compositions that are variously joyous, reflective, tormented, and beseeching. The voices of men and women from dozens of countries and Jewish sub-traditions around the world are joined here. While the intent of this book is to maximize opportunities for reflection and spiritual growth, it also celebrates the breadth and depth of Jewish civilization. Some of the poetry is transparent in its meaning from the very first reading, other liturgical compositions continue to yield fresh meaning as they are mined over and over again. All of these words, however, must be balanced by silence, wordless melody, and thoughts shared by those gathered in worship if the High Holy Day season is to have the meaning for worshippers that our tradition suggests is possible.

The sections that follow in this introduction should help the service leader to understand some of the unique choices in this *mahzor* and how to utilize them.

SELIHOT. This short Saturday night service ushers in the High Holy Day season. For many it serves as a re-introduction not only to the season's great themes, but also to the words of the *mahzor* and indeed the book itself. In light of this fact, the *Selihot* service is built into this *mahzor*, but designed to encourage a substantial paging through the volume. This is an excellent

evening for introducing music that will enhance the community's High Holy Day experience, for studying the liturgy, or discussing in personal terms the closing of the old year and the opening of the new. Thus the outline in the *mahzor* is not meant to be slavishly followed. There should be significant variations from year to year. There is no single standard *minhag*/custom for the *Selihot* service; your community may well evolve customs of its own.

KABBALAT HASHANAH. Parallel to the traditional *Kabbalat Shabbat* and the new *Kabbalat Hag* for pilgrimage festivals in the Shabbat and Festival volume of the *Kol Haneshamah* prayerbook series, *Kabbalat Hashanah* serves as an introduction to the High Holy Day season in general and Rosh Hashanah in particular. The original Rosh Hashanah evening service is short because it was traditionally recited before dinner. The fuller service in this prayerbook assumes an after-dinner service, so those communities with an early service will need to use this material very judiciously.

TORAH READINGS. For several hundred years, considerable variety has existed regarding the Torah readings for the *Yamim Nora'im*. This reflects many factors. A distancing from the recitation of a sacrifice offered in the Temple during these holy days has resulted in changes in the *Maftir* portions as well as in the Torah reading for Yom Kippur morning. A different aesthetic sense has resulted in some communities changing the reading for the first day of Rosh Hashanah to the telling of the story of creation, an appropriate theme for celebrating the world's birthday. A rejection of some moral assertions has resulted in many communities changing the reading for Yom Kippur afternoon. This *mahzor* supplies several alternatives, each of which can be used in a variety of ways. Therefore, it is critically important that the Torah readings for the entirety of the High Holy Day season be determined well in advance and publicized

to every Torah reader, *gabay* and *darshan*/speaker. Otherwise, confusion and embarrassment may result.

SHOFAR BLOWING AND ROSH HASHANAH MUSAF (ADDITIONAL SERVICE). For many communities, the highlight of Rosh Hashanah is the sounding of the shofar. In other communities, the three great themes of *Musaf* (*Malḥuyot, Ziḥronot*, and *Shofarot*) provide the most elevated liturgical moment. In those emphasizing the shofar blowing, the *Musaf* themes are often interwoven, and a separate *Musaf* eliminated. Other communities choose to follow the shofar blowing solely by reciting the *Musaf* Amidah aloud; still others choose to include a silent Amidah as well. And some communities move the *Musaf* themes into the *Shaḥarit* Amidah. This *maḥzor* provides guiding rubrics for all these possibilities. Communities may well find that their practices in this regard evolve over the years. In all communities the shofar blowing and the *Musaf* choices for Rosh Hashanah will vary between the first and second days.

TASHLIḤ. The *Tashliḥ* ritual, traditionally performed at an open body of water on Rosh Hashanah afternoon, has only a few core prayers. It is these alone that appear in this *maḥzor* on pages 675-676. While it is possible to substantially embellish these with songs, meditations and commentary, this happy and informal event can be stifled by efforts to create an over-substantial liturgy for the occasion. Walking after a heavy festive meal, chatting with friends, and enjoying creation on the world's birthday are as important to the success of *Tashliḥ* as the casting of sin-laden crumbs into the sea.

YIZKOR. *Yizkor* in this *maḥzor* is designed to be a free-standing liturgical unit. Some communities may choose to place it after the *Haftarah* in the morning service. Increasingly, *Yizkor* is moved to a location between *Musaf* and the afternoon service when attendance would otherwise be at a low ebb in order to accommodate the large number of people who come only to say

Yizkor. Because there is much flexibility in the placement of *Yizkor,* this choice will reflect space concerns and other practical considerations as well as local custom.

YOM KIPPUR MUSAF, AVODAH SERVICE, ELEH EZKERAH (MARTYROLOGY). Many Jews experience these three liturgical units as separate from each other, in which case the recitation of the order of the liturgy in the Temple often seems irrelevant. The martyrology, while usually deeply moving, seems to have no relationship to the rest of what happens on Yom Kippur. These difficulties prompted our restructuring of this portion of the Yom Kippur liturgy.

The progression of the *Avodah* from the High Priest to his family to his tribe to the whole Jewish people occasioned the overall framing of this *Musaf,* which progresses from concern with self to family to the Jewish people to all of humanity. The theme of self is embedded in the introductory portion of the *Musaf,* while the theme of humanity is part of the last section of the Amidah, which has peace as its theme. The Jewish people are described in the Torah as a nation of priests. In this service, we each take responsibility for performing the priestly role of navigating the concentric circles of expiation.

The martyrology has become part of the section on the Jewish people. The original martyrology assumed a knowledge of the importance of the great Jewish sages whose death it recorded. Such knowledge can no longer be taken for granted, and the struggle to teach, learn and create Torah in subsequent generations is for us an important part of the tale. Therefore, the three alternative martyrologies not only recount different examples of suffering; they tell of great teaching, as well. Thus this section of the service should provide an opportunity not only for marveling at the heroism of those who have sacrificed their very lives for Judaism and the Jewish people, but also studying the rich moral and spiritual legacy they have left us.

These insights provide an additional opportunity for reflection about the meaning of our lives and the thoughts and actions that can uplift them.

This *maḥzor* provides the liturgy for the full penitential season. Drawing from the living wellsprings of the Jewish past, it does not stand complete in itself. It invites the addition of prayer, poetry and insight that will continually renew these words. Most of all, it invites the active engagement of mind and open-hearted encounter that will lift these words off the page and allow them to soar. May you be uplifted each year by this encounter and each year retain a part of that elevation so that you start the next year a little higher on the mountain. We who have labored to produce a timeless Jewish liturgy that speaks to our time have found growth and nurture in the task. May your efforts at prayer find similar reward.

DAVID A. TEUTSCH
Chair, Prayerbook Commission
June 1998

NOTES ON USAGE

Hebrew Pronunciation. The pronunciation in this book follows current Israeli usage. Accordingly, Hebrew words are accented on the final syllable unless otherwise noted. Where the stress is not on the last syllable of a word, the stressed syllable is marked with a caret (x̌). In biblical passages where there are cantillation marks, those marks replace the caret in marking the stressed syllable. *The kamatz katan* (pronounced "o" as in "store") is marked with this sign: x̣.

Transliteration. Where Hebrew words are not accented on the final syllable, this is indicated by underlining the accented syllable in the transliteration. Use of periods and capital letters roughly follows Hebrew sentence structure. Generally, no other punctuation will occur. Below is a table of Hebrew letters and vowels with their English equivalents.

Consonants

א	(not pronounced)	ל	l
בּ	b	מ ם	m
ב	v	נ ן	n
ג	g (as in "go")	ס	s
ד	d	ע	(not pronounced)
ה	h	פּ	p
ו	v	פ ף	f
ז	z (as in "Zion")	צ ץ	tz (as in "mitzvah")
ח	ḥ (as in "*ḥazan*")	ק	k
ט	t	ר	r
י	y	שׁ	sh
כּ ךּ	k	שׂ	s
כ ך	ḥ (as in "*baruḥ*")	ת ת	t

Vowels

אֶ / אֱ / אֵ / אְ	e (as in "bed")
אַ / אֲ / אָ	a (as in "are")
או / אׂ / אָ / אֳ	o (as in "store")
או / אֻ	u (as in "put")
אִי / אִ	i (as in "sit")

Diphthongs and Glides

אֵי / אֶא / אֶה	ey (as in "they")
אַי	ay (as in "bayou")
וּי	uwi (u + i, pronounced rapidly together)
וׂי	oy (as in "toy")

Those transliterations that have become accepted as standard or familiar English have not been changed. Examples: Shabbat, siddur, sukkah, Kiddush. In these cases the doubling of the middle consonant has been kept even though the system of transliteration used here does not require it.

* Indicates where it is traditional for the cantor or service leader to begin chanting in a prayer.

← and ↩ indicate that a prayer continues on the next page.

הִגָּיוֹן הַלֵּב

MEDITATIONS

היכי דמי בעל תשובה אמר רבי יהודה כגון שבאת לידו דבר
עבירה פעם ראשונה ושניה וניצלה הימנה:

How is one proved a repentant sinner? Rav Judah said, "If the
object which caused the original transgression comes before the
repentant sinner on two occasions and the sinner keeps away
from it."

Talmud Yoma 86b

৵

הלא תראה החוט של משי כמה הוא חזק כשיכפיל פעמים רבות
וכבר ידעת כי עיקרו מחלוש שבדברים והוא ריר התולעת ונראה
החבל הגדול של ספינה כשמשמשין בו זמן ארוך הולך הלוך
וחסור עד אשר יפסק וישוב חלוש מכל חלוש וכמו כן ענין
הקטנות והגדלות בעבירות עם ההתמדה ובקשת המחילה. ועל
כן דמה אותם הכתוב בו כמו שנאמר (ישעיה ה) הוי משכי העון
בחבלי השוא וכעבות העגלה חטאה:

Observe a silken cord. How strong it becomes when it is
doubled over many times, though its origin is the weakest of
things—a worm's mucus. Note also how a ship's cable, when
used for a long time, becomes the weakest of the weak. So it is
with the grave and light character of transgressions. They
become grave only if one persists in them and light if one
beseeches forgiveness for them. Thus it says in Scripture, "Woe
to them who draw iniquity with cords of vanity, and sin as it
were with a cart rope." (Isaiah 5:18)

Bahya ibn Pakuda, Hovot Halevavot, 7.7

৵

Sin involves a disturbance in the relation between us and God, and atonement implies the poise, solace and encouragement that come with the restoration to a better relationship. From the point of view of ethical religion, the same remains true. If we identify God with that aspect of reality which confers meaning and value on life and elicits from us those ideals that determine the course of human progress, then the failure to live up to the best that is in us means that our souls are not attuned to the divine, that we have betrayed God.

Mordecai M. Kaplan

The sacramental efficacy of the ritual of atonement is nil, and its symbolic power of no value, unless the sense of sin leads us to seek the reconstruction of our personalities in accordance with highest ethical possibilities of human nature; only then can we experience *teshuvah*, the sense of returning to God.

Mordecai M. Kaplan

And you wait, await the one thing
that will infinitely increase your life;
the gigantic, the stupendous,
the awakening of stones,
depths turned round toward you.

The volumes in brown and gold
flicker dimly on the bookshelves;
and you think of lands traveled through,
of paintings, of the garments
of women found and lost.

And then all at once you know: that was it.
You rise, and there stands before you
the fear and prayer and shape
of a vanished year.

Rainer Maria Rilke

Awe is an intuition for the creaturely dignity of all things and their preciousness to God; a realization that things not only are what they are but also stand, however remotely, for something absolute. Awe is a sense for the transcendent, for the reference everywhere to God, who is beyond all things. Awe enables us to perceive in the world intimations of the divine, to sense in small things the beginning of infinite significance, to sense the ultimate in the common and the simple; to feel in the rush of the passing the stillness of the eternal.

Abraham Joshua Heschel (Adapted)

∽

On this day, let us be like Moses, heavy of tongue, who had to struggle over each sound. On this day when we shall say more words than on any other day in the year, we strive to find one sentence, phrase, word, or letter that will begin here on earth and reach to the heavens.

Michael Strassfeld

∽

אֲנִי מִתְפַּלֵּל מִתּוֹךְ הַלֵּב סָדוּר
קָרוּעַ שׁוּלַיִם וְכָל הַמִּלִּים הַחֲסֵרוֹת אֲנִי
רוֹאָן מִתְעוֹפְפוֹת כְּבָר זְמַן רַב מִתְעוֹפְפוֹת
וּמְבַקְשׁוֹת מָנוֹחַ לְכַף הָרֶגֶל אֵיךְ
אָבִיא לָהֶן מָזוֹר וְלֵב
סִדּוּרִי אֲכוּל שׁוּלַיִם
אָזֵל וְעָרֹם

I pray a siddur from my heart,
one with torn edges, and all its missing words
I see have long since vanished, flying away
and seeking a resting-place. How
shall I bring a bandage for them
when my heart's siddur with eaten edges
still goes naked?

Amir Gilboa

∽

Forgiveness opens a series of questions, painful questions, that constitute the central challenge within human life. All of the apparent dilemmas, however, finally meet in a single issue: Will I be in relation to others, or will I refuse that relation?

All religious traditions declare that forgiveness is always a possibility. In the words of one *hadith*: "One who approaches near to me one span, I will approach one cubit; and one who approaches near to me one cubit, I will approach one fathom; and whoever approaches me walking, I will come running, and one who meets me with sins equivalent to the whole world, I will greet with forgiveness equal to it." (From the *Mishkat al-masabih* quoted in *Islamic Spirituality*, Seyyed Hossein Nasr, ed.) What is the way to that approach? And why does the open door appear to us as shut?

It is the closed door, of course, that brings the need for forgiveness. Estrangement makes us feel the loss of bonds we may hardly have noticed before. The loss of friendship or alienation from a family member—that sense of being cut off from the vital current of life—creates suffering.

This suffering can be the fire that refines, that brings the drives of the ego in contact with a deeper self, that ultimately starts us "walking," bringing us to the first steps of the exchange that is called forgiveness.

Experiencing the pain of the estrangement without and the fragmentation within is an integral part of forgiveness. This pain must not be avoided. Avoidance of any part of our lives on any level leads away from the unifying grace of forgiveness. Rage and sadness have to be faced in order to forgive, yet people try to live without facing that. Indeed a person cannot find redemption until she/he sees the flaws in her/his soul and tries to efface

them. Nor can a people be redeemed until it sees the flaws in its soul and tries to efface them. But whether it be a person or a people, whoever shuts out the realization of her/his flaws is shutting out redemption.

A person chooses death by not forgiving. There is a sense in which you can destroy yourself by not saying yes to the reality that actually exists. Forgiveness is the great yes. Acting in accordance with the highest ideals of our tradition, I do not have a choice whether or not I should forgive you, I only have a choice whether or not I will. And I must if I want to be alive.

Lorraine Kisly and Martin Buber (Adapted)

"O God, create for me a pure heart, and renew within me a just spirit."

Psalms 51:12

With the New Year, we have a chance for newness within our hearts, a newness that can change the course of our lives. But change is often frightening, and sometimes we are not sure that we are indeed ready for it. "What will this new heart be like?" we wonder. "How will this purified heart change the persons we are?" "Will the very structure of our lives change as our spirits are renewed?" So much uncertainty comes with change. As we stand at the threshold of a New Year, we pray for the valor to face uncertainty, the courage to truly change what needs to be changed, and the faith to welcome the new spirit that is within us.

Leila Gal Berner

A Reconstructionist Understanding of Sin and Salvation

What are we to do about our sins? In the first place, we must not permit them to lead to self-hate or self-contempt. We must be able to see good in ourselves. We must believe that we have within us something that reflects the goodness that exists in the world. Most of our moral failures are due to a distrust of our capacity for virtue. We, all of us, have ideals of the man or woman we should like to be. Let us see in the very fact that we project that ideal for ourselves the evidence that it must have some affinity with what we really are. This is the image of God in us. Though it may be obscured by our sins, if we can see it at all, we must come to live that ideal so much that we find satisfaction in removing the moral stains which obscure it.

Nothing that we can say or think can really undo what has been done. The past can never be relived and it always conditions the present and future. Therein lies the inexorable reality of sin. Having failed, however, does not mean that we are failures, for the future lies before us with its infinite possibilities.

In our discouragement, many of us brood over our incapacity for good behavior, instead of trying to find out what bad consequences of our acts make them sinful, and how we may put our conduct on the right track so that it will not lead to wreckage of our abiding purposes. If, instead of thinking of our sin as though it were a taint on our ego, we regard it as a form of bad behavior in our relations to the world about us, a disposition to wrong-doing rather than wrong-being, we will not brood about what has already been done, but try to learn from our experience how to do better.

In this way we answer the paradox of sin by a sort of paradox of salvation. We use our experience of sin in order to attain virtue. The power of *teshuvah*, that is turning in the direction of the will to moral achievement, converts what were willful sins into virtues.

Mordecai M. Kaplan

◌◌

Understand the words of Hillel as a guide for entry into the New Year:

אִם אֵין אֲנִי לִי מִי לִי?

"If I am not for myself, who is for me?..." This may refer to *tikun haneshamah*/repair of the soul. If I do not engage in the deeply personal work of inward turning (*teshuvah*), no one else can do it for me.

וּכְשֶׁאֲנִי לְעַצְמִי מָה אֲנִי?

"And when I am only for myself, what am I?..." This may refer to *tikun ha'olam*/repair of the world. If each of us is *only* self-focused, then ultimately what are we? What makes us human is our relationship to others; what make us human is our "response-ability," our understanding of responsibility—to ourselves and to the world.

וְאִם לֹא עַכְשָׁיו אֵימָתַי?

"And if not now, when?" What better time than at the birth of a New Year to begin the journey toward self-repair (*tikun haneshamah*) and world-repair (*tikun ha'olam*).

Leila Gal Berner

છ

The theme of the *Yamim Nora'im* is *teshuvah*/turning. This suggests being in motion, in process. Our deepest efforts to redirect our lives require sustained attention and vigilance; how much easier to have a single defining moment of change! But Rosh Hashanah is the beginning of the new year, not the year itself. Today we begin to move.

Richard Hirsh

છ

Repentance is one of the ultimate spiritual realities at the core of Jewish faith. Its significance goes far beyond the narrow meaning of contrition or regret for sin, and it embraces a number of concepts considered to be fundamental to the very existence of the world.

Certain sages go so far as to include repentance among the entities created before the world itself. The implication of this remarkable statement is that repentance is a universal, primordial phenomenon; in such a context it has two meanings. One is that it is embedded in the root structure of the world; the other, that before we were created, we were given the possibility of changing the course of our lives. In this latter sense repentance is the highest expression of our capacity to choose freely—it is a manifestation of the divine in us. By repenting, we can extricate ourselves from the binding web of our lives, from the chain of causality that otherwise compels us to follow a path of no return.

Repentance also comprises the notion that we have a measure of control over our existence in all dimensions, including time. Time flows in one direction; it is impossible to undo or even to alter an action after it has occurred and become an "event," an objective fact. However, even though the past is "fixed," repentance admits of an ascendancy over it, of the possibility of changing its significance in the context of the present and the future. This is why repentance has been presented as something created before the world itself. In a world of the inexorable flow of time, in which all objects and events are interconnected in a relationship of cause and effect, repentance is the exception: it is the potential for something else.

Adin Steinsaltz

The Maggid of Dubno taught his disciples that ritual performance alone was insufficient for *teshuvah*. Specifically, listening to the sound of the shofar is but a means to a higher end. To illustrate this point, he told the following parable:

A man came to a big city for the first time and lodged in an inn overnight. Awakened in the middle of the night by the loud beating of drums, he inquired drowsily, "What is this all about?" Informed that a fire had broken out and that the drum beating was the city's fire alarm, he turned over and went back to sleep.

He reported the incident to the village authorities on his return home. "They have a wonderful system in the big city. When a fire breaks out, people beat their drums and before long the fire burns out." Excited, they ordered a supply of drums and distributed them to the population. Several weeks later, when a fire broke out in the village, there was a deafening explosion of beating drums, and while the people waited expectantly for the flames to subside, their homes burned to the ground.

A visitor passing through the village, when told the reason for the ear-splitting din, mocked the simple residents. "Idiots! Do you think that a fire can be put out by beating drums? The drums are no more than an alarm for people to wake up and extinguish the fire themselves."

The Maggid continued. "So it is with us. We sound the shofar to extinguish the fires of sin and evil that burn within us. But the shofar is merely an alarm to rouse us from our moral slumber. Our task is to search our deeds and turn from our accustomed ways to remake our lives ourselves."

Alexander A. Steinbach (Adapted)

According to tradition, Rosh Hashanah and Yom Kippur are *Yamim Nora'im*, days of awe, solemn days. The Jews who label themselves "secularist" or "agnostic" are baffled by these holidays. The basic trouble is that the very terminology of the Holy Days—sin, repentance, forgiveness, sovereignty of God—sounds alien to the secularist. It is, at best, an echo out of the remote past. And the fact is that for many in the synagogue, too, these words are no longer meaningful and do not correspond to genuine experience. But if there is an ethical-humanist dimension to Rosh Hashanah and Yom Kippur, then it should be possible to invest this terminology with contemporary significance and provide a reason for regarding these Holy Days as a common possession of all Jews.

There is a wonderful Hebrew-Yiddish phrase, *ḥeshbon hanefesh*. The phrase connotes a taking stock of one's soul, an inner accounting, a sitting-in-judgment upon oneself. As we make our *ḥeshbon hanefesh*, we confess our failure to span the gap between conscience and conduct, between the standards we profess and the actions we perform. We remember what we should have done and did not do. This chasm between *believing* and *living* may or may not always be surmountable, but the refusal to try to span it is *sin*, and the will to bridge it, or at least to narrow it, is *atonement* and *redemption*. Sin is the gap between our promise and our conduct, between our standards and our actions.

The Sovereignty of God is symbolic of the oneness of humanity in freedom, righteousness, and dignity. And if God is what is best and highest within us, reaching out to what is best and highest in the universe, then God is not in Heaven, but is a power in the world and in us for transforming ourselves and the world in preparation for the Kingdom.

Israel Knox (Adapted)

∾

פעם אחת אמר רבינו משל. אדם תעה כמה ימים ביער ולא היה
יודע איזוהי דרך נכונה. פתאום ראה אדם אחר הולך לקראתו.
באה שמחה גדולה בלבו, עתה בוודאי ידע הדרך הנכונה. כיון
שפגעו זה בזה שאל אותו אחי אמור לי היכן הדרך הנכונה, זה
כמה ימים אני תועה. אמר לו אחי אף אני איני יודע, שאף אני
תועה כאן כבר ימים הרבה, אלא אומר לך בדרך שהלכתי אני אל
תלך אתה, שבדרך זו תועים. ועכשיו נחפש דרך חדשה. כן
אנחנו, דבר זה אני יכול לומר לכם, שבדרך שהלכנו עד עכשיו
אין לנו ללכת, שבדרך זו תועים. אלא עכשיו נחפש דרך חדשה.

Rabbi Ḥayim of Zans was wont to tell the following parable:

A sojourner had been wandering about in a forest for several
days, not knowing which was the right way out. Suddenly he
saw someone approaching him. His heart was filled with
anticipation. "Now I will learn which is the right way," he
thought. When they neared one another, he asked, "Please, tell
me which is the right way out of this forest. I have been
wandering about for several days."

Said the other to him, "I do not know the way out either, for I
too have been wandering about here for many, many days. But
this I can tell you: do not take the way I have been going, for that
will lead you astray. Now let us look for a new way together."

S. Y. Agnon

෨෨

רְשׁוּת לְכָל אָדָם נְתוּנָה, אִם רָצָה לְהַטּוֹת עַצְמוֹ לְדֶרֶךְ טוֹבָה וְלִהְיוֹת צַדִּיק, הָרְשׁוּת בְּיָדוֹ: וְאִם רָצָה לְהַטּוֹת עַצְמוֹ לְדֶרֶךְ רָעָה וְלִהְיוֹת רָשָׁע, הָרְשׁוּת בְּיָדוֹ: הוּא שֶׁכָּתוּב בַּתּוֹרָה: "הֵן הָאָדָם הָיָה כְּאַחַד מִמֶּנּוּ לָדַעַת טוֹב וָרָע": אֶלָּא כָּל אָדָם רָאוּי לוֹ לִהְיוֹת.... צַדִּיק כְּמֹשֶׁה רַבֵּנוּ אוֹ רָשָׁע כְּיָרָבְעָם אוֹ חָכָם אוֹ סָכָל אוֹ רַחֲמָן אוֹ אַכְזָרִי אוֹ כִּילַי אוֹ שׁוֹעַ... וְאֵין לוֹ מִי שֶׁיִּכְפֵּהוּ וְלֹא גּוֹזֵר עָלָיו וְלֹא מִי שֶׁמּוֹשְׁכוֹ לְאֶחָד מִשְּׁנֵי הַדְּרָכִים.... זֶה הַחוֹטֵא הוּא הִפְסִיד אֶת עַצְמוֹ:

אָסוּר לְאָדָם לְהַנְהִיג עַצְמוֹ בְּדִבְרֵי חֲלָקוֹת וּפִתּוּי וְלֹא יִהְיֶה אֶחָד בַּפֶּה וְאֶחָד בַּלֵּב — אֶלָּא תּוֹכוֹ כְּבָרוֹ וְהָעִנְיָן שֶׁבַּלֵּב הוּא הַדָּבָר שֶׁבַּפֶּה: וְאָסוּר לִגְנֹב דַּעַת הַבְּרִיּוֹת וַאֲפִלּוּ דַּעַת הַנָּכְרִי: כֵּיצַד ?... לֹא יִסְרַהֵב בַּחֲבֵרוֹ שֶׁיֹּאכַל אֶצְלוֹ וְהוּא יוֹדֵעַ שֶׁאֵינוֹ אוֹכֵל; וְלֹא יַרְבֶּה לוֹ בְּתִקְרֹבֶת וְהוּא יוֹדֵעַ שֶׁאֵינוֹ מְקַבֵּל; וְלֹא יִפְתַּח לוֹ חָבִיּוֹת שֶׁהוּא צָרִיךְ לְפָתְחָן לְמָכְרָן כְּדֵי לְפַתּוֹתוֹ שֶׁבִּשְׁבִיל כְּבוֹדוֹ פָּתַח וְכֵן כָּל כַּיּוֹצֵא בּוֹ:... אֶלָּא שְׂפַת אֱמֶת וְרוּחַ נָכוֹן וְלֵב טָהוֹר:

Free will is given to every human being. If we wish to incline ourselves toward goodness and righteousness, we are free to do so; and if we wish to incline ourselves towards evil, we are also free to do that. As the Torah says (Genesis 3:22), "Humanity is unique in knowing good and evil...." We each decide whether to make ourselves...learned or ignorant, compassionate or cruel, generous or miserly....No one forces us, no one decides for us, no one drags us along one path or the other....Those who err must take responsibility for themselves.

Smooth speech and deception are forbidden to us. Our words must not differ from our thoughts; the inner and outer person must be the same. What is in the heart should be on the lips. We are forbidden to deceive anyone, Jew or non-Jew, about ↵

anything. For example, one must not urge food on another knowing that the other cannot eat it. One must not offer gifts that cannot be accepted. A storekeeper opening a bottle in order to sell its contents must not pretend to be opening it in honor of a particular person, and the like....Honest speech, integrity and a pure heart—that is what is required of us.

Moses Maimonides (Hilḥot Teshuvah 5:1-2, Hilḥot De'ot 2:6)

๛

כיון דחב בר נש קמי קודשא בריך הוא זמנא חדא, עביד רשימו. וכד חב ביה זמנא תניינא, אתתקף ההוא רשימו יתיר. חב ביה זמנא תליתאה, אתפשט ההוא כתמא.

A sin leaves a mark; repeated, it deepens the mark; when committed a third time, the mark becomes a stain.   Zohar

๛

אם משים אדם נגד אור השמש בחלון מחיצות קלות וקלושות לרוב מאד הן מאפילות כמו מחיצה אחת עבה ויותר: וככה ממש הוא בנמשל בכל עונות שאדם דש בעקביו ומכל שכן המפורסמות מדברי רבינו זכרונם לברכה שהן ממש כעבודה זרה וגילוי עריות ושפיכות דמים: והמספר בגנות חבירו היא לשון הרע השקולה כעבודה זרה וגילוי עריות ושפיכות דמים: וכל הכועס כאילו עובד עבודה זרה וכן מי שיש בו גסות הרוח:

If one places many thin and threadbare sheets in front of the window, they have the same effect in screening the light of the sun as one heavy blanket. Similarly it is not only the serious sins such as idolatry, debauchery, and bloodshed which act as a screen between the Divine Light and the soul, but also the lesser offenses, such as indulging in slanderous talk, flying into a rage, pride, and many such offenses.

Shneur Zalman

אַל תּאמַר שֶׁאֵין תְּשׁוּבָה אֶלָּא מֵעֲבֵרוֹת שֶׁיֵּשׁ בָּהֶן מַעֲשֶׂה כְּגוֹן זְנוּת
וְגָזֵל וּגְנֵבָה:
אֶלָּא כְּשֵׁם שֶׁצָּרִיךְ אָדָם לָשׁוּב מֵאֵלּוּ כָּךְ הוּא צָרִיךְ לְחַפֵּשׂ בְּדֵעוֹת
רָעוֹת שֶׁיֵּשׁ לוֹ וְלָשׁוּב מִן הַכַּעַס וּמִן הָאֵיבָה וּמִן הַקִּנְאָה וּמִן
הַהִתּוּל וּמֵרְדִיפַת הַמָּמוֹן וְהַכָּבוֹד וּמֵרְדִיפַת הַמַּאֲכָלוֹת: מִן הַכֹּל
צָרִיךְ לַחֲזֹר בִּתְשׁוּבָה:
וְאֵלּוּ הָעֲוֹנוֹת קָשִׁים מֵאוֹתָן שֶׁיֵּשׁ בָּהֶן מַעֲשֶׂה שֶׁבִּזְמַן שֶׁאָדָם נִשְׁקָע
בְּאֵלּוּ קָשֶׁה הוּא לִפְרֹשׁ מֵהֶם: וְכֵן הוּא אוֹמֵר: "יַעֲזֹב רָשָׁע דַּרְכּוֹ
וְאִישׁ אָוֶן מַחְשְׁבֹתָיו":

Do not think that people are obliged to repent only for
transgressions involving acts, such as stealing and robbing and
promiscuity. Just as individuals must turn in repentance from
such acts, so must they personally search out their evil thoughts
and turn in repentance from anger, from hatred, from jealousy,
from mocking thoughts, from over-concern with money or
prestige, and from gluttony. From all these thoughts a person
must turn in repentance. They are more serious than
transgressions involving acts, for when a person is addicted to
them, it is difficult to give them up. Thus it is said: "Let the
wicked forsake their way, the unrighteous their thoughts."
(Isaiah 55:7)

Moses Maimonides (Hilḥot Teshuvah 7:3)

∾

Teshuvah/turning need not be a dramatically large change to be
significant. A subtle shift now, of even just a fraction of a degree
out of 360, can take one on a vastly different path over the
course of a life's trajectory.

Betsy Platkin Teutsch

∾

לְעוֹלָם יִרְאֶה אָדָם עַצְמוֹ כְּאִילוּ חֶצְיוֹ חַיָּיב וְחֶצְיוֹ זַכַּאי עָשָׂה מִצְוָה
אַחַת אַשְׁרָיו שֶׁהִכְרִיעַ עַצְמוֹ לְכַף זְכוּת עָבַר עֲבֵירָה אַחַת אוֹי לוֹ
שֶׁהִכְרִיעַ אֶת עַצְמוֹ לְכַף חוֹבָה.... רַבִּי אֶלְעָזָר בְּרַבִּי שִׁמְעוֹן אוֹמֵר
לְפִי שֶׁהָעוֹלָם נִידוֹן אַחַר רוּבּוֹ וְהַיָּחִיד נִידוֹן אַחַר רוּבּוֹ עָשָׂה מִצְוָה
אַחַת אַשְׁרָיו שֶׁהִכְרִיעַ אֶת עַצְמוֹ וְאֶת כָּל הָעוֹלָם לְכַף זְכוּת עָבַר
עֲבֵירָה אַחַת אוֹי לוֹ שֶׁהִכְרִיעַ אֶת עַצְמוֹ וְאֶת כָּל הָעוֹלָם לְכַף
חוֹבָה:

Each one of us should always consider ourselves evenly
balanced, that is, half sinful and half righteous. If we perform
one mitzvah we should be joyous, for we have tilted the scales
towards righteousness. If we commit one sin we should be
remorseful, for we have tilted the scale toward sinfulness....

Rabbi Elazar ben Shimon said: "Inasmuch as the world is judged
in accordance with the majority of *its* deeds, and we individuals
are judged in accordance with *our* deeds, if we perform one
mitzvah, happy are we, for we have tipped our own scales and
the scales of the world toward merit. If we commit one sin, woe
unto us, for we have tipped the scales toward sinfulness for
ourselves and for the world."

Talmud Kiddushin 40a,b

෨෪

מְכַסֶּה פְשָׁעָיו לֹא יַצְלִיחַ וּמוֹדֶה וְעֹזֵב יְרֻחָם:

One who covers up transgressions will not prosper, but one who
confesses and forsakes them shall obtain mercy.

Proverbs 28:13

෨෪

רַחֲצוּ הִזַּכּוּ הָסִירוּ רֹעַ מַעַלְלֵיכֶם:... דִּרְשׁוּ מִשְׁפָּט אַשְּׁרוּ חָמוֹץ שִׁפְטוּ יָתוֹם רִיבוּ אַלְמָנָה:... אִם יִהְיוּ חֲטָאֵיכֶם כַּשָּׁנִים כַּשֶּׁלֶג יַלְבִּינוּ אִם־יַאְדִּימוּ כַתּוֹלָע כַּצֶּמֶר יִהְיוּ:

Put away your evil doings.... Seek justice, relieve the oppressed, judge the fatherless, plead for the widow.... Though your sins be like scarlet, they shall be white as snow; though red like crimson, they shall be as wool.

Isaiah 1:16-18

જ્

שׁוּבוּ אֵלַי וְאָשׁוּבָה אֲלֵיכֶם אָמַר יהוה צְבָאוֹת....

Return to me, and I will return to you, says the GOD of hosts....

Malachi 3:7

જ્

חַטָּאת וְאָשָׁם וַדַּאי מְכַפְּרִין מִיתָה וְיוֹם הַכִּפּוּרִים מְכַפְּרִין עִם הַתְּשׁוּבָה: הַתְּשׁוּבָה מְכַפֶּרֶת עַל עֲבֵרוֹת הַקַּלּוֹת עַל עֲשֵׂה וְעַל לֹא תַעֲשֶׂה וְעַל הַחֲמוּרוֹת הִיא תוֹלָה עַד שֶׁיָּבֹא יוֹם הַכִּפּוּרִים וִיכַפֵּר:

Repentance accomplishes atonement for lesser transgressions against both positive and negative commands in the Torah, while for graver transgressions it suspends punishment until Yom Kippur comes and accomplishes atonement.

Mishnah Yoma 8:8

જ્

הָאוֹמֵר: אֶחֱטָא וְאָשׁוּב, אֶחֱטָא וְאָשׁוּב — אֵין מַסְפִּיקִין בְּיָדוֹ לַעֲשׂוֹת תְּשׁוּבָה; אֶחֱטָא, וְיוֹם הַכִּפּוּרִים מְכַפֵּר — אֵין יוֹם הַכִּפּוּרִים מְכַפֵּר: עֲבֵרוֹת שֶׁבֵּין אָדָם לַמָּקוֹם — יוֹם הַכִּפּוּרִים מְכַפֵּר; עֲבֵרוֹת שֶׁבֵּין אָדָם לַחֲבֵרוֹ — אֵין יוֹם הַכִּפּוּרִים מְכַפֵּר עַד שֶׁיְּרַצֶּה אֶת חֲבֵרוֹ:

If one says, "I will sin and repent, sin and repent," there will be no repentance. "I will sin and Yom Kippur will accomplish atonement," then Yom Kippur will accomplish no atonement. For transgressions between a person and God, Yom Kippur accomplishes atonement, but for transgressions between two people, Yom Kippur accomplishes atonement only if the offender has appeased the offended person...

Mishnah Yoma 8:9

అ

אָמַר הַקָּדוֹשׁ בָּרוּךְ הוּא לְיִשְׂרָאֵל בָּנַי פִּתְחוּ לִי פֶּתַח אֶחָד שֶׁל תְּשׁוּבָה כְּחֻדָּהּ שֶׁל מַחַט וַאֲנִי פוֹתֵחַ לָכֶם פְּתָחִים שֶׁיִּהְיוּ עֲגָלוֹת וּקְרוֹנִיּוֹת נִכְנָסוֹת בּוֹ:

The *Kadosh Baruḥ Hu* said to Israel, "My children, show me an opening of repentance no larger than the eye of a needle, and I will widen it into openings through which wagons and carriages can pass."

Song of Songs Rabbah 5:2.2

అ

Four main reasons are given for the command to fast on Yom Kippur.

Fasting as a penance. By fasting on Yom Kippur, we show contrition for the wrong we have done and good we have failed to do.... When we fast for our sins, we are saying in so many words, we do not want to be let off lightly; we deserve to be punished.

Fasting as self-discipline. Fasting on Yom Kippur serves a potent reminder of the need of the self-discipline which leads to self-improvement.

Fasting as a means of focusing the mind on the spiritual. By fasting on Yom Kippur, the needs of the body are left unattended for twenty-four hours and Jews give all their concentration to the things of the spirit.

Fasting as a means of awakening compassion. By fasting we are moved to think of the needs of others and to alleviate their suffering.

Louis Jacobs

ख

Every time I listen to your pain
instead of telling you how to fix it
I make a sacrifice.
I used to be a magician
who diverted himself from his problems
by focusing on someone else's.
You might have been impressed by my cleverness
but it did not help either of us.
At last I have been reduced to silence.
My silence can be a mirror for you.
May this offering of emptiness
give you room to heal.

Seth D. Riemer

ख

As scholars have often noted, there is a basic difference between the orientation of the biblical *Yom Hakippurim* and Yom Kippur after the destruction of the Temples. In biblical times, Yom Kippur served the function of cleansing the Sanctuary, the abode of God, of any impurity....

Our Yom Kippur focuses on the behavior of the individual in his or her personal life and on the interaction of the community of Jews. Nevertheless, the motivation behind the biblical Yom Kippur is worth holding in mind. We must scrutinize our own lives carefully at least once each year so that we do not allow unwanted behavior to become so rigid that it will be too difficult to undo. We must repair the wounds we have inflicted before they develop into permanent ones. We must recharge our communities with a devotion to that which is godly and holy lest we lose all sight of our purpose.   Edward Greenstein

❧

The Talmud records these words of Rabbi Yehudah Hanasi: "One person may acquire eternal life after many years of effort, and another acquires it in a single instant."

For some of us, the road to reconciliation is incremental: we assign a series of tasks to ourselves, and gradually but steadily accomplish one after another after another, until we reach our goal.

For some of us, years of self-neglect, complacency, and defeat are suddenly overcome in one moment of insight, in one experience of the holy, in one unexpected moment of victory, in one unanticipated moment of anguish.

Each life is a story of moments: a moment in which a chance remark awakens an unexpected insight; a moment of solitude that results in a renewed sense of responsibility; a moment of atonement that yields eternity; and a moment of awareness that yields hope.   Richard Hirsh

❧

When asked the reason for his leniency in permitting the sick to eat during Yom Kippur, Rabbi Ḥayim of Brisk replied, "It's not that I am lenient when it comes to Yom Kippur, but I am strict when it comes to saving a life." For those who are physically well, fasting on Yom Kippur is a mitzvah that nourishes our souls. However, for those of us who are physically frail, the mitzvah incumbent upon us is to nourish our bodies, so that we may live. *Teshuvah* (inward turning) can only occur where life allows for the turning.

Leila Gal Berner

ᔔ

Repentance is not just a psychological phenomenon, a storm within a human teacup, but is a process that can effect real change in the world, in all the worlds. Every human action elicits certain inevitable results that extend beyond their immediate context, passing from one level of existence to another, from one aspect of reality to another. The act of repentance is, in the first place, a severance of the chain of cause and effect in which one transgression follows inevitably upon another. Beyond this, it is an attempt to nullify and even to alter the past. This can only be achieved when we subjectively shatter the order of our own existence. The thrust of repentance is to break through the ordinary limits of the self. Obviously this cannot take place within the routine of life; it [must] be an ongoing activity throughout life. Repentance is thus something that persists; it is an ever-renewed extrication from causality and limitation.

Adin Steinsaltz

Kabbalat Hashanah, pages 23-57, provides a broad variety of options for introducing the Yamim Nora'im/Days of Awe on the evening of Rosh Hashanah. This new liturgical feature can take a variety of forms to reflect the needs of the sheliaḥ tzibur/*service leader and community.*
Choose from the following:

This is the moment that the world changes; at this instant one year ends, the other begins. The air is cluttered with the past and potent with new possibilities.

This night as the New Year begins,
We come together as a community;
Yet each of us is strangely solitary.

Each of us comes here with special hopes and dreams;
Each of us bears our own worries and concerns.

Each of us has a story no one else can tell;
Each of us brings praise no one else can offer.

Each of us feels joy no one else can share;
Each of us has regrets that others cannot know.

And so, at this sacred time, we pray:
If we are weary, may we find strength;
If we are discouraged, may we find hope.

If we have forgotten how to share, may we teach each other
and learn together.
If we have been careless with one another, may we
seek forgiveness.

If our hearts have been chilled by indifference,
May we be warmed by renewed purpose,
inspired by the spirit of this holy night.

Sidney Greenberg (Adapted)

This Rosh Hashanah, each of us enters this sanctuary with a different need.

Some hearts are full of gratitude and joy:
They are overflowing with the happiness of love
and the joy of life;
they are eager to confront the day, to make the world
more fair;
they are recovering from illness or have escaped misfortune.
And we rejoice with them.

Some hearts ache with sorrow:
Disappointments weigh heavily upon them, and they have
tasted despair; families have been broken;
loved ones lie on a bed of pain;
death has taken those whom they cherished.
May our presence and sympathy bring them comfort.

Some hearts are embittered:
They have sought answers in vain;
have had their ideals mocked and betrayed;
life has lost its meaning and value.
May the knowledge that we too are searching
restore their hope that there is something to find.

Some spirits hunger:
They long for friendship; they crave understanding;
they yearn for warmth.

May we in our common need gain strength from one another;
sharing our joys, lightening each other's burdens, and praying
for the welfare of our community.

Chaim Stern

✺

Our noisy year has now descended with the sun beyond our sight, and in the silence of this praying place, we close the door upon the hectic joys and fears, the accomplishments and anguish, of the year that we have left behind. What was but moments ago the substance of our life has now become its memory, and what we did must now be woven into what we are. On this day we shall not do, but be; we are to walk the outer limits of our humanity, no longer ride unseeing through a world we only vaguely sense beneath our cushioned wheels. On this day, heat and warmth and light must come from deep within ourselves; no longer can we tear apart the world to make our fire. On this day, but a breath away from our creation, we are to breathe in a world from which we may no longer feel apart, but as close as eye to blossom, and ear to the singing in the night.

We are here, on this Rosh Hashanah Eve, poised somewhere between what we have been and what we wish to be. We are here at this season of *teshuvah*, of turning, of returning to the self we have covered up behind the roles and masks with which we have learned to protect ourselves. We are here in celebration and in search, in judgment and embrace, ready to confront ourselves and the world in which we find ourselves this night. We seek to open wide the windows behind which we have hidden, and to send forth hand and heart to learn where we have come, what we have become, and what we hope to be.

Richard N. Levy (Adapted)

∾

אָדָם בֶּאֱמֶת אֵינוֹ צָרִיךְ

אָדָם בֶּאֱמֶת אֵינוֹ צָרִיךְ אֶלָּא לְסֵפֶר אֶחָד בְּחַיָּיו
כַּאֲשֶׁר כָּל חַיָּיו נִקְבָּצִים לְעֵינָיו בַּסֵּפֶר הַפָּתוּחַ לְעֵינָיו
כַּאֲשֶׁר הוּא קוֹרֵא בּוֹ דַּף אַחַר דַּף וְרוֹאֶה לְעֵינָיו
אֵיךְ יוֹם אַחַר יוֹם רָדַף כְּמוֹ דַּף אַחַר דַּף
בַּסֵּפֶר הַפָּתוּחַ לְעֵינָיו.
וְאַף לֹא אֶחָד נֶעֱזָב וּבְרַחֲמִים רַבִּים נֶאֱסָף
דַּף אַחַר דַּף
בַּסֵּפֶר הַפָּתוּחַ לְעֵינָיו
כִּי רוֹאֶה לְעֵינָיו
פָּתוּחַ סֵפֶר חַיָּיו
בְּרַחֲמִים רַבִּים נֶעֱזָב.

Human beings need but one book in their life,
when my whole life is gathered like an open book
before my eyes, when I read it page by page
seeing with my own eyes how day has followed day,
flown like page has followed page
in the open book before my eyes.
And yet not even one is left behind;
in great mercy it is gathered
page by page,
like a book open before my eyes.
how, in great mercy
my open book of life
is left behind.

Amir Gilboa

HADLAKAT NEROT /
CANDLELIGHTING FOR ROSH HASHANAH

Candles are traditionally lit in the home. Many communities also light candles together at the beginning of the **Kabbalat Hashanah** *service.*

Blessed are you, SOURCE OF LIGHT, our God, the sovereign of all worlds, who has made us holy with your mitzvot, and commanded us to kindle the (Shabbat and) festival light.

Blessed are you, ETERNAL ONE, our God, the sovereign of all worlds, who gave us life, and kept us strong, and brought us to this time.

Many contemporary Jews are reciting *berahot*/blessings in ways that reflect their theological outlooks and ethical concerns. At any place where a blessing occurs in the liturgy, the following elements can be combined to create alternative formulas for *berahot*. This can be done by selecting one phrase from each group to form the introductory clause.

I	Baruh atah adonay	בָּרוּךְ אַתָּה יהוה	Blessed are you Adonay
	Beruhah at yah	בְּרוּכָה אַתְּ יָהּ	Blessed are you Yah
	Nevareh et	נְבָרֵךְ אֶת	Let us bless
II	eloheynu	אֱלֹהֵינוּ	our God
	hashehinah	הַשְּׁכִינָה	Shehinah
	eyn hahayim	עֵין הַחַיִּים	Source of Life
III	meleh ha'olam	מֶלֶךְ הָעוֹלָם	Sovereign of all worlds
	hey ha'olamim	חֵי הָעוֹלָמִים	Life of all the worlds
	ru'ah ha'olam	רוּחַ הָעוֹלָם	Spirit of the world

The phrase *"Nevareh et eyn hahayim"* was originally formulated by poet Marcia Falk (see SOURCES, p. 1248).

הַדְלָקַת 🕯 נֵרוֹת 🕯 לְרֹאשׁ הַשָּׁנָה

בָּרוּךְ אַתָּה יהוה אֱלֹהֵינוּ מֶלֶךְ הָעוֹלָם אֲשֶׁר קִדְּשָׁנוּ בְּמִצְוֹתָיו וְצִוָּנוּ
לְהַדְלִיק נֵר שֶׁל (שַׁבָּת וְ) יוֹם טוֹב:

Baruḥ atah adonay eloheynu meleḥ ha'olam asher kideshanu
bemitzvotav vetzivanu lehadlik ner shel (shabbat ve) yom tov.

בָּרוּךְ אַתָּה יהוה אֱלֹהֵינוּ מֶלֶךְ הָעוֹלָם שֶׁהֶחֱיָנוּ וְקִיְּמָנוּ וְהִגִּיעָנוּ
לַזְּמַן הַזֶּה:

Baruḥ atah adonay eloheynu meleḥ ha'olam sheheḥeyanu
vekiyemanu vehigi'anu lazeman hazeh.

MA'ASEY BEREYSHIT / A HYMN OF CREATION

Bless, O my spirit, THE ETERNAL ONE!
O LIVING ONE, my God, how vast you are!
In majesty and splendor you are clothed,
wearing the light of heaven as your shawl,
and stretching forth your canopy of sky,
you pitch the rafters of your chambers on the waters,
making the clouds your chariot,
surveying all on wings of air,
making the winds your messengers;
your servants, fire and flame.

And there was evening, there was morning: a single day.

GUIDED MEDITATION. Sit comfortably in your chair, legs uncrossed. Close
your eyes. Breathe in and out slowly for a minute or two. Pay attention to
the order and strength in your body. Remember your connection with all
living creatures.

Picture yourself on a small boat slowly floating along the banks of a river.
You feel a quiet sense of calm. As you slowly drift along, you see on the
riverbank the people you have connected with over this past year. They
appear one by one, beginning from last Rosh Hashanah right on through
to the present. Allow yourself time to review these connections as they
occurred throughout the year. Let the images gradually emerge. Keep in
mind that you can only accept from others what you have space to receive
within yourself. As you end your ride, beach your boat and get out. Think
about what you want to take with you. Put in the boat what you want to
leave behind. Take a few minutes and enjoy the sun on the riverbank.
How do you feel? When you are ready, open your eyes.   D.B.

We remember the creation of the world even as we strive to recreate it.

בָּרְכִי נַפְשִׁי אֶת־יהוה   יהוה אֱלֹהַי גָּדַלְתָּ מְּאֹד

הוֹד וְהָדָר לָבָשְׁתָּ:   עֹטֶה־אוֹר כַּשַּׂלְמָה

נוֹטֶה שָׁמַיִם כַּיְרִיעָה: הַמְקָרֶה בַמַּיִם עֲלִיּוֹתָיו

הַשָּׂם־עָבִים רְכוּבוֹ   הַמְהַלֵּךְ עַל־כַּנְפֵי־רֽוּחַ:

עֹשֶׂה מַלְאָכָיו רוּחוֹת   מְשָׁרְתָיו אֵשׁ לֹהֵט:

וַיְהִי־עֶרֶב וַיְהִי־בֹקֶר יוֹם אֶחָד:

Vayehi erev vayehi voker yom ehad.

Who made the world?
Who made the swan and the black bear?
Who made the grasshopper?
The grasshopper, I mean—
the one who has flung herself out of the grass,
the one who is eating sugar out of my hand,
who is moving her jaws back and forth instead of up and down—
who is gazing around with her enormous and complicated eyes.
Now she lifts her pale forearms and thoroughly washes her face.
Now she snaps her wings open, and floats away.
I don't know exactly what a prayer is.
I do know how to pay attention, how to fall down
into the grass, how to kneel down in the grass,
how to be idle and blessed, how to stroll through the fields,
which is what I have been doing all day.
Tell me, what else should I have done?
Doesn't everything die at last, and too soon?
Tell me, what is it you plan to do
with your one wild and precious life?

Mary Oliver

You place the earth on its foundations,
never to topple for as long as time endures.
You cover it with ocean for its garment;
the waters rise up on the mountains of the ocean floor.
You speak, they scurry to obey,
hastening in fright before your voice's roar;
they ascend the mountains, and descend into the depths;
to the places you have readied for them.

And you set a boundary that they cannot cross;
and never can they overrun the earth again.

And there was evening, there was morning: a second day.

You make the fountains of the deep gush forth their waters;
down between the hills they make their course.
And they give drink to every living creature,
slaking the thirst of every wild beast.
Beside them dwell the birds that fill the skies,
calling their song amid the foliage. ↩

יָסַד־אֶרֶץ עַל־מְכוֹנֶיהָ:   בַּל־תִּמּוֹט עוֹלָם וָעֶד:

תְּהוֹם כַּלְבוּשׁ כִּסִּיתוֹ:   עַל־הָרִים יַעַמְדוּ־מָיִם:

מִן־גַּעֲרָתְךָ יְנוּסוּן: מִן־קוֹל רַעַמְךָ יֵחָפֵזוּן:

יַעֲלוּ הָרִים יֵרְדוּ בְקָעוֹת: אֶל־מְקוֹם זֶה יָסַדְתָּ לָהֶם:

גְּבוּל־שַׂמְתָּ בַּל־יַעֲבֹרוּן: בַּל־יְשׁוּבוּן לְכַסּוֹת הָאָרֶץ:

וַיְהִי־עֶרֶב וַיְהִי־בֹקֶר יוֹם שֵׁנִי:

Vayehi erev vayehi voker yom sheni.

הַמְשַׁלֵּחַ מַעְיָנִים בַּנְּחָלִים   בֵּין הָרִים יְהַלֵּכוּן:

יַשְׁקוּ כָּל־חַיְתוֹ שָׂדָי   יִשְׁבְּרוּ פְרָאִים צְמָאָם:

עֲלֵיהֶם עוֹף־הַשָּׁמַיִם יִשְׁכּוֹן   מִבֵּין עֳפָאִים יִתְּנוּ־קוֹל: ⟵

COMMENTARY. This *piyut* was structured by Michael Strassfeld to reflect the Jewish understanding that Rosh Hashanah is the birthday of the world. Its intention is to remind us of the wonder of nature, which is reflected in each day of the biblical story of creation. As we re-experience the glorious complexity and astounding unity of our world, our quest for our place and purpose is renewed. In wonder and humility we celebrate the world's unity and mystery and acknowledge our lack of mastery.

D.A.T.

From your upper chambers you give water to the mountains,
replenishing the earth with your creation's fruits.
You make grains to grow, to feed the cattle,
vegetation for the human beings to till,
to bring forth bread out of the earth,
and wine for gladdening the human heart,
and oil for brightening the face,
and food for sustenance and life.

And there was evening, there was morning: a third day.

You make the moon for measuring the seasons,
the sun which knows its time to set.
You appoint the dark, and night arrives,
when forest animals awake and stir about,
the lions roaring for their prey,
seeking their food from God.

When sun gives forth its rays, they're gathered
to their lairs and make their beds,
and humans go out to their labors,
working till the evening comes.

And there was evening, there was morning: a fourth day.

מַשְׁקֶה הָרִים מֵעֲלִיּוֹתָיו   מִפְּרִי מַעֲשֶׂיךָ תִּשְׂבַּע הָאָרֶץ:
מַצְמִיחַ חָצִיר לַבְּהֵמָה   וְעֵשֶׂב לַעֲבֹדַת הָאָדָם
לְהוֹצִיא לֶחֶם מִן־הָאָרֶץ: וְיַיִן יְשַׂמַּח לְבַב־אֱנוֹשׁ
לְהַצְהִיל פָּנִים מִשָּׁמֶן   וְלֶחֶם לְבַב־אֱנוֹשׁ יִסְעָד:

וַיְהִי־עֶרֶב וַיְהִי־בֹקֶר יוֹם שְׁלִישִׁי:

Vayehi erev vayehi voker yom shelishi.

עָשָׂה יָרֵחַ לְמוֹעֲדִים   שֶׁמֶשׁ יָדַע מְבוֹאוֹ:
תָּשֶׁת־חֹשֶׁךְ וִיהִי לָיְלָה   בּוֹ־תִרְמֹשׂ כָּל־חַיְתוֹ־יָעַר:
הַכְּפִירִים שֹׁאֲגִים לַטָּרֶף   וּלְבַקֵּשׁ מֵאֵל אָכְלָם:
תִּזְרַח הַשֶּׁמֶשׁ יֵאָסֵפוּן   וְאֶל־מְעוֹנֹתָם יִרְבָּצוּן:
יֵצֵא אָדָם לְפָעֳלוֹ   וְלַעֲבֹדָתוֹ עֲדֵי־עָרֶב:

וַיְהִי־עֶרֶב וַיְהִי־בֹקֶר יוֹם רְבִיעִי: ←

Vayehi erev vayehi voker yom revi'i.

The trees of THE ALMIGHTY drink their fill,
cedars of Lebanon, which God has planted,
where the birds have made their nests;
and junipers make shelter for the stork.
The lofty mountains are for wild goats;
the crannies of their stones, the badgers' homes.

Behold the sea in its immensity:
its teeming creatures dwell there beyond number,
living things both great and small;
and there the ships travel about; as does
Leviathan, whom you created for your sport.

And there was evening, there was morning: a fifth day.

How great is your Creation, FOUNT OF LIFE,
and all of it you made in wisdom!
How the earth abounds with all your creatures!
And all of them are looking toward you,
to give them food in time of need.
You give your sustenance for them to gather;
open your hand, and satisfy them well.

Should you conceal your presence, they are frightened;
should you take away their breath, they perish
and return to dust.
Send back your breath, and they revive;
earth's living face is thus renewed. ↩

יִשְׂבְּעוּ עֲצֵי יְהֹוָה   אַרְזֵי לְבָנוֹן אֲשֶׁר נָטָע:

אֲשֶׁר־שָׁם צִפֳּרִים יְקַנֵּנוּ   חֲסִידָה בְּרוֹשִׁים בֵּיתָהּ:

הָרִים הַגְּבֹהִים לַיְּעֵלִים   סְלָעִים מַחְסֶה לַשְׁפַנִּים:

זֶה הַיָּם גָּדוֹל וּרְחַב יָדָיִם   שָׁם־רֶמֶשׂ וְאֵין מִסְפָּר

חַיּוֹת קְטַנּוֹת עִם־גְּדֹלוֹת:

שָׁם אֳנִיּוֹת יְהַלֵּכוּן   לִוְיָתָן זֶה־יָצַרְתָּ לְשַׂחֶק־בּוֹ:

וַיְהִי־עֶרֶב וַיְהִי־בֹקֶר יוֹם חֲמִישִׁי:

Vayehi erev vayehi voker yom ḥamishi.

מָה־רַבּוּ מַעֲשֶׂיךָ יהוה   כֻּלָּם בְּחָכְמָה עָשִׂיתָ מָלְאָה הָאָרֶץ קִנְיָנֶךָ:

כֻּלָּם אֵלֶיךָ יְשַׂבֵּרוּן   לָתֵת אָכְלָם בְּעִתּוֹ:

תִּתֵּן לָהֶם יִלְקֹטוּן   תִּפְתַּח יָדְךָ יִשְׂבְּעוּן טוֹב:

תַּסְתִּיר פָּנֶיךָ יִבָּהֵלוּן   תֹּסֵף רוּחָם יִגְוָעוּן וְאֶל־עֲפָרָם יְשׁוּבוּן:

תְּשַׁלַּח רוּחֲךָ יִבָּרֵאוּן   וּתְחַדֵּשׁ פְּנֵי אֲדָמָה: ←—

Let the glory of THE ANCIENT ONE endure forever;
may you, THE SOURCE OF ALL, rejoice in your creation,
you, whose very gaze makes all life tremble,
whose touch upon the mountains sets them rumbling with
  smoke.
I sing to you, CREATOR, all my life,
make melody to you, my God, while I yet live.
May my prayer be pleasing to you;
for in THE BOUNTIFUL do I rejoice.
Let wrongdoing be finished from the earth!
May evildoers cease, and be no more!

And bless, O my soul, THE ONE WHO IS! Halleluyah!

Based on Psalm 104 and Genesis 1

෴

We are still in the midst of the sixth day. We are created, we have
eaten of the tree of knowledge, been banished from Eden, loved,
given birth, hated, killed and yet the sixth day is not over. Our
human story repeated in endless generations is incomplete. God
has called upon us to finish the work of creation and thus to say
of the work of our hands *ki tov*/it is good.

Then will *vayehi erev vayehi voker*/And there was evening, there
was morning, the sixth day, be immediately followed by *vayehulu*
and then the work ceased, and the universe was complete, and
all rested on the seventh day.

יְהִי כְבוֹד יהוה לְעוֹלָם   יִשְׂמַח יהוה בְּמַעֲשָׂיו:
הַמַּבִּיט לָאָרֶץ וַתִּרְעָד   יִגַּע בֶּהָרִים וְיֶעֱשָׁנוּ:
אָשִׁירָה לַיהוה בְּחַיָּי   אֲזַמְּרָה לֵאלֹהַי בְּעוֹדִי:
יֶעֱרַב עָלָיו שִׂיחִי   אָנֹכִי אֶשְׂמַח בַּיהוה:
יִתַּמּוּ חַטָּאִים מִן־הָאָרֶץ   וּרְשָׁעִים עוֹד אֵינָם
בָּרֲכִי נַפְשִׁי אֶת־יהוה   **הַלְלוּיָהּ**

Ashirah ladonay beḥayay azamerah leylohay be'odi.
ye'erav alav siḥi anoḥi esmaḥ badonay.
Yitamu ḥata'im min ha'aretz uresha'im od eynam
bareḥi nafshi et adonay haleluyah.

For the chief musician, to a Gathite melody; by Asaph.

Sing joyful song to God, our strength,
make joyous sounds for Jacob's God!

Raise up a song, and strike the tambourine,
pluck sweetly on the strings, accompanied by harp.

Blast piercing notes upon the shofar for the New Moon,
for the full moon, for our festive holiday.

For it is Israel's law,
a statute of the God of Jacob.

God established it in Joseph's clans,
when going forth against the land of Egypt;
I heard a language that I didn't know.

"I have relieved their shoulders from their burdens,
their hands are freed from carrying the basket.

In sorrow you called out, and I released you,
I answered from my hidden place where thunder rolls,
I tried you at Meribah's waters. So it was! ↵

לַמְנַצֵּחַ עַל הַגִּתִּית לְאָסָף:

הַרְנִינוּ לֵאלֹהִים עוּזֵּנוּ הָרִיעוּ לֵאלֹהֵי יַעֲקֹב:

שְׂאוּ־זִמְרָה וּתְנוּ־תֹף כִּנּוֹר נָעִים עִם־נָבֶל:

תִּקְעוּ בַחֹדֶשׁ שׁוֹפָר בַּכֶּסֶה לְיוֹם חַגֵּנוּ:

כִּי חֹק לְיִשְׂרָאֵל הוּא מִשְׁפָּט לֵאלֹהֵי יַעֲקֹב:

עֵדוּת בִּיהוֹסֵף שָׂמוֹ בְּצֵאתוֹ עַל־אֶרֶץ מִצְרָיִם שְׂפַת לֹא־יָדַעְתִּי אֶשְׁמָע:

הֲסִירוֹתִי מִסֵּבֶל שִׁכְמוֹ כַּפָּיו מִדּוּד תַּעֲבֹרְנָה:

בַּצָּרָה קָרָאתָ וָאֲחַלְּצֶךָּ אֶעֶנְךָ בְּסֵתֶר רָעַם אֶבְחָנְךָ עַל־מֵי מְרִיבָה סֶלָה: ←

NOTE. This appellation "For the chief musician, to a Gathite melody" occurs dozens of times at the beginning of psalms, as at the end of the book of Habakuk. Often it occurs alongside references to Asaph, the clan of Levite singers. This suggests that the choir leader either composed or directed the performance of these compositions.   D.A.T.

Listen, my people, I admonish you!
Israel, if you only would pay heed to me!

Let you not have among you alien gods,
let you not bow down to exotic gods.

I am THE REDEEMING ONE, your God,
who brings you up out of the land of Egypt.
Open up your mouth, and I shall fill it!

But my people did not listen to my voice,
no, Israel did not care for me.

So I sent away the people in their stubbornness of heart,
I let them go according to their own devices.

Would that my people might listen to me,
yes, would that Israel walked according to my ways!

How quickly would I crush their enemies,
on their oppressors would I cast my hand.

Those who hate GOD would cringe before my people;
I would stand beside them always.

God would feed them from the choicest wheat.
Yes, from the rock I'd feed you honey in abundance."

Psalm 81

שְׁמַע עַמִּי וְאָעִ֫ידָה בָּךְ יִשְׂרָאֵל אִם־תִּשְׁמַע־לִי:
לֹא־יִהְיֶה בְךָ אֵל זָר וְלֹא תִשְׁתַּחֲוֶה לְאֵל נֵכָר:
אָנֹכִי יהוה אֱלֹהֶיךָ הַמַּעַלְךָ מֵאֶרֶץ מִצְרָיִם הַרְחֶב־פִּיךָ וַאֲמַלְאֵהוּ:
וְלֹא־שָׁמַע עַמִּי לְקוֹלִי וְיִשְׂרָאֵל לֹא־אָבָה לִי:
וָאֲשַׁלְּחֵהוּ בִּשְׁרִירוּת לִבָּם יֵלְכוּ בְּמוֹעֲצוֹתֵיהֶם:
לוּ עַמִּי שֹׁמֵעַ לִי יִשְׂרָאֵל בִּדְרָכַי יְהַלֵּכוּ:
כִּמְעַט אוֹיְבֵיהֶם אַכְנִיעַ וְעַל־צָרֵיהֶם אָשִׁיב יָדִי:
מְשַׂנְאֵי יהוה יְכַחֲשׁוּ־לוֹ וִיהִי עִתָּם לְעוֹלָם:
וַיַּאֲכִילֵהוּ מֵחֵלֶב חִטָּה וּמִצּוּר דְּבַשׁ אַשְׂבִּיעֶךָ:

COMMENTARY. Psalm 81 was identified as the psalm for the day of Rosh
Hashanah by the Gaon of Vilna (eighteenth-century spiritual and
intellectual leader). The psalm's contrasting moods of joyous celebration
and quiet contemplation make it especially suited for such use. Two
important symbols of the holiday appear here—the shofar, which awakens
us from our everyday complacency, and the honey, reflecting our hopes for
a sweet new year.   R.S.

A Song for the Ascents.

I lift my eyes up to the hills.
From where does my help come?

My help is from THE UNSEEN ONE,
the maker of the heavens and the earth,

who will not cause your foot to fail.
Your protector never slumbers.

Behold the one who slumbers not, who never sleeps,
the guardian of Israel.

THE ABUNDANT ONE preserves you,
THE WATCHFUL ONE, your shelter, at your right hand a support.

By day, the sun will not afflict you,
nor the moonlight by the night.

THE VIGILANT shall guard you from all evil,
and will keep your lifebreath safe.

THE SHEPHERD guard your going out and coming in,
from now unto eternity.

Psalm 121

שִׁיר לַמַּעֲלוֹת אֶשָּׂא עֵינַי אֶל־הֶהָרִים מֵאַיִן יָבֹא עֶזְרִי:

עֶזְרִי מֵעִם יהוה עֹשֵׂה שָׁמַיִם וָאָרֶץ:

אַל־יִתֵּן לַמּוֹט רַגְלֶךָ אַל־יָנוּם שֹׁמְרֶךָ:

הִנֵּה לֹא־יָנוּם וְלֹא יִישָׁן שׁוֹמֵר יִשְׂרָאֵל:

יהוה שֹׁמְרֶךָ יהוה צִלְּךָ עַל־יַד יְמִינֶךָ:

יוֹמָם הַשֶּׁמֶשׁ לֹא־יַכֶּכָּה וְיָרֵחַ בַּלָּיְלָה:

יהוה יִשְׁמָרְךָ מִכָּל־רָע יִשְׁמֹר אֶת־נַפְשֶׁךָ:

יהוה יִשְׁמָר־צֵאתְךָ וּבוֹאֶךָ מֵעַתָּה וְעַד־עוֹלָם:

Esa eynay el heharim me'ayin yavo ezri.
Ezri me'im adonay oseh shamayim va'aretz.

KAVANAH. Often prayer seeks to turn our thoughts towards God; at other times it directs our attention towards ourselves, and sometimes these two poles are held in intimate relation, as in the opening outcry of the psalm: "I lift my eyes up to the hills. From where does my help come?" Had the life-sustaining force we call God not been with us, how could we possibly have survived calumny and contempt, pogroms and persecutions? Given the perils and pains of Jewish history, our continued existence as a people is not easy to account for in the usual reasoned terms of causal explanation.

Might we then succumb, if only for a moment, to the cry of the psalmist, and give voice to our astonished recognition that our existence is surely by the grace of God, a gift that surpasses explanation.   E.G.

Now, bless THE LIVING ONE, all servants of THE ONE MOST
HIGH.

You who stand assembled in the house of THE ETERNAL in
the evenings,

raise up your hands in holiness, and bless THE FOUNT OF
LIFE.

May THE ETERNAL ONE, creator of the heavens and the
earth, bless you from Zion's mount.

By day, THE BOUNTIFUL sends love to guard me,

and by night, God's song is with me.

My prayer is to the living God.

THE CREATOR of the heavens' multitudes is with us,

a stronghold for us, truly, is the God of Jacob!

O CREATOR of the hosts of heaven, happy is the one who
trusts in you!

ETERNAL ONE, send help!

Let the sovereign of the world give answer when we call.

Psalms 134; 42:9; 46:8; 84:13; 20:10

הִנֵּה בָּרֲכוּ אֶת־יהוה כָּל־עַבְדֵי יהוה
הָעֹמְדִים בְּבֵית־יהוה בַּלֵּילוֹת:
שְׂאוּ־יְדֵכֶם קֹדֶשׁ וּבָרֲכוּ אֶת־יהוה:
יְבָרֶכְךָ יהוה מִצִּיּוֹן עֹשֵׂה שָׁמַיִם וָאָרֶץ:
יוֹמָם יְצַוֶּה יהוה חַסְדּוֹ וּבַלַּיְלָה שִׁירֹה עִמִּי תְּפִלָּה לְאֵל חַיָּי:
יהוה צְבָאוֹת עִמָּנוּ מִשְׂגָּב־לָנוּ אֱלֹהֵי יַעֲקֹב סֶלָה:
יהוה צְבָאוֹת אַשְׁרֵי אָדָם בֹּטֵחַ בָּךְ:
יהוה הוֹשִׁיעָה הַמֶּלֶךְ יַעֲנֵנוּ בְיוֹם־קָרְאֵנוּ:

Select from among the following songs:

Who is the person who wishes to live,
who desires days to behold life's good?
Preserve your tongue from evil,
and your lips from uttering deceit.
Turn away from evil, and do good,
seek peace, and follow after it.

Psalms 34:13–15

෨

All the world before us
is a very narrow bridge,
and the main thing
is not to fear at all.

Attributed to Rabbi Naḥman of Bratzlav

෨

Pour out your heart like water
in the presence of THE LIVING GOD.

Lamentations 2:19

෨

Find words in you to offer
and return to THE COMPASSIONATE.

Hosea 14:3

מִי־הָאִישׁ הֶחָפֵץ חַיִּים אֹהֵב יָמִים לִרְאוֹת טוֹב:

נֹצֹר לְשׁוֹנְךָ מֵרָע וּשְׂפָתֶיךָ מִדַּבֵּר מִרְמָה:

סוּר מֵרָע וַעֲשֵׂה־טוֹב בַּקֵּשׁ שָׁלוֹם וְרָדְפֵהוּ:

Mi ha'ish heḥafetz ḥayim ohev yamim lirot tov.
Netzor leshoneḥa mera usfateḥa midaber mirmah.
Sur mera va'asey tov bakesh shalom verodfehu.

∝

כָּל־הָעוֹלָם כֻּלּוֹ גֶּשֶׁר צַר מְאֹד וְהָעִקָּר לֹא לְפַחֵד כְּלָל:

Kol ha'olam kulo gesher tzar me'od
veha'ikar lo lefaḥed kelal.

∝

שִׁפְכִי כַמַּיִם לִבֵּךְ נֹכַח פְּנֵי אֲדֹנָי:

Shifḥi ḥamayim libeḥ noḥaḥ peney adonay.

∝

קְחוּ עִמָּכֶם דְּבָרִים וְשׁוּבוּ אֶל־יהוה:

Keḥu imaḥem devarim veshuvu el adonay.

Open to me, O you gateways of justice,
Yes, let me come in, and give thanks unto Yah!

This is the gateway to ONE EVERLASTING,
let all who are righteous come in.   Psalms 118:19-20

❧

Behold, the days are coming,
that I shall send forth hunger in the Land,
not hunger for bread,
nor thirst for water,
but desire to hear the words of THE ETERNAL ONE.   Amos 8:11

❧

Return us, PRECIOUS ONE, let us return!
Renew our days, as you have done of old!   Lamentations 5:2

❧

I lift my eyes up to the hills.
From where does my help come?   Psalms 121:1-2

❧

And as for me, my prayer is for you, GENTLE ONE,
may it be for you a time of desire,
O God, in the abundance of your love,
respond to me in truth with your help.   Psalms 69:14

❧

פִּתְחוּ־לִי שַׁעֲרֵי־צֶדֶק   אָבֹא־בָם אוֹדֶה יָהּ׃
זֶה־הַשַּׁעַר לַיהוה   צַדִּיקִים יָבֹאוּ בוֹ׃

Pithu li sha'arey tzedek avo vam odeh yah.
Zeh hasha'ar ladonay tzadikim yavo'u vo.

הִנֵּה יָמִים בָּאִים... וְהִשְׁלַחְתִּי רָעָב בָּאָרֶץ
לֹא־רָעָב לַלֶּחֶם וְלֹא־צָמָא לַמַּיִם כִּי אִם־לִשְׁמֹעַ אֵת דִּבְרֵי יהוה׃

Hiney yamim ba'im vehishlaḥti ra'av ba'aretz
lo ra'av laleḥem velo tzama lamayim
ki im lishmo'a et divrey adonay.

❧

הֲשִׁיבֵנוּ יהוה אֵלֶיךָ וְנָשׁוּבָה חַדֵּשׁ יָמֵינוּ כְּקֶדֶם׃

Hashivenu adonay eleḥa venashuva ḥadesh yameynu kekedem.

❧

אֶשָּׂא עֵינַי אֶל־הֶהָרִים מֵאַיִן יָבֹא עֶזְרִי׃

Esa eynay el heharim me'ayin yavo ezri.

❧

וַאֲנִי תְפִלָּתִי־לְךָ יהוה עֵת רָצוֹן אֱלֹהִים בְּרָב־חַסְדֶּךָ עֲנֵנִי בֶּאֱמֶת
יִשְׁעֶךָ׃

Va'ani tefilati leḥa adonay et ratzon elohim berov ḥasdeḥa aneni
be'emet yisheḥa.

❧

לֹא רעב ללחם ולא צמא למים כי אם לשמוע את דברי יהוה/not hunger for bread, nor thirst for water, but desire to hear the words of THE ETERNAL ONE. In ten days, we will observe the fast of Yom Kippur, denying ourselves both food and drink. These words of Amos anticipate that fast and remind us that there are other deprivations, both physical and spiritual, whose impact is no less difficult, and whose duration can be more devastating.   R.H.

The following two psalms are customarily added when Rosh Hashanah falls on Shabbat.

A psalm. A song for the day of Shabbat.

A good thing to give thanks to THE ETERNAL
to sing out to your name supreme,

to tell about your kindness in the morning,
and your faithfulness at night,

on ten-stringed lyre and on flute,
with melodies conceived on harp,

for you, ALMIGHTY ONE, elate me with your deeds,
I'll sing about the actions of your hands.

How great your deeds have been, SUPERNAL ONE.
your thoughts exceedingly profound.

Of this the foolish person cannot know,
of this the shallow cannot understand. ↩

NOTE. Psalms 92 and 93 express the motifs of wholeness, joy, and rest in Shabbat. Psalm 92 has been associated with Shabbat since biblical times. According to the midrash,* Shabbat itself stood up and recited this psalm at Creation, thus exulting in the role given it as the day of inner joy for all of God's creatures.   A.G.

*Midrash is a genre of interpretative commentary that derives its name from the root דרש: to search out. The activity of expounding midrash is one of elucidation through creative expansion of words, verses, or whole stories that are ambiguous in the biblical text. These provide fertile ground for imaginative explanation. Midrashic literature dates back to the period of the early Amoraic rabbis, ca. 400 C.E., and is still being created today.
                                                                                    M.P.

מִזְמוֹר שִׁיר לְיוֹם הַשַּׁבָּת:

וּלְזַמֵּר לְשִׁמְךָ עֶלְיוֹן: טוֹב לְהֹדוֹת לַיהוה

וֶאֱמוּנָתְךָ בַּלֵּילוֹת: לְהַגִּיד בַּבֹּקֶר חַסְדֶּךָ

עֲלֵי הִגָּיוֹן בְּכִנּוֹר: עֲלֵי־עָשׂוֹר וַעֲלֵי־נָבֶל

בְּמַעֲשֵׂי יָדֶיךָ אֲרַנֵּן: כִּי שִׂמַּחְתַּנִי יהוה בְּפָעֳלֶךָ

מְאֹד עָמְקוּ מַחְשְׁבֹתֶיךָ:   מַה־גָּדְלוּ מַעֲשֶׂיךָ יהוה

← וּכְסִיל לֹא־יָבִין אֶת־זֹאת: אִישׁ־בַּעַר לֹא יֵדָע

Mizmor shir leyom hashabbat.
Tov lehodot ladonay ulzamer leshimeha elyon.
Lehagid baboker hasdeha ve'emunateha baleylot.
Aley asor va'aley navel aley higayon behinor.

May these hours of rest and renewal
open my heart to joy and my mind to truth.
May all who struggle find rest on this day.
May all who suffer find solace on this day.
May all who hurt find healing on this day.
May all who despair find purpose on this day.
May all who hunger find fulfillment on this day.

And may I live my life in such a way
that this day may fulfill its promise.   R.M.S.

DERASH. On a Rosh Hashanah that coincided with Shabbat, the Hasidic master Levi Yitzhak made the following appeal to God: "Master of the Universe! Today is the New Year when you inscribe the Jews either in the Book of Life or in the Book of Death. Today is also *Shabbos*. Inasmuch as it is forbidden to write on *Shabbos*, how will it be possible for you to inscribe the Jewish people for the coming year? There is only one solution. If you will inscribe your people for a year of life, it is permissible for you to write, in accordance with the teaching of our Sages that the obligation of saving even a single life supersedes all the laws of *Shabbos*."

For though the wicked multiply like weeds,
and evildoers sprout up all around,

it is for their destruction for all time,
but you, MAJESTIC ONE, are lifted high eternally,

behold your enemies, RESPLENDENT ONE,
behold, your enemies are lost,

all evildoers shall be scattered.

You raise my horn like that of the triumphant ox;
I am anointed with fresh oil.

My eye shall gaze in victory on my enemies,
on all who rise against me to do harm

my ears shall hear of their demise.

The righteous flourish like the palm trees,
like cedars of Lebanon they grow,

implanted in the house of THE ALL-KNOWING ONE
amid the courtyards of our God they bear fruit.

In their old age, they'll put forth seed,
fleshy and fresh they'll ever be,

to tell the uprightness of THE ONE ALONE,
my Rock, in whom no fault resides.

Psalm 92

בִּפְרֹחַ רְשָׁעִים כְּמוֹ־עֵשֶׂב   וַיָּצִיצוּ כָּל־פֹּעֲלֵי אָוֶן

לְהִשָּׁמְדָם עֲדֵי־עַד:

וְאַתָּה מָרוֹם לְעֹלָם יהוה:

כִּי הִנֵּה אֹיְבֶיךָ יהוה   כִּי־הִנֵּה אֹיְבֶיךָ יֹאבֵדוּ

יִתְפָּרְדוּ כָּל־פֹּעֲלֵי אָוֶן:

וַתָּרֶם כִּרְאֵים קַרְנִי   בַּלֹּתִי בְּשֶׁמֶן רַעֲנָן:

וַתַּבֵּט עֵינִי בְּשׁוּרָי   בַּקָּמִים עָלַי מְרֵעִים

תִּשְׁמַעְנָה אָזְנָי:

* צַדִּיק כַּתָּמָר יִפְרָח   כְּאֶרֶז בַּלְּבָנוֹן יִשְׂגֶּה:

שְׁתוּלִים בְּבֵית יהוה   בְּחַצְרוֹת אֱלֹהֵינוּ יַפְרִיחוּ:

עוֹד יְנוּבוּן בְּשֵׂיבָה   דְּשֵׁנִים וְרַעֲנַנִּים יִהְיוּ:

לְהַגִּיד כִּי־יָשָׁר יהוה   צוּרִי וְלֹא־עַוְלָתָה בּוֹ:

Tzadik katamar yifraḥ, ke'erez balvanon yisgeh.
Shetulim beveyt adonay, beḥatzrot eloheynu yafriḥu.
Od yenuvun beseyvah, deshenim vera'ananim yihyu.
Lehagid ki yashar adonay, tzuri velo avlatah bo.

THE ETERNAL reigns, is clothed in majesty,
THE INVISIBLE is clothed, is girded up with might.

> The world is now established,
> it cannot give way.

Your throne was long ago secured,
beyond eternity are you.

The rivers raise, O MIGHTY ONE,
the rivers raise a roaring sound,

> the floods raise up torrential waves,

but louder than the sound of mighty waters,
more exalted than the breakers of the sea,

> raised up on high are you, THE SOURCE.

Your precepts have retained their truth,
and holiness befits your house,

THE ETERNAL ONE, forever and a day.

Psalm 93

יְהֹוָה מָלָךְ גֵּאוּת לָבֵשׁ לָבֵשׁ יהוה עֹז הִתְאַזָּר
אַף־תִּכּוֹן תֵּבֵל בַּל־תִּמּוֹט:

מֵעוֹלָם אָתָּה: נָכוֹן כִּסְאֲךָ מֵאָז
נָשְׂאוּ נְהָרוֹת קוֹלָם   נָשְׂאוּ נְהָרוֹת יהוה
יִשְׂאוּ נְהָרוֹת דָּכְיָם:

אַדִּירִים מִשְׁבְּרֵי־יָם   מִקֹּלוֹת מַיִם רַבִּים
אַדִּיר בַּמָּרוֹם יהוה:

לְבֵיתְךָ נַאֲוָה־קֹּדֶשׁ   * עֵדֹתֶיךָ נֶאֶמְנוּ מְאֹד
יהוה לְאֹרֶךְ יָמִים:

COMMENTARY. Psalm 93 concludes *Kabbalat Shabbat* by retelling the ancient tale of Creation. The waters raised a great shout, showing their power to overwhelm the dry land as it first emerged. So do the forces of chaos and destruction threaten the islands of peace and security we manage to create in our lives. The psalmist assures us, however, that the voice of God is greater than that of even the fiercest storm tides of the ocean. With God's throne firmly established, the peace of Shabbat is now triumphant. A.G.

KAVANAH. This psalm, recited when Rosh Hashanah falls on Shabbat, celebrates our ancestors' vision of the enthronement of God, a metaphor of majesty particularly appropriate to Rosh Hashanah. Against the ever changing flow of the waters, God remains constant; against the ever changing flow of our lives, we return each year to the ideals and aspirations that orient us anew. R.H.

As the days of twelve long months have slipped beneath the ocean with the waning sun, and the heavy lights of old things have gone glimmering into blackness, we have come to this place of prayer and study to seek out one another, and to feel the presence of our people. Each of us has met that people in a different house—a warm, accepting one; a shifting, fettered one; a concerned, empathic one; a defensive, bitter one. Yet from these diverse houses in which our spirits grew, there was fashioned in us a common recognition that we are related intimately and personally to the Jewish people. However we might reach out to others, to embrace all men and women, a part of us remains with that special people even as we sometimes struggle to find our place within it.

We seek that place once more on this new night, not alone in the direction of our single lives, but together in celebration and in search, in judgment and embrace, to begin again to confront ourselves and the ever-becoming world.

Richard Levy (Adapted)

ḤATZI KADDISH / SHORT KADDISH

Reader: Let God's name be made great and holy in the world that was created as God willed. May God complete the holy realm in your own lifetime, in your days, and in the days of all the house of Israel, quickly and soon. And say: Amen.

Congregation: May God's great name be blessed, forever and as long as worlds endure.

Reader: May it be blessed, and praised, and glorified, and held in honor, viewed with awe, embellished, and revered; and may the blessed name of holiness be hailed, though it be higher by far than all the blessings, songs, praises and consolations that we utter in this world. And say: Amen.

חֲצִי קַדִּישׁ

יִתְגַּדַּל וְיִתְקַדַּשׁ שְׁמֵהּ רַבָּא בְּעָלְמָא דִּי בְרָא כִרְעוּתֵהּ וְיַמְלִיךְ
מַלְכוּתֵהּ בְּחַיֵּיכוֹן וּבְיוֹמֵיכוֹן וּבְחַיֵּי דְכָל בֵּית יִשְׂרָאֵל בַּעֲגָלָא וּבִזְמַן
קָרִיב וְאִמְרוּ אָמֵן:
יְהֵא שְׁמֵהּ רַבָּא מְבָרַךְ לְעָלַם וּלְעָלְמֵי עָלְמַיָּא:
יִתְבָּרַךְ וְיִשְׁתַּבַּח וְיִתְפָּאַר וְיִתְרוֹמַם וְיִתְנַשֵּׂא וְיִתְהַדָּר וְיִתְעַלֶּה
וְיִתְהַלָּל שְׁמֵהּ דְּקֻדְשָׁא בְּרִיךְ הוּא
לְעֵלָּא לְעֵלָּא מִכָּל בִּרְכָתָא וְשִׁירָתָא תֻּשְׁבְּחָתָא וְנֶחֱמָתָא דַּאֲמִירָן
בְּעָלְמָא וְאִמְרוּ אָמֵן:

Reader: Yitgadal veyitkadash shemey raba
be'alma divra hirutey veyamlih malhutey
behayeyhon uvyomeyhon uvhayey dehol beyt yisra'el
ba'agala uvizman kariv ve'imru amen.

Congregation: Yehey shemey raba mevarah le'alam
ulalmey almaya.

Reader: Yitbarah veyishtabah veyitpa'ar veyitromam
veyitnasey veyit-hadar veyitaleh veyit-halal
shemey dekudsha berih hu
le'ela le'ela mikol birhata veshirata
tushbehata venehemata da'amiran be'alma ve'imru amen.

COMMENTARY. Several forms of kaddish exist. The best known is *kaddish
yatom*/mourner's kaddish. Thematically, the kaddish emphasizes God's
holiness and our desire that consciousness of the divine holiness should
become transformatively present in all people. Functionally, the kaddish
serves as a divider in the service. The *hatzi kaddish*/short kaddish divides
parts of the service from each other. *Kaddish derabanan*/the sages' kaddish
marks the end of study. *Kaddish titkabal*/kaddish for completion of prayer
follows the recitation of the Amidah, the central prayer of the liturgy.

D.A.T.

Bless THE INFINITE, the blessed One!
Blessed is THE INFINITE, the blessed One, now and forever.

ASHER BIDVARO / GOD IN NATURE

TRADITIONAL VERSION

Blessed are you, ETERNAL ONE our God, sovereign of all worlds, by whose word the evenings fall. In wisdom you open heaven's gates. With divine discernment you make seasons change, causing the times to come and go, and ordering the stars on their appointed paths through heaven's dome, all according to your will. Creator of the day and night, you roll back light before the dark, and dark before the light. ↵

COMMENTARY. This is the time when one day ends and another begins, but the moment of transition is imperceptible. So too Rosh Hashanah begins as the borders of the old and new years touch. What we accomplished in the year that is ending blends into the year that begins; what we hope for in the year that is starting illuminates what we must leave behind.   R.H.

COMMENTARY. Much as Jews are immersed in history, we also live in the cycles of time. The light of the fading day rolls away, and with the evening a new day is born. So too do the seasons roll by, bringing the green of spring and the flowering and warmth of summer. Now as the cooler, shorter days of autumn come upon us, the old year fades, and a new year begins. In these cycles we feel the inexorable passage of time, looking through the growing darkness to brighter days ahead, through the coolness to new flowering and rebirth. As the year cycles, we weigh the progress in our lives, in our communities, in human history.

We struggle with the light and the dark within ourselves, hoping to bring more light into the new year.   D.A.T.

בָּרְכוּ אֶת יהוה הַמְבֹרָךְ:
בָּרוּךְ יהוה הַמְבֹרָךְ לְעוֹלָם וָעֶד:

Barehu et adonay hamvorah.
Baruh adonay hamvorah le'olam va'ed.

אֲשֶׁר בִּדְבָרוֹ

בָּרוּךְ אַתָּה יהוה אֱלֹהֵינוּ מֶלֶךְ הָעוֹלָם אֲשֶׁר בִּדְבָרוֹ מַעֲרִיב עֲרָבִים
בְּחָכְמָה פּוֹתֵחַ שְׁעָרִים וּבִתְבוּנָה מְשַׁנֶּה עִתִּים וּמַחֲלִיף אֶת הַזְּמַנִּים
וּמְסַדֵּר אֶת־הַכּוֹכָבִים בְּמִשְׁמְרוֹתֵיהֶם בָּרָקִיעַ כִּרְצוֹנוֹ: בּוֹרֵא יוֹם
וָלַיְלָה גּוֹלֵל אוֹר מִפְּנֵי חֹשֶׁךְ וְחֹשֶׁךְ מִפְּנֵי אוֹר: ←

COMMENTARY. The two *berahot* that precede the Shema set the stage for its evening recitation. The first *berahah* praises God for the wonders of creation that are visible at twilight: the shifting patterns of the stars, the rhythm of the seasons, the regular passage from day to night. All of these are a nightly reminder of the unchanging plan of creation.

The second *berahah* praises God, whose instruction is a special token of love for Israel. Israel responds by meditating upon God's teaching "day and night," "when we lie down and when we rise." This phrasing recalls the preceding *berahah*, adding Israel's study of Torah to the natural order: The sun sets, the stars shine, and Israel studies—as regularly as day and night. The phrase "when we lie down and when we rise" anticipates the Shema, which follows. This interplay between the *berahot* and the Shema suggests that the Shema is Israel's morning and evening Torah study. At the same time, it is Israel's declaration of the oneness of the power that makes for the natural order and for learning, for creation and human creativity.   S.S.

Please look, and answer me, FORGIVING ONE, my God,
　　please give light to my eyes, lest I should sleep
　　　　the sleep of death,
for even darkness is not dark for you,
　　and nighttime shines like light,
　　　　and darkness and the light are one.
So now, our God, please listen to your servants' prayer,
　　and to our supplication.
Cause your face to shine upon your holy place,
　　which now lies desolate.
　　　　Act for your sake!
Send forth your light, and your truth,
　　and let them be my guide,
and let them bring me to your holy mountain,
　　to the places where your presence dwells,
for with you is the fount of life,
　　in your light do we behold the light. ↵

COMMENTARY. In speaking of *your holy place, which now lies desolate*, this prayer alludes to the ruins of the ancient Temple, whose famous Western Wall (the sole part of the original structure that still stands) has remained a place of pilgrimage for Jews through the centuries, even to our own day. Even among Jews who do not hope for a literal restoration of Solomon's Temple, this site is an important link to biblical Israel—a symbol of its ancient sovereignty and independence, as well as the sovereignty and independence of the present-day State of Israel. It is also as a *ruin* that the site speaks most meaningfully as a reminder of the all-too-frequent eclipse of Jewry in the world, and so a memorial to the many who have suffered or died for being Jewish.　　　　　　　　　　　　　J.R.

הַבִּיטָה עֲנֵנִי יהוה אֱלֹהָי הָאִירָה עֵינַי פֶּן־אִישַׁן הַמָּוֶת:

גַּם־חֹשֶׁךְ לֹא־יַחְשִׁיךְ מִמֶּךָ וְלַיְלָה כַּיּוֹם יָאִיר כַּחֲשֵׁיכָה כָּאוֹרָה:

וְעַתָּה שְׁמַע אֱלֹהֵינוּ אֶל־תְּפִלַּת עַבְדְּךָ וְאֶל־תַּחֲנוּנָיו

וְהָאֵר פָּנֶיךָ עַל־מִקְדָּשְׁךָ הַשָּׁמֵם לְמַעַן אֲדֹנָי:

שְׁלַח־אוֹרְךָ וַאֲמִתְּךָ הֵמָּה יַנְחוּנִי

יְבִיאוּנִי אֶל־הַר־קָדְשְׁךָ וְאֶל־מִשְׁכְּנוֹתֶיךָ:

כִּי־עִמְּךָ מְקוֹר חַיִּים בְּאוֹרְךָ נִרְאֶה־אוֹר: ←

Ki imeḥa mekor ḥayim be'orḥa nireh or.

DERASH. Light is the stuff of creation. "And God said: 'Let there be light.'" The great spiritual paradox consists of this: to our eyes, the world contains both darkness and light. Indeed, the ultimate light of creation casts ever shifting shadows that appear as antagonistic forces, shades, and grades of light and darkness. Oftentimes we cannot tell the shadows from true darkness. But our ability to choose is the light that guides our steps through life. We seek God's light, the light of creation that transcends the conditions of the moment and partakes of eternity. By consciously choosing love, justice and truth, we draw sustenance from that light and unite with the Source. S.P.W.

COMMENTARY. Within the *matbe'a shel tefilah*, the required outline of the prayer service, lies considerable flexibility. The thematic outline and order of the prayers remain unchanged throughout the year. Yet we need to give voice to the themes of the day, season, and year. For almost two thousand years, poets have written insertions to accomplish this. In the Creation section of the service that immediately follows *Bareḥu* / the call to prayer, these additions are known as *yotzerot* in the morning service and *ma'arevot* in the evening service, reflecting the names of these sections taken from their concluding *beraḥot* / blessings. Thus, the added prayers here conform to a practice hallowed by tradition. D.A.T.

For you illuminate the lamps of THE ETERNAL,
   you, my God, shine brightly on my darkness.
The lamp of THE CREATOR is the breath of human life,
   it searches all the recesses within.
For you have saved my soul from death,
   truly, my foot from stumbling,
that I might walk about amid God's presence
   in the light of life.
Yes, all of these are things that God can do
   for someone, even two times, even three,
to bring one's spirit back from lowest depths,
   into light, the light of life.

Psalms 13:4; 139:12; Daniel 9:17; Psalms 43:3; 36:10; 18:29; Proverbs 20:27; Psalms 56:14; Job 33:29-30

You make day pass away and bring on night, dividing between
day and night. The Leader of the Throngs of Heaven is your
name! Living and enduring God, rule over us, now and always.
Blessed are you, ALMIGHTY ONE, who makes the evening fall.

KAVANAH. When we deny the existence of death, we are pretending our
lives are something other than what they are. Living a full life—
acknowledging and relishing all of who we are—requires both the
recognition that the spark of life within each of us transcends us, and that
the time will come when our bodies return to the dust. Loving and caring,
struggling and losing, building and celebrating, nurturing and mourning,
allow us to transcend our deaths while we live, but not to escape death. In
our time, escaping death has become an overwhelming preoccupation of
medical technology and legal intervention. Let me live the fullness of my
days, and when my time comes, die with dignity.   D.A.T.

אֱלֹהַי יַגִּיהַּ חָשְׁכִּי: כִּי־אַתָּה תָּאִיר נֵרִי יהוה
חֹפֵשׂ כָּל־חַדְרֵי־בָטֶן: נֵר יהוה נִשְׁמַת אָדָם
הֲלֹא רַגְלַי מִדֶּחִי כִּי הִצַּלְתָּ נַפְשִׁי מִמָּוֶת
בְּאוֹר הַחַיִּים: לְהִתְהַלֵּךְ לִפְנֵי אֱלֹהִים
פַּעֲמַיִם שָׁלוֹשׁ עִם־גָּבֶר: הֶן־כָּל־אֵלֶּה יִפְעַל־אֵל
לְאוֹר בְּאוֹר הַחַיִּים: לְהָשִׁיב נַפְשׁוֹ מִנִּי־שָׁחַת

* וּמַעֲבִיר יוֹם וּמֵבִיא לָיְלָה וּמַבְדִּיל בֵּין יוֹם וּבֵין לָיְלָה יהוה
צְבָאוֹת שְׁמוֹ: אֵל חַי וְקַיָּם תָּמִיד יִמְלֹךְ עָלֵינוּ לְעוֹלָם וָעֶד: בָּרוּךְ
אַתָּה יהוה הַמַּעֲרִיב עֲרָבִים:

El ḥay vekayam tamid yimloḥ aleynu le'olam va'ed.
Baruḥ atah adonay hama'ariv aravim.

ALTERNATIVE VERSIONS: ASHER BIDVARO

It Is Not You Alone Who Pray

It is not you alone who pray,
or we, or those others;
all things pray, and all things
pour forth their souls.

The heavens pray, the earth prays,
every creature and every living thing.
In all life, there is longing.

Creation is itself but a longing,
a kind of prayer to the Almighty.
What are the clouds,
the rising and the setting
of the sun,
the soft radiance of the moon
and the gentleness of the night?

What are the flashes of the human mind
and the storms of the human heart?
They are all prayers—
the outpouring of
boundless longing for God.

Michah Joseph Berdyczewski

∾

God The Life of Nature

Our ancestors acclaimed the God
Whose handiwork they read
In the mysterious heavens above,
And in the varied scene of earth below,
In the orderly march of days and nights,
Of seasons and years,
And in the checkered fate of humankind.

Night reveals the limitless caverns of space,
Hidden by the light of day,
And unfolds horizonless vistas
Far beyond imagination's ken.
The mind is staggered,
Yet soon regains its poise,
And peering through the boundless dark,
Orients itself anew
By the light of distant suns
Shrunk to glittering sparks.
The soul is faint,
Yet soon revives,
And learns to spell once more the name of God
Across the newly visioned firmament.

  Lift your eyes, look up;
  Who made these stars?

God is the oneness
That spans the fathomless deeps of space
And the measureless eons of time,
Binding them together in deed,
As we do in thought. ⮐

God is the sameness
In the elemental substance of stars and planets,
Of this our earthly abode
And of all that it holds.

God is the unity
Of all that is,
The uniformity of all that moves,
The rhythm of all things
And the nature of their interaction.

God is the mystery of life,
Enkindling inert matter
With inner drive and purpose.

God is the creative flame
That transfigures lifeless substance,
Leaping into ever higher realms of being,
Brightening into the radiant glow of feeling,
Till it runs into the white fire of thought.

And though no sign of living things
Breaks the eternal silence of the spheres,
We cannot deem this earth,
This tiny speck in the infinitude,
Alone instinct with God.

By that token
Which unites the worlds in bonds of matter
Are all the worlds bound
In the bond of Life.

God is in the faith
By which we overcome
The fear of loneliness, of helplessness,
Of failure and of death. ↰

God is in the hope
Which, like a shaft of light,
Cleaves the dark abysms
Of sin, of suffering, and of despair.

God is in the love
Which creates, protects, forgives.

It is God's spirit
That broods upon the chaos we have wrought,
Disturbing its static wrongs,
And stirring into life the formless beginnings
Of the new and better world.

Mordecai M. Kaplan (Adapted)

AHAVAT OLAM / GOD'S LOVE IN TORAH

TRADITIONAL VERSION

With everlasting love, you love the house of Israel. Torah and mitzvot, laws and justice you have taught us. And so, DEAR ONE our God, when we lie down and when we rise, we reflect upon your laws; we take pleasure in your Torah's words and your mitzvot, now and always. Truly, they are our life, our length of days. On them we meditate by day and night. ↩

KAVANAH. The שמע/Shema is wrapped in אהבה/ahavah/love. The blessing preceding the Shema concludes, "who loves your people Israel." This prayer begins "ואהבת/ve'ahavta, And you must love יהוה!" First you are loved, then you respond with love. Love is central to Jewish life. Love means commitment and limitations—Torah and mitzvot. That is so both in our relationships with each other and in our relationship with God.

L.W.K.

אַהֲבַת עוֹלָם בֵּית יִשְׂרָאֵל עַמְּךָ אָהָבְתָּ: תּוֹרָה וּמִצְוֹת חֻקִּים
וּמִשְׁפָּטִים אוֹתָנוּ לִמַּדְתָּ: עַל כֵּן יהוה אֱלֹהֵינוּ בְּשָׁכְבֵּנוּ וּבְקוּמֵנוּ
נָשִׂיחַ בְּחֻקֶּיךָ וְנִשְׂמַח בְּדִבְרֵי תוֹרָתֶךָ וּבְמִצְוֹתֶיךָ לְעוֹלָם וָעֶד כִּי הֵם
חַיֵּינוּ וְאֹרֶךְ יָמֵינוּ וּבָהֶם נֶהְגֶּה יוֹמָם וָלָיְלָה: ←

Ahavat olam beyt yisra'el ameḥa aḥavta.
Torah umitzvot ḥukim umishpatim otanu limadeta.
Al ken adonay eloheynu beshoḥbenu uvkumenu nasi'aḥ
    beḥukeḥa
venismaḥ bedivrey torateḥa uvmitzvoteḥa le'olam va'ed
ki hem ḥayeynu ve'oreḥ yameynu
uvahem nehgeh yomam valaylah.

THE ETERNAL is my light and help;
whom, then, should I fear?
Bless, O my soul, THE BOUNTIFUL!
ETERNAL ONE my God, magnificent are you;
in glory and in splendor you are clothed!
You spread your light out like a garment,
stretching out the heavens like exquisite drapery,
your word a lamp before my feet,
your light establishing my path.
The teachings of THE FOUNT OF WISDOM are just,
they make the heart rejoice.
The mitzvah of THE LAWGIVER is pure,
it gives light to the eyes.
For truly, mitzvah is a lamp,
and Torah, light.

Psalms 27:1; 104:1-2; 119:105; 19:9; Proverbs 6:23

Your love will never depart from us as long as worlds endure.
Blessed are you, BELOVED ONE, who loves your people Israel.

לעולמים/as long as worlds endure. According to rabbinic tradition, creation is not a one-time event; God must constantly create in order to sustain the world. On Rosh Hashanah we celebrate the rebirth of the world, marvel at God's constancy manifested in creation, and anticipate the future possibilities.　　　R.H.

יהוה אוֹרִי וְיִשְׁעִי מִמִּי אִירָא׃
בָּרֲכִי נַפְשִׁי אֶת־יהוה אֱלֹהַי גָּדַֽלְתָּ מְּאֹד
הוֹד וְהָדָר לָבָֽשְׁתָּ׃ עֹֽטֶה־אוֹר כַּשַּׂלְמָה
נוֹטֶה שָׁמַֽיִם כַּיְרִיעָה׃

נֵר־לְרַגְלִי דְבָרֶֽךָ   וְאוֹר לִנְתִיבָתִי׃
פִּקּוּדֵי יהוה יְשָׁרִים   מְשַׂמְּחֵי־לֵב
מִצְוַת יהוה בָּרָה   מְאִירַת עֵינָֽיִם׃
כִּי נֵר מִצְוָה וְתוֹרָה אוֹר׃

וְאַהֲבָתְךָ לֹא תָסוּר מִמֶּֽנּוּ לְעוֹלָמִים׃
בָּרוּךְ אַתָּה יהוה אוֹהֵב עַמּוֹ יִשְׂרָאֵל׃

Ve'ahavateḥa lo tasur mimenu le'olamim.
Baruḥ atah adonay ohev amo yisra'el.

COMMENTARY. The custom on the High Holy Days as well as on other festivals has been to expand key sections of the service by adding poetic material linking the theme of that section to the theme of the day. Michael Strassfeld followed that custom here by creating a *piyut* comprised of biblical verses. It links divine light, natural light, and the light of Torah, thereby linking the creation themes of Rosh Hashanah with the ideas of love and revelation characteristic of the blessing preceding the Shema.

D.A.T.

ואהבתך לא תסור. Our text follows the Sephardic version, in the declarative model ("Your love will never depart from us.") rather than the imperative ("Never remove your love from us!"). Divine love is unconditional. It is available to every one of us when we fashion our lives into channels to receive and share it. The Jewish people together experiences that eternal love as reflected in our love for the study of Torah—a wisdom lovingly received, shared, and passed on enriched by each generation.

A.G.

שְׁמַע יִשְׂרָאֵל יְהוָה אֱלֹהֵינוּ יְהוָה אֶחָד

SHEMA

Listen, Israel: THE ETERNAL is our God,
   THE ETERNAL ONE alone!

Blessed be the name and glory of God's realm, forever!

And you must love THE ONE, your God, with your whole heart,
with every breath, with all you have. Take these words that I
command you now to heart. Teach them intently to your
children. Speak them when you sit inside your house or walk
upon the road, when you lie down and when you rise. And bind
them as a sign upon your hand, and keep them visible before
your eyes. Inscribe them on the doorposts of your house and on
your gates. ↵

שְׁמַע ... וּבִשְׁעָרֶיךָ / Listen ... gates (Deuteronomy 6:4-9).

DERASH. The Shema is called *kabbalat ol malḥut shamayim*. We "receive
upon ourselves the yoke of the sovereignty of Heaven." To proclaim God
as ours and as one is to acknowledge fealty to the divine will—and the
Shema is a time to listen. We listen in order to discover God's will.

D.A.T.

וְאָהַבְתָּ אֵת יְהוָה / love יהוה your God. Abbaye said, "Let the love of God be
spread through your activities. If a person studies and helps others to do
so, if one's business dealings are decent and trustworthy—what do people
say? 'Happy is the one who studied Torah, and the one who teaches Torah!
Have you seen the one who studied Torah? How beautiful! What a fine
person!' Thus, the Torah says, 'You are my servant Israel; I will be
glorified by you.'" (Isaiah 49:3)   Talmud Yoma 86a

שְׁמַע יִשְׂרָאֵל יהוה אֱלֹהֵינוּ יהוה אֶחָד:

בָּרוּךְ שֵׁם כְּבוֹד מַלְכוּתוֹ לְעוֹלָם וָעֶד:

וְאָהַבְתָּ אֵת יהוה אֱלֹהֶיךָ בְּכָל־לְבָבְךָ וּבְכָל־נַפְשְׁךָ וּבְכָל־מְאֹדֶךָ: וְהָיוּ הַדְּבָרִים הָאֵלֶּה אֲשֶׁר אָנֹכִי מְצַוְּךָ הַיּוֹם עַל־לְבָבֶךָ: וְשִׁנַּנְתָּם לְבָנֶיךָ וְדִבַּרְתָּ בָּם בְּשִׁבְתְּךָ בְּבֵיתֶךָ וּבְלֶכְתְּךָ בַדֶּרֶךְ וּבְשָׁכְבְּךָ וּבְקוּמֶךָ: וּקְשַׁרְתָּם לְאוֹת עַל־יָדֶךָ וְהָיוּ לְטֹטָפֹת בֵּין עֵינֶיךָ: וּכְתַבְתָּם עַל־מְזֻזוֹת בֵּיתֶךָ וּבִשְׁעָרֶיךָ:

Shema yisra'el adonay oheynu adonay eḥad.
Baruḥ shem kevod malḥuto le'olam va'ed.

Ve'ahavta et adonay eloheha
beḥol levaveha uveḥol nafsheha uveḥol me'odeha.
Vehayu hadevarim ha'eleh asher anoḥi metzaveha hayom al
levaveha.
Veshinantam levaneha vedibarta bam
beshivteha beveyteha uvelehteha vadereḥ uveshohbeha
uvekumeha.
Ukeshartam le'ot al yadeha vehayu letotafot beyn eyneha.
Uḥetavtam al mezuzot beyteha uvishareha.

COMMENTARY. The Shema—six words in all—bears multiple meanings. *"Shema"* can mean "hear," "listen," or "understand." *"Eḥad"* can mean "one," "unique," or "alone/only." Our translation captures the sense of fidelity to the Sovereign. But do we need to be reminded to Whom we are loyal? Do we still need to assert one God in a world that has largely heard the message of monotheism? Perhaps the issue for our generation is more the nature of Godliness: what can we identify as uniquely divine in our world and within ourselves, and how can we envision and articulate that uniqueness?   R.H.

For the second paragraph of the Shemà, read either the version below or the biblical section beginning on page 81, then continue with the third paragraph, page 83.

BIBLICAL SELECTION I

It came to pass, and will again,
that if you truly listen
to the voice of THE ETERNAL ONE, your God,
being sure to do whatever has been asked of you today,
THE ONE, your God, will make of you a model
for all nations of the earth,
and there will come upon you all these blessings,
as you listen to the call of THE ABUNDANT ONE, your God:
Blessed be you in the city,
blessed be you upon the field.
Blessed be the fruit of your womb,
the fruit of your land, the fruit of your cattle,
the calving of your oxen, and the lambing of your sheep.
Blessed be your basket and your kneading-trough.
Blessed be you when you come home,
and blessed be you when you go forth.

See, I have placed in front of you today
both life and good, both death and ill,
commanding you today to love THE BOUNDLESS ONE, your God,
to walk in ways I have ordained,
keeping the commandments, laws, and judgments,
so that you survive and multiply.
THE BOUNTIFUL, your God, will bless you
on the land you are about to enter and inherit. ↵

עליון אלהיך...ונתנך/**your God will make of you a model.** A literal translation of this phrase might render it: "Your God will raise you above all the nations of the earth," but viewed in context, with the first half of the verse demanding obedience to the divine voice and fulfillment of the mitzvot, it is clear that the intent is to separate Israel by virtue of its vocation. Thus, the translation here, "make of you a model for all nations of the earth," is a more accurate, if less literal, rendering.   D.A.T.

For the second paragraph of the Shema, read either the version below or the biblical section beginning on page 82, then continue with the third paragraph, page 84.

BIBLICAL SELECTION I

וְהָיָה אִם־שָׁמֹעַ תִּשְׁמַע בְּקוֹל יהוה אֱלֹהֶיךָ לִשְׁמֹר לַעֲשׂוֹת
אֶת־כָּל־מִצְוֹתָיו אֲשֶׁר אָנֹכִי מְצַוְּךָ הַיּוֹם וּנְתָנְךָ יהוה אֱלֹהֶיךָ עֶלְיוֹן
עַל כָּל־גּוֹיֵי הָאָרֶץ: וּבָאוּ עָלֶיךָ כָּל־הַבְּרָכוֹת הָאֵלֶּה וְהִשִּׂיגֻךָ כִּי
תִשְׁמַע בְּקוֹל יהוה אֱלֹהֶיךָ: בָּרוּךְ אַתָּה בָּעִיר וּבָרוּךְ אַתָּה בַּשָּׂדֶה:
בָּרוּךְ פְּרִי־בִטְנְךָ וּפְרִי אַדְמָתְךָ וּפְרִי בְהֶמְתֶּךָ שְׁגַר אֲלָפֶיךָ
וְעַשְׁתְּרוֹת צֹאנֶךָ: בָּרוּךְ טַנְאֲךָ וּמִשְׁאַרְתֶּךָ: בָּרוּךְ אַתָּה בְּבֹאֶךָ
וּבָרוּךְ אַתָּה בְּצֵאתֶךָ:

רְאֵה נָתַתִּי לְפָנֶיךָ הַיּוֹם אֶת־הַחַיִּים וְאֶת־הַטּוֹב וְאֶת־הַמָּוֶת
וְאֶת־הָרָע: אֲשֶׁר אָנֹכִי מְצַוְּךָ הַיּוֹם לְאַהֲבָה אֶת־יהוה אֱלֹהֶיךָ
לָלֶכֶת בִּדְרָכָיו וְלִשְׁמֹר מִצְוֹתָיו וְחֻקֹּתָיו וּמִשְׁפָּטָיו וְחָיִיתָ וְרָבִיתָ
וּבֵרַכְךָ יהוה אֱלֹהֶיךָ בָּאָרֶץ אֲשֶׁר־אַתָּה בָא־שָׁמָּה לְרִשְׁתָּהּ: ←

COMMENTARY. The traditional wording of Biblical Selection II (page 81) presents detailed bountiful or devastating consequences of Israel's collective relationship to the mitzvot. That biblical section (Deuteronomy 11:13-21) offers a supernatural theology that many contemporary Jews find difficult. The biblical section on this page (Deuteronomy 28:1-6, 30:15-19) was included in the 1945 Reconstructionist siddur. It begins by encouraging observance in the same language, but concentrates on the positive ways in which observance of mitzvot focuses our attention on God's presence as perceived through productivity and the pursuit of abundant life.   S.S.

KAVANAH. The doctrine of the unity of God calls for the integration of all life's purposes into a consistent pattern of thought and conduct.   M.M.K.

But if your heart should turn away,
and you not heed, and go astray,
and you submit to other gods and serve them,
I declare to you today that you shall be
destroyed completely; you shall not live out
a great expanse of days upon the land
that you now cross the Jordan to possess.
I call as witnesses concerning you
both heaven and earth, both life and death,
that I have placed in front of you
a blessing and a curse.
Choose life, that you may live,
you and your seed!

Continue with page 83.

COMMENTARY. The statement of God's oneness unifies not only the context of the Shema but the text as well—three scriptural paragraphs specified in the Mishnah (a second-century codification of Jewish law). The powerful declaration of God's unity fuses the responsibility to love God and to study God's teachings (first paragraph) with the lesson that their fulfillment confirms God's presence (second and third paragraphs). Hence, the unity of God as idea and presence.   S.S.

וְאִם־יִפְנֶה לְבָבְךָ וְלֹא תִשְׁמָע וְנִדַּחְתָּ וְהִשְׁתַּחֲוִיתָ לֵאלֹהִים אֲחֵרִים
וַעֲבַדְתָּם: הִגַּדְתִּי לָכֶם הַיּוֹם כִּי אָבֹד תֹּאבֵדוּן לֹא־תַאֲרִיכֻן יָמִים
עַל־הָאֲדָמָה אֲשֶׁר אַתָּה עֹבֵר אֶת־הַיַּרְדֵּן לָבֹא שָׁמָּה לְרִשְׁתָּהּ:
הַעִדֹתִי בָכֶם הַיּוֹם אֶת־הַשָּׁמַיִם וְאֶת־הָאָרֶץ הַחַיִּים וְהַמָּוֶת נָתַתִּי
לְפָנֶיךָ הַבְּרָכָה וְהַקְּלָלָה וּבָחַרְתָּ בַּחַיִּים לְמַעַן תִּחְיֶה אַתָּה וְזַרְעֶךָ:

Continue with וַיֹּאמֶר, page 84.

DERASH. God is the assumption that there is enough in the world to meet
our needs but not to meet our greed for power and pleasure.

M.M.K. (Adapted)

In the handwritten scroll of the Torah
The word "Shema" of "Shema Yisra'el"
Ends with an oversized *ayin*,
And the word "Ehad"
Ends with an oversized *dalet*.
Taken together
These two letters
Spell "Ed," meaning "witness."
> Whenever we recite the Shema
> We bear witness
> To our awareness
> Of God's presence.

H.M.

BIBLICAL SELECTION II

And if you truly listen to my bidding, as I bid you now—loving THE FOUNT OF LIFE, your God, and serving God with all your heart, with every breath—then I will give you rain upon your land in its appointed time, the early rain and later rain, so you may gather in your corn, your wine and oil. And I will give you grass upon your field to feed your animals, and you will eat and be content. Beware, then, lest your heart be led astray, and you go off and worship other gods, and you submit to them, so that the anger of THE MIGHTY ONE should burn against you, and seal up the heavens so no rain would fall, so that the ground would not give forth her produce, and you be forced to leave the good land I am giving you.

So place these words upon your heart, into your lifebreath. Bind them as a sign upon your hand, and let them rest before your eyes. Teach them to your children, speaking of them when you sit at home, and when you walk upon the road, when you lie down, and when you rise. Inscribe them on the doorposts of your house and on your gates—so that your days and your children's days be many on the land THE FAITHFUL ONE promised to give your ancestors, as long as heaven rests above the earth.

Continue on page 83.

לבבך/*levaveha*/your heart. The לב/*lev*/heart was seen as the source of emotions and intellect. Feelings and reason are complementary partners, not conflicting parts, of the human psyche. The double ב of לבב teaches that a love of God must contain all dualities (e.g., the good and bad in you). L.W.K.

DERASH. This warning against idolatry has ecological significance. If we continue to pollute the environment—and thus display contempt for the integrity of God's creation—pure rain will cease to fall, and the ground will cease to give forth its produce. M.L.

וְהָיָ֗ה אִם־שָׁמֹ֤עַ תִּשְׁמְעוּ֙ אֶל־מִצְוֺתַ֔י אֲשֶׁ֧ר אָנֹכִ֛י מְצַוֶּ֥ה אֶתְכֶ֖ם
הַיּ֑וֹם לְאַהֲבָ֞ה אֶת־יהו֤ה אֱלֹֽהֵיכֶם֙ וּלְעׇבְד֔וֹ בְּכׇל־לְבַבְכֶ֖ם וּבְכׇל־
נַפְשְׁכֶֽם: וְנָתַתִּ֧י מְטַֽר־אַרְצְכֶ֛ם בְּעִתּ֖וֹ יוֹרֶ֣ה וּמַלְק֑וֹשׁ וְאָסַפְתָּ֣ דְגָנֶ֔ךָ
וְתִירֹֽשְׁךָ֖ וְיִצְהָרֶֽךָ: וְנָתַתִּ֛י עֵ֥שֶׂב בְּשָׂדְךָ֖ לִבְהֶמְתֶּ֑ךָ וְאָכַלְתָּ֖ וְשָׂבָֽעְתָּ:
הִשָּׁמְר֣וּ לָכֶ֔ם פֶּ֥ן יִפְתֶּ֖ה לְבַבְכֶ֑ם וְסַרְתֶּ֗ם וַעֲבַדְתֶּם֙ אֱלֹהִ֣ים אֲחֵרִ֔ים
וְהִשְׁתַּחֲוִיתֶ֖ם לָהֶֽם: וְחָרָ֨ה אַף־יהו֜ה בָּכֶ֗ם וְעָצַ֤ר אֶת־הַשָּׁמַ֙יִם֙
וְלֹֽא־יִהְיֶ֣ה מָטָ֔ר וְהָ֣אֲדָמָ֔ה לֹ֥א תִתֵּ֖ן אֶת־יְבוּלָ֑הּ וַאֲבַדְתֶּ֣ם מְהֵרָ֗ה
מֵעַל֙ הָאָ֣רֶץ הַטֹּבָ֔ה אֲשֶׁ֥ר יהו֖ה נֹתֵ֥ן לָכֶֽם:

וְשַׂמְתֶּם֙ אֶת־דְּבָרַ֣י אֵ֔לֶּה עַל־לְבַבְכֶ֖ם וְעַֽל־נַפְשְׁכֶ֑ם וּקְשַׁרְתֶּ֨ם אֹתָ֤ם
לְאוֹת֙ עַל־יֶדְכֶ֔ם וְהָי֥וּ לְטוֹטָפֹ֖ת בֵּ֣ין עֵינֵיכֶֽם: וְלִמַּדְתֶּ֥ם אֹתָ֛ם
אֶת־בְּנֵיכֶ֖ם לְדַבֵּ֣ר בָּ֑ם בְּשִׁבְתְּךָ֤ בְּבֵיתֶ֙ךָ֙ וּבְלֶכְתְּךָ֣ בַדֶּ֔רֶךְ וּֽבְשׇׁכְבְּךָ֖
וּבְקוּמֶֽךָ: וּכְתַבְתָּ֛ם עַל־מְזוּז֥וֹת בֵּיתֶ֖ךָ וּבִשְׁעָרֶֽיךָ: לְמַ֨עַן יִרְבּ֤וּ יְמֵיכֶם֙
וִימֵ֣י בְנֵיכֶ֔ם עַ֚ל הָֽאֲדָמָ֔ה אֲשֶׁ֨ר נִשְׁבַּ֧ע יהו֛ה לַאֲבֹֽתֵיכֶ֖ם לָתֵ֣ת לָהֶ֑ם
כִּימֵ֥י הַשָּׁמַ֖יִם עַל־הָאָֽרֶץ: ←—

Continue on page 84.

DERASH. The traditional second paragraph of the Shema (Deuteronomy
11:13-21) offers an account of the natural process by which the blessings
of God themselves lead to pride, self-satisfaction, and ingratitude on the
part of those who receive them. Ironically, the more we are blessed, so
seems, the less grateful and aware of blessing we become. It is when we
are most sated, Scripture warns us, that we should be most careful.
Fullness can lead to ingratitude, and ingratitude to idolatry—primarily in
the form of worship of our own accomplishments. Then, indeed, "the
heavens might close up and no rain fall." For once we begin to worship
our achievements, we will never find satisfaction.   A.G.

THE BOUNDLESS ONE told Moses: Speak to the Israelites—tell them to make themselves *tzitzit* upon the corners of their clothes, throughout their generations. Have them place upon the corner *tzitzit* a twine of royal blue. This is your *tzitzit*. Look at it and remember all the mitzvot of the ETERNAL ONE. And do them, so you won't go off after the lusts of your heart or after what catches your eye, so that you remember to do all my mitzvot and be holy for your God. I am THE FAITHFUL ONE, your God, who brought you from Mitzrayim to be for you a God. I am THE INFINITE, your God.

ויאמר יהוה . . . אלהיכם / THE BOUNDLESS ONE . . . God (Numbers 15:37-41).

COMMENTARY. In the ancient Near East, free people wore fringes, or *tzitzit*, on the hems of their everyday clothes. Since only free people wore *tzitzit*, they were a form of identification. Business transactions were sealed by kissing the *tzitzit*.

The mitzvah of *tzitzit* is based on that ancient sign of freedom. The fringes remind us that we voluntarily follow the way of God, who freed us from Egyptian slavery. It is, literally, a string tied around our finger.

Today, many Jews who recite the Shema gather the four corners of their *tallitot* (prayer shawls), hold the *tzitzit*, and kiss them at each mention of the word ציצית/*tzitzit*. This custom shows that we take these words seriously, like a legal contract.   L.W.K.

מצרים/*Mitzrayim* was the escaping Hebrews', not the Egyptians', name for the land of Egypt: perhaps a slave-term, and probably not of Semitic origin, it has associations with the root צרר, to be in distress, constricted, in anguish, or in dire straits. This word powerfully evokes the choking oppression of slavery. As the psalmist wrote: מן המצר קראתי יה/From the depths I called to Yah.   M.P.

Transliteration can be found on page 312.

וַיֹּאמֶר יְהוָה אֶל־מֹשֶׁה לֵּאמֹר: דַּבֵּר אֶל־בְּנֵי יִשְׂרָאֵל וְאָמַרְתָּ
אֲלֵהֶם וְעָשׂוּ לָהֶם צִיצִת עַל־כַּנְפֵי בִגְדֵיהֶם לְדֹרֹתָם וְנָתְנוּ
עַל־צִיצִת הַכָּנָף פְּתִיל תְּכֵלֶת: וְהָיָה לָכֶם לְצִיצִת וּרְאִיתֶם אֹתוֹ
וּזְכַרְתֶּם אֶת־כָּל־מִצְוֺת יְהוָה וַעֲשִׂיתֶם אֹתָם וְלֹא תָתוּרוּ אַחֲרֵי
לְבַבְכֶם וְאַחֲרֵי עֵינֵיכֶם אֲשֶׁר־אַתֶּם זֹנִים אַחֲרֵיהֶם: לְמַעַן תִּזְכְּרוּ
וַעֲשִׂיתֶם אֶת־כָּל־מִצְוֺתָי וִהְיִיתֶם קְדֹשִׁים לֵאלֹהֵיכֶם: אֲנִי יְהוָה
אֱלֹהֵיכֶם אֲשֶׁר הוֹצֵאתִי אֶתְכֶם מֵאֶרֶץ מִצְרַיִם לִהְיוֹת לָכֶם
לֵאלֹהִים אֲנִי יְהוָה אֱלֹהֵיכֶם: **אֱמֶת:**

אחרי עיניכם / after what catches your eye, that is, the physical and material
temptations you see. The Baal Shem Tov had a method for dealing with
distractions, especially sexual ones. If you can't get the person out of your
thoughts, remember that beauty is a reflection of God's image. Redirect
that energy towards God. L.W.K.

תכלת is Sidon blue, which is obtained from a shellfish. Sidon or royal blue
is associated with majesty—even today the British queen wears a blue sash.
The Jews were so oppressed at the time of Bar Kohba that indigo, a vegetable dye, replaced Sidon blue on their *tzitzit*. The Romans banned the
blue fringe because of its symbolism. During the nineteenth century the
Radziner *hasidim* reintroduced its use. Now other Jews have also begun to
use it. The long *tehelet* thread intertwined with short white ones is a
complex and powerful image that hints at the interplay between majesty
and subject within our own hearts. E.M.

EMET VE'EMUNAH / REDEMPTION

Our faith and truth rest on all this, which is binding upon us:
That THE BOUNDLESS ONE alone is our divinity
and that no divinity exists but One;
that we are Israel, community of God;
that it is God who saves us from the hand
of governments, the very palm of tyrants;
who enacts great deeds without measure,
and wondrous deeds beyond all count;
who puts our souls amid the living,
and who keeps our feet from giving way;
who breaks apart the schemes of those who hate us,
confounds the thoughts of any bearing us ill-will;
that it is God who made miracles for us in Egypt,
signs and wonders in Ham's children's land.
From one generation to the next, God is our guarantor,
and even on a day that turned to night,
God stayed with us when death's deep shadow fell.
And even in our age of orphans and survivors,
God's loving acts have not abandoned us,
and God has brought together our scattered kin
from the distant corners of the earth. ﬩

אמת ואמונה / *Emet Ve'emunah*. The blessing immediately following the Shema
deals with the theme of divine redemption. The present text, a rewritten
version, includes references to the Holocaust, from which there was no
redemption, and the return to Zion, a fulfillment of Israel's ancient dream.
The same divine spirit that gave Israel the courage to seek freedom from
Egypt in ancient times inspired those who fought for Israel's freedom in
our own day. At the same time, this version omits those portions of the
text that glory in the enemy's fall or see in God a force for vengeance. All
humans are God's beloved children, as were the Egyptians who drowned
at the sea.   A.G.

אֱמֶת וֶאֱמוּנָה

אֱמֶת. וֶאֱמוּנָה כָּל־זֹאת וְקַיָּם עָלֵינוּ
כִּי הוּא יהוה אֱלֹהֵינוּ וְאֵין זוּלָתוֹ
וַאֲנַחְנוּ יִשְׂרָאֵל עַמּוֹ:
הַפּוֹדֵנוּ מִיַּד מְלָכִים
הַגּוֹאֲלֵנוּ מִכַּף עָרִיצִים
הָעוֹשֶׂה גְדוֹלוֹת אֵין חֵקֶר
וְנִפְלָאוֹת אֵין מִסְפָּר:
הַשָּׂם נַפְשֵׁנוּ בַּחַיִּים
וְלֹא נָתַן לַמּוֹט רַגְלֵנוּ:
הַמֵּפֵר עֲצַת אוֹיְבֵינוּ
וְהַמְקַלְקֵל מַחְשְׁבוֹת שׂוֹנְאֵינוּ:
הָעוֹשֶׂה לָּנוּ נִסִּים בְּמִצְרַיִם
אוֹתוֹת וּמוֹפְתִים בְּאַדְמַת בְּנֵי חָם:
מִדּוֹר לְדוֹר הוּא גוֹאֲלֵנוּ:
וּבַיּוֹם שֶׁהָפַךְ לְלַיְלָה
עִמָּנוּ הָיָה בְּגֵיא צַלְמָוֶת:
גַּם בְּדוֹר יְתוֹמִים
לֹא עֲזָבוּנוּ חֲסָדָיו
וַיְקַבֵּץ נִדָּחֵינוּ מִקְצוֹת תֵּבֵל: ←

KAVANAH. What are miracles? The blooming of a flower, the hatching of an egg, indeed every creative act in nature, is a miracle. Moments in history that move us toward freedom, goodness and truth feel like miracles to me. In recognizing these moments, I feel the world's unity and goodness calling me toward my highest self.   D.A.T.

As then, so now,
God brings the people Israel forth
from every place of menace, to a lasting freedom.

And the pathway of the just is like the light of dawn,
growing lighter steadily until the day is full.
And light is planted for the righteous like a seed,
and joy for those upright of heart.
Rejoice, you righteous, in THE OMNIPRESENT,
be thankful for the traces of God's holiness!
A people walking in the darkness
have beheld a wondrous light.
Those dwelling in a land of gloomy shadows
find the light of dawn upon them.
[When plague of darkness fell on Egypt,]
no one could behold another person,
none could go forth from their house, none could go forth
    for three days
but all the Israelites had light
wherever they were dwelling.
Arise and shine, for truly light has dawned for you,
the glory of THE OMNIPRESENT shines upon you.
House of Jacob, come, let us go forth
amid the light of THE ETERNAL ONE!

God is the one who brought the Israelites
through a divided Sea of Reeds.
There, they beheld divine might;
they praised and thanked the Name,
and willingly accepted for themselves
God's rule. ↰

כְּאָז גַּם עַתָּה
מוֹצִיא אֶת עַמּוֹ יִשְׂרָאֵל
מִכַּף כָּל אוֹיְבָיו
לְחֵרוּת עוֹלָם:

וְאֹרַח צַדִּיקִים כְּאוֹר נֹגַהּ   הוֹלֵךְ וָאוֹר עַד־נְכוֹן הַיּוֹם:
אוֹר זָרֻעַ לַצַּדִּיק   וּלְיִשְׁרֵי־לֵב שִׂמְחָה:
שִׂמְחוּ צַדִּיקִים בַּיהוה   וְהוֹדוּ לְזֵכֶר קָדְשׁוֹ:
הָעָם הַהֹלְכִים בַּחֹשֶׁךְ   רָאוּ אוֹר גָּדוֹל
יֹשְׁבֵי בְּאֶרֶץ צַלְמָוֶת   אוֹר נָגַהּ עֲלֵיהֶם:
לֹא־רָאוּ אִישׁ אֶת־אָחִיו   וְלֹא־קָמוּ אִישׁ מִתַּחְתָּיו

שְׁלֹשֶׁת יָמִים

וּלְכָל־בְּנֵי יִשְׂרָאֵל   הָיָה אוֹר בְּמוֹשְׁבֹתָם:
קוּמִי אוֹרִי כִּי בָא אוֹרֵךְ   וּכְבוֹד יהוה עָלַיִךְ זָרַח:
בֵּית יַעֲקֹב לְכוּ וְנֵלְכָה   בְּאוֹר יהוה:

הַמַּעֲבִיר בָּנָיו בֵּין גִּזְרֵי יַם סוּף
שָׁם רָאוּ אֶת גְּבוּרָתוֹ
שִׁבְּחוּ וְהוֹדוּ לִשְׁמוֹ*
וּמַלְכוּתוֹ בְרָצוֹן קִבְּלוּ עֲלֵיהֶם: ←

Or zarua latzadik uleyishrey lev simḥah.
Simeḥu tzadikim badonay vehodu lezeḥer kodsho.

ואַרח...יהוה / The pathway...ONE (Proverbs 4:18; Psalms 97:11-12; Isaiah 9:1; Exodus 10:23; Isaiah 60:1, 2:5).

COMMENTARY. The biblical verses added by Michael Strassfeld here pick up on the theme of rejoicing at the sea and link it to the rejoicing of the righteous in the light of the divine.   D.A.T.

Moses, Miriam, and all the Israelites
broke out in song, abundant in their joy,
and, all as one, they said:

"Who among the mighty can compare
to you, WISE ONE?
    Who can compare to you,
        adorned in holiness,
            awesome in praises,
                acting wondrously!"

Your children saw you in your majesty,
splitting the sea in front of Moses.
"This is my God!" they cried, and said:

"THE HOLY ONE will reign forever!"

And it was said:

"Yes, THE REDEEMING ONE has rescued Jacob,
    saved him from a power stronger than his own!"

Blessed are you, THE GUARDIAN, Israel's redeeming power!

COMMENTARY. Two beautiful *berahot* complete the liturgical framework of
the Shema in the evening service. The first of these is called *Ge'ulah*—
"Redemption." Recalling the Exodus from Egypt, it thematically echoes
the third paragraph of the Shema. Moreover, it identifies the sovereign
God, named in the Shema's credo, as the power that freed Israel from
slavery. Its vivid, here-and-now recollection of the escape from Egyptian
bondage invites and challenges Israel to claim the redemption as a personal
experience in each generation and to hear echoes of that ancient triumph
over tyranny in each modern-day struggle for freedom, in every attempt to
move toward the messianic future.   S.S.

DERASH. The passage through the Sea of Reeds was the birthing of the
Jewish people. Our first act as a people, as a community...was to sing! Not
to pray, not to enact law, not to organize...but to sing!   R.H.

מֹשֶׁה וּמִרְיָם וּבְנֵי יִשְׂרָאֵל לְךָ עָנוּ שִׁירָה בְּשִׂמְחָה רַבָּה וְאָמְרוּ כֻלָּם:
מִי־כָמֹכָה בָּאֵלִם יהוה מִי כָּמֹכָה נֶאְדָּר בַּקֹּדֶשׁ
נוֹרָא תְהִלֹּת עֹשֵׂה פֶלֶא:
מַלְכוּתְךָ רָאוּ בָנֶיךָ בּוֹקֵעַ יָם לִפְנֵי מֹשֶׁה זֶה אֵלִי עָנוּ וְאָמְרוּ:
יהוה יִמְלֹךְ לְעֹלָם וָעֶד:
וְנֶאֱמַר: כִּי פָדָה יהוה אֶת־יַעֲקֹב וּגְאָלוֹ מִיַּד חָזָק מִמֶּנּוּ: בָּרוּךְ אַתָּה
יהוה גָּאַל יִשְׂרָאֵל:

Mi ḥamoḥah ba'elim adonay. Mi kamoḥah nedar bakodesh
nora tehilot osey feleh.
Malḥuteḥa ra'u vaneḥa boke'a yam lifney mosheh.
Zeh eli anu ve'ameru. Adonay yimloḥ le'olam va'ed.
Vene'emar ki fadah adonay et ya'akov ugalo miyad ḥazak
mimenu. Baruḥ atah adonay ga'al yisra'el.

בוקע ים לפני משה. This maḥzor reinstates reference to the splitting of the
sea as a sign of God's redeeming power. The earlier Reconstructionist
prayerbook omitted that reference because of its emphasis on supernatural
intervention. As myth, however, the ancient tale of wonder underscores
the sense of daily miracle in our lives. Even those of us who cannot affirm
a God who intervenes in the natural process, and thus cannot accept the
literal meaning of the tale, can appreciate its human message. According to
the midrash, the sea did not split until one Israelite, Naḥshon ben
Aminadav, had the courage to walk upright into the water. Perhaps it was
the divine spirit in Naḥshon, rather than the magic of Moses's wand, that
caused the sea to split.   A.G.

NOTE. Biblical references include Exodus 15:11, 18 and Jeremiah 31:11.

DERASH. Rabbi Judah said: [At the sea] each tribe said to the other, "You
go into the sea first!" As they stood there bickering, Naḥshon ben
Aminadav jumped into the water. Meanwhile Moses was praying. God said
to him, "My friend is drowning—and you pray!" "What can I do?" Moses
asked. [God responded as it says in the text,] "Speak to the people of
Israel and tell them to go! Raise your staff...."   Talmud Sotah 37a

בָּרוּךְ אַתָּה יהוה הַפּוֹרֵשׂ סֻכַּת שָׁלוֹם

HASHKIVENU / DIVINE HELP

Help us to lie down, DEAR ONE, our God, in peace, and let us rise again, our sovereign, to life. Spread over us the shelter of your peace. Decree for us a worthy daily lot, and redeem us for the sake of your great name, and enfold us in the wings of your protection, for you are our redeeming guardian. Truly, a sovereign, gracious, and compassionate God are you. Guard our going forth each day for life and peace, now and always. Spread over us the shelter of your peace.

Blessed are you, COMPASSIONATE ONE, who spreads your canopy of peace over all your people Israel and over Jerusalem.

On weekdays continue on page 97. On Shabbat continue on page 95.

עָלֵינוּ וְעַל כָּל־עַמּוֹ יִשְׂרָאֵל וְעַל יְרוּשָׁלַם

הַשְׁכִּיבֵנוּ

Transliteration and commentary follow on pages 93-94.

הַשְׁכִּיבֵנוּ יְהוָה אֱלֹהֵינוּ לְשָׁלוֹם וְהַעֲמִידֵנוּ מַלְכֵּנוּ לְחַיִּים וּפְרוֹשׂ עָלֵינוּ סֻכַּת שְׁלוֹמֶךָ: וְתַקְּנֵנוּ בְּעֵצָה טוֹבָה מִלְּפָנֶיךָ וְהוֹשִׁיעֵנוּ לְמַעַן שְׁמֶךָ: וּבְצֵל כְּנָפֶיךָ תַּסְתִּירֵנוּ כִּי אֵל שׁוֹמְרֵנוּ וּמַצִּילֵנוּ אָתָּה כִּי אֵל מֶלֶךְ חַנּוּן וְרַחוּם אָתָּה: וּשְׁמֹר צֵאתֵנוּ וּבוֹאֵנוּ לְחַיִּים וּלְשָׁלוֹם מֵעַתָּה וְעַד עוֹלָם: וּפְרֹשׂ עָלֵינוּ סֻכַּת שְׁלוֹמֶךָ:

בָּרוּךְ אַתָּה יְהוָה הַפּוֹרֵשׂ סֻכַּת שָׁלוֹם עָלֵינוּ וְעַל כָּל־עַמּוֹ יִשְׂרָאֵל וְעַל יְרוּשָׁלָיִם:

On weekdays continue on page 98. On Shabbat continue on page 96.

COMMENTARY. *Hashkivenu*/Help us lie down [in peace]—is the final prescribed part of the Shema. It recalls the Shema by expressing the hope that we will "lie down...in peace" and "rise again...to life." An extension of *Emet Ve'emunah*, *Hashkivenu* joins the vivid recollection of past redemption to a prayer for present protection and future peace. By calling God "guardian" and "protector" but also "redeemer," Israel recognizes new dimensions of the power that makes for freedom. The blessing is unique to the evening service. Perhaps responding to the cold, dark uncertainty of night, we invoke God's dwelling of peace. 　　　　　　　　　　S.S.

KAVANAH. Enable us, God, to behold meaning in the chaos of life about us and purpose in the chaos of life within us. Deliver us from the sense of futility in our strivings toward the light and the truth. Give us strength to ride safely through the maelstrom of petty cares and anxieties. May we behold things in their proper proportions and see life in its wholeness and its holiness. 　　　　　　　　　　M.M.K. (Adapted)

NOTE. For our ancestors, the future of Jerusalem was not just about the future of the Jewish people. Jerusalem, in the biblical vision, will become the capital of the whole world. Praying for the peace of Jerusalem is the same as praying for the unity of all humanity and peace throughout the world. 　　　　　　　　　　D.A.T.

KAVANAH. As we enter the dark of evening, we face the unknown. Earlier, in *Asher Bidvaro* (the Creation section immediately following *Barehu*), we affirmed the power that transforms night into day and day into night. Now we call for protection from the shadows that lengthen around us— shadows of fear and guilt, the uncharted future, the ever pursuing past. We ask that the shadows of God's wings envelop us with love and mercy. The unknown night, like the unknown tomorrow, can only be met with faith in the power of infinite compassion to care for us. 　　　　　　S.P.W.

KAVANAH. Dear God, when we go to sleep at night, wrap our tired bodies in a starry blanket. All night fill us with warmth and wonder, and comfort us with peaceful thoughts. Let our brightest dreams come true in the morning, when we pray all people we meet will come near in friendship, those we love will share in our happiness, and no harm will come our way. Merciful one, we are always in your care. You are like a parent to us, and we feel that you'll keep us safe, and guard us from danger, and teach us to be caring. 　　　　　　　　　　S.D.R.

Hashkivenu adonay eloheynu leshalom veha'amidenu malkenu lehayim ufros aleynu sukkat shelomeha. Vetakenenu ve'etzah tovah milefaneha vehoshi'enu lema'an shemeha. Uvtzel kenafeha tastirenu ki el shomrenu umatzilenu atah ki el meleh hanun verahum atah. Ushmor tzeytenu uvo'enu lehayim ulshalom me'atah ve'ad olam. Ufros aleynu sukkat shelomeha. Baruh atah adonay hapores sukkat shalom aleynu ve'al kol amo yisra'el ve'al yerushalayim.

On weekdays continue on page 97. On Shabbat continue on the next page.

COMMENTARY. The version presented here follows certain Sephardic versions by deleting the series of petitions for protection. Such petition is considered inappropriate on Shabbat and holidays, times of fulfillment and appreciation for the many blessings we have. These days are themselves a sukkah of peace. We pray that real and complete peace be the lot of Israel and Jerusalem, so torn by strife in recent memory. Our tradition sees Jerusalem as the center of the world. Creation began there, according to the rabbis. So may the peace that begins there radiate forth and bless all earth's peoples. The peace of Jerusalem, the "heart of the world," is also the peace of every human heart.   A.G.

When fears multiply
And danger threatens;
When sickness comes,
When death confronts us—
It is God's blessing of shalom
That sustains us
And upholds us.

Lightening our burden,
Dispelling our worry,
Restoring our strength,
Renewing our hope—
Reviving us.   H.M.

On Friday evening add:

VESHAMERU / OBSERVING SHABBAT

Let Israel's descendants keep Shabbat, making Shabbat throughout all their generations, as an eternal bond. Between me and Israel's descendants shall it be a sign eternally. For in six days THE FASHIONER OF ALL made skies and earth, and on the seventh day God ceased and drew a breath of rest.

NOTE. The placement of *Veshameru* after *Hashkivenu* suggests an aspect of the agreement between God and Israel: God guards Israel, and Israel guards Shabbat, which is a reminder and foretaste of peace in our world.

S.S.

KAVANAH. The recitations of *Veshameru* preceding the Amidah and of *Vayehulu* following it on Friday evening are acts of witnessing. In keeping Shabbat, Israel bears testimony to the fact that ours is a created world. For us this means that divinity fills the universe. Our task is to treat all living things with respect, and so enhance the divine light in them. Only by this way of living is the testimony of Shabbat made real.

A.G.

On Friday evening add:

וְשָׁמְרוּ

וְשָׁמְרוּ בְנֵי־יִשְׂרָאֵל אֶת־הַשַּׁבָּת לַעֲשׂוֹת אֶת־הַשַּׁבָּת לְדֹרֹתָם
בְּרִית עוֹלָם: בֵּינִי וּבֵין בְּנֵי יִשְׂרָאֵל אוֹת הִיא לְעוֹלָם כִּי־שֵׁשֶׁת
יָמִים עָשָׂה יהוה אֶת־הַשָּׁמַיִם וְאֶת־הָאָרֶץ וּבַיּוֹם הַשְּׁבִיעִי שָׁבַת
וַיִּנָּפַשׁ:

Veshameru veney yisra'el et hashabbat
la'asot et hashabbat ledorotam berit olam.
Beyni uveyn beney yisra'el ot hi le'olam.
Ki sheshet yamim asah adonay et hashamayim ve'et ha'aretz
uvayom hashevi'i shavat vayinafash.

ושמרו...וינפש / Let...rest (Exodus 31:16-17).

NOTE. At this point in the service the theme of the day is recalled by quoting a biblical verse. *Veshameru*, recited here on Shabbat, reminds us of the Shabbat themes in the Amidah. This is particularly important on holidays, when the Shabbat theme is less prominent in the Amidah itself. When Shabbat and a holiday coincide, the verses for both are recited.

D.A.T.

TIKU SHOFAR /
ANNOUNCING ROSH HASHANAH

Blast piercing notes upon the shofar for the New Moon,
for the full moon, for our festive holiday.

For it is Israel's law,
a statute of the God of Jacob.

COMMENTARY. Most of the biblical contexts make it clear that the shofar
was sounded primarily to announce the beginning of the special day,
especially the new moon: "Sound on the new moon the shofar, at the
darkening of the moon, the day of our festival; for it is a statute for Israel,
a ruling of the God of Jacob" (Psalms 81:4-5). Rosh Hashanah is the
seventh, and thus a special, new moon. Two of the shofar's other
associations in the Torah make it appropriate to Rosh Hashanah. The
shofar heralds the nearing of God at the Sinai revelation (Exodus 19). On
Rosh Hashanah we turn ourselves back toward the ways of God that the
Torah teaches. In addition, the shofar is sounded on *Yom Hakippurim*, the
tenth day of the seventh month, to announce the Jubilee Year, the fiftieth
year, in which land, estates, and freedom that people had lost in the forty-
nine (7×7) preceding years will be restored: "Declare independence in the
land for all its inhabitants" (Leviticus 25:10). Rosh Hashanah promises a
new lease on life, a shot at redemption, to all those who are moved by the
sounding of the shofar to do *teshuvah*.   E.L.G.

DERASH. How can the law be both Israel's and God's? We Jews have
discovered, shaped and created our tradition. When our tradition reveals
the divinity at work within the world, it speaks both in our voice, and in
God's.   R.H.

תִּקְעוּ בַחֹדֶשׁ שׁוֹפָר בַּכֶּסֶה לְיוֹם חַגֵּנוּ:
כִּי חֹק לְיִשְׂרָאֵל הוּא מִשְׁפָּט לֵאלֹהֵי יַעֲקֹב:

Tiku vahodesh shofar bakeseh leyom hagenu
Ki hok leyisra'el hu mishpat leylohey ya'akov.

תקעו...יעקב / Blast...Jacob (Psalms 81:4-5).

DERASH. *Keseh*, the Hebrew word for "full moon," is similar to the Hebrew word for covering or hiding (*kisah*). The rabbis suggest that here, *keseh*, instead of meaning the full moon, reflects the fact that the moon is covered on Rosh Hashanah. Mystics have proposed that because Rosh Hashanah occurs at the beginning of the month, when the moon's light is obscured, the darkness of judgment can block out the divine light of mercy. The shofar sound arouses the quality of mercy and subdues judgment, thereby permitting light to shine through. Similarly, self-judgment, shame, and acts of wrongdoing can cover or cloud over our own light, while *teshuvah* and forgiveness, evoked by the sound of the shofar, can reveal our light. C.B.

COMMENTARY. On Shabbat and festivals, biblical verses introducing the theme of the day serve as a bridge between the Shema with its blessings and the Amidah. *Tiku vahodesh shofar*/Blast piercing notes upon the shofar for the New Moon announces Rosh Hashanah through its heralding of the shofar blasts, the most distinctive feature of the Rosh Hashanah liturgy. This announcement of the first day of the year captures ancient origins, sounding a challenge to contemporary complacency. D.A.T.

ḤATZI KADDISH/SHORT KADDISH

Reader: Let God's name be made great and holy in the world that was created as God willed. May God complete the holy realm in your own lifetime, in your days, and in the days of all the house of Israel, quickly and soon. And say: Amen.

Congregation: May God's great name be blessed, forever and as long as worlds endure.

Reader: May it be blessed, and praised, and glorified, and held in honor, viewed with awe, embellished, and revered; and may the blessed name of holiness be hailed, though it be higher by far than all the blessings, songs, praises and consolations that we utter in this world. And say: Amen.

COMMENTARY. Holiness is the quality or value that things or persons have when they help people to become fully human.   M.M.K. (Adapted)

COMMENTARY. During this season of the year, we struggle with images of God as judge and sovereign even as we see God as source of forgiveness and return. The repetition at this time of year of the word לעלא/higher by far reminds us on the one hand that only true change on our part can reach through the many intervening layers to reconnect us with the divine in ourselves and in our world. The liturgical repetition also reminds us how important, powerful, and redeeming that reconnection can be. "Go higher!" "Settle for nothing less!" It beckons us not to quit during the strenuous climb. True change is not easy, but saving our lives depends on it.   D.A.T.

חֲצִי קַדִּישׁ

יִתְגַּדַּל וְיִתְקַדַּשׁ שְׁמֵהּ רַבָּא בְּעָלְמָא דִּי בְרָא כִרְעוּתֵהּ וְיַמְלִיךְ
מַלְכוּתֵהּ בְּחַיֵּיכוֹן וּבְיוֹמֵיכוֹן וּבְחַיֵּי דְכָל בֵּית יִשְׂרָאֵל בַּעֲגָלָא וּבִזְמַן
קָרִיב וְאִמְרוּ אָמֵן:
יְהֵא שְׁמֵהּ רַבָּא מְבָרַךְ לְעָלַם וּלְעָלְמֵי עָלְמַיָּא:
יִתְבָּרַךְ וְיִשְׁתַּבַּח וְיִתְפָּאַר וְיִתְרוֹמַם וְיִתְנַשֵּׂא וְיִתְהַדָּר וְיִתְעַלֶּה
וְיִתְהַלָּל שְׁמֵהּ דְּקֻדְשָׁא בְּרִיךְ הוּא
לְעֵלָּא לְעֵלָּא מִכָּל בִּרְכָתָא וְשִׁירָתָא תֻּשְׁבְּחָתָא וְנֶחֱמָתָא דַּאֲמִירָן
בְּעָלְמָא וְאִמְרוּ אָמֵן:

Reader: Yitgadal veyitkadash shemey raba
be'alma divra ḥirutey veyamliḥ malḥutey
behayeyḥon uvyomeyḥon uvḥayey deḥol beyt yisra'el
ba'agala uvizman kariv ve'imru amen.

Congregation: Yehey shemey raba mevaraḥ le'alam
ulalmey almaya.

Reader: Yitbaraḥ veyishtabaḥ veyitpa'ar veyitromam
veyitnasey veyit-hadar veyitaleh veyit-halal
shemey dekudsha beriḥ hu
le'ela le'ela mikol birḥata veshirata
tushbeḥata veneḥemata da'amiran be'alma ve'imru amen.

You do not have to leave the room.
Remain standing in your place and listen.
Do not even listen, simply wait.
Do not even wait.
Be quiet, still and solitary.
The world will freely offer itself to you.
To be unmasked.
It has no choice.
It will roll in ecstasy at your feet.   Franz Kafka

Autumn

Inside me the season is autumn,
the chill is in me, you can see through me,
and I am sad, but not altogether cheerless,
and filled with humility and goodness.

But if I rage sometimes,
then I am the one whose rage is shedding my leaves,
and the simple thought comes sadly to me
that raging isn't really what is needed.

The main need is that I should be able
to see myself and the struggling, shocked world
in autumnal nakedness,
when even you, and the world, can be seen right through.

Flashes of insight are the children of silence.
It doesn't matter, if we don't rage aloud.
We must calmly cast off all mere noise
in the name of the new foliage.

Something has apparently happened to me,
and I am relying on nothing but silence,
when the leaves laying themselves one on another
inaudibly become the earth.

And you can see it all, as if from a height,
when you can shed your leaves at the right time
when without passion inner autumn
lays its airy fingers on your forehead....

Y. Yevtushenko

עלמא ולעלב

Drawn by your
love, I come
into your house

RENEW OUR DAYS

שויתי

ואני ברב חסדך
אבוא ביתך:

היום הרת עולם.

ותאמר שובו
בני־אדם:למנות
ימינו כן הוד ע ונביא
לבב חכמה:שובה
יהוה עד־מתי והנחם
על־עבדיך:שבענו
בבקר חסדך ונרננה
ונשמחה בכל־ימינו
ויהי נעם ה' עלינו

RETURN US, ETERNAL ONE!

השיבנו
יהוה
אליך

היום הרת עולם.

A sovereign on high,
Great power who
reigns, who calls to
each era, reveals
hidden things, the
purest of speech, who
discern in heaven's
spheres, who guides
constellations, and seasons, and years.

AS YOU HAVE DONE OF OLD!

ונשובה
חדש
ימינו
כקדם

היום הרת עולם:

מלך עליון
גבור כגבורות
קורא הדורות
גולה נסתרות
אמרותי טהורות
יודע ספרות
לתוצאות מזרות
לעדי־עד ימלך
מלך עליון

RENEW OUR DAYS

LET US RETURN!

השיבנו
יהוה
אליך

היום הרת עולם.

RETURN US, ETERNAL ONE!

Before you
every secret is
uncovered, the
whole multitude of
mysteries since the
world began. All is
revealed and known
before you
your watchful eye
reaches beyond all generations.

לנגדי
תמיד

יהוה

ונשובה
חדש
ימינו
כקדם

יום הרת עולם

Today the world is born

AMIDAH

The traditional Amidah follows here. Meditations begin on page 127. The Amidah is traditionally recited while standing, beginning with three short steps forward and bowing left and right, a reminder of our entry into the divine presence.

Open my lips, BELOVED ONE,
and let my mouth declare your praise.

1. AVOT VE'IMOT / ANCESTORS

Blessed are you, ANCIENT ONE, our God, God of our ancestors,

God of Abraham	God of Sarah
God of Isaac	God of Rebekah
God of Jacob	God of Rachel
	and God of Leah; ⤶

COMMENTARY. A. J. Heschel has said, "The term, 'God of Abraham, Isaac and Jacob' is semantically different from a term such as 'the God of truth, goodness and beauty.' Abraham, Isaac and Jacob do not signify ideas, principles or abstract values. Nor do they stand for teachers or thinkers, and the term is not to be understood like that of 'the God of Kant, Hegel and Schelling.' Abraham, Isaac and Jacob are not principles to be comprehended but lives to be continued. The life of one who joins the covenant of Abraham continues the life of Abraham. For the present is not apart from the past. 'Abraham is still standing before God' (Genesis 18:22). Abraham endures forever. We are Abraham, Isaac and Jacob." In this same spirit, we are also Sarah and Rebekah, Rachel and Leah.   L.W.K.

KAVANAH. The introductory words (Psalms 51:17) of the Amidah contain a paradox of divine and human power. Our ability to be whole, upright, free, and fully alive grows as we acknowledge and appreciate an infinitely higher source of power in the universe. This allows us to be receptive. By acknowledging our human vulnerability, we open our hearts to the support, compassion, and faithfulness available around us.   S.P.W.

עֲמִידָה

The traditional Amidah follows here. Meditations begin on page 127. The Amidah is traditionally recited while standing, beginning with three short steps forward and bowing left and right, a reminder of our entry into the divine presence.

אֲדֹנָי שְׂפָתַי תִּפְתָּח וּפִי יַגִּיד תְּהִלָּתֶֽךָ:

 אָבוֹת וְאִמּוֹת

בָּרוּךְ אַתָּה יהוה אֱלֹהֵֽינוּ וֵאלֹהֵי אֲבוֹתֵֽינוּ וְאִמּוֹתֵֽינוּ

אֱלֹהֵי שָׂרָה	אֱלֹהֵי אַבְרָהָם
אֱלֹהֵי רִבְקָה	אֱלֹהֵי יִצְחָק
אֱלֹהֵי רָחֵל	אֱלֹהֵי יַעֲקֹב
← וֵאלֹהֵי לֵאָה:	

COMMENTARY. Throughout the centuries the pursuit of meaningful communal prayer has led to variations in the Amidah. These variations reflect the attitudes and beliefs of different prayer communities. Changes have been introduced into this Amidah, most notably in the first two *berahot*. The first *berahah* has been expanded to include the matriarchs along with the patriarchs as exemplars of God's presence in human lives. By concentrating on examples of healing forces and life-sustaining rains, the second *berahah* acknowledges God as the power that sustains life. The traditional emphasis on God's ability to resurrect the dead has been replaced here by a celebration of God as the power that sustains all life.

S.S.

COMMENTARY. On Rosh Hashanah we celebrate renewal, but we hope to live our lives without endlessly repeating ourselves. Instead, through the process of *teshuvah*/turning, we attempt to change a bit each year. We pray that when we return to the beginning in the cycle of the year, we will stand at a higher point, our lives an ascending spiral over our years. This *shiviti* (page 102) plays on that theme of spiraling, and also hints at the double helix, another spiraling mystery of life.

B.P.T.

great, heroic, awesome God, supreme divinity,
imparting deeds of kindness, begetter of all;
mindful of the loyalty of Israel's ancestors,
bringing, with love, redemption to their children's children
for the sake of the divine name.

Remember us for life,
sovereign who wishes us to live,
and write us in the Book of Life,
for your sake, ever-living God.

Regal One, our help, salvation, and protector:
Blessed are you, KIND ONE,
the shield of Abraham and help of Sarah. ↵

COMMENTARY. Near the beginning of the Amidah, an insertion states our
heartfelt hope in facing the new year—that we should be remembered for
life. In describing God as one who desires life, we connect our hopes to
the divine purpose. Thus we can ask that our names be recorded in the
Book of Life for God's sake. But as the Amidah progresses, we move
beyond our personal needs to a grander vision encompassing the meaning
and purpose of all life.   E.M.

הָאֵל הַגָּדוֹל הַגִּבּוֹר וְהַנּוֹרָא אֵל עֶלְיוֹן גּוֹמֵל חֲסָדִים טוֹבִים וְקוֹנֵה הַכֹּל וְזוֹכֵר חַסְדֵי אָבוֹת וְאִמּוֹת וּמֵבִיא גְאֻלָּה לִבְנֵי בְנֵיהֶם לְמַעַן שְׁמוֹ בְּאַהֲבָה:

זָכְרֵנוּ לְחַיִּים מֶלֶךְ חָפֵץ בַּחַיִּים וְכָתְבֵנוּ בְּסֵפֶר הַחַיִּים לְמַעַנְךָ אֱלֹהִים חַיִּים:

מֶלֶךְ עוֹזֵר וּמוֹשִׁיעַ וּמָגֵן: בָּרוּךְ אַתָּה יהוה מָגֵן אַבְרָהָם וְעֶזְרַת שָׂרָה: ←

עזרת שרה / *ezrat sarah*. The biblical term *ezer* has two meanings, "rescue" and "be strong." It is commonly translated as "aid" or "help." It also has the sense of power and strength. In Deuteronomy 33:29, *ezer* is parallel to גאוה, majesty. Eve is described as Adam's *ezer kenegdo*, a power equal to him, a strength and majesty to match his. Thus *magen avraham* (shield of Abraham) and *ezrat sarah* (help of Sarah) are parallel images of power and protection.   R.S.A.

KAVANAH. God is experienced as עוזר / helper, every time our thought of God furnishes us an escape from the sense of frustration and supplies us with a feeling of permanence in the midst of universal flux.

M.M.K. (Adapted)

2. GEVUROT / DIVINE POWER

You are forever powerful, ALMIGHTY ONE, abundant in your saving acts. You send down the dew. In loyalty you sustain the living, nurturing the life of every living thing, upholding those who fall, healing the sick, freeing the captive, and remaining faithful to all life held dormant in the earth. Who can compare to you, almighty God, who can resemble you, the source of life and death, who makes salvation grow? Who can compare to you, source of all mercy, remembering all creatures mercifully, decreeing life! Faithful are you in giving life to every living thing. Blessed are you, THE FOUNT OF LIFE, who gives and renews life.

During Minḥah, *continue on the following page when chanting aloud. Otherwise, continue below.*

3. KEDUSHAT HASHEM / HALLOWING GOD'S NAME

Recited when praying silently:

Holy are you. Your name is holy.
And all holy beings hail you each day.

Continue on page 111.

KAVANAH. How awesome is divine creation, how splendid the unfolding of nature, how comforting the seasons' cycles—dew in the summer and wind and rain in the fall. As we acknowledge cycles—life and death, birth and renewal—we thank the Sustainer of Life and we embrace death as part of life. Consider the cycles of your own life as you enter the New Year. Consider your age and the condition of your body. What "season" are you in now at the dawn of the New Year?   L.G.B.

ב 2 **גְּבוּרוֹת**

אַתָּה גִּבּוֹר לְעוֹלָם אֲדֹנָי רַב לְהוֹשִׁיעַ: מוֹרִיד הַטָּל: מְכַלְכֵּל חַיִּים
בְּחֶֽסֶד מְחַיֵּה כָּל חַי בְּרַחֲמִים רַבִּים סוֹמֵךְ נוֹפְלִים וְרוֹפֵא חוֹלִים
וּמַתִּיר אֲסוּרִים וּמְקַיֵּם אֱמוּנָתוֹ לִישֵׁנֵי עָפָר: מִי כָמֽוֹךָ בַּֽעַל גְּבוּרוֹת
וּמִי דּֽוֹמֶה לָּךְ מֶֽלֶךְ מֵמִית וּמְחַיֵּה וּמַצְמִֽיחַ יְשׁוּעָה: מִי כָמֽוֹךָ אַב
הָרַחֲמִים זוֹכֵר יְצוּרָיו לְחַיִּים בְּרַחֲמִים: וְנֶאֱמָן אַתָּה לְהַחֲיוֹת כָּל חָי:
בָּרוּךְ אַתָּה יהוה מְחַיֵּה כָּל חָי:

During Minḥah, continue on the following page when chanting aloud. Otherwise, continue below.

ג 3 **קְדֻשַּׁת הַשֵּׁם**

Recited when praying silently:

אַתָּה קָדוֹשׁ וְשִׁמְךָ קָדוֹשׁ וּקְדוֹשִׁים בְּכָל יוֹם יְהַלְלֽוּךָ סֶּֽלָה:

Continue on page 112.

DERASH. The second blessing of the Amidah is called *Gevurot—Power/ Mightiness.* It acknowledges God's vast power in contrast with our limited power. This orientation, born of our own vulnerability and fear of death, leads immediately to the awareness that life and death are indivisible. In fact, the process of renewal is built into the universe. S.P.W.

כל חי/every living thing, gives and renews life. The traditional siddur affirms מחיה מתים/revival of the dead. We substitute כל חי, demonstrating an understanding that all of life is rooted in the world's divine order and avoiding affirmation of life after death. We cannot know what happens to us after we die, but we can, by our thought and action, affirm the possibility of this-worldly salvation. D.A.T.

This Kedushah *is inserted only when this Amidah is used for* Minḥah *and chanted aloud.*

We sanctify your name throughout this world,
as it is sanctified in the heavens above,
as it is written by your prophet:
"And each celestial being calls to another, and declares:
Holy, holy, holy is THE RULER of the Multitudes of Heaven!
All the world is filled with divine glory!"
And they are answered with a blessing:
"Blessed is the glory of THE HOLY ONE,
wherever God may dwell!"
And as is written in your sacred words of psalm:
"May THE ETERNAL reign forever,
your God, O Zion, from one generation to the next.
Halleluyah!"
From one generation to the next may we declare your greatness,
and for all eternities may we affirm your holiness,
And may your praise, our God, never be absent from our
    mouths now and forever.
For you are a great and holy God. ↩

וקרא...כבודו / And...glory (Isaiah 6:3).
ברוך...ממקומו / Blessed...dwell (Ezekiel 3:12).
ימלך...הלליה / May...Halleluyah (Psalms 146:10).

נְקַדֵּשׁ אֶת שִׁמְךָ בָּעוֹלָם כְּשֵׁם שֶׁמַּקְדִּישִׁים אוֹתוֹ בִּשְׁמֵי מָרוֹם כַּכָּתוּב
עַל יַד נְבִיאֶךָ : וְקָרָא זֶה אֶל זֶה וְאָמַר

קָדוֹשׁ קָדוֹשׁ קָדוֹשׁ

יהוה צְבָאוֹת מְלֹא כָל הָאָרֶץ כְּבוֹדוֹ :
לְעֻמָּתָם בָּרוּךְ יֹאמֵרוּ :
בָּרוּךְ כְּבוֹד יהוה מִמְּקוֹמוֹ : וּבְדִבְרֵי קָדְשְׁךָ כָּתוּב לֵאמֹר :
יִמְלֹךְ יהוה לְעוֹלָם אֱלֹהַיִךְ צִיּוֹן לְדֹר וָדֹר הַלְלוּיָהּ :
לְדוֹר וָדוֹר נַגִּיד גָּדְלֶךָ וּלְנֵצַח נְצָחִים קְדֻשָּׁתְךָ נַקְדִּישׁ וְשִׁבְחֲךָ
אֱלֹהֵינוּ מִפִּינוּ לֹא יָמוּשׁ לְעוֹלָם וָעֶד כִּי אֵל מֶלֶךְ גָּדוֹל וְקָדוֹשׁ אָתָּה : ←

Nekadesh et shimeḥa ba'olam keshem shemakdishim oto
bishmey marom kakatuv al yad nevi'eḥa. Vekara zeh el zeh
ve'amar.
Kadosh kadosh kadosh adonay tzeva'ot melo ḥol ha'aretz kevodo.
Le'umatam baruḥ yomeru:
Baruḥ kevod adonay mimekomo.
Uvdivrey kodsheḥa katuv lemor.
Yimloḥ adonay le'olam elohayiḥ tziyon ledor vador halleluyah.
Ledor vador nagid godleḥa ulenetzaḥ netzaḥim kedushateḥa
nakdish veshivḥaḥa eloheynu mipinu lo yamush le'olam va'ed ki
el meleḥ gadol vekadosh atah. ↰

And therefore, HOLY ONE, let awe of you
infuse the whole of your Creation,
and let knowledge of your presence
dwell in all your creatures.
And let every being worship you,
and each created life pay homage to your rule.
Let all of them, as one, enact your bidding
with a whole and peaceful heart.
For we have always known, ALMIGHTY ONE,
that all authority to rule belongs to you,
all strength is rooted in your arm,
all mighty deeds have emanated from your hand.
Your name alone is the source of awe
that surges through all life.

And therefore, HOLY ONE, let awe of you
infuse your people, let the praise of you
ring out from all who worship you.
Let hope enliven all who seek you,
and let all who look to you with hope
find strength to speak.
Grant joy throughout your Land,
let happiness resound throughout your holy city,
soon, and in our days.

And therefore, let the just behold your peace,
let them rejoice and celebrate,
let all who follow in your path sing out with glee,
let all who love you dance with joy,
and may your power overwhelm all treachery,
so that it vanish wholly from the earth like smoke.
Then shall the power of injustice pass away! ⤶

וּבְכֵן תֵּן פַּחְדְּךָ יהוה אֱלֹהֵינוּ עַל כָּל־מַעֲשֶׂיךָ וְאֵימָתְךָ עַל כָּל־מַה־שֶּׁבָּרָאתָ וְיִירָאוּךָ כָּל־הַמַּעֲשִׂים וְיִשְׁתַּחֲווּ לְפָנֶיךָ כָּל־הַבְּרוּאִים וְיֵעָשׂוּ כֻלָּם אֲגֻדָּה אַחַת לַעֲשׂוֹת רְצוֹנְךָ בְּלֵבָב שָׁלֵם כְּמוֹ שֶׁיָּדַעְנוּ יהוה אֱלֹהֵינוּ שֶׁהַשִּׁלְטוֹן לְפָנֶיךָ עֹז בְּיָדְךָ וּגְבוּרָה בִּימִינֶךָ וְשִׁמְךָ נוֹרָא עַל כָּל־מַה־שֶּׁבָּרָאתָ:

וּבְכֵן תֵּן כָּבוֹד יהוה לְעַמֶּךָ תְּהִלָּה לִירֵאֶיךָ וְתִקְוָה לְדוֹרְשֶׁיךָ וּפִתְחוֹן פֶּה לַמְיַחֲלִים לָךְ שִׂמְחָה לְאַרְצֶךָ וְשָׂשׂוֹן לְעִירֶךָ בִּמְהֵרָה בְיָמֵינוּ:

וּבְכֵן צַדִּיקִים יִרְאוּ וְיִשְׂמָחוּ וִישָׁרִים יַעֲלֹזוּ וַחֲסִידִים בְּרִנָּה יָגִילוּ וְעוֹלָתָה תִּקְפָּץ־פִּיהָ וְכָל־הָרִשְׁעָה כֻּלָּהּ כְּעָשָׁן תִּכְלֶה כִּי תַעֲבִיר מֶמְשֶׁלֶת זָדוֹן מִן הָאָרֶץ: ←

COMMENTARY. Our text diverges from the traditional text for *uveḥen ten kavod*, which continues with a prayer for renewed strength to the seed of David—a clear appeal for the restoration of the Davidic monarchy through a God-chosen Messiah. Most Jews of the modern era do not expect or desire a divinely appointed royal personage to come and solve our problems for us. But in rejecting the *literal* Messiah we do not have to abandon the messianic passion—the commitment of "all who look to you with hope" and "find strength to speak." We need to take responsibility for bringing messianic days by enthusiastically advancing the ideals of human freedom, dignity, and creativity.   S.D.R.

COMMENTARY. The *uveḥen* paragraphs are among the most ancient of the High Holy Day liturgy. They link divine sovereignty, holiness and unity with awareness of divine power. They then express the hope that awareness of God will bring us to general reverence and awe. When humanity experiences this awe, the righteous will rejoice in God made manifest in our transformation.   D.A.T.

May you alone be sovereign over all of your Creation,
and Mt. Zion be the seat and symbol of your glory,
and Jerusalem, your holy city—
as is written in your holy scriptures:
"THE ETERNAL ONE shall reign forever,
your God, O Zion, through all generations!
Halleluyah!"

Holy are you,
and awe-inspiring is your name,
and there is no God apart from you,
as it is written: "THE CREATOR of the hosts of heaven
shall be exalted through the rule of law,
and God, the Holy One, made holy by the reign of justice."
Blessed are you, ETERNAL ONE,
the holy sovereign power. ⤺

וְתִמְלֹךְ אַתָּה יהוה לְבַדֶּךָ עַל כָּל־מַעֲשֶׂיךָ בְּהַר צִיּוֹן מִשְׁכַּן כְּבוֹדֶךָ
וּבִירוּשָׁלַיִם עִיר קָדְשֶׁךָ: כַּכָּתוּב בְּדִבְרֵי קָדְשֶׁךָ:
יִמְלֹךְ יהוה לְעוֹלָם אֱלֹהַיִךְ צִיּוֹן לְדֹר וָדֹר הַלְלוּיָהּ:

קָדוֹשׁ אַתָּה וְנוֹרָא שְׁמֶךָ וְאֵין אֱלוֹהַּ מִבַּלְעָדֶיךָ: כַּכָּתוּב: וַיִּגְבַּהּ יהוה
צְבָאוֹת בַּמִּשְׁפָּט וְהָאֵל הַקָּדוֹשׁ נִקְדַּשׁ בִּצְדָקָה: בָּרוּךְ אַתָּה יהוה
הַמֶּלֶךְ הַקָּדוֹשׁ: →

הללויה...ימלך / THE ETERNAL ONE...Hallelujah! (Psalms 146:10).
בצדקה...ויגבה / THE CREATOR...justice (Isaiah 5:16).

4. KEDUSHAT HAYOM / THE DAY'S HOLINESS

You have loved us, and have taken pleasure in us, and have made us holy with your mitzvot, and you have brought us, sovereign one, near to your service, and have called us to the shelter of your great and holy name.

On Saturday evening, add the following:
(You have given us as heritage the seasons of rejoicing, the appointed times of holiness, the holidays for giving of ourselves, and you have made a part of that inheritance the holiness of Shabbat, the honor of the Festival, and celebration of the ancient pilgrimage. You have divided, HOLY ONE, our God, between the holy and the ordinary, between daylight and the dark, between the seventh day and the first six days of Creation. You have set a boundary between the holiness of Shabbat and the holiness of Festivals, and raised to holiness the seventh day, above the first six days of the Creation. And you have enabled holiness to grow within your people Israel, a holiness that emanates from you alone.)

On Shabbat, add words in parenthesis.

And you have given us, ALMIGHTY ONE, our God in love this Day of (Shabbat and of) Remembrance, a day to heed the Shofar blast, (with love), a holy convocation, a remembrance of the going-out from Egypt.

Our God, our ancients' God, may our prayer arise and come to you, and be beheld, and be acceptable. Let it be heard, acted upon, remembered—the memory of us and all our needs, the memory of our ancestors, the memory of messianic hopes, memory of Jerusalem your holy city, and the memory of all your kin, the house of Israel, all surviving in your presence. Act for goodness and grace, for love and care; for life, well-being and peace, on this Day of Remembrance. ⤺

קְדֻשַּׁת הַיּוֹם

אַתָּה אֲהַבְתָּנוּ וְרָצִיתָ בָּנוּ וְקִדַּשְׁתָּנוּ בְּמִצְוֹתֶיךָ וְקֵרַבְתָּנוּ מַלְכֵּנוּ לַעֲבוֹדָתֶךָ וְשִׁמְךָ הַגָּדוֹל וְהַקָּדוֹשׁ עָלֵינוּ קָרָאתָ:

On Saturday evening add the following:

(וַתִּתֶּן־לָנוּ זְמַנֵּי שָׂשׂוֹן וּמוֹעֲדֵי קֹדֶשׁ וְחַגֵּי נְדָבָה וַתּוֹרִישֵׁנוּ קְדֻשַּׁת שַׁבָּת וּכְבוֹד מוֹעֵד וַחֲגִיגַת הָרֶגֶל: וַתַּבְדֵּל יהוה אֱלֹהֵינוּ בֵּין קֹדֶשׁ לְחוֹל בֵּין אוֹר לְחֹשֶׁךְ בֵּין יוֹם הַשְּׁבִיעִי לְשֵׁשֶׁת יְמֵי הַמַּעֲשֶׂה בֵּין קְדֻשַּׁת שַׁבָּת לִקְדֻשַּׁת יוֹם טוֹב הִבְדַּלְתָּ וְאֶת־יוֹם הַשְּׁבִיעִי מִשֵּׁשֶׁת יְמֵי הַמַּעֲשֶׂה קִדַּשְׁתָּ הִבְדַּלְתָּ וְקִדַּשְׁתָּ אֶת־עַמְּךָ יִשְׂרָאֵל בִּקְדֻשָּׁתֶךָ:)

On Shabbat add the words in parenthesis.

וַתִּתֶּן לָנוּ יהוה אֱלֹהֵינוּ בְּאַהֲבָה אֶת־יוֹם (הַשַּׁבָּת הַזֶּה וְאֶת־יוֹם) הַזִּכָּרוֹן הַזֶּה יוֹם (זִכְרוֹן) תְּרוּעָה (בְּאַהֲבָה) מִקְרָא קֹדֶשׁ זֵכֶר לִיצִיאַת מִצְרָיִם:

אֱלֹהֵינוּ וֵאלֹהֵי אֲבוֹתֵינוּ וְאִמּוֹתֵינוּ יַעֲלֶה וְיָבֹא וְיַגִּיעַ וְיֵרָאֶה וְיֵרָצֶה וְיִשָּׁמַע וְיִפָּקֵד וְיִזָּכֵר זִכְרוֹנֵנוּ וּפִקְדוֹנֵנוּ וְזִכְרוֹן אֲבוֹתֵינוּ וְאִמּוֹתֵינוּ וְזִכְרוֹן יְמוֹת הַמָּשִׁיחַ וְזִכְרוֹן יְרוּשָׁלַיִם עִיר קָדְשֶׁךָ וְזִכְרוֹן כָּל עַמְּךָ בֵּית יִשְׂרָאֵל לְפָנֶיךָ לִפְלֵיטָה וּלְטוֹבָה וּלְחֵן וּלְחֶסֶד וּלְרַחֲמִים לְחַיִּים וּלְשָׁלוֹם בְּיוֹם הַזִּכָּרוֹן הַזֶּה:

MEDITATION. Take a moment to find your pulse. Can you feel it? Can you hear it? Is it quick? Slow? Your pulse is your timepiece, your clock, expressing the flow, literally, of your life. Can you feel the regular beat? Feel that pulse of time. What is an accomplishment of this last year that you are proud of? What happened this year that gave you joy? What was a significant challenge of this past year? Where have you traveled? Look at your hands. Feel your hands. What have your hands accomplished this year? What have they held? What have they touched? How do you use them every day? Bless the work of your hands. Clench them. Relax them. Realize your power. Where do you want to go in the year ahead?

Leora R. Zeitlin (Adapted)

Remember us this day, ALL-KNOWING ONE, our God, for goodness. Favor us this day with blessing. Preserve us this day for life. With your redeeming nurturing word, be kind and generous. Act tenderly on our behalf, and grant us victory over all our trials. Truly, our eyes turn toward you, for you are a providing God; gracious and merciful are you.

Our God, our ancients' God; May it be your will that a heavenly inspiration be awakened in us on this holy day to rebuild the Land of Israel, to renew it and to make it holy for your service, and may peace prevail there as well as freedom, justice, and the rule of Law, as it is written by your prophet: "Truly, Torah shall go forth from Zion, and the word of the ETERNAL from Jerusalem!" And it is said: "Let none do harm, let none destroy, throughout my holy mountain, for the earth is filled with knowledge of the OMNIPRESENT, as the waters fill the sea."

Our God, our ancients' God, rule over all the world in its entirety, by showing forth your glory, and be raised up over all the earth in your beloved presence. And let the wondrous aura of your reign be manifest in all who dwell upon the earth— let every creature know that you are its creator, let every living thing discern that you have fashioned it, let everyone who draws the breath of life declare that you, THE ANCIENT ONE, reign supreme, and that your sovereignty embraces all. כ

KAVANAH. One part of the human psyche in each of us encourages the hubris of claiming we are God. The arrogance of power and authority, however, dissolves before the recognition that we are but short-lived glimmers of the Eternal One. When we all share that humility, our world will be transformed.   J.A.S.

כי...ירושלים / Truly...Jerusalem (Isaiah 2:3).
לא...מכסים / Let...sea (Isaiah 11:9).

זָכְרֵנוּ יהוה אֱלֹהֵינוּ בּוֹ לְטוֹבָה: וּפָקְדֵנוּ בוֹ לִבְרָכָה וְהוֹשִׁיעֵנוּ בוֹ
לְחַיִּים: וּבִדְבַר יְשׁוּעָה וְרַחֲמִים חוּס וְחָנֵּנוּ וְרַחֵם עָלֵינוּ וְהוֹשִׁיעֵנוּ
כִּי אֵלֶיךָ עֵינֵינוּ כִּי אֵל מֶלֶךְ חַנּוּן וְרַחוּם אָתָּה:

אֱלֹהֵינוּ וֵאלֹהֵי אֲבוֹתֵינוּ וְאִמּוֹתֵינוּ יְהִי רָצוֹן מִלְּפָנֶיךָ שֶׁיֵּעָרֶה עָלֵינוּ
רוּחַ מִמָּרוֹם בַּיוֹם הַקָּדוֹשׁ הַזֶּה לְכוֹנֵן אֶת־אֶרֶץ יִשְׂרָאֵל לְחַדֵּשׁ
וּלְקַדֵּשׁ אוֹתָהּ לַעֲבוֹדָתֶךָ וְשָׁכַן בָּאָרֶץ שָׁלוֹם חֹפֶשׁ צֶדֶק וּמִשְׁפָּט
כַּכָּתוּב עַל־יַד נְבִיאֶךָ: כִּי מִצִּיּוֹן תֵּצֵא תוֹרָה וּדְבַר־יהוה מִירוּשָׁלָיִם:
וְנֶאֱמַר: לֹא־יָרֵעוּ וְלֹא־יַשְׁחִיתוּ בְּכָל־הַר קָדְשִׁי כִּי־מָלְאָה הָאָרֶץ
דֵּעָה אֶת־יהוה כַּמַּיִם לַיָּם מְכַסִּים:

אֱלֹהֵינוּ וֵאלֹהֵי אֲבוֹתֵינוּ וְאִמּוֹתֵינוּ מְלֹךְ עַל כָּל־הָעוֹלָם כֻּלּוֹ בִּכְבוֹדֶךָ
וְהִנָּשֵׂא עַל כָּל־הָאָרֶץ בִּיקָרֶךָ וְהוֹפַע בַּהֲדַר גְּאוֹן עֻזֶּךָ עַל כָּל־יוֹשְׁבֵי
תֵבֵל אַרְצֶךָ וְיֵדַע כָּל־פָּעוּל כִּי אַתָּה פְעַלְתּוֹ וְיָבִין כָּל־יְצוּר כִּי אַתָּה
יְצַרְתּוֹ וְיֹאמַר כֹּל אֲשֶׁר נְשָׁמָה בְּאַפּוֹ: יהוה וּמַלְכוּתוֹ בַּכֹּל מָשָׁלָה: ←

COMMENTARY. The shofar is always sounded on Rosh Hashanah, except,
according to tradition, on Shabbat. Following the ban on playing musical
instruments outside the Temple on Shabbat, most rabbis forbade the
sounding of the shofar because this might result in the shofar being
carried, a Shabbat violation. Furthermore, not sounding the shofar on
Shabbat differentiated the practice of the Temple from that of the
synagogue, giving the synagogue a lessened standing. Silencing musical
instruments on Shabbat also acts as a זכר לחרבן/remembrance of the
destruction of the Temple. In our time, some congregations have begun to
sound the shofar on Shabbat. This custom began in Reform congregations
that celebrated only a single day of Rosh Hashanah. Some see no problem
in carrying on Shabbat and have no desire to elevate the Temple sacrificial
practices or hope for their reinstitution. They often support this practice
because the shofar is so central to Rosh Hashanah. There is a diversity of
practice among Reconstructionist communities. Some refrain from
blowing the shofar in order to teach the sanctity of Shabbat on a day
when many are present in the synagogue.   D.A.T.

Our God, our ancients' God, (take pleasure in our rest,) enable us to realize holiness through your mitzvot, give us our portion in your Torah, let us enjoy the good things of your world, and gladden us with your salvation. (And help us to perpetuate, ETERNAL ONE, our God, with love and with desire, your holy Shabbat, and may all your people Israel, all who treat your name as holy, find rest and peace upon this day.) Refine our hearts to serve you truthfully, for you are a God of truth, and your word is truthful and endures forever. Blessed are you, ETERNAL ONE, the sovereign power over all the earth, who raises up to holiness (Shabbat,) the people Israel and the Day of Remembrance.

5. AVODAH / WORSHIP

Take pleasure, GRACIOUS ONE, our God, in Israel your people; lovingly accept their fervent prayer. May Israel's worship always be acceptable to you.

And may our eyes behold your homecoming, with merciful intent, to Zion. Blessed are you, THE FAITHFUL ONE, who brings your presence home to Zion. ↩

KAVANAH. *Avodah*: Service and prayer. In ancient times, we Jews brought sacrificial offerings to God at the Temple in Jerusalem. Now we are in relationship with the Divine through the meditations of our hearts and the ways in which we choose to act in the world.　　　　L.G.B.

להב תפלתם/their fervent prayer. The word להב literally means "flame," but has come to mean "fervor." The traditional version of the prayer speaks of אשי ישראל—the rekindled flames of animal sacrifice. This prayerbook, by referring to להב תפלתם/their fervent prayer maintains the fire imagery, but changes the flames into the spiritual flames of the heart.　　　　J.A.S.

אֱלֹהֵינוּ וֵאלֹהֵי אֲבוֹתֵינוּ וְאִמּוֹתֵינוּ (רְצֵה בִמְנוּחָתֵנוּ) קַדְּשֵׁנוּ בְּמִצְוֹתֶיךָ וְתֵן חֶלְקֵנוּ בְּתוֹרָתֶךָ שַׂבְּעֵנוּ מִטּוּבֶךָ וְשַׂמְּחֵנוּ בִּישׁוּעָתֶךָ (וְהַנְחִילֵנוּ יהוה אֱלֹהֵינוּ בְּאַהֲבָה וּבְרָצוֹן שַׁבַּת קָדְשֶׁךָ וְיָנוּחוּ בָה יִשְׂרָאֵל מְקַדְּשֵׁי שְׁמֶךָ) וְטַהֵר לִבֵּנוּ לְעָבְדְּךָ בֶּאֱמֶת כִּי אַתָּה אֱלֹהִים אֱמֶת וּדְבָרְךָ אֱמֶת וְקַיָּם לָעַד: בָּרוּךְ אַתָּה יהוה מֶלֶךְ עַל כָּל־הָאָרֶץ מְקַדֵּשׁ (הַשַּׁבָּת וְ) יִשְׂרָאֵל וְיוֹם הַזִּכָּרוֹן: ←

ה ‏5 עֲבוֹדָה

רְצֵה יהוה אֱלֹהֵינוּ בְּעַמְּךָ יִשְׂרָאֵל וְלַהַב תְּפִלָּתָם בְּאַהֲבָה תְקַבֵּל בְּרָצוֹן וּתְהִי לְרָצוֹן תָּמִיד עֲבוֹדַת יִשְׂרָאֵל עַמֶּךָ: וְתֶחֱזֶינָה עֵינֵינוּ בְּשׁוּבְךָ לְצִיּוֹן בְּרַחֲמִים: בָּרוּךְ אַתָּה יהוה הַמַּחֲזִיר שְׁכִינָתוֹ לְצִיּוֹן: ←

DERASH. The term Sheḥinah implies that God is not aloof from human life with all its defeats and triumphs. God is in the very midst of life. The rabbis say that when people suffer for their sins, the Sheḥinah cries out. The Sheḥinah thus moves from Israel to all humanity. M.M.K. (Adapted)

COMMENTARY. On Rosh Hashanah and Yom Kippur we add to this prayer the phrase, "You are a God of truth, and your word is truthful and endures forever." This reminds us of the penitential season's task—getting back in touch with what is ultimately important, the changeless ground of meaning in human life. At this turning of the seasons when we celebrate the birthday of the world and become so very conscious of change in our lives, we sense that we can understand change only when we are in touch with the unchanging verities in life. D.A.T.

6. HODA'AH / THANKS

We give thanks to you that you are THE ALL-MERCIFUL, our God,
God of our ancestors, today and always. A firm, enduring source
of life, a shield to us in time of trial, you are ever there, from age
to age. We acknowledge you, declare your praise, and thank you
for our lives entrusted to your hand, our souls placed in your
care, for your miracles that greet us every day, and for your
wonders and the good things that are with us every hour,
morning, noon, and night. GOOD ONE, whose kindness never
stops, KIND ONE, whose loving acts have never failed—always
have we placed our hope in you.

For all these things, your name be blessed
and raised in honor always, sovereign of ours, forever.

And write down for a good life all the people of your covenant.

Let all of life acknowledge you! May all beings
praise your name in truth. O God, our rescue and our aid.
Blessed are you, THE GRACIOUS ONE,
whose name is good, to whom all thanks are due. ↲

הוֹדָאָה

מוֹדִים אֲנַחְנוּ לָךְ שָׁאַתָּה הוּא יהוה אֱלֹהֵינוּ וֵאלֹהֵי אֲבוֹתֵינוּ
וְאִמּוֹתֵינוּ לְעוֹלָם וָעֶד צוּר חַיֵּינוּ מָגֵן יִשְׁעֵנוּ אַתָּה הוּא לְדוֹר וָדוֹר:
נוֹדֶה לְּךָ וּנְסַפֵּר תְּהִלָּתֶךָ עַל חַיֵּינוּ הַמְּסוּרִים בְּיָדֶךָ וְעַל נִשְׁמוֹתֵינוּ
הַפְּקוּדוֹת לָךְ וְעַל נִסֶּיךָ שֶׁבְּכָל יוֹם עִמָּנוּ וְעַל נִפְלְאוֹתֶיךָ וְטוֹבוֹתֶיךָ
שֶׁבְּכָל־עֵת עֶרֶב וָבֹקֶר וְצָהֳרָיִם: הַטּוֹב כִּי לֹא כָלוּ רַחֲמֶיךָ וְהַמְרַחֵם
כִּי לֹא תַמּוּ חֲסָדֶיךָ מֵעוֹלָם קִוִּינוּ לָךְ:

וְעַל כֻּלָּם יִתְבָּרַךְ וְיִתְרוֹמַם שִׁמְךָ מַלְכֵּנוּ תָּמִיד לְעוֹלָם וָעֶד:

וּכְתֹב לְחַיִּים טוֹבִים כָּל־בְּנֵי בְרִיתֶךָ:

וְכֹל הַחַיִּים יוֹדוּךָ סֶּלָה וִיהַלְלוּ אֶת שִׁמְךָ בֶּאֱמֶת הָאֵל יְשׁוּעָתֵנוּ
וְעֶזְרָתֵנוּ סֶלָה: בָּרוּךְ אַתָּה יהוה הַטּוֹב שִׁמְךָ וּלְךָ נָאֶה לְהוֹדוֹת: ⟶

COMMENTARY. The attitude of thankfulness portrayed in the *modim* prayer above comes near the end of the Amidah as if to say that by this time we should be ready to acknowledge how much is outside of our control, how many gifts we receive, how much we have to be grateful for. On the High Holy Days we ask that "all the people of your covenant" be written down for a good life. To be part of the covenant is to accept the obligation of a stance of thankfulness, which itself conveys the possibility of leading a good life.

D.A.T.

7. BIRKAT HASHALOM / BLESSING FOR PEACE

Grant abundant peace eternally for Israel, your people. For you are the sovereign source of all peace. So, may it be a good thing in your eyes to bless your people Israel, and all who dwell on earth, in every time and hour, with your peace.

In the book of life, blessing, peace, and proper sustenance, may we be remembered and inscribed, we and all your people, the house of Israel, for a good life and for peace.

Blessed are you, COMPASSIONATE ONE, maker of peace. ⤶

The Amidah traditionally concludes with bowing and taking three steps back.

ואת כל יושבי תבל/and all who dwell on earth. According to the sages, every Amidah must conclude with a prayer for peace and an acknowledgment of God as the power that makes for peace. Inclusion of the words "and all who dwell on earth" proclaims that Israel desires the blessing of peace, not for itself alone, but for all humanity.   S.S.

KAVANAH. God is shalom. God's name is shalom, everything is held together by shalom.   Zohar

בספר חיים...ופרנסה טובה/In the book of life...and proper sustenance. This insertion into the closing benediction of the Amidah is unique to the *Yamim Nora'im*. The mythic imagery is of a celestial "Book of Life," in which our ancestors imagined their fate was inscribed. On Rosh Hashanah we celebrate creation, pray for repentance, ask for a world of peace, and seek the assurance of life. Worthy goals, and serious subjects. But the quiet courage of the petition for "proper sustenance," for a daily routine of labor that confers integrity and dignity and neither shames nor humiliates us is the foundation of these larger hopes.   R.H.

KAVANAH. Try to imagine a time of true peace and tranquility, and think about your part in helping this time to come. How will you be a peacemaker? Can you help to bring peace when conflict arises in your community? Can you find peace within yourself?   L.G.B.

שָׁלוֹם רָב עַל יִשְׂרָאֵל עַמְּךָ תָּשִׂים לְעוֹלָם: כִּי אַתָּה הוּא מֶלֶךְ אָדוֹן
לְכָל הַשָּׁלוֹם: וְטוֹב בְּעֵינֶיךָ לְבָרֵךְ אֶת עַמְּךָ יִשְׂרָאֵל וְאֶת כָּל־יוֹשְׁבֵי
תֵבֵל בְּכָל עֵת וּבְכָל שָׁעָה בִּשְׁלוֹמֶךָ:

בְּסֵפֶר חַיִּים בְּרָכָה וְשָׁלוֹם וּפַרְנָסָה טוֹבָה נִזָּכֵר וְנִכָּתֵב לְפָנֶיךָ אֲנַחְנוּ
וְכָל עַמְּךָ בֵּית יִשְׂרָאֵל לְחַיִּים טוֹבִים וּלְשָׁלוֹם: בָּרוּךְ אַתָּה יהוה
עוֹשֶׂה הַשָּׁלוֹם: ←

Shalom rav al yisra'el ameḥa tasim le'olam.
Ki atah hu meleḥ adon leḥol hashalom.
Vetov be'eyneḥa levareḥ et ameḥa yisra'el
ve'et kol yoshvey tevel
beḥol et uvḥol sha'ah bishlomeḥa.

Besefer ḥayim beraḥah veshalom ufarnasah tovah
nizaḥer venikatev lefaneḥa
anaḥnu veḥol ameḥa beyt yisra'el
leḥayim tovim ulshalom.
Baruḥ atah adonay osey hashalom. ⤵

The Amidah traditionally concludes with bowing and taking three steps back.

עושה השלום/Maker of peace. This ancient version of the prayer for peace
in its most universal form was assigned in the traditional liturgy to the ten
days of *teshuvah*. During the year the text read, "who blesses your people
Israel with peace." In our times, when life has been transformed by the
constant threat of global destruction, the need of the hour calls for the
more universal form of the prayer throughout the year.   A.G.

ELOHAY NETZOR /
A CONCLUDING MEDITATION

Dear God, protect my tongue from evil,
and my lips from telling lies.
May I turn away from evil
and do what is good in your sight.
Let me be counted among those who seek peace.
May my words of prayer
and my heart's meditation be seen favorably,
BELOVED ONE, my rock and my redeemer.
May the one who creates harmony above
make peace
for us and for all Israel,
and for all who dwell on earth.
And say: Amen.

On Shabbat continue on page 131.
On all other days turn to page 137.

COMMENTARY. The Talmud lists examples of twelve personal meditations that could follow the Amidah. If this one does not speak to you, compose your own, or stand or sit in silent meditation. L.W.K.

NOTE. Like the opening verse of the Amidah, this prayer employs the singular and deals with the power of words. But here the concern is for words between people, not for those directed to God. Some people find it easier to talk to God than to talk to others. L.W.K.

KAVANAH. Sin is the failure to live up to the best that is in us. It means that our souls are not attuned to the divine—that we have betrayed God.
M.M.K. (Adapted)

יהיו ... וגואלי / May... redeemer (Psalms 19:15).

אֱלֹהַי נְצוֹר

אֱלֹהַי נְצוֹר לְשׁוֹנִי מֵרָע
וּשְׂפָתַי מִדַּבֵּר מִרְמָה:

יְהִי רָצוֹן שֶׁאָסוּר מֵרָע
וְהַטּוֹב בְּעֵינֶיךָ אֶעֱשֶׂה
יְהִי חֶלְקִי עִם מְבַקְשֵׁי שָׁלוֹם וְרוֹדְפָיו:

יִהְיוּ לְרָצוֹן אִמְרֵי פִי
וְהֶגְיוֹן לִבִּי לְפָנֶיךָ
יהוה צוּרִי וְגוֹאֲלִי:

עוֹשֶׂה שָׁלוֹם בִּמְרוֹמָיו
הוּא יַעֲשֶׂה שָׁלוֹם
עָלֵינוּ וְעַל כָּל יִשְׂרָאֵל
וְעַל כָּל יוֹשְׁבֵי תֵבֵל
וְאִמְרוּ אָמֵן:

Yihyu leratzon imrey fi
vehegyon libi lefaneha
adonay tzuri vego'ali.

Oseh shalom bimromav
hu ya'aseh shalom
aleynu ve'al kol yisra'el
ve'al kol yoshvey tevel
ve'imru amen.

On Shabbat continue on page 132.
On all other days turn to page 137.

MEDITATIONS / AMIDAH ALTERNATIVES

Something is very gently,
invisibly, silently,
pulling at me—a thread
or net of threads
finer than cobweb and as
elastic. I haven't tried
the strength of it. No barbed hook
pierced and tore me. Was it
not long ago this thread
began to draw me? Or
way back? Was I
born with its knot about my
neck, a bridle? Not fear
but a stirring
of wonder makes me
catch my breath when I feel
the tug of it when I thought
it had loosened itself and gone.

Denise Levertov

The day has come
To take an accounting of my life.

Have I dreamed of late
Of the person I want to be,
Of the changes I would make
In my daily habits,
In the way I am with others,
In the friendship I show companions,
Woman friends, man friends, my partner,
In the regard I show my father and mother,
Who brought me out of childhood? ↵

I have remained enchained too often to less than what I am.
But the day has come to take an accounting of my life.

Have I renewed of late
My vision of the world I want to live in,
Of the changes I would make
In the way my friends are with each other
The way we find out whom we love
The way we grow to educated people
The way in which the many kinds of needy people
Grope their way to justice?

I, who am my own kind of needy person, have been afraid
    of visions.
But the day has come to take an accounting of my life.

Have I faced up of late
To the needs I really have—
Not for comforts which shelter my unsureness,
Not for honors which paper over my (really tawdry) self,
Not for handsome beauty, in which my weakness masquerades,
Nor for unattractiveness in which my strengths hide out—

I need to be loved.
Do I deserve to be?
I need to love another.

Can I commit my love?
Perhaps its object will be less than my visions
(And then I would be less)
Perhaps I am not brave enough
To find new vision
Through a real and breathing person. ↵

I need to come in touch with my own power,
Not with titles,
Not possessions, money, high praise,
But with the power that is mine
As a child, of the Power that is the universe
To be a comfort, a source of honor,
Handsome and beautiful from the moment I awoke this
   morning
So strong
That I can risk the love of someone else
So sure
That I can risk to change the world
And know that even if it all comes crashing down
I shall survive it all—
Saddened a bit, shaken perhaps,
Not unvisited by tears
But my dreams shall not crash down
My visions not go glimmering.
So long as I have breath
I know I have the strength
To transform what I can be
To what I am.
                    Richard N. Levy

"Where is the place of God's glory?" :אַיֵּה מְקוֹם כְּבוֹדוֹ
"Where is the dwelling of God?"
This is the question with which the Rabbi of Kotzk surprised a number of learned Jews who happened to be visiting him.

They laughed at him: "What a thing to ask! Is not the whole world full of God's glory?"
Then he answered his own question:
"God dwells wherever people let God in."

Martin Buber (Adapted)

We Jews are a community based on memory. A common memory has kept us together and enabled us to survive. This does not mean that we based our life on any one particular past, even on the loftiest of pasts; it simply means that one generation passed on to the next a memory which gained in scope—for new destiny and new emotional life were constantly accruing to it—and which realized itself in a way we can call organic. This expanding memory was more than a spiritual motif; it was a power which sustained, fed, and quickened Jewish existence itself.

Martin Buber

According to the Kabbalah, redemption is not an event that will take place all at once at "the end of days" nor is it something that concerns the Jewish people alone. It is a continual process, taking place at every moment. The good deeds of men and women are single acts in the long drama of redemption, and not only the people Israel but the whole universe must be redeemed.

There is longing for peace in the hearts of men and women. But peace is not the same as the absence of war. Peace among people depends upon a relationship of reverence for each other. Peace will not come until people return out of their exile from each other, and Sarah and Hagar, Jacob and Esau, can embrace upon peaceful shores. Peace will not come until we search out the holy sparks of godliness that have gone astray in the wicked, and bring them back to their true selves.

Peace will not come until we see the flaws in our own selves and struggle to efface them, until each of us realizes our individual uniqueness, and we each attune our very special selves to their perfection.

Peace will not come until we renounce excessive self-concern and allow our hearts to be moved enough by the misery of our fellows to dare what must be dared.

Abraham Joshua Heschel (Excerpted and Adapted)

Additional meditations may be found on pages 1-20.

On Shabbat continue here.
On weekdays turn to page 137.

VAYḤULU / CREATION COMPLETED

Heaven, earth, and all their beings were finished. God completed on the seventh day the work that had been done, and ceased upon the seventh day from all the work that had been done. God blessed the seventh day and set it apart. For on it God had ceased from all the work that had been done in carrying out Creation.

ME'EYN SHEVA / REPRISE OF THE AMIDAH

Blessed are you, THE ANCIENT ONE, our God, God of our ancestors,

God of Abraham
God of Isaac
God of Jacob

God of Sarah
God of Rebekah
God of Rachel
and God of Leah;

great, heroic, awesome God, supreme divinity,
who creates the heavens and the earth. ⤸

KAVANAH. Shabbat represents the affirmation that life is not vain or futile, but supremely worthwhile.   M.M.K. (Adapted)

ויכלו ... לעשות / Heaven ... Creation (Genesis 2:1-3).

On *Shabbat* continue here.
On weekdays turn to page 137.

וַיְכֻלּוּ

וַיְכֻלּוּ הַשָּׁמַיִם וְהָאָרֶץ וְכָל־צְבָאָם: וַיְכַל אֱלֹהִים בַּיּוֹם הַשְּׁבִיעִי
מְלַאכְתּוֹ אֲשֶׁר עָשָׂה וַיִּשְׁבֹּת בַּיּוֹם הַשְּׁבִיעִי מִכָּל־מְלַאכְתּוֹ אֲשֶׁר
עָשָׂה: וַיְבָרֶךְ אֱלֹהִים אֶת־יוֹם הַשְּׁבִיעִי וַיְקַדֵּשׁ אֹתוֹ כִּי בוֹ שָׁבַת
מִכָּל־מְלַאכְתּוֹ אֲשֶׁר־בָּרָא אֱלֹהִים לַעֲשׂוֹת:

בָּרוּךְ אַתָּה יהוה אֱלֹהֵינוּ וֵאלֹהֵי אֲבוֹתֵינוּ וְאִמּוֹתֵינוּ:

אֱלֹהֵי שָׂרָה   אֱלֹהֵי אַבְרָהָם
אֱלֹהֵי רִבְקָה   אֱלֹהֵי יִצְחָק
אֱלֹהֵי רָחֵל   אֱלֹהֵי יַעֲקֹב
וֵאלֹהֵי לֵאָה:

← הָאֵל הַגָּדוֹל הַגִּבּוֹר וְהַנּוֹרָא אֵל עֶלְיוֹן קוֹנֵה שָׁמַיִם וָאָרֶץ:

Vayhulu hashamayim veha'aretz vehol tzeva'am
vayhal elohim bayom hashevi'i melahto asher asah
vayishbot bayom hashevi'i mikol melahto asher asah.
Vayvareh elohim et yom hashevi'i vaykadesh oto
ki vo shavat mikol melahto asher bara elohim la'asot.

Baruh atah adonay eloheynu veylohey avoteynu ve'imoteynu
elohey avraham, elohey sarah
elohey yitzhak, elohey rivkah
elohey ya'akov, elohey rahel
veylohey le'ah
ha'el hagadol hagibor vehanora
el elyon
koney shamayim va'aretz. כ

Shielding our ancestors with a word,
a speech enlivening all beings,
the holy Sovereign,
to whom no being can compare,
who gives this people rest upon the holy Shabbat—
yes, God is pleased to give them rest!
We stand in the divine presence, awed and trembling,
and offer up continually our thankful prayer,
our expression of praise.
God to whom all thanks are due,
the source of peace, who sanctifies Shabbat,
who blesses the seventh day
and gives rest in holiness
to a people steeped in Shabbat joy,
in memory of Creation in the beginning. ↵

מגן אבות / *Magen Avot* summarizes the Shabbat Amidah. It refers to each of
the seven blessings in order: shielding ancestors, giving life, providing
holiness, ordaining Shabbat, allowing worship, inspiring thanks, blessing
with peace. Perhaps once an alternative Amidah, *Magen Avot* today provides
a joyous communal reprise of the themes first invoked in the privacy of
the Amidah.   D.A.T.

מֵעֵין שֶׁבַע

מָגֵן אָבוֹת בִּדְבָרוֹ מְחַיֵּה כָּל חַי בְּמַאֲמָרוֹ הַמֶּלֶךְ הַקָּדוֹשׁ שֶׁאֵין
כָּמוֹהוּ הַמֵּנִיחַ לְעַמּוֹ בְּיוֹם שַׁבַּת קָדְשׁוֹ כִּי בָם רָצָה לְהָנִיחַ לָהֶם:
לְפָנָיו נַעֲבֹד בְּיִרְאָה וָפַחַד וְנוֹדֶה לִשְׁמוֹ בְּכָל יוֹם תָּמִיד מֵעֵין
הַבְּרָכוֹת: אֵל הַהוֹדָאוֹת אֲדוֹן הַשָּׁלוֹם מְקַדֵּשׁ הַשַּׁבָּת וּמְבָרֵךְ שְׁבִיעִי
וּמֵנִיחַ בִּקְדֻשָּׁה לְעַם מְדֻשְּׁנֵי־עֹנֶג זֵכֶר לְמַעֲשֵׂה בְרֵאשִׁית: ←

Magen avot bidvaro
mehayey kol hay bema'amaro.
hameleh hakadosh she'eyn kamohu
hameniah le'amo beyom shabbat kodsho
ki vam ratzah lehani'ah lahem.
Lefanav na'avod beyirah vafahad
venodeh lishmo behol yom tamid
me'eyn haberahot.
El hahoda'ot adon hashalom
mekadesh hashabbat umvareh shevi'i
umeniah bikdushah le'am medusheney oneg
zeher lema'asey vereyshit. ⸂

TRADITIONAL VERSION

Our God, our ancients' God, take pleasure in our rest. Make us holy through your mitzvot. Make us a part of Torah. Let us enjoy the good things of your world and rejoice in all your saving acts. Refine our hearts to serve you honestly. Help us to perpetuate, with love and joy, your holy Shabbat. Let all Israel, and all who treat your name as holy, rest upon this day. Blessed are you, BELOVED ONE, source of the holiness of Shabbat.

ALTERNATIVE VERSION

Shabbat of holiness, beloved and blessed,
may your glory dwell amidst the people of your holy place.
In you, our queen, we find our rest.
And in your holy mitzvot our souls rejoice.
With your goodness we are content.
In you our hearts grow pure,
and in your Shabbat rest we find true worship.
Holy Shabbat, source of blessing,
may you, too, be blessed in our rest.
And blessed are you, ETERNAL ONE, who makes Shabbat holy.

שבת קדש האהובה / Shabbat of holiness. This original Hebrew text addresses Shabbat in feminine language, as bride and as queen. She is the subject of our affection and the source of our sustenance. We ask that her blessing dwell in our midst for peace and joy. We ask, too, that the Jewish people bless Shabbat with their love and devotion.   M.P.

TRADITIONAL VERSION

אֱלֹהֵינוּ וֵאלֹהֵי אֲבוֹתֵינוּ וְאִמּוֹתֵינוּ רְצֵה בִמְנוּחָתֵנוּ קַדְּשֵׁנוּ בְּמִצְוֹתֶיךָ
וְתֵן חֶלְקֵנוּ בְּתוֹרָתֶךָ שַׂבְּעֵנוּ מִטּוּבֶךָ וְשַׂמְּחֵנוּ בִּישׁוּעָתֶךָ וְטַהֵר לִבֵּנוּ
לְעָבְדְּךָ בֶּאֱמֶת: וְהַנְחִילֵנוּ יהוה אֱלֹהֵינוּ בְּאַהֲבָה וּבְרָצוֹן שַׁבַּת
קָדְשֶׁךָ: וְיָנוּחוּ בָהּ כָּל יִשְׂרָאֵל מְקַדְּשֵׁי שְׁמֶךָ: בָּרוּךְ אַתָּה יהוה
מְקַדֵּשׁ הַשַּׁבָּת:

Eloheynu veylohey avoteynu ve'imoteynu
retzey vimnuhatenu.
Kadeshenu bemitzvoteha
veten helkenu betorateha.
Sabe'enu mituveha
vesamehenu bishu'ateha
vetaher libenu le'ovdeha be'emet.
Vehanhilenu adonay eloheynu
be'ahavah uvratzon shabbat kodsheha
veyanuhu vah yisra'el mekadeshey shemeha.
Baruh atah adonay mekadesh hashabbat.

ALTERNATIVE VERSION

שַׁבָּת קֹדֶשׁ הָאֲהוּבָה וְהַבְּרוּכָה
יִשְׁכּוֹן כְּבוֹדֵךְ בְּלֵב עַם מְקַדְּשֵׁךְ:
בָּךְ נִמְצָא מְנוּחָתֵנוּ
וּבְמִצְוֹת קְדֻשָּׁתֵךְ תָּגֵל נַפְשֵׁנוּ:
בְּטוּבֵךְ נִשְׂבַּע וּבָךְ יִטְהַר לִבֵּנוּ
וּבִמְנוּחָתֵךְ נָבוֹא לַעֲבוֹדַת אֱמֶת:
שַׁבָּת קֹדֶשׁ מְקוֹר הַבְּרָכָה
הִתְבָּרְכִי גַּם אַתְּ בִּמְנוּחָתֵנוּ
בָּרוּךְ אַתָּה יהוה מְקַדֵּשׁ הַשַּׁבָּת:

Each year should be the best year I have yet lived.
Each year we are more learned in the ways of life.
Each year we are wiser than the year before.
Each year our eyes know better the sights to seek.
Each year our ears listen with a finer tuning.
Every happening is a jewel, wrought about the fancy of time.
All that we understand of the universe is the setting for each
    sight and sound of the day.

The child looks with gladness each year to be one year
    older.
Should not this welcome pursue us all our years?
The piling of the years is a richness like the piling of gold.
Our years are coins with which we can purchase more wisely
    at the bazaars of each new season.
Our love is more pliant and patient having been taught by
    time.
This new year is one year older than the last.
The earth is more abounding in its growth.
The creatures have moved another step in their unfolding.
Humankind has left us one more year of art for our
    contemplation.
History is one year more resonant with lessons.
The sunrises are one year more familiar and promising.
The sunsets are one year less fearful, and the peace of the
    night is one year closer.

Kenneth L. Patton

Concluding prayers begin on page 1195.

BIRḤOT HASHAḤAR / MORNING BLESSINGS

How lovely are your tents, O Ya'akov,
how fine your encampments, Yisrael!

And as for me, drawn by your love,
I come into your house.

I lay me down in a humble surrender,
before your holy shrine in awe.

GREAT ONE, how I love your house's site,
adore your Glory's dwelling place.

And as for me, I fall in prayer,
my body I bend down,

I greet, I bless, I bend the knee,
before THE ONE who fashions me.

And as for me, my prayer is for you, GENTLE ONE,
may it be for you a time of desire,

O God, in the abundance of your love,
respond to me in truth with your help.

NOTE. The *Mah Tovu* prayer is composed entirely of biblical verses: Numbers 24:5; Psalms 5:8, 26:8, 95:6 (adapted) and 69:14.

COMMENTARY. *Mah Tovu* begins with a historical progression—the tents of our earliest ancestors, then the sanctuary of the years of wandering in the wilderness, then the Temple in Jerusalem. Each of these is linked to the synagogue, for it too is "your house." And I, the contemporary soul, seeking the right moment to encounter the divine there, am thus not alone. I am a link in the chain of tradition bearing the truth of your salvation.   D.A.T.

בִּרְכוֹת הַשַּׁחַר

מַה טֹּבוּ אֹהָלֶיךָ יַעֲקֹב מִשְׁכְּנֹתֶיךָ יִשְׂרָאֵל: וַאֲנִי בְּרֹב חַסְדְּךָ אָבוֹא בֵיתֶךָ אֶשְׁתַּחֲוֶה אֶל הֵיכַל קָדְשְׁךָ בְּיִרְאָתֶךָ: יהוה אָהַבְתִּי מְעוֹן בֵּיתֶךָ וּמְקוֹם מִשְׁכַּן כְּבוֹדֶךָ: וַאֲנִי אֶשְׁתַּחֲוֶה וְאֶכְרָעָה אֶבְרְכָה לִפְנֵי יהוה עֹשִׂי: וַאֲנִי תְפִלָּתִי לְךָ יהוה עֵת רָצוֹן אֱלֹהִים בְּרָב חַסְדֶּךָ עֲנֵנִי בֶּאֱמֶת יִשְׁעֶךָ:

Mah tovu ohaleha ya'akov mishkenoteha yisra'el. Va'ani berov hasdeha avo veyteha eshtahaveh el heyhal kodsheha beyirateha. Adonay ahavti me'on beyteha umkom mishkan kevodeha. Va'ani eshtahaveh ve'ehra'ah evrehah lifney adonay osi. Va'ani tefilati leha adonay et ratzon elohim berov hasdeha aneni be'emet yisheha.

KAVANAH. Torah tells us that a Moabite soothsayer, Balaam, had come to curse the Israelite people, but when he stood on a hill viewing the Israelites' peaceful encampment, "the spirit of God came upon him," and he exclaimed in wonder—"How lovely are your tents, O Yaakov, how fine your encampments, Yisrael!" (Numbers 24:5)

As we enter the New Year together, may this dwelling place we share together be "lovely." May the "tent" and shelter we build together at the dawn of this New Year be filled with harmony and peace, trust, strength and love—so our lips, too, may offer blessing.   L.G.B.

ואני תפלתי/as for me, my prayer is for you. The Hebrew text has often been creatively misread to mean "I am my prayer." All I have to offer in prayer is myself. We begin our prayers with a feeling of humility, knowing that the vaunted words we are about to speak are no greater than the person who speaks them. Most of the prayers in our liturgy are phrased in the first person plural, in which *we* as a community stand before the Divine presence. But here they are introduced in the halting and somewhat unsure voice of the individual, expressing some of that inadequacy that each of us feels as we enter the place and hour of prayer.   A.G.

ATIFAT TALLIT / DONNING THE TALLIT

It is customary to wrap oneself in the tallit before reciting the blessing that follows. After the blessing is recited, the tallit is placed across the shoulders. In some congregations the blessing is said in unison.

Bless, O my soul, THE ONE!
ABUNDANT ONE, my God, how great you grow!
In majesty and beauty you are dressed,
wrapping yourself in light as in a garment,
stretching out the heavens like a shawl!   Psalms 104:1-2

Blessed are You, VEILED ONE, our God, the sovereign of all worlds, who has made us holy with your mitzvot, and commanded us to wrap ourselves amid the fringed tallit. ↵

COMMENTARY. According to rabbinic tradition, Psalms 104:1-2 describes how God, robed in splendor, wrapped in light, began to create the world. The radiance of God's light-robe (one source says that God donned a white tallit) illumined the world before the creation of sun, moon, and stars. This meditation invites the worshipper to consider the act of donning the tallit to be the first step in the daily renewal of the world. God's wrapping in light becomes Israel's enlightened wrapping at the outset of a new day. It encourages Israel to celebrate world-renewing creativity as an unfailing sign of the divine presence within humankind.

S.S.

DERASH. The tallit is a very personal ritual object. Usually I wrap it around myself when joining in a prayer community. For the tallit both creates a private space for me and links me with Jewish tradition. It emphasizes my connection to my people while also offering me spiritual privacy. I am alone and in community at the same time.   L.G.B.

עֲטִיפַת טַלִּית

It is customary to wrap oneself in the tallit before reciting the blessing that follows. After the blessing is recited, the tallit is placed across the shoulders. In some congregations the blessing is said in unison.

בָּרְכִי נַפְשִׁי אֶת־יהוה יהוה אֱלֹהַי גָּדַלְתָּ מְּאֹד הוֹד וְהָדָר לָבָשְׁתָּ:
עֹטֶה־אוֹר כַּשַּׂלְמָה נוֹטֶה שָׁמַיִם כַּיְרִיעָה:

בָּרוּךְ אַתָּה יהוה אֱלֹהֵינוּ מֶלֶךְ הָעוֹלָם
אֲשֶׁר קִדְּשָׁנוּ בְּמִצְוֹתָיו
וְצִוָּנוּ לְהִתְעַטֵּף בַּצִּיצִית: —←

Baruḥ atah adonay eloheynu meleḥ ha'olam
asher kideshanu bemitzvotav
vetzivanu lehitatef batzitzit.

Many contemporary Jews are reciting *beraḥot*/blessings in ways that reflect their theological outlooks and ethical concerns. At any place where a blessing occurs in the liturgy, the following elements can be combined to create alternative formulas for *beraḥot*. This can be done by selecting one phrase from each group to form the introductory clause.

I	Baruḥ atah adonay	בָּרוּךְ אַתָּה יהוה	Blessed are you Adonay
	Beruḥah at yah	בְּרוּכָה אַתְּ יָהּ	Blessed are you Yah
	Nevareḥ et	נְבָרֵךְ אֶת	Let us bless
II	eloheynu	אֱלֹהֵינוּ	our God
	hashehinah	הַשְּׁכִינָה	Sheḥinah
	eyn haḥayim	עֵין הַחַיִּים	Source of Life
III	meleḥ ha'olam	מֶלֶךְ הָעוֹלָם	Sovereign of all worlds
	ḥey ha'olamim	חֵי הָעוֹלָמִים	Life of all the worlds
	ru'aḥ ha'olam	רוּחַ הָעוֹלָם	Spirit of the world

The phrase *nevareḥ et eyn haḥayim* was originally formulated by poet Marcia Falk (see SOURCES, p. 1248).

מַה יָּקָר חַסְדְּךָ אֱלֹהִים וּבְנֵי אָדָם בְּצֵל כְּנָפֶיךָ יֶחֱסָיוּן

How precious is your love, O God,
when earthborn find the shelter of your wing!
They're nourished from the riches of your house.
Give drink to them from your Edenic stream.
For with you is the fountain of all life,
in your Light do we behold all light.
Extend your love to those who know you,
and your justice to those honest in their hearts.   Psalms 36:8-11

COMMENTARY. The wearing of the tallit has its origins in the biblical commandment (Numbers 15:37-41) that a tassel should be attached to each corner of a garment to remind the Israelites of the mitzvot. This garment, resembling a poncho, was the basic garment worn every day. When clothing without such defined corners came to be customary, the tallit became a special ritual garment. In our time, a large tallit is worn only during the morning prayer, while traditional Jews wear a small tallit, also known as *arba kanfot*/four corners, underneath their outer clothes. In the biblical commandment the fringe included a color called תכלת/*tehelet*, a particular shade of purple-blue. When this was no longer available, the rabbis ruled that the tassels should be an undyed white. Some contemporary Jews have reinstituted the inclusion of blue in the fringe. Today in Reconstructionist congregations, women are encouraged to wear tallitot as well.   D.A.T.

מַה יָּקָר חַסְדְּךָ אֱלֹהִים וּבְנֵי אָדָם בְּצֵל כְּנָפֶיךָ יֶחֱסָיוּן

מַה־יָּקָר חַסְדְּךָ אֱלֹהִים וּבְנֵי אָדָם בְּצֵל כְּנָפֶיךָ יֶחֱסָיוּן:
יִרְוְיֻן מִדֶּשֶׁן בֵּיתֶךָ וְנַחַל עֲדָנֶיךָ תַשְׁקֵם:
כִּי־עִמְּךָ מְקוֹר חַיִּים בְּאוֹרְךָ נִרְאֶה־אוֹר:
מְשֹׁךְ חַסְדְּךָ לְיֹדְעֶיךָ וְצִדְקָתְךָ לְיִשְׁרֵי־לֵב:

כי עמך מקור חיים / For with you is the fountain of all life, in your light do we behold all light. The flow of light represented by the tallit is joined to the blessing of life itself. God is described here in the psalmist's most delicate and abstract phrasing. We reach forth to the source of life and are bathed in its light as it flows forth to meet us. A.G.

DERASH. The tallit is a "garment of brightness." It links us with the whole universe, with the whole of Nature. The blue thread within it (Numbers 15:37–41) reminds us that heaven and earth can touch, that the elements of our universe are all wondrously connected. L.G.B.

SHIREY SHAḤAR/MORNING SONGS

One of the following introductory poems may be added here.

I

Morning I will seek you,
  my fortress rock, each day.
My song of dawn and dusk
  before you I shall lay.
I stand before your greatness,
  with trembling I'm fraught,
because your eyes can enter
  my heart's most secret way.

What can be done, by heart
  or tongue, what can one do or say?
And how much strength lies deep
  within my body as I pray?
And yet you find it good
  —mere human song—and so,
I thank you for as long as shall
  your lifebreath in me play.

Solomon ibn Gabirol

One of the following introductory poems may be added here.

I

שַׁחַר אֲבַקֶּשְׁךָ צוּרִי וּמִשְׂגַּבִּי
אֶעֱרֹךְ לְפָנֶיךָ שַׁחְרִי וְגַם עַרְבִּי:
לִפְנֵי גְדֻלָּתָךְ אֶעֱמֹד וְאֶבָּהֵל
כִּי עֵינְךָ תִרְאֶה כָּל־מַחְשְׁבוֹת לִבִּי:

מַה־זֶּה אֲשֶׁר יוּכַל הַלֵּב וְהַלָּשׁוֹן לַעֲשׂוֹת
וּמַה־כֹּחַ רוּחִי בְּתוֹךְ קִרְבִּי:
הִנֵּה לְךָ תִיטַב זִמְרַת אֱנוֹשׁ עַל־כֵּן
אוֹדְךָ בְּעוֹד תִּהְיֶה נִשְׁמַת אֱלוֹהַּ בִּי:

שחר אבקשך/Morning I will seek you. The *Shaharit* service, as its name implies, was originally meant to be recited at dawn. Our tradition views the two daily times of change of light as sacred hours to be appreciated with prayer and inner quiet. Though our morning service usually begins long after sunrise, we should try to preserve something of that special memory of dawn's quiet blessing as we begin our prayer. A.G.

II

My heart's a place for you, as you are mine.
Remembering you, I hail, nighttime, daytime,
I praise you, Holy One, my crown divine,
    cure of my soul, to my thirst quench sublime.

I walk amid your light, unto your room,
    and from your precious glow my clothes I find,
and, happy serving you, my place assume,
    in dread filled joy of you, perfect and kind.

My God, glory and love around me bloom,
    my wish is seeing you, outside dream's time,
for you my passion burns, my whole life through,
    my want is to ascend, these heavens climb.

Anonymous

לבבי מקומך /My heart's a place for you, as you are mine. The journey to
God is a journey inward rather than upward. We think more easily of a
God who dwells within the human soul than we do of one in the sky or
on a mountain. Here the poet reminds us that while God is indeed in us,
we are also "inside" God. The Hebrew word *makom* or "place" is one of
our ancient names for the divine. "God is the place of the world," said the
rabbis, "but the world is not God's place," meaning that the divine cannot
be contained within the finite. In the spirit of this poem, we might choose
to say that the inwardness with which we seek God and the inwardness
with which the divine seeks us is the same inwardness.   A.G.

II

לְבָבִי מְקוֹמָךְ וְאַתָּה מְקוֹמִי
בְּזִכְרָךְ אֲהַלֵּל בְּלֵילִי וְיוֹמִי:
שְׁבָחָךְ קְדוֹשִׁי עֲטֶרֶת לְרֹאשִׁי
וְרִפְאוּת לְנַפְשִׁי וְשִׁקּוּי לְעַצְמִי:

מְהַלֵּךְ בְּאוֹרָךְ לְנֹכַח דְּבִירָךְ
וּמֵהוֹד יְקָרָךְ לְבוּשִׁי וְעָצְמִי:
וְאֶשְׂמַח בְּעָבְדָךְ בְּעָמְדִי לְנֶגְדָּךְ
וְאֶשְׂמַח בְּפַחְדָּךְ בְּחַסְדָּךְ שְׁלוֹמִי:

אֱלֹהַי כְּבוֹדָךְ סְבִיבִי וְחַסְדָּךְ
וְחֶפְצִי רְאוֹתָךְ וְלֹא בַחֲלוֹמִי:
לָךְ תַּאֲוָתִי בְּחַיַּי וּמוֹתִי
וְחֶפְצִי עֲלוֹתִי לְגָבְהֵי מְרוֹמִי:

III

You knew me long before you fashioned me,
and as long as your breath lives in me, you shall
   preserve me.
Would I have any place to stand were you to push me on?
Would I have power to walk were you to hold me back?
What can I say other than thoughts your hand has shaped
   in me?
What can I do unless you shall enable me?
I seek you in this hour of desire: Please answer me!
May your desire, like a shield, surround me.
So raise me up to hasten early to your dwelling place,
to bless your Name alone, please waken me!

Yehudah Halevi

III

יְדַעְתָּֽנִי בְּטֶֽרֶם תִּצְּרֵֽנִי   וְכָל עוֹד רוּחֲךָ בִּי תִּצְּרֵֽנִי

הֲיֵשׁ לִי מַעֲמָד אִם תֶּהְדְּפֵֽנִי   וְאִם לִי מַהֲלָךְ אִם תַּעְצְרֵֽנִי

וּמָה אֹמַר וּמַחְשָׁבִי בְיָדֶךָ   וּמָה אוּכַל עֲשׂה עַד תַּעְזְרֵֽנִי

דְּרַשְׁתִּֽיךָ בְּעֵת רָצוֹן עֲנֵֽנִי   וְכַצְּנָה רְצוֹנְךָ תַעְטְרֵֽנִי

הֲקִימֵֽנִי לְשַׁחֵר אֶת־דְּבִירְךָ   וְאֶת שִׁמְךָ לְבָרֵךְ עוֹרְרֵֽנִי׃

DERASH. Each of us is bombarded daily with messages that if we accomplish this or buy that, we will become who we want to be. Such messages belie another reality about our lives. Sickness, accident, war, randomness, and hundreds of other circumstances are at least partly beyond our control. When we are honest with ourselves, we recognize not only our own power, but our finitude, the extraordinary contemporary achievements from which we benefit, and our fragility. Often, I am not in control of my own destiny. Passing through the valley of fear, I come to seek hope and trust. In my smallness, I seek the Source of all life. Now I am ready to begin!

D.A.T.

IV

I call to you, please answer me, divine one!
Incline your ear to me, and listen to my prayer.
May I, with justice, come to see your face,
May I awake with satisfaction to behold your form!

For I have trusted in you, GUIDING ONE,
and I have said: You are my God!
Please hear my supplication when I call to you,
when I raise up my hands in homage to your holy place.
ETERNAL ONE, my God, I have cried out to you,
and you have healed me.
To you, RESTORING ONE, I call,
to my protector I lay out my supplication.

Let your face's light shine on your servant,
help me with your love!
For in you, ABUNDANT ONE, I place my hope,
may you give answer, sovereign one, my God.
Please hear my prayer, ETERNAL ONE, please hearken to my
    cry,
and to my tearful plea do not be deaf!
Hear, O HIDDEN ONE, deal graciously with me,
SUPERNAL ADVOCATE, become a help for me.

I rejoiced when people said to me:
Let's go forth to the house of GOD!
I take joy in all that you have said,
like one who comes into great wealth.
Please hear, my sovereign, my God,
the sound of my prayer's cry,
for truly, I now pray to you.
ILLUMINATOR of the dawn, please hear my voice;
my morning prayer I offer you, and wait with expectation. ↵

אֲנִי קְרָאתִיךָ כִי־תַעֲנֵנִי אֵל הַט־אָזְנְךָ לִי שְׁמַע אִמְרָתִי:

אֲנִי בְּצֶדֶק אֶחֱזֶה פָנֶיךָ אֶשְׂבְּעָה בְהָקִיץ תְּמוּנָתֶךָ:

וַאֲנִי עָלֶיךָ בָטַחְתִּי יהוה אָמַרְתִּי אֱלֹהַי אָתָּה:

שְׁמַע קוֹל תַּחֲנוּנַי בְּשַׁוְּעִי אֵלֶיךָ בְּנָשְׂאִי יָדַי אֶל־דְּבִיר קָדְשֶׁךָ:

יהוה אֱלֹהָי שִׁוַּעְתִּי אֵלֶיךָ וַתִּרְפָּאֵנִי:

אֵלֶיךָ יהוה אֶקְרָא וְאֶל־אֲדֹנָי אֶתְחַנָּן:

הָאִירָה פָנֶיךָ עַל־עַבְדֶּךָ הוֹשִׁיעֵנִי בְחַסְדֶּךָ:

כִּי־לְךָ יהוה הוֹחָלְתִּי אַתָּה תַעֲנֶה אֲדֹנָי אֱלֹהָי:

שָׁמְעָה תְפִלָּתִי יהוה וְשַׁוְעָתִי הַאֲזִינָה אֶל־דִּמְעָתִי אַל־תֶּחֱרָשׁ:

שְׁמַע־יהוה וְחָנֵּנִי יהוה הֱיֵה עֹזֵר לִי:

שָׂמַחְתִּי בְּאֹמְרִים לִי בֵּית יהוה נֵלֵךָ:

שָׂשׂ אָנֹכִי עַל־אִמְרָתֶךָ כְּמוֹצֵא שָׁלָל רָב:

הַקְשִׁיבָה לְקוֹל שַׁוְעִי מַלְכִּי וֵאלֹהָי כִּי־אֵלֶיךָ אֶתְפַּלָּל:

יהוה בֹּקֶר תִּשְׁמַע קוֹלִי בֹּקֶר אֶעֱרָךְ־לְךָ וַאֲצַפֶּה: ←

Eleḥa adonay ekra ve'el adonay ethanan.
Shema adonay veḥoneni adonay heyey ozer li. ←

I cry out to you that you might answer, God.
Incline your ear to me, and listen to my utterance.
My feet are standing on the straight path,
and in company of others I now bless THE OMNIPRESENT.

Psalms 17:6, 15; 31:15; 28:2; 30:3, 9; 31:7; 38:16; 39:13; 30:11; 122:1; 119:162; 5:3-4; 26:12

KAVANAH. Public worship aids us by liberating personality from the confining walls of the individual ego. Imprisoned in self, we easily fall prey to morbid broodings. Interference with career, personal disappointment and disillusionment, hurts to vanity, the fear of death—all these tend so to dominate our attention that our minds move in a fixed and narrow system of ideas, which we detest but from which we see no escape. With a whole wide world of boundless opportunities about us, we permit our minds, as it were, to pace up and down within the narrow cell of their ego-prisons. But participation in public worship breaks through the prison of the ego and lets in the light and air of the world. Instead of living but one small and petty life, we now share the multitudinous life of our people. Against the wider horizons that now open to our ken, personal cares do not loom so large. Life becomes infinitely more meaningful and worthwhile when we become aware, through our participation in public worship, of a common life that transcends our individual selves.

M.M.K. (Adapted)

אֲנִי קְרָאתִ֫יךָ כִי־תַעֲנֵ֫נִי אֵל הַט־אָזְנְךָ לִי שְׁמַע אִמְרָתִי:
רַגְלִי עָמְדָה בְמִישׁוֹר בְּמַקְהֵלִים אֲבָרֵךְ יהוה:

שמחתי באמרים לי בית יהוה נלך /I rejoiced when people said to me: Let's go
forth to the house of GOD! This is indeed how we want to feel when
given the opportunity to attend synagogue and be part of a community of
prayer. Yet there are so many reasons why we stay away: a lack of
knowledge or skill that makes us feel incompetent, the press of other
responsibilities or opportunities, the difficulty in becoming spiritually
engaged through public worship, and simply falling out of the habit.
Then, when it comes time "to go forth to the house of GOD," instead of
rejoicing we experience anxiety. This is a season for seeking a path that
will led toward rejoicing at the opportunity to worship.   R.H.

KAVANAH. When we worship in public we know our life is part of a larger
life, a wave of an ocean of being—the first-hand experience of that larger
life which is God.   M.M.K.

V

My God, you have prepared my tongue,
  and in your wisdom you have placed
into my mouth these prayerful songs,
  surpassing every worldly craft in grace.
And you have given me a singer's throat,
  with which I call out sweetly, never hoarse;
since dawn of life, you have prepared my foot
  toward you alone to set its course.
My every instinct you have purified
  like wool as white as snow,
and never have you cast aside
  my heart to wander as sleepwalkers go.
Be now my refuge, and my secret place,
  as yesterday, and every future day.
Protect me now, in your abundant grace,
  my God, do not delay!

Solomon ibn Gabirol

לְשׁוֹנִי כּוֹנַנְתָּ   אֱלֹהַי וַתִּבְחַר
בְּשִׁירִים שֶׁשַּׂמְתָּ   בְּפִי טוֹב מִמִּסְחָר
וְלִי גָרוֹן תַּתָּה   בְּקָרְאִי לֹא נִחָר
וְנֶגְדְּךָ כּוֹנַנְתָּ   צְעָדַי מִמִּשְׁחָר
וְיִצְרִי הִלְבַּנְתָּ   כְּמוֹ צֶמֶר צָחַר
וְלָכֵן לֹא שַׁתָּה   לְבָבִי בִּי סְחַרְחָר
הֱיֵה סִתְרִי עַתָּה   כְּאֶתְמוֹל וּכְמָחָר
מָגִנִּי אַתָּה   אֱלֹהַי אַל תְּאַחַר׃

NOTE. Solomon ibn Gabirol was an eleventh-century Sephardic poet and philosopher.

VI

As the heart yearns for the waters of a brook,
so yearns my heart for you, O God.
My soul now thirsts for God, the living God.
When might I come to see the face of God?
My tears have been my food both day and night,
whenever people said to me: "Where is your God?"
These things I call to mind, and I pour out my soul,
as I now pass amid the crowd,
making my way with them up to the house of God,
amid the sound of jubilation and thanksgiving,
amid the roar of celebration.
Why are you downcast, my soul,
why do you sigh within me?
Place hope in God!
For soon I shall again give thanks
to God, whose presence is my saving force!

Psalms 42:2-6

VI

כְּאַיָּל תַּעֲרֹג עַל־אֲפִיקֵי־מָיִם
כֵּן נַפְשִׁי תַעֲרֹג אֵלֶיךָ אֱלֹהִים׃
צָמְאָה נַפְשִׁי לֵאלֹהִים לְאֵל חָי
מָתַי אָבוֹא וְאֵרָאֶה פְּנֵי אֱלֹהִים׃
הָיְתָה־לִּי דִמְעָתִי לֶחֶם יוֹמָם וָלָיְלָה
בֶּאֱמֹר אֵלַי כָּל־הַיּוֹם אַיֵּה אֱלֹהֶיךָ׃
אֵלֶּה אֶזְכְּרָה וְאֶשְׁפְּכָה עָלַי נַפְשִׁי
כִּי אֶעֱבֹר בַּסָּךְ אֶדַּדֵּם עַד־בֵּית אֱלֹהִים
בְּקוֹל־רִנָּה וְתוֹדָה הָמוֹן חוֹגֵג׃
מַה־תִּשְׁתּוֹחֲחִי נַפְשִׁי
וַתֶּהֱמִי עָלָי
הוֹחִילִי לֵאלֹהִים כִּי עוֹד אוֹדֶנּוּ
יְשׁוּעֹת פָּנָיו׃

KAVANAH. As the pilgrim in the psalm ascends toward the Temple, surrounded by a celebrating throng, loneliness and sadness well up from within. While the pilgrim longs for a sense of serenity, meaning and security as the time for making an offering draws near, an inner struggle takes place—a struggle to feel hope, become ready to offer real thanks, and experience the possibility of redemption. "Let my thirst be quenched," the psalmist cries, "by the waters of salvation." H.L./D.A.T.

For the sake of the union of the blessed Holy One with the Shehinah, I stand here, ready in body and mind, to take upon myself the mitzvah, "You shall love your fellow human being as yourself," and by this merit may I open up my mouth:

COMMENTARY. This *kavanah* before the morning service was introduced by the kabbalists of Safed. Only by accepting upon ourselves the obligation to love others as ourselves are we allowed to enter the human community of prayer. It is as members of that community and, specifically, as Jews that we come before God in worship.   A.G.

KAVANAH. Before we can effect reconciliation with God, we must first become reconciled with those from whom we are estranged.

Mishnah Yoma 8.9 (Adapted)

ואהבת...כמוך / You shall...yourself (Leviticus 19:18)

לְשֵׁם יִחוּד קוּדְשָׁא בְּרִיךְ הוּא וּשְׁכִינְתֵּיהּ

Men say:

הִנְנִי מוּכָן וּמְזוּמָּן

Women say:

הִנְנִי מוּכָנָה וּמְזוּמֶּנֶת

לְקַבֵּל עָלַי מִצְוַת עֲשֵׂה שֶׁל

וְאָהַבְתָּ לְרֵעֲךָ כָּמוֹךָ

וּבִזְכוּת זֶה אֶפְתַּח פִּי:

Some communities add Yigdal *(page 1225-1226)*, Adon Olam *(page 1223-1224)*, and/ or Psalm 27 *(page 1217-1218)* here.

BIRHOT HASHAHAR / MORNING BLESSINGS

Blessed are you, AWAKENER, our God, life of all the worlds, who removes sleep from my eyes, and slumber from my eyelids.

DERASH. The "worlds" to which *hey ha'olamim* refers may be the many universes that each of us inhabits, the vast spaces that surround our world, or the infinite depths that fill the human heart. We proclaim that God is the single flow of life that inhabits and unifies them all.   A.G.

COMMENTARY. This sequence of blessings is the central portion of *Birhot Hashahar*. It was designed by the talmudic sages to celebrate such acts of awakening as focusing the eyes, sitting up, stretching, standing, etc. The transference of these blessings to the public worship service (ninth century) disengaged the blessing and the particular act of awakening with which it was joined. In their public setting the morning blessings took on a new level of meaning. Removed from the acts of awakening, individual activities became metaphors for godly action. The blessing "who clothes the naked" ceased to be a pointed acknowledgment of personal possessions and personal protection. Instead it became a celebration of God as the power that prompts the care and nurturance of humankind. The blessing "who raises the lowly" ceased to be a blessing over the renewal of physical mobility and became a blessing of the divine presence manifest in actions that raise the bodies and elevate the spirits of those who are low.   S.S.

COMMENTARY. The order of *Birhot Hashahar* varies from prayerbook to prayerbook because this was not a set part of the public service. Individuals originally recited these blessings as they went about rising, washing and dressing in the morning. Later they were recited privately as a prelude to public prayer. The order of the blessings here begins with the universal act of waking up and becoming aware of the world. It continues with greater wakefulness, addressing sight, clothing, and the act of standing upright. It then shifts to particulars reflecting Jewish uniqueness. Only then does it turn to the full awareness of the mind and spirit expressed in *Elohay Neshamah*.   D.A.T.

Some communities add Yigdal *(page 1225-1226),* Adon Olam *(page 1223-1224), and/ or* Psalm 27 *(page 1217-1218) here.*

בִּרְכוֹת הַשַּׁחַר

בָּרוּךְ אַתָּה יהוה אֱלֹהֵינוּ חֵי הָעוֹלָמִים
הַמַּעֲבִיר שֵׁנָה מֵעֵינַי וּתְנוּמָה מֵעַפְעַפָּי: ←

Baruḥ atah adonay eloheynu ḥey ha'olamim
hama'avir shenah me'eynay utnumah me'afapay. ﬤ

COMMENTARY. The familiar introductory formula for blessings including the phrase *meleḥ ha'olam* / sovereign of the world, was adopted by the rabbis during the talmudic era and universally accepted by later Jews. Substituting another rabbinic phrase, *ḥey ha'olamim* / life of all the worlds, expresses the idea that as Judaism continues to evolve, alternatives to the ancient metaphor of God as divine ruler should emerge. This alternative blessing formulation may be used throughout the siddur by those who prefer it, just as the traditional *meleḥ ha'olam* may be substituted here.

A.G.

COMMENTARY. Various editions of the prayerbook offer different orders of the morning blessings. Here the first blessing is that on awakening. Then comes a blessing on the sounds of dawn, followed by the return of waking consciousness ("who establishes the dry land upon the waters"), and then the blessing on opening our eyes and seeing our world, freshly created with the dawn, around us. The cycle is completed with the blessing "who gives strength to the weary" as we begin our day. A.G.

DERASH. When we are about to say: "Blessed are you, our God, sovereign of all worlds," and prepare to utter the first word "blessed," we should do so with all our strength, so that we will have no strength left to say, "are you." And this is the meaning of the verse in the Scriptures: "But they that wait for God shall exchange their strength." What we are really saying is: "Source of life, I am giving you all the strength that is within me in that very first word; now will you, in exchange, give me an abundance of new strength, so that I can go on with my prayer." M.B. (Adapted)

Blessed are you, THE PROVIDENT, our God, life of all the worlds, who gives the bird of dawn discernment to tell day from night.

Blessed are you, THE FASHIONER, our God, life of all the worlds, who stretches forth the earth upon the waters.

Blessed are you, THE LAMP, our God, life of all the worlds, who makes the blind to see.

Blessed are you, THE COMPASSIONATE, our God, life of all the worlds, who clothes the naked.

Blessed are you, REDEEMING ONE, our God, life of all the worlds, who makes the captive free.

Blessed are you, THE HELPING HAND, our God, life of all the worlds, who raises up the humble. ⤶

KAVANAH. We give thanks that we are restored whole and healthy to consciousness and to an orderly universe. That is why, in the second blessing, we give thanks that when we stepped out of bed, our feet encountered not the watery chaos which preceded creation, but the solid earth which God spread over the waters. The daily emergence from unconsciousness reminds us of our fragility as human creatures and our need for support and care.   R.A.

DERASH. For whom do we recite blessings? If God is beyond blessing, then we must be reciting them for ourselves. Each *berahah* urges us to avoid taking the world for granted. Each contains a vision of the creative or redemptive power in the world. Jewish tradition teaches that living up to our heritage as beings created *betzelem elohim*, in the image of God, requires us to "imitate God." Thus each *berahah* can teach us something about living our lives in consonance with the divine. Blessings tell us not so much about a God "out there somewhere," they teach us how to make manifest the godly in ourselves.   D.A.T.

זוקֵף כפופים / who raises up the humble: literally, makes upright those bent down. The phrase could suggest either those suffering a physical deformity or those humbled by adverse circumstances.   J.R.

בָּרוּךְ אַתָּה יהוה אֱלֹהֵינוּ חֵי הָעוֹלָמִים
הַנּוֹתֵן לַשֶּׂכְוִי בִינָה לְהַבְחִין בֵּין יוֹם וּבֵין לָיְלָה:

בָּרוּךְ אַתָּה יהוה אֱלֹהֵינוּ חֵי הָעוֹלָמִים רוֹקַע הָאָרֶץ עַל הַמָּיִם:

בָּרוּךְ אַתָּה יהוה אֱלֹהֵינוּ חֵי הָעוֹלָמִים פּוֹקֵחַ עִוְרִים:

בָּרוּךְ אַתָּה יהוה אֱלֹהֵינוּ חֵי הָעוֹלָמִים מַלְבִּישׁ עֲרֻמִּים:

בָּרוּךְ אַתָּה יהוה אֱלֹהֵינוּ חֵי הָעוֹלָמִים מַתִּיר אֲסוּרִים:

בָּרוּךְ אַתָּה יהוה אֱלֹהֵינוּ חֵי הָעוֹלָמִים זוֹקֵף כְּפוּפִים: ⟵

Baruḥ atah adonay eloheynu ḥey ha'olamim
   hanoten lasehvi vinah lehavḥin beyn yom uveyn laylah.

Baruḥ atah adonay eloheynu ḥey ha'olamim
   roka ha'aretz al hamayim.

Baruḥ atah adonay eloheynu ḥey ha'olamim poke'aḥ ivrim.

Baruḥ atah adonay eloheynu ḥey ha'olamim malbish arumim.

Baruḥ atah adonay eloheynu ḥey ha'olamim matir asurim.

Baruḥ atah adonay eloheynu ḥey ha'olamim zokef kefufim. ⟵

שכוי / bird of dawn has been variously rendered as "rooster," "watchman," "celestial appearance," or "meteor." In an urban setting, the earliest sound of life we are likely to hear at dawn is the chirping of sparrows. *Sehvi* is thus rendered differently from *gever*, rooster, here to capture some of the ambiguity of the word.   J.R.

KAVANAH. Those of us who live in plenty are grateful for the clothing on our bodies, the warmth of a garment that shields us from the elements. We pray for a time when this blessing may be spoken by *all* people, a time when *all* humans are "clothed" with warmth and safety, enwrapped in God's love.   L.G.B.

Blessed are you, THE WAY, our God, life of all the worlds, who makes firm a person's steps.

Blessed are you, THE GENEROUS, our God, life of all the worlds, who acts for all my needs.

Blessed are you, THE MIGHTY ONE, our God, life of all the worlds, who girds Israel with strength.

Blessed are you, THE BEAUTIFUL, our God, life of all the worlds, who crowns Israel with splendor. ⤶

DERASH. המכין מצעדי גבר/who makes firm a person's steps. An interpretive translation of Psalms 37:23-24: "When one's steps follow the divine path, they bring delight along the way." The Baal Shem Tov noted in this connection that wherever one goes and whatever one does each day should have a deeper spiritual significance that parallels the mundane reality of everyday existence. In bringing to our lives this deeper significance, we find new delight in the firmness of our steps.   L.G.B.

DERASH. Rabbi Abraham Joshua Heschel once said that when he marched with the Reverend Martin Luther King, Jr., in Selma, Alabama, his "feet were praying."

בָּרוּךְ אַתָּה יהוה אֱלֹהֵינוּ חֵי הָעוֹלָמִים
הַמֵּכִין מִצְעֲדֵי גָֽבֶר:

בָּרוּךְ אַתָּה יהוה אֱלֹהֵינוּ חֵי הָעוֹלָמִים
שֶׁעָשָׂה לִי כָּל־צָרְכִּי:

בָּרוּךְ אַתָּה יהוה אֱלֹהֵינוּ חֵי הָעוֹלָמִים
אוֹזֵר יִשְׂרָאֵל בִּגְבוּרָה:

בָּרוּךְ אַתָּה יהוה אֱלֹהֵינוּ חֵי הָעוֹלָמִים
עוֹטֵר יִשְׂרָאֵל בְּתִפְאָרָה: ⟵

Baruḥ atah adonay eloheynu ḥey ha'olamim
hameḥin mitzadey gaver.

Baruḥ atah adonay eloheynu ḥey ha'olamim
she'asah li kol tzorki.

Baruḥ atah adonay eloheynu ḥey ha'olamim
ozer yisra'el bigvurah.

Baruḥ atah adonay eloheynu ḥey ha'olamim
oter yisra'el betifarah. ⤵

Blessed are you, THE IMAGELESS, our God, life of all the worlds, who made me in your image.

Blessed are you, THE FREE, our God, life of all the worlds, who made me free.

Blessed are you, THE ANCIENT ONE, our God, life of all the worlds, who made me of the people Israel.

Blessed are you, RENEWING ONE, our God, life of all the worlds, who gives strength to the weary.

COMMENTARY. Once we are awake, we return to full consciousness of who we are. In the rigidly stratified society in which these prayers originated, people were less conscious of identity than of status. Thus, the original forms of these prayers expressed the thankfulness of the most privileged members of the community—free Jewish males—that they did not have the less privileged status of women, slaves or non-Jews.

The blessings we now use affirm that since we embody the divine image, we are all intrinsically valuable. To degrade or enslave others is to deface the image of God. We were created free just as our creator is free. We are capable of choice, of invention and of transformation in our lives and in our world. We also give thanks for our particular identity as Jews. God who creates our common humanity, also cherishes human diversity. Each people is unique and precious.   R.A.

NOTE. "THE IMAGELESS...who made me in your image." This paradoxical rendering enables us to understand that our being made "in the divine image" (Genesis 1:26-27) encompasses other than physical attributes: speech, will, reason, spirituality, kindness, freedom of action, moral sense.

J.R.

בָּרוּךְ אַתָּה יהוה אֱלֹהֵינוּ חֵי הָעוֹלָמִים
שֶׁעָשַׂנִי בְּצַלְמוֹ:

בָּרוּךְ אַתָּה יהוה אֱלֹהֵינוּ חֵי הָעוֹלָמִים
שֶׁעָשַׂנִי בֶּן / בַּת חוֹרִין:

בָּרוּךְ אַתָּה יהוה אֱלֹהֵינוּ חֵי הָעוֹלָמִים
שֶׁעָשַׂנִי יִשְׂרָאֵל:

בָּרוּךְ אַתָּה יהוה אֱלֹהֵינוּ חֵי הָעוֹלָמִים
הַנּוֹתֵן לַיָּעֵף כֹּחַ:

Baruḥ atah adonay eloheynu ḥey ha'olamim
she'asani betzalmo.

Baruḥ atah adonay eloheynu ḥey ha'olamim
she'asani ben/bat ḥorin.

Baruḥ atah adonay eloheynu ḥey ha'olamim
she'asani yisra'el.

Baruḥ atah adonay eloheynu ḥey ha'olamim
hanoten laya'ef ko'aḥ.

שעשני בצלמו / who made me in your image. When a human being is slain, the very image of God is shattered. We revere human life because it is a spark of the life that animates the universe. Only after we have acquired the principle of reverence for each person is it possible to love each other as we should love, not merely "as thyself" but as a reflection of the divine. "Beloved are human beings," said R. Akiba, "for they were made in the image of God." M.M.K. (Adapted)

Blessed are you, THE ARCHITECT, our God, the sovereign of all worlds, who shaped the human being with wisdom, making for us all the openings and vessels of the body. It is revealed and known before your Throne of Glory that if one of these passageways be open when it should be closed, or blocked up when it should be free, one could not stay alive or stand before you. Blessed are you, MIRACULOUS, the wondrous healer of all flesh.

COMMENTARY. This blessing expresses wonder at the simple but necessary functioning of the human body. We do not need to stand before any greater wonder of nature than our own bodies in order to appreciate the intricacy and beauty with which our world is endowed. A sense of awe at our own creation is a starting point of prayer. A.G.

בָּרוּךְ אַתָּה יהוה אֱלֹהֵינוּ מֶלֶךְ הָעוֹלָם אֲשֶׁר יָצַר אֶת־הָאָדָם בְּחָכְמָה
וּבָרָא בוֹ נְקָבִים נְקָבִים חֲלוּלִים חֲלוּלִים:
גָּלוּי וְיָדוּעַ לִפְנֵי כִסֵּא כְבוֹדֶךָ שֶׁאִם יִפָּתֵחַ אֶחָד מֵהֶם אוֹ יִסָּתֵם אֶחָד
מֵהֶם אִי אֶפְשָׁר לְהִתְקַיֵּם וְלַעֲמֹד לְפָנֶיךָ:
בָּרוּךְ אַתָּה יהוה רוֹפֵא כָל־בָּשָׂר וּמַפְלִיא לַעֲשׂוֹת:

Baruh atah adonay eloheynu meleh ha'olam asher yatzar et
ha'adam behohmah uvara vo nekavim nekavim halulim
halulim. Galuwi veyadu'a lifney hisey hevodeha she'im yipate'ah
ehad mehem o yisatem ehad mehem i efshar lehitkayem
vela'amod lefaneha. Baruh atah adonay rofey hol basar umafli
la'asot.

נקבים נקבים/all the openings. We regularly perceive by contrast: light and
shadow, height and depth, loudness and softness. Often we become aware
of health only after illness has replaced it. This brief paragraph of praise
for the wondrous workings of the human organism encourages recognition of the blessing of health in its presence, not its absence. Every
moment we are healing! E.G.

My God, the soul you gave to me is pure. You have created it, you shaped it, and you breathed it into me, and you preserve it deep inside of me. And someday you will take it from me, restoring it to everlasting life. ⮐

COMMENTARY. The word *neshamah*, which means both "breath" and "soul," provides a linguistic connection between the blessings for body and soul. The blessing for the soul uses the vocabulary of the Creation story, especially Genesis 2:6, which describes how God created the human form and then animated it with the breath of life. Hence, the language of celebrating each awakening carries an echo of the primal joining of human form to life force. Every awakening is nothing less than a rehearsal of the mystery of creation.

The traditional version of the blessing for the soul acknowledges the daily renewal of life as a recollection of creation and also as a foretaste of resurrection. The current version concludes instead by acknowledging God as the power that renews life each day.   S.S.

DERASH. This short and beautiful prayer starts each day and offers comfort in times of stress. Self-esteem is a precious gift. Even though we may lose it in the tragedies of the present, it will be restored to us in our future. God, the healer, returns our souls to us.   E.M.

נשמה שנתת בי טהורה היא /the soul you gave to me is pure. This elegant and eloquent affirmation of the eternal purity of the soul and the possibility of personal renewal is especially appropriate at this season of *teshuvah*.   R.H.

KAVANAH. Even on these days, when we are most focused on our shortcomings and faults, this prayer reminds us that our souls are pure. The task of these ten days is to turn towards that purity.

Adina Abramowitz

אַתָּה בְרָאתָהּ אַתָּה יְצַרְתָּהּ אַתָּה נְפַחְתָּהּ בִּי וְאַתָּה מְשַׁמְּרָהּ בְּקִרְבִּי
וְאַתָּה עָתִיד לִטְּלָהּ מִמֶּנִּי לְחַיֵּי עוֹלָם: ←

Elohay neshamah shena<u>ta</u>ta bi tehorah hi.

לחיי עולם/restoring [the soul] to everlasting life. The traditional Hebrew
text says, "and restore it to me in the future to come." The text in our
siddur, rather than stressing the traditional notion of individual afterlife, or
of personal resurrection in the messianic End of Days, reverses the
emphasis: the soul, having sojourned in the physical life, is restored to the
everlasting stream of life—to the continuum of being that is the sum-total
of all transitory lives, when viewed from the perspective of eternity.   J.R.

GUIDED MEDITATION. In the Hebrew of אלהי נשמה/My God, the soul,
many of the words end with the sound "*ah*," spelled "הָ". When this
prayer is chanted slowly, you breathe these words. Thus this prayer
suggests an opportunity, through breathing, to explore the connection
between *neshamah* as breath and as soul:

Sit comfortably with your eyes closed, feet uncrossed, and hands loosely
on your lap. Take a series of slow, relaxed breaths. Don't try to control
them. Just let them come and go freely. Focus your concentration on your
breath. Let the thoughts you have flow through you. Don't try to control
them. Each time you end a thought, return your focus to your breath. Do
this for several minutes. As you follow your breath, reflect on the divine
energy it contains.   L.W.K./D.B.

As long as spirit breathes in me, I offer thanks before you, BREATH DIVINE, my God, God of my ancestors, the master of all deeds, and source of every life. Blessed are you, THE HOLY SPIRIT, in whose possession is the breath of every living thing, the animation of all flesh.

KAVANAH. We are each created in the image of God. When we allow the reflections of our own beings to illuminate the universe, when we understand that we carry God *within us*, we are closer to doing the work that will eventually perfect the world. When we each accept the purity of our own souls and the purity of the souls of others, *tikun olam* will have been achieved.　　　　　　　　　　　　　　　　　　　　　L.G.B.

KAVANAH. "Sleep is one sixtieth a part of death" (Talmud Berahot 57b), and waking is a kind of rebirth.　　　　　　　　　　　　　　　L.W.K.

כָּל זְמַן שֶׁהַנְּשָׁמָה בְקִרְבִּי מוֹדֶה / מוֹדָה אֲנִי לְפָנֶֽיךָ יהוה אֱלֹהַי
וֵאלֹהֵי אֲבוֹתַי וְאִמּוֹתַי רִבּוֹן כָּל הַמַּעֲשִׂים אֲדוֹן כָּל הַנְּשָׁמוֹת: בָּרוּךְ
אַתָּה יהוה אֲשֶׁר בְּיָדוֹ נֶֽפֶשׁ כָּל חָי וְרֽוּחַ כָּל בָּשָׂר:

אשר בידו נפש כל חי /in whose possession is the breath of every living thing. We gratefully acknowledge God as the source of life itself and of the constant renewal of our spirit. The traditional formula of this blessing, referring to the future resurrection of the dead, has been emended. As Reconstructionists, we accept both the finality of death and the infinite wondrousness of life. Our religion is about the balancing of these two realities, neither of which may be allowed to negate the other.   A.G.

BIRKAT LIMUD TORAH/
BLESSING PRECEDING TORAH STUDY

Blessed are you, THE ONE OF SINAI, our God, the sovereign of all worlds, who made us holy with your mitzvot, and commanded us to occupy ourselves with words of Torah. ⤸

COMMENTARY. The three blessings on pages 170, 174, and 176 constitute a meditation on body, soul and intellect. The first blessing reflects the intricate workings of our physiology. We recognize the wondrous system of arteries, organs and glands that comprise the "human machine." We then celebrate the purity of the soul that is implanted within us, we feel the "wind-spirit" of our own breath, our *anima* filled with air. As we breathe, all the systems of our bodies are also filled with life-sustaining oxygen. Finally, we rejoice in our intellects—in our ability to study and grapple with words of Torah, to reflect on them and our capacity to teach them to future generations. L.G.B.

בִּרְכַּת לְמוּד תּוֹרָה

בָּרוּךְ אַתָּה יהוה אֱלֹהֵינוּ מֶלֶךְ הָעוֹלָם אֲשֶׁר קִדְּשָׁנוּ בְּמִצְוֹתָיו וְצִוָּנוּ לַעֲסֹק בְּדִבְרֵי תוֹרָה: ←

Baruḥ atah adonay eloheynu meleḥ ha'olam asher kideshanu bemitzvotav vetzivanu la'asok bedivrey torah. ⮌

לעסק בדברי תורה / to occupy ourselves with words of Torah. The Hebrew words here do not say "to study Torah," but rather to "be engaged" or "to be busy with" the study of Torah. We study Torah not as an intellectual exercise alone. Rather, we understand our "engagement" with Torah more holistically—as an every day, every moment activity. We also understand that to be fully "engaged" with Torah is to wrestle with Torah—to challenge our tradition while loving it, to question while celebrating it.

L.G.B.

Transmit to us, WISE ONE, our God, your Torah's words, into our mouths, and to the mouths of all the House of Israel, who called you kin. May we, and our children, and all the children of your people, the House of Israel, all of us, be knowers of your Name and learners of your Torah, for its sake alone. Blessed are you, THE SAGE, who teaches Torah to your people Israel.

Study selections on the themes of the High Holy Days from biblical and rabbinic literature follow. Other selections could, of course, be used.

COMMENTARY. Blessings and texts for Torah study are a traditional part of *Birhot Hashahar.* Like body and soul, Torah study is a daily part of Jewish living. Rabbinic literature records more than a half dozen versions of Torah blessings. The ornate Torah blessing in our text (pages 175-178) both begins and ends with the formula *"Baruh atah."* In the first instance, the formula of the blessing acknowledges that Torah study is essential to Jewish life. The concluding phrase of blessing praises God as the teacher of Torah. From a Reconstructionist perspective, the metaphor of God as teacher is an invitation and challenge to discern the divine presence in learning. A talmudic passage appears between the two blessings. It offers the hope that we, the people Israel, will always see Torah as an intrinsic part of ourselves.   S.S.

וְהַעֲרֶב־נָא יהוה אֱלֹהֵינוּ אֶת דִּבְרֵי תוֹרָתְךָ בְּפִינוּ וּבְפִי עַמְּךָ בֵּית
יִשְׂרָאֵל וְנִהְיֶה אֲנַחְנוּ וְצֶאֱצָאֵינוּ וְצֶאֱצָאֵי עַמְּךָ בֵּית יִשְׂרָאֵל כֻּלָּנוּ
יוֹדְעֵי שְׁמֶךָ וְלוֹמְדֵי תוֹרָתְךָ לִשְׁמָהּ:
בָּרוּךְ אַתָּה יהוה הַמְלַמֵּד תּוֹרָה לְעַמּוֹ יִשְׂרָאֵל:

Veha'arev na adonay eloheynu et divrey torateha befinu uvefi
ameha beyt yisra'el venihyeh anahnu vetze'etza'eynu
vetze'etza'ey ameha beyt yisra'el kulanu yodey shemeha
velomdey torateha lishmah. Baruh atah adonay hamlamed
torah le'amo yisra'el.

*Study selections on the themes of the High Holy Days from biblical and rabbinic literature
follow. Other selections could, of course, be used.*

DERASH. We must study the Torah with a view toward discerning the great
traits of Jewish consciousness that struggled to become articulate in its
traditions, laws, prophecies, psalms and wisdom. We should study all of its
traditions with the purpose of finding out their bearing on Israel's destiny
and duty in the world and then seek to make that destiny and duty our
own.   M.M.K. (Adapted)

BIBLICAL VERSES ON EVIL AND
ITS CONSEQUENCES

Woe to those who say of evil, "It is good,"
   and of good, "It is evil,"
who put darkness in the place of light,
   and light in the place of darkness,
who put bitterness in the place of sweetness
   and sweetness in the place of bitterness.
Woe to those who see themselves as wise,
   and who account themselves as clever.
Woe to those who become mighty when they're full of wine,
   and think themselves heroic when they've mixed
   their drink,
who give preference to the wicked for a bribe,
   and withhold justice from the good.

They have a mouth, but cannot speak,
   they have eyes, but cannot see.
They have ears, but cannot hear,
   they have a nose, but cannot smell.
They have rebelled against the light,
   and have not recognized its path,
   and have not dwelt along its roads.
To all of them, the morning is a darkness,
   truly, they are intimate with terror's shade.

But evil's light shall be extinguished,
   its fire's flame shall never shine,
the light shall darken in its tent,
   its lamp shall go dead where it shines.
The wicked grope in darkness where no light exists,
   they cast about like drunkards in a haze. ↵

הוֹי הָאֹמְרִים לָרַע טוֹב וְלַטּוֹב רָע
שָׂמִים חֹשֶׁךְ לְאוֹר וְאוֹר לְחֹשֶׁךְ שָׂמִים מַר לְמָתוֹק
וּמָתוֹק לְמָר:

הוֹי חֲכָמִים בְּעֵינֵיהֶם וְנֶגֶד פְּנֵיהֶם נְבֹנִים:
הוֹי גִּבּוֹרִים לִשְׁתּוֹת יָיִן וְאַנְשֵׁי־חַיִל לִמְסֹךְ שֵׁכָר:
מַצְדִּיקֵי רָשָׁע עֵקֶב שֹׁחַד וְצִדְקַת צַדִּיקִים יָסִירוּ מִמֶּנּוּ:

פֶּה־לָהֶם וְלֹא יְדַבֵּרוּ עֵינַיִם לָהֶם וְלֹא יִרְאוּ:
אָזְנַיִם לָהֶם וְלֹא יִשְׁמָעוּ אַף לָהֶם וְלֹא יְרִיחוּן:
הֵמָּה הָיוּ בְּמֹרְדֵי־אוֹר לֹא הִכִּירוּ דְרָכָיו
וְלֹא יָשְׁבוּ בִּנְתִיבֹתָיו:
כִּי יַחְדָּו בֹּקֶר לָמוֹ צַלְמָוֶת כִּי־יַכִּיר בַּלְהוֹת צַלְמָוֶת:

גַּם אוֹר רְשָׁעִים יִדְעָךְ וְלֹא־יִגַּהּ שְׁבִיב אִשּׁוֹ:
אוֹר חָשַׁךְ בְּאָהֳלוֹ וְנֵרוֹ עָלָיו יִדְעָךְ:
יְמַשְׁשׁוּ־חֹשֶׁךְ וְלֹא־אוֹר וַיַּתְעֵם כַּשִּׁכּוֹר: ←

COMMENTARY. The rabbis often created new prayers by anthologizing biblical verses. Michael Strassfeld employed this technique in creating this *piyut*-like meditation on human evil and its consequences.   D.A.T.

And I shall banish from their midst
   the voice of joy, the voice of happiness,
the voice of the bridegroom and the voice of the bride,
   the sound of the handmill and the light of the lamp.
Yes, all the lights amid the heavens
   I shall blacken over you,
and I shall place a darkness on your land,
   says THE ALMIGHTY God.
So listen, you who cannot hear,
   and you who cannot see, lift up your gaze.

Isaiah 5:20-23; Psalms 115:5-6; Job 24:13, 17; 18:5-6; 12:25; Jeremiah 25:10; Ezekiel 32:8; Isaiah 42:18.

וְהַאֲבַדְתִּי מֵהֶם   קוֹל שָׂשׂוֹן וְקוֹל שִׂמְחָה
קוֹל חָתָן וְקוֹל כַּלָּה   קוֹל רֵחַיִם וְאוֹר נֵר:
כָּל־מְאוֹרֵי אוֹר בַּשָּׁמַיִם   אַקְדִּירֵם עָלֶיךָ
וְנָתַתִּי חֹשֶׁךְ עַל אַרְצֶךָ   נְאֻם אֲדֹנָי יְהוָה:
הַחֵרְשִׁים שְׁמָעוּ   וְהַעִוְרִים הַבִּיטוּ לִרְאוֹת:

TESHUVAH IN MIDRASH

One who says, time after time,
"I'll sin, but later I'll do *teshuvah*,"
will not have the opportunity to do *teshuvah*.
Or: "I'll sin, but Yom Kippur will bring atonement,"
Yom Kippur will not effect atonement.
For wrongful acts that one has done toward God,
Yom Kippur will bring atonement,
but for a wrongful act between one person and another,
Yom Kippur will not effect atonement
till one gains forgiveness from the person wronged.
Rabbi Eleazar ben Azariah explained this verse of Torah:
"From all your wrongful acts
before the FOUNT OF MERCY
you shall be cleansed"—   Leviticus 16:30
for wrongful acts that one has done toward God,
Yom Kippur will bring atonement,
but for a wrongful act between one person and another,
Yom Kippur will not effect atonement
till one gains forgiveness from the person wronged.

Rabbi Akiba said: Happy are you, O people Israel!
Who is the one before whom you are cleansed?
Who is the one who cleanses you?
It is your heavenly Creator!
As is written: "I shall sprinkle over you
pure waters, and you shall be clean.
From all of your impurities, from all of your idolatries,
I'll make you clean."   Ezekiel 36:25
And it is written:
"The hope of Israel / Israel's purifying water
is THE FOUNT OF LIFE!"   Jeremiah 17:13
Just as waters of a mikvah purify your sins,
so does the blessed Holy One wash clean
the people Israel.
                                               Mishnah Yoma 8:9

BIRḤOT HASHAḤAR / MORNING BLESSINGS / 183

תְּשׁוּבָה

הָאוֹמֵר: "אֶחֱטָא וְאָשׁוּב, אֶחֱטָא וְאָשׁוּב" — אֵין מַסְפִּיקִין בְּיָדוֹ לַעֲשׂוֹת תְּשׁוּבָה; אֶחֱטָא וְיוֹם־הַכִּפּוּרִים מְכַפֵּר — אֵין יוֹם־הַכִּפּוּרִים מְכַפֵּר. עֲבֵרוֹת שֶׁבֵּין אָדָם לַמָּקוֹם — יוֹם־הַכִּפּוּרִים מְכַפֵּר, עֲבֵרוֹת שֶׁבֵּין אָדָם לַחֲבֵרוֹ — אֵין יוֹם־הַכִּפּוּרִים מְכַפֵּר, עַד שֶׁיְּרַצֶּה אֶת־חֲבֵרוֹ. אֶת זוֹ דָרַשׁ רַבִּי אֶלְעָזָר בֶּן־עֲזַרְיָה: "מִכֹּל חַטֹּאתֵיכֶם לִפְנֵי יהוה תִּטְהָרוּ" — עֲבֵרוֹת שֶׁבֵּין אָדָם לַמָּקוֹם יוֹם־הַכִּפּוּרִים מְכַפֵּר, עֲבֵרוֹת שֶׁבֵּין אָדָם לַחֲבֵרוֹ — אֵין יוֹם־הַכִּפּוּרִים מְכַפֵּר, עַד שֶׁיְּרַצֶּה אֶת־חֲבֵרוֹ.

אָמַר רַבִּי עֲקִיבָא: אַשְׁרֵיכֶם, יִשְׂרָאֵל, לִפְנֵי מִי אַתֶּם מִטַּהֲרִים וּמִי מְטַהֵר אֶתְכֶם? — אֲבִיכֶם שֶׁבַּשָּׁמָיִם! שֶׁנֶּאֱמַר: "וְזָרַקְתִּי עֲלֵיכֶם מַיִם טְהוֹרִים וּטְהַרְתֶּם מִכֹּל טֻמְאוֹתֵיכֶם וּמִכָּל־גִּלּוּלֵיכֶם אֲטַהֵר אֶתְכֶם"; וְאוֹמֵר: "מִקְוֵה יִשְׂרָאֵל יהוה" — מַה מִּקְוֶה מְטַהֵר אֶת־הַטְּמֵאִים, אַף הַקָּדוֹשׁ־בָּרוּךְ־הוּא מְטַהֵר אֶת־יִשְׂרָאֵל.

Rabbi Abbahu bar Ze'ira said:
Great is *teshuvah*,
for it existed in the world before Creation,
as it says: "Before the mountains came to birth,
you, God, gave the human being ability to change
and to be humble."

Soḥar Tov 90; Genesis Rabbah 1.4 (quoting Psalms 90:23)

Two things are both near to you and far,
both far from you and near:
Teshuvah is near to you, yet far,
and far from you, yet near.
And death is near to you, yet far,
and far from you, yet near.

Ecclesiastes Rabbah 8.18

"Open up to me my sister!"—
Rabbi Yasa said: "The blessed Holy One
declared to Israel: Open up to me, my children,
a gate of *teshuvah* narrow as a needle's eye,
and I shall open up for you a gateway
wide enough for wagons and for coaches to come through.

Song of Songs Rabbah 25.2; Yalkut Shimoni on Song of Songs 5:2

"Outside, the stranger need not lodge."—
or the blessed Holy One views no being as unworthy;
rather, all are received by God.
In every hour, the gates are open,
and whoever seeks to enter may come in.

Exodus Rabbah 19.4 (quoting Job 31:32)

אָמַר רַבִּי אַבָּהוּ בַּר זְעִירָא: גְּדוֹלָה תְּשׁוּבָה שֶׁקָּדְמָה לִבְרִיאַת הָעוֹלָם שֶׁנֶּאֱמַר בְּטֶרֶם הָרִים יֻלָּדוּ... תָּשֵׁב אֱנוֹשׁ עַד־דַּכָּא:

שְׁנֵי דְבָרִים קְרוֹבִים לְךָ וּרְחוֹקִים מִמֶּךָ רְחוֹקִים מִמְּךָ וּקְרוֹבִים לָךְ: תְּשׁוּבָה קְרוֹבָה לְךָ וּרְחוֹקָה מִמֶּךָ רְחוֹקָה מִמְּךָ וּקְרוֹבָה לָךְ מִיתָה קְרוֹבָה לְךָ וּרְחוֹקָה מִמֶּךָ רְחוֹקָה מִמְּךָ וּקְרוֹבָה לָךְ:

רַבִּי יֵסָא אָמַר: אָמַר הַקָּדוֹשׁ־בָּרוּךְ־הוּא לְיִשְׂרָאֵל: בָּנַי פִּתְחוּ לִי פֶּתַח שֶׁל תְּשׁוּבָה כְּחֻדָּהּ שֶׁל מַחַט וַאֲנִי פוֹתֵחַ לָכֶם פֶּתַח שֶׁיִּהְיוּ עֲגָלוֹת וּקְרוֹנוֹת נִכְנָסוֹת בּוֹ:

"בַּחוּץ לֹא־יָלִין גֵּר" — שֶׁאֵין הַקָּדוֹשׁ־בָּרוּךְ־הוּא פּוֹסֵל לִבְרִיָּה אֶלָּא לַכֹּל הוּא מְקַבֵּל: הַשְּׁעָרִים נִפְתָּחִין בְּכָל־שָׁעָה וְכָל־מִי שֶׁהוּא מְבַקֵּשׁ לִכָּנֵס יִכָּנֵס:

Rabbi Ḥama son of Rabbi Ḥaninah said:
Great is *teshuvah*, for it brings healing to the world,
as it is said: "I shall heal their affliction [*meshuvatam*],
yes, willingly I'll show them love!"

Talmud Yoma 86a (quoting Hosea 14:5)

Rabbi Abbahu said:
In a place where people doing *teshuvah* stand,
even the wholly righteous cannot stand,
as it is said: "Shalom! Shalom!"
Peace be to all, both far and near!"
—first to those who are far,
and only afterward, to those who are near.

Talmud Beraḥot 34b (quoting Isaiah 57:19)

תְּשׁוּבָה

אָמַר רַבִּי חָמָא בְּרַבִּי חֲנִינָא: גְּדוֹלָה תְשׁוּבָה שֶׁמְּבִיאָה רְפָאוּת לָעוֹלָם שֶׁנֶּאֱמַר אֶרְפָּא מְשׁוּבָתָם אֹהֲבֵם נְדָבָה:

רַב אַבָּהוּ אָמַר: בִּמְקוֹם שֶׁבַּעֲלֵי־תְשׁוּבָה עוֹמְדִים צַדִּיקִים גְּמוּרִים אֵינָם עוֹמְדִים שֶׁנֶּאֱמַר שָׁלוֹם שָׁלוֹם לָרָחוֹק וְלַקָּרוֹב — לָרָחוֹק תְּחִלָּה וְאַחַר־כָּךְ לַקָּרוֹב:

COMMENTARY. A controversy existed among the rabbis about who is closer to God—Jews who have not sinned or those who have sinned and done *teshuvah*. Perhaps for some of the rabbis Ḥama's *midrash* was just a bit of hyperbole to motivate the discouraged to action. But how close to God can one stand who has never been tempted and therefore never developed the broken-heartedness, honesty and strength of will that true turning requires? The act of *teshuvah* brings a self-awareness that can create intimate new links to the divine.   D.A.T.

KADDISH DERABANAN / THE SAGES' KADDISH

Reader: Let God's name be made great and holy in the world that was created as God willed. May God complete the holy realm in your own lifetime, in your days, and in the days of all the house of Israel, quickly and soon. And say: Amen.

Congregation: May God's great name be blessed, forever and as long as worlds endure.

Reader: May it be blessed, and praised, and glorified, and held in honor, viewed with awe, embellished and revered; and may the blessed name of holiness be hailed, though it be higher by far than all the blessings, songs, praises and consolations that we utter in this world. And say: Amen.

For Israel and her sages, for their pupils and all pupils of their pupils, and for all who occupy themselves with Torah, whether in this place or any other place, may God grant them and you abundant peace, and grace, and love, and mercy, and long life, and ample sustenance, and saving acts, all flowing from divine abundance in the worlds beyond. And say: Amen.

May heaven grant a universal peace and life for us and for all Israel. And say: Amen.

May the one who creates harmony above make peace for us, and for all Israel, and for all who dwell on earth. And say: Amen.

DERASH. When we recite the Kaddish Derabanan, we are thankful for the teachings of Torah (in its widest sense). We have received from those who have come before us—and we accept our own place as links in the chain of tradition. Every student becomes a teacher—what we have learned we will teach. We celebrate our sense of accomplishment, our feeling that we have gained richness from our study. With this Kaddish we re-affirm the honorable endeavor in which we have been engaged. We are a people of study and learning, teaching and receiving—*this* is critical to our collective Jewish life.   L.G.B.

קַדִּישׁ דְּרַבָּנָן

יִתְגַּדַּל וְיִתְקַדַּשׁ שְׁמֵהּ רַבָּא בְּעָלְמָא דִּי בְרָא כִרְעוּתֵהּ וְיַמְלִיךְ מַלְכוּתֵהּ בְּחַיֵּיכוֹן וּבְיוֹמֵיכוֹן וּבְחַיֵּי דְכָל בֵּית יִשְׂרָאֵל בַּעֲגָלָא וּבִזְמַן קָרִיב וְאִמְרוּ אָמֵן:

יְהֵא שְׁמֵהּ רַבָּא מְבָרַךְ לְעָלַם וּלְעָלְמֵי עָלְמַיָּא:

יִתְבָּרַךְ וְיִשְׁתַּבַּח וְיִתְפָּאַר וְיִתְרוֹמַם וְיִתְנַשֵּׂא וְיִתְהַדָּר וְיִתְעַלֶּה וְיִתְהַלָּל שְׁמֵהּ דְּקֻדְשָׁא בְּרִיךְ הוּא לְעֵלָּא לְעֵלָּא מִכָּל בִּרְכָתָא וְשִׁירָתָא תֻּשְׁבְּחָתָא וְנֶחֱמָתָא דַּאֲמִירָן בְּעָלְמָא וְאִמְרוּ אָמֵן:

עַל יִשְׂרָאֵל וְעַל רַבָּנָן וְעַל תַּלְמִידֵיהוֹן וְעַל כָּל תַּלְמִידֵי תַלְמִידֵיהוֹן וְעַל כָּל מָאן דְּעָסְקִין בְּאוֹרַיְתָא דִּי בְּאַתְרָא הָדֵין וְדִי בְּכָל אֲתַר וַאֲתַר יְהֵא לְהוֹן וּלְכוֹן שְׁלָמָא רַבָּא חִנָּא וְחִסְדָּא וְרַחֲמִין וְחַיִּין אֲרִיכִין וּמְזוֹנֵי רְוִיחֵי וּפֻרְקָנָא מִן קֳדָם אֲבוּהוֹן דִּבִשְׁמַיָּא וְאַרְעָא וְאִמְרוּ אָמֵן:

יְהֵא שְׁלָמָא רַבָּא מִן שְׁמַיָּא וְחַיִּים עָלֵינוּ וְעַל כָּל יִשְׂרָאֵל וְאִמְרוּ אָמֵן: עוֹשֶׂה שָׁלוֹם בִּמְרוֹמָיו הוּא יַעֲשֶׂה שָׁלוֹם עָלֵינוּ וְעַל כָּל יִשְׂרָאֵל וְעַל כָּל יוֹשְׁבֵי תֵבֵל וְאִמְרוּ אָמֵן:

From the cowardice that shrinks from new truth,
From the laziness that is content with half-truths,
From the arrogance that thinks it knows all truth,
O God of truth, deliver us.   M.M.K.

COMMENTARY. Most scholars agree that Kaddish Derabanan is the most ancient form of the kaddish prayer. It was used at the conclusion of study long before the kaddish became a prayer for mourners. Its prayer is that the efforts of both students and teachers bring holiness and a sense of the divine presence into the world. This in turn should help them formulate a vision of peace that they can spread to all Israel, and ultimately to all the world. Kaddish Derabanan, like all forms of the kaddish, thus brings us in touch with the central purpose of prayer.   D.A.T.

A psalm. A song for dedication of the house. Of David.

I exalt you, GLORIOUS ONE, because you have delivered me; you gave my enemies no joy on my account.

DEAR ONE, my God, I have cried out to you, and you have made me whole.

REDEEMER, you have raised my spirit from the land of no return, you revived me from among those fallen in a pit.

Sing out to THE ALMIGHTY, fervent souls, be thankful when you call God's holiness to mind.

For God is angry for a moment, but shows favor for a lifetime; though one goes to bed in weeping, one awakes in song.

And I, how I exclaimed in my security: I cannot fail!

PROTECTOR, when you wished, you raised my mountain's strength, and when you hid your face, I was afraid.

To you, THE FOUNT OF LIFE, I used to call, and from my benefactor I sought help unmerited:

"What use in my blood's waste?
What benefit, my going down into the pit?
Can dust acknowledge you? Can it declare your truth?

Hear, O HIDDEN ONE, deal graciously with me,
SUPERNAL ADVOCATE, become a help for me!"

You changed my mourning to ecstatic dance,
you loosed my sackcloth, and girded me with joy,

that glory might sing out to you, and not be still!
To you, ABUNDANT ONE my God, I always shall give thanks.

Psalm 30

שִׁיר־חֲנֻכַּת הַבַּיִת לְדָוִד:

אֲרוֹמִמְךָ יהוה כִּי דִלִּיתָנִי וְלֹא־שִׂמַּחְתָּ אֹיְבַי לִי:

יהוה אֱלֹהָי שִׁוַּעְתִּי אֵלֶיךָ וַתִּרְפָּאֵנִי:

יהוה הֶעֱלִיתָ מִן־שְׁאוֹל נַפְשִׁי חִיִּיתַנִי מִיָּרְדִי־בוֹר:

זַמְּרוּ לַיהוה חֲסִידָיו וְהוֹדוּ לְזֵכֶר קָדְשׁוֹ:

כִּי רֶגַע בְּאַפּוֹ חַיִּים בִּרְצוֹנוֹ בָּעֶרֶב יָלִין בֶּכִי וְלַבֹּקֶר רִנָּה:

וַאֲנִי אָמַרְתִּי בְשַׁלְוִי בַּל־אֶמּוֹט לְעוֹלָם:

יהוה בִּרְצוֹנְךָ הֶעֱמַדְתָּה לְהַרְרִי עֹז הִסְתַּרְתָּ פָנֶיךָ הָיִיתִי נִבְהָל:

אֵלֶיךָ יהוה אֶקְרָא וְאֶל־אֲדֹנָי אֶתְחַנָּן:

מַה־בֶּצַע בְּדָמִי בְּרִדְתִּי אֶל שָׁחַת הֲיוֹדְךָ עָפָר הֲיַגִּיד אֲמִתֶּךָ:

שְׁמַע־יהוה וְחָנֵּנִי יהוה הֱיֵה־עֹזֵר לִי:

הָפַכְתָּ מִסְפְּדִי לְמָחוֹל לִי פִּתַּחְתָּ שַׂקִּי וַתְּאַזְּרֵנִי שִׂמְחָה:

* לְמַעַן יְזַמֶּרְךָ כָבוֹד וְלֹא יִדֹּם יהוה אֱלֹהַי לְעוֹלָם אוֹדֶךָּ:

Eleḥa adonay ekra ve'el adonay et-ḥanan.
Shema adonay veḥoneni adonay heyey ozer li.

KAVANAH. Focus on one of the psalms, one image, one verse or one word. Savor it. Let its fullness move you. Move at your own speed, easing yourself into the psalmist's vision. Let it become yours. L.W.K.

DERASH. "A song for dedication of the house." Prayer communities often find themselves in someone else's "house" for the *Yamim Nora'im*. We make these spaces holy through our presence and intentions, prayers and song. It is up to us to create holy space. R.H.

PESUKEY DEZIMRA / VERSES OF PRAISE

Blessed is the one who spoke and all things came to be!
  Blessed are you!
Blessed, who created all in the beginning!
  Blessed is your name!
Blessed is the one who speaks and acts!
  Blessed are you!
Blessed, who determines and fulfills!
  Blessed is your name!
Blessed, who deals kindly with the world!
  Blessed are you! ‿

COMMENTARY. The God affirmed in the words of *Baruḥ She'amar* may be understood in either concrete anthropomorphic terms or in a more abstract manner. It is the latter view with which we Reconstructionists are most comfortable. Our God is not a person who promises and fulfills as a human being would. In speaking of a God who fulfills promises, we express our basic trust in life and our affirmation that goodness and godliness have their own reward.   A.G.

KAVANAH. The opening passage of the Torah describes how God created the world by calling, or speaking, it into being. "Blessed is the one who spoke and all things came to be." This teaches that language is a powerful creative force. Later in the Torah we read that God commands destruction (for example, the flood), which takes place exactly as God wills. Anything that has the power to create also has the power to destroy. We are created in God's image; our words, like God's, have the power to both create and destroy. Words can hurt or heal, depending on our use of them. The gift of language is thus an awesome responsibility entrusted to us, and we must learn to be more mindful of its powers. Let us use our words for the sake of kindness and never to injure other human beings. Rabbi Levi said: "God says, if you bear false witness against your neighbor, I regard it as if you had declared that I had not created the world."   S.D.R.

פְּסוּקֵי דְזִמְרָה

בָּרוּךְ שֶׁאָמַר וְהָיָה הָעוֹלָם   בָּרוּךְ הוּא:

בָּרוּךְ עוֹשֶׂה בְרֵאשִׁית   בָּרוּךְ שְׁמוֹ:

בָּרוּךְ אוֹמֵר וְעוֹשֶׂה   בָּרוּךְ הוּא:

בָּרוּךְ גּוֹזֵר וּמְקַיֵּם   בָּרוּךְ שְׁמוֹ:

בָּרוּךְ מְרַחֵם עַל הָאָרֶץ   בָּרוּךְ הוּא: ←

Baruḥ she'amar vehayah ha'olam.   Baruḥ hu.

Baruḥ oseh vereyshit.   Baruḥ shemo.

Baruḥ omer ve'oseh.   Baruḥ hu.

Baruḥ gozer umkayem.   Baruḥ shemo.

Baruḥ meraḥem al ha'aretz.   Baruḥ hu. ←

Blessed is the one who spoke and the world became.

Blessed is the one.

Blessed is the one who in the beginning gave birth.

Blessed is the one who says and performs.

Blessed is the one who declares and fulfills.

Blessed is the one whose womb covers the earth.

Blessed is the one whose womb protects all creatures.

Blessed is the one who nourishes those who are in awe of Her.

Blessed is the one who lives forever, and exists eternally.

Blessed is the one who redeems and saves.

Blessed is God's name.

Naomi Janowitz and Margaret Moers Wenig

Blessed, who acts kindly toward all creatures!
    Blessed is your name!
Blessed, who responds with good to those in awe!
    Blessed are you!
Blessed, who removes the dark and brings the light!
    Blessed is your name!
Blessed is the one who lives eternally and lasts forever!
    Blessed are you!
Blessed, who delivers and redeems!
    Blessed are you and your name! ↰

COMMENTARY. *Baruh She'amar* is the rabbinic composition that introduces *Pesukey Dezimra*/Verses of Praise, which traditionally is compiled from biblical passages, primarily from Psalms.

The focus of *Birhot Hashaḥar* is on physical awakening. In *Pesukey Dezimra* the kaleidoscopic imagery awakens our emotions. Just as we find our own pace walking through art museums, so *Pesukey Dezimra* invites each of us to wander amidst its visions. On different days, different imagery comes to life. *Pesukey Dezimra* moves us toward prayerfulness, toward readiness to join in spiritual community.   D.A.T.

DERASH. *Pesukey Dezimra* begins with an apology for verbal prayer. It is only because God "spoke the world into being" that we dare to assume that words can serve as the vehicles for our deepest prayers. In participating in verbal prayer, we somehow partake of that same act of Divine word-power through which the world was created. A Hasidic comment on the opening line of *Baruh She'amar* translates it: "A *baruh* (blessing) that is said and creates a world—that's a *baruh*!"   A.G.

בָּרוּךְ מְרַחֵם עַל־הַבְּרִיּוֹת   בָּרוּךְ שְׁמוֹ:
בָּרוּךְ מְשַׁלֵּם שָׂכָר טוֹב לִירֵאָיו   בָּרוּךְ הוּא:
בָּרוּךְ מַעֲבִיר אֲפֵלָה וּמֵבִיא אוֹרָה   בָּרוּךְ שְׁמוֹ:
בָּרוּךְ חַי לָעַד וְקַיָּם לָנֶצַח   בָּרוּךְ הוּא:
בָּרוּךְ פּוֹדֶה וּמַצִּיל   בָּרוּךְ הוּא וּבָרוּךְ שְׁמוֹ: ←

Baruḥ meraḥem al haberiyot.	Baruḥ shemo.
Baruḥ meshalem saḥar tov lire'av.	Baruḥ hu.
Baruḥ ma'avir afelah umevi orah.	Baruḥ shemo.
Baruḥ ḥay la'ad vekayam lanetzaḥ	Baruḥ hu.
Baruḥ podeh umatzil.	Baruḥ hu uvaruḥ shemo. ↵

ברוך מרחם על הבריות /Blessed, who acts kindly toward all creatures.
As God nurtures and cares, so should we.

Avot De Rabbi Natan 11a (Adapted by L.W.K.)

COMMENTARY. According to the Mishnah, some Jews regularly meditated for an hour before beginning public prayer. As the public prayer service expanded, this time of personal preparation became filled with a collection of psalms and other biblical selections that became known as *Pesukey Dezimra*—"Verses of Song." Rabbinic literature records many variations of *Pesukey Dezimra*, but common to all versions are selections from Psalms 146-150, known as the "Hallel Psalms" because they feature variations of that term as a praise of God. Another important Hallel psalm, 136, is also a traditional part of this section. The central importance of these psalms indicates that the major theme of *Pesukey Dezimra* is the praise (*hallel*) of God. Indeed, the Talmud sometimes refers to *Pesukey Dezimra* as the daily Hallel.   S.S.

Blessed are you, THE EVERLASTING ONE, our God, the sovereign of all worlds. Divine one, who gave birth to all, the merciful, subject of praise upon our people's mouths, lauded and glorified upon the tongues of all who love and serve you. And through these, the songs sung by your servant David, may we hail you, SOURCE OF BEING. With praises and with melodies we celebrate your greatness, and we praise you, glorify you, call to mind your Name, and crown you as our sovereign, God of ours, the only one, the living one, throughout all worlds. The one who reigns, lauded and glorified unto the end of time, whose name is ever great. Blessed are you, THE ONE, the sovereign hailed in songs of praise.

COMMENTARY. Although the patchwork of psalms and praises known as *Pesukey Dezimra* is said to have evolved centuries after the prayer service itself, one can sense in this preface to the service an important echo of worship in biblical times—both the daily service of priests and Levites in the Temple, and the prayers of pilgrims ascending to the Holy City for the seasonal festivals. This bold appropriation of historical memory, undertaken in a period of exile and dispersion, affirms the continuity of biblical Israel with the later people Israel—in effect, inscribing the image of the former upon the latter. All of the themes and moods of the service are present in *Pesukey Dezimra*.

J.R.

בָּרוּךְ אַתָּה יהוה אֱלֹהֵינוּ מֶלֶךְ הָעוֹלָם: הָאֵל הָאָב הָרַחֲמָן הַמְהֻלָּל בְּפִי עַמּוֹ: מְשֻׁבָּח וּמְפֹאָר בִּלְשׁוֹן חֲסִידָיו וַעֲבָדָיו: וּבְשִׁירֵי דָוִד עַבְדֶּךָ נְהַלֶּלְךָ יהוה אֱלֹהֵינוּ: בִּשְׁבָחוֹת וּבִזְמִירוֹת נְגַדֶּלְךָ וּנְשַׁבֵּחֲךָ וּנְפָאֶרְךָ וְנַזְכִּיר שִׁמְךָ וְנַמְלִיכְךָ מַלְכֵּנוּ אֱלֹהֵינוּ *יָחִיד חֵי־הָעוֹלָמִים: מֶלֶךְ מְשֻׁבָּח וּמְפֹאָר עֲדֵי־עַד שְׁמוֹ הַגָּדוֹל: בָּרוּךְ אַתָּה יהוה מֶלֶךְ מְהֻלָּל בַּתִּשְׁבָּחוֹת:

Baruḥ atah adonay eloheynu meleḥ ha'olam. Ha'el ha'av haraḥaman hamhulal befi amo. Meshubaḥ umfo'ar bilshon ḥasidav va'avadav. Uvshirey david avdeḥa nehaleleḥa adonay eloheynu. Bishvaḥot uvizmirot negadeleḥa unshabeḥaḥa unfa'ereḥa venazkir shimeḥa venamliḥeḥa malkenu eloheynu yaḥid ḥey ha'olamim. Meleḥ meshubaḥ umfo'ar adey ad shemo hagadol. Baruḥ atah adonay meleḥ mehulal batishbaḥot.

DERASH. Rabbi Simlay said: "A person should arrange praise of the Holy One and then pray." (Talmud Beraḥot 32a) *Pesukey Dezimra* is a preparation. It helps our transition into prayer. L.W.K. (Adapted)

Give thanks to THE MAGNIFICENT, call on the name,
make known among all peoples God's great deeds.

Sing songs of God, make melody for God,
converse about God's wondrous acts.

Celebrate the holy name,
God will delight the heart of those who seek THE ONE.

Inquire of THE HOLY ONE and gather strength,
search out the divine presence always.

Call to mind the wondrous things God did,
the acts of wonderment, the judgments of God's mouth.

Sing to THE INCOMPARABLE throughout the earth,
bring news, from one day to the next, of divine help.

Tell among the nations of God's glory,
amid all peoples, of God's wondrous acts.

For great is THE ETERNAL, celebrated mightily,
and awesome, above all false gods,

for all the gods of popular imaginings are mere idols,
but THE CREATOR alone made the heavens.

I Chronicles 16:8-12, 23-26

הוֹדוּ | לַיהוה קִרְאוּ בִשְׁמוֹ הוֹדִיעוּ בָעַמִּים עֲלִילוֹתָיו:
שִׁירוּ לוֹ זַמְּרוּ־לוֹ שִׂיחוּ בְּכָל־נִפְלְאוֹתָיו:
הִתְהַלְלוּ בְּשֵׁם קָדְשׁוֹ יִשְׂמַח לֵב מְבַקְשֵׁי יהוה:
דִּרְשׁוּ יהוה וְעֻזּוֹ בַּקְּשׁוּ פָנָיו תָּמִיד:
זִכְרוּ נִפְלְאֹתָיו אֲשֶׁר עָשָׂה מֹפְתָיו וּמִשְׁפְּטֵי־פִיהוּ:

שִׁירוּ לַיהוה כָּל־הָאָרֶץ בַּשְּׂרוּ מִיּוֹם־אֶל־יוֹם יְשׁוּעָתוֹ:
סַפְּרוּ בַגּוֹיִם אֶת־כְּבוֹדוֹ בְּכָל־הָעַמִּים נִפְלְאוֹתָיו:
כִּי גָדוֹל יהוה וּמְהֻלָּל מְאֹד וְנוֹרָא הוּא עַל־כָּל־אֱלֹהִים:
* כִּי כָּל־אֱלֹהֵי הָעַמִּים אֱלִילִים וַיהוה שָׁמַיִם עָשָׂה:

בקשו פניו תמיד /search out the divine presence always. The Hebrew
literally reads "Seek His face always." The religious person is one who
knows in each situation how to seek "the face of God." Whatever befalls
us and wherever life may lead, we find ourselves still seeking. Each unique
human situation calls upon us to find God's presence and act upon it in a
unique way.   A.G.

DERASH. The service of gratitude is eternal. As the Rabbis put it (Leviticus
Rabbah 9), though in the time to come all sacrifices will cease, the thank-
offering will never cease. It will last on in eternity; thanksgiving will never
become obsolete in the realms of spiritual bliss. A world full of praise—
how near to heaven it would be! We must bring ourselves into line with
such ideals. Our worship must not be impatient supplication, but patient
praise. We must think less of what we lack, more of what we have.

                                                              M.M.K./M.S.

A song of triumph. A psalm of David.

The skies recount the glory of divinity,
God's handiwork the heavens' dome declares.

Day after day pours forth its evidence,
night after night expresses knowledge of it,

yet without speech and without words,
without their voice being heard.

Through all the earth their chord goes forth,
and to the farthest reaches of the globe, their phrase.

For the sun a tent is placed in their domain,

and it is like a bridegroom stepping from his canopy,
rejoicing like a mighty runner on his course,

the borders of the heavens are his starting point,
his orbit runs beyond their other edge,
with nothing hidden from his warmth. ↵

השמים מספרים כבוד אל / The skies recount the glory of divinity. The
Hebrew verb *mesaperim* ("recount") is associated by the rabbis with the
word "sapphire." The verse would then mean, "The heavens shine like
sapphire with the glory of God."   A.G.

קום / their chord, literally, their line/chord, here understood as a musical
chord. Belief in "the music of the spheres," a notion shared by many
cultures in the ancient and medieval world, is perhaps reflected here, and
it bears interesting resonance with conceptions of the cosmos advanced in
modern physics and astronomy. The music of the spheres and that of the
psalmist stand in a certain parallel.   J.R.

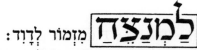

לַמְנַצֵּחַ מִזְמוֹר לְדָוִד:

הַשָּׁמַיִם מְסַפְּרִים כְּבוֹד־אֵל וּמַעֲשֵׂה יָדָיו מַגִּיד הָרָקִיעַ:

יוֹם לְיוֹם יַבִּיעַ אֹמֶר וְלַיְלָה לְּלַיְלָה יְחַוֶּה־דָּעַת:

אֵין אֹמֶר וְאֵין דְּבָרִים בְּלִי נִשְׁמָע קוֹלָם:

בְּכָל־הָאָרֶץ יָצָא קַוָּם וּבִקְצֵה תֵבֵל מִלֵּיהֶם לַשֶּׁמֶשׁ שָׂם אֹהֶל בָּהֶם:

וְהוּא כְּחָתָן יֹצֵא מֵחֻפָּתוֹ יָשִׂישׂ כְּגִבּוֹר לָרוּץ אֹרַח:

מִקְצֵה הַשָּׁמַיִם מוֹצָאוֹ וּתְקוּפָתוֹ עַל־קְצוֹתָם וְאֵין נִסְתָּר מֵחַמָּתוֹ: ←

Nature is God's *niggun*,
a wordless melody of unfolding Life.
To awaken to God we must hear the *niggun*.
To awaken to God we must listen in deep silence.
Silence arises when thinking ceases.
If we would know God
we must quiet the mind,
cease the chatter that passes for knowledge
when in fact it only flatters the foolish.
We cannot live without words
but let us not imagine that words are sufficient.
As a symphony needs rest to lift music out of noise,
so we need Silence to lift Truth out of words.　　　　R.M.S.

KAVANAH. There are two things that fill my soul with holy reverence and ever-growing wonder—the spectacle of the starry sky that virtually annihilates us as physical beings, and the Moral Law that raises us to infinite dignity as intelligent agents.　　　　Immanuel Kant

The Torah of THE ONE is flawless, it restores the soul,
the testimony of THE ONE is true, it makes wise the simple,

precepts of THE ONE are sure, they make the heart rejoice,
the mitzvah of THE ONE is clear, it gives light to the eyes,

fear of THE ONE is pure, it stands eternally,
the judgments of THE ONE are true, together they are just,

desired more than gold, and greater than the purest gold,
sweeter than honey, than the nectar of a honeycomb!

Your servant, too, is being enlightened by them,
in their preservation is great consequence.

Our petty failures, who can understand?
From hidden faults declare me clean!

And from premeditated ones, as well, protect your servant.
Do not let them govern me!

Then might I be perfect, cleared of grave wrongdoing.

May the utterances of my mouth be pleasing,
the conceptions of my heart, before you,
PRECIOUS ONE, my rock, my champion.

Psalm 19

COMMENTARY. Rabbi Kaplan used to say that if you want to discover the
truth of a statement about God, you must invert it. He would then state,
"The Torah of God is flawless, restoring the soul" should be read,
"Whatever restores the soul is the Torah of God."   M.S.

מְשִׁיבַת נָפֶשׁ   תּוֹרַת יהוה תְּמִימָה

מַחְכִּימַת פֶּתִי: עֵדוּת יהוה נֶאֱמָנָה

מְשַׂמְּחֵי־לֵב   פִּקּוּדֵי יהוה יְשָׁרִים

מְאִירַת עֵינָיִם: מִצְוַת יהוה בָּרָה

עוֹמֶדֶת לָעַד   יִרְאַת יהוה טְהוֹרָה

צָדְקוּ יַחְדָּו: מִשְׁפְּטֵי־יהוה אֱמֶת

הַנֶּחֱמָדִים מִזָּהָב וּמִפַּז רָב וּמְתוּקִים מִדְּבַשׁ וְנֹפֶת צוּפִים:

גַּם־עַבְדְּךָ נִזְהָר בָּהֶם בְּשָׁמְרָם עֵקֶב רָב:

שְׁגִיאוֹת מִי־יָבִין מִנִּסְתָּרוֹת נַקֵּנִי:

גַּם מִזֵּדִים חֲשֹׂךְ עַבְדֶּךָ אַל־יִמְשְׁלוּ־בִי אָז אֵיתָם וְנִקֵּיתִי מִפֶּשַׁע רָב:

* יִהְיוּ לְרָצוֹן אִמְרֵי־פִי וְהֶגְיוֹן לִבִּי לְפָנֶיךָ יהוה צוּרִי וְגֹאֲלִי:

Torat adonay temimah meshivat nafesh
edut adonay ne'emanah mahkimat peti.
Pikudey adonay yesharim mesamehey lev
mitzvat adonay barah me'irat eynayim.
Yirat adonay tehorah omedet la'ad
mishpetey adonay emet tzadeku yahdav.

אז איתם / Then might I be perfect—the phrase is rendered in a subjunctive mood ("might" instead of "shall") to express the uncertainty and wishfulness—perhaps even wistfulness—of the speaker, who knows that even with God's help, total human perfection is unattainable.

מפשע רב / mipesha rav / of grave wrongdoing is a wordplay on the boldly contrasting umipaz rav, "and greater than the purest gold," eight lines earlier, expressing the sharp difference between the perfection of divine utterance and the human imperfection of the psalm's speaker.   J.R.

A psalm of David, when he changed his appearance feigning madness before the Philistine king Avimeleḥ, who sent him on his way.

A blessing shall I speak for THE ALMIGHTY, at all times,
  always is God's praise upon my mouth.
By THE INCOMPARABLE shall my soul celebrate,
  and may the humble hear it and rejoice.
Give greatness to THE ONE along with me,
  and let us elevate the divine name in unison.
Deeply have I searched for THE INEFFABLE,
  and in all my trials, God has rescued me.
Have eyes turned toward God and be enlightened!
  Oh, let not your faces darken in confusion!
Zero this person had, but when he called, GOD listened,
  and in all his troubles, he was helped!
He had an angel of THE ONE stationed around him,
  as around all those who fear GOD and are freed.
Taste then, and see how good THE FOUNT can be,
  how happy is the person who finds refuge there.
You holy beings, have awe of THE DIVINE
  there is no lack for those who tremble at it.
Cubs of the lion are at times in need and hungry,
  but those who ask of GOD shall never lack the good.
Listen children, hear me out,
  an awe for THE MYSTERIOUS I'll teach to you. ⤺

COMMENTARY. Rabbi Kaplan used to say that we can only know God through the direct experience of the world. He would then cite the verse, טעמו וראו כי טוב יהוה / Taste, then and see how good THE FOUNT can be (Psalms 34:9). Buber made the same point when he said, "One who truly goes out to meet the world goes out also to God" (I and Thou).   M.S.

לְדָוִד בְּשַׁנּוֹתוֹ אֶת־טַעְמוֹ לִפְנֵי אֲבִימֶלֶךְ וַיְגָרְשֵׁהוּ וַיֵּלַךְ:

אֲבָרְכָה אֶת־יהוה בְּכָל־עֵת תָּמִיד תְּהִלָּתוֹ בְּפִי:

בַּיהוה תִּתְהַלֵּל נַפְשִׁי יִשְׁמְעוּ עֲנָוִים וְיִשְׂמָחוּ:

גַּדְּלוּ לַיהוה אִתִּי וּנְרוֹמְמָה שְׁמוֹ יַחְדָּו:

דָּרַשְׁתִּי אֶת־יהוה וְעָנָנִי וּמִכָּל־מְגוּרוֹתַי הִצִּילָנִי:

הִבִּיטוּ אֵלָיו וְנָהָרוּ וּפְנֵיהֶם אַל־יֶחְפָּרוּ:

זֶה עָנִי קָרָא וַיהוה שָׁמֵעַ וּמִכָּל־צָרוֹתָיו הוֹשִׁיעוֹ:

חֹנֶה מַלְאַךְ־יהוה סָבִיב לִירֵאָיו וַיְחַלְּצֵם:

טַעֲמוּ וּרְאוּ כִּי־טוֹב יהוה אַשְׁרֵי הַגֶּבֶר יֶחֱסֶה־בּוֹ:

יְראוּ אֶת־יהוה קְדֹשָׁיו כִּי־אֵין מַחְסוֹר לִירֵאָיו:

כְּפִירִים רָשׁוּ וְרָעֵבוּ וְדֹרְשֵׁי יהוה לֹא־יַחְסְרוּ כָל־טוֹב:

לְכוּ־בָנִים שִׁמְעוּ־לִי יִרְאַת יהוה אֲלַמֶּדְכֶם: ←

NOTE. "He" has been used in the translation of several verses in this psalm because they refer specifically to King David. R.S.

COMMENTARY. In the opening sentence of this psalm, the Hebrew idiom for "feigning madness" means literally to "change one's taste." And this is what David did. He began to physically taste that God is good, as the psalm says: טעמו וראו כי־טוב יהוה / Taste then, and see how good THE FOUNT can be. And he proclaimed that the tongue that has tasted sweetness—confirming God's goodness—may no longer speak evil or deceit. To Avimeleḥ, the powerful Philistine ruler, this surely appeared to be madness. To us, it resounds as a challenge. J.A.S.

Might there be a person who wants life,
   who desires days of seeking good?
Never let your tongue speak evil,
   nor your lips pronounce deceit!
Swerve away from evil, perform good,
   seek peace, and follow after it.
Eyes of THE ONE look toward the righteous,
   divine ears are trained upon their cry.

Present is GOD when evildoers act,
   to ban them from the land of memory,
ZION'S GOD will listen when you cry
   and from all your troubles God will save.
Quite near is THE OASIS to the broken-hearted,
   and the despairing it will help.
Righteous one may be, with many troubles,
   but from all of them THE LIVING WATERS save.
Showing care down to a person's bones,
   God will not let a single one of them be broken.
The wicked ones will perish in their evil,
   haters of the righteous will be summoned to account.
Powerful redeemer is THE ONE to those who serve,
   all who trust in THE ETERNAL triumph over guilt.

Psalm 34

COMMENTARY. This psalm is an alphabetical acrostic. The English equivalents of the initial letters are based on the Hebrew, rather than the English, alphabet. The Tetragrammaton appears in this psalm, as in Psalm 29, eighteen times, the numerical equivalent of life.   J.R.

אֹהֵב יָמִים לִרְאוֹת טוֹב: מִי־הָאִישׁ הֶחָפֵץ חַיִּים

וּשְׂפָתֶיךָ מִדַּבֵּר מִרְמָה: נְצֹר לְשׁוֹנְךָ מֵרָע

בַּקֵּשׁ שָׁלוֹם וְרָדְפֵהוּ:   סוּר מֵרָע וַעֲשֵׂה־טוֹב

וְאָזְנָיו אֶל־שַׁוְעָתָם: עֵינֵי יהוה אֶל־צַדִּיקִים

לְהַכְרִית מֵאֶרֶץ זִכְרָם: פְּנֵי יהוה בְּעֹשֵׂי רָע

וּמִכָּל־צָרוֹתָם הִצִּילָם: צָעֲקוּ וַיהוה שָׁמֵעַ

וְאֶת־דַּכְּאֵי־רוּחַ יוֹשִׁיעַ:   קָרוֹב יהוה לְנִשְׁבְּרֵי־לֵב

וּמִכֻּלָּם יַצִּילֶנּוּ יהוה: רַבּוֹת רָעוֹת צַדִּיק

אַחַת מֵהֵנָּה לֹא נִשְׁבָּרָה: שֹׁמֵר כָּל־עַצְמוֹתָיו

וְשֹׂנְאֵי צַדִּיק יֶאְשָׁמוּ:   תְּמוֹתֵת רָשָׁע רָעָה

וְלֹא יֶאְשְׁמוּ כָּל־הַחֹסִים בּוֹ:   * פּוֹדֶה יהוה נֶפֶשׁ עֲבָדָיו

Mi ha'ish hehafetz hayim ohev yamim lirot tov.
Netzor leshoneha mera usfateha midaber mirmah.
Sur mera va'asey tov bakesh shalom verodfehu.

COMMENTARY. "Will be summoned to account"..."triumph over guilt"—
the Hebrew verb is the same in both verses: *yeshamu...lo yeshemu*. The
rendering of these phrases is meant to capture the paradoxical theological
and psychological implications of guilt: considered as a condition of
responsibility before God, the concept of guilt is an important cornerstone
of religious belief; considered as an emotion that can, sometimes
inappropriately, lead a person into despair or self-hatred, a sense of guilt
can sometimes be dangerous and wrong. Those who "triumph over" guilt
master the crippling effects of guilt as an emotion; they will, however,
retain their sense of right and wrong, and continue to hold themselves
responsible before God.   J.R.

A prayer of Moses, the man of God.

My protector, you are our abode,
one generation to the next,

since before the mountains came to birth,
before the birthpangs of the land and world.

From eternity unto eternity, you are divine.

You return a person unto dust.
You say: Return, O children of humanity!

Truly, a thousand years are in your eyes
like yesterday—so quickly does it pass—
or like the watchman's nighttime post.

You pour upon them sleep, they sleep.
When morning comes, it vanishes like chaff.

At dawn, life blossoms and renews itself,
at dusk, it withers and dries up.

Truly, we are consumed amid your anger,
and amid your wrath are made to tremble. ↵

COMMENTARY. Psalm 90 could be called a wisdom psalm. Its message is that the very eternity of God forces us to confront the shortness of human life and our own mortality. The psalmist calls out for the wisdom "to assess our days" and thus to gain an understanding heart. Facing mortality squarely and honestly, the psalmist, with great poignancy, calls out for as many joyous days as those we have experienced suffering and pain. The human capacity to arise from suffering and experience joy again is one of the greatest testimonies to God's presence.   A.G.

אֲדֹנָי מָעוֹן אַתָּה הָיִיתָ לָּנוּ   בְּדֹר וָדֹר:

בְּטֶרֶם הָרִים יֻלָּדוּ   וַתְּחוֹלֵל אֶרֶץ וְתֵבֵל

וּמֵעוֹלָם עַד־עוֹלָם אַתָּה אֵל:

תָּשֵׁב אֱנוֹשׁ עַד־דַּכָּא   וַתֹּאמֶר שׁוּבוּ בְנֵי־אָדָם:

כִּי אֶלֶף שָׁנִים בְּעֵינֶיךָ   כְּיוֹם אֶתְמוֹל כִּי יַעֲבֹר

וְאַשְׁמוּרָה בַלָּיְלָה:

זְרַמְתָּם שֵׁנָה יִהְיוּ   בַּבֹּקֶר כֶּחָצִיר יַחֲלֹף:

בַּבֹּקֶר יָצִיץ וְחָלָף   לָעֶרֶב יְמוֹלֵל וְיָבֵשׁ:

כִּי־כָלִינוּ בְאַפֶּךָ   וּבַחֲמָתְךָ נִבְהָלְנוּ: ←

NOTE. Psalm 90. תפלה למשה איש האלהים /A prayer of Moses, the man of God—A number of psalms are traditionally ascribed to authors other than David. This is the only one ascribed to Moses. The identification may rest on the psalmist's extreme humility before God, the psalm's desertlike mood, its stress on the nothingness of humanity and nature, and its pleading on behalf of human beings in the face of divine wrath.   J.R.

COMMENTARY. תשב אנוש עד דכא / ותאמר שובו /You return a person unto dust. You say: Return...—This couplet captures, with some irony, two values of the word "return": physical return of the human being to dust is suggested first, and the line that follows could allude to it as well; or God's call could mean, "Repent, do *teshuvah*!" When the word appears again some verses later, its meaning is deepened further: "Return, FOUNTAIN OF LIGHT!"—Here, the prayer calls upon God to return from hiding or from anger, and be reconciled with humanity. Human and divine repentance mirror each other. The psalmist prays for this mutual return.   J.R.

You have placed our sins before your presence,
our hidden faults into the lamplight of your face.

Yes, all our days are emptied in your fire,
our years are finished off as but a murmur.

Years of our lifetime are but seventy
—perhaps, among the strongest, eighty years—

and most of them are toil and fatigue,
then quickly it all ends, we fly away.

Who knows the full strength of your fury?
Is our fear of you the equal of your wrath?

Oh, let us know how to assess our days,
how we may bring the heart some wisdom.

Return, FOUNTAIN OF LIGHT! How long?
Be reconciled with your servants!

Give us, at daybreak, the plenty of your love,
enable us to dance and to rejoice throughout our days.

Regale us for as many days as you have tortured us,
as many years as we have witnessed evil.

Let your accomplishments be visible to those who serve you,
let your beauty rest upon their children,

let our divine protector's pleasure be upon us,
and the labor of our hands, make it secure,

the labor of our hands ensure!

Psalm 90

שַׁתָּ עֲוֹנֹתֵינוּ לְנֶגְדֶּ֑ךָ   עֲלֻמֵ֗נוּ לִמְא֥וֹר פָּנֶֽיךָ:
כִּי כָל־יָמֵ֗ינוּ פָּנ֣וּ בְעֶבְרָתֶ֑ךָ   כִּלִּ֖ינוּ שָׁנֵ֣ינוּ כְמוֹ־הֶֽגֶה:
יְמֵי־שְׁנוֹתֵ֨ינוּ בָהֶם שִׁבְעִ֥ים שָׁנָ֗ה   וְאִ֤ם בִּגְבוּרֹ֨ת שְׁמוֹנִ֥ים שָׁנָ֗ה
וְ֭רָהְבָּם עָמָ֣ל וָאָ֑וֶן   כִּי־גָ֥ז חִ֗ישׁ וַנָּעֻֽפָה:
מִֽי־יוֹדֵ֗עַ עֹ֥ז אַפֶּ֑ךָ   וּ֝כְיִרְאָ֥תְךָ עֶבְרָתֶֽךָ:
לִמְנ֣וֹת יָ֭מֵינוּ כֵּ֣ן הוֹדַ֑ע   וְ֝נָבִ֗א לְבַ֣ב חָכְמָֽה:
שׁוּבָ֣ה יְ֭הוה עַד־מָתָ֑י   וְ֝הִנָּחֵ֗ם עַל־עֲבָדֶֽיךָ:
שַׂבְּעֵ֣נוּ בַבֹּ֣קֶר חַסְדֶּ֑ךָ   וּֽנְרַנְּנָ֥ה וְ֝נִשְׂמְחָ֗ה בְּכָל־יָמֵֽינוּ:
שַׂ֭מְּחֵנוּ כִּימ֣וֹת עִנִּיתָ֑נוּ   שְׁ֝נ֗וֹת רָאִ֥ינוּ רָעָֽה:
יֵרָאֶ֣ה אֶל־עֲבָדֶ֣יךָ פָעֳלֶ֑ךָ   וַ֝הֲדָרְךָ֗ עַל־בְּנֵיהֶֽם:
*וִיהִ֤י נֹ֤עַם אֲדֹנָ֥י אֱלֹהֵ֗ינוּ עָ֫לֵ֥ינוּ   וּמַעֲשֵׂ֣ה יָ֭דֵינוּ כּוֹנְנָ֥ה עָלֵ֑ינוּ
וּֽמַעֲשֵׂ֥ה יָ֝דֵ֗ינוּ כּוֹנְנֵֽהוּ:

For the chief musician, to a Gathite melody; by Asaph.

Sing joyful song to God, our strength,
make joyous sounds for Jacob's God!

Raise up a song, and strike the tambourine,
pluck sweetly on the strings, accompanied by harp.

Blast piercing notes upon the shofar for the New Moon,
for the full moon, for our festive holiday.

For it is Israel's law,
a statute of the God of Jacob.

God established it in Joseph's clans,
when going forth against the land of Egypt;
I heard a language that I didn't know.

"I have relieved their shoulders of their burdens,
their hands are freed from carrying the basket.

In sorrow you called out, and I released you,
I answered from my hidden place where thunder rolls,
I tried you at Meribah's waters. So it was! ⤺

לַמְנַצֵּחַ

עַל־הַגִּתִּית לְאָסָף׃

הַרְנִינוּ לֵאלֹהִים עוּזֵּנוּ הָרִיעוּ לֵאלֹהֵי יַעֲקֹב׃

שְׂאוּ־זִמְרָה וּתְנוּ־תֹף כִּנּוֹר נָעִים עִם־נָבֶל׃

תִּקְעוּ בַחֹדֶשׁ שׁוֹפָר בַּכֶּסֶה לְיוֹם חַגֵּנוּ׃

כִּי חֹק לְיִשְׂרָאֵל הוּא מִשְׁפָּט לֵאלֹהֵי יַעֲקֹב׃

עֵדוּת בִּיהוֹסֵף שָׂמוֹ בְּצֵאתוֹ עַל־אֶרֶץ מִצְרָיִם שְׂפַת לֹא־יָדַעְתִּי אֶשְׁמָע׃

הֲסִירוֹתִי מִסֵּבֶל שִׁכְמוֹ כַּפָּיו מִדּוּד תַּעֲבֹרְנָה׃

בַּצָּרָה קָרָאתָ וָאֲחַלְּצֶךָּ אֶעֶנְךָ בְּסֵתֶר רַעַם אֶבְחָנְךָ עַל־מֵי מְרִיבָה סֶלָה׃ ←

NOTE. This appellation "For the chief musician, to a Gathite melody," occurs dozens of times at the beginning of psalms, as at the end of the book of Habakuk. Often it occurs alongside references to Asaph, the clan of Levite singers. This suggests that the choir leader either composed or directed the performance of these compositions. D.A.T.

Listen, my people, I admonish you!
Israel, if you only would pay heed to me!

Let you not have among you alien gods,
let you not bow down to exotic gods.

I am THE REDEEMING ONE, your God,
who brings you up out of the land of Egypt.
Open up your mouth, and I shall fill it!

But my people did not listen to my voice.
no, Israel did not care for me.

So I sent away the people in their stubbornness of heart,
I let them go according to their own devices.

Would that my people might listen to me,
yes, would that Israel walked according to my ways!

How quickly would I crush their enemies,
on their oppressors would I cast my hand.

Those who hate GOD would cringe before my people;
I would stand beside them always.

God would feed them from the choicest wheat.
Yes, from the rock I'd feed you honey in abundance."

Psalm 81

שְׁמַע עַמִּי וְאָעִידָה בָּךְ יִשְׂרָאֵל אִם־תִּשְׁמַע־לִי:
לֹא־יִהְיֶה בְךָ אֵל זָר וְלֹא תִשְׁתַּחֲוֶה לְאֵל נֵכָר:
אָנֹכִי יהוה אֱלֹהֶיךָ הַמַּעַלְךָ מֵאֶרֶץ מִצְרָיִם הַרְחֶב־פִּיךָ וַאֲמַלְאֵהוּ:
וְלֹא־שָׁמַע עַמִּי לְקוֹלִי וְיִשְׂרָאֵל לֹא־אָבָה לִי:
וָאֲשַׁלְּחֵהוּ בִּשְׁרִירוּת לִבָּם יֵלְכוּ בְּמוֹעֲצוֹתֵיהֶם:
לוּ עַמִּי שֹׁמֵעַ לִי יִשְׂרָאֵל בִּדְרָכַי יְהַלֵּכוּ:
כִּמְעַט אוֹיְבֵיהֶם אַכְנִיעַ וְעַל־צָרֵיהֶם אָשִׁיב יָדִי:
מְשַׂנְאֵי יהוה יְכַחֲשׁוּ־לוֹ וִיהִי עִתָּם לְעוֹלָם:
* וַיַּאֲכִילֵהוּ מֵחֵלֶב חִטָּה וּמִצּוּר דְּבַשׁ אַשְׂבִּיעֶךָ:

COMMENTARY. Psalm 81 is divided into two sections reflecting the
contrasting moods we experience on Rosh Hashanah. The first eight
verses emphasize our joy in praising God and our gratitude at no longer
finding ourselves in the narrow places in our lives represented by
Mitzrayim/Egypt. The many references to joyous song and instrumental
music-making communicate our sense of celebration, as we anticipate the
opportunity for a new beginning presented by the new year. Verses 9-16
reflect the more somber and contemplative aspect of the Days of Awe.
These verses are punctuated by forms of the verb *shema*/listen. On Rosh
Hashanah and Yom Kippur we strain to listen for God's message in the
world, as well as to our innermost selves. The tension between the psalm's
two moods is resolved in the final words, "from the rock I feed you honey
in abundance." The rock simultaneously refers back to the agonizing trial
at Meribah when Moses strikes a rock to extract water for the complaining
Israelites; and to God, the Rock of Israel. These words also give substance
to the vague promise, "open your mouth wide, and I will fill it." In
opening ourselves to God's presence, we free ourselves from the
oppressors and alien gods of our own Egypt. Only then can our mouths
be truly filled with both joyous prayer and the sweetness of (Rosh
Hashanah) honey.

R.S.

For Rosh Hashanah:

A song of triumph, to a Gathite melody. Of David.

ALMIGHTY ONE, our sovereign, how glorious is your name
  throughout the earth,
you whose splendor is stretched forth across the heavens!

Even from the mouths of infants and of nurselings
  you have drawn foundation for your power,
in order to confound your enemies,
in order to frustrate your foe and to enact your justice.

When I behold your heavens, which your hands have wrought,
the moon and stars you have created,
what are human beings that you should think of them,
the children of humanity that you take note of them?

For you have made them only slightly less than divine beings,
and have crowned them with your glory and your splendor.

You have given us authority over your handiwork,
all things you make dependent on our power—
the sheep and cattle, all of them,
even the wild mountain beasts,
birds of the skies, fish of the sea,
all that travel through the ocean currents.

Our FOUNT OF LIFE, our God, how glorious is your name
  throughout the earth!

Psalm 8

לַ**מְנַצֵּחַ** עַל־הַגִּתִּית מִזְמוֹר לְדָוִד׃

יהוה אֲדֹנֵינוּ מָה־אַדִּיר שִׁמְךָ בְּכָל־הָאָרֶץ

אֲשֶׁר־תְּנָה הוֹדְךָ עַל־הַשָּׁמָיִם׃

מִפִּי עוֹלְלִים וְיֹנְקִים יִסַּדְתָּ עֹז לְמַעַן צוֹרְרֶיךָ

לְהַשְׁבִּית אוֹיֵב וּמִתְנַקֵּם׃

כִּי־אֶרְאֶה שָׁמֶיךָ מַעֲשֵׂה אֶצְבְּעֹתֶיךָ

יָרֵחַ וְכוֹכָבִים אֲשֶׁר כּוֹנָנְתָּה׃

מָה־אֱנוֹשׁ כִּי־תִזְכְּרֶנּוּ וּבֶן־אָדָם כִּי תִפְקְדֶנּוּ׃

וַתְּחַסְּרֵהוּ מְּעַט מֵאֱלֹהִים וְכָבוֹד וְהָדָר תְּעַטְּרֵהוּ׃

תַּמְשִׁילֵהוּ בְּמַעֲשֵׂי יָדֶיךָ כֹּל שַׁתָּה תַחַת־רַגְלָיו׃

צֹנֶה וַאֲלָפִים כֻּלָּם וְגַם בַּהֲמוֹת שָׂדָי׃

צִפּוֹר שָׁמַיִם וּדְגֵי הַיָּם עֹבֵר אָרְחוֹת יַמִּים׃

יהוה אֲדֹנֵינוּ מָה־אַדִּיר שִׁמְךָ בְּכָל־הָאָרֶץ׃

For Yom Kippur:

[A psalm] of David.
A poem of contemplation.

Happy is the one whose wrong has been forgiven,
whose transgression has been cleared!

Happy is the one whose error is no longer reckoned
   by THE GOD OF MERCY,
and no treachery remains within that person's soul.

While I was silent, I wore out my bones
   with anguished roaring through the day,
yes, day and night your hand was heavy over me.
My strength was ravaged as in summer drought.
How difficult it was!

But then I made my errors known to you,
   and I did not conceal my wrongful acts.
I said: "I shall confess to you, exalted God,
   all my injustices, FORGIVING ONE."
And you forgave my wrongs, and cleared my sins.
   How glad I was!

Because of this, all those who love you
   pray to you, whenever sin is found,
so that a flood of great torrential waters
   will not overwhelm them.

You are my shelter, you protect me from distress;
you surround me with the joys of your deliverance.
   How fortunate I am! ↰

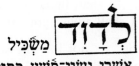 מַשְׂכִּיל

אַשְׁרֵי נְשׂוּי־פֶּשַׁע כְּסוּי חֲטָאָה:

אַשְׁרֵי־אָדָם לֹא יַחְשֹׁב יהוה לוֹ עָוֹן
וְאֵין בְּרוּחוֹ רְמִיָּה:

כִּי־הֶחֱרַשְׁתִּי בָּלוּ עֲצָמָי בְּשַׁאֲגָתִי כָּל־הַיּוֹם:
כִּי יוֹמָם וָלַיְלָה תִּכְבַּד עָלַי יָדֶךָ
נֶהְפַּךְ לְשַׁדִּי בְּחַרְבֹנֵי קַיִץ סֶלָה:

חַטָּאתִי אוֹדִיעֲךָ וַעֲוֹנִי לֹא־כִסִּיתִי
אָמַרְתִּי אוֹדֶה עֲלֵי פְשָׁעַי לַיהוה
וְאַתָּה נָשָׂאתָ עֲוֹן חַטָּאתִי סֶלָה:

עַל־זֹאת יִתְפַּלֵּל כָּל־חָסִיד אֵלֶיךָ לְעֵת מְצֹא
רַק לְשֵׁטֶף מַיִם רַבִּים אֵלָיו לֹא יַגִּיעוּ:

אַתָּה סֵתֶר לִי מִצַּר תִּצְּרֵנִי רָנֵּי פַלֵּט תְּסוֹבְבֵנִי סֶלָה: —←

"I shall instruct you," [you have said,]
"I shall light up for you the road on which you tread,
I shall advise you, and my eye is watchful over you.

So, act not like the senseless horse or mule,
whose petulance is curbed by bridle and by reins
   before one can approach."

Great are the torments of the wicked,
but the one who trusts in GOD is ringed by loving-kindness.
Have joy in THE ETERNAL ONE; rejoice, you who are just!
Cry out for joy, all who are upright!

Psalm 32

אַשְׂכִּילְךָ וְאוֹרְךָ בְּדֶרֶךְ־זוּ תֵלֵךְ
אִיעֲצָה עָלֶיךָ עֵינִי:

אַל־תִּהְיוּ כְּסוּס כְּפֶרֶד אֵין הָבִין
בְּמֶתֶג־וָרֶסֶן עֶדְיוֹ לִבְלוֹם בַּל קְרֹב אֵלֶיךָ:

רַבִּים מַכְאוֹבִים לָרָשָׁע וְהַבּוֹטֵחַ בַּיהוה חֶסֶד יְסוֹבְבֶנּוּ:
שִׂמְחוּ בַיהוה וְגִילוּ צַדִּיקִים וְהַרְנִינוּ כָּל־יִשְׁרֵי־לֵב:

COMMENTARY. The Hebrew exclamation *selah!* has no exact translation, but it completes the thought of a verse by making it more emphatic. In this psalm, it exercises an important function, marking three key moments in the worshipper's evolving awareness: the past state of sin; the turning-point, when repentance occurred; and the present state of trust in God. The translation therefore substitutes three appropriate exclamatory phrases ("How difficult it was!" "How glad I was!" "How fortunate I am!") where the word occurs in order to capture the trajectory of the worshipper's spiritual progress.   J.R.

For Yom Kippur:

A Prayer of David.

Listen, GOD of justice, hearken to my song of joy,
give ear, please, to my prayer, here spoken without guile.

Your judgment of my case comes forth,
your gaze is so direct!

You prove my heart, you visit in the night,
you test me, and find nothing wrong,
my mouth does not transgress.

As for the deeds of human beings,
guided by your words,
I've kept myself away from lawless paths.

My feet held firm,
along your winding trails, my steps did not give way.

I have called out to you, that you, divinity, might answer me;
extend your ear to me, and listen to my utterance.

Act wondrously with loving deeds,
redeeming those who trust in you,
preserving from aggressors with your mighty hand.

Protect me like the pupil of an eye,
conceal me in the shelter of your wings

from evildoers who despoil me,
from mortal enemies who have surrounded me.

Their inner substance is closed off,
their mouths have spoken arrogance.

תְּפִלָּה לְדָוִד

שִׁמְעָה יהוה צֶדֶק הַקְשִׁיבָה רִנָּתִי הַאֲזִינָה תְפִלָּתִי
בְּלֹא שִׂפְתֵי מִרְמָה:
מִלְּפָנֶיךָ מִשְׁפָּטִי יֵצֵא עֵינֶיךָ תֶּחֱזֶינָה מֵישָׁרִים:
בָּחַנְתָּ לִבִּי פָּקַדְתָּ לַּיְלָה צְרַפְתַּנִי בַל־תִּמְצָא זַמֹּתִי
בַּל־יַעֲבָר־פִּי:
לִפְעֻלּוֹת אָדָם בִּדְבַר שְׂפָתֶיךָ
אֲנִי שָׁמַרְתִּי אָרְחוֹת פָּרִיץ:
תָּמֹךְ אֲשֻׁרַי בְּמַעְגְּלוֹתֶיךָ בַּל־נָמוֹטוּ פְעָמָי:
אֲנִי־קְרָאתִיךָ כִי־תַעֲנֵנִי אֵל הַט־אָזְנְךָ לִי שְׁמַע אִמְרָתִי:
הַפְלֵה חֲסָדֶיךָ מוֹשִׁיעַ חוֹסִים מִמִּתְקוֹמְמִים בִּימִינֶךָ:
שָׁמְרֵנִי כְּאִישׁוֹן בַּת־עָיִן בְּצֵל כְּנָפֶיךָ תַּסְתִּירֵנִי:
מִפְּנֵי רְשָׁעִים זוּ שַׁדּוּנִי אֹיְבַי בְּנֶפֶשׁ יַקִּיפוּ עָלָי:
חֶלְבָּמוֹ סָגְרוּ פִּימוֹ דִּבְּרוּ בְגֵאוּת: ←

COMMENTARY. The psalmist describes himself as having clean hands and a pure heart, as a person walking a godly path. With this claim on God, the psalmist asks for protection from evil doers and enemies. Then moving beyond worldly, everyday concerns, the psalmist makes the ultimate request—to be worthy of directly encountering the divine. Jews on Yom Kippur, with their struggle for complete goodness, can see the first part of the psalm as a portrayal of the ideal toward which they are aspiring. As the order of the psalm makes clear, while there may be some temporal rewards for leading the good life, the ultimate reward is spiritual. D.A.T.

Our feet they have hemmed in,
their eyes they have set roaming in the land.

The enemy is like a lion eager to attack,
a youthful lion crouching in its hiding-place.

Arise, REDEEMING ONE, go forth to meet the foe and
   to subdue.
Rescue my life from evil with your power,

from those made mortal by your hand, ALMIGHTY ONE,
from mortal ones whose share in life is brief.

But as for those in your protection, satisfy their hunger,
let their children enjoy plenty,
and in turn pass on abundance to their young.

May I, with justice, come to see your face,
may I awake with satisfaction to behold your form!

Psalm 17

אַשֻּׁרֵ֫נוּ עַתָּה סְבָב֥וּנוּ עֵינֵיהֶ֥ם יָ֝שִׁ֗יתוּ לִנְט֥וֹת בָּאָֽרֶץ׃

דִּמְיֹנ֗וֹ כְּ֭אַרְיֵה יִכְס֣וֹף לִטְר֑וֹף וְ֝כִכְפִ֗יר יֹשֵׁ֥ב בְּמִסְתָּרִֽים׃

ק֘וּמָ֤ה יְהוָ֗ה קַדְּמָ֣ה פָ֭נָיו הַכְרִיעֵ֑הוּ פַּלְּטָ֥ה נַ֝פְשִׁ֗י מֵרָשָׁ֥ע חַרְבֶּֽךָ׃

מִֽמְתִ֥ים יָדְךָ֨ ׀ יְהוָ֡ה מִֽמְתִ֬ים מֵחֶ֗לֶד חֶלְקָ֥ם בַּֽחַיִּים֮

וּֽצְפוּנְךָ֮ תְּמַלֵּ֪א בִ֫טְנָ֥ם יִשְׂבְּע֥וּ בָנִ֑ים

וְהִנִּ֥יחוּ יִ֝תְרָ֗ם לְעֽוֹלְלֵיהֶֽם׃

אֲנִ֗י בְּ֭צֶדֶק אֶחֱזֶ֣ה פָנֶ֑יךָ אֶשְׂבְּעָ֥ה בְ֝הָקִ֗יץ תְּמוּנָתֶֽךָ׃

A song of the Ascents:

From amid the depths, I have cried out, REDEEMING ONE,
so hearken, my protector, to my voice,
and let your ears be attentive to my call of prayer.
Were you, O God, to keep exact accounting of our sins,
who, my sovereign, could survive?
For you possess the power to forgive;
for this, the awe of you is stirred.
I hope for you, ABUNDANT ONE, my soul has hoped,
and for God's word I wait with expectation.
My spirit longs for its protector
more than those who wait for dawn,
those who wait for day to break.
So Israel hopes for THE ABUNDANT ONE,
for with THE FOUNT OF MERCY is the power of love,
with God, the power to redeem.
God is the one who shall release
the people Israel from their sins.

Psalm 130

שִׁיר הַמַּעֲלוֹת
מִמַּעֲמַקִּים קְרָאתִיךָ יהוה: אֲדֹנָי שִׁמְעָה בְקוֹלִי
תִּהְיֶינָה אָזְנֶיךָ קַשֻּׁבוֹת לְקוֹל תַּחֲנוּנָי:
אִם־עֲוֹנוֹת תִּשְׁמָר־יָהּ אֲדֹנָי מִי יַעֲמֹד:
כִּי־עִמְּךָ הַסְּלִיחָה לְמַעַן תִּוָּרֵא:
קִוִּיתִי יהוה קִוְּתָה נַפְשִׁי וְלִדְבָרוֹ הוֹחָלְתִּי:
נַפְשִׁי לַאדֹנָי מִשֹּׁמְרִים לַבֹּקֶר שֹׁמְרִים לַבֹּקֶר:
יַחֵל יִשְׂרָאֵל אֶל־יהוה
כִּי־עִם־יהוה הַחֶסֶד וְהַרְבֵּה עִמּוֹ פְדוּת:
וְהוּא יִפְדֶּה אֶת־יִשְׂרָאֵל מִכֹּל עֲוֹנֹתָיו:

Dwelling in the secret of the Highest,
in the shade of the Almighty does one lodge.

I say to THE ETERNAL ONE: My roof, my fortress tower,
my God, in whom I trust!

For One shall shelter you from trapper's snare,
from the disease that sweeps the villages.

Inside divine wings you are nestled,
beneath God's pinions you are housed,
a shield embracing is God's truth.

You shall not fear from nighttime terror,
from the arrow that soars by day,

from pestilence that stalks the gloom,
from feverish demon of the noon.

A thousand dangers fall away beside you,
yes, ten thousand of them, at your right.
To you, they can't draw near.

Just cast your eyes around,
the payment of the wicked you shall see.

For you, PRESENCE, are canopy to me,
Supernal One, you've offered your abode. ↵

בְּצֵל שַׁדַּי יִתְלוֹנָן: יֹשֵׁב בְּסֵתֶר עֶלְיוֹן

אֱלֹהַי אֶבְטַח־בּוֹ:   אֹמַר לַיהוה מַחְסִי וּמְצוּדָתִי

מִדֶּבֶר הַוּוֹת: כִּי הוּא יַצִּילְךָ מִפַּח יָקוּשׁ

וְתַחַת־כְּנָפָיו תֶּחְסֶה   בְּאֶבְרָתוֹ יָסֶךְ לָךְ

צִנָּה וְסֹחֵרָה אֲמִתּוֹ:

מֵחֵץ יָעוּף יוֹמָם: לֹא־תִירָא מִפַּחַד לָיְלָה

מִקֶּטֶב יָשׁוּד צָהֳרָיִם: מִדֶּבֶר בָּאֹפֶל יַהֲלֹךְ

וּרְבָבָה מִימִינֶךָ   יִפֹּל מִצִּדְּךָ אֶלֶף

אֵלֶיךָ לֹא יִגָּשׁ:

וְשִׁלֻּמַת רְשָׁעִים תִּרְאֶה: רַק בְּעֵינֶיךָ תַבִּיט

עֶלְיוֹן שַׂמְתָּ מְעוֹנֶךָ: ←   כִּי־אַתָּה יהוה מַחְסִי

NOTE. This psalm revels in the many words for the enclave of divine protection: secret [place], shade, fortress tower, wings, pinions, embracing, shield, canopy, abode, tent, angels, divine hands.   J.R.

No evil shall befall you,
nor shall any plague approach your tent.

For God shall bid the angels to you,
to protect you upon all your paths.

On divine hands you shall be carried,
lest your foot should strike the rock.

On roaring lion and on python you shall tread,
you'll trample cub and crocodile.

Yes, in Me is her desire, I help her to survive,
I shall exalt her, for she knows my name.

He calls to Me, I answer him,
with him am I in time of trial.
I release him, and I pay him honor.

Long are the days I satisfy her with,
I look upon her with my saving help.

Long are the days I satisfy him with,
I look upon him with my saving help.

Psalm 91

NOTE. To achieve gender balance, the translator has exercised poetic license in choosing pronouns here.   D.A.T.

וְנֶגַע לֹא־יִקְרַב בְּאָהֳלֶךָ:	לֹא־תְאֻנֶּה אֵלֶיךָ רָעָה
לִשְׁמָרְךָ בְּכָל־דְּרָכֶיךָ:	כִּי מַלְאָכָיו יְצַוֶּה־לָּךְ
פֶּן־תִּגֹּף בָּאֶבֶן רַגְלֶךָ:	עַל־כַּפַּיִם יִשָּׂאוּנְךָ
תִּרְמֹס כְּפִיר וְתַנִּין:	עַל־שַׁחַל וָפֶתֶן תִּדְרֹךְ
אֲשַׂגְּבֵהוּ כִּי־יָדַע שְׁמִי:	כִּי בִי חָשַׁק וַאֲפַלְּטֵהוּ
עִמּוֹ־אָנֹכִי בְצָרָה	יִקְרָאֵנִי וְאֶעֱנֵהוּ

אֲחַלְּצֵהוּ וַאֲכַבְּדֵהוּ:

וְאַרְאֵהוּ בִּישׁוּעָתִי:	* אֹרֶךְ יָמִים אַשְׂבִּיעֵהוּ
וְאַרְאֵהוּ בִּישׁוּעָתִי:	אֹרֶךְ יָמִים אַשְׂבִּיעֵהוּ

Oreḥ yamim asbi'ehu ve'arehu bishu'ati.

COMMENTARY. The function of angels in the Bible was primarily that of messengers as reflected in the Hebrew term *malaḥ*. Though the Bible does refer to other kinds of angels, their function is quite sketchy. In the second Temple period, the lore about angels grew quite rapidly. At several points the Hebrew liturgy utilizes biblical excerpts in ways that reflect the later understanding of angels. This is particularly the case in the three forms of *Kedushah* found in the Shabbat and Festival morning service.   D.A.T.

Acknowledge THE ETERNAL, who is good,
   God's love is everlasting,
praise the God of all the gods,
   Ki le'olam ḥasdo,
give thanks to the most powerful of powers,
   God's love is everlasting,
who alone performs great, wondrous deeds,
   Ki le'olam ḥasdo,
maker of the heavens with sublime discernment,
   God's love is everlasting,
founder of the earth upon the waters,
   Ki le'olam ḥasdo,
maker of the great light orbs,
   God's love is everlasting,
sunlight for dominion of the day,
   Ki le'olam ḥasdo,
moon and stars to rule the night,
   God's love is everlasting,
who, amid our lowliness, remembered,
   Ki le'olam ḥasdo,
who unyoked us from our troubles,
   God's love is everlasting,
who gives sustenance to all of flesh,
   Ki le'olam ḥasdo!
Praises to the heavens' God,
   God's love is everlasting!

                                    Selected from Psalm 136

COMMENTARY. הודו ליהוה / Acknowledge THE ETERNAL. Psalm 136 is
sometimes called the Great Hallel. Its resounding chorus of praise was
probably sung by the Levites on festive occasions during Second Temple
times. The stanzas of the psalm combine mention of the wonders of
Creation and the history of Israel as signs of God's faithfulness.   A.G.

כִּי לְעוֹלָם חַסְדּוֹ:
כִּי לְעוֹלָם חַסְדּוֹ:
כִּי לְעוֹלָם חַסְדּוֹ:
כִּי לְעוֹלָם חַסְדּוֹ:
כִּי לְעוֹלָם חַסְדּוֹ:
כִּי לְעוֹלָם חַסְדּוֹ:
כִּי לְעוֹלָם חַסְדּוֹ:
כִּי לְעוֹלָם חַסְדּוֹ:
כִּי לְעוֹלָם חַסְדּוֹ:
כִּי לְעוֹלָם חַסְדּוֹ:
כִּי לְעוֹלָם חַסְדּוֹ:
כִּי לְעוֹלָם חַסְדּוֹ:
כִּי לְעוֹלָם חַסְדּוֹ:

הוֹדוּ לַיהוה כִּי־טוֹב

הוֹדוּ לֵאלֹהֵי הָאֱלֹהִים
הוֹדוּ לַאֲדֹנֵי הָאֲדֹנִים
לְעֹשֵׂה נִפְלָאוֹת גְּדֹלוֹת לְבַדּוֹ
לְעֹשֵׂה הַשָּׁמַיִם בִּתְבוּנָה
לְרֹקַע הָאָרֶץ עַל־הַמָּיִם
לְעֹשֵׂה אוֹרִים גְּדֹלִים
אֶת־הַשֶּׁמֶשׁ לְמֶמְשֶׁלֶת בַּיּוֹם
אֶת־הַיָּרֵחַ וְכוֹכָבִים לְמֶמְשְׁלוֹת בַּלָּיְלָה
שֶׁבְּשִׁפְלֵנוּ זָכַר לָנוּ
וַיִּפְרְקֵנוּ מִצָּרֵינוּ
נֹתֵן לֶחֶם לְכָל־בָּשָׂר
הוֹדוּ לְאֵל הַשָּׁמָיִם

Hodu ladonay ki tov   Ki le'olam ḥasdo.
Hodu leylohey ha'elohim   Ki le'olam ḥasdo.
Hodu la'adoney ha'adonim   Ki le'olam ḥasdo.
Le'osey nifla'ot gedolot levado   Ki le'olam ḥasdo.
Le'osey hashamayim bitvunah   Ki le'olam ḥasdo.
Leroka ha'aretz al hamayim   Ki le'olam ḥasdo.
Le'osey orim gedolim   Ki le'olam ḥasdo.
Et hashemesh lememshelet bayom   Ki le'olam ḥasdo.
Et hayare'aḥ vehoḥavim lememshelot balaylah   Ki le'olam ḥasdo.
Shebeshiflenu zaḥar lanu   Ki le'olam ḥasdo.
Vayifrekenu mitzareynu   Ki le'olam ḥasdo.
Noten leḥem leḥol basar   Ki le'olam ḥasdo.
Hodu le'el hashamayim   Ki le'olam ḥasdo.

Rejoice, you just ones, in THE SOURCE,
you who are upright, it is fitting to sing praise.

Give thanks to THE INCOMPARABLE upon the harp,
by ten-stringed lute, make melody for God,

yes, sing a new song to the One,
play heartily a melody with hornblast,

for the word of THE SUPERNAL ONE is true,
whose every deed is done in faith,

who loves the righteous and the just.
THE PROVIDER'S kindness fills the earth!

By THE CREATOR'S word the skies were made,
by breath of divine speaking all their host,

who gathered in a heap the ocean's waters,
placing into chambers all the deep.

Have awe of THE UNSEEN ONE, all the earth,
have dread of God, all dwellers of the globe,

for here was one who spoke and all things were,
who gave command and everything arose,

REDEEMER, who makes void the plans of nations,
who subverts the scheming among peoples.

The counsel of THE ETERNAL ONE shall stand forever,
God's meditations, from one generation to the next. ↵

צַדִּיקִים בַּיהוה   לַיְשָׁרִים נָאוָה תְהִלָּה׃

הוֹדוּ לַיהוה בְּכִנּוֹר   בְּנֵבֶל עָשׂוֹר זַמְּרוּ־לוֹ׃

שִׁירוּ־לוֹ שִׁיר חָדָשׁ   הֵיטִיבוּ נַגֵּן בִּתְרוּעָה׃

כִּי־יָשָׁר דְּבַר־יהוה   וְכָל־מַעֲשֵׂהוּ בֶּאֱמוּנָה׃

אֹהֵב צְדָקָה וּמִשְׁפָּט   חֶסֶד יהוה מָלְאָה הָאָרֶץ׃

בִּדְבַר יהוה שָׁמַיִם נַעֲשׂוּ   וּבְרוּחַ פִּיו כָּל־צְבָאָם׃

כֹּנֵס כַּנֵּד מֵי הַיָּם   נֹתֵן בְּאוֹצָרוֹת תְּהוֹמוֹת׃

יִּירְאוּ מֵיהוה כָּל־הָאָרֶץ   מִמֶּנּוּ יָגוּרוּ כָּל־יֹשְׁבֵי תֵבֵל׃

כִּי הוּא אָמַר וַיֶּהִי   הוּא־צִוָּה וַיַּעֲמֹד׃

יהוה הֵפִיר עֲצַת־גּוֹיִם   הֵנִיא מַחְשְׁבוֹת עַמִּים׃

עֲצַת יהוה לְעוֹלָם תַּעֲמֹד   מַחְשְׁבוֹת לִבּוֹ לְדֹר וָדֹר׃ —←

What is a new song?
When we break our habits of heart and mind
We step out of the past and into the Present.
What is new is what is no longer habitual.
What is new is what arises out of the Moment.

R.M.S.

Happy is the nation who has THIS ONE for its God,
the people who has chosen this inheritance.

Far from the heavens does THE KEEPER watch,
beholds all children of humanity,

surveying, from the seat of rule,
all dwellers of the earth,

who fashions all their hearts as one,
who understands their every deed.

A king cannot be saved, however great his force,
no mighty one whose great strength can redeem.

His horse proves false for rescuing,
in the abundance of his force he can't be saved.

But see! GOD'S eye looks toward the awestruck,
those who yearn for divine love,

for saving of their souls from death,
and giving them, amid their hunger, life.

Our spirit has awaited THE ETERNAL,
who is for us a help and shield.

Through One alone our heart rejoices,
in whose holy name we place our trust.

May your kindness be upon us,
just as we have placed our hope in you.

Psalm 33

אַשְׁרֵי הַגּוֹי אֲשֶׁר־יְהוָה אֱלֹהָיו   הָעָם בָּחַר לְנַחֲלָה לוֹ׃
מִשָּׁמַיִם הִבִּיט יְהוָה   רָאָה אֶת־כָּל־בְּנֵי הָאָדָם׃
מִמְּכוֹן־שִׁבְתּוֹ הִשְׁגִּיחַ   אֶל כָּל־יֹשְׁבֵי הָאָרֶץ׃
הַיֹּצֵר יַחַד לִבָּם   הַמֵּבִין אֶל־כָּל־מַעֲשֵׂיהֶם׃
אֵין הַמֶּלֶךְ נוֹשָׁע בְּרָב־חָיִל   גִּבּוֹר לֹא־יִנָּצֵל בְּרָב־כֹּחַ׃
שֶׁקֶר הַסּוּס לִתְשׁוּעָה   וּבְרֹב חֵילוֹ לֹא יְמַלֵּט׃
הִנֵּה עֵין יְהוָה אֶל־יְרֵאָיו   לַמְיַחֲלִים לְחַסְדּוֹ׃
לְהַצִּיל מִמָּוֶת נַפְשָׁם   וּלְחַיּוֹתָם בָּרָעָב׃
נַפְשֵׁנוּ חִכְּתָה לַיהוָה   עֶזְרֵנוּ וּמָגִנֵּנוּ הוּא׃
* כִּי־בוֹ יִשְׂמַח לִבֵּנוּ   כִּי בְשֵׁם קָדְשׁוֹ בָטָחְנוּ׃
יְהִי־חַסְדְּךָ יְהוָה עָלֵינוּ   כַּאֲשֶׁר יִחַלְנוּ לָךְ׃

A psalm. A song for the day of Shabbat.

A good thing to give thanks to THE ETERNAL,
to sing out to your name supreme,

to tell about your kindness in the morning,
and your faithfulness at night,

on ten-stringed lyre and on flute,
with melodies conceived on harp,

for you, ALMIGHTY ONE, elate me with your deeds,
I'll sing about the actions of your hands.

How great your deeds have been, SUPERNAL ONE,
your thoughts exceedingly profound.

Of this the foolish person cannot know,
of this the shallow cannot understand.

For though the wicked multiply like weeds,
and evildoers sprout up all around,

it is for their destruction for all time,
but you, MAJESTIC ONE, are lifted high eternally, ↵

It is good to give thanks.
Why? Does God need our praise?
No.
We do.
To awaken to Wonder
to holiness
to God.
It is good to give thanks
for through thanksgiving comes awakening.

R.M.S.

מִזְמוֹר שִׁיר לְיוֹם־הַשַּׁבָּת:

וּלְזַמֵּר לְשִׁמְךָ עֶלְיוֹן: טוֹב לְהֹדוֹת לַיהוה

וֶאֱמוּנָתְךָ בַּלֵּילוֹת: לְהַגִּיד בַּבֹּקֶר חַסְדֶּךָ

עֲלֵי הִגָּיוֹן בְּכִנּוֹר: עֲלֵי־עָשׂוֹר וַעֲלֵי־נָבֶל

בְּמַעֲשֵׂי יָדֶיךָ אֲרַנֵּן: כִּי שִׂמַּחְתַּנִי יהוה בְּפָעֳלֶךָ

מְאֹד עָמְקוּ מַחְשְׁבֹתֶיךָ: מַה־גָּדְלוּ מַעֲשֶׂיךָ יהוה

וּכְסִיל לֹא־יָבִין אֶת־זֹאת: אִישׁ־בַּעַר לֹא יֵדָע

וַיָּצִיצוּ כָּל־פֹּעֲלֵי אָוֶן בִּפְרֹחַ רְשָׁעִים כְּמוֹ־עֵשֶׂב

לְהִשָּׁמְדָם עֲדֵי־עַד:

—: וְאַתָּה מָרוֹם לְעֹלָם יהוה

Mizmor shir leyom hashabbat.

Tov lehodot ladonay   ulzamer leshimeḥa elyon.

Lehagid baboker ḥasdeḥa   ve'emunateḥa baleylot.

Aley asor va'aley navel   aley higayon beḥinor.

COMMENTARY. Beautiful in many respects, this twice-recited (evening and morning) Sabbath psalm also contains affirmations which do not flow easily from our lips: the wicked, despite their apparent success, are destined to perish (verses 8-10), while the righteous are destined to flourish (verses 13-15). Who, observing the vast human traumas of this century, can say these words with full conviction?

Isn't this psalm facile, smug? At moments of harassment or discouragement, so it may seem; but during the composed times of quiet reflection, such as Shabbat, it appears closer to the truth than its cynical opposite. Historically, a good case can be made that evil eventually destroys itself; philosophically, it can be convincingly argued that evil contains its own self-destruction, its own internal contradiction.

Yet this vision is far from our present reality, especially when applied to individual cases. With reason Rashi construes the phrase *leyom hashabbat* for the Sabbath Day in the first verse of the psalm as referring to *olam shekulo Shabbat*, a world-in-the-making when all will be serene.   E.G.

behold your enemies, RESPLENDENT ONE,
behold, your enemies are lost,

all evildoers shall be scattered.

You raise my horn like that of the triumphant ox;
I am anointed with fresh oil.

My eye shall gaze in victory on my enemies,
on all who rise against me to do harm;

my ears shall hear of their demise.

The righteous flourish like the palm trees,
like cedars of Lebanon they grow,

implanted in the house of THE ALL KNOWING ONE
amid the courtyards of our God they bear fruit.

In their old age, they'll put forth seed,
fleshy and fresh they'll ever be,

to tell the uprightness of ONE ALONE,
my Rock, in whom no fault resides.

Psalm 92

כִּי הִנֵּה אֹיְבֶיךָ יהוה   כִּי־הִנֵּה אֹיְבֶיךָ יֹאבֵדוּ

יִתְפָּרְדוּ כָּל־פֹּעֲלֵי אָוֶן:

וַתָּרֶם כִּרְאֵים קַרְנִי   בַּלֹּתִי בְּשֶׁמֶן רַעֲנָן:

וַתַּבֵּט עֵינִי בְּשׁוּרָי   בַּקָּמִים עָלַי מְרֵעִים

תִּשְׁמַעְנָה אָזְנָי:

צַדִּיק כַּתָּמָר יִפְרָח   כְּאֶרֶז בַּלְּבָנוֹן יִשְׂגֶּה:

שְׁתוּלִים בְּבֵית יהוה   בְּחַצְרוֹת אֱלֹהֵינוּ יַפְרִיחוּ:

* עוֹד יְנוּבוּן בְּשֵׂיבָה   דְּשֵׁנִים וְרַעֲנַנִּים יִהְיוּ:

לְהַגִּיד כִּי־יָשָׁר יהוה   צוּרִי וְלֹא־עַוְלָתָה בּוֹ:

Tzadik katamar yifraḥ ke'erez balvanon yisgeh.
Shetulim beveyt adonay beḥatzrot eloheynu yafriḥu.
Od yenuvun beseyvah deshenim vera'ananim yihyu.
Lehagid ki yashar adonay tzuri velo avlatah bo.

COMMENTARY. צדיק כתמר יפרח / The righteous flourish like the palm trees. Unlike other trees, the palm brings forth each new branch from its very heart. So, too, the *tzadik: tzadikim* reach outward from their very depths. There are no superficial branches on their trees. The righteous are as open as palms, as strong and straight as cedars. Such people remain fresh and fruitful even in their old age.   A.G.

THE ETERNAL reigns, is clothed in majesty,
THE INVISIBLE is clothed, is girded up with might.

  The world is now established,
  it cannot give way.

Your throne was long ago secured,
beyond eternity are you.

The rivers raise, O MIGHTY ONE,
the rivers raise a roaring sound,

  the floods raise up torrential waves,

but louder than the sound of mighty waters,
more exalted than the breakers of the sea,

  raised up on high are you, THE SOURCE.

Your precepts have retained their truth,
and holiness befits your house,

ETERNAL ONE, forever and a day.

Psalm 93

Some communities recite Ashrey *(Psalm 145, page 593) here.*

| יְהֹוָה | מָלָךְ גֵּאוּת לָבֵשׁ | לָבֵשׁ יהוה עֹז הִתְאַזָּר |

אַף־תִּכּוֹן תֵּבֵל בַּל־תִּמּוֹט:

נָכוֹן כִּסְאֲךָ מֵאָז   מֵעוֹלָם אָתָּה:

נָשְׂאוּ נְהָרוֹת יהוה   נָשְׂאוּ נְהָרוֹת קוֹלָם

יִשְׂאוּ נְהָרוֹת דָּכְיָם:

מִקֹּלוֹת מַיִם רַבִּים   אַדִּירִים מִשְׁבְּרֵי־יָם

אַדִּיר בַּמָּרוֹם יהוה:

* עֵדֹתֶיךָ נֶאֶמְנוּ מְאֹד   לְבֵיתְךָ נָאֲוָה־קֹּדֶשׁ

יהוה לְאֹרֶךְ יָמִים:

Some communities recite Ashrey (Psalm 145, page 594) here.

COMMENTARY. How often it feels that the chaos in our world—and the chaotic feelings in our hearts—could overwhelm us! The central Jewish article of faith that God is one and that the world is therefore one, that the world makes sense, stands as an assertion that the forces of chaos will not ultimately prevail. The floods raise up torrential waves, but we listen for the one reality that can overwhelm the mighty waters.   D.A.T.

A Song for the Ascents.

I lift my eyes up to the hills.
From where does my help come?

My help is from THE UNSEEN ONE,
the maker of the heavens and the earth,

who will not cause your foot to fail.
Your protector never slumbers.

Behold the one who slumbers not, who never sleeps,
the guardian of Israel.

THE ABUNDANT ONE preserves you,
THE WATCHFUL ONE, your shelter, at your right hand a support.

By day, the sun will not afflict you,
nor the moonlight by the night.

THE VIGILANT shall guard you from all evil,
and will keep your lifebreath safe.

THE SHEPHERD guard your going out and coming in,
from now unto eternity.

Psalm 121

לא ינום ולא יישן/slumbers not, who never sleeps. Many are the metaphors for God: Ruler, Spouse, Parent. Here the psalmist imagines God as a parent who remains ever alert to a child's call in the night. How comforting to remember a time when no matter the hour, our cries would be heard.

R.H.

אֶשָּׂא עֵינַי אֶל־הֶהָרִים מֵאַיִן יָבֹא עֶזְרִי:

עֶזְרִי מֵעִם יהוה עֹשֵׂה שָׁמַיִם וָאָרֶץ:

אַל־יִתֵּן לַמּוֹט רַגְלֶךָ אַל־יָנוּם שֹׁמְרֶךָ:

הִנֵּה לֹא־יָנוּם וְלֹא יִישָׁן שׁוֹמֵר יִשְׂרָאֵל:

יהוה שֹׁמְרֶךָ יהוה צִלְּךָ עַל־יַד יְמִינֶךָ:

יוֹמָם הַשֶּׁמֶשׁ לֹא־יַכֶּכָּה וְיָרֵחַ בַּלָּיְלָה:

יהוה יִשְׁמָרְךָ מִכָּל־רָע יִשְׁמֹר אֶת־נַפְשֶׁךָ:

יהוה יִשְׁמָר־צֵאתְךָ וּבוֹאֶךָ מֵעַתָּה וְעַד־עוֹלָם:

Esa eynay el heharim me'ayin yavo ezri.
Ezri me'im adonay oseh shamayim va'aretz.

מאין יבא עזרי /me'ayin yavo ezri/ From where does my help come. *Ayin* can be read as meaning Nothing, a reference to the Eyn Sof, the infinite, unknowable One. My help is from that Emptiness which is prior to all creation, and which makes room for me to creatively change the universe.

J.A.S.

KAVANAH. Often prayer seeks to turn our thoughts towards God; at other times it directs our attention towards ourselves, and sometimes these two poles are held in intimate relation, as in the opening outcry of the psalm: "I lift my eyes up to the hills. From where does my help come?" Had the life-sustaining force we call God not been with us, how could we possibly have survived calumny and contempt, pogroms and persecutions? Given the perils and pains of Jewish history, our continued existence as a people is not easy to account for in the usual reasoned terms of causal explanation.

Might we then succumb, if only for a moment, to the cry of the psalmist, and give voice to our astonished recognition that our existence is surely by the grace of God, a gift that surpasses explanation.

E.G.

A Song of Ascents. Of David.

I rejoiced whenever people said to me,
let's journey to the house of THE UNSEEN!

Our feet would stand
inside your gates, Jerusalem,

Jerusalem, built up, a city
where all things converge,

the place to which the tribes would climb,
the tribes of Yah,

the place of Israel's witness,
for acknowledging the name of THE ETERNAL.

For there the seats of justice dwell,
the thrones of David's house.

So, let us say: Shalom, Yerushalayim,
and let all who love you be consoled,

great solace be upon your force,
salvation's rest amid your halls,

for all my kin, for all my friends,
may I now speak: Shalom to you!

And for the house of THE INDWELLING ONE, our God,
I only seek your good.

Psalm 122

COMMENTARY. Psalms 121 and 122 are included from the Sephardic rite. They are part of a group of pilgrims' songs, sung by our ancestors as they went up to the Temple. These two psalms, simple in their language and strong in their faith, are classics of our ancient religious literature.   A.G.

שִׁיר הַמַּעֲלוֹת לְדָוִד

שָׂמַחְתִּי בְּאֹמְרִים לִי בֵּית יהוה נֵלֵךְ:

עֹמְדוֹת הָיוּ רַגְלֵינוּ בִּשְׁעָרַיִךְ יְרוּשָׁלָ͏ִם:

יְרוּשָׁלַ͏ִם הַבְּנוּיָה כְּעִיר שֶׁחֻבְּרָה־לָּהּ יַחְדָּו:

שֶׁשָּׁם עָלוּ שְׁבָטִים שִׁבְטֵי־יָהּ עֵדוּת לְיִשְׂרָאֵל לְהֹדוֹת לְשֵׁם יהוה:

כִּי שָׁמָּה יָשְׁבוּ כִסְאוֹת לְמִשְׁפָּט כִּסְאוֹת לְבֵית דָּוִד:

שַׁאֲלוּ שְׁלוֹם יְרוּשָׁלָ͏ִם יִשְׁלָיוּ אֹהֲבָיִךְ:

יְהִי־שָׁלוֹם בְּחֵילֵךְ שַׁלְוָה בְּאַרְמְנוֹתָיִךְ:

לְמַעַן אַחַי וְרֵעָי אֲדַבְּרָה־נָּא שָׁלוֹם בָּךְ:

* לְמַעַן בֵּית־יהוה אֱלֹהֵינוּ אֲבַקְשָׁה טוֹב לָךְ:

Sha'alu shelom yerushalayim yishlayu ohavayih.
Yehi shalom beheyleh shalvah be'armenotayih.
Lema'an ahay vere'ay adaberah–na shalom bah.
Lema'an beyt adonay eloheynu avakshah tov lah.

COMMENTARY. Psalms 121 and 122 are selections from the Psalms of Ascent or the Psalms of Degrees, originally sung in the Temple. The beginning of the upward path exists in the recognition of God's loving, helpful presence in our lives (Psalm 121). God is with us when we behold nature in its perfection and we become ready to acknowledge the possibility of communion with the power of Creation. Awareness of our access to God offers us protection no matter how often we enter and leave the ascending journey.   S.P.W.

Halleluyah!

Hail, my soul, THE OMNIPRESENT!

I hail THE INNERMOST my whole life through,
I sing out to my God as long as I endure.

Trust not in human benefactors,
in mortal beings, who have no power to help.

Their spirit leaves, they go back to the ground,
on that day, all their thoughts are lost.

Happy is the one who has the God of Jacob for a help,
whose hopeful thought is for THE LIVING ONE, our God,

the maker of the heavens and the earth,
the seas and all that they contain,

the world's true guardian, ↩

DERASH. The God of religion is the God we can know and experience
every time we choose to act in the spirit of moral responsibility by being
loyal, honest, just, sympathetic and creative.   M.M.K. (Adapted)

אל־תבטחו בנדיבים / "Trust not in human benefactors..." Judaism bequeathed
a gift to humanity: the hope for the future embodied in the mythic figure
of the messiah. Yet how often has this hope been distorted and
disappointed as each pretender to the title has proven false. As
Reconstructionists, we affirm a messianic era, not a messiah. We are also
cautioned by the psalmist not to be overconfident, or to overestimate the
possibilities of our bringing the messianic era to fruition. Improvement,
rather than perfection, is a more realistic though more humble aspiration
in light of the horrors of the 20th century.   R.H.

הַלְלוּיָהּ

הַלְלִי נַפְשִׁי אֶת־יהוה: אֲהַלְלָה יהוה בְּחַיָּי

אֲזַמְּרָה לֵאלֹהַי בְּעוֹדִי: אַל־תִּבְטְחוּ בִנְדִיבִים

בְּבֶן־אָדָם שֶׁאֵין לוֹ תְשׁוּעָה: תֵּצֵא רוּחוֹ יָשֻׁב לְאַדְמָתוֹ

בַּיּוֹם הַהוּא אָבְדוּ עֶשְׁתֹּנֹתָיו: אַשְׁרֵי שֶׁאֵל יַעֲקֹב בְּעֶזְרוֹ

שִׂבְרוֹ עַל־יהוה אֱלֹהָיו: עֹשֶׂה שָׁמַיִם וָאָרֶץ

אֶת־הַיָּם וְאֶת־כָּל־אֲשֶׁר־בָּם

הַשֹּׁמֵר אֱמֶת לְעוֹלָם: ⟵

DERASH. אהללה יהוה בחיי אזמרה לאלהי בעודי /I shall praise the Eternal One with my life, I shall sing to my God with my virtue/talent/gift. (Rabbi Naḥman of Bratzlav's rendering)

Why do we find it so difficult to pray? What prevents us from praising God? Our lists would most likely emphasize intellectual and theological obstacles; few would include Rabbi Naḥman's audacious suggestion that a key to the silence of our souls is that we think too little of ourselves. Our low self-regard makes us feel inwardly unworthy to praise the beneficent bestower of blessings upon humankind.

So, recommends Rabbi Naḥman, begin your preparation for prayer by focusing on your עוד /od, on something worthy about yourself, a virtue, a talent, a personal quality perhaps overlooked or unappreciated. Concentrate even a little on this עוד /od, and your sense of unworthiness will be diminished. In touch with this element of value in yourself—and even the worst of sinners possesses goodness as well, Naḥman assures—you'll find that this merit, this עוד /od, recognized, will help you sing God's praises, and that your life itself will utter a hymn of praise to God.   E.G.

who musters justice on behalf of the oppressed,
who gives bread to the hungry,

ADVOCATE, who sets the captive free,

THE UNSEEN ONE, who makes the blind to see,
SUPPORTING ONE, who helps the lame to stand,

THE WATCHFUL ONE, who loves the just,

THE BOUNTIFUL, protector of the stranger,
and in whom the orphan and the widow find their strength,

By whom the evildoers' route is set awry.

The ALL-EMBRACING reigns eternally,
your God, O Zion, from one generation to the next.
Halleluyah!

Psalm 146

עֹשֶׂה מִשְׁפָּט לַעֲשׁוּקִים נֹתֵן לֶחֶם לָרְעֵבִים

יהוה מַתִּיר אֲסוּרִים:

יהוה פֹּקֵחַ עִוְרִים יהוה זֹקֵף כְּפוּפִים

יהוה אֹהֵב צַדִּיקִים:

יהוה שֹׁמֵר אֶת־גֵּרִים יָתוֹם וְאַלְמָנָה יְעוֹדֵד

וְדֶרֶךְ רְשָׁעִים יְעַוֵּת:

*יִמְלֹךְ יהוה לְעוֹלָם אֱלֹהַיִךְ צִיּוֹן לְדֹר וָדֹר

הַלְלוּיָהּ׃

COMMENTARY. The latter part of this psalm lists divine actions worthy of human emulation. The approach of predicate theology treats divine attributes as models for human conduct. In praising God this way we are not attempting to make factual statements about God's conduct. We are stating values that we hope to make manifest through the way we lead our lives.   D.A.T.

Halleluyah! How good it is to sing out to our God!
How much a pleasure and how fitting is our praise!

The builder of Jerusalem is ZION'S GOD,
may those of Israel gone astray be gathered there.

The healer of the broken-hearted,
the one who bandages their bones,

who alone reckons the number of the stars,
while giving names to every one of them—

how great is our protector, and how powerful,
whose understanding has no limit!

THE COMPASSIONATE encourages the humble,
and brings down the wicked to the earth,

sing choruses of thanks to THE MAGNIFICENT,
sing out to our God with instrument of strings,

the one who covers up the sky with clouds,
who prepares the rainfall for the earth,

who causes grass to sprout upon the mountains,

who gives the beast its sustenance,
young ravens, what they clamor for,

who is indifferent to the horse's power,
who takes no pleasure in the muscle's might,

הַלְלוּיָהּ

כִּי־טוֹב זַמְּרָה אֱלֹהֵינוּ   כִּי־נָעִים נָאוָה תְהִלָּה:

בּוֹנֵה יְרוּשָׁלַיִם יהוה   נִדְחֵי יִשְׂרָאֵל יְכַנֵּס:

הָרוֹפֵא לִשְׁבוּרֵי לֵב   וּמְחַבֵּשׁ לְעַצְּבוֹתָם:

מוֹנֶה מִסְפָּר לַכּוֹכָבִים   לְכֻלָּם שֵׁמוֹת יִקְרָא:

גָּדוֹל אֲדוֹנֵינוּ וְרַב־כֹּחַ   לִתְבוּנָתוֹ אֵין מִסְפָּר:

מְעוֹדֵד עֲנָוִים יהוה   מַשְׁפִּיל רְשָׁעִים עֲדֵי־אָרֶץ:

עֱנוּ לַיהוה בְּתוֹדָה   זַמְּרוּ לֵאלֹהֵינוּ בְכִנּוֹר:

הַמְכַסֶּה שָׁמַיִם בְּעָבִים   הַמֵּכִין לָאָרֶץ מָטָר

הַמַּצְמִיחַ הָרִים חָצִיר:

נוֹתֵן לִבְהֵמָה לַחְמָהּ   לִבְנֵי עֹרֵב אֲשֶׁר יִקְרָאוּ:

לֹא בִגְבוּרַת הַסּוּס יֶחְפָּץ   לֹא־בְשׁוֹקֵי הָאִישׁ יִרְצֶה: ⟵

COMMENTARY. Psalm 147 has three majestic interlacing themes. The divine is present in the ordered universe of galaxies and creatures. The divine is present, too, in the broken human heart, in those humbled by loss and disappointment. Finally, the divine is present in the capacity of our senses and in our ability to appreciate the world around us.   S.P.W.

THE JUST ONE values only those in awe of God,
only the ones who yearn for God's kind love.

Give praise, Jerusalem, to THE ETERNAL,
hail your God, O Zion.

For God has fortified the bars upon your gates,
has blessed your brood amid your breast,

and sets your borderlands at peace,
and satisfies you with the choicest wheat,

the one who sends an utterance to earth,
whose word runs swiftest in the world,

the giver of a snow like fleece,
who strews a frost like frigid ash,

who casts down hail like crumbs of bread
—before such chill, who can endure?—

but who, with but a word, can melt them all,
and by whose breath the waters flow.

God tells the words to Jacob,
laws and judgments to the people Israel.

Has God not done so for all nations?
Are there any who do not know such laws?

Halleluyah!

Psalm 147

רוֹצֶה יהוה אֶת־יְרֵאָיו אֶת־הַמְיַחֲלִים לְחַסְדּוֹ:
שַׁבְּחִי יְרוּשָׁלַיִם אֶת־יהוה הַלְלִי אֱלֹהַיִךְ צִיּוֹן:
כִּי־חִזַּק בְּרִיחֵי שְׁעָרָיִךְ בֵּרַךְ בָּנַיִךְ בְּקִרְבֵּךְ:
הַשָּׂם־גְּבוּלֵךְ שָׁלוֹם חֵלֶב חִטִּים יַשְׂבִּיעֵךְ:
הַשֹּׁלֵחַ אִמְרָתוֹ אָרֶץ עַד־מְהֵרָה יָרוּץ דְּבָרוֹ:
הַנֹּתֵן שֶׁלֶג כַּצָּמֶר כְּפוֹר כָּאֵפֶר יְפַזֵּר:
מַשְׁלִיךְ קַרְחוֹ כְפִתִּים לִפְנֵי קָרָתוֹ מִי יַעֲמֹד:
יִשְׁלַח דְּבָרוֹ וְיַמְסֵם יַשֵּׁב רוּחוֹ יִזְּלוּ־מָיִם:
* מַגִּיד דְּבָרָיו לְיַעֲקֹב חֻקָּיו וּמִשְׁפָּטָיו לְיִשְׂרָאֵל:
לֹא עָשָׂה כֵן לְכָל־גּוֹי וּמִשְׁפָּטִים בַּל־יְדָעוּם

הַלְלוּיָה:

Halleluyah!

Hail! THE OMNIPRESENT from the heavens,
praise God in the heights,

sing out your praises, all you angels,
praise God, all you multitudes,

give praise to God, you sun and moon,
praise God, all you stars of light,

praise God, heavens upon heavens,
and you, the waters up above the heavens!

Let all praise the name of THE ETERNAL,
who commanded, and all things became,

who raised them up forever and an aeon,
who affixed a limit none could pass. ⤶

הַלְלוּיָהּ

הַלְלוּ אֶת־יהוה מִן־הַשָּׁמַ֫יִם הַלְלוּהוּ בַּמְּרוֹמִים:

הַלְלוּהוּ כָּל־מַלְאָכָיו הַלְלוּהוּ כָּל־צְבָאָיו:

הַלְלוּהוּ שֶׁמֶשׁ וְיָרֵחַ הַלְלוּהוּ כָּל־כּוֹכְבֵי אוֹר:

הַלְלוּהוּ שְׁמֵי הַשָּׁמָיִם וְהַמַּיִם אֲשֶׁר מֵעַל הַשָּׁמָיִם:

יְהַלְלוּ אֶת־שֵׁם יהוה כִּי הוּא צִוָּה וְנִבְרָאוּ:

וַיַּעֲמִידֵם לָעַד לְעוֹלָם חָק־נָתַן וְלֹא יַעֲבוֹר: ←

COMMENTARY. This psalm and the tradition it represents stand as an important counterweight to the first chapter in Genesis. That chapter gives us the impression that humans are separate from the world around us, we alone having been created in God's image as "the crown of creation." Here we see a different vision. The human community is an integral part of the natural realm. "You young men, and you maidens, elders sitting with the young," sing and dance before God as do mountains and hills, fruit trees and cedars. A.G.

Give praise to THE ALL-POWERFUL throughout the earth,
you dragons and torrential depths,

you fire and hail and snow and smoke,
you raging wind, all acting by God's word,

you mountains, all you hills,
you fruit trees, bearing every seed,

you wild animals, and every beast,
you creeping thing, and bird of wing,

you rulers of the earth, and all the nations,
nobles, and you judges of the land,

you young men, and you maidens,
elders sitting with the young!

Let all bless the name of THE ETERNAL,
for God's name alone is to be exalted.

God's majesty is in the earth and heavens,

God has raised the fortunes of our people,
praises for the fervent ones,

for Israel's children, people near to God,
Halleluyah!

Psalm 148

הַלְלוּ אֶת־יהוה מִן־הָאָרֶץ   תַּנִּינִים וְכָל־תְּהֹמוֹת:

אֵשׁ וּבָרָד שֶׁלֶג וְקִיטוֹר   רוּחַ סְעָרָה עֹשָׂה דְבָרוֹ:

הֶהָרִים וְכָל־גְּבָעוֹת   עֵץ פְּרִי וְכָל־אֲרָזִים:

הַחַיָּה וְכָל־בְּהֵמָה   רֶמֶשׂ וְצִפּוֹר כָּנָף:

מַלְכֵי־אֶרֶץ וְכָל־לְאֻמִּים   שָׂרִים וְכָל־שֹׁפְטֵי אָרֶץ:

בַּחוּרִים וְגַם־בְּתוּלוֹת   זְקֵנִים עִם־נְעָרִים:

יְהַלְלוּ אֶת־שֵׁם יהוה   כִּי־נִשְׂגָּב שְׁמוֹ לְבַדּוֹ

הוֹדוֹ עַל־אֶרֶץ וְשָׁמָיִם:

* וַיָּרֶם קֶרֶן לְעַמּוֹ   תְּהִלָּה לְכָל־חֲסִידָיו

לִבְנֵי יִשְׂרָאֵל עַם קְרֹבוֹ:

הַלְלוּיָהּ.

Hallelu/Yah!
Call out to Yah in Heaven's holy place!
Boom out to Yah across the firmament!
Shout out for Yah, for all God's mighty deeds!
Cry out for Yah, as loud as God is great!
Blast out for Yah with piercing shofar note!
Pluck out for Yah with lute and violin!
Throb out for Yah with drum and writhing dance!
Sing out for Yah with strings and husky flute!
Ring out for Yah with cymbals that resound!
Clang out for Yah with cymbals that rebound!
Let every living thing Yah's praises sing, Hallelu/Yah!
Let every living thing Yah's praises sing, Hallelu/Yah!

Psalm 150

Blessed is THE ONE eternally.
Amen! Amen!
Blessed is THE OMNIPRESENT,
dwelling in Jerusalem, Halleluyah!
Blessed is THE MIGHTY ONE divine,
The God of Israel who alone works wonders,
and blessed is the glorious name forever,
and may God's glory fill the earth.
Amen! Amen!

COMMENTARY. Psalm 150 as it appears in the biblical text does not repeat
its concluding line as it does in the liturgy. The repetition here makes this
concluding verse parallel to all the preceding ones, allowing it to fit a
variety of musical settings. The repetition also emphasizes the psalm's
essential message.   D.A.T.

הַלְלוּ־אֵל בְּקָדְשׁוֹ הַלְלוּהוּ בִּרְקִיעַ עֻזּוֹ:

הַלְלוּהוּ בִגְבוּרֹתָיו הַלְלוּהוּ כְּרֹב גֻּדְלוֹ:

הַלְלוּהוּ בְּתֵקַע שׁוֹפָר הַלְלוּהוּ בְּנֵבֶל וְכִנּוֹר:

הַלְלוּהוּ בְתֹף וּמָחוֹל הַלְלוּהוּ בְּמִנִּים וְעֻגָב:

הַלְלוּהוּ בְצִלְצְלֵי שָׁמַע הַלְלוּהוּ בְּצִלְצְלֵי תְרוּעָה:

* כֹּל הַנְּשָׁמָה תְּהַלֵּל יָהּ הַלְלוּיָהּ:

כֹּל הַנְּשָׁמָה תְּהַלֵּל יָהּ **הַלְלוּיָהּ:**

Halleluyah halelu el bekodsho. Haleluhu birki'a uzo.

Haleluhu vigvurotav. Haleluhu kerov gudlo.

Haleluhu beteka shofar.

Haleluhu benevel vehinor.

Haleluhu betof umahol.

Haleluhu beminim ve'ugav.

Haleluhu betziltzeley shama.

Haleluhu betziltzeley teru'ah.

Kol haneshamah tehalel yah. Halleluyah.

בָּרוּךְ יהוה לְעוֹלָם אָמֵן וְאָמֵן: בָּרוּךְ יהוה מִצִּיּוֹן שֹׁכֵן יְרוּשָׁלָיִם הַלְלוּיָהּ: בָּרוּךְ יהוה אֱלֹהִים אֱלֹהֵי יִשְׂרָאֵל עֹשֵׂה נִפְלָאוֹת לְבַדּוֹ:

* וּבָרוּךְ שֵׁם כְּבוֹדוֹ לְעוֹלָם וְיִמָּלֵא כְבוֹדוֹ אֶת־כָּל־הָאָרֶץ אָמֵן וְאָמֵן:

וימלא כבודו את כל הארץ /and may God's glory fill the earth. The meaning of the Hebrew phrase is rich in ambiguity. All earth is filled with divine glory, but divine glory itself is filled up with earthliness. It is the reality of this world that fills God's presence, as it is the presence that gives the world its glory.   A.G.

ברוך...ואמן /Blessed...Amen! (Psalms 89:53, 135:21, 72:18-19).

The soul of every living thing shall bless your name, ETERNAL ONE, our God, the spirit of all flesh shall glorify and hold in reverence continually the memory of you, our sovereign one. From one eternity to another, you alone are God. For without you, we have no ruler, no redeemer, none to champion our cause, none to rescue or to save, none to nourish or to nurture us, whatever be the hour, or the trouble, or the need. ↵

COMMENTARY. *Nishmat Kol Hay* consists of three sections. The first section presents God's unity as that unity is declared with every breath of creation. The second section gives thanks for timely rains and declares God to be beyond creation's collective ability to praise. Even if we could enlist nature's greatest capacities in the service of praising God, they would still fall short. Praise "as great as all outdoors" is still inadequate.

In the third section of *Nishmat Kol Hay*, Israel's unique praises reflect its historical experiences of God as the power that brings redemption. *Nishmat Kol Hay* begins with a universal chorus of praise, moves to the particular praise of Israel, and then speaks of the many ways that individual actions serve as praise. Praises arise from the universe *within* the self just as they fill the universe *without*. Verses from the psalms illustrate aspects of body and breath/soul contributing praises that fill worlds.

Pesukey Dezimra ends with this rabbinic composition reassembling individual voices into a chorus of adoration and thanksgiving. The final paragraphs are a reprise of the first blessing of *Pesukey Dezimra* in *Baruh She'amar* (page 194). Thus, the entire collection beginning with *Baruh She'amar* and ending before the Kaddish (which separates *Pesukey Dezimra* from *Shaharit*) becomes a well defined literary whole.   S.S.

Nishmat is the song of the wave
awakening to the ocean,
seeing that the wave is the ocean and the ocean the wave,
recognizing the interdependence of all things and
discovering the awesome wonder that is our reality.   R.M.S.

נִשְׁמַת כָּל־חַי תְּבָרֵךְ אֶת־שִׁמְךָ יהוה אֱלֹהֵינוּ וְרוּחַ כָּל־בָּשָׂר תְּפָאֵר
וּתְרוֹמֵם זִכְרְךָ מַלְכֵּנוּ תָּמִיד: מִן־הָעוֹלָם וְעַד־הָעוֹלָם אַתָּה אֵל
וּמִבַּלְעָדֶיךָ אֵין לָנוּ מֶלֶךְ גּוֹאֵל וּמוֹשִׁיעַ פּוֹדֶה וּמַצִּיל וּמְפַרְנֵס
וּמְרַחֵם בְּכָל־עֵת צָרָה וְצוּקָה אֵין לָנוּ מֶלֶךְ אֶלָּא אָתָּה: ←

Nishmat kol ḥay tevareḥ et shimeḥa adonay eloheynu.

DERASH. *Nefesh, ruaḥ, neshamah:* these three Hebrew terms are often
translated as soul or spirit. They were originally terms for breath. This
relation between soul and breathing is found in other sacred languages as
well: *atman* in Sanskrit, *pneuma* in Greek, *anima* and *spiritus* in Latin are all
terms for soul. All in origin refer to breath and breathing. Literally, then,
this prayer asserts that the breath of all living creatures proclaims God's
blessing. In what sense might this be so?

Breath is the prerequisite of life and speech, of existence and communication, and it is a gift requiring no conscious attention except in cases of
illness. If each inhalation required a direct order, each exhalation a
conscious command, how should we find energy or attention for anything
else? How should we sleep? In truth, we do not breathe; we are breathed.
At this moment of my writing, at this moment of your reading, at
succeeding moments of our praying, breath enters and leaves our lungs
without our conscious intervention. Truly we are breathed.   E.G.

נשמת כל חי / The soul of every living thing. This ancient and grand
rabbinic closing to the morning psalms follows the biblical view that
refuses to make any distinction between matter and spirit. God is the
breath that resides in all of life, the spirit that animates all flesh. It is this
corporeal world that is the locus of divinity. We need only develop the eyes
to see it.   A.G.

KAVANAH. Prayer is not just words. It is actions; it is our very breathing.
Nishmat asserts that—with *kavanah*, proper intent—the act of breathing
and living can itself become a prayer to God.   S.D.R.

God of the first things and the last, the deity of every creature, power over all that comes to be, the subject of all praises through the multitude of laudatory songs, who guides the universe in love, all creatures with compassion. THE WATCHFUL ONE will never slumber, never sleep! To you who wakens all who sleep and stirs all those who slumber, who gives speech to those who cannot speak, who frees the captive and upholds the falling, who makes upright those bent down—to you alone we offer thanks.

And were our mouths oceans of song, our tongues alive with exultation like the waters' waves, our lips filled full of praises like the heaven's dome, our eyes lit up like sun and moon, our hands spread out like eagle's wings, our feet as light as those of the gazelle—we would never have sufficient praise for you, ABUNDANT ONE, our God, God of our ancestors, nor could we bless your name enough for even one small measure of the thousands upon thousands of the times of goodness, when you acted for our ancestors and us. ↩

COMMENTARY. This passage invokes Creation—the separation of sky and water, the fixing of the heavenly lights, the creation of winged creatures and fleet-footed animals. The poet imagines human beings with the best qualities of all the rest of creation. Even then our most elaborate praises would not suffice to express the immensity of the blessing we receive. We are therefore urged to honor our good fortune in God's creative power with every organ of our bodies and with every imaginable verbal variation—that is all we can do in the face of the multiplicity of God's wonders.

R.S.

אֱלֹהֵי הָרִאשׁוֹנִים וְהָאַחֲרוֹנִים אֱלוֹהַּ כָּל־בְּרִיּוֹת אֲדוֹן כָּל־תּוֹלָדוֹת הַמְהֻלָּל בְּרֹב הַתִּשְׁבָּחוֹת הַמְנַהֵג עוֹלָמוֹ בְּחֶסֶד וּבְרִיּוֹתָיו בְּרַחֲמִים: וַיהוה לֹא־יָנוּם וְלֹא־יִישָׁן הַמְעוֹרֵר יְשֵׁנִים וְהַמֵּקִיץ נִרְדָּמִים וְהַמֵּשִׂיחַ אִלְּמִים וְהַמַּתִּיר אֲסוּרִים וְהַסּוֹמֵךְ נוֹפְלִים וְהַזּוֹקֵף כְּפוּפִים לְךָ לְבַדְּךָ אֲנַחְנוּ מוֹדִים:

אִלּוּ פִינוּ מָלֵא שִׁירָה כַיָּם וּלְשׁוֹנֵנוּ רִנָּה כַּהֲמוֹן גַּלָּיו וְשִׂפְתוֹתֵינוּ שֶׁבַח כְּמֶרְחֲבֵי רָקִיעַ וְעֵינֵינוּ מְאִירוֹת כַּשֶּׁמֶשׁ וְכַיָּרֵחַ וְיָדֵינוּ פְרוּשׂוֹת כְּנִשְׁרֵי שָׁמָיִם וְרַגְלֵינוּ קַלּוֹת כָּאַיָּלוֹת אֵין אֲנַחְנוּ מַסְפִּיקִים לְהוֹדוֹת לְךָ יהוה אֱלֹהֵינוּ וֵאלֹהֵי אֲבוֹתֵינוּ וְאִמּוֹתֵנוּ וּלְבָרֵךְ אֶת־שִׁמְךָ עַל־ אַחַת מֵאֶלֶף אֶלֶף אַלְפֵי אֲלָפִים וְרִבֵּי רְבָבוֹת פְּעָמִים הַטּוֹבוֹת שֶׁעָשִׂיתָ עִם־אֲבוֹתֵינוּ וְעִמָּנוּ: —←

Ilu finu maley shirah kayam.

KAVANAH. מעורר ישנים / who wakens all who sleep. Our faith awakens us from the sleep of our unawareness and calls us to release the bound, to raise up the fallen, and to uplift those who are bent over. In this we are doing godly work, serving as the limbs of the divine presence in this world. It is only through our acting in this way that God's work is done in the human community. And it is only by recognizing such acts as God's work that we transcend ourselves and our own needs in fulfilling them.

A.G.

From Egypt you redeemed us, ANCIENT ONE, our God, and from the house of servitude you rescued us. When we were hungry, you provided us with food. With satisfaction you have nurtured us, and from the sword you have delivered us, and during pestilence you gave us refuge, and from dreadful and persistent sicknesses you've set us free. Down to the present day, your kindnesses have been a help to us, your loving acts have not forsaken us.

So never more abandon us, FOUNT OF COMPASSION.

Therefore, the limbs that you have molded for us, breath and spirit you have breathed into our nostrils, tongue that you have placed into our mouths—behold, they shall give thanks, and bless, and praise, and glorify, exalt, admire, sanctify, and crown your name our sovereign power. For every mouth will offer thanks to you, each tongue swear oath; each knee will bend, each upright body will bow down; and every heart will be in awe of you, and every inner organ sing out to your name—as it is written: "Let all my bones declare: THE INFINITE! Who is like you? You, who save the poor from those of greater strength, the destitute and the oppressed from their exploiters." The wail of the downtrodden you will hear, and to the cry of the unfortunate you hearken and come forth with help. Who resembles you, who can be your equal, who can estimate your worth? Divinity so great, so mighty, and so awesome, supreme God, creator of the heavens and the earth!

We hail you, and we praise you, and we glorify you, and we bless your holy name, as it is said by David: "Bless, O my soul, THE ONE, and all my inner strength, God's holy name."

Divinity so consummate in strength, so abundant in the glory of your name, so great unto eternity, so awesome in your awe-inspiring deeds.

מִמִּצְרַיִם גְּאַלְתָּנוּ יהוה אֱלֹהֵינוּ וּמִבֵּית עֲבָדִים פְּדִיתָנוּ בְּרָעָב זַנְתָּנוּ
וּבְשָׂבָע כִּלְכַּלְתָּנוּ מֵחֶרֶב הִצַּלְתָּנוּ וּמִדֶּבֶר מִלַּטְתָּנוּ וּמֵחֳלָיִים רָעִים
וְנֶאֱמָנִים דִּלִּיתָנוּ: עַד־הֵנָּה עֲזָרוּנוּ רַחֲמֶיךָ וְלֹא־עֲזָבוּנוּ חֲסָדֶיךָ וְאַל־
תִּטְּשֵׁנוּ יהוה אֱלֹהֵינוּ לָנֶצַח:

עַל־כֵּן אֵבָרִים שֶׁפִּלַּגְתָּ בָּנוּ וְרוּחַ וּנְשָׁמָה שֶׁנָּפַחְתָּ בְּאַפֵּינוּ וְלָשׁוֹן
אֲשֶׁר שַׂמְתָּ בְּפִינוּ הֵן הֵם יוֹדוּ וִיבָרְכוּ וִישַׁבְּחוּ וִיפָאֲרוּ וִירוֹמְמוּ
וְיַעֲרִיצוּ וְיַקְדִּישׁוּ וְיַמְלִיכוּ אֶת־שִׁמְךָ מַלְכֵּנוּ: כִּי כָל־פֶּה לְךָ יוֹדֶה
וְכָל־לָשׁוֹן לְךָ תִשָּׁבַע וְכָל־בֶּרֶךְ לְךָ תִכְרַע וְכָל־קוֹמָה לְפָנֶיךָ
תִשְׁתַּחֲוֶה וְכָל־לְבָבוֹת יִירָאוּךָ וְכָל־קֶרֶב וּכְלָיוֹת יְזַמְּרוּ לִשְׁמֶךָ כַּדָּבָר
שֶׁכָּתוּב: כָּל־עַצְמוֹתַי תֹּאמַרְנָה יהוה מִי כָמוֹךָ: מַצִּיל עָנִי מֵחָזָק
מִמֶּנּוּ וְעָנִי וְאֶבְיוֹן מִגֹּזְלוֹ: שַׁוְעַת עֲנִיִּים אַתָּה תִשְׁמַע צַעֲקַת הַדַּל
תַּקְשִׁיב וְתוֹשִׁיעַ מִי יִדְמֶה־לָּךְ וּמִי יִשְׁוֶה־לָּךְ וּמִי יַעֲרָךְ־לָךְ הָאֵל
הַגָּדוֹל הַגִּבּוֹר וְהַנּוֹרָא אֵל עֶלְיוֹן קוֹנֵה שָׁמַיִם וָאָרֶץ:

*נְהַלֶּלְךָ וּנְשַׁבֵּחֲךָ וּנְפָאֶרְךָ וּנְבָרֵךְ אֶת־שֵׁם קָדְשֶׁךָ כָּאָמוּר לְדָוִד
בָּרְכִי נַפְשִׁי אֶת־יהוה וְכָל־קְרָבַי אֶת־שֵׁם קָדְשׁוֹ: הָאֵל בְּתַעֲצֻמוֹת
עֻזֶּךָ הַגָּדוֹל בִּכְבוֹד שְׁמֶךָ הַגִּבּוֹר לָנֶצַח וְהַנּוֹרָא בְּנוֹרְאוֹתֶיךָ:

כל עצמותי תאמרנה / Let all my bones declare (Psalms 35:10). It is the whole
self that calls out the praises of God, not just the lips or the mind. The act
of prayer is one that calls upon the entire person. This is why traditional
Jewish prayer may involve the rhythmic swaying of the body. There is
preserved in this ancient and largely unconscious movement an element of
ritual dance in which bodily movement was joined to speech in calling out
God's glory.   A.G.

ברכי נפשי...קדשו / Bless...name (Psalms 103:1).

The sovereign one, presiding on your lofty and exalted throne!

COMMENTARY. When we are brushed by the magic of the world's splendor, when we catch a hint of the mysteries of the universe, when we behold nature in all its wild beauty, we are embraced by a majesty that both takes our breath away and restores it to us in an inspiring rush. At that moment, the "lofty and exalted throne" shines before us. We are humble—and joyful.   L.G.B.

KAVANAH. Praised be to absolutes, to the truths planted deep within us. Praised be these inner sovereigns and our ability to revere them, to hold them sacred, so that we can act in their name.   D.B.

COMMENTARY. Rosh Hashanah is the descendant of ancient Near Eastern ceremonies celebrating the annual re-enthronement of the local king and deity. In the ancient mythologies, this enthronement was associated with the defeat of chaos. We too have a need to re-enthrone meaning in the face of the chaos of our lives.   J.A.S.

DERASH. On a hospital bed in an intensive-care unit, a critically ill patient was heard to say, "I'm ready. If God calls me now, I'm ready to go." This acknowledgment of our basic human frailty, mortality and ultimate lack of control is an essential aspect of addressing God as *Hameleḥ*/the Sovereign. We live life for as long as we have it, doing godly acts as long as we are able. When our time comes, may we be ready.   Carl S. Choper

On the High Holy Days in some communities, the ḥazan or a second sheliaḥ tzibur/ prayer leader begins here.

הַמֶּלֶךְ
יוֹשֵׁב עַל כִּסֵּא רָם וְנִשָּׂא:

Hameleḥ
yoshev al kisey ram venisa.

The traditional liturgy subtly underlines the changes in mood and meaning from weekday to Shabbat to Holiday to High Holy Day by its shifts in *nusaḥ*, the melodic liturgical line. Such a shift occurs at this juncture. On weekdays much of this passage is omitted, and the person who will chant the main part of שחרית/the morning service begins simply—"ישתבח שמך לעד/your name will always be praised." On Shabbat the new service leader emphasizes the stative, restful nature of Shabbat and its grandeur by beginning "שוכן עד מרום/forever dwelling in the highest heights." On the Pilgrimage Festivals the new leader emphasizes the historical origins of the festivals and their connection to revelation and redemption by beginning "האל בתעצומות עזך/divinity so consummate in strength." On the High Holy Days the leader leads us toward the primary struggle of this season, the effort to re-enthrone the divine in our lives, by beginning, "המלך/the Sovereign."   D.A.T.

Forever dwelling in the heights, forever holy is God's name! And it is written: "Sing joyously, you fervent ones, about THE FOUNT OF LIFE, for, from the upright, praise is fitting!"

By the mouths of all the upright you are raised!
And in the words of all the just ones you are blessed!
And on the tongues of all the fervent you are sanctified!
And in the midst of all the saintly, you are praised ↵

שׁוֹכֵן עַד מָרוֹם וְקָדוֹשׁ שְׁמוֹ:
וְכָתוּב: רַנְּנוּ צַדִּיקִים בַּיהוה לַיְשָׁרִים נָאוָה תְהִלָּה:

בְּפִי	יְשָׁרִים	תִּתְרוֹמָם
וּבְדִבְרֵי	צַדִּיקִים	תִּתְבָּרַךְ
וּבִלְשׁוֹן	חֲסִידִים	תִּתְקַדָּשׁ
וּבְקֶרֶב	קְדוֹשִׁים	תִּתְהַלָּל ←

Shohen ad marom vekadosh shemo.
Vehatuv: Ranenu tzadikim badonay laysharim navah tehilah.
Befi yesharim titromam
uvdivrey tzadikim titbarah.
uvlishon hasidim titkadash
uvkerev kedoshim tit-halal

רננו...תהלה / Sing...fitting! (Psalms 33:1).

And in the congregations of the tens of thousands of your people, the House of Israel, through joyful song, your name is glorified, our sovereign, in each and every generation. Thus is the obligation of all creatures in your presence, HOLY ONE, our God, God of our ancestors, to thank, to hail, to praise, to glorify, to hold aloft, and to embellish, and to bless, and to exalt, and to revere, beyond all words of song and praise sung by your servant David son of Jesse, your anointed one.

Your name be praised eternally, our sovereign, you who are divine, and powerful, and great, and holy, throughout all the heavens and the earth. For unto you, RESPLENDENT ONE, our God, our ancients' God, it is appropriate to offer song, and to ascribe all greatness, might, and praise, all splendor, holiness, and royalty, all blessings and all thanks, from now unto eternity. Blessed are you, ETERNAL ONE, the sovereign divine, so great in praises, God of all thanksgiving, source of wondrous deeds, who takes pleasure in our song and melody. Blessed is the one who lives eternally!

חי העולמים / who lives eternally. The Hebrew phrase literally means life of the worlds. This prayerbook also uses the rich and ambiguous phrase for the morning blessings. The word *olam* can refer either to space or to time. A God who is "the life of the *olamim*" can be one who lives eternally, one who inhabits all of many worlds, or one who joins space and time together. Space and time are the two essential categories that are sanctified by religion. Our tradition declares both certain times and particular places to be especially holy. It is through our reverence for these that we learn to treat life as a whole with the reverence of *kedushah*. It is our understanding of God as *ḥey ha'olamim* that cuts through the distinction between space and time and binds them together in cosmic oneness. A.G.

וּבְמַקְהֲלוֹת רִבְבוֹת עַמְּךָ בֵּית יִשְׂרָאֵל בְּרִנָּה יִתְפָּאֵר שִׁמְךָ מַלְכֵּנוּ בְּכָל־דּוֹר וָדוֹר שֶׁכֵּן חוֹבַת כָּל־הַיְצוּרִים לְפָנֶיךָ יהוה אֱלֹהֵינוּ וֵאלֹהֵי אֲבוֹתֵנוּ וְאִמּוֹתֵנוּ *לְהוֹדוֹת לְהַלֵּל לְשַׁבֵּחַ לְפָאֵר לְרוֹמֵם לְהַדֵּר לְבָרֵךְ לְעַלֵּה וּלְקַלֵּס עַל כָּל־דִּבְרֵי שִׁירוֹת וְתִשְׁבְּחוֹת דָּוִד בֶּן־יִשַׁי עַבְדְּךָ מְשִׁיחֶךָ:

*יִשְׁתַּבַּח שִׁמְךָ לָעַד מַלְכֵּנוּ הָאֵל הַמֶּלֶךְ הַגָּדוֹל וְהַקָּדוֹשׁ בַּשָּׁמַיִם וּבָאָרֶץ כִּי לְךָ נָאֶה יהוה אֱלֹהֵינוּ וֵאלֹהֵי אֲבוֹתֵינוּ וְאִמּוֹתֵינוּ שִׁיר וּשְׁבָחָה הַלֵּל וְזִמְרָה עֹז וּמֶמְשָׁלָה נֶצַח גְּדֻלָּה וּגְבוּרָה תְּהִלָּה וְתִפְאֶרֶת קְדֻשָּׁה וּמַלְכוּת *בְּרָכוֹת וְהוֹדָאוֹת מֵעַתָּה וְעַד עוֹלָם: בָּרוּךְ אַתָּה יהוה אֵל מֶלֶךְ גָּדוֹל בַּתִּשְׁבָּחוֹת אֵל הַהוֹדָאוֹת אֲדוֹן הַנִּפְלָאוֹת הַבּוֹחֵר בְּשִׁירֵי זִמְרָה מֶלֶךְ אֵל חֵי הָעוֹלָמִים:

עבדך משיחך / your servant...your anointed one. David was anointed as ruler over Israel by Samuel, according to I Samuel 16. Anointment, the pouring of olive oil over the head of a chosen leader of Israel, was a symbol of elevation to kingship. Eventually, "Anointed One" (*mashiah*) came to refer to *the* Messiah, the descendant of King David who would rule Israel and the world at the End of Days. The rule of David, at least for the people of the southern kingdom, Judah, symbolized an idyllic time of unity and sovereignty in Israel. Belief in a Messiah became more intense when Israel's unity and sovereignty ended. Here, the term refers simply to the anointing event in David's lifetime.   J.R.

ḤATZI KADDISH / SHORT KADDISH

Reader: Let God's name be made great and holy in the world that was created as God willed. May God complete the holy realm in your own lifetime, in your days, and in the days of all the house of Israel, quickly and soon. And say: Amen.

Congregation: May God's great name be blessed, forever and as long as worlds endure.

Reader: May it be blessed, and praised, and glorified and held in honor, viewed with awe, embellished and revered; and may the blessed name of holiness be hailed, though it be higher by far than all the blessings, songs, praises and consolations that we utter in this world. And say: Amen.

COMMENTARY. Holiness is the quality or value that things or persons have when they help people to become fully human.   M.M.K. (Adapted)

COMMENTARY. Kaddish is thematically similar to the *Aleynu* prayer. It is at heart a prayer for the inflow of divine presence, which it is imagined will bring true fulfillment to our lives. The prayer thus reminds us that the small sparks of holiness we manage to discover in our everyday lives are but *hints* of the holiness our efforts can help to make manifest.   D.A.T.

חֲצִי קַדִּישׁ

יִתְגַּדַּל וְיִתְקַדַּשׁ שְׁמֵהּ רַבָּא בְּעָלְמָא דִּי בְרָא כִרְעוּתֵהּ וְיַמְלִיךְ
מַלְכוּתֵהּ בְּחַיֵּיכוֹן וּבְיוֹמֵיכוֹן וּבְחַיֵּי דְכָל בֵּית יִשְׂרָאֵל בַּעֲגָלָא וּבִזְמַן
קָרִיב וְאִמְרוּ: אָמֵן:
יְהֵא שְׁמֵהּ רַבָּא מְבָרַךְ לְעָלַם וּלְעָלְמֵי עָלְמַיָּא:
יִתְבָּרַךְ וְיִשְׁתַּבַּח וְיִתְפָּאַר וְיִתְרוֹמַם וְיִתְנַשֵּׂא וְיִתְהַדָּר וְיִתְעַלֶּה
וְיִתְהַלָּל שְׁמֵהּ דְּקֻדְשָׁא בְּרִיךְ הוּא
לְעֵלָּא לְעֵלָּא מִכָּל בִּרְכָתָא וְשִׁירָתָא תֻּשְׁבְּחָתָא וְנֶחֱמָתָא דַּאֲמִירָן
בְּעָלְמָא וְאִמְרוּ: אָמֵן:

Reader: Yitgadal veyitkadash shemey raba
be'alma di vera ḥirutey veyamliḥ malḥutey
beḥayeyhon uvyomeyhon uvḥayey deḥol beyt yisra'el
ba'agala uvizman kariv ve'imru amen.

Congregation: Yehey shemey raba mevaraḥ le'alam ulalmey almaya.

Reader: Yitbaraḥ veyishtabaḥ veyitpa'ar veyitromam veyitnasey
veyit-hadar veyitaleh veyit-halal shemey dekudsha beriḥ hu le'ela
le'ela mikol birḥata veshirata tushbeḥata veneḥemata da'amiran
be'alma ve'imru amen.

THE SHEMA AND ITS BLESSINGS

When a minyan is present, the Barehu is said. The congregation rises and faces the ark. It is customary to bow. The reader chants the first line, and the congregation responds with the second.

Bless THE INFINITE, the blessed One!
Blessed is THE INFINITE, the blessed One, now and forever!

KAVANAH. As we bless the Source of Life,
so we are blessed.
And the blessing gives us strength
and makes our visions clear.
And the blessing gives us peace,
and the courage to dare.

Faith Rogow

COMMENTARY. *Barehu* calls the congregation together for formal worship. The sections that precede it in the morning service, *Birhot Hashahar* and *Pesukey Dezimra*, brought individuals gradually closer together until they could reach the mutual connection needed for joining together in prayer. The emotional stirring and heightened awareness brought by these earlier sections now become focused in the tighter intellectual structure of the Shema and its blessings and the Amidah.

D.A.T.

When a minyan is present, the Barehu *is said. The congregation rises and faces the ark. It is customary to bow. The reader chants the first line, and the congregation responds with the second.*

בָּרְכוּ אֶת יהוה הַמְבֹרָךְ:
בָּרוּךְ יהוה הַמְבֹרָךְ לְעוֹלָם וָעֶד:

Barehu et adonay hamvorah.
Baruh adonay hamvorah le'olam va'ed.

Many contemporary Jews are reciting *berahot*/blessings in ways that reflect their theological outlooks and ethical concerns. At any place where a blessing occurs in the liturgy, the following elements can be combined to create alternative formulas for *berahot*. This can be done by selecting one phrase from each group to form the introductory clause.

I	Baruh atah adonay	בָּרוּךְ אַתָּה יהוה	Blessed are you Adonay
	Beruhah at yah	בְּרוּכָה אַתְּ יָהּ	Blessed are you Yah
	Nevareh et	נְבָרֵךְ אֶת	Let us bless
II	eloheynu	אֱלֹהֵינוּ	our God
	hashehinah	הַשְּׁכִינָה	Shehinah
	eyn hahayim	עֵין הַחַיִּים	Source of Life
III	meleh ha'olam	מֶלֶךְ הָעוֹלָם	Sovereign of all worlds
	hey ha'olamim	חֵי הָעוֹלָמִים	Life of all the worlds
	ru'ah ha'olam	רוּחַ הָעוֹלָם	Spirit of the world

The phrase *nevareh et eyn hahayim* was originally formulated by poet Marcia Falk. (see SOURCES, p. 1248).

YOTZER/GOD IN NATURE

Blessed are you, ETERNAL ONE, our God,
the sovereign of all worlds,

On Yom Kippur add:

(You who open up for us the gates of mercy,
and who light with your forgiveness
the eyes of those who love you)

who fashion light and create darkness, maker of peace
and creator of all.
Light of the world,
amid light's storehouse, light out of darkness—
God spoke, and all was born!

On weekdays continue on the following page. On Shabbat continue on page 283.

COMMENTARY. *Or olam*/Light of the world. This line, which the rabbis added here only for Rosh Hashanah and Yom Kippur, expresses in a highly nuanced way the general themes of creation and light. Here, God's word and the light become synonymous. Since light in our tradition also signifies Torah and redemption, the divine creative word links the power of creation to revelation and redemption, suggesting that redemption through *teshuvah* is as natural a divine gift as each sunrise, and just as sure.

D.A.T.

יוֹצֵר

בָּרוּךְ אַתָּה יהוה אֱלֹהֵינוּ מֶלֶךְ הָעוֹלָם

Baruḥ atah adonay eloheynu meleḥ ha'olam

On Yom Kippur add:

(הַפּוֹתֵחַ לָנוּ שַׁעֲרֵי רַחֲמִים וּמֵאִיר עֵינֵי הַמְחַכִּים לִסְלִיחָתוֹ)

(hapote'aḥ lanu sha'arey raḥamim ume'ir eyney hameḥakim liseliḥato)

יוֹצֵר אוֹר וּבוֹרֵא חֹשֶׁךְ עֹשֶׂה שָׁלוֹם וּבוֹרֵא אֶת־הַכֹּל:
אוֹר עוֹלָם בְּאוֹצַר חַיִּים אוֹרוֹת מֵאֹפֶל אָמַר וַיֶּהִי:

yotzer or uvorey ḥosheḥ oseh shalom uvorey et hakol.
Or olam be'otzar ḥayim orot mey'ofel amar vayehi.

On weekdays continue on the following page. On Shabbat continue on page 284.

עשה שלום ובורא את הכל/maker of peace and creator of all. This phrase, taken from Isaiah, appears there as "maker of peace and creator of evil" (Isaiah 45:7). The ancient rabbinic authorities who crafted the prayerbook adjusted the language as part of the ongoing struggle to reconcile the existence of evil with that of God.   R.H.

On weekdays:

You who in your mercy give light to the earth and its inhabitants, and in your goodness do perpetually renew each day Creation's wondrous work, how great your deeds, ETERNAL ONE! In wisdom you have made them all. The earth is filled with your accomplishments. You are the world's sole sovereign, dwelling in the highest heights before the dawn of time, praised and magnified and held in awe from days of old. God of the world, in your abundant mercy, care for us. Source of our strength, our stronghold rock, our shield of help, the fortress over us! All-powerful and blessed, great in discernment, you have prepared and wrought the sunlight's healing rays; true good you have created; luminaries you have made, in honor of your name, surrounding for divine omnipotence; your principal celestial ones, quaking in holiness, revere the shaker of the heavens, to eternity. They tell of divine glory and the holiness of God. Be blessed, redeeming power, in celebration of your handiwork, and for the luminaries that you made. Let all declare your greatness!

Continue on page 291.

On weekdays:

הַמֵּאִיר לָאָרֶץ וְלַדָּרִים עָלֶיהָ בְּרַחֲמִים וּבְטוּבוֹ מְחַדֵּשׁ בְּכָל־יוֹם
תָּמִיד מַעֲשֵׂה בְרֵאשִׁית: מָה־רַבּוּ מַעֲשֶׂיךָ יהוה כֻּלָּם בְּחָכְמָה עָשִׂיתָ
מָלְאָה הָאָרֶץ קִנְיָנֶךָ: הַמֶּלֶךְ הַמְרוֹמָם לְבַדּוֹ מֵאָז הַמְשֻׁבָּח וְהַמְפֹאָר
וְהַמִּתְנַשֵּׂא מִימוֹת עוֹלָם אֱלֹהֵי עוֹלָם בְּרַחֲמֶיךָ הָרַבִּים רַחֵם עָלֵינוּ
אֲדוֹן עֻזֵּנוּ צוּר מִשְׂגַּבֵּנוּ מָגֵן יִשְׁעֵנוּ מִשְׂגָּב בַּעֲדֵנוּ: אֵל בָּרוּךְ גְּדוֹל
דֵּעָה הֵכִין וּפָעַל זָהֳרֵי חַמָּה טוֹב יָצַר כָּבוֹד לִשְׁמוֹ מְאוֹרוֹת נָתַן
סְבִיבוֹת עֻזּוֹ פִּנּוֹת צְבָאָיו קְדוֹשִׁים רוֹמְמֵי שַׁדַּי תָּמִיד
מְסַפְּרִים כְּבוֹד־אֵל וּקְדֻשָּׁתוֹ: *תִּתְבָּרַךְ יהוה אֱלֹהֵינוּ עַל־שֶׁבַח
מַעֲשֵׂה יָדֶיךָ וְעַל־מְאוֹרֵי אוֹר שֶׁעָשִׂיתָ יְפָאֲרוּךָ סֶּלָה:

Continue on page 291.

NOTE. An early acrostic version of the *Yotzer* became a part of this expanded rabbinic text. In both Hebrew and English, bold letters here indicate the location of the acrostic.　　　D.A.T

COMMENTARY. The first major theme following *Barehu* is that of Creation. We wonder at the order, the complexity, the vastness of our world. Struck by our own smallness, we are nonetheless also caught up in the grace of having a home amidst the splendor that is nature. Our wonder and our sense of smallness give way to thankfulness for the gift of life in this world.　　　D.A.T.

On Shabbat continue here:

Let all beings acknowledge you, all cry praise to you, and all declare: There is none as holy as THE ONE! Let all beings hold you in the highest reverence, you, the fashioner of all. The God who opens up each day the doors and gateways of the East, who bursts open the windows of the heavens' dome, bringing forth the sunlight from its place and moonlight from its seat of rest, providing light for the entire world and for its creatures—all of whom divinity, in boundless love, brought into being. Bringer of light, with tender care, upon the earth and its inhabitants, in goodness you renew each day perpetually Creation's wondrous work.

You are the world's sole sovereign, dwelling in the highest heights before the dawn of time, praised and magnified and held in awe since the primordial days. God of the world, in your abundant mercy care for us. Source of our strength, our fortress rock, our shield of help, the shelter over us! None like you exists, no God apart from you. Beside you there is nothing. Who resembles you? None like you exists, ETERNAL ONE, our God, within this world, no God apart from you, our sovereign, in any future world. Beside you, our redeeming power, there is nothing in the days to come. None resembles you, our saving force, throughout all lifetimes and all worlds.

COMMENTARY. A sense of God's excesses seems to characterize this outburst of hymns in praise of the creator of the cosmic lights. The verses seem also to reflect a sense of divine energy overflowing through the world, filling the Universe with limitless luminosity. To proclaim this plenitude is a special human privilege, made possible for many of us by these radiant words of prayer.   E.G.

On Shabbat continue here:

הַכֹּל יוֹדֽוּךָ וְהַכֹּל יְשַׁבְּחֽוּךָ וְהַכֹּל יֹאמְרוּ אֵין קָדוֹשׁ כַּיהוה: הַכֹּל
יְרוֹמְמֽוּךָ סֶּֽלָה יוֹצֵר הַכֹּל: הָאֵל הַפּוֹתֵֽחַ בְּכָל־יוֹם דַּלְתוֹת שַׁעֲרֵי
מִזְרָח וּבוֹקֵֽעַ חַלּוֹנֵי רָקִֽיעַ מוֹצִיא חַמָּה מִמְּקוֹמָהּ וּלְבָנָה מִמְּכוֹן
שִׁבְתָּהּ וּמֵאִיר לָעוֹלָם כֻּלּוֹ וּלְיוֹשְׁבָיו שֶׁבְּרָא בְּמִדַּת הָרַחֲמִים:
הַמֵּאִיר לָאָֽרֶץ וְלַדָּרִים עָלֶֽיהָ בְּרַחֲמִים וּבְטוּבוֹ מְחַדֵּשׁ בְּכָל־יוֹם
תָּמִיד מַעֲשֵׂה בְרֵאשִׁית:

הַמֶּֽלֶךְ הַמְרוֹמָם לְבַדּוֹ מֵאָז הַמְשֻׁבָּח וְהַמְפֹאָר וְהַמִּתְנַשֵּׂא מִימוֹת
עוֹלָם: אֱלֹהֵי עוֹלָם בְּרַחֲמֶֽיךָ הָרַבִּים רַחֵם עָלֵֽינוּ אֲדוֹן עֻזֵּֽנוּ צוּר
מִשְׂגַּבֵּֽנוּ מָגֵן יִשְׁעֵֽנוּ מִשְׂגָּב בַּעֲדֵֽנוּ: אֵין כְּעֶרְכְּךָ וְאֵין זוּלָתֶֽךָ אֶֽפֶס
בִּלְתֶּֽךָ וּמִי דֽוֹמֶה לָּךְ: אֵין כְּעֶרְכְּךָ יהוה אֱלֹהֵֽינוּ בָּעוֹלָם הַזֶּה וְאֵין
זוּלָתְךָ מַלְכֵּֽנוּ לְחַיֵּי הָעוֹלָם הַבָּא: אֶֽפֶס בִּלְתְּךָ גּוֹאֲלֵֽנוּ לִימוֹת
הַמָּשִֽׁיחַ וְאֵין דּֽוֹמֶה־לְּךָ מוֹשִׁיעֵֽנוּ לְחַיֵּי עוֹלָמִים:

מחדש בכל יום תמיד מעשה בראשית/you renew each day perpetually
Creation's wondrous work. Rabbi Simḥah Bunam taught, "The Holy One
created the world in a state of beginning. The universe is always in an
uncompleted state, in the form of its beginning. It is not like a vessel at
which the master works until it is finished; it requires continuous labor
and unceasing renewal by creative forces. Were there a second's pause by
these forces, the universe would return to primeval chaos."   Hasidic

לימות המשיח/limot hamashiaḥ/in the days to come. This phrase literally
means "in the days of the messiah," but it is more accurately understood
as "messianic days." We do not refer here to an anointed individual, but
rather to the peace and harmony toward which we strive.   D.A.T.

This translation can be sung to the same melody as the Hebrew.
Transliteration can be found on page 288.

An essence reigns supreme above all created beings,
Blessed one, whom everyone with breath of life must bless,
Great one, whose abundant goodness fills the world,
Discerning one, whose knowledge fills all space and
emptiness.
How proudly does God shine above the holy beings!
O, beautiful in glory! O, chariot divine!
Zealous in your merit, your justice fills the throne,
Heaven's love and tender care the glory ever shines.
The lights our God created are filled with every good,
You, O God, have fashioned them with knowledge and with
care,
Kindling amid their heart your awesome might and power,
Leaving them to govern night and day forevermore.
Magnificent your brightness, your beams so radiant,
Now all is luminescent, all space they now do fill. ⤶

Transliteration can be found on page 288.

אֵל אָדוֹן עַל כָּל־הַמַּעֲשִׂים | בָּרוּךְ וּמְבֹרָךְ בְּפִי כָּל־נְשָׁמָה:
גָּדְלוֹ וְטוּבוֹ מָלֵא עוֹלָם | דַּעַת וּתְבוּנָה סֹבְבִים אֹתוֹ:
הַמִּתְגָּאֶה עַל חַיּוֹת הַקֹּדֶשׁ | וְנֶהְדָּר בְּכָבוֹד עַל־הַמֶּרְכָּבָה:
זְכוּת וּמִישׁוֹר לִפְנֵי כִסְאוֹ | חֶסֶד וְרַחֲמִים לִפְנֵי כְבוֹדוֹ:
טוֹבִים מְאוֹרוֹת שֶׁבָּרָא אֱלֹהֵינוּ | יְצָרָם בְּדַעַת בְּבִינָה וּבְהַשְׂכֵּל:
כֹּחַ וּגְבוּרָה נָתַן בָּהֶם | לִהְיוֹת מוֹשְׁלִים בְּקֶרֶב תֵּבֵל:
מְלֵאִים זִיו וּמְפִיקִים נֹגַהּ | נָאֶה זִיוָם בְּכָל־הָעוֹלָם:
שְׂמֵחִים בְּצֵאתָם וְשָׂשִׂים בְּבוֹאָם | עֹשִׂים בְּאֵימָה רְצוֹן קוֹנָם:
פְּאֵר וְכָבוֹד נוֹתְנִים לִשְׁמוֹ | צָהֳלָה וְרִנָּה לְזֵכֶר מַלְכוּתוֹ:
קָרָא לַשֶּׁמֶשׁ וַיִּזְרַח אוֹר | רָאָה וְהִתְקִין צוּרַת הַלְּבָנָה:

שֶׁבַח נוֹתְנִים לוֹ כָּל־צְבָא מָרוֹם
תִּפְאֶרֶת וּגְדֻלָּה שְׂרָפִים וְאוֹפַנִּים וְחַיּוֹת הַקֹּדֶשׁ:

Continue on page 290.

So joyous in emergence, so happy in return,
Obedient in dread of their creator's awesome will.
Pride and glory they proclaim befitting of God's name,
Circling in joyous dance, proclaiming divine rule:
Call, O God, upon the sun, enable it to shine!
Reach your gaze unto the moon, reshape that comely jewel!
Showing praise to God, the heavens' hosts now sing,
The holy angels thronging 'round, how beautiful they ring!

Continue on page 289.

COMMENTARY. "An essence...Blessed one...Great one..." This hymn, drawing upon the prophetic visions of Ezekiel 1-2 and Isaiah 6, is an alphabetical acrostic written by one of the *Merkavah* ("Chariot") mystics of the early post-talmudic era. The translation recreates the acrostic pattern according to the Hebrew, rather than the English alphabet.   J.R.

El adon al kol hama'asim

Godlo vetuvo maley olam
Hamitga'eh al hayot hakodesh

Zehut umishor lifney hiso

Tovim me'orot shebara
eloheynu
Ko'ah ugevurah natan bahem
Meley'im ziv umefikim nogah
Semehim betzeytam vesasim
bevo'am
Pe'er vehavod notnim lishmo

Kara lashemesh vayizrah or

Baruh umevorah befi kol
neshamah.
Da'at utevunah sovevim oto.
Venedar behavod al
hamerkavah.
Hesed verahamim lifney
hevodo.
Yetzaram beda'at bevinah
uvehaskel.
Lihyot moshlim bekerev tevel.
Na'eh zivam behol ha'olam.
Osim be'eymah retzon konam.

Tzoholah verinah lezeher
malhuto.
Ra'ah vehitkin tzurat
halevanah.

Shevah notnim lo kol tzeva marom
Tiferet ugedulah serafim ve'ofanim vehayot hakodesh.

Continue on page 290.

COMMENTARY. This expansive acrostic hymn of praise is especially appropriate for the Sabbath, the holy day that celebrates creation. We are reminded that we inhabit a brilliant yet orderly universe. This song sees the primary substance of the universe as light emanating from divine goodness. On Shabbat, we take the time to bask in the illumination of God's healing, loving light.   S.P.W.

Praises to God, who rested from all labors of Creation! On the seventh day did God ascend, returning to the throne of glory. With splendor God adorned the day of rest, calling Shabbat a time of pleasure. This is the distinction of the seventh day, for on it the divine one ceased from all creation's work. The seventh day itself offers its praise, calling out "a psalm of the Shabbat: It is good to give thanks to THE ETERNAL..." Therefore, let all God's creatures offer laudatory blessing! Praise, appreciation and greatness may they give to God, the sovereign creator of all things, who in great holiness has given an inheritance of rest unto the people Israel, upon Shabbat, the holy day. May your name, DEAR ONE, our God, be declared holy; and your memory, our sovereign, be magnified both in the skies above and on the earth below. Be blessed, redeeming power, in celebration of your handiwork, and for the luminaries that you made. Let all declare your greatness!

לָאֵל אֲשֶׁר שָׁבַת מִכָּל־הַמַּעֲשִׂים בַּיּוֹם הַשְּׁבִיעִי הִתְעַלָּה וְיָשַׁב עַל־
כִּסֵּא כְבוֹדוֹ: תִּפְאֶרֶת עָטָה לְיוֹם הַמְּנוּחָה עֹנֶג קָרָא לְיוֹם הַשַּׁבָּת:
זֶה שֶׁבַח שֶׁל־יוֹם הַשְּׁבִיעִי שֶׁבּוֹ שָׁבַת אֵל מִכָּל־מְלַאכְתּוֹ וְיוֹם
הַשְּׁבִיעִי מְשַׁבֵּחַ וְאוֹמֵר מִזְמוֹר שִׁיר לְיוֹם הַשַּׁבָּת טוֹב לְהֹדוֹת
לַיהוה: לְפִיכָךְ יְפָאֲרוּ וִיבָרְכוּ לָאֵל כָּל־יְצוּרָיו שֶׁבַח יְקָר וּגְדֻלָּה יִתְּנוּ
לָאֵל מֶלֶךְ יוֹצֵר כֹּל הַמַּנְחִיל מְנוּחָה לְעַמּוֹ יִשְׂרָאֵל בִּקְדֻשָּׁתוֹ בְּיוֹם
שַׁבַּת קֹדֶשׁ: שִׁמְךָ יהוה אֱלֹהֵינוּ יִתְקַדַּשׁ וְזִכְרְךָ מַלְכֵּנוּ יִתְפָּאֵר
בַּשָּׁמַיִם מִמַּעַל וְעַל־הָאָרֶץ מִתָּחַת: תִּתְבָּרַךְ מוֹשִׁיעֵנוּ עַל־שֶׁבַח
מַעֲשֵׂה יָדֶיךָ וְעַל־מְאוֹרֵי אוֹר שֶׁעָשִׂיתָ יְפָאֲרוּךָ סֶּלָה:

DERASH. The principle of *imitatio dei*—that we are to imitate the attributes of God—applies to this prayer. The text imagines God finishing the work of creation on Friday evening and returning to the throne of glory. I learn from this that there is godliness in treating ourselves royally on Shabbat.

J.A.S.

White butterflies, with single
black fingerpaint eyes on their wings
dart and settle, eddy and mate
over the green tangle of vines
in Labor Day morning steam.

The year grinds into ripeness
and rot, grapes darkening,
pears yellowing, the first
Virginia creeper twining crimson,
the grasses, dry straw to burn.

The New Year rises, beckoning
across the umbrellas on the sand.
I begin to reconsider my life.
What is the yield of my impatience?
What is the fruit of my resolve?

I turn from frantic white dance
over the jungle of productivity
and slowly a niggun slides
cold water down my throat.
I rest on a leaf spotted red.

Now is the time to let the mind
search backwards like the raven loosed
to see what can feed us. Now,
the time to cast the mind forward
to chart an aerial map of the months.

The New Year is a great door
that stands across the evening and Yom
Kippur is the second door. Between them
are song and silence, stone and clay pot
to be filled from within myself.

I will find there both ripeness and rot,
What I have done and undone,
What I must let go with the waning days
and what I must take in. With the last
tomatoes, we harvest the fruit of our lives.

Marge Piercy

COMMENTARY. It is a long-standing custom to write special liturgical
poems, *piyutim*, that tie each part of the service to the theme of the day.
This custom has become less common in recent years because most
piyutim reflect sensibilities and styles so far removed from our own. This
poem by Marge Piercy reflects both the theme of this part of the service—
wonder at the beauty, power and unity of creation—and the theme of this
High Holy Day season. In that sense, it is the contemporary equivalent of
a *piyut*.   D.A.T.

May you be blessed, our rock, our sovereign, our champion, creator of the holy beings, and let your name be praised eternally, majestic one, the fashioner of ministering angels. All of them are standing in the heavens' highest realms, and giving voice, in awestruck unison, to words of the living God, the sovereign of all worlds. All of them adored, all brilliant in light, all great and mighty—all of them perform, in awe and dread, the will of their creator. And all open their mouths in holiness and purity. With song and melody, they bless, they praise, they magnify, they raise aloft, and sanctify, and proclaim sovereign: ↩

COMMENTARY. This passage pictures an angelic chorus singing God's praises. In Jewish tradition, angels have had a long and varied history— messengers warning Abraham of Sodom's destruction, the heavenly choir of Isaiah, the Talmud's host of heavenly functionaries, the impersonal forces of medieval philosophy, the presences of the Kabbalists. The tradition leaves ample room for each generation to understand angels as it will, whether as natural forces or revealing moments in our lives, the divine in the people we meet, or manifestations of the goodness in our world or in the inner workings of the human heart. D.A.T.

On both Shabbat and weekdays continue here.

תִּתְבָּרַךְ צוּרֵנוּ מַלְכֵּנוּ וְגוֹאֲלֵנוּ בּוֹרֵא קְדוֹשִׁים יִשְׁתַּבַּח שִׁמְךָ לָעַד
מַלְכֵּנוּ יוֹצֵר מְשָׁרְתִים וַאֲשֶׁר מְשָׁרְתָיו כֻּלָּם עוֹמְדִים בְּרוּם עוֹלָם
וּמַשְׁמִיעִים בְּיִרְאָה יַחַד בְּקוֹל דִּבְרֵי אֱלֹהִים חַיִּים וּמֶלֶךְ עוֹלָם *כֻּלָּם
אֲהוּבִים כֻּלָּם בְּרוּרִים כֻּלָּם גִּבּוֹרִים וְכֻלָּם עֹשִׂים בְּאֵימָה וּבְיִרְאָה רְצוֹן
קוֹנָם וְכֻלָּם פּוֹתְחִים אֶת־פִּיהֶם בִּקְדֻשָּׁה וּבְטָהֳרָה בְּשִׁירָה וּבְזִמְרָה
וּמְבָרְכִים וּמְשַׁבְּחִים וּמְפָאֲרִים וּמַעֲרִיצִים וּמַקְדִּישִׁים וּמַמְלִיכִים ←

Who are holy beings?
They are beloved, clear of mind and courageous.
Their will and God's are one.
Raising their voices in constant gratitude
    they marvel at every detail of life,
Granting each other loving permission to be exactly who they are.
When we listen for their sweet voices, we can hear the echo within our
    own souls.   S.P.W.

The name of God, the regal, grand, and awesome one! Holy is God! And all of them receive upon themselves, from each to each, the yoke of heaven's rule, and lovingly they give to one another the permission to declare their maker holy. In an ecstasy of spirit, with pure speech and holy melody, all of them respond in awe as one, and cry: "Holy, holy, holy is THE RULER of the Multitudes of Heaven. The whole world overflows with divine glory!

The angels of the chariot and holy creatures of the heavens, in great quaking, rise to face the seraphim. And, facing them, they sing in praise, and cry: "Blessed be the glory of THE ONE, wherever God may dwell!"

NOTE. Several forms of *kedushah* exist in our liturgy. Here we have the *Kedushah Diyeshivah*, which we recite without standing. We remember that, according to the Bible, the angels proclaim God's holiness, but we do not yet rise to do so ourselves. Proclaiming the holiness of the divine unity takes more preparation and concentration. We strive to be ready to move from remembering to proclaiming when we recite the *Kedushah* of the Amidah.

D.A.T.

מלא כל הארץ כבודו Literally, the fullness of the earth is God's glory. In this we recognize that there are barren places and empty lives. When we turn despair to hope, cry out for justice, pursue peace, we fill the earth with what is holy, and then the fullness of the earth is God's glory.

S.E.S.

אֶת שֵׁם הָאֵל הַמֶּלֶךְ הַגָּדוֹל הַגִּבּוֹר וְהַנּוֹרָא קָדוֹשׁ הוּא *וְכֻלָּם
מְקַבְּלִים עֲלֵיהֶם עֹל מַלְכוּת שָׁמַיִם זֶה מִזֶּה וְנוֹתְנִים בְּאַהֲבָה רְשׁוּת
זֶה לָזֶה לְהַקְדִּישׁ לְיוֹצְרָם בְּנַחַת רוּחַ בְּשָׂפָה בְרוּרָה וּבִנְעִימָה קְדֻשָּׁה
כֻּלָּם כְּאֶחָד עוֹנִים וְאוֹמְרִים בְּיִרְאָה:

קָדוֹשׁ קָדוֹשׁ קָדוֹשׁ

יהוה צְבָאוֹת מְלֹא כָל הָאָרֶץ כְּבוֹדוֹ:

* וְהָאוֹפַנִּים וְחַיּוֹת הַקֹּדֶשׁ בְּרַעַשׁ גָּדוֹל מִתְנַשְּׂאִים לְעֻמַּת שְׂרָפִים
לְעֻמָּתָם מְשַׁבְּחִים וְאוֹמְרִים:

בָּרוּךְ כְּבוֹד יהוה מִמְּקוֹמוֹ:

Kadosh kadosh kadosh adonay tzeva'ot melo ḥol ha'aretz kevodo.

Baruḥ kevod adonay mimekomo.

ונותנים באהבה/and lovingly they give to one another the permission. Here
our text follows the Sephardic version by adding the word *be'ahavah* (in
love). It is only in our love for one another that we are truly capable of
granting to each other "permission" to pray. A community of Jews who
stand together in real prayer must be one where each individual is known
and cared for as a person. Only when such love exists among us are we a
community whose members can truly "grant permission" to one another
to seek or to sanctify God. A.G.

To blessed God they offer melodies. To the sovereign and enduring God they utter songs, and make their praises heard, for God alone is holy and revered, enactor of all mighty deeds, the fashioner of all new things, the seeder of all righteousness, the grower of all saving acts, creator of all healing, awesome in praises, source of every wonder, who renews each day, with constant good, Creation's work—as it is said: "The maker of the skies' great lights, whose love is everlasting!"

Let a new light shine forever upon Zion. Soon, may everyone of us be worthy of its light. Blessed are you, ETERNAL ONE, the shaper of the heavens' lights.

זורע צדקות מצמיח ישועות / the seeder of all righteousness, the grower of all saving acts. What the prayer says about God applies also to us: For salvation to grow, we must sow צדקות—righteous and just acts.   J.A.S.

לָאֵל בָּרוּךְ נְעִימוֹת יִתֵּנוּ לַמֶּלֶךְ אֵל חַי וְקַיָּם זְמִירוֹת יֹאמֵרוּ
וְתִשְׁבָּחוֹת יַשְׁמִיעוּ כִּי הוּא לְבַדּוֹ מָרוֹם וְקָדוֹשׁ פּוֹעֵל גְּבוּרוֹת עוֹשֶׂה
חֲדָשׁוֹת זוֹרֵעַ צְדָקוֹת מַצְמִיחַ יְשׁוּעוֹת בּוֹרֵא רְפוּאוֹת נוֹרָא תְהִלּוֹת
אֲדוֹן הַנִּפְלָאוֹת הַמְחַדֵּשׁ בְּטוּבוֹ בְּכָל יוֹם תָּמִיד מַעֲשֵׂה בְרֵאשִׁית
כָּאָמוּר: לְעֹשֵׂה אוֹרִים גְּדֹלִים כִּי לְעוֹלָם חַסְדּוֹ:
* אוֹר חָדָשׁ עַל צִיּוֹן תָּאִיר וְנִזְכֶּה כֻלָּנוּ בִּמְהֵרָה לְאוֹרוֹ. בָּרוּךְ אַתָּה
יהוה יוֹצֵר הַמְּאוֹרוֹת:

Or ḥadash al tziyon ta'ir venizkeh ḥulanu bimherah le'oro.
Baruḥ atah adonay yotzer hame'orot.

לעשה...חסדו / The maker...everlasting (Psalms 136:7).

Every day, Creation is renewed.
Wake up and see unfolding
In the spreading light of dawn,
The world and all it contains
Coming into being, new, fresh,
Filled with divine goodness
And love.
Every day, Creation is renewed.
Reflected in the great lights
We see a new day,
One precious day,
Eternity.

S.P.W.

AHAVAH RABAH / LOVE AND TORAH

With an abounding love, you love us, NURTURER, our God; with great compassion do you care for us. Our source, our sovereign, just as our ancestors placed their trust in you, and you imparted to them laws of life, so be gracious to us, too, and teach us. Our fount, our loving parent, caring one, be merciful with us, and place into our hearts ability to understand, to see, to hear, to learn, to teach, to keep, to do, and to uphold with love all that we study of your Torah. ⤺

אהבה רבה / With an abounding love, you love us. *Ahavah Rabah* may be called the quintessentially Jewish prayer. In boundless love for Israel, God gives the greatest gift imaginable: teachings that will help us to live. What more could we want from the loving parent, combining attributes of both father and mother, who here becomes the compassionate teacher, sharing the gift of true knowledge with children who have become disciples? We pray that we may have the open and understanding heart to receive these teachings, to make them real by our deeds, and to pass them on to others. This is our response to God's love: a commitment to study, to live the life of Torah, and to carry it forward to future generations.   A.G.

COMMENTARY. אבותינו ואמותינו שבטחו בך / just as our ancestors placed their trust in you. Every Jew, including Jews by choice and Jews from families that have been non-observant for several generations, can claim such ancestors as Abraham and Sarah, models of trust in God. Torah is our living inheritance because from that time until this in every generation, there have been Jews who trusted, learned, taught, and added their words and lives to the unfolding process of Torah. We have inherited their words, their deeds, and their trust. The challenge to learn, teach and do—to trust in God—is their challenge to us and our challenge to future generations.   R.H.

אַהֲבָה רַבָּה אֲהַבְתָּנוּ יהוה אֱלֹהֵינוּ חֶמְלָה גְדוֹלָה וִיתֵרָה חָמַלְתָּ
עָלֵינוּ: אָבִינוּ מַלְכֵּנוּ בַּעֲבוּר אֲבוֹתֵינוּ וְאִמּוֹתֵינוּ שֶׁבָּטְחוּ בְךָ
וַתְּלַמְּדֵם חֻקֵּי חַיִּים כֵּן תְּחָנֵּנוּ וּתְלַמְּדֵנוּ: אָבִינוּ הָאָב הָרַחֲמָן
הַמְרַחֵם רַחֵם עָלֵינוּ וְתֵן בְּלִבֵּנוּ לְהָבִין וּלְהַשְׂכִּיל לִשְׁמֹעַ לִלְמֹד
וּלְלַמֵּד לִשְׁמֹר וְלַעֲשׂוֹת וּלְקַיֵּם אֶת כָּל דִּבְרֵי תַלְמוּד תּוֹרָתֶךָ
בְּאַהֲבָה: ←

Ahavah rabah ahavtanu adonay eloheynu ḥemlah gedolah viterah
ḥamalta aleynu. Avinu malkenu ba'avur avoteynu ve'imoteynu
shebateḥu veḥa vatelamdem ḥukey ḥayim ken teḥonenu
utelamdenu. Avinu ha'av haraḥaman hamraḥem raḥem aleynu
veten belibenu lehavin ulehaskil lishmo'a lilmod ulelamed
lishmor vela'asot ulekayem et kol divrey talmud torateha
be'ahavah. ⟵

COMMENTARY. In the preceding pages (279-298) we offered an extended
blessing for Creation. We accepted our creatureliness, our place in nature.
Now we shift to concern with what gives our creaturely lives transcendent
meaning.

We learn of our own significance through the love that is freely offered to
us first by parents and later by others as well. We learn our ultimate worth
in this love, which is rooted in the divine love. This is truly essential
teaching! This love teaches us what to do with our lives, how to serve
others, how to do the divine bidding. Thus loving and learning are
inseparable parts of our tie to the divine.   D.A.T.

KAVANAH. In my personal practice, I have replaced אבינו מלכנו/our Father
our King with אבינו אמנו/our Father our Mother because it is through the
teaching of my parents that I have come to see God.   J.A.S.

Enlighten us with your Torah, cause our hearts to cling to your mitzvot. Make our hearts one, to love your name and be in awe of it. Keep us from shame, and from humiliation, and from stumbling, today and always. For we have trusted in your holy, great, and awesome name. May we be glad, rejoicing in your saving power, and may you reunite our people from all corners of the earth, leading us proudly independent to our land. For you are the redeeming God and have brought us near to your great name, to offer thanks to you, and lovingly declare your unity. Blessed are you, ABUNDANT ONE, who lovingly cares for your people Israel.

KAVANAH. In gathering together the four corners of the tallit, we gather our scattered thoughts and focus on unity—uniting our people, uniting the disparate elements of our lives, uniting with the oneness that links all that is. This inner unity is the place out of which our hearts speak the Shema.

D.A.T.

וליחדך באהבה/lovingly declare your unity. We could also translate this phrase, "declare your unity through love." When we recite the Shema, our affirmation of the ETERNAL ONE is complete not when we say, "אחד/ alone," but when we accept the mitzvah of "ואהבת/you must love."

J.A.S.

NOTE. Jews traditionally have gathered in the four tzitziyot at the corners of their tallitot when they reach vehavi'enu/reunite. The tzitziyot are then held throughout the Shema.

וְהָאֵר עֵינֵינוּ בְּתוֹרָתֶךָ וְדַבֵּק לִבֵּנוּ בְּמִצְוֹתֶיךָ וְיַחֵד לְבָבֵנוּ לְאַהֲבָה וּלְיִרְאָה אֶת שְׁמֶךָ וְלֹא נֵבוֹשׁ וְלֹא נִכָּלֵם וְלֹא נִכָּשֵׁל לְעוֹלָם וָעֶד: כִּי בְשֵׁם קָדְשְׁךָ הַגָּדוֹל וְהַנּוֹרָא בָּטָחְנוּ: נָגִילָה וְנִשְׂמְחָה בִּישׁוּעָתֶךָ:

* וַהֲבִיאֵנוּ לְשָׁלוֹם מֵאַרְבַּע כַּנְפוֹת הָאָרֶץ וְתוֹלִיכֵנוּ קוֹמְמִיּוּת לְאַרְצֵנוּ: כִּי אֵל פּוֹעֵל יְשׁוּעוֹת אָתָּה: וְקֵרַבְתָּנוּ לְשִׁמְךָ הַגָּדוֹל סֶלָה בֶּאֱמֶת: לְהוֹדוֹת לְךָ וּלְיַחֶדְךָ בְּאַהֲבָה: בָּרוּךְ אַתָּה יהוה אוֹהֵב עַמּוֹ יִשְׂרָאֵל:

Veha'er eyneynu betorateha vedabek libenu bemitzvoteha veyahed levavenu le'ahavah uleyirah et shemeha. Velo nevosh velo nikalem velo nikashel le'olam va'ed. Ki veshem kodsheha hagadol vehanora batahnu. Nagilah venismehah bishu'ateha.

Vahavi'enu leshalom me'arba kanfot ha'aretz vetolihenu komemiyut le'artzenu. Ki el po'el yeshu'ot atah. Vekeravtanu leshimeha hagadol selah be'emet. Lehodot leha uleyahedeha be'ahavah. Baruh atah adonay ohev amo yisra'el.

KAVANAH. When we feel as distant from others as the four corners of the earth are from each other, when our alienation and obsession with self make us belligerent, gather us together; bring us to peace. Help us to become aware of your wholeness; let us be whole. J.A.S.

שְׁמַע יִשְׂרָאֵל יְהֹוָה אֱלֹהֵינוּ יְהֹוָה אֶחָד

SHEMA

Listen, Israel: THE ETERNAL is our God,
THE ETERNAL ONE alone!

Blessed be the name and glory of God's realm forever!

And you must love THE ONE, your God, with your whole heart,
with every breath, with all you have. Take these words that I
command you now to heart. Teach them intently to your
children. Speak them when you sit inside your house or walk
upon the road, when you lie down and when you rise. And bind
them as a sign upon your hand, and keep them visible before
your eyes. Inscribe them on the doorposts of your house and on
your gates. ↩

שְׁמַע יִשְׂרָאֵל / Listen, Israel. The core of our worship is not a prayer at all,
but a cry to our fellow-Jews and fellow-humans. In it we declare that God
is one—which is also to say that humanity is one, that life is one, that joys
and sufferings are all one—for God is the force that binds them all
together. There is nothing obvious about this truth, for life as we experience it seems infinitely fragmented. Human beings seem isolated from one
another, divided by all the fears and hatreds that make up human history.
Even within a single life, one moment feels cut off from the next, memories of joy and fullness offering us little consolation when we are depressed
or lonely. To assert that all is one in God is our supreme act of faith. No
wonder that the Shema, the first "prayer" we learn in childhood, is also
the last thing we are to say before we die. The memory of these words on
the lips of martyrs deepens our faith as we call them out each day.   A.G.

COMMENTARY. From recognition of our place in nature in the first blessing
of this part of the service, we shifted to concern with our moral place in
the second blessing. As creatures made conscious of our ultimate worth by
love, we recite the Shema. We thereby enter into a partnership aimed at
transforming the world and ourselves in the light of that vision of ultimate
worth.
D.A.T.

שְׁמַע יִשְׂרָאֵל יהוה אֱלֹהֵינוּ יהוה אֶחָד׃

בָּרוּךְ שֵׁם כְּבוֹד מַלְכוּתוֹ לְעוֹלָם וָעֶד׃

וְאָהַבְתָּ אֵת יהוה אֱלֹהֶיךָ בְּכָל־לְבָבְךָ וּבְכָל־נַפְשְׁךָ וּבְכָל־מְאֹדֶךָ׃
וְהָיוּ הַדְּבָרִים הָאֵלֶּה אֲשֶׁר אָנֹכִי מְצַוְּךָ הַיּוֹם עַל־לְבָבֶךָ׃ וְשִׁנַּנְתָּם
לְבָנֶיךָ וְדִבַּרְתָּ בָּם בְּשִׁבְתְּךָ בְּבֵיתֶךָ וּבְלֶכְתְּךָ בַדֶּרֶךְ וּבְשָׁכְבְּךָ
וּבְקוּמֶךָ׃ וּקְשַׁרְתָּם לְאוֹת עַל־יָדֶךָ וְהָיוּ לְטֹטָפֹת בֵּין עֵינֶיךָ׃
וּכְתַבְתָּם עַל־מְזֻזוֹת בֵּיתֶךָ וּבִשְׁעָרֶיךָ׃

Shema yisra'el adonay eloheynu adonay eḥad.
Baruḥ shem kevod malḥuto le'olam va'ed.

Ve'ahavta et adonay eloheḥa
beḥol levaveḥa uveḥol nafsheḥa uveḥol me'odeḥa.
Vehayu hadevarim ha'eleh asher anoḥi metzaveḥa hayom al
levaveḥa,
Veshinantam levaneḥa vedibarta bam
beshivteḥa beveyteḥa uveleḥteḥa vadereḥ uveshoḥbeḥa
uvekumeḥa.
Ukeshartam le'ot al yadeḥa vehayu letotafot beyn eyneḥa.
Uḥtavtam al mezuzot beyteḥa uvishareḥa.

GUIDED MEDITATION: Think of someone who loves you. Feel his or her presence. Take a deep breath and open up to the love that is coming to you. Focus on that feeling of love.   L.W.K.

ואהבת/And you must love. You shall love your God intellectually, emotionally and with all your deeds. Whatever you love most in these ways is your god. For the Jewish people, the deepest love should be for freedom, justice and peace.   M.M.K./M.S.

שמע...ובשעריך/Listen...gates (Deuteronomy 6:4-9).

For the second paragraph of the Shema, read either the version below or the biblical selection beginning on page 309, then continue with the third paragraph, page 311.

BIBLICAL SELECTION I

It came to pass, and will again,
that if you truly listen
to the voice of THE ETERNAL ONE, your God,
being sure to do whatever has been asked of you today,
THE ONE, your God, will make of you a model
for all nations of the earth,
and there will come upon you all these blessings,
as you listen to the call of THE ABUNDANT ONE, your God:
Blessed be you in the city,
blessed be you upon the field.
Blessed be the fruit of your womb,
the fruit of your land, the fruit of your cattle,
the calving of your oxen, and the lambing of your sheep.
Blessed be your basket and your kneading-trough.
Blessed be you when you come home,
and blessed be you when you go forth.

See, I have placed in front of you today
both life and good, both death and ill,
commanding you today to love THE BOUNDLESS ONE, your God,
to walk in ways I have ordained,
keeping the commandments, laws, and judgments,
so that you survive and multiply.
THE BOUNTIFUL, your God, will bless you
on the land you are about to enter and inherit. ↵

For the second paragraph of the Shema, read either the version below or the biblical selection beginning on page 310, then continue with the third paragraph, page 312.

BIBLICAL SELECTION I

וְהָיָה אִם־שָׁמֹעַ תִּשְׁמַע בְּקוֹל יהוה אֱלֹהֶיךָ לִשְׁמֹר לַעֲשׂוֹת
אֶת־כָּל־מִצְוֹתָיו אֲשֶׁר אָנֹכִי מְצַוְּךָ הַיּוֹם וּנְתָנְךָ יהוה אֱלֹהֶיךָ עֶלְיוֹן
עַל כָּל־גּוֹיֵי הָאָרֶץ: וּבָאוּ עָלֶיךָ כָּל־הַבְּרָכוֹת הָאֵלֶּה וְהִשִּׂיגֻךָ כִּי
תִשְׁמַע בְּקוֹל יהוה אֱלֹהֶיךָ: בָּרוּךְ אַתָּה בָּעִיר וּבָרוּךְ אַתָּה בַּשָּׂדֶה:
בָּרוּךְ פְּרִי־בִטְנְךָ וּפְרִי אַדְמָתְךָ וּפְרִי בְהֶמְתֶּךָ שְׁגַר אֲלָפֶיךָ
וְעַשְׁתְּרוֹת צֹאנֶךָ: בָּרוּךְ טַנְאֲךָ וּמִשְׁאַרְתֶּךָ: בָּרוּךְ אַתָּה בְּבֹאֶךָ
וּבָרוּךְ אַתָּה בְּצֵאתֶךָ:

רְאֵה נָתַתִּי לְפָנֶיךָ הַיּוֹם אֶת־הַחַיִּים וְאֶת־הַטּוֹב וְאֶת־הַמָּוֶת
וְאֶת־הָרָע: אֲשֶׁר אָנֹכִי מְצַוְּךָ הַיּוֹם לְאַהֲבָה אֶת־יהוה אֱלֹהֶיךָ
לָלֶכֶת בִּדְרָכָיו וְלִשְׁמֹר מִצְוֹתָיו וְחֻקֹּתָיו וּמִשְׁפָּטָיו וְחָיִיתָ וְרָבִיתָ
וּבֵרַכְךָ יהוה אֱלֹהֶיךָ בָּאָרֶץ אֲשֶׁר־אַתָּה בָא־שָׁמָּה לְרִשְׁתָּהּ: ⟵

COMMENTARY. The traditional wording of Biblical Selection II presents detailed bountiful or devastating consequences of Israel's collective relationship to the mitzvot. That biblical section (Deuteronomy 11:13-21) offers a supernatural theology that many contemporary Jews find difficult. The biblical selection on this page (Deuteronomy 28:1-6, 30:15-19) was included in the 1945 Reconstructionist siddur. It begins by encouraging observance in the same language, but concentrates on the positive ways in which observance of mitzvot focuses our attention on God's presence as perceived through productivity and the pursuit of abundant life.   S.S.

DERASH. A person must acquire a religious faith, not by being reasoned to about God, but by experiencing God's power in making life worthwhile.
M.M.K. (Adapted)

306 / SHEMA

But if your heart should turn away,
and you not heed, and go astray,
and you submit to other gods and serve them,
I declare to you today that you shall be
destroyed completely; you shall not live out
a great expanse of days upon the land
that you now cross the Jordan to possess.
I call as witnesses concerning you
both heaven and earth, both life and death,
that I have placed in front of you
a blessing and a curse.
Choose life, that you may live,
you and your seed!

Continue on page 311.

וְאִם־יִפְנֶ֤ה לְבָבְךָ֙ וְלֹ֣א תִשְׁמָ֔ע וְנִדַּחְתָּ֗ וְהִשְׁתַּחֲוִ֛יתָ לֵאלֹהִ֥ים אֲחֵרִ֖ים וַעֲבַדְתָּֽם: הִגַּ֤דְתִּי לָכֶם֙ הַיּ֔וֹם כִּ֥י אָבֹ֖ד תֹּאבֵד֑וּן לֹא־תַאֲרִיכֻ֤ן יָמִים֙ עַל־הָ֣אֲדָמָ֔ה אֲשֶׁ֨ר אַתָּ֜ה עֹבֵ֧ר אֶת־הַיַּרְדֵּ֛ן לָבֹ֥א שָׁ֖מָּה לְרִשְׁתָּֽהּ: הַעִדֹ֨תִי בָכֶ֣ם הַיּוֹם֮ אֶת־הַשָּׁמַ֣יִם וְאֶת־הָאָרֶץ֒ הַחַיִּ֤ים וְהַמָּ֙וֶת֙ נָתַ֣תִּי לְפָנֶ֔יךָ הַבְּרָכָ֖ה וְהַקְּלָלָ֑ה וּבָֽחַרְתָּ֙ בַּֽחַיִּ֔ים לְמַ֥עַן תִּֽחְיֶ֖ה אַתָּ֥ה וְזַרְעֶֽךָ:

Continue with וַיֹּאמֶר*, page 312.*

לְמַעַן תִּחְיֶה אַתָּה וְזַרְעֶךָ/that you may live, you and your seed. These biblical words, so tempting in their simplicity, reveal a complex view of history once endorsed by some of our ancestors. Obey the mitzvot, and peace and prosperity are yours; transgress the commandments, and punishment—specifically, exile from the Land of Israel—will befall you.

For many generations, this "adaptive myth"—that exile was a consequence of our own failings—helped Jews explain and sustain themselves through periods of oppression. But for many in our generation, such answers are inadequate. We can no longer believe that whatever evil befalls us, individually or collectively, results from sin or transgression; bad things do happen to good people, and the punishment does not always fit the crime.

In the shadow of the Holocaust, perhaps the best we can do—perhaps the right thing to do—is to *respond* to evil, rather than seek explanations for its existence. In the words of the Talmud, we cannot explain either the prosperity of the wicked or the suffering of the just. But our tradition teaches that God is on the side of good, freedom, justice and righteousness, and as we affirm and work for those values, we deny the ascendency of evil.

R.H.

BIBLICAL SELECTION II

And if you truly listen to my bidding, as I bid you now—loving THE FOUNT OF LIFE, your God, and serving God with all your heart, with every breath—then I will give you rain upon your land in its appointed time, the early rain and later rain, so you may gather in your corn, your wine and your oil. And I will give you grass upon your field to feed your animals, and you will eat and be content. Beware, then, lest your heart be led astray, and you go off and worship other gods, and you submit to them, so that the anger of THE MIGHTY ONE should burn against you, and seal up the heavens so no rain would fall, so that the ground would not give forth her produce, and you be forced to leave the good land I am giving you.

So place these words upon your heart, into your lifebreath. Bind them as a sign upon your hand, and let them rest before your eyes. Teach them to your children, speaking of them when you sit at home, and when you walk upon the road, when you lie down, and when you rise. Inscribe them on the doorposts of your house and on your gates—so that your days and your children's days be many on the land THE FAITHFUL ONE promised to give your ancestors, as long as heaven rests above the earth. ↵

DERASH. The traditional second paragraph of the Shema (Deuteronomy 11:13-21) offers an account of the natural process by which the blessings of God themselves lead to pride, self-satisfaction, and ingratitude on the part of those who receive them. Ironically, the more we are blessed, so it seems, the less grateful and aware of blessing we become. It is when we are most sated, Scripture warns us, that we should be most careful. Fullness can lead to ingratitude, and ingratitude to idolatry—primarily in the form of worship of our own accomplishments. Then, indeed, "the heavens might close up and no rain fall." For, once we begin to worship our achievements, we will never find satisfaction.   A.G.

BIBLICAL SELECTION II

וְהָיָה אִם־שָׁמֹעַ תִּשְׁמְעוּ אֶל־מִצְוֹתַי אֲשֶׁר אָנֹכִי מְצַוֶּה אֶתְכֶם
הַיּוֹם לְאַהֲבָה אֶת־יהוה אֱלֹהֵיכֶם וּלְעָבְדוֹ בְּכָל־לְבַבְכֶם וּבְכָל־
נַפְשְׁכֶם: וְנָתַתִּי מְטַר־אַרְצְכֶם בְּעִתּוֹ יוֹרֶה וּמַלְקוֹשׁ וְאָסַפְתָּ דְגָנֶךָ
וְתִירֹשְׁךָ וְיִצְהָרֶךָ: וְנָתַתִּי עֵשֶׂב בְּשָׂדְךָ לִבְהֶמְתֶּךָ וְאָכַלְתָּ וְשָׂבָעְתָּ:
הִשָּׁמְרוּ לָכֶם פֶּן־יִפְתֶּה לְבַבְכֶם וְסַרְתֶּם וַעֲבַדְתֶּם אֱלֹהִים אֲחֵרִים
וְהִשְׁתַּחֲוִיתֶם לָהֶם: וְחָרָה אַף־יהוה בָּכֶם וְעָצַר אֶת־הַשָּׁמַיִם
וְלֹא־יִהְיֶה מָטָר וְהָאֲדָמָה לֹא תִתֵּן אֶת־יְבוּלָהּ וַאֲבַדְתֶּם מְהֵרָה
מֵעַל הָאָרֶץ הַטֹּבָה אֲשֶׁר יהוה נֹתֵן לָכֶם:

וְשַׂמְתֶּם אֶת־דְּבָרַי אֵלֶּה עַל־לְבַבְכֶם וְעַל־נַפְשְׁכֶם וּקְשַׁרְתֶּם אֹתָם
לְאוֹת עַל־יֶדְכֶם וְהָיוּ לְטוֹטָפֹת בֵּין עֵינֵיכֶם: וְלִמַּדְתֶּם אֹתָם
אֶת־בְּנֵיכֶם לְדַבֵּר בָּם בְּשִׁבְתְּךָ בְּבֵיתֶךָ וּבְלֶכְתְּךָ בַדֶּרֶךְ וּבְשָׁכְבְּךָ
וּבְקוּמֶךָ: וּכְתַבְתָּם עַל־מְזוּזוֹת בֵּיתֶךָ וּבִשְׁעָרֶיךָ: לְמַעַן יִרְבּוּ יְמֵיכֶם
וִימֵי בְנֵיכֶם עַל הָאֲדָמָה אֲשֶׁר נִשְׁבַּע יהוה לַאֲבֹתֵיכֶם לָתֵת לָהֶם
כִּימֵי הַשָּׁמַיִם עַל־הָאָרֶץ: ←

COMMENTARY. What human action could result in the destruction of the
rains, the onset of crop failure and famine? Abuse of the eco-system upon
which our very lives depend. And how could such an event occur? When
we lose sight of our place in the world and the wondrous gift in all that is.
The traditional second paragraph of the Shema was replaced by another
biblical selection in earlier Reconstructionist liturgy because the traditional
paragraph was understood as literal reward and punishment. However,
today in the light of our awareness of the human abuse of the environment, we recognize that often this reward and punishment rest in our own
hands. This ancient and yet vital message of the Torah urges us to choose
life.

D.A.T.

THE BOUNDLESS ONE told Moses: Speak to the Israelites—tell them to make themselves *tzitzit* upon the corners of their clothes, throughout their generations. Have them place upon the corner *tzitzit* a twine of royal blue. This is your *tzitzit*. Look at it and remember all the mitzvot of the ETERNAL ONE. And do them, so you won't go off after the lusts of your heart or after what catches your eye, so that you remember to do all my mitzvot and be holy for your God. I am THE FAITHFUL ONE, your God, who brought you from Mitzrayim to be for you a God. I am THE INFINITE, your God.

למען תזכרו /so that you remember. The *tzitzit*, like all the forms of religion, are there as reminders for us as we go about our daily lives. All of us have had moments when we most became ourselves, liberated from the bonds holding us back, or when we discovered those great inner truths that lend meaning to our lives. But such moments are forgotten, covered over by the petty angers and frustrations of daily living, by the hard shell we think we need about us to protect our most precious feelings.

Our tradition calls upon us to bring such moments back to mind and make them part of our worship. Our own innermost liberation is our "coming out of Egypt"; our own moment of deepest truth is our "standing before Sinai." Let us remember these as we look at our *tzitzit*, and join them to the ancient memories of our people. A.G.

DERASH. The four *tzitziyot* represent the four corners of the world. The divine presence spans the entire area from one corner of the world to the other. So too are the inescapable moral obligations which extend throughout our lives no matter where we are. D.A.T.

ויאמר...אלהיכם / THE BOUNDLESS ONE...God (Numbers 15:37-41).

וַיֹּאמֶר יְהוָֹה אֶל־מֹשֶׁה לֵּאמֹר: דַּבֵּר אֶל־בְּנֵי יִשְׂרָאֵל וְאָמַרְתָּ
אֲלֵהֶם וְעָשׂוּ לָהֶם צִיצִת עַל־כַּנְפֵי בִגְדֵיהֶם לְדֹרֹתָם וְנָתְנוּ
עַל־צִיצִת הַכָּנָף פְּתִיל תְּכֵלֶת: וְהָיָה לָכֶם לְצִיצִת וּרְאִיתֶם אֹתוֹ
וּזְכַרְתֶּם אֶת־כָּל־מִצְוֹת יְהוֹה וַעֲשִׂיתֶם אֹתָם וְלֹא תָתוּרוּ אַחֲרֵי
לְבַבְכֶם וְאַחֲרֵי עֵינֵיכֶם אֲשֶׁר־אַתֶּם זֹנִים אַחֲרֵיהֶם: לְמַעַן תִּזְכְּרוּ
וַעֲשִׂיתֶם אֶת־כָּל־מִצְוֹתָי וִהְיִיתֶם קְדֹשִׁים לֵאלֹהֵיכֶם: אֲנִי יְהוָֹה
אֱלֹהֵיכֶם אֲשֶׁר הוֹצֵאתִי אֶתְכֶם מֵאֶרֶץ מִצְרַיִם לִהְיוֹת לָכֶם
לֵאלֹהִים אֲנִי יְהוָֹה אֱלֹהֵיכֶם: **אֱמֶת:**

Vayomer adonay el moshe leymor. Daber el beney yisra'el
ve'amarta aleyhem ve'asu lahem tzitzit al kanfey vigdeyhem
ledorotam venatenu al tzitzit hakanaf petil teḥelet. Vehayah
laḥem letzitzit uritem oto uzḥartem et kol mitzvot adonay
va'asitem otam velo taturu aharey levaveḥem ve'aḥarey
eyneyḥem asher atem zonim aḥareyhem. Lema'an tizkeru
va'asitem et kol mitzvotay vihe-yitem kedoshim leyloheyḥem.
Ani adonay eloheyḥem asher hotzeyti eteḥem me'eretz
mitzrayim lihyot laḥem leylohim ani adonay eloheyḥem.
Adonay eloheyḥem emet.

DERASH. Torah instructs me:
"Put *tzitzit* on the corners of your garment
and weave a thread of blue to the fringes.
These shall remind you to live
justly,
lovingly, and
simply.
Look upon them and remember:
Be holy!
for the Source and Substance of Life is holy."

R.M.S.

EMET VEYATZIV / TRUE AND ESTABLISHED

True, and established, and correct,
enduring and straightforward,
steadfast, good, and beautiful
one fundamental principle shall be—
as for our ancestors so for us
and for the generations after us
and for all the generations that the seed of Israel,
your servants, shall exist—
the truth for early eras and for later ones,
a thing most excellent and real,
forever and as long as time endures,
a true and faithful law that cannot pass away.
The truth is that you are THE ETERNAL ONE,
our God, our ancients' God,
our sovereign one, our ancients' sovereign one,
our champion, our ancients' champion,
our rock, the rock of our salvation;
our redeemer and our rescuer,
your name has always been,
there is no God but you.
Help of our ancestors you have always been,
shield and savior to their children after them,
in each and every generation.
In heaven's heights your dwelling sits,
but your judgments and your justice
fill the farthest reaches of the earth.
Happy is the one who pays heed to your mitzvot,
who takes your Torah and your word to heart!
True it is that you are sovereign to your people,
and a mighty ruler who is quick to plead their cause.↩

אֱמֶת וְיַצִּיב וְנָכוֹן וְקַיָּם וְיָשָׁר וְנֶאֱמָן וְאָהוּב וְחָבִיב וְנֶחְמָד וְנָעִים וְנוֹרָא וְאַדִּיר וְמְתֻקָּן וּמְקֻבָּל וְטוֹב וְיָפֶה הַדָּבָר הַזֶּה:

* עַל אֲבוֹתֵינוּ וְעַל אִמּוֹתֵינוּ וְעָלֵינוּ וְעַל בָּנֵינוּ וְעַל דּוֹרוֹתֵינוּ וְעַל כָּל־דּוֹרוֹת זֶרַע יִשְׂרָאֵל עֲבָדֶיךָ:

עַל הָרִאשׁוֹנִים וְעַל הָאַחֲרוֹנִים דָּבָר טוֹב וְקַיָּם לְעוֹלָם וָעֶד אֱמֶת וֶאֱמוּנָה חֹק וְלֹא יַעֲבוֹר: *אֱמֶת שָׁאַתָּה הוּא יהוה אֱלֹהֵינוּ וֵאלֹהֵי אֲבוֹתֵינוּ וְאִמּוֹתֵינוּ מַלְכֵּנוּ מֶלֶךְ אֲבוֹתֵינוּ גּוֹאֲלֵנוּ גּוֹאֵל אִמּוֹתֵינוּ צוּרֵנוּ צוּר יְשׁוּעָתֵנוּ פּוֹדֵנוּ וּמַצִּילֵנוּ מֵעוֹלָם הוּא שְׁמֶךָ: אֵין אֱלֹהִים זוּלָתֶךָ:

עֶזְרַת אֲבוֹתֵינוּ וְאִמּוֹתֵינוּ אַתָּה הוּא מֵעוֹלָם מָגֵן וּמוֹשִׁיעַ לִבְנֵיהֶם אַחֲרֵיהֶם בְּכָל דֹּר וָדֹר: בְּרוּם עוֹלָם מוֹשָׁבֶךָ וּמִשְׁפָּטֶיךָ וְצִדְקָתְךָ עַד אַפְסֵי־אָרֶץ: אַשְׁרֵי אִישׁ שֶׁיִּשְׁמַע לְמִצְוֹתֶיךָ וְתוֹרָתְךָ וּדְבָרְךָ יָשִׂים עַל לִבּוֹ: אֱמֶת אַתָּה הוּא אָדוֹן לְעַמֶּךָ וּמֶלֶךְ גִּבּוֹר לָרִיב רִיבָם: ⟵

DERASH. *Emet Veyatziv* is an affirmation of the Shema. We join the last words of the Shema to אמת as a statement of our ongoing commitment to their truth. Both אמת/truth and אמן/Amen are derived from a root meaning "strong" or "firm." It has also been noted that the three letters of אמת span the Hebrew alphabet; they are its beginning, middle and end. In contrast, the letters of שקר/lie are all huddled together in a single corner of the alphabet. Truth is broad and all-encompassing; we have to expand our minds in order to embrace it. Lies, like gossip and malicious talk, bring out the narrowness within us. Let us commit ourselves, in affirming the Shema, to breadth of vision and the ongoing search for truth.

L.W.K./A.G.

True it is that you are first and last,
and without you, we have no ruler, champion, or savior.
From servitude and bondage you redeemed us, BOUNDLESS ONE,
  our God,
and from a house of slavery you set us free.
For this your loved ones celebrated you,
and held divinity in reverence,
and your beloved ones gave forth their melodies,
their songs and exaltations, blessings and thanks,
to the sovereign, living, and enduring God,
the lofty, the exalted, and the awesome one,
who casts the prideful down, and lifts the lowly,
who sets the captive free, and saves the humble,
and who helps the poor, responding to our people
when they cry aloud to God. ↵

Each second we live is a new and unique moment of the universe, a
moment that never was before and will never be again—and what do we
teach our children? We teach them that two and two is four, and that Paris
is the capital of France. When will we also teach them what they are? We
should say to each of them, "Do you know what you are? You are a
marvel! You are unique. In all of the world there is no other child exactly
like you. In the millions of years that have passed there has never been
another child like you. And look at your body...what a wonder it is. You
may become a Shakespeare, a Michelangelo, a Beethoven. You have the
capacity for anything. Yes, you are a marvel. And when you grow up, can
you then harm another who is like you, a marvel? You must cherish one
another. You must work—we all must work—to make this world worthy
of its children."

Pablo Casals

אֱמֶת אַתָּה הוּא רִאשׁוֹן וְאַתָּה הוּא אַחֲרוֹן וּמִבַּלְעָדֶיךָ אֵין לָנוּ מֶלֶךְ גּוֹאֵל וּמוֹשִׁיעַ: מִמִּצְרַיִם גְּאַלְתָּנוּ יהוה אֱלֹהֵינוּ וּמִבֵּית עֲבָדִים פְּדִיתָנוּ:

עַל־זֹאת שִׁבְּחוּ אֲהוּבִים וְרוֹמְמוּ אֵל: וְנָתְנוּ יְדִידִים זְמִירוֹת שִׁירוֹת וְתִשְׁבָּחוֹת בְּרָכוֹת וְהוֹדָאוֹת לְמֶלֶךְ אֵל חַי וְקַיָּם: רָם וְנִשָּׂא גָּדוֹל וְנוֹרָא מַשְׁפִּיל גֵּאִים וּמַגְבִּיהַּ שְׁפָלִים מוֹצִיא אֲסִירִים וּפוֹדֶה עֲנָוִים וְעוֹזֵר דַּלִּים וְעוֹנֶה וְעוֹנֶה לְעַמּוֹ בְּעֵת שַׁוְּעָם אֵלָיו: ←

COMMENTARY. The sequence of this part of the service moves from Creation (*Yotzer*) to love and revelation (*Ahavah Rabah*), to affirmation of our commitment (Shema) and now to redemption. In this way the idea is expressed that redemption becomes possible only if we participate in making it happen.

The symbol of redemption in the mythic life of the Jewish people is the crossing of the Sea. In the rabbinic imagination, the ancient Israelites slog through mud up to their knees, their waists, even their chests. It falls to us to continue the task of redemption—to face the contemporary morass and find the resolve to wade through it with waves threatening to submerge us on either hand. We wade toward a future that at our darkest moments seems but a dim hope. The hint of the Promised Land is in our loving moments.

We join in singing what the Israelites proclaimed after they had successfully crossed the Sea and find in their redemption the strength to seek our own. This struggle carries us into the Amidah, a prayer of becoming, of transformation, of divine-human partnership that brings grace into our lives and into our world.   D.A.T.

Give praises
to the highest God! Blessed is God, the one to bless!
So Moses, Miriam and the Israelites came forth with
song to you,
in boundless happiness, and they all cried:
    "Who among the mighty can compare
        to you, ETERNAL ONE?
            Who can compare to you,
                adorned in holiness,
                    awesome in praises,
                        acting wondrously!"

A new song did the redeemed ones sing out to your name,
    beside the Sea.
Together, all of them gave thanks, declared your sovereignty,
    and said:
"THE HOLY ONE will reign forever!"

Rock of Israel, rise up to the help of Israel,
redeem, according to your word, Judah and Israel.
Blessed are you, ETERNAL ONE, the champion of Israel.

On Rosh Hashanah, continue with the Amidah on the next page.
For the silent Yom Kippur Amidah, turn to page 739.
If the Yom Kippur Amidah is being recited aloud through the Kedushah, *turn to page 387.*

GUIDED MEDITATION. The astounding moment of awe and thanksgiving
experienced by the Israelites upon the crossing of the Red Sea has parallels
in all of our lives. We have all had difficult crossings, experiences that we
struggled through in spite of the pain they caused us. Thus completion
afforded us a sublime sense of inner joy and peace. Take a moment to
recall one of those times. Allow the feelings of celebration to envelop you.
Hold on to those feelings as you recite the *Mi Hamohah.*   D.B.

* תְּהִלּוֹת לְאֵל עֶלְיוֹן בָּרוּךְ הוּא וּמְבוֹרָךְ מֹשֶׁה וּמִרְיָם וּבְנֵי יִשְׂרָאֵל
לְךָ עָנוּ שִׁירָה בְּשִׂמְחָה רַבָּה וְאָמְרוּ כֻלָּם:
מִי־כָמֹכָה בָּאֵלִם יהוה מִי כָּמֹכָה נֶאְדָּר בַּקֹּדֶשׁ
נוֹרָא תְהִלֹּת עֹשֵׂה פֶלֶא:
* שִׁירָה חֲדָשָׁה שִׁבְּחוּ גְאוּלִים לְשִׁמְךָ עַל־שְׂפַת הַיָּם:
יַחַד כֻּלָּם הוֹדוּ וְהִמְלִיכוּ וְאָמְרוּ:
יהוה יִמְלֹךְ לְעֹלָם וָעֶד:
* צוּר יִשְׂרָאֵל קוּמָה בְּעֶזְרַת יִשְׂרָאֵל: וּפְדֵה כִנְאֻמֶךָ יְהוּדָה וְיִשְׂרָאֵל:
גֹּאֲלֵנוּ יהוה צְבָאוֹת שְׁמוֹ קְדוֹשׁ יִשְׂרָאֵל:
בָּרוּךְ אַתָּה יהוה גָּאַל יִשְׂרָאֵל:

Mi ḥamoḥah ba'elim adonay. Mi kamoḥah nedar bakodesh
nora tehilot osey feleh.
Shirah ḥadashah shibeḥu ge'ulim leshimeḥa al sefat hayam.
Yaḥad kulam hodu vehimliḥu ve'ameru.
Adonay yimloḥ le'olam va'ed.
Tzur yisra'el kumah be'ezrat yisra'el. Ufedey ḥinumeḥa yehudah
veyisrael. Go'aleynu adonay tzeva'ot shemo kedosh yisra'el.
Baruḥ atah adonay ga'al yisra'el.

On Rosh Hashanah, continue with the Amidah on the next page.
For the silent Yom Kippur Amidah, turn to page 740.
If the Yom Kippur Amidah is being recited aloud through the Kedushah, turn to
page 388.

DERASH. Rabbi Judah said: [At the sea] each tribe said to the other, "You
go into the sea first!" As they stood there bickering, Naḥshon ben
Aminadav jumped into the water. God said to Moses, who had been
praying, "My friend is drowning—and you pray!" "What can I do?" Moses
asked. God responded, "Speak to the people of Israel and tell them to go!
Raise your staff..."   Talmud Sotah 37a

DERASH. Most congregations stand at *tzur yisra'el* rather than waiting for
the blessing. Thus we are already on our feet when we request that God
קוּמָה/arise. We cannot ask God to rise up to help Israel unless we have
done so ourselves.   E.M.

PRELUDE TO THE AMIDAH

Prayers I

Don't let me fall
Like a stone that drops on the hard ground.
And don't let my hands become dry
As the twigs of a tree
When the wind beats down the last leaves.
And when the storm rips dust from the earth
Angry and howling,
Don't let me become the last fly
Trembling terrified on a windowpane.
Don't let me fall.
I have so much prayer,
But as a blade of Your grass in a distant, wild field
Loses a seed in the lap of the earth
And dies away,
Sow in me Your living breath,
As You sow a seed in the earth.

Kadya Molodowsky
(translated by Kathryn Hellerstein)

∽

...And I have felt
A presence that disturbs me with the joy
Of elevated thoughts; a sense sublime
Of something far more deeply interfused,
Whose dwelling is the light of setting suns,
And the round ocean and the living air,
And the blue sky, and the mind of man;
A motion and a spirit, that impels
All thinking things, all objects of all thought,
And rolls through all things....

William Wordsworth

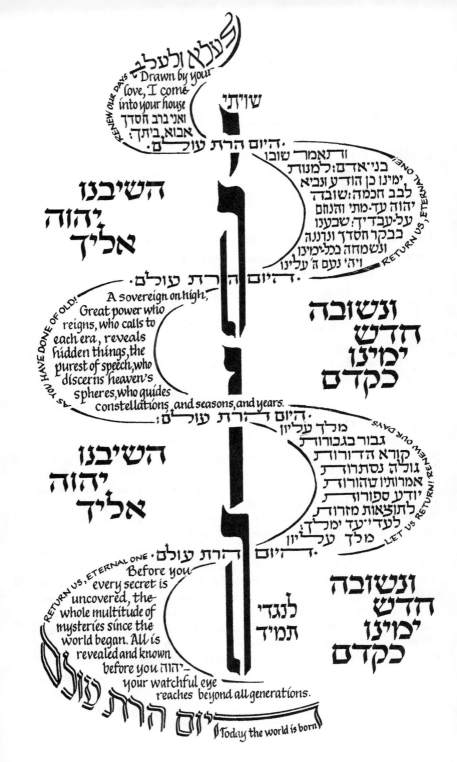

The following Introduction to the Amidah is recited when chanting part or all of the Amidah aloud. If both a Shaḥarit and Musaf Amidah will be chanted aloud, this introduction is used for Musaf.

The silent Amidah begins on the next page.

OḤILAH LA'EL /
INTRODUCTION TO THE AMIDAH

I yearn for God,
I seek God's face,
I ask of God the power of expression, so that
I might sing, amid my people, of God's power.
I express my joy in God's creative acts.
I know that thoughts are human, but that poetry belongs to
   God.
I ask of you, my sovereign, open my lips—then shall
I tell your glory!
May my words of prayer, and my heart's meditation
   be seen favorably, PRECIOUS ONE, my rock, my champion.

COMMENTARY. Our search for a Jewish way in which to speak about life as an ongoing religious quest inevitably brings us back to the psalmist, and especially to those passages where the author of the Psalms cries out to "seek My face," "to behold the beauty of God," or "to dwell in God's courts." We shudder, of course, at such a fully anthropomorphic concept of God. If God has a face, we tend to believe, surely it is a projection of the human face. It is we who take the mysterious and faceless One of the universe and make it into a humanlike deity. But I also do not believe the matter is quite that simple. *Our need to create God, I believe, comes out of the deepest recesses of ourselves, the place within us that also knows, in a way we cannot fully articulate, that God created us.* We are but an effulgence of the One, a ray of that light called Y-H-W-H. From deep within us, there wells up a need to testify to that truth, to construct a reality that will remind us of our hidden source. We are created in the image of God, if you will, and we are obliged to return the favor. *So the face is our gift to God. But the light that shines forth from that face and radiates with love—that surely is God's gift to us.*

A.G. (Adapted)

The following Introduction to the Amidah is recited when chanting part or all of the Amidah aloud. If both a Shaḥarit *and* Musaf *Amidah will be chanted aloud, this introduction is used for* Musaf.

The silent Amidah begins on the next page.

אוֹחִילָה לָאֵל

אוֹחִֽילָה לָאֵל

אֲחַלֶּה פָנָיו

אֶשְׁאֲלָה מִמֶּֽנּוּ מַעֲנֵה לָשׁוֹן:

אֲשֶׁר בִּקְהַל עָם אָשִֽׁירָה עֻזּוֹ

אַבִּֽיעָה רְנָנוֹת בְּעַד מִפְעָלָיו:

לְאָדָם מַעַרְכֵי־לֵב וּמֵיהוה מַעֲנֵה לָשׁוֹן:

אֲדֹנָי שְׂפָתַי תִּפְתָּח וּפִי יַגִּיד תְּהִלָּתֶֽךָ:

יִהְיוּ לְרָצוֹן אִמְרֵי־פִי וְהֶגְיוֹן לִבִּי לְפָנֶֽיךָ יהוה צוּרִי וְגֹאֲלִי:

KAVANAH. In the Hebrew original, all but two lines of this prayer commence with the letter *aleph*—the marker in future-tense verbs of the first-person subject, "I." Even when the speaker of the Hebrew text is not referring directly to the self, the self persists, so to speak, as an echo—in a sense, as the necessary precondition of all prayer. Here, the worshipper struggles to make his or her private prayer *public*, knowing that even this public utterance will be stamped with the indelible marks of the self. But only when the prayer achieves true mutuality, only when it is completed and received by the One addressed, whose name is likewise *Aleph*, can the worshipper truly say: "I am." J.R.

אדני...תהלתך /I ask of you...glory! (Psalms 51:17).
יהיו לרצון...וגאלי /May...champion (Psalms 19:15).

This Amidah can be used for both Shaḥarit *and* Musaf, *and can be read silently or chanted aloud. Rubrics guiding the reader for these choices are placed throughout the Amidah.*

AMIDAH FOR ROSH HASHANAH MORNING

The Amidah is traditionally recited while standing, beginning with three steps forward and bowing, left and right, a reminder of our entry into the divine presence. The traditional Amidah follows here. Directed Meditations begin on page 1, and an alternative Amidah can be found on page 383.

Open my lips, BELOVED ONE,
and let my mouth declare your praise.

1. AVOT VE'IMOT / ANCESTORS

Blessed are you, THE ANCIENT ONE our God, God of our ancestors,

God of Abraham	God of Sarah
God of Isaac	God of Rebekah
God of Jacob	God of Rachel
	and God of Leah; ⤸

DERASH. Acknowledging our ancestors reminds us that what we are is shaped by who they were. Just as an acorn is shaped by the oak that preceded it and yet gives birth to a tree uniquely its own, so we are shaped by our ancestors yet give rise to a Judaism all our own.   R.M.S.

KAVANAH. The opening of the Amidah calls to mind previous generations, near as well as distant. Take a few moments to think about your parents, your grandparents, and other relatives about whom you may have heard stories. What is your connection with them?   L.G.B.

NOTE. The choreography of the Amidah is modeled on the approach of subjects before their sovereign. We take three steps forward, bow, offer praise, deliver our petition, offer thanks, and take three steps back. On Rosh Hashanah we are especially mindful of the metaphor of monarchy.

          R.H.

אדוני...תהלתך / Open...praise (Psalms 51:17).

This Amidah can be used for both Shaharit and Musaf, and can be read silently or chanted aloud. Rubrics guiding the reader for these choices are placed throughout the Amidah.

עֲמִידָה

The Amidah is traditionally recited while standing, beginning with three steps forward and bowing, left and right, a reminder of our entry into the divine presence. The traditional Amidah follows here. Directed Meditations begin on page 1, and an alternative Amidah can be found on page 383.

אֲדֹנָי שְׂפָתַי תִּפְתָּח וּפִי יַגִּיד תְּהִלָּתֶךָ:

אָבוֹת וְאִמּוֹת

בָּרוּךְ אַתָּה יהוה אֱלֹהֵֽינוּ וֵאלֹהֵי אֲבוֹתֵֽינוּ וְאִמּוֹתֵֽינוּ

אֱלֹהֵי שָׂרָה	אֱלֹהֵי אַבְרָהָם
אֱלֹהֵי רִבְקָה	אֱלֹהֵי יִצְחָק
אֱלֹהֵי רָחֵל	אֱלֹהֵי יַעֲקֹב
וֵאלֹהֵי לֵאָה: ←	

Baruh atah adonay eloheynu veylohey avoteynu ve'imoteynu

elohey avraham	elohey sarah
elohey yitzhak	elohey rivkah
elohey ya'akov	elohey rahel
	veylohey le'ah

NOTE. The traditional liturgy evolved gradually. It contains thousands of variant or alternative versions. Reconstructionist liturgy has eliminated references to traditional beliefs that Jews are the chosen people, that there is individual reward and punishment, that the Temple should be rebuilt, that there will be a personal Messiah and that there will be bodily resurrection. The Reconstructionist commitment to equality for women has resulted in additional changes. Our liturgy reflects an understanding of God as the Source of goodness, the Life of nature, and the Power that makes for salvation.   D.A.T.

great, heroic, awesome God, supreme divinity,
imparting deeds of kindness, begetter of all;
mindful of the loyalty of Israel's ancestors,
bringing, with love, redemption to their children's children
for the sake of the divine name.

The lines that follow are chanted aloud by the service leader. They are omitted when praying silently.

By the counsel of the sages and the wise,
and by the knowledge of those learned in our ways,
I open up my mouth in prayer and supplication,
to entreat mercy from the sovereign of all Creation. ↵

COMMENTARY. Abraham Joshua Heschel used to teach that the reason graven images are forbidden by the Torah is not that God has no image, but because God has but one image: that of every living, breathing, human being. You may not fashion an image of God in any medium other than that of your entire life—that is the message of the Torah.

To be a religious Jew is to walk the tightrope between knowing the invisibility of God and seeing the face of God everywhere. YHWH is but a breath, utterly without form, the essence of abstraction itself. And yet that same abstraction is the face of God that "peers out from the windows, peeks through the lattice-work." That face contains within it all the faces of humanity, and each of them contains the face of God. God is *ruah kol basar*, the spirit that resides in all flesh. That presence may be brought to consciousness in the mind of every human who is open to it, as it may be blocked out and negated entirely by the closing of the human heart, by cruelty, or by the denial of God's image. The *Shehinah*, the divine presence in our world, does not dwell where she is not wanted.   A.G. (Adapted)

הָאֵל הַגָּדוֹל הַגִּבּוֹר וְהַנּוֹרָא אֵל עֶלְיוֹן גּוֹמֵל חֲסָדִים טוֹבִים וְקוֹנֵה הַכֹּל וְזוֹכֵר חַסְדֵי אָבוֹת וְאִמּוֹת וּמֵבִיא גְאֻלָּה לִבְנֵי בְנֵיהֶם לְמַעַן שְׁמוֹ בְּאַהֲבָה:

The lines that follow are chanted aloud by the service leader. They are omitted when praying silently.

מִסּוֹד חֲכָמִים וּנְבוֹנִים וּמִלֶּמֶד דַּעַת מְבִינִים אֶפְתְּחָה פִּי בִתְפִלָּה וּבְתַחֲנוּנִים לְחַלּוֹת וּלְחַנֵּן פְּנֵי מֶלֶךְ מַלְכֵי הַמְּלָכִים וַאֲדוֹנֵי הָאֲדוֹנִים: ←

Ha'el hagadol hagibor vehanora el elyon gomel ḥasadim tovim vekoney hakol vezoḥer ḥasdey avot ve'imot umevi ge'ulah livney veneyhem lema'an shemo be'ahavah.

Misod ḥaḥamim unevonim umil_emed _da'at mevinim efteḥah fi bitefilah uvetaḥanunim leḥalot uleḥanen peney _meleḥ malḥey hamelaḥim va'adoney ha'adonim.

MEDITATION. On this holy day, I come to this most personal prayer aware of my own imperfection, my difficulty in saying what is truly in my heart, my doubt that I can really bring myself to change so that the effort of this moment of prayer will be justified. At this moment, it takes *hutzpah* to begin to pray at all. And so, not yet having found the words of my heart, I fall back on words of the tradition. Thus does the Amidah always start with the reminder that we stand on the merit, insight and teaching of our ancestors. During the High Holy Days, however, even this seems to be not quite enough, and so beyond the invocation of the patriarchs and matriarchs, we have the invocation of the learned and the wise. I am reminded that I need not know yet what is in my heart. I can take the guidance of those who came before me, and begin in the Amidah to walk their path. In so doing, I put myself into their words, and let their words lead me to my own.   D.A.T.

Remember us for life,
our sovereign, who wishes us to live,
and write us in the Book of Life,
for your sake, ever-living God.

Regal One, our help, salvation, and protector:
Blessed are you, KIND ONE,
the shield of Abraham and help of Sarah. ⤺

KAVANAH. May our deeds be deeds of life. May our lives be lived for the
sake of the God of life. Then our own hands will enter our names in the
book of life.
                                                                    J.A.S.

וכתבנו בספר החיים/and write us in the Book of Life. The persistence of
mythic motifs such as a heavenly ledger suggest that for all our intellectual
advances over our ancestors, we remain emotionally rooted in the language
and images they created. We no longer believe that Someone is deciding
today if we are entered in the Book of Life, yet no less than our ancestors
do we desire that we be granted the gift of being here next Rosh Hashanah!
                                                                    R.H.

זָכְרֵנוּ לְחַיִּים מֶלֶךְ חָפֵץ בַּחַיִּים וְכָתְבֵנוּ בְּסֵפֶר הַחַיִּים לְמַעַנְךָ אֱלֹהִים חַיִּים:

מֶלֶךְ עוֹזֵר וּמוֹשִׁיעַ וּמָגֵן: בָּרוּךְ אַתָּה יהוה מָגֵן אַבְרָהָם וְעֶזְרַת שָׂרָה: ←

Zoḥrenu leḥayim meleḥ ḥafetz baḥayim veḥotvenu besefer haḥayim lema'aneḥa elohim ḥayim.

Meleḥ ozer umoshi'a umagen. Baruḥ atah adonay magen avraham ve'ezrat sarah. ↵

COMMENTARY. This version of the first beraḥah in the Amidah includes the matriarchs as well as the patriarchs. The phrase "help of Sarah," ezrat sarah, comes from a Hebrew root (עזר) which can mean either "save" or "be strong." This parallels the meaning of magen/shield. The biblical text says that Abraham experienced God as a shield and that Sarah experienced God as a helper. Their experience and the example of their lives can enrich our own. Just as Abraham and Sarah found the strength to face the unknown physical and spiritual dangers of their journey, so we seek to find the courage and inspiration to meet the challenges of our own time.

R.S.

2. GEVUROT / DIVINE POWER

You are forever powerful, ALMIGHTY ONE,
abundant in your saving acts. You send down the dew.

In loyalty you sustain the living,
nurturing the life of every living thing,
upholding those who fall,
healing the sick, freeing the captive,
and remaining faithful to all life
held dormant in the earth.
Who can compare to you, almighty God,
who can resemble you, the source of life and death,
who makes salvation grow?

Who can compare to you, source of all mercy,
remembering all creatures mercifully, decreeing life!

Faithful are you in giving life to every living thing.
Blessed are you, THE FOUNT OF LIFE,
who gives and renews life.

When reciting the Amidah silently, continue on the next page.

When chanting aloud with a minyan, continue with the Kedushah. *The* Kedushah *on page 359 should be used in* Shaḥarit *if a Kedushah will be recited in both* Shaḥarit *and* Musaf. *If only one Kedushah will be recited, and for the* Musaf *Kedushah if both will be recited, continue on page 333.*

DERASH. In the *Gevurot*, I address the power that underlies all change when I say: *atah gibor*/you—power! Then I name the manifestations of change inherent in my observation of nature and humanity: the blowing wind and the falling rain, those who fall down and need support, the sick who are becoming well, the bound who become free. Though aware of loss, we shift our focus to the power of renewal. We call this power "Flowering of Hope"—*matzmiaḥ yeshu'ah*.   S.P.W.

אַתָּה גִבּוֹר לְעוֹלָם אֲדֹנָי רַב לְהוֹשִׁיעַ: מוֹרִיד הַטָּל:

מְכַלְכֵּל חַיִּים בְּחֶֽסֶד מְחַיֵּה כָּל חַי בְּרַחֲמִים רַבִּים סוֹמֵךְ נוֹפְלִים וְרוֹפֵא חוֹלִים וּמַתִּיר אֲסוּרִים וּמְקַיֵּם אֱמוּנָתוֹ לִישֵׁנֵי עָפָר: מִי כָמֽוֹךָ בַּֽעַל גְּבוּרוֹת וּמִי דֽוֹמֶה לָךְ מֶֽלֶךְ מֵמִית וּמְחַיֶּה וּמַצְמִֽיחַ יְשׁוּעָה:

מִי כָמֽוֹךָ אַב הָרַחֲמִים זוֹכֵר יְצוּרָיו לְחַיִּים בְּרַחֲמִים:

‎← וְנֶאֱמָן אַתָּה לְהַחֲיוֹת כָּל חָי: בָּרוּךְ אַתָּה יהוה מְחַיֵּה כָּל חָי: ‎—

Atah gibor le'olam adonay rav lehoshi'a. Morid hatal.

Mehalkel hayim behesed mehayey kol hay berahamim rabim someh noflim verofey holim umatir asurim umekayem emunato lisheney afar. Mi hamoha ba'al gevurot umi domeh lah meleh memit umehayeh umatzmi'ah yeshu'ah.

Mi hamoha av harahamim zoher yetzurav lehayim berahamim. Vene'eman atah lehahayot kol hay. Baruh atah adonay mehayey kol hay. ‎⤺

When reciting the Amidah silently, continue on the next page.

When chanting aloud with a minyan, continue with the Kedushah. The Kedushah on page 360 should be used in Shaharit if a Kedushah will be recited in both Shaharit and Musaf. If only one Kedushah will be recited, and for the Musaf Kedushah if both will be recited, continue on page 334.

3. KEDUSHAT HASHEM / HALLOWING GOD'S NAME

Recited when praying silently:

Holy are you. Your name is holy.
And all holy beings hail you each day.

Continue on page 363.

KAVANAH. קדשת השם /Hallowing God's Name. The act of naming gives us power, for in naming that which is holy to us we draw the outlines of our relationship with the Divine. There are as many names and images for the Divine as there are imaginative human beings. Where do you find holiness?

L.G.B.

Recited when praying silently:

אַתָּה קָדוֹשׁ וְשִׁמְךָ קָדוֹשׁ וּקְדוֹשִׁים בְּכָל יוֹם יְהַלְלוּךָ סֶּלָה:

Continue on page 364.

KAVANAH. You are eternal, the life of all that lives, the love in all that loves. You animate lifeless matter. You are the courage of those who conquer adversity. You are in the health of those who overcome sickness. You are the hope of those who now sleep in the dust. Yet you are more than all these, O master of life and death and salvation. You are holy, and those who strive after holiness worship you.   M.M.K. (Adapted)

GUIDED MEDITATION. Breathe in and out, feeling the purity of your breath coming into your body. Breathe out slowly, allowing all impurities to leave you. Experience the wholeness and completeness of each breath. Feel its circularity, its roundness, its holiness. God's Name is in each breath. Breathe deeply, allowing your breath to enter and soften all the sore, cramped places in your soul. As your breath fills you, an exaltation enters your being! You truly know your source in the One. Through *your* loving justice and compassion, God's *kedushah*/holiness enters the world.   M.P.

Continue here during Musaf *when the* Kedushah *is recited and during* Shaḥarit *when only one* Kedushah *will be recited.*

May THE ETERNAL reign forever,
your God, O Zion, from one generation to the next.
Halleluyah!
For you, O God, are holy, you are enthroned amid the praises
sung by Israel.

The ark is opened.

All-Embracing One, You are our God,
Blessed in heaven, and upon earth,
Greatest in might, revered beyond worth,
Distinction surpassing, above all acclaim,
Who uttered a word, and all things became,
Who gave a command, and Creation arose—
So shall your name outlast all the worlds!
How all that has life is infused with your Being,
The clearest of sight, all-knowing, all-seeing!
You dwell beyond all, in mystery concealed,
Crown of salvation, redemption revealed.
Law is your garment, and justice your way,
Mighty your zeal—all creatures obey.
Now and forever is judgment your crown,
So hidden in honor, yet great in renown.
On all of Creation your faith radiates,
Perfect in deeds, in truth and in grace,
Stronghold of justice, upright without peer,
Creation calls out, and you are near—
Revered and adored by all of Creation,
Seated on high in your heavenly station.
The earth you suspended upon the abyss,
Forever you live, in awe and in holiness!

NOTE. This *piyut* is a Hebrew acrostic. Each line of the translation begins
with the English sound closest to the Hebrew letter.

Continue here during Musaf *when the* Kedushah *is recited and during* Shaḥarit *when only one* Kedushah *will be recited.*

יִמְלֹךְ יהוה לְעוֹלָם אֱלֹהַיִךְ צִיּוֹן לְדֹר וָדֹר הַלְלוּיָהּ:

וְאַתָּה קָדוֹשׁ יוֹשֵׁב תְּהִלּוֹת יִשְׂרָאֵל:

The ark is opened.

אֵל נָא אַתָּה הוּא אֱלֹהֵינוּ

גּ בּוֹר וְנַעֲרָץ	בַּשָּׁמַיִם וּבָאָרֶץ
ה וּא שָׂח וַיֶּהִי	דָּגוּל מֵרְבָבָה
ז כְּרוֹ לָנֶצַח	וְ צִוָּה וְנִבְרָאוּ
ט הוֹר עֵינַיִם:	חַי עוֹלָמִים
כְּ תְרוֹ יְשׁוּעָה	י וֹשֵׁב סֵתֶר
מַ עֲטֵהוּ קִנְאָה	לְבוּשׁוֹ צְדָקָה
ס תְרוֹ יֹשֶׁר	נְ אְפַּד נְקָמָה
פְּ עֻלָּתוֹ אֱמֶת	עֲ צָתוֹ אֱמוּנָה
קָ רוֹב לְקוֹרְאָיו בֶּאֱמֶת	צַ דִּיק וְיָשָׁר
שׁ וֹכֵן שְׁחָקִים	רָ ם וּמִתְנַשֵּׂא

תּוֹלֶה אֶרֶץ עַל בְּלִימָה:

חַי וְקַיָּם נוֹרָא וּמָרוֹם וְקָדוֹשׁ:

El na atah hu eloheynu
bashama̲yim uva'a̲retz gibor vena'aratz
dagul merevavah hu saḥ vaye̲hi
vetzivra'u zi̲ḥro lane̲tzaḥ
ḥay olamim tehor eyna̲yim
yoshev se̲ter kitro yeshu'ah
levusho tzedakah ma'a̲tehu kinah
nepad nekamah sitro yo̲sher
atzato emunah pe'ulato emet
tzadik veyashar karov lekorav be'emet
ram umitnasey shoḥen sheḥakim
to̲leh a̲retz al belimah
ḥay vekayam nora umarom vekadosh.

Awesomeness, truth absolute,
  the life of all the worlds.
Boundless knowledge, blessing all,
  the life of all the worlds.
Great in eminence, greatness itself,
  the life of all the worlds.
Divine in knowledge, speech divine,
  the life of all the worlds.
Heaven's splendor, beauty's height,
  the life of all the worlds.
Wisdom's summit, world's first being,
  the life of all the worlds.
Zeal of purity, zealous in light,
  the life of all the worlds.
Hand of power, holding might,
  the life of all the worlds.
Truth's array, absence of taint,
  the life of all the worlds.
Unity, and awesome yoke,
  the life of all the worlds. ⤶

COMMENTARY. This hymn, which is a classic text of *Merkavah* mysticism, seems to depict the choruses of praise sung by the angels to God. The song is an alphabetical acrostic; in the translation, the initial letter or sound of each line corresponds to a letter of the Hebrew alphabet, and is also echoed later in the line.   J.R.

DERASH. What is the point of calling God by all these exalted names over and over again? Are we not invoking the best and the highest in our historical imagination in order to bring ourselves closer to those qualities? These hymns are incantations or affirmations. We hope that the words, recited with attention, will bring the spirit of strength, power, goodness, truth and compassion into our personal and collective lives.   S.P.W.

הָאַדֶּרֶת וְהָאֱמוּנָה	לְחַי עוֹלָמִים:
הַבִּינָה וְהַבְּרָכָה	לְחַי עוֹלָמִים:
הַגַּאֲוָה וְהַגְּדֻלָּה	לְחַי עוֹלָמִים:
הַדֵּעָה וְהַדִּבּוּר	לְחַי עוֹלָמִים:
הַהוֹד וְהֶהָדָר	לְחַי עוֹלָמִים:
הַוַּעַד וְהַוָּתִיקוּת	לְחַי עוֹלָמִים:
הַזֹּךְ וְהַזֹּהַר	לְחַי עוֹלָמִים:
הַחַיִל וְהַחֹסֶן	לְחַי עוֹלָמִים:
הַטֶּכֶס וְהַטֹּהַר	לְחַי עוֹלָמִים:
הַיִּחוּד וְהַיִּרְאָה	לְחַי עוֹלָמִים: ←

Ha'aderet veha'emunah	lehay olamim.
Habina vehaberahah	lehay olamim.
Haga'avah vehagedulah	lehay olamim.
Hade'ah vehadibur	lehay olamim.
Hahod vehehadar	lehay olamim.
Hava'ad vehavatikut	lehay olamim.
Hazoh vehazohar	lehay olamim.
Hahayil vehahosen	lehay olamim.
Hatehes vehatohar	lehay olamim.
Hayihud vehayirah	lehay olamim.

Crown of glory, light to come,
  the life of all the worlds.
Lesson, and enlivening,
  the life of all the worlds.
Majesty of rule and might,
  the life of all the worlds.
New in beauty, never-ending,
  the life of all the worlds.
Sublime, exalted, seated high,
  the life of all the worlds.
Overwhelming, one most humble,
  the life of all the worlds.
Power to save, in power proud,
  the life of all the worlds.
Splendor bright and steady justice,
  the life of all the worlds.
Quest and call, holy quintessence,
  the life of all the worlds.
Rejoicing song, subject revered,
  the life of all the worlds.
Song of the world, subject of praise,
  the life of all the worlds.
Theme of all talk, the one, sublime,
  the life of all the worlds.

COMMENTARY. This ancient hymn originated in the Rosh Hashanah morning service. It may be sung to any of several tunes used for *Adon Olam* or *El Adon*. This simple list of attributes for "the life of all the worlds" harks back to the most primitive forms of religious poetry. Following a double acrostic pattern—here repeated in the English translation—the author calls forth the qualities we associate with God.

"Do you want to know the One we worship?" the poet seems to say. "Then know all these qualities, for it is in them that God, 'the life of all the worlds,' may be said to dwell." The poem may thus be seen as an early expression of predicate theology, a way of approaching a definition of God by listing the qualities we associate with divinity. A.G.

לְחַי עוֹלָמִים:	הַכֶּתֶר וְהַכָּבוֹד
לְחַי עוֹלָמִים:	הַלֶּקַח וְהַלִּבּוּב
לְחַי עוֹלָמִים:	הַמְּלוּכָה וְהַמֶּמְשָׁלָה
לְחַי עוֹלָמִים:	הַנּוֹי וְהַנֵּצַח
לְחַי עוֹלָמִים:	הַסִּגּוּי וְהַשֶּׂגֶב
לְחַי עוֹלָמִים:	הָעֹז וְהָעֲנָוָה
לְחַי עוֹלָמִים:	הַפְּדוּת וְהַפְּאֵר
לְחַי עוֹלָמִים:	הַצְּבִי וְהַצֶּדֶק
לְחַי עוֹלָמִים:	הַקְּרִיאָה וְהַקְּדֻשָׁה
לְחַי עוֹלָמִים:	הָרֹן וְהָרוֹמֵמוֹת
לְחַי עוֹלָמִים:	הַשִּׁיר וְהַשֶּׁבַח
לְחַי עוֹלָמִים:	הַתְּהִלָּה וְהַתִּפְאֶרֶת

Haketer vehakavod	leḥay olamim
Halekaḥ vehalibuv	leḥay olamim
Hameluḥah vehamemshalah	leḥay olamim
Hanoy vehanetzaḥ	leḥay olamim
Hasiguwi vehasegev	leḥay olamim
Ha'oz veha'anavah	leḥay olamim
Hapedut vehape'er	leḥay olamim
Hatzevi vehatzedek	leḥay olamim
Hakeri'ah vehakedushah	leḥay olamim
Haron veharomemot	leḥay olamim
Hashir vehashevaḥ	leḥay olamim
Hatehilah vehatiferet	leḥay olamim

MELEḤ ELYON / A SOVEREIGN ON HIGH

And so, there was a sovereign in Yeshurun!

A sovereign on high, Almighty and revered,
  raised up over all, respected and feared,
    appointer of rulers on each nation's throne,
      who reigns for eternity, one God alone.

A sovereign on high, Great power who reigns
  who calls to each era, reveals hidden things,
    the purest of speech, who discerns heaven's spheres,
      who guides constellations, and seasons, and years.

A sovereign on high, Held in honor by all,
  All-knowing, all-loving, giving life unto all,
    though hidden from all, God surveys all as one,
      and reigns for eternity, one God alone.

A sovereign on high, Seeing all that's concealed,
  probes conscience and memory, the forgotten revealed.
    with eyes ever open, declaring our thought,
      the God of all lifebreath, whose wisdom is sought.

A sovereign on high, The purest above,
  surpassing the angels, arousing their love,
    setting boundaries for oceans, and quieting seas,
      God's reign is forever, through all eternities.

A sovereign on high, Containing the deep,
  who stirs mighty storms, then puts their raging to sleep,
    who cries out "Enough!" lest a flood fill the world,
      who banishes the waves the abyss has unfurled. ↩

‏וּבְכֵן‎ וַיְהִי בִישֻׁרוּן מֶלֶךְ:

מֶלֶךְ עֶלְיוֹן אַמִּיץ הַמְנֻשָּׂא לְכָל־רֹאשׁ מִתְנַשֵּׂא אוֹמֵר וְעוֹשֶׂה מָעוֹז
וּמַחְסֶה נִשָּׂא וְנוֹשֵׂא מוֹשִׁיב מְלָכִים לַכִּסֵּא
לַעֲדֵי־עַד יִמְלוֹךְ:

מֶלֶךְ עֶלְיוֹן גִּבּוֹר בִּגְבוּרוֹת קוֹרֵא הַדּוֹרוֹת גּוֹלֶה נִסְתָּרוֹת אִמְרוֹתָיו
טְהוֹרוֹת יוֹדֵעַ סְפוֹרוֹת לְתוֹצָאוֹת מַזָּרוֹת
לַעֲדֵי־עַד יִמְלוֹךְ:

מֶלֶךְ עֶלְיוֹן הַמְפֹאָר בְּפִי כֹל וְהוּא כֹל יָכוֹל הַמְרַחֵם אֶת כֹּל וְנוֹתֵן
מִחְיָה לַכֹּל וְנֶעְלָם מֵעֵין כֹּל וְעֵינָיו מְשׁוֹטְטוֹת בַּכֹּל
לַעֲדֵי־עַד יִמְלוֹךְ:

מֶלֶךְ עֶלְיוֹן זוֹכֵר נִשְׁכָּחוֹת חוֹקֵר טוּחוֹת עֵינָיו פְּקוּחוֹת מַגִּיד שֵׁחוֹת
אֱלֹהֵי הָרוּחוֹת אִמְרוֹתָיו נְכוֹחוֹת
לַעֲדֵי־עַד יִמְלוֹךְ:

מֶלֶךְ עֶלְיוֹן טָהוֹר בִּזְבוּלָיו אוֹת הוּא בְּאֶרְאֶלָּיו אֵין עֲרוֹךְ אֵלָיו
לִפְעוֹל כְּמִפְעָלָיו חוֹל שָׁם גְּבוּלָיו בַּהֲמוֹת יָם לְגַלָּיו
לַעֲדֵי־עַד יִמְלוֹךְ:

מֶלֶךְ עֶלְיוֹן כּוֹנֵס מֵי הַיָּם רוֹגַע גַּלֵּי יָם סוֹעֵר שְׁאוֹן דָּכְיָם מְלֹא
הָעוֹלָם דַּיָּם מַשְׁבִּיחָם בַּעְיָם וְשָׁבִים אָחוֹר וְאַיָּם
← ‏לַעֲדֵי־עַד יִמְלוֹךְ:‎

COMMENTARY. In the original form of this *piyut*, the structure consisted of alternating stanzas, one describing ‏מלך עליון‎/*meleḥ elyon*/sovereign on high and the next describing ‏מלך אביון‎/*meleḥ evyon*/inconsequential earthly ruler. Over time, the disparaging comments about the limitedness, helplessness and weakness of earthly rulers came to be omitted. Our version is a lofty meditation on divine sovereignty without any negative comment on us who stand in awe of it.   D.A.T.

‏ויהי בישרון מלך‎/there was a sovereign in Yeshurun (Deuteronomy 33:5).

A sovereign on high, whose Might does not fail,
 whose road is the wind, whose path is the gale,
  whose garment is light, making night like the day,
   who reigns in dark mystery with luminous array.

A sovereign on high, Sequestered in cloud,
 fiery angels and cherubs bear a Chariot proud,
  the lightning and stars, and heavenly signs,
   forever with praises, God's rule they enshrine.

A sovereign on high, Provider whose hand
 is eternally open, raining wealth on the land,
  while day after day expresses earth's praise
   of the One who shall reign beyond all the days.

A sovereign on high, the Quintessence of awe,
 whose holiness surpasses all natural law,
  who spoke, and who measured the world's cornerstone,
   who created all things for God's glory alone.

A sovereign on high, Showing kindness in need,
 to prayer and supplication ever willing to heed,
  abundant in kindness, and sparing of wrath,
   may God reign forever, the first and the last!

מֶלֶךְ עֶלְיוֹן מוֹשֵׁל בִּגְבוּרָה דַּרְכּוֹ סוּפָה וּסְעָרָה עוֹטֶה אוֹרָה לַיְלָה כַּיּוֹם לְהָאִירָה עֲרָפֶל לוֹ סִתְרָה וְעָמֵּהּ שְׁרֵא נְהוֹרָא

לַעֲדֵי־עַד יִמְלֹךְ:

מֶלֶךְ עֶלְיוֹן סִתְרוֹ עָבִים סְבִיבָיו לְהָבִים רְכוּבוֹ כְּרוּבִים מְשָׁרְתָיו שְׁבִיבִים מַזָּלוֹת וְכוֹכָבִים הִלּוּלוּ מַרְבִּים

לַעֲדֵי־עַד יִמְלֹךְ:

מֶלֶךְ עֶלְיוֹן פּוֹתֵחַ יָד וּמַשְׂבִּיעַ צוֹרֵר מַיִם וּמַנְבִּיעַ יַבֶּשֶׁת לְהַטְבִּיעַ לִשְׁלִישׁ וְלִרְבִּיעַ יוֹם לְיוֹם יַבִּיעַ שִׁבְחוֹ לְהַבִּיעַ

לַעֲדֵי־עַד יִמְלֹךְ:

מֶלֶךְ עֶלְיוֹן קָדוֹשׁ וְנוֹרָא בְּמוֹפֵת וּבְמוֹרָא מִמַּדֵּי אֶרֶץ קָרָא וְאֶבֶן פִּנָּתָהּ יָרָה וְכָל־הַנִּבְרָא לִכְבוֹדוֹ בָרָא

לַעֲדֵי־עַד יִמְלֹךְ:

מֶלֶךְ עֶלְיוֹן שׁוֹמֵעַ אֶל אֶבְיוֹנִים וּמַאֲזִין חַנּוּנִים מַאֲרִיךְ רְצוֹנִים וּמְקַצֵּר חֲרוֹנִים רִאשׁוֹן לָרִאשׁוֹנִים וְאַחֲרוֹן לָאַחֲרוֹנִים

לַעֲדֵי־עַד יִמְלֹךְ:

And so, let all proclaim the sovereignty
   of God, who judges all with justice,
one who plumbs the heart upon the day of justice,
   who reveals what is concealed, with justice;
one who speaks the truth upon the day of justice,
   drawing out our inner thoughts with justice.
Ancient one, who has compassion on the day of justice,
   and who calls to mind the covenant of justice;
one who spares Creation on the day of justice,
   and who cleanses those who seek the God of justice;
one who knows all thoughts upon the day of justice,
   who holds back from anger, though enacting justice;
who is clad in righteousness upon the day of justice,
   and is merciful toward wrongdoing, with justice;
one awesome in praises on the day of justice,
   and forgiving to those burdened with the weight of justice;
answering whoever calls upon the day of justice,
   and acting mercifully in pursuit of justice;
one who searches out the hidden on the day of justice,
   and who calls to service in enacting justice;
one who is loving to our people on the day of justice,
   who keeps safe whoever loves the God of justice,
and supports whoever seeks perfection on the day of justice!

וּבְכֵן לְךָ הַכֹּל יַכְתִּירוּ

לְאֵל עוֹרֵךְ דִּין

לְגוֹלֶה עֲמֻקוֹת בַּדִּין:	לְבוֹחֵן לְבָבוֹת בְּיוֹם דִּין
לְהוֹגֶה דֵעוֹת בַּדִּין:	לְדוֹבֵר מֵישָׁרִים בְּיוֹם דִּין
לְזוֹכֵר בְּרִיתוֹ בַּדִּין:	לְוָתִיק וְעוֹשֶׂה חֶסֶד בְּיוֹם דִּין
לְטַהֵר חוֹסָיו בַּדִּין:	לְחוֹמֵל מַעֲשָׂיו בְּיוֹם דִּין
לְכוֹבֵשׁ כַּעְסוֹ בַּדִּין:	לְיוֹדֵעַ מַחֲשָׁבוֹת בְּיוֹם דִּין
לְמוֹחֵל עֲוֹנוֹת בַּדִּין:	לְלוֹבֵשׁ צְדָקוֹת בְּיוֹם דִּין
לְסוֹלֵחַ לַעֲמוּסָיו בַּדִּין:	לְנוֹרָא תְהִלּוֹת בְּיוֹם דִּין
לְפוֹעֵל רַחֲמָיו בַּדִּין:	לְעוֹנֶה לְקוֹרְאָיו בְּיוֹם דִּין
לְקוֹנֶה עֲבָדָיו בַּדִּין:	לְצוֹפֶה נִסְתָּרוֹת בְּיוֹם דִּין
לְשׁוֹמֵר אוֹהֲבָיו בַּדִּין:	לְרַחֵם עַמּוֹ בְּיוֹם דִּין

לְתוֹמֵךְ תְּמִימָיו בְּיוֹם דִּין:

COMMENTARY. Jewish liturgy has been formed over time by the layering of each era's experiences, hopes, fears, beliefs and aspirations. The language and literary form of each piece of liturgy casts light onto Jewish lives and visions obscured by their distance in time. The medieval *piyutim* are the liturgical poems that form the bulk of the traditional High Holiday liturgy. This *piyut*, composed by Shimon ben Yitzhak of Mayence in the eleventh century, reflects the experience of those who have been ruled by flawed mortal kings. He envisions the sovereign on high as the flawless and eternal ruler who knows the most hidden secrets of the human heart, guarantees justice throughout the world and provides for the needs of every creature. This grand vision of the divine monarch not only makes vivid the imagined re-enthronement of God at the mythic center of Rosh Hashanah; it also creates a guarantor of justice whose standard we can use to measure our conduct and explore our motivations. Internalizing this author's vision provides us with the challenge of measuring ourselves by those visionary standards.   D.A.T.

INTERPRETIVE VERSION: UNETANEH TOKEF

When we really begin a new year it is decided,
And when we actually repent, it is determined;

> Who shall be truly alive, and who shall merely exist;
> Who shall be happy, and who miserable;

Who shall be tormented by the fire of ambition,
And whose hopes shall be quenched by the waters of failure;

> Who shall be pierced by the sharp sword of envy,
> And who shall be torn by the wild beast of resentment;

Who shall hunger for companionship,
And who shall thirst for approval;

> Who shall be shattered by storms of change,
> And who shall be plagued by the pressures of conformity;

Who shall be strangled by insecurity,
And who shall be beaten into submission;

> Who shall be content with their lot,
> And who shall wander in search of satisfaction;

Who shall be serene,
And who shall be distraught;

> Who shall be at ease,
> And who shall be afflicted with anxiety;

Who shall be poor in their own eyes,
And who shall be rich in tranquility.

> But *teshuvah, tefilah* and *tzedakah*
> Have the power to change the character of our lives.

May we resolve, then, to turn from our accustomed ways
And to behave righteously
So that we may truly begin a new year.

Stanley Rabinowitz (Adapted)

INTERPRETIVE VERSION: UNETANEH TOKEF

Let us ask ourselves hard questions
For this is the time for truth.

> How much time did we waste
> In the year that is now gone?

Did we fill our days with life
Or were they dull and empty?

> Was there love inside our home
> Or was the affectionate word left unsaid?

Was there a real companionship with our children
Or was there a living together and a growing apart?

> Were we a help to our mates
> Or did we take them for granted?

How was it with our friends:
Were we there when they needed us or not?

> The kind deed: did we perform it or postpone it?
> The unnecessary gibe: did we say it or hold it back?

Did we live by false values?
Did we deceive others?
Did we deceive ourselves?

> Were we sensitive to the rights and feelings
> Of those who worked for us?

Did we acquire only possessions
Or did we acquire new insights as well?

> Did we fear what the crowd would say
> And keep quiet when we should have spoken out?

Did we mind only our own business
Or did we feel the heartbreak of others?

> Did we live right,
> And if not,
> Then have we learned, and will we change?

Jack Riemer

UNETANEH TOKEF/NOW, WE DECLARE...

And so, let holiness arise to you,
for you, God, are our sovereign,

The ark is opened.

Now, we declare the sacred power of this day,
which is the most awesome and solemn of days,
when your rule is established over all,
and your throne set in place by the power of love,
and you come forth to govern in truth.

True it is that you are our judge,
you alone can reprove, you alone can know,
you alone are witness to all deeds.

It is you who shall write,
you who shall seal what is written,
you who shall read,
and you who shall number all souls.
You alone can remember what we have forgotten;
it is you who shall open the Book of Remembrance,
but its contents shall speak for themselves,
for it bears the imprint of us all,
which our deeds and our lives have inscribed.

And when the great shofar is sounded,
a small, quiet voice can be heard,
and the heavenly beings are thrown into fright,
and, seized by a terrible dread, they declare:

"Behold, the Day of Judgment has arrived,
when even those in heaven's court are judged,
for none can be exempt from justice's eyes!"

וּבְכֵן לְךָ תַעֲלֶה קְדֻשָּׁה כִּי אַתָּה אֱלֹהֵינוּ מֶלֶךְ:

The ark is opened.

וּנְתַנֶּה תֹּקֶף קְדֻשַּׁת הַיּוֹם כִּי הוּא נוֹרָא וְאָיֹם: וּבוֹ תִנָּשֵׂא מַלְכוּתֶךְ
וְיִכּוֹן בְּחֶסֶד כִּסְאֶךָ וְתֵשֵׁב עָלָיו בֶּאֱמֶת: אֱמֶת כִּי אַתָּה הוּא דַיָּן
וּמוֹכִיחַ וְיוֹדֵעַ וָעֵד וְכוֹתֵב וְחוֹתֵם וְסוֹפֵר וּמוֹנֶה וְתִזְכֹּר כָּל־
הַנִּשְׁכָּחוֹת וְתִפְתַּח אֶת־סֵפֶר הַזִּכְרוֹנוֹת וּמֵאֵלָיו יִקָּרֵא וְחוֹתָם יַד כָּל־
אָדָם בּוֹ:

וּבְשׁוֹפָר גָּדוֹל יִתָּקַע וְקוֹל דְּמָמָה דַקָּה יִשָּׁמַע. וּמַלְאָכִים יֵחָפֵזוּן
וְחִיל וּרְעָדָה יֹאחֵזוּן וְיֹאמְרוּ הִנֵּה יוֹם הַדִּין: לִפְקֹד עַל צְבָא מָרוֹם
בַּדִּין כִּי לֹא יִזְכּוּ בְעֵינֶיךָ בַּדִּין →

KAVANAH. *Unetaneh tokef* refers to the awesome and threatening power of
this day. Our ancestors saw themselves as if exposed to divine retribution
for their sins. They pictured punishment from God mainly in terms of
natural disasters to life and livelihood—plagues, wars and other woes that
can swoop down on us, physically maiming us, ruining our stores and
crops, starving our families. While that feeling—the sense that life's
tragedies are largely externally imposed—may linger, another way of
understanding this prayer, and the whole of these "days of awe," is to
recognize how small and hidden from sight is the nature of so much
misfortune that we experience. The splitting of an atom, which we cannot
see, unleashes terrors of dreadful, almost unimaginable proportions.
Similarly, we should not regard lightly the little wounds to the spirit
which happen daily. Every insult uttered, every belittling gesture, every lie
or rejection or unfair accusation is a punishment to a society that does not
value the spirit of respect, the necessity of truth, or the power of love. If
we pay better attention to each other's feelings, the small cruelties and
hidden meannesses that are tearing us apart from within will no longer
threaten. Let us resolve to heal the environment of suspicion, in which
promises are broken, wills are broken and hearts are broken. Let us no
longer make excuses for selfishness that causes such injuries to the human
spirit, made in God's image.   S.D.R.

And all who come into the world
pass before you like sheep for the shepherd—
for, just as a shepherd numbers the flock,
passing the herd by the staff,
so do you make us pass by before you,
and number, and count, and determine the life,
one by one, of all who have lifebreath within.
You decide for each creature its cycles of life,
and you write down its destined decree.

On Rosh Hashanah, all is written and revealed,
and on Yom Kippur, the course of every life is sealed!

—how many pass on, how many shall thrive,
who shall live on, and who shall die,
whose death is timely, and whose is not,
who dies by fire, and who shall be drowned,
who by the sword, and who by the beast,
who by hunger, and who by thirst,
who by an earthquake, who by a plague,
who shall be strangled, and who shall be stoned,
who dwells in peace, and who is uprooted,
who shall live safely, and who shall be harmed,
whose life is tranquil, and whose is tormented,
who shall be poor, and who shall be rich,
who shall be humbled, and who is raised up! ↵

וְכָל־בָּאֵי עוֹלָם יַעַבְרוּן לְפָנֶיךָ כִּבְנֵי מָרוֹן: כְּבַקָּרַת רוֹעֶה עֶדְרוֹ
מַעֲבִיר צֹאנוֹ תַּחַת שִׁבְטוֹ כֵּן תַּעֲבִיר וְתִסְפֹּר וְתִמְנֶה וְתִפְקֹד נֶפֶשׁ
כָּל־חָי וְתַחְתֹּךְ קִצְבָּה לְכָל־בְּרִיָּה וְתִכְתֹּב אֶת־גְּזַר דִּינָם:

בְּרֹאשׁ הַשָּׁנָה יִכָּתֵבוּן וּבְיוֹם צוֹם כִּפּוּר יֵחָתֵמוּן

Kevakarat ro'eh edro ma'avir tzono taḥat shivto ken ta'avir
vetispor vetimneh vetifkod nefesh kol ḥay vetaḥtoḥ kitzbah
leḥol beriyah vetiḥtov et gezar dinam.

Berosh hashanah yikatevun uveyom tzom kipur yeḥatemun

כַּמָּה יַעַבְרוּן וְכַמָּה יִבָּרֵאוּן מִי יִחְיֶה וּמִי יָמוּת
מִי בְקִצּוֹ וּמִי לֹא בְקִצּוֹ מִי בָאֵשׁ וּמִי בַמַּיִם
מִי בַחֶרֶב וּמִי בַחַיָּה מִי בָרָעָב וּמִי בַצָּמָא
מִי בָרַעַשׁ וּמִי בַמַּגֵּפָה מִי בַחֲנִיקָה וּמִי בַסְּקִילָה
מִי יָנוּחַ וּמִי יָנוּעַ מִי יִשָּׁקֵט וּמִי יִטָּרֵף
מִי יִשָּׁלֵו וּמִי יִתְיַסָּר מִי יֵעָנִי וּמִי יֵעָשֵׁר
מִי יִשָּׁפֵל וּמִי יָרוּם: →

The glory and agony of being human rousing us
entreating us to wake up!
To know that we who have no power
can be filled with power.
When we wake up to our transparent nature,
divine forgiveness shines through us.
When we forget our names,
we become part of God's name.
When we learn to act and yield, act and yield,
we smash the contradiction of existence.   S.P.W.

But *teshuvah*, and *tefilah*, and *tzedakah*
make easier what God may decree,
make easier what life holds in store,
make easier facing the world,
make easier facing ourselves.

For, as is your name, so is your praise—
slow to be angry, quick to forgive;
you do not desire a person to die,
but only to change and to live.
Down to a person's last day of life,
the person is given the chance to return,
and all who return, and resolve to be just,
are welcomed by you straight-away.

For truly you are their creator,
and you know their innermost nature,
and they know they are flesh and blood. ↵

COMMENTARY. But *teshuvah*, and *tefilah*, and *tzedakah*.... These meritorious acts, says the original Hebrew text, "cause the evil of the decree to pass away" (*ma'avirin et ro'a hagezerah*). The English rendition seeks to encompass several ways that we are likely to feel ourselves facing a decree on the Day of Judgment: by God, by the events of our lives, by the world around us, and, of course, by ourselves. The power of repentance, prayer, and acts of giving to turn "judgment," in all its forms, from an alien and arbitrary event to a shaping force of our life and our identity is the subject of these lines. We cannot will away either what happens to us or what happens around us, but we may have it in our power to turn it into something quite other than "evil." J.R.

מעבירין את רע הגזרה / make easier what God may decree. We cannot change the decree. But sometimes our *tzedakah*, by providing food for the hungry, shelter for the homeless, or peace for the embattled, reduces רע הגזרה / the severe effects of the decree. We can make easier what "God may decree" by living lives of meaning in the face of apparently meaningless events. J.A.S.

ROSH HASHANAH MORNING / 351

וּתְשׁוּבָה וּתְפִלָּה וּצְדָקָה

מַעֲבִירִין אֶת רֹעַ הַגְּזֵרָה:

כִּי כְּשִׁמְךָ כֵּן תְּהִלָּתֶךָ קָשֶׁה לִכְעֹס וְנוֹחַ לִרְצוֹת כִּי לֹא תַחְפֹּץ בְּמוֹת הַמֵּת כִּי אִם בְּשׁוּבוֹ מִדַּרְכּוֹ וְחָיָה: וְעַד יוֹם מוֹתוֹ תְּחַכֶּה־לּוֹ אִם יָשׁוּב מִיָּד תְּקַבְּלוֹ: אֱמֶת כִּי אַתָּה הוּא יוֹצְרָם וְאַתָּה יוֹדֵעַ יִצְרָם כִּי הֵם בָּשָׂר וָדָם: ←

Uteshuvah utefilah utzedakah
ma'avirin et ro'a hagezerah.

Ki heshimeha ken tehilateha kasheh lihos venoah lirtzot. Ki lo tahpotz bemot hamet ki im beshuvo midarko vehayah. Ve'ad yom moto tehakeh lo im yashuv miyad tekabelo. Emet ki atah hu yotzram ve'atah yode'a yitzram ki hem basar vadam. ←

ותשובה ותפילה וצדקה מעבירין את רע הגזרה/But *teshuvah*, and *tefilah*, and *tzedakah* make easier what God may decree. After the fierce determinism of the first half of *Unetaneh Tokef*—suggesting that nothing is within our control, and all is decreed—we are suddenly presented with a note of encouragement: How we act can, in some way, affect how we live.

Reconstructionism rejects the superstitious dimensions of prayer, and we do not believe either that "all is decreed" or that "*teshuvah*, and *tefilah*, and *tzedakah*" can magically mitigate what may happen. But we do accept, as this prayer suggests, that though there are things beyond our control, we do retain control over how we react to those things.

A Reconstructionist interpretation of the Hebrew might yield: "Direction (*teshuvah*), Reflection (*tefilah*) and Connection (*tzedakah*) make it possible to live within boundaries not of our making and beyond our control." *Teshuvah*, or turning-to-God/liness, is the process of deciding the *direction* of our lives. *Tefilah*, or prayer, can be a *reflection* on who we are, where we are, and where we are going. *Tzedakah*, both charity and acts of justice, *connect* us to others, reminding us that our own salvation or self-fulfillment cannot exist apart from those with whom we share past, present and future. R.H.

All of humanity is founded on dust—
of dust they are made, and to dust they return;
as long as they live, they strive for their bread.
Like vessels of clay, they can break.
Like grass they can wither, like flowers they fade,
like shadows they pass, like clouds they are emptied,
like wind their strength is exhausted,

like dust they are scattered about,
like a dream they shall vanish from sight.
But you, holy one, your reign is eternal,
the God who lives and endures!

No limit exists to the years of your life,
no end is assigned to the length of your days,
no measure contains the array of your glory,
your name is beyond all translation.

Your name is the perfect expression of you,
and you have, in turn, embodied your name,
and have called us, as well, by your name.

The ark is closed, and we remain standing.

אָדָם יְסוֹדוֹ מֵעָפָר וְסוֹפוֹ לֶעָפָר: בְּנַפְשׁוֹ יָבִיא לַחְמוֹ: מָשׁוּל כַּחֶרֶס הַנִּשְׁבָּר כֶּחָצִיר יָבֵשׁ וּכְצִיץ נוֹבֵל כְּצֵל עוֹבֵר וּכְעָנָן כָּלָה וּכְרֽוּחַ נוֹשָׁבֶת וּכְאָבָק פּוֹרֵֽחַ וְכַחֲלוֹם יָעוּף:

וְאַתָּה הוּא מֶֽלֶךְ אֵל חַי וְקַיָּם:

Adam yesodo me'afar vesofo le'afar. Benafsho yavi laḥmo. Mashul kaḥeres hanishbar keḥatzir yavesh uḥetzitz novel ketzel over uḥe'anan kaleh uḥeruaḥ noshavet uḥe'avak pore'aḥ vehaḥalom ya'uf.

Ve'atah hu meleḥ el ḥay vekayam.

אֵין קִצְבָּה לִשְׁנוֹתֶֽיךָ וְאֵין קֵץ לְאֹֽרֶךְ יָמֶֽיךָ וְאֵין שִׁעוּר לְמַרְכְּבוֹת כְּבוֹדֶֽךָ וְאֵין פֵּרוּשׁ לְעֵילוֹם שְׁמֶֽךָ: שִׁמְךָ נָאֶה לְךָ וְאַתָּה נָאֶה לִשְׁמֶֽךָ וּשְׁמֵֽנוּ קָרָֽאתָ בִּשְׁמֶֽךָ:

The ark is closed, and we remain standing.

ושמנו קראת בשמך /and have called us, as well, by your name. This refers to the godly quality that is inherent in all people. If our name and God's name are intertwined, then our calling to God and God's calling to us are reciprocal actions. We speak God's voice as well as listen for it. God is within each of us. As we call out to God, God calls out to us.   M.B.K.

Act for the sake of your name,
and make your name holy
over all who now declare
the holiness of your great name.
Act for the glory of your name,
which is uplifted and made holy
by the hidden utterance of holy seraphim,
who, bathed in holiness, proclaim the holiness
of your great name,
joining those who dwell above
with those who dwell on earth,
as it is written by your prophet's hand:
"And they call out, one to another, and declare:

Holy, holy, holy is THE CREATOR of the Multitudes of Heaven!
All the world is filled with divine glory!"

God's glory fills the world,
as the ministering angels ask, one to another,
"What place could contain God's holiness?"
And they are answered with a blessing:
"Blessed is the glory of THE OMNIPRESENT,
wherever God may dwell!"

And from God's place, God mercifully turns
bestowing graciousness upon the people
who declare the oneness of the divine name
evening and morning, each day continually,
as twice a day they say with love: "Shema!"
"Listen, Israel: THE ETERNAL is our God,
THE ETERNAL ONE alone!" ↰

וקרא...כבודו / And...glory! (Isaiah 6:3).

ברוך...ממקומו / Blessed...dwell! (Ezekiel 3:12).

שמע...אחד / Listen...alone! (Deuteronomy 6:4).

עֲשֵׂה לְמַעַן שְׁמֶךָ וְקַדֵּשׁ אֶת־שְׁמֶךָ עַל מַקְדִּישֵׁי שְׁמֶךָ בַּעֲבוּר כְּבוֹד
שְׁמֶךָ הַנַּעֲרָץ וְהַנִּקְדָּשׁ כְּסוֹד שִֽׂיחַ שַׂרְפֵי־קֹֽדֶשׁ הַמַּקְדִּישִׁים שְׁמֶךָ
בַּקֹּֽדֶשׁ דָּרֵי מַֽעְלָה עִם דָּרֵי מַֽטָּה כַּכָּתוּב עַל יַד נְבִיאֶֽךָ וְקָרָא זֶה
אֶל זֶה וְאָמַר

קָדוֹשׁ קָדוֹשׁ קָדוֹשׁ

יהוה צְבָאוֹת מְלֹא כָל־הָאָֽרֶץ כְּבוֹדוֹ:

כְּבוֹדוֹ מָלֵא עוֹלָם מְשָׁרְתָיו שׁוֹאֲלִים זֶה לָזֶה אַיֵּה מְקוֹם כְּבוֹדוֹ
לְעֻמָּתָם בָּרוּךְ יֹאמֵֽרוּ:

בָּרוּךְ כְּבוֹד יהוה מִמְּקוֹמוֹ:

מִמְּקוֹמוֹ הוּא יִֽפֶן בְּרַחֲמִים וְיָחֹן עַם הַמְיַחֲדִים שְׁמוֹ עֶֽרֶב וָבֹֽקֶר בְּכָל
יוֹם תָּמִיד פַּעֲמַֽיִם בְּאַהֲבָה שְׁמַע אוֹמְרִים:

שְׁמַע יִשְׂרָאֵל יהוה אֱלֹהֵֽינוּ יהוה אֶחָד: ←

Asey lema'an shemeha vekadesh et shimeha al makdishey shemcha
ba'avur kevod shimeha hana'aratz vehanikdash kesod siah sarfey
kodesh hamakdishim shimeha bakodesh darey malah im darey
matah kakatuv al yad nevi'eha vekarah zeh el zeh ve'amar:
Kadosh kadosh kadosh adonay tzeva'ot melo hol ha'aretz kevodo.
Kevodo maley olam mesharetav sho'alim zeh lazeh ayey mekom
kevodo le'umatam baruh yomeru:
Baruh kevod adonay mimekomo.
Mimekomo hu yifen berahamim veyahon am hamyahadim
shemo erev vavoker behol yom tamid pa'amayim be'ahavah
shema omrim:
Shema yisra'el adonay eloheynu adonay ehad. ↵

COMMENTARY. The structure of the *Kedushah* rests upon myths in Jewish
tradition about angelic choruses praising God. By standing at attention and
singing words ascribed to the angelic chorus, we become imitators of the
heavenly chorus. Jews traditionally rock upward on their toes each time
the word קדוש / *kadosh* / holy is chanted here. It is as if we were straining
upward to join the heavenly choir in praise.   D.A.T.

This is our God.
This is our source.
This is our sovereign.
This is our saving power.
And this one, mercifully,
shall declare a second time,
for every living being to hear,
confirming God's divinity for you:
"I am the OMNIPRESENT ONE, your God!"

O, mighty one, our mighty one,
THE SOVEREIGN who watches over us,
how mighty is your name throughout the earth!
The time shall come that GOD will reign
throughout the earth. On that day
shall THE FOUNT OF LIFE be one,
the divine name be one.
And as is written in your sacred words of psalm:
"May THE ETERNAL reign forever,
your God, O Zion, from one generation to the next. Halleluyah!"

From one generation to the next
may we declare your greatness,
and for all eternities may we affirm your holiness,
And may your praise, our God,
never be absent from our mouths
now and forever.
For you are a great and holy God.

Continue on page 363.

אני...אלהיכם / I...God! (Numbers 15:41).
יהוה אדנינו...הארץ / The SOVEREIGN...earth! (Psalms 8:10).
והיה יהוה...אחד / The time...be one (Zechariah 14:9).
ימלך...הללויה / May...Halleluyah! (Psalms 146:10).

הוּא אֱלֹהֵינוּ הוּא אָבִינוּ הוּא מַלְכֵּנוּ הוּא מוֹשִׁיעֵנוּ וְהוּא יַשְׁמִיעֵנוּ
בְּרַחֲמָיו שֵׁנִית לְעֵינֵי כָּל חָי: לִהְיוֹת לָכֶם לֵאלֹהִים:
אֲנִי יהוה אֱלֹהֵיכֶם:

אַדִּיר אַדִּירֵנוּ יהוה אֲדֹנֵינוּ מָה־אַדִּיר שִׁמְךָ בְּכָל־הָאָרֶץ: וְהָיָה יהוה
לְמֶלֶךְ עַל־כָּל־הָאָרֶץ בַּיּוֹם הַהוּא יִהְיֶה יהוה אֶחָד וּשְׁמוֹ אֶחָד:
וּבְדִבְרֵי קָדְשְׁךָ כָּתוּב לֵאמֹר:

יִמְלֹךְ יהוה לְעוֹלָם אֱלֹהַיִךְ צִיּוֹן לְדֹר וָדֹר הַלְלוּיָהּ:
לְדוֹר וָדוֹר נַגִּיד גָּדְלֶךָ וּלְנֵצַח נְצָחִים קְדֻשָּׁתְךָ נַקְדִּישׁ וְשִׁבְחֲךָ
אֱלֹהֵינוּ מִפִּינוּ לֹא יָמוּשׁ לְעוֹלָם וָעֶד כִּי אֵל מֶלֶךְ גָּדוֹל וְקָדוֹשׁ אָתָּה:

Continue on page 364.

Hu eloheynu hu avinu hu malkeynu hu moshi'eynu vehu
yashmi'enu berahamav shenit le'eyney kol hay lihyot lahem
leylohim ani adonay eloheyhem.

Adir adirenu adonay adoneynu mah adir shimeha behol ha'aretz.

Vehayah adonay lemeleh al kol ha'aretz bayom hahu yihyeh
adonay ehad ushemo ehad.

Uvedivrey kodsheha katuv lemor.

Yimloh adonay le'olam elohayih tziyon ledor vador halleluyah.

Ledor vador nagid godleha ulenetzah netzahim kedushateha
nakdish veshivhaha eloheynu mipinu lo yamush le'olam va'ed ki
el meleh gadol vekadosh atah.

COMMENTARY. On the pilgrimage festivals and Days of Awe, the paragraph
אדיר אדירנו / adir adireynu! / O mighty one is added to the Kedushah. This
provides an additional opportunity to emphasize not only divine
sovereignty, but the hope that God's rule will become permanently
manifest throughout the earth. Its placement here in the middle of the
Kedushah stands as a reminder that holiness is only complete when human
beings live lives that bring them into harmony with the divine. Thus the
prayer for divine sovereignty is a prayer we are meant to take personally as
we strive to be holy.   D.A.T.

We sanctify your name throughout this world,
as it is sanctified in the heavens above,
as it is written by your prophet:
"And each celestial being calls to another, and exclaims
Holy, holy, holy is THE RULER of the Multitudes of Heaven!
All the world is filled with divine glory!"

And then, with quaking noises,
so overwhelming in their power,
they raise up their voices,
rise to face the seraphim,
and, facing them, they say:
"Blessed is the glory of THE HOLY ONE,
wherever God may dwell!" ⤶

DERASH. Holiness is the manner in which we react to persons, objects, places and events which we regard as indispensable to human welfare and self-realization.

M.M.K.

 וקרא...כבודו / And...glory! (Isaiah 6:3).
ברוך...ממקומו / Blessed...dwell! (Ezekiel 3:12).

This version of the Kedushah should be used for Shaḥarit *when a* Kedushah *will be recited in both* Shaḥarit *and* Musaf.

נְקַדֵּשׁ אֶת־שִׁמְךָ בָּעוֹלָם כְּשֵׁם שֶׁמַּקְדִּישִׁים אוֹתוֹ בִּשְׁמֵי מָרוֹם:
כַּכָּתוּב עַל־יַד נְבִיאֶךָ: וְקָרָא זֶה אֶל־זֶה וְאָמַר

קָדוֹשׁ קָדוֹשׁ קָדוֹשׁ

יהוה צְבָאוֹת מְלֹא כָל־הָאָרֶץ כְּבוֹדוֹ:
אָז בְּקוֹל רַעַשׁ גָּדוֹל אַדִּיר וְחָזָק מַשְׁמִיעִים קוֹל מִתְנַשְּׂאִים לְעֻמַּת
שְׂרָפִים לְעֻמָּתָם בָּרוּךְ יֹאמֵרוּ:

⟵ בָּרוּךְ כְּבוֹד יהוה מִמְּקוֹמוֹ:

Nekadesh et shimeḥa ba'olam keshem
shemakdishim oto bishmey marom
kakatuv al yad nevi'eḥa vekara zeh el zeh ve'amar:
Kadosh kadosh kadosh adonay tzeva'ot
melo ḥol ha'aretz kevodo.
Az bekol ra'ash gadol adir veḥazak
mashmi'im kol mitnasim le'umat
serafim le'umatam baruḥ yomeru:
Baruḥ kevod adonay mimekomo ⤸

And from your dwelling-place,
our sovereign, appear
and reign among us,
for we wait for you.
When will you reign in Zion?
Soon, and in our lifetime,
may you come to dwell eternally!
May your greatness and your holiness be realized
in Jerusalem, your city,
from one generation to the next,
and throughout all eternities.
And may our eyes behold your realm,
as has been prophesied in songs about your power:
"May THE ETERNAL reign forever,
your God, O Zion, from one generation to the next. Halleluyah!"
From one generation to the next may we declare your greatness,
    and for all eternities may we affirm your holiness,
And may your praise, our God, never be absent from our
    mouths, now and forever.
For you are a great and holy God. ⤶

הללויה...יִמְלֹךְ / May...Halleluyah! (Psalms 146:10).

DERASH. This prayer affirms that God will appear "from your dwelling-place...." Where is God's place? God is called *Makom*, Place itself. We affirm, then, the possibility of God's emergence from God's very self. Some of the rabbis understood a spark of the divine to be present in everything. To appear "from your dwelling place" thus could also mean that we hope to see that which is godly within each thing. Together these interpretations suggest that we pray that God emerge out of the divine spark in each thing in order to manifest that this world is God's Place.

S.P.W.

מִמְּקוֹמְךָ מַלְכֵּנוּ תוֹפִיעַ וְתִמְלֹךְ עָלֵינוּ כִּי מְחַכִּים אֲנַחְנוּ לָךְ: מָתַי
תִּמְלוֹךְ בְּצִיּוֹן בְּקָרוֹב בְּיָמֵינוּ לְעוֹלָם וָעֶד תִּשְׁכֹּן: תִּתְגַּדַּל וְתִתְקַדַּשׁ
בְּתוֹךְ יְרוּשָׁלַיִם עִירְךָ לְדוֹר וָדוֹר וּלְנֵצַח נְצָחִים: וְעֵינֵינוּ תִרְאֶינָה
מַלְכוּתֶךָ כַּדָּבָר הָאָמוּר בְּשִׁירֵי עֻזֶּךָ:

יִמְלֹךְ יהוה לְעוֹלָם אֱלֹהַיִךְ צִיּוֹן לְדֹר וָדֹר הַלְלוּיָהּ:

לְדוֹר וָדוֹר נַגִּיד גָּדְלֶךָ וּלְנֵצַח נְצָחִים קְדֻשָּׁתְךָ נַקְדִּישׁ וְשִׁבְחֲךָ
אֱלֹהֵינוּ מִפִּינוּ לֹא יָמוּשׁ לְעוֹלָם וָעֶד כִּי אֵל מֶלֶךְ גָּדוֹל וְקָדוֹשׁ אָתָּה: —←

Mimekomeḥa malkenu tofi'a vetimloḥ aleynu ki meḥakim anaḥnu laḥ. Matay timloḥ betziyon bekarov beyameynu le'olam va'ed tishkon. Titgadal vetitkadash betoḥ yerushalayim ireḥa ledor vador uleneẓaḥ netzaḥim. Ve'eyneynu tirenah malḥuteḥa kadavar ha'amur beshirey uzeḥa:

Yimloḥ adonay le'olam elohayiḥ tziyon ledor vador halleluyah.

Ledor vador nagid godleḥa uleneẓaḥ netzaḥim kedushateḥa nakdish veshivḥaḥa eloheynu mipinu lo yamush le'olam va'ed ki el meleḥ gadol vekadosh atah. ↩

And therefore, HOLY ONE, let awe of you
infuse the whole of your Creation,
and let knowledge of your presence
dwell in all your creatures.
And let every being worship you,
and each created life pay homage to your rule.
Let all of them, as one, enact your bidding
with a whole and peaceful heart.
For we have always known, ALMIGHTY ONE,
that all authority to rule belongs to you,
all strength is rooted in your arm,
all mighty deeds have emanated from your hand.
Your name alone is the source of awe
that surges through all life.

And therefore, HOLY ONE, let awe of you
infuse your people, let the praise of you
ring out from all who worship you.
Let hope enliven all who seek you,
and let all who look to you with hope
find strength to speak.
Grant joy throughout your Land,
let happiness resound throughout your holy city,
soon, and in our days. ↩

The Amidah continues here.

If the remainder of the Amidah is being read silently, it is customary to remain standing. If the remainder of the Amidah is being chanted aloud (חזרת הש״ץ / reader's repetition), it is customary to be seated here.

וּבְכֵן תֵּן פַּחְדְּךָ יהוה אֱלֹהֵינוּ עַל כָּל־מַעֲשֶׂיךָ וְאֵימָתְךָ עַל כָּל־מַה־שֶּׁבָּרָאתָ וְיִירָאוּךָ כָּל־הַמַּעֲשִׂים וְיִשְׁתַּחֲווּ לְפָנֶיךָ כָּל־הַבְּרוּאִים וְיֵעָשׂוּ כֻלָּם אֲגֻדָּה אַחַת לַעֲשׂוֹת רְצוֹנְךָ בְּלֵבָב שָׁלֵם כְּמוֹ שֶׁיָּדַעְנוּ יהוה אֱלֹהֵינוּ שֶׁהַשִּׁלְטוֹן לְפָנֶיךָ עֹז בְּיָדְךָ וּגְבוּרָה בִּימִינֶךָ וְשִׁמְךָ נוֹרָא עַל כָּל־מַה־שֶּׁבָּרָאתָ:

וּבְכֵן תֵּן כָּבוֹד יהוה לְעַמֶּךָ תְּהִלָּה לִירֵאֶיךָ וְתִקְוָה לְדוֹרְשֶׁיךָ וּפִתְחוֹן פֶּה לַמְיַחֲלִים לָךְ שִׂמְחָה לְאַרְצֶךָ וְשָׂשׂוֹן לְעִירֶךָ בִּמְהֵרָה בְיָמֵינוּ: ←

COMMENTARY. *Uveḥen* / And therefore is repeated three times. Each repetition alludes to one of the three sections we will encounter later in the service, *Malḥuyot, Ziḥronot* and *Shofarot*. The first *Uveḥen*, corresponding to *Malḥuyot*/Sovereignty, calls us to acknowledge ourselves as created beings living in a world where we are not completely in charge. It is terrifying, and we acknowledge our fear at the absence of control in our lives. We also share our awareness with each other. The second *Uveḥen*, corresponding to *Ziḥronot* / Memory, confirms and reminds us that we have a group (human / Jewish / God-seeker) identity and relationship with the source of all. We have been created in such a way that we can enter into relationship with our creator. We can be God's people. In the third *Uveḥen*, corresponding to *Shofarot*/Redemption, we envision our future and the great happiness that will accompany our waking up to who we really are.

S.P.W.

And therefore, let the just behold your peace,
let them rejoice and celebrate,
let all who follow in your path sing out with glee,
let all who love you dance with joy,
and may your power overwhelm all treachery,
so that it vanish wholly from the earth like smoke.
Then shall the power of injustice pass away!

May you alone be sovereign over all of your Creation,
and Mt. Zion be the seat and symbol of your glory,
and Jerusalem, your holy city—
as is written in your holy scriptures:
"The Eternal One shall reign forever,
your God, O Zion, through all generations!
Halleluyah!"

Holy are you,
and awe-inspiring is your name,
and there is no God apart from you,
as it is written: "The Creator of the hosts of heaven
shall be exalted through the rule of law,
and God, the Holy One, made holy by the reign of justice."
Blessed are you, Eternal One,
the holy sovereign power. ‿ↄ

בֵן צַדִּיקִים ‬ יִרְאוּ וְיִשְׂמָחוּ וִישָׁרִים יַעֲלֹזוּ וַחֲסִידִים בְּרִנָּה יָגִילוּ וְעוֹלָתָה תִּקְפָּץ־פִּיהָ וְכָל־הָרִשְׁעָה כֻּלָּהּ כְּעָשָׁן תִּכְלֶה כִּי תַעֲבִיר מֶמְשֶׁלֶת זָדוֹן מִן הָאָרֶץ:

וְתִמְלֹךְ אַתָּה יהוה לְבַדֶּךָ עַל כָּל־מַעֲשֶׂיךָ בְּהַר צִיּוֹן מִשְׁכַּן כְּבוֹדֶךָ וּבִירוּשָׁלַיִם עִיר קָדְשֶׁךָ: כַּכָּתוּב בְּדִבְרֵי קָדְשֶׁךָ: יִמְלֹךְ יהוה לְעוֹלָם אֱלֹהַיִךְ צִיּוֹן לְדֹר וָדֹר הַלְלוּיָהּ:

קָדוֹשׁ אַתָּה וְנוֹרָא שְׁמֶךָ וְאֵין אֱלוֹהַּ מִבַּלְעָדֶיךָ: כַּכָּתוּב: וַיִּגְבַּהּ יהוה צְבָאוֹת בַּמִּשְׁפָּט וְהָאֵל הַקָּדוֹשׁ נִקְדַּשׁ בִּצְדָקָה: בָּרוּךְ אַתָּה יהוה הַמֶּלֶךְ הַקָּדוֹשׁ: ⟵

COMMENTARY. The liturgy for the *Yamim Nora'im* is characterized by the insertion of special prayer units, often in groups of three. The smallest tripartite unit for these days occurs here in the third blessing of the Amidah, in the section known as *Uvehen*/And therefore. These three paragraphs articulate a perennial polarity of Judaism: universalism and particularism. The first paragraph involves "the whole of your creation," the second asks that the awe of God "infuse your people," and the final paragraph speaks of "the just." Our prayer, *uvehen*, illuminates the dual dimension of Rosh Hashanah as "*Harat Olam*/The Birthday of the Entire World" as well as "*Yom Hazikaron*/A Day of Remembrance" of the particular actions of the Jewish people.   R.H.

ימלך...הללויה / THE ETERNAL...Halleluyah (Psalms 146:10).
ויגבה...בצדקה / THE CREATOR...justice (Isaiah 5:16).

4. KEDUSHAT HAYOM / THE DAY'S HOLINESS

On Shabbat add the words in parenthesis.

You have loved us, and have taken pleasure in us,
and have made us holy with your mitzvot,
and you have brought us, sovereign one,
near to your service,
and have called us to the shelter of your great and holy name.

And you have given us, ALMIGHTY ONE, our God
in love this Day of (Shabbat and of) Remembrance,
a day to heed the (the memory of) shofar blast,
(with love,) a holy convocation,
A remembrance of the going out from Egypt. ꜀

For Shaḥarit, continue on the following page. For Musaf, continue on page 371.

KAVANAH. The traditional *Kedushat Hayom* states that the people Israel were exiled "because of our sins." But what exile is meant? Exile from Jerusalem? From the Temple? Because of what sin that we in this generation have committed? Perhaps our sin is our exile from ourselves. The end of our exile would consist not in the rebuilding of a physical Temple, but in the rebuilding of an inner reserve of spiritual integrity. An end to denying who we are demands that we face the dangers and challenges ahead as Jews with courage and creativity, that we join our fellow Jews in affirming the importance, vitality and guiding vision of our Jewish heritage. S.D.R.

קְדֻשַּׁת הַיּוֹם

On Shabbat add the words in parenthesis.

אַתָּה אֲהַבְתָּנוּ וְרָצִיתָ בָּנוּ וְקִדַּשְׁתָּנוּ בְּמִצְוֹתֶיךָ וְקֵרַבְתָּנוּ מַלְכֵּנוּ לַעֲבוֹדָתֶךָ וְשִׁמְךָ הַגָּדוֹל וְהַקָּדוֹשׁ עָלֵינוּ קָרָאתָ: וַתִּתֶּן לָנוּ יהוה אֱלֹהֵינוּ בְּאַהֲבָה אֶת־יוֹם (הַשַּׁבָּת הַזֶּה וְאֶת־יוֹם) הַזִּכָּרוֹן הַזֶּה יוֹם (זִכְרוֹן) תְּרוּעָה (בְּאַהֲבָה) מִקְרָא קֹדֶשׁ זֵכֶר לִיצִיאַת מִצְרָיִם: ←

Atah ahavtanu veratzita banu vekidashtanu bemitzvoteha vekeravtanu malkenu la'avodateha veshimeha hagadol vehakadosh aleynu karata. Vatiten lanu adonay eloheynu be'ahavah et yom (hashabbat hazeh ve'et yom) hazikaron hazeh yom (zihron) teruah (be'ahavah) mikra kodesh zeher litzi'at mitzrayim. ⟵

For Shaḥarit continue on the following page. For Musaf, continue on page 372.

Our God, our ancients' God, may our prayer arise and come to you, and be beheld, and be acceptable. Let it be heard, acted upon, remembered—the memory of us and all our needs, the memory of our ancestors, the memory of messianic hopes, the memory of Jerusalem your holy city, and the memory of all your kin, the house of Israel, all surviving in your presence. Act for goodness and grace, for love and care, for life, well-being and peace, on this Day of Remembrance.

Remember us this day, ALL-KNOWING ONE, our God, for goodness. Favor us this day with blessing. Preserve us this day for life. With your redeeming nurturing word, be kind and generous. Act tenderly on our behalf, and grant us victory over all our trials. Truly, our eyes turn toward you, for you are a providing God; gracious and merciful are you. ⤶

אֱלֹהֵֽינוּ וֵאלֹהֵי אֲבוֹתֵֽינוּ וְאִמּוֹתֵֽינוּ יַעֲלֶה וְיָבוֹא וְיַגִּֽיעַ וְיֵרָאֶה וְיֵרָצֶה
וְיִשָּׁמַע וְיִפָּקֵד וְיִזָּכֵר זִכְרוֹנֵֽנוּ וּפִקְדוֹנֵֽנוּ וְזִכְרוֹן אֲבוֹתֵֽינוּ וְאִמּוֹתֵֽינוּ
וְזִכְרוֹן יְמוֹת הַמָּשִֽׁיחַ וְזִכְרוֹן יְרוּשָׁלַֽיִם עִיר קָדְשֶֽׁךָ וְזִכְרוֹן כָּל עַמְּךָ
בֵּית יִשְׂרָאֵל לְפָנֶֽיךָ לִפְלֵיטָה וּלְטוֹבָה וּלְחֵן וּלְחֶֽסֶד וּלְרַחֲמִים לְחַיִּים
וּלְשָׁלוֹם בְּיוֹם הַזִּכָּרוֹן הַזֶּה:

זָכְרֵֽנוּ יהוה אֱלֹהֵֽינוּ בּוֹ לְטוֹבָה: וּפָקְדֵֽנוּ בוֹ לִבְרָכָה: וְהוֹשִׁיעֵֽנוּ בוֹ
לְחַיִּים: וּבִדְבַר יְשׁוּעָה וְרַחֲמִים חוּס וְחָנֵּֽנוּ וְרַחֵם עָלֵֽינוּ וְהוֹשִׁיעֵֽנוּ
כִּי אֵלֶֽיךָ עֵינֵֽינוּ כִּי אֵל מֶֽלֶךְ חַנּוּן וְרַחוּם אָֽתָּה: ←——

Our God, our ancients' God,
may it be your will that a heavenly inspiration
be awakened in us on this holy day
to renew the Land of Israel,
and to make it holy for your service,
and may peace prevail there
as well as freedom, justice, and the rule of Law,
as it is written by your prophet:
"Truly, Torah shall go forth from Zion,
and the word of the ETERNAL from Jerusalem!"
And it is said: "Let none do harm,
let none destroy, throughout my holy mountain,
for the earth is filled with knowledge of the OMNIPRESENT,
as the waters fill the sea."

Our God, our ancients' God,
have mercy for our kindred of the House of Israel
who are dwelling in distress. Please bring them forth
from darkness into light,
and accept with mercy and compassion
the prayers of your people Israel,
wherever they may dwell,
as they pour out their hearts before you
(on this Shabbat, and) on this Day of Remembrance.

When Rosh Hashanah coincides with Shabbat, add:
(Those who keep Shabbat enjoy your realm,
they call Shabbat the summit of delight.
A people that observes the holy seventh day
enjoys abundant goodness and delight.

The seventh day you favored and made holy,
you have called it the most loved of days,
a sign you made of it eternally,
in memory of Creation's works and days.) ـכ

During Shaḥarit *continue on the next page. During* Musaf *continue on page 611.*

אֱלֹהֵֽינוּ וֵאלֹהֵי אֲבוֹתֵֽינוּ וְאִמּוֹתֵֽינוּ יְהִי רָצוֹן מִלְּפָנֶֽיךָ שֶׁיֵּעָרֶה עָלֵֽינוּ
רֽוּחַ מִמָּרוֹם בַּיּוֹם הַקָּדוֹשׁ הַזֶּה לְכוֹנֵן אֶת־אֶֽרֶץ יִשְׂרָאֵל לְחַדֵּשׁ
וּלְקַדֵּשׁ אוֹתָהּ לַעֲבוֹדָתֶֽךָ וְשָׁכַן בָּאָֽרֶץ חֹֽפֶשׁ שָׁלוֹם צֶֽדֶק וּמִשְׁפָּט
כַּכָּתוּב עַל־יַד נְבִיאֶֽךָ: כִּי מִצִּיּוֹן תֵּצֵא תוֹרָה וּדְבַר־יהוה מִירוּשָׁלָֽיִם:
וְנֶאֱמַר לֹא־יָרֵֽעוּ וְלֹא־יַשְׁחִֽיתוּ בְּכָל־הַר קָדְשִׁי כִּי־מָלְאָה הָאָֽרֶץ דֵּעָה
אֶת־יהוה כַּמַּֽיִם לַיָּם מְכַסִּים:

אֱלֹהֵֽינוּ וֵאלֹהֵי אֲבוֹתֵֽינוּ וְאִמּוֹתֵֽינוּ רַחֵם עַל אַחֵֽינוּ בֵּית יִשְׂרָאֵל
הַנְּתוּנִים בְּצָרָה וְהוֹצִיאֵם מֵאֲפֵלָה לְאוֹרָה וְקַבֵּל בְּרַחֲמִים אֶת־תְּפִלַּת
עַמְּךָ יִשְׂרָאֵל בְּכָל־מְקוֹמוֹת מוֹשְׁבוֹתֵיהֶם הַשּׁוֹפְכִים אֶת־לִבָּם לְפָנֶֽיךָ
(בְּיוֹם הַשַּׁבָּת הַזֶּה וּ)בְיוֹם הַזִּכָּרוֹן הַזֶּה:

When Rosh Hashanah coincides with Shabbat, add:

(יִשְׂמְחוּ בְמַלְכוּתְךָ שׁוֹמְרֵי שַׁבָּת וְקֽוֹרְאֵי עֹֽנֶג: עַם מְקַדְּשֵׁי שְׁבִיעִי
כֻּלָּם יִשְׂבְּעוּ וְיִתְעַנְּגוּ מִטּוּבֶֽךָ: וְהַשְּׁבִיעִי רָצִֽיתָ בּוֹ וְקִדַּשְׁתּוֹ: חֶמְדַּת
יָמִים אוֹתוֹ קָרָֽאתָ זֵֽכֶר לְמַעֲשֵׂה בְרֵאשִׁית:) ←

(Yismehu vemalhuteha shomrey shabbat vekorey oneg. Am
mekadeshey shevi'i kulam yisbe'u veyitanegu mituveha.
Vehashevi'i ratzita bo vekidashto. Hemdat yamim oto karata
zeher lema'asey vereyshit.) ↵

During Shaharit continue on the next page. During Musaf, continue on page 612.

COMMENTARY. The weekday Amidah consists of nineteen blessings. On
Shabbat and holidays, the middle thirteen of these are omitted because
they consist of workaday petitions, and a single blessing about the day is
substituted except on Rosh Hashanah. Traditionally during *Musaf*, in the
place of the single middle blessing are three blessings—*Malhuyot*/
Sovereignty, *Zihronot*/Remembrance, and *Shofarot*/Redemption. These
themes, which with the shofar blasts, define the Rosh Hashanah liturgy,
are often moved either into *Shaharit* or into the Shofar service in
contemporary communities.   D.A.T.

כי...ירושלים / Truly...Jerusalem (Isaiah 2:3).
לא...מכסים / Let...sea (Isaiah 11:9).

Our God, our ancients' God,
rule over all the world in its entirety,
by showing forth your glory,
and be raised up over all the earth
in your beloved presence.
And let the wondrous aura of your reign
be manifest in all who dwell upon the earth—
let every creature know that you are its creator,
let every living thing discern that you have fashioned it,
let everyone who draws the breath of life declare
that you, THE ANCIENT ONE, reign supreme,
and that your sovereignty embraces all.

On Shabbat, add the words in parenthesis.

Our God, our ancients' God,
(take pleasure in our rest,)
enable us to realize holiness through your mitzvot,
give us our portion in your Torah,
let us enjoy the good things of your world,
and gladden us with your salvation.
(And help us to perpetuate, ETERNAL ONE, our God,
with love and with desire,
your holy Shabbat,
and may all your people Israel,
all who treat your name as holy,
find rest and peace upon this day.)
Refine our hearts to serve you truthfully,
for you are a God of truth,
and your word is truthful
and endures forever.
Blessed are you, ETERNAL ONE,
the sovereign power over all the earth,
who raises up to holiness (Shabbat,)
the people Israel
and the Day of Memory. ﬤ

אֱלֹהֵינוּ וֵאלֹהֵי אֲבוֹתֵינוּ וְאִמּוֹתֵינוּ מְלֹךְ עַל כָּל־הָעוֹלָם כֻּלּוֹ בִּכְבוֹדֶךָ וְהִנָּשֵׂא עַל כָּל הָאָרֶץ בִּיקָרֶךָ וְהוֹפַע בַּהֲדַר גְּאוֹן עֻזֶּךָ עַל כָּל־יוֹשְׁבֵי תֵבֵל אַרְצֶךָ וְיֵדַע כָּל־פָּעוּל כִּי אַתָּה פְעַלְתּוֹ וְיָבִין כָּל־יָצוּר כִּי אַתָּה יְצַרְתּוֹ וְיֹאמַר כֹּל אֲשֶׁר נְשָׁמָה בְאַפּוֹ: יהוה מֶלֶךְ וּמַלְכוּתוֹ בַּכֹּל מָשָׁלָה:

On Shabbat, add the words in parenthesis.

אֱלֹהֵינוּ וֵאלֹהֵי אֲבוֹתֵינוּ וְאִמּוֹתֵינוּ (רְצֵה בִמְנוּחָתֵנוּ) קַדְּשֵׁנוּ בְּמִצְוֹתֶיךָ וְתֵן חֶלְקֵנוּ בְּתוֹרָתֶךָ שַׂבְּעֵנוּ מִטּוּבֶךָ וְשַׂמְּחֵנוּ בִּישׁוּעָתֶךָ (וְהַנְחִילֵנוּ יהוה אֱלֹהֵינוּ בְּאַהֲבָה וּבְרָצוֹן שַׁבַּת קָדְשֶׁךָ וְיָנוּחוּ בָהּ יִשְׂרָאֵל מְקַדְּשֵׁי שְׁמֶךָ) וְטַהֵר לִבֵּנוּ לְעָבְדְּךָ בֶּאֱמֶת כִּי אַתָּה אֱלֹהִים אֱמֶת וּדְבָרְךָ אֱמֶת וְקַיָּם לָעַד: בָּרוּךְ אַתָּה יהוה מֶלֶךְ עַל כָּל־הָאָרֶץ מְקַדֵּשׁ (הַשַּׁבָּת וְ) יִשְׂרָאֵל וְיוֹם הַזִּכָּרוֹן: ←

meleḥ al kol ha'aretz mekadesh (hashabbat ve) yisrael veyom hazikaron.

5. AVODAH / WORSHIP

Take pleasure GRACIOUS ONE, our God, in Israel your people; lovingly accept their fervent prayer. May Israel's worship always be acceptable to you.

And may our eyes behold your homecoming, with merciful intent, to Zion. Blessed are you, THE FAITHFUL ONE, who brings your presence home to Zion.

6. HODA'AH / THANKS

We give thanks to you that you are THE ALL-MERCIFUL, our God, God of our ancestors, today and always. A firm, enduring source of life, a shield to us in time of trial, you are ever there, from age to age. We acknowledge you, declare your praise, and thank you for our lives entrusted to your hand, our souls placed in your care, for your miracles that greet us every day, and for your wonders and the good things that are with us every hour, morning, noon, and night. Good One, whose kindness never stops, Kind One, whose loving acts have never failed—always have we placed our hope in you.

For all these things, your name be blessed and raised in honor always, sovereign of ours, forever. And write down for a good life all the people of your covenant.

Let all of life acknowledge you! May all beings praise your name in truth, O God, our rescue and our aid. Blessed are you, THE GRACIOUS ONE, whose name is good, to whom all thanks are due. ↵

רְצֵה יהוה אֱלֹהֵינוּ בְּעַמְּךָ יִשְׂרָאֵל וְלִתְפִלָּתָם תִּפְלָּתָם בְּאַהֲבָה תְקַבֵּל בְּרָצוֹן וּתְהִי לְרָצוֹן תָּמִיד עֲבוֹדַת יִשְׂרָאֵל עַמֶּךָ:

וְתֶחֱזֶינָה עֵינֵינוּ בְּשׁוּבְךָ לְצִיּוֹן בְּרַחֲמִים: בָּרוּךְ אַתָּה יהוה הַמַּחֲזִיר שְׁכִינָתוֹ לְצִיּוֹן:

‏6‏ הוֹדָאָה

מוֹדִים אֲנַחְנוּ לָךְ שָׁאַתָּה הוּא יהוה אֱלֹהֵינוּ וֵאלֹהֵי אֲבוֹתֵינוּ וְאִמּוֹתֵינוּ לְעוֹלָם וָעֶד צוּר חַיֵּינוּ מָגֵן יִשְׁעֵנוּ אַתָּה הוּא לְדוֹר וָדוֹר: נוֹדֶה לְּךָ וּנְסַפֵּר תְּהִלָּתֶךָ עַל חַיֵּינוּ הַמְּסוּרִים בְּיָדֶךָ וְעַל נִשְׁמוֹתֵינוּ הַפְּקוּדוֹת לָךְ וְעַל נִסֶּיךָ שֶׁבְּכָל יוֹם עִמָּנוּ וְעַל נִפְלְאוֹתֶיךָ וְטוֹבוֹתֶיךָ שֶׁבְּכָל עֵת עֶרֶב וָבֹקֶר וְצָהֳרָיִם: הַטּוֹב כִּי לֹא כָלוּ רַחֲמֶיךָ וְהַמְרַחֵם כִּי לֹא תַמּוּ חֲסָדֶיךָ מֵעוֹלָם קִוִּינוּ לָךְ:

וְעַל כֻּלָּם יִתְבָּרַךְ וְיִתְרוֹמַם שִׁמְךָ מַלְכֵּנוּ תָּמִיד לְעוֹלָם וָעֶד: וּכְתֹב לְחַיִּים טוֹבִים כָּל־בְּנֵי בְרִיתֶךָ:

וְכֹל הַחַיִּים יוֹדוּךָ סֶּלָה וִיהַלְלוּ אֶת שִׁמְךָ בֶּאֱמֶת הָאֵל יְשׁוּעָתֵנוּ וְעֶזְרָתֵנוּ סֶלָה: בָּרוּךְ אַתָּה יהוה הַטּוֹב שִׁמְךָ וּלְךָ נָאֶה לְהוֹדוֹת: ←

KAVANAH. So often we use our spare moments to reflect on the unpleasant places in our lives, our resentments, vindictiveness, pain, victimization. We need to create a litany of our blessings. Take a minute. Close your eyes. Think of seven blessings in your life. Create this menorah of thankfulness. Whenever you say *modim anaḥnu laḥ* or light the Sabbath candles or have a spare moment, recite the blessings on your menorah of thankfulness.

Z.S.S.

7. BIRKAT HASHALOM / BLESSING FOR PEACE

The following paragraph is said only when the Amidah is recited aloud.

Our God, our ancients' God,
bless us with the threefold blessing
spoken from the mouth of Aaron and his sons, as is said:
May THE ETERNAL bless you
and protect you.   Let it be God's will!
May THE ETERNAL'S face give light
to you, and show you favor.   Let it be God's will!
May THE ETERNAL'S face be lifted
toward you, and bestow upon you
peace.   Let it be God's will!

COMMENTARY. Traditionally the Priestly Blessing was done by the male descendants of the *kohanim.* In some congregations the *sheliaḥ tzibur* (service leader) recites the blessing, and the congregation responds with "*Ken yehi ratzon.*" In other communities all the members of the congregation wrap arms and tallitot around each other and recite the blessing together. Another way to enact the Priestly Blessing is for each congregant to turn to a neighbor and recite the first half of each blessing, while the neighbor responds with the second half of the blessing. Michael M. Cohen

COMMENTARY. Rabbi Lavy Becker of Montreal noticed that when this blessing was pronounced in the synagogue of Pisa, all the children gathered under the sheltering wings of their fathers' tallitot to receive it. He recognized this "as a reconstruction of the ancient priestly ceremony." He modified that custom so that those wearing a tallit share it with their neighbors and all are under the sheltering wings of the Sheḥinah as we bless each other. It is now an established part of Canadian Reconstructionist practice. E.M.

יברכך...שלום / May...peace (Numbers 6:24-26).

The following paragraph is said only when the Amidah is recited aloud.

אֱלֹהֵֽינוּ וֵאלֹהֵי אֲבוֹתֵֽינוּ וְאִמוֹתֵֽינוּ בָּרְכֵֽנוּ בַּבְּרָכָה הַמְשֻׁלֶּֽשֶׁת הָאֲמוּרָה מִפִּי אַהֲרֹן וּבָנָיו כָּאָמוּר:

יְבָרֶכְךָ יהוה וְיִשְׁמְרֶֽךָ.

כֵּן יְהִי רָצוֹן:

יָאֵר יהוה פָּנָיו אֵלֶֽיךָ וִיחֻנֶּֽךָּ:

כֵּן יְהִי רָצוֹן:

יִשָּׂא יהוה פָּנָיו אֵלֶֽיךָ וְיָשֵׂם לְךָ שָׁלוֹם:

כֵּן יְהִי רָצוֹן:

Eloheynu veylohey avoteynu ve'imoteynu
bare<u>h</u>enu babera<u>h</u>ah hamshule<u>sh</u>et
ha'amurah mipi aharon uvanav ka'amur:

Yevare<u>h</u>e<u>h</u>a adonay veyishmere<u>h</u>a.   Ken yehi ratzon.
Ya'er adonay panav ele<u>h</u>a vi<u>h</u>une<u>h</u>a.   Ken yehi ratzon.
Yisa adonay panav ele<u>h</u>a veyasem le<u>h</u>a shalom.   Ken yehi ratzon.

Grant peace, goodness and blessing in the world,
grace, love, and mercy
over us and over all your people Israel.
Bless us, source of being, all of us, as one
amid your light,
for by your light,
WISE ONE, our God, you give to us
Torah of life, and love of kindness,
justice, blessing, mercy, life, and peace.
So may it be a good thing in your eyes,
to bless your people Israel, and all peoples,
with abundant strength and peace.

In the book of life, blessing, and peace, and proper sustenance,
may we be remembered and inscribed,
we and all your people, the house of Israel,
for a good life and for peace.

Blessed are you, COMPASSIONATE ONE, maker of peace.

The silent Amidah traditionally concludes with bowing and taking three steps back.
When chanting aloud, continue with Avinu Malkenu, *page 451, except on Shabbat, when*
the service continues on page 461.

KAVANAH. Try to imagine a time of true peace and tranquility, and think
about your part in helping this time to come about. What can you do?
What can you commit to? How will *you* be a peacemaker?   L.G.B.

שִׂים שָׁלוֹם טוֹבָה וּבְרָכָה בָּעוֹלָם חֵן וָחֶסֶד וְרַחֲמִים עָלֵינוּ וְעַל כָּל־
יִשְׂרָאֵל עַמֶּךָ: בָּרְכֵנוּ אָבִינוּ כֻּלָּנוּ כְּאֶחָד בְּאוֹר פָּנֶיךָ: כִּי בְאוֹר פָּנֶיךָ
נָתַתָּ לָּנוּ יהוה אֱלֹהֵינוּ תּוֹרַת חַיִּים וְאַהֲבַת חֶסֶד וּצְדָקָה וּבְרָכָה
וְרַחֲמִים וְחַיִּים וְשָׁלוֹם: וְטוֹב בְּעֵינֶיךָ לְבָרֵךְ אֶת־עַמְּךָ יִשְׂרָאֵל וְאֶת־
כָּל־הָעַמִּים בְּרָב־עֹז וְשָׁלוֹם:

בְּסֵפֶר חַיִּים בְּרָכָה וְשָׁלוֹם וּפַרְנָסָה טוֹבָה נִזָּכֵר וְנִכָּתֵב לְפָנֶיךָ אֲנַחְנוּ
וְכָל־עַמְּךָ בֵּית יִשְׂרָאֵל לְחַיִּים טוֹבִים וּלְשָׁלוֹם:
בָּרוּךְ אַתָּה יהוה עוֹשֵׂה הַשָּׁלוֹם:

Sim shalom tovah uveraḥah ba'olam ḥen vaḥesed veraḥamim
aleynu ve'al kol yisra'el ameḥa. Bareḥenu avinu kulanu ke'eḥad
be'or paneḥa. Ki ve'or paneḥa natata lanu adonay eloheynu torat
ḥayim ve'ahavat ḥesed utzedakah uveraḥah veraḥamim veḥayim
veshalom. Vetov be'eyneyḥa levareḥ et ameḥa yisra'el ve'et kol
ha'amim berov oz veshalom.
Besefer ḥayim beraḥah veshalom ufarnasah tovah nizaḥer
venikatev lefaneḥa anaḥnu veḥol ameḥa beyt yisra'el leḥayim
tovim uleshalom.
Baruḥ atah adonay osey hashalom.

The silent Amidah traditionally concludes with bowing and taking three steps back.
When chanting aloud, continue with Avinu Malkenu, *page 452, except on Shabbat, when*
the service continues on page 462.

RIBONO SHEL OLAM /
CONCLUDING MEDITATION

Sovereign of the universe,
fulfill my heart's petitions for the good.
Let me be worthy to perform your will with a whole heart.
Deliver me from the inclination to do evil,
and give me my portion in your Torah.
May I merit, with all Israel, your people,
that your Presence dwell upon us.
Make evident among us
the spirit of wisdom and understanding,
the spirit of counsel and strength,
the spirit of knowledge and the awe of THE CREATOR.
May divine love surround the one
who trusts in THE ETERNAL.

May my words of prayer, and my heart's meditation
be seen favorably, PRECIOUS ONE,
my rock, my champion.

May the one who creates harmony above
make peace for us and for all Israel,
and for all who dwell on earth.
And say: Amen.

רִבּוֹנוֹ שֶׁל עוֹלָם

רִבּוֹנוֹ שֶׁל עוֹלָם מַלֵּא מִשְׁאֲלוֹת לִבִּי לְטוֹבָה וְזַכֵּנִי לַעֲשׂוֹת רְצוֹנְךָ
בְּלֵבָב שָׁלֵם: מַלְּטֵנִי מִיֵּצֶר הָרָע וְתֵן חֶלְקִי בְּתוֹרָתֶךָ: זַכֵּנִי עִם כָּל
יִשְׂרָאֵל עַמֶּךָ שֶׁתִּשְׁרֶה שְׁכִינָתְךָ עָלֵינוּ וְהוֹפַע עָלֵינוּ רוּחַ חָכְמָה
וּבִינָה רוּחַ עֵצָה וּגְבוּרָה רוּחַ דַּעַת וְיִרְאַת יהוה:
וְהַבּוֹטֵחַ בַּיהוה חֶסֶד יְסוֹבְבֶנּוּ.
יִהְיוּ לְרָצוֹן אִמְרֵי פִי וְהֶגְיוֹן לִבִּי לְפָנֶיךָ יהוה צוּרִי וְגוֹאֲלִי:

עוֹשֶׂה שָׁלוֹם בִּמְרוֹמָיו הוּא יַעֲשֶׂה שָׁלוֹם עָלֵינוּ וְעַל כָּל יִשְׂרָאֵל וְעַל
כָּל יוֹשְׁבֵי תֵבֵל וְאִמְרוּ אָמֵן:

שכינתך / *sheḥinateḥa* / your Presence. This term is one of the most frequent
ways of speaking of God in rabbinic and mystical tradition. The term
derives from Exodus 25:8: "And I shall dwell in their midst (*veshaḥanti
betoḥam*)." God's Presence coming to dwell in the Tabernacle was believed
to be the normal outcome of the priestly sacrificial labors. When Israel's
Second Temple was destroyed, the belief arose that God continues to
dwell among Israelites during study and prayer. "If two sit and there are
words of Torah between them, the Sheḥinah dwells with them" (Pirkey
Avot 3:3). J.R.

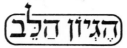

MEDITATIONS / AMIDAH ALTERNATIVES

In the time of your life, live—so that in that good time there shall be no ugliness or death for yourself or for any life your life touches.

Seek goodness everywhere, and when it is found, bring it out of its hiding place and let it be free and unashamed.

Place in matter and in flesh the least of the values, for these are the things that hold death and must pass away.

Discover in all things that which shines and is beyond corruption.

Encourage virtue in whatever heart it may have been driven into secrecy and sorrow by the shame and terror of the world.

Ignore the obvious, for it is unworthy of the clear eye and the kindly heart.

Be the inferior of no one, nor of anyone be the superior. Remember that everyone is a variation of yourself. No one's guilt is not yours, nor is anyone's innocence a thing apart....

In the time of your life, live—so that in that wondrous time you shall not add to the misery and sorrow of the world, but shall smile to the infinite delight and mystery of it.

William Saroyan

A man went from village to village, everywhere asking the same question, "Where can I find God?" He journeyed from rabbi to rabbi, and nowhere was he satisfied with the answers he received, so he would pack his bags, and hurry on to the next village. Some of the rabbis replied, "Pray, and you will find God." But the man had tried to pray, and knew that he could not. And some replied, "Study and you will find God." But the more he read, the more confused he became, and the further he seemed from God. Others replied, "Forget your quest. God is within you." But the man had tried to find God within himself and failed. ⤺

One day, the man arrived wearily at a very small village set in the middle of a forest. He approached a woman who was tending some chickens. She asked whom he could be looking for in such a small place, and she did not seem surprised when he told her that he was looking for God. She showed him to the rabbi's house.

When he went in, the rabbi was studying. He waited a moment, but impatient to be off to the next village if he could not be satisfied, he interrupted. "Rabbi—how do I find God?" The rabbi paused, and the man wondered which of the many answers he had already received he would be told this time. But the rabbi simply said, "You have come to the right place. God is in this village. Why don't you stay a few days; you might find God here."

The man was puzzled. He did not understand what the rabbi could mean. But the answer was unusual, and so he stayed. For several days, he strode round and round, asking all the villagers where God was that morning, but they would only smile and ask him to have a meal with them. Gradually, he got to know them and even helped with some of the village work. Every now and then he would see the rabbi by chance, and the rabbi would ask him, "Have you met God yet?" The man would smile, and sometimes he understood and sometimes he did not understand. For months he stayed in the village, and then for years. He became part of the village and shared in all its life. He went to *shul* with the villagers every Friday night. Sometimes he knew why he prayed, and sometimes he didn't. And sometimes he really said prayers, and sometimes only words. And then he would return with one of them for a *Shabbos* meal, and when they talked about God, he was always assured that God was in the village, though he wasn't quite sure where or when God could be found. Gradually, he too began to believe that God was in the village, though he wasn't quite sure where. He knew, however, that sometimes he had encountered God. ⤺

Time passed and the rabbi came to him and said, "You have met God now, have you not?" And the man responded, "I think that I have. But I am not sure why I met God, or how, or when. And why is God in this village only?"

So the rabbi replied, "God is not a person or a thing. You cannot meet God in that way. When you came to our village, you were so absorbed in your question that you could not recognize an answer when you heard it. Nor could you recognize God when you met God, because you were not really looking for God. Now that you have stopped pursuing God, you have found God. Now you can return to your town if you wish."

So, the man went back to his town, and God went with him. And the man knew that God was within himself and within other people. And other people knew it too, and sometimes they would ask him, "Where can we find God?" And the man would always answer, "You have come to the right spot. God is in this place."

Jeffrey Newman

If you have no past you have no future either, you are a foundling in this world, with no father or mother, without tradition, without duties to what comes after you, the future, the eternal. If you serve only yourself, you measure and weigh everything against yourself—there is nothing for you to strive towards. You have moods, but no character; desires, but no will—no great love, no great hate—you [merely] flirt with life....

I. L. Peretz

Our commitment to the redeeming deed applies, in the first place, to life within the human community. We take it as our task to enhance each person's potential for realizing the divine image, remembering that each of us bears a portrait unique and vital to the wholeness of God. But how clear can that portrait be when its bearer is suffering from hunger? Or from political oppression? Or from domestic bondage? Or when the person is hurting self and others, due to a compulsion from which it seems impossible to break free? If we are going to enhance the divine image in this world, we must work to maximize human freedom, always remembering that it was only after we came out of bondage that we were able to look toward God's mountain.

That commitment to freedom also includes helping people to create the sorts of lives and social structures to allow that freedom a lasting and secure home. Our Judaism lives in those two essential moments when we discover God. *We celebrate (and guard) our freedom, knowing God at the Sea, and we build a community that lives in God's presence, knowing God at the mountain...*Religious humanism, as I understand it, means a realization that the task is ours to do; we no longer wait for the divine hand, separate from our own, to come and save. This acceptance of responsibility is itself a sacred act for us. We seek to accept, with deeply humbling gratitude, the role of actor for divine compassion in the world of physical reality. The voice of God *does* speak to us at Sinai, but it is none other than the voice of Moses. The hands and feet of God *do* bring redemption, but they are none other than our own limbs, offered by us to our Maker in order to fulfill their true purpose.

Arthur Green

Additional meditations can be found on pages 1-20.
Avinu Malkenu *is on page 451,* Kaddish Titkabal *is on page 461.*

AMIDAH CHANTED ON YOM KIPPUR MORNING

The Yom Kippur morning service begins with Birhot Hashahar *(page 139) and* Pesukey Dezimra. *It continues with the Shema and its blessings (page 277). Some communities continue by chanting the Amidah that follows here. Others continue with a silent Amidah (page 739) and then continue here. The Amidah is traditionally recited while standing, beginning with three steps forward and bowing, left and right, a reminder of our entry into the divine presence.*

Open my lips, BELOVED ONE,
and let my mouth declare your praise.

1. AVOT VE'IMOT / ANCESTORS

Blessed are you, ANCIENT ONE, our God, God of our ancestors,

God of Abraham	God of Sarah
God of Isaac	God of Rebekah
God of Jacob	God of Rachel
	and God of Leah;

DERASH. Acknowledging our ancestors reminds us that what we are is shaped by who they were. Just as an acorn is shaped by the oak that preceded it and yet gives birth to a tree uniquely its own, so we are shaped by our ancestors yet give rise to a Judaism all our own.   R.M.S.

COMMENTARY. Throughout the centuries the pursuit of meaningful communal prayer has led to variations in the Amidah. These variations reflect the attitudes and beliefs of different prayer communities. In the ongoing pursuit of meaningful prayer, changes have been introduced into the Amidah, most notably in the first two of the seven *berahot* which comprise the Yom Kippur Amidah. The first *berahah* includes the matriarchs along with the patriarchs as exemplars of God's presence in human lives. By concentrating on examples of healing forces and life-sustaining rains, the second *berahah* acknowledges God as the power that sustains life. The traditional emphasis on God's ability to resurrect the dead has been replaced here by a celebration of God as the power that sustains all life.   S.S.

עֲמִידָה

The Yom Kippur morning service begins with Birhot Hashahar *(page 140) and* Pesukey Dezimra. *It continues with the Shema and its blessings (page 278). Some communities continue by chanting the Amidah that follows here. Others continue with a silent Amidah (page 740) and then continue here. The Amidah is traditionally recited while standing, beginning with three steps forward and bowing, left and right, a reminder of our entry into the divine presence.*

אֲדֹנָי שְׂפָתַי תִּפְתָּח וּפִי יַגִּיד תְּהִלָּתֶךָ:

אָבוֹת וְאִמּוֹת

בָּרוּךְ אַתָּה יהוה אֱלֹהֵינוּ וֵאלֹהֵי אֲבוֹתֵינוּ וְאִמּוֹתֵינוּ

אֱלֹהֵי שָׂרָה	אֱלֹהֵי אַבְרָהָם
אֱלֹהֵי רִבְקָה	אֱלֹהֵי יִצְחָק
אֱלֹהֵי רָחֵל	אֱלֹהֵי יַעֲקֹב
וֵאלֹהֵי לֵאָה: ←	

Baruh atah adonay eloheynu veylohey avoteynu ve'imoteynu
> elohey avraham   elohey sarah
> elohey yitzhak   elohey rivkah
> elohey ya'akov   elohey rahel
>   veylohey le'ah

KAVANAH. The opening of the Amidah calls to mind previous generations, near as well as distant. Take a few moments to think about your parents, your grandparents, other relatives about whom you may have heard stories. What is your connection with them?   L.G.B.

אדוני...תהלתך / Open...praise (Psalms 51:17).

COMMENTARY. Invoking our ancestors: some communities link the names of the patriarchs and matriarchs, others recite the names of the men and then the women, or the women and then the men. There is value, as well as conflict, in each model. Linking the ancestors reminds us of the importance of relationships, in time and space. Separating them reminds us of the significance of preserving our individuality.   R.H.

great, heroic, awesome God, supreme divinity,
imparting deeds of kindness, begetter of all;
mindful of the loyalty of Israel's ancestors,
bringing, with love, redemption to their children's children
for the sake of the divine name.

By the counsel of the sages and the wise,
and by the knowledge of all learned in our ways,
may my mouth be opened, and my prayers arise,
to entreat the sovereign full of mercy and compassion,
who forgives and pardons all transgression.

Remember us for life,
our sovereign, who wishes us to live,
and write us in the Book of Life,
for your sake, ever-living God.

Regal One, our help, salvation, and protector:
Blessed are you, KIND ONE,
the shield of Abraham and help of Sarah. ↵

כתבנו בספר החיים/and write us in the Book of Life. The persistence of
mythic motifs such as a heavenly ledger suggests that for all our
intellectual advances over our ancestors, we remain emotionally rooted in
the language and images they created. We no longer believe that Someone
is deciding today if we are entered in the Book of Life, yet no less than
our ancestors do we desire that we be granted the gift of being here next
Yom Kippur!   R.H.

COMMENTARY. This version of the first berahah in the Amidah includes the
matriarchs as well as the patriarchs. The phrase "help of Sarah," ezrat
sarah, comes from a Hebrew root (עזר) which can mean either "save" or
"be strong." This parallels the meaning of magen/shield. The biblical text
says that Abraham experienced God as a shield and that Sarah experienced
God as a helper. Their experience and the example of their lives can
enrich our own. Just as Abraham and Sarah found the strength to face the
unknown physical and spiritual dangers of their journey, so we seek to
find the courage and inspiration to meet the challenges of own time.
                                                                  R.S.

הָאֵל הַגָּדוֹל הַגִּבּוֹר וְהַנּוֹרָא אֵל עֶלְיוֹן גּוֹמֵל חֲסָדִים טוֹבִים וְקוֹנֶה הַכֹּל וְזוֹכֵר חַסְדֵי אָבוֹת וְאִמּוֹת וּמֵבִיא גְאֻלָּה לִבְנֵי בְנֵיהֶם לְמַעַן שְׁמוֹ בְּאַהֲבָה:

מִסּוֹד חֲכָמִים וּנְבוֹנִים וּמִלֶּמֶד דַּעַת מְבִינִים אֶפְתְּחָה פִּי בִּתְפִלָּה וּבְתַחֲנוּנִים לְחַלּוֹת וּלְחַנֵּן פְּנֵי מֶלֶךְ מָלֵא רַחֲמִים מוֹחֵל וְסוֹלֵחַ לַעֲוֹנִים:

זָכְרֵנוּ לְחַיִּים מֶלֶךְ חָפֵץ בַּחַיִּים וְכָתְבֵנוּ בְּסֵפֶר הַחַיִּים לְמַעַנְךָ אֱלֹהִים חַיִּים:

מֶלֶךְ עוֹזֵר וּמוֹשִׁיעַ וּמָגֵן: בָּרוּךְ אַתָּה יהוה מָגֵן אַבְרָהָם וְעֶזְרַת שָׂרָה: ←

Ha'el hagadol hagibor vehanora el elyon gomel ḥasadim tovim vekoney hakol vezoḥer ḥasdey avot ve'imot umevi ge'ulah livney veneyhem lema'an shemo be'ahavah.

Misod ḥaḥamim unevonim umilemed da'at mevinim efteḥah fi bitefilah uvetaḥanunim leḥalot uleḥanen peney meleḥ maley raḥamim moḥel vesole'aḥ la'avonim.

Zoḥrenu leḥayim meleḥ ḥafetz baḥayim veḥotvenu besefer haḥayim lema'aneḥa elohim ḥayim.

Meleḥ ozer umoshi'a umagen. Baruḥ atah adonay magen avraham ve'ezrat sarah. ↵

2. GEVUROT / DIVINE POWER

You are forever powerful, ALMIGHTY ONE,
abundant in your saving acts. You send down the dew.
In loyalty you sustain the living,
nurturing the life of every living thing,
upholding those who fall,
healing the sick, freeing the captive,
and remaining faithful to all life
held dormant in the earth.
Who can compare to you, almighty God,
who can resemble you, the source of life and death,
who makes salvation grow?

Who can compare to you, source of all mercy,
remembering all creatures mercifully, decreeing life!

Faithful are you in giving life to every living thing.
Blessed are you, THE FOUNT OF LIFE,
who gives and renews life. ⤶

DERASH. In the *Gevurot*, I address the power that underlies all change when I say: *atah gibor* /you—power! Then I name the manifestations of change inherent in my observation of nature and humanity: the blowing wind and the falling rain, those who fall down and need support, the sick who are becoming well, the bound who become free. Though aware of loss, we shift our focus to the power of renewal. We call this power "Flowering of Hope"—*Matzmiah yeshu'ah.*   S.P.W.

אַתָּה גִבּוֹר לְעוֹלָם אֲדֹנָי רַב לְהוֹשִׁיעַ: מוֹרִיד הַטָּל: מְכַלְכֵּל חַיִּים
בְּחֶסֶד מְחַיֶּה כָּל חַי בְּרַחֲמִים רַבִּים סוֹמֵךְ נוֹפְלִים וְרוֹפֵא חוֹלִים
וּמַתִּיר אֲסוּרִים וּמְקַיֵּם אֱמוּנָתוֹ לִישֵׁנֵי עָפָר: מִי כָמוֹךָ בַּעַל גְּבוּרוֹת
וּמִי דוֹמֶה לָּךְ מֶלֶךְ מֵמִית וּמְחַיֶּה וּמַצְמִיחַ יְשׁוּעָה:

מִי כָמוֹךָ אַב הָרַחֲמִים זוֹכֵר יְצוּרָיו לְחַיִּים בְּרַחֲמִים:

וְנֶאֱמָן אַתָּה לְהַחֲיוֹת כָּל חָי: בָּרוּךְ אַתָּה יהוה מְחַיֶּה כָּל חָי: ←

Atah gibor le'olam adonay rav lehoshi'a.
Morid hatal.
Mehalkel hayim behesed mehayey kol hay berahamim rabim
someh noflim verofey holim umatir asurim umekayem emunato
lisheney afar. Mi hamoha ba'al gevurot umi domeh lah meleh
memit umehayeh umatzmi'ah yeshu'ah.

Mi hamoha av harahamim zoher yetzurav lehayim berahamim.
Vene'eman atah lehahayot kol hay. Baruh atah adonay mehayey
kol hay. ↵

3. KEDUSHAT HASHEM /
HALLOWING GOD'S NAME

And so, raise up the name of THE ETERNAL ONE, our God,
  bow down before God's holy mount,
    for holy is THE AWESOME ONE, our God!

Raise up the name of the **A**lmighty one,
  the one who dwells in awe,
    for God is holy,
      By God's breath the heavens came to birth!

Raise up the name of **G**reatness,
  all you congregation of the just,
    for God is holy,
      and **D**eclares just things, relating mighty deeds!

Raise up the name of **H**oliness,
  of the exalted one on high, for God is holy,
    One whose every act is awesome to the world!

Raise up the name of the all-mindful one,
  who **Z**ealously has kept our covenant of old,
    for God is holy,
      Hewing mightily the flames of heavenly fire!

Raise up the name of one **T**otally pure,
  the one who hurls forth thunderbolts,
    for God is holy,
      Joining together the foundation of the earth! ↵

וּבְכֵן רוֹמְמוּ יהוה אֱלֹהֵינוּ וְהִשְׁתַּחֲווּ לְהַר קָדְשׁוֹ
כִּי קָדוֹשׁ יהוה אֱלֹהֵינוּ:

אַדִּיר וְנוֹרָא	רוֹמְמוּ
בְּרוּחוֹ שָׁמַיִם שִׁפְרָה:	כִּי קָדוֹשׁ הוּא
גְּדֻלָּתוֹ בִּקְהַל יְשָׁרִים	רוֹמְמוּ
דּוֹבֵר צְדָקוֹת מַגִּיד מֵישָׁרִים:	כִּי קָדוֹשׁ הוּא
הַנַּעֲרָץ בִּקְדֻשָּׁה	רוֹמְמוּ
וְהִלּוּכוֹ בִּקְדֻשָּׁה:	כִּי קָדוֹשׁ הוּא
זוֹכֵר בְּרִית אָבוֹת	רוֹמְמוּ
חוֹצֵב לֶהָבוֹת:	כִּי קָדוֹשׁ הוּא
טָהוֹר שׁוֹלֵחַ בְּרָקִים	רוֹמְמוּ
יוֹסֵד אֲרָקִים: ←	כִּי קָדוֹשׁ הוּא

רוֹמְמוּ יהוה...יהוה אלהנו / raise up the name of the ETERNAL ONE...AWESOME
ONE, our God! (Psalms 99:9).

Raise up the name of the Creator's throne,
  which God has founded in the heights,
    for God is holy,
      Linking the wise by artful plan, amassing wisdom
      in the world!

Raise up the name of the all-Merciful,
  who makes wrongdoing vanish like a cloud,
    for God is holy,
      Nobly holding out a hand to all who stray!

Raise up the name of a divinity
  So ancient that the world can never reckon by its years,
    for God is holy,
      Examining the hearts of everything that lives!

Raise up the name of saving Power,
  who redeems all those who serve in faith,
    for God is holy,
      Sources of righteousness and truth to all created
      in the world!

Raise up the name of the Creator of the heavens and the earth,
  for God is holy,
    one whose gaze can Reach the farthest corners
    of the world!

Raise up the name of the Sovereign eternal one,
  for God is holy, and
    The name and fame of God are one!

רוֹמְמוּ   כִּסְאוֹ הֵכִין בִּשְׁמֵי רוּמָה

כִּי קָדוֹשׁ הוּא   לוֹכֵד חֲכָמִים בְּעָרְמָה:

רוֹמְמוּ   מוֹחֶה כָעָב פְּשָׁעִים

כִּי קָדוֹשׁ הוּא   נוֹתֵן יָד לַפּוֹשְׁעִים:

רוֹמְמוּ   שַׂגִּיא שָׁנָיו לְאֵין חֵקֶר

כִּי קָדוֹשׁ הוּא   עֶשְׁתּוֹנוֹת חוֹקֵר:

רוֹמְמוּ   פּוֹדֶה נֶפֶשׁ עֲבָדָיו

כִּי קָדוֹשׁ הוּא   צַדִּיק קוֹשְׁט מַעֲבָדָיו:

רוֹמְמוּ   קוֹנֵה שָׁמַיִם וָאָרֶץ

כִּי קָדוֹשׁ הוּא   רָם הַמַּבִּיט לְקַצְוֹת הָאָרֶץ:

רוֹמְמוּ   שׁוֹכֵן עַד וְקָדוֹשׁ שְׁמוֹ

כִּי קָדוֹשׁ הוּא   תְּהִלָּתוֹ כִּשְׁמוֹ:

And so, the holy reaches up to you,
for you are our God.

All-knowing God! To whom can I compare you?
No being can resemble you.
By what metaphor can I describe you?
Your imprint is inscribed in all of nature.
Greater by far than any chariot that bears you,
more rarified than any medium of thought.
Does any person's word suffice to capture you?
Whose tongue could possibly encompass you?
Who fully comprehends your counsel?
No god precedes you in the world.
This world is witness to your being alone.
There is no reality apart from you.
How visible your wisdom in all things!
A sign of you is present in all life.
The world had not yet come to be,
the pillars of the skies had not yet stood,
yet you were there already, dwelling everywhere,
before the heights and depths were yet defined.
Containing everything, and being contained by none,
you filled the universe, nothing encompassed you.
Let hearts and minds exhaust their store of words,
and tongues grow weary trying to explain. ﬤ

וּלְךָ תַּעֲלֶה קְדֻשָּׁה כִּי אַתָּה אֱלֹהֵינוּ:

אֱלֹהִים אֶל־מִי אֲמַשִּׁילֶךָ	וְאֵין עֲרוֹךְ אֵלֶיךָ:
בַּמָּה אֲדַמֶּךָ	וְכָל־דְּמוּת טֶבַע חוֹתָמֶךְ:
גָּבַהְתָּ מִכָּל־מֶרְכָּבָה	וְגָאִיתָ מִכָּל־מַחֲשָׁבָה:
דִּבֵּר מִי יְכַלְכְּלֶךָ	וּלְשׁוֹן מִי תְּכִילֶךָ:
הֲיֵשׁ לֵבָב יְגוּרְךָ	וְיֵשׁ עַיִן תְּשׁוּרֶךָ:
וְאֶת־מִי נוֹעַצְתָּ וַיְבִינֶךָ	וְלֹא נוֹצַר אֵל לְפָנֶיךָ:
זֶה עוֹלָמְךָ יְעִידֶךָ	כִּי אֵין בִּלְעָדֶיךָ:
חָכְמָתְךָ בַּכֹּל מְבֹאֶרֶת	וְאוֹת חוֹתָמְךָ נִכֶּרֶת:
טֶרֶם הָרִים יֻלָּדוּ	וְעַמּוּדֵי־שַׁחַק עָמָדוּ:
יָשַׁבְתָּ מוֹשַׁב אֱלֹהִים	וְאֵין עֲמָקִים וְאֵין גְּבוֹהִים:
כִּלְכַּלְתָּ הַכֹּל וְלֹא יְכַלְכְּלוּךָ	וּמִלֵּאתָ הַכֹּל וְלֹא יְכִלוּךְ:
לִבָּבוֹת עָמְדוּ מִלִּדְרוֹשׁ	וּלְשׁוֹנוֹת נִלְאוּ מִלְּפָרֵשׁ: ←

COMMENTARY. This acrostic illustrates the paradox of our relationship with God in its form and content. God is repeatedly addressed as you—a most tender, intimate, relational term. This is the form of the prayer. It is a conversation between familiars. The content emphasizes the otherness of God, the unattainability of divine perfection, the unknowability of divine depth, scope, strength and splendor. It is in the human experience of godliness, in the realization of godly attributes of righteousness and faith, that the bridge between form and content is constructed. This bridge is known as *kedushah*—holiness. S.P.W.

Multitudes of sages are confounded,
ideas so quickly fail to capture what you are.
"Noble and awesome" you are called in songs of praise,
but you remain beyond all praise.
So great in strength, how wondrous is your life!
You fill the heavens and the earth.
Outreaching every depth and height, beyond all distances,
no one can capture the dimensions of your being.
Perhaps through deeds alone can you be known,
by faith, in holy congregations, are you grasped.
Chiefly through your justice are you heard or understood,
and through your Torah are your ways made known.
Close by are you, and intimate, to those who turn to you,
though far from those who go astray.
Readily have those who purify themselves beheld you,
they do not need a lamp to seek you out.
Surely they have heard you with the ears of mind and spirit,
even when their hearing has grown dim.
Throughout all time do they proclaim your holiness:
"Holy, holy, holy, THE CREATOR of all worlds!"

Today—as life and death are being written
in the Book of Memory—
Arise!
Please waken!
Please be stirred!
Please stand!
Please come forward!
Please get up!
Please pray!
For this soul,
implore now
the attention
of the One who dwells above!

מַחְשְׁבוֹת חֲכָמִים יִתְמָֽהוּ   וְרַעְיוֹנֵי מְהִירִים יִתְמַהְמָֽהוּ:

נוֹרָא תְהִלּוֹת נִקְרֵֽאתָ   וְעַל כָּל־תְּהִלָּה נַעֲלֵֽיתָ:

שַׂגִּיא כֹחַ אֵיךְ נִפְלֵֽאתָ   וְהַשָּׁמַֽיִם וְהָאָֽרֶץ מָלֵֽאתָ:

עֹמֶק עָמֹק מִי יִמְצָאֶֽנּוּ   וְרָחוֹק רָחוֹק מִי יִרְאֶֽנּוּ:

פְּעָלֶֽיךָ הֵם הַדְּרוּשִׁים   אַף אֱמוּנָתְךָ בִּקְהַל קְדוֹשִׁים:

צִדְקָתְךָ הִיא הַנִּשְׁמָֽעַת   וְתוֹרָתְךָ הִיא הַנּוֹדָֽעַת:

קָרְבָתְךָ קְרוּבָה לַשָּׁבִים   וּרְחוֹקָה מְאֹד מִן הַשּׁוֹבָבִים:

רָאוֹךְ הַנְּשָׁמוֹת הַטְּהוֹרוֹת   וְלֹא נִצְרְכוּ לִמְאוֹרוֹת:

שְׁמָעֽוּךָ בְּאָזְנֵי רַעְיוֹנֵיהֶם   כִּי תֶחֱרַֽשְׁנָה אָזְנֵיהֶם:

תָּמִיד קְדֻשָּׁתְךָ קוֹרְאוֹת   קָדוֹשׁ קָדוֹשׁ קָדוֹשׁ יהוה צְבָאוֹת:

הַיּוֹם יִכָּתֵב בְּסֵֽפֶר הַזִּכְרוֹנוֹת הַחַיִּים וְהַמָּֽוֶת: אָֽנָּא כַנֶּה עֽוּרִי נָא הִתְעוֹרְרִי נָא עִמְדִי נָא הִתְיַצְּבִי נָא קֽוּמִי נָא חַלִּי נָא בְּעַד הַנֶּֽפֶשׁ חֲנִי נָא פְּנֵי דַר עֶלְיוֹן:

And so, let all proclaim the sovereignty
   of God, the arbiter of justice;
who brings soul-searching on the day of justice,
   going into hidden places with the eye of justice;
who demands accounting on the day of justice,
   holding up our thoughts to scrutiny in justice;
wise one, who is loving on the day of justice,
   seeking our redemption in the covenant of justice;
having mercy for all creatures on the day of justice,
   thoroughly renewing those who trust in justice;
informed of every thought upon the day of justice,
   keeping wrath away while governing in justice;
like one clad in righteousness upon the day of justice,
   merciful toward wrongdoing, though bringing justice;
noble and awesome on the day of justice,
   sparing all those burdened with the weight of justice;
answering whoever calls upon the day of justice,
   putting kindness foremost, though enacting justice;
searching hidden virtues on the day of justice,
   calling forth the willingness to serve in justice;
redeeming lovingly God's people on the day of justice,
   showing love and mercy in pursuit of justice,
tenderly supporting all who seek perfection
   on the day of justice!

לָאֵל עוֹרֵךְ דִּין

לְגוֹלֶה עֲמֻקּוֹת בַּדִּין	לְבוֹחֵן לְבָבוֹת בְּיוֹם דִּין
לְהוֹגֶה דֵעוֹת בַּדִּין	לְדוֹבֵר מֵישָׁרִים בְּיוֹם דִּין
לְזוֹכֵר בְּרִיתוֹ בַּדִּין	לְוָתִיק וְעוֹשֶׂה חֶסֶד בְּיוֹם דִּין
לְטַהֵר חוֹסָיו בַּדִּין	לְחוֹמֵל מַעֲשָׂיו בְּיוֹם דִּין
לְכוֹבֵשׁ כַּעְסוֹ בַּדִּין	לְיוֹדֵעַ מַחֲשָׁבוֹת בְּיוֹם דִּין
לְמוֹחֵל עֲוֹנוֹת בַּדִּין	לְלוֹבֵשׁ צְדָקוֹת בְּיוֹם דִּין
לְסוֹלֵחַ לַעֲמוּסָיו בַּדִּין	לְנוֹרָא תְהִלּוֹת בְּיוֹם דִּין
לְפוֹעֵל רַחֲמָיו בַּדִּין	לְעוֹנֶה לְקוֹרְאָיו בְּיוֹם דִּין
לְקוֹנֶה עֲבָדָיו בַּדִּין	לְצוֹפֶה נִסְתָּרוֹת בְּיוֹם דִּין
לְשׁוֹמֵר אוֹהֲבָיו בַּדִּין	לְרַחֵם עַמּוֹ בְּיוֹם דִּין

לְתוֹמֵךְ תְּמִימָיו בְּיוֹם דִּין:

Uveḥen leḥa hakol yaḥtiru
le'el oreḥ din

levoḥen levavot beyom din
ledover meysharim beyom din
levatik ve'oseh ḥesed beyom din
leḥomel ma'asav beyom din
leyode'a mahashavot beyom din
lelovesh tzedakot beyom din
lenora tehilot beyom din
le'oneh lekorav beyom din
letzofeh nistarot beyom din
leraḥem amo beyom din

legoleh amukot badin
lehogeh de'ot badin
lezoḥer berito badin
letaher ḥosav badin
leḥovesh kaso badin
lemoḥel avonot badin
lesoleaḥ la'amusav badin
lefo'el raḥamav badin
lekoneh avadav badin
leshomer ohavav badin

letomeḥ temimav beyom din.

We exalt you and declare you holy,
according to the mystery of the murmurings
of the holy seraphim,
who declare the holiness of your Name,
as it is written by your prophets:
"And each celestial being calls to another and exclaims:
Holy, holy, holy is THE CREATOR of the Multitudes of Heaven!
All the world is filled with divine glory!"

God's glory fills the world,
as the ministering angels ask, one to another,
"What place could contain God's holiness?"
And they are answered with a blessing:
"Blessed is the glory of THE OMNIPRESENT,
wherever God may dwell!"

And from God's place, God mercifully turns,
bestowing graciousness upon the people
who declare the oneness of the divine name
evening and morning, each day continually,
as twice a day they say, with love: "Shema!"
"Listen, Israel: THE ETERNAL is our God,
THE ETERNAL ONE alone!" ↵

וקרא...כבודו / And...glory! (Isaiah 6:3).
ברוך...ממקומו / Blessed...dwell! (Ezekiel 3:12).
שמע...אחד / Listen...alone! (Deuteronomy 6:4).

נַעֲרִיצְךָ וְנַקְדִּישְׁךָ כְּסוֹד שִׂיחַ שַׂרְפֵי קֹדֶשׁ הַמַּקְדִּישִׁים שִׁמְךָ בַּקֹּדֶשׁ כַּכָּתוּב עַל יַד נְבִיאֶךָ: וְקָרָא זֶה אֶל זֶה וְאָמַר

קָדוֹשׁ קָדוֹשׁ קָדוֹשׁ

יהוה צְבָאוֹת מְלֹא כָל־הָאָרֶץ כְּבוֹדוֹ:
כְּבוֹדוֹ מָלֵא עוֹלָם מְשָׁרְתָיו שׁוֹאֲלִים זֶה לָזֶה אַיֵּה מְקוֹם כְּבוֹדוֹ לְעֻמָּתָם בָּרוּךְ יֹאמֵרוּ:
בָּרוּךְ כְּבוֹד יהוה מִמְּקוֹמוֹ:
מִמְּקוֹמוֹ הוּא יִפֶן בְּרַחֲמִים וְיָחֹן עַם הַמְיַחֲדִים שְׁמוֹ עֶרֶב וָבֹקֶר בְּכָל יוֹם תָּמִיד פַּעֲמַיִם בְּאַהֲבָה שְׁמַע אוֹמְרִים:
← שְׁמַע יִשְׂרָאֵל יהוה אֱלֹהֵינוּ יהוה אֶחָד:

Na'aritzeha venakdisheha kesod si'ah sarfey kodesh hamakdishim shimeha bakodesh kakatuv al yad nevi'eha vekara zeh el zeh ve'amar:
Kadosh kadosh kadosh adonay tzeva'ot melo hol ha'aretz kevodo.
Kevodo maley olam mesharetav sho'alim zeh lazeh ayey mekom kevodo le'umatam baruh yomeru:
Baruh kevod adonay mimekomo.
Mimekomo hu yifen berahamim veyahon am hamyahadim shemo erev vavoker behol yom tamid pa'amayim be'ahavah shema omrim:
Shema yisra'el adonay eloheynu adonay ehad. ⤸

COMMENTARY. The structure of the *Kedushah* rests upon myths in Jewish tradition about angelic choruses praising God. By standing at attention and singing words ascribed to the angelic chorus, we imitate the heavenly chorus. Jews traditionally rock upward on their toes each time the word קדוש/*kadosh*/holy is chanted here. It is as if we were straining upward to join the heavenly choir in the purity of our praise for God. D.A.T.

This is our God.
This is our source.
This is our sovereign.
This is our saving power.
And this one, mercifully,
shall declare a second time,
for every living being to hear,
confirming God's divinity for you:
"I am the OMNIPRESENT ONE, your God!"

O, mighty one, our mighty one,
THE SOVEREIGN who watches over us,
how mighty is your name throughout the earth!
The time shall come that GOD will reign
throughout the earth. On that day
shall THE FOUNT OF LIFE be one,
the divine name be one.
And as is written in your sacred words of psalm:
"May THE ETERNAL reign forever,
your God, O Zion, from one generation to the next. Halleluyah!"

From one generation to the next
may we declare your greatness,
and for all eternities may we affirm your holiness,
And may your praise, our God,
never be absent from our mouths
now and forever.
For you are a great and holy God. ↩

אני...אלהיכם / I...God! (Numbers 15:41).
יהוה אדנינו...הארץ / The SOVEREIGN...earth! (Psalms 8:10).
והיה יהוה...אחד / The time...be one (Zechariah 14:9).
ימלך...הללויה / May...Halleluyah! (Psalms 146:10).

הוּא אֱלֹהֵינוּ הוּא אָבִינוּ הוּא מַלְכֵּנוּ הוּא מוֹשִׁיעֵנוּ וְהוּא יַשְׁמִיעֵנוּ בְּרַחֲמָיו שֵׁנִית לְעֵינֵי כָּל חָי: לִהְיוֹת לָכֶם לֵאלֹהִים

אֲנִי יהוה אֱלֹהֵיכֶם:

אַדִּיר אַדִּירֵנוּ יהוה אֲדֹנֵינוּ מָה־אַדִּיר שִׁמְךָ בְּכָל־הָאָרֶץ: וְהָיָה יהוה לְמֶלֶךְ עַל־כָּל־הָאָרֶץ בַּיּוֹם הַהוּא יִהְיֶה יהוה אֶחָד וּשְׁמוֹ אֶחָד: וּבְדִבְרֵי קָדְשְׁךָ כָּתוּב לֵאמֹר:

יִמְלֹךְ יהוה לְעוֹלָם אֱלֹהַיִךְ צִיּוֹן לְדֹר וָדֹר הַלְלוּיָהּ:

לְדוֹר וָדוֹר נַגִּיד גָּדְלֶךָ וּלְנֵצַח נְצָחִים קְדֻשָּׁתְךָ נַקְדִּישׁ וְשִׁבְחֲךָ אֱלֹהֵינוּ מִפִּינוּ לֹא יָמוּשׁ לְעוֹלָם וָעֶד כִּי אֵל מֶלֶךְ גָּדוֹל וְקָדוֹשׁ אָתָּה: ←

Hu eloheynu hu avinu hu malkeynu hu moshi'eynu vehu yashmi'enu berahamav shenit le'eyney kol hay lihyot lahem leylohim ani adonay eloheyhem.
Adir adirenu adonay adoneynu mah adir shimeha behol ha'aretz vehayah adonay lemeleh al kol ha'aretz bayom hahu yihyeh adonay ehad ushemo ehad.
Uvdivrey kodsheha katuv lemor.
Yimloh adonay le'olam elohayih tziyon ledor vador halleluyah.
Ledor vador nagid godleha ulnetzah netzahim kedushateha nakdish veshivhaha eloheynu mipinu lo yamush le'olam va'ed ki el meleh gadol vekadosh atah. ↵

If the remainder of the Amidah is being read silently, it is customary to remain standing until the completion of the Amidah. If the remainder of the Amidah is being chanted aloud, it is customary to be seated here.

And therefore, HOLY ONE, let awe of you
infuse the whole of your Creation,
and let knowledge of your presence
dwell in all your creatures.
And let every being worship you,
and each created life pay homage to your rule.
Let all of them, as one, enact your bidding
with a whole and peaceful heart.
For we have always known, ALMIGHTY ONE,
that all authority to rule belongs to you,
all strength is rooted in your arm,
all mighty deeds have emanated from your hand.
Your name alone is the source of awe
that surges through all life.

And therefore, HOLY ONE, let awe of you
infuse your people, let the praise of you
ring out from all who worship you.
Let hope enliven all who seek you,
and let all who look to you with hope
find strength to speak.
Grant joy throughout your Land,
let happiness resound throughout your holy city,
soon, and in our days.

And therefore, let the just behold your peace,
let them rejoice and celebrate,
let all who follow in your path sing out with glee,
let all who love you dance with joy,
and may your power overwhelm all treachery,
so that it vanishes wholly from the earth like smoke.
Then shall the power of injustice pass away!

If the remainder of the Amidah is being read silently, it is customary to remain standing until the completion of the Amidah. If the remainder of the Amidah is being chanted aloud, it is customary to be seated here.

וּבְכֵן תֵּן פַּחְדְּךָ יהוה אֱלֹהֵינוּ עַל כָּל־מַעֲשֶׂיךָ וְאֵימָתְךָ עַל כָּל־מַה־שֶּׁבָּרָאתָ וְיִירָאוּךָ כָּל־הַמַּעֲשִׂים וְיִשְׁתַּחֲווּ לְפָנֶיךָ כָּל־הַבְּרוּאִים וְיֵעָשׂוּ כֻלָּם אֲגֻדָּה אַחַת לַעֲשׂוֹת רְצוֹנְךָ בְּלֵבָב שָׁלֵם כְּמוֹ שֶׁיָּדַעְנוּ יהוה אֱלֹהֵינוּ שֶׁהַשִּׁלְטוֹן לְפָנֶיךָ עֹז בְּיָדְךָ וּגְבוּרָה בִּימִינֶךָ וְשִׁמְךָ נוֹרָא עַל כָּל־מַה־שֶּׁבָּרָאתָ:

וּבְכֵן תֵּן כָּבוֹד יהוה לְעַמֶּךָ תְּהִלָּה לִירֵאֶיךָ וְתִקְוָה לְדוֹרְשֶׁיךָ וּפִתְחוֹן פֶּה לַמְיַחֲלִים לָךְ שִׂמְחָה לְאַרְצֶךָ וְשָׂשׂוֹן לְעִירֶךָ בִּמְהֵרָה בְיָמֵינוּ:

וּבְכֵן צַדִּיקִים יִרְאוּ וְיִשְׂמָחוּ וִישָׁרִים יַעֲלֹזוּ וַחֲסִידִים בְּרִנָּה יָגִילוּ וְעוֹלָתָה תִּקְפָּץ־פִּיהָ וְכָל־הָרִשְׁעָה כֻּלָּהּ כְּעָשָׁן תִּכְלֶה כִּי תַעֲבִיר מֶמְשֶׁלֶת זָדוֹן מִן הָאָרֶץ: ←

COMMENTARY. The *Uveḥen* prayer speaks out of an awareness that the Divine holiness can reach its fullness only when it is allowed to infuse the entire world. This will be possible only when the vision of Yom Kippur—each human being transformed in thought and deed by an awareness of God's presence and demand—takes hold not only within every Jew, but within all who inhabit our world. Thus even on Yom Kippur we experience only a part of the Divine holiness. This prayer asks of us that we rededicate ourselves not only to our own holiness but to that of our world. D.A.T.

May you alone be sovereign over all of your Creation,
and Mt. Zion be the seat and symbol of your glory,
and Jerusalem, your holy city—
as is written in your holy scriptures:
"The Eternal One shall reign forever,
your God, O Zion, through all generations!
Halleluyah!"

Holy are you,
and awe-inspiring is your name,
and there is no God apart from you,
as it is written: "The Creator of the hosts of heaven
shall be exalted through the rule of law,
and God, the Holy One, made holy by the reign of justice."
Blessed are you, Eternal One,
the holy sovereign power. ↵

It is customary to be seated here.

וְתִמְלֹךְ אַתָּה יהוה לְבַדֶּךָ עַל כָּל־מַעֲשֶׂיךָ בְּהַר צִיּוֹן מִשְׁכַּן כְּבוֹדֶךָ
וּבִירוּשָׁלַיִם עִיר קָדְשֶׁךָ: כַּכָּתוּב בְּדִבְרֵי קָדְשֶׁךָ:

יִמְלֹךְ יהוה לְעוֹלָם אֱלֹהַיִךְ צִיּוֹן לְדֹר וָדֹר הַלְלוּיָהּ:

קָדוֹשׁ אַתָּה וְנוֹרָא שְׁמֶךָ וְאֵין אֱלוֹהַּ מִבַּלְעָדֶיךָ: כַּכָּתוּב: וַיִּגְבַּהּ יהוה
צְבָאוֹת בַּמִּשְׁפָּט וְהָאֵל הַקָּדוֹשׁ נִקְדַּשׁ בִּצְדָקָה: בָּרוּךְ אַתָּה יהוה
הַמֶּלֶךְ הַקָּדוֹשׁ: ←

It is customary to be seated here.

הללויה...יְמלֹך / THE ETERNAL...Halleluyah! (Psalms 146:10).
בצדקה...ויגבה / THE CREATOR...justice (Isaiah 5:16).

4. KEDUSHAT HAYOM / THE DAY'S HOLINESS

On Shabbat add the words in parenthesis.

You have loved us, and have taken pleasure in us,
and have made us holy with your mitzvot,
and you have brought us, sovereign one,
near to your service,
and have called us to the shelter of your great and holy name.
And you gave us, HOLY ONE, our God, with love,
(this day of Shabbat, for holiness and rest, and)
this Day of Atonement,
for pardon, for forgiveness, and for atonement,
a day for pardoning all of our wrongful acts,
(with love,)
a holy convocation,
a remembrance of the going out from Egypt.

Our God, our ancients' God, may our prayer arise and come to you, and be beheld, and be acceptable. Let it be heard, acted upon, remembered—the memory of us and all our needs, the memory of our ancestors, the memory of messianic hopes, the memory of Jerusalem your holy city, and the memory of all your kin, the house of Israel, all surviving in your presence. Act for goodness and grace, for love and care; for life, well-being and peace, on this Day of Atonement.

Remember us this day, ALL-KNOWING ONE, our God, for goodness. Favor us this day with blessing. Preserve us this day for life. With your redeeming nurturing word, be kind and generous. Act tenderly on our behalf, and grant us victory over all our trials. Truly, our eyes turn toward you, for you are a providing God; gracious and merciful are you.

קְדֻשַּׁת הַיּוֹם

On Shabbat add the words in parenthesis.

אַתָּה אֲהַבְתָּנוּ וְרָצִיתָ בָּנוּ וְקִדַּשְׁתָּנוּ בְּמִצְוֹתֶיךָ וְקֵרַבְתָּנוּ מַלְכֵּנוּ לַעֲבוֹדָתֶךָ וְשִׁמְךָ הַגָּדוֹל וְהַקָּדוֹשׁ עָלֵינוּ קָרָאתָ:

וַתִּתֶּן־לָנוּ יהוה אֱלֹהֵינוּ בְּאַהֲבָה אֶת־יוֹם (הַשַּׁבָּת הַזֶּה לִקְדֻשָּׁה וְלִמְנוּחָה וְאֶת־יוֹם) הַכִּפּוּרִים הַזֶּה לִמְחִילָה וְלִסְלִיחָה וּלְכַפָּרָה וְלִמְחָל־בּוֹ אֶת־כָּל־עֲוֹנוֹתֵינוּ (בְּאַהֲבָה) מִקְרָא קֹדֶשׁ זֵכֶר לִיצִיאַת מִצְרָיִם:

אֱלֹהֵינוּ וֵאלֹהֵי אֲבוֹתֵינוּ וְאִמּוֹתֵינוּ יַעֲלֶה וְיָבוֹא וְיַגִּיעַ וְיֵרָאֶה וְיֵרָצֶה וְיִשָּׁמַע וְיִפָּקֵד וְיִזָּכֵר זִכְרוֹנֵנוּ וּפִקְדוֹנֵנוּ וְזִכְרוֹן אֲבוֹתֵינוּ וְאִמּוֹתֵינוּ וְזִכְרוֹן יְמוֹת הַמָּשִׁיחַ וְזִכְרוֹן יְרוּשָׁלַיִם עִיר קָדְשֶׁךָ וְזִכְרוֹן כָּל עַמְּךָ בֵּית יִשְׂרָאֵל לְפָנֶיךָ לִפְלֵיטָה וּלְטוֹבָה וּלְחֵן וּלְחֶסֶד וּלְרַחֲמִים לְחַיִּים וּלְשָׁלוֹם בְּיוֹם הַכִּפּוּרִים הַזֶּה:

זָכְרֵנוּ יהוה אֱלֹהֵינוּ בּוֹ לְטוֹבָה: וּפָקְדֵנוּ בוֹ לִבְרָכָה וְהוֹשִׁיעֵנוּ בוֹ לְחַיִּים: וּבִדְבַר יְשׁוּעָה וְרַחֲמִים חוּס וְחָנֵּנוּ וְרַחֵם עָלֵינוּ וְהוֹשִׁיעֵנוּ כִּי אֵלֶיךָ עֵינֵינוּ כִּי אֵל מֶלֶךְ חַנּוּן וְרַחוּם אָתָּה:

Remember, for our sake,
the ancestral covenant, as you have promised:

"And I shall remember my covenant with Jacob,
and, as well, my covenant with Isaac,
and, as well, my covenant with Abraham,
I shall remember them, and shall recall
the Land I promised them."

Leviticus 26:42

Remember, for our sake,
the covenant of former times, as you have promised:

"And I shall remember, for their sake,
the covenant of former times,
whereby I brought them from the land of Egypt,
in the sight of all the nations,
to become their God,
I am THE LAWGIVER!"

Leviticus 26:45

Have mercy on us, and do not destroy us, as it is written:

"For THE FOUNT OF MERCY is a God compassionate,
who shall not let you wither, and shall not destroy you,
nor shall God forget the covenant made with your ancestors,
the one promised by oath to them."

Deuteronomy 4:31

Open up our hearts to love and to revere your name,
as it is written:

"THE BOUNTIFUL, your God, shall circumcise your hearts,
and your children's hearts,
to love THE FOUNT OF LIFE, your God,
with all your heart, with all your soul,
that you might live."

Deuteronomy 30:6

זְכָר־לָֽנוּ בְּרִית אָבוֹת כַּאֲשֶׁר אָמַֽרְתָּ:
וְזָכַרְתִּי אֶת־בְּרִיתִי יַעֲקוֹב וְאַף אֶת־בְּרִיתִי יִצְחָק וְאַף אֶת־בְּרִיתִי אַבְרָהָם אֶזְכֹּר וְהָאָֽרֶץ אֶזְכֹּר:

זְכָר־לָֽנוּ בְּרִית רִאשׁוֹנִים כַּאֲשֶׁר אָמַֽרְתָּ:
וְזָכַרְתִּי לָהֶם בְּרִית רִאשׁוֹנִים אֲשֶׁר הוֹצֵֽאתִי־אֹתָם מֵאֶֽרֶץ מִצְרַֽיִם לְעֵינֵי הַגּוֹיִם לִהְיוֹת לָהֶם לֵאלֹהִים אֲנִי יהוה:

רַחֵם עָלֵֽינוּ וְאַל תַּשְׁחִיתֵֽנוּ כְּמָה שֶׁכָּתוּב:
כִּי אֵל רַחוּם יהוה אֱלֹהֶֽיךָ לֹא יַרְפְּךָ וְלֹא יַשְׁחִיתֶֽךָ וְלֹא יִשְׁכַּח אֶת־בְּרִית אֲבֹתֶֽיךָ אֲשֶׁר נִשְׁבַּע לָהֶם:

מוֹל אֶת־לְבָבֵֽנוּ לְאַהֲבָה אֶת שְׁמֶֽךָ כְּמָה שֶׁכָּתוּב:
וּמָל יהוה אֱלֹהֶֽיךָ אֶת־לְבָבְךָ וְאֶת־לְבַב זַרְעֶֽךָ לְאַהֲבָה אֶת־יהוה אֱלֹהֶֽיךָ בְּכָל־לְבָבְךָ וּבְכָל־נַפְשְׁךָ לְמַֽעַן חַיֶּֽיךָ: ←

COMMENTARY. How can we be in a covenant with the Creator of all? How do we dare ask to be remembered with compassion? Where in our hearts is the capacity to reach out beyond the known, the limited, the failures of our lives to imagine something different? Our ancestors have bequeathed it all to us—the covenant, the memory, the compassion and the imagination. Do we dare accept our inheritance?   S.P.W.

COMMENTARY. ומל יהוה אלהיך את לבבך/your God shall circumcise your hearts. Jewish tradition links circumcision to covenantal commitment and to purification. The heart, which the rabbis understood to be the seat of the intellect, is not physically circumcised but, through divine will, purified and rededicated to covenantal service. The act of circumcision creates a wound and makes the one who is circumcised vulnerable. The poet here freely offers our vulnerability, our openness to transformation, as part of our Yom Kippur prayer for purification.   D.A.T.

Be present for us when we call on you, as it is written:

> "And you shall seek out THE BELOVED ONE, your God,
> from where you are, and you shall find God,
> provided that you search for God
> with all your heart, and all your soul."
>
> Deuteronomy 4:29

Blot out our sins upon this day, and purify us,
as it is written:

> "For on this day, atonement shall be made for you,
> to make you clean from all your wrongdoings.
> Before THE FOUNT OF MERCY, you shall all be clean."
>
> Leviticus 16:30

∽

Return us, BLESSED ONE, let us return!
Renew our days, as you have done of old! Lamentations 5:21

הַמָּצֵא לָנוּ בְּבַקָּשָׁתֵנוּ כְּמָה שֶׁכָּתוּב:

וּבִקַּשְׁתֶּם מִשָּׁם אֶת־יהוה אֱלֹהֶיךָ וּמָצָאתָ כִּי תִדְרְשֶׁנּוּ בְּכָל־לְבָבְךָ
וּבְכָל־נַפְשֶׁךָ:

כַּפֵּר חַטָּאֵינוּ בַּיּוֹם הַזֶּה וְטַהֲרֵנוּ כְּמָה שֶׁכָּתוּב:

כִּי־בַיּוֹם הַזֶּה יְכַפֵּר עֲלֵיכֶם לְטַהֵר אֶתְכֶם מִכֹּל חַטֹּאתֵיכֶם לִפְנֵי יהוה
תִּטְהָרוּ:

⁂

הֲשִׁיבֵנוּ יהוה אֵלֶיךָ וְנָשׁוּבָה חַדֵּשׁ יָמֵינוּ כְּקֶדֶם:

Hashivenu adonay eleha venashuva ḥadesh yameynu kekedem.

Hear our voices, ETERNAL ONE, our God,
and accept our prayer with mercy and good will.
Turn us, ANCIENT ONE, toward you, let us return.
Renew our days like days of old.
Do not cast us away
from dwelling in your presence,
and do not remove your holy spirit from our midst.
And do not cast us off as we grow old;
do not forsake us when our strength departs.
Do not forsake us, GENTLE ONE, our God,
do not withdraw from us.
Give us a sign of blessing,
so that anyone who bears us ill
shall hesitate to harm us.
For truly, you, ETERNAL ONE,
have always helped us and consoled us.
Hear now our words, GOD OF COMPASSION,
and behold our contemplation.
May our words of prayer,
and meditations of our hearts,
be seen favorably, PRECIOUS ONE, our rock, our champion.
For we place our hope in you, ETERNAL ONE,
so may you answer us, Almighty One, our God.

COMMENTARY. This is one of the most well known and dramatic prayers of the High Holy Day liturgy, yet it is fraught with problematic images—a God who might reject the infirm, who might cast out the aged, who might ignore our vulnerability were it not for our pleading. This *piyut* is popular not for what it implies about God but for what it says about us: I am weaker than I usually admit. I fear the inevitable loss of power that comes with getting older. I fear my vulnerability. I need the support of others to compensate for my frailty. I need the protection of others to compensate for my foolishness. I need the community of others for my legacy to live when my life is gone. You who are here praying with me can make possible this, my redemption. We pray for the strength to make God present for each other, that the weakest, oldest, frailest might find consolation and a sign of blessing.   D.A.T.

יהוה אֱלֹהֵינוּ חוּס וְרַחֵם עָלֵינוּ וְקַבֵּל בְּרַחֲמִים

וּבְרָצוֹן אֶת־תְּפִלָּתֵנוּ:

הֲשִׁיבֵנוּ יהוה אֵלֶיךָ וְנָשׁוּבָה חַדֵּשׁ יָמֵינוּ כְּקֶדֶם:

אַל תַּשְׁלִיכֵנוּ מִלְּפָנֶיךָ וְרוּחַ קָדְשְׁךָ אַל תִּקַּח מִמֶּנּוּ:

אַל תַּשְׁלִיכֵנוּ לְעֵת זִקְנָה כִּכְלוֹת כֹּחֵנוּ אַל תַּעַזְבֵנוּ:

אַל תַּעַזְבֵנוּ יהוה אֱלֹהֵינוּ אַל תִּרְחַק מִמֶּנּוּ:

עֲשֵׂה עִמָּנוּ אוֹת לְטוֹבָה וְיִרְאוּ שׂוֹנְאֵינוּ וְיֵבֹשׁוּ

כִּי אַתָּה יהוה עֲזַרְתָּנוּ וְנִחַמְתָּנוּ:

אֲמָרֵינוּ הַאֲזִינָה יהוה בִּינָה הֲגִיגֵנוּ:

יִהְיוּ לְרָצוֹן אִמְרֵי־פִינוּ וְהֶגְיוֹן לִבֵּנוּ לְפָנֶיךָ יהוה צוּרֵנוּ וְגוֹאֲלֵנוּ:

כִּי לְךָ יהוה הוֹחָלְנוּ אַתָּה תַעֲנֶה אֲדֹנָי אֱלֹהֵינוּ:

Shema kolenu adonay eloheynu ḥus veraḥem aleynu
vekabel beraḥamim uveratzon et tefilatenu.
Hashivenu adonay eleḥa venashuvah ḥadesh yameynu kekedem.
Al tashliḥenu milefaneḥa veru'aḥ kodsheḥa al tikaḥ mimenu.
Al tashliḥenu le'et ziknah kiḥlot koḥenu al ta'azvenu.
Al ta'azvenu adonay eloheynu al tirḥak mimenu.
Asey imanu ot letovah veyiru soneynu veyevoshu
ki atah adonay azartanu veniḥamtanu.
Amareynu ha'azinah adonay binah hagigenu.
Yihyu leratzon imrey finu vehegyon libenu lefaneḥa adonay
tzurenu vego'alenu.
Ki leḥa adonay hoḥalnu atah ta'aneh adonay eloheynu.

NOTE. After the first verse *Shema Kolenu* is composed of biblical verses
adapted by the poet.   M.B.K.

Our God, our ancients' God,
do not forsake us, and do not turn us away,
and do not cause us shame,
and do not nullify your covenant with us,
but bring us nearer to your Torah,
teach us your mitzvot,
instruct us in your ways.
Incline our hearts to treat your name with awe,
and open up our inner nature to your love,
and bring us back to you in truth,
with whole and peaceful heart.
And for the sake of your great name,
be merciful, and grant forgiveness for our wrongs,
as it is written in your prophet's words:

"For the sake of your great name, ETERNAL ONE,
forgive my wrongdoing, for I have done much wrong."

Our God, our ancients' God,
forgive us, pardon us, help us atone—
for we are your people, and you are our God,
we are your children, and you are our creator,
we are your servants, and you are our sovereign,
we are your community, and you are our portion,
we are your possession, and you are our fate,
we are your sheep, and you are our shepherd,
we are your vineyard, and you are our keeper,
we are your creation, and you are our fashioner,
we are your loved ones, and you are our beloved,
we are your treasure, and you are our kin,
we are your people, and you are our ruler,
we are your faithful, and you our source of faith! ↵

אֱלֹהֵינוּ וֵאלֹהֵי אֲבוֹתֵינוּ וְאִמּוֹתֵינוּ אַל תַּעַזְבֵנוּ וְאַל תִּטְּשֵׁנוּ וְאַל
תַּכְלִימֵנוּ וְאַל תָּפֵר בְּרִיתְךָ אִתָּנוּ קָרְבֵנוּ לְתוֹרָתֶךָ לַמְּדֵנוּ מִצְוֹתֶיךָ
הוֹרֵנוּ דְרָכֶיךָ הַט לִבֵּנוּ לְיִרְאָה אֶת־שְׁמֶךָ וּמוֹל אֶת־לְבָבֵנוּ לְאַהֲבָתֶךָ
וְנָשׁוּב אֵלֶיךָ בֶּאֱמֶת וּבְלֵב שָׁלֵם וּלְמַעַן שִׁמְךָ הַגָּדוֹל תִּמְחַל וְתִסְלַח
לַעֲוֹנֵינוּ כַּכָּתוּב בְּדִבְרֵי קָדְשֶׁךָ: לְמַעַן שִׁמְךָ יהוה וְסָלַחְתָּ לַעֲוֹנִי כִּי
רַב הוּא:

אֱלֹהֵינוּ וֵאלֹהֵי אֲבוֹתֵינוּ וְאִמּוֹתֵינוּ סְלַח לָנוּ: מְחַל לָנוּ: כַּפֶּר־לָנוּ:

אָנוּ בָנֶיךָ וְאַתָּה אָבִינוּ:	כִּי אָנוּ עַמֶּךָ וְאַתָּה אֱלֹהֵינוּ:
אָנוּ עֲבָדֶיךָ וְאַתָּה חֶלְקֵנוּ:	אָנוּ קְהָלֶךָ וְאַתָּה אֲדוֹנֵינוּ:
אָנוּ צֹאנֶךָ וְאַתָּה רוֹעֵנוּ:	אָנוּ נַחֲלָתֶךָ וְאַתָּה גוֹרָלֵנוּ:
אָנוּ פְעֻלָּתֶךָ וְאַתָּה יוֹצְרֵנוּ:	אָנוּ כַרְמֶךָ וְאַתָּה נוֹטְרֵנוּ:
אָנוּ סְגֻלָּתֶךָ וְאַתָּה קְרוֹבֵנוּ:	אָנוּ רַעְיָתֶךָ וְאַתָּה דוֹדֵנוּ:
אָנוּ מַאֲמִירֶךָ וְאַתָּה מַאֲמִירֵנוּ: ←	אָנוּ עַמֶּךָ וְאַתָּה מַלְכֵּנוּ:

Eloheynu velohey avoteynu ve'imoteynu selaḥ lanu. Meḥal lanu.
Kaper lanu.
Ki anu ameḥa ve'atah eloheynu. Anu vaneḥa ve'atah avinu.
Anu avadeḥa ve'atah adoneynu. Anu kehaleḥa ve'atah ḥelkenu.
Anu naḥalateḥa ve'atah goralenu. Anu tzoneḥa ve'atah ro'enu.
Anu ḥarmeḥa ve'atah notrenu. Anu fe'ulateḥa ve'atah yotzrenu.
Anu rayateḥa ve'atah dodenu. Anu segulateḥa ve'atah kerovenu.
Anu ameḥa ve'atah malkenu. Anu ma'amireḥa ve'atah ma'amirenu.

למען...רב הוא / For the sake of...wrong (Psalms 25:11).

This prayer sings of the exquisite mutuality between the Jewish people
and the Divine. One without the other has no meaningful existence. A
lover does not have reality without a beloved, and so it is with all the pairs
of mutuality. The Jewish people without a relationship to our God
(however we understand that term) may be no more than a scattered
collection of individuals. The Divine, cut off from a community of the
faithful, may be nothing more than a meaningless abstraction. S.P.W.

We are strong-willed and stubborn,
but you are merciful and gracious.
We are stiff-necked, but you are slow to anger.
We are full of error, but you are full of mercy.
We—our days are like a passing shadow,
but you are one whose years shall never end.
Our God, our ancients' God,
may our prayer come before you.
Hide not from our supplication,
for we are not so insolent and stubborn
as to say, here in your presence,
"HOLY ONE, God of our fathers and our mothers,
we are righteous, and we have not sinned,"
for we indeed have sinned. ↩

אָנוּ עַזֵּי פָנִים וְאַתָּה רַחוּם וְחַנּוּן: אָנוּ קְשֵׁי עֹרֶף וְאַתָּה אֶרֶךְ אַפַּיִם:
אָנוּ מְלֵאֵי עָוֹן וְאַתָּה מָלֵא רַחֲמִים: אָנוּ יָמֵינוּ כְּצֵל עוֹבֵר וְאַתָּה הוּא
וּשְׁנוֹתֶיךָ לֹא יִתַּמּוּ:

אֱלֹהֵינוּ וֵאלֹהֵי אֲבוֹתֵינוּ וְאִמּוֹתֵינוּ תָּבוֹא לְפָנֶיךָ תְּפִלָּתֵנוּ וְאַל
תִּתְעַלַּם מִתְּחִנָּתֵנוּ שֶׁאֵין אֲנַחְנוּ עַזֵּי פָנִים וּקְשֵׁי עֹרֶף לוֹמַר לְפָנֶיךָ
יהוה אֱלֹהֵינוּ וֵאלֹהֵי אֲבוֹתֵינוּ וְאִמּוֹתֵינוּ צַדִּיקִים אֲנַחְנוּ וְלֹא חָטָאנוּ
אֲבָל אֲנַחְנוּ חָטָאנוּ: ←

The community rises.

We have acted wrongly,
we have been untrue,
and we have gained unlawfully
and have defamed.
We have harmed others,
we have wrought injustice,
we have zealously transgressed,
and we have hurt
and have told lies.
We have improperly advised,
and we have covered up the truth,
and we have laughed in scorn.
We have misused responsibility
and have neglected others.
We have stubbornly rebelled.
We have offended,
we have perverted justice,
we have stirred up enmity,
and we have kept ourselves from change.
We have reached out to evil,
we have shamelessly corrupted
and have treated others with disdain.
Yes, we have thrown ourselves off course,
and we have tempted and misled. ↰

The community rises.

אָשַׁמְנוּ: בָּגַדְנוּ: גָּזַלְנוּ: דִּבַּרְנוּ דֹפִי:
הֶעֱוִינוּ: וְהִרְשַׁעְנוּ: זַדְנוּ: חָמַסְנוּ:
טָפַלְנוּ שֶׁקֶר: יָעַצְנוּ רָע: כִּזַּבְנוּ: לַצְנוּ:
מָרַדְנוּ: נִאַצְנוּ: סָרַרְנוּ: עָוִינוּ:
פָּשַׁעְנוּ: צָרַרְנוּ: קִשִּׁינוּ עֹרֶף: רָשַׁעְנוּ:
שִׁחַתְנוּ: תִּעַבְנוּ: תָּעִינוּ: תִּעְתָּעְנוּ: —←

Ashamnu. Bagadnu. Gazalnu. Dibarnu dofi.
He'evinu. Vehirshanu. Zadnu. Hamasnu.
Tafalnu shaker. Ya'atznu ra. Kizavnu. Latznu.
Maradnu. Ni'atznu. Sararnu. Avinu.
Pashanu. Tzararnu. Kishinu oref. Rashanu.
Shihatnu. Ti'avnu. Ta'inu. Titanu. ←

COMMENTARY. The *Ashamnu*, the short alphabetic acrostic confession, precedes the *Al Het*, the longer catalogue of sins for which we seek forgiveness. It is no easy task to confront our failings, still more daunting to name them, perhaps most difficult to speak them. We are first given the opportunity, as it were, to practice; we chant together a short series of statements of a general nature. As we draw our voices together, we move on to the lengthier and more specific listing of sins, strengthened by the presence of others who, like us, have also failed.   R.H.

424 / AMIDAH/VIDUI/CONFESSIONAL

We have turned away from your mitzvot,
and from your righteous laws,
as if it did not matter to us.
And you are just, whatever comes upon us,
for what you do is truth,
and we have done much wrong.

We have done wrong, and have rebelled.
And so, we were not ready for your help.
Place into our hearts the will
to leave behind the path of evil,
and so hasten our redemption and renewal—
as is written by your prophet's hand:
"Let the wicked leave behind their unjust way,
let the unworthy cast away their plans,
let them return to THE COMPASSIONATE, who will be merciful,
returning to our God, who shall abundantly forgive."

סַרְנוּ מִמִּצְוֹתֶיךָ וּמִמִּשְׁפָּטֶיךָ הַטּוֹבִים וְלֹא שָׁוָה לָנוּ: וְאַתָּה צַדִּיק עַל
כָּל־הַבָּא עָלֵינוּ כִּי־אֱמֶת עָשִׂיתָ וַאֲנַחְנוּ הִרְשָׁעְנוּ:

הִרְשַׁעְנוּ וּפָשַׁעְנוּ לָכֵן לֹא נוֹשָׁעְנוּ וְתֵן בְּלִבֵּנוּ לַעֲזֹב דֶּרֶךְ רֶשַׁע וְחִישׁ
לָנוּ יֶשַׁע כַּכָּתוּב עַל יַד נְבִיאֶךָ: יַעֲזֹב רָשָׁע דַּרְכּוֹ וְאִישׁ אָוֶן
מַחְשְׁבֹתָיו וְיָשֹׁב אֶל יהוה וִירַחֲמֵהוּ וְאֶל־אֱלֹהֵינוּ כִּי־יַרְבֶּה לִסְלוֹחַ:

ואתה...הרשענו / And...wrong (Nehemiah 9:33).
יעזב...לסלוח / Let...forgive (Isaiah 55:7).

What can we say before you,
you who dwell on high?
What can we tell you,
you who inhabit heaven's heights?
Are you not one who knows all things,
both hidden and revealed?

From eternity you have been called
"the One who passes over transgression."
So hear our cry as we stand here
in prayer before you.
Pass over the transgression
of a people who return from their transgressing.
Erase our guilt from before your eyes.

You know the secrets of the universe,
the most hidden recesses of all that lives.
You search the chambers of our inner being,
you examine the conscience and the heart.
There is nothing hidden from you,
nothing is concealed before your eyes.
So, let it be your will,
ETERNAL ONE, our God, God of our ancestors,
that you may grant forgiveness to us for all of our sins,
and be merciful to us for all of our injustices,
and let us atone for all we have done wrong: ⤶

מַה נֹּאמַר לְפָנֶיךָ יוֹשֵׁב מָרוֹם וּמַה נְּסַפֵּר לְפָנֶיךָ שׁוֹכֵן שְׁחָקִים: הֲלֹא
כָל הַנִּסְתָּרוֹת וְהַנִּגְלוֹת אַתָּה יוֹדֵעַ: שִׁמְךָ מֵעוֹלָם עוֹבֵר עַל פֶּשַׁע:
שַׁוְעָתֵנוּ תַאֲזִין בְּעָמְדֵנוּ לְפָנֶיךָ בִתְפִלָּה: תַּעֲבֹר עַל פֶּשַׁע לְעַם שָׁבֵי
פֶשַׁע: תִּמְחֶה פְּשָׁעֵינוּ מִנֶּגֶד עֵינֶיךָ:
אַתָּה יוֹדֵעַ רָזֵי עוֹלָם וְתַעֲלוּמוֹת סִתְרֵי כָל חָי: אַתָּה חוֹפֵשׂ כָּל חַדְרֵי
בָטֶן וּבוֹחֵן כְּלָיוֹת וָלֵב: אֵין דָּבָר נֶעְלָם מִמֶּךָ וְאֵין נִסְתָּר מִנֶּגֶד
עֵינֶיךָ: וּבְכֵן יְהִי רָצוֹן מִלְּפָנֶיךָ יהוה אֱלֹהֵינוּ וֵאלֹהֵי אֲבוֹתֵינוּ
וְאִמּוֹתֵינוּ שֶׁתִּסְלַח לָנוּ עַל כָּל חַטֹּאתֵינוּ וְתִמְחָל לָנוּ עַל כָּל עֲוֹנוֹתֵינוּ
וּתְכַפֶּר לָנוּ עַל כָּל פְּשָׁעֵינוּ: →

For the wrong that we have done before you
in the closing of the heart,
and for the wrong that we have done before you
without knowing what we do.
For the wrong that we have done before you
whether open or concealed,
and for the wrong that we have done before you
knowingly and by deceit.
For the wrong that we have done before you
through the prompting of the heart,
and for the wrong that we have done before you
through the influence of others.
For the wrong that we have done before you
whether by intention or mistake,
and for the wrong that we have done before you
by the hand of violence.
For the wrong that we have done before you
through our foolishness of speech,
and for the wrong that we have done before you
through an evil inclination.

And for them all, God of forgiveness,
please forgive us, pardon us, help us atone!

For the wrong that we have done before you
in the palming of a bribe,
and for the wrong that we have done before you
by expressions of contempt.
For the wrong that we have done before you
through misuse of food and drink,
and for the wrong that we have done before you
by our avarice and greed. ↩

וְעַל חֵטְא שֶׁחָטָאנוּ לְפָנֶיךָ בִּבְלִי דָעַת:

עַל חֵטְא שֶׁחָטָאנוּ לְפָנֶיךָ בַּגָּלוּי וּבַסֵּתֶר:

וְעַל חֵטְא שֶׁחָטָאנוּ לְפָנֶיךָ בְּדַעַת וּבְמִרְמָה:

עַל חֵטְא שֶׁחָטָאנוּ לְפָנֶיךָ בְּהַרְהוֹר הַלֵּב:

וְעַל חֵטְא שֶׁחָטָאנוּ לְפָנֶיךָ בִּוְעִידַת זְנוּת:

עַל חֵטְא שֶׁחָטָאנוּ לְפָנֶיךָ בְּזָדוֹן וּבִשְׁגָגָה:

וְעַל חֵטְא שֶׁחָטָאנוּ לְפָנֶיךָ בְּחֹזֶק יָד:

עַל חֵטְא שֶׁחָטָאנוּ לְפָנֶיךָ בְּטִפְשׁוּת פֶּה:

וְעַל חֵטְא שֶׁחָטָאנוּ לְפָנֶיךָ בְּיֵצֶר הָרָע:

וְעַל כֻּלָּם אֱלוֹהַּ סְלִיחוֹת סְלַח לָנוּ: מְחַל לָנוּ: כַּפֶּר־לָנוּ:

Ve'al kulam eloha seliḥot selaḥ lanu. Meḥal lanu. Kaper lanu.

עַל חֵטְא שֶׁחָטָאנוּ לְפָנֶיךָ בְּכַפַּת שֹׁחַד:

וְעַל חֵטְא שֶׁחָטָאנוּ לְפָנֶיךָ בְּלָצוֹן:

עַל חֵטְא שֶׁחָטָאנוּ לְפָנֶיךָ בְּמַאֲכָל וּבְמִשְׁתֶּה:

וְעַל חֵטְא שֶׁחָטָאנוּ לְפָנֶיךָ בְּנֶשֶׁךְ וּבְמַרְבִּית: ←

COMMENTARY. Often Jews mistakenly dismiss the reality of sin, substituting the gentler but weaker image of "missing the mark." This suggests that sin lies only in failing to do what we should rather than in failing to be who we should be.

Reducing sin to the status of an almost inadvertent error hardly seems tenable in the light of our awareness of the horrors of which humans, individually as well as collectively, have proved capable. The very nature of human nature lies before us as an open question.

There is a dark side to human nature, an impulse to evil which distorts and corrupts our best intentions. Rabbinic tradition teaches that each of us has a good as well as an evil inclination, the *yetzer hatov* and the *yetzer hara*. Sin is not only what we do, or do not do; it is also a question of who we are. In order to confess sin, we must first confront sin. R.H.

For the wrong that we have done before you
   through offensive gaze,
and for the wrong that we have done before you
   through a condescending glance.

And for them all, God of forgiveness,
   please forgive us, pardon us, help us atone!

For the wrong that we have done before you
   by our quickness to oppose,
and for the wrong that we have done before you
   by deception of a friend.
For the wrong that we have done before you
   by unwillingness to change,
and for the wrong that we have done before you
   by running to embrace an evil act.
For the wrong that we have done before you
   by our groundless hatred,
and for the wrong that we have done before you
   in the giving of false pledges.

And for them all, God of forgiveness,
   please forgive us, pardon us, help us atone! ↩

עַל חֵטְא שֶׁחָטָאנוּ לְפָנֶיךָ בְּשִׁקּוּר עָיִן:

וְעַל חֵטְא שֶׁחָטָאנוּ לְפָנֶיךָ בְּעֵינַיִם רָמוֹת:

וְעַל כֻּלָּם אֱלוֹהַּ סְלִיחוֹת סְלַח לָנוּ: מְחַל לָנוּ: כַּפֶּר-לָנוּ:

Ve'al kulam eloha seliḥot selaḥ lanu. Meḥal lanu. Kaper lanu.

עַל חֵטְא שֶׁחָטָאנוּ לְפָנֶיךָ בִּפְלִילוּת:

וְעַל חֵטְא שֶׁחָטָאנוּ לְפָנֶיךָ בִּצְדִיַּת רֵעַ:

עַל חֵטְא שֶׁחָטָאנוּ לְפָנֶיךָ בְּקַשְׁיוּת עֹרֶף:

וְעַל חֵטְא שֶׁחָטָאנוּ לְפָנֶיךָ בְּרִיצַת רַגְלַיִם לְהָרַע:

עַל חֵטְא שֶׁחָטָאנוּ לְפָנֶיךָ בִּשְׂנְאַת חִנָּם:

וְעַל חֵטְא שֶׁחָטָאנוּ לְפָנֶיךָ בִּתְשׂוּמֶת יָד:

וְעַל כֻּלָּם אֱלוֹהַּ סְלִיחוֹת סְלַח לָנוּ: מְחַל לָנוּ: כַּפֶּר-לָנוּ: ←

Ve'al kulam eloha seliḥot selaḥ lanu. Meḥal lanu. Kaper lanu. ↵

COMMENTARY. Why tap our hearts as we recite the *Vidui*? To remind ourselves that the collective responsibility for the wrongdoing in our community rests on each one of us. As we tap our chests, we might ask how we will make things different in our community this coming year.

D.A.T.

And for mitzvot that call on us to act,
and for mitzvot that bid us not to act,
for mitzvot that say: "Arise, and do...!"
and for mitzvot that do not say: "Arise, and do...!"
for those that are made known to us,
and those that are not known to us.

Those that are known to us
are things we have acknowledged
and confessed before you,
but those that are not known to us
are things revealed and known only to you,
as it is said: "The hidden things
belong to THE ETERNAL ONE, our God.
What is revealed belongs to us and to our children,
always and forever—all the matters
of this Torah that are ours to carry out."
For you are the source of all forgiveness,
the fount of mercy for each and every generation,
and apart from you we have no sovereign
so full of mercy and forgiveness, none but you.

The community is seated.
Continue on page 437.

וְעַל מִצְוַת עֲשֵׂה וְעַל מִצְוַת לֹא תַעֲשֶׂה בֵּין שֶׁיֵּשׁ־בָּהּ קוּם עֲשֵׂה וּבֵין שֶׁאֵין בָּהּ קוּם עֲשֵׂה אֶת־הַגְּלוּיִים לָנוּ וְאֶת־שֶׁאֵינָם גְּלוּיִים לָנוּ: אֶת־הַגְּלוּיִים לָנוּ כְּבָר אֲמַרְנוּם לְפָנֶיךָ וְהוֹדִינוּ לְךָ עֲלֵיהֶם וְאֶת־שֶׁאֵינָם גְּלוּיִים לָנוּ לְפָנֶיךָ הֵם גְּלוּיִים וִידוּעִים כַּדָּבָר שֶׁנֶּאֱמַר: הַנִּסְתָּרֹת לַיהוה אֱלֹהֵינוּ וְהַנִּגְלֹת לָנוּ וּלְבָנֵינוּ עַד עוֹלָם לַעֲשׂוֹת אֶת־כָּל־דִּבְרֵי הַתּוֹרָה הַזֹּאת כִּי אַתָּה סָלְחָן לְכָל־דּוֹר וָדוֹר וּמִבַּלְעָדֶיךָ אֵין לָנוּ מֶלֶךְ מוֹחֵל וְסוֹלֵחַ אֶלָּא אָתָּה:

The community is seated.
Continue on page 438.

הנסתרות...הזאת / The hidden...out (Deuteronomy 29:28).

ALTERNATIVE AL ḤET

We sin against God when we sin against ourselves;
for our failures of truth, we ask forgiveness;
for pretending to emotions we do not feel;
for using the sins of others to excuse our own;
for denying our responsibility for our own misfortunes;
for refusing to admit our share in the troubles of others;
for condemning in our children the faults we tolerate in
   ourselves;
for condemning in our parents the faults we tolerate in
   ourselves;
for passing judgment without knowledge of the facts;
for remembering the price of things but forgetting their
   value;
for teaching our children everything but the meaning of life;
for loving our egos better than the truth.

וְעַל כֻּלָּם אֱלֽוֹהַּ סְלִיחוֹת סְלַח לָֽנוּ: מְחַל לָֽנוּ: כַּפֶּר־לָֽנוּ:

Ve'al kulam eloha seliḥot selaḥ lanu. Meḥal lanu. Kaper lanu.

We sin against God when we sin against ourselves;
  for our failures of love we ask forgiveness;
for using people as stepping stones to advancement;
for confusing love and lust;
for withholding love to control those we claim to love;
for hiding from others behind an armor of mistrust;
for treating with arrogance people weaker than ourselves;
for condescending towards those whom we regard as inferiors;
for shunting aside those whose age is an embarrassment to us;
for giving ourselves the fleeting pleasure of inflicting lasting
  hurts;
for cynicism which eats away our faith in the possibility of love.

וְעַל כֻּלָּם אֱלֽוֹהַּ סְלִיחוֹת סְלַח לָֽנוּ: מְחַל לָֽנוּ: כַּפֶּר־לָֽנוּ:

Ve'al kulam eloha seliḥot selaḥ lanu. Meḥal lanu. Kaper lanu.

Chaim Stern (Adapted)

The community is seated.

And through the love, ETERNAL ONE, our God,
with which you love your people Israel,
and through compassion you have shown
to all who share your covenant,
you gave us, BLESSED ONE,
(this day of Shabbat for holiness and for rest and)
this Day of Atonement,
for forgiveness of our sins,
for pardoning our transgressions,
and for atonement of the wrong that we have done.

You overlook your people's wrongdoing,
as it is written by your prophet's hand:
"Who is a God like you?
—forgiving sin, absolving the transgressions
of the remnant of your heritage,
you who do not cling to anger,
but desire only kindness,
you who act mercifully once again,
subduing the effects of our transgressions,
casting all our wrongs to the waters of the sea."

All the wrongs done by your people Israel
you hereby cast into oblivion.
Those deeds shall not be dwelt on any further,
nor shall they come to mind again.

DERASH. Can we truly experience Yom Kippur as a gift of God's love and
deep compassion for us? This day is not a punishment. It is not a trial. It
is not an endurance contest. It is a precious gift. It is a protected cove in
our year, a harbor of silence and song, hours empty of demand and need.
It is a day of touching our hearts with forgiveness, immersing in the pool
of purity and innocence and emerging with the profound awareness and
acceptance that leads to change.   S.P.W.

וּמֵאַהֲבָתְךָ יהוה אֱלֹהֵינוּ שֶׁאָהַבְתָּ אֶת יִשְׂרָאֵל עַמֶּֽךָ וּמֵחֶמְלָתְךָ
מַלְכֵּֽנוּ שֶׁחָמַֽלְתָּ עַל בְּנֵי בְרִיתֶֽךָ נָתַֽתָּ לָּֽנוּ יהוה אֱלֹהֵֽינוּ אֶת (יוֹם
הַשַּׁבָּת הַזֶּה לִקְדֻשָּׁה וְלִמְנוּחָה וְאֶת) יוֹם הַכִּפֻּרִים הַזֶּה לִמְחִילַת
חֵטְא וְלִסְלִיחַת עָוֹן וּלְכַפָּרַת פָּֽשַׁע:

תַּעֲבוֹר עַל פֶּֽשַׁע לְעַם שָׁבֵי פֶֽשַׁע כַּכָּתוּב עַל יַד נְבִיאֶֽךָ: מִי־אֵל
כָּמֽוֹךָ נֹשֵׂא עָוֹן וְעֹבֵר עַל־פֶּֽשַׁע לִשְׁאֵרִית נַחֲלָתוֹ לֹא־הֶחֱזִיק לָעַד
אַפּוֹ כִּי־חָפֵץ חֶֽסֶד הוּא: יָשׁוּב יְרַחֲמֵֽנוּ יִכְבּוֹשׁ עֲוֹנֹתֵֽינוּ וְתַשְׁלִיךְ
בִּמְצֻלוֹת יָם כָּל־חַטֹּאותָם: וְכָל חַטֹּאת עַמְּךָ בֵּית יִשְׂרָאֵל תַּשְׁלִיךְ
בִּמְקוֹם אֲשֶׁר לֹא יִזָּכְרוּ וְלֹא יִפָּקְדוּ וְלֹא יַעֲלוּ עַל לֵב לְעוֹלָם: ←

COMMENTARY. בני בריתך/all who share your covenant. In the biblical
account, Abraham voluntarily enters into a covenant with God. At Sinai,
the whole people Israel joins in the renewal and expansion of that
covenant. Both God and Israel act voluntarily. Yet, according to the
midrash, God held Mount Sinai over the Israelites' heads and said, "If you
accept the covenant, well and good; and if not I will drop this mountain
on your heads." Thus, at least some of the rabbis saw the covenant as
voluntary for God and *involuntary* for Israel. For those who were born and
raised as Jews in an earlier era, the covenantal commitment to Judaism
could hardly have been experienced as a totally free choice. For us, who
have easy access to secular opportunities and to assimilation, entering into
the covenant is a voluntary action. We are all Jews by choice, and it is God
who has ceased to be the "chooser." We are not only upholders of the
covenant, but the definers of the covenant. We have committed ourselves
to the task of striving to be a holy people, upholding justice, redeeming
the downtrodden. We have covenanted to make God manifest in our time.
We do not intend or wish to be alone in this among the peoples of the
world. We make no exclusive covenantal claim. We speak only of our own
choosing, and we hope that others will speak of theirs.   D.A.T.

תעבור...קדם / You...old (based on Micah 7:18-20).

"You show faithfulness to Jacob,
love to Abraham,
as you have promised to our ancestors
from days of old."

On Shabbat add the words in parenthesis.

Our God, our ancients' God,
forgive us our transgressions
this Day (of Shabbat and) of Atonement,
blot out and cause to pass away
our wrongdoings and our errors
from before your eyes, as it is said:
"I, yes I, shall be the one
who blots out your wrongdoing, for my sake;
your errors I shall not remember any more!"
And it is said: "I have made your sins
vanish like a storm cloud
and, like a mist, the things you have done wrong.
Return to me, for it is I who have redeemed you!"
And it is said: "For on this day,
atonement shall be made for you,
to make you clean from all of your wrongdoings.
Before THE FOUNT OF MERCY, you shall all be clean." ↵

תִּתֵּן אֱמֶת לְיַעֲקֹב חֶסֶד לְאַבְרָהָם אֲשֶׁר־נִשְׁבַּעְתָּ לַאֲבוֹתֵינוּ מִימֵי
קֶדֶם:

On Shabbat add the words in parenthesis.

אֱלֹהֵינוּ וֵאלֹהֵי אֲבוֹתֵינוּ וְאִמּוֹתֵינוּ מְחַל לַעֲוֹנוֹתֵינוּ בְּיוֹם (הַשַּׁבָּת
הַזֶּה וּבְיוֹם) הַכִּפֻּרִים הַזֶּה: מְחֵה וְהַעֲבֵר פְּשָׁעֵינוּ וְחַטֹּאתֵינוּ מִנֶּגֶד
עֵינֶיךָ: כָּאָמוּר: אָנֹכִי אָנֹכִי הוּא מֹחֶה פְשָׁעֶיךָ לְמַעֲנִי וְחַטֹּאתֶיךָ לֹא
אֶזְכֹּר: וְנֶאֱמַר: מָחִיתִי כָעָב פְּשָׁעֶיךָ וְכֶעָנָן חַטֹּאתֶיךָ שׁוּבָה אֵלַי כִּי
גְאַלְתִּיךָ: וְנֶאֱמַר: כִּי־בַיּוֹם הַזֶּה יְכַפֵּר עֲלֵיכֶם לְטַהֵר אֶתְכֶם מִכֹּל
חַטֹּאתֵיכֶם לִפְנֵי יהוה תִּטְהָרוּ: ←

אנכי...אזכר / I, yes...more! (Isaiah 43:25).

מחיתי...גאלתיך / I have...you! (Isaiah 44:22).

כי ביום...תטהרו / For on...clean (Leviticus 16:30).

MEDITATION. Visualize your defects, your cravings and your willfulness.
Visualize the negative patterns that keep you from God and from the
fullest expression of human love.

However they appear to you, let them be transformed into clouds in the
wide expanse of sky. See these troubling parts of yourself as vapors, gray
and white puffs of smoke passing in the sky. Watch them pass, watch them
change design, watch them lose form. Watch them vanish.   S.P.W.

Our God, our ancients' God (take pleasure in our rest,)
enable us to realize holiness with your mitzvot,
give us our portion in your Torah,
let us enjoy the good things of your world,
and gladden us with your salvation,
(and help us to perpetuate, ETERNAL ONE, our God,
your holy Shabbat, with love and joy,
and let all Israel, and all who treat your name as holy,
rest upon this day,) and refine our hearts
to serve you truthfully.
For you are a forgiving God to Israel,
and compassionate to all the tribes of Yeshurun
in each and every generation,
and apart from you we have no sovereign,
none full of compassion and forgiveness,
except you.
Blessed are you, FORGIVING ONE,
sovereign of mercy and forgiveness
for our wrongdoings and for those
of all your kin, the house of Israel,
you who make our guilt to pass away,
year after year,
the sovereign power over all the earth
who raises up to holiness
(Shabbat,) the people Israel
and the Day of Atonement.

אֱלֹהֵינוּ וֵאלֹהֵי אֲבוֹתֵינוּ וְאִמּוֹתֵינוּ (רְצֵה בִמְנוּחָתֵנוּ) קַדְּשֵׁנוּ
בְּמִצְוֹתֶיךָ וְתֵן חֶלְקֵנוּ בְּתוֹרָתֶךָ: שַׂבְּעֵנוּ מִטּוּבֶךָ וְשַׂמְּחֵנוּ בִּישׁוּעָתֶךָ:
(וְהַנְחִילֵנוּ יהוה אֱלֹהֵינוּ בְּאַהֲבָה וּבְרָצוֹן שַׁבַּת קָדְשֶׁךָ וְיָנוּחוּ בָה
יִשְׂרָאֵל מְקַדְּשֵׁי שְׁמֶךָ) וְטַהֵר לִבֵּנוּ לְעָבְדְּךָ בֶּאֱמֶת: כִּי אַתָּה סָלְחָן
לְיִשְׂרָאֵל וּמָחֳלָן לְשִׁבְטֵי יְשֻׁרוּן בְּכָל־דּוֹר וָדוֹר וּמִבַּלְעָדֶיךָ אֵין לָנוּ
מֶלֶךְ מוֹחֵל וְסוֹלֵחַ אֶלָּא אָתָּה: בָּרוּךְ אַתָּה יהוה מֶלֶךְ מוֹחֵל וְסוֹלֵחַ
לַעֲוֹנוֹתֵינוּ וְלַעֲוֹנוֹת עַמּוֹ בֵּית יִשְׂרָאֵל וּמַעֲבִיר אַשְׁמוֹתֵינוּ בְּכָל־שָׁנָה
וְשָׁנָה מֶלֶךְ עַל־כָּל־הָאָרֶץ מְקַדֵּשׁ (הַשַּׁבָּת וְ)יִשְׂרָאֵל וְיוֹם הַכִּפֻּרִים: ←

5. AVODAH / WORSHIP

Take pleasure, GRACIOUS ONE, our God, in Israel your people; lovingly accept their fervent prayer. May Israel's worship always be acceptable to you.

And may our eyes behold your homecoming, with merciful intent, to Zion. Blessed are you, THE FAITHFUL ONE, who brings your presence home to Zion.

6. HODA'AH / THANKS

We give thanks to you that you are THE ALL-MERCIFUL, our God, God of our ancestors, today and always. A firm, enduring source of life, a shield to us in time of trial, you are ever there, from age to age. We acknowledge you, declare your praise, and thank you for our lives entrusted to your hand, our souls placed in your care, for your miracles that greet us every day, and for your wonders and the good things that are with us every hour, morning, noon, and night. Good One, whose kindness never stops, Kind One, whose loving acts have never failed—always have we placed our hope in you.

For all these things, your name be blessed and raised in honor always, sovereign of ours, forever. ↵

‏עֲבוֹדָה‏ 5

רְצֵה יהוה אֱלֹהֵינוּ בְּעַמְּךָ יִשְׂרָאֵל וְלִתְפִלָּתָם בְּאַהֲבָה תְּקַבֵּל בְּרָצוֹן וּתְהִי לְרָצוֹן תָּמִיד עֲבוֹדַת יִשְׂרָאֵל עַמֶּךָ:

וְתֶחֱזֶינָה עֵינֵינוּ בְּשׁוּבְךָ לְצִיּוֹן בְּרַחֲמִים: בָּרוּךְ אַתָּה יהוה הַמַּחֲזִיר שְׁכִינָתוֹ לְצִיּוֹן:

‏הוֹדָאָה‏ 6

מוֹדִים אֲנַחְנוּ לָךְ שָׁאַתָּה הוּא יהוה אֱלֹהֵינוּ וֵאלֹהֵי אֲבוֹתֵינוּ וְאִמּוֹתֵינוּ לְעוֹלָם וָעֶד צוּר חַיֵּינוּ מָגֵן יִשְׁעֵנוּ אַתָּה הוּא לְדוֹר וָדוֹר: נוֹדֶה לְּךָ וּנְסַפֵּר תְּהִלָּתֶךָ עַל חַיֵּינוּ הַמְּסוּרִים בְּיָדֶךָ וְעַל נִשְׁמוֹתֵינוּ הַפְּקוּדוֹת לָךְ וְעַל נִסֶּיךָ שֶׁבְּכָל יוֹם עִמָּנוּ וְעַל נִפְלְאוֹתֶיךָ וְטוֹבוֹתֶיךָ שֶׁבְּכָל־עֵת עֶרֶב וָבֹקֶר וְצָהֳרָיִם: הַטּוֹב כִּי לֹא כָלוּ רַחֲמֶיךָ וְהַמְרַחֵם כִּי לֹא תַמּוּ חֲסָדֶיךָ מֵעוֹלָם קִוִּינוּ לָךְ:

← וְעַל כֻּלָּם יִתְבָּרַךְ וְיִתְרוֹמַם שִׁמְךָ מַלְכֵּנוּ תָּמִיד לְעוֹלָם וָעֶד:

Our creator, our sovereign,
remember your love for us,
and banish pestilence and war,
and famine, and captivity, and slaughter,
and crime, and violence, and plague,
and terrible disaster,
and every kind of illness,
and every kind of tragic accident,
and every kind of strife,
and all the forms of retribution,
and all evil decrees,
and groundless hatred.
Remove them from our midst,
and from the midst of all
who dwell on earth.
And write down for a good life
all who share your covenant.

Let all of life acknowledge you! May all beings praise your name in truth, O God, our rescue and our aid. Blessed are you, THE GRACIOUS ONE, whose name is good, to whom all thanks are due. ⤶

אָבִינוּ מַלְכֵּנוּ זְכֹר רַחֲמֶיךָ וְכַלֵּה דֶּבֶר וְחֶרֶב וְרָעָב וּשְׁבִי וּמַשְׁחִית וְעָוֹן וּשְׁמָד וּמַגֵּפָה וּפֶגַע רַע וְכָל־מַחֲלָה וְכָל־תְּקָלָה וְכָל־קְטָטָה וְכָל־מִינֵי פֻרְעָנִיּוֹת וְכָל־גְּזֵרָה רָעָה וְשִׂנְאַת חִנָּם מֵעָלֵינוּ וּמֵעַל כָּל־בְּנֵי עוֹלָמֶךָ:

וּכְתֹב לְחַיִּים טוֹבִים כָּל־בְּנֵי בְרִיתֶךָ:

וְכֹל הַחַיִּים יוֹדוּךָ סֶּלָה וִיהַלְלוּ אֶת שִׁמְךָ בֶּאֱמֶת הָאֵל יְשׁוּעָתֵנוּ וְעֶזְרָתֵנוּ סֶלָה: בָּרוּךְ אַתָּה יהוה הַטּוֹב שִׁמְךָ וּלְךָ נָאֶה לְהוֹדוֹת: ←

7. BIRKAT HASHALOM / BLESSING FOR PEACE

Our God, our ancients' God,
bless us with the threefold blessing
spoken from the mouth of Aaron and his sons, as is said:
May THE ETERNAL bless you
    and protect you.   Let it be God's will!
May THE ETERNAL'S face give light
    to you, and show you favor.   Let it be God's will!
May THE ETERNAL'S face be lifted
    toward you, and bestow upon you
    peace.   Let it be God's will!

COMMENTARY. Traditionally the Priestly Blessing was done by the male descendants of the *kohanim*. In some congregations the *sheliah tzibur* (service leader) recites the blessing, and the congregation responds with *"Ken yehi ratzon."* In other communities all the members of the congregation wrap arms and tallitot around each other and recite the blessing together. Another way to enact the Priestly Blessing is for each congregant to turn to a neighbor and recite the first half of each blessing, while the neighbor responds with the second half of the blessing. Michael M. Cohen

COMMENTARY. Rabbi Lavy Becker of Montreal noticed that when this blessing was pronounced in the synagogue of Pisa, all the children gathered under the sheltering wings of their fathers' tallitot to receive it. He recognized this "as a reconstruction of the ancient priestly ceremony." He modified that custom so that those wearing a tallit share it with their neighbors and all are under the sheltering wings of the Shehinah as we bless each other. It is now an established part of Canadian Reconstructionist practice. E.M.

יברכך...שלום / May...peace (Numbers 6:24-26).

בִּרְכַּת הַשָּׁלוֹם

אֱלֹהֵינוּ וֵאלֹהֵי אֲבוֹתֵינוּ וְאִמּוֹתֵינוּ בָּרְכֵנוּ בַּבְּרָכָה הַמְשֻׁלֶּשֶׁת
הָאֲמוּרָה מִפִּי אַהֲרֹן וּבָנָיו כָּאָמוּר:

יְבָרֶכְךָ יְהוָה וְיִשְׁמְרֶךָ.

כֵּן יְהִי רָצוֹן:

יָאֵר יהוה פָּנָיו אֵלֶיךָ
וִיחֻנֶּךָ:

כֵּן יְהִי רָצוֹן:

יִשָּׂא יהוה פָּנָיו אֵלֶיךָ
וְיָשֵׂם לְךָ שָׁלוֹם:

כֵּן יְהִי רָצוֹן:

Eloheynu veylohey avoteynu ve'imoteynu
barehenu baberahah hamshuleshet
ha'amurah mipi aharon uvanav ka'amur:
Yevareheha adonay veyishmereha.   Ken yehi ratzon.
Ya'er adonay panav eleha vihuneka.   Ken yehi ratzon.
Yisa adonay panav eleha veyasem leha shalom.   Ken yehi ratzon.

Grant peace, goodness and blessing in the world,
grace, love, and mercy
over us and over all your people Israel.
Bless us, source of being, all of us, as one
amid your light,
for by your light,
WISE ONE, our God, you give to us
Torah of life, and love of kindness,
justice, blessing, mercy, life, and peace.
So may it be a good thing in your eyes,
to bless your people Israel, and all peoples,
with abundant strength and peace.

In the book of life, blessing, and peace, and proper sustenance,
may we be remembered and inscribed,
we and all your people, the house of Israel,
for a good life and for peace.

Blessed are you, COMPASSIONATE ONE, maker of peace.

On Shabbat continue on page 461.

KAVANAH. Try to imagine a time of true peace and tranquility, and think about your part in helping this time to come about. What can you do? What can you commit to? How will *you* be a peacemaker?　　　　L.G.B.

שִׂים שָׁלוֹם טוֹבָה וּבְרָכָה בָּעוֹלָם חֵן וָחֶסֶד וְרַחֲמִים עָלֵינוּ וְעַל
כָּל־יִשְׂרָאֵל עַמֶּךָ: בָּרְכֵנוּ אָבִינוּ כֻּלָּנוּ כְּאֶחָד בְּאוֹר פָּנֶיךָ: כִּי בְאוֹר
פָּנֶיךָ נָתַתָּ לָּנוּ יהוה אֱלֹהֵינוּ תּוֹרַת חַיִּים וְאַהֲבַת חֶסֶד וּצְדָקָה
וּבְרָכָה וְרַחֲמִים וְחַיִּים וְשָׁלוֹם: וְטוֹב בְּעֵינֶיךָ לְבָרֵךְ אֶת־עַמְּךָ
יִשְׂרָאֵל וְאֶת־כָּל־הָעַמִּים בְּרָב־עֹז וְשָׁלוֹם.

בְּסֵפֶר חַיִּים בְּרָכָה וְשָׁלוֹם וּפַרְנָסָה טוֹבָה נִזָּכֵר וְנִכָּתֵם לְפָנֶיךָ אֲנַחְנוּ
וְכָל־עַמְּךָ בֵּית יִשְׂרָאֵל לְחַיִּים טוֹבִים וּלְשָׁלוֹם:

בָּרוּךְ אַתָּה יהוה עוֹשֶׂה הַשָּׁלוֹם:

Sim shalom tovah uveraḥah ba'olam ḥen vaḥesed veraḥamim
aleynu ve'al kol yisrael ameḥa. Bareḥenu avinu kulanu ke'eḥad
be'or paneḥa. Ki ve'or paneḥa natata lanu adonay eloheynu torat
ḥayim ve'ahavat ḥesed utzedakah uveraḥah veraḥamim veḥayim
veshalom. Vetov be'eyneḥa levareḥ et ameḥa yisra'el ve'et kol
ha'amim berov oz veshalom.

Besefer ḥayim beraḥah veshalom ufarnasah tovah nizaḥer
veneḥatem lefaneḥa anaḥnu veḥol ameḥa beyt yisra'el leḥayim
tovim uleshalom.

Baruḥ atah adonay osey hashalom.

On Shabbat continue on page 462.

AVINU MALKENU/
OUR CREATOR, OUR SOVEREIGN

The ark is opened.

Most communities follow tradition in not reciting Avinu Malkenu *when Rosh Hashanah or Yom Kippur falls on Shabbat because of the prayer's petitionary nature. For an alternative version see pages 457-460. For an interpretive version see page 456.*

Our creator, our sovereign, we have done wrong in your presence.

Our creator, our sovereign, we have no one to rule over us but you.

Our creator, our sovereign, help us for the honor of your name.

Our creator, our sovereign, renew for us a good year.

Our creator, our sovereign, nullify the plans of any who may seek to do us harm.

Our creator, our sovereign, grant forgiveness and atonement for all of our transgressions.

Our creator, our sovereign, help us to return wholeheartedly into your presence.

Our creator, our sovereign, send thorough healing to all those who ail.

Our creator, our sovereign, inscribe us for good fortune in the Book of Life.

Our creator, our sovereign, inscribe us in the Book of Redemption and Salvation.

Our creator, our sovereign, inscribe us in the Book of Sustenance and Livelihood.

Our creator, our sovereign, inscribe us in the Book of Merit.

Our creator, our sovereign, inscribe us in the Book of Forgiveness and Atonement.

Our creator, our sovereign, let grow for us the tree of imminent redemption. ↶

DERASH. The *Avinu Malkenu* prayer gives us permission to open up our deepest yearnings to the Universal One. By allowing our yearnings, often hidden even from ourselves, to emerge, we are taking a first step toward achieving an inner balance which will enable us to move forward toward wholeness.

D.B.

אָבִינוּ מַלְכֵּנוּ

The ark is opened.

Most communities follow tradition in not reciting Avinu Malkenu *when Rosh Hashanah or Yom Kippur falls on Shabbat because of the prayer's petitionary nature. For an alternative version see pages 457-460. For an interpretive version see page 456.*

אָבִֽינוּ מַלְכֵּֽנוּ חָטָֽאנוּ לְפָנֶֽיךָ:

אָבִֽינוּ מַלְכֵּֽנוּ אֵין לָֽנוּ מֶֽלֶךְ אֶלָּא אָֽתָּה:

אָבִֽינוּ מַלְכֵּֽנוּ עֲשֵׂה עִמָּֽנוּ לְמַֽעַן שְׁמֶֽךָ:

אָבִֽינוּ מַלְכֵּֽנוּ חַדֵּשׁ עָלֵֽינוּ שָׁנָה טוֹבָה:

אָבִֽינוּ מַלְכֵּֽנוּ הָפֵר עֲצַת אוֹיְבֵֽינוּ:

אָבִֽינוּ מַלְכֵּֽנוּ סְלַח וּמְחַל לְכָל־עֲוֹנוֹתֵֽינוּ:

אָבִֽינוּ מַלְכֵּֽנוּ הַחֲזִירֵֽנוּ בִּתְשׁוּבָה שְׁלֵמָה לְפָנֶֽיךָ:

אָבִֽינוּ מַלְכֵּֽנוּ שְׁלַח רְפוּאָה שְׁלֵמָה לַחוֹלִים:

אָבִֽינוּ מַלְכֵּֽנוּ כָּתְבֵֽנוּ בְּסֵֽפֶר חַיִּים טוֹבִים:

אָבִֽינוּ מַלְכֵּֽנוּ כָּתְבֵֽנוּ בְּסֵֽפֶר גְּאֻלָּה וִישׁוּעָה:

אָבִֽינוּ מַלְכֵּֽנוּ כָּתְבֵֽנוּ בְּסֵֽפֶר פַּרְנָסָה וְכַלְכָּלָה:

אָבִֽינוּ מַלְכֵּֽנוּ כָּתְבֵֽנוּ בְּסֵֽפֶר זְכֻיּוֹת:

אָבִֽינוּ מַלְכֵּֽנוּ כָּתְבֵֽנוּ בְּסֵֽפֶר סְלִיחָה וּמְחִילָה:

אָבִֽינוּ מַלְכֵּֽנוּ הַצְמַח לָֽנוּ יְשׁוּעָה בְּקָרוֹב: ←—

COMMENTARY. Jews have traditionally not recited *Avinu Malkenu* on Shabbat because Shabbat is a day of rest, a day focused on appreciation of what we are and what we have. Work and need, and all discussions of them, including petitionary prayer, are out of place on Shabbat. Since *Avinu Malkenu* is entirely petitionary and specifically refers to *parnasah*, earning a living, its use on Shabbat was excluded as early as the time of the Mishnah (around the third century C.E.). D.A.T.

Our creator, our sovereign, remember us, though we are made of dust.

Our creator, our sovereign, be merciful to us and to all our offspring.

Our creator, our sovereign, act in memory of all those who have been killed while honoring your name.

Our creator, our sovereign, act in honor of your great and mighty, awe-inspiring name, which has been called out over us for our protection.

Our creator, our sovereign, be gracious with us and respond to us, for we have no deeds to justify us; deal with us in righteousness and love, and save us now.

Continue on page 461.

COMMENTARY. Perhaps more than any other prayer, *Avinu Malkenu* invokes the image of a long-bearded king sitting in judgment upon his throne. How many are the ways that this image can trouble us! Some Jews are struggling to recover from the harsh judgments of parents or peers, or from harsh self-judgments. Some are struggling to escape the transcendent imagery of God and replace it with the divine within. Some have trouble with the maleness of the image.

Despite these very real difficulties, there is a powerful core of truth in the *Avinu Malkenu* that transcends the trouble many of us have with its imagery: we must grapple with standards of justice that are external to us. Social responsibility is not merely a matter of personal conscience. Chanting the *Avinu Malkenu* reminds us of standards by which we ought to judge ourselves.

Furthermore, it reminds us of forces infinitely greater than ourselves upon which our very lives depend. While our lives depend upon our inner resources, we cannot exist without the aid of natural and social forces. Knowing who we are means accepting the limits of our power and knowledge and the inevitability of our dependency.   D.A.T.

אָבִֽינוּ מַלְכֵּֽנוּ זְכוֹר כִּי עָפָר אֲנָֽחְנוּ:

אָבִֽינוּ מַלְכֵּֽנוּ חֲמוֹל עָלֵֽינוּ וְעַל־עוֹלָלֵֽינוּ וְטַפֵּֽינוּ:

אָבִֽינוּ מַלְכֵּֽנוּ עֲשֵׂה לְמַֽעַן הֲרוּגִים עַל־שֵׁם קָדְשֶֽׁךָ:

אָבִֽינוּ מַלְכֵּֽנוּ עֲשֵׂה לְמַֽעַן שִׁמְךָ הַגָּדוֹל הַגִּבּוֹר וְהַנּוֹרָא שֶׁנִּקְרָא
עָלֵֽינוּ:

אָבִֽינוּ מַלְכֵּֽנוּ חָנֵּֽנוּ וַעֲנֵֽנוּ כִּי אֵין בָּֽנוּ מַעֲשִׂים עֲשֵׂה עִמָּֽנוּ צְדָקָה
וָחֶֽסֶד וְהוֹשִׁיעֵֽנוּ:

Avinu malkenu honenu va'anenu ki eyn banu ma'asim
asey imanu tzedakah vahesed vehoshi'enu.

Continue on page 462.

COMMENTARY. In *Avinu Malkenu* we seek the strength to do justice, the inner harmony needed to find forgiveness, and the acceptance of the small place we have amidst the tumult of the world. It is in that context that we express the hopes embodied in this prayer. Whether or not the worshipper chooses to change the words of *Avinu Malkenu*, the fervently expressed pleas it contains transcend the constraints of time and place.   D.A.T.

DERASH. Divine love, חסד/*hesed*, makes it possible to take the next personal step of continuing our efforts after finding that our deeds have once again failed to measure up to our own expectations. It is in taking that step, made possible by חסד/love, that we find salvation.   J.A.S.

אָבִינוּ מַלְכֵּנוּ, מְקוֹרֵנוּ אֱלֹהֵינוּ

חָנֵּנוּ וַעֲנֵנוּ
כִּי אֵין בָּנוּ מַעֲשִׂים

עֲשֵׂה עִמָּנוּ
צְדָקָה וָחֶסֶד

Deal with us in righteousness

וְהוֹשִׁיעֵנוּ

and love and save us.

A Woman's Meditation

When men were children, they thought of God as a father;
When men were slaves, they thought of God as a master;
When men were subjects, they thought of God as a king.
But I am a woman, not a slave, not a subject,
not a child who longs for God as father or mother.

I might imagine God as teacher or friend, but those images,
like king, master, father or mother, are too small for me now.

God is the force of motion and light in the universe;
God is the strength of life on our planet;
God is the power moving us to do good;
God is the source of love springing up in us.
God is far beyond what we can comprehend.

Ruth Brin

AVINU MALKENU/
OUR SOURCE, OUR GOD

Our source, our God, we have done wrong in your presence.

Our source, our God, we have no one to rule over us but you.

Our source, our God, help us for the honor of your name.

Our source, our God, renew for us a good year.

Our source, our God, nullify the plans of any who may seek to do us harm.

Our source, our God, grant forgiveness and atonement for all of our transgressions.

Our source, our God, help us to return wholeheartedly into your presence.

Our source, our God, send thorough healing to all those who ail.

Our source, our God, inscribe us for good fortune in the Book of Life.

Our source, our God, inscribe us in the Book of Redemption and Salvation.

Our source, our God, inscribe us in the Book of Sustenance and Livelihood. ↵

אָבִינוּ מַלְכֵּנוּ

מְקוֹרֵנוּ אֱלֹהֵינוּ חָטָאנוּ לְפָנֶיךָ:

מְקוֹרֵנוּ אֱלֹהֵינוּ אֵין לָנוּ מֶלֶךְ אֶלָּא אָתָּה:

מְקוֹרֵנוּ אֱלֹהֵינוּ עֲשֵׂה עִמָּנוּ לְמַעַן שְׁמֶךָ:

מְקוֹרֵנוּ אֱלֹהֵינוּ חַדֵּשׁ עָלֵינוּ שָׁנָה טוֹבָה:

מְקוֹרֵנוּ אֱלֹהֵינוּ הָפֵר עֲצַת אוֹיְבֵינוּ:

מְקוֹרֵנוּ אֱלֹהֵינוּ סְלַח וּמְחַל לְכָל־עֲוֹנוֹתֵינוּ:

מְקוֹרֵנוּ אֱלֹהֵינוּ הַחֲזִירֵנוּ בִּתְשׁוּבָה שְׁלֵמָה לְפָנֶיךָ:

מְקוֹרֵנוּ אֱלֹהֵינוּ שְׁלַח רְפוּאָה שְׁלֵמָה לַחוֹלִים:

מְקוֹרֵנוּ אֱלֹהֵינוּ כָּתְבֵנוּ בְּסֵפֶר חַיִּים טוֹבִים:

מְקוֹרֵנוּ אֱלֹהֵינוּ כָּתְבֵנוּ בְּסֵפֶר גְּאֻלָּה וִישׁוּעָה:

מְקוֹרֵנוּ אֱלֹהֵינוּ כָּתְבֵנוּ בְּסֵפֶר פַּרְנָסָה וְכַלְכָּלָה: ⟵

NOTE. מקורנו אלהינו /*Mekorenu Eloheynu*/Our source, our God. This alternative version changes the first two words of each line from "Our creator, our sovereign" to "Our source, our God." Many other versions can be constructed to reflect different theological outlooks and ethical concerns. This can be done by selecting one word from each group below to form the introductory phrase.

I	Imeynu	אִמֵּינוּ	Our mother
	Eloheynu	אֱלֹהֵינוּ	Our God
	Mekorenu	מְקוֹרֵנוּ	Our source
	Avinu	אָבִינוּ	Our creator (literally, father)
	Sheḥinatenu	שְׁכִינָתֵנוּ	Our presence
II	Malkatenu	מַלְכָּתֵנוּ	Our queen
	Shebashamayim	שֶׁבַּשָּׁמַיִם	In heaven
	Atartenu	עֲטַרְתֵּנוּ	Our crown
	Sheḥinatenu	שְׁכִינָתֵנוּ	Our presence
	Malkenu	מַלְכֵּנוּ	Our sovereign

Our source, our God, inscribe us in the Book of Merit.

Our source, our God, inscribe us in the Book of Forgiveness and Atonement.

Our source, our God, let grow for us the tree of imminent redemption.

Our source, our God, remember us, though we are made of dust.

Our source, our God, be merciful to us and to all our offspring.

Our source, our God, act in memory of all those who have been killed while honoring your name.

Our source, our God, act in honor of your great, mighty, and awe-inspiring name, which has been called out over us for our protection.

Our creator, our sovereign, be gracious with us and respond to us, for we have no deeds to justify us; deal with us in righteousness and love, and save us now.

KAVANAH. Our father/mother/parent evokes a mood of closeness, caring and intimacy. Our king/queen/ruler elicits the qualities of power, distance and setting limits. We pour out our hearts in the hope that tender concern will balance with the exercise of power, that they will join on our behalf to heal us, our community, our world.   S.P.W.

מְקוֹרֵֽנוּ אֱלֹהֵֽינוּ כָּתְבֵֽנוּ בְּסֵֽפֶר זְכִיּוֹת:

מְקוֹרֵֽנוּ אֱלֹהֵֽינוּ כָּתְבֵֽנוּ בְּסֵֽפֶר סְלִיחָה וּמְחִילָה:

מְקוֹרֵֽנוּ אֱלֹהֵֽינוּ הַצְמַח לָֽנוּ יְשׁוּעָה בְּקָרוֹב:

מְקוֹרֵֽנוּ אֱלֹהֵֽינוּ זְכוֹר כִּי עָפָר אֲנָֽחְנוּ:

מְקוֹרֵֽנוּ אֱלֹהֵֽינוּ חֲמוֹל עָלֵֽינוּ וְעַל־עוֹלָלֵֽינוּ וְטַפֵּֽנוּ:

מְקוֹרֵֽנוּ אֱלֹהֵֽינוּ עֲשֵׂה לְמַֽעַן הֲרוּגִים עַל־שֵׁם קָדְשֶֽׁךָ:

מְקוֹרֵֽנוּ אֱלֹהֵֽינוּ עֲשֵׂה לְמַֽעַן שְׁמְךָ הַגָּדוֹל הַגִּבּוֹר וְהַנּוֹרָא שֶׁנִּקְרָא עָלֵֽינוּ:

אָבִֽינוּ מַלְכֵּֽנוּ חָנֵּֽנוּ וַעֲנֵֽנוּ כִּי אֵין בָּֽנוּ מַעֲשִׂים עֲשֵׂה עִמָּֽנוּ צְדָקָה וָחֶֽסֶד וְהוֹשִׁיעֵֽנוּ:

Avinu malkenu ḥonenu va'anenu ki eyn banu ma'asim asey imanu tzedakah vaḥesed vehoshi'enu.

KADDISH TITKABAL / KADDISH FOR THE COMPLETION OF PRAYER

Reader: Let God's name be made great and holy in the world that was created as God willed. May God complete the holy realm in your own lifetime, in your days, and in the days of all the house of Israel, quickly and soon. And say: Amen.

Congregation: May God's great name be blessed forever and as long as worlds endure.

Reader: May it be blessed, and praised, and glorified, and held in honor, viewed with awe, embellished, and revered; and may the blessed name of holiness be hailed, though it be higher by far than all the blessings, songs, praises, and consolations that we utter in this world. And say: Amen.

And may the prayer and supplication of the whole house of Israel be acceptable to their creator in the heavens. And say: Amen.

May Heaven grant a universal peace, and life for us, and for all Israel. And say: Amen.

May the one who creates harmony above make peace for us and for all Israel, and for all who dwell on earth. And say: Amen.

קַדִּישׁ תִּתְקַבַּל

יִתְגַּדַּל וְיִתְקַדַּשׁ שְׁמֵהּ רַבָּא בְּעָלְמָא דִּי בְרָא כִרְעוּתֵהּ וְיַמְלִיךְ
מַלְכוּתֵהּ בְּחַיֵּיכוֹן וּבְיוֹמֵיכוֹן וּבְחַיֵּי דְכָל בֵּית יִשְׂרָאֵל בַּעֲגָלָא וּבִזְמַן
קָרִיב וְאִמְרוּ אָמֵן:
יְהֵא שְׁמֵהּ רַבָּא מְבָרַךְ לְעָלַם וּלְעָלְמֵי עָלְמַיָּא:
יִתְבָּרַךְ וְיִשְׁתַּבַּח וְיִתְפָּאַר וְיִתְרוֹמַם וְיִתְנַשֵּׂא וְיִתְהַדָּר וְיִתְעַלֶּה
וְיִתְהַלָּל שְׁמֵהּ דְּקֻדְשָׁא בְּרִיךְ הוּא
לְעֵלָּא לְעֵלָּא מִכָּל בִּרְכָתָא וְשִׁירָתָא תֻּשְׁבְּחָתָא וְנֶחֱמָתָא דַּאֲמִירָן
בְּעָלְמָא וְאִמְרוּ אָמֵן:
תִּתְקַבַּל צְלוֹתְהוֹן וּבָעוּתְהוֹן דְּכָל בֵּית יִשְׂרָאֵל קֳדָם אֲבוּהוֹן דִּי
בִשְׁמַיָּא וְאִמְרוּ אָמֵן:
יְהֵא שְׁלָמָא רַבָּא מִן שְׁמַיָּא וְחַיִּים עָלֵינוּ וְעַל כָּל יִשְׂרָאֵל וְאִמְרוּ
אָמֵן:
עוֹשֶׂה שָׁלוֹם בִּמְרוֹמָיו הוּא יַעֲשֶׂה שָׁלוֹם עָלֵינוּ וְעַל כָּל יִשְׂרָאֵל וְעַל
כָּל יוֹשְׁבֵי תֵבֵל וְאִמְרוּ אָמֵן:

Yehey shemey raba mevaraḥ le'alam ulalmey almaya.

Oseh shalom bimromav hu ya'aseh shalom aleynu ve'al kol
yisra'el ve'al kol yoshvey tevel ve'imru amen.

HOTZA'AT SEFER TORAH /
THE TORAH SERVICE

There is none like you among the powerful, ETERNAL ONE,
and there are no deeds like your deeds.
Your realm embraces all the worlds,
your reign encompasses all generations.
THE ETERNAL ONE reigns!
THE ETERNAL ONE has always reigned!
THE ETERNAL ONE shall reign beyond all time.
THE ETERNAL ONE gives strength to our people.
May THE ETERNAL ONE bless our people with enduring peace.

Source of all mercy,
deal kindly and in good will with Zion.
Rebuild the walls of Jerusalem,
For in you alone we place our trust,
God, sovereign, high and revered,
the life of all the worlds.

COMMENTARY. We approach the Torah slowly. First we open the ark so that
the Torah is visible. We look at the Torah but refrain from touching. Next,
the Torah is removed from the ark and held by the service leader. Later the
Torah is carried through the congregation, and everyone can touch the
Torah. This demonstrates that the Torah is not the property of those
leading the services; the Torah belongs to the Jewish community. Finally,
the coverings of the Torah scroll are removed, allowing us a privileged
intimacy with the words we hear.

In the words of the Torah we hear our ancestors' experience of the divine.
We communicate with generations past and, perhaps on occasion, we hear
Torah as the voice of God refracted through human speech.   D.E.

COMMENTARY. ועד...מלך יהוה מלך יהוה / THE ETERNAL ONE reigns...has
always reigned...shall reign beyond all time. The divinity we discover
within human existence is eternal; it is the same Power that our ancestors
named יהוה, that the talmudic rabbis knew as *Hamakom*/ The Place, that
the mystical Kabbalists knew as *Eyn Sof*/ Without End, and that we now
seek to name.   R.H.

הוֹצָאַת סֵפֶר תּוֹרָה

אֵין כָּמֽוֹךָ בָאֱלֹהִים אֲדֹנָי וְאֵין כְּמַעֲשֶֽׂיךָ:
מַלְכוּתְךָ מַלְכוּת כָּל־עֹלָמִים וּמֶמְשַׁלְתְּךָ בְּכָל־דּוֹר וָדוֹר:
יהוה מֶֽלֶךְ יהוה מָלָךְ יהוה יִמְלֹךְ לְעוֹלָם וָעֶד:
יהוה עֹז לְעַמּוֹ יִתֵּן יהוה יְבָרֵךְ אֶת־עַמּוֹ בַשָּׁלוֹם:

אַב הָרַחֲמִים הֵטִֽיבָה בִרְצוֹנְךָ אֶת־צִיּוֹן תִּבְנֶה חוֹמוֹת יְרוּשָׁלָֽיִם:
כִּי בְךָ לְבַד בָּטָֽחְנוּ מֶֽלֶךְ אֵל רָם וְנִשָּׂא אֲדוֹן עוֹלָמִים:

Eyn kamoha va'elohim adonay ve'eyn kema'aseha.
Malhuteha malhut kol olamim umemshalteha behol dor vador.
Adonay meleh adonay malah adonay yimloh le'olam va'ed.
Adonay oz le'amo yiten adonay yevareh et amo vashalom.
Av harahamim hetivah virtzoneha et tziyon tivneh homot
    yerushalayim.
Ki veha levad batahnu meleh el ram venisa adon olamim.

אֵין...יְרוּשׁלים / There is none...Jerusalem. This section of the service is
composed of selections from Psalms 86, 145, 93, 29, and 51, and Exodus
15:18.

יהוה מלך...ימלך לעולם ועד / THE ETERNAL ONE reigns...shall reign beyond
all time. The assertion of God's sovereignty is a challenge to human
beings—it is we who are called upon to crown God. In declaring God's
sovereignty, we dedicate the daily deeds of our lives to making the earth a
divine realm.   D.E.

תבנה חומות ירושלים / Rebuild the walls of Jerusalem. How different these
words must have sounded before there was a sovereign, living state of
Israel! No longer do we merely dream of a distant rebuilding. The walls
are rising before our eyes. Like our ancestors, we must be concerned with
building both the earthly Jerusalem and the heavenly Jerusalem.   D.E.

The ark is opened.

One of the following may be sung:

(1)

And it happened, when the Ark began its journey,
that Moses said: Arise, ASCENDANT ONE,
and may your enemies be scattered,
May the ones who oppose you
Be afraid of your might!
Behold, out of Zion emerges our Torah,
and the word of THE WISE ONE from Jerusalem's heights.
Blessed is God who has given us Torah,
to Israel, our people, with holy intent.

(2)

Open to me, O you gateways of justice,
Yes, let me come in, and give thanks unto Yah!
This is the gateway to ONE EVERLASTING,
let all who are righteous come in.

KAVANAH. Whenever the ark was moved, this signaled to the Israelites that
it was time to break camp and move on. In our religious life, we can never
be sure when the command to get up and move will reverberate in our
minds and hearts. This is the threat and meaning in openness to religious
experience, for it can transform who we are and lead us on a journey
whose destination we do not know as we set out. All we need is the
courage to listen.   R.H.

The ark is opened.

One of the following may be sung:

(1)

וַיְהִי בִּנְסֹעַ הָאָרֹן וַיֹּאמֶר מֹשֶׁה קוּמָה יהוה וְיָפֻצוּ אֹיְבֶיךָ וְיָנֻסוּ
מְשַׂנְאֶיךָ מִפָּנֶיךָ:
כִּי מִצִּיּוֹן תֵּצֵא תוֹרָה וּדְבַר יהוה מִירוּשָׁלָיִם:
בָּרוּךְ שֶׁנָּתַן תּוֹרָה לְעַמּוֹ יִשְׂרָאֵל בִּקְדֻשָּׁתוֹ:

Vayhi binso'a ha'aron vayomer mosheh kumah adonay veyafutzu
oyveha veyanusu mesaneha mipaneha.
Ki mitziyon tetzey torah udvar adonay mirushalayim.
Baruh shenatan torah le'amo yisra'el bikdushato.

(2)

פִּתְחוּ־לִי שַׁעֲרֵי־צֶדֶק אָבֹא־בָם אוֹדֶה יָהּ:
זֶה־הַשַּׁעַר לַיהוה צַדִּיקִים יָבֹאוּ בוֹ:

Pithu li sha'arey tzedek avo vam odeh yah.
Zeh hasha'ar ladonay tzadikim yavo'u vo.

ויהי...מפניך /And...might! (Numbers 10:35).
כי...ירושלים /Behold...Jerusalem's heights (Isaiah 2:3).
פתחו...בו /Open...come in (Psalms 118:19-20).

The Torah of THE ONE is flawless, it restores the soul.
The testimony of THE ONE is true, it makes wise the simple.

The precepts of THE ONE are sure, they make the heart rejoice.
The mitzvah of THE ONE is clear, it gives light to the eyes.

Fear of THE ONE is pure, it stands eternally.
The judgments of THE ONE are true, together they are just.

The following paragraph is omitted on Shabbat.

ADONAY ADONAY, God loving and gracious,
patient, and abundant in kindness and truth,
keeping kindness for a thousand ages,
forgiving sin and rebellion and transgression,
making pure!

And as for me, my prayer is for you, GENTLE ONE,
may it be for you a time of desire.
O God, in the abundance of your love,
respond to me in truth with your help.

צדקו יחדיו...תורת יהוה / The Torah...together they are just (Psalms 19:8-10).

ואני...ישעך / And as for me...your help (Psalms 69:14).

יהוה...ונקה / ADONAY...pure! It is customary to recite Exodus 34:6-7 on the High Holy Days. Kabbalists beginning with Isaac Luria (sixteenth-century Safed) understood these verses to contain the thirteen attributes of God. Reciting the attributes celebrates God's presence as vividly experienced in the observance of the Days of Awe.   D.A.T.

תּוֹרַת יהוה תְּמִימָה   מְשִׁיבַת נָפֶשׁ:
עֵדוּת יהוה נֶאֱמָנָה   מַחְכִּימַת פֶּתִי:
פִּקּוּדֵי יהוה יְשָׁרִים   מְשַׂמְּחֵי לֵב:
מִצְוַת יהוה בָּרָה   מְאִירַת עֵינָיִם:
יִרְאַת יהוה טְהוֹרָה   עוֹמֶדֶת לָעַד:
מִשְׁפְּטֵי יהוה אֱמֶת   צָדְקוּ יַחְדָּיו:

Torat adonay temimah meshivat nafesh.
Edut adonay ne'emanah mahkimat peti.
Pikudey adonay yesharim mesamehey lev.
Mitzvat adonay barah me'irat eynayim.
Yirat adonay tehorah omedet la'ad.
Mishpetey adonay emet tzadeku yahdav.

The following paragraph is omitted on Shabbat.

יהוה יהוה אֵל רַחוּם וְחַנּוּן אֶרֶךְ אַפַּיִם וְרַב־חֶסֶד וֶאֱמֶת נֹצֵר חֶסֶד
לָאֲלָפִים נֹשֵׂא עָוֹן וָפֶשַׁע וְחַטָּאָה וְנַקֵּה:

וַאֲנִי תְפִלָּתִי־לְךָ יהוה עֵת רָצוֹן אֱלֹהִים בְּרָב־חַסְדֶּךָ עֲנֵנִי בֶּאֱמֶת
יִשְׁעֶךָ:

Adonay adonay el rahum vehanun ereh apayim verav hesed
ve'emet notzer hesed la'alafim nosey avon vafesha vehata'ah
venakey.

Va'ani tefilati leha adonay et ratzon elohim berov hasdeha aneni
be'emet yisheha.

The leader takes out the Torah and recites each line, followed by the congregation:

Listen, Israel: THE ETERNAL is our God, THE ETERNAL is one!

One is our God, great is our sovereign,
holy and awesome is God's name.

The leader faces the ark, bows and says:

Declare with me the greatness of THE INFINITE,
together let us raise God's name.

The leader carries the Torah around the room as the leader and congregation sing:

To you, ETERNAL ONE, is all majesty,
and might, and splendor, and eternity, and power!
For everything that is, in the heavens and the earth,
is yours, ALMIGHTY ONE, as is all sovereignty,
and highest eminence above all beings.
Exalt THE MIGHTY ONE our God,
Bow down before God's footstool.
God is holy!
Exalt the name of THE INEFFABLE,
Bow down before God's holy mount,
For holy is THE AWESOME ONE, our God!

The Torah reading for the first day of Rosh Hashanah begins on page 481 or page 491; for the second day of Rosh Hashanah, page 503; for Yom Kippur, page 517.

להדם רגליו / before God's footstool. According to tradition, in the Jerusalem Temple there were two cherubim whose wings joined to form a seat. In other ancient Near Eastern temples, an idol was seated in such a chair. In Jerusalem, the chair remained empty with the ark below. The ark was seen as God's footstool, and the Temple as God's entry point into the world. We hope our worship brings God into the world.   D.E.

The leader takes out the Torah and recites each line, followed by the congregation:

שְׁמַע יִשְׂרָאֵל יהוה אֱלֹהֵינוּ יהוה אֶחָד:

Shema yisra'el adonay eloheynu adonay eḥad.

אֶחָד אֱלֹהֵינוּ גָּדוֹל אֲדוֹנֵינוּ קָדוֹשׁ וְנוֹרָא שְׁמוֹ:

Eḥad eloheynu gadol adoneynu kadosh venora shemo.

The leader faces the ark, bows and says:

גַּדְּלוּ לַיהוה אִתִּי וּנְרוֹמְמָה שְׁמוֹ יַחְדָּו:

Gadelu ladonay iti unromemah shemo yaḥdav.

The leader carries the Torah around the room as the leader and congregation sing:

לְךָ יהוה הַגְּדֻלָּה וְהַגְּבוּרָה וְהַתִּפְאֶרֶת וְהַנֵּצַח וְהַהוֹד כִּי־כֹל בַּשָּׁמַיִם
וּבָאָרֶץ לְךָ יהוה הַמַּמְלָכָה וְהַמִּתְנַשֵּׂא לְכֹל לְרֹאשׁ:
רוֹמְמוּ יהוה אֱלֹהֵינוּ וְהִשְׁתַּחֲווּ לַהֲדֹם רַגְלָיו קָדוֹשׁ הוּא:
רוֹמְמוּ יהוה אֱלֹהֵינוּ וְהִשְׁתַּחֲווּ לְהַר קָדְשׁוֹ כִּי־קָדוֹשׁ יהוה אֱלֹהֵינוּ:

Leḥa adonay hagedulah vehagevurah vehatiferet vehanetzaḥ
vehahod ki ḥol bashamayim uva'aretz leḥa adonay hamamlaḥah
vehamitnasey leḥol lerosh.
Romemu adonay eloheynu vehishtaḥavu lahadom raglav kadosh
hu.
Romemu adonay eloheynu vehishtaḥavu lehar kodsho ki kadosh
adonay eloheynu.

The Torah reading for the first day of Rosh Hashanah begins on page 482 or page 492; for the second day of Rosh Hashanah, page 504; for Yom Kippur, page 518.

גדלו...יחדו / Declare...name (Psalms 34:4).
לך...לראש / To you...beings (I Chronicles 29:11).
רוממו...אלהינו / Exalt...our God! (Psalms 99:5,9).

The Torah is placed on the reading table and opened. The gabay *says:*

May God help, protect, and save
all who seek refuge in God's shelter,
and let us say: Amen.
Let everyone declare the greatness of our God,
let all give honor to the Torah.
May _____ arise,
as the first (second, third, . . . seventh) one called up to the Torah.
Blessed is the One who has given Torah to the people Israel! ↵

COMMENTARY. The public reading of the Torah is a form of ritualized study designed to actively engage the participants. During the Torah reading, one person reads from the scroll. There are also two *gabayim*. One *gabay* assigns the Torah honors, calls people up to the Torah, and recites additional prayers, including the *mi sheberah* prayers. The second *gabay* follows the Torah reading closely and corrects errors.

Traditionally, seven adult Jews were called on Shabbat morning, six on Yom Kippur, five on Pilgrimage Festivals and Rosh Hashanah, four on Rosh Hodesh and three on weekdays, Hanukah and Shabbat afternoon. On days when the *haftarah* is chanted, an additional *aliyah*, known as the *maftir*, is given to the person who reads the *haftarah*. In many contemporary synagogues, there are fewer *aliyot* on Shabbat and holidays. D.A.T.

The Torah is placed on the reading table and opened. The gabay *says:*

וְיַעֲזוֹר וְיָגֵן וְיוֹשִׁיעַ לְכָל הַחוֹסִים בּוֹ וְנֹאמַר אָמֵן:
הַכֹּל הָבוּ גֹדֶל לֵאלֹהֵינוּ וּתְנוּ כָבוֹד לַתּוֹרָה:

יַעֲמוֹד/תַּעֲמוֹד/יַעֲמְדוּ _____ בֶּן/בַּת _____ לָעֲלִיָּה/לַמַּפְטִיר
[הָרִאשׁוֹנָה, הַשֵּׁנִית, הַשְּׁלִישִׁית, הָרְבִיעִית, הַחֲמִישִׁית, הַשִּׁשִּׁית,
הַשְּׁבִיעִית, הוֹסָפָה]
בָּרוּךְ שֶׁנָּתַן תּוֹרָה לְעַמּוֹ יִשְׂרָאֵל בִּקְדֻשָּׁתוֹ: ←——

NOTE. The biblical texts used in this *mahzor* for all Torah and *haftarah* readings follow the Masoretic vocalization and trope, and therefore differ from the liturgical Hebrew in the rest of the book.

And you who cling to THE ETERNAL ONE your God,
are all alive today!

COMMENTARY. The 1945 Reconstructionist prayerbook eliminated all references to Jewish chosenness for both ideological and moral reasons. Chosenness posits a God who chooses, and it supports claims of national superiority. Thus, that prayerbook's Torah blessings replace *baḥar banu mikol ha'amim*/who has chosen us from all the peoples, with *asher kervanu la'avodato*/who has drawn us to your service. This prayerbook follows the 1945 version but provides alternatives in the commentary on the facing page.

D.A.T.

COMMENTARY. The *aliyah* is the public enactment of an individual's commitment to Judaism, reiterated in the words of the hallowed formula. It is an enactment of belonging and an enactment of belief.

The *aliyah* is always a numinous moment when the experience of divinity is strong. Even though this numinous quality often is dimmed by repetition or by our increased informality, we still experience the power of standing on the *bimah* before the Torah ark, *ner tamid* (eternal light), Jewish officiants, and fellow Jews. The act links us in the living moment to the mythic event of God's calling the Jewish people at Sinai, as well as to all other moments of calling in Jewish and human experience. When we chant new words, rather than the words of the tradition, we are doing more than merely changing a formula of words; we are enacting our own calling to a new and no longer traditional way of being Jewish. Whereas saying *asher baḥar banu* links us to the biblical drama at Sinai, chanting *asher kervanu* links us both to that drama and to the Reconstructionist movement's root metaphor of Judaism as an evolving religious civilization.

Robin Goldberg

ואתם הדבקים...היום/And you who cling...today (Deuteronomy 4:4). The people to whom this verse was originally spoken live on through their place in the chain of tradition. We touch the past by bringing the ancient words to life. And when future generations recite this verse, we, who have kept the chain alive, will be present. You who cleave to Adonay your God, you are *all* alive today.

D.E.

וְאַתֶּם הַדְּבֵקִים בַּיהוה אֱלֹהֵיכֶם חַיִּים כֻּלְּכֶם הַיּוֹם:

Ve'atem hadevekim badonay eloheyhem ḥayim kuleḥem hayom.

The last part of the blessing preceding the Torah reading has been the subject of considerable discussion. Below are several current variants. You can use these by selecting one from section I, one from II, and then III:

I.   בָּרוּךְ אַתָּה יהוה אֱלֹהֵֽינוּ מֶֽלֶךְ הָעוֹלָם   Blessed are you, ETERNAL ONE,
Baruḥ atah adonay eloheynu meleḥ   our God, sovereign of all worlds
ha'olam

בָּרוּךְ אַתָּה יהוה אֱלֹהֵֽינוּ חֵי הָעוֹלָמִים   Blessed are you, ETERNAL ONE,
Baruḥ atah adonay eloheynu ḥey   our God, life of all the worlds
ha'olamim

נְבָרֵךְ אֶת עֵין הַחַיִּים   Let us bless the source of life
Nevareḥ et eyn haḥayim

II.   אֲשֶׁר קֵרְבָֽנוּ לַעֲבוֹדָתוֹ וְנָֽתַן לָֽנוּ   who has drawn us to your service,
אֶת תּוֹרָתוֹ:   and given us your Torah.
asher kervanu la'avodato venatan
lanu et torato.

אֲשֶׁר בָּחַר בָּֽנוּ מִכָּל הָעַמִּים וְנָֽתַן לָֽנוּ   who has singled us out from all
אֶת תּוֹרָתוֹ:   the peoples and given us your
asher baḥar banu mikol ha'amim   Torah.
venatan lanu et torato.

III.   בָּרוּךְ אַתָּה יהוה נוֹתֵן הַתּוֹרָה: Blessed are you, ETERNAL ONE,
Baruḥ atah adonay noten hatorah.   giver of the Torah.

The phrase *nevareḥ et eyn haḥayim* was originally formulated by poet Marcia Falk (see SOURCES, p. 1248).

BIRHOT HATORAH / TORAH BLESSINGS

Those who receive an aliyah to the Torah say the following blessings:

Bless THE INFINITE, the blessed One!

Congregation:

Blessed is THE INFINITE, the blessed One, now and forever!

The response of the congregation is repeated, and the blessing continued as follows (For alternative versions, see page 474):

Blessed are you, ETERNAL ONE, our God, the sovereign of all worlds, who has drawn us to your service, and has given us your Torah. Blessed are you, ETERNAL ONE, who gives the Torah.

After the section of the Torah is read, the following blessing is recited:

Blessed are you, ETERNAL ONE, our God, the sovereign of all worlds, who has given us a Torah of truth, and planted in our midst eternal life. Blessed are you, ETERNAL ONE, who gives the Torah.

COMMENTARY. Group *aliyot* provide an opportunity for including more people in public roles on the *Yamim Nora'im*. In this season of transition, many communities focus group *aliyot* on beginnings (births and adoptions, new homes, jobs, new committed relationships, weddings, new schools), endings (loss of loved ones, retirements, graduations), and milestones (trips to Israel, *beney mitzvah*). Some communities use one day to mark the past year's accomplishments (*tikun olam*, Jewish learning, leading worship, offering hospitality, communal leadership, *tzedakah*, adult bar/bat mitzvah). Some use a day for marking similar new commitments. Other *aliyot* might be used for those who are healing or who have recovered from life-threatening illness, or those new to the community.   B.P.T./R.S./D.A.T.

COMMENTARY. The blessing over the Torah recalls the *Barehu*, the call to worship, the beginning of the morning and evening services recited only in the presence of the minyan, ten adult Jews. The blessing encircles the Torah reading in a familiar liturgical pattern of blessing and study. Through blessing, study, and community we manifest God, Torah and Israel.   S.P.W.

בִּרְכוֹת הַתּוֹרָה

Those who receive an aliyah to the Torah say the following blessings:

בָּרְכוּ אֶת יהוה הַמְבֹרָךְ:

Barehu et adonay hamevorah.

Congregation:

בָּרוּךְ יהוה הַמְבֹרָךְ לְעוֹלָם וָעֶד:

Baruh adonay hamevorah le'olam va'ed.

The response of the congregation is repeated and the blessing continued as follows
(for alternative versions, see page 474):

בָּרוּךְ אַתָּה יהוה אֱלֹהֵינוּ מֶלֶךְ הָעוֹלָם אֲשֶׁר קֵרְבָנוּ לַעֲבוֹדָתוֹ
וְנָתַן־לָנוּ אֶת־תּוֹרָתוֹ: בָּרוּךְ אַתָּה יהוה נוֹתֵן הַתּוֹרָה:

Baruh atah adonay eloheynu meleh ha'olam asher kervanu
la'avodato venatan lanu et torato.
Baruh atah adonay noten hatorah.

After the section of the Torah is read, the following blessing is recited:

בָּרוּךְ אַתָּה יהוה אֱלֹהֵינוּ מֶלֶךְ הָעוֹלָם אֲשֶׁר נָתַן־לָנוּ תּוֹרַת אֱמֶת
וְחַיֵּי עוֹלָם נָטַע בְּתוֹכֵנוּ: בָּרוּךְ אַתָּה יהוה נוֹתֵן הַתּוֹרָה:

Baruh atah adonay eloheynu meleh ha'olam asher natan lanu
torat emet vehayey olam nata betoheynu.
Baruh atah adonay noten hatorah.

DERASH. *Aliyah* is ascent. We ascend to the Torah to acknowledge that we
choose to live under its laws and principles. We ascend to the Torah to
affirm that we are part of a people and a story that is much greater than
ourselves. We ascend to the Torah to represent those who remain below.
We ascend to the Torah to risk receiving an honor, to risk being known
and seen, to risk being at Sinai again. We ascend to the Torah with slow
steps, or in haste, with enthusiasm or reluctance, in awe or in fear, in hope
and in love.
                                                                    S.P.W.

BIRKAT HAGOMEL / BLESSING FOR DELIVERANCE AND GOOD FORTUNE

If the person called up to the Torah has recently escaped danger or returned safely from a journey, he or she recites as follows:

Blessed are you, ABUNDANT ONE, our God, the sovereign of all worlds, who bestows good things on those in debt to you, and who has granted me all good.

Congregational response to one who offers this blessing:

Amen. And may the one who has bestowed upon you good, continue to bestow upon you good.

For a mi sheberah *for an individual or for a group, see pages 479-480. For other* mi sheberah *prayers, see* Kol Haneshamah: Shabbat Vehagim, *pages 685-693.*

COMMENTARY. *Mi sheberah* prayers announce to the whole community individual times of joy and need. When *birkat hagomel* or a *mi sheberah* is recited, it is customary to contribute to *tzedakah*. Often this offering is directed to the synagogue. On happy occasions this serves as an offering of thanksgiving. A *mi sheberah* in the form of petition, such as a prayer for healing, was traditionally offered in the hope that a good deed would encourage divine intervention. More recently the act of *tzedakah* has been understood as a tangible way of expressing gratitude for the support and good wishes of the community. Just as the community supports the individual in times of need, so does the community depend upon the support of each individual.

D.A.T.

בִּרְכַּת הַגּוֹמֵל

If the person called up to the Torah has recently escaped danger or returned safely from a journey, he or she recites as follows:

בָּרוּךְ אַתָּה יהוה אֱלֹהֵינוּ מֶלֶךְ הָעוֹלָם הַגּוֹמֵל לְחַיָּבִים טוֹבוֹת
שֶׁגְּמָלַנִי כָּל טוֹב:

Baruḥ atah adonay eloheynu meleḥ ha'olam hagomel leḥayavim tovot shegemalani kol tov.

Congregational response to a man who offers this blessing:

אָמֵן. מִי שֶׁגְּמָלְךָ טוֹב הוּא יִגְמָלְךָ כָּל טוֹב סֶלָה:

Amen. Mi shegemaleḥa tov hu yigmolḥa kol tov selah.

Congregational response to a woman who offers this blessing:

אָמֵן. מִי שֶׁגְּמָלֵךְ טוֹב הוּא יִגְמָלֵךְ כָּל טוֹב סֶלָה:

Amen. Mi shegemaleḥ tov hu yigmoleḥ kol tov selah.

COMMENTARY. At the mysterious edges of life we seek the embrace of our community past and present. Hence individuals marking recovery from illness or the birth of a child are blessed before the open Torah. This process can build community as news is communicated and support mobilized. Most significantly it counteracts the devastating possibility of isolation in times of vulnerability. The practice gives voice to gratitude and anxiety in a forum where it can be shared and transformed into connectedness and faith.   S.P.W.

INDIVIDUAL MI SHEBERAH

מִי שֶׁבֵּרַךְ

Male

מִי שֶׁבֵּרַךְ אֲבוֹתֵֽינוּ אַבְרָהָם יִצְחָק וְיַעֲקֹב וְאִמּוֹתֵֽינוּ שָׂרָה רִבְקָה רָחֵל
וְלֵאָה הוּא יְבָרֵךְ אֶת _____ בֶּן _____ וְ _____ שֶׁעָלָה לִכְבוֹד
הַמָּקוֹם וְלִכְבוֹד הַתּוֹרָה (וְלִכְבוֹד הַשַּׁבָּת) וְלִכְבוֹד יוֹם הַדִּין:* הַקָּדוֹשׁ
בָּרוּךְ הוּא יְחַיֵּֽיהוּ וְיִשְׁמְרֵֽהוּ מִכָּל־צָרָה וְצוּקָה וּמִכָּל־נֶֽגַע וּמַחֲלָה
וְיִשְׁלַח בְּרָכָה וְהַצְלָחָה בְּכָל מַעֲשֵׂה יָדָיו וְיִכְתְּבֵהוּ וְיַחְתְּמֵֽהוּ לְחַיִּים
טוֹבִים בְּזֶה יוֹם הַדִּין עִם־כָּל־יִשְׂרָאֵל אֶחָיו וְאַחְיוֹתָיו וְנֹאמַר אָמֵן:

Female

מִי שֶׁבֵּרַךְ אֲבוֹתֵֽינוּ אַבְרָהָם יִצְחָק וְיַעֲקֹב וְאִמּוֹתֵֽינוּ שָׂרָה רִבְקָה
רָחֵל וְלֵאָה הוּא יְבָרֵךְ אֶת _____ בַּת _____ וְ _____
שֶׁעָלְתָה לִכְבוֹד הַמָּקוֹם וְלִכְבוֹד הַתּוֹרָה (וְלִכְבוֹד הַשַּׁבָּת) וְלִכְבוֹד
יוֹם הַדִּין:* וְלִכְבוֹד הַקָּדוֹשׁ בָּרוּךְ הוּא יְחַיֶּֽיהָ וְיִשְׁמְרֶֽהָ מִכָּל־צָרָה
וְצוּקָה וּמִכָּל־נֶֽגַע וּמַחֲלָה וְיִשְׁלַח בְּרָכָה וְהַצְלָחָה בְּכָל מַעֲשֵׂה יָדֶֽיהָ
וְיִכְתְּבֶהָ וְיַחְתְּמֶהָ לְחַיִּים טוֹבִים בְּזֶה יוֹם הַדִּין עִם־כָּל־יִשְׂרָאֵל
אַחֶֽיהָ וְאַחְיוֹתֶֽיהָ וְנֹאמַר אָמֵן:

May the one who blessed our ancestors, Abraham, Isaac, and
Jacob, Sarah, Rebekah, Rachel, and Leah, bless _____
who has risen today in honor of the SOURCE OF ALL and in
honor of the Torah (and Shabbat) and in honor of this Day of
Awe.* May he/she be granted life and kept from every trouble
and affliction, and from every harm and sickness. May he/she be
granted blessing and success in all his/her labors, and may he/
she be written and sealed for good life on this Day of Awe along
with all of Israel, and let us say: Amen.

---

*At this point in the *mi sheberah*, an additional phrase can easily be added.
The *gabay* may choose to chant part or all of the *mi sheberah* in English.
When Hebrew alone is used, an English announcement of the occasion is
appropriate.

D.A.T.

COLLECTIVE BLESSING FOR THOSE WHO HAVE RECEIVED ALIYOT

מִי שֶׁבֵּרַךְ אֲבוֹתֵֽינוּ אַבְרָהָם יִצְחָק וְיַעֲקֹב וְאִמּוֹתֵֽינוּ שָׂרָה רִבְקָה רָחֵל
וְלֵאָה הוּא יְבָרֵךְ אֶת כָּל אֵֽלֶּה שֶׁעָלוּ הַיּוֹם לִכְבוֹד הַמָּקוֹם לִכְבוֹד
הַתּוֹרָה (וְלִכְבוֹד הַשַּׁבָּת וְ) יוֹם הַדִּין בִּשְׂכַר זֶה הַקָּדוֹשׁ בָּרוּךְ הוּא
יְחַיֵּים וְיִשְׁמְרֵם מִכָּל צָרָה וְצוּקָה וּמִכָּל נֶֽגַע וּמַחֲלָה וְיִשְׁלַח בְּרָכָה
וְהַצְלָחָה בְּכָל מַעֲשֵׂה יְדֵיהֶם וְיִכְתְּבֵם וְיַחְתְּמֵם לְחַיִּים טוֹבִים בְּזֶה
יוֹם הַדִּין עִם כָּל יִשְׂרָאֵל אַחֵיהֶם וְאַחְיוֹתֵיהֶם וְנֹאמַר אָמֵן:

May the one who blessed our ancestors, Abraham, Isaac and
Jacob, Sarah, Rebekah, Rachel and Leah, bless all those here who
have risen today in honor of the Omnipresent, and in honor of
the Torah, (and in honor of Shabbat,) and in honor of this Day
of Awe. And by this merit, may they be granted life and kept
from all trouble and affliction, and from every harm or sickness,
and may they find blessing and success in all their labors, and
may they be written and sealed for good life on this Day of Awe,
along with all of Israel, all their brothers and their sisters, and let
us say: Amen.

Some communities read the traditional Torah portion about the birth of Isaac (Genesis 21:1-34) on the first day of Rosh Hashanah, in which case the recommended reading from the second Sefer Torah is about creation (Genesis 1:1-5, page 491). Others first read the entire creation story (Genesis 1:1-2:3), in which case they read the beginning of the story of Isaac's birth (Genesis 21:1-4) for Maftir. A few communities read the traditional Maftir, Numbers 29:1-6, which we have placed as the Maftir for the second day, page 547.

TORAH READING FOR THE FIRST DAY OF ROSH HASHANAH

First Aliyah

THE FOUNT OF LIFE took note of Sarah, as was promised;
thus did THE CREATOR do for Sarah, as was spoken:
She conceived and bore to Abraham a son in his old age,
at the appointed time God had declared.
And Abraham called the child born to him by Sarah: "Yitzḥak."
And Abraham, upon the eighth day, circumcised his son,
as God commanded him.

Genesis 21:1-4

Rosh Hashanah as the birthday of the world recalls for us God's creation of the world in the beginning of time. Strikingly, the traditional Torah reading for Rosh Hashanah is not the story of creation (Genesis 1:1) but rather the birth of Isaac, and the *haftarah* concerns the birth of Samuel—both tales of long-desired births to barren women. In fact, there is a tradition that Rosh Hashanah is *not* the day the world was created. *Pesikta Rabati*, an early rabbinic midrashic work, states that the world was created on the twenty-fifth of Elul. Rosh Hashanah then is the sixth day of creation, the day on which humans were created. For the beginning of humanity marks the real beginning of creation. It is the beginning of history and most of all the beginning of the relationship between the human and the divine. Rosh Hashanah thus affirms the importance of human life, even of one single birth, as equivalent to God's creating the world. By stressing life, it calls upon us to examine the quality of our lives as we prepare for Yom Kippur—the day when life is to be judged.

Michael Strassfeld

Some communities read the traditional Torah portion about the birth of Isaac (Genesis 21:1-34) on the first day of Rosh Hashanah, in which case the recommended reading from the second Sefer Torah is about creation (Genesis 1:1-5, page 492). Others first read the entire creation story (Genesis 1:1-2:3), in which case they read the beginning of the story of Isaac's birth (Genesis 21:1-4) for Maftir. A few communities read the traditional Maftir, Numbers 29:1-6, which we have placed as the Maftir for the second day, page 548.

First Aliyah

וַיהוָה פָּקַד אֶת־שָׂרָה כַּאֲשֶׁר אָמָר וַיַּעַשׂ יהוה לְשָׂרָה כַּאֲשֶׁר דִּבֵּר:
וַתַּהַר וַתֵּלֶד שָׂרָה לְאַבְרָהָם בֵּן לִזְקֻנָיו לַמּוֹעֵד אֲשֶׁר־דִּבֶּר אֹתוֹ
אֱלֹהִים: וַיִּקְרָא אַבְרָהָם אֶת־שֶׁם־בְּנוֹ הַנּוֹלַד־לוֹ אֲשֶׁר־יָלְדָה־לוֹ
שָׂרָה יִצְחָק: וַיָּמָל אַבְרָהָם אֶת־יִצְחָק בְּנוֹ בֶּן־שְׁמֹנַת יָמִים כַּאֲשֶׁר
צִוָּה אֹתוֹ אֱלֹהִים:

DERASH. There is a profound philosophical truth to the rabbinic insight that the world does not begin until the sixth day of Creation and the appearance on that day of the human being. So far as we know, there would be no world, nor God, without the perception of the world by human minds—one might go so far as to say by my human mind. Theoretically, God and the rest of the world might have existed, but like the famous falling tree in the forest that makes no sound without an ear to hear it, without a human mind to perceive God and the world, who would know? God certainly can only be recognized by human beings—God depends on us for that much, at least.   E.L.G.

Second Aliyah

And Abraham was then one hundred years of age
when Yitzḥak, his child, was born to him.
And Sarah said: "God has brought me laughter—*tzeḥok!*—
and all who hear of it will share my laughter, too!"
And she added: "Who would have said to Abraham
that Sarah would be nursing children,
or that I would bear a child in his old age!"

And the child grew, and then was weaned.
And Abraham prepared a splendid feast of celebration
on the day Yitzḥak was weaned.   Genesis 21:5-8

(On Shabbat, Third Aliyah)

But Sarah saw the son that the Egyptian woman, Hagar,
had born to Abraham, and he was mocking—*metzaḥek*.
She said to Abraham: "Cast out this servant-woman
and her son! For this servant-woman's child
shall not inherit with my child, with Yitzḥak!"
And this matter was of grave concern in Abraham's eyes,
for after all, it was his child.
But God told Abraham: "Don't let this matter
of your child and servant-woman be improper in your sight.
Whatever Sarah tells you, listen to her voice,
because through Yitzḥak shall your seed be called.   Genesis 21:9-12

וְאַבְרָהָם בֶּן־מְאַת שָׁנָה בְּהִוָּלֶד לוֹ אֵת יִצְחָק בְּנוֹ: וַתֹּאמֶר שָׂרָה
צְחֹק עָשָׂה לִי אֱלֹהִים כָּל־הַשֹּׁמֵעַ יִצְחַק־לִי: וַתֹּאמֶר מִי מִלֵּל
לְאַבְרָהָם הֵינִיקָה בָנִים שָׂרָה כִּי־יָלַדְתִּי בֵן לִזְקֻנָיו: וַיִּגְדַּל הַיֶּלֶד
וַיִּגָּמַל וַיַּעַשׂ אַבְרָהָם מִשְׁתֶּה גָדוֹל בְּיוֹם הִגָּמֵל אֶת־יִצְחָק:

וַתֵּרֶא שָׂרָה אֶת־בֶּן־הָגָר הַמִּצְרִית אֲשֶׁר־יָלְדָה לְאַבְרָהָם מְצַחֵק:
וַתֹּאמֶר לְאַבְרָהָם גָּרֵשׁ הָאָמָה הַזֹּאת וְאֶת־בְּנָהּ כִּי לֹא יִירַשׁ בֶּן־
הָאָמָה הַזֹּאת עִם־בְּנִי עִם־יִצְחָק: וַיֵּרַע הַדָּבָר מְאֹד בְּעֵינֵי אַבְרָהָם
עַל אוֹדֹת בְּנוֹ: וַיֹּאמֶר אֱלֹהִים אֶל־אַבְרָהָם אַל־יֵרַע בְּעֵינֶיךָ
עַל־הַנַּעַר וְעַל־אֲמָתֶךָ כֹּל אֲשֶׁר תֹּאמַר אֵלֶיךָ שָׂרָה שְׁמַע בְּקֹלָהּ כִּי
בְיִצְחָק יִקָּרֵא לְךָ זָרַע:

Third Aliyah (On Shabbat, Fourth Aliyah)

Besides, the servant-woman's child
I shall make a nation, too; for he, too is your child."
And Abraham arose early the next morning,
and he took a bread loaf and a water sack,
and he gave them to Hagar
—placing them upon her shoulder—
and the child,
and he sent her on her way. She went
and wandered in the desert of Be'er Sheva,
and the water in the water sack was emptied,
and she left the child in the shadow of a bush,
and went and sat a bowshot's length across from him.
"Let me not look upon the child's death," she said,
then raised her voice and wept.
God heard the child's voice,
and God's angel called out to Hagar from heaven,
saying to her: "What's wrong with you, Hagar?
Don't be afraid. For God has heard the child's voice
from where he sits.
                                                        Genesis 21:13-17

COMMENTARY. The word באשר, referring to both time and space, provides
a key to understanding Ishmael's situation. We can understand God's voice
reaching Ishmael באשר הוא שם/where he sits, as a metaphor for Ishmael's
experiences of God's redemptive power. Situating Ishmael in this way
suggests some important insights about the process of *teshuvah* in which
we are engaged. If we seek to understand and forgive, we must forget our
own expectations and assumptions, encountering others as they are at a
particular moment. Similarly, by honestly recognizing and accepting
myself for who I am at this particular time and place in my life, by
honestly engaging in the "stock-taking of the soul" known as *heshbon
hanefesh*, I can find the strength to change the direction of my life.
Becoming conscious of who I am in my essence frees me to improve my
life, my relationships and my world. In meeting others and ourselves
"where they/we are," we follow God's example in the Ishmael story,
finding hope and opportunity for growth and transformation in places and
times that otherwise might be filled with hopelessness and despair. R.S.

FIRST DAY ROSH HASHANAH / 485

וְגַם אֶת־בֶּן־הָאָמָה לְגוֹי אֲשִׂימֶנּוּ כִּי זַרְעֲךָ הוּא: וַיַּשְׁכֵּם אַבְרָהָם ׀
בַּבֹּקֶר וַיִּקַּח־לֶחֶם וְחֵמַת מַיִם וַיִּתֵּן אֶל־הָגָר שָׂם עַל־שִׁכְמָהּ
וְאֶת־הַיֶּלֶד וַיְשַׁלְּחֶהָ וַתֵּלֶךְ וַתֵּתַע בְּמִדְבַּר בְּאֵר שָׁבַע: וַיִּכְלוּ הַמַּיִם
מִן־הַחֵמֶת וַתַּשְׁלֵךְ אֶת־הַיֶּלֶד תַּחַת אַחַד הַשִּׂיחִם: וַתֵּלֶךְ וַתֵּשֶׁב
לָהּ מִנֶּגֶד הַרְחֵק כִּמְטַחֲוֵי קֶשֶׁת כִּי אָמְרָה אַל־אֶרְאֶה בְּמוֹת הַיָּלֶד
וַתֵּשֶׁב מִנֶּגֶד וַתִּשָּׂא אֶת־קֹלָהּ וַתֵּבְךְּ: וַיִּשְׁמַע אֱלֹהִים אֶת־קוֹל
הַנַּעַר וַיִּקְרָא מַלְאַךְ אֱלֹהִים ׀ אֶל־הָגָר מִן־הַשָּׁמַיִם וַיֹּאמֶר לָהּ
מַה־לָּךְ הָגָר אַל־תִּירְאִי כִּי־שָׁמַע אֱלֹהִים אֶל־קוֹל הַנַּעַר בַּאֲשֶׁר
הוּא־שָׁם:

Communities have a history—in an important sense they are constituted by their past—and for this reason we can speak of a real community as a "community of memory," one that does not forget its past. In order not to forget that past, a community is involved in retelling its story, its constitutive narrative, and in so doing, it offers examples of the men and women who have embodied and exemplified the meaning of the community. These stories of collective history and exemplary individuals are an important part of the tradition that is so central to a community of memory.

The stories that make up a tradition contain conceptions of character, of what a good person is like, and of the virtues that define such character. But the stories are not all exemplary, not all about successes and achievements. A genuine community of memory will also tell painful stories of shared suffering that sometimes creates deeper identities than success...And if the community is completely honest, it will remember stories not only of suffering received but of suffering inflicted—dangerous memories, for they call the community to alter ancient evils.

The communities of memory that tie us to the past also turn us toward the future as communities of hope. They carry a context of meaning that can allow us to connect our aspirations for ourselves and those closest to us with aspirations of a larger whole and see our own efforts as being, in part, contributions to a common good. Robert N. Bellah

(On Shabbat, Fifth Aliyah)

Arise now, take the boy,
and hold him with your hand,
for I shall make him a great nation!"
And God opened up her eyes.
She saw a well of water,
and she went and filled the sack with water,
and she gave water to the boy.
And God was with the boy,
and he grew up, and settled in the desert,
and became a shooter of the bow.
He dwelt in Paran's desert,
and his mother got for him a wife from Egypt.

Fourth Aliyah (On Shabbat, Sixth Aliyah)

And it happened at that time
that Abimeleh and Phicol, chief of his army,
said to Abraham: "God is with you in whatever you may do!
Now, swear to me by God right here
that you shall not deal falsely with me,
or with any of my offspring or posterity,
but you shall act, toward me
and toward the land in which you dwell,
according to the kindness I have shown you."
And Abraham replied: "I'll swear it."
But Abraham complained to Abimeleh
about the water Abimeleh's servants stole,
And Abimeleh said: "I didn't know!
Who did this thing? You never told me!
I myself have never heard of it before today."
And Abraham took sheep and cattle,
and he gave them to Abimeleh,
and the two of them cut a covenant.

Genesis 21:18-27

FIRST DAY ROSH HASHANAH / 487

קוּמִי שְׂאִי אֶת־הַנַּעַר וְהַחֲזִיקִי אֶת־יָדֵךְ בּוֹ כִּי־לְגוֹי גָּדוֹל אֲשִׂימֶנּוּ: וַיִּפְקַח אֱלֹהִים אֶת־עֵינֶיהָ וַתֵּרֶא בְּאֵר מָיִם וַתֵּלֶךְ וַתְּמַלֵּא אֶת־הַחֵמֶת מַיִם וַתַּשְׁקְ אֶת־הַנָּעַר: וַיְהִי אֱלֹהִים אֶת־הַנַּעַר וַיִּגְדָּל וַיֵּשֶׁב בַּמִּדְבָּר וַיְהִי רֹבֶה קַשָּׁת: וַיֵּשֶׁב בְּמִדְבַּר פָּארָן וַתִּקַּח־לוֹ אִמּוֹ אִשָּׁה מֵאֶרֶץ מִצְרָיִם:

Fourth Aliyah (On Shabbat, Sixth Aliyah)

וַיְהִי בָּעֵת הַהִוא וַיֹּאמֶר אֲבִימֶלֶךְ וּפִיכֹל שַׂר־צְבָאוֹ אֶל־אַבְרָהָם לֵאמֹר אֱלֹהִים עִמְּךָ בְּכֹל אֲשֶׁר־אַתָּה עֹשֶׂה: וְעַתָּה הִשָּׁבְעָה לִּי בֵאלֹהִים הֵנָּה אִם־תִּשְׁקֹר לִי וּלְנִינִי וּלְנֶכְדִּי כַּחֶסֶד אֲשֶׁר־עָשִׂיתִי עִמְּךָ תַּעֲשֶׂה עִמָּדִי וְעִם־הָאָרֶץ אֲשֶׁר־גַּרְתָּה בָּהּ: וַיֹּאמֶר אַבְרָהָם אָנֹכִי אִשָּׁבֵעַ: וְהוֹכִחַ אַבְרָהָם אֶת־אֲבִימֶלֶךְ עַל־אֹדוֹת בְּאֵר הַמַּיִם אֲשֶׁר גָּזְלוּ עַבְדֵי אֲבִימֶלֶךְ: וַיֹּאמֶר אֲבִימֶלֶךְ לֹא יָדַעְתִּי מִי עָשָׂה אֶת־הַדָּבָר הַזֶּה וְגַם־אַתָּה לֹא־הִגַּדְתָּ לִּי וְגַם אָנֹכִי לֹא שָׁמַעְתִּי בִּלְתִּי הַיּוֹם: וַיִּקַּח אַבְרָהָם צֹאן וּבָקָר וַיִּתֵּן לַאֲבִימֶלֶךְ וַיִּכְרְתוּ שְׁנֵיהֶם בְּרִית:

COMMENTARY. The text says not that a well suddenly appeared, but that Hagar's eyes were opened so that she could now see it. The miracle is spiritual rather than physical or supernatural. The well had always been there, but Hagar, paralyzed by fear, despair, and her own sense of powerlessness, was blinded to the possibility of salvation. In calling out to God, she finds the strength to discover what she needs to do. Only then does Hagar see the well.

Hagar's example can serve as a comfort and an inspiration when the pain and difficulty of our own lives seem too overwhelming, when taking the next step seems impossible. We are reminded that there are always unseen possibilities. As we call out in prayer during the *Yamim Nora'im*, we, too, can reorient our vision, see new possibilities in our lives and adjust our attitudes and actions. R.S.

Fifth Aliyah (On Shabbat, Seventh Aliyah)

Abraham set seven ewes apart. And Abimeleḥ asked:
"What are these seven ewes which you have set apart?"
And he replied: "Here: take these seven ewes from me
by way of testimony that I dug this well."

Therefore one now calls that place
"Be'er Sheva—Well of Oath."

For there the two of them declared an oath,
and made a covenant at Be'er Sheva.
Then Abimeleḥ, and Phicol, chief of his army, rose,
and they returned home to the country of the Philistines.
And [Abraham] planted a tamarisk at Be'er Sheva,
and he called out there the name
of THE ETERNAL ONE, God of the world,
and Abraham lived near the country of the Philistines
for many days.

Genesis 21:28-34

DERASH. The Hebrew for tamarisk is אשל. Its three letters signify the essentials of Abraham's hospitality: א for אכילה / food, ש for שתיה / drink, and ל for לויה / escort.

Genesis Rabbah 54.6

DERASH. Why, immediately after making a contract with King Abimeleḥ, does Abraham call on "the name of THE ETERNAL ONE, God of the world?" To emphasize that no earthly authority should be allowed to obscure our ultimate allegiance.

J.A.S./D.A.T.

וַיַּצֵּב אַבְרָהָם אֶת־שֶׁבַע כִּבְשֹׂת הַצֹּאן לְבַדְּהֶן: וַיֹּאמֶר אֲבִימֶלֶךְ
אֶל־אַבְרָהָם מָה הֵנָּה שֶׁבַע כְּבָשֹׂת הָאֵלֶּה אֲשֶׁר הִצַּבְתָּ לְבַדָּנָה:
וַיֹּאמֶר כִּי אֶת־שֶׁבַע כְּבָשֹׂת תִּקַּח מִיָּדִי בַּעֲבוּר תִּהְיֶה־לִּי לְעֵדָה כִּי
חָפַרְתִּי אֶת־הַבְּאֵר הַזֹּאת: עַל־כֵּן קָרָא לַמָּקוֹם הַהוּא בְּאֵר שָׁבַע
כִּי שָׁם נִשְׁבְּעוּ שְׁנֵיהֶם: וַיִּכְרְתוּ בְרִית בִּבְאֵר שָׁבַע וַיָּקָם אֲבִימֶלֶךְ
וּפִיכֹל שַׂר־צְבָאוֹ וַיָּשֻׁבוּ אֶל־אֶרֶץ פְּלִשְׁתִּים: וַיִּטַּע אֶשֶׁל בִּבְאֵר
שָׁבַע וַיִּקְרָא־שָׁם בְּשֵׁם יהוה אֵל עוֹלָם: וַיָּגָר אַבְרָהָם בְּאֶרֶץ
פְּלִשְׁתִּים יָמִים רַבִּים:

ALTERNATIVE TORAH READING FOR THE FIRST DAY OF ROSH HASHANAH

First Aliyah

When God at first created the heavens and the earth,
the earth was waste and wildness,
with darkness on the face of ocean depths.
The breath of God was hovering
upon the water's face.
God said: Let there be light! And there was light.
God saw the light, that it was good,
and God divided between light and darkness.
And God called light "day";
and darkness God called "night."
And there was evening; there was morning:
One day.

Genesis 1:1-5

When recited as a Maftir *portion, the reading concludes here, and the service continues with lifting and tying the scroll, followed by the* haftarah, *page 551.*

COMMENTARY. With regard to Creation, there are mitzvot on several levels that derive from our commitment to the retelling of the tale. Faith in Creation makes demands in the areas of both those mitzvot that lead to the personal fulfillment of divinity in our lives, and those that lead to the greater realization of the divine presence in the universe as a whole. The first mitzvah that proceeds from our faith in Creation is that of awareness itself. The obligation to remain aware of divine presence is the foundation of all religious life. The second mitzvah of Creation is that of treating every human being as the image of God. Every person is entitled to the esteem and reverence in which we hold the face of God. A third mitzvah that Creation calls upon us to fulfill is that of the Sabbath. A fourth mitzvah is that of acting with concern for the healthy survival of Creation itself. The rabbis tell us that shortly after Adam was created, God walked him around the Garden of Eden and told him to take care to guard the world that he was being given. "If you destroy this world," he was told, "there is no one to come and set it right after you." Such an *aggadah* has a level of intense meaning in our age that the early rabbis could hardly have foretold. Telling the tale of Creation is itself a statement of love of the natural world. It needs to be accompanied by actions that bear witness to that love—without these it is false testimony.

A.G.

ALTERNATIVE TORAH READING FOR THE FIRST DAY OF ROSH HASHANAH

First Aliyah

בְּרֵאשִׁית בָּרָא אֱלֹהִים אֵת הַשָּׁמַיִם וְאֵת הָאָרֶץ: וְהָאָרֶץ הָיְתָה
תֹהוּ וָבֹהוּ וְחֹשֶׁךְ עַל־פְּנֵי תְהוֹם וְרוּחַ אֱלֹהִים מְרַחֶפֶת עַל־פְּנֵי
הַמָּיִם: וַיֹּאמֶר אֱלֹהִים יְהִי אוֹר וַיְהִי־אוֹר: וַיַּרְא אֱלֹהִים אֶת־
הָאוֹר כִּי־טוֹב וַיַּבְדֵּל אֱלֹהִים בֵּין הָאוֹר וּבֵין הַחֹשֶׁךְ: וַיִּקְרָא
אֱלֹהִים ׀ לָאוֹר יוֹם וְלַחֹשֶׁךְ קָרָא לָיְלָה וַיְהִי־עֶרֶב וַיְהִי־בֹקֶר יוֹם
אֶחָד:

When recited as a Maftir portion, the reading concludes here, and the service continues with lifting and tying the scroll, followed by the haftarah, page 552.

DERASH. In the Torah we learn that light comes from God. "God said, 'Let there be light.' And there was light. God saw the light, that it was good." Our mystics believe that each human soul is a divine spark, a small piece of God. When you put all the small sparks together, you increase light. By working together for justice, we bring more light into the world. S.D.R.

בראשית ברא / When God at first created. God created the world in a permanent state of ראשית /beginning. The universe is always incomplete. Continuous creative effort is needed to renew the world, to keep it from sinking again into primeval chaos. Simḥah Bunam of Przysucha

DERASH. God sought to create a partnership with people, to be one with them. Thus, the text says, "A day of oneness" (יום אחד). Similarly, the first day of making offerings to God in the sanctuary was like the first day of creation, for on that day we drew near to God. On a day when we seek oneness with God, God proclaims, "It is like the day that I created my world"—we are made one with God again. Genesis Rabbah 3:9 (Adapted)

Second Aliyah

And God said: "Let there be a dome amid the waters,
and let it separate between the waters!"
And God made the dome, and thus divided
between the waters that were beneath the dome
and the waters that were above the dome.
And it was so.
And God called the dome "Heaven."
And there was evening; there was morning:
a second day.

(On Shabbat, Third Aliyah)

And God said: "Let the waters underneath the heavens
be gathered to a single place,
and let dry land appear!"
And it was so.
And God called the dry land "Earth,"
and where the waters gathered up
God called them "Oceans."
And God saw that it was good.
And God said: "Let the earth grow grasses
putting forth their seed,
and fruit trees yielding fruit
according to their kinds, their seed within them,
all across the earth!"
And it was so.
The earth brought forth the grasses
putting forth their seed according to their kinds,
and trees yielding fruits, their seed within them,
each according to its kind.
God saw that it was good.
And there was evening; there was morning:
a third day.

Genesis 1:6-13

וַיֹּאמֶר אֱלֹהִים יְהִי רָקִיעַ בְּתוֹךְ הַמָּיִם וִיהִי מַבְדִּיל בֵּין מַיִם לָמָיִם: וַיַּעַשׂ אֱלֹהִים אֶת־הָרָקִיעַ וַיַּבְדֵּל בֵּין הַמַּיִם אֲשֶׁר מִתַּחַת לָרָקִיעַ וּבֵין הַמַּיִם אֲשֶׁר מֵעַל לָרָקִיעַ וַיְהִי־כֵן: וַיִּקְרָא אֱלֹהִים לָרָקִיעַ שָׁמָיִם וַיְהִי־עֶרֶב וַיְהִי־בֹקֶר יוֹם שֵׁנִי:

(*On Shabbat, Third Aliyah*)

וַיֹּאמֶר אֱלֹהִים יִקָּווּ הַמַּיִם מִתַּחַת הַשָּׁמַיִם אֶל־מָקוֹם אֶחָד וְתֵרָאֶה הַיַּבָּשָׁה וַיְהִי־כֵן: וַיִּקְרָא אֱלֹהִים ׀ לַיַּבָּשָׁה אֶרֶץ וּלְמִקְוֵה הַמַּיִם קָרָא יַמִּים וַיַּרְא אֱלֹהִים כִּי־טוֹב: וַיֹּאמֶר אֱלֹהִים תַּדְשֵׁא הָאָרֶץ דֶּשֶׁא עֵשֶׂב מַזְרִיעַ זֶרַע עֵץ פְּרִי עֹשֶׂה פְּרִי לְמִינוֹ אֲשֶׁר זַרְעוֹ־ בוֹ עַל־הָאָרֶץ וַיְהִי־כֵן: וַתּוֹצֵא הָאָרֶץ דֶּשֶׁא עֵשֶׂב מַזְרִיעַ זֶרַע לְמִינֵהוּ וְעֵץ עֹשֶׂה־פְּרִי אֲשֶׁר זַרְעוֹ־בוֹ לְמִינֵהוּ וַיַּרְא אֱלֹהִים כִּי־ טוֹב: וַיְהִי־עֶרֶב וַיְהִי־בֹקֶר יוֹם שְׁלִישִׁי:

COMMENTARY. The first chapter of Genesis indicates that there is an underlying unity to the universe, a unity which is then divided into its parts by the divine act of naming. Other religious traditions have also expressed this idea. For example, the Tao Te Ching says that "the nameless is the beginning of heaven and earth; the named is the mother of ten thousand things." The religious impulse in all of us involves becoming aware that the many are also one.   J.A.S.

Why is the second day the only day not described as "good?" Rabbi Ḥanina said, "It is because on that day schism was created, as it is said, 'God...divided between the waters....' Rabbi Tavyomi added, "If a schism that improved the world is not described as 'good,' then how much the more so a schism that detracts from it."   Genesis Rabbah 4:6

Third Aliyah (On Shabbat, Fourth Aliyah)

And God said: "Let there be luminaries
in the dome of heaven,
to divide between the day and night,
and they shall serve for signs and seasons,
and for days and years.
And let them serve as lamps
amid the dome of heaven,
to give light upon the earth!"
And it was so.
God made the two great luminaries,
the larger one to rule the day,
the smaller one to rule the night, together with the stars.
God placed them in the dome of heaven,
to give light upon the earth,
to rule the day and night,
and to divide between the light and darkness.
And God saw that it was good.
And there was evening; there was morning: a fourth day.

(On Shabbat, Fifth Aliyah)

And God said: "Let the waters teem
with swarming creatures and the breath of life,
and let birds fly above the earth across the face of heaven's dome!"
And God created the great sea-beasts,
and all the animals that move about,
with which the waters teemed according to their kinds,
and every winged bird according to its kind.
God saw that it was good.
And God blessed them, saying:
"Be fruitful and increase,
and fill the waters of the seas,
and let birds multiply throughout the earth!"
And there was evening; there was morning: a fifth day.

Genesis 1:14-23

FIRST DAY ROSH HASHANAH / 495

Third Aliyah (On Shabbat, Fourth Aliyah)

וַיֹּ֣אמֶר אֱלֹהִ֗ים יְהִ֤י מְאֹרֹת֙ בִּרְקִ֣יעַ הַשָּׁמַ֔יִם לְהַבְדִּ֕יל בֵּ֥ין הַיּ֖וֹם וּבֵ֣ין הַלָּ֑יְלָה וְהָי֤וּ לְאֹתֹת֙ וּלְמ֣וֹעֲדִ֔ים וּלְיָמִ֖ים וְשָׁנִֽים: וְהָי֤וּ לִמְאוֹרֹת֙ בִּרְקִ֣יעַ הַשָּׁמַ֔יִם לְהָאִ֖יר עַל־הָאָ֑רֶץ וַֽיְהִי־כֵֽן: וַיַּ֣עַשׂ אֱלֹהִ֔ים אֶת־שְׁנֵ֥י הַמְּאֹרֹ֖ת הַגְּדֹלִ֑ים אֶת־הַמָּא֤וֹר הַגָּדֹל֙ לְמֶמְשֶׁ֣לֶת הַיּ֔וֹם וְאֶת־הַמָּא֤וֹר הַקָּטֹן֙ לְמֶמְשֶׁ֣לֶת הַלַּ֔יְלָה וְאֵ֖ת הַכּֽוֹכָבִֽים: וַיִּתֵּ֥ן אֹתָ֛ם אֱלֹהִ֖ים בִּרְקִ֣יעַ הַשָּׁמָ֑יִם לְהָאִ֖יר עַל־הָאָֽרֶץ: וְלִמְשֹׁל֙ בַּיּ֣וֹם וּבַלַּ֔יְלָה וּֽלְהַבְדִּ֔יל בֵּ֥ין הָא֖וֹר וּבֵ֣ין הַחֹ֑שֶׁךְ וַיַּ֥רְא אֱלֹהִ֖ים כִּי־טֽוֹב: וַֽיְהִי־עֶ֥רֶב וַֽיְהִי־בֹ֖קֶר י֥וֹם רְבִיעִֽי:

(On Shabbat, Fifth Aliyah)

וַיֹּ֣אמֶר אֱלֹהִ֔ים יִשְׁרְצ֣וּ הַמַּ֔יִם שֶׁ֖רֶץ נֶ֣פֶשׁ חַיָּ֑ה וְעוֹף֙ יְעוֹפֵ֣ף עַל־הָאָ֔רֶץ עַל־פְּנֵ֖י רְקִ֥יעַ הַשָּׁמָֽיִם: וַיִּבְרָ֣א אֱלֹהִ֔ים אֶת־הַתַּנִּינִ֖ם הַגְּדֹלִ֑ים וְאֵ֣ת כָּל־נֶ֣פֶשׁ הַֽחַיָּ֣ה ׀ הָֽרֹמֶ֡שֶׂת אֲשֶׁר֩ שָׁרְצ֨וּ הַמַּ֜יִם לְמִֽינֵהֶ֗ם וְאֵ֤ת כָּל־ע֤וֹף כָּנָף֙ לְמִינֵ֔הוּ וַיַּ֥רְא אֱלֹהִ֖ים כִּי־טֽוֹב: וַיְבָ֧רֶךְ אֹתָ֛ם אֱלֹהִ֖ים לֵאמֹ֑ר פְּר֣וּ וּרְב֗וּ וּמִלְא֤וּ אֶת־הַמַּ֨יִם֙ בַּיַּמִּ֔ים וְהָע֖וֹף יִ֥רֶב בָּאָֽרֶץ: וַֽיְהִי־עֶ֥רֶב וַֽיְהִי־בֹ֖קֶר י֥וֹם חֲמִישִֽׁי:

Fourth Aliyah (On Shabbat, Sixth Aliyah)

And God said: "Let the earth bring forth
land animals according to their kinds—
the cattle and the roving creatures,
and the wild beasts, according to their kind!"
And it was so.
God made the wild beasts according to their kind
and cattle according to its kind,
and all the swarming creatures of the earth
according to their kind!
God saw that it was good.
And God said: "Let us make a human being
in our image, and according to our likeness,
and let the humans rule the fishes of the sea,
the birds across the skies,
and creatures of the earth,
and every creeping thing that creeps upon the land."
And God created the human being
in God's image—
in the image of divinity did God create it;
both male and female God created them.
And God blessed them, and God said to them:
"Be fruitful and increase,
and fill the earth, and be responsible for it,
and rule the fishes of the sea,
the birds across the skies,
and every living thing that moves upon the earth."
And God said: "See, I hereby give to you
all the grasses putting forth their seed
across the face of all the earth,
and every tree, within which is a tree-fruit
putting forth its seed—it shall be food for you.
And for every living creature of the earth,
and every bird across the skies,
and everything that moves about upon the earth,

Fourth Aliyah (On Shabbat, Sixth Aliyah)

וַיֹּאמֶר אֱלֹהִים תּוֹצֵא הָאָרֶץ נֶפֶשׁ חַיָּה לְמִינָהּ בְּהֵמָה וָרֶמֶשׂ
וְחַיְתוֹ־אֶרֶץ לְמִינָהּ וַיְהִי־כֵן: וַיַּעַשׂ אֱלֹהִים אֶת־חַיַּת הָאָרֶץ לְמִינָהּ
וְאֶת־הַבְּהֵמָה לְמִינָהּ וְאֵת כָּל־רֶמֶשׂ הָאֲדָמָה לְמִינֵהוּ וַיַּרְא
אֱלֹהִים כִּי־טוֹב: וַיֹּאמֶר אֱלֹהִים נַעֲשֶׂה אָדָם בְּצַלְמֵנוּ כִּדְמוּתֵנוּ
וְיִרְדּוּ בִדְגַת הַיָּם וּבְעוֹף הַשָּׁמַיִם וּבַבְּהֵמָה וּבְכָל־הָאָרֶץ וּבְכָל־
הָרֶמֶשׂ הָרֹמֵשׂ עַל־הָאָרֶץ: וַיִּבְרָא אֱלֹהִים | אֶת־הָאָדָם בְּצַלְמוֹ
בְּצֶלֶם אֱלֹהִים בָּרָא אֹתוֹ זָכָר וּנְקֵבָה בָּרָא אֹתָם: וַיְבָרֶךְ אֹתָם
אֱלֹהִים וַיֹּאמֶר לָהֶם אֱלֹהִים פְּרוּ וּרְבוּ וּמִלְאוּ אֶת־הָאָרֶץ וְכִבְשֻׁהָ
וּרְדוּ בִּדְגַת הַיָּם וּבְעוֹף הַשָּׁמַיִם וּבְכָל־חַיָּה הָרֹמֶשֶׂת עַל־הָאָרֶץ:
וַיֹּאמֶר אֱלֹהִים הִנֵּה נָתַתִּי לָכֶם אֶת־כָּל־עֵשֶׂב | זֹרֵעַ זֶרַע אֲשֶׁר עַל־
פְּנֵי כָל־הָאָרֶץ וְאֶת־כָּל־הָעֵץ אֲשֶׁר־בּוֹ פְרִי־עֵץ זֹרֵעַ זָרַע לָכֶם
יִהְיֶה לְאָכְלָה: וּלְכָל־חַיַּת הָאָרֶץ וּלְכָל־עוֹף הַשָּׁמַיִם וּלְכֹל | ←

DERASH. When God was about to create the first people, God saw that
both righteous and wicked would be among the descendants of Adam and
Eve. God said, "If I create Adam, wicked people will descend from him,
but if I do not create Adam, the righteous will not descend from him." So
God momentarily ignored the ways of the wicked, and with divine mercy
created the first people.   Genesis Rabbah 8:4

DERASH. When a flesh-and-blood ruler stamps an image on a coin, every
coin looks alike, but even though the sovereign of all made each of us in
the divine image, no two of us are alike.   Mishnah Sanhedrin 4:5

DERASH. Why does the Torah say that Adam—a single person—was created
first? For the sake of peace, for no one can say, my ancestor was greater
than yours.   Mishnah Sanhedrin 4:5

COMMENTARY. The rabbis taught that every bit of creation is essential. Not
even the mosquito, that annoying little creature, is superfluous. Even
snakes and frogs are manifestations of divine will!
                                          Genesis Rabbah 10:7 (Adapted)

498 / ALTERNATIVE MORNING TORAH READING

whatever has the breath of life within,
all grass and vegetation shall be food."
And it was so.
And God saw all that had been made,
and truly it was very good.
And there was evening; there was morning:
the sixth day.

Genesis 1:24-31

Fifth Aliyah (On Shabbat, Seventh Aliyah)

And the heavens and the earth, and all their beings
were finished. And God finished on the seventh day
the work that had been done.
God rested on the seventh day
from all the labors God had done.
God blessed the seventh day,
and made it holy,
for on it God had rested from all work
that God had done in carrying out Creation.

Genesis 2:1-3

When the Creation story has been read from the first scroll, the Ḥatzi Kaddish, *page 543, is recited here.*

רוֹמֵשׂ עַל־הָאָרֶץ אֲשֶׁר־בּוֹ נֶפֶשׁ חַיָּה אֶת־כָּל־יֶרֶק עֵשֶׂב לְאָכְלָה וַיְהִי־כֵן: וַיַּרְא אֱלֹהִים אֶת־כָּל־אֲשֶׁר עָשָׂה וְהִנֵּה־טוֹב מְאֹד וַיְהִי־עֶרֶב וַיְהִי־בֹקֶר יוֹם הַשִּׁשִּׁי:

Fifth Aliyah (On Shabbat, Seventh Aliyah)

וַיְכֻלּוּ הַשָּׁמַיִם וְהָאָרֶץ וְכָל־צְבָאָם: וַיְכַל אֱלֹהִים בַּיּוֹם הַשְּׁבִיעִי מְלַאכְתּוֹ אֲשֶׁר עָשָׂה וַיִּשְׁבֹּת בַּיּוֹם הַשְּׁבִיעִי מִכָּל־מְלַאכְתּוֹ אֲשֶׁר עָשָׂה: וַיְבָרֶךְ אֱלֹהִים אֶת־יוֹם הַשְּׁבִיעִי וַיְקַדֵּשׁ אֹתוֹ כִּי בוֹ שָׁבַת מִכָּל־מְלַאכְתּוֹ אֲשֶׁר־בָּרָא אֱלֹהִים לַעֲשׂוֹת:

When the Creation story has been read from the first scroll, the Ḥatzi Kaddish, page 544, is recited here.

DERASH. Traditional education in physics begins with pulleys, levers and inclined planes, continues with trajectories and motion, and electricity and magnetism. After studying relativity, $E=Mc^2$, and Heisenberg uncertainty one can begin to unravel the big bang and other cosmologies. Similarly traditional Jewish study of Ḥumash begins not with Genesis, but with the Levitical codes of sin and sacrifice, then the book of Numbers, and the miracles of the Exodus. After studying the Ten Commandments and the sermons of Deuteronomy, as well as Codes, Mishnah, Maimonides, and Talmud, one can truly begin to unravel the deep mysteries of *Bereyshit Bara Elohim*.... In choosing to read Genesis on Rosh Hashanah we set for ourselves both a standard and a goal. The text, like the creation it describes, is incredibly complex. We must learn much to begin to understand it, and what we have already learned is just the Beginning....

E.M.

וכבשה /*vehivshuha* / be responsible. Literally, "subdue it." Human beings have extraordinary powers for reshaping the world, taming animals, growing crops, even for creating and destroying whole species. The biblical text acknowledges this power. Our translation suggests that we have our power as stewards of God's will. It is up to us to act responsibly.   D.A.T.

A PRAYER FOR CHILDREN

We pray for the children who put chocolate fingers on everything, who love to be tickled, who stomp in puddles and ruin their new pants, who eat candy before supper and who can never find their shoes in the morning. And we also pray for those who stare at photographers from behind barbed wire, who have never bounded down the street in a new pair of shoes, and who are born in places that we would not be caught dead in and that they will be.

We pray for the children who give us sticky kisses and fistfuls of dandelions, who sleep with their dogs and who bury their goldfish, who hug us so tightly and who forget their lunch money, who squeeze toothpaste all over the sink, who watch their fathers shave, and who slurp their soup. And we also pray for those who will never get dessert, who watch their fathers suffer, who cannot find any bread to steal, who do not have any rooms to clean up, whose pictures are on milk cartons instead of on dressers, and whose monsters are real.

We pray for the children who spend all of their allowance by Tuesday, who pick at their food, who love ghost stories, who shove dirty clothes under the bed and who never rinse the bathtub, who love visits from the tooth fairy, even after they find out who it really is, who do not like to be kissed in front of the school bus, and who squirm during services.

And we also pray for those children whose nightmares occur in the daytime, who live in the gunsights of their brothers and sisters, who will eat anything, who have never seen a dentist, who are not spoiled by anyone, who go to bed hungry and wake up hungry, whose bodies consume themselves, who live and move and have no address. We pray for those who will grab the hand of anyone kind enough to offer it, and for those who find no hand to grab.

For all these children, we pray today, for they are all so precious.

Ina J. Hughs (Adapted)

ROSH HASHANAH / 501

ON ROSH HASHANAH:
WELCOMING THE NEWBORN

Parents who have welcomed children into their homes are invited with them to the Bimah.

Reader: When the people of Israel stood at Mount Sinai ready to receive the Torah, God said to them, "Bring me good securities to guarantee that you will keep my Way, and then I will give Torah to you." They said, "Our ancestors are our securities." God said, "I have faults to find with your ancestors..." They said, "Our prophets will be our securities." God said, "I have faults to find with your prophets...." They said, "Our children will be our securities." And God replied, "Indeed, they are good securities. For their sake will I give you my Torah." Song of Songs Rabbah 1:4

Congregation: For the sake of the children, for the sake of the unfolding was Torah given to Israel. Let us welcome the newborn of our people and the children who have come into our midst this year, bringing special joy. Let us welcome the children, that they might become our guarantors, reminding us that we receive Torah only to teach Torah. And that we teach Torah only when we do Torah: here, now and always.

Parents: We are humbled by this moment. Through our love, we raise this child in love. The mystery of beginnings is with us, and we acknowledge its presence.

בָּרוּךְ אַתָּה יהוה אֱלֹהֵינוּ מֶלֶךְ הָעוֹלָם שֶׁהֶחֱיָנוּ וְקִיְּמָנוּ וְהִגִּיעָנוּ לַזְּמָן הַזֶּה:

Blessed is the FOUNTAIN OF BEING whose power enlivens us, sustains us, and enables us to reach this moment of joy.

Reader: There is grace in every dawn, loveliness in every fresh morning. We will endure, we will prevail—we the children of Hope, children of the One who crowds the heavens with stars, endows the earth with glory, and fills the mind with wonder!

Chaim Stern (Adapted)

Parents and children are seated.

TORAH READING FOR THE SECOND DAY OF ROSH HASHANAH

First Aliyah

After these things, God tested Abraham.
He said to him, "Abraham." And Abraham replied: "I'm here."
God said: "Take, now, your child,
your only child, your beloved Yitzḥak,
and go forth to the land of Moriah,
and offer him up there as a burnt-offering
upon one of the mountains I shall indicate to you."

And Abraham arose early the next morning,
and saddled his donkey,
and he took with him two servant-boys,
and Yitzḥak, his child,
and he split the wood of the burnt-offering,
and he arose, and went off to the place God told him of.

Genesis 22:1-3

KAVANAH. Beware the person who says, "I know exactly what this verse of Torah means!" For meaning has many layers, and the last one we uncover sheds new light on the first.   D.A.T.

COMMENTARY. When God first said, "לך לך /go forth," Abraham did as he was told, separating himself from his family and land of origin and embarking on his life's adventure. Here the same words call Abraham to go forth again, this time to the culmination of that journey.

Samson Raphael Hirsch (Adapted)

וַיְהִ֗י אַחַר֙ הַדְּבָרִ֣ים הָאֵ֔לֶּה וְהָ֣אֱלֹהִ֔ים נִסָּ֖ה אֶת־אַבְרָהָ֑ם וַיֹּ֣אמֶר
אֵלָ֔יו אַבְרָהָ֖ם וַיֹּ֥אמֶר הִנֵּֽנִי: וַיֹּ֡אמֶר קַח־נָ֠א אֶת־בִּנְךָ֙ אֶת־יְחִֽידְךָ֤
אֲשֶׁר־אָהַ֙בְתָּ֙ אֶת־יִצְחָ֔ק וְלֶךְ־לְךָ֔ אֶל־אֶ֖רֶץ הַמֹּרִיָּ֑ה וְהַעֲלֵ֤הוּ שָׁם֙
לְעֹלָ֔ה עַ֚ל אַחַ֣ד הֶֽהָרִ֔ים אֲשֶׁ֖ר אֹמַ֥ר אֵלֶֽיךָ: וַיַּשְׁכֵּ֨ם אַבְרָהָ֜ם בַּבֹּ֗קֶר
וַֽיַּחֲבֹשׁ֙ אֶת־חֲמֹר֔וֹ וַיִּקַּ֞ח אֶת־שְׁנֵ֤י נְעָרָיו֙ אִתּ֔וֹ וְאֵ֖ת יִצְחָ֣ק בְּנ֑וֹ וַיְבַקַּע֙
עֲצֵ֣י עֹלָ֔ה וַיָּ֣קָם וַיֵּ֔לֶךְ אֶל־הַמָּק֖וֹם אֲשֶׁר־אָֽמַר־ל֥וֹ הָאֱלֹהִֽים:

COMMENTARY. For our ancestors, the narrative of the *Akedah*, binding of
Isaac, was a model of patriarchal piety. Abraham's willingness to sacrifice
his son coupled with Isaac's passive participation were painfully consoling
to generations of Jews for whom martyrdom was decreed.

Our experience is different; we would not collaborate with a God who
demands the life of our children as the condition of the Covenant. We
resonate instead with the Abraham of Sodom and Gemorah, who dares
God: "Shall not the Judge of all the earth act justly?"

Yet despite our difficulties with the story, we evade it at our peril. There is,
after all, a dark side to human life, to religious life. There are impulses of
aggression within each of us, dormant perhaps, under control we hope,
but always ready to be released.

The *Akedah* challenges us not to emulate the cruel faith of Abraham, but
to recognize in his actions our own potential to harm, even destroy, those
we love.   R.H.

COMMENTARY. What a difference between Abraham as public figure and
private person! Abraham is a shrewd general, clever negotiator, covenantor
with God, and generous host to strangers. Yet he never reconciles with his
parents, cannot resolve the tension between Sarah and Hagar, fails to
defend Sarah, and sends Hagar and Ishmael out into the desert. I believe
that the test of Abraham contained in the binding of Isaac is the inevitable
outcome of the dissonance between the public and private Abraham. Our
public and private actions can only move toward harmony when we do
teshuvah, the turning that unites our inner and outer lives. We need not be
shocked into change by the near-sacrifice of our children. "Let the hearts
of parents be turned to their children, and the hearts of children turned to
their parents". (Malachi 3:24)   E.M.

504 / MORNING TORAH READING

Second Aliyah

And on the third day of the journey,
Abraham raised up his eyes,
and saw the place from far away.
And Abraham said to his servants:
"Wait here with the donkey.
I and the boy will go up to that place
and worship, and we shall return to you."
And Abraham picked up the wood of the burnt-offering,
and placed it on Yitzhak, his child,
and he took the firebrand in his hand, and the sacrificial knife,
and the two of them went on together.
And Yitzhak spoke to Abraham, his father.
"Father," said he. "I'm here, my son," he answered.
"Behold," he asked, "here are the firebrand and the wood,
but where's the lamb for the burnt-offering?"
And Abraham replied: "God will provide the lamb
for the burnt-offering, my son."
And the two of them went on together.

Genesis 22:4-8

COMMENTARY. Picture the young Isaac, roused by his father. Abraham's preparation and motivation for this excursion are hidden from Isaac's young consciousness. He begins to walk after the adult. As they travel, he catches up and sees what Abraham is carrying in front of him. He notes the knife, the wood on the donkey, the flame. "We are going to sacrifice, to pray," he realizes. But he sees that there is no animal. So he says, "I see the fire and the wood, but where is the animal to be sacrificed?" As the son now strides easily next to the old man, the father replies, "God will show us how to use what we have brought and exactly what we will sacrifice." And indeed, Isaac now turns from Abraham and looks ahead into the unknowable future, as he now knows his father has done since hearing the voice saying, "Go now from the place you know to one I will show you." "And they walked together side by side." The child follows behind the parent, unaware that the parent is walking ahead into an unknown. The child grows, catches up, the two look together into the uncertain future; the child becomes an adult.   Daniel Siegel

SECOND DAY ROSH HASHANAH / 505

בַּיּוֹם הַשְּׁלִישִׁי וַיִּשָּׂא אַבְרָהָם אֶת־עֵינָיו וַיַּרְא אֶת־הַמָּקוֹם מֵרָחֹק:
וַיֹּאמֶר אַבְרָהָם אֶל־נְעָרָיו שְׁבוּ־לָכֶם פֹּה עִם־הַחֲמוֹר וַאֲנִי וְהַנַּעַר
נֵלְכָה עַד־כֹּה וְנִשְׁתַּחֲוֶה וְנָשׁוּבָה אֲלֵיכֶם: וַיִּקַּח אַבְרָהָם אֶת־עֲצֵי
הָעֹלָה וַיָּשֶׂם עַל־יִצְחָק בְּנוֹ וַיִּקַּח בְּיָדוֹ אֶת־הָאֵשׁ וְאֶת־הַמַּאֲכֶלֶת
וַיֵּלְכוּ שְׁנֵיהֶם יַחְדָּו: וַיֹּאמֶר יִצְחָק אֶל־אַבְרָהָם אָבִיו וַיֹּאמֶר אָבִי
וַיֹּאמֶר הִנֶּנִּי בְנִי וַיֹּאמֶר הִנֵּה הָאֵשׁ וְהָעֵצִים וְאַיֵּה הַשֶּׂה לְעֹלָה:
וַיֹּאמֶר אַבְרָהָם אֱלֹהִים יִרְאֶה־לּוֹ הַשֶּׂה לְעֹלָה בְּנִי וַיֵּלְכוּ שְׁנֵיהֶם
יַחְדָּו:

DERASH. Even as God is the dominant Father and Abraham a trusting and obedient son, so in the purely human realm Abraham appears as the dominant father and Isaac as the archetype of the submissive son. Only once does Isaac speak and ask the fateful question; thereafter he is a mere object of the drama. Abraham, the prince and Patriarch, the honored and aged friend of God, overawes his timid son, whose will to independence may well have been crippled by doting and protective parents. He has no personality apart from his father. As one they walk together to the sacrifice, and silently Isaac submits to the dreadful act.

The story may thus be read as a paradigm of a father-and-son relationship. In a way every parent seeks to dominate his child and is in danger of seeking to sacrifice him to his parental plans or hopes. In the biblical story, God is present and can therefore stay the father's hand. In all too many repetitions of the scene God is absent and the knife falls. Thus is the *Akedah* repeated forever, with its test and its terror.   Gunther Plaut

Third Aliyah

They came up to the place that God had told him of,
and Abraham built there the sacrificial altar.
He arranged the wood, and there he bound Yitzḥak, his child,
and put him on the sacrificial place, atop the wood,
and he stretched forth his hand and took the sacrificial
knife to slay his child. ↩

DERASH. Perhaps the *Akedah* is really the story of Isaac, who needed to find
God. He had grown up spoiled in a home affluent for those times. He had
experienced neither the soul searching of his father nor the anguish of his
mother, who waited almost a lifetime to have a child. It may have taken a
traumatic experience to force him to look within himself. His close brush
with death may have been the event that preceded his discovery of God.
He then went off into the wilderness alone in order to transform himself
into the leader he was destined to become. How else could we say in the
Amidah: The God of Abraham, the God of Sarah, the God of Isaac? In
every time, in every place, we each need to find our own God as the
matriarchs and patriarchs did. This is the challenge of Rosh Hashanah.

M.J.K.

וַיָּבֹ֜אוּ אֶֽל־הַמָּק֗וֹם אֲשֶׁ֣ר אָֽמַר־ל֣וֹ הָֽאֱלֹהִים֮ וַיִּ֧בֶן שָׁ֣ם אַבְרָהָ֣ם אֶת־
הַמִּזְבֵּ֗חַ וַיַּֽעֲרֹךְ֙ אֶת־הָ֣עֵצִ֔ים וַֽיַּעֲקֹד֙ אֶת־יִצְחָ֣ק בְּנ֔וֹ וַיָּ֤שֶׂם אֹתוֹ֙
עַל־הַמִּזְבֵּ֔חַ מִמַּ֖עַל לָֽעֵצִֽים׃ וַיִּשְׁלַ֤ח אַבְרָהָם֙ אֶת־יָד֔וֹ וַיִּקַּ֖ח אֶת־
הַֽמַּאֲכֶ֑לֶת לִשְׁחֹ֖ט אֶת־בְּנֽוֹ׃ ←

COMMENTARY. What happened to Isaac in the terrible silence on Moriah as he looked up from where he was bound on the sacrificial altar to see the sunlight glinting off the knife-blade held firmly in his father's hand? Even with all the love and trust a son gives to a father, Isaac was shattered by the knowledge that Abraham would have sacrificed him in obedience to God. And it is not insignificant that the Torah makes no mention of Isaac coming down from the mountain. "Abraham then returned to his servants and they departed together for Be'er Sheva."

I imagine Isaac sitting on the mountain, rubbing the rope burns on his wrists and arms, massaging his limbs to restore circulation as the burning sacrifice makes a sweet savour unto God. He looks at Abraham, the echoes of the wings of death reverberating in his ears, and with anguished tears and a breaking voice, says, "How could you do this to me? How could you put me through something like this? And for what? Just so you could prove something to God? What kind of God would play games with my life? I don't want to have anything to do with you or your God." And he tells his father to go, to leave him.

I imagine Isaac leaving the mountain and going into the desert and there he finds his half-brother, Ishmael. He too knows something about anger, despair and mistrust. He too was subjected to a life-threatening trial and was saved only by divine intervention. I imagine Isaac and Ishmael sitting around a desert campfire in the chill of the evening, sharing with each other the ordeal of being their father's sons, and in sharing that ordeal (and with whom else could they share it but each other), they become brothers. In other words, they learn to love each other.

Julius Lester (Adapted)

And an angel of THE OMNIPRESENT ONE
called out to him from heaven, saying: "Abraham! Abraham!"
And he replied: "I'm here."
The angel said: "Do not put forth your hand upon the boy,
and do not cause him any harm!
For now I know that you are one in awe of God,
for you did not withhold your child, your only child, from me!"
And Abraham raised up his eyes and saw—behold!—
a ram in the back, ensnared within the bushes by its horns.
And Abraham went out, and he took the ram,
and offered it as a burnt offering
in place of his own child.

And Abraham would call that place: "ADONAY-Yireh" (GOD
Sees!),
as it is said today: "Upon the Mount of THE ETERNAL ONE
let one be seen!"

Genesis 22:9-14

Fourth Aliyah

And the angel of THE OMNIPRESENT ONE
called out to Abraham a second time from heaven,
saying: "By myself I swear, proclaiming my ETERNAL WILL,
because you have performed this task,
and did not spare even your child, your only child,
that I shall greatly bless you
and shall surely multiply your seed,
like stars upon the heavens,
and like sands upon the seashore,
and your offspring shall possess
the gateway of their foes. ⤺

וַיִּקְרָא אֵלָיו מַלְאַךְ יהוה מִן־הַשָּׁמַיִם וַיֹּאמֶר אַבְרָהָם | אַבְרָהָם
וַיֹּאמֶר הִנֵּנִי: וַיֹּאמֶר אַל־תִּשְׁלַח יָדְךָ אֶל־הַנַּעַר וְאַל־תַּעַשׂ לוֹ
מְאוּמָה כִּי | עַתָּה יָדַעְתִּי כִּי־יְרֵא אֱלֹהִים אַתָּה וְלֹא חָשַׂכְתָּ אֶת־
בִּנְךָ אֶת־יְחִידְךָ מִמֶּנִּי: וַיִּשָּׂא אַבְרָהָם אֶת־עֵינָיו וַיַּרְא וְהִנֵּה־אַיִל
אַחַר נֶאֱחַז בַּסְּבַךְ בְּקַרְנָיו וַיֵּלֶךְ אַבְרָהָם וַיִּקַּח אֶת־הָאַיִל וַיַּעֲלֵהוּ
לְעֹלָה תַּחַת בְּנוֹ: וַיִּקְרָא אַבְרָהָם שֵׁם־הַמָּקוֹם הַהוּא יהוה | יִרְאֶה
אֲשֶׁר יֵאָמֵר הַיּוֹם בְּהַר יהוה יֵרָאֶה:

Fourth Aliyah

וַיִּקְרָא מַלְאַךְ יהוה אֶל־אַבְרָהָם שֵׁנִית מִן־הַשָּׁמָיִם: וַיֹּאמֶר בִּי
נִשְׁבַּעְתִּי נְאֻם־יהוה כִּי יַעַן אֲשֶׁר עָשִׂיתָ אֶת־הַדָּבָר הַזֶּה וְלֹא
חָשַׂכְתָּ אֶת־בִּנְךָ אֶת־יְחִידֶךָ: כִּי־בָרֵךְ אֲבָרֶכְךָ וְהַרְבָּה אַרְבֶּה אֶת־
זַרְעֲךָ כְּכוֹכְבֵי הַשָּׁמַיִם וְכַחוֹל אֲשֶׁר עַל־שְׂפַת הַיָּם וְיִרַשׁ זַרְעֲךָ אֵת
שַׁעַר אֹיְבָיו: ⟵

DERASH. The ram was "ensnared within the bushes by its horns." Was
Abraham able to totally extricate the ram, or were the ram's horns left
there in the bushes, severed from the sacrificial animal? After everyone has
left the scene, I picture the shofar/ram's horn still ensnared in the bushes.
The passing wind blows a shrill cry from the ensnared ram's horn, a cry
that we repeat today.   J.A.S.

DERASH. Did the blessing come to Abraham because he did not withhold
his son from the possibility of dying on the altar, or because he listened to
the angel and did not withhold him from further living? It seems to me
that Abraham would withhold Isaac from God's presence by slaying him,
not by allowing him to live. It is Abraham's willingness to heed the call of
the angel of mercy, not his willingness to sacrifice his son, that is the basis
of the ensuing blessing.   J.A.S.

And all the nations of the earth
shall bless themselves by your posterity,
because you listened to my voice!"

And Abraham went back then to his servant-boys,
and they arose, and went together to Be'er Sheva,
and Abraham dwelt in Be'er Sheva.

Genesis 22:15-19

Fifth Aliyah

And it happened, after these things,
that it was told to Abraham: "Behold,
Milkah—she, too!—has given birth to children
to Naḥor, your brother: Utz, firstborn,
and Buz, his brother, and Kemuel
(who one day would become the father of Aram),
and Kesed, and Ḥazo, and Pildash and Yidlaf,
and Betuel. (And Betuel would one day father Rivkah!)"
These eight children Milkah bore to Naḥor,
brother of Abraham.
And Naḥor's concubine, whose name was Re'umah,
she, too, became the mother of Tevaḥ,
and Gaḥam, and Taḥash, and Ma'aḥah.

Genesis 22:20-24

וְהִתְבָּרֲכוּ בְזַרְעֲךָ כֹּל גּוֹיֵי הָאָרֶץ עֵקֶב אֲשֶׁר שָׁמַעְתָּ בְּקֹלִי: וַיָּשָׁב אַבְרָהָם אֶל־נְעָרָיו וַיָּקֻמוּ וַיֵּלְכוּ יַחְדָּו אֶל־בְּאֵר שָׁבַע וַיֵּשֶׁב אַבְרָהָם בִּבְאֵר שָׁבַע:

Fifth Aliyah

וַיְהִי אַחֲרֵי הַדְּבָרִים הָאֵלֶּה וַיֻּגַּד לְאַבְרָהָם לֵאמֹר הִנֵּה יָלְדָה מִלְכָּה גַם־הִוא בָּנִים לְנָחוֹר אָחִיךָ: אֶת־עוּץ בְּכֹרוֹ וְאֶת־בּוּז אָחִיו וְאֶת־קְמוּאֵל אֲבִי אֲרָם: וְאֶת־כֶּשֶׂד וְאֶת־חֲזוֹ וְאֶת־פִּלְדָּשׁ וְאֶת־יִדְלָף וְאֵת בְּתוּאֵל: וּבְתוּאֵל יָלַד אֶת־רִבְקָה שְׁמֹנָה אֵלֶּה יָלְדָה מִלְכָּה לְנָחוֹר אֲחִי אַבְרָהָם: וּפִילַגְשׁוֹ וּשְׁמָהּ רְאוּמָה וַתֵּלֶד גַּם־הִוא אֶת־טֶבַח וְאֶת־גַּחַם וְאֶת־תַּחַשׁ וְאֶת־מַעֲכָה:

The real hero of the sacrifice was the ram
who knew nothing of the plot among the others.
He sort of volunteered
to die in Isaac's place.

I want to sing a song in his memory—
of curly wool, of the human eyes,
of the horns, so still in his living head—
and they turned them into trumpets
after the kill
to sound their war-cry
to sound their crude joy.

I like to see the last scene
as a photo in a glossy fashion magazine
the young man, tan and pampered
in his designer suit,
and the angel by his side in a
long silk receiving gown,
and both of them empty-eyed,
glancing at two empty places.

And behind them, as a colorful background, the ram
caught in a thicket before the kill,
and the thicket his last friend.

The angel went home,
Isaac went home,
and Abraham and God went home,

But the real hero of the sacrifice
is the ram.

Yehuda Amichai

Inheritance

The ram came last.
And Abraham did not know
that it answered the question
that had come first
in the sunset of his life.

When he raised his white head
he saw he was not dreaming;
when he saw the angel
the knife dropped from his hand.

The boy who was unbound
saw the back of his father.

Isaac, it is told, was not sacrificed.
He had a long life, a good life,
until his eyes went dark.

But that hour
he bequeathed to his descendants
still to be born
a knife
in the heart.

Haim Guri

Yitzhak

Toward morning, the sun took a walk in the forest,
together with me, and with Abba,
with my right hand in his left.

Like lightning, a knife was flashing through the trees,
and I was struck with fear at my eyes' terror
at the blood upon the leaves.

Abba, Abba, hurry up and save Yitzhak,
so no one will be missing from the noonday feast.

It's I who am the slaughtered one, my son,
my blood already on the leaves.
And Abba's voice was stifled,
and his face was white.

And I wanted to cry out, I writhed not to believe,
ripping my eyes open,
and I awoke,

my right hand drained of blood.

Amir Gilboa

יִצְחָק

לִפְנוֹת בֹּקֶר טִיְלָה שֶׁמֶשׁ בְּתוֹךְ הַיַּעַר
יַחַד עִמִּי וְעִם אַבָּא
וִימִינִי בִּשְׂמֹאלוֹ.

כִּבְרָק לֶהָבָה מַאֲכֶלֶת בֵּין הָעֵצִים.
וַאֲנִי יָרֵא כָּל־כָּךְ אֶת פַּחַד עֵינַי מוּל דָּם עַל הֶעָלִים.

אַבָּא אַבָּא מַהֵר וְהַצִּילָה אֶת יִצְחָק
וְלֹא יֶחְסַר אִישׁ בִּסְעֻדַּת הַצָּהֳרַיִם.

זֶה אֲנִי הַנִּשְׁחָט, בְּנִי.
וּכְבָר דָּמִי עַל הֶעָלִים.
וְאַבָּא נִסְתַּם קוֹלוֹ.
וּפָנָיו חִוְרִים.

וְרָצִיתִי לִצְעֹק, מְפַרְפֵּר לֹא לְהַאֲמִין
וְקוֹרֵעַ הָעֵינַיִם.
וְנִתְעוֹרַרְתִּי.

וְאָזְלַת־דָּם הָיְתָה יַד יָמִין

TORAH READING FOR YOM KIPPUR SHAHARIT

The traditional Torah reading for Yom Kippur morning (Leviticus 16) summarizes the service in the Temple on Yom Kippur. This dramatic reading, repeated in part during the Avodah sections of Musaf, does not have the same impact upon many contemporary listeners as it did over the generations. As a consequence, some communities prefer to read Nitzavim (Deuteronomy 29:9-30:20), the alternative Torah reading, on pages 531-542.

First Aliyah

THE ALMIGHTY spoke to Moses,
after the death of two of Aaron's sons
when they drew near before THE HOLY ONE and died.
GOD said to Moses: Speak to Aaron your brother,
tell him he cannot come at will into the holy place,
inside the curtain in the presence of the cover
that is on the Ark, lest he might die—
for I appear over the cover, in a cloud.
Aaron shall come into the sanctuary thus:
with a male ox as an atonement offering,
and a ram for sacrificial fire.

Leviticus 16:1-3

(On Shabbat, Second Aliyah)

A linen tunic he shall wear,
with linen breeches—
they will be upon his flesh.
And he shall gird himself with linen sash,
and a linen turban shall he don.
These will be holy garments.
He shall wash his body, and shall put them on.
And from the congregation of the Israelites,
let him take two kid goats:
one for an atonement offering,
and one for offering up by fire. ⤸

The traditional Torah reading for Yom Kippur morning (Leviticus 16) summarizes the service in the Temple on Yom Kippur. This dramatic reading, repeated in part during the Avodah sections of Musaf, does not have the same impact upon many contemporary listeners as it did over the generations. As a consequence, some communities prefer to read Nitzavim (Deuteronomy 29:9-30:20), the alternative Torah reading, on pages 531-542.

First Aliyah

וַיְדַבֵּר יהוה אֶל־מֹשֶׁה אַחֲרֵי מוֹת שְׁנֵי בְּנֵי אַהֲרֹן בְּקָרְבָתָם לִפְנֵי־
יהוה וַיָּמֻתוּ: וַיֹּאמֶר יהוה אֶל־מֹשֶׁה דַּבֵּר אֶל־אַהֲרֹן אָחִיךָ וְאַל־
יָבֹא בְכָל־עֵת אֶל־הַקֹּדֶשׁ מִבֵּית לַפָּרֹכֶת אֶל־פְּנֵי הַכַּפֹּרֶת אֲשֶׁר
עַל־הָאָרֹן וְלֹא יָמוּת כִּי בֶּעָנָן אֵרָאֶה עַל־הַכַּפֹּרֶת: בְּזֹאת יָבֹא
אַהֲרֹן אֶל־הַקֹּדֶשׁ בְּפַר בֶּן־בָּקָר לְחַטָּאת וְאַיִל לְעֹלָה:

(On Shabbat, Second Aliyah)

כְּתֹנֶת־בַּד קֹדֶשׁ יִלְבָּשׁ וּמִכְנְסֵי־בַד יִהְיוּ עַל־בְּשָׂרוֹ וּבְאַבְנֵט בַּד יַחְגֹּר
וּבְמִצְנֶפֶת בַּד יִצְנֹף בִּגְדֵי־קֹדֶשׁ הֵם וְרָחַץ בַּמַּיִם אֶת־בְּשָׂרוֹ וּלְבֵשָׁם:
וּמֵאֵת עֲדַת בְּנֵי יִשְׂרָאֵל יִקַּח שְׁנֵי־שְׂעִירֵי עִזִּים לְחַטָּאת ←

COMMENTARY. Why are instructions given to Aaron "after the death of two of Aaron's sons?" Rav Azaria compares this to a doctor who visits a sick person and says, "Do not eat anything cold, and do not lie in a damp place." Another doctor says, "Do not eat anything cold, and do not lie in a damp place so that you do not die like John Doe died." The second doctor made a stronger case than the first.

Rashi

כי בענן אראה /For I appear...in a cloud. Since God appears there in a pillar of cloud, and since the revelation of God's *Shehinah* is there, Aaron should be careful not to enter at will. The rabbis comment that he should enter only with the cloud of incense and only on Yom Kippur (Talmud *Yoma* 53a).

Rashi

כתנת בד קדש /ketonet bad kodesh/linen tunic. The high priest had two sets of clothes – בגדי זהב /bigdey zahav/golden clothing and בגדי לבן /bigdey lavan/white clothing. The Mishnah (*Yoma* 7:4) points out that on Yom Kippur the white clothing was worn only when the high priest entered the Holy of Holies. The simple white garment was worn in the Holy of Holies, and the gold was worn before the multitude gathered at the Temple. What affects how you dress?

M.B.K./D.A.T.

And Aaron shall sacrifice the ox
as offering for his sins.
He shall atone both for himself and for his household.

Leviticus 16:4-6

Second Aliyah (On Shabbat, Third Aliyah)

And he shall take the two kid goats,
and stand them up before THE OMNIPRESENT,
at the Tent of Meeting's entranceway.
And then let Aaron place a lot
upon each of the two goats:
one lot for THE HOLY ONE,
and one for Azazel.
Aaron shall offer up the goat
the lot has designated for THE HOLY ONE,
and he shall make it an atonement offering.
And the goat the lot has marked for Azazel
shall be presented live before THE OMNIPRESENT,
for atonement, when the goat is sent to Azazel,
into the wilderness.
Aaron shall sacrifice the ox
as offering for his sins.
He shall atone both for himself and for his household,
by slaughtering his offering for sins.

Leviticus 16:7-11

וְאַיִל אֶחָד לְעֹלָה: וְהִקְרִיב אַהֲרֹן אֶת־פַּר הַחַטָּאת אֲשֶׁר־לוֹ וְכִפֶּר בַּעֲדוֹ וּבְעַד בֵּיתוֹ:

Second Aliyah (On Shabbat, Third Aliyah)

וְלָקַח אֶת־שְׁנֵי הַשְּׂעִירִם וְהֶעֱמִיד אֹתָם לִפְנֵי יהוה פֶּתַח אֹהֶל מוֹעֵד: וְנָתַן אַהֲרֹן עַל־שְׁנֵי הַשְּׂעִירִם גֹּרָלוֹת גּוֹרָל אֶחָד לַיהוה וְגוֹרָל אֶחָד לַעֲזָאזֵל: וְהִקְרִיב אַהֲרֹן אֶת־הַשָּׂעִיר אֲשֶׁר עָלָה עָלָיו הַגּוֹרָל לַיהוה וְעָשָׂהוּ חַטָּאת: וְהַשָּׂעִיר אֲשֶׁר עָלָה עָלָיו הַגּוֹרָל לַעֲזָאזֵל יָעֳמַד־חַי לִפְנֵי יהוה לְכַפֵּר עָלָיו לְשַׁלַּח אֹתוֹ לַעֲזָאזֵל הַמִּדְבָּרָה: וְהִקְרִיב אַהֲרֹן אֶת־פַּר הַחַטָּאת אֲשֶׁר־לוֹ וְכִפֶּר בַּעֲדוֹ וּבְעַד בֵּיתוֹ וְשָׁחַט אֶת־פַּר הַחַטָּאת אֲשֶׁר־לוֹ:

COMMENTARY. The Torah reading reflects this holiday's theme, in the emphasis on expiation of sins through the ritual of the two goats and by direct mention of Yom Kippur as an occasion on which to "practice self-denial." To make sense of the reading's elaborate instructions for sacrifice, we must begin by recognizing that biblical religion was based in large measure on a popular belief that relinquishing to God precious possessions (such as livestock and grain) gave people credit and approval in God's eyes. We may regard the sacrifices as naive and primitive. But they had the same value in their time as our forms of altruistic giving have in ours.

Is it wrong to donate money to charitable causes or the State of Israel? No. But in a thousand years our descendants will probably wonder what we had in mind by these telethons, fundraising brunches and letter-writing campaigns. Perhaps they'll have figured out more efficient strategies to achieve justice and will regard what *we* do as rather primitive, foolish and wasteful.   S.D.R.

.

Third Aliyah (On Shabbat, Fourth Aliyah)

And he shall take his censer,
filled with burning coals,
lit from the altar fire
before THE HOLY ONE.
And he shall take two handfuls
of an aromatic incense, finely ground,
and bring it to the inside of the altar curtain,
and offer up the incense on the fire,
in the presence of THE HOLY ONE.
And when the cloud of incense
covers up the altar-cover,
which lies atop the Ark of Covenant,
he shall not die.

And he shall take some of the ox's blood,
and sprinkle with his fingers on the surface
of the altar-cover, on the east side.
Before the altar-cover, let him sprinkle
with the blood upon his fingers seven times.
And he shall slay the goat of offering
for the people's sins, and bring the blood
inside the altar-curtain,
and he shall do with its blood as he had done
beforehand with the ox's blood—sprinkling the blood
upon the altar-cover as he stands before it. ↩

Third Aliyah (On Shabbat, Fourth Aliyah)

וְלָקַח מְלֹא־הַמַּחְתָּה גַּחֲלֵי־אֵשׁ מֵעַל הַמִּזְבֵּחַ מִלִּפְנֵי יהוה וּמְלֹא
חָפְנָיו קְטֹרֶת סַמִּים דַּקָּה וְהֵבִיא מִבֵּית לַפָּרֹכֶת: וְנָתַן אֶת־הַקְּטֹרֶת
עַל־הָאֵשׁ לִפְנֵי יהוה וְכִסָּה ׀ עֲנַן הַקְּטֹרֶת אֶת־הַכַּפֹּרֶת אֲשֶׁר עַל־
הָעֵדוּת וְלֹא יָמוּת: וְלָקַח מִדַּם הַפָּר וְהִזָּה בְאֶצְבָּעוֹ עַל־פְּנֵי
הַכַּפֹּרֶת קֵדְמָה וְלִפְנֵי הַכַּפֹּרֶת יַזֶּה שֶׁבַע־פְּעָמִים מִן־הַדָּם
בְּאֶצְבָּעוֹ: וְשָׁחַט אֶת־שְׂעִיר הַחַטָּאת אֲשֶׁר לָעָם וְהֵבִיא אֶת־דָּמוֹ
אֶל־מִבֵּית לַפָּרֹכֶת וְעָשָׂה אֶת־דָּמוֹ כַּאֲשֶׁר עָשָׂה לְדַם —←

מלפני יהוה / *milifney adonay* / before the OMNIPRESENT. This clearly refers to
the location where the Israelites believed the divine presence came to rest
in the tent.

The rabbis were uncomfortable with the anthropomorphic imagery
referring to God that appears within the Torah, so they interpreted
milifney adonay as a directional phrase meaning "toward the altar." This
method of interpretation has continued today, as evidenced in classical
Reconstructionist thought, which has moved away from the idea of God as
a person.   D.A.T./M.B.K.

He shall make atonement for the sanctuary,
for the Israelites' uncleanness,
and for their misdeeds, and all their sins.
He shall likewise make atonement
for the Tent of Meeting that now dwells among them,
unclean though they be.
And no one shall be present in the Tent of Meeting,
when he comes there to atone in holiness,
until he comes out.
And he shall make atonement,
for himself, and for his household,
and for the whole assembly of the Israelites.

Leviticus 16:12-17

Fourth Aliyah (On Shabbat, Fifth Aliyah)

And he shall go forth to the altar,
which is before THE HOLY ONE,
and he shall make atonement for it.
And let him take some of the ox's blood,
and some of the goat's blood,
and place it on the altar horns around the altar,
sprinkling with the blood upon his fingers
seven times, thus purifying it,
making it holy, from Israel's uncleanness.

And when he has completed the atonement,
for the Tent of Meeting and the holy place,
he shall dedicate the live goat: ⮌

הַפָּר וְהִזָּה אֹתוֹ עַל־הַכַּפֹּרֶת וְלִפְנֵי הַכַּפֹּרֶת: וְכִפֶּר עַל־הַקֹּדֶשׁ מִטֻּמְאֹת בְּנֵי יִשְׂרָאֵל וּמִפִּשְׁעֵיהֶם לְכָל־חַטֹּאתָם וְכֵן יַעֲשֶׂה לְאֹהֶל מוֹעֵד הַשֹּׁכֵן אִתָּם בְּתוֹךְ טֻמְאֹתָם: וְכָל־אָדָם לֹא־יִהְיֶה ן בְּאֹהֶל מוֹעֵד בְּבֹאוֹ לְכַפֵּר בַּקֹּדֶשׁ עַד־צֵאתוֹ וְכִפֶּר בַּעֲדוֹ וּבְעַד בֵּיתוֹ וּבְעַד כָּל־קְהַל יִשְׂרָאֵל:

Fourth Aliyah (On Shabbat, Fifth Aliyah)

וְיָצָא אֶל־הַמִּזְבֵּחַ אֲשֶׁר לִפְנֵי־יהוה וְכִפֶּר עָלָיו וְלָקַח מִדַּם הַפָּר וּמִדַּם הַשָּׂעִיר וְנָתַן עַל־קַרְנוֹת הַמִּזְבֵּחַ סָבִיב: וְהִזָּה עָלָיו מִן־הַדָּם בְּאֶצְבָּעוֹ שֶׁבַע פְּעָמִים וְטִהֲרוֹ וְקִדְּשׁוֹ מִטֻּמְאֹת בְּנֵי יִשְׂרָאֵל: וְכִלָּה מִכַּפֵּר אֶת־הַקֹּדֶשׁ וְאֶת־אֹהֶל מוֹעֵד וְאֶת־הַמִּזְבֵּחַ וְהִקְרִיב אֶת־ הַשָּׂעִיר הֶחָי: ←

COMMENTARY. In order to carry out the rituals of purification, Aaron entered the Tent of Meeting, the most sacred space in the portable sanctuary. Curiously, all of the dramatic rituals of Yom Kippur were then carried out in private, rather than in sight of the people, who depended on Aaron's efficacy for their own expiation.

However isolated the members of the community might have been from direct participation, they were nonetheless included in the rituals transpiring within the Tent of Meeting. The individual acts carried out by Aaron were not executed for his own sake, but by him on behalf of the community. What appeared to be a supreme moment of solitude was an event of the entire people. These rituals derive their meaning from the intersection of the personal and the public; the solitary act takes on meaning when carried out in the context of the community.   R.H.

Aaron shall place his two hands
on the live goat's head,
and make confession, for himself,
and for the Israelites' transgressions,
and for all their wrongs,
and all their sins.
And he shall place them
on the scapegoat's head,
and he shall send it,
by the hand of an appointed messenger,
into the wilderness.
The goat shall bear upon itself
all of their sins,
into a land cut off from settlement.
Thus shall he send the goat
into the wild.

And Aaron shall come into the Tent of Meeting,
and remove the linen garments he has worn
in his approach into the sanctuary,
and he shall leave them there.
And he shall bathe his flesh with water
in the holy place, and wash his garments,
and go forth and offer up his offering
and those of the people.
He shall make atonement,
for himself and for the people.

Leviticus 16:18-24

וְסָמַךְ אַהֲרֹן אֶת־שְׁתֵּי יָדָו עַל־רֹאשׁ הַשָּׂעִיר הַחַי וְהִתְוַדָּה עָלָיו אֶת־כָּל־עֲוֺנֹת בְּנֵי יִשְׂרָאֵל וְאֶת־כָּל־פִּשְׁעֵיהֶם לְכָל־חַטֹּאתָם וְנָתַן אֹתָם עַל־רֹאשׁ הַשָּׂעִיר וְשִׁלַּח בְּיַד־אִישׁ עִתִּי הַמִּדְבָּרָה: וְנָשָׂא הַשָּׂעִיר עָלָיו אֶת־כָּל־עֲוֺנֹתָם אֶל־אֶרֶץ גְּזֵרָה וְשִׁלַּח אֶת־הַשָּׂעִיר בַּמִּדְבָּר: וּבָא אַהֲרֹן אֶל־אֹהֶל מוֹעֵד וּפָשַׁט אֶת־בִּגְדֵי הַבָּד אֲשֶׁר לָבַשׁ בְּבֹאוֹ אֶל־הַקֹּדֶשׁ וְהִנִּיחָם שָׁם: וְרָחַץ אֶת־בְּשָׂרוֹ בַמַּיִם בְּמָקוֹם קָדוֹשׁ וְלָבַשׁ אֶת־בְּגָדָיו וְיָצָא וְעָשָׂה אֶת־עֹלָתוֹ וְאֶת־עֹלַת הָעָם וְכִפֶּר בַּעֲדוֹ וּבְעַד הָעָם:

בני ישראל ומפשעיהם לכל חטאתם/For the Israelites' uncleanness and for their misdeeds. This is for those who entered the sanctuary unclean but did not know it, for *ḥatot* are sins done inadvertently. Misdeeds, *pesha'im*, involve those who entered the sanctuary knowing they were unclean. Through the ritual of Yom Kippur, atonement is available to both groups.

Rashi

Fifth Aliyah (On Shabbat, Sixth Aliyah)

And the fat part of the offering for sins
he shall cast upon the altar-fire as incense.
And the appointed messenger,
who shall convey the goat to Azazel,
shall wash his clothes,
and bathe his flesh with water,
and afterwards, he may re-enter the encampment.
And the cattle offering for sins,
and the goat offering for sins,
whose blood had been brought in
to make atonement for the holy place,
let him convey outside the camp,
and they shall burn their hides,
their flesh parts, and their waste.
The one who burns them shall wash his clothes,
and bathe his flesh with water,
and afterward, he may re-enter the encampment.

And it shall be for you an everlasting statute:
in the seventh month, upon the tenth day of the month,
you shall afflict your souls.
No work shall you perform,
both homeborn and the stranger in your midst,
for on this day atonement shall be made for you,
to make you clean from all of your wrongdoing.
Before THE FOUNT OF LIFE,
you shall be clean.

Leviticus 16:25-30

וְאֵת חֵלֶב הַחַטָּאת יַקְטִיר הַמִּזְבֵּחָה: וְהַמְשַׁלֵּחַ אֶת־הַשָּׂעִיר֙
לַעֲזָאזֵ֔ל יְכַבֵּס בְּגָדָיו וְרָחַץ אֶת־בְּשָׂר֖וֹ בַּמָּיִם וְאַחֲרֵי־כֵן יָב֖וֹא
אֶל־הַמַּחֲנֶה: וְאֵת֩ פַּ֨ר הַחַטָּאת וְאֵ֣ת ׀ שְׂעִיר הַחַטָּאת אֲשֶׁ֤ר הוּבָא
אֶת־דָּמָם֙ לְכַפֵּ֣ר בַּקֹּ֔דֶשׁ יוֹצִ֖יא אֶל־מִח֣וּץ לַֽמַּחֲנֶ֑ה וְשָׂרְפ֣וּ בָאֵ֔שׁ
אֶת־עֹרֹתָ֥ם וְאֶת־בְּשָׂרָ֖ם וְאֶת־פִּרְשָֽׁם: וְהַשֹּׂרֵ֣ף אֹתָ֔ם יְכַבֵּ֣ס בְּגָדָ֗יו
וְרָחַ֧ץ אֶת־בְּשָׂר֛וֹ בַּמָּ֖יִם וְאַחֲרֵי־כֵ֥ן יָב֖וֹא אֶל־הַֽמַּחֲנֶֽה: וְהָיְתָ֥ה לָכֶ֖ם
לְחֻקַּ֣ת עוֹלָ֑ם בַּחֹ֣דֶשׁ הַשְּׁבִיעִ֣י בֶּֽעָשׂ֣וֹר לַחֹ֗דֶשׁ תְּעַנּ֣וּ אֶת־נַפְשֹֽׁתֵיכֶ֗ם
וְכָל־מְלָאכָה֙ לֹ֣א תַֽעֲשׂ֔וּ הָֽאֶזְרָ֔ח וְהַגֵּ֖ר הַגָּ֥ר בְּתֽוֹכְכֶֽם: כִּֽי־בַיּ֥וֹם הַזֶּ֛ה
יְכַפֵּ֥ר עֲלֵיכֶ֖ם לְטַהֵ֣ר אֶתְכֶ֑ם מִכֹּל֙ חַטֹּ֣אתֵיכֶ֔ם לִפְנֵ֥י יְהוָ֖ה תִּטְהָֽרוּ:

יכבס...ורחץ / *yiḥabes...veraḥatz* / wash...and bathe. The act of handling the
goat, metaphorically driving Israel's sins out of the camp, made the
handler unclean. The very act needed to purify the community made the
purifier impure! The necessary tasks of spiritual healing and moral
confrontation purified the community even while they could damage and
even sully the community leader. Just as the handler of the goat must then
seek individual purification, so must contemporary leaders, too, find ways
to heal and purify themselves, if they are to provide long-term morally
vigorous leadership.   D.A.T.

Sixth Aliyah (On Shabbat, Seventh Aliyah)

A Shabbat of Shabbaton—complete cessation—
it shall be for you. You shall afflict your souls.
It is an everlasting statute.
The priest whom one anoints
to serve the priesthood in his father's place
shall make atonement,
and he shall wash the linen garments,
and the garments of the holy service.
He shall make atonement,
for the sanctuary's holy place—
and for the Tent of Meeting,
and for the altar, he shall make atonement.
And for the priests,
and for the whole assembly of the people,
he shall make atonement.
And this shall be for you
an everlasting law: to make atonement
for the Israelites from all their sins,
on one day of the year.
And it was done as God commanded Moses.

Leviticus 16:31-34

Continue on page 543.

COMMENTARY. The final sentence of this passage does not say "Moses did..." but rather "it was done" (literally "one did")—suggesting that it is not Moses who is the subject of the sentence but in fact the future generations of the people Israel, who would carry out this ritual whether in deed or, later, in memory, through annual public recitation on the Day of Atonement.

J.R.

Sixth Aliyah (On Shabbat, Seventh Aliyah)

שַׁבַּ֨ת שַׁבָּת֥וֹן הִיא֙ לָכֶ֔ם וְעִנִּיתֶ֖ם אֶת־נַפְשֹׁתֵיכֶ֑ם חֻקַּ֖ת עוֹלָ֑ם: וְכִפֶּ֣ר
הַכֹּהֵ֗ן אֲשֶׁר־יִמְשַׁ֣ח אֹתוֹ֮ וַאֲשֶׁ֣ר יְמַלֵּא֙ אֶת־יָד֔וֹ לְכַהֵ֖ן תַּ֣חַת אָבִ֑יו
וְלָבַ֛שׁ אֶת־בִּגְדֵ֥י הַבָּ֖ד בִּגְדֵ֥י הַקֹּֽדֶשׁ: וְכִפֶּר֙ אֶת־מִקְדַּ֣שׁ הַקֹּ֔דֶשׁ וְאֶת־
אֹ֤הֶל מוֹעֵד֙ וְאֶת־הַמִּזְבֵּ֣חַ יְכַפֵּ֑ר וְעַ֧ל הַכֹּהֲנִ֛ים וְעַל־כָּל־עַ֥ם הַקָּהָ֖ל
יְכַפֵּֽר: וְהָיְתָה־זֹּ֨את לָכֶ֜ם לְחֻקַּ֣ת עוֹלָ֗ם לְכַפֵּ֞ר עַל־בְּנֵ֤י יִשְׂרָאֵל֙
מִכָּל־חַטֹּאתָ֔ם אַחַ֖ת בַּשָּׁנָ֑ה וַיַּ֕עַשׂ כַּאֲשֶׁ֛ר צִוָּ֥ה יְהוָ֖ה אֶת־מֹשֶֽׁה:

Continue on page 544.

שבת שבתון /*shabbat shabbaton*. One of the most ancient names for Yom
Kippur is the "sabbath of sabbaths." Jewish tradition understands Shabbat
to be holier than other holidays of the year and Yom Kippur to be the
holiest of all. On Shabbat we withdraw from labor to enjoy and restore
ourselves. The regulations for Yom Kippur are based in part on those of
Shabbat but are more rigorous in several ways. This emphasizes the
further withdrawal from physical aspects of living and creates a suitable
structure for this most spiritual of days.   D.A.T.

NITZAVIM: ALTERNATIVE YOM KIPPUR TORAH READING

This Torah reading can be used as an alternative reading for Yom Kippur morning or afternoon. The first aliyah can also be used as the maftir reading. This Torah reading serves as an alternative because it vividly conveys that on this day we stand to be judged, and we seek to renew our covenantal commitment.

First Aliyah

You stand here, all of you, today,
before THE FOUNT OF LIFE, your God—
your leaders and your tribes,
your elders, your officials,
every person of the people Israel,
your children and your spouses,
and the stranger in your midst where you encamp,
those who cut wood, those who draw water—
all of you, prepared to enter into covenant
with THE ETERNAL ONE, your God, into the oath
that THE ETERNAL ONE, your God, concludes
with you today.

Deuteronomy 29:9-11

Second Aliyah

And God will raise you up
to be a people dedicated to divinity,
and God, in turn, shall pledge
to be your God, as God has promised you,
according to the oath God made with your ancestors,
with Abraham, with Isaac, and with Jacob.
Not with you alone do I now make this covenant and oath,
but, in addition to whoever stands with us today
before THE FOUNT OF LIFE, our God,
all those who are not here with us today.

Deuteronomy 29:12-14

ALTERNATIVE YOM KIPPUR TORAH READING

פָּרָשַׁת נִצָּבִים

This Torah reading can be used as an alternative reading for Yom Kippur morning or afternoon. The first aliyah can also be used as the maftir reading. This Torah reading serves as an alternative because it vividly conveys that on this day we stand to be judged, and we seek to renew our covenantal commitment.

First Aliyah

אַתֶּם נִצָּבִים הַיּוֹם כֻּלְּכֶם לִפְנֵי יהוה אֱלֹהֵיכֶם רָאשֵׁיכֶם שִׁבְטֵיכֶם זִקְנֵיכֶם וְשֹׁטְרֵיכֶם כֹּל אִישׁ יִשְׂרָאֵל: טַפְּכֶם נְשֵׁיכֶם וְגֵרְךָ אֲשֶׁר בְּקֶרֶב מַחֲנֶיךָ מֵחֹטֵב עֵצֶיךָ עַד שֹׁאֵב מֵימֶיךָ: לְעׇבְרְךָ בִּבְרִית יהוה אֱלֹהֶיךָ וּבְאָלָתוֹ אֲשֶׁר יהוה אֱלֹהֶיךָ כֹּרֵת עִמְּךָ הַיּוֹם:

Second Aliyah

לְמַעַן הָקִים־אֹתְךָ הַיּוֹם ׀ לוֹ לְעָם וְהוּא יִהְיֶה־לְּךָ לֵאלֹהִים כַּאֲשֶׁר דִּבֶּר־לָךְ וְכַאֲשֶׁר נִשְׁבַּע לַאֲבֹתֶיךָ לְאַבְרָהָם לְיִצְחָק וּלְיַעֲקֹב: וְלֹא אִתְּכֶם לְבַדְּכֶם אָנֹכִי כֹּרֵת אֶת־הַבְּרִית הַזֹּאת וְאֶת־הָאָלָה הַזֹּאת: כִּי אֶת־אֲשֶׁר יֶשְׁנוֹ פֹּה עִמָּנוּ עֹמֵד הַיּוֹם לִפְנֵי יהוה אֱלֹהֵינוּ וְאֵת אֲשֶׁר אֵינֶנּוּ פֹּה עִמָּנוּ הַיּוֹם:

COMMENTARY. Who owns Torah? This Torah portion proclaims that it is not just the learners, scholars and officials. It is everyone—the young and the old, the water haulers and the elders, men, women and children. Each of us stands before God, shares a responsibility for the covenant, teaches its importance through our own actions.　　　　　　　　D.A.T.

COMMENTARY. If it is people's task to make God manifest in the world, then our failure to do so will result in God's hiddenness. When we pass down the covenant, a torch of divine light linking the generations, we connect the next generation to Sinai by virtue of this shared enlightenment. Thus we can all stand at Sinai; we can all make God present in the world.　　　　　　　　D.A.T.

Third Aliyah (For Minḥah, Second Aliyah)

For you have known how we have dwelt
inside the land of Egypt, how we traveled
through the nations in whose midst you passed.
And you have seen their futile forms of worship
and their idols—fetishes of wood and stone,
of silver and of gold, which they cherished as their own.
Perhaps among you there are some—
a man, a woman, or a family, or a tribe—
whose heart still yearns to turn away
from THE ETERNAL ONE, our God,
who yearns to go and worship as those nations do.
Or perhaps among you there is still
the root of poison weed or wormwood.

And should they hear these solemn words of promise,
and should think themselves more fortunate
in claiming: "It is better I should go
according to the prompting of my heart
for better or for worse, whatever the result"—
then THE ALMIGHTY ONE shall not forgive.
But rather, then God's anger will be kindled,
and all the punishments recorded in this scroll
shall fall upon them, and their names shall be erased
from heaven's book.

And THE ALMIGHTY ONE shall mark them for misfortune
from among all Israel's tribes, according to the oaths
of covenant recorded in this scroll.
And a later generation from among your children
who will rise up after you, and the stranger
who will come from a remote land and behold
the afflictions and diseases of your land,
which GOD will cause to come upon it— ↩

כִּי־אַתֶּם יְדַעְתֶּם אֵת אֲשֶׁר־יָשַׁבְנוּ בְּאֶרֶץ מִצְרָיִם וְאֵת אֲשֶׁר־עָבַרְנוּ
בְּקֶרֶב הַגּוֹיִם אֲשֶׁר עֲבַרְתֶּם: וַתִּרְאוּ אֶת־שִׁקּוּצֵיהֶם וְאֵת גִּלֻּלֵיהֶם
עֵץ וָאֶבֶן כֶּסֶף וְזָהָב אֲשֶׁר עִמָּהֶם: פֶּן־יֵשׁ בָּכֶם אִישׁ אוֹ־אִשָּׁה אוֹ
מִשְׁפָּחָה אוֹ־שֵׁבֶט אֲשֶׁר לְבָבוֹ פֹנֶה הַיּוֹם מֵעִם יהוה אֱלֹהֵינוּ
לָלֶכֶת לַעֲבֹד אֶת־אֱלֹהֵי הַגּוֹיִם הָהֵם פֶּן־יֵשׁ בָּכֶם שֹׁרֶשׁ פֹּרֶה רֹאשׁ
וְלַעֲנָה: וְהָיָה בְּשָׁמְעוֹ אֶת־דִּבְרֵי הָאָלָה הַזֹּאת וְהִתְבָּרֵךְ בִּלְבָבוֹ
לֵאמֹר שָׁלוֹם יִהְיֶה־לִּי כִּי בִּשְׁרִרוּת לִבִּי אֵלֵךְ לְמַעַן סְפוֹת הָרָוָה
אֶת־הַצְּמֵאָה: לֹא־יֹאבֶה יהוה סְלֹחַ לוֹ כִּי אָז יֶעְשַׁן אַף־יהוה
וְקִנְאָתוֹ בָּאִישׁ הַהוּא וְרָבְצָה בּוֹ כָּל־הָאָלָה הַכְּתוּבָה בַּסֵּפֶר הַזֶּה
וּמָחָה יהוה אֶת־שְׁמוֹ מִתַּחַת הַשָּׁמָיִם: וְהִבְדִּילוֹ יהוה לְרָעָה מִכֹּל
שִׁבְטֵי יִשְׂרָאֵל כְּכֹל אָלוֹת הַבְּרִית הַכְּתוּבָה בְּסֵפֶר הַתּוֹרָה הַזֶּה:
וְאָמַר הַדּוֹר הָאַחֲרוֹן בְּנֵיכֶם אֲשֶׁר יָקוּמוּ מֵאַחֲרֵיכֶם וְהַנָּכְרִי אֲשֶׁר
יָבֹא מֵאֶרֶץ רְחוֹקָה וְרָאוּ אֶת־מַכּוֹת הָאָרֶץ הַהִוא וְאֶת־תַּחֲלֻאֶיהָ
אֲשֶׁר־חִלָּה יהוה בָּהּ: ←—

COMMENTARY. How should we understand blessings and curses if we
reject a God who keeps score and rewards and punishes? The rewards
that flow from living in a just, compassionate, and productive community
are both material and spiritual in nature. The inner rewards that come
from a life of spiritual discipline and moral engagement are not easily
measured because they are not translatable into dollars or other material
rewards, but they are at least as real. And the curses? We know all too
much about the physical horrors and spiritual disasters we are capable of
visiting upon each other. Regardless of our theologies, we still live daily
with the possibility of blessings and curses. It is still up to us to choose
life.   D.A.T.

a land ablaze with salt and sulphur,
where no seed can dwell, no plant can sprout,
no grass can grow, like the upheaval
of Sodom and Gomorrah, Admah and Tzevoyim,
which THE ALMIGHTY ONE had overturned
in anger and in fury—all the nations
then will ask: "Why has God done this
to the land? Why this great fury of God's anger?"
And they shall be told: "Because they have forsaken
the covenant of THE ETERNAL ONE, God of their ancestors,
which God had sworn with them when they were brought forth
from the land of Egypt." For they have gone and worshipped
other powers, have bowed to things they never knew,
which they were never meant to serve.

GOD's anger has been kindled at their land,
to bring upon them all the curses written in this scroll.
And THE ALMIGHTY has uprooted them from where they dwell,
with anger, and with terror and great wrath,
and cast them out to other lands this very day.

The hidden things are for THE HOLY ONE, our God,
but those that are revealed are ours to do,
and for our children, to eternity,
in order that this Torah shall be carried out.

Deuteronomy 29:15-28

גָּפְרִית וָמֶלַח שְׂרֵפָה כָל־אַרְצָהּ לֹא תִזָּרַע וְלֹא תַצְמִחַ וְלֹא־יַעֲלֶה בָהּ כָּל־עֵשֶׂב כְּמַהְפֵּכַת סְדֹם וַעֲמֹרָה אַדְמָה וּצְבֹיִים אֲשֶׁר הָפַךְ יְהוֹה בְּאַפּוֹ וּבַחֲמָתוֹ: וְאָמְרוּ כָּל־הַגּוֹיִם עַל־מֶה עָשָׂה יְהוֹה כָּכָה לָאָרֶץ הַזֹּאת מֶה חֳרִי הָאַף הַגָּדוֹל הַזֶּה: וְאָמְרוּ עַל אֲשֶׁר עָזְבוּ אֶת־בְּרִית יְהוֹה אֱלֹהֵי אֲבֹתָם אֲשֶׁר כָּרַת עִמָּם בְּהוֹצִיאוֹ אֹתָם מֵאֶרֶץ מִצְרָיִם: וַיֵּלְכוּ וַיַּעַבְדוּ אֱלֹהִים אֲחֵרִים וַיִּשְׁתַּחֲווּ לָהֶם אֱלֹהִים אֲשֶׁר לֹא־יְדָעוּם וְלֹא חָלַק לָהֶם: וַיִּחַר־אַף יְהוֹה בָּאָרֶץ הַהִוא לְהָבִיא עָלֶיהָ אֶת־כָּל־הַקְּלָלָה הַכְּתוּבָה בַּסֵּפֶר הַזֶּה: וַיִּתְּשֵׁם יְהוֹה מֵעַל אַדְמָתָם בְּאַף וּבְחֵמָה וּבְקֶצֶף גָּדוֹל וַיַּשְׁלִכֵם אֶל־אֶרֶץ אַחֶרֶת כַּיּוֹם הַזֶּה: הַנִּסְתָּרֹת לַיהוֹה אֱלֹהֵינוּ וְהַנִּגְלֹת לָנוּ וּלְבָנֵינוּ עַד־עוֹלָם לַעֲשׂוֹת אֶת־כָּל־דִּבְרֵי הַתּוֹרָה הַזֹּאת:

NOTE. It is customary to read this lengthy list of curses (Deuteronomy 29:19-27) at a high speed and in a soft voice because the curses were considered almost too horrible to contemplate.

COMMENTARY. An interpretation from Midrash *Tanhumah* asks why the section of blessings (Deuteronomy 30:1-10) is attached to the long list of curses that precedes it. The *midrash* imagines that when the Israelites heard these curses, their faces began to turn green, and they said, "Who can stand up before all of these curses?" Moses comforted them saying, "You are standing here today! Although you have greatly angered God in the past, God did not destroy you. You still exist before God." Rashi

COMMENTARY. Rashi, an eleventh century French commentator, teaches that והתברך / *vehitbareh*, the reflexive verb for blessing oneself (Deuteronomy 29:18), means that one should offer a blessing of peace in one's heart. I should believe that the curses of others will not affect me, that I shall have peace. The verb is reflexive because we bless ourselves. M.B.K.

COMMENTARY. Nahmanides, a fourteenth century commentator, explains that the hidden things belong to God because the community cannot be blamed for what an individual does secretly. The community must take responsibility for public acts that are publicly known. Acts done in secrecy are not the public's affair—they are between the individual and God. D.A.T./M.B.K.

Fourth Aliyah (For Minḥah, Third Aliyah)

When all these things have come upon you,
both the blessing and the curse
that I have placed before you,
you shall take to heart what I have said,
when you are dwelling among all the nations
where THE ALMIGHTY ONE, your God has driven you—
then shall you return to THE ALL-MERCIFUL, your God,
and listen to God's voice,
fulfilling all that I have commanded you today,
you and your children,
with all your heart, and with all your soul.
Then THE ETERNAL ONE, your God,
will restore you from captivity
and love you, gathering you again from all the nations
where THE ALMIGHTY ONE, your God, has scattered you.
Even if GOD scattered you to the ends of the horizon,
THE ALL-MERCIFUL, your God, will gather you from there
and bring you back. And THE REDEEMING ONE, your God,
will bring you to the land your ancestors inherited,
and you shall have possession of it once again,
and God will bring good fortune on you,
making you more numerous than your ancestors.
And THE REDEEMING ONE, your God, will open up your hearts,
yours and your children's, to love THE BOUNTIFUL, your God,
with all your heart and all your soul,
that you may live.

Deuteronomy 30:1-6

Minḥah *Torah reading concludes here.*

COMMENTARY. הנסתרות /*hanistarot*/ The hidden things. People should not be suspicious or assume wrongdoing by their neighbor without evidence. Acts not publicly known are between God and the individual, not between people.

Rashi

Fourth Aliyah (For Minḥah, Third Aliyah)

וְהָיָה כִי־יָבֹאוּ עָלֶיךָ כָּל־הַדְּבָרִים הָאֵלֶּה הַבְּרָכָה וְהַקְּלָלָה אֲשֶׁר
נָתַתִּי לְפָנֶיךָ וַהֲשֵׁבֹתָ אֶל־לְבָבֶךָ בְּכָל־הַגּוֹיִם אֲשֶׁר הִדִּיחֲךָ יהוה
אֱלֹהֶיךָ שָׁמָּה: וְשַׁבְתָּ עַד־יהוה אֱלֹהֶיךָ וְשָׁמַעְתָּ בְקֹלוֹ כְּכֹל אֲשֶׁר־
אָנֹכִי מְצַוְּךָ הַיּוֹם אַתָּה וּבָנֶיךָ בְּכָל־לְבָבְךָ וּבְכָל־נַפְשֶׁךָ: וְשָׁב יהוה
אֱלֹהֶיךָ אֶת־שְׁבוּתְךָ וְרִחֲמֶךָ וְשָׁב וְקִבֶּצְךָ מִכָּל־הָעַמִּים אֲשֶׁר
הֱפִיצְךָ יהוה אֱלֹהֶיךָ שָׁמָּה: אִם־יִהְיֶה נִדַּחֲךָ בִּקְצֵה הַשָּׁמָיִם מִשָּׁם
יְקַבֶּצְךָ יהוה אֱלֹהֶיךָ וּמִשָּׁם יִקָּחֶךָ: וֶהֱבִיאֲךָ יהוה אֱלֹהֶיךָ אֶל־
הָאָרֶץ אֲשֶׁר־יָרְשׁוּ אֲבֹתֶיךָ וִירִשְׁתָּהּ וְהֵיטִבְךָ וְהִרְבְּךָ מֵאֲבֹתֶיךָ: וּמָל
יהוה אֱלֹהֶיךָ אֶת־לְבָבְךָ וְאֶת־לְבַב זַרְעֶךָ לְאַהֲבָה אֶת־יהוה
אֱלֹהֶיךָ בְּכָל־לְבָבְךָ וּבְכָל־נַפְשְׁךָ לְמַעַן חַיֶּיךָ:

Minḥah *Torah reading concludes here*

COMMENTARY. In the thirtieth chapter of Deuteronomy, we are given a
glimpse of the dance of *teshuvah*. The text reads: "...then shall you return
to THE ALL-MERCIFUL, your God, and listen to God's voice" (verse 2).
Thus the first step is taken by us. "Then THE ETERNAL ONE, your God,
will restore you from captivity and love you" (verse 3)." Once we have
taken the initial step, we find God turning to meet us with compassion.
"God will return rejoicing."   R.H.

COMMENTARY. "The hidden things are for THE HOLY ONE, our God, but
those that are revealed are ours to do, and for our children, to eternity."
This Hebrew text is marked with dots to emphasize that Torah is a human
possession. Nonetheless, no matter how learned and knowledgeable we
are, our understanding of our world remains profoundly limited. We are
responsible for ethical living and teaching based on the limited amount we
know. We need to acquire moral courage to cope with our inevitable
uncertainty. The hidden things are God's. We live with that which is
revealed; we seek trust in God for the strength to acknowledge what
remains hidden from us.   D.A.T.

NOTE. The verse ומל יהוה...לבבך /open up your heart, literally circumcise
your heart (30:6) provides a central theme of the *piyut* found on page 805.

Fifth Aliyah

And THE ALMIGHTY ONE, your God, shall cast
all of the curses mentioned here upon your enemies,
on those who hate you and have persecuted you,
and you shall come to listen once again
to the voice of THE ETERNAL,
doing what God asks of you, as I command you here today.
THE BOUNTIFUL, your God, will grant abundance
for the labor of your hands
and for the fruit of your womb,
and for the offspring of your cattle
and the produce of your land.
It will go well with you,
for truly, THE REDEEMING ONE will once again rejoice
in your well-being, just as THE ETERNAL ONE
had taken joy in your ancestors,
for you shall listen to the voice
of THE ALL-MERCIFUL, your God,
to keep the mitzvot and laws recorded in this scroll of Torah.
Yes, you shall return to THE ETERNAL ONE, your God,
with all your heart and all your soul.   Deuteronomy 30:7-10

(On Shabbat morning, Sixth Aliyah)

For this mitzvah, which I enjoin on you today,
is not too puzzling for you, nor too remote.
It is not something high up in the heavens,
so that you might say:
"Who shall go up to the sky for us, and bring it to us
and make it understandable to us?—then we might do it!"
It is not beyond the ocean, so that you might say:
"Who shall cross the ocean for us, and bring it to us,
and enable us to hear it—then we might do it!"
But rather it is very close to you,
upon your mouth and in your heart—it can be done!

                                        Deuteronomy 30:11-14

וְנָתַן֩ יְהֹוָ֨ה אֱלֹהֶ֜יךָ אֵ֣ת כָּל־הָאָל֣וֹת הָאֵ֗לֶּה עַל־אֹיְבֶ֛יךָ וְעַל־שֹׂנְאֶ֖יךָ
אֲשֶׁ֣ר רְדָפ֑וּךָ: וְאַתָּ֣ה תָשׁ֗וּב וְשָׁמַעְתָּ֙ בְּק֣וֹל יְהֹוָ֔ה וְעָשִׂ֨יתָ֙ אֶת־כָּל־
מִצְוֺתָ֔יו אֲשֶׁ֛ר אָנֹכִ֥י מְצַוְּךָ֖ הַיּֽוֹם: וְהוֹתִֽירְךָ֩ יְהֹוָ֨ה אֱלֹהֶ֜יךָ בְּכֹ֣ל ׀
מַעֲשֵׂ֣ה יָדֶ֗ךָ בִּפְרִ֨י בִטְנְךָ֜ וּבִפְרִ֧י בְהֶמְתְּךָ֛ וּבִפְרִ֥י אַדְמָתְךָ֖ לְטֹבָ֑ה כִּ֣י ׀
יָשׁ֣וּב יְהֹוָ֗ה לָשׂ֤וּשׂ עָלֶ֨יךָ֙ לְט֔וֹב כַּאֲשֶׁר־שָׂ֖שׂ עַל־אֲבֹתֶֽיךָ: כִּ֣י תִשְׁמַ֗ע
בְּקוֹל֙ יְהֹוָ֣ה אֱלֹהֶ֔יךָ לִשְׁמֹ֤ר מִצְוֺתָיו֙ וְחֻקֹּתָ֔יו הַכְּתוּבָ֕ה בְּסֵ֖פֶר
הַתּוֹרָ֣ה הַזֶּ֑ה כִּ֤י תָשׁוּב֙ אֶל־יְהֹוָ֣ה אֱלֹהֶ֔יךָ בְּכָל־לְבָבְךָ֖ וּבְכָל־נַפְשֶֽׁךָ:

(On Shabbat morning, Sixth Aliyah)

כִּ֚י הַמִּצְוָ֣ה הַזֹּ֔את אֲשֶׁ֛ר אָנֹכִ֥י מְצַוְּךָ֖ הַיּ֑וֹם לֹא־נִפְלֵ֥את הִוא֙ מִמְּךָ֔
וְלֹ֥א רְחֹקָ֖ה הִֽוא: לֹ֥א בַשָּׁמַ֖יִם הִ֑וא לֵאמֹ֗ר מִ֣י יַעֲלֶה־לָּ֤נוּ הַשָּׁמַ֨יְמָה֙
וְיִקָּחֶ֣הָ לָּ֔נוּ וְיַשְׁמִעֵ֥נוּ אֹתָ֖הּ וְנַעֲשֶֽׂנָּה: וְלֹֽא־מֵעֵ֥בֶר לַיָּ֖ם הִ֑וא לֵאמֹ֗ר
מִ֣י יַעֲבָר־לָ֜נוּ אֶל־עֵ֤בֶר הַיָּם֙ וְיִקָּחֶ֣הָ לָּ֔נוּ וְיַשְׁמִעֵ֥נוּ אֹתָ֖הּ וְנַעֲשֶֽׂנָּה:
כִּֽי־קָר֥וֹב אֵלֶ֛יךָ הַדָּבָ֖ר מְאֹ֑ד בְּפִ֥יךָ וּבִלְבָבְךָ֖ לַעֲשֹׂתֽוֹ:

לא בשמים / *lo bashamayim* / not something high up in the heavens. If Torah
were in heaven, humans could not engage in study in this world.   Rashi

Sixth Aliyah (On Shabbat morning, Seventh Aliyah)

Behold, I set in front of you today
both life and good, both death and evil.
I ask of you today to love THE FOUNT OF LIFE, your God,
walk in God's ways, and keep what God commands,
God's statutes and God's justice—
that you may live and multiply,
and THE ETERNAL ONE your God will bless you
in the Land that you are coming to inherit.
But if your heart should turn away,
and fail to hear, and be misled,
and if you bow to other powers
and become enslaved to them,
I tell you now that you shall surely perish,
and shall not prolong your days upon the Land
that you are now about to cross the Jordan to possess.
I call as witnesses for you today
the heavens and the earth:
both life and death I place before you now,
both blessing and a curse.
Choose life, that you may live,
you and the seed of life within you,
loving THE FOUNT OF LIFE, your God,
hearing God's voice, and clinging to divinity.
For that is your life, your length of days—
to dwell upon the ground that THE ETERNAL ONE
has promised to your ancestors,
to Abraham, to Isaac, and to Jacob,
to give to them.

Deuteronomy 30:15-20

Sixth Aliyah (On Shabbat morning, Seventh Aliyah)

רְאֵה נָתַתִּי לְפָנֶיךָ הַיּוֹם אֶת־הַחַיִּים וְאֶת־הַטּוֹב וְאֶת־הַמָּוֶת וְאֶת־
הָרָע: אֲשֶׁר אָנֹכִי מְצַוְּךָ הַיּוֹם לְאַהֲבָה אֶת־יהוה אֱלֹהֶיךָ לָלֶכֶת
בִּדְרָכָיו וְלִשְׁמֹר מִצְוֹתָיו וְחֻקֹּתָיו וּמִשְׁפָּטָיו וְחָיִיתָ וְרָבִיתָ וּבֵרַכְךָ
יהוה אֱלֹהֶיךָ בָּאָרֶץ אֲשֶׁר־אַתָּה בָא־שָׁמָּה לְרִשְׁתָּהּ: וְאִם־יִפְנֶה
לְבָבְךָ וְלֹא תִשְׁמָע וְנִדַּחְתָּ וְהִשְׁתַּחֲוִיתָ לֵאלֹהִים אֲחֵרִים וַעֲבַדְתָּם:
הִגַּדְתִּי לָכֶם הַיּוֹם כִּי אָבֹד תֹּאבֵדוּן לֹא־תַאֲרִיכֻן יָמִים עַל־
הָאֲדָמָה אֲשֶׁר אַתָּה עֹבֵר אֶת־הַיַּרְדֵּן לָבֹא שָׁמָּה לְרִשְׁתָּהּ: הַעִדֹתִי
בָכֶם הַיּוֹם אֶת־הַשָּׁמַיִם וְאֶת־הָאָרֶץ הַחַיִּים וְהַמָּוֶת נָתַתִּי לְפָנֶיךָ
הַבְּרָכָה וְהַקְּלָלָה וּבָחַרְתָּ בַּחַיִּים לְמַעַן תִּחְיֶה אַתָּה וְזַרְעֶךָ:
לְאַהֲבָה אֶת־יהוה אֱלֹהֶיךָ לִשְׁמֹעַ בְּקֹלוֹ וּלְדָבְקָה־בוֹ כִּי הוּא חַיֶּיךָ
וְאֹרֶךְ יָמֶיךָ לָשֶׁבֶת עַל־הָאֲדָמָה אֲשֶׁר נִשְׁבַּע יהוה לַאֲבֹתֶיךָ
לְאַבְרָהָם לְיִצְחָק וּלְיַעֲקֹב לָתֵת לָהֶם:

COMMENTARY. Often Torah is dismissed as abstruse, inaccessible and other-worldly learning. Dismissing it in this way allows a convenient avoidance of the powerful messages it offers for our daily lives. As if in response, this passage proclaims the simplicity of the Torah's message: Love God, walk a godly path, seek to do what is required of you. Making a commitment to follow this simple message can become a source of teaching about how to make Torah study more accessible. If we treat Torah as our own, its paths become the intimate byways of our lives. What at a distance seems so obscure grows clear as we draw near to it.   D.A.T.

COMMENTARY. The terms שמים וארץ/shamayim va'aretz/heaven and earth are a biblical literary pairing. These terms when used together do not refer to two specific places, but rather define the boundaries of the witnesses. Everything in the universe bears witness in this new covenant. The cosmos from top to bottom is in the zone of the covenant.   M.B.K.

COMMENTARY. The mythic structure here makes heaven and earth the witnesses to God's judgment in the trial of the Jewish people. The covenantal violation before this court casts the people in the role of actor and God in the role of the aggrieved party. It is in this court-like context that we are told that all will be forgiven if we choose life—caring, commitment, love and fidelity, lives lived with God in mind. Heaven and earth are only witnesses. We are the ones with the power to choose.
     D.A.T.

ḤATZI KADDISH / SHORT KADDISH

Ḥatzi Kaddish is recited at the conclusion of the Torah reading from the first scroll. Both scrolls are placed on the reading table.

Reader: Let God's name be made great and holy in the world that was created as God willed. May God complete the holy realm in your own lifetime, in your days, and in the days of all the house of Israel, quickly and soon. And say: Amen.

Congregation: May God's great name be blessed, forever and as long as worlds endure.

Reader: May it be blessed, and praised, and glorified, and held in honor, viewed with awe, embellished, and revered; and may the blessed name of holiness be hailed, though it be higher by far than all the blessings, songs, praises, and consolations that we utter in this world. And say: Amen.

חֲצִי קַדִּישׁ

Ḥatzi Kaddish is recited at the conclusion of the Torah reading from the first scroll. Both scrolls are placed on the reading table.

יִתְגַּדַּל וְיִתְקַדַּשׁ שְׁמֵהּ רַבָּא בְּעָלְמָא דִּי בְרָא כִרְעוּתֵהּ וְיַמְלִיךְ
מַלְכוּתֵהּ בְּחַיֵּיכוֹן וּבְיוֹמֵיכוֹן וּבְחַיֵּי דְכָל בֵּית יִשְׂרָאֵל בַּעֲגָלָא וּבִזְמַן
קָרִיב וְאִמְרוּ אָמֵן:

יְהֵא שְׁמֵהּ רַבָּא מְבָרַךְ לְעָלַם וּלְעָלְמֵי עָלְמַיָּא:

יִתְבָּרַךְ וְיִשְׁתַּבַּח וְיִתְפָּאַר וְיִתְרוֹמַם וְיִתְנַשֵּׂא וְיִתְהַדָּר וְיִתְעַלֶּה וְיִתְהַלָּל
שְׁמֵהּ דְּקֻדְשָׁא בְּרִיךְ הוּא לְעֵלָּא לְעֵלָּא מִכָּל בִּרְכָתָא וְשִׁירָתָא
תֻּשְׁבְּחָתָא וְנֶחֱמָתָא דַּאֲמִירָן בְּעָלְמָא וְאִמְרוּ אָמֵן:

Reader: Yitgadal veyitkadash shemey raba
be'alma divra ḥirutey veyamliḥ malḥutey
behayeyhon uvyomeyhon uvḥayey deḥol beyt yisra'el
ba'agala uvizman kariv ve'imru amen.

Congregation: Yehey shemey raba mevaraḥ le'alam
ulalmey almaya.

Reader: Yitbaraḥ veyishtabaḥ veyitpa'ar veyitromam
veyitnasey veyit-hadar veyitaleh veyit-halal
shemey dekudsha beriḥ hu
le'ela le'ela mikol birḥata veshirata
tushbeḥata veneḥemata da'amiran be'alma ve'imru amen.

This is the Torah.

It is a Tree of Life to those who hold fast to it.

Those who uphold it may be counted fortunate!

This is the Torah which Moses placed before the children of
Israel,

by the word of THE ALMIGHTY ONE, and by the hand of Moses.

The second reading takes place here. After that, the second scroll is lifted as indicated above.

COMMENTARY. The 1945 Reconstructionist Prayerbook put "*Etz ḥayim hi /*
It is a tree of life" in place of "*asher sam mosheh lifney beney yisra'el /* which
Moses placed before the children of Israel." Earlier Reconstructionists
were concerned that it be made clear that while affirming the holiness of
Torah, they did not believe that it was given to Moses at Mount Sinai.
Many current Reconstructionists believe the evolutionary nature of the
Torah to be self-evident and have returned to the traditional line for the
sake of its rich mythic imagery. Both options are included here.   D.A.T.

עץ חיים היא / It is a Tree of Life. The book of Genesis tells us that the tree
of life is in the garden of Eden. The Torah is our tree of life; it is our way
back to the garden.   D.E.

The Torah is lifted, and one of the following is recited:

וְזֹאת הַתּוֹרָה עֵץ־חַיִּים הִיא לַמַּחֲזִיקִים בָּהּ וְתֹמְכֶיהָ מְאֻשָּׁר:

Vezot hatorah etz ḥayim hi lamaḥazikim bah vetomḥeha me'ushar.

◦◦◦

וְזֹאת הַתּוֹרָה אֲשֶׁר־שָׂם מֹשֶׁה לִפְנֵי בְּנֵי יִשְׂרָאֵל עַל־פִּי יהוה בְּיַד־מֹשֶׁה:

Vezot hatorah asher sam mosheh lifney beney yisra'el al pi adonay beyad mosheh.

The second reading takes place here. After that, the second scroll is lifted as indicated above.

עץ...מאשר / It...fortunate! (Proverbs 3:18).
וזאת...ישראל / This...Israel (Deuteronomy 4:44).
על...משה / by...Moses (Numbers 9:23).

MAFTIR TORAH READING FOR THE SECOND DAY OF ROSH HASHANAH

And in the seventh month,
upon the first day of the month,
a holy convocation you shall have.
No task of work shall you perform.
A day announced by shofar blasts it shall be for you.

And you shall make a burnt offering
of sweet-scented smoke:
one calf of cattle,
one ram, and seven yearling lambs
without a blemish,
and an offering of grain—
fine flour mixed with oil:
a three-tenths measure for the calf,
and two-tenths for the ram,
and one-tenth for each of the seven lambs.
And there shall be one goat as an offering for sin,
for your atonement,
along with a burnt-offering for the New Moon,
with its offering of meal,
the regular burnt-offering and its offering of meal,
with their libations as prescribed by law,
a fire of sweet savor to THE HOLY ONE.

Numbers 29:1-6

The second Torah scroll is lifted and tied while Vezot Hatorah *is recited.*
That is followed by the haftarah, *page 551.*

MAFTIR TORAH READING FOR THE SECOND
DAY OF ROSH HASHANAH

וּבַחֹ֨דֶשׁ הַשְּׁבִיעִ֜י בְּאֶחָ֣ד לַחֹ֗דֶשׁ מִֽקְרָא־קֹ֙דֶשׁ֙ יִהְיֶ֣ה לָכֶ֔ם כָּל־
מְלֶ֥אכֶת עֲבֹדָ֖ה לֹ֣א תַעֲשֻׂ֑ו י֥וֹם תְּרוּעָ֖ה יִהְיֶ֥ה לָכֶֽם: וַעֲשִׂיתֶ֨ם עֹלָ֜ה
לְרֵ֤יחַ נִיחֹ֙חַ֙ לַֽיהֹוָ֔ה פַּ֧ר בֶּן־בָּקָ֛ר אֶחָ֖ד אַ֣יִל אֶחָ֑ד כְּבָשִׂ֧ים בְּנֵֽי־שָׁנָ֛ה
שִׁבְעָ֖ה תְּמִימִֽם: וּמִנְחָתָ֗ם סֹ֤לֶת בְּלוּלָ֣ה בַשֶּׁ֔מֶן שְׁלֹשָׁ֣ה עֶשְׂרֹנִ֗ים
לַפָּ֞ר שְׁנֵ֤י עֶשְׂרֹנִים֙ לָאָ֔יִל: וְעִשָּׂר֣וֹן אֶחָ֔ד לַכֶּ֖בֶשׂ הָאֶחָ֑ד לְשִׁבְעַ֖ת
הַכְּבָשִֽׂים: וּשְׂעִיר־עִזִּ֥ים אֶחָ֖ד חַטָּ֑את לְכַפֵּ֖ר עֲלֵיכֶֽם: מִלְּבַד֙ עֹלַ֣ת
הַחֹ֗דֶשׁ וּמִנְחָתָ֔הּ וְעֹלַ֤ת הַתָּמִיד֙ וּמִנְחָתָ֔הּ וְנִסְכֵּיהֶ֖ם כְּמִשְׁפָּטָ֑ם
לְרֵ֣יחַ נִיחֹ֔חַ אִשֶּׁ֖ה לַֽיהֹוָֽה:

The second Torah scroll is lifted and tied while Vezot Hatorah *is recited.*
That is followed by the haftarah, *page 552.*

Some communities that read the traditional Torah reading for Yom Kippur morning prefer an alternative to the traditional maftir reading, which is also about the sacrifices. The first aliyah from Nitzavim (Deuteronomy 29:9-11) serves this purpose. See page 531.

MAFTIR TORAH READING FOR YOM KIPPUR

And on the tenth day of the seventh month,
you will have a holy convocation,
and you will afflict your souls.
No work will you perform.
And you will offer a burnt-offering:
a sacrifice of sweet aroma,
one male of cattle oxen,
one ram, and seven lambs,
a year old and unblemished,
you will have,
along with *minḥah*-offering
of finest flour, mixed with oil,
three tenths of a measure for the bull,
and two tenths for the ram,
and seven tenths apiece for the seven lambs.
A goat kid shall be an offering for sins,
apart from the sin-offering for the atonement,
and the perpetual burnt-offering,
its *minḥah* offering, and its libations.

Numbers 29:7-11

The second Torah scroll is lifted and tied while Vezot Hatorah *is recited. That is followed by the* haftarah, *page 551.*

MAFTIR TORAH READING FOR YOM KIPPUR

Some communities that read the traditional Torah reading for Yom Kippur morning prefer an alternative to the traditional maftir reading, which is also about the sacrifices. The first aliyah from Nitzavim (Deuteronomy 29:9-11) serves this purpose. See page 532.

וּבֶעָשׂוֹר֩ לַחֹ֨דֶשׁ הַשְּׁבִיעִ֜י הַזֶּ֗ה מִקְרָא־קֹ֙דֶשׁ֙ יִהְיֶ֣ה לָכֶ֔ם וְעִנִּיתֶ֖ם
אֶת־נַפְשֹׁתֵיכֶ֑ם כָּל־מְלָאכָ֖ה לֹ֥א תַעֲשֽׂוּ׃ וְהִקְרַבְתֶּ֨ם עֹלָ֤ה לַֽיהוה֙
רֵ֣יחַ נִיחֹ֔חַ פַּ֧ר בֶּן־בָּקָ֛ר אֶחָ֖ד אַ֣יִל אֶחָ֑ד כְּבָשִׂ֧ים בְּנֵֽי־שָׁנָ֛ה שִׁבְעָ֖ה
תְּמִימִ֥ם יִהְי֖וּ לָכֶֽם׃ וּמִ֨נְחָתָ֔ם סֹ֖לֶת בְּלוּלָ֣ה בַשָּׁ֑מֶן שְׁלֹשָׁ֣ה עֶשְׂרֹנִים֩
לַפָּ֨ר שְׁנֵ֤י עֶשְׂרֹנִים֙ לָאַ֣יִל הָאֶחָֽד׃ עִשָּׂרֹ֤ון עִשָּׂרֹון֙ לַכֶּ֣בֶשׂ הָֽאֶחָ֔ד
לְשִׁבְעַ֖ת הַכְּבָשִֽׂים׃ שְׂעִיר־עִזִּ֥ים אֶחָ֖ד חַטָּ֑את מִלְּבַ֞ד חַטַּ֣את
הַכִּפֻּרִים֙ וְעֹלַ֣ת הַתָּמִ֔יד וּמִנְחָתָ֖הּ וְנִסְכֵּיהֶֽם׃

The second Torah scroll is lifted and tied while Vezot Hatorah is recited.
That is followed by the haftarah blessing, page 552, and the haftarah, page 570.

COMMENTARY. The *maftir* presents a command to "afflict your souls" on Yom Kippur. The word for "afflict" is related to the Hebrew word for "poverty"—a disease that afflicts the soul of our society. We afflict ourselves today to be reminded of the affliction of others. Empathy ought to lead to action. The *haftarah*, which follows, thus stresses the importance of making this a time to resolve that we will feed the hungry, bring the homeless to our houses, clothe the naked, and not hide ourselves from our fellow human beings.   S.D.R.

ועניתם את נפשתיכם /*ve'initem et nafshoteyhem*/You will afflict your souls. The self-denial practiced on Yom Kippur, for example, by foregoing food and drink, and avoiding bathing, is all physical self-denial. How should we understand this text's suggestion that it is our souls that are meant to be affected? One way of understanding this is that the soul mirrors the body, so that there is an inner chastening that comes from the outer action. A second way to understand the phrase is that the physical forebearances create a space within which the ritual and liturgical actions of the day can have a powerful inner impact. The impact here is to simplify and humble—to rid ourselves of the layers that have built up on us and prevented us from being fully ourselves. The act of chastening or purification can thus be understood as an act of renewal.   D.A.T.

BIRKAT HAFTARAH / HAFTARAH BLESSING

Blessed are you, ETERNAL ONE, our God, the sovereign of all worlds, who has called upon the righteous prophets and desired their words, spoken in truth. Blessed are you, WISE ONE, who takes pleasure in the Torah, and in Moses, servant of God, and in the prophets of truth and justice.

On the first day of Rosh Hashanah, continue below. On the second day continue on page 563. On Yom Kippur, continue on page 569.

HAFTARAH FOR THE FIRST DAY OF ROSH HASHANAH

There was a certain man from Ramatayim-Tzofim
amid the mountains of Ephraim,
and his name was Elkanah the son of Yeroham,
who was the son of Eliahu, who was the son of Tohu,
who was the son of Tzuf, an Ephratite.
He had two wives: the first one's name was Hannah;
the second one was called Peninah.
And Peninah had two sons; but Hannah had no sons.

That man would go up from his town,
from time to time, to worship and to offer sacrifice
to THE CREATOR of the Multitudes of Heaven, at Shiloh.
There, were Eli's two sons, Hophni and Pinḥas,
priests to THE ETERNAL ONE. And on that occasion,
Elkanah would offer sacrifice, and give gifts
to Peninah, and to all his sons and daughters.
But to Hannah he would give a double portion,
for he loved Hannah, though GOD had closed her womb.
Her rival used to taunt her and provoke her
for the sake of causing her distress
about the fact that GOD had closed her womb. ↵

בִּרְכַּת הַפְטָרָה

בָּרוּךְ אַתָּה יהוה אֱלֹהֵֽינוּ מֶֽלֶךְ הָעוֹלָם אֲשֶׁר בָּחַר בִּנְבִיאִים טוֹבִים
וְרָצָה בְדִבְרֵיהֶם הַנֶּאֱמָרִים בֶּאֱמֶת: בָּרוּךְ אַתָּה יהוה הַבּוֹחֵר בַּתּוֹרָה
וּבְמֹשֶׁה עַבְדּוֹ וּבְנְבִיאֵי הָאֱמֶת וָצֶֽדֶק:

On the first day of Rosh Hashanah, continue below. On the second day continue on page 564. On Yom Kippur, continue on page 570.

הַפְטָרָה

וַיְהִי אִישׁ אֶחָד מִן־הָרָמָתַֽיִם צוֹפִים מֵהַר אֶפְרָֽיִם וּשְׁמוֹ אֶלְקָנָה
בֶּן־יְרֹחָם בֶּן־אֱלִיהוּא בֶּן־תֹּחוּ בֶן־צוּף אֶפְרָתִי: וְלוֹ שְׁתֵּי נָשִׁים שֵׁם
אַחַת חַנָּה וְשֵׁם הַשֵּׁנִית פְּנִנָּה וַיְהִי לִפְנִנָּה יְלָדִים וּלְחַנָּה אֵין
יְלָדִים: וְעָלָה הָאִישׁ הַהוּא מֵעִירוֹ מִיָּמִים | יָמִֽימָה לְהִשְׁתַּחֲוֹת
וְלִזְבֹּחַ לַיהוה צְבָאוֹת בְּשִׁלֹה וְשָׁם שְׁנֵי בְנֵי־עֵלִי חָפְנִי וּפִנְחָס
כֹּהֲנִים לַיהוה: וַיְהִי הַיּוֹם וַיִּזְבַּח אֶלְקָנָה וְנָתַן לִפְנִנָּה אִשְׁתּוֹ
וּלְכָל־בָּנֶֽיהָ וּבְנוֹתֶֽיהָ מָנוֹת: וּלְחַנָּה יִתֵּן מָנָה אַחַת אַפָּֽיִם כִּי אֶת־
חַנָּה אָהֵב וַיהוה סָגַר רַחְמָהּ: וְכִעֲסַֽתָּה צָרָתָהּ גַּם־כַּֽעַס בַּעֲבוּר
הַרְּעִמָהּ כִּי־סָגַר יהוה בְּעַד רַחְמָהּ: ←

COMMENTARY. This *haftarah* describes a would-be mother's pain leading to
the miraculous birth of Samuel—though is not every birth miraculous?
The parallel between the birth of Isaac in the traditional Torah portion and
the birth of Samuel in the *haftarah* is an obvious one. Perhaps less obvious
is the implication that each individual life has a place in the divine plan.
On this holy day the *haftarah* challenges us to discover our own calling.

D.A.T.

And so it happened, year by year:
whenever she went up to the house of THE ETERNAL ONE,
her rival would provoke her, and she wept and would not eat.
Her husband, Elkanah, would say to her,
"Why are you weeping, Hannah, and why won't you eat?
And why is your heart troubled?
Am I not worth more to you than ten children?"

And once, after she ate and drank at Shiloh, Hannah arose,
and Eli the priest was sitting at his station at the doorway
of the house of THE ETERNAL ONE.
And she was in a bitter mood,
and prayed to THE ETERNAL, while she wept and wept.
She made a vow, and said:
"CREATOR of the Multitudes of Heaven,
if truly you behold your servant's state of need,
if you remember me, and don't forget your servant,
if you give your servant-woman human seed,
then I shall dedicate my child to THE ETERNAL
for a lifelong service, and no shears
shall touch his head of hair."

And while she prayed at length before THE OMNIPRESENT ONE,
Eli caught sight of her moving her lips.
Because Hannah was speaking to herself, and only her lips were moving
while her voice could not be heard, Eli mistook her for a drunk.

COMMENTARY. The prayer of Hannah is an example of private rather than public worship. She has gone to pour out her heart before God in the holy place. As important as the role of community was to the rabbinic view of prayer, the rabbis also understood that prayer at its core is a matter of the heart alone. The depth and sincerity of Hannah's prayer became a model for them. This apparently included the very strong and seemingly audacious way in which Hannah spoke both to Eli and to God. The model of prayer offered here is hardly one of submission and entreaty. Hannah stood up to both human and divine authority, demanding that she be treated justly and recognized for the wronged person she was.   A.G.

FIRST DAY ROSH HASHANAH / 553

וְכֵן יַעֲשֶׂה שָׁנָה בְשָׁנָה מִדֵּי עֲלֹתָהּ בְּבֵית יהוה כֵּן תַּכְעִסֶנָּה וַתִּבְכֶּה וְלֹא תֹאכַל: וַיֹּאמֶר לָהּ אֶלְקָנָה אִישָׁהּ חַנָּה לָמֶה תִבְכִּי וְלָמֶה לֹא תֹאכְלִי וְלָמֶה יֵרַע לְבָבֵךְ הֲלוֹא אָנֹכִי טוֹב לָךְ מֵעֲשָׂרָה בָּנִים: וַתָּקָם חַנָּה אַחֲרֵי אָכְלָה בְשִׁלֹה וְאַחֲרֵי שָׁתֹה וְעֵלִי הַכֹּהֵן יֹשֵׁב עַל־הַכִּסֵּא עַל־מְזוּזַת הֵיכַל יהוה: וְהִיא מָרַת נָפֶשׁ וַתִּתְפַּלֵּל עַל־יהוה וּבָכֹה תִבְכֶּה: וַתִּדֹּר נֶדֶר וַתֹּאמַר יהוה צְבָאוֹת אִם־רָאֹה תִרְאֶה ׀ בָּעֳנִי אֲמָתֶךָ וּזְכַרְתַּנִי וְלֹא־תִשְׁכַּח אֶת־אֲמָתֶךָ וְנָתַתָּה לַאֲמָתְךָ זֶרַע אֲנָשִׁים וּנְתַתִּיו לַיהוה כָּל־יְמֵי חַיָּיו וּמוֹרָה לֹא־יַעֲלֶה עַל־רֹאשׁוֹ: וְהָיָה כִּי הִרְבְּתָה לְהִתְפַּלֵּל לִפְנֵי יהוה וְעֵלִי שֹׁמֵר אֶת־פִּיהָ: וְחַנָּה הִיא מְדַבֶּרֶת עַל־לִבָּהּ רַק שְׂפָתֶיהָ נָּעוֹת וְקוֹלָהּ לֹא יִשָּׁמֵעַ וַיַּחְשְׁבֶהָ עֵלִי לְשִׁכֹּרָה: ←

And Eli said to her:
"How can you be drunk like this?
Put away your wine!"
But Hannah answered, saying,
"No, my lord, I am a woman sore in spirit,
and no wine or liquor have I drunk.
For I was only pouring out my soul to GOD.
Do not mistake your servant for a wanton woman,
for I was just now speaking
out of great preoccupation and distress."

And Eli answered: "Go in peace,
and may the God of Israel give you what you ask—
whatever you request from God."
And she replied: "So may your servant-woman
merit favor in your eyes."
The woman then departed on her way.
She ate, and no longer was she troubled.

And they arose early the next morning,
and they worshipped before THE OMNIPRESENT ONE,
and they returned back to their house in Ramah.
And Elkanah was intimate with Hannah, his wife,
and GOD remembered her.

I Samuel 1:1-19

Some communities conclude here.

וַיֹּ֤אמֶר אֵלֶ֙יהָ֙ עֵלִ֔י עַד־מָתַ֖י תִּשְׁתַּכָּרִ֑ין הָסִ֥ירִי אֶת־יֵינֵ֖ךְ מֵעָלָֽיִךְ׃

וַתַּ֨עַן חַנָּ֤ה וַתֹּ֙אמֶר֙ לֹ֣א אֲדֹנִ֔י אִשָּׁ֤ה קְשַׁת־ר֙וּחַ֙ אָנֹ֔כִי וְיַ֥יִן וְשֵׁכָ֖ר לֹ֣א שָׁתִ֑יתִי וָאֶשְׁפֹּ֥ךְ אֶת־נַפְשִׁ֖י לִפְנֵ֥י יְהוָֽה׃ אַל־תִּתֵּן֙ אֶת־אֲמָ֣תְךָ֔ לִפְנֵ֖י בַּת־בְּלִיָּ֑עַל כִּֽי־מֵרֹ֥ב שִׂיחִ֛י וְכַעְסִ֖י דִּבַּ֥רְתִּי עַד־הֵֽנָּה׃ וַיַּ֧עַן עֵלִ֛י וַיֹּ֥אמֶר לְכִ֖י לְשָׁל֑וֹם וֵאלֹהֵ֣י יִשְׂרָאֵ֗ל יִתֵּן֙ אֶת־שֵׁ֣לָתֵ֔ךְ אֲשֶׁ֥ר שָׁאַ֖לְתְּ מֵעִמּֽוֹ׃ וַתֹּ֕אמֶר תִּמְצָ֧א שִׁפְחָתְךָ֛ חֵ֖ן בְּעֵינֶ֑יךָ וַתֵּ֨לֶךְ הָאִשָּׁ֤ה לְדַרְכָּהּ֙ וַתֹּאכַ֔ל וּפָנֶ֥יהָ לֹא־הָיוּ־לָ֖הּ עֽוֹד׃ וַיַּשְׁכִּ֣מוּ בַבֹּ֗קֶר וַיִּֽשְׁתַּחֲווּ֙ לִפְנֵ֣י יְהוָ֔ה וַיָּשֻׁ֛בוּ וַיָּבֹ֥אוּ אֶל־בֵּיתָ֖ם הָרָמָ֑תָה וַיֵּ֤דַע אֶלְקָנָה֙ אֶת־חַנָּ֣ה אִשְׁתּ֔וֹ וַיִּֽזְכְּרֶ֖הָ יְהוָֽה׃

Some communities conclude here.

And at the turning of the season,
Hannah became pregnant, and she later bore a child,
and she called him "Samuel" (Sought-from-God)
—for (as she would say): "I sought him—*she'iltiv*—
from THE OMNIPRESENT ONE."
The man, Elkanah, went up with his entire household
to sacrifice to GOD the offering of the season,
and to commemorate his vow.
But Hannah did not go up, but told her husband:
"I shall wait until the boy is weaned,
and then shall bring him to appear
before THE OMNIPRESENT ONE,
and he shall dwell there permanently."
And Elkanah, her husband, said to her:
"Do what is proper in your eyes;
stay here until you wean him,
just as long as GOD's will can be done."
And his wife remained there,
nursing her child until his weaning.
Then she brought him with her, after she weaned him,
bringing three offerings of cattle,
an ephah of flour, and a flask of wine.
She brought him to the house of GOD at Shiloh,
and the boy was just a youth.
They slaughtered the cattle offering,
and brought the boy to Eli,
and she said: "Please, my lord,
may your soul thrive, my lord. I am the woman
who had stood before you here, praying to GOD.
I prayed to have this boy,
and GOD answered the request which I had made.
And so, I hereby lend him back to GOD,
for as many days as he might be required by GOD!"
And they worshipped there to THE ETERNAL ONE.

Some communities conclude here.   I Samuel 1:20-28

וַיְהִי֙ לִתְקֻפ֣וֹת הַיָּמִ֔ים וַתַּ֥הַר חַנָּ֖ה וַתֵּ֣לֶד בֵּ֑ן וַתִּקְרָ֤א אֶת־שְׁמוֹ֙
שְׁמוּאֵ֔ל כִּ֥י מֵיהֹוָ֖ה שְׁאִלְתִּֽיו: וַיַּ֨עַל הָאִ֤ישׁ אֶלְקָנָה֙ וְכָל־בֵּית֔וֹ לִזְבֹּ֧חַ
לַיהֹוָ֛ה אֶת־זֶ֥בַח הַיָּמִ֖ים וְאֶת־נִדְרֽוֹ: וְחַנָּ֖ה לֹ֣א עָלָ֑תָה כִּי־אָמְרָ֣ה
לְאִישָׁ֗הּ עַ֣ד יִגָּמֵ֤ל הַנַּ֙עַר֙ וַהֲבִאֹתִ֔יו וְנִרְאָה֙ אֶת־פְּנֵ֣י יְהֹוָ֔ה וְיָ֥שַׁב שָׁ֖ם
עַד־עוֹלָֽם: וַיֹּ֣אמֶר לָהּ֩ אֶלְקָנָ֨ה אִישָׁ֜הּ עֲשִׂ֧י הַטּ֣וֹב בְּעֵינַ֗יִךְ שְׁבִי֙ עַד־
גׇּמְלֵ֣ךְ אֹת֔וֹ אַ֛ךְ יָקֵ֥ם יְהֹוָ֖ה אֶת־דְּבָר֑וֹ וַתֵּ֤שֶׁב הָֽאִשָּׁה֙ וַתֵּ֣ינֶק אֶת־בְּנָ֔הּ
עַד־גׇמְלָ֖הּ אֹתֽוֹ: וַתַּעֲלֵ֨הוּ עִמָּ֜הּ כַּאֲשֶׁ֣ר גְּמָלַ֗תּוּ בְּפָרִ֤ים שְׁלֹשָׁה֙
וְאֵיפָ֨ה אַחַ֥ת קֶ֙מַח֙ וְנֵ֣בֶל יַ֔יִן וַתְּבִאֵ֥הוּ בֵית־יְהֹוָ֖ה שִׁל֑וֹ וְהַנַּ֖עַר נָֽעַר:
וַֽיִּשְׁחֲט֖וּ אֶת־הַפָּ֑ר וַיָּבִ֥יאוּ אֶת־הַנַּ֖עַר אֶל־עֵלִֽי: וַתֹּ֙אמֶר֙ בִּ֣י אֲדֹנִ֔י חֵ֥י
נַפְשְׁךָ֖ אֲדֹנִ֑י אֲנִ֣י הָאִשָּׁ֗ה הַנִּצֶּ֤בֶת עִמְּכָה֙ בָּזֶ֔ה לְהִתְפַּלֵּ֖ל אֶל־יְהֹוָֽה:
אֶל־הַנַּ֥עַר הַזֶּ֖ה הִתְפַּלָּ֑לְתִּי וַיִּתֵּ֨ן יְהֹוָ֥ה לִי֙ אֶת־שְׁאֵ֣לָתִ֔י אֲשֶׁ֥ר
שָׁאַ֖לְתִּי מֵעִמּֽוֹ: וְגַ֣ם אָנֹכִ֗י הִשְׁאִלְתִּ֙הוּ֙ לַֽיהֹוָ֔ה כׇּל־הַיָּמִים֙ אֲשֶׁ֣ר
הָיָ֔ה ה֥וּא שָׁא֖וּל לַֽיהֹוָ֑ה וַיִּשְׁתַּ֥חוּ שָׁ֖ם לַיהֹוָֽה:

Some communities conclude here.

Some communities begin here.

And Hannah prayed and said:
"My heart rejoices in THE FAITHFUL ONE,
my fortunes have been raised up by THE FOUNT OF LIFE!
My utterance is powerful against my foes,
yes, truly I am joyful in your victory!
There is none as holy as THE OMNIPRESENT ONE,
for none exists apart from you, O God!
—nor is there any stronghold like our God.

Have done, my foes, with all your endless boastful talk,
let insolence no longer come forth from your mouth!
For THE UNSEEN ONE is a crafty God
by whom much mischief is contrived:
The bows of mighty ones are smashed,
but they who once had stumbled have grown strong.
Those well-fed now hire themselves out for bread,
and those once hungry are not hungry any more.
The barren woman has borne seven,
the mother of many is forlorn.
THE POWER OF UPHEAVAL slays and brings to life,
brings down into the earth, and raises up!
THE GOD OF CHANGE both disinherits and makes rich,
both humbles and exalts, ↵

Some communities begin here.

וַתִּתְפַּלֵּל חַנָּה֮ וַתֹּאמַר֒ עָלַ֤ץ לִבִּי֙ בַּיהֹוָ֔ה רָ֥מָה קַרְנִ֖י בַּֽיהֹוָ֑ה רָ֤חַב פִּי֙
עַל־אֹ֣ויְבַ֔י כִּ֥י שָׂמַ֖חְתִּי בִּישׁוּעָתֶֽךָ׃ אֵין־קָד֥וֹשׁ כַּיהֹוָ֖ה כִּֽי־אֵ֣ין בִּלְתֶּ֑ךָ
וְאֵ֥ין צ֖וּר כֵּֽאלֹהֵֽינוּ׃ אַל־תַּרְבּ֤וּ תְדַבְּרוּ֙ גְּבֹהָ֣ה גְבֹהָ֔ה יֵצֵ֥א עָתָ֖ק
מִפִּיכֶ֑ם כִּ֣י אֵ֤ל דֵּעוֹת֙ יְהֹוָ֔ה וְלֹ֥א נִתְכְּנ֖וּ עֲלִלֽוֹת׃ קֶ֥שֶׁת גִּבֹּרִ֖ים
חַתִּ֑ים וְנִכְשָׁלִ֖ים אָ֥זְרוּ חָֽיִל׃ שְׂבֵעִ֤ים בַּלֶּ֨חֶם֙ נִשְׂכָּ֔רוּ וּרְעֵבִ֖ים חָדֵ֑לּוּ
עַד־עֲקָרָה֙ יָלְדָ֣ה שִׁבְעָ֔ה וְרַבַּ֥ת בָּנִ֖ים אֻמְלָֽלָה׃ יְהֹוָ֖ה מֵמִ֣ית וּמְחַיֶּ֑ה
מוֹרִ֥יד שְׁא֖וֹל וַיָּֽעַל׃ יְהֹוָ֖ה מוֹרִ֣ישׁ וּמַעֲשִׁ֑יר מַשְׁפִּ֖יל אַף־מְרוֹמֵֽם׃ ⟵

raises the pauper from the dust,
and from the dungheap lifts the destitute,
seating them among the noble-born,
according them a chair of honor.
THE OMNIPRESENT owns the pillars of the earth,
on which the world was placed.
God guards the steps of those who act in lovingkindness,
while evildoers are undone amid the dark.
For no one can prevail by might alone.
ALMIGHTY ONE! Your enemies shall break apart against you!
THE OMNIPRESENT, thundering in the heavens,
shall judge the farthest reaches of the earth,
establishing the rule of God,
raising the power of redemption."

I Samuel 2:1-10

For the concluding haftarah *blessings, see page 575.*

COMMENTARY. Hannah's prayer expresses one of the most fundamental
ideas of biblical literature—that the God of Israel is a God of surprise,
working out divine will in human affairs through sometimes devious
means, and often turning the tables on those who think themselves mighty
and prosperous. At the same time, this is a message of comfort to those in
need—the pauper, the oppressed, the childless—urging them not to give
up hope that their downtrodden state can be quickly reversed. Since
Hannah gave birth to Samuel, the greatest leader of Israel between Moses
and King David, her song is also a way of saying that Israel's destiny is
often served by those who have thought themselves the most peripheral to
it. This song was an affirmation of revolutionary change, voiced at a time
when Israel's survival as a nation was in doubt, therefore a time when
Israel was most in need of a God of Change.   J.R.

מֵקִים מֵעָפָר דָּל מֵאַשְׁפֹּת יָרִים אֶבְיוֹן לְהוֹשִׁיב עִם־נְדִיבִים וְכִסֵּא
כָבוֹד יַנְחִלֵם כִּי לַיהוה מְצֻקֵי אֶרֶץ וַיָּשֶׁת עֲלֵיהֶם תֵּבֵל: רַגְלֵי
חֲסִידָו יִשְׁמֹר וּרְשָׁעִים בַּחֹשֶׁךְ יִדָּמּוּ כִּי־לֹא בְכֹחַ יִגְבַּר־
אִישׁ: יהוה יֵחַתּוּ מְרִיבָו עָלָו בַּשָּׁמַיִם יַרְעֵם יהוה יָדִין אַפְסֵי־אָרֶץ
וְיִתֶּן־עֹז לְמַלְכּוֹ וְיָרֵם קֶרֶן מְשִׁיחוֹ:

For the concluding haftarah *blessings, see page 576.*

HAFTARAH FOR THE SECOND DAY OF ROSH HASHANAH

Thus says THE OMNIPRESENT ONE:
"They find favor in the wilderness,
this people who escaped the sword,
the people Israel heading to a place of rest."

From afar, THE GOD OF ISRAEL was made manifest to me:
"I loved you with an everlasting love;
therefore have I continued in my kindness toward you.
Once again, I shall rebuild you, maiden Israel,
you shall be rebuilt. Again shall you take up your timbrels,
and go forth in joyous dance and playful leaping,
again shall you replant your vineyards
on the mountains of Shomron,
the sowers shall replant, and taste their fruits!"

Truly, the day is coming when the sentinels
shall call out on Mt. Ephraim:
"Arise, let us go up to Zion,
to THE REDEEMING ONE, our God!"
For thus says THE FOUNT OF LIFE:
"Dance joyously for Jacob,
call in rapture at the crossroad of the nations,
make known, give praise, declare:
'O, GOD OF ZION, save your people,
save the remnant of the people Israel!'
And behold, I bring them from a northern land,
I gather them from the remote recesses of the earth.
Among them are the blind, the lame,
the pregnant mothers giving birth,
yes, all of them together,
a great community returning home! ↩

HAFTARAH FOR THE SECOND DAY OF
ROSH HASHANAH

כֹּה אָמַר יהוה מָצָא חֵן בַּמִּדְבָּר עַם שְׂרִידֵי חָרֶב הָלוֹךְ לְהַרְגִּיעוֹ
יִשְׂרָאֵל: מֵרָחוֹק יהוה נִרְאָה לִי וְאַהֲבַת עוֹלָם אֲהַבְתִּיךְ עַל־כֵּן
מְשַׁכְתִּיךְ חָסֶד: עוֹד אֶבְנֵךְ וְנִבְנֵית בְּתוּלַת יִשְׂרָאֵל עוֹד תַּעְדִּי
תֻפַּיִךְ וְיָצָאת בִּמְחוֹל מְשַׂחֲקִים: עוֹד תִּטְּעִי כְרָמִים בְּהָרֵי שֹׁמְרוֹן
נָטְעוּ נֹטְעִים וְחִלֵּלוּ: כִּי יֶשׁ־יוֹם קָרְאוּ נֹצְרִים בְּהַר אֶפְרָיִם קוּמוּ
וְנַעֲלֶה צִיּוֹן אֶל־יהוה אֱלֹהֵינוּ: כִּי־כֹה | אָמַר יהוה רָנּוּ לְיַעֲקֹב
שִׂמְחָה וְצַהֲלוּ בְּרֹאשׁ הַגּוֹיִם הַשְׁמִיעוּ הַלְלוּ וְאִמְרוּ הוֹשַׁע יהוה
אֶת־עַמְּךְ אֵת שְׁאֵרִית יִשְׂרָאֵל: הִנְנִי מֵבִיא אוֹתָם מֵאֶרֶץ צָפוֹן
וְקִבַּצְתִּים מִיַּרְכְּתֵי־אָרֶץ בָּם עִוֵּר וּפִסֵּחַ הָרָה וְיֹלֶדֶת יַחְדָּו קָהָל
גָּדוֹל יָשׁוּבוּ הֵנָּה: ←

COMMENTARY. This people who escaped the sword—that could be any Jewish generation! The near sacrifice of Isaac could have been the sacrificing of the entire future of the Jewish people. Instead Isaac finds life anew with Rebekah, and Jewish life goes on. This *haftarah*, too, recalls a moment when our people escaped the sword and found new life and new love in the wilderness. Perhaps more miraculous than the myriad of near misses of Jewish history is the faith of the Jewish people, who have, in the face of every sword and moment of desolation, reasserted new life and new love.   D.A.T.

They come with weeping and with supplication,
as I bring them, lead them by a straight road
to the flowing rivers, and they stumble not
—for I am like a loving parent to the people Israel,
and Ephraim is my first-born child."

Hear the word of THE ABUNDANT ONE, you nations!
Tell it in the islands far away!
Tell how the one who scattered Israel
now is reuniting them,
preserves them as a shepherd keeps the flock.
For THE LOVING ONE has rescued Jacob,
saved the people from a hand more powerful than they.
And they have come rejoicing on the heights of Zion,
flowing with the bounty of THE FOUNT OF LIFE,
with corn, and wine, and oil,
with flocks, and cattle.
Their spirit overflowing like a blessed garden,
and no longer shall they live in lamentation.

Then shall the maiden celebrate with dance,
the young and old together shall rejoice.
"For I shall turn their mourning into gladness,
and I shall console them, make their happiness
much greater than their suffering of old.
I'll saturate their priests with spiritual abundance,
and shall satisfy my people with my goodness."
So says THE POWER OF RENEWAL! Jeremiah 31:1-13

Some communities end here.

Thus proclaims THE GOD OF ZION:
"A voice is sounded in Ramah,
a wailing, bitter weeping,
Rachel weeping for her children. ⤶

בִּבְכִי יָבֹאוּ וּבְתַחֲנוּנִים אוֹבִילֵם אוֹלִיכֵם אֶל־נַחֲלֵי מַיִם בְּדֶרֶךְ יָשָׁר
לֹא יִכָּשְׁלוּ בָּהּ כִּי־הָיִיתִי לְיִשְׂרָאֵל לְאָב וְאֶפְרַיִם בְּכֹרִי הוּא:
שִׁמְעוּ דְבַר־יהוה גּוֹיִם וְהַגִּידוּ בָאִיִּים מִמֶּרְחָק וְאִמְרוּ מְזָרֵה
יִשְׂרָאֵל יְקַבְּצֶנּוּ וּשְׁמָרוֹ כְּרֹעֶה עֶדְרוֹ: כִּי־פָדָה יהוה אֶת־יַעֲקֹב
וּגְאָלוֹ מִיַּד חָזָק מִמֶּנּוּ: וּבָאוּ וְרִנְּנוּ בִמְרוֹם־צִיּוֹן וְנָהֲרוּ אֶל־טוּב
יהוה עַל־דָּגָן וְעַל־תִּירֹשׁ וְעַל־יִצְהָר וְעַל־בְּנֵי־צֹאן וּבָקָר וְהָיְתָה
נַפְשָׁם כְּגַן רָוֶה וְלֹא־יוֹסִיפוּ לְדַאֲבָה עוֹד: אָז תִּשְׂמַח בְּתוּלָה
בְּמָחוֹל וּבַחֻרִים וּזְקֵנִים יַחְדָּו וְהָפַכְתִּי אֶבְלָם לְשָׂשׂוֹן וְנִחַמְתִּים
וְשִׂמַּחְתִּים מִיגוֹנָם: וְרִוֵּיתִי נֶפֶשׁ הַכֹּהֲנִים דֶּשֶׁן וְעַמִּי אֶת־טוּבִי
יִשְׂבָּעוּ נְאֻם־יהוה:

Some communities end here.

כֹּה | אָמַר יהוה קוֹל בְּרָמָה נִשְׁמָע נְהִי בְּכִי תַמְרוּרִים רָחֵל מְבַכָּה
עַל־בָּנֶיהָ מֵאֲנָה לְהִנָּחֵם עַל־בָּנֶיהָ כִּי אֵינֶנּוּ: ←

She has refused to be consoled
about her children, for they are no longer."
Thus says THE GOD OF ISRAEL:
"Hold back your voice from weeping,
and your eyes from tears.
For a reward awaits your labors,"
says THE OMNIPRESENT ONE.
"Your children are returning
from the land of their oppressor;
hope arises for your future,"
says THE POWER OF REDEMPTION,
"for your children are returning to their home.
Yes, I have heard the wandering Ephraim:
'You've chastised me, and I was made to suffer,
like a calf that lacks instruction.
But bring me back, let me return,
for you are THE REDEEMING ONE, my God!
For, as I change, I have rethought my life,
and now that I know more, I'm stricken deep within,
I am ashamed, I feel disgrace,
I bear in pain the errors of my youth.'

Is Ephraim not my dearest child,
a source of joy to me?
Truly, whenever I make mention of it,
I am flooded with memories.
Therefore, I fill with yearning,
and am overcome with love."
So says THE ANCIENT ONE!

Jeremiah 31:14-20

Continue with the haftarah *blessings on page 575.*

כֹּה ׀ אָמַ֣ר יְהֹוָ֗ה מִנְעִ֤י קוֹלֵךְ֙ מִבֶּ֔כִי וְעֵינַ֖יִךְ מִדִּמְעָ֑ה כִּי֩ יֵ֨שׁ שָׂכָ֤ר
לִפְעֻלָּתֵךְ֙ נְאֻם־יְהֹוָ֔ה וְשָׁ֖בוּ מֵאֶ֥רֶץ אוֹיֵֽב: וְיֵשׁ־תִּקְוָ֥ה לְאַחֲרִיתֵ֖ךְ
נְאֻם־יְהֹוָ֑ה וְשָׁ֥בוּ בָנִ֖ים לִגְבוּלָֽם: שָׁמ֣וֹעַ שָׁמַ֗עְתִּי אֶפְרַ֨יִם֙ מִתְנוֹדֵ֔ד
יִסַּרְתַּ֨נִי֙ וָֽאִוָּסֵ֔ר כְּעֵ֖גֶל לֹ֣א לֻמָּ֑ד הֲשִׁיבֵ֣נִי וְאָשׁ֔וּבָה כִּ֥י אַתָּ֖ה יְהֹוָ֥ה
אֱלֹהָֽי: כִּֽי־אַחֲרֵ֤י שׁוּבִי֙ נִחַ֔מְתִּי וְאַֽחֲרֵי֙ הִוָּ֣דְעִ֔י סָפַ֖קְתִּי עַל־יָרֵ֑ךְ
בֹּ֚שְׁתִּי וְגַם־נִכְלַ֔מְתִּי כִּ֥י נָשָׂ֖אתִי חֶרְפַּ֥ת נְעוּרָֽי: הֲבֵן֩ יַקִּ֨יר לִ֜י אֶפְרַ֗יִם
אִ֚ם יֶ֣לֶד שַׁעֲשֻׁעִ֔ים כִּֽי־מִדֵּ֤י דַבְּרִי֙ בּ֔וֹ זָכֹ֥ר אֶזְכְּרֶ֖נּוּ ע֑וֹד עַל־כֵּ֗ן הָמ֤וּ
מֵעַי֙ ל֔וֹ רַחֵ֥ם אֲרַֽחֲמֶ֖נּוּ נְאֻם־יְהֹוָֽה:

Continue with the haftarah *blessings on page 576.*

HAFTARAH FOR YOM KIPPUR MORNING

And God has said: Prepare, prepare
the road—yes, clear a thoroughfare,
remove the stumbling block
from my people's way!
For thus says God, lofty and revered
who dwells forever, and whose name is holy:
Exalted and holy shall I dwell among you!
As for the downtrodden and destitute,
I shall revive the spirit of the lowly,
and the heart of the depressed I shall restore.
Indeed, not for all time shall I be quarrelsome,
not for eternity shall I seethe with rage,
but from me shall my spirit drip like dew.
I shall create the breath of life.

For my people's sinful deed I was enraged,
I struck them, and I turned away in wrath,
and they, for their part, pursued foolish ways.
But I have seen their folly, and shall heal them.
I shall guide them, and console them,
and for the mourners in their midst,
I shall create comforting words
—Shalom, shalom, to far and near!—
and I shall heal them.
But the wicked are like a troubled sea,
they cannot be at peace,
their waters stir with mire and mud.
There is no peace for them, says God,
none for the wicked.

Cry from the throat, do not relent,
raise up your voices like a shofar,
tell my people their transgression,
the house of Jacob, their mistakes. ↵

הַפְטָרָה

וְאָמַר סֹלּוּ־סֹלּוּ פַּנּוּ־דָרֶךְ הָרִימוּ מִכְשׁוֹל מִדֶּרֶךְ עַמִּי: כִּי כֹה אָמַר רָם וְנִשָּׂא שֹׁכֵן עַד וְקָדוֹשׁ שְׁמוֹ מָרוֹם וְקָדוֹשׁ אֶשְׁכּוֹן וְאֶת־דַּכָּא וּשְׁפַל־רוּחַ לְהַחֲיוֹת רוּחַ שְׁפָלִים וּלְהַחֲיוֹת לֵב נִדְכָּאִים: כִּי לֹא לְעוֹלָם אָרִיב וְלֹא לָנֶצַח אֶקְּצוֹף כִּי־רוּחַ מִלְּפָנַי יַעֲטוֹף וּנְשָׁמוֹת אֲנִי עָשִׂיתִי: בַּעֲוֹן בִּצְעוֹ קָצַפְתִּי וְאַכֵּהוּ הַסְתֵּר וְאֶקְצֹף וַיֵּלֶךְ שׁוֹבָב בְּדֶרֶךְ לִבּוֹ: דְּרָכָיו רָאִיתִי וְאֶרְפָּאֵהוּ וְאַנְחֵהוּ וַאֲשַׁלֵּם נִחֻמִים לוֹ וְלַאֲבֵלָיו: בּוֹרֵא נִיב שְׂפָתָיִם שָׁלוֹם | שָׁלוֹם לָרָחוֹק וְלַקָּרוֹב אָמַר יְהוָה וּרְפָאתִיו: וְהָרְשָׁעִים כַּיָּם נִגְרָשׁ כִּי הַשְׁקֵט לֹא יוּכָל וַיִּגְרְשׁוּ מֵימָיו רֶפֶשׁ וָטִיט: אֵין שָׁלוֹם אָמַר אֱלֹהַי לָרְשָׁעִים: קְרָא בְגָרוֹן אַל־תַּחְשֹׂךְ כַּשּׁוֹפָר הָרֵם קוֹלֶךָ וְהַגֵּד לְעַמִּי פִּשְׁעָם וּלְבֵית יַעֲקֹב חַטֹּאתָם: ←

COMMENTARY. This *haftarah* criticizes those who believe that fasting and prayer alone can bring about true atonement. For Isaiah, ritual action without moral action is not meaningful. Ritual acts and conduct supporting social justice become constant parts of our lives only when they reinforce each other through the way each is allowed to interpret and enhance the other.   M.B.K.

COMMENTARY. The choice of this *haftarah*, which emphasizes the ease with which the ritual and the moral can be unhooked from each other, reflects the fact that carefully observing Yom Kippur and then returning to everyday affairs with unaltered conduct was an ancient problem just as it is a modern one. Ultimately, each of us can only answer for ourselves the question, "How much will I change this year?" Do I really want the ritual of this day to have a transformative effect on my life? I have today to contemplate that question. This is preparation for the challenge beginning tomorrow.   D.A.T.

For they seek me out, day by day,
they yearn for knowledge of my way.
Like a people righteous in their deeds,
who have not left behind the justice of their God,
they ask of me the laws of righteousness,
they yearn for nearness to their God.
"Why, when we fasted, did you not see it?
Our souls we have afflicted, do you not know?"
Behold, while you are fasting, you engage in business,
and your workers you continue to oppress!
Behold, you fast in strife and quarrelling,
and with a meanly clenched fist you strike.
Today, you do not fast in such a way
as to make your voice heard on high.
Is this the kind of fast I delight in?
A fast merely to deprive one's body?
Is it bowing the head like the willows,
or reclining in sackcloth and ash?
Do you call that a fast,
a day in which THE HOLY ONE delights?
Is not the fast that I desire
the unlocking of the chains of wickedness,
the loosening of exploitation,
the freeing of all those oppressed,
the breaking of the yoke of servitude?
Is it not the sharing of your bread with those who starve,
the bringing of the wretched poor into your house,
or clothing someone you see who is naked,
and not hiding from your kin in their need?
Then shall your light burst forth like the dawn,
your waters of healing soon flourish again,
your righteousness will travel before you,
and the glory of THE ALMIGHTY will encompass you.
Then will you call and THE ETERNAL ONE will answer,
you will cry out, and God will respond: Here am I! ↵

וְאוֹתִ֣י י֣וֹם ׀ י֗וֹם יִדְרֹשׁ֘וּן֘ וְדַ֣עַת דְּרָכַ֣י יֶחְפָּצ֔וּן כְּג֞וֹי אֲשֶׁר־צְדָקָ֣ה עָשָׂ֗ה וּמִשְׁפַּ֤ט אֱלֹהָיו֙ לֹ֣א עָזָ֔ב יִשְׁאָל֙וּנִי֙ מִשְׁפְּטֵי־צֶ֔דֶק קִרְבַ֥ת אֱלֹהִ֖ים יֶחְפָּצֽוּן׃ לָ֤מָּה צַּמְנוּ֙ וְלֹ֣א רָאִ֔יתָ עִנִּ֥ינוּ נַפְשֵׁ֖נוּ וְלֹ֣א תֵדָ֑ע הֵ֣ן בְּי֤וֹם צֹֽמְכֶם֙ תִּמְצְאוּ־חֵ֔פֶץ וְכָל־עַצְּבֵיכֶ֖ם תִּנְגֹּֽשׂוּ׃ הֵ֣ן לְרִ֤יב וּמַצָּה֙ תָּצ֔וּמוּ וּלְהַכּ֖וֹת בְּאֶגְרֹ֣ף רֶ֑שַׁע לֹא־תָצ֣וּמוּ כַיּ֔וֹם לְהַשְׁמִ֥יעַ בַּמָּר֖וֹם קוֹלְכֶֽם׃ הֲכָזֶ֗ה יִֽהְיֶה֙ צ֣וֹם אֶבְחָרֵ֔הוּ י֛וֹם עַנּ֥וֹת אָדָ֖ם נַפְשׁ֑וֹ הֲלָכֹ֨ף כְּאַגְמֹ֜ן רֹאשׁ֗וֹ וְשַׂ֤ק וָאֵ֙פֶר֙ יַצִּ֔יעַ הֲלָזֶה֙ תִּקְרָא־צ֔וֹם וְי֖וֹם רָצ֥וֹן לַיהוָֽה׃ הֲל֣וֹא זֶ֗ה צ֤וֹם אֶבְחָרֵ֙הוּ֙ פַּתֵּ֙חַ֙ חַרְצֻבּ֣וֹת רֶ֔שַׁע הַתֵּ֖ר אֲגֻדּ֣וֹת מוֹטָ֑ה וְשַׁלַּ֤ח רְצוּצִים֙ חָפְשִׁ֔ים וְכָל־מוֹטָ֖ה תְּנַתֵּֽקוּ׃ הֲל֨וֹא פָרֹ֤ס לָֽרָעֵב֙ לַחְמֶ֔ךָ וַעֲנִיִּ֥ים מְרוּדִ֖ים תָּ֣בִיא בָ֑יִת כִּֽי־תִרְאֶ֤ה עָרֹם֙ וְכִסִּית֔וֹ וּמִבְּשָׂרְךָ֖ לֹ֥א תִתְעַלָּֽם׃ אָ֣ז יִבָּקַ֤ע כַּשַּׁ֙חַר֙ אוֹרֶ֔ךָ וַאֲרֻכָתְךָ֖ מְהֵרָ֣ה תִצְמָ֑ח וְהָלַ֤ךְ לְפָנֶ֙יךָ֙ צִדְקֶ֔ךָ כְּב֥וֹד יְהוָ֖ה יַֽאַסְפֶֽךָ׃ אָ֤ז תִּקְרָא֙ וַֽיהוָ֣ה יַֽעֲנֶ֔ה תְּשַׁוַּ֖ע וְיֹאמַ֥ר הִנֵּֽנִי ←

COMMENTARY. This *haftarah* poses the question of what it will take to create a world transformed. Its answer posits a society governed justly, interpersonal relationships characterized by caring, and religious life that points us toward ultimate meaning. Isaiah suggests that if we achieve all this, God will intervene to bring a society transformed. But if we achieve all this, society will have already been transformed.   D.A.T.

COMMENTARY. The *haftarah* is linked to the Torah reading in a daring way. The prophet *Yeshayahu* / Isaiah questions the value of fasting while we pursue business as usual. It is thus a critique of religious hypocrisy, and it remains to this day a challenge for the Jewish community in our effort to link ethics with ritual practice.   S.D.R.

If you banish oppression from your midst,
the menacing hand and tainted speech,
if you give of yourself to the hungry,
fulfilling the needs of the poor—
then shall your light shine in darkness,
and your darkness shall be like the noon.
THE RIGHTEOUS ONE will guide you always,
will satisfy your thirst in desert wastes,
will give your bones new life,
and you'll be like a well-watered garden,
like a spring whose waters do not fail.
And those among you will rebuild ancient ruins,
foundations long dormant you'll restore.
You shall be called the repairer of bridges,
the restorer of settlement roads.

If you refrain from trampling the Sabbath,
from doing your business on my holy day,
if you call the Sabbath your delight,
and honor THE CREATOR's holy day,
then shall you take pleasure in GOD EVERLASTING,
and I shall convey you on high,
and feed you with Jacob's inheritance—
for the mouth of THE ETERNAL ONE has spoken!

Isaiah 57:14-58:14

אִם־תָּסִיר מִתּוֹכְךָ֙ מוֹטָ֔ה שְׁלַ֥ח אֶצְבַּ֖ע וְדַבֶּר־אָֽוֶן: וְתָפֵ֤ק לָֽרָעֵב֙ נַפְשֶׁ֔ךָ וְנֶ֥פֶשׁ נַעֲנָ֖ה תַּשְׂבִּ֑יעַ וְזָרַ֤ח בַּחֹ֙שֶׁךְ֙ אוֹרֶ֔ךָ וַאֲפֵלָתְךָ֖ כַּֽצָּהֳרָֽיִם: וְנָחֲךָ֣ יְהוָה֮ תָּמִיד֒ וְהִשְׂבִּ֤יעַ בְּצַחְצָחוֹת֙ נַפְשֶׁ֔ךָ וְעַצְמֹתֶ֖יךָ יַחֲלִ֑יץ וְהָיִ֙יתָ֙ כְּגַ֣ן רָוֶ֔ה וּכְמוֹצָ֣א מַ֔יִם אֲשֶׁ֥ר לֹא־יְכַזְּב֖וּ מֵימָֽיו: וּבָנ֤וּ מִמְּךָ֙ חָרְב֣וֹת עוֹלָ֔ם מוֹסְדֵ֥י דוֹר־וָד֖וֹר תְּקוֹמֵ֑ם וְקֹרָ֤א לְךָ֙ גֹּדֵ֣ר פֶּ֔רֶץ מְשֹׁבֵ֥ב נְתִיב֖וֹת לָשָֽׁבֶת: אִם־תָּשִׁ֤יב מִשַּׁבָּת֙ רַגְלֶ֔ךָ עֲשׂ֥וֹת חֲפָצֶ֖יךָ בְּי֣וֹם קָדְשִׁ֑י וְקָרָ֣אתָ לַשַּׁבָּ֣ת עֹ֗נֶג לִקְד֤וֹשׁ יְהוָה֙ מְכֻבָּ֔ד וְכִבַּדְתּוֹ֙ מֵעֲשׂ֣וֹת דְּרָכֶ֔יךָ מִמְּצ֥וֹא חֶפְצְךָ֖ וְדַבֵּ֣ר דָּבָֽר: אָ֗ז תִּתְעַנַּג֙ עַל־יְהוָ֔ה וְהִרְכַּבְתִּ֖יךָ עַל־בָּ֣מֳותֵי אָ֑רֶץ וְהַאֲכַלְתִּ֗יךָ נַחֲלַת֙ יַעֲקֹ֣ב אָבִ֔יךָ כִּ֛י פִּ֥י יְהוָ֖ה דִּבֵּֽר:

CONCLUDING HAFTARAH BLESSINGS

After the haftarah is chanted, the following blessings are said:

Blessed are you ETERNAL ONE, our God, the sovereign of all worlds, the rock of all the worlds, the righteous one throughout all generations, the faithful God, whose word is deed, who speaks and fulfills, whose words are truth and justice.

Faithful are you, ETERNAL ONE, our God, and faithful are your words; not a single word of yours is unfulfilled, for you are a sovereign God, faithful and merciful. Blessed are you, ETERNAL ONE, the God faithful in all your words.

Be merciful to Zion, which is the house of life to us, and be a help to Israel, your people, soon and in our days. Blessed are you, ETERNAL ONE, who gives joy to Zion through her children.

Give us joy, ETERNAL ONE, our God, in Elijah, your prophet and your servant. Soon may redemption come and give joy to our hearts. May God turn the hearts of the parents to their children, and the hearts of the children to their parents. And may your house be called a house of prayer for all peoples. Blessed are you, ETERNAL ONE, who brings an everlasting peace. ⟵

ולעמך ישראל תושיע / be a help to Israel your people. The traditional phrase here, *aluvat nefesh* / cast-down soul, reflected the Jewish people's exile from their land. With the establishment of the State of Israel, we are no longer "cast down." This fundamental change in Jewish life is reflected in the revised language here.

D.A.T.

After the haftarah is chanted, the following blessings are said:

בָּרוּךְ אַתָּה יהוה אֱלֹהֵינוּ מֶלֶךְ הָעוֹלָם צוּר כָּל הָעוֹלָמִים צַדִּיק בְּכָל
הַדּוֹרוֹת הָאֵל הַנֶּאֱמָן הָאוֹמֵר וְעוֹשֶׂה הַמְדַבֵּר וּמְקַיֵּם שֶׁכָּל דְּבָרָיו
אֱמֶת וָצֶדֶק:

נֶאֱמָן אַתָּה הוּא יהוה אֱלֹהֵינוּ וְנֶאֱמָנִים דְּבָרֶיךָ וְדָבָר אֶחָד מִדְּבָרֶיךָ
אָחוֹר לֹא יָשׁוּב רֵיקָם כִּי אֵל מֶלֶךְ נֶאֱמָן וְרַחֲמָן אָתָּה: בָּרוּךְ אַתָּה
יהוה הָאֵל הַנֶּאֱמָן בְּכָל דְּבָרָיו:

רַחֵם עַל צִיּוֹן כִּי הִיא בֵּית חַיֵּינוּ וּלְעֲמַךְ יִשְׂרָאֵל תּוֹשִׁיעַ בִּמְהֵרָה
בְיָמֵינוּ: בָּרוּךְ אַתָּה יהוה מְשַׂמֵּחַ צִיּוֹן בְּבָנֶיהָ:

שַׂמְּחֵנוּ יהוה אֱלֹהֵינוּ בְּאֵלִיָּהוּ הַנָּבִיא עַבְדֶּךְ בִּמְהֵרָה יָבוֹא וְיָגֵל
לִבֵּנוּ: וְהֵשִׁיב לֵב אָבוֹת עַל בָּנִים וְלֵב בָּנִים עַל אֲבוֹתָם וּבֵיתְךָ בֵּית
תְּפִלָּה יִקָּרֵא לְכָל הָעַמִּים: בָּרוּךְ אַתָּה יהוה מֵבִיא שָׁלוֹם לָעַד: ←

COMMENTARY. Most liturgists agree that the practice of reciting a *haftarah*, generally a selection from the prophets, probably developed during a time when public reading of the Torah was banned. A selection roughly paralleling a major theme from the week's Torah portion was therefore selected. When public reading of the Torah became possible again, the popular custom of chanting the *haftarah* continued. The *haftarah* is usually chanted, utilizing a *trope* or cantillation system that has numerous variations. In modern times the bar/bat mitzvah has often taken on this responsibility as a sign of committed membership in the adult community.
D.A.T.

COMMENTARY. This version of the *haftarah* blessing eliminates the Davidic references and the hopes for a literal messiah that they invoke. In their place are Malachi 3:24 and a slightly altered version of Isaiah 56:7. Here Elijah is pictured coming to herald messianic days by uniting families, communities, and peoples through mutal understanding.
D.A.T.

On Rosh Hashanah, continue here:

For the Torah and for worship, and for the prophets (and for this day of Shabbat), and for this Day of Remembrance which you have given us, ETERNAL ONE, our God, (for holiness and for rest,) for happiness and joy, for honor and for splendor—for everything, WISE ONE, our God, we offer thanks to you and bless you. May your name be blessed continually by every living being, forever and eternally, for you are a God of truth, and your word is truthful and endures forever. Blessed are you, ETERNAL ONE, source of the holiness of (Shabbat,) the people Israel and the Day of Remembrance.

On Yom Kippur, continue here:

For the Torah, and for worship, for the prophets (and for this day of Shabbat), and for this Day of Atonement, which you have given us, ABUNDANT ONE, our God, for holiness and for rest, for pardon, for forgiveness, and for atonement, for honor and for splendor—for everything, WISE ONE, our God, we offer thanks to you, and bless you. May your name be blessed continually by every living being, forever and eternally. Your word is truth, and stands forever. Blessed are you, ETERNAL ONE, the sovereign of mercy and forgiveness for our wrongdoing, and for that of all your people, the House of Israel, you who make our guilt to pass away year after year—the sovereign over all the earth, source of the holiness of (Shabbat,) Israel and the Day of Atonement.

The service continues with the Prayer for the Country, page 579; Prayer for the State of Israel, page 581; or Prayers for Peace, pages 583 and 584. On Rosh Hashanah the Shofar service follows, page 585. On Yom Kippur, continue with Ashrey, page 593, or Returning the Torah to the Ark, page 597.

On Rosh Hashanah, *continue here:*

עַל הַתּוֹרָה וְעַל הָעֲבוֹדָה וְעַל הַנְּבִיאִים (וְעַל יוֹם הַשַּׁבָּת הַזֶּה) וְעַל יוֹם הַזִּכָּרוֹן הַזֶּה שֶׁנָּתַתָּ לָּנוּ יהוה אֱלֹהֵינוּ (לִקְדֻשָּׁה וְלִמְנוּחָה) לְכָבוֹד וּלְתִפְאָרֶת: עַל הַכֹּל יהוה אֱלֹהֵינוּ אֲנַחְנוּ מוֹדִים לָךְ וּמְבָרְכִים אוֹתָךְ: יִתְבָּרַךְ שִׁמְךָ בְּפִי כָּל חַי תָּמִיד לְעוֹלָם וָעֶד וּדְבָרְךָ אֱמֶת וְקַיָּם לָעַד: בָּרוּךְ אַתָּה יהוה מֶלֶךְ עַל כָּל הָאָרֶץ מְקַדֵּשׁ (הַשַּׁבָּת וְ) יִשְׂרָאֵל וְיוֹם הַזִּכָּרוֹן:

On Yom Kippur, *continue here:*

עַל הַתּוֹרָה וְעַל הָעֲבוֹדָה וְעַל הַנְּבִיאִים וְעַל יוֹם (הַשַּׁבָּת הַזֶּה וְעַל יוֹם) הַכִּפּוּרִים הַזֶּה שֶׁנָּתַתָּ לָּנוּ יהוה אֱלֹהֵינוּ (לִקְדֻשָּׁה וְלִמְנוּחָה) לִמְחִילָה וְלִסְלִיחָה וּלְכַפָּרָה וְלִמְחָל־בּוֹ אֶת כָּל עֲוֹנוֹתֵינוּ לְכָבוֹד וּלְתִפְאָרֶת: עַל הַכֹּל יהוה אֱלֹהֵינוּ אֲנַחְנוּ מוֹדִים לָךְ וּמְבָרְכִים אוֹתָךְ: יִתְבָּרַךְ שִׁמְךָ בְּפִי כָּל חַי תָּמִיד לְעוֹלָם וָעֶד וּדְבָרְךָ אֱמֶת וְקַיָּם לָעַד: בָּרוּךְ אַתָּה יהוה מֶלֶךְ מוֹחֵל וְסוֹלֵחַ לַעֲוֹנוֹתֵינוּ וְלַעֲוֹנוֹת עַמּוֹ בֵּית יִשְׂרָאֵל וּמַעֲבִיר אַשְׁמוֹתֵינוּ בְּכָל שָׁנָה וְשָׁנָה מֶלֶךְ עַל כָּל הָאָרֶץ מְקַדֵּשׁ (הַשַּׁבָּת וְ) יִשְׂרָאֵל וְיוֹם הַכִּפּוּרִים:

The service continues with the Prayer for the Country, page 580; Prayer for the State of Israel, page 582; or Prayers for Peace, pages 583 and 584. On Rosh Hashanah the Shofar service follows, page 585. On Yom Kippur, continue with Ashrey, page 594, or Returning the Torah to the Ark, page 598.

TEFILAH LAMEMSHALAH / PRAYER FOR THE COUNTRY

Sovereign of the universe, mercifully receive our prayer for our land and its government. Let your blessing pour out on this land and on all officials of this country who are occupied, in good faith, with the public needs. Instruct them from your Torah's laws, enable them to understand your principles of justice, so that peace and tranquility, happiness and freedom, might never turn away from our land. Please, WISE ONE, God of the lifebreath of all flesh, waken your spirit within all inhabitants of our land, and plant among the peoples of different nationalities and faiths who dwell here, love and brotherhood, peace and friendship. Uproot from their hearts all hatred and enmity, all jealousy and vying for supremacy. Fulfill the yearning of all the people of our country to speak proudly in its honor. Fulfill their desire to see it become a light to all nations.

Therefore, may it be your will, that our land should be a blessing to all inhabitants of the globe. Cause friendship and freedom to dwell among all peoples. And soon fulfill the vision of your prophet: "Nation shall not lift up sword against nation. Let them learn no longer ways of war." And let us say: Amen.

COMMENTARY. On the eve of the destruction of the First Temple in 586 B.C.E., the prophet Jeremiah called on his people to "pray for the peace of the land to which I am exiling you." We Jews have recognized the importance of just government in the lands where we have lived because we have fared better in societies guided by principles of justice, equality and law. Today, in North America, where we strive to fulfill the opportunities inherent in living in two civilizations, our motivation must go beyond what is good for us to what is right for all.   R.H.

תְּפִלָּה לַמֶּמְשָׁלָה

רִבּוֹן הָעוֹלָם קַבֵּל נָא בְּרַחֲמִים אֶת־תְּפִלָּתֵנוּ בְּעַד אַרְצֵנוּ וּמֶמְשַׁלְתָּהּ
הָרֵק אֶת־בִּרְכָתְךָ עַל הָאָרֶץ הַזֹּאת וְעַל כָּל שָׂרֵי הַמְּדִינָה הַזֹּאת
הָעוֹסְקִים בְּצָרְכֵי צִבּוּר בֶּאֱמוּנָה: הוֹרֵם מֵחֻקֵּי תוֹרָתֶךָ הֲבִינֵם
מִשְׁפְּטֵי צִדְקֶךָ לְמַעַן לֹא יָסוּרוּ מֵאַרְצֵנוּ שָׁלוֹם וְשַׁלְוָה אֲשֶׁר וָחֹפֶשׁ
כָּל־הַיָּמִים: אָנָּא יהוה אֱלֹהֵי הָרוּחוֹת לְכָל־בָּשָׂר הַעֲרֵה רוּחֲךָ עַל
כָּל־תּוֹשְׁבֵי אַרְצֵנוּ וְטַע בֵּין בְּנֵי הָאֻמּוֹת וְהָאֱמוּנוֹת הַשּׁוֹנוֹת
הַשּׁוֹכְנִים בָּהּ אַהֲבָה וְאַחֲוָה שָׁלוֹם וְרֵעוּת וַעֲקֹר מִלִּבָּם כָּל שִׂנְאָה
וְאֵיבָה קִנְאָה וְתַחֲרוּת לְמַלְּאוֹת מַשָּׂא־נֶפֶשׁ בָּנֶיהָ הַמִּתְפָּאֲרִים
בִּכְבוֹדָהּ וְהַמִּשְׁתּוֹקְקִים לִרְאוֹתָהּ אוֹר לְכָל־הַגּוֹיִים:
וְכֵן יְהִי רָצוֹן מִלְּפָנֶיךָ שֶׁתְּהֵא אַרְצֵנוּ בְּרָכָה לְכָל־יוֹשְׁבֵי תֵבֵל וְתַשְׁרֶה
בֵּינֵיהֶם רֵעוּת וְחֵרוּת וְקַיֵּם בִּמְהֵרָה חֲזוֹן נְבִיאֶךָ לֹא־יִשָּׂא גוֹי אֶל־גּוֹי
חֶרֶב וְלֹא־יִלְמְדוּ עוֹד מִלְחָמָה וְנֹאמַר אָמֵן:

Lo yisa goy el goy herev velo yilmedu od milhamah.

לֹא...מִלחמה / Nation...war (Isaiah 2:4).

What do I desire for my country? How do I vision the land I love?
Let it be a land where knowledge is free,
Where the mind is without fear, and men and women hold their heads
   high,
Where words come out from the depth of truth,
Where the world has not been broken up into fragments by narrow
   domestic walls,
Where tireless striving stretches its arms toward perfection,
Where the clear stream of reason has not lost its way in the dreamy
   desert sand of dead habit,
Where the mind is led forward into ever-widening thought and action,
Into that heaven of freedom let my country awake.

Rabindranath Tagore (Adapted)

TEFILAH LIMDINAT YISRA'EL /
PRAYER FOR THE STATE OF ISRAEL

Rock and champion of Israel, please bless the state of Israel, first fruit of the flourishing of our redemption. Guard it in the abundance of your love. Spread over it the shelter of your peace. Send forth your light and truth to those who lead and judge it, and to those who hold elective office. Establish in them, through your presence, wise counsel, that they might walk in the way of justice, freedom and integrity. Strengthen the hands of those who guard our holy land. Let them inherit salvation and life. And give peace to the land, and perpetual joy to its inhabitants. Appoint for a blessing all our kindred of the house of Israel in all the lands of their dispersion. Plant in their hearts a love of Zion. And for all our people everywhere, may God be with them, and may they have the opportunity to go up to the land. Cause your spirit's influence to emanate upon all dwellers of our holy land. Remove from their midst hatred and enmity, jealousy and wickedness. Plant in their hearts love and kinship, peace and friendship. And soon fulfill the vision of your prophet: "Nation shall not lift up sword against nation. Let them learn no longer ways of war." And let us say: Amen.

תְּפִלָּה לִמְדִינַת יִשְׂרָאֵל

צוּר יִשְׂרָאֵל וְגוֹאֲלוֹ בָּרֵךְ נָא אֶת מְדִינַת יִשְׂרָאֵל רֵאשִׁית צְמִיחַת
גְּאֻלָּתֵנוּ הָגֵן עָלֶיהָ בְּרֹב חַסְדֶּךָ וּפְרֹשׂ עָלֶיהָ סֻכַּת שְׁלוֹמֶךָ שְׁלַח אוֹרְךָ
וַאֲמִתְּךָ לְרָאשֶׁיהָ לְשׁוֹפְטֶיהָ וּלְנִבְחָרֶיהָ וְתַקְּנֵם בְּעֵצָה טוֹבָה מִלְּפָנֶיךָ
לְמַעַן יֵלְכוּ בְּדֶרֶךְ הַצֶּדֶק הַחֹפֶשׁ וְהַיֹּשֶׁר: חַזֵּק אֶת־יְדֵי מְגִנֵּי אֶרֶץ
קָדְשֵׁנוּ וְהַנְחִילֵם יְשׁוּעָה וְחַיִּים וְנָתַתָּ שָׁלוֹם בָּאָרֶץ וְשִׂמְחַת עוֹלָם
לְיוֹשְׁבֶיהָ: פְּקָד־נָא לִבְרָכָה אֶת אַחֵינוּ בֵּית יִשְׂרָאֵל בְּכָל־אַרְצוֹת
פְּזוּרֵיהֶם טַע בְּלִבָּם אַהֲבַת צִיּוֹן וּמִי־בָהֶם מִכָּל־עַמּוֹ יְהִי אֱלֹהָיו
עִמּוֹ וְיָעַל: הָאֲצֵל מֵרוּחֲךָ עַל כָּל יוֹשְׁבֵי אֶרֶץ קָדְשֵׁנוּ הָסֵר מִקִּרְבָּם
שִׂנְאָה וְאֵיבָה קִנְאָה וְרִשְׁעוּת וְטַע בְּלִבָּם אַהֲבָה וְאַחֲוָה שָׁלוֹם
וְרֵעוּת וְקַיֵּם בִּמְהֵרָה חֲזוֹן נְבִיאֶךָ לֹא יִשָּׂא גוֹי אֶל־גּוֹי חֶרֶב וְלֹא־
יִלְמְדוּ עוֹד מִלְחָמָה וְנֹאמַר אָמֵן:

Lo yisa goy el goy ḥerev velo yilmedu od milḥamah.

מי...וְיָעַל / may...to the land. This is a slightly altered version of Ezra 1:3.
לא...מלחמה / Nation...war (Isaiah 2:4).

We pray for Israel.
Both the mystic ideal of our ancestors' dreams.
And the living miracle, here and now,
Built of heart, muscle, and steel.

May she endure and guard her soul,
Surviving the relentless, age-old hatreds.
The cynical concealment of diplomatic deceit.
And the rumblings that warn of war.

May Israel continue to be the temple that magnetizes
The loving eyes of Jews in all corners:

Jews in lands of affluence and relative peace
Who forget the glory and pain of their being
And Jews in lands of oppression whose bloodied fists
Beat in anguish and pride
Against the cage of their imprisonment.

May Israel yet embrace her homeless, her own,
And bind the ingathered into one people.

May those who yearn for a society built on human concern
Find the vision of the prophets realized in her.
May her readiness to defend
Never diminish her search for peace.

May we always dare to hope
That in our day the antagonism will end,
That all the displaced, Arab and Jew, will be rooted again,
That within Israel and across her borders
All God's children will touch hands in peace.

Nahum Waldman

The man under his fig tree telephoned the man under his vine:
"Tonight they definitely might come. Assign
positions, armor-plate the leaves, secure the tree,
tell the dead to report home immediately."

The white lamb leaned over, said to the wolf:
"Humans are bleating, and my heart aches with grief.
I'm afraid they'll get to gunpoint, to bayonets in the dust.
At our next meeting this matter will be discussed."

All the nations (united) will flow to Jerusalem
to see if the Torah has gone out. And then,
inasmuch as it's spring, they'll come down
and pick flowers from all around.

And they'll beat swords into plowshares and plowshares into
     swords,
and so on and so on, and back and forth.

Perhaps from being beaten thinner and thinner,
the iron of hatred will vanish, forever.

Yehuda Amichai

SHOFAR SERVICE: READINGS

Select from among the following readings:

Even though sounding the shofar is an unexplained biblical decree, it seems to bear a message: Wake up sleepers! Examine your ways! Return to yourselves and repent.

ॐ

Waking up is a common act like breathing or eating, something you do every day without reflection. It is also a turning point. If sleep is like death, then awakening is like resurrection. If sleep entails losing the world, awakening means regaining it. While the world into which you wake is resistantly old, impervious to the implications of dawn, a strong awakener knows the day which begins in starry darkness nonetheless is new.

We resist waking up. We yearn for a trance-like numbness, the uninterrupted flow of imagination. We choose to stumble through our days as if in a dream, for we are inertial beings given to drifting with the tide, heedless of our destination.

While Jews have been visionaries, we are not bound to our visions. While we continue to dream, we remain committed to interpretation. We sense we cannot see God and live, but we can hear God and awaken—as Abraham awoke from his terrible vision atop Mount Moriah where clasping the knife of imagination, he nearly slashed the tender neck of reality. "Abraham!" he heard the angel call. And he stopped. It takes an outside force to stun us. Surprised, jolted, disarmed, he awoke and discovered a ram caught by its horn in a thicket.

Abraham descending Moriah embodies the way of the Jew: Jews are interrupters, disenchanters, spell-breakers, committed to dreaming but with eyes open, committed to restful awareness, hallowed after "six days" of productivity.

Beginning again, re-newing the old, re-membering the sounds, re-calling the words, re-creating the world—this is the stuff of Torah, the business of the Jew.   James Ponet (Adapted)

עוּרוּ יְשֵׁנִים מִשְּׁנַתְכֶם וְנִרְדָּמִים הָקִיצוּ מִתַּרְדֵּמַתְכֶם וְחַפְּשׂוּ
בְּמַעֲשֵׂיכֶם וְחִזְרוּ בִּתְשׁוּבָה וְזִכְרוּ בּוֹרַאֲכֶם: אֵלּוּ הַשׁוֹכְחִים אֶת
הָאֱמֶת בְּהַבְלֵי הַזְּמַן וְשׁוֹגִים כָּל שְׁנָתָם בְּהֶבֶל וָרִיק אֲשֶׁר לֹא יוֹעִיל
וְלֹא יַצִּיל — הַבִּיטוּ לְנַפְשׁוֹתֵיכֶם וְהֵיטִיבוּ דַרְכֵיכֶם וּמַעַלְלֵיכֶם
וְיַעֲזֹב כָּל אֶחָד מִכֶּם דַּרְכּוֹ הָרָעָה וּמַחֲשַׁבְתּוֹ אֲשֶׁר לֹא טוֹבָה:

Awake from your slumber and rouse yourselves from your
lethargy. Scrutinize your deeds and turn in repentance.
Remember what is true, you who forget eternal truth in the
trifles of the hour, you who go astray all your years after vain
illusions that neither profit nor deliver. Look well into yourselves
and mend your ways and your actions; forsake the evil path and
unworthy purpose, and turn to God. Moses Maimonides

୬

There are sounds which first we heard as children which have
engraved themselves, like ancient riverbeds long dry, into our
inner ear. Years later, when we've grown, those early sounds will
open up those ancient streams, and the place and moment of
that early music will flow again across our memory, and we are
at once transported there, splashing in the cooling spray like the
children we still are, with all the joy and playfulness and awe we
thought had dried up in our long-sought maturity. Buried even
deeper in us than our childhood is the childhood of our people,
when we were wandering and playing at the foot of Sinai, full of
wonder and confusion, as the cloud appeared, and holy fire, and
thunder voices out of heaven, and the sounds of a shofar. Each
year when the shofar sounds for us again, the cloud appears
above the riverbed of memory, and we know that if sufficient
wonder and confusion fill our minds, the holy fire will burn
once more, and voices from our modest shofar will thunder out
of heaven once again. If only we can listen, the moment and the
place will flow again, and we can splash with the child our
people was at the beginning, in the stream. Richard Levy

The blowing of the shofar is the only special biblical ritual for Rosh Hashanah. The symbolism of the shofar is not made explicit in the Torah. Whether it is meant to arouse our slumbering souls or as a clarion call to war against the worst part of our natures, the primitive sound of the shofar blast stirs something deep within us. There is a sense of expectation in the silence before the shofar sound, followed by unease evoked by the various blasts. Part of its sense of mystery lies in the interplay of the silence, the piercing sound, and the hum of people praying. On its most basic level, the shofar can be seen to express what we cannot find the right words to say. The blasts are the wordless cries of the people of Israel. The shofar is the instrument that sends those cries of pain and longing hurtling across the vast distance toward the Other.

There are three shofar sounds: *tekiyah*—one blast; *shevarim*—three short blasts; and *teruah*—nine staccato blasts. The Torah does not state explicitly how many shofar blasts are required, but the rabbis (based on a complicated exegesis of Leviticus 25:9 and 23:24 and Numbers 20:1) derive the necessity to have three blasts of *teruah* preceded by and followed by *tekiyah*. The only question for the rabbis is what constitutes a *teruah*. One opinion is that it should sound like groaning (our *shevarim* sound); another is that it should sound like sobbing (what we call *teruah*); and a third opinion is that it should sound like both together (our *shevarim teruah*). Therefore, we have the pattern of *tekiyah teruah tekiyah, tekiyah shevarim tekiyah, tekiyah shevarim teruah tekiyah* to cover all possibilities.

Michael Strassfeld

The pattern of the shofar blasts mirrors the inner drama we experience as we take stock of our souls and our lives during the *Yamim Nora'im*. We begin Rosh Hashanah with a certain degree of inner wholeness and self-satisfaction reflected in the single drawn out note of *tekiyah*. During the course of the *Yamim Nora'im* we may experience anguish and broken-heartedness as we attempt to come to terms with our own shortcomings. This brokenness of heart and soul, a necessary part of the *teshuvah* process, is reflected in the moaning, sobbing sounds of the broken *teruah* and *shevarim* blasts. Just as these broken cries are followed by the renewed wholeness of the *tekiyah gedolah*—the longest shofar blast of all, so we hope to emerge from our days of introspection and prayer with a new sense of inner wholeness. The healing process of *teshuvah* can take place only after we honestly come to terms with the lack of completeness in our lives and our world. By the time of the *tekiyah gedolah*, may we find the strength and wholeness of heart and soul to go forth into a troubled and imperfect world with the will to bring wholeness and peace.   Reena M. Spicehandler

Isaac Arama sees the three shofar notes as symbolizing different approaches to three different kinds of people:

The *tekiyah*, with its simple and straightforward sound, is intended for the righteous, arousing feelings of confidence and inner peace.

The *teruah*, with its wailing sound, is aimed at the wicked, moving them to fear and trembling.

The *shevarim*, with its broken and uncertain sound, is designed for the average person, neither saint not sinner, who may find in it a message of either hope or despair.   Herman Kieval

SOUNDING THE SHOFAR

God has ascended amid cries of joy,
THE OMNIPRESENT ONE, amid the shofar blast.
Sing out to God, sing out,
sing to the sovereign one, sing out!
For God is sovereign over all the earth;
Sing out a song of praise.

Psalms 47:6-8

From the depths, I called out: "Yah!"
God answered, bringing great relief.

Psalms 118:5

You heard my call; don't close your ear
to my outcry, my plea for comfort.

Lamentations 3:56

The beginning of your word is truth,
and all your righteous judgments are eternal.

Psalms 119:160

Please stand in pledge for my release,
don't let the lawless have me in their grasp!

Psalms 119:122

I take pleasure in your utterance,
like one who finds great treasure.

Psalms 119:162

In knowledge and good judgment teach me—
truly, I have faith in your mitzvot.

Psalms 119:66

Please favor now my voluntary prayer,
and teach me now the justice of your ways.

Psalms 119:108

Some communities repeat the singing of Min Hametzar *between sections of the Shofar Blowing on the following page.*

COMMENTARY. Psalm 118 literally reads: "From a narrow place I called out to God, but God answered me from an open place." This is to teach that calling out for God's help allows even the most narrow-minded, "uptight" person to break out of closed-mindedness into a more broad-minded, compassionate understanding. The shofar—with its narrow end through which we blow and wide end from which sound emerges—symbolizes the process of spiritual liberation through divine inspiration.   S.D.R.

עֲלָה אֱלֹהִים בִּתְרוּעָה יהוה בְּקוֹל שׁוֹפָר:

זַמְּרוּ אֱלֹהִים זַמֵּרוּ זַמְּרוּ לְמַלְכֵּנוּ זַמֵּרוּ:

כִּי מֶלֶךְ כָּל־הָאָרֶץ אֱלֹהִים זַמְּרוּ מַשְׂכִּיל:

מִן־הַמֵּצַר קָרָאתִי יָּהּ עָנָנִי בַמֶּרְחָב יָהּ:

קוֹלִי שָׁמָעְתָּ אַל־תַּעְלֵם אָזְנְךָ לְרַוְחָתִי לְשַׁוְעָתִי:

רֹאשׁ־דְּבָרְךָ אֱמֶת וּלְעוֹלָם כָּל־מִשְׁפַּט צִדְקֶךָ:

עֲרֹב עַבְדְּךָ לְטוֹב אַל־יַעַשְׁקֻנִי זֵדִים:

שָׂשׂ אָנֹכִי עַל־אִמְרָתֶךָ כְּמוֹצֵא שָׁלָל רָב:

טוּב טַעַם וָדַעַת לַמְּדֵנִי כִּי בְמִצְוֺתֶיךָ הֶאֱמָנְתִּי:

נִדְבוֹת פִּי רְצֵה־נָא יהוה וּמִשְׁפָּטֶיךָ לַמְּדֵנִי:

Min hametzar karati yah anani vamerhav yah.

Some communities repeat the singing of Min Hametzar *between sections of the Shofar Blowing on the following page.*

NOTE. Sounding the shofar on behalf of the community is a sacred task. It has traditionally been delegated to an upright and humble person who has learned the proper technique. The meaning and responsibility that rest in the skills and intentions of the shofar blower shape a memorable moment of this awesome day, underlying the need for careful personal and musical preparation.   D.A.T.

COMMENTARY. The traditional liturgy includes all of Psalm 47 here. It is a natural choice because of the way it heralds God with shofar blasts and cries of joy. Our *mahzor* includes only verses 6-8 in keeping with our commitment to eliminate references to chosenness and to celebrations marking the destruction or subjugation of other peoples.   D.A.T.

We stand for the Shofar Blowing.

Blessed are you, ETERNAL ONE, our God, the sovereign of all worlds, who raises us to holiness with your mitzvot, and has commanded us to hear the shofar sound.

Blessed are you THE ETERNAL ONE, our God, the sovereign of all worlds, who gave us life, and kept us strong, and brought us to this time.

The shofar is sounded. We are then seated.

Some communities that do not recite a Musaf *Amidah continue with* Malḥuyot *(page 607) here. In that case, they return the Torah to the ark after* Shofarot *(page 597).*

DERASH. The shofar sound represents prayer beyond words, an intensity of longing that can only be articulated in a wordless shout. But the order of the sounds, according to one old interpretation, contains the message in quite explicit terms. Each series of shofar blasts begins with *tekiyah,* a whole sound. It is followed by *shevarim,* a tripartite broken sound whose very name means "breakings." "I started off whole," the shofar speech says, "and I became broken." Then follows *teruah,* a staccato series of blast fragments, saying: "I was entirely smashed to pieces." But each series has to end with a new *tekiyah,* promising wholeness once more. The shofar cries out a hundred times on Rosh Hashanah: "I was whole, I was broken, even smashed to bits, but I shall be whole again!"   A.G.

COMMENTARY. Several models are available for the shofar blowing. The traditional model is for the shofar blowing to be done by one unamplified voice. Another model is for all the people who have *shofarot* to participate in the shofar blowing simultaneously. All the other congregants, led by a caller, call out *tekiyah.* This creates a powerful dialogue. It has been my custom in the last few years to have the first set of sounds (*tekiyah shevarim teruah tekiyah*) done by one shofar and all the other sets blown in unison by all the people who have *shofarot.* A model for the *tekiyah gedolah* is for all the shofar blowers to line up. The first one begins, and when he or she is out of breath, the next one continues to blow. This is a real *tekiyah gedolah.*   Z.S.S.

ROSH HASHANAH SHAḤARIT / 591

בָּרוּךְ אַתָּה יהוה אֱלֹהֵינוּ מֶלֶךְ הָעוֹלָם
אֲשֶׁר קִדְּשָׁנוּ בְּמִצְוֹתָיו וְצִוָּנוּ לִשְׁמֹעַ קוֹל שׁוֹפָר:

בָּרוּךְ אַתָּה יהוה אֱלֹהֵינוּ מֶלֶךְ הָעוֹלָם
שֶׁהֶחֱיָנוּ וְקִיְּמָנוּ וְהִגִּיעָנוּ לַזְּמַן הַזֶּה:

תְּקִיעָה	תְּרוּעָה	שְׁבָרִים	תְּקִיעָה
תְּקִיעָה	תְּרוּעָה	שְׁבָרִים	תְּקִיעָה
תְּקִיעָה	תְּרוּעָה	שְׁבָרִים	תְּקִיעָה

תְּקִיעָה	שְׁבָרִים	תְּקִיעָה
תְּקִיעָה	שְׁבָרִים	תְּקִיעָה
תְּקִיעָה	שְׁבָרִים	תְּקִיעָה

תְּקִיעָה	תְּרוּעָה	תְּקִיעָה
תְּקִיעָה	תְּרוּעָה	תְּקִיעָה
תְּקִיעָה גְדוֹלָה	תְּרוּעָה	תְּקִיעָה

We are seated. Some communities that do not recite a Musaf Amidah *continue with* Malḥuyot *(page 607) here. In that case, they return the Torah to the ark after* Shofarot *(page 598).*

KAVANAH. The song of the shofar penetrates through our walls of fear. Thrilled by its intensity, we open up to its powerful reminder of the inner song in each of us. The shofar proclaims that all of our holy songs can join together as one.   D.B.

COMMENTARY. Like an alarm clock the shofar unsettles us. Yet some people sleep through the alarm clock's jolting rings. The appeal to conscience is clear and direct enough, yet all too often we ignore it. What does it take for us to hear the shofar's call? Perhaps a different way of understanding our social obligations. Every time you witness the suffering of another human being, or of any living thing, realize that your own heart is crying out in pain but that you just can't hear it.   S.D.R.

592 / SOUNDING THE SHOFAR

On Yom Kippur, some communities recite Yizkor (pages 1004-1034) here.
The following couplet is recited only on Rosh Hashanah.

Happy are the people who know the shofar blast, ETERNAL ONE!
They walk about in the light of your presence.

Happy are they who dwell within your house,
  may they continue to give praise to you.
Happy is the people for whom life is thus,
  happy is the people with THE EVERLASTING for its God!

A Psalm of David
    All exaltations do I raise to you, my sovereign God,
      and I give blessing to your name, forever and eternally.
    Blessings do I offer you each day,
      I hail your name, forever and eternally.
    Great is THE ETERNAL, to be praised emphatically,
      because God's greatness has no measure.
    Declaring praises for your deeds one era to the next,
      people describe your mighty acts.
    Heaven's glorious splendor is my song,
      words of your miracles I eagerly pour forth.
    Wondrous are your powers—people tell of them,
      and your magnificence do I recount.
    Signs of your abundant goodness they express,
      and in your justice they rejoice.
    How gracious and how merciful is THE ABUNDANT ONE,
      slow to anger, great in love.
    To all God's creatures, goodness flows,
      on all creation, divine love.
    Your creatures all give thanks to you,
      your fervent ones bless you emphatically. ↵

אשרי...יהלכון / Happy...presence (Psalms 89:16).
אשרי...סלה / Happy...you (Psalms 84:5).
אשרי...אלהיו / Happy...God (Psalms 144:15).

On Yom Kippur, some communities recite Yizkor (pages 1004-1034) here.
The following line is recited only on Rosh Hashanah:

אַשְׁרֵי

הָעָם יוֹדְעֵי תְרוּעָה יהוה בְּאוֹר־פָּנֶיךָ יְהַלֵּכוּן:

Ashrey ha'am yodey teruah adonay be'or paneḥa yehaleḥun.

עוֹד יְהַלְלוּךָ סֶּלָה:	אַשְׁרֵי יוֹשְׁבֵי בֵיתֶךָ
אַשְׁרֵי הָעָם שֶׁיהוה אֱלֹהָיו:	אַשְׁרֵי הָעָם שֶׁכָּכָה לּוֹ
תְּהִלָּה לְדָוִד	
וַאֲבָרְכָה שִׁמְךָ לְעוֹלָם וָעֶד:	אֲרוֹמִמְךָ אֱלֹהַי הַמֶּלֶךְ
וַאֲהַלְלָה שִׁמְךָ לְעוֹלָם וָעֶד:	בְּכָל־יוֹם אֲבָרְכֶךָּ
וְלִגְדֻלָּתוֹ אֵין חֵקֶר:	גָּדוֹל יהוה וּמְהֻלָּל מְאֹד
וּגְבוּרֹתֶיךָ יַגִּידוּ:	דּוֹר לְדוֹר יְשַׁבַּח מַעֲשֶׂיךָ
וְדִבְרֵי נִפְלְאֹתֶיךָ אָשִׂיחָה:	הֲדַר כְּבוֹד הוֹדֶךָ
וּגְדֻלָּתְךָ אֲסַפְּרֶנָּה:	וֶעֱזוּז נוֹרְאֹתֶיךָ יֹאמֵרוּ
וְצִדְקָתְךָ יְרַנֵּנוּ:	זֵכֶר רַב־טוּבְךָ יַבִּיעוּ
אֶרֶךְ אַפַּיִם וּגְדָל־חָסֶד:	חַנּוּן וְרַחוּם יהוה
וְרַחֲמָיו עַל־כָּל־מַעֲשָׂיו:	טוֹב־יהוה לַכֹּל
וַחֲסִידֶיךָ יְבָרְכוּכָה: ⟵	יוֹדוּךָ יהוה כָּל־מַעֲשֶׂיךָ

Ashrey yoshvey veyteḥa od yehaleluḥa selah.
Ashrey ha'am shekaḥah lo ashrey ha'am she'adonay elohav.
Tehilah ledavid.
Aromimeḥa elohay hameleḥ va'avareḥah shimeḥa le'olam va'ed.
Beḥol yom avareḥeka va'ahalela shimeḥa le'olam va'ed.
Gadol adonay umhulal me'od veligdulato eyn ḥeker.
Dor ledor yeshabaḥ ma'aseḥa ugevuroteḥa yagidu.
Hadar kevod hodeḥa vedivrey nifle'oteḥa asiḥah.
Ve'ezuz noroteḥa yomeru ugedulateḥa asaperenah.
Zeḥer rav tuveḥa yabi'u vetzidkateḥa yeranenu.
Ḥanun veraḥum adonay ereḥ apayim ugedol ḥased.
Tov adonay lakol veraḥamav al kol ma'asav.
Yoduḥa adonay kol ma'aseḥa vehasideḥa yevareḥuḥah. ⟳

Calling out the glory of your sovereignty,
  of your magnificence they speak,
Letting all people know your mighty acts,
  and of your sovereignty's glory and splendor.
May your sovereignty last all eternities,
  your dominion for era after era.
Strong support to all who fall,
  God raises up the humble and the lame.
All hopeful gazes turn toward you,
  as you give sustenance in its appointed time.
Providing with your open hand,
  you satisfy desire in all life.
So just is God in every way,
  so loving amid all the divine deeds.
Close by is God to all who call,
  to all who call to God in truth.
Responding to the yearning of all those who fear,
  God hears their cry and comes to rescue them.
Showing care to all who love God, THE ETERNAL
  brings destruction to all evildoers.
The praise of THE ALL-KNOWING does my mouth declare,
  and all flesh give blessing to God's holy name,
    unto eternity.

Psalm 145

And as for us, we bless the name of Yah,
  from now until the end of time. Halleluyah!

ואנחנו...הללויה / And...Halleluyah! (Psalms 115:18).

COMMENTARY. Psalm 145 is an alphabetical acrostic. The translation roughly preserves the sound of the Hebrew initials of each line. The line for the letter *nun* is missing from this psalm, for unknown reasons. J.R.

כְּבוֹד מַלְכוּתְךָ יֹאמֵרוּ   וּגְבוּרָתְךָ יְדַבֵּרוּ:
לְהוֹדִיעַ לִבְנֵי הָאָדָם גְּבוּרֹתָיו   וּכְבוֹד הֲדַר מַלְכוּתוֹ:
מַלְכוּתְךָ מַלְכוּת כָּל־עֹלָמִים   וּמֶמְשַׁלְתְּךָ בְּכָל־דּוֹר וָדוֹר:
סוֹמֵךְ יהוה לְכָל־הַנֹּפְלִים   וְזוֹקֵף לְכָל־הַכְּפוּפִים:
עֵינֵי־כֹל אֵלֶיךָ יְשַׂבֵּרוּ   וְאַתָּה נוֹתֵן־לָהֶם אֶת־אָכְלָם בְּעִתּוֹ:
פּוֹתֵחַ אֶת־יָדֶךָ   וּמַשְׂבִּיעַ לְכָל־חַי רָצוֹן:
צַדִּיק יהוה בְּכָל־דְּרָכָיו   וְחָסִיד בְּכָל־מַעֲשָׂיו:
קָרוֹב יהוה לְכָל־קֹרְאָיו   לְכֹל אֲשֶׁר יִקְרָאֻהוּ בֶאֱמֶת:
רְצוֹן יְרֵאָיו יַעֲשֶׂה   וְאֶת־שַׁוְעָתָם יִשְׁמַע וְיוֹשִׁיעֵם:
שׁוֹמֵר יהוה אֶת־כָּל־אֹהֲבָיו   וְאֵת כָּל־הָרְשָׁעִים יַשְׁמִיד:
* תְּהִלַּת יהוה יְדַבֶּר פִּי   וִיבָרֵךְ כָּל־בָּשָׂר שֵׁם קָדְשׁוֹ לְעוֹלָם וָעֶד:
וַאֲנַחְנוּ נְבָרֵךְ יָהּ   מֵעַתָּה וְעַד־עוֹלָם הַלְלוּיָהּ:

Kevod malḥuteḥa yomeru ugevurateḥa yedaberu.
Lehodi'a livney ha'adam gevurotav uḥevod hadar malḥuto.
Malḥuteḥa malḥut kol olamim umemshalteḥa beḥol dor vador.
Someḥ adonay leḥol hanofelim vezokef leḥol hakefufim.
Eyney ḥol eleḥa yesaberu
    ve'atah noten lahem et oḥlam be'ito.
Pote'aḥ et yadeḥa umasbi'a leḥol ḥay ratzon.
Tzadik adonay beḥol deraḥav vehasid beḥol ma'asav.
Karov adonay leḥol korav leḥol asher yikra'uhu ve'emet.
Retzon yere'av ya'aseh ve'et shavatam yishma veyoshi'em.
Shomer adonay et kol ohavav ve'et kol haresha'im yashmid.
Tehilat adonay yedaber pi
    vivareḥ kol basar shem kodsho le'olam va'ed.
Va'anaḥnu nevareḥ yah me'atah ve'ad olam halleluyah.

HAHNASAT SEFER TORAH / RETURNING THE TORAH TO THE ARK

Let all bless the name of THE ETERNAL,
for it alone is to be exalted.

God's splendor dwells on earth and in the heavens,
God has lifted up our people's strength.
Praise to all God's fervent ones,
to the children of Israel, people near to God.
Halleluyah!

Traditionally the Torah is carried around the room, although some congregations immediately place it in the ark and continue with Etz Hayim Hi, page 605.

הַכְנָסַת סֵפֶר תּוֹרָה

יְהַלְלוּ אֶת־שֵׁם יהוה כִּי־נִשְׂגָּב שְׁמוֹ לְבַדּוֹ

הוֹדוֹ עַל־אֶרֶץ וְשָׁמָיִם: וַיָּרֶם קֶרֶן לְעַמּוֹ תְּהִלָּה לְכָל־חֲסִידָיו לִבְנֵי
יִשְׂרָאֵל עַם קְרוֹבוֹ הַלְלוּיָה:

Yehalelu et shem adonay ki nisgav shemo levado
Hodo al eretz veshamayim vayarem keren le'amo tehilah lehol
hasidav livney yisra'el am kerovo halleluyah.

Traditionally the Torah is carried around the room, although some congregations immediately place it in the ark and continue with Etz Ḥayim Hi, *page 606.*

יהללו...הללויה /Let...Halleluyah! (Psalms 148:13-14).

On Shabbat, substitute Psalm 29 (page 603).

The world belongs to GOD in all its fullness,
the earth, and all who dwell on it,
for God has founded it upon the waters,
on the torrents, God established it.
Who can ascend the mount of THE ETERNAL?
Who rises to the holy place of God?
The one whose hands are clean, whose heart is pure,
whose soul has not been vainly self-excusing,
the one who never swore deceitfully.

That person reaps a blessing from THE ALL-KNOWING ONE,
justice from the God of help.
For many generations now,
the family of Jacob has sought your presence.
You city gates, open your bolts,
eternal gates, be lifted up,
and let the sovereign of glory come! ↩

לא־נשא לשוא נפשי / Whose soul has not been vainly self-excusing. Literally, "who has not lifted up the soul in vain." The psalm turns on repetitions of the key verb, "lift up," playing on its many meanings. Compare: "That person reaps [literally, lifts up] a blessing....You city gates, open [literally, lift up] your gates, etc." The pilgrim, ascending the steep slopes toward the Temple Mount, contemplates, through this interplay of associations, the fundamental act of pilgrimage: an offering-up to God.   J.R.

NOTE. This psalm asks and answers several questions, suggesting that it was sung antiphonally in ancient times with the congregation singing the responses.   D.A.T.

On Shabbat, substitute Psalm 29 (page 604).

לְדָוִד מִזְמוֹר

לַיהוה הָאָרֶץ וּמְלוֹאָהּ   תֵּבֵל וְיֹשְׁבֵי בָהּ׃

כִּי־הוּא עַל־יַמִּים יְסָדָהּ   וְעַל־נְהָרוֹת יְכוֹנְנֶהָ׃

מִי־יַעֲלֶה בְהַר־יהוה   וּמִי־יָקוּם בִּמְקוֹם קָדְשׁוֹ׃

נְקִי כַפַּיִם וּבַר־לֵבָב   אֲשֶׁר לֹא־נָשָׂא לַשָּׁוְא נַפְשִׁי

וְלֹא נִשְׁבַּע לְמִרְמָה׃

יִשָּׂא בְרָכָה מֵאֵת יהוה   וּצְדָקָה מֵאֱלֹהֵי יִשְׁעוֹ׃

זֶה דּוֹר דֹּרְשָׁיו   מְבַקְשֵׁי פָנֶיךָ יַעֲקֹב סֶלָה׃

שְׂאוּ שְׁעָרִים רָאשֵׁיכֶם   וְהִנָּשְׂאוּ פִּתְחֵי עוֹלָם

וְיָבוֹא מֶלֶךְ הַכָּבוֹד׃ ←

Ledavid mizmor.

Ladonay ha'aretz umlo'ah tevel veyoshvey vah.

Ki hu al yamim yesadah ve'al neharot yeḥoneneha.

Mi ya'aleh behar adonay umi yakum bimkom kodsho.

Neki ḥapayim uvar levav asher lo nasa lashav nafshi velo nishba
    lemirmah.

Yisa veraḥah me'et adonay utzedakah me'elohey yisho.

Zeh dor dorshav mevakshey faneḥa ya'akov selah.

Se'u she'arim resheyḥem vehinasu pitḥey olam veyavo meleḥ
    hakavod. ↵

Who is the sovereign of glory?
THE MAGNIFICENT, so powerful and mighty!
THE ETERNAL ONE, a champion in battle!
You city gates, open your bolts;
eternal gates, be lifted up,
and let the sovereign of glory come!
Who is this one, the sovereign of glory?
THE RULER of the Multitudes of Heaven,
the sovereign of glory.

Psalm 24

Continue on page 605.

מִי זֶה מֶלֶךְ הַכָּבוֹד יהוה עִזּוּז וְגִבּוֹר
יהוה גִּבּוֹר מִלְחָמָה:
שְׂאוּ שְׁעָרִים רָאשֵׁיכֶם וּשְׂאוּ פִּתְחֵי עוֹלָם
וְיָבוֹא מֶלֶךְ הַכָּבוֹד:
מִי הוּא זֶה מֶלֶךְ הַכָּבוֹד יהוה צְבָאוֹת הוּא
מֶלֶךְ הַכָּבוֹד סֶלָה:

Mi zeh meleḥ hakavod adonay izuz vegibor adonay gibor
milḥamah.
Se'u she'arim rasheyḥem use'u pitḥey olam veyavo meleḥ
hakavod.
Mi hu zeh meleḥ hakavod adonay tzeva'ot hu meleḥ hakavod
selah.

Continue on page 606.

A psalm of David: Give to THE ONE WHO IS, you so-called gods, give to THE INDIVISIBLE glory and strength!

Give to THE UNSEEN ONE the glory of the divine Name, worship THE ANCIENT ONE with holy ornament.

The voice of THE UNENDING on the waters,
God in full Glory thundering,

THE ONE WHO CALLS over many waters,

yes, the voice of THE REVEALED ONE in full strength,
voice of THE TRUTHFUL in full beauty,

voice of THE ETERNAL ONE breaking the cedars,
THE ALL-KNOWING smashing the cedars of Lebanon,

making them skip about like calves,
yes, Lebanon and Sirion, like offspring of the wild ox.

The voice of THE JUST ONE hewing flames of fire,
the voice of THE ANOINTER making the desert writhe,
of THE REVIVER, giving birthpangs to the wastelands of Kadesh,

the voice of THE CREATOR, convulsing all the deer,
stripping the forests,
while amid God's palace all declare: "The Glory!"

THE REDEEMER, prevailing at the Sea,
THE PRESENCE, presiding for the world,

THE WANDERER, imparting strength to Israel,
GIVER OF WORDS, blessing the people in their peace.

Psalm 29

מִזְמוֹר לְדָוִד

הָבוּ לַיהוה כָּבוֹד וָעֹז: הָבוּ לַיהוה בְּנֵי אֵלִים

הִשְׁתַּחֲווּ לַיהוה בְּהַדְרַת־קֹדֶשׁ: הָבוּ לַיהוה כְּבוֹד שְׁמוֹ

אֵל הַכָּבוֹד הִרְעִים קוֹל יהוה עַל־הַמָּיִם

יהוה עַל־מַיִם רַבִּים:

קוֹל יהוה בֶּהָדָר: קוֹל־יהוה בַּכֹּחַ

וַיְשַׁבֵּר יהוה אֶת־אַרְזֵי הַלְּבָנוֹן: קוֹל יהוה שֹׁבֵר אֲרָזִים

לְבָנוֹן וְשִׂרְיוֹן כְּמוֹ בֶן־רְאֵמִים: וַיַּרְקִידֵם כְּמוֹ־עֵגֶל

קוֹל־יהוה חֹצֵב לַהֲבוֹת אֵשׁ:

יָחִיל יהוה מִדְבַּר קָדֵשׁ: קוֹל יהוה יָחִיל מִדְבָּר

וַיֶּחֱשֹׂף יְעָרוֹת קוֹל יהוה יְחוֹלֵל אַיָּלוֹת

וּבְהֵיכָלוֹ כֻּלּוֹ אֹמֵר כָּבוֹד:

וַיֵּשֶׁב יהוה מֶלֶךְ לְעוֹלָם: יהוה לַמַּבּוּל יָשָׁב

יהוה יְבָרֵךְ אֶת־עַמּוֹ בַשָּׁלוֹם: יהוה עֹז לְעַמּוֹ יִתֵּן

Mizmor ledavid.

Havu ladonay beney elim havu ladonay kavod va'oz.

Havu ladonay kevod shemo hishtaḥavu ladonay behadrat
  kodesh.

Kol adonay al hamayim el hakavod hirim adonay al mayim rabim.

Kol adonay bako'aḥ kol adonay behadar.

Kol adonay shover arazim vayshaber adonay et arzey
  halevanon.

Vayarkidem kemo egel levanon vesiryon kemo ven re'emim.

Kol adonay ḥotzev lahavot esh.

Kol adonay yaḥil midbar yaḥil adonay midbar kadesh.

Kol adonay yeḥolel ayalot vayeḥesof ye'arot uveheyḥalo kulo
  omer kavod.

Adonay lamabul yashav vayeshev adonay meleḥ le'olam.

Adonay oz le'amo yiten adonay yevareḥ et amo vashalom.

604 / RETURNING THE TORAH TO THE ARK

The ark is opened and the Torah placed inside.

And when the Ark was set at rest, they would proclaim:
Restore, ETERNAL ONE, the many thousand troops of Israel!

For it is a precious teaching I have given you,
my Torah: Don't abandon it!

It is a Tree of Life to those that hold fast to it,
all who uphold it may be counted fortunate.

Its ways are ways of pleasantness,
and all its paths are peace.

Return us, PRECIOUS ONE, let us return!
Renew our days, as you have done of old!

The ark is closed.

COMMENTARY. "Renew our days as you have done of old."
We may read:
Renew our days as when we were young.
Revive us with the wonder of your world,
    with the enthusiasm of our youth.
Help us to recover something of the child within
    that knew you in the desert
    and trembled at the foot of the mountain.
Grant us, once again, the sacred vision
    and the courage of new beginnings.
Do not return us to days past:
Renew our days as when we were young.   S.E.S.

The ark is opened and the Torah placed inside.

וּבְנֻחֹה יֹאמַר שׁוּבָה יהוה רִבְבוֹת אַלְפֵי יִשְׂרָאֵל:
כִּי לֶקַח טוֹב נָתַתִּי לָכֶם תּוֹרָתִי אַל־תַּעֲזֹבוּ:
עֵץ־חַיִּים הִיא לַמַּחֲזִיקִים בָּהּ וְתֹמְכֶיהָ מְאֻשָּׁר:
דְּרָכֶיהָ דַרְכֵי־נֹעַם וְכָל־נְתִיבוֹתֶיהָ שָׁלוֹם:
הֲשִׁיבֵנוּ יהוה אֵלֶיךָ וְנָשׁוּבָה חַדֵּשׁ יָמֵינוּ כְּקֶדֶם:

Etz ḥayim hi lamaḥazikim bah vetomḥeha me'ushar.
Deraḥeha darḥey no'am veḥol netivoteha shalom.
Hashivenu adonay eleḥa venashuvah ḥadesh yameynu
    kekedem.

The ark is closed.

ובנחה...ישראל / And...Israel (Numbers 10:36).
כי...תעזבו / For...it (Proverbs 4:2).
עץ...מאשר / It...fortunate (Proverbs 3:18).
דרכיה...שלום / Its...peace (Proverbs 3:17).
השיבנו...כקדם / Return...old (Lamentations 5:21).

עץ חיים היא / It is a Tree of Life. At the end of the Garden story, Adam and
Eve are forbidden access to the mysterious Tree of Life, whose fruit
confers immortality. Yet over the generations to follow, humankind itself
becomes a Tree of Life. The Torah is handed on from one generation to
another, binding the generations in a commonwealth of time and conferring
the norms on which the survival of civilization depends. Thus the Torah is
compared to the Tree of Life.   J.R.

INTRODUCTION TO MALHUYOT/
ZIHRONOT/SHOFAROT

The three major themes of the Rosh Hashanah *Musaf* are most frequently spoken of as reflecting three important aspects of God and theology. The first, *Malhuyot*—sovereignty—proclaims God's sovereignty over the world and humanity. The second—*Zihronot*—remembrance—tells us that God cares about the world and remembers all our deeds, both the good and the bad. The third, *Shofarot*, reminds us of the revelation of God at Sinai and of the final redemption still to come. Together they "describe" a god who is omniscient and omnipotent and who is actively involved in this world on a continuing basis.

These three aspects are also part of our lives, for we are created *betzelem elohim*—in the image of God. We are to reflect in our lives aspects of the Divine, or as the rabbinic principle states: You should be merciful as God is merciful, you should be just, etc. Looking at these three themes in this manner gives us a different perspective. *Malhuyot* focuses on control—control over others and over ourselves. *Zihronot* has to do with memory and thought. Remembering is what the covenant is based on, for we are to remember what God did for us in Egypt and elsewhere. Remembering, too, is what all human relationships are based on, for without memory of past events and feelings, there is no way to deepen emotional attachments; each meeting becomes the first; whether for love or hate, no one has any more meaning to you than anyone else. *Shofarot*, the third, has to do with sound and thus with communication and speech.

Appropriately for Rosh Hashanah, these three themes are reflected in the three creation stories at the beginning of Genesis—that is, the Garden, the Flood and the Tower of Babel.

For the story of the tree in the Garden is a story of controls—of self-control and of curbing desire. Both God and humans learn from the Garden that there is no self-control without tasting of ↵

knowledge; without at least partial understanding of who we are and the consequences of our deeds, there is no motivation to curb desire. Both God and humanity learn that self-control will be difficult for humans.

The second creation story is that of the Flood, which is quoted in the liturgy of *Ziḥronot* as follows: "Remember us as You remembered Noah in love, graciously saving him when You released the flood to destroy all creatures because of their evil deeds...." The liturgy continues with a quotation (Genesis 8:1) from the Noah story. God *remembers* Noah and saves him. Later God remembers the people of Israel in Egypt and decides to redeem them. It is out of memory, out of cognition, that God acts, that God saves, and that God establishes or reestablishes relationships with humans.

We, too, are meant to remember the Noahs amid the floodwater and reach out to save them. We are to remember and emphasize the good in others in order to relate to them, not focus on their faults. We are also meant to remember the past and not live only in the present. Remembering the past gives us a proper sense of our place in the universe and, even more important, makes us cognizant of a future that we must be engaged in creating.

The third creation story is that of the Tower of Babel, in which we learn the power of speech and its danger. Today, we remain confounded by the diversity of languages, but even more by the difficulty of really communicating rather than just speaking.

Self-control, thinking/remembering, and speech are what make us human. To realize our full potential, we must strive with each of these aspects of our humanity, which in themselves are only reflections of the Divine.

Michael Strassfeld

Choose from the following songs:

וּבָא לְצִיּוֹן גּוֹאֵל וּלְשָׁבֵי פֶּשַׁע בְּיַעֲקֹב נְאֻם יהוה:

Uva letzion go'el uleshavey <u>fe</u>sha beya'akov ne'um adonay.

And a redeemer shall come to Zion, and to those of Jacob
who return from their transgression, says THE GOD OF ISRAEL.

❧

עִבְדוּ אֶת־יהוה בְּשִׂמְחָה בֹּאוּ לְפָנָיו בִּרְנָנָה:

Ivdu et adonay besim<u>h</u>ah <u>bo</u>'u lefanav birnanah.

Serve God with happiness,
come into God's presence
with a joyful song!

❧

יִשְׂרָאֵל וְאוֹרַיְתָא קֻדְשָׁא בְּרִיךְ הוּא חַד הוּא:
תּוֹרָה אוֹרָה הַלְלוּיָהּ:

Yisra'el ve'orayta kudsha beri<u>h</u> hu <u>h</u>ad hu.
Torah orah halleluyah.

Israel, Torah, and the Blessed Holy One are one. Torah is light.
Halleluyah!

וּבָא...יהוה / And...THE GOD OF ISRAEL (Isaiah 59:20).
עבדו...ברננה / Serve...song (Psalms 100:2).

ישראל ואורייתא / *Yisra'el ve'orayta.* This song is a popular adaptation of a
phrase attributed to the *Zohar* by the eighteenth-century Italian moralist
Moshe Ḥayim Luzzatto.

R.S.

ROSH HASHANAH MUSAF / 609

The three sections—*Malḥuyot, Ziḥronot* and *Shofarot*—follow a logical progression. The first section proclaims God Creator and Monarch. As author of the universe, God is the one of absolute power, bringing life and death, awesome and holy. Emphasized here is the majesty of God's kingdom, along with the promise that God's true rule will one day be perceived by all. The God of *Malḥuyot* remains distant, however, enshrined in a holiness that seems far beyond our reach. *Ziḥronot* balances that awesome monarchy; indeed, God may be Monarch, but God is one who cares. God remembered Noah, the one who was spared in the hour of God's greatest wrath. So God remembered Israel in Egypt, the righteous in their trials, and the life of each individual human being. The awesome Ruler has entered into a covenant with humanity (again, through Noah, not with Israel alone), a covenant that promises God will take cognizance of each individual human life, of every human cry. *Shofarot* then tells us of the acts of God: God who rules and remembers will also act. God has given us the gift of self-revelation at Sinai, and God will reveal a mighty hand yet again, at the end of time. These three sections of the liturgy should be read as a single unit, a summation of world history as seen from the perspective of Israel's faith.

Arthur Green (Adapted)

DERASH. *Malḥuyot*/sovereignties, challenges us to get our priorities straight. When the ruler calls, everything else falls by the wayside. We do not usually order our priorities with awareness of the presence of the *Meleḥ*/ Sovereign. As a result we often get means and ends confused. *Meleḥ* helps us remember not to give the means preponderance over the ends.   Z.S.S.

Some communities begin Musaf *with* Malhuyot *and therefore continue below. Others begin* Musaf *with a silent Amidah or the Amidah chanted aloud, beginning on page 323, and then continue here.*

MALHUYOT / SOVEREIGNTY

We rise for Aleynu. It is customary to bow or prostrate at "bend the knee."
Choose one of the following:

It is up to us to offer praises to the Source of all,
to declare the greatness of the author of Creation,
who gave us teachings of truth
and planted eternal life within us.

❧

It is up to us to offer praises to the Source of all,
to declare the greatness of the author of Creation,
who created heaven's heights and spread out its expanse,
who laid the earth's foundation and brought forth its offspring,
giving life to all its peoples,
the breath of life to all who walk about. ⤶

COMMENTARY. This siddur offers several versions of the *Aleynu*. The first, from the 1945 Reconstructionist siddur, emphasizes that the gift of Torah or teaching demands our committed response. The second version, by Rabbi Max D. Klein based on Isaiah 42:5, emphasizes that our obligation to God flows from our role as part of Creation. The traditional *Aleynu* that appears below the line has troubled Reconstructionist Jews because it implies the inferiority of other faiths and peoples.   D.A.T.

COMMENTARY. The *Aleynu* prayer was originally composed for use on Rosh Hashanah in the *Malhuyot* section of the *Musaf*. Its trumpeting of divine sovereignty and the anticipated recognition of that sovereignty by all of humanity is central to the liturgy of Rosh Hashanah. The world's birthday and the re-enthronement of God have been linked themes as early as anyone can discover. Thus, the Mishnah knows only this location for *Aleynu*. Because of its power and centrality in Jewish thought and feeling, *Aleynu* eventually came to be included in Shabbat and daily worship as well.   D.A.T.

Some communities begin Musaf *with* Malhuyot *and therefore continue below. Others begin Musaf with a silent Amidah or the Amidah chanted aloud, beginning on page 324, and then continue here.*

מַלְכִיּוֹת

We rise for Aleynu. It is customary to bow or prostrate at "korim." Choose one of the following:

Aleynu leshabe'ah la'adon hakol

latet gedulah leyotzer bereyshit

shenatan lanu torat emet

vehayey olam nata betohenu.

עָלֵינוּ לְשַׁבֵּחַ לַאֲדוֹן הַכֹּל

לָתֵת גְּדֻלָּה לְיוֹצֵר בְּרֵאשִׁית

שֶׁנָּתַן לָנוּ תּוֹרַת אֱמֶת

וְחַיֵּי עוֹלָם נָטַע בְּתוֹכֵנוּ:

Continue on page 614.

∾

Aleynu leshabe'ah la'adon hakol

latet gedulah leyotzer bereyshit.

bore hashamayim venoteyhem

roka ha'aretz vetze'etza'eha

noten neshamah la'am aleha

veru'ah laholehim bah.

עָלֵינוּ לְשַׁבֵּחַ לַאֲדוֹן הַכֹּל

לָתֵת גְּדֻלָּה לְיוֹצֵר בְּרֵאשִׁית

בּוֹרֵא הַשָּׁמַיִם וְנוֹטֵיהֶם

רֹקַע הָאָרֶץ וְצֶאֱצָאֶיהָ

נֹתֵן נְשָׁמָה לָעָם עָלֶיהָ

וְרוּחַ לַהֹלְכִים בָּהּ: ←

עָלֵינוּ לְשַׁבֵּחַ לַאֲדוֹן הַכֹּל לָתֵת גְּדֻלָּה
לְיוֹצֵר בְּרֵאשִׁית שֶׁלֹּא עָשָׂנוּ כְּגוֹיֵי
הָאֲרָצוֹת וְלֹא שָׂמָנוּ כְּמִשְׁפְּחוֹת הָאֲדָמָה
שֶׁלֹּא שָׂם חֶלְקֵנוּ כָּהֶם וְגוֹרָלֵנוּ כְּכָל
הֲמוֹנָם:

It is up to us to offer praises to the Source of all, to declare the greatness of the author of Creation, who has made us different from the other nations of the earth, and situated us in quite a different spot, and made our daily lot another kind from theirs, and given us a destiny uncommon in this world.

And so, we bend the knee and bow,
acknowledging the sovereign who rules
above all those who rule, the blessed Holy One,
who stretched out the heavens and founded the earth,
whose realm embraces heaven's heights,
whose mighty presence stalks celestial ramparts.
This is our God; there is none else besides,
as it is written in the Torah:
"You shall know this day, and bring it home
inside your heart, that THE SUPREME ONE is God
in the heavens above and on the earth below.
There is no other God." ⤺

DERASH. Every person and people that feel they have something to live for,
and that are bent on living that life in righteousness, are true witnesses of
God.
                                                                M.M.K.

KAVANAH. As the hand held before the eye hides the tallest mountain, so
this small earthly life hides from our gaze the vast radiance and secrets of
which the world is full, and if we can take life from before our eyes, as
one takes away one's hand, we will see the great radiance within the
world.
                                                                M.B. (Adapted)

עוד...וידעת / You...other God (Deuteronomy 4:39).

וַאֲנַחְנוּ כּוֹרְעִים וּמִשְׁתַּחֲוִים וּמוֹדִים לִפְנֵי מֶֽלֶךְ מַלְכֵי הַמְּלָכִים
הַקָּדוֹשׁ בָּרוּךְ הוּא:
שֶׁהוּא נוֹטֶה שָׁמַֽיִם וְיוֹסֵד אֶֽרֶץ וּמוֹשַׁב יְקָרוֹ בַּשָּׁמַֽיִם מִמַּֽעַל וּשְׁכִינַת
עֻזּוֹ בְּגָבְהֵי מְרוֹמִים: הוּא אֱלֹהֵֽינוּ אֵין עוֹד: אֱמֶת מַלְכֵּֽנוּ אֶֽפֶס
זוּלָתוֹ כַּכָּתוּב בְּתוֹרָתוֹ: וְיָדַעְתָּ הַיּוֹם וַהֲשֵׁבֹתָ אֶל־לְבָבֶֽךָ כִּי יהוה
הוּא הָאֱלֹהִים בַּשָּׁמַֽיִם מִמַּֽעַל וְעַל־הָאָֽרֶץ מִתַּֽחַת אֵין עוֹד: —←

Va'anaḥnu korim umishtaḥavim umodim
lifney meleḥ malḥey hamelaḥim hakadosh baruḥ hu.

Shehu noteh shamayim veyosed aretz umoshav yekaro
bashamayim mima'al
usheḥinat uzo begovhey meromim.
Hu eloheynu eyn od.
Emet malkenu efes zulato kakatuv betorato.
Veyadata hayom vahashevota el levaveḥa
ki adonay hu ha'elohim bashamayim mima'al ve'al ha'aretz
mitaḥat eyn od.

And so, we put our hope in you,
THE EMINENCE, our God,
that soon we may behold
the full splendor of your might,
and see idolatry vanish from the earth,
and all material gods be swept away,
and the power of your rule repair the world,
and all creatures of flesh call on your name,
and all the wicked of the earth turn back to you.
Let all who dwell upon the globe perceive and know
that to you each knee must bend, each tongue swear oath,
and let them give the glory of your name its precious due.
Let all of them take upon themselves your rule.
Reign over them, soon and for always.
For this is all your realm, throughout all worlds, across all
   time—
as it is written in your Torah:
"THE ETERNAL ONE will reign now and forever."

DERASH. God does not stand apart from humanity and issue commands to
people. God's presence is evidenced in those qualities of the human
personality and of society by which the evils of life are overcome, and
latent good brought to realization. By ascribing primacy to these qualities
we acclaim the sovereignty of God.   M.M.K.

עַל כֵּן נְקַוֶּה לְּךָ יהוה אֱלֹהֵינוּ לִרְאוֹת מְהֵרָה בְּתִפְאֶרֶת עֻזֶּךָ לְהַעֲבִיר גִּלּוּלִים מִן הָאָרֶץ וְהָאֱלִילִים כָּרוֹת יִכָּרֵתוּן לְתַקֵּן עוֹלָם בְּמַלְכוּת שַׁדַּי: וְכָל בְּנֵי בָשָׂר יִקְרְאוּ בִשְׁמֶךָ: לְהַפְנוֹת אֵלֶיךָ כָּל רִשְׁעֵי אָרֶץ: יַכִּירוּ וְיֵדְעוּ כָּל יוֹשְׁבֵי תֵבֵל כִּי לְךָ תִּכְרַע כָּל בֶּרֶךְ תִּשָּׁבַע כָּל־לָשׁוֹן: לְפָנֶיךָ יהוה אֱלֹהֵינוּ יִכְרְעוּ וְיִפֹּלוּ וְלִכְבוֹד שִׁמְךָ יְקָר יִתֵּנוּ וִיקַבְּלוּ כֻלָּם אֶת עֹל מַלְכוּתֶךָ וְתִמְלֹךְ עֲלֵיהֶם מְהֵרָה לְעוֹלָם וָעֶד: כִּי הַמַּלְכוּת שֶׁלְּךָ הִיא וּלְעוֹלְמֵי עַד תִּמְלֹךְ בְּכָבוֹד:

DERASH. When senseless hatred reigns on earth and people hide their faces from one another, then heaven is forced to hide its face. But when love comes to rule the earth and people reveal their faces to one another, then the splendor of God will be revealed.   M.B. (Adapted)

DERASH. It is not the seeking after God that divides but the claim to have found God and to have discovered the only proper way of obeying God and communing with God.   M.M.K. (Adapted)

As it is written in your Torah,
"THE HOLY ONE will reign forever!"

Exodus 15:18

And it is said:
"God found no fault in Jacob,
and beheld no evil deed in Israel,
for THE FOUNT OF RIGHTEOUSNESS is with them,
and there the horn-blast
sounds the sovereignty of God!"

Numbers 23:21

And it is said:
"God's sovereignty arose in Yeshurun,
when leaders of the people
came together with the tribes of Israel!"

Deuteronomy 33:5

And in your holy Scripture's words,
the following is written:
"For to GOD belongs all power to rule,
to God alone the governance of nations!"

Psalms 22:29

And it is said:
"THE ETERNAL reigns, is clothed in majesty,
THE INVISIBLE is clothed, is girded up with might,
The world is now established,
it cannot give way!"

Psalms 93:1

כַּכָּתוּב בְּתוֹרָתֶךָ:
יהוה יִמְלֹךְ לְעֹלָם וָעֶד:

וְנֶאֱמַר:
לֹא־הִבִּיט אָוֶן בְּיַעֲקֹב וְלֹא־רָאָה עָמָל בְּיִשְׂרָאֵל
יהוה אֱלֹהָיו עִמּוֹ וּתְרוּעַת מֶלֶךְ בּוֹ:

וְנֶאֱמַר:
וַיְהִי בִישֻׁרוּן מֶלֶךְ
בְּהִתְאַסֵּף רָאשֵׁי עָם יַחַד שִׁבְטֵי יִשְׂרָאֵל:

וּבְדִבְרֵי קָדְשְׁךָ כָּתוּב לֵאמֹר:
כִּי לַיהוה הַמְּלוּכָה וּמֹשֵׁל בַּגּוֹיִם:

וְנֶאֱמַר:
יהוה מָלָךְ גֵּאוּת לָבֵשׁ לָבֵשׁ יהוה עֹז הִתְאַזָּר
אַף־תִּכּוֹן תֵּבֵל בַּל־תִּמּוֹט: ←——

And it is said:
"You city gates, raise up your bolts,
you gates to the eternal, open up,
and let the sovereign of glory come!

Who is the sovereign of glory?
THE FOUNT OF RIGHTEOUSNESS, so powerful and mighty!
THE ETERNAL ONE, the champion in strife!

You city gates, raise up your bolts,
you gates to the eternal, open up,
and let the sovereign of glory come!

Who is this one, the sovereign of glory?
THE CREATOR of all beings,
the sovereign of glory. It is so!" Psalms 24:7-10

And by your servants' hands, the prophets,
the following is written:
"Thus says THE HOLY ONE,
the people Israel's sovereign and redeemer,
THE CREATOR of all beings:
I am the first and last,
apart from me there is no God!" Isaiah 44:6

And it is said:
"Redemption has arisen for Mount Zion,
Justice for the Mount of Esau,
for all sovereignty belongs to THE ETERNAL ONE!" Obadiah 1:21

And it is said:
"THE EVERLASTING ONE will reign
as sovereign over all the earth.
On that day shall THE MANY-NAMED be one,
God's name be one!" Zechariah 14:9

As it is written in your Torah:
"Listen, Israel: THE ETERNAL is our God, THE ETERNAL ONE
alone!" Deuteronomy 6:4

וְנֶאֱמַר:
שְׂאוּ שְׁעָרִים רָאשֵׁיכֶם וְהִנָּשְׂאוּ פִּתְחֵי עוֹלָם
וְיָבוֹא מֶלֶךְ הַכָּבוֹד:
מִי זֶה מֶלֶךְ הַכָּבוֹד יהוה עִזּוּז וְגִבּוֹר יהוה גִּבּוֹר מִלְחָמָה:
שְׂאוּ שְׁעָרִים רָאשֵׁיכֶם וּשְׂאוּ פִּתְחֵי עוֹלָם וְיָבֹא מֶלֶךְ הַכָּבוֹד:
מִי הוּא זֶה מֶלֶךְ הַכָּבוֹד יהוה צְבָאוֹת הוּא מֶלֶךְ הַכָּבוֹד סֶלָה:

וְעַל יְדֵי עֲבָדֶיךָ הַנְּבִיאִים כָּתוּב לֵאמֹר:
כֹּה־אָמַר יהוה מֶלֶךְ־יִשְׂרָאֵל וְגֹאֲלוֹ יהוה צְבָאוֹת
אֲנִי רִאשׁוֹן וַאֲנִי אַחֲרוֹן וּמִבַּלְעָדַי אֵין אֱלֹהִים:

וְנֶאֱמַר:
וְעָלוּ מוֹשִׁעִים בְּהַר צִיּוֹן לִשְׁפֹּט אֶת־הַר עֵשָׂו
וְהָיְתָה לַיהוה הַמְּלוּכָה:

וְנֶאֱמַר:
וְהָיָה יהוה לְמֶלֶךְ עַל־כָּל־הָאָרֶץ
בַּיּוֹם הַהוּא יִהְיֶה יהוה אֶחָד וּשְׁמוֹ אֶחָד:

וּבְתוֹרָתְךָ כָּתוּב לֵאמֹר:
שְׁמַע יִשְׂרָאֵל יהוה אֱלֹהֵינוּ יהוה אֶחָד:

NOTE. The recitation of the *Shema* implies a commitment to be bound by the commandments. The rabbis therefore called the *Shema* קבלת עול מלכות שמים / the acceptance of the yoke of divine sovereignty. This explains why the *Shema* was included in the *Malḥuyot* verses, which otherwise include explicit references to God as מלך / sovereign. J.A.S.

ADIREY AYUMAH / AWESOMELY NOBLE

THE ETERNAL ONE now reigns!
   THE ETERNAL ONE has always reigned!
     THE ETERNAL ONE shall ever reign!

Awesomely noble in their awe, the angels cry aloud:
   THE ETERNAL ONE now reigns!
Born of the lightning bolts, they bless aloud:
   THE ETERNAL ONE has always reigned!
Great ones on high, God's greatness they declare aloud:
   THE ETERNAL ONE shall ever reign!

THE ETERNAL ONE now reigns!
   THE ETERNAL ONE has always reigned!
     THE ETERNAL ONE shall ever reign!

Dashing about in fiery awe, they all declare aloud:
   THE ETERNAL ONE now reigns!
Hailing God on high, now hear them say aloud:
   THE ETERNAL ONE has always reigned!
Voices in unison, vast multitudes give voice aloud:
   THE ETERNAL ONE shall ever reign!

THE ETERNAL ONE now reigns!
   THE ETERNAL ONE has always reigned!
     THE ETERNAL ONE shall ever reign!

Zealous in remembering, behold their song aloud:
   THE ETERNAL ONE now reigns!
Heaven's mysteries and beauties shape their call aloud:
   THE ETERNAL ONE has always reigned!
The scribes of heaven's orbs, they offer praise aloud:
   THE ETERNAL ONE shall ever reign!

THE ETERNAL ONE now reigns!
   THE ETERNAL ONE has always reigned!
     THE ETERNAL ONE shall ever reign! �

יהוה מֶלֶךְ יהוה מָלָךְ יהוה יִמְלֹךְ לְעֹלָם וָעֶד׃

יהוה מֶלֶךְ׃	יַאְדִּירוּ בְקוֹל	אַדִּירֵי אֲיֻמָּה
יהוה מָלָךְ׃	יְבָרְכוּ בְקוֹל	בְּרוּאֵי בָרָק
יהוה יִמְלֹךְ׃	יַגְבִּירוּ בְקוֹל	גִּבּוֹרֵי גֹבַהּ

יהוה מֶלֶךְ יהוה מָלָךְ יהוה יִמְלֹךְ לְעֹלָם וָעֶד׃

יהוה מֶלֶךְ׃	יְדוֹבְבוּ בְקוֹל	דּוֹהֲרֵי דוֹלְקִים
יהוה מָלָךְ׃	יְהַלְלוּ בְקוֹל	הֲמוֹנֵי הַמֻּלָּה
יהוה יִמְלֹךְ׃	יַוַעֲדוּ בְקוֹל	וְחַיָּלִים וְחַיּוֹת

יהוה מֶלֶךְ יהוה מָלָךְ יהוה יִמְלֹךְ לְעֹלָם וָעֶד׃

יהוה מֶלֶךְ׃	יְזַמְּרוּ בְקוֹל	זוֹכְרֵי זְמִירוֹת
יהוה מָלָךְ׃	יְחַסְּנוּ בְקוֹל	חַכְמֵי חִידוֹת
יהוה יִמְלֹךְ׃	יְטַכְּסוּ בְקוֹל	טַפְסְרֵי טְפוּחִים

יהוה מֶלֶךְ יהוה מָלָךְ יהוה יִמְלֹךְ לְעֹלָם וָעֶד׃ ←

Adonay meleḥ Adonay malaḥ Adonay yimloḥ le'olam va'ed.

Jubilant heirs of divine glory, in joy all cry aloud:
THE ETERNAL ONE now reigns!
Compelling in their mighty voice, they crown divinity aloud:
THE ETERNAL ONE has always reigned!
Luminously clad in flame, they lovingly declare aloud:
THE ETERNAL ONE shall ever reign!

THE ETERNAL ONE now reigns!
THE ETERNAL ONE has always reigned!
THE ETERNAL ONE shall ever reign!

Mellifluous of utterance, they mouth their words aloud:
THE ETERNAL ONE now reigns!
Now sparking with celestial light, a new song call aloud:
THE ETERNAL ONE has always reigned!
Seraphim surround the Throne and sing in praise aloud:
THE ETERNAL ONE shall ever reign!

THE ETERNAL ONE now reigns!
THE ETERNAL ONE has always reigned!
THE ETERNAL ONE shall ever reign!

Ordering their song of might, all answering aloud:
THE ETERNAL ONE now reigns!
Powerfully struck with awe, a psalm they call aloud:
THE ETERNAL ONE has always reigned!
Celestial army, faithful flock, send chiming song aloud:
THE ETERNAL ONE shall ever reign!

THE ETERNAL ONE now reigns!
THE ETERNAL ONE has always reigned!
THE ETERNAL ONE shall ever reign! ↵

יהוה מֶלֶךְ:	יַיְשִׁירוּ בְקוֹל	יוֹרְשֵׁי יְקָרָה
יהוה מָלָךְ:	יַכְתִּירוּ בְקוֹל	כַּבִּירֵי כֹחַ
יהוה יִמְלֹךְ:	יְלַבְּכוּ בְקוֹל	לְבוּשֵׁי לֶהָבוֹת

יהוה מֶלֶךְ יהוה מָלָךְ יהוה יִמְלֹךְ לְעֹלָם וָעֶד:

יהוה מֶלֶךְ:	יְמַלְלוּ בְקוֹל	מַנְעִימֵי מֶלֶל
יהוה מָלָךְ:	יְנַצְּחוּ בְקוֹל	נוֹצְצֵי נֹגַהּ
יהוה יִמְלֹךְ:	יְסַלְסְלוּ בְקוֹל	שְׂרָפִים סוֹבְבִים

יהוה מֶלֶךְ יהוה מָלָךְ יהוה יִמְלֹךְ לְעֹלָם וָעֶד:

יהוה מֶלֶךְ:	יַעֲנוּ בְקוֹל	עוֹרְכֵי עֹז
יהוה מָלָךְ:	יִפְצְחוּ בְקוֹל	פְּחוּדֵי פְלָאֲךְ
יהוה יִמְלֹךְ:	יְצַלְצְלוּ בְקוֹל	צִבְאוֹת צֹאנְךְ

יהוה מֶלֶךְ יהוה מָלָךְ יהוה יִמְלֹךְ לְעֹלָם וָעֶד: ⟶

Adonay meleḥ Adonay malaḥ Adonay yimloḥ le'olam va'ed.

Communities of holiness, cry holiness of God aloud:
THE ETERNAL ONE now reigns!
Resounding thousands upon thousands ring aloud:
THE ETERNAL ONE has always reigned!
Shimmering with heaven's fire, they shout aloud:
THE ETERNAL ONE shall ever reign!

THE ETERNAL ONE now reigns!
THE ETERNAL ONE has always reigned!
THE ETERNAL ONE shall ever reign!

Their devotion they sustain, God's rule perpetuate aloud:
THE ETERNAL ONE now reigns!
Trumpeting your splendor, your perfection they extol aloud:
THE ETERNAL ONE has always reigned!
Tested and attested true, your glory all shall teach aloud!
THE ETERNAL ONE shall ever reign!

THE ETERNAL ONE now reigns!
THE ETERNAL ONE has always reigned!
THE ETERNAL ONE shall ever reign!

יהוה מֶלֶךְ:	יַקְדִּישׁוּ בְקוֹל	קְהִלּוֹת קֹדֶשׁ
יהוה מָלָךְ:	יְרַנְּנוּ בְקוֹל	רִבְבוֹת רְבָבָה
יהוה יִמְלֹךְ:	יְשַׁנְּנוּ בְקוֹל	שְׁבִיבֵי שַׁלְהָבוֹת

יהוה מֶלֶךְ יהוה מָלָךְ יהוה יִמְלֹךְ לְעֹלָם וָעֶד:

יהוה מֶלֶךְ:	יַתְמִידוּ בְקוֹל	תּוֹמְכֵי תְהִלּוֹת
יהוה מָלָךְ:	יַתְמִימוּ בְקוֹל	תּוֹקְפֵי תִפְאַרְתֶּךָ
יהוה יִמְלֹךְ:	יִתְּנוּ בְקוֹל	תְּמִימֵי תְעוּדָה

יהוה מֶלֶךְ יהוה מָלָךְ יהוה יִמְלֹךְ לְעֹלָם וָעֶד:

Adonay meleḥ Adonay malaḥ Adonay yimloḥ le'olam va'ed.

KAVANAH. This alphabetical acrostic hymn by Rabbi Eleazar Kallir, a sixth-century Palestinian poet and mystic, tells of the infinite varieties of divine praise sung by the angels on high. But the chorus lines of the song, relentlessly affirming God's rule from all eternity past to all eternity ahead, are the same words sung by the people Israel in their houses of worship as they enthrone the rule of God in the world on the Days of Awe. The Talmud says that the angels wait on high each morning to hear Israel begin their prayers—and so, by proclaiming this ecstatic hymn, Jews not only try on the "angelic" perspective but also, in effect, arouse and empower the heavenly multitudes to sing their own declaration of God's sovereignty. For this reason, perhaps, the poem can simultaneously be read two ways: as a description of the angels singing to God in their infinite choruses on high *and* as a description of Jews borrowing the fire and fervor of the angels to make their own prayers audible to Heaven's ear.   J.R.

Our God, our ancients' God,
rule over all the world in its entirety
by showing forth your glory,
and be raised up over all the earth
in your beloved presence.
And let the wondrous aura of your reign
be manifest in all who dwell upon the earth—
let every creature know that you are its creator,
let every living thing discern that you have fashioned it,
let everyone who draws the breath of life declare
that you, THE ANCIENT ONE, reign supreme,
and that your sovereignty embraces all.

On Shabbat, add the words in parenthesis.

Our God, our ancients' God,
(take pleasure in our rest,)
enable us to realize holiness through your mitzvot,
give us our portion in your Torah,
let us enjoy the good things of your world,
and gladden us with your salvation.
(And help us to perpetuate, ETERNAL ONE, our God,
with love and with desire,
your holy Shabbat,
and may all your people Israel,
all who treat your name as holy,
find rest and peace upon this day.) ↩

אֱלֹהֵֽינוּ וֵאלֹהֵי אֲבוֹתֵֽינוּ וְאִמּוֹתֵֽינוּ מְלֹךְ עַל כָּל הָעוֹלָם כֻּלּוֹ בִּכְבוֹדֶֽךָ וְהִנָּשֵׂא עַל כָּל הָאָֽרֶץ בִּיקָרֶֽךָ וְהוֹפַע בַּהֲדַר גְּאוֹן עֻזֶּֽךָ עַל כָּל יוֹשְׁבֵי תֵבֵל אַרְצֶֽךָ וְיֵדַע כָּל פָּעוּל כִּי אַתָּה פְעַלְתּוֹ וְיָבִין כָּל יְצוּר כִּי אַתָּה יְצַרְתּוֹ וְיֹאמַר כֹּל אֲשֶׁר נְשָׁמָה בְאַפּוֹ : יהוה מֶֽלֶךְ וּמַלְכוּתוֹ בַּכֹּל מָשָֽׁלָה : אֱלֹהֵֽינוּ וֵאלֹהֵי אֲבוֹתֵֽינוּ וְאִמּוֹתֵֽינוּ (רְצֵה בִמְנוּחָתֵֽנוּ) קַדְּשֵֽׁנוּ בְּמִצְוֹתֶֽיךָ וְתֵן חֶלְקֵֽנוּ בְּתוֹרָתֶֽךָ שַׂבְּעֵֽנוּ מִטּוּבֶֽךָ וְשַׂמְּחֵֽנוּ בִּישׁוּעָתֶֽךָ (וְהַנְחִילֵֽנוּ יהוה אֱלֹהֵֽינוּ בְּאַהֲבָה וּבְרָצוֹן שַׁבַּת קָדְשֶֽׁךָ וְיָנֽוּחוּ בוֹ כָּל יִשְׂרָאֵל מְקַדְּשֵׁי שְׁמֶֽךָ :)

MALHUYOT READING 1

We cannot actually picture goodness. It is not a being; it is a force, like electricity. Nobody ever actually saw electricity, but we can see and feel what electricity does. If we have an electric heater and connect it, we get heat. We get to know what electricity is by what it does. In the same way, we get to know what God is by what God makes us do: when people are, so to speak, connected with God, they do good things. We call those people godly people, and their acts, godly acts. Whenever this force is active, we say that God has exercised influence and power.

Belief in God, therefore, has to do...with human nature, with the way individual men and women act, with their attitudes, their ideals. Belief in God has to do with our attitude towards life itself. Do we find life good? Is life worthwhile? If we believe that life is good, that, in spite of sickness and accidents, in spite of poverty and war, in spite of all the sad and difficult conditions in the world, the world is a wonderful place to live in and can be made a still better place, then we believe in God. When we believe in God, we cannot be discouraged because we believe that all the misery in the world is due, not to the fact that misery is a necessary part of life, but to the fact that we have not yet discovered how to do away with that misery. Ira Eisenstein (Adapted)

MALHUYOT READING 2

Our life is a faint tracing on the surface of mystery. [This] surface is not smooth, any more than the planet is smooth; not even a single hydrogen atom is smooth, let alone a [tree]. Nor does it fit together; not even the chlorophyll and hemoglobin molecules are a perfect match....Nature seems to exult in abounding radicality, extremism, anarchy. If we were to judge nature by its common sense or likelihood, we wouldn't believe the world existed. In nature, improbabilities are the one stock in trade. The whole creation is one lunatic fringe. No claims of any and all revelations could be so far-fetched as a single giraffe. If creation had been left up to me, I'm sure I wouldn't have had the imagination or courage to do more than shape a single, reasonably sized atom, smooth as a snowball, and let it go at that.

The wonder is—given the errant nature of freedom and the burgeoning of texture in time—the wonder is that all the forms are not monsters, that there is beauty at all, grace gratuitous, pennies found, like a mockingbird's free fall. Beauty itself is the fruit of the creator's exuberance that grew such a tangle, and the grotesques and horrors bloom from that same free growth, that intricate scramble and twine up and down the conditions of time.

This, then is the extravagant landscape of the world, given, given with pizzazz, given in good measure, pressed down, shaken together, and running over.

Annie Dillard

MALHUYOT READING 3

Where shall I find you?
Your glory fills the world.
Behold, I find You
Where we earn our bread by the sweat of our brows,
Among the lonely and the poor, the lowly, the lost,
You are with us in blazing heat and shattering storm.

Behold, I find You
In the mind free to sail by its own star,
In words that spring from the depth of truth.
Wherever we struggle for justice and freedom.
Where we toil to unravel the secrets of Your world.
Where we make beauty out of words,
　　Wherever noble deeds are done.

Behold, I find You
In the merry shouts of children at their play;
In the sleep falling on their infant eyelids,
　　And in the smile that dances on their sleeping lips.

Let me find the strength not to cast off one in need.
Not to bend the knee before a haughty tyrant.
Give me strength to lift my spirits above the trivial,
To bear lightly my joys and sorrows.

Rabindranath Tagore (Adapted)

I was brought up to believe in free will. Although I came to
doubt all revelation, I can never accept the idea that the universe
is a physical or chemical accident, a result of blind evolution.
Even though I learned to recognize the lies, the clichés, and the
idolatries of the human mind, I still cling to some truths which I
think all of us might accept someday. There must be a way for
us to attain all possible pleasures, all the powers and knowledge
that nature can grant us and still serve God—a God who speaks
in deeds, not in words, and whose vocabulary is the universe.

Isaac Bashevis Singer (Adapted)

COMMENTARY. When we become aware of our dependence upon the laws
of nature, we acknowledge the rulership of a Power greater than and
beyond us that determines the conditions under which human life is lived.
This awareness, properly understood, leads to humility and a recognition
of the limits of human power.　　　Ira Eisenstein

Refine our hearts to serve you truthfully,
for you are a God of truth,
and your word is truthful
and endures forever.
Blessed are you, ETERNAL ONE,
the sovereign power over all the earth,
who raises up to holiness
(Shabbat,) the people Israel
and the Day of Memory.

We rise. The shofar is sounded.

May what our lips express
be pleasing in your presence
God exalted and sublime!
You who discern and listen,
you who keep watch, and hearken
to our shofar blast,
may you receive with mercy and with favor
this arrangement of our holy Scripture's
declaration of your rule.

COMMENTARY. How do I want to inscribe myself into the Book of Life for the coming year? What do I want my script to be? The *Areshet Sefateynu* reminds us that we are writing our script in partnership with God. It challenges us to write a good script.   Z.S.S.

וְטַהֵר לִבֵּנוּ לְעָבְדְּךָ בֶּאֱמֶת כִּי אַתָּה אֱלֹהִים אֱמֶת וּדְבָרְךָ אֱמֶת וְקַיָּם
לָעַד : בָּרוּךְ אַתָּה יהוה מֶלֶךְ עַל כָּל הָאָרֶץ מְקַדֵּשׁ (הַשַּׁבָּת וְ)יִשְׂרָאֵל
וְיוֹם הַזִּכָּרוֹן:

We rise.

תְּקִיעָה שְׁבָרִים תְּרוּעָה תְּקִיעָה Tekiyah Shevarim Teruah Tekiyah

תְּקִיעָה שְׁבָרִים תְּרוּעָה תְּקִיעָה Tekiyah Shevarim Teruah Tekiyah

תְּקִיעָה שְׁבָרִים תְּרוּעָה תְּקִיעָה Tekiyah Shevarim Teruah Tekiyah

אֲרֶשֶׁת שְׂפָתֵינוּ יֶעֱרַב לְפָנֶיךָ אֵל רָם וְנִשָּׂא מֵבִין וּמַאֲזִין מַבִּיט
וּמַקְשִׁיב לְקוֹל תְּקִיעָתֵנוּ וּתְקַבֵּל בְּרַחֲמִים וּבְרָצוֹן סֵדֶר מַלְכִיּוֹתֵינוּ:

meleh al kol ha'aretz mekadesh (hashabbat ve) yisrael veyom
hazikaron.

Areshet sefateynu ye'erav lefaneha el ram venisa mevin uma'azin
mabit umakshiv lekol tekiyatenu utekabel berahamim uveratzon
seder malhuyoteynu.

COMMENTARY. The sounding of the shofar, the most ancient rite in the
observance of Rosh Hashanah, has been interpreted as a summons to the
soul to present itself before the judgment seat of God. It has also been
construed as *teruat meleh*, the salute of the Sovereign, with all its
implications of fealty and allegiance. It has functioned, and should still
function, in the life of the Jewish people as an invitation to the individual
Jew to renew the oath of unqualified allegiance and loyalty to those ideals,
the realization of which would convert human society into a kingdom of
God.   M.M.K.

הַיּוֹם הֲרַת עוֹלָם

הַיּוֹם יַעַמְדוּ כָּל יְצוּרֵי עוֹלָמִים
כְּאֲגוּדָה אֶחָת לַעֲשׂוֹת רְצוֹנְךָ בְּלֵבָב שָׁלֵם
לְהִתְחַדֵּשׁ עִם בּוֹרְאָם עוֹלָם קָדוֹשׁ:

Hayom harat olam
Hayom ya'amdu kol yetzurey olamim
ke'agudah aḥat la'asot retzoneḥa belevav shalem
lehitḥadesh im boram olam kadosh.

Today, the world is born!
Today shall stand before you
all the beings of the cosmos, as one community,
to do your will with perfect heart,
to be renewed with their Creator
in the universal sacredness of life!

We are seated.

KAVANAH. "The whole notion of time as an arrow shooting inexorably forward has been shattered forever in the complex geometries of quantum space, where multidimensional strings and loops carry time in all directions and even bring it to a halt." (Deepak Chopra) Our ancestors intuited this understanding when they wrote: "Today the world was born." They did not say "the anniversary of the world's birth," but literally, "Today the world was conceived." This means that we can connect in this moment to the precise energy present at creation. This awareness can lead us to identify with a reality that is not bounded by time.   S.P.W.

The essence [of the Jewish conception of life]...seems to me to lie in an affirmative attitude to the life of all creation. The life of the individual has meaning only insofar as it aids in making the life of every living thing nobler and more beautiful. Life is sacred—that is to say, it is the supreme value, to which all other values are subordinate. The hallowing of the supra-individual life brings in its train a reverence for everything spiritual—a particularly characteristic feature of the Jewish tradition.

But the Jewish tradition also contains something else, something which finds splendid expression in many of the psalms, namely, a sort of intoxicated joy and amazement at the beauty and grandeur of this world, of which we can just form a faint notion. It is the feeling from which true scientific research draws its spiritual sustenance, but which also seems to find expression in the song of birds.

Albert Einstein (Adapted)

Hail the hand that scattered space with stars,
Wrapped whirling world in bright blue blanket, air,
Made worlds within worlds, elements in earth,
Souls within skins, every one a teeming universe,
Every tree a system of semantics, and pushed
Beyond probability to place consciousness
On this cooling crust of burning rock.

Oh praise that hand, mind, heart, soul, power or force
That so inclosed, separated, limited planets, trees, humans
Yet breaks all bounds and borders
To lavish on us light, love, life
This trembling glory.

Ruth Brin

ZIḤRONOT / REMEMBERING

You remember all that you have made within your world,
consider every creature fashioned since Creation.
Before you every secret is uncovered,
the whole multitude of mysteries since the world began.
Nothing is forgotten in the presence of your Throne of Glory,
and nothing hidden from before your eyes.
You remember each completed act and each created being—
none escapes your gaze.
All is revealed and known before you, ANCIENT ONE,
your watchful eye reaches beyond all generations,
for you bring the claim of memory into the world,
the power by which all breath and spirit must be reckoned.
All of your many works,
your mass of living creatures,
the vast infinity of beings—
each has its place within your memory and thought.
And so have you made known since the Beginning,
this you have made clear from days of old!

This very day marks the beginning of your Creation,
a memorial of the world's first day—
for it is Israel's law, a statute of the God of Jacob.
And on it, every nation stands in judgment:
which one destined for the sword, which for peace,
which for famine, which for plenty. ↵

DERASH. On the first day, the day of the world's birth, the whole world
was in a state of pure potential. Contemplating that newborn world, we
feel awe at the fact of creation. On Rosh Hashanah we are reminded that
today is a first day. We still contain within us the awesome and godly
potential of our creation. That potential is in our hands.   J.A.S.

אַתָּה זוֹכֵר מַעֲשֵׂה עוֹלָם וּפוֹקֵד כָּל־יְצוּרֵי קֶדֶם: לְפָנֶיךָ נִגְלוּ כָּל־
תַּעֲלוּמוֹת וַהֲמוֹן נִסְתָּרוֹת שֶׁמִּבְּרֵאשִׁית: כִּי אֵין שִׁכְחָה לִפְנֵי כִסֵּא
כְבוֹדֶךָ וְאֵין נִסְתָּר מִנֶּגֶד עֵינֶיךָ: אַתָּה זוֹכֵר אֶת־כָּל־הַמִּפְעָל וְגַם כָּל־
הַיְצוּר לֹא נִכְחָד מִמֶּךָ: הַכֹּל גָּלוּי וְיָדוּעַ לְפָנֶיךָ יהוה אֱלֹהֵינוּ צוֹפֶה
וּמַבִּיט עַד סוֹף כָּל־הַדּוֹרוֹת כִּי תָבִיא חֹק זִכָּרוֹן לְהִפָּקֵד כָּל־רוּחַ
וָנֶפֶשׁ לְהִזָּכֵר מַעֲשִׂים רַבִּים וַהֲמוֹן בְּרִיּוֹת לְאֵין תַּכְלִית: מֵרֵאשִׁית
כָּזֹאת הוֹדַעְתָּ וּמִלְּפָנִים אוֹתָהּ גִּלִּיתָ: זֶה הַיּוֹם תְּחִלַּת מַעֲשֶׂיךָ זִכָּרוֹן
לְיוֹם רִאשׁוֹן: כִּי חֹק לְיִשְׂרָאֵל הוּא מִשְׁפָּט לֵאלֹהֵי יַעֲקֹב: וְעַל
הַמְּדִינוֹת בּוֹ יֵאָמֵר: אֵיזוֹ לַחֶרֶב וְאֵיזוֹ לַשָּׁלוֹם אֵיזוֹ לָרָעָב וְאֵיזוֹ
לַשֹּׂבַע: ←

COMMENTARY. The *Ziḥronot* section is meant to bring to awareness that "You remember everything, there is no forgetting before You." This is a place of great awareness and enlightenment. *Ziḥronot* challenges us to create ongoing mindfulness of values, soul, truth, dedication. It prods us to be aware of impulsive reaction and to transform it with conscious memory.

Z.S.S.

DERASH. This people had [a] sense of history. It had a gift uniting the artistic and the moral, a receptivity through which some of eternity enters the human essence. This ability so rare in human beings came to be the possession of this people through its gradual growth: it was able to have time. This people's Sabbath and festivals are not just ancient institutions, but they are evidences of a fundamental power, an ability which is as artistic as it is moral. This power was both the commandment and the ability of this people to take a step backward, as artists do, to view the totality of their work. This people stepped back from the work of days in order to see the path of the weeks, from the events of the months to see the journey of the years, and from the customs of the era in order to comprehend the enduring task. From this it gained the knowledge and the ability to possess time, to own time for its own life. It acquired the ability to think in generations and live in generations, to look backward into the far reaches and to look forward into the great distances. Through history, this people came to be what it is: the people of the great memory and the great expectation.

Leo Baeck (Adapted)

On it, every living thing is summoned to account,
brought into memory, for life or death.
Who can escape the claims of memory on this day?
For the memory of every creature comes before you:
each person's acts, each person's history,
every deed—each step a mortal takes, each thought,
each plan, each inclination, and each consequence.

Happy is the person who does not forget you,
or the human being who gains courage through your help!
For those who seek you out shall never stumble,
they who trust in you shall never suffer shame.
For the memory of all created beings comes before you,
and you read carefully the deeds of all.
And so, with love, did you remember Noah,
and appoint him for a fate of mercy and redemption,
even as you brought the Flood upon the world,
destroying all flesh, due to the evil of their deeds.
And thus, REDEEMING ONE, our God,
did Noah come before you in your thoughts.
He was remembered,
and allowed to multiply his seed on earth—
as many as the grains of dust upon the land,
descendants numbering as the sands beside the sea. ↩

DERASH. When we pray for God to remember, we are reciting a list of
things that we then collectively remember. This remembering of past good
deeds and good intentions for future actions inspires us to higher thoughts
and deeds. In praying for God to remember, we need to take responsibility
for becoming the vehicles by which our prayer can become reality. It is
only our subsequent actions that can prove our prayers are not in vain.

D.A.T.

וּבְרִיּוֹת בּוֹ יִפָּקֵדוּ לְהַזְכִּירָם לַחַיִּים וְלַמָּוֶת: מִי לֹא נִפְקַד כְּהַיּוֹם הַזֶּה כִּי זֵכֶר כָּל־הַיְצוּר לְפָנֶיךָ בָּא מַעֲשֵׂה אִישׁ וּפְקֻדָּתוֹ וַעֲלִילוֹת מִצְעֲדֵי־ גָבֶר מַחְשְׁבוֹת אָדָם וְתַחְבּוּלוֹתָיו וְיִצְרֵי מַעַלְלֵי־אִישׁ:

אַשְׁרֵי אִישׁ שֶׁלֹּא יִשְׁכָּחֶךָּ וּבֶן־אָדָם יִתְאַמֶּץ־בָּךְ כִּי דוֹרְשֶׁיךָ לְעוֹלָם לֹא יִכָּשֵׁלוּ וְלֹא יִכָּלְמוּ לָנֶצַח כָּל־הַחוֹסִים בָּךְ: כִּי זֵכֶר כָּל־הַמַּעֲשִׂים לְפָנֶיךָ בָּא וְאַתָּה דוֹרֵשׁ מַעֲשֵׂה כֻלָּם: וְגַם אֶת־נֹחַ בְּאַהֲבָה זָכַרְתָּ וַתִּפְקְדֵהוּ בִּדְבַר יְשׁוּעָה וְרַחֲמִים בַּהֲבִיאֲךָ אֶת־מֵי הַמַּבּוּל לְשַׁחֵת כָּל־בָּשָׂר מִפְּנֵי רֹעַ מַעַלְלֵיהֶם: עַל כֵּן זִכְרוֹנוֹ בָּא לְפָנֶיךָ יהוה אֱלֹהֵינוּ לְהַרְבּוֹת זַרְעוֹ כְּעַפְרוֹת תֵּבֵל וְצֶאֱצָאָיו כְּחוֹל הַיָּם:

COMMENTARY. Who is it who remembers? Once we believed it was the father/king God, sitting above the small world and noting our behaviors in His great book. And now, when life is cheap and things are thrown away after one use and there is no heaven above the earth, who is it who notes and remembers? That our behaviors are recorded in God's book means that our actions have significance. It is our choice whether to dedicate what we do to supporting redemption or resisting it. Each separate thing we do, no matter how trivial it seems, can be a vehicle for furthering this redemptive process. Yet we discard so many opportunities each day, as though what we do doesn't matter. Each day we live, each act we perform, contributes to the flow of history toward salvation. Thus each thing we do really is recorded and preserved in the world. If we act on behalf of God, so it is written.   Daniel Siegel

DERASH. What are we affirming about God when we speak of God's memory? In the biblical pattern, God's remembering is followed by, or even implies, God's saving action—for example, God remembers Noah, Sarah, and the enslaved Israelites. We can find God in the feeling that we who are adrift, barren or oppressed are not alone, and in the possibility inherent in the universe for a transformed future.   J.A.S.

As it is written in your Torah:
"God remembered Noah and every living thing,
and all the beasts with him upon the Ark,
and God caused a breeze to pass throughout the earth,
and all the floodwaters withdrew."

Genesis 8:1

And it is said:
"And God heard [Israel's] cry of pain,
and God remembered the covenant with Abraham,
with Isaac, and with Jacob."

Exodus 2:24

And it is said:
"And I remember now my covenant with Jacob—
and my covenant with Isaac
and my covenant with Abraham
I shall remember.
And the earth I shall recall."

Leviticus 26:42

And in your holy Scriptures,
the following is written:
"God's wondrous deeds were made to be remembered,
gracious and merciful is THE ETERNAL ONE."

Psalms 111:4

And it is said:
"God gave sustenance
to those in awe of the divine,
God keeps the covenant in mind for all eternity."

Psalms 111:5

כַּכָּתוּב בְּתוֹרָתֶךָ:

וַיִּזְכֹּר אֱלֹהִים אֶת־נֹחַ וְאֵת כָּל־הַחַיָּה וְאֶת־כָּל־הַבְּהֵמָה אֲשֶׁר אִתּוֹ
בַּתֵּבָה וַיַּעֲבֵר אֱלֹהִים רוּחַ עַל הָאָרֶץ וַיָּשֹׁכּוּ הַמָּיִם:

וְנֶאֱמַר: וַיִּשְׁמַע אֱלֹהִים אֶת־נַאֲקָתָם וַיִּזְכֹּר אֱלֹהִים אֶת־בְּרִיתוֹ אֶת־
אַבְרָהָם אֶת־יִצְחָק וְאֶת־יַעֲקֹב:

וְנֶאֱמַר: וְזָכַרְתִּי אֶת־בְּרִיתִי יַעֲקוֹב וְאַף אֶת־בְּרִיתִי יִצְחָק וְאַף אֶת־
בְּרִיתִי אַבְרָהָם אֶזְכֹּר וְהָאָרֶץ אֶזְכֹּר:

וּבְדִבְרֵי קָדְשְׁךָ כָּתוּב לֵאמֹר:
זֵכֶר עָשָׂה לְנִפְלְאֹתָיו חַנּוּן וְרַחוּם יהוה:

וְנֶאֱמַר: טֶרֶף נָתַן לִירֵאָיו יִזְכֹּר לְעוֹלָם בְּרִיתוֹ: ⟵

COMMENTARY. It was ancient Israel that first assigned a decisive
significance to history. "The heavens," in the words of the psalmist,
might still "declare the glory of God," but it was human history that
revealed God's will and purpose. This novel perception was not the result
of philosophical speculation, but of the peculiar nature of Israelite faith. It
emerged out of an intuitive and revolutionary understanding of God, and
was refined through profoundly felt historical experiences. However it
came about, in retrospect the consequences are manifest. Suddenly, the
crucial encounter between humanity and the divine shifted away from the
realm of nature and the cosmos to the plane of history, conceived now in
terms of divine challenge and human response. The pagan conflict of the
gods with the forces of chaos, or with one another, was replaced by a
drama of a different and more poignant order: the paradoxical struggle
between the divine will of an omnipotent Creator and the free will of
God's creatures, people, in the course of history; a tense dialectic of
obedience and rebellion.   Yosef Hayim Yerushalmi (Adapted)

And it is said:
"And God remembered the covenant with them,
and, with great love,
relented from stern justice."

Psalms 106:45

And by your servants' hands, the prophets,
the following is written:
"Go, and proclaim to Jerusalem's ears,
Thus says THE GOD OF ISRAEL: I recall
the love you showed me in your youth,
the time when you betrothed yourself to me,
following after me across a barren land."

Jeremiah 2:2

And it is said:
"I remember my covenant with you,
in days when you were young,
and I shall now create for you,
an everlasting covenant."

Ezekiel 16:60

And it is said:
"Is Ephraim not my dearest child,
a source of joy to me?
Truly, whenever I make mention of it,
I am flooded with memories.
Therefore, I fill with yearning,
and am overcome with love.
So says THE ANCIENT ONE!"

Jeremiah 31:19

וְנֶאֱמַר: וַיִּזְכֹּר לָהֶם בְּרִיתוֹ וַיִּנָּחֵם כְּרֹב חֲסָדָיו:

וְעַל יְדֵי עֲבָדֶיךָ הַנְּבִיאִים כָּתוּב לֵאמֹר:

הָלֹךְ וְקָרָאתָ בְאָזְנֵי יְרוּשָׁלַיִם לֵאמֹר: כֹּה אָמַר יהוה זָכַרְתִּי לָךְ חֶסֶד נְעוּרַיִךְ אַהֲבַת כְּלוּלֹתָיִךְ לֶכְתֵּךְ אַחֲרַי בַּמִּדְבָּר בְּאֶרֶץ לֹא זְרוּעָה:

וְנֶאֱמַר: וְזָכַרְתִּי אֲנִי אֶת־בְּרִיתִי אוֹתָךְ בִּימֵי נְעוּרָיִךְ וַהֲקִימוֹתִי לָךְ בְּרִית עוֹלָם:

וְנֶאֱמַר: הֲבֵן יַקִּיר לִי אֶפְרַיִם אִם יֶלֶד שַׁעֲשׁוּעִים כִּי־מִדֵּי דַבְּרִי בּוֹ זָכֹר אֶזְכְּרֶנּוּ עוֹד עַל־כֵּן הָמוּ מֵעַי לוֹ רַחֵם אֲרַחֲמֶנּוּ נְאֻם־יהוה:

Our God, our ancients' God,
remember us, be mindful of our good,
we who stand before you.
Please designate us for a fate of mercy
and salvation, decreed from heaven's
highest, primordial heights.
And remember for our sake the covenant,
the love, the promise that you swore
to Abraham, our ancestor, on Mount Moriah.
Envisage once again the gift of Abraham,
our ancestor, as he bound and dedicated
at the place of sacrifice, his child Isaac,
reining in his love to do your will
with perfect heart.
So may your love restrain strict justice,
removing anger's burdens from us.
In your great goodness, let wrath be turned away
from us, your people, from your Holy City,
and from the Land of Israel, your inheritance.
Fulfill for us, ALL-MINDFUL ONE, our God,
the promise that you made in your Torah,
through your servant Moses,
from your glorious Presence,
as was said: ↩

אֱלֹהֵינוּ וֵאלֹהֵי אֲבוֹתֵֽינוּ וְאִמּוֹתֵֽינוּ זָכְרֵֽנוּ בְּזִכְרוֹן טוֹב לְפָנֶֽיךָ וּפָקְדֵֽנוּ בִּפְקֻדַּת יְשׁוּעָה וְרַחֲמִים מִשְּׁמֵי שְׁמֵי קֶֽדֶם וּזְכָר־לָֽנוּ יהוה אֱלֹהֵֽינוּ אֶת־הַבְּרִית וְאֶת־הַחֶֽסֶד וְאֶת־הַשְּׁבוּעָה אֲשֶׁר נִשְׁבַּֽעְתָּ לְאַבְרָהָם אָבִֽינוּ בְּהַר הַמּוֹרִיָּה וְתֵרָאֶה לְפָנֶֽיךָ עֲקֵדָה שֶׁעָקַד אַבְרָהָם אָבִֽינוּ אֶת־יִצְחָק בְּנוֹ עַל גַּב הַמִּזְבֵּֽחַ וְכָבַשׁ רַחֲמָיו לַעֲשׂוֹת רְצוֹנְךָ בְּלֵבָב שָׁלֵם: כֵּן יִכְבְּשׁוּ רַחֲמֶֽיךָ אֶת־כַּעַסְךָ מֵעָלֵֽינוּ וּבְטוּבְךָ הַגָּדוֹל יָשׁוּב חֲרוֹן אַפְּךָ מֵעַמְּךָ וּמֵעִירְךָ וּמִנַּחֲלָתֶֽךָ וְקַיֶּם־לָֽנוּ יהוה אֱלֹהֵֽינוּ אֶת־הַדָּבָר שֶׁהִבְטַחְתָּֽנוּ בְּתוֹרָתֶֽךָ עַל יְדֵי מֹשֶׁה עַבְדְּךָ מִפִּי כְבוֹדֶֽךָ כָּאָמוּר: ←

We are part of God's memory,
because nothing precious is ever lost in the universe,
and love is more precious than anything.
Love's promise and love's fulfillment are never lost.
They always turn up.
They are our inheritance,
if we remember.   S.P.W.

DERASH. The Torah states that God remembers our deeds and holds us
accountable for our wrongdoings. Yet few of us believe in a God who takes
a personal interest in humankind. Not many of us think of God as a
person at all. Does it still make sense to follow the tradition and speak of
"divine remembrance?" What we do in the world can cause good or evil
that stretches vastly beyond our imagining. Our actions shape the world's
memory. The genetic structure of various life forms has been shown—in
places like Hiroshima and Chernobyl—to bear the impact of human
misuse of the atom. Indeed, our contempt for the ecosystem that we share
with other life forms is unforgettably etched onto the very landscape and
will be visibly recalled with shame for generations to come. We cause good
and evil that become a part of universal memory. By beginning to heal the
wounds that we ourselves have caused, we will be remembered for a
blessing. *Adonay*, you remember all things forgotten. For you there is no
forgetting.   S.D.R.

"I have remembered, for your sake,
the covenant of former generations,
whom I brought forth from the land of Egypt,
in the eyes of all the nations
to become their God,
I, THE GOD OF ISRAEL."

For you are a God who can remember
all that is forgotten, since eternity.
Nothing is forgotten in the presence
of your Throne of Glory.
So may you remember now
the sacrifice of Isaac,
and be merciful to his posterity,
who are alive today.
Blessed are you, ETERNAL ONE,
who keeps the covenant in mind.

וְזָכַרְתִּי לָהֶם בְּרִית רִאשֹׁנִים אֲשֶׁר הוֹצֵאתִי־אֹתָם מֵאֶרֶץ מִצְרַ֫יִם לְעֵינֵי הַגּוֹיִם לִהְיוֹת לָהֶם לֵאלֹהִים אֲנִי יהוה: כִּי זוֹכֵר כָּל־הַנִּשְׁכָּחוֹת אַתָּה הוּא מֵעוֹלָם וְאֵין שִׁכְחָה לִפְנֵי כִסֵּא כְבוֹדֶ֫ךָ: וַעֲקֵדַת יִצְחָק לְזַרְעוֹ הַיּוֹם בְּרַחֲמִים תִּזְכֹּר. בָּרוּךְ אַתָּה יהוה זוֹכֵר הַבְּרִית:

וזכרתי...יהוה / I...THE GOD OF ISRAEL (Leviticus 26:45).

ZIḤRONOT READING 1

Remember! All our ancestors live in us. Though their tongues are silent, they speak with ours. Though their hands are still, they labor through us.

The past lives in us, in our very bodies. The structure of our organs, the energy that moves our muscles, the nerves and brain wherewith we apprehend our world, all are an inheritance from generations that have passed.

Remember! The past lives in our worlds, in our ability to reason, to communicate thought and feeling, to work, to love.

Remember! The past lives in the world's wealth and resources. We eat the fruit of trees planted by forebears long gone. With metals stored in the earth we forge our tools. Through skills and devices conceived by vanished generations, we survive in the world.

Remember! The past lives in our society and our folkways. Others before us originated government to make us secure, courts to administer justice and protect our liberties, ritual to enhance our days.

May we cherish justice and freedom in the affairs of our land, peace and equality among the peoples, that our children after us may not revile us for bequeathing a heritage of evil.

May we be true to our past as Jews, seeking to fulfill the unrealized ideals of our prophets and sages. May we fit ourselves to be their successors, and to impart to our children the vision of a godly kingdom.

Milton Steinberg (Adapted)

ZIHRONOT READING 2

Humans differ from the rest of living creation mainly in the possession of self-consciousness. Other creatures live from moment to moment. If they have memories, they are not aware that those are memories. If the future in any way determines their actions, they have no mental picture of that future. The consciousness of history is the consciousness of that larger self which one shares with one's fellows. Individuals are centuries, if not millennia, older than their chronological ages. But people who have a historical consciousness actually feel that the life they live extends far beyond the actual life of their bodies. Conscious of the experiences of the past, attached by a kind of umbilical cord to the history, the culture, the civilization of centuries, the individual's being becomes coextensive with the being of their peoples. The individual enjoys, as it were, an earthly immortality.

Mordecai M. Kaplan (Adapted)

ZIHRONOT READING 3

Judaism does not command us to believe; it commands us to remember. The commandment of faith in the Torah is *Remember*: "that you may remember the day of your departure from the land of Egypt as long as you live."

There is a slow and silent stream, a stream not of oblivion but of memory, from which we must constantly drink before entering the realm of faith....The substance of our very being is memory, our way of living is retaining the reminders, articulating memory.

The true story of the mind is not preserved in learned volumes, but in the living mental organism of everyone...The riches of a soul are stored up in its memory. This is the test of character— not whether an individual follows the daily fashion, but whether the past is alive in the present. When we want to understand ourselves, to find out what is most precious in our lives, we search our memory. Memory is the soul's witness to the capricious mind.

We are a people in whom the past endures, in whom the present is inconceivable without moments gone by. The vision of the prophets lasted a moment, a moment enduring forever. What happened once upon a time happens all the time.

Jews have not preserved the ancient monuments, they have retained the ancient moments. The light kindled in their history was never extinguished. With sustaining vitality the past survives in their thoughts, hearts, rituals. Recollection is a holy act: we sanctify the present by remembering the past.

Abraham Joshua Heschel (Collected & Adapted)

ZIHRONOT READING 4

So there is nothing new under the sun. I accept that. That is my challenge. There is beauty enough and ugliness enough and love enough and hate enough for any one of us to select from and shape our own absolutely personal combinations. But this shaping must be a conscious thing: a reaching back and forward for those details that create patterns and form and motif in a life. To see living as connection is to bevel the rough edges, miter the corners, blur the divisions so that time becomes a chain of always accessible segments, not fragments, of knowledge and experience.

Faye Moskowitz

ZIḤRONOT READING 5

Out of the debris of dying stars,
this rain of particles
that waters the waste with brightness;

the sea-wave of atoms hurrying home,
collapse of the giant,
unstable guest who cannot stay;

the sun's heart reddens and expands,
his mighty aspiration is lasting,
as the shell of his substance
one day will be white with frost.

In the radiant field of Orion
great hordes of stars are forming,
just as we see every night
fiery and faithful to the end.

Out of the cold and fleeing dust
that is never and always,
the silence and waste to come—
this arm, this hand,
my voice, your face, this love.

John Haines

We rise. The shofar is sounded.

May what our lips express
be pleasing in your presence,
God exalted and sublime!
You who discern and listen,
you who keep watch, and hearken
to our shofar blast,
may you receive with mercy and with favor
this arrangement of our holy Scripture's
declarations of the power of memory.

Today, the world is born!
Today shall stand before you
all the beings of the cosmos,
whether as your children
or your servants.
If as your children, show them mercy,
like a mother toward her children.
If as your servants,
then our eyes are turned toward you
in great anticipation,
that you may be gracious,
rendering judgment for the good, on our behalf,
as clear as light of day.

We are seated.

COMMENTARY. The central theme of New Year's Day is the power of memory itself. Memory defies oblivion, breaks the coils of the present, establishes the continuity of the generations, and rescues human life and effort from futility. It affords the only true resurrection of the dead. The act of remembering is thus in itself redemptive. If, on the one hand, it involves a chastening assessment, it involves, on the other, a comforting reassurance. New Year's Day is at once a day of judgment and a new beginning. If it looks backward, it does so only on the way forward; and its symbol is the trumpet of an eternal reveille. Theodore H. Gaster (Adapted)

Tekiyah	Shevarim	Tekiyah	תְּקִיעָה	שְׁבָרִים	תְּקִיעָה
Tekiyah	Shevarim	Tekiyah	תְּקִיעָה	שְׁבָרִים	תְּקִיעָה
Tekiyah	Shevarim	Tekiyah	תְּקִיעָה	שְׁבָרִים	תְּקִיעָה

אֲרֶֽשֶׁת שְׂפָתֵֽינוּ יֶעֱרַב לְפָנֶֽיךָ אֵל רָם וְנִשָּׂא מֵבִין וּמַאֲזִין מַבִּיט
וּמַקְשִׁיב לְקוֹל תְּקִיעָתֵֽנוּ וּתְקַבֵּל בְּרַחֲמִים וּבְרָצוֹן סֵֽדֶר זִכְרוֹנוֹתֵֽינוּ:

Areshet sefateynu ye'erav lefaneḥa el ram venisa mevin uma'azin
mabit umakshiv lekol tekiyatenu utekabel beraḥamim uveratzon
seder ziḥronoteynu.

הַיּוֹם הֲרַת עוֹלָם

הַיּוֹם יַעֲמִיד בַּמִּשְׁפָּט כָּל יְצוּרֵי עוֹלָמִים
אִם כְּבָנִים אִם כַּעֲבָדִים
אִם כְּבָנִים רַחֲמֵֽנוּ כְּרַחֵם אֵם עַל בָּנִים
וְאִם כַּעֲבָדִים עֵינֵֽינוּ לְךָ תְלוּיוֹת
עַד שֶׁתְּחָנֵּֽנוּ וְתוֹצִיא כָאוֹר מִשְׁפָּטֵֽנוּ אָיֹם קָדוֹשׁ:

SHOFAROT / CALLING

You revealed yourself
amid your cloud of glory,
to a holy people, to converse with them.
From heaven did you make your voice heard,
as you revealed yourself
through heaven's radiant mists.
And the entire world was shaken by your presence,
the beings you created trembled at your coming forth.
As you, our sovereign, became manifest upon Mt. Sinai,
to teach your people Torah and mitzvot,
You made heard the splendor of your voice,
your holy utterances, through flames of fire.
With thunder and lightning, you were shown to them,
amid the shofar's call to them did you appear.

As it is written in your Torah:
"And it happened on the third day, when morning came,
that there were thundering sounds and lightning,
and thick clouds upon the mountain,
and the shofar's great and mighty voice was heard,
and all the people trembled in their encampment."

Exodus 19:16

And it is said:
"And as the shofar's call grew louder and more forceful,
Moses spoke, and THE ALMIGHTY answered him aloud." ↵

Exodus 19:19

אַתָּה נִגְלֵיתָ בַּעֲנַן כְּבוֹדֶךָ עַל עַם קָדְשְׁךָ לְדַבֵּר עִמָּם: מִן הַשָּׁמַיִם הִשְׁמַעְתָּם קוֹלֶךָ וְנִגְלֵיתָ עֲלֵיהֶם בְּעַרְפְלֵי טֹהַר: גַּם כָּל־הָעוֹלָם כֻּלּוֹ חָל מִפָּנֶיךָ וּבְרִיּוֹת בְּרֵאשִׁית חָרְדוּ מִמֶּךָ בְּהִגָּלוֹתְךָ מַלְכֵּנוּ עַל הַר סִינַי לְלַמֵּד לְעַמְּךָ תּוֹרָה וּמִצְוֹת וַתַּשְׁמִיעֵם אֶת־הוֹד קוֹלֶךָ וְדִבְּרוֹת קָדְשְׁךָ מִלַּהֲבוֹת אֵשׁ: בְּקוֹלוֹת וּבְרָקִים עֲלֵיהֶם נִגְלֵיתָ וּבְקוֹל שׁוֹפָר עֲלֵיהֶם הוֹפָעְתָּ:

כַּכָּתוּב בְּתוֹרָתֶךָ:

וַיְהִי בַיּוֹם הַשְּׁלִישִׁי בִּהְיֹת הַבֹּקֶר וַיְהִי קֹלֹת וּבְרָקִים וְעָנָן כָּבֵד עַל־הָהָר וְקֹל שֹׁפָר חָזָק מְאֹד וַיֶּחֱרַד כָּל־הָעָם אֲשֶׁר בַּמַּחֲנֶה:

וְנֶאֱמַר: וַיְהִי קוֹל הַשּׁוֹפָר הוֹלֵךְ וְחָזֵק מְאֹד מֹשֶׁה יְדַבֵּר וְהָאֱלֹהִים יַעֲנֶנּוּ בְקוֹל:

DERASH. Maimonides speaks of the shofar as an awakener. We want to awaken to a higher awareness that gives us a perspective from which we can see the flaws in the routines of life and how they can be improved. The word shofar can be derived from *leshaper*, fixing or improving. *Shapru ma'asehem*: Shofarot encourages us to repair our deeds. The awareness provided by the shofar blast enhances our experience of this reflective day.

Z.S.S.

DERASH. Our ancestors imagined the divine voice as sometimes booming amidst the fire and thunder, sometimes whispering in the desert wind. When they were able to hear the divine command, a place deep inside them trembled, the place that sometimes trembles when we hear the shofar blast.

J.A.S.

And it is said:

"And all the people then beheld the thunder's voices,
the flaming torches, the sound of the shofar,
and the mountain smoldering with smoke.
And the people were afraid, and wavered,
but they stood and viewed it from afar."

Exodus 20:15

And in your holy scriptures
the following is written:
"God ascended amid horn-blasts,
THE REDEEMER by the call of the shofar."

Psalms 47:6

And it is said:

"With trumpets and the shofar's call,
sound forth before the sovereign one,
THE GOD OF ISRAEL!"

Psalms 98:6

And it is said:

"Blast piercing notes upon the shofar for the New Moon,
for the full moon, for our festive holiday!
For it is Israel's law,
a statute of the God of Jacob!"

Psalms 81:4-5

COMMENTARY. "The people then beheld the thunder's voices, the flaming torches, the sound of the shofar." How can people see the sound of the shofar? By "see" does it mean all sensory perception including listening? What is most important here is the fear felt by the people in light of what they experienced—the apprehension caused by what they apprehended.

D.A.T.

וְנֶאֱמַר: וְכָל־הָעָם רֹאִים אֶת־הַקּוֹלֹת וְאֶת־הַלַּפִּידִם וְאֵת קוֹל הַשֹּׁפָר וְאֶת־הָהָר עָשֵׁן וַיַּרְא הָעָם וַיָּנֻעוּ וַיַּעַמְדוּ מֵרָחֹק:

וּבְדִבְרֵי קָדְשְׁךָ כָּתוּב לֵאמֹר:
עָלָה אֱלֹהִים בִּתְרוּעָה יהוה בְּקוֹל שׁוֹפָר:

וְנֶאֱמַר: בַּחֲצֹצְרוֹת וְקוֹל שׁוֹפָר הָרִיעוּ לִפְנֵי הַמֶּלֶךְ יהוה:

וְנֶאֱמַר: תִּקְעוּ בַחֹדֶשׁ שׁוֹפָר בַּכֵּסֶה לְיוֹם חַגֵּנוּ כִּי חֹק לְיִשְׂרָאֵל הוּא מִשְׁפָּט לֵאלֹהֵי יַעֲקֹב: ⟵

COMMENTARY. Consider the word שופר/shofar. Its letters also spell the world *shefer*/beauty. Reorder those letters, and you have the word *refesh*/mud. We blow through the shofar's narrow end, but the sound comes out the broad end. The soul of each person is like a shofar: each of us has a capacity for broadmindedness and courage, and for narrow-mindedness and cowardice. Our task in doing *teshuvah*/repentance, as in blowing the shofar, is to move from narrowness towards broadness, from our earthly mire toward divine beauty. Each of us is both mud and spirit—lowly creatures of the earth and children of the Most High. The shofar sounds rise upward, challenging us to follow. S.D.R.

And by your servants' hands, the prophets,
the following is written:
"All you who dwell upon the globe,
all the earth's inhabitants,
when the signal has been raised upon the mountaintops,
behold, and listen to the shofar's piercing call!"   Isaiah 18:3

And it is said:
"And it shall happen on that day,
upon the sounding of the great shofar,
that all lost souls throughout Assyria,
and all forlorn throughout the land of Egypt,
shall bow down to THE REDEEMING ONE,
upon the holy mountain of Jerusalem!"   Isaiah 27:13

And it is said:
"And THE INEFFABLE shall then be seen by you,
God's arrow shall go forth like lightning.
The sovereign God, emerging
with the shofar's piercing call,
shall tread the storms of Yemen,
THE CREATOR of all beings
shielding you from harm!"   Zechariah 9:14-15

So may you shield your people Israel,
with your everlasting peace!

Our God, our ancients' God,
sound the great shofar for our freedom. ↩

וְעַל יְדֵי עֲבָדֶיךָ הַנְּבִיאִים כָּתוּב לֵאמֹר:

כָּל־יֹשְׁבֵי תֵבֵל וְשֹׁכְנֵי אָרֶץ כִּנְשֹׂא־נֵס הָרִים תִּרְאוּ וְכִתְקֹעַ שׁוֹפָר תִּשְׁמָעוּ:

וְנֶאֱמַר: וְהָיָה בַּיּוֹם הַהוּא יִתָּקַע בְּשׁוֹפָר גָּדוֹל וּבָאוּ הָאֹבְדִים בְּאֶרֶץ אַשּׁוּר וְהַנִּדָּחִים בְּאֶרֶץ מִצְרָיִם וְהִשְׁתַּחֲווּ לַיהוה בְּהַר הַקֹּדֶשׁ בִּירוּשָׁלָיִם:

וְנֶאֱמַר: וַיהוה עֲלֵיהֶם יֵרָאֶה וְיָצָא כַבָּרָק חִצּוֹ וַאדֹנָי יהוה בַּשּׁוֹפָר יִתְקָע וְהָלַךְ בְּסַעֲרוֹת תֵּימָן: יהוה צְבָאוֹת יָגֵן עֲלֵיהֶם:

כֵּן תָּגֵן עַל עַמְּךָ יִשְׂרָאֵל בִּשְׁלוֹמֶךָ:

אֱלֹהֵינוּ וֵאלֹהֵי אֲבוֹתֵינוּ וְאִמּוֹתֵינוּ תְּקַע בְּשׁוֹפָר גָּדוֹל לְחֵרוּתֵנוּ:

COMMENTARY. God is sovereign. This means that nothing else, no political system, no authority figure, no flesh and blood monarch can ultimately claim one's allegiance. God as ruler is a great motivator for radical challenging of the political status quo. The metaphor allows us to realize that even the most powerful system, law, ruler, or institution is not absolute.

S.P.W.

וְנֶאֱמַר

הַלְלוּיָהּ הַלְלוּ אֵל בְּקָדְשׁוֹ הַלְלוּהוּ בִּרְקִיעַ עֻזּוֹ:
הַלְלוּהוּ בִגְבוּרֹתָיו הַלְלוּהוּ כְּרֹב גֻּדְלוֹ:
הַלְלוּהוּ בְּתֵקַע שׁוֹפָר הַלְלוּהוּ בְּנֵבֶל וְכִנּוֹר:
הַלְלוּהוּ בְּתֹף וּמָחוֹל הַלְלוּהוּ בְּמִנִּים וְעֻגָב:
הַלְלוּהוּ בְּצִלְצְלֵי־שָׁמַע הַלְלוּהוּ בְּצִלְצְלֵי תְרוּעָה:
כֹּל הַנְּשָׁמָה תְּהַלֵּל יָהּ הַלְלוּיָהּ:
כֹּל הַנְּשָׁמָה תְּהַלֵּל יָהּ הַלְלוּיָהּ

Halleluyah halelu el bekodsho. Haleluhu birki'a uzo.
Haleluhu vigvurotav. Haleluhu kerov gudlo.
Haleluhu beteka shofar.
Haleluhu benevel vehinor.
Haleluhu betof umahol.
Haleluhu beminim ve'ugav.
Haleluhu betziltzeley shama.
Haleluhu betziltzeley teru'ah.
Kol haneshamah tehalel yah. Halleluyah.

Hallelu/Yah!
Call out to Yah in Heaven's holy place!
Boom out to Yah across the firmament!
Shout out for Yah, for all God's mighty deeds!
Cry out for Yah, as loud as God is great!
Blast out for Yah with piercing shofar note!
Pluck out for Yah with lute and violin!
Throb out for Yah with drum and writhing dance!
Sing out for Yah with strings and husky flute!
Ring out for Yah with cymbals that resound!
Clang out for Yah with cymbals that rebound!
Let every living thing Yah's praises sing, Hallelu/Yah!

Psalm 150

ROSH HASHANAH MUSAF / 659

SHOFAROT READING 1

For untold generations, our ancestors listened as we do at this season to the sound of the shofar. What did they hear in its piercing tones? What solemn truth did they detect in its melodies, that stirred them to improve the world? What does it say to us, who stand between two years, groping for a light to guide us?

> *Tekiyah!* Awake! Awake! The shofar calls. Let not the torpor of habit dull your minds to the heroism of humanity, human yearnings and aspirations! Let us heed the *tekiyah* of the shofar, and rouse ourselves from our thoughtlessness, lest we waste our lives in the search for wealth that avails not, and pleasures in which there is no peace.

Shevarim! Hear the accents of the *shevarim*, the broken refrain, the hesitant melody which echoes the sighing and weeping of an unhappy humanity.

> Many who might be alive today moulder on battlefields, vain sacrifices, forgotten by all except those hearts that will never be joyous again for want of them. Many who love sunlight and cleanliness must dwell in the foul darkness of hovels.

Many who toil faithfully go hungry for want of bread and naked for lack of clothing. Many who could be strong are frail in body because of hardship, twisted in limb because of cruelty of their fellows.

> Let us heed the *shevarim* of the shofar. Let us open our ears to the cry of suffering humanity, our hearts to compassion and love. ↩

Have we heard the tragic wail of pain-racked bodies and bitter hearts? And are our souls sad? Then listen now to the trumpet-blast of the *teruah*, the call to battle.

These evils need not be. Give of your bread to those who hunger, and of your strength to those who fail; give of your energies to justice and truth; then will the evils that oppress humanity pass away. In our hearts, and in our minds, we hold the means whereby these scourges can be banished from the earth forever.

Milton Steinberg (Adapted)

SHOFAROT READING 2

Beat! beat! drums—blow! bugles! blow!
Through the windows—through doors—burst like a ruthless force,
Into the solemn place, and scatter the congregation,
Into the school where the scholar is studying;
Leave not the bridegroom quiet—no happiness must he have now with his bride,
Nor the peaceful farmer any place, ploughing the field or gathering the grain,
So fierce you whirr and pound you drums—so shrill you bugles blow,

Beat! beat! drums—blow! bugles! blow!
Over the traffic of cities—over the rumble of wheels in the streets;
Are beds prepared for sleepers at night in the houses? No sleepers must sleep in those beds,
No bargainers' bargains by day—no brokers or speculators—would they continue?
Would the talkers be talking? would the singer attempt to sing?
Would the lawyer rise in the court to state his case before the judge? ↰

Then rattle quicker, heavier drums—you bugles wilder blow.

Beat! beat! drums!—blow! bugles! blow!
Make no parley—stop for no expostulation,
Mind not the timid—mind not the weeper or prayer,
Mind not the old man beseeching the young man,
Let not the child's voice be heard, nor the mother's entreaties,
Make even the trestles to shake the dead where they lie awaiting
the hearses,
So strong you thump O terrible drums—so loud you bugles
blow.

Walt Whitman (Adapted)

SHOFAROT READING 3

Connections are made slowly, sometimes they grow
underground.
You cannot tell always by looking what is happening.
More than half a tree is spread out in the soil under your feet.
Penetrate quietly as the earthworm that blows no trumpet.
Fight persistently as the creeper that brings down the tree.
Spread like the squash plant that overruns the garden.
Gnaw in the dark and use the sun to make sugar.

Weave real connections, create real nodes, build real houses.
Live a life you can endure: make love that is loving.
Keep a tangling and interweaving and taking more in,
a thicket and bramble wilderness to the outside but to us
interconnected with rabbit runs and burrows and lairs.

Live as if you liked yourself, and it may happen:
reach out, keep reaching out, keep bringing in.
This is how we are going to live for a long time: not always,
for every gardener knows that after the digging, after the
planting,
after the long season of tending and growth, the harvest comes.

Marge Piercy

Raise up the banner for the gathering-in of those in exile,
and bring near to you all those dispersed among the nations.
Let all our scattered people, as if by miracle,
be reunited from the earth's remotest lands,
and bringing us forth to Zion, to your City,
to Jerusalem, rejoicing where your presence
comes to rest. For there our ancestors
made offerings to you, their gifts
of reconciliation.
As is written in your Torah:
"Upon the day of your rejoicing, your appointed times,...
on your New Moons,
you shall sound a piercing note on trumpets,
you shall make memorial celebration
in the presence of your God,
I am THE FOUNT OF LIFE, your God!"

For you are the one who listens to the shofar's call
and hearkens to its blast,
and there is none like you.

We rise for the sounding of the shofar.

Blessed are you, ALMIGHTY ONE,
who listens mercifully to your people Israel's call.

May what our lips express
be pleasing in your presence,
God exalted and sublime!
You who discern and listen,
you who keep watch, and hearken
to our shofar blast,
may you receive with mercy and with favor
this arrangement of our holy Scripture's
verses of the shofar's call.

We are seated.

וביום...אלהיכם / Upon...God! (Numbers 10:10).

וְשָׂא נֵס לְקַבֵּץ גָּלִיּוֹתֵֽינוּ וְקָרֵב פְּזוּרֵֽינוּ מִבֵּין הַגּוֹיִם וּנְפוּצוֹתֵֽינוּ כַּנֵּס מִיַּרְכְּתֵי־אָֽרֶץ: וַהֲבִיאֵֽנוּ לְצִיּוֹן עִירְךָ בְּרִנָּה וְלִירוּשָׁלַֽיִם בֵּית מִקְדָּשְׁךָ בְּשִׂמְחַת עוֹלָם שֶׁשָּׁם עָשׂוּ אֲבוֹתֵֽינוּ וְאִמּוֹתֵֽינוּ לְפָנֶֽיךָ אֶת־עוֹלוֹתֵיהֶם וְאֶת־זִבְחֵי שַׁלְמֵיהֶם: וְכֵן כָּתוּב בְּתוֹרָתֶֽךָ:

וּבְיוֹם שִׂמְחַתְכֶם וּבְמוֹעֲדֵיכֶם וּבְרָאשֵׁי חָדְשֵׁכֶם וּתְקַעְתֶּם בַּחֲצֹצְרֹת וְהָיוּ לָכֶם לְזִכָּרוֹן לִפְנֵי אֱלֹהֵיכֶם אֲנִי יהוה אֱלֹהֵיכֶם:

כִּי אַתָּה שׁוֹמֵֽעַ קוֹל שׁוֹפָר וּמַאֲזִין תְּרוּעָה וְאֵין דּֽוֹמֶה לָּךְ: בָּרוּךְ אַתָּה יהוה שׁוֹמֵֽעַ קוֹל תְּרוּעַת עַמּוֹ יִשְׂרָאֵל בְּרַחֲמִים:

We rise.

Tekiyah Teruah Tekiyah	תְּקִיעָה תְּרוּעָה תְּקִיעָה
Tekiyah Teruah Tekiyah	תְּקִיעָה תְּרוּעָה תְּקִיעָה
Tekiyah Teruah Tekiyah (gedolah)	(גְּדוֹלָה) תְּקִיעָה תְּרוּעָה תְּקִיעָה

אֲרֶֽשֶׁת שְׂפָתֵֽינוּ יֶעֱרַב לְפָנֶֽיךָ אֵל רָם וְנִשָּׂא מֵבִין וּמַאֲזִין מַבִּיט וּמַקְשִׁיב לְקוֹל תְּקִיעָתֵֽנוּ וּתְקַבֵּל בְּרַחֲמִים וּבְרָצוֹן סֵֽדֶר שׁוֹפְרוֹתֵֽינוּ:

Areshet sefate̲ynu ye'erav lefane̲ha el ram venisa mevin uma'azin mabit umakshiv lekol tekiyate̲nu utekabel bera̲hamim uveratzon se̲der shofrote̲ynu.

We are seated.

והביאנו לציון / bringing us forth to Zion; not only to Eretz Yisrael. In the imagery of the classical prophets, *Zion* is a symbolic term which connotes the Jewish people settled in safety in their homeland in a world without war. We pray to be "restored" not only as residents of our ancestral homeland, but as citizens of a planet of peace.   R.H.

NOTE. The *tekiyah gedolah*, the extra-long blast at the end of the day's shofar blowing, sometimes occurs here, unless it is the custom of the community to blow the shofar as part of *Kaddish Titkabal*, page 1196.

INTERPRETIVE HAYOM HARAT OLAM

Have you ever seen
anything
in your life
more wonderful

than the way the sun,
every evening,
relaxed and easy,
floats toward the horizon

and into the clouds or the hills,
or the rumpled sea,
and is gone—
and how it slides again

out of the blackness
every morning,
on the other side of the world,
like a red flower

streaming upward on its heavenly oils,
say, on a morning in early summer,
at its perfect imperial distance—
and have you ever felt for anything

such wild love—
do you think there is anywhere, in any language,
a word billowing enough
for the pleasure
that fills you
as the sun
reaches out,
as it warms you—

(Continued on the facing page)

as you stand there,
empty-handed—
or have you too
turned from this world—

or have you too
gone crazy
for power,
for things?

Mary Oliver

הַיּוֹם הֲרַת עוֹלָם

הַיּוֹם יַאֲזִין כָּל יְצוּרֵי עוֹלָמִים לְקוֹל שׁוֹפָר קוֹל קוֹרֵא לְתַקֵּן עוֹלָם
בְּמַלְכוּת שַׁדַּי קוֹל הוֹלֵךְ וְחָזֵק מְאֹד וְלָנוּ לְדַבֵּר וְלַעֲשׂוֹת וְהָאֱלֹהִים
יַעֲנֶנּוּ בְּקוֹל אָיֹם וְקָדוֹשׁ׃

This is the birthday of the world!
Today, all beings of the cosmos
listen to the shofar's call.
Its voice proclaims the world's repair,
through sovereignty of THE ALMIGHTY ONE—
a voice that grows in strength as it proceeds.
All we need do is speak and act,
and God will answer us,
a voice awesome and holy.

Communities that conclude with the final blessings of the Amidah continue on the following page. Others continue with Kaddish Titkabal (page 1196), Aleynu (page 1201), Psalm 27 (page 1217), or Mourner's Kaddish (page 1215).

7. AVODAH / WORSHIP

Take pleasure, GRACIOUS ONE, our God, in Israel your people; lovingly accept their fervent prayer. May Israel's worship always be acceptable to you.

And may our eyes behold your homecoming, with merciful intent, to Zion. Blessed are you, THE FAITHFUL ONE, who brings your presence home to Zion.

8. HODA'AH / THANKS

We give thanks to you that you are THE ALL-MERCIFUL, our God, God of our ancestors, today and always. A firm, enduring source of life, a shield to us in time of trial, you are ever there, from age to age. We acknowledge you, declare your praise, and thank you for our lives entrusted to your hand, our souls placed in your care, for your miracles that greet us every day, and for your wonders and the good things that are with us every hour, morning, noon and night. GOOD ONE, whose kindness never stops, KIND ONE, whose loving acts have never failed—always have we placed our hope in you.

For all these things, your name be blessed and raised in honor always, sovereign of ours, forever. And write down for a good life all the people of your covenant.

Let all of life acknowledge you! May all beings praise your name in truth. O God, our rescue and our aid. Blessed are you, THE GRACIOUS ONE whose name is good, to whom all thanks are due. ↵

עֲבוֹדָה

רְצֵה יהוה אֱלֹהֵינוּ בְּעַמְּךָ יִשְׂרָאֵל וְלִתְפִלָּתָם תִּפְלָתָם בְּאַהֲבָה תְקַבֵּל בְּרָצוֹן וּתְהִי לְרָצוֹן תָּמִיד עֲבוֹדַת יִשְׂרָאֵל עַמֶּךָ:

וְתֶחֱזֶינָה עֵינֵינוּ בְּשׁוּבְךָ לְצִיּוֹן בְּרַחֲמִים: בָּרוּךְ אַתָּה יהוה הַמַּחֲזִיר שְׁכִינָתוֹ לְצִיּוֹן:

הוֹדָאָה

מוֹדִים אֲנַחְנוּ לָךְ שָׁאַתָּה הוּא יהוה אֱלֹהֵינוּ וֵאלֹהֵי אֲבוֹתֵינוּ וְאִמּוֹתֵינוּ לְעוֹלָם וָעֶד צוּר חַיֵּינוּ מָגֵן יִשְׁעֵנוּ אַתָּה הוּא לְדוֹר וָדוֹר: נוֹדֶה לְּךָ וּנְסַפֵּר תְּהִלָּתֶךָ עַל חַיֵּינוּ הַמְּסוּרִים בְּיָדֶךָ וְעַל נִשְׁמוֹתֵינוּ הַפְּקוּדוֹת לָךְ וְעַל נִסֶּיךָ שֶׁבְּכָל יוֹם עִמָּנוּ וְעַל נִפְלְאוֹתֶיךָ וְטוֹבוֹתֶיךָ שֶׁבְּכָל־עֵת עֶרֶב וָבֹקֶר וְצָהֳרָיִם: הַטּוֹב כִּי לֹא כָלוּ רַחֲמֶיךָ וְהַמְרַחֵם כִּי לֹא תַמּוּ חֲסָדֶיךָ מֵעוֹלָם קִוִּינוּ לָךְ:

וְעַל כֻּלָּם יִתְבָּרַךְ וְיִתְרוֹמַם שִׁמְךָ מַלְכֵּנוּ תָּמִיד לְעוֹלָם וָעֶד:

וּכְתֹב לְחַיִּים טוֹבִים כָּל־בְּנֵי בְרִיתֶךָ:

וְכֹל הַחַיִּים יוֹדוּךָ סֶּלָה וִיהַלְלוּ אֶת שִׁמְךָ בֶּאֱמֶת הָאֵל יְשׁוּעָתֵנוּ וְעֶזְרָתֵנוּ סֶלָה: בָּרוּךְ אַתָּה יהוה הַטּוֹב שִׁמְךָ וּלְךָ נָאֶה לְהוֹדוֹת: ←

9. BIRKAT HASHALOM / BLESSING FOR PEACE

Our God, our ancients' God,
bless us with the threefold blessing
spoken from the mouth of Aaron and his sons, as is said:

May THE ETERNAL bless you
  and protect you.   Let it be God's will!
May THE ETERNAL'S face give light
  to you, and show you favor.   Let it be God's will!
May THE ETERNAL'S face be lifted
  toward you, and bestow upon you
  peace.   Let it be God's will! ↩

COMMENTARY. Traditionally the Priestly Blessing was done by the male descendants of the *kohanim*. In some congregations the *sheliah tzibur* (service leader) recites the blessing, and the congregation responds with "*Ken yehi ratzon.*" In other communities all the members of the congregation wrap arms and tallitot around each other and recite the blessing together. Another way to enact the Priestly Blessing is for each congregant to turn to a neighbor and recite the first half of each blessing, while the neighbor responds with the second half of the blessing. Michael M. Cohen

COMMENTARY. Rabbi Lavy Becker of Montreal noticed that when this blessing was pronounced in the synagogue of Pisa, all the children gathered under the sheltering wings of their fathers' tallitot to receive it. He recognized this "as a reconstruction of the ancient priestly ceremony." He modified that custom so that those wearing a tallit share it with their neighbors and all are under the sheltering wings of the Shehinah as we bless each other. It is now an established part of Canadian Reconstructionist practice. E.M.

יברכך...שלום / May...peace (Numbers 6:24-26).

בִּרְכַּת הַשָּׁלוֹם

אֱלֹהֵינוּ וֵאלֹהֵי אֲבוֹתֵינוּ וְאִמּוֹתֵינוּ בָּרְכֵנוּ בַּבְּרָכָה הַמְשֻׁלֶּשֶׁת הָאֲמוּרָה מִפִּי אַהֲרֹן וּבָנָיו כָּאָמוּר:

יְבָרֶכְךָ יהוה וְיִשְׁמְרֶךָ

כֵּן יְהִי רָצוֹן:

יָאֵר יהוה פָּנָיו אֵלֶיךָ וִיחֻנֶּךָּ:

כֵּן יְהִי רָצוֹן:

יִשָּׂא יהוה פָּנָיו אֵלֶיךָ וְיָשֵׂם לְךָ שָׁלוֹם:

כֵּן יְהִי רָצוֹן:

Eloheynu veylohey avoteynu ve'imoteynu
barehenu baberahah hamshuleshet
ha'amurah mipi aharon uvanav ka'amur:

Yevareheha adonay veyishmereha.   Ken yehi ratzon.
Ya'er adonay panav eleha vihuneka.   Ken yehi ratzon.
Yisa adonay panav eleha veyasem leha shalom. Ken yehi ratzon.

Grant peace, goodness and blessing in the world,
grace, love, and mercy
over us and over all your people Israel.
Bless us, source of being, all of us, as one
amid your light,
for by your light,
WISE ONE, our God, you give to us
Torah of life, and love of kindness,
justice, blessing, mercy, life, and peace.
So may it be a good thing in your eyes,
to bless your people Israel, and all peoples,
with abundant strength and peace.

In the book of life, blessing and peace, and proper sustenance,
may we be remembered and inscribed,
we and all your people, the house of Israel,
for a good life and for peace.

Blessed are you, COMPASSIONATE ONE, maker of peace.

KAVANAH. Try to imagine a time of true peace and tranquility, and think
about your part in helping this time to come about. What can you do?
What can you commit to? How will *you* be a peacemaker?   L.G.B.

שִׂים שָׁלוֹם טוֹבָה וּבְרָכָה בָּעוֹלָם חֵן וָחֶסֶד וְרַחֲמִים עָלֵינוּ וְעַל
כָּל־יִשְׂרָאֵל עַמֶּךְ: בָּרְכֵנוּ אָבִינוּ כֻּלָּנוּ כְּאֶחָד בְּאוֹר פָּנֶיךָ: כִּי בְאוֹר
פָּנֶיךָ נָתַתָּ לָּנוּ יהוה אֱלֹהֵינוּ תּוֹרַת חַיִּים וְאַהֲבַת חֶסֶד וּצְדָקָה
וּבְרָכָה וְרַחֲמִים וְחַיִּים וְשָׁלוֹם: וְטוֹב בְּעֵינֶיךָ לְבָרֵךְ אֶת עַמְּךָ יִשְׂרָאֵל
וְאֶת כָּל הָעַמִּים בְּרָב־עֹז וְשָׁלוֹם.

בְּסֵפֶר חַיִּים בְּרָכָה וְשָׁלוֹם וּפַרְנָסָה טוֹבָה נִזָּכֵר וְנִכָּתֵב לְפָנֶיךָ אֲנַחְנוּ
וְכָל־עַמְּךָ בֵּית יִשְׂרָאֵל לְחַיִּים טוֹבִים וּלְשָׁלוֹם:
בָּרוּךְ אַתָּה יהוה עוֹשֵׂה הַשָּׁלוֹם:

Sim shalom tovah uverahah ba'olam hen vahesed verahamim
aleynu ve'al kol yisra'el ameha. Barehenu avinu kulanu ke'ehad
be'or paneha. Ki ve'or paneha natata lanu adonay eloheynu torat
hayim ve'ahavat hesed utzedakah uverahah verahamim vehayim
veshalom. Vetov be'eyneha levareh et ameha yisra'el ve'et kol
ha'amim berov oz veshalom.

Besefer hayim berahah veshalom ufarnasah tovah nizaher
venikatev lefaneha anahnu vehol ameha beyt yisra'el lehayim
tovim uleshalom.

Baruh atah adonay osey hashalom.

The ark is opened.

Today, give us courage and strength.
   Amen!
Today, give us blessing.
   Amen!
Today, give us goodness.
   Amen!
Today, seek our welfare and good.
   Amen!
Today, write us down for a good life.
   Amen!
Today, please hearken to our cry.
   Amen!
Today, accept with mercy and good will our prayer.
   Amen!
Today, may your right hand keep us safe.
   Amen!

The ark is closed.

On a day like today,
may you bring us, joyful and glad,
to the completion of our reconstruction.
As is written by your prophet's hand:
"And I shall bring you to my holy mountain,
and you shall celebrate there
inside my house of prayer...
For my house shall then be called
a house of prayer for all peoples!"

And may we and all the people Israel,
and all who dwell on earth,
enjoy justice and blessing,
lovingkindness, life, and peace,
until eternity.

Concluding prayers begin on page 1195.

והביאותים...לכל־העמים /And I...peoples! (Isaiah 56:7).

אָמֵן:	הַיּוֹם תְּאַמְּצֵנוּ:
אָמֵן:	הַיּוֹם תְּבָרְכֵנוּ:
אָמֵן:	הַיּוֹם תְּגַדְּלֵנוּ:
אָמֵן:	הַיּוֹם תִּדְרְשֵׁנוּ לְטוֹבָה:
אָמֵן:	הַיּוֹם תִּכְתְּבֵנוּ לְחַיִּים טוֹבִים:
אָמֵן:	הַיּוֹם תִּשְׁמַע שַׁוְעָתֵנוּ:
אָמֵן:	הַיּוֹם תְּקַבֵּל בְּרַחֲמִים וּבְרָצוֹן אֶת־תְּפִלָּתֵנוּ:
אָמֵן:	הַיּוֹם תִּתְמְכֵנוּ בִּימִין צִדְקֶךָ:

Hayom te'amtzenu.	Amen.
Hayom tevarhenu.	Amen.
Hayom tegadlenu.	Amen.
Hayom tidreshenu letovah.	Amen.
Hayom tihtevenu lehayim tovim.	Amen.
Hayom tishma shavatenu.	Amen.
Hayom tekabel berahamim uveratzon et tefilatenu.	Amen.
Hayom titmehenu bimin tzidkeha.	Amen.

כְּהַיּוֹם הַזֶּה תְּבִיאֵנוּ שָׂשִׂים וּשְׂמֵחִים בְּבִנְיַן שָׁלֵם כַּכָּתוּב עַל יַד
נְבִיאֶךָ: וַהֲבִיאוֹתִים אֶל הַר קָדְשִׁי וְשִׂמַּחְתִּים בְּבֵית תְּפִלָּתִי... כִּי
בֵיתִי בֵּית תְּפִלָּה יִקָּרֵא לְכָל־הָעַמִּים: וּצְדָקָה וּבְרָכָה וְרַחֲמִים וְחַיִּים
וְשָׁלוֹם יִהְיֶה־לָּנוּ וּלְכָל־יִשְׂרָאֵל וּלְכֹל יוֹשְׁבֵי תֵבֵל עַד עוֹלָם:

Concluding prayers begin on page 1196.

NOTE. Genesis tells us that we are each made in the divine image. We come to the sanctuary/holy place on Rosh Hashanah to be reminded of the divine holiness within. Only when we unlock the door to the holiness deep within ourselves do we begin to fulfill our purpose in coming to this physical sanctuary. We can only become wholly a part of holy community when we become open to the holiness within ourselves. D.A.T.

TASHLIḤ

Tashliḥ is recited on the afternoon of the first day of Rosh Hashanah unless the first day falls on Shabbat, in which case it is recited on the second day. Its name comes from שלך / *cast out. Our task at this season of the year is to cast out transgressions and seek greater strength and clarity of purpose in the year ahead. This task of casting out is carried out symbolically at a body of water such as a stream, lake or ocean, where bread crumbs are cast onto the water while the following verses are said. Songs and prayers can be added.*

Cast off all your transgressions from yourselves
and make for yourselves a new heart and a new spirit.

Who is a God like you?
—forgiving sin, absolving the transgressions
of the remnant of your heritage,
you who do not cling to anger,
but desire only kindness,
you who act mercifully once again,
subduing the effects of our transgressions,
casting to the ocean waters all our wrongs.
You show faithfulness to Jacob,
love to Abraham,
as you have sworn to Abraham
from days of old.

None shall do harm, none shall destroy
throughout my holy mountain,
truly shall the world be filled with knowledge
of the FOUNT OF LIFE,
like waters of the ocean covering the earth.

תַּשְׁלִיךְ

Tashlih *is recited on the afternoon of the first day of Rosh Hashanah unless the first day falls on Shabbat, in which case it is recited on the second day. Its name comes from* שלך / *cast out. Our task at this season of the year is to cast out transgressions and seek greater strength and clarity of purpose in the year ahead. This task of casting out is carried out symbolically at a body of water such as a stream, lake or ocean, where bread crumbs are cast onto the water while the following verses are said. Songs and prayers can be added.*

הַשְׁלִיכוּ מֵעֲלֵיכֶם אֶת־כָּל־פִּשְׁעֵיכֶם אֲשֶׁר פְּשַׁעְתֶּם בָּם וַעֲשׂוּ לָכֶם
לֵב חָדָשׁ וְרוּחַ חֲדָשָׁה:

מִי־אֵל כָּמוֹךָ נֹשֵׂא עָוֹן וְעֹבֵר עַל־פֶּשַׁע לִשְׁאֵרִית נַחֲלָתוֹ
לֹא־הֶחֱזִיק לָעַד אַפּוֹ כִּי־חָפֵץ חֶסֶד הוּא:
יָשׁוּב יְרַחֲמֵנוּ יִכְבֹּשׁ עֲוֹנֹתֵינוּ
וְתַשְׁלִיךְ בִּמְצֻלוֹת יָם כָּל־חַטֹּאתָם:
תִּתֵּן אֱמֶת לְיַעֲקֹב חֶסֶד לְאַבְרָהָם
אֲשֶׁר־נִשְׁבַּעְתָּ לַאֲבֹתֵינוּ מִימֵי קֶדֶם:

לֹא־יָרֵעוּ וְלֹא־יַשְׁחִיתוּ בְּכָל־הַר קָדְשִׁי
כִּי־מָלְאָה הָאָרֶץ דֵּעָה אֶת־יהוה כַּמַּיִם לַיָּם מְכַסִּים:

השליכו...חדשה / Cast...spirit (Ezekiel 18:31).
מי...קדם / Who...old (Micah 7:18-20).
לא...מכסים / None...earth (Isaiah 11:9).

COMMENTARY. The core of the *Tashlih* service is Micah 7:18-20, whose verses correspond to the Thirteen Attributes that are read during the Rosh Hashanah service, and where the reference to "casting sins into the sea" can be found. The origin of the *Tashlih* ritual is unknown. The Maharil (Jacob ben Moses Moellin), a leading European 15th-century Talmudist, first mentioned the custom.   M.B.K.

ROSH HASHANAH MINḤAH

Uva letziyon *may be preceded by* Ashrey, *page 593.*

And a redeemer shall come to Zion, and to those of Jacob
who return from their transgression, says THE GOD OF ISRAEL,
and as for me, this shall be my covenant with them, says
THE REDEEMING ONE: my spirit, which is in your midst,
and my words which I have placed into your mouths shall
never cease from there,
nor from your seed, nor from the mouths of all born out of
them, says GOD, henceforth and for eternity.
And you, O God, are holy, you are enthroned amid the praises
sung by Israel,
as they call to one another and declare:
"Holy, holy, holy is THE CREATOR of the Multitudes of Heaven,
the world is filled to overflowing with God's glory!"

And they all draw strength from one another, and declare:
"Holy in the highest heavens, where God's presence dwells,
holy on the earth, where all God's deeds resound,
holy to eternity, through all eternities,
THE CREATOR of the Multitudes of Heaven,
yes, the world is overflowing with the splendor of God's light!"

COMMENTARY. And they all draw strength...and declare...And a divine
wind. These and the ensuing lines intersperse Hebrew and Aramaic
descriptions of the same events, based on the prophetic visions of Isaiah
6:3, Ezekiel 3:12, and Exodus 15:18. The Aramaic paraphrases, typically,
are more detailed and expansive, bordering on midrash.   J.R.

מִנְחָה לְרֹאשׁ הַשָּׁנָה

Uva letziyon *may be preceded by* Ashrey, *page 594.*

וּבָא לְצִיּוֹן גּוֹאֵל וּלְשָׁבֵי פֶשַׁע בְּיַעֲקֹב נְאֻם יהוה: וַאֲנִי זֹאת בְּרִיתִי
אוֹתָם אָמַר יהוה רוּחִי אֲשֶׁר עָלֶיךָ וּדְבָרַי אֲשֶׁר־שַׂמְתִּי בְּפִיךָ לֹא־
יָמוּשׁוּ מִפִּיךָ וּמִפִּי זַרְעֲךָ וּמִפִּי זֶרַע זַרְעֲךָ אָמַר יהוה מֵעַתָּה וְעַד־
עוֹלָם: וְאַתָּה קָדוֹשׁ יוֹשֵׁב תְּהִלּוֹת יִשְׂרָאֵל: וְקָרָא זֶה אֶל־זֶה וְאָמַר:
קָדוֹשׁ קָדוֹשׁ קָדוֹשׁ יהוה צְבָאוֹת מְלֹא כָל־הָאָרֶץ כְּבוֹדוֹ: וּמְקַבְּלִין
דֵּין מִן דֵּין וְאָמְרִין: קַדִּישׁ בִּשְׁמֵי מְרוֹמָא עִלָּאָה בֵּית שְׁכִינְתֵּהּ קַדִּישׁ
עַל אַרְעָא עוֹבַד גְּבוּרְתֵּהּ קַדִּישׁ לְעָלַם וּלְעָלְמֵי עָלְמַיָּא יהוה צְבָאוֹת
מַלְיָא כָל־אַרְעָא זִיו יְקָרֵהּ:

DERASH. The covenant described in this prayer binds God to constant
accessibility. Thus we have the power to make God manifest through our
minds, our mouths and our shared experience. So it has been throughout
our generations. In this prayer Israel enthrones God—keeps God
sovereign—through our declaration of God's holiness. The task of lighting
the world with the divine splendor is one we fulfill by declaring God's
praises. We thereby create the bonds that join us in holiness and make
God manifest in the world. It lies in the power of religious life to take
ordinary individuals and join us into a holy people. This is truly a
covenant—in continually making ourselves holy, we make God eternally
sovereign.   D.A.T.

ובא...עולם/And...eternity (Isaiah 59:20-21).
ואתה...ישראל/And you...Israel (Psalms 22:4).
וקרא...כבודו/As...glory (Isaiah 6:3).

And a divine wind lifted me aloft; I heard a voice, speaking
with great emotion:

"Blessed is the glory of THE LIVING GOD, wherever God may
dwell!"

And the spirit lifted me; I heard behind me a great,
tumultuous sound from those who sang out praises
and declared:

"Blessed is the precious aura of THE OMNIPRESENT, from the
place where the Shehinah dwells!

THE ETERNAL ONE shall reign forever,
the kingdom of THE FOUNT OF LIFE shall last eternally,
through all eternities!"

When Rosh Hashanah falls on Shabbat, continue with removing the Torah from the ark,
page 463. Deuteronomy 32:1-12 (on the following page) is read. The Torah is then returned
to the ark, page 597. Continue with Hatzi Kaddish, page 735. On all other days,
Uva letziyon is immediately followed by Hatzi Kaddish (page 735), the Amidah (pages
739-774), Avinu Malkenu, Kaddish Titkabal, Aleynu, and Mourner's Kaddish.

וַתִּשָּׂאֵנִי רוּחַ וָאֶשְׁמַע אַחֲרַי קוֹל רַעַשׁ גָּדוֹל: בָּרוּךְ כְּבוֹד יהוה
מִמְּקוֹמוֹ וּנְטָלַתְנִי רוּחָא וְשִׁמְעִית בַּתְרַי קָל זִיעַ סַגִּיא דִּמְשַׁבְּחִין
וְאָמְרִין: בְּרִיךְ יְקָרָא דַיהוה מֵאֲתַר בֵּית שְׁכִינְתֵּהּ: יהוה יִמְלֹךְ
לְעוֹלָם וָעֶד יהוה מַלְכוּתֵהּ קָאֵים לְעָלַם וּלְעָלְמֵי עָלְמַיָּא:

When Rosh Hashanah falls on Shabbat, continue with removing the Torah from the ark,
page 464. Deuteronomy 32:1-12 (on the following page) is read. The Torah is then returned
to the ark, page 598. Continue with Hatzi Kaddish, page 736. On all other days,
Uva letziyon is immediately followed by Hatzi Kaddish (page 736), the Amidah (pages
739-774), Avinu Malkenu, Kaddish Titkabal, Aleynu, and Mourner's Kaddish.

ברוך...ממקומו / Blessed is the glory...dwell! (Ezekiel 3:12).

TORAH READING FOR ROSH HASHANAH
SHABBAT MINHAH: HA'AZINU

First Aliyah

Hearken you skies, that I may speak,
and listen, dwellers of the earth,
to my mouth's utterance!
Let my teaching fall like dewdrops,
my speech like showers on the sprouting vegetation,
and like droplets on the grass.
When I call out the name of THE ALMIGHTY ONE,
give glory to our God!

Deuteronomy 32:1-3

Second Aliyah

The Rock! God's deed is perfect!
Truly, every word of God is just,
and God is a divinity of truth,
in whom there is no flaw,
This is a just and righteous God!

God's children have misused divinity,
theirs is the blame, not God's!
They are a generation that is crooked and perverse.
Shall you deal this way with God,
you people foolish and unwise?
Is not God the one who brought you into being,
your Creator who has fashioned you, who gave you life?

Deuteronomy 32:4-6

First Aliyah

הַאֲזִינוּ הַשָּׁמַיִם וַאֲדַבֵּרָה
יַעֲרֹף כַּמָּטָר לִקְחִי
כִּשְׂעִירִם עֲלֵי־דֶשֶׁא
כִּי שֵׁם יהוה אֶקְרָא

וְתִשְׁמַע הָאָרֶץ אִמְרֵי־פִי:
תִּזַּל כַּטַּל אִמְרָתִי
וְכִרְבִיבִים עֲלֵי־עֵשֶׂב:
הָבוּ גֹדֶל לֵאלֹהֵינוּ:

Second Aliyah

הַצּוּר תָּמִים פָּעֳלוֹ
אֵל אֱמוּנָה וְאֵין עָוֶל
שִׁחֵת לוֹ לֹא בָּנָיו מוּמָם
הֲלַיהוה תִּגְמְלוּ־זֹאת
הֲלוֹא־הוּא אָבִיךָ קָּנֶךָ

כִּי כָל־דְּרָכָיו מִשְׁפָּט
צַדִּיק וְיָשָׁר הוּא:
דּוֹר עִקֵּשׁ וּפְתַלְתֹּל:
עַם נָבָל וְלֹא חָכָם
הוּא עָשְׂךָ וַיְכֹנְנֶךָ: ←

Third Aliyah

Consider days of old,
study the history of each generation.
Ask your parents—they will tell you!
Ask your grandparents—they will say it to you!
When the Supernal One gave nations their inheritance,
when God divided up humanity, fixing the boundaries
of the peoples and establishing the numbers
of the people Israel,
truly each people was a part of THE ETERNAL ONE—
thus did the seed of Jacob share in God's inheritance.

God found them in the wilderness,
amid a howling wasteland.
God surrounded them, watched over them, protected them
as if they were the pupil of God's eye.
Just like an eagle keeping watch over its nest—
it hovers, spreads its wings,
bears up its young upon its pinions—
so was God alone a guide for them,
no alien god was there to help.

Deuteronomy 32:7-12

Continue on page 597, returning the Torah to the ark, then Ḥatzi Kaddish *(page 735)*, *the Amidah (pages 739-774)*, Avinu Malkenu, Kaddish Titkabal, Aleynu, *and* Mourner's Kaddish.

זְכֹר יְמוֹת עוֹלָם   בִּינוּ שְׁנוֹת דֹּר־וָדֹר

שְׁאַל אָבִיךָ וְיַגֵּדְךָ   זְקֵנֶיךָ וְיֹאמְרוּ לָךְ:

בְּהַנְחֵל עֶלְיוֹן גּוֹיִם   בְּהַפְרִידוֹ בְּנֵי אָדָם

יַצֵּב גְּבֻלֹת עַמִּים   לְמִסְפַּר בְּנֵי יִשְׂרָאֵל:

כִּי חֵלֶק יהוה עַמּוֹ   יַעֲקֹב חֶבֶל נַחֲלָתוֹ:

יִמְצָאֵהוּ בְּאֶרֶץ מִדְבָּר   וּבְתֹהוּ יְלֵל יְשִׁמֹן

יְסֹבְבֶנְהוּ יְבוֹנְנֵהוּ   יִצְּרֶנְהוּ כְּאִישׁוֹן עֵינוֹ:

כְּנֶשֶׁר יָעִיר קִנּוֹ   עַל־גּוֹזָלָיו יְרַחֵף

יִפְרֹשׂ כְּנָפָיו יִקָּחֵהוּ   יִשָּׂאֵהוּ עַל־אֶבְרָתוֹ:

יהוה בָּדָד יַנְחֶנּוּ   וְאֵין עִמּוֹ אֵל נֵכָר:

Continue on page 598, returning the Torah to the ark, then Ḥatzi Kaddish *(page 736), the* Amidah *(pages 739-774),* Avinu Malkenu, Kaddish Titkabal, Aleynu, *and* Mourner's Kaddish.

מַעֲרִיב
לְיוֹם כִּפּוּר

LIGHTING OF A MEMORIAL CANDLE

We light this candle in the memory of all our loved ones. May their memory be a blessing!

We light this candle in the memory of the soldiers of the Israel Defense Force, all those who sacrificed their lives for the sanctification of God, and all those who died in the Holocaust. May their memory be a blessing!

The memorial candle is now lit.

LIGHTING OF YOM KIPPUR CANDLES

The festival candles are lit.

Blessed are you, ETERNAL ONE, our God,
the sovereign of all worlds,
who has made us holy with your mitzvot,
and commanded us to kindle
the light of (Shabbat and of)
the Day of Atonement.

May it be your will, ETERNAL ONE, our God,
and God of our ancestors, that these candles
light up the pathway of return
on this your holy *Shabbat Shabbaton*
a Sabbath of complete cessation.
By their light may your light be seen.
And let us say: Amen.

DERASH. Why Day of Atonements—*Yom Hakippurim*—and not Day of Atonement—*Yom Kippur*? Here we speak in the plural, despite this being a day of solitude and singularity. I come knowing that I will be asked to confess sins, an intimidating, even frightening prospect. We are strengthened in the task as we realize that those with whom we have come to pray are engaged in the same process. Not for each of us alone is this a "Day of Atonement," but for all of us together: a "Day of Atonements."

R.H.

הַדְלָקַת נֵר 🕯 זִכָּרוֹן

נֵר זֶה אָנוּ מַדְלִיקִים לְזִכְרָם שֶׁל כָּל הָאֲהוּבִים שֶׁלָּנוּ: יְהִי זִכְרָם
בָּרוּךְ:

נֵר זֶה אָנוּ מַדְלִיקִים לְזִכְרָם שֶׁל חַיָּלֵי צְבָא הַהֲגָנָה לְיִשְׂרָאֵל וְכָל־
אֵלֶּה שֶׁמָּסְרוּ אֶת־נַפְשָׁם עַל־קִדּוּשׁ הַשֵּׁם וְשֶׁנֶּהֶרְגוּ בַּשּׁוֹאָה: יְהִי
זִכְרָם בָּרוּךְ:

The memorial candle is now lit.

הַדְלָקַת 🕯 נֵרוֹת 🕯 לְיוֹם כִּפּוּר

The festival candles are lit.

בָּרוּךְ אַתָּה יהוה אֱלֹהֵינוּ מֶלֶךְ הָעוֹלָם אֲשֶׁר קִדְּשָׁנוּ בְּמִצְוֹתָיו וְצִוָּנוּ
לְהַדְלִיק נֵר שֶׁל (שַׁבָּת וְ) יוֹם הַכִּפּוּרִים:

Baruḥ atah adonay eloheynu meleḥ ha'olam asher kideshanu
bemitzvotav vetzivanu lehadlik ner shel (shabbat ve) yom
hakippurim.

יְהִי רָצוֹן מִלְּפָנֶיךָ יהוה אֱלֹהֵינוּ וֵאלֹהֵי אֲבוֹתֵינוּ וְאִמּוֹתֵינוּ שֶׁיָּאִירוּ
נֵרוֹת אֵלֶּה אֶת דַּרְכֵי הַתְּשׁוּבָה בְּיוֹם שַׁבָּת שַׁבָּתוֹן קָדְשֶׁךָ: לְאוֹרָם
נִרְאֶה אוֹר וְנֹאמַר אָמֵן:

COMMENTARY. Those who recite *Yizkor* in memory of loved ones
traditionally light a *Yizkor* candle at home before joining the community
for *Kol Nidrey*. This is also done on the anniversary of the death of a loved
one. For this home ritual, see *Kol Haneshamah: Shirim Uvraḥot* [pages 136-
137]. The communal lighting of a *Yizkor* candle here commemorates the
losses suffered by our community as a whole—not only those who once
lived among us, but also our people's martyrs, those who died for the
upbuilding of the land of Israel, and those we lost in the Holocaust. We
define ourselves in part by whom we choose to remember. May their
memory be a blessing for us.
D.A.T.

ATIFAT TALLIT / DONNING THE TALLIT

It is customary to wrap oneself in the tallit before reciting the blessing that follows.

Blessed are You, VEILED ONE, our God, the sovereign of all worlds, who has made us holy with your mitzvot, and commanded us to wrap ourselves amid the fringed tallit.

COMMENTARY. The *Kol Nidrey* service is the only time we are obligated to wear a tallit in the evening. Some wear a simple white robe (*kittel*) as well. These constitute the traditional costume of burial. Yom Kippur reminds us of our mortality even as the cessation from food, drink, sex, bathing, and other everyday activities serves as a rehearsal for death. The tallit is also a shelter: a secure place in which we wrap ourselves for this day's journey.

R.H.

עֲטִיפַת טַלִּית

It is customary to wrap oneself in the tallit before reciting the blessing that follows.

בָּרוּךְ אַתָּה יהוה אֱלֹהֵינוּ מֶלֶךְ הָעוֹלָם
אֲשֶׁר קִדְּשָׁנוּ בְּמִצְוֹתָיו
וְצִוָּנוּ לְהִתְעַטֵּף בַּצִּיצִית:

Baruḥ atah adonay eloheynu meleḥ ha'olam
asher kideshanu bemitzvotav
vetzivanu lehitatef batzitzit.

NOTE. The tallit is normally not worn at night, when the fringes cannot easily be seen. Jewish tradition understands Yom Kippur as one long day filled with light. Therefore on Yom Kippur the tallit is worn by the whole congregation beginning with the evening service. The *beraḥah*, which is recited only once each day, is recited here before the tallit is put on and therefore not in the morning service.　　　　　　　D.A.T.

KOL NIDREY/ALL VOWS

By the authority of all who congregate above
and all who congregate on earth,
and with permission of the omnipresent One,
and by consent of this assembly,
we accept into our midst whoever seeks to pray.
Whether righteous or unrighteous,
all shall pray as one community. ⮌

KAVANAH. Worlds are joined in this opening recitation. Upper and lower
worlds are joined. The divine and the human are joined. We and they—
those who have crossed the boundary to leave the we—are joined. This
reveals our intention in seeking atonement: at-one-ment. We seek
unification, the dissolution of barriers, the merging and unity that will
culminate at the end of Yom Kippur.   S.P.W.

DERASH. It is we who are the righteous, granting permission to participate
in prayer. It is also we who are the unrighteous, seeking readmission to the
community of holy beings. Realizing that each of us is both righteous and
transgressor is the first step in *teshuvah*.   J.A.S.

DERASH. The Kabbalist Isaac Luria taught that we can build our personal
sanctuary (*mishkan*) with God one year at a time. The task of Yom Kippur
is to build our *mishkan* in time, to build a relationship with God that will
last for the year. Yom Kippur is a return to the source to reconstruct our
interior.   Z.S.S.

COMMENTARY. This prayer has long been associated with the Hidden
Jews—the Jews in Spain who converted to Christianity during the
Inquisition and kept their Jewish life secret in order to survive. This
prayer allowed them to pray as Jews by forgiving the vows they had made
to another religion, another system of beliefs. What a deep resonance this
interpretation has for gay and lesbian Jews who are living hidden, secret
lives! For those in the closet about their gay identity in their Jewish
communities and those in the closet about their Jewish lives in the gay
community, this prayer recognizes the pain of hidden and split identities
and offers the hope for integration and healing.   Adina Abramowitz

בִּישִׁיבָה שֶׁל מַעְלָה וּבִישִׁיבָה שֶׁל מַטָּה
עַל דַּעַת הַמָּקוֹם וְעַל דַּעַת הַקָּהָל
אָנוּ מַתִּירִין לְהִתְפַּלֵּל עִם הָעֲבַרְיָנִים: ←

בישיבה / By the authority of all who congregate. Originally a legal formula, *Kol Nidrey* is introduced by this meditation in which an imaginary court is invoked to validate the liturgical proceeding. The parallelism is striking: "who congregate above/the Omnipresent One" and "who congregates on earth/this assembly." We stand *before* God and *among* our community—we require the permission and participation of both.　　　　　　R.H.

Anu matirin lehitpalel im ha'avaryanim / Whether righteous or unrighteous, all shall pray as one community. There is a Jewish folk legend that suggests that in the *Kol Nidrey* chant, the word עברינים/*avaryanim* (transgressors) was actually a code for the word, *Iberyanim* (Iberians or Spaniards), referring to death-fearing Spanish Jews who had converted to Christianity during the Inquisition, but who secretly continued to practice Judaism. According to the legend, in embracing these crypto-Jews within the community of believers and sinners, the *Kol Nidrey* chant reminds us that we all wear masks, we all hide our true essence—and we all enjoy the possibility of God's forgiveness.　　　　　　L.G.B.

DERASH. The setting for *Kol Nidrey* is that of two courts joined. The earthly court, composed of the ḥazan and two people holding Torah scrolls, reflects the heavenly court where God sits in judgment. The imagery of the court is further emphasized by the legalistic style of the *Kol Nidrey* prayer itself. In this introductory prayer to *Kol Nidrey*, "we" are granted permission to pray with sinners. But since no human being is without sin, this permission must be understood as a mutual act. We can only become a community when we begin to forgive ourselves and each other.　　　　　　D.A.T.

All vows,
and formulas of prohibition, and declarations of taboo,
and promises of abstinence, and names of God,
and pledges one assumes on penalty, and oaths,
whatever we have vowed and then forgot,
whatever we have sworn but not upheld,
whatever we declared taboo that went amiss,
whatever prohibitions we assumed upon ourselves to no avail,
from the last Day of Atonement to this Day of Atonement
– may the day come upon us for the good! –

from all of them we now request release.
Let their burden be dissolved, and lifted off, and canceled,
and made null and void, bearing no force and no reality.
Those vows shall not be binding vows,
those prohibitions not be binding prohibitions,
those oaths shall not be binding oaths.

COMMENTARY. Part of the awesome power of *Kol Nidrey* comes from the gathering of so many Jews in community. Although we may have theological hesitations regarding *Kol Nidrey's* annulment of vows, these pale in comparison to the fulfillment of our one shared commitment: to be here together.

J.A.S.

COMMENTARY. Despite generations of commentary, the peculiar paradox of *Kol Nidrey* remains—that even as we prepare to swear loyalty to our resolutions, we declare that unkept pledges are absolved. In the early years of the original Reconstructionist synagogue (the Society for the Advancement of Judaism), Rabbi Mordecai Kaplan attempted to avoid this problem by substituting Psalm 130 for the words of *Kol Nidrey* while chanting the traditional melody. The reaction of the congregants was strongly negative: while they may not have been able to make sense of *Kol Nidrey's* words, the emotional appeal determined the outcome. Today we remain moved by the solemnity of the moment, the plaintive chant, and the orchestrated overture to the Day of Atonement—even when the purpose of the words escapes us. In the realm of the spirit, the heart often speaks louder than the head.

R.H.

כָּל נִדְרֵי וֶאֱסָרֵי וּשְׁבוּעֵי וַחֲרָמֵי וְקוֹנָמֵי וְקִנּוּסֵי וְכִנּוּיֵי דְּנִדְּרָנָא
וּדְאִשְׁתַּבַּעְנָא וּדְאַחֲרִימְנָא וּדְאָסַרְנָא עַל נַפְשָׁתָנָא מִיּוֹם כִּפּוּרִים
שֶׁעָבַר עַד יוֹם כִּפּוּרִים זֶה הַבָּא עָלֵינוּ לְטוֹבָה כֻּלְּהוֹן אִחֲרַטְנָא בְהוֹן
כֻּלְּהוֹן יְהוֹן שָׁרָן שְׁבִיקִין שְׁבִיתִין בְּטֵלִין וּמְבֻטָּלִין לָא שְׁרִירִין וְלָא
קַיָּמִין: נִדְרַ֫נָא לָא נִדְרֵי וֶאֱסָרַ֫נָא לָא אֱסָרֵי וּשְׁבוּעָתַ֫נָא לָא שְׁבוּעוֹת: ←

Kol nidrey ve'esarey ushevu'ey vaharamey vekonamey vekinusey
veḥ inuyey dindarna ude'ishtabana ude'aharimna ude'asarena
al nafshatana miyom kippurim she'avar ad yom kippurim zeh
haba aleynu letovah kulehon iharatna vehon kulehon yehon
sheran shevikin shevitin beteylin umevutalin la sheririn vela
kayamin. Nidrana la nidrey ve'esarana la esarey ushevu'atana
la shevu'ot. ↵

COMMENTARY. The *Kol Nidrey* is at once a legal declaration and a prayer. In
the careful language of a contract it marks out the territory of prayer,
introspection, and personal resolve as a domain beyond law. This is a
realm where the promptings of the heart and utterances in the passion of
the moment are allowed a certain freedom, privacy, and momentum,
irrespective of their realization or completion in practice. By declaring
such utterances null and void, one both affirms their importance and
limits their force. Let the heart be free, says this prayer, to promise what it
will, to aspire where it will, even to call itself to task in the harsh language
of law—but let us be at peace with our past failures or resolve and get on
with our lives as best we can. *Kol Nidrey* inevitably calls to mind all that
we have done, or not done, since the previous *Kol Nidrey*. Indeed, it is that
previous declaration that now reaches into the present, and releases us to
pray and to change—and to assume our role in our community of prayer.

J.R.

KAVANAH. At this Yom Kippur, we seek to deal kindly but honestly with
ourselves, to take care that our commitment to ideals does not entail the
destruction of our own souls, our own worlds. We freely admit our
failings and create our atonements. No excuse, no escape, just an honest
seeing into the truth, that we might correct our path and set off once more
toward the good each of us seeks.

R.M.S.

694 / **KOL NIDREY**

"And there shall be atonement
for the whole community of Israel,
and the stranger dwelling in their midst
—indeed, for an entire people that has gone astray." Numbers 15:26

"Grant forgiveness, then,
for the transgression of this people,
as the abundance of your love demands,
and as you have always lifted from disfavor
these, your people, from the time of Egypt until now,"
as it is told: Numbers 14:19

"THE FOUNT OF MERCY said:
I grant forgiveness, as you ask." Numbers 14:20

Blessed are you, ETERNAL ONE, the sovereign of all worlds,
who has given us life,
and has sustained us,
and has brought us to this time.

סלחתי כדבריך /I grant forgiveness as you ask. The words, from Numbers 14:20, are portrayed as God's speech following the rebellious report of the spies sent by Moses to scout out the Promised Land. Moses implores God not to eradicate the Israelite people. "Thus, I [God] grant forgiveness as you [Moses] ask." On Yom Kippur, each of us brings our own rebellious report: We have scouted out our own Promised Land and declared ourselves unable to secure it. Despite the promise of God's presence, we have squandered the opportunity to advance. But tonight, each of us becomes like Moses; each of us asks for ourselves: "Grant forgiveness as I ask." We do not expect to reach the Promised Land—only to be allowed to continue on the journey. R.H.

DERASH. According to the *midrash*, Yom Kippur plays a part in the Exodus year. On Shavuot, Moshe goes up to receive the tablets. He comes down and breaks them on the seventeenth of Tammuz. For forty days he argues with God to forgive. He goes up again on Rosh Ḥodesh Elul, and comes down on Yom Kippur reciting *salaḥti kidvareḥa*. So the Torah that was actually received was not the Torah of Shavuot but the Torah of Yom Kippur. Our law is one that was given with *salaḥti kidvareḥa*. It contains the built-in possibility of *teshuvah*. Z.S.S.

YOM KIPPUR MA'ARIV / 695

וְנִסְלַח לְכָל־עֲדַת בְּנֵי יִשְׂרָאֵל וְלַגֵּר הַגָּר בְּתוֹכָם כִּי לְכָל־הָעָם
בִּשְׁגָגָה:

סְלַח־נָא לַעֲוֺן הָעָם הַזֶּה כְּגֹדֶל חַסְדֶּךָ וְכַאֲשֶׁר נָשָׂאתָה לָעָם הַזֶּה
מִמִּצְרַיִם וְעַד־הֵנָּה: וְשָׁם נֶאֱמַר:

וַיֹּאמֶר יהוה: סָלַחְתִּי כִּדְבָרֶךָ:

בָּרוּךְ אַתָּה יהוה אֱלֹהֵינוּ מֶלֶךְ הָעוֹלָם שֶׁהֶחֱיָנוּ וְקִיְּמָנוּ וְהִגִּיעָנוּ
לַזְּמַן הַזֶּה:

Venislaḥ leḥol-adat beney yisra'el velager hagar betoḥam ki leḥol-ha'am bishgagah.

Selaḥ-na la'avon ha'am hazeh kegodel ḥasdeḥa veha'asher nasatah la'am hazeh mimitzrayim ve'ad heynah. Vesham ne'emar:

Vayomer adonay: Salaḥti kidevareḥa.

Baruḥ atah adonay eloheynu meleḥ ha'olam sheheḥeyanu vekiyemanu vehigi'anu lazeman hazeh.

DERASH. These verses from the book of Numbers appear in the story of the Israelite spies in Canaan. Later we will recite the Thirteen Attributes of God's compassion, also part of the wilderness story of human failure. The disasters during the wandering in the wilderness are part of the Torah's paradigm for forgetting purpose, losing awareness, faith and truth. The people seek a product of their own making, a god of gold to worship in place of the living God that is beyond their full comprehension and mastery. Our stumbling and falling often occurs when we substitute an immediate and known gratification for a transcendent value. Through the inclusion of the Thirteen Attributes in the stories of the wilderness wanderings, divine forgiveness and mercy are inextricably linked with this story of failure. It teaches us about the universality of error and forgetfulness and the eternal possibility of realizing God's loving presence in our lives.   S.P.W.

All the vows on our lips,
The burdens in our hearts,
The pent-up regrets
About which we brooded and spoke
Through prayers without end
On last Atonement Day
Did not change our way of life,
Did not bring deliverance
In the year that has gone.
From mountain peaks of fervor
We fell to common ways
At the close of the fast.

Will You hear our regret?
Will You open our prison,
Release us from shackles of habit?
Will You answer our prayers,
Forgive our wrongs,
Though we sin again and again?
In moments of weakness
We do not remember
Promises of Atonement Day.
Look past forgetfulness,
Take only from our hearts.
Forgive us, pardon us.

Ze'ev Falk (Translated by Stanley Schachter)

On Shabbat continue on the following page. On all other days turn to page 705.

כָּל־נִדְרֵי שְׂפָתֵֽינוּ, קַבָּלוֹת שֶׁבְּלִבֵּֽנוּ
וְהִרְהוּרֵי הַתְּשׁוּבָה שֶׁהָגִֽינוּ וּבִטֵּֽאנוּ
בְּאַלְפֵי תְפִלּוֹתֵֽינוּ בְּיוֹם כִּפּוּר שֶׁהָיָה
לֹא שִׁנּוּ אֹֽרַח חַיֵּֽינוּ,
לֹא הֵבִֽיאוּ גְאֻלָּתֵֽנוּ
בַּשָּׁנָה שֶׁנִּסְתַּיְּמָה:
מִמְּרוֹמֵי הִתְלַהֲבוּתֵֽנוּ
אֶל חַלִּין הֶרְגֵּלֵֽנוּ
שַֽׁבְנוּ מִיָּד עִם נְעִילָה:

הֲתִשְׁמַע חֲרָטָתֵֽנוּ, אִם תַּתִּיר אֶת־מַאֲסָרֵֽנוּ
בִּידֵי יֵֽצֶר שֶׁל שִׁגְרָה?

הֲתִרְצֶה תְפִלָּתֵֽנוּ לְכַפֵּר עַל פְּשָׁעֵֽינוּ
אַף אִם נָשׁוּב וְנֶחֱטָא?
דַּע כִּי בִּשְׁעַת חֻלְשָׁתֵֽנוּ לֹא נִזְכֹּר מוֹדָעָתֵֽנוּ
מִיּוֹם כִּפּוּר שֶׁהָיָה:
תִּתְחַשֵּׁב בְּשִׁכְחָתֵֽנוּ וּתְקַבֵּל כַּוָּנוֹתֵֽינוּ
לִסְלִיחָה וְלִמְחִילָה:

On Shabbat continue on the following page. On all other days turn to page 706.

COMMENTARY. Often we are confronted with moral or religious decisions where the right choice does not seem immediately clear. We make our choices as best we can despite not being entirely certain. At *Kol Nidrey* we look back at the year and hope our decisions have been correct. However, if they were not correct and we are now aware of it, we pray that we will be forgiven by whomever we may have offended, and that our consciences can be clear.

Carl S. Choper

The following two psalms are customarily added when Yom Kippur falls on Shabbat.

A psalm. A song for the day of Shabbat.

A good thing to give thanks to THE ETERNAL
to sing out to your name supreme,

to tell about your kindness in the morning,
and your faithfulness at night,

on ten-stringed lyre and on flute,
with melodies conceived on harp,

for you, ALMIGHTY ONE, elate me with your deeds,
I'll sing about the actions of your hands.

How great your deeds have been, SUPERNAL ONE,
your thoughts exceedingly profound.

Of this the foolish person cannot know,
of this the shallow cannot understand. ↩

NOTE. Psalms 92 and 93 express the motifs of wholeness, joy and rest in Shabbat. Psalm 92 has been associated with Shabbat since biblical times. According to the *midrash*, Shabbat itself stood up and recited this psalm at Creation, thus exulting in the role given it as the day of inner joy for all of God's creatures.   A.G.

The following two psalms are customarily added when Yom Kippur falls on Shabbat.

מִזְמוֹר שִׁיר לְיוֹם הַשַּׁבָּת:

טוֹב לְהֹדוֹת לַיהוה

לְהַגִּיד בַּבֹּקֶר חַסְדֶּךָ

עֲלֵי־עָשׂוֹר וַעֲלֵי־נָבֶל

כִּי שִׂמַּחְתַּנִי יהוה בְּפָעֳלֶךָ

מַה־גָּדְלוּ מַעֲשֶׂיךָ יהוה

אִישׁ־בַּעַר לֹא יֵדָע

וּלְזַמֵּר לְשִׁמְךָ עֶלְיוֹן:

וֶאֱמוּנָתְךָ בַּלֵּילוֹת:

עֲלֵי הִגָּיוֹן בְּכִנּוֹר:

בְּמַעֲשֵׂי יָדֶיךָ אֲרַנֵּן:

מְאֹד עָמְקוּ מַחְשְׁבֹתֶיךָ:

וּכְסִיל לֹא־יָבִין אֶת־זֹאת: ←

Mizmor shir leyom hashabbat.
Tov lehodot ladonay ulezamer leshimeha elyon.
Lehagid baboker hasdeha ve'emunateha baleylot.
Aley asor va'aley navel aley higayon behinor.

COMMENTARY. Beautiful in many respects, this twice-recited (evening and morning) Sabbath psalm also contains affirmations which do not flow easily from our lips: the wicked, despite their apparent success, are destined to perish (verses 8-10), while the righteous are destined to flourish (verses 13-15). Who, observing the vast human traumas of this century, can say these words with full conviction?

Isn't this psalm facile, smug? At moments of harassment or discouragement, so it may seem; but during the composed times of quiet reflection, such as Shabbat, it appears closer to the truth than its cynical opposite. Historically, a good case can be made that evil eventually destroys itself; philosophically, it can be convincingly argued that evil contains its own self-destruction, its own internal contradiction.

Yet this vision is far from our present reality, especially when applied to individual cases. With reason Rashi construes the phrase *leyom hashabbat* for the Sabbath Day in the first verse of the psalm as referring to *olam shekulo shabbat*, a world-in-the-making when all will be serene.   E.G.

For though the wicked multiply like weeds,
and evildoers sprout up all around,

> it is for their destruction for all time,
> but you, MAJESTIC ONE, are lifted high eternally,

behold your enemies, RESPLENDENT ONE,
behold, your enemies are lost,

> all evildoers shall be scattered.

You raise my horn like that of the triumphant ox;
I am anointed with fresh oil.

My eye shall gaze in victory on my enemies,
on all who rise against me to do harm;

> my ears shall hear of their demise.

The righteous flourish like the palm trees,
like cedars of Lebanon they grow,

implanted in the house of THE ALL-KNOWING ONE
amid the courtyards of our God they bear fruit.

In their old age, they'll put forth seed,
fleshy and fresh they'll ever be,

to tell the uprightness of THE ONE ALONE,
my Rock, in whom no fault resides.

Psalm 92

בִּפְרֹחַ רְשָׁעִים כְּמוֹ־עֵשֶׂב וַיָּצִיצוּ כָּל־פֹּעֲלֵי אָוֶן
לְהִשָּׁמְדָם עֲדֵי־עַד:
וְאַתָּה מָרוֹם לְעֹלָם יהוה:
כִּי הִנֵּה אֹיְבֶיךָ יהוה כִּי־הִנֵּה אֹיְבֶיךָ יֹאבֵדוּ
יִתְפָּרְדוּ כָּל־פֹּעֲלֵי אָוֶן:
וַתָּרֶם כִּרְאֵים קַרְנִי בַּלֹּתִי בְּשֶׁמֶן רַעֲנָן:
וַתַּבֵּט עֵינִי בְּשׁוּרָי בַּקָּמִים עָלַי מְרֵעִים
תִּשְׁמַעְנָה אָזְנָי:
* צַדִּיק כַּתָּמָר יִפְרָח כְּאֶרֶז בַּלְּבָנוֹן יִשְׂגֶּה:
שְׁתוּלִים בְּבֵית יהוה בְּחַצְרוֹת אֱלֹהֵינוּ יַפְרִיחוּ:
עוֹד יְנוּבוּן בְּשֵׂיבָה דְּשֵׁנִים וְרַעֲנַנִּים יִהְיוּ:
לְהַגִּיד כִּי־יָשָׁר יהוה צוּרִי וְלֹא־עַוְלָתָה בּוֹ:

Tzadik katamar yifraḥ ke'erez balvanon yisgeh.
Shetulim beveyt adonay beḥatzrot eloheynu yafriḥu.
Od yenuvun beseyvah deshenim vera'ananim yihyu.
Lehagid ki yashar adonay tzuri velo avlatah bo.

DERASH. On this night of confession, when we number our sins, we stand in sharp contrast to God "in whom no fault resides." Whatever our conception of God, it must include standards of ethical perfection against which we measure our accomplishments and failures. R.H.

THE ETERNAL reigns, is clothed in majesty,
THE INVISIBLE is clothed, is girded up with might.

> The world is now established,
> it cannot give way.

Your throne was long ago secured,
beyond eternity are you.

The rivers raise, O MIGHTY ONE,
the rivers raise a roaring sound,

> the floods raise up torrential waves,

but louder than the sound of mighty waters,
more exalted than the breakers of the sea,

> raised up on high are you, THE SOURCE.

Your precepts have retained their truth,
and holiness befits your house,

THE ETERNAL ONE, forever and a day.

Psalm 93

DERASH. Why does this psalm (93) follow the psalm for Shabbat (92)? In it God watches the seas. The *midrash* notes that just as earth was created by parting the waters, so was Redemption created by parting the waters. In Creation land was redeemed from the waters. In Redemption human freedom is created. The creation of Shabbat planted the seed of human redemption. The experience of Shabbat nurtures that seed, giving us the strength to quell the floods in our time.   D.A.T./S.D.R.

יְ֖הֹוָ֣ה מָלָךְ֮ גֵּא֢וּת לָ֫בֵ֥שׁ לָבֵ֣שׁ יהוה עֹ֣ז הִתְאַזָּ֑ר
אַף־תִּכּ֥וֹן תֵּבֵ֝ל בַּל־תִּמּֽוֹט:

נָכ֣וֹן כִּסְאֲךָ֣ מֵאָ֑ז מֵעוֹלָ֣ם אָֽתָּה:
נָשְׂא֤וּ נְהָר֨וֹת יהוה נָשְׂא֣וּ נְהָר֣וֹת קוֹלָ֑ם
יִשְׂא֖וּ נְהָר֣וֹת דָּכְיָֽם:

מִקֹּל֨וֹת מַ֤יִם רַבִּ֗ים אַדִּירִ֣ים מִשְׁבְּרֵי־יָ֑ם
אַדִּ֖יר בַּמָּר֣וֹם יהוה:
* עֵֽדֹתֶ֨יךָ נֶֽאֶמְנ֬וּ מְאֹ֗ד לְבֵיתְךָ֥ נָֽאֲוָה־קֹּ֑דֶשׁ
יהוה לְאֹ֣רֶךְ יָמִֽים:

COMMENTARY. Psalm 93 retells the ancient tale of Creation. The waters raised a great shout, showing their power to overwhelm the dry land as it first emerged. So do the forces of chaos and destruction threaten the islands of peace and security we manage to create in our lives. The psalmist assures us, however, that the voice of God is greater than that of even the fiercest storm tides of the ocean. With God's throne firmly established, the peace of Shabbat is now triumphant. A.G.

A Song of the Ascents

From the depths I have called out to you, REDEEMING ONE,
please listen, my provider, to my voice!
May you hearken to my voice of supplication.
Were you to pay careful attention to a person's sins,
who could endure, almighty one?
With you alone originates all power to forgive;
for this you are revered.
So I have hoped, MERCIFUL ONE! My soul has hoped,
and for your word I have looked forward in my yearning.
My spirit yearns for my protector more than people watch for
daybreak,
truly, more than watching for the dawn.
So does Israel eagerly anticipate THE MERCIFUL,
for from THE MERCIFUL all kindness comes,
from God alone comes all deliverance,
yes, God alone delivers Israel from its wrongful acts.

Psalm 130

COMMENTARY. The psalmist yearns for the appearance of God and resulting release from sin like the night watchman eagerly hopes for the coming dawn—not only a source of beauty, light, and the lifting of a heavy burden, but of loving redemption as well. While we are in the dark, it is a matter of faith and hope that the light will come. But faith and hope also express our previous experience. Dawn's glory does come daily. And so we pray for release from the power of our previous transgressions.   D.A.T.

מִמַּעֲמַקִּים קְרָאתִיךָ יהוה: אֲדֹנָי שִׁמְעָה בְקוֹלִי
תִּהְיֶינָה אָזְנֶיךָ קַשֻּׁבוֹת לְקוֹל תַּחֲנוּנָי:
אִם־עֲוֹנוֹת תִּשְׁמָר־יָהּ אֲדֹנָי מִי יַעֲמֹד:
כִּי־עִמְּךָ הַסְּלִיחָה לְמַעַן תִּוָּרֵא:
קִוִּיתִי יהוה קִוְּתָה נַפְשִׁי וְלִדְבָרוֹ הוֹחָלְתִּי:
נַפְשִׁי לַאדֹנָי מִשֹּׁמְרִים לַבֹּקֶר שֹׁמְרִים לַבֹּקֶר:
יַחֵל יִשְׂרָאֵל אֶל־יהוה
כִּי־עִם־יהוה הַחֶסֶד וְהַרְבֵּה עִמּוֹ פְדוּת:
וְהוּא יִפְדֶּה אֶת־יִשְׂרָאֵל מִכֹּל עֲוֹנוֹתָיו

DERASH. Why does Yom Kippur follow Rosh Hashanah? Should it not be the other way around—first a settling of accounts for the previous year and then a celebration of a new year with its promise of change and its potential for betterment? Is it not necessary to clear away the old, to repent for the past, before we can really welcome the new?

The hope for a *new* year must precede a systematic review of the old, for it shakes us awake to the possibility of renewal. The new year calls on us to join in the struggle to transform ourselves. The shofar blasts are meant to arouse our slothful selves to the new possibilities that await us. Once conscious of the new year and what it offers, we are ready to look back at our past. Conscious that life can be as sweet as apples dipped in honey, that the barren woman can bear fruit even in old age, and that the descending knife can be halted in midair, we approach Yom Kippur with the hope for growth and change....   Michael Strassfeld

THE SHEMA AND ITS BLESSINGS

When a minyan is present, the Barehu *is said. The congregation rises and faces the ark. It is customary to bow.*

Bless THE INFINITE, the blessed One!

Blessed is THE INFINITE, the blessed One, now and forever!

KAVANAH. Public worship aids us by liberating personality from the confining walls of the individual ego. Imprisoned in self, we easily fall prey to morbid broodings. Interference with career, personal disappointment and disillusionment, hurts to vanity, the fear of death—all these tend so to dominate our attention that our minds move in a fixed and narrow system of ideas, which we detest but from which we see no escape. With a whole wide world of boundless opportunities about us, we permit our minds, as it were, to pace up and down within the narrow cell of their ego-prisons. But participation in public worship breaks through the prison of the ego and lets in the light and air of the world. Instead of living but one small and petty life, we now share the multitudinous life of our people. Against the wider horizons that now open to our ken, personal cares do not loom so large. Life becomes infinitely more meaningful and worthwhile when we become aware, through our participation in public worship, of a common life that transcends our individual selves.

M.M.K. (Adapted)

When a minyan is present, the Barehu *is said. The congregation rises and faces the ark. It is customary to bow.*

בָּרְכוּ אֶת יהוה הַמְבֹרָךְ:
בָּרוּךְ יהוה הַמְבֹרָךְ לְעוֹלָם וָעֶד:

Barehu et adonay hamvorah.
Baruh adonay hamvorah le'olam va'ed.

KAVANAH. When we worship in public we know our life is part of a larger life, a wave of an ocean of being—the first-hand experience of that larger life which is God. M.M.K.

KAVANAH. The main part of the evening service begins with the customary prayers: *Barehu, Asher Bidvaro, Ahavat Olam, Shema*....There is something reassuring about the familiarity of the liturgy, a security in knowing that even as we embark on the day of atoning, we travel a liturgical road which is remarkably similar to the one a Jew can walk every day of the year. The other days of the year lead us to Yom Kippur, and a bit of Yom Kippur's call to return is contained in the everyday. R.H.

ASHER BIDVARO / GOD IN NATURE

Blessed are you, ETERNAL ONE our God, sovereign of all worlds, by whose word the evenings fall. In wisdom you open heaven's gates. With divine discernment you make seasons change, causing the times to come and go, and ordering the stars on their appointed paths through heaven's dome, all according to your will. Creator of the day and night, who rolls back light before the dark, and dark before the light, who makes day pass away and brings on night, dividing between day and night: CREATOR of the Multitudes of Heaven is your name! Living and enduring God, rule over us, now and always. Blessed are you, ALMIGHTY ONE, who makes the evenings fall.

DERASH. When we are about to say, "Blessed are you, our God, sovereign of all worlds" and prepare to utter the first word "blessed," we should do so with all our strength, so that we will have no strength left to say, "are you." And this is the meaning of the verse in the Scriptures: "But they that wait for God shall exchange their strength." What we are really saying is: "Source of life, I am giving you all the strength that is within me in that very first word; now will you, in exchange, give me an abundance of new strength, so that I can go on with my prayer."   M.B. (Adapted)

אור, חושך, אור / light, dark, light. The words roll into each other just as day rolls into night. They are not separate realms. They mix together. God rules both light and darkness. בין / beyn: between. Related to בינה / binah and תבונה / tevunah: understanding. Wisdom is the ability to distinguish between things, to make sense out of confusion.   L.W.K.

KAVANAH. In looking to the past and future, we pray that as God "in wisdom opens heaven's gates" so God will in mercy open human hearts.
          R.H.

אֲשֶׁר בִּדְבָרוֹ

בָּרוּךְ אַתָּה יהוה אֱלֹהֵינוּ מֶלֶךְ הָעוֹלָם אֲשֶׁר בִּדְבָרוֹ מַעֲרִיב עֲרָבִים
בְּחָכְמָה פּוֹתֵחַ שְׁעָרִים וּבִתְבוּנָה מְשַׁנֶּה עִתִּים וּמַחֲלִיף אֶת הַזְּמַנִּים
וּמְסַדֵּר אֶת־הַכּוֹכָבִים בְּמִשְׁמְרוֹתֵיהֶם בָּרָקִיעַ כִּרְצוֹנוֹ: בּוֹרֵא יוֹם
וָלַיְלָה גּוֹלֵל אוֹר מִפְּנֵי חֹשֶׁךְ וְחֹשֶׁךְ מִפְּנֵי אוֹר: *וּמַעֲבִיר יוֹם וּמֵבִיא
לַיְלָה וּמַבְדִּיל בֵּין יוֹם וּבֵין לַיְלָה יהוה צְבָאוֹת שְׁמוֹ: אֵל חַי וְקַיָּם
תָּמִיד יִמְלֹךְ עָלֵינוּ לְעוֹלָם וָעֶד: בָּרוּךְ אַתָּה יהוה הַמַּעֲרִיב עֲרָבִים:

El ḥay vekayam tamid yimloḥ aleynu le'olam va'ed.
Baruḥ atah adonay hama'ariv aravim.

אשר בדברו מעריב ערבים / By whose word the evenings fall. The word plays
a central role in the Jewish imagination. Our liturgy fantasizes that God
brings on evening each night by saying "Evening!" Thus we repeat each
day the original act of Creation that took place by means of the divine
word. It is only because we affirm a God who so values language that we
feel ourselves able to use words in prayer. Our word, perhaps like God's,
gives expression to a depth that goes beyond language, but that can be
shared only through the symbolic power of speech.   A.G.

COMMENTARY. The two *beraḥot* which precede the Shema set the stage for
its evening recitation. The first *beraḥah* praises God for the wonders of
creation that are visible at twilight: the shifting patterns of the stars, the
rhythm of the seasons, the regular passage from day to night. All of these
are a nightly reminder of the unchanging plan of creation.

The second *beraḥah* praises God, whose instruction is a special token of
love for Israel. Israel responds by meditating upon God's teaching "day
and night," "when we lie down and when we rise." This phrasing recalls
the preceding *beraḥah*, adding Israel's study of Torah to the natural order:
The sun sets, the stars shine, and Israel studies—as regularly as day and
night. The phrase "when we lie down and when we rise" anticipates the
Shema, which follows. This interplay between the *beraḥot* and the Shema
suggests that the Shema is Israel's morning and evening Torah study. At
the same time, it is Israel's declaration of the oneness of the power that
makes for the natural order and for learning, for creation and human
creativity.   S.S.

AHAVAT OLAM / GOD'S LOVE IN TORAH

With everlasting love, you love the house of Israel. Torah and mitzvot, laws and justice you have taught us. And so, DEAR ONE our God, when we lie down and when we rise, we reflect upon your laws; we take pleasure in your Torah's words and your mitzvot, now and always. Truly, they are our life, our length of days. On them we meditate by day and night. Your love will never depart from us as long as worlds endure. Blessed are you, BELOVED ONE, who loves your people Israel.

KAVANAH. The שמע/Shema is wrapped in אהבה/ahavah/love. The blessing preceding the Shema concludes, "who loves your people Israel." This prayer begins "ואהבת/ve'ahavta, And you must love יהוה!" First you are loved, then you respond with love. Love is central to Jewish life. Love means commitment and limitations—Torah and mitzvot. That is so both in our relationships with each other and in our relationship with God.

L.W.K.

אַהֲבַת עוֹלָם

אַהֲבַת עוֹלָם בֵּית יִשְׂרָאֵל עַמְּךָ אָהָבְתָּ: תּוֹרָה וּמִצְוֹת חֻקִּים
וּמִשְׁפָּטִים אוֹתָנוּ לִמַּדְתָּ: עַל כֵּן יהוה אֱלֹהֵינוּ בְּשָׁכְבֵנוּ וּבְקוּמֵנוּ
נָשִׂיחַ בְּחֻקֶּיךָ וְנִשְׂמַח בְּדִבְרֵי תוֹרָתֶךָ וּבְמִצְוֹתֶיךָ לְעוֹלָם וָעֶד כִּי הֵם
חַיֵּינוּ וְאֹרֶךְ יָמֵינוּ וּבָהֶם נֶהְגֶּה יוֹמָם וָלָיְלָה: וְאַהֲבָתְךָ לֹא תָסוּר
מִמֶּנּוּ לְעוֹלָמִים: בָּרוּךְ אַתָּה יהוה אוֹהֵב עַמּוֹ יִשְׂרָאֵל:

Ahavat olam beyt yisra'el ameha ahavta.
Torah umitzvot hukim umishpatim otanu limadeta.
Al ken adonay eloheynu beshohbenu uvkumenu nasi'ah
    behukeha
venismah bedivrey torateha uvmitzvoteha le'olam va'ed
ki hem hayeynu ve'oreh yameynu
uvahem nehgeh yomam valaylah.
Ve'ahavateha lo tasur mimenu le'olamim.
Baruh atah adonay ohev amo yisra'el.

ואהבתך לא תסור . Our text follows the Sephardic version, in the declarative
model ("Your love will never depart from us.") rather than the imperative
("Never remove your love from us!"). Divine love is unconditional. It is
available to every one of us when we fashion our lives into channels to
receive and share it. The Jewish people together experiences that eternal
love as reflected in our love for the study of Torah—a wisdom lovingly
received, shared, and passed on enriched by each generation.   A.G.

שְׁמַע יִשְׂרָאֵל יְהֹוָה אֱלֹהֵינוּ יְהֹוָה אֶחָד

SHEMA

Listen, Israel: THE ETERNAL is our God,
THE ETERNAL ONE alone!

Blessed be the name and glory of God's realm, forever!

And you must love THE ONE, your God, with your whole heart,
with every breath, with all you have. Take these words that I
command you now to heart. Teach them intently to your
children. Speak them when you sit inside your house or walk
upon the road, when you lie down and when you rise. And bind
them as a sign upon your hand, and keep them visible before
your eyes. Inscribe them on the doorposts of your house and on
your gates. ↲

שמע ... ובשעריך / Listen ... gates (Deuteronomy 6:4-9).

DERASH. The Shema is called *kabbalat ol malḥut shamayim.* We "receive
upon ourselves the yoke of the sovereignty of Heaven." To proclaim God
as ours and as one is to acknowledge fealty to the divine will—and the
Shema is a time to listen. We listen in order to discover God's will.

D.A.T.

ואהבת את יהוה . Love יהוה your God. Abbaye said, "Let the love of God be
spread through your activities. If a person studies and helps others to do
so, if one's business dealings are decent and trustworthy—what do people
say? 'Happy is the one who studied Torah, and the one who teaches Torah!
Have you seen the one who studied Torah? How beautiful! What a fine
person!' Thus, the Torah says, 'You are my servant Israel; I will be
glorified by you' (Isaiah 49:3)." Talmud Yoma 86a

KAVANAH. The Shema challenges us to be fully conscious. True hearing
involves an awareness of what is. A moment of full consciousness
illuminates our false perceptions and opens us up to new possibilities. It is
a courageous and honest encounter with the now. D.B.

שְׁמַע יִשְׂרָאֵל יהוה אֱלֹהֵינוּ יהוה אֶחָד:

The following line is recited aloud on Yom Kippur.

בָּרוּךְ שֵׁם כְּבוֹד מַלְכוּתוֹ לְעוֹלָם וָעֶד:

וְאָהַבְתָּ אֵת יהוה אֱלֹהֶיךָ בְּכָל־לְבָבְךָ וּבְכָל־נַפְשְׁךָ וּבְכָל־מְאֹדֶךָ:
וְהָיוּ הַדְּבָרִים הָאֵלֶּה אֲשֶׁר אָנֹכִי מְצַוְּךָ הַיּוֹם עַל־לְבָבֶךָ: וְשִׁנַּנְתָּם
לְבָנֶיךָ וְדִבַּרְתָּ בָּם בְּשִׁבְתְּךָ בְּבֵיתֶךָ וּבְלֶכְתְּךָ בַדֶּרֶךְ וּבְשָׁכְבְּךָ
וּבְקוּמֶךָ: וּקְשַׁרְתָּם לְאוֹת עַל־יָדֶךָ וְהָיוּ לְטֹטָפֹת בֵּין עֵינֶיךָ:
וּכְתַבְתָּם עַל־מְזֻזוֹת בֵּיתֶךָ וּבִשְׁעָרֶיךָ:

Shema yisra'el adonay eloheynu adonay eḥad.
Baruḥ shem kevod malḥuto le'olam va'ed.

Ve'ahavta et adonay eloheha
beḥol levaveha uveḥol nafsheha uveḥol me'odeha.
Vehayu hadevarim ha'eleh asher anoḥi metzaveha hayom al
levaveha.
Veshinantam levaneha vedibarta bam
beshivteha beveyteha uveleḥteha vadereḥ uveshohbeha
uvekumeha.
Ukeshartam le'ot al yadeha vehayu letotafot beyn eyneha.
Uḥetavtam al mezuzot beyteha uvishareha.

לבבך /*levaveha*/ your heart. The לב /*lev*/ heart, was seen as the source of emotions and intellect. Feelings and reason are complementary partners, not conflicting parts, of the human psyche. The double ב of לבב teaches that a love of God must contain all dualities (e.g., the good and bad in you).   L.W.K.

Listen! Israel, listen!
Still the mind's chatter, quiet the heart's desire
The rush of life flows through me.
The heart of eternity beats in my own chest. Listen.
I am the fingers of a divine and infinite hand.
I am the thoughts of a divine and infinite mind.
There is only one reality, the Singular Source and Substance
of all diversity. This One alone is God.   R.M.S.

For the second paragraph of the Shema, read either the version below or the biblical section beginning on page 719, then continue with the third paragraph, page 721.

BIBLICAL SELECTION I

It came to pass, and will again,
that if you truly listen
to the voice of THE ETERNAL ONE, your God,
being sure to do whatever has been asked of you today,
THE ONE, your God, will make of you a model
for all nations of the earth,
and there will come upon you all these blessings,
as you listen to the call of THE ABUNDANT ONE, your God:
Blessed be you in the city,
blessed be you upon the field.
Blessed be the fruit of your womb,
the fruit of your land, the fruit of your cattle,
the calving of your oxen, and the lambing of your sheep.
Blessed be your basket and your kneading-trough.
Blessed be you when you come home,
and blessed be you when you go forth.

See, I have placed in front of you today
both life and good, both death and ill,
commanding you today to love THE BOUNDLESS ONE, your God,
to walk in ways I have ordained,
keeping the commandments, laws, and judgments,
so that you survive and multiply.
THE BOUNTIFUL, your God, will bless you
on the land you are about to enter and inherit. ↵

For the second paragraph of the Shema, read either the version below or the biblical section beginning on page 720, then continue with the third paragraph, page 722.

BIBLICAL SELECTION I

וְהָיָה אִם־שָׁמֹעַ תִּשְׁמְעוּ בְּקוֹל יהוה אֱלֹהֶיךָ לִשְׁמֹר לַעֲשׂוֹת
אֶת־כָּל־מִצְוֹתָיו אֲשֶׁר אָנֹכִי מְצַוְּךָ הַיּוֹם וּנְתָנְךָ יהוה אֱלֹהֶיךָ עֶלְיוֹן
עַל כָּל־גּוֹיֵי הָאָרֶץ: וּבָאוּ עָלֶיךָ כָּל־הַבְּרָכוֹת הָאֵלֶּה וְהִשִּׂיגֻךָ כִּי
תִשְׁמַע בְּקוֹל יהוה אֱלֹהֶיךָ: בָּרוּךְ אַתָּה בָּעִיר וּבָרוּךְ אַתָּה בַּשָּׂדֶה:
בָּרוּךְ פְּרִי־בִטְנְךָ וּפְרִי אַדְמָתְךָ וּפְרִי בְהֶמְתֶּךָ שְׁגַר אֲלָפֶיךָ
וְעַשְׁתְּרוֹת צֹאנֶךָ: בָּרוּךְ טַנְאֲךָ וּמִשְׁאַרְתֶּךָ: בָּרוּךְ אַתָּה בְּבֹאֶךָ
וּבָרוּךְ אַתָּה בְּצֵאתֶךָ:

רְאֵה נָתַתִּי לְפָנֶיךָ הַיּוֹם אֶת־הַחַיִּים וְאֶת־הַטּוֹב וְאֶת־הַמָּוֶת
וְאֶת־הָרָע: אֲשֶׁר אָנֹכִי מְצַוְּךָ הַיּוֹם לְאַהֲבָה אֶת־יהוה אֱלֹהֶיךָ
לָלֶכֶת בִּדְרָכָיו וְלִשְׁמֹר מִצְוֹתָיו וְחֻקֹּתָיו וּמִשְׁפָּטָיו וְחָיִיתָ וְרָבִיתָ
וּבֵרַכְךָ יהוה אֱלֹהֶיךָ בָּאָרֶץ אֲשֶׁר־אַתָּה בָא־שָׁמָּה לְרִשְׁתָּהּ: ←

COMMENTARY. The traditional wording of Biblical Selection II presents detailed bountiful or devastating consequences of Israel's collective relationship to the mitzvot. That biblical section (Deuteronomy 11:13-21) offers a supernatural theology that many contemporary Jews find difficult. The biblical section on this page (Deuteronomy 28:1-6, 30:15-19) was included in the 1945 Reconstructionist siddur. It begins by encouraging observance in the same language, but concentrates on the positive ways in which observance of mitzvot focuses our attention on God's presence as perceived through productivity and the pursuit of abundant life.   S.S.

KAVANAH. The doctrine of the unity of God calls for the integration of all life's purposes into a consistent pattern of thought and conduct.   M.M.K.

But if your heart should turn away,
and you not heed, and go astray,
and you submit to other gods and serve them,
I declare to you today that you shall be
destroyed completely; you shall not live out
a great expanse of days upon the land
that you now cross the Jordan to possess.
I call as witnesses concerning you
both heaven and earth, both life and death,
that I have placed in front of you
a blessing and a curse.
Choose life, that you may live,
you and your seed!

Continue with page 721.

וְאִם־יִפְנֶה לְבָבְךָ וְלֹא תִשְׁמָע וְנִדַּחְתָּ וְהִשְׁתַּחֲוִיתָ לֵאלֹהִים אֲחֵרִים וַעֲבַדְתָּם: הִגַּדְתִּי לָכֶם הַיּוֹם כִּי אָבֹד תֹּאבֵדוּן לֹא־תַאֲרִיכֻן יָמִים עַל־הָאֲדָמָה אֲשֶׁר אַתָּה עֹבֵר אֶת־הַיַּרְדֵּן לָבֹא שָׁמָּה לְרִשְׁתָּהּ: הַעִדֹתִי בָכֶם הַיּוֹם אֶת־הַשָּׁמַיִם וְאֶת־הָאָרֶץ הַחַיִּים וְהַמָּוֶת נָתַתִּי לְפָנֶיךָ הַבְּרָכָה וְהַקְּלָלָה וּבָחַרְתָּ בַּחַיִּים לְמַעַן תִּחְיֶה אַתָּה וְזַרְעֶךָ:

Continue with וַיֹּאמֶר, *page 722.*

In the handwritten scroll of the Torah
The word "*Shema*" of "*Shema Yisra'el*"
Ends with an oversized *ayin*,
And the word "*Eḥad*"
Ends with an oversized *dalet*.
Taken together
These two letters
Spell "*Ed*," meaning "witness."
    Whenever we recite the Shema
    We bear witness
    To our awareness
    Of God's presence.   H.M.

BIBLICAL SELECTION II

And if you truly listen to my bidding, as I bid you now—loving THE FOUNT OF LIFE, your God, and serving God with all your heart, with every breath—then I will give you rain upon your land in its appointed time, the early rain and later rain, so you may gather in your corn, your wine and oil. And I will give you grass upon your field to feed your animals, and you will eat and be content. Beware, then, lest your heart be led astray, and you go off and worship other gods, and you submit to them, so that the anger of THE MIGHTY ONE should burn against you, and seal up the heavens so no rain would fall, so that the ground would not give forth her produce, and you be forced to leave the good land I am giving you.

So place these words upon your heart, into your lifebreath. Bind them as a sign upon your hand, and let them rest before your eyes. Teach them to your children, speaking of them when you sit at home, and when you walk upon the road, when you lie down, and when you rise. Inscribe them on the doorposts of your house and on your gates—so that your days and your children's days be many on the land THE FAITHFUL ONE promised to give your ancestors, as long as heaven rests above the earth. ↩

DERASH. God is the assumption that there is enough in the world to meet our needs but not to meet our greed for power and pleasure.

M.M.K. (Adapted)

COMMENTARY. The statement of God's oneness unifies not only the context of Shema but the text as well—three scriptural paragraphs specified in the Mishnah (a second-century codification of Jewish law). The powerful declaration of God's unity fuses the responsibility to love God and to study God's teachings (first paragraph) with the lesson that their fulfillment confirms God's presence (second and third paragraphs). Hence, the unity of God as idea and presence.

S.S.

BIBLICAL SELECTION II

וְהָיָ֗ה אִם־שָׁמֹ֤עַ תִּשְׁמְעוּ֙ אֶל־מִצְוֺתַ֔י אֲשֶׁ֧ר אָנֹכִ֛י מְצַוֶּ֥ה אֶתְכֶ֖ם
הַיּ֑וֹם לְאַהֲבָ֞ה אֶת־יהוה אֱלֹֽהֵיכֶם֙ וּלְעָבְד֔וֹ בְּכָל־לְבַבְכֶ֖ם וּבְכָל־
נַפְשְׁכֶֽם: וְנָתַתִּ֧י מְטַֽר־אַרְצְכֶ֛ם בְּעִתּ֖וֹ יוֹרֶ֣ה וּמַלְק֑וֹשׁ וְאָסַפְתָּ֣ דְגָנֶ֔ךָ
וְתִירֹֽשְׁךָ֖ וְיִצְהָרֶֽךָ: וְנָתַתִּ֛י עֵ֥שֶׂב בְּשָׂדְךָ֖ לִבְהֶמְתֶּ֑ךָ וְאָכַלְתָּ֖ וְשָׂבָֽעְתָּ:
הִשָּֽׁמְר֣וּ לָכֶ֔ם פֶּ֥ן יִפְתֶּ֖ה לְבַבְכֶ֑ם וְסַרְתֶּ֗ם וַעֲבַדְתֶּם֙ אֱלֹהִ֣ים אֲחֵרִ֔ים
וְהִשְׁתַּחֲוִיתֶ֖ם לָהֶֽם: וְחָרָ֨ה אַף־יהוה֙ בָּכֶ֔ם וְעָצַ֣ר אֶת־הַשָּׁמַ֗יִם
וְלֹא־יִהְיֶ֣ה מָטָ֔ר וְהָ֣אֲדָמָ֔ה לֹ֥א תִתֵּ֖ן אֶת־יְבוּלָ֑הּ וַאֲבַדְתֶּ֣ם מְהֵרָ֗ה
מֵעַל֙ הָאָ֣רֶץ הַטֹּבָ֔ה אֲשֶׁ֥ר יהוה נֹתֵ֖ן לָכֶֽם:

וְשַׂמְתֶּם֙ אֶת־דְּבָרַ֣י אֵ֔לֶּה עַל־לְבַבְכֶ֖ם וְעַל־נַפְשְׁכֶ֑ם וּקְשַׁרְתֶּ֨ם אֹתָ֤ם
לְאוֹת֙ עַל־יֶדְכֶ֔ם וְהָי֥וּ לְטוֹטָפֹ֖ת בֵּ֥ין עֵינֵיכֶֽם: וְלִמַּדְתֶּ֥ם אֹתָ֛ם
אֶת־בְּנֵיכֶ֖ם לְדַבֵּ֣ר בָּ֑ם בְּשִׁבְתְּךָ֤ בְּבֵיתֶ֙ךָ֙ וּבְלֶכְתְּךָ֣ בַדֶּ֔רֶךְ וּֽבְשָׁכְבְּךָ֖
וּבְקוּמֶֽךָ: וּכְתַבְתָּ֛ם עַל־מְזוּז֥וֹת בֵּיתֶ֖ךָ וּבִשְׁעָרֶֽיךָ: לְמַ֨עַן֙ יִרְבּ֣וּ יְמֵיכֶ֗ם
וִימֵ֣י בְנֵיכֶ֔ם עַ֚ל הָֽאֲדָמָ֔ה אֲשֶׁ֨ר נִשְׁבַּ֧ע יהוה לַאֲבֹֽתֵיכֶ֖ם לָתֵ֣ת לָהֶ֑ם
כִּימֵ֥י הַשָּׁמַ֖יִם עַל־הָאָֽרֶץ: ⟵

DERASH. This warning against idolatry has ecological significance. If we
continue to pollute the environment—and thus display contempt for the
integrity of God's creation—pure rain will cease to fall, and the ground
will cease to give forth its produce.   M.L.

DERASH. The traditional second paragraph of the Shema (Deuteronomy
11:13-21) offers an account of the natural process by which the blessings
of God themselves lead to pride, self-satisfaction, and ingratitude on the
part of those who receive them. Ironically, the more we are blessed, so it
seems, the less grateful and aware of blessing we become. It is when we
are most sated, Scripture warns us, that we should be most careful.
Fullness can lead to ingratitude, and ingratitude to idolatry—primarily in
the form of worship of our own accomplishments. Then, indeed, "the
heavens might close up and no rain fall." For, once we begin to worship
our achievements, we will never find satisfaction.   A.G.

THE BOUNDLESS ONE told Moses: Speak to the Israelites—tell them to make themselves *tzitzit* upon the corners of their clothes, throughout their generations. Have them place upon the corner *tzitzit* a twine of royal blue. This is your *tzitzit*. Look at it and remember all the mitzvot of the ETERNAL ONE. And do them, so you won't go off after the lusts of your heart or after what catches your eye, so that you remember to do all my mitzvot and be holy for your God. I am THE FAITHFUL ONE, your God, who brought you from Mitzrayim to be for you a God. I am THE INFINITE, your God.

תכלת is Sidon blue, which is obtained from a shellfish. Sidon or royal blue is associated with majesty—even today the British queen wears a blue sash. The Jews were so oppressed at the time of Bar Koḥba that indigo, a vegetable dye, replaced Sidon blue on their *tzitzit*. The Romans banned the blue fringe because of its symbolism. During the nineteenth century the Radziner *ḥasidim* reintroduced its use. Now other Jews have also begun to use it. The long *teḥelet* thread intertwined with short white ones is a complex and powerful image that hints at the interplay between majesty and subject within our own hearts.   E.M.

אחרי עיניכם / after what catches your eye, that is, the physical and material temptations you see. The Baal Shem Tov had a method for dealing with distractions, especially sexual ones. If you can't get the person out of your thoughts, remember that beauty is a reflection of God's image. Redirect that energy towards God.   L.W.K.

וַיֹּאמֶר יְהוָה אֶל־מֹשֶׁה לֵּאמֹר: דַּבֵּר אֶל־בְּנֵי יִשְׂרָאֵל וְאָמַרְתָּ
אֲלֵהֶם וְעָשׂוּ לָהֶם צִיצִת עַל־כַּנְפֵי בִגְדֵיהֶם לְדֹרֹתָם וְנָתְנוּ
עַל־צִיצִת הַכָּנָף פְּתִיל תְּכֵלֶת: וְהָיָה לָכֶם לְצִיצִת וּרְאִיתֶם אֹתוֹ
וּזְכַרְתֶּם אֶת־כָּל־מִצְוֹת יְהוָה וַעֲשִׂיתֶם אֹתָם וְלֹא תָתוּרוּ אַחֲרֵי
לְבַבְכֶם וְאַחֲרֵי עֵינֵיכֶם אֲשֶׁר־אַתֶּם זֹנִים אַחֲרֵיהֶם: לְמַעַן תִּזְכְּרוּ
וַעֲשִׂיתֶם אֶת־כָּל־מִצְוֹתָי וִהְיִיתֶם קְדֹשִׁים לֵאלֹהֵיכֶם: אֲנִי יְהוָה
אֱלֹהֵיכֶם אֲשֶׁר הוֹצֵאתִי אֶתְכֶם מֵאֶרֶץ מִצְרַיִם לִהְיוֹת לָכֶם
לֵאלֹהִים אֲנִי יְהוָה אֱלֹהֵיכֶם: **אֱמֶת:**

Vayomer adonay el mosheh leymor. Daber el beney yisra'el
ve'amarta aleyhem ve'asu lahem tzitzit al kanfey vigdeyhem
ledorotam venatenu al tzitzit hakanaf petil teḥelet. Vehayah
laḥem letzitzit uritem oto uzḥartem et kol mitzvot adonay
va'asitem otam velo taturu aḥarey levaveḥem ve'aḥarey
eyneyḥem asher atem zonim aḥareyhem. Lema'an tizkeru
va'asitem et kol mitzvotay vihe-yitem kedoshim leyloheyḥem.
Ani adonay eloheyḥem asher hotzeyti etḥem me'eretz mitzrayim
lihyot laḥem leylohim ani adonay eloheyḥem.

ויאמר...אלהיכם / THE BOUNDLESS ONE...God (Numbers 15:37-41).

מצרים / *Mitzrayim* was the escaping Hebrews', not the Egyptians', name for
the land of Egypt: perhaps a slave-term, and probably not of Semitic
origin, it has associations with the root צרר, to be in distress, constricted,
in anguish, or in dire straits. This word powerfully evokes the choking
oppression of slavery. As the psalmist wrote: מן המצר קראתי יה / From the
depths I called to Yah.   M.P.

EMET VE'EMUNAH / REDEMPTION

The translation of the Ge'ulah *is on this page; an interpretive version begins on page 725.*

Our faith and truth rest on all this, which is binding upon us:
That THE BOUNDLESS ONE alone is our divinity
and that no divinity exists but One;
that we are Israel, community of God;
that it is God who saves us from the hand
of governments, the very palm of tyrants;
who enacts great deeds without measure,
and wondrous deeds beyond all count;
who puts our souls amid the living,
and who keeps our feet from giving way;
who breaks apart the schemes of those who hate us,
confounds the thoughts of any bearing us ill-will;
that it is God who made miracles for us in Egypt,
signs and wonders in Ham's children's land.
From one generation to the next, God is our guarantor,
and even on a day that turned to night,
God stayed with us when death's deep shadow fell.
And even in our age of orphans and survivors,
God's loving acts have not abandoned us,
and God has brought together our scattered kin
from the distant corners of the earth.

                        As then, so now,
God brings the people Israel forth
from every place of menace, to a lasting freedom.
God is the one who brought the Israelites
through a divided Sea of Reeds.
There, they beheld divine might;
they praised and thanked the Name,
and willingly accepted for themselves
God's rule.

Moses, Miriam and the Israelites came forth
with song to you in joy, and they all cried:
Continue on page 727.

אֱמֶת וֶאֱמוּנָה כָּל זֹאת וְקַיָּם עָלֵינוּ
כִּי הוּא יהוה אֱלֹהֵינוּ וְאֵין זוּלָתוֹ
וַאֲנַחְנוּ יִשְׂרָאֵל עַמּוֹ:
הַפּוֹדֵנוּ מִיַּד מְלָכִים
הַגּוֹאֲלֵנוּ מִכַּף עָרִיצִים
הָעוֹשֶׂה גְדוֹלוֹת אֵין חֵקֶר
וְנִפְלָאוֹת אֵין מִסְפָּר:
הַשָּׂם נַפְשֵׁנוּ בַּחַיִּים
וְלֹא נָתַן לַמּוֹט רַגְלֵנוּ:
הַמֵּפֵר עֲצַת אוֹיְבֵינוּ
וְהַמְקַלְקֵל מַחְשְׁבוֹת שׂוֹנְאֵינוּ:
הָעוֹשֶׂה לָּנוּ נִסִּים בְּמִצְרַיִם
אוֹתוֹת וּמוֹפְתִים בְּאַדְמַת בְּנֵי חָם:
מִדּוֹר לְדוֹר הוּא גוֹאֲלֵנוּ:
וּבַיּוֹם שֶׁהָפַךְ לְלָיְלָה
עִמָּנוּ הָיָה בְּגֵיא צַלְמָוֶת:

Continue on page 726.

COMMENTARY. The blessing immediately following the Shema deals with the theme of divine redemption. The present text, a rewritten version, includes references to the Holocaust, from which there was no redemption, and the return to Zion, a fulfillment of Israel's ancient dream. The same divine spirit that gave Israel the courage to seek freedom from Egypt in ancient times inspired those who fought for Israel's freedom in our own day. At the same time, this version omits those portions of the text that glory in the enemy's fall or see in God a force for vengeance. All humans are God's beloved children, as were the Egyptians who drowned at the sea.   A.G.

INTERPRETIVE VERSION

We acknowledge as true and trustworthy that there is but one universal God, and that to God's service Israel stands eternally committed.

We recognize in God the power that has enabled us to triumph over defeat, persecution and oppression.

It was God who redeemed us from Egyptian bondage, and delivered us from the despotism of the pharaohs.

For God wills that we be free to use our powers in holy service, and be not bound to the arbitrary rule of any mortal.

Whenever human rulers usurp divine authority, and exploit the people, those tyrants' hearts are hardened, their own arrogance writes their doom.

Therefore we will never be discouraged nor dismayed when unrighteous powers rise up to destroy us.

Though enemy hosts pursue us, we shall remember how our ancestors were saved at the Sea of Reeds.

We therefore repeat the words of triumph with which they gave thanks for their deliverance: 1945 Reconstructionist Prayer Book (Adapted)

(Congregation sings מי כמכה, *page 727)*

COMMENTARY. Two beautiful *berahot* complete the liturgical framework of the Shema in the evening service. The first of these is called *Ge'ulah*— "Redemption." Recalling the Exodus from Egypt, it thematically echoes the third paragraph of the Shema. Moreover, it identifies the sovereign God, named in the Shema's credo, as the power that freed Israel from slavery. Its vivid, here-and-now recollection of the escape from Egyptian bondage invites and challenges Israel to claim the redemption as a personal experience in each generation and to hear echoes of that ancient triumph over tyranny in each modern-day struggle for freedom, in every attempt to move toward the messianic future.   S.S.

גַּם בְּדוֹר יְתוֹמִים
לֹא עֲזָבוּנוּ חֲסָדָיו
וַיְקַבֵּץ נִדָּחֵינוּ מִקְצוֹת תֵּבֵל:
כְּאָז גַּם עַתָּה
מוֹצִיא אֶת עַמּוֹ יִשְׂרָאֵל
מִכַּף כָּל אוֹיְבָיו
לְחֵרוּת עוֹלָם:
הַמַּעֲבִיר בָּנָיו בֵּין גִּזְרֵי יַם סוּף
שָׁם רָאוּ אֶת גְּבוּרָתוֹ
שִׁבְּחוּ וְהוֹדוּ לִשְׁמוֹ
וּמַלְכוּתוֹ בְרָצוֹן קִבְּלוּ עֲלֵיהֶם:

מֹשֶׁה וּמִרְיָם וּבְנֵי יִשְׂרָאֵל לְךָ עָנוּ שִׁירָה בְּשִׂמְחָה רַבָּה וְאָמְרוּ כֻלָּם:

DERASH. Rabbi Judah said: [At the sea] each tribe said to the other, "You go into the sea first!" As they stood there bickering, Naḥshon ben Aminadav jumped into the water. Meanwhile Moses was praying. God said to him, "My friend is drowning—and you pray!" "What can I do?" Moses asked. [God responded as it says in the text,] "Speak to the people of Israel and tell them to go! Raise your staff...."   Talmud Sotah 37a

NOTE. Biblical references include Job 9:10, Psalms 66:9.

"Who among the mighty can compare
to you, WISE ONE?
Who can compare to you,
adorned in holiness,
awesome in praises,
acting wondrously!"

Your children saw you in your majesty,
splitting the sea in front of Moses.
"This is my God!" they cried, and said:

"THE HOLY ONE will reign forever!"

And it was said:

"Yes, THE REDEEMING ONE has rescued Jacob,
saved him
from a power
stronger than his own!"

Blessed are you, THE GUARDIAN, Israel's redeeming power!

When our ancestors
beheld these truths
they proclaimed:
Among all the gods
we can name,
who can compare to the
One Beyond Naming?

Among all the quantities
we can label, number,
mark and measure,
which compares to the
Mystery
at the Heart of Reality?

R.M.S.

פדה יהוה את יעקב וגאלו מיד חזק ממנו / The Redeeming One has rescued
Jacob, saved him from a power stronger than his own. Traditional
commentators differ about which event in the life of Jacob the verse
describes. I believe it is the nocturnal struggle from which Jacob emerges
limping but alive, the wrestle from which he emerges with the new name
"Israel." Our own struggles echo those of Jacob. Our formidable
adversary, the rabbis teach, is our *yetzer hara*, our "evil inclination." Often
this power seems "stronger than our own impulse to do good." How then
to resist, to survive, to triumph? Through faith in the redeeming power
that enables us to transcend who we are now and to strive for what we
may yet become! R.H.

מִי־כָמֹכָה בָּאֵלִם יהוה מִי כָּמֹכָה נֶאְדָּר בַּקֹּדֶשׁ
נוֹרָא תְהִלֹּת עֹשֵׂה פֶלֶא:
מַלְכוּתְךָ רָאוּ בָנֶיךָ בּוֹקֵעַ יָם לִפְנֵי מֹשֶׁה זֶה אֵלִי עָנוּ וְאָמְרוּ:
יהוה יִמְלֹךְ לְעֹלָם וָעֶד:
וְנֶאֱמַר: כִּי־פָדָה יהוה אֶת־יַעֲקֹב וּגְאָלוֹ מִיַּד חָזָק מִמֶּנּוּ: בָּרוּךְ אַתָּה
יהוה גָּאַל יִשְׂרָאֵל:

Mi ḥamoḥah ba'elim adonay.
Mi kamoḥah nedar bakodesh
nora tehilot osey fele.
Malḥuteḥa ra'u vaneḥa boke'a yam lifney mosheh.
Zeh eli anu ve'ameru.
Adonay yimloḥ le'olam va'ed.
Vene'emar ki fadah adonay et ya'akov ugalo miyad ḥazak
mimenu.
Baruḥ atah adonay ga'al yisra'el.

COMMENTARY. This *maḥzor* reinstates reference to the splitting of the sea
as a sign of God's redeeming power. The earlier Reconstructionist
prayerbook omitted that reference because of its emphasis on supernatural
intervention. As myth, however, the ancient tale of wonder underscores
the sense of daily miracle in our lives. Even those of us who cannot affirm
a God who intervenes in the natural process, and thus cannot accept the
literal meaning of the tale, can appreciate its human message. According to
the *midrash*, the sea did not split until one Israelite, Naḥshon ben
Aminadav, had the courage to walk upright into the water. Perhaps it was
the divine spirit in Naḥshon, rather than the magic of Moses' wand, that
caused the sea to split.   A.G.

NOTE. Biblical references include Exodus 15:11, 18 and Jeremiah 31:11.

בָּרוּךְ אַתָּה יהוה הַפּוֹרֵשׂ סֻכַּת שָׁלוֹם

HASHKIVENU / DIVINE HELP

Transliteration and commentary follow on pages 731-732.

Help us to lie down, DEAR ONE, our God, in peace, and let us rise again, our sovereign, to life. Spread over us the shelter of your peace. Decree for us a worthy daily lot, and redeem us for the sake of your great name, and enfold us in the wings of your protection, for you are our redeeming guardian. Truly, a sovereign, gracious, and compassionate God are you. Guard our going forth each day for life and peace, now and always. Spread over us the shelter of your peace.

Blessed are you, COMPASSIONATE ONE, who spreads your canopy of peace over all your people Israel and over Jerusalem.

הַשְׁכִּיבֵנוּ

Transliteration and commentary follow on pages 731-732.

הַשְׁכִּיבֵנוּ יהוה אֱלֹהֵינוּ לְשָׁלוֹם וְהַעֲמִידֵנוּ מַלְכֵּנוּ לְחַיִּים וּפְרוֹשׂ
עָלֵינוּ סֻכַּת שְׁלוֹמֶךָ: וְתַקְּנֵנוּ בְּעֵצָה טוֹבָה מִלְּפָנֶיךָ וְהוֹשִׁיעֵנוּ לְמַעַן
שְׁמֶךָ: וּבְצֵל כְּנָפֶיךָ תַּסְתִּירֵנוּ כִּי אֵל שׁוֹמְרֵנוּ וּמַצִּילֵנוּ אָתָּה כִּי אֵל
מֶלֶךְ חַנּוּן וְרַחוּם אָתָּה: וּשְׁמֹר צֵאתֵנוּ וּבוֹאֵנוּ לְחַיִּים וּלְשָׁלוֹם
מֵעַתָּה וְעַד עוֹלָם: וּפְרוֹשׂ עָלֵינוּ סֻכַּת שְׁלוֹמֶךָ:

בָּרוּךְ אַתָּה יהוה הַפּוֹרֵשׂ סֻכַּת שָׁלוֹם עָלֵינוּ וְעַל כָּל־עַמּוֹ יִשְׂרָאֵל
וְעַל יְרוּשָׁלָיִם:

COMMENTARY. *Hashkivenu* / Help us lie down [in peace]—is the final prescribed part of the Shema. It recalls the Shema by expressing the hope that we will "lie down...in peace" and "rise again...to life." An extension of *Emet Ve'emunah*, *Hashkivenu* joins the vivid recollection of past redemption to a prayer for present protection and future peace. By calling God "guardian" and "protector" but also "redeemer," Israel recognizes new dimensions of the power that makes for freedom. The final acknowledgment of God as the one who "spreads the sukkah of peace over us, over Israel, and over Jerusalem" conjures up a future time when Israel, its people, and its holy city will dwell in peace. The blessing is unique to the evening service. Perhaps responding to the cold, dark uncertainty of night, we invoke God's dwelling of peace.   S.S.

KAVANAH. Enable us, God, to behold meaning in the chaos of life about us and purpose in the chaos of life within us. Deliver us from the sense of futility in our strivings toward the light and the truth. Give us strength to ride safely through the maelstrom of petty cares and anxieties. May we behold things in their proper proportions and see life in its wholeness and its holiness.   M.M.K. (Adapted)

NOTE. For our ancestors, the future of Jerusalem was not just about the future of the Jewish people. Jerusalem, in the biblical vision, will become the capital of the whole world. Praying for the peace of Jerusalem is the same as praying for the unity of all humanity and peace throughout the world.   D.A.T.

COMMENTARY. The version presented here follows certain Sephardic versions by deleting the series of petitions for protection. Such petition is considered inappropriate on Shabbat and holidays, days of fulfillment and appreciation for the many blessings we have. These days are themselves a sukkah of peace. We pray that real and complete peace be the lot of Israel and Jerusalem, so torn by strife in recent memory. Our tradition sees Jerusalem as the center of the world. Creation began there, according to the rabbis. So may the peace that begins there radiate forth and bless all earth's peoples. The peace of Jerusalem, the "heart of the world," is also the peace of every human heart.   A.G.

Hashkivenu adonay eloheynu leshalom veha'amidenu malkenu
lehayim ufros aleynu sukkat shelomeha. Vetakenenu ve'etzah
tovah milefaneha vehoshi'enu lema'an shemeha. Uevtzel
kenafeha tastirenu ki el shomrenu umatzilenu atah ki el
meleh hanun verahum atah. Ushmor tzeytenu uvo'enu
lehayim uleshalom me'atah ve'ad olam. Ufros aleynu sukkat
shelomeha. Baruh atah adonay hapores sukkat shalom aleynu
ve'al kol amo yisra'el ve'al yerushalayim.

KAVANAH. On Yom Kippur we say the everyday *Hashkivenu*, though on this
awe-filled night it has added meaning. The fears and terrors of our
exposed hearts are added to our natural primordial night-fears. Desiring
atonement, we have just opened our hearts before the stern Judge. In
Hashkivenu, we ask that same merciful Judge, in the same words we use
every day, to "spread the canopy of peace" in order that we may "lie down
in peace" on this night of nights, and that we, who are judged this night,
will "awaken to life."   E.M.

When fears multiply
And danger threatens;
When sickness comes,
When death confronts us—
It is God's blessing of shalom
That sustains us
And upholds us.
Lightening our burden,
Dispelling our worry,
Restoring our strength,
Renewing our hope—
Reviving us.   H.M.

On Friday evening, add this paragraph:

VESHAMERU / OBSERVING SHABBAT

Let Israel's descendants keep Shabbat, making Shabbat throughout all their generations, as an eternal bond. Between me and Israel's descendants shall it be a sign eternally. For in six days THE FASHIONER OF ALL made skies and earth, and on the seventh day God ceased and drew a breath of rest.

MAKING ATONEMENT/
YOM KIPPUR PURIFICATION

For on this day, atonement shall be made for you, to make you clean from all of your wrongdoings. Before THE FOUNT OF MERCY, you shall all be clean.

KAVANAH. Yom Kippur reenacts the yearly rituals that achieved atonement in biblical times. Something is really supposed to happen on this day. Can we open our beings to the possibility of a spiritual cleansing, a moral death and rebirth, a true letting go of hurtful patterns and habits that besmirch our relationship with self, others and the world? What is our hope for this day?

S.P.W.

יכפר עליכם /atonement shall be made for you. This brief quotation from Leviticus 16:30 is followed in the Torah by the words "And the *kohen*/priest...shall make atonement." (Leviticus 16:32). Today, in the absence of the priesthood and the cultic rituals of cleansing, each Jew becomes a priest. Only through your own actions "shall atonement be made for you."

R.H.

On Friday evening, add this paragraph:

וְשָׁמְרוּ

וְשָׁמְרוּ בְנֵי־יִשְׂרָאֵל אֶת־הַשַּׁבָּת לַעֲשׂוֹת אֶת־הַשַּׁבָּת לְדֹרֹתָם בְּרִית
עוֹלָם: בֵּינִי וּבֵין בְּנֵי יִשְׂרָאֵל אוֹת הִיא לְעוֹלָם כִּי־שֵׁשֶׁת יָמִים עָשָׂה
יהוה אֶת־הַשָּׁמַיִם וְאֶת־הָאָרֶץ וּבַיּוֹם הַשְּׁבִיעִי שָׁבַת וַיִּנָּפַשׁ:

Veshameru veney yisra'el et hashabbat
la'asot et hashabbat ledorotam berit olam.
Beyni uveyn beney yisra'el ot hi le'olam.
Ki sheshet yamim asah adonay et hashamayim ve'et ha'aretz
uvayom hashevi'i shavat vayinafash.

יְכַפֵּר עֲלֵיכֶם

כִּי־בַיּוֹם הַזֶּה יְכַפֵּר עֲלֵיכֶם לְטַהֵר אֶתְכֶם
מִכֹּל חַטֹּאתֵיכֶם לִפְנֵי יהוה תִּטְהָרוּ:

Ki vayom hazeh yehaper aleyhem letaher et'hem
mikol hatoteyhem lifney adonay tit'haru.

וְשָׁמְרוּ...וַיִּנָּפַשׁ / Let...rest (Exodus 31:16-17).
כִּי...תִּטְהָרוּ / For...clean (Leviticus 16:30).

ḤATZI KADDISH / SHORT KADDISH

Reader: Let God's name be made great and holy in the world that was created as God willed. May God complete the holy realm in your own lifetime, in your days, and in the days of all the house of Israel, quickly and soon. And say: Amen.

Congregation: May God's great name be blessed, forever and as long as worlds endure.

Reader: May it be blessed, and praised, and glorified, and held in honor, viewed with awe, embellished, and revered; and may the blessed name of holiness be hailed, though it be higher by far than all the blessings, songs, praises, and consolations that we utter in this world. And say: Amen.

COMMENTARY. Holiness is the quality or value that things or persons have when they help people to become fully human.   M.M.K. (Adapted)

COMMENTARY. During this season of the year, we struggle with images of God as judge and sovereign even as we see God as source of forgiveness and return. The repetition at this time of year of the word לעלא / *higher by far* reminds us that only true change on our part can reach through the many intervening layers to reconnect us with the divine in ourselves and in our world. The liturgical repetition also reminds us how important, powerful, and redeeming that reconnection can be. "Go higher!" "Settle for nothing less!" It beckons us not to quit during the effortful climb. Real change is not easy, but saving our lives depends on it.   D.A.T.

חֲצִי קַדִּישׁ

יִתְגַּדַּל וְיִתְקַדַּשׁ שְׁמֵהּ רַבָּא בְּעָלְמָא דִּי בְרָא כִרְעוּתֵהּ וְיַמְלִיךְ
מַלְכוּתֵהּ בְּחַיֵּיכוֹן וּבְיוֹמֵיכוֹן וּבְחַיֵּי דְכָל בֵּית יִשְׂרָאֵל בַּעֲגָלָא וּבִזְמַן
קָרִיב וְאִמְרוּ אָמֵן:
יְהֵא שְׁמֵהּ רַבָּא מְבָרַךְ לְעָלַם וּלְעָלְמֵי עָלְמַיָּא:
יִתְבָּרַךְ וְיִשְׁתַּבַּח וְיִתְפָּאַר וְיִתְרוֹמַם וְיִתְנַשֵּׂא וְיִתְהַדָּר וְיִתְעַלֶּה
וְיִתְהַלָּל שְׁמֵהּ דְּקֻדְשָׁא בְּרִיךְ הוּא
לְעֵלָּא לְעֵלָּא מִכָּל בִּרְכָתָא וְשִׁירָתָא תֻּשְׁבְּחָתָא וְנֶחֱמָתָא דַּאֲמִירָן
בְּעָלְמָא וְאִמְרוּ אָמֵן:

Reader: Yitgadal veyitkadash shemey raba
be'alma divra ḥirutey veyamliḥ malḥutey
behayeyḥon uvyomeyḥon uvḥayey deḥol beyt yisra'el
ba'agala uvizman kariv ve'imru amen.

Congregation: Yehey shemey raba mevaraḥ le'alam
                ulalmey almaya.

Reader: Yitbaraḥ veyishtabaḥ veyitpa'ar veyitromam
veyitnasey veyit-hadar veyitaleh veyit-halal
shemey dekudsha beriḥ hu
le'ela le'ela mikol birḥata veshirata
tushbeḥata veneḥemata da'amiran be'alma ve'imru amen.

May the words of my mouth and the longing of my heart be acceptable to you, God... לְפָנֶיךָ יְהֹוָה צוּרִי...

הַשְּׁעָרִים נִפְתָּחִין
The gates are open,
בְּכָל־שָׁעָה
in every hour;
וְכָל־מִי שֶׁמְּבַקֵּשׁ לִיכָּנֵס
and whoever seeks to enter
תִּכָּנֵס:
may come in.

שִׁוִּיתִי
יְהֹוָה

Remember us for life

Let hope enliven all who seek you and let all who look to you with hope find strength to speak

Find words in you to offer and return to THE COMPASSIONATE.

You know, the universe's mystery

AMIDAH

The traditional Amidah follows here. Meditations begin on page 1. The Amidah is traditionally recited while standing, beginning with three short steps forward and bowing left and right, a reminder of our entry into the divine presence.

Open my lips, BELOVED ONE,
and let my mouth declare your praise.

1. AVOT VE'IMOT / ANCESTORS

Blessed are you, THE ANCIENT ONE, our God, God of our ancestors,

God of Abraham   God of Sarah
God of Isaac   God of Rebekah
God of Jacob   God of Rachel
                           and God of Leah;

COMMENTARY. A. J. Heschel has said, "The term, 'God of Abraham, Isaac and Jacob' is semantically different from a term such as 'the God of truth, goodness, and beauty.' Abraham, Isaac and Jacob do not signify ideas, principles or abstract values. Nor do they stand for teachers or thinkers, and the term is not to be understood like that of 'the God of Kant, Hegel and Schelling.' Abraham, Isaac and Jacob are not principles to be comprehended but lives to be continued. The life of one who joins the covenant of Abraham continues the life of Abraham. For the present is not apart from the past. 'Abraham is still standing before God' (Genesis 18:22). Abraham endures forever. We are Abraham, Isaac and Jacob." In this same spirit, we are also Sarah and Rebekah, Rachel and Leah.   L.W.K.

KAVANAH. The introductory words (Psalms 51:17) of the Amidah contain a paradox of divine and human power. Our ability to be whole, upright, free, and fully alive grows as we acknowledge and appreciate an infinitely higher source of power in the universe. This allows us to be receptive. By acknowledging our human vulnerability, we open our hearts to the support, compassion and faithfulness available around us.   S.P.W.

KAVANAH. Silence can come from a breakdown in communication or from an intimacy that makes other forms of communication temporarily unnecessary. Let our silence say what words can't express. Let us use this silent prayer-time as an opportunity to meet the divine presence, to experience God's cosmic power and awe-inspiring, fathomless depth. S.D.R.

The traditional Amidah follows here. Meditations begin on page 1. The Amidah is traditionally recited while standing, beginning with three short steps forward and bowing left and right, a reminder of our entry into the divine presence.

אֲדֹנָי שְׂפָתַי תִּפְתָּח וּפִי יַגִּיד תְּהִלָּתֶֽךָ:

 אָבוֹת וְאִמּוֹת

בָּרוּךְ אַתָּה יהוה אֱלֹהֵֽינוּ וֵאלֹהֵי אֲבוֹתֵֽינוּ וְאִמּוֹתֵֽינוּ

אֱלֹהֵי שָׂרָה	אֱלֹהֵי אַבְרָהָם
אֱלֹהֵי רִבְקָה	אֱלֹהֵי יִצְחָק
אֱלֹהֵי רָחֵל	אֱלֹהֵי יַעֲקֹב
וֵאלֹהֵי לֵאָה: ←	

DERASH. So often the power of our lips is limited by our fears and self-doubt. When we say "Open our lips," we are also saying, "God, help me to open up and see beyond my current limits, so that I can recognize and accept the myriad of possibilities in my life."   D.B.

NOTE. The traditional liturgy evolved gradually. It contains thousands of variant or alternative versions. Reconstructionist liturgy has eliminated reference to traditional beliefs that Jews are the Chosen People, that there is individual reward and punishment, that the Temple should be rebuilt, that there will be a personal Messiah and that there will be bodily resurrection. The Reconstructionist commitment to equality for women has resulted in additional changes. Our understanding of God as the Source of goodness, the Life of nature, and the Power that makes for salvation replaces some more anthropomorphic and anthropopathic traditional imagery.   D.A.T.

אדוני...תהלתך/Open...praise (Psalms 51:17).

great, heroic, awesome God, supreme divinity,
imparting deeds of kindness, begetter of all;
mindful of the loyalty of Israel's ancestors,
bringing, with love, redemption to their children's children
for the sake of the divine name.

Remember us for life,
sovereign who wishes us to live,
and write us in the Book of Life,
for your sake, ever-living God.

Regal One, our help, salvation, and protector:
Blessed are you, KIND ONE,
the shield of Abraham and help of Sarah. ↵

עזרת שרה / *ezrat sarah*. The biblical term *ezer* has two meanings, "rescue"
and "be strong." It is commonly translated as "aid" or "help." It also has
the sense of power and strength. In Deuteronomy 33:29, *ezer* is parallel to
גאוה, majesty. Eve is described as Adam's *ezer kenegdo*, a power equal to
him, a strength and majesty to match his. Thus *magen avraham* (shield of
Abraham) and *ezrat sarah* (help of Sarah) are parallel images of power and
protection.

R.S.A.

KAVANAH. God is experienced as עוזר / helper, every time our thought of
God furnishes us an escape from the sense of frustration and supplies us
with a feeling of permanence in the midst of universal flux.

M.M.K. (Adapted)

DERASH. *Ḥayim*, the Hebrew word for life, is a plural noun. We seek life
brimming with fullness. Our resentments and hatreds, our lies and games
lead us to forget how rich and varied our lives can be. To be written in the
book of life refers to our participation in the ever changing, birthing and
passing, gaining and losing moments that compose life. S.P.W.

KAVANAH. Is the book of life a ledger, in which we settle for being
mentioned? Or is it a book of living, in which we write our chapter by
living our story?

R.H.

הָאֵל הַגָּדוֹל הַגִּבּוֹר וְהַנּוֹרָא אֵל עֶלְיוֹן גּוֹמֵל חֲסָדִים טוֹבִים וְקוֹנֵה
הַכֹּל וְזוֹכֵר חַסְדֵי אָבוֹת וְאִמּוֹת וּמֵבִיא גְאֻלָּה לִבְנֵי בְנֵיהֶם לְמַעַן
שְׁמוֹ בְּאַהֲבָה:

זָכְרֵנוּ לְחַיִּים מֶלֶךְ חָפֵץ בַּחַיִּים וְכָתְבֵנוּ בְּסֵפֶר הַחַיִּים לְמַעַנְךָ אֱלֹהִים
חַיִּים:

מֶלֶךְ עוֹזֵר וּמוֹשִׁיעַ וּמָגֵן: בָּרוּךְ אַתָּה יהוה מָגֵן אַבְרָהָם וְעֶזְרַת
שָׂרָה: ←

In each age
we receive and transmit
Torah.
At each moment
we are addressed by the
World.
In each age
we are challenged
by our ancient teaching.
At each moment
we stand face to Face with
Truth.
In each age
we add our wisdom
to that which has gone before.
At each moment
the knowing heart
is filled with wonder.
In each age
the children of Torah
become its builders
and seek to set the world firm
on a foundation of Truth.

R.M.S.

2. GEVUROT / DIVINE POWER

You are forever powerful, ALMIGHTY ONE, abundant in your saving acts. You send down the dew. In loyalty you sustain the living, nurturing the life of every living thing, upholding those who fall, healing the sick, freeing the captive, and remaining faithful to all life held dormant in the earth. Who can compare to you, almighty God, who can resemble you, the source of life and death, who makes salvation grow?

Who can compare to you, source of all mercy, remembering all creatures mercifully, decreeing life!

Faithful are you in giving life to every living thing. Blessed are you, THE FOUNT OF LIFE, who gives and renews life.

3. KEDUSHAT HASHEM / HALLOWING GOD'S NAME

Holy are you. Your name is holy.
And all holy beings hail you each day.⤺

DERASH. The *maḥzor* proclaims God as *memit umeḥayeh* / source of life and death. What is Yom Kippur, after all, if not a day of death and rebirth? And what is God, after all, if not the Power that enables what has died—our hopes, our dreams, our plans—to come back to life? Thus God is called *Elohim ḥayim* / God of Life! R.H.

ב 2 גְּבוּרוֹת

אַתָּה גִבּוֹר לְעוֹלָם אֲדֹנָי רַב לְהוֹשִׁיעַ: מוֹרִיד הַטָּל: מְכַלְכֵּל חַיִּים בְּחֶסֶד מְחַיֶּה כָּל חַי בְּרַחֲמִים רַבִּים סוֹמֵךְ נוֹפְלִים וְרוֹפֵא חוֹלִים וּמַתִּיר אֲסוּרִים וּמְקַיֵּם אֱמוּנָתוֹ לִישֵׁנֵי עָפָר: מִי כָמוֹךָ בַּעַל גְּבוּרוֹת וּמִי דּוֹמֶה לָּךְ מֶלֶךְ מֵמִית וּמְחַיֶּה וּמַצְמִיחַ יְשׁוּעָה:

מִי כָמוֹךָ אַב הָרַחֲמִים זוֹכֵר יְצוּרָיו לְחַיִּים בְּרַחֲמִים:

וְנֶאֱמָן אַתָּה לְהַחֲיוֹת כָּל חָי: בָּרוּךְ אַתָּה יהוה מְחַיֵּה כָּל חָי:

ג 3 קְדֻשַּׁת הַשֵּׁם

אַתָּה קָדוֹשׁ וְשִׁמְךָ קָדוֹשׁ וּקְדוֹשִׁים בְּכָל יוֹם יְהַלְלוּךָ סֶּלָה: ←

מחיה כל חי/who gives and renews life. The traditional *maḥzor* affirms מחיה מתים/reviving of the dead. We substitute כל חי, demonstrating an understanding that all of life is rooted in the world's divine order and avoiding affirmation of bodily resurrection. We cannot know what happens to us after we die, but we can, by our thought and action, affirm the possibility of this-worldly salvation.   D.A.T.

מחיה כל חי/who gives and renews life. All the vast powers of the universe are rooted in the divine. In the face of that vast power we feel small and vulnerable. We fear death. But that power also contains the possibility of life and renewal. In celebrating this Power, we waken again to life. S.P.W.

And therefore, HOLY ONE, let awe of you
infuse the whole of your Creation,
and let knowledge of your presence
dwell in all your creatures.
And let every being worship you,
and each created life pay homage to your rule.
Let all of them, as one, enact your bidding
with a whole and peaceful heart.
For we have always known, ALMIGHTY ONE,
that all authority to rule belongs to you,
all strength is rooted in your arm,
all mighty deeds have emanated from your hand.
Your name alone is the source of awe
that surges through all life.

And therefore, HOLY ONE, let awe of you
infuse your people, let the praise of you
ring out from all who worship you.
Let hope enliven all who seek you,
and let all who look to you with hope
find strength to speak.
Grant joy throughout your land,
let happiness resound throughout your holy city,
soon, and in our days.

And therefore, let the just behold your peace,
let them rejoice,
let all who follow in your path sing out with joy,
let all who love you dance in celebration,
and may your power overwhelm all treachery,
so that it vanish wholly from the earth like smoke.
Then shall the power of injustice pass away! ↵

וּבְכֵן תֵּן פַּחְדְּךָ יהוה אֱלֹהֵינוּ עַל כָּל־מַעֲשֶׂיךָ וְאֵימָתְךָ עַל כָּל־מַה־שֶּׁבָּרָאתָ וְיִירָאוּךָ כָּל־הַמַּעֲשִׂים וְיִשְׁתַּחֲווּ לְפָנֶיךָ כָּל־הַבְּרוּאִים וְיֵעָשׂוּ כֻלָּם אֲגֻדָּה אַחַת לַעֲשׂוֹת רְצוֹנְךָ בְּלֵבָב שָׁלֵם כְּמוֹ שֶׁיָּדַעְנוּ יהוה אֱלֹהֵינוּ שֶׁהַשִּׁלְטוֹן לְפָנֶיךָ עֹז בְּיָדְךָ וּגְבוּרָה בִּימִינֶךָ וְשִׁמְךָ נוֹרָא עַל כָּל־מַה־שֶּׁבָּרָאתָ:

וּבְכֵן תֵּן כָּבוֹד יהוה לְעַמֶּךָ תְּהִלָּה לִירֵאֶיךָ וְתִקְוָה לְדוֹרְשֶׁיךָ וּפִתְחוֹן פֶּה לַמְיַחֲלִים לָךְ שִׂמְחָה לְאַרְצֶךָ וְשָׂשׂוֹן לְעִירֶךָ בִּמְהֵרָה בְיָמֵינוּ:

וּבְכֵן צַדִּיקִים יִרְאוּ וְיִשְׂמָחוּ וִישָׁרִים יַעֲלֹזוּ וַחֲסִידִים בְּרִנָּה יָגִילוּ וְעוֹלָתָה תִּקְפָּץ־פִּיהָ וְכָל־הָרִשְׁעָה כֻּלָּהּ כְּעָשָׁן תִּכְלֶה כִּי תַעֲבִיר מֶמְשֶׁלֶת זָדוֹן מִן הָאָרֶץ: ←

COMMENTARY. Our text diverges from the traditional text for *uveḥen ten kavod* which continues with a prayer for renewed strength to the seed of David—a clear appeal for the restoration of the Davidic monarchy through a God-chosen Messiah. Most Jews of the modern era do not expect or desire a divinely appointed royal personage to come and solve our problems for us. But in rejecting the *literal* Messiah we do not have to abandon the messianic passion—the commitment of "all who look to you with hope" and "find strength to speak." We need to take responsibility for bringing messianic days by enthusiastically advancing the ideals of human freedom, dignity, and creativity.   S.D.R.

KAVANAH. Sovereignty belongs to the Power that makes for liberation. Maintaining hope in our God depends on our acts as liberators. May we find the courage to speak truth to earthly power. And in struggling against oppressive power, may we find contentment and joy.   J.A.S.

May you alone be sovereign over all of your Creation,
and Mount Zion be the seat and symbol of your glory,
and Jerusalem, your holy city—
as is written in your holy scriptures:
"THE ETERNAL ONE shall reign forever,
your God, O Zion, through all generations!
Halleluyah!"

Holy are you,
and awe-inspiring is your name,
and there is no God apart from you,
as it is written: "THE CREATOR of the hosts of heaven
shall be exalted through the rule of law,
and God, the Holy One, made holy by the reign of justice."
Blessed are you, ETERNAL ONE,
the holy sovereign power.

4. KEDUSHAT HAYOM / THE DAY'S HOLINESS

You have loved us, and have taken pleasure in us,
and have made us holy with your mitzvot,
and you have brought us, sovereign one,
near to your service,
and have called us to the shelter of your great and holy name
and you have given us, ALMIGHTY ONE, our God, in love ↵

ימלך...הללויה / THE ETERNAL ONE...Halleluyah! (Psalms 146).
ויגבה...בצדקה / THE CREATOR...justice (Isaiah 5:16).

וְתִמְלֹךְ אַתָּה יהוה לְבַדֶּךָ עַל כָּל־מַעֲשֶׂיךָ בְּהַר צִיּוֹן מִשְׁכַּן כְּבוֹדֶךָ וּבִירוּשָׁלַיִם עִיר קָדְשֶׁךָ: כַּכָּתוּב בְּדִבְרֵי קָדְשֶׁךָ: יִמְלֹךְ יהוה לְעוֹלָם אֱלֹהַיִךְ צִיּוֹן לְדֹר וָדֹר הַלְלוּיָהּ:

קָדוֹשׁ אַתָּה וְנוֹרָא שְׁמֶךָ וְאֵין אֱלוֹהַּ מִבַּלְעָדֶיךָ: כַּכָּתוּב: וַיִּגְבַּהּ יהוה צְבָאוֹת בַּמִּשְׁפָּט וְהָאֵל הַקָּדוֹשׁ נִקְדַּשׁ בִּצְדָקָה: בָּרוּךְ אַתָּה יהוה הַמֶּלֶךְ הַקָּדוֹשׁ:

4 קְדֻשַּׁת הַיּוֹם

אַתָּה אֲהַבְתָּנוּ וְרָצִיתָ בָּנוּ וְקִדַּשְׁתָּנוּ בְּמִצְוֹתֶיךָ וְקֵרַבְתָּנוּ מַלְכֵּנוּ לַעֲבוֹדָתֶךָ. וְשִׁמְךָ הַגָּדוֹל וְהַקָּדוֹשׁ עָלֵינוּ קָרָאתָ: וַתִּתֶּן לָנוּ יהוה אֱלֹהֵינוּ בְּאַהֲבָה ←

COMMENTARY. If God is One and God of all, how can this universal Presence reside, as it were, in the particular place of the Jewish people, Mount Zion? Religion is not an abstract idea, but a lived reality, requiring a people, a place, and a program. To speak of religion in general is like speaking of language in general; one can only speak a given language, not language itself. Similarly, each people needs to translate the universal intuition of the Divine into the particular words, places, rituals, and concepts of its own religion.   R.H.

On Shabbat add the words in parenthesis:

This day of (Shabbat for holiness and for rest
and this Day of) Atonement,
for pardoning, forgiveness, and atonement,
on which you pardon us for all of our transgressions
(with love), a holy convocation,
a remembrance of the going-out from Egypt.

Our God, our ancients' God, may our prayer arise and come to
you, and be beheld, and be acceptable. Let it be heard, acted
upon, remembered—the memory of us and all our needs, the
memory of our ancestors, the memory of messianic hopes, the
memory of Jerusalem your holy city, and the memory of all your
kin, the house of Israel, all surviving in your presence. Act for
goodness and grace, for love and care; for life, well-being and
peace, on this Day of Atonement.

Remember us this day, ALL-KNOWING ONE, our God, for
goodness. Favor us this day with blessing. Preserve us this day
for life. With your redeeming, nurturing word, be kind and
generous. Act tenderly on our behalf, and grant us victory over
all our trials. Truly, our eyes turn toward you, for you are a
providing God; gracious and merciful are you.

Our God, our ancients' God,
forgive us our transgressions,
this day (of Shabbat, and Day) of Atonement,
blot out and cause to pass away
our wrongdoings and our errors
from before your eyes, as it is said:
"I, yes I, shall be the one
who blots out your wrongdoing, for my sake;
your errors I shall not remember any more!" ↵

אֶת יוֹם (הַשַּׁבָּת הַזֶּה וְלִקְדֻשָׁה וְלִמְנוּחָה וְאֶת יוֹם) הַכִּפּוּרִים הַזֶּה
לִמְחִילָה וְלִסְלִיחָה וּלְכַפָּרָה וְלִמְחָל־בּוֹ אֶת כָּל עֲוֹנוֹתֵינוּ (בְּאַהֲבָה)
מִקְרָא קֹדֶשׁ זֵכֶר לִיצִיאַת מִצְרָיִם:

אֱלֹהֵינוּ וֵאלֹהֵי אֲבוֹתֵינוּ וְאִמּוֹתֵינוּ יַעֲלֶה וְיָבוֹא וְיַגִּיעַ וְיֵרָאֶה וְיֵרָצֶה
וְיִשָּׁמַע וְיִפָּקֵד וְיִזָּכֵר זִכְרוֹנֵנוּ וּפִקְדוֹנֵנוּ וְזִכְרוֹן אֲבוֹתֵינוּ וְאִמּוֹתֵינוּ
וְזִכְרוֹן יְמוֹת הַמָּשִׁיחַ וְזִכְרוֹן יְרוּשָׁלַיִם עִיר קָדְשֶׁךָ וְזִכְרוֹן כָּל עַמְּךָ
בֵּית יִשְׂרָאֵל לְפָנֶיךָ לִפְלֵיטָה וּלְטוֹבָה לְחֵן וּלְחֶסֶד וּלְרַחֲמִים לְחַיִּים
וּלְשָׁלוֹם בְּיוֹם הַכִּפּוּרִים הַזֶּה:

זָכְרֵנוּ יהוה אֱלֹהֵינוּ בּוֹ לְטוֹבָה: וּפָקְדֵנוּ לִבְרָכָה וְהוֹשִׁיעֵנוּ בּוֹ
לְחַיִּים: וּבִדְבַר יְשׁוּעָה וְרַחֲמִים חוּס וְחָנֵּנוּ וְרַחֵם עָלֵינוּ וְהוֹשִׁיעֵנוּ
כִּי אֵלֶיךָ עֵינֵינוּ כִּי אֵל מֶלֶךְ חַנּוּן וְרַחוּם אָתָּה:

אֱלֹהֵינוּ וֵאלֹהֵי אֲבוֹתֵינוּ וְאִמּוֹתֵינוּ מְחַל לַעֲוֹנוֹתֵינוּ בְּיוֹם (הַשַּׁבָּת
הַזֶּה וּבְיוֹם) הַכִּפּוּרִים הַזֶּה: מְחֵה וְהַעֲבֵר פְּשָׁעֵינוּ וְחַטֹּאתֵינוּ מִנֶּגֶד
עֵינֶיךָ: כָּאָמוּר: אָנֹכִי אָנֹכִי הוּא מֹחֶה פְשָׁעֶיךָ לְמַעֲנִי וְחַטֹּאתֶיךָ לֹא
אֶזְכֹּר: ←

זכר ליציאת מצרים/a remembrance of the going-out from Egypt. The
Pilgrimage Festivals are obviously tied to the exodus from Egypt and the
wandering in the desert. But why connect Shabbat or Yom Kippur with
the exodus? Because the very existence of these holy days depended on the
Israelites going forth from Egypt. Each Shabbat, each Yom Kippur, is a
moment in time to appreciate our freedom to seek God and to do the
divine will. So it is that our observance today renews our gratitude and
reconnects us to our history of redemption.   D.A.T.

אנכי...אזכר/I, yes...more! (Isaiah 43:25).

And it is said: "I have made your sins
vanish like a stormcloud,
and, like a mist, the things you have done wrong.
Return to me, for it is I who have redeemed you!"
And it is said: "For on this day,
atonement shall be made for you,
to make you clean from all of your wrongdoings.
Before THE FOUNT OF MERCY, you shall all be clean."

Our God, our ancients' God (take pleasure in our rest),
enable us to realize holiness with your mitzvot,
give us our portion in your Torah,
let us enjoy the good things of your world,
and gladden us with your salvation,
(and help us to perpetuate, ETERNAL ONE, our God,
your holy Shabbat, with love and joy,
and let all Israel, and all who treat your name as holy,
rest upon this day,) and refine our hearts
to serve you truthfully.
For you are a forgiving God to Israel,
and compassionate to all the tribes of Yeshurun
in each and every generation,
and apart from you we have no sovereign,
none full of compassion and forgiveness,
except you.
Blessed are you, FORGIVING ONE,
sovereign of mercy and forgiveness
for our wrongdoings and for those
of all your kin, the house of Israel,
you who make our guilt to pass away,
year after year,
the sovereign power over all the earth
who raises up to holiness
(Shabbat,) the people Israel
and the Day of Atonement.

וְנֶאֱמַר: מָחִיתִי כָעָב פְּשָׁעֶיךָ וְכֶעָנָן חַטֹּאותֶיךָ שׁוּבָה אֵלַי כִּי גְאַלְתִּיךָ: וְנֶאֱמַר: כִּי בַיּוֹם הַזֶּה יְכַפֵּר עֲלֵיכֶם לְטַהֵר אֶתְכֶם מִכֹּל חַטֹּאתֵיכֶם לִפְנֵי יהוה תִּטְהָרוּ:

אֱלֹהֵינוּ וֵאלֹהֵי אֲבוֹתֵינוּ וְאִמּוֹתֵינוּ (רְצֵה בִמְנוּחָתֵנוּ) קַדְּשֵׁנוּ בְּמִצְוֹתֶיךָ וְתֵן חֶלְקֵנוּ בְּתוֹרָתֶךָ שַׂבְּעֵנוּ מִטּוּבֶךָ וְשַׂמְּחֵנוּ בִּישׁוּעָתֶךָ (וְהַנְחִילֵנוּ יהוה אֱלֹהֵינוּ בְּאַהֲבָה וּבְרָצוֹן שַׁבַּת קָדְשֶׁךָ וְיָנוּחוּ בָהּ יִשְׂרָאֵל מְקַדְּשֵׁי שְׁמֶךָ) וְטַהֵר לִבֵּנוּ לְעָבְדְּךָ בֶּאֱמֶת כִּי אַתָּה סָלְחָן לְיִשְׂרָאֵל וּמָחֳלָן לְשִׁבְטֵי יְשֻׁרוּן בְּכָל דּוֹר וָדוֹר וּמִבַּלְעָדֶיךָ אֵין לָנוּ מֶלֶךְ מוֹחֵל וְסוֹלֵחַ אֶלָּא אָתָּה: בָּרוּךְ אַתָּה יהוה מֶלֶךְ מוֹחֵל וְסוֹלֵחַ לַעֲוֹנוֹתֵינוּ וְלַעֲוֹנוֹת עַמּוֹ בֵּית יִשְׂרָאֵל וּמַעֲבִיר אַשְׁמוֹתֵינוּ בְּכָל שָׁנָה וְשָׁנָה מֶלֶךְ עַל כָּל הָאָרֶץ מְקַדֵּשׁ (הַשַּׁבָּת וְ) יִשְׂרָאֵל וְיוֹם הַכִּפּוּרִים: ←

ומעביר אשמותינו בכל שנה ושנה / who make our guilt to pass away year after year. Being human means being imperfect. None of us can ever succeed at our goal of living a transgression-free life—not even for a year. And yet, we are not at liberty to abandon that goal. Just imagine the horror of a world inhabited by people who have stopped striving to be good! And so every year we do the best we can. Every year we succeed in new small ways, and sometimes in large ones, at the task of bringing goodness into the world. And every year we fail in small ways, and sometimes in large ones. Every year we must face our errors in order to let go of them. And we can only let go when we find forgiveness. Our guilt passes away as we strive again toward perfection.   D.A.T.

מחיתי...גאלתיך / I have...you! (Isaiah 44:22).

כי ביום...תטהרו / For on...clean (Leviticus 16:30).

5. AVODAH / WORSHIP

Take pleasure, GRACIOUS ONE, our God, in Israel your people; lovingly accept their fervent prayer. May Israel's worship always be acceptable to you.

And may our eyes behold your homecoming, with merciful intent, to Zion. Blessed are you, THE FAITHFUL ONE, who brings your presence home to Zion.

6. HODA'AH / THANKS

We give thanks to you that you are THE ALL-MERCIFUL, our God, God of our ancestors, today and always. A firm, enduring source of life, a shield to us in time of trial, you are ever there, from age to age. We acknowledge you, declare your praise, and thank you for our lives entrusted to your hand, our souls placed in your care, for your miracles that greet us every day, and for your wonders and the good things that are with us every hour, morning, noon, and night. Good One, whose kindness never stops, Kind One, whose loving acts have never failed—always have we placed our hope in you.

For all these things, your name be blessed and raised in honor always, sovereign of ours, forever.

And write down for a good life all who share your covenant.

Let all of life acknowledge you! May all beings praise your name in truth, O God, our rescue and our aid. Blessed are you, THE GRACIOUS ONE, whose name is good, to whom all thanks are due. ↰

רְצֵה יהוה אֱלֹהֵינוּ בְּעַמְּךָ יִשְׂרָאֵל וְלִהַב תְּפִלָּתָם בְּאַהֲבָה תְקַבֵּל בְּרָצוֹן וּתְהִי לְרָצוֹן תָּמִיד עֲבוֹדַת יִשְׂרָאֵל עַמֶּךָ:

וְתֶחֱזֶינָה עֵינֵינוּ בְּשׁוּבְךָ לְצִיּוֹן בְּרַחֲמִים: בָּרוּךְ אַתָּה יהוה הַמַּחֲזִיר שְׁכִינָתוֹ לְצִיּוֹן:

הוֹדָאָה 6

מוֹדִים אֲנַחְנוּ לָךְ שָׁאַתָּה הוּא יהוה אֱלֹהֵינוּ וֵאלֹהֵי אֲבוֹתֵינוּ וְאִמּוֹתֵינוּ לְעוֹלָם וָעֶד צוּר חַיֵּינוּ מָגֵן יִשְׁעֵנוּ אַתָּה הוּא לְדוֹר וָדוֹר: נוֹדֶה לְךָ וּנְסַפֵּר תְּהִלָּתֶךָ עַל חַיֵּינוּ הַמְּסוּרִים בְּיָדֶךָ וְעַל נִשְׁמוֹתֵינוּ הַפְּקוּדוֹת לָךְ וְעַל נִסֶּיךָ שֶׁבְּכָל יוֹם עִמָּנוּ וְעַל נִפְלְאוֹתֶיךָ וְטוֹבוֹתֶיךָ שֶׁבְּכָל־עֵת עֶרֶב וָבֹקֶר וְצָהֳרָיִם: הַטּוֹב כִּי לֹא כָלוּ רַחֲמֶיךָ וְהַמְרַחֵם כִּי לֹא תַמּוּ חֲסָדֶיךָ מֵעוֹלָם קִוִּינוּ לָךְ:

וְעַל כֻּלָּם יִתְבָּרַךְ וְיִתְרוֹמַם שִׁמְךָ מַלְכֵּנוּ תָּמִיד לְעוֹלָם וָעֶד:

וּכְתֹב לְחַיִּים טוֹבִים כָּל־בְּנֵי בְרִיתֶךָ:

וְכֹל הַחַיִּים יוֹדוּךָ סֶּלָה וִיהַלְלוּ אֶת שִׁמְךָ בֶּאֱמֶת הָאֵל יְשׁוּעָתֵנוּ וְעֶזְרָתֵנוּ סֶלָה: בָּרוּךְ אַתָּה יהוה הַטּוֹב שִׁמְךָ וּלְךָ נָאֶה לְהוֹדוֹת: ←

וכתוב לחיים טובים כל בני בריתך/And write down for a good life all who share your covenant. A "good" life? A life of doing good? Feeling good? Being good? With devotional *hutzpah*, our prayer goes beyond the raw request for life over death, and implores God to grant a "good life." In this season, it is our challenge to ask ourselves again what we believe a good life is.

R.H.

During evening service continue below. During all other services continue on page 757.

7. BIRKAT HASHALOM / BLESSING FOR PEACE

Grant abundant peace eternally for Israel, your people. For you are the sovereign source of all peace. So, may it be a good thing in your eyes to bless your people Israel, and all who dwell on earth, in every time and hour, with your peace.

In the book of life, blessing, peace, and proper sustenance, may we be remembered and inscribed, we and all your people, the house of Israel, for a good life and for peace.

Blessed are you, COMPASSIONATE ONE, maker of peace. ↩

We continue silently with the confessional prayers on page 759.

ואת כל יושבי תבל/and all who dwell on earth. According to the sages, every *Amidah* must conclude with a prayer for peace and an acknowledgement of God as the power that makes for peace. Inclusion of the words "and all who dwell on earth" proclaims that Israel desires the blessing of peace, not for itself alone, but for all humanity.   S.S.

KAVANAH. God is shalom. God's name is shalom, everything is held together by shalom.   Zohar

COMMENTARY. *Besefer ḥayim...ufarnasah tovah*/In the book of life...and proper sustenance. This insertion into the closing benediction of the Amidah is unique to the *Yamim Nora'im*. The mythic imagery is of a celestial "Book of Life," in which our ancestors imagined their fate was inscribed. On Yom Kippur, we pray for repentance, we ask for a world of peace, and we seek the assurance of life. Worthy goals, and serious subjects. But the quiet courage of the petition for "proper sustenance," for a daily routine of labor that confers integrity and dignity, and neither shames nor humiliates us, is the foundation of these larger hopes.   R.H.

During evening service continue below. During all other services continue on page 758.

בִּרְכַּת הַשָּׁלוֹם

שָׁלוֹם רָב עַל יִשְׂרָאֵל עַמְּךָ תָּשִׂים לְעוֹלָם: כִּי אַתָּה הוּא מֶלֶךְ אָדוֹן
לְכָל הַשָּׁלוֹם: וְטוֹב בְּעֵינֶיךָ לְבָרֵךְ אֶת עַמְּךָ יִשְׂרָאֵל וְאֶת כָּל־יוֹשְׁבֵי
תֵבֵל בְּכָל עֵת וּבְכָל שָׁעָה בִּשְׁלוֹמֶךָ:

בְּסֵפֶר חַיִּים בְּרָכָה וְשָׁלוֹם וּפַרְנָסָה טוֹבָה נִזָּכֵר וְנִכָּתֵב לְפָנֶיךָ אֲנַחְנוּ
וְכָל עַמְּךָ בֵּית יִשְׂרָאֵל לְחַיִּים טוֹבִים וּלְשָׁלוֹם:

בָּרוּךְ אַתָּה יהוה עוֹשֶׂה הַשָּׁלוֹם: —←

Shalom rav al yisra'el ameḥa tasim le'olam.
Ki atah hu meleḥ adon leḥol hashalom.
Vetov be'eyneḥa levareḥ et ameḥa yisra'el
ve'et kol yoshvey tevel
beḥol et uvḥol sha'ah vishlomeḥa.

Besefer ḥayim beraḥah veshalom ufarnasah tovah
nizaḥer venikatev lefaneḥa
anaḥnu veḥol ameḥa beyt yisra'el
leḥayim tovim uleshalom.

Baruḥ atah adonay osey hashalom.

We continue silently with the confessional prayers on page 760.

עושה השלום/Maker of peace. This ancient version of the prayer for peace
in its most universal form was assigned in the traditional liturgy to the ten
days of *teshuvah*. During the year the text read, "who blesses your people
Israel with peace." In our times, when life has been transformed by the
constant threat of global destruction, the need of the hour calls for the
more universal form of the prayer throughout the year.   A.G.

Grant peace, goodness and blessing in the world,
grace, love, and mercy
over us and over all your people Israel.
Bless us, source of being, all of us, as one
amid your light,
for by your light,
WISE ONE, our God, you give to us
Torah of life, and love of kindness,
justice, blessing, mercy, life, and peace.
So may it be a good thing in your eyes,
to bless your people Israel, and all peoples,
with abundant strength and peace.

In the book of life, blessing, peace, and proper sustenance,
may we be remembered and inscribed,
we and all your people, the house of Israel,
for a good life and for peace.

Blessed are you, COMPASSIONATE ONE, maker of peace.

During all services except Ma'ariv, recite the following paragraph:

שִׂים שָׁלוֹם טוֹבָה וּבְרָכָה בָּעוֹלָם חֵן וָחֶסֶד וְרַחֲמִים עָלֵינוּ וְעַל כָּל־
יִשְׂרָאֵל עַמֶּךָ: בָּרְכֵנוּ אָבִינוּ כֻּלָּנוּ כְּאֶחָד בְּאוֹר פָּנֶיךָ: כִּי בְאוֹר פָּנֶיךָ
נָתַתָּ לָּנוּ יהוה אֱלֹהֵינוּ תּוֹרַת חַיִּים וְאַהֲבַת חֶסֶד וּצְדָקָה וּבְרָכָה
וְרַחֲמִים וְחַיִּים וְשָׁלוֹם: וְטוֹב בְּעֵינֶיךָ לְבָרֵךְ אֶת עַמְּךָ יִשְׂרָאֵל וְאֶת
כָּל הָעַמִּים בְּרָב־עֹז וְשָׁלוֹם:

בְּסֵפֶר חַיִּים בְּרָכָה וְשָׁלוֹם וּפַרְנָסָה טוֹבָה נִזָּכֵר וְנִכָּתֵב לְפָנֶיךָ אֲנַחְנוּ
וְכָל־עַמְּךָ בֵּית יִשְׂרָאֵל לְחַיִּים טוֹבִים וּלְשָׁלוֹם:
בָּרוּךְ אַתָּה יהוה עוֹשֶׂה הַשָּׁלוֹם:

KAVANAH. Try to imagine a time of true peace and tranquility, and think about your part in helping this time to come about. What can you do? What can you commit to? How will *you* be a peacemaker?   L.G.B.

May it be your will, ETERNAL ONE, my God,
that you not place your servant
under the strictest form of judgment,
for no creature can truly be considered just,
when standing in your presence.
Who am I? What is my life?
I am like a piece of straw before a fire,
like dried and withered trees before a raging flame,
like silver waiting to be purged of baser metals,
the emptiest of empty things,
in whom no substance dwells.
How can I hope to face you, HOLY ONE, my God?
What healing can I hope to seek from you?

What you hold unimportant I have overvalued,
what you have held important I have overlooked.
What you have held as precious I have pushed away,
what you have kept away from you I have drawn close.
I never did intend to make you angry,
but now, presumptuous as it may seem,
I come to ask your mercy,
and forgiveness, and atonement.
I have put on my boldest face like flintrock,
I know I shall not suffer shame.
Truly, in you I trust, KIND ONE.

I have declared: "You are my God!"
I have relied on your abundant love,
because I know you are
a gentle God, gracious and compassionate,
slow to grow angry, overflowing in your love,
and ready always to do good. ⤴

יְהִי רָצוֹן מִלְּפָנֶיךָ יהוה אֱלֹהַי וֵאלֹהֵי אֲבוֹתַי וְאִמּוֹתַי שֶׁלֹּא תָבוֹא בְמִשְׁפָּט אֶת עַבְדֶּךָ כִּי לֹא יִצְדַּק לְפָנֶיךָ כָל־חָי: מָה־אֲנִי מֶה־חַיַּי אֲנִי כְקַשׁ לִפְנֵי אֵשׁ וּכְעֵצִים יְבֵשִׁים לִפְנֵי הָאוֹר בֶּסֶף סִיגִים מְצֻפֶּה עַל חָרֶשׂ הֲבֵל הֲבָלִים שֶׁאֵין בּוֹ מַמָּשׁ: בַּמֶּה אֲקַדֵּם פָּנֶיךָ יהוה אֱלֹהַי אוֹ מָה רְפוּאָה אֲבַקֵּשׁ מִמֶּךָ:

אֶת־אֲשֶׁר הֵקַלְתָּ הֶחֱמַרְתִּי וְאֶת־אֲשֶׁר הֶחֱמַרְתָּ הֵקַלְתִּי: אֶת־אֲשֶׁר קֵרַבְתָּ הִרְחַקְתִּי וְאֶת־אֲשֶׁר הִרְחַקְתָּ קֵרַבְתִּי: אַךְ לֹא לְהַכְעִיסְךָ נִתְכַּוַּנְתִּי: וּבְעַזּוּת מֵצַח בָּאתִי לְבַקֵּשׁ מִלְּפָנֶיךָ מְחִילָה וּסְלִיחָה וְכַפָּרָה: שַׂמְתִּי פָנַי כַּחַלָּמִישׁ וָאֵדַע כִּי לֹא אֵבוֹשׁ כִּי עָלֶיךָ בָטָחְתִּי יהוה אָמַרְתִּי אֱלֹהַי אָתָּה: וְנִשְׁעַנְתִּי עַל רֹבֵּי חֲסָדֶיךָ כִּי יָדַעְתִּי כִּי אַתָּה אֵל חַנּוּן וְרַחוּם אֶרֶךְ אַפַּיִם וְרַב־חֶסֶד וּמַרְבֶּה לְהֵיטִיב: ←

COMMENTARY. Repentance, like deepened spirituality, emerges from inner brokenness. I can put on a brave front, denying that I have done wrong, and evading my own inner knowledge of transgression and loneliness, doubt and failure. But in doing so I have failed to tap the insight and recognize the brokenness that can bring me to humility. Only from the place of humility can I sense the redemptive power in the Transcendent Unity that brings release and healing.   D.A.T.

It is traditional to tap one's chest when reciting each transgression in the Vidui. *In doing so, we are acknowledging individual responsibility for communal transgression.*

Our God, our ancients' God,
may our prayer come before you.
Hide not from our supplication,
for we are not so insolent and stubborn
as to say, here in your presence,
"HOLY ONE, God of our fathers and our mothers,
We are righteous, and we have not sinned,"
for we indeed have sinned.

We have acted wrongly,
we have been untrue,
and we have gained unlawfully
and have defamed.
We have harmed others,
we have wrought injustice,
we have zealously transgressed,
and we have hurt
and have told lies.
We have improperly advised,
and we have covered up the truth,
and we have laughed in scorn.
We have misused responsibility
and have neglected others
and have stubbornly rebelled.
We have offended,
we have perverted justice,
we have stirred up enmity,
and we have kept ourselves from change.
We have reached out to evil,
we have shamelessly corrupted
and have treated others with disdain.
Yes, we have thrown ourselves off course,
and we have tempted and misled. ↵

YOM KIPPUR / 761

It is traditional to tap one's chest when reciting each transgression in the Vidui. *In doing so, we are acknowledging individual responsibility for communal transgression.*

אֱלֹהֵינוּ וֵאלֹהֵי אֲבוֹתֵינוּ וְאִמּוֹתֵינוּ תָּבוֹא לְפָנֶיךָ תְּפִלָּתֵנוּ וְאַל תִּתְעַלַּם מִתְּחִנָּתֵנוּ שֶׁאֵין אֲנַחְנוּ עַזֵּי פָנִים וּקְשֵׁי עֹרֶף לוֹמַר לְפָנֶיךָ יהוה אֱלֹהֵינוּ וֵאלֹהֵי אֲבוֹתֵינוּ וְאִמּוֹתֵינוּ צַדִּיקִים אֲנַחְנוּ וְלֹא חָטָאנוּ אֲבָל אֲנַחְנוּ חָטָאנוּ:

אָשַׁמְנוּ: בָּגַדְנוּ: גָּזַלְנוּ: דִּבַּרְנוּ דֹפִי:
הֶעֱוִינוּ: וְהִרְשַׁעְנוּ: זַדְנוּ: חָמַסְנוּ:
טָפַלְנוּ שֶׁקֶר: יָעַצְנוּ רָע: כִּזַּבְנוּ: לַצְנוּ:
מָרַדְנוּ: נִאַצְנוּ: סָרַרְנוּ: עָוִינוּ:
פָּשַׁעְנוּ: צָרַרְנוּ: קִשִּׁינוּ עֹרֶף: רָשַׁעְנוּ:
שִׁחַתְנוּ: תִּעַבְנוּ: תָּעִינוּ: תִּעְתָּעְנוּ: ←

COMMENTARY. This alphabetical acrostic serves an interesting function. By limiting the range of sins—setting boundaries by the ends of the alphabet—we are forced to define the essential categories of sin that we need to address. The tendency to extend our list of failures often leads to a sense of spiritual defeat...a list without end! By defining here the basic categories, we set for ourselves a reasonable agenda for atonement. R.H.

DERASH. Master of the Universe, the ways of your righteous court are not the ways of this world's courts. In a human court, one who totally denies a debt may go free, but one who admits to a debt is required to pay. In the divine court, woe to those who deny what they have done! Yet those who confess their guilt and make a break with their former actions are shown mercy and saved. S.D.R.

COMMENTARY. *Teshuvah* begins when I acknowledge that I have done wrong, that I have harmed another. After this, I come to understand that the wrong I have done also damages me and pains my own soul. The traditional tapping of the chest that accompanies the confessional prayers can be understood as an outward sign and reminder of this inward pain. But *teshuvah* does not end there. My soul does not need to carry this self-inflicted pain. My soul can return to its original purity, to acts of love and justice. I have the capacity to heal and be healed. J.A.S.

We have turned away from your mitzvot,
and from your righteous laws,
as if it did not matter to us.
And you are just,
whatever comes upon us,
for what you do is truth,
and we have done much wrong.
What can we say before you,
you who dwell on high?
What can we tell you,
you who inhabit heaven's heights?
Are you not one who knows all things,
both hidden and revealed?

You know the universe's mysteries,
the most hidden secrets of all living beings.
You search a person's innermost recesses,
and you probe the depths of conscience and of thought.
Nothing is hidden from you,
nothing is concealed before your gaze.

So, let it be your will,
ETERNAL ONE, our God, God of our ancestors,
that you may grant forgiveness to us for all of our sins,
and pardon us for all of our injustices,
and let us atone for all we have done wrong:

For the wrong that we have done before you
   by compulsion or by will,
and for the wrong that we have done before you
   by the utterance of our lips. ↩

סָרְנוּ מִמִּצְוֹתֶיךָ וּמִמִּשְׁפָּטֶיךָ הַטּוֹבִים וְלֹא שָׁוָה לָנוּ: וְאַתָּה צַדִּיק עַל
כָּל־הַבָּא עָלֵינוּ כִּי אֱמֶת עָשִׂיתָ וַאֲנַחְנוּ הִרְשָׁעְנוּ:
מַה נֹּאמַר לְפָנֶיךָ יוֹשֵׁב מָרוֹם וּמַה נְּסַפֵּר לְפָנֶיךָ שׁוֹכֵן שְׁחָקִים הֲלֹא
כָּל הַנִּסְתָּרוֹת וְהַנִּגְלוֹת אַתָּה יוֹדֵעַ:

אַתָּה יוֹדֵעַ רָזֵי עוֹלָם וְתַעֲלוּמוֹת סִתְרֵי כָל חָי: אַתָּה חוֹפֵשׂ כָּל חַדְרֵי
בָטֶן וּבוֹחֵן כְּלָיוֹת וָלֵב: אֵין דָּבָר נֶעְלָם מִמֶּךָ וְאֵין נִסְתָּר מִנֶּגֶד
עֵינֶיךָ: וּבְכֵן יְהִי רָצוֹן מִלְּפָנֶיךָ יהוה אֱלֹהֵינוּ וֵאלֹהֵי אֲבוֹתֵינוּ
וְאִמּוֹתֵינוּ שֶׁתִּסְלַח לָנוּ עַל כָּל חַטֹּאתֵינוּ וְתִמְחַל לָנוּ עַל כָּל עֲוֹנוֹתֵינוּ
וּתְכַפֶּר לָנוּ עַל כָּל פְּשָׁעֵינוּ:

עַל חֵטְא שֶׁחָטָאנוּ לְפָנֶיךָ בְּאֹנֶס וּבְרָצוֹן:
וְעַל חֵטְא שֶׁחָטָאנוּ לְפָנֶיךָ בְּבִטּוּי שְׂפָתָיִם: ←

KAVANAH. Tonight we concern ourselves with *teshuvah*, turning:
Turning from ignorance to truth,
from darkness to light,
from evil to good,
from conceit to compassion,
from self to Life.
Turning is the key to survival.
The seasons, the planets, the galaxies—
all maintain their existence through turning.
Our turning, too, is in the natural order of things,
holding the key to our survival by returning us to holiness.   R.M.S.

ואתה...הרשענו/And...wrong (Nehemiah 9:33).

For the wrong that we have done before you
through misuse of sex,
and for the wrong that we have done before you
by the speaking of our mouths.
For the wrong that we have done before you
by the shaming of our neighbor,
and for the wrong that we have done before you
by an insincere confession.
For the wrong that we have done before you
by scoffing at our parents and our teachers,
and for the wrong that we have done before you
by the profanation of your name.
For the wrong that we have done before you
in impurity of lips,
and for the wrong that we have done before you
whether knowingly or not.

And for them all, God of forgiveness,
please forgive us, pardon us, help us atone! ↩

KAVANAH. Rabbi Sholom Rokeaḥ of Belz taught that the worst kind of
exile occurs when one is alienated from oneself. Then, one is "both captor
and captive, in exile within oneself." On Yom Kippur, we are given the gift
of forgiveness, yet some of us cannot accept the gift; some of us cannot let
go of guilt and shame. Yom Kippur offers us God's faith in us—and
demands from us faith in ourselves.   L.G.B.

COMMENTARY. It is customary for people to gently tap their chests with
their fists once for each transgression of the *Vidui*. Even though the *Vidui*
is stated in the plural, this tapping reminds us that each of us must ask
ourselves not only which of these sins we have committed, but which of
these sins we have failed to prevent others from committing.   D.A.T.

עַל חֵטְא שֶׁחָטָאנוּ לְפָנֶיךָ בְּגִלּוּי עֲרָיוֹת:

וְעַל חֵטְא שֶׁחָטָאנוּ לְפָנֶיךָ בְּדִבּוּר פֶּה:

עַל חֵטְא שֶׁחָטָאנוּ לְפָנֶיךָ בְּהוֹנָאַת רֵעַ:

וְעַל חֵטְא שֶׁחָטָאנוּ לְפָנֶיךָ בְּוִדּוּי פֶּה:

עַל חֵטְא שֶׁחָטָאנוּ לְפָנֶיךָ בְּזִלְזוּל הוֹרִים וּמוֹרִים:

וְעַל חֵטְא שֶׁחָטָאנוּ לְפָנֶיךָ בְּחִלּוּל הַשֵּׁם:

עַל חֵטְא שֶׁחָטָאנוּ לְפָנֶיךָ בְּטֻמְאַת שְׂפָתָיִם:

וְעַל חֵטְא שֶׁחָטָאנוּ לְפָנֶיךָ בְּיוֹדְעִים וּבְלֹא יוֹדְעִים:

וְעַל כֻּלָּם אֱלוֹהַּ סְלִיחוֹת סְלַח לָנוּ: מְחַל לָנוּ: כַּפֶּר לָנוּ: ←

COMMENTARY. A large portion of the *hata'im*/sins listed refer to a part of the body (mouth, lips, tongue, eyes, throat, neck) for two reasons. First, our bodies need to know the nature of our wrongs. We need to experience the pain of our behavior viscerally before we are willing to change. Our confession and acknowledgment cannot remain a purely intellectual activity. We must feel, in our guts, the ill we cause ourselves and others, or we will not be motivated to really change. Second, most of the *hata'im* derive from forgetting our connection to the whole. We imagine that we can act as if there were no consequences, as if we were loose limbs and eyes and mouths divorced from a larger body, the body of our fellow human beings, the body of organic life on earth, the body of all life. Most *hata'im* derive from our separation and isolation from past and future. Most *hata'im* spring from the illusion of separateness. We think we can get away with it. But there is no getting away. There is no forgetfulness. All is remembered. All is related.   S.P.W.

For the wrong that we have done before you
  through deceiving and through lies.
and for the wrong that we have done before you
  by speaking ill of others.
For the wrong that we have done before you
  by false dealings in our work,
and for the wrong that we have done before you
  by our arrogance and pride.
For the wrong that we have done before you
  through abusive speech,
and for the wrong that we have done before you
  by refusing compromise.

And for them all, God of forgiveness,
  please forgive us, pardon us, help us atone!

For the wrong that we have done before you
  by rebellious acts,
and for the wrong that we have done before you
  by the envy in our eye.
For the wrong that we have done before you
  by triviality of thought,
and for the wrong that we have done before you
  by our gossiping and rumoring.
And for the wrong that we have done before you
  by our empty promises,
and for the wrong that we have done before you
  through confusion of the heart.

And for them all, God of forgiveness,
  please forgive us, pardon us, help us atone! ↵

עַל חֵטְא שֶׁחָטָאנוּ לְפָנֶיךָ בְּכַחַשׁ וּבְכָזָב:

וְעַל חֵטְא שֶׁחָטָאנוּ לְפָנֶיךָ בְּלָשׁוֹן הָרָע:

עַל חֵטְא שֶׁחָטָאנוּ לְפָנֶיךָ בְּמַשָּׂא וּבְמַתָּן:

וְעַל חֵטְא שֶׁחָטָאנוּ לְפָנֶיךָ בִּנְטִיַּת גָּרוֹן:

עַל חֵטְא שֶׁחָטָאנוּ לְפָנֶיךָ בְּשִׂיחַ שִׂפְתוֹתֵינוּ:

וְעַל חֵטְא שֶׁחָטָאנוּ לְפָנֶיךָ בְּעַזּוּת מֶצַח:

וְעַל כֻּלָּם אֱלוֹהַּ סְלִיחוֹת סְלַח לָנוּ: מְחַל לָנוּ: כַּפֶּר לָנוּ:

עַל חֵטְא שֶׁחָטָאנוּ לְפָנֶיךָ בִּפְרִיקַת עֹל:

וְעַל חֵטְא שֶׁחָטָאנוּ לְפָנֶיךָ בִּצְרוּת עָיִן:

עַל חֵטְא שֶׁחָטָאנוּ לְפָנֶיךָ בְּקַלּוּת רֹאשׁ:

וְעַל חֵטְא שֶׁחָטָאנוּ לְפָנֶיךָ בִּרְכִילוּת:

עַל חֵטְא שֶׁחָטָאנוּ לְפָנֶיךָ בִּשְׁבוּעַת שָׁוְא:

וְעַל חֵטְא שֶׁחָטָאנוּ לְפָנֶיךָ בְּתִמְהוֹן לֵבָב:

וְעַל כֻּלָּם אֱלוֹהַּ סְלִיחוֹת סְלַח לָנוּ: מְחַל לָנוּ: כַּפֶּר לָנוּ: ←—

DERASH. *Teshuvah* means a remaking of the self, a new ordering of priorities, so that something which seemed irresistibly important to us before is now seen as much less important. Repentance means becoming virtually a new person in terms of our values and priorities. That is why the classic test of repentance in Judaism resides in finding yourself in the same situation to which you had formerly responded weakly, that is, sinfully, and meeting it differently this time—because your understanding of what you stand for as a person has changed. *Teshuvah* means changing our values, altering our patterns of response, the way we allocate our time, and thus it means becoming new people, no longer burdened by the bad habits of the past.   Harold Kushner

And for mitzvot that call on us to act,
and for mitzvot that bid us not to act,
for mitzvot that say: "Arise, and do...!"
and for mitzvot that do not say: "Arise, and do...!"
for those that are made known to us,
and those that are not known to us.

Those that are known to us
are things we have acknowledged
and confessed before you,
but those that are not known to us
are things revealed and known only to you,
as it is said: "The hidden things
belong to THE ETERNAL ONE, our God.
What is revealed belongs to us and to our children,
always and forever—all the matters
of this Torah that are ours to carry out."
For you are the source of all forgiveness,
the fount of mercy for each and every generation,
and apart from you we have no sovereign.
so full of mercy and forgiveness, none but you. ↵

וְעַל מִצְוֹת עֲשֵׂה וְעַל מִצְוֹת לֹא תַעֲשֶׂה בֵּין שֶׁיֵּשׁ־בָּהּ קוּם עֲשֵׂה וּבֵין
שֶׁאֵין בָּהּ קוּם עֲשֵׂה אֶת־הַגְּלוּיִים לָנוּ וְאֶת־שֶׁאֵינָם גְּלוּיִים לָנוּ: אֶת־
הַגְּלוּיִים לָנוּ כְּבָר אֲמַרְנוּם לְפָנֶיךָ וְהוֹדִינוּ לְךָ עֲלֵיהֶם וְאֶת־שֶׁאֵינָם
גְּלוּיִים לָנוּ לְפָנֶיךָ הֵם גְּלוּיִים וִידוּעִים כַּדָּבָר שֶׁנֶּאֱמַר: הַנִּסְתָּרֹת
לַיהוה אֱלֹהֵינוּ וְהַנִּגְלֹת לָנוּ וּלְבָנֵינוּ עַד־עוֹלָם לַעֲשׂוֹת אֶת־כָּל־דִּבְרֵי
הַתּוֹרָה הַזֹּאת: כִּי אַתָּה סָלְחָן לְכָל־דּוֹר וָדוֹר וּמִבַּלְעָדֶיךָ אֵין לָנוּ
מֶלֶךְ מוֹחֵל וְסוֹלֵחַ אֶלָּא אָתָּה: ←

COMMENTARY. Judaism is concerned with seeking forgiveness. Up to three times, one must sincerely approach a person one has offended to make amends. If one is rebuffed after making recompense for damages and seeking forgiveness three times, one is regarded as forgiven. There is a tradition for seeking forgiveness regarding persons we have wronged who are unable to grant it—infants, those with severe mental illness, those whom we are unable to locate, and those who died before we could ask their forgiveness. We seek atonement not from them but from God by adding during the silent *Al Ḥet*, "For the wrong that we have done before You in the matter of [name of the person]." E.M.

DERASH. Our prayer speaks in three categories: *seliḥah* / forgiveness, *meḥilah* / pardon, and *kaparah* / atonement. One way of understanding the process of Yom Kippur—or any moment of *teshuvah* / turning-to-God—is to see these three as sequential. The first stage, *seliḥah*, implies the act of approaching, of coming to ask forgiveness. If our contrition is accepted, we are granted *meḥilah*, or pardon. The one we have offended accepts our apology and meets it with reconciliation. This brings the change we seek within ourselves—the sense of making atonement, of having purged and purified ourselves of those things which pollute and distort our convictions and commitments. R.H.

הנסתרת...הזאת / The hidden...one (Deuteronomy 29:28).

My God, before I was created,
I was not worthy to receive the gift of life,
and now that I have been created,
it is as if I never was.
While yet I live, I am but dust;
how much the more so when I die!
May it be your will, ETERNAL ONE,
my God, my ancients' God,
that I not go astray again,
and whatever the wrongdoing
I have done before you,
may you, in your great mercy,
purge it from me,
but not by means of grievous suffering
or terrible disease.

Dear God, protect my tongue from evil,
and my lips from telling lies.
And toward my adversaries may my spirit remain tranquil,
and I always remain ready for the needs of others.
Open my heart toward your Torah,
let my spirit seek to do all that you ask of me.
Let all who bear me animosity
be brought to reconsider their ill-will.
Act for the sake of your name.
Act for the sake of your deeds.
Act for the sake of your holiness.
Act for the sake of your Torah.
So that all those dear to you may find release,
let your right hand bring deliverance, and answer me.
May my words of prayer
and my heart's meditation be seen favorably,
PRECIOUS ONE, my rock, my champion.
May the one who creates harmony above
make peace for us and for all Israel,
and for all who dwell on earth. And say: Amen.

אֱלֹהַי עַד שֶׁלֹּא נוֹצַרְתִּי אֵינִי כְדַי וְעַכְשָׁו שֶׁנּוֹצַרְתִּי כְּאִלּוּ לֹא
נוֹצַרְתִּי: עָפָר אֲנִי בְּחַיַּי קַל וָחֹמֶר בְּמִיתָתִי: יְהִי רָצוֹן מִלְּפָנֶיךָ יהוה
אֱלֹהַי וֵאלֹהֵי אֲבוֹתַי וְאִמּוֹתַי שֶׁלֹּא אֶחֱטָא עוֹד וּמַה־שֶּׁחָטָאתִי לְפָנֶיךָ
מָרֵק בְּרַחֲמֶיךָ הָרַבִּים אֲבָל לֹא עַל יְדֵי יִסּוּרִים וָחֳלָיִים רָעִים:

אֱלֹהַי נְצֹר לְשׁוֹנִי מֵרָע וּשְׂפָתַי מִדַּבֵּר מִרְמָה וְלִמְקַלְלַי נַפְשִׁי תִדֹּם
וְנַפְשִׁי כֶּעָפָר לַכֹּל תִּהְיֶה: פְּתַח לִבִּי בְּתוֹרָתֶךָ וּבְמִצְוֹתֶיךָ תִּרְדֹּף נַפְשִׁי
וְכָל הַחוֹשְׁבִים עָלַי רָעָה מְהֵרָה הָפֵר עֲצָתָם וְקַלְקֵל מַחֲשַׁבְתָּם:
עֲשֵׂה לְמַעַן שְׁמֶךָ עֲשֵׂה לְמַעַן יְמִינֶךָ עֲשֵׂה לְמַעַן קְדֻשָּׁתֶךָ עֲשֵׂה
לְמַעַן תּוֹרָתֶךָ: לְמַעַן יֵחָלְצוּן יְדִידֶיךָ הוֹשִׁיעָה יְמִינְךָ וַעֲנֵנִי: יִהְיוּ
לְרָצוֹן אִמְרֵי פִי וְהֶגְיוֹן לִבִּי לְפָנֶיךָ יהוה צוּרִי וְגוֹאֲלִי: עֹשֶׂה שָׁלוֹם
בִּמְרוֹמָיו הוּא יַעֲשֶׂה שָׁלוֹם עָלֵינוּ וְעַל כָּל יִשְׂרָאֵל וְעַל כָּל יוֹשְׁבֵי
תֵבֵל וְאִמְרוּ אָמֵן:

COMMENTARY. Life begins as an unearned gift. While we possess it, we live
with the reality that our ultimate destiny is death. We return to dust. So
what can give meaning to our lives? This poem suggests that meaning
flows from our connection to the Eternal. Sin, which pulls us away from
the Eternal, is a foretaste of the bitterness of death. When we search for
meaning, we purge ourselves of that bitterness and cling again to the
Eternal. The gift of life is renewed.   D.A.T.

COMMENTARY. Act for the sake of your name...your deeds...your holiness...your Torah. These beseechings trace the course of Israel's history:
first, the ancestors of Israel knew only of God's name; then, in the Exodus
from Egypt, Israel learned of God's deeds (literally, "right hand"); in the
days of the desert Tabernacle, they learned of God's holiness and the
demands placed upon a holy people; finally, at the edge of the Promised
Land, a new generation was exhorted to hand on Torah from one
generation to another.   J.R.

אלהי נצור...וגואלי / Dear...champion. Based on a prayer in Beraḥot 17a.
למען...וענני / So...me (Psalms 60:7 and 108:7).

Master of the World, I now forgive all who have angered me or sinned against me whether through my body, my possessions, my honor or anything that is mine, whether by accident or by intention, knowingly or unknowingly, word or deed. Let no one be punished on my account. My God and the God of my ancestors, may it be your will that I sin no more and that I not again do what is evil in your sight. In your great mercy, wipe away my sins without requiring my suffering. May the words of my mouth and the longing of my heart be acceptable to you, THE LISTENER, my rock and my redeemer.

On Shabbat during Ma'ariv, continue on the following page. Otherwise during Ma'ariv, turn to page 781. During Shaḥarit, turn to page 387. During Musaf, turn to page 843. During Minḥah, turn to page 1075.

יהיו...וגואלי / May...redeemer (Psalms 19:15).

רִבּוֹנוֹ שֶׁל עוֹלָם הֲרֵינִי מוֹחֵל לְכָל־מִי שֶׁהִכְעִיס וְהִקְנִיט אוֹתִי אוֹ
שֶׁחָטָא כְּנֶגְדִּי בֵּין בְּגוּפִי בֵּין בְּמָמוֹנִי בֵּין בִּכְבוֹדִי בֵּין בְּכָל־אֲשֶׁר לִי
בֵּין בְּאֹנֶס בֵּין בְּרָצוֹן בֵּין בְּשׁוֹגֵג בֵּין בְּמֵזִיד בֵּין בְּדִבּוּר בֵּין בְּמַעֲשֶׂה
לְכָל־בֶּן־אָדָם. וְלֹא יֵעָנֵשׁ שׁוּם אָדָם בְּסִבָּתִי: יְהִי רָצוֹן מִלְּפָנֶיךָ יהוה
אֱלֹהַי וֵאלֹהֵי אֲבוֹתַי וְאִמּוֹתַי שֶׁלֹּא אֶחֱטָא עוֹד וְלֹא אֶחֱזֹר בָּהֶם וְלֹא
אָשׁוּב עוֹד לְהַכְעִיסֶךָ וְלֹא אֶעֱשֶׂה הָרַע בְּעֵינֶיךָ וּמַה־שֶּׁחָטָאתִי
לְפָנֶיךָ מְחֹק בְּרַחֲמֶיךָ הָרַבִּים אֲבָל לֹא עַל יְדֵי יִסּוּרִים וָחֳלָיִים רָעִים:
יִהְיוּ לְרָצוֹן אִמְרֵי־פִי וְהֶגְיוֹן לִבִּי לְפָנֶיךָ יהוה צוּרִי וְגֹאֲלִי:

On Shabbat during Ma'ariv, continue on the following page. Otherwise during Ma'ariv, turn to page 782. During Shaharit, *turn to page 388. During Musaf, turn to page 844. During* Minhah, *turn to page 1076.*

KAVANAH. We have just completed the Amidah, silent, intense and personal. Now we have an opportunity to do what we may have been trying to do for hours, days, weeks, or even months. We have an opportunity to forgive those who have hurt or have wronged us. We might be willing to do it for their sake, but if not, we should be willing to do it for our own. Resentment, grudge-bearing and antique anger contaminate our lives. Forgiving those who have wronged me allows me to jettison the pollutants of my soul. If this Amidah has given me the strength to accomplish this task, then it has served its purpose.

D.A.T.

On Shabbat continue here. On weekdays turn to page 781.

VAYHULU / CREATION COMPLETED

Heaven, earth, and all their beings were finished. God completed on the seventh day the work that had been done, and ceased upon the seventh day from all the work that had been done. God blessed the seventh day and set it apart. For on it God had ceased from all the work that had been done in carrying out Creation.

ME'EYN SHEVA / REPRISE OF THE AMIDAH

Blessed are you, ANCIENT ONE, our God, God of our ancestors,

God of Abraham	God of Sarah
God of Isaac	God of Rebekah
God of Jacob	God of Rachel
	and God of Leah;

great, heroic, awesome God, supreme divinity,
who creates the heavens and the earth. ⮌

KAVANAH. Shabbat represents the affirmation that life is not vain or futile, but supremely worthwhile.   M.M.K. (Adapted)

ויכלו...לעשות /Heaven...Creation (Genesis 2:1-3).

On Shabbat continue here. On weekdays turn to page 782.

וַיְכֻלּוּ

וַיְכֻלּוּ הַשָּׁמַיִם וְהָאָרֶץ וְכָל־צְבָאָם: וַיְכַל אֱלֹהִים בַּיּוֹם הַשְּׁבִיעִי
מְלַאכְתּוֹ אֲשֶׁר עָשָׂה וַיִּשְׁבֹּת בַּיּוֹם הַשְּׁבִיעִי מִכָּל־מְלַאכְתּוֹ אֲשֶׁר
עָשָׂה: וַיְבָרֶךְ אֱלֹהִים אֶת־יוֹם הַשְּׁבִיעִי וַיְקַדֵּשׁ אֹתוֹ כִּי בוֹ שָׁבַת
מִכָּל־מְלַאכְתּוֹ אֲשֶׁר־בָּרָא אֱלֹהִים לַעֲשׂוֹת:

בָּרוּךְ אַתָּה יהוה אֱלֹהֵינוּ וֵאלֹהֵי אֲבוֹתֵינוּ וְאִמּוֹתֵינוּ:

אֱלֹהֵי שָׂרָה	אֱלֹהֵי אַבְרָהָם
אֱלֹהֵי רִבְקָה	אֱלֹהֵי יִצְחָק
אֱלֹהֵי רָחֵל	אֱלֹהֵי יַעֲקֹב
וֵאלֹהֵי לֵאָה:	

הָאֵל הַגָּדוֹל הַגִּבּוֹר וְהַנּוֹרָא אֵל עֶלְיוֹן קוֹנֵה שָׁמַיִם וָאָרֶץ: ←——

Vayḥulu hashamayim veha'aretz veḥol tzeva'am
vayḥal elohim bayom hashevi'i melaḥto asher asah
vayishbot bayom hashevi'i mikol melaḥto asher asah.
Vayvareḥ elohim et yom hashevi'i vaykadesh oto
ki vo shavat mikol melaḥto asher bara elohim la'asot.

Baruḥ atah adonay eloheynu veylohey avoteynu ve'imoteynu
elohey avraham   elohey sarah
elohey yitzḥak   elohey rivkah
elohey ya'akov   elohey raḥel
veylohey le'ah
ha'el hagadol hagibor vehanora
el elyon
koney shamayim va'aretz. ↰

Shielding our ancestors with a word,
a speech enlivening all beings,
the holy Sovereign,
to whom no being can compare,
who gives this people rest upon the holy Shabbat—
yes, God is pleased to give them rest!
We stand in the divine presence, awed and trembling,
and offer up continually our thankful prayer,
our expression of praise.
God to whom all thanks are due,
the source of peace, who sanctifies Shabbat,
who blesses the seventh day
and gives rest in holiness
to a people steeped in Shabbat joy,
in memory of Creation in the beginning. ↵

מגן אבות / *Magen Avot* summarizes the Shabbat Amidah. It refers to each of
the seven blessings in order: shielding ancestors, giving life, providing
holiness, ordaining Shabbat, allowing worship, inspiring thanks, blessing
with peace. When *Magen Avot* is recited on a holiday, it conveys Shabbat
themes that are largely obscured by the nature of the festival Amidah.

D.A.T.

מֵעֵין שֶׁבַע

מָגֵן אָבוֹת בִּדְבָרוֹ מְחַיֵּה כָּל חַי בְּמַאֲמָרוֹ הַמֶּלֶךְ הַקָּדוֹשׁ שֶׁאֵין
כָּמֽוֹהוּ הַמֵּנִֽיחַ לְעַמּוֹ בְּיוֹם שַׁבַּת קָדְשׁוֹ כִּי בָם רָצָה לְהָנִֽיחַ לָהֶם:
לְפָנָיו נַעֲבֹד בְּיִרְאָה וָפַֽחַד וְנוֹדֶה לִשְׁמוֹ בְּכָל יוֹם תָּמִיד מֵעֵין
הַבְּרָכוֹת: אֵל הַהוֹדָאוֹת אֲדוֹן הַשָּׁלוֹם מְקַדֵּשׁ הַשַּׁבָּת וּמְבָרֵךְ שְׁבִיעִי
וּמֵנִֽיחַ בִּקְדֻשָּׁה לְעַם מְדֻשְּׁנֵי־עֹֽנֶג זֵֽכֶר לְמַעֲשֵׂה בְרֵאשִׁית: ←

Magen avot bidvaro
meḥayey kol ḥay bema'amaro.
hameleḥ hakadosh she'eyn kamohu
hameniaḥ le'amo beyom shabbat kodsho
ki vam ratzah lehani'aḥ lahem.
Lefanav na'avod beyirah vafaḥad
venodeh lishmo beḥol yom tamid
me'eyn haberaḥot.
El hahoda'ot adon hashalom
mekadesh hashabbat umevareḥ shevi'i
umeniaḥ bikdushah le'am medusheney oneg
zeḥer lema'asey vereyshit. ⤺

TRADITIONAL VERSION

Our God, our ancients' God, take pleasure in our rest. Make us holy through your mitzvot. Make us a part of Torah. Let us enjoy the good things of your world and rejoice in all your saving acts. Refine our hearts to serve you honestly. Help us to perpetuate, with love and joy, your holy Shabbat. Let all Israel, and all who treat your name as holy, rest upon this day. Blessed are you, BELOVED ONE, source of the holiness of Shabbat.

ALTERNATIVE VERSION

Shabbat of holiness, beloved and blessed,
may your glory dwell amidst the people of your holy place.
In you, our queen, we find our rest.
And in your holy mitzvot our souls rejoice.
With your goodness we are content.
In you our hearts grow pure,
and in your Shabbat rest we find true worship.
Holy Shabbat, source of blessing,
may you, too, be blessed in our rest.
And blessed are you, ETERNAL ONE, who makes Shabbat holy.

שבת קדש האהובה /Shabbat of holiness. This original Hebrew text addresses Shabbat in feminine language, as bride and as queen. She is the subject of our affection and the source of our sustenance. We ask that her blessing dwell in our midst for peace and joy. We ask, too, that the Jewish people bless Shabbat with their love and devotion.   M.P.

TRADITIONAL VERSION

אֱלֹהֵינוּ וֵאלֹהֵי אֲבוֹתֵינוּ וְאִמּוֹתֵינוּ רְצֵה בִמְנוּחָתֵנוּ קַדְּשֵׁנוּ בְּמִצְוֹתֶיךָ
וְתֵן חֶלְקֵנוּ בְּתוֹרָתֶךָ שַׂבְּעֵנוּ מִטּוּבֶךָ וְשַׂמְּחֵנוּ בִּישׁוּעָתֶךָ וְטַהֵר לִבֵּנוּ
לְעָבְדְּךָ בֶּאֱמֶת: וְהַנְחִילֵנוּ יהוה אֱלֹהֵינוּ בְּאַהֲבָה וּבְרָצוֹן שַׁבַּת
קָדְשֶׁךָ: וְיָנוּחוּ בָה כָּל יִשְׂרָאֵל מְקַדְּשֵׁי שְׁמֶךָ: בָּרוּךְ אַתָּה יהוה
מְקַדֵּשׁ הַשַּׁבָּת:

Eloheynu veylohey avoteynu ve'imoteynu
retzey vimnuhatenu.
Kadeshenu bemitzvoteha
veten helkenu betorateha.
Sabe'enu mituveha
vesamehenu bishu'ateha
vetaher libenu le'ovdeha be'emet.
Vehanhilenu adonay eloheynu
be'ahavah uveratzon shabbat kodsheha
veyanuhu vah yisra'el mekadeshey shemeha.
Baruh atah adonay mekadesh hashabbat.

ALTERNATIVE VERSION

שַׁבָּת קֹדֶשׁ הָאֲהוּבָה וְהַבְּרוּכָה
יִשְׁכֹּן כְּבוֹדֵךְ בְּלֵב עַם מְקַדְּשֶׁךְ:
בָּךְ נִמְצָא מְנוּחָתֵנוּ
וּבְמִצְוֹת קְדֻשָּׁתֵךְ תָּגֵל נַפְשֵׁנוּ:
בְּטוּבֵךְ נִשְׂבַּע וּבָךְ יִטְהַר לִבֵּנוּ
וּבִמְנוּחָתֵךְ נָבוֹא לַעֲבוֹדַת אֱמֶת:
שַׁבָּת קֹדֶשׁ מְקוֹר הַבְּרָכָה
הִתְבָּרְכִי גַּם אַתְּ בִּמְנוּחָתֵנוּ
בָּרוּךְ אַתָּה יהוה מְקַדֵּשׁ הַשַּׁבָּת:

SELIḤOT/PRAYERS FOR FORGIVENESS

May our prayers rise at evening hour,
and may our cry come forth from the dawn,
and may our song be pleasing through the day.

May our voices rise at evening hour,
and may our merit come forth from the dawn,
and may our prayer redeem us through the day.

May our searching rise at evening hour,
and may our plea for pardon come at dawn,
and may our sigh reach you through the day.

May refuge rise at evening hour,
and may it come, for your sake, with the dawn,
and may atonement reach us through the day.

May salvation rise at evening hour,
and may our cleansing come forth with the dawn,
and may we plead for grace throughout the day.

May our memory rise at evening hour,
and may confession come forth with the dawn,
and may our glory ring out through the day.

May urgent prayer rise at evening hour,
and may rejoicing come forth with the dawn,
and may our plea be heard throughout the day.

May our weeping rise at evening hour,
and may it come forth to you with the dawn,
and may it find your favor through the day.

We long for transformation
as we cast our voices upward
on the wings of the day.
Words pile on words,
creating a ladder,
ascending to the heart of prayer.

S.P.W.

יַעֲלֶה תַחֲנוּנֵנוּ מֵעֶרֶב   וְיָבוֹא שַׁוְעָתֵנוּ מִבֹּקֶר
וְיֵרָאֶה רִנּוּנֵנוּ עַד עָרֶב:

יַעֲלֶה קוֹלֵנוּ מֵעֶרֶב   וְיָבוֹא צִדְקָתֵנוּ מִבֹּקֶר
וְיֵרָאֶה פִּדְיוֹנֵנוּ עַד עָרֶב:

יַעֲלֶה עִנּוּיֵנוּ מֵעֶרֶב   וְיָבוֹא סְלִיחָתֵנוּ מִבֹּקֶר
וְיֵרָאֶה נַאֲקָתֵנוּ עַד עָרֶב:

יַעֲלֶה מְנוּסֵנוּ מֵעֶרֶב   וְיָבוֹא לְמַעֲנוֹ מִבֹּקֶר
וְיֵרָאֶה כִּפּוּרֵנוּ עַד עָרֶב:

יַעֲלֶה יִשְׁעֵנוּ מֵעֶרֶב   וְיָבוֹא טָהֳרֵנוּ מִבֹּקֶר
וְיֵרָאֶה חִנּוּנֵנוּ עַד עָרֶב:

יַעֲלֶה זִכְרוֹנֵנוּ מֵעֶרֶב   וְיָבוֹא וְעוּדֵנוּ מִבֹּקֶר
וְיֵרָאֶה הַדְרָתֵנוּ עַד עָרֶב:

יַעֲלֶה דָפְקֵנוּ מֵעֶרֶב   וְיָבוֹא גִילֵנוּ מִבֹּקֶר
וְיֵרָאֶה בַקָשָׁתֵנוּ עַד עָרֶב:

יַעֲלֶה אָנְקָתֵנוּ מֵעֶרֶב   וְיָבוֹא אֵלֶיךָ מִבֹּקֶר
וְיֵרָאֶה אֵלֵינוּ עַד עָרֶב:

Ya'aleh taḥanunenu me'erev
veyavo shavatenu miboker
veyera'eh rinunenu ad arev.

NOTE. This is a reverse alphabetical acrostic.

You who hear prayer,
let all flesh come to you,   Psalms 65:3
let all flesh come to worship before you,
FOUNT OF MERCY.   based on Isaiah 66:23
Let them bow down
to you, great sovereign power.
Let them pay honor to your name.   Psalms 86:9
Come, let us bow down in worship,
let us give blessing in the presence
of THE ABUNDANT ONE, who made us all.   Psalms 95:6
Enter God's gates with thankful prayer,
God's courtyards with a song of praise.
Acknowledge God, and bless God's name.   Psalms 100:4
Behold, all servants of THE ANCIENT ONE
give blessing to the name of THE ETERNAL,
you who stand in THE ALMIGHTY'S house
at evenings,
lift up your hands in holiness,
and bless THE OMNIPRESENT   Psalms 134:1-2
And as for us, eternal one,
in the abundance of your love,
may you enable us to come into your house.   based on Psalms 5:8
Let us bow down in awe of you,
amid your holy sanctuary;
enable us to worship at your holy sanctuary;
and give thankful prayer in your name,
acknowledging your love and truth,
for you have made your name and utterance
supreme throughout the earth. ﬤ   Psalms 138:2

שְׁמַע תְּפִלָּה עָדֶיךָ כָּל־בָּשָׂר יָבֹאוּ: יָבוֹא כָל־בָּשָׂר לְהִשְׁתַּחֲוֹת לְפָנֶיךָ
יהוה: יָבֹאוּ וְיִשְׁתַּחֲווּ לְפָנֶיךָ אֲדֹנָי וִיכַבְּדוּ לִשְׁמֶךָ: בֹּאוּ נִשְׁתַּחֲוֶה
וְנִכְרָעָה נִבְרְכָה לִפְנֵי־יהוה עֹשֵׂנוּ: בֹּאוּ שְׁעָרָיו בְּתוֹדָה חֲצֵרֹתָיו
בִּתְהִלָּה הוֹדוּ־לוֹ בָּרְכוּ שְׁמוֹ: הִנֵּה בָּרְכוּ אֶת־יהוה כָּל־עַבְדֵי יהוה
הָעֹמְדִים בְּבֵית־יהוה בַּלֵּילוֹת: שְׂאוּ יְדֵיכֶם קֹדֶשׁ וּבָרְכוּ אֶת־יהוה:
וַאֲנַחְנוּ בְּרֹב חַסְדְּךָ נָבוֹא בֵיתֶךָ נִשְׁתַּחֲוֶה אֶל־הֵיכַל־קָדְשְׁךָ בְּיִרְאָתֶךָ:
נִשְׁתַּחֲוֶה אֶל־הֵיכַל קָדְשְׁךָ וְנוֹדֶה אֶת־שְׁמֶךָ עַל־חַסְדְּךָ וְעַל־אֲמִתֶּךָ
כִּי־הִגְדַּלְתָּ עַל־כָּל־שִׁמְךָ אִמְרָתֶךָ: ←—

Come, let us rejoice in THE ETERNAL,
shout joyfully for the Rock of our salvation!   Psalms 95:1-2
Hurry forth in thanks before the Presence,
shouting in song to God.
Justice and righteousness
are the foundation of your throne,
love and truth go forth ahead of you,   Psalms 89:15
and all of us in unison
sing sweetly of your mystery.
Amid the house of God we go about with fervor,   Psalms 55:15
God, to whom belongs the sea and the dry land
shaped by the divine hand, in whose great hand is held
the breath of every living thing, the spirit of all flesh.   Job 12:10

The soul is yours,
the body is your handiwork,
be sparing, please,
to all that you have made.
The soul is yours,
the body, yours,
O, FOUNT OF MERCY, act
in keeping with your name.

We come in honor of your name,
ETERNAL ONE—please act
in keeping with your name,
and for the glory of your name,
for you are called
a God gracious and kind.
And for the sake of your great name,
MERCIFUL ONE, may you forgive
our wrongdoing, for it abounds. ↩

לְכוּ נְרַנְּנָה לַיהוה נָרִיעָה לְצוּר יִשְׁעֵנוּ:
נְקַדְּמָה פָנָיו בְּתוֹדָה בִּזְמִרוֹת נָרִיעַ לוֹ:
צֶדֶק וּמִשְׁפָּט מְכוֹן כִּסְאֶךָ חֶסֶד וֶאֱמֶת יְקַדְּמוּ פָנֶיךָ:
אֲשֶׁר יַחְדָּו נַמְתִּיק סוֹד בְּבֵית אֱלֹהִים נְהַלֵּךְ בְּרָגֶשׁ:
אֲשֶׁר־לוֹ הַיָּם וְהוּא עָשָׂהוּ וְיַבֶּשֶׁת יָדָיו יָצָרוּ:
אֲשֶׁר בְּיָדוֹ נֶפֶשׁ כָּל־חָי וְרוּחַ כָּל־בְּשַׂר־אִישׁ:

Leḥu neranenah ladonay nari'ah letzur yisheṇu.
Nekademah fanav betodah bizmirot nari'ah lo.

הַנְּשָׁמָה לָךְ וְהַגּוּף פָּעֳלָךְ חוּסָה עַל עֲמָלָךְ:
הַנְּשָׁמָה לָךְ וְהַגּוּף שֶׁלָּךְ יהוה עֲשֵׂה לְמַעַן שְׁמֶךָ:

אָתָנוּ עַל שִׁמְךָ יהוה עֲשֵׂה לְמַעַן שְׁמֶךָ:
בַּעֲבוּר כְּבוֹד שִׁמְךָ כִּי אֵל חַנּוּן וְרַחוּם שְׁמֶךָ:
לְמַעַן שִׁמְךָ יהוה וְסָלַחְתָּ לַעֲוֺנֵנוּ כִּי רַב הוּא: ←

Haneshamah laḥ vehaguf po'olaḥ ḥusah al amalaḥ.

למען...הוא / And...abounds (Psalms 25:11).

Our God, it is your way
to be reluctant to grow angry,
whether toward the wicked or the righteous.
That is one reason you are praised.
For your sake, God, not for our own,
please act—behold us standing here
in need and desolation.

May you favor patience
toward a windblown leaf,
be reconciled to us,
who are but dust and ash.
Cast off our wrongs,
show grace to your Creation.
Appear among us,
for there is none to plead our cause.
Deal justly now, on our behalf. ↵

דַּרְכְּךָ אֱלֹהֵינוּ לְהַאֲרִיךְ אַפֶּךָ לָרָעִים וְלַטּוֹבִים וְהִיא תְהִלָּתֶךָ: לְמַעַנְךָ אֱלֹהֵינוּ עֲשֵׂה וְלֹא לָנוּ: רְאֵה עֲמִידָתֵנוּ דַּלִּים וְרֵיקִים:

תַּעֲלֶה אֲרוּכָה לְעָלֶה נִדָּף: תְּנַחֵם עַל עָפָר וָאֵפֶר: תַּשְׁלִיךְ חֲטָאֵינוּ וְתָחֹן מַעֲשֶׂיךָ: תֵּרֶא כִּי אֵין אִישׁ עֲשֵׂה עִמָּנוּ צְדָקָה: ←

DERASH. Divinity is made manifest in the world when we act in a godly way. When we become mired in wrongdoing, we dim God's presence. For the sake of God's name—*lema'an shimeha*—we need to seek forgiveness.

J.A.S.

Bless, O my soul, THE OMNIPRESENT ONE,
and all my inner self, God's holy name!
Bless, O my soul, THE FOUNT OF LIFE,
do not forget the gifts God has bestowed
—the one who pardons all your wrongs,
who heals all your afflictions,
who restores your life from peril of destruction,
who adorns you with a crown of love and mercy,
who fills you with the beauty of God's goodness,
so that, like the phoenix, you are renewed,
your youth restored.
THE ALMIGHTY ONE acts righteously,
brings justice to all who are oppressed.
God made known to Moses the ways of God,
to all children of Israel, divine deeds.
Merciful and gracious is THE ANCIENT ONE,
slow to grow angry, great in lovingkindness.
God does not quarrel with us long,
nor bear a grudge forever.
God does not deal with us according to our wrongs,
and not according to our sins does God bestow our lot.
But rather, as high as heaven is above the earth,
so does God's love abound for those in awe.
As far as East from West has God removed from us
the stigma of our wrongs.
Like the love of parent for a child, so is the love
of THE ABUNDANT ONE for those in awe of God.
For God knows our inner nature,
remembering that we are made of dust.
The human being's days are like the chaff,
like flowers of the field—one blossoms for a time,
but when the fury of the wind comes over us,
the very ground disowns us. ↵

בָּרְכִי נַפְשִׁי אֶת־יהוה וְכָל־קְרָבַי אֶת־שֵׁם קָדְשׁוֹ:

בָּרְכִי נַפְשִׁי אֶת־יהוה וְאַל־תִּשְׁכְּחִי כָּל־גְּמוּלָיו:

הַסֹּלֵחַ לְכָל־עֲוֹנֵכִי הָרֹפֵא לְכָל־תַּחֲלוּאָיְכִי:

הַגּוֹאֵל מִשַּׁחַת חַיָּיְכִי הַמְעַטְּרֵכִי חֶסֶד וְרַחֲמִים:

הַמַּשְׂבִּיעַ בַּטּוֹב עֶדְיֵךְ תִּתְחַדֵּשׁ כַּנֶּשֶׁר נְעוּרָיְכִי:

עֹשֵׂה צְדָקוֹת יהוה וּמִשְׁפָּטִים לְכָל־עֲשׁוּקִים:

יוֹדִיעַ דְּרָכָיו לְמֹשֶׁה לִבְנֵי יִשְׂרָאֵל עֲלִילוֹתָיו:

רַחוּם וְחַנּוּן יהוה אֶרֶךְ אַפַּיִם וְרַב־חָסֶד:

לֹא־לָנֶצַח יָרִיב וְלֹא לְעוֹלָם יִטּוֹר:

לֹא כַחֲטָאֵינוּ עָשָׂה לָנוּ וְלֹא כַעֲוֹנוֹתֵינוּ גָּמַל עָלֵינוּ:

כִּי כִגְבֹהַּ שָׁמַיִם עַל הָאָרֶץ גָּבַר חַסְדּוֹ עַל־יְרֵאָיו:

כִּרְחֹק מִזְרָח מִמַּעֲרָב הִרְחִיק מִמֶּנּוּ אֶת־פְּשָׁעֵינוּ:

כְּרַחֵם אָב עַל־בָּנִים רִחַם יהוה עַל־יְרֵאָיו:

כִּי־הוּא יָדַע יִצְרֵנוּ זָכוּר כִּי־עָפָר אֲנָחְנוּ:

אֱנוֹשׁ כֶּחָצִיר יָמָיו כְּצִיץ הַשָּׂדֶה כֵּן יָצִיץ:

כִּי רוּחַ עָבְרָה־בּוֹ וְאֵינֶנּוּ וְלֹא־יַכִּירֶנּוּ עוֹד מְקוֹמוֹ: ←

Barehi nafshi et adonay vehol keravay et shem kodsho.

COMMENTARY. This psalm begins with praise of God for salvation that the author has experienced. While reflecting on God's greatness, the psalmist becomes aware of human smallness and frailty, then comes to the recognition that divine love allows us to transcend our frailty. God's love is an invitation to partake in eternity. The psalmist accepts the invitation and concludes as he began, but with the meaning of the praise transformed.

J.A.S.

Yet the kindness of THE EVERLASTING ONE
toward those in awe of God
endures from one eternity to another,
God's righteousness persists throughout all generations,
for those who keep God's covenant,
those who remember and enact what God has taught.
THE OMNIPRESENT ONE in heaven has prepared a seat of rule,
God's sovereignty has come to reign in every place.
Bless THE OMNIPRESENT, you who serve and struggle
on behalf of God, you who do God's will,
you who listen to God's word as it is voiced.
Bless THE OMNIPRESENT, all you multitudes of heaven,
you who minister to God, and enact God's will.
Let all God's creatures bless THE OMNIPRESENT,
in every place, affirm God's rule.
Bless, O my soul, THE OMNIPRESENT ONE!

Psalm 103

༄

Find words in you to offer
and return to THE COMPASSIONATE.

וְחֶסֶד יהוה מֵעוֹלָם וְעַד־עוֹלָם עַל־יְרֵאָיו וְצִדְקָתוֹ לִבְנֵי בָנִים
לְשֹׁמְרֵי בְרִיתוֹ וּלְזֹכְרֵי פִקֻּדָיו לַעֲשׂוֹתָם:
יהוה בַּשָּׁמַיִם הֵכִין כִּסְאוֹ וּמַלְכוּתוֹ בַּכֹּל מָשָׁלָה:
בָּרְכוּ יהוה מַלְאָכָיו גִּבֹּרֵי כֹחַ עֹשֵׂי דְבָרוֹ
לִשְׁמֹעַ בְּקוֹל דְּבָרוֹ:
בָּרְכוּ יהוה כָּל־צְבָאָיו מְשָׁרְתָיו עֹשֵׂי רְצוֹנוֹ:
בָּרְכוּ יהוה כָּל־מַעֲשָׂיו בְּכָל־מְקֹמוֹת מֶמְשַׁלְתּוֹ
בָּרְכִי נַפְשִׁי אֶת־יהוה:

თ

קְחוּ עִמָּכֶם דְּבָרִים וְשׁוּבוּ אֶל־יהוה:

Keḥu imaḥem devarim veshuvu el adonay.

קחו...יהוה / Find...COMPASSIONATE (Hosea 14:3).

All-merciful and gracious God:
  We have done wrong before you—
  please be kind to us!

Atonement's fount and source,
Bold searcher of the heart,
Going deep into all things,
Deliberate and just are your words.

  We have done wrong before you—
  please be kind to us!

How lovely are your wonders,
Wonderful, your deeds!
Zealous in memory of your covenant,
How carefully you search the inner self!

  We have done wrong before you—
  please be kind to us.

The Good One who bestows all good,
You know all hidden things,
Conquering our wrongful acts.
Law and justice are your garb.

  We have done wrong before you—
  please be kind to us. ⏎

רַחוּם וְחַנּוּן

חָטָאנוּ לְפָנֶיךָ רַחֵם עָלֵינוּ:

אֲדוֹן הַסְּלִיחוֹת

בּוֹחֵן לְבָבוֹת

גּוֹלֶה עֲמוּקוֹת

דּוֹבֵר צְדָקוֹת

חָטָאנוּ לְפָנֶיךָ רַחֵם עָלֵינוּ:

הָדוּר בְּנִפְלָאוֹת

וָתִיק הָעֲלִילִיּוֹת

זוֹכֵר בְּרִית אָבוֹת

חוֹקֵר כְּלָיוֹת

חָטָאנוּ לְפָנֶיךָ רַחֵם עָלֵינוּ:

טוֹב וּמֵטִיב לַבְּרִיּוֹת

יוֹדֵעַ כָּל־נִסְתָּרוֹת

כּוֹבֵשׁ עֲוֹנוֹת

לוֹבֵשׁ צְדָקוֹת

חָטָאנוּ לְפָנֶיךָ רַחֵם עָלֵינוּ: ←

COMMENTARY. Saying we have done wrong is not only an acknowledgment
of failure. It also contains the recognition that we know what is right.
Living in a community concerned with doing good, being good, and trying
to do better, we each internalize a moral compass that can guide us if we
are prepared to listen for its still, small voice. The still, small voice inside
us connects us to the transcendent reality that is far beyond us. In
addressing the Transcendent One, we honor and validate our moral
compass. We have done wrong. We are prepared to be directed by our
compass toward atonement.   D.A.T.

Majestic, filled with good,
Nothing but awesome is your praise,
So ready to forgive are you,
One who responds in time of trial.

   We have done wrong before you—
   please be kind to us!

Power of all saving deeds,
Surveying all that is to be,
Calling to generations yet to come.
Roaming the heaven's cloud-filled heights,
Sure to hearken to all prayers,
Thorough and flawless your knowledge of all!

   We have done wrong before you—
   please be kind to us!

מָלֵא זָכִיּוֹת
נוֹרָא תְהִלּוֹת
סוֹלֵחַ עֲוֹנוֹת
עוֹנֶה בַצָּרוֹת

חָטָאנוּ לְפָנֶיךָ רַחֵם עָלֵינוּ:

פּוֹעֵל יְשׁוּעוֹת
צוֹפֶה עֲתִידוֹת
קוֹרֵא הַדּוֹרוֹת
רוֹכֵב עֲרָבוֹת
שׁוֹמֵעַ תְּפִלּוֹת
תְּמִים דֵּעוֹת.

חָטָאנוּ לְפָנֶיךָ רַחֵם עָלֵינוּ:

Gentle God, you are reluctant to grow angry,
rightly are you called a God of mercy.
You have shown the path of *teshuvah*,
of return to you.

May you remember the abundance
of your mercy and your lovingkindness,
today and every day,
for the seed of those who love you.

May you turn in mercy toward us,
for you hold all the mercy in the world.
May we rush to seek your presence with our prayers,
according to what you made known of old.

Return to us, leaving behind your anger,
as it is written in your Torah,
and may we find refuge in your sheltering presence,
as on the day when THE ETERNAL ONE descended in a cloud.

May you pass over our transgressions,
and erase our guilt, as on the day
when your Presence became manifest
to Moses in the second giving
of the Tablets of your Law.

May you hear our cry,
and hearken to our utterance of prayer,
as, on that day, you called the name of THE ETERNAL,
as it is told:

"THE OMNIPRESENT passed before him and declared..."

אֵל אֶֽרֶךְ אַפַּֽיִם אַתָּה וּבַֽעַל הָרַחֲמִים נִקְרֵֽאתָ וְדֶֽרֶךְ תְּשׁוּבָה הוֹרֵֽיתָ: גְּדֻלַּת רַחֲמֶֽיךָ וַחֲסָדֶֽיךָ תִּזְכֹּר הַיּוֹם וּבְכָל־יוֹם לְזֶֽרַע יְדִידֶֽיךָ: תֵּֽפֶן אֵלֵֽינוּ בְּרַחֲמִים כִּי אַתָּה הוּא בַּֽעַל הָרַחֲמִים:

בְּתַחֲנוּן וּבִתְפִלָּה פָּנֶֽיךָ נְקַדֵּם כְּהוֹדַֽעְתָּ לֶעָנָו מִקֶּֽדֶם: מֵחֲרוֹן אַפְּךָ שׁוּב כְּמוֹ בְּתוֹרָתְךָ כָּתוּב וּבְצֵל כְּנָפֶֽיךָ נֶחֱסֶה וְנִתְלוֹנָן כְּיוֹם וַיֵּֽרֶד יהוה בֶּעָנָן: תַּעֲבֹר עַל פֶּֽשַׁע וְתִמְחֶה אָשָׁם כְּיוֹם וַיִּתְיַצֵּב עִמּוֹ שָׁם תַּאֲזִין שַׁוְעָתֵֽנוּ וְתַקְשֵׁב מֶֽנּוּ מַאֲמָר כְּיוֹם וַיִּקְרָא בְשֵׁם יהוה: וְשָׁם נֶאֱמַר: וַיַּעֲבֹר יהוה עַל־פָּנָיו וַיִּקְרָא ←

ובצל...נחסה / and may...presence. Based on Psalms 36:8.

וירד יהוה בענן / THE ETERNAL ONE descended in a cloud. This refers to the events of Exodus 34: 1-7, when God gave Moses the Ten Commandments for a second time, and proclaimed the Thirteen Attributes of Divine Mercy. These lines are a principal motif throughout the High Holiday services because they stress the slowness of God to anger, the willingness of THE ETERNAL ONE to extend mercy to the thousandth generation of those who love the divine and follow in God's ways. Occurring as they do not long after the sin of the Golden Calf (Exodus 32), these verses thus stress, in the High Holiday context, God's readiness to forgive even a grievous wrongdoing if one's repentance is genuine. The rabbinic excerpting pointedly omitted the second half of Exodus 34:7, which, like Exodus 20:5, had been a more admonitory warning of punishment "up to the third and fourth generation" for those who sin (changing venakkeh lo' yenakkeh, "but will not hold innocent," to venakkeh, "and making clean"), thus radically revising the biblical concept of retributive justice to a far more unconditional emphasis on God's unlimited power to forgive. J.R.

ויעבר...ויקרא / THE OMINIPRESENT...declared (Exodus 34:6).

We rise.

ADONAY ADONAY, God loving and gracious,
patient, and abundant in kindness and truth,
keeping kindness for a thousand ages,
forgiving sin and rebellion and transgression,
making pure!

May you forgive our sins and our wrongdoing,
may you claim us as your own!

THE FOUNT OF LIFE!
    I am the One before the human being goes astray.
THE FOUNT OF MERCY!
    I am the One after the human being goes astray,
God!
    My quality of mercy is extended to all nations.
Merciful!
    To one who merits it.
And gracious!
    Even toward one who does not merit it.
Slow to grow angry!
    Delaying anger even toward the wicked, who can change.
Abundant in my love!
    To those in need of love.
And truth!
    To reward the ones who do My will.
Keeping love until the thousandth generation!
    When a person does good deeds.
Forgiving sin!
    Even for one who acts deliberately.
And wrongdoing!
    Even for those rebelling, and provoking God.
And transgression!
    For the one who acts merely by oversight.
Making clean!
    For those who turn toward God. ↩

We rise.

יְהוה יְהוה אֵל רַחוּם וְחַנּוּן אֶֽרֶךְ אַפַּֽיִם וְרַב־חֶֽסֶד וֶאֱמֶת נֹצֵר חֶֽסֶד
לָאֲלָפִים נֹשֵׂא עָוֹן וָפֶֽשַׁע וְחַטָּאָה וְנַקֵּה:

וְסָלַחְתָּ לַעֲוֺנֵֽנוּ וּלְחַטָּאתֵֽנוּ וּנְחַלְתָּֽנוּ:

אֲנִי הוּא קֹֽדֶם שֶׁיֶּחֱטָא הָאָדָם	יְהוה
אֲנִי הוּא לְאַחַר שֶׁיֶּחֱטָא הָאָדָם	יְהוה
מִדַּת הָרַחֲמִים גַּם לַגּוֹיִם	אֵל
לְמִי שֶׁיֵּשׁ לוֹ זְכוּת	רַחוּם
לְמִי שֶׁאֵין לוֹ זְכוּת	וְחַנּוּן
מַאֲרִיךְ אַף לָרְשָׁעִים אוּלַי יְשׁוּבוּן	אֶֽרֶךְ אַפַּֽיִם
לִנְצְרֵכֵי חֶֽסֶד	וְרַב חֶֽסֶד
לְשַׁלֵּם שָׂכָר לְעוֹשֵׂי רְצוֹנוֹ	וֶאֱמֶת
כְּשֶׁאָדָם עוֹשֶׂה טוֹב	נֹצֵר חֶֽסֶד לָאֲלָפִים
לְעוֹשֶׂה בְזָדוֹן	נֹשֵׂא עָוֹן
הַמּוֹרְדִים לְהַכְעִיס	וָפֶֽשַׁע
הָעוֹשֶׂה בִשְׁגָגָה	וְחַטָּאָה
לַשָּׁבִים ←	וְנַקֵּה

Adonay adonay el raḥum veḥanun ereḥ apayim verav ḥesed
ve'emet notzer ḥesed la'alafim nosey avon vafesha veḥata'ah
venakey. ᵌ

NOTE. This prayer was first placed in this location by Jules Harlow in the
1972 Rabbinical Assembly *maḥzor*. The Hebrew, by Mosheh Hakohen
Niral of the 18th century, uses rabbinic sources, including Talmud Rosh
Hashanah 17b. The prayer is a commentary on the thirteen attributes of
God (Exodus 34:6-7) that are a major refrain throughout the liturgy of the
Days of Awe. The commentary explores the connection between the
verses, the process of *teshuvah* and the nature of God.   D.A.T.

ונחלתנו...יהוה / ADONAY...own (Exodus 34:6-7, 9).

Forgive us, our creator, for we have done wrong,
grant pardon to us, sovereign, for we have transgressed
for you, ETERNAL ONE, are good and merciful,
abundant in your steadfast love
to all who call on you!

We are seated.

༄

Just like the lump of clay
held in the sculptor's hands:
at will, the sculptor stretches it,
at will, the sculptor makes it small.
And so are we in your hands,
and so let love preserve;
look to your covenant,
and do not let your anger serve.

Just like the piece of stone
held in the mason's hands:
at will, the mason picks it up,
at will, the mason cuts.
And so are we in your hands,
you give life and take it away;
look to your covenant,
and do not let your anger sway.

Just like the axe's blade
held in the blacksmith's hands:
at will, it is plunged into the fire,
at will, it is taken out.
And so are we in your hands;
you feed the needy and the poor,
look to your covenant,
and let your anger rule no more. ↵

סְלַח לָנוּ אָבִינוּ כִּי חָטָאנוּ מְחַל לָנוּ מַלְכֵּנוּ כִּי פָשָׁעְנוּ: כִּי־אַתָּה
אֲדֹנָי טוֹב וְסַלָּח וְרַב־חֶסֶד לְכָל־קוֹרְאֶיךָ:

We are seated.

∾

כִּי הִנֵּה כַחֹמֶר בְּיַד הַיּוֹצֵר בִּרְצוֹתוֹ מַרְחִיב וּבִרְצוֹתוֹ מְקַצֵּר: כֵּן
אֲנַחְנוּ בְיָדְךָ חֶסֶד נוֹצֵר   לַבְּרִית הַבֵּט וְאַל תֵּפֶן לַיֵּצֶר:

כִּי הִנֵּה כָאֶבֶן בְּיַד הַמְסַתֵּת בִּרְצוֹתוֹ אוֹחֵז וּבִרְצוֹתוֹ מְכַתֵּת: כֵּן
אֲנַחְנוּ בְיָדְךָ מְחַיֶּה וּמְמוֹתֵת   לַבְּרִית הַבֵּט וְאַל תֵּפֶן לַיֵּצֶר:

כִּי הִנֵּה כַגַּרְזֶן בְּיַד הֶחָרָשׁ בִּרְצוֹתוֹ דִּבֵּק לָאוּר וּבִרְצוֹתוֹ פֵּרֵשׁ: כֵּן
אֲנַחְנוּ בְיָדְךָ תּוֹמֵךְ עָנִי וָרָשׁ   לַבְּרִית הַבֵּט וְאַל תֵּפֶן לַיֵּצֶר: ←

כי אתה...לכל־קוראיך /for...you! (Psalms 86:5).

KAVANAH. The image of God as potter and humans as unmolded clay is problematic for some of us. We humans don't want to think of ourselves as so unformed, so susceptible to manipulation by an inscrutable and distant God. But if we consider this prayer as a metaphor for partnership, we note that any artisan, no matter how skilled, cannot produce a thing of beauty unless the raw material is good. If we think of God as helping us to make our lives a thing of beauty, we may joyfully offer the raw material that is ourselves to God.

L.G.B.

COMMENTARY. A Hebrew pun in this hymn connects *yotzer*/creator with *yetzer*/anger. Powerful forces in creative hands can bring out beauty and meaning. In anger these hands can deform or crush. We pray that the powerful connection/covenant linking us to the divine source will overpower our potential for evil and bring to light our ultimate worth.

Adina Abramowitz

DERASH. Like the raw materials of nature, we each possess potential and resistance to developing that potential. This poem invokes the power that will shape our potential for the greatest beauty, service, and goodness. We ask that the resistance to that unfolding be overcome through loving and creative relationship.

S.P.W.

Just like the wheel of the ship
held in the pilot's hands:
at will, the pilot turns it in,
at will, the pilot turns it out.
And so are we in your hands,
O, God who blesses and forgives;
look to your covenant,
and in your mercy let us live.

Just like the glass
held in the glassmaker's hands:
at will, it is given form,
at will, it is melted down.
And so are we in your hands;
you make wrongdoing pass away,
look to your covenant,
and don't let anger have its way.

Just like the curtain's cloth
held in the embroiderer's hands:
at will, it is made to lie flat,
at will, it is gathered up.
And so are we in your hands,
O, God of justice and of zeal;
look to your covenant,
and let your anger be concealed.

Just like the silver
held in the smelter's hands:
at will, it is blended with a metal,
at will, it is purified.
And so are we in your hands,
you who give healing to all ills;
look to your covenant,
and let not anger shape your will.

כִּי הִנֵּה כַחֹמֶר בְּיַד הַמַּלָּח בִּרְצוֹתוֹ אוֹחֵז וּבִרְצוֹתוֹ שִׁלַּח: כֵּן אֲנַחְנוּ
בְיָדְךָ אֵל טוֹב וְסַלָּח   לַבְּרִית הַבֵּט וְאַל הֵפֶן לַיֵּצֶר:

כִּי הִנֵּה כִזְכוּכִית בְּיַד הַמְזַגֵּג בִּרְצוֹתוֹ חוֹגֵג וּבִרְצוֹתוֹ מְמוֹגֵג: כֵּן
אֲנַחְנוּ בְיָדְךָ מַעֲבִיר זָדוֹן וְשָׁגֵג   לַבְּרִית הַבֵּט וְאַל הֵפֶן לַיֵּצֶר:

כִּי הִנֵּה כַיְרִיעָה בְּיַד הָרוֹקֵם בִּרְצוֹתוֹ מְיַשֵּׁר וּבִרְצוֹתוֹ מְעַקֵּם: כֵּן
אֲנַחְנוּ בְיָדְךָ אֵל קַנָּא וְנוֹקֵם   לַבְּרִית הַבֵּט וְאַל הֵפֶן לַיֵּצֶר:

כִּי הִנֵּה כַכֶּסֶף בְּיַד הַצּוֹרֵף בִּרְצוֹתוֹ מְסַגְסֵג וּבִרְצוֹתוֹ מְצָרֵף: כֵּן
אֲנַחְנוּ בְיָדְךָ מַמְצִיא לְמָזוֹר תֶּרֶף   לַבְּרִית הַבֵּט וְאַל הֵפֶן לַיֵּצֶר:

COMMENTARY. In hundreds of ways we receive the message that we are independent individuals, that private thought and personal conscience can make us whatever we want to be. But thought and conscience are profoundly shaped by the limits and opportunities contained in the language we speak, the historical circumstances in which we live and the communities of which we are a part. So vast are the forces that shape us! We are indeed molded like clay, shaped like molten metal, chipped at like stone. However, we do have the ability to choose communities, learn languages and seek meaning. The challenge is to become aware of what is molding us so that we can place ourselves where we can be shaped by forces of transcendence and goodness.   D.A.T.

COMMENTARY. This poem suggests, in a series of beautiful images, that our destiny is not ultimately shaped by our own efforts, but by a Power that often supports us and sometimes overwhelms us. So many things remain beyond our control; so many circumstances, unplanned and unanticipated, have brought us to this time, this place, this season. Before this reality, our posture is one of humility.   R.H.

Remember, for our sake,
the ancestral covenant, as you have promised:

"And I shall remember my covenant with Jacob,
and, as well, my covenant with Isaac,
and, as well, my covenant with Abraham;
I shall remember them, and shall recall
the Land I promised them."   Leviticus 26:42

Remember, for our sake,
the covenant of former times, as you have promised:

"And I shall remember, for their sake,
the covenant of former times,
whereby I brought them from the land of Egypt,
in the sight of all the nations,
to become their God,
I am THE LAWGIVER!"   Leviticus 26:45

Have mercy on us, and do not destroy us, as it is written:

"For THE FOUNT OF MERCY is a God compassionate,
who shall not let you wither, and shall not destroy you,
nor shall God forget the covenant made with your ancestors,
the one promised by oath to them."   Deuteronomy 4:31

Open up our hearts to love and to revere your name,
as it is written:

"THE BOUNTIFUL, your God, shall circumcise your hearts,
and your children's hearts,
to love THE FOUNT OF LIFE, your God,
with all your heart, with all your soul,
that you might live."   Deuteronomy 30:6

זְכָר־לָנוּ בְּרִית אָבוֹת כַּאֲשֶׁר אָמַרְתָּ׃
וְזָכַרְתִּי אֶת־בְּרִיתִי יַעֲקוֹב וְאַף אֶת־בְּרִיתִי יִצְחָק וְאַף אֶת־בְּרִיתִי
אַבְרָהָם אֶזְכֹּר וְהָאָרֶץ אֶזְכֹּר׃

זְכָר־לָנוּ בְּרִית רִאשׁוֹנִים כַּאֲשֶׁר אָמַרְתָּ׃
וְזָכַרְתִּי לָהֶם בְּרִית רִאשׁוֹנִים אֲשֶׁר הוֹצֵאתִי־אֹתָם מֵאֶרֶץ מִצְרַיִם
לְעֵינֵי הַגּוֹיִם לִהְיוֹת לָהֶם לֵאלֹהִים אֲנִי יהוה׃

רַחֵם עָלֵינוּ וְאַל תַּשְׁחִיתֵנוּ כְּמָה שֶׁכָּתוּב׃
כִּי אֵל רַחוּם יהוה אֱלֹהֶיךָ לֹא יַרְפְּךָ וְלֹא יַשְׁחִיתֶךָ וְלֹא יִשְׁכַּח אֶת־
בְּרִית אֲבֹתֶיךָ אֲשֶׁר נִשְׁבַּע לָהֶם׃

מוֹל אֶת־לְבָבֵנוּ לְאַהֲבָה אֶת שְׁמֶךָ כְּמָה שֶׁכָּתוּב׃
וּמָל יהוה אֱלֹהֶיךָ אֶת־לְבָבְךָ וְאֶת־לְבַב זַרְעֶךָ לְאַהֲבָה אֶת־יהוה
אֱלֹהֶיךָ בְּכָל־לְבָבְךָ וּבְכָל־נַפְשְׁךָ לְמַעַן חַיֶּיךָ׃ ←

COMMENTARY. How can we be in a covenant with the Creator of all? How do we dare ask to be remembered with compassion? Where in our hearts is the capacity to reach out beyond the known, the limited, the failures of our lives to imagine something different? Our ancestors have bequeathed it all to us—the covenant, the memory, the compassion and the imagination. Do we dare accept our inheritance?　　　　S.P.W.

COMMENTARY. ומל יהוה אלהיך את לבבך/your God shall circumcise your hearts. Jewish tradition links circumcision to covenantal commitment and to purification. The heart, which the rabbis understood to be the seat of the intellect, is not physically circumcised but, through divine will, purified and rededicated to covenantal service. The act of circumcision creates a wound and makes the one who is circumcised vulnerable. The poet here freely offers our vulnerability, our openness to transformation, as part of our Yom Kippur prayer for purification.　　　　D.A.T.

Be present for us when we call on you, as it is written:

"And you shall seek out THE BELOVED ONE, your God,
from where you are, and you shall find God,
provided that you search for God
with all your heart and all your soul." Deuteronomy 4:29

Blot out our sins upon this day, and purify us, as it is written:

"For on this day, atonement shall be made for you,
to make you clean from all your wrongdoings.
Before THE FOUNT OF MERCY, you shall all be clean."

Leviticus 16:30

༄

Pour out your heart like water
in the presence of THE LIVING GOD. Lamentations 2:19

༄

Return us, PRECIOUS ONE, let us return!
Renew our days, as you have done of old! Lamentations 5:21

הַמָּצֵא לָֽנוּ בְּבַקָּשָׁתֵֽנוּ כְּמָה שֶׁכָּתוּב:
וּבִקַּשְׁתֶּם מִשָּׁם אֶת־יהוה אֱלֹהֶֽיךָ וּמָצָֽאתָ כִּי תִדְרְשֶֽׁנּוּ בְּכָל־לְבָבְךָ
וּבְכָל־נַפְשֶֽׁךָ:

כַּפֵּר חַטָּאֵֽינוּ בַּיּוֹם הַזֶּה וְטַהֲרֵֽנוּ כְּמָה שֶׁכָּתוּב:
כִּי־בַיּוֹם הַזֶּה יְכַפֵּר עֲלֵיכֶם לְטַהֵר אֶתְכֶם מִכֹּל חַטֹּאתֵיכֶם לִפְנֵי יהוה
תִּטְהָֽרוּ:

&

שִׁפְכִי כַמַּֽיִם לִבֵּךְ נֹֽכַח פְּנֵי אֲדֹנָי:

Shifḥi ḥamayim libeḥ noḥaḥ peney adonay.

&

הֲשִׁיבֵֽנוּ יהוה אֵלֶֽיךָ וְנָשֽׁוּבָה חַדֵּשׁ יָמֵֽינוּ כְּקֶֽדֶם:

Hashivenu adonay eleḥa venashuvah ḥadesh yameynu kekedem.

O, sovereign God, presiding on the Throne of Mercy,
you whose way is to be loving,
you who grant forgiveness
for transgressions of your people,
you who readily ignore the first misdeeds,
abundant in forgiveness for our shortcomings,
and quick to pardon those who have done wrong,
enacting justice for all flesh and spirit,
yet reluctant to requite their evil deeds in kind,
you, God, who instructed us,
declaring thirteen attributes of God,
remember us today, and call to mind
your covenant of thirteen qualities of mercy,
as you once taught your humble prophet in days past—
for thus is written: "And THE ETERNAL ONE
came down amid the cloud, and stood before him there,
and called the name of THE COMPASSIONATE,
and THE ALL-MERCIFUL passed by before him and declared: ↵

אֵל מֶלֶךְ יוֹשֵׁב עַל כִּסֵּא רַחֲמִים מִתְנַהֵג בַּחֲסִידוּת מוֹחֵל עֲוֹנוֹת עַמּוֹ מַעֲבִיר רִאשׁוֹן רִאשׁוֹן מַרְבֶּה מְחִילָה לְחַטָּאִים וּסְלִיחָה לְפוֹשְׁעִים עוֹשֶׂה צְדָקוֹת עִם כָּל־בָּשָׂר וָרוּחַ וְלֹא כְרָעָתָם תִּגְמֹל:

אֵל הוֹרֵיתָ לָּנוּ לוֹמַר שְׁלֹשׁ עֶשְׂרֵה זְכָר־לָנוּ הַיּוֹם בְּרִית שְׁלֹשׁ עֶשְׂרֵה כְּהוֹדַעְתָּ לֶעָנָו מִקֶּדֶם וְכֵן כָּתוּב: וַיֵּרֶד יהוה בֶּעָנָן וַיִּתְיַצֵּב עִמּוֹ שָׁם וַיִּקְרָא בְשֵׁם יהוה: וַיַּעֲבֹר יהוה עַל־פָּנָיו וַיִּקְרָא: ←

וירד...ונחלתנו/And THE ETERNAL ONE...own! (Exodus 34:5-7, 9).

We rise.

ADONAY ADONAY, God loving and gracious,
patient, and abundant in kindness and truth,
keeping kindness for a thousand ages,
forgiving sin and rebellion and transgression,
making pure!

May you forgive our sins and our wrongdoing,
may you claim us as your own!

Forgive us, our creator, for we have done wrong,
grant pardon to us, sovereign, for we have transgressed,
for you, ETERNAL ONE, are good and merciful,
abundant in your steadfast love
to all who call on you! ↵

DERASH. Those who believe that God will punish wrongdoing with
directed thunderbolts understand divine forgiveness as a reprieve from
thunderbolts. What do we, who do not believe in divine thunderbolts,
mean by divine forgiveness? Divine forgiveness is manifest in our coming
to understand that wrongdoing is not part of our essence. We are forgiven
when we once again understand that our source is in the divine and that
we can act accordingly. This is why the process that leads to forgiveness is
called *teshuvah*/returning; we return to our own godly essence.   J.A.S.

We rise.

יהוה יהוה אֵל רַחוּם וְחַנּוּן אֶרֶךְ אַפַּיִם וְרַב־חֶסֶד וֶאֱמֶת נֹצֵר חֶסֶד
לָאֲלָפִים נֹשֵׂא עָוֹן וָפֶשַׁע וְחַטָּאָה וְנַקֵּה:

וְסָלַחְתָּ לַעֲוֹנֵנוּ וּלְחַטָּאתֵנוּ וּנְחַלְתָּנוּ:

סְלַח לָנוּ אָבִינוּ כִּי חָטָאנוּ מְחַל לָנוּ מַלְכֵּנוּ כִּי פָשָׁעְנוּ: כִּי־אַתָּה
אֲדֹנָי טוֹב וְסַלָּח וְרַב־חֶסֶד לְכָל־קוֹרְאֶיךָ: ←

Adonay adonay el raḥum veḥanun ereḥ apayim verav ḥesed
ve'emet notzer ḥesed la'alafim nosey avon vafesha veḥata'ah
venakey. ↵

SHEMA KOLENU / HEAR OUR VOICE

Hear our voice, ETERNAL ONE, our God,
and accept our prayer with mercy and good will.
Turn us, ANCIENT ONE, toward you,
that we might be enabled to return.
Renew our days like days of old.
Do not cast us away from dwelling in your presence,
and do not remove your holy spirit from our midst.
And do not cast us off as we grow old;
do not forsake us when our strength departs.
Do not forsake us, GENTLE ONE, our God,
do not withdraw from us.
Give us a sign of blessing, so that anyone who bears us ill
shall hesitate to harm us.
For truly you, ETERNAL ONE,
have always helped us and consoled us.
Hear now our words, GOD OF COMPASSION,
and behold our contemplation.
May our words of prayer and meditations of our hearts
be seen favorably, PRECIOUS ONE, our rock, our champion.
For we place our hope in you, ETERNAL ONE,
so may you answer us, Almighty One, our God. ↵

We are seated.

אל תשליכנו לעת זקנה / Do not cast us off as we grow old. Torah teaches, "You shall rise before the aged and show deference to the old" (Leviticus 19:32). Ben Sira 25:6 teaches, "Wise advice comes from the elders."

NOTE. *Shema Kolenu* after its introductory line is composed entirely of biblical verses adapted by the poet from singular to plural form: Lamentations 5:21, Psalms 51:13, Psalms 71:9, Psalms 38:22, Psalms 86:17, Psalms 5:2, Psalms 19:15, Psalms 38:16.   M.B.K.

יהוה אֱלֹהֵינוּ חוּס וְרַחֵם עָלֵינוּ

וְקַבֵּל בְּרַחֲמִים וּבְרָצוֹן אֶת־תְּפִלָּתֵנוּ:

הֲשִׁיבֵנוּ יהוה אֵלֶיךָ וְנָשׁוּבָה חַדֵּשׁ יָמֵינוּ כְּקֶדֶם:

אַל־תַּשְׁלִיכֵנוּ מִלְּפָנֶיךָ וְרוּחַ קָדְשְׁךָ אַל־תִּקַּח מִמֶּנּוּ:

אַל־תַּשְׁלִיכֵנוּ לְעֵת זִקְנָה כִּכְלוֹת כֹּחֵנוּ אַל־תַּעַזְבֵנוּ:

אַל־תַּעַזְבֵנוּ יהוה אֱלֹהֵינוּ אַל־תִּרְחַק מִמֶּנּוּ:

עֲשֵׂה־עִמָּנוּ אוֹת לְטוֹבָה וְיִרְאוּ שׂוֹנְאֵינוּ וְיֵבֹשׁוּ

כִּי־אַתָּה יהוה עֲזַרְתָּנוּ וְנִחַמְתָּנוּ:

אֲמָרֵינוּ הַאֲזִינָה יהוה בִּינָה הֲגִיגֵנוּ:

יִהְיוּ לְרָצוֹן אִמְרֵי־פִינוּ וְהֶגְיוֹן לִבֵּנוּ לְפָנֶיךָ יהוה צוּרֵנוּ וְגוֹאֲלֵנוּ:

כִּי־לְךָ יהוה הוֹחָלְנוּ אַתָּה תַעֲנֶה אֲדֹנָי אֱלֹהֵינוּ: ←

We are seated.

Shema ko__le__nu adonay elo__he__ynu ḥus veraḥem a__le__ynu
vekabel beraḥamim uveratzon et tefila__te__nu.

Hashi__ve__nu adonay ele__ḥa__ venashuvah ḥadesh ya__me__ynu ke__ke__dem.

Al tashli__ḥe__nu milefa__ne__ḥa veru'aḥ kodshe__ḥa al tikaḥ mi__me__nu.

Al tashli__ḥe__nu le'et ziknah ki__ḥlot ko__ḥe__nu al ta'az__ve__nu.

Al ta'az__ve__nu adonay elo__he__ynu al tirḥak mi__me__nu.

Asey i__ma__nu ot letovah veyiru so__ne__ynu veye__vo__shu
ki atah adonay azar__ta__nu veniḥam__ta__nu.

Ama__re__ynu ha'azi__nah adonay __bi__nah hagi__ge__nu.

Yihyu leratzon imrey __fi__nu vehegyon li__be__nu lefa__ne__ḥa adonay
tzu__re__nu vego'a__le__nu.

Ki le__ḥa__ adonay hoḥalnu atah ta'aneh adonay elo__he__ynu. ↵

אל תשליכנו לעת זקנה/do not cast us off when we are old. In a world that worships youth and physical strength, old age is often viewed as a curse. In this prayer we ask God not to abandon us as we age. The whole community hears this plea, for the Torah teaches that "you shall rise before the aged and show deference to the old" (Leviticus 19:32, which is read on Yom Kippur afternoon). Our tradition asks us to do right by those who have cared for us and sees the experience, memories and wisdom of our elders as an invaluable resource for us.   L.G.B.

Our God, our ancients' God,
do not forsake us, and do not turn away,
and do not cause us shame,
and do not nullify your covenant with us,
but bring us nearer to your Torah,
teach us your mitzvot,
instruct us in your ways.
Incline our hearts to treat your name with awe,
and open up our inner nature to your love,
and bring us back to you in truth,
with whole and peaceful heart.
And for the sake of your great name,
be merciful, and grant forgiveness for our wrongs,
as it is written in your prophets' words:
"For the sake of your great name, ETERNAL ONE,
forgive my wrongdoing, for I have done much wrong."

Our God, our ancients' God,
forgive us, pardon us, help us atone—
for we are your people, and you are our God,
we are your children, and you are our creator,
we are your servants, and you are our sovereign,
we are your community, and you are our portion,
we are your possession, and you are our fate,
we are your sheep, and you are our shepherd,
we are your vineyard, and you are our keeper,
we are your creation, and you are our fashioner,
we are your loved ones, and you are our beloved,
we are your treasure, and you are our kin,
we are your people, and you are our ruler,
we are your faithful, and you our source of faith! ↩

למען...הוא / For...wrong (Psalms 25:11).

אֱלֹהֵינוּ וֵאלֹהֵי אֲבוֹתֵינוּ וְאִמּוֹתֵנוּ אַל תַּעַזְבֵנוּ וְאַל תִּטְּשֵׁנוּ וְאַל
תַּכְלִימֵנוּ וְאַל תָּפֵר בְּרִיתְךָ אִתָּנוּ קָרְבֵנוּ לְתוֹרָתֶךָ לַמְּדֵנוּ מִצְוֹתֶיךָ
הוֹרֵנוּ דְרָכֶיךָ הַט לִבֵּנוּ לְיִרְאָה אֶת־שְׁמֶךָ וּמוֹל אֶת־לְבָבֵנוּ לְאַהֲבָתֶךָ
וְנָשׁוּב אֵלֶיךָ בֶּאֱמֶת וּבְלֵב שָׁלֵם וּלְמַעַן שִׁמְךָ הַגָּדוֹל תִּמְחַל וְתִסְלַח
לַעֲוֺנֵנוּ כַּכָּתוּב בְּדִבְרֵי קָדְשֶׁךָ: לְמַעַן־שִׁמְךָ יהוה וְסָלַחְתָּ לַעֲוֺנִי כִּי
רַב־הוּא:

אֱלֹהֵינוּ וֵאלֹהֵי אֲבוֹתֵינוּ וְאִמּוֹתֵינוּ סְלַח לָנוּ: מְחַל לָנוּ: כַּפֶּר לָנוּ:

אָנוּ בָנֶיךָ וְאַתָּה אָבִינוּ:	כִּי אָנוּ עַמֶּךָ וְאַתָּה אֱלֹהֵינוּ:
אָנוּ קְהָלֶךָ וְאַתָּה חֶלְקֵנוּ:	אָנוּ עֲבָדֶיךָ וְאַתָּה אֲדוֹנֵינוּ:
אָנוּ צֹאנֶךָ וְאַתָּה רוֹעֵנוּ:	אָנוּ נַחֲלָתֶךָ וְאַתָּה גוֹרָלֵנוּ:
אָנוּ פְעֻלָּתֶךָ וְאַתָּה יוֹצְרֵנוּ:	אָנוּ כַרְמֶךָ וְאַתָּה נוֹטְרֵנוּ:
אָנוּ סְגֻלָּתֶךָ וְאַתָּה קְרוֹבֵנוּ:	אָנוּ רַעְיָתֶךָ וְאַתָּה דוֹדֵנוּ:
אָנוּ מַאֲמִירֶךָ וְאַתָּה מַאֲמִירֵנוּ: ←	אָנוּ עַמֶּךָ וְאַתָּה מַלְכֵּנוּ:

Eloheynu velohey avoteynu ve'imoteynu selaḥ lanu. Meḥal lanu.
Kaper lanu.
Ki anu ameḥa ve'atah eloheynu. Anu vaneḥa ve'atah avinu.
Anu avadeḥa ve'atah adoneynu. Anu kehaleḥa ve'atah ḥelkenu.
Anu naḥalateḥa ve'atah goralenu. Anu tzoneḥa ve'atah ro'enu.
Anu ḥarmeḥa ve'atah notrenu. Anu fe'ulateḥa ve'atah yotzrenu.
Anu rayateḥa ve'atah dodenu. Anu segulateḥa ve'atah kerovenu.
Anu ameḥa ve'atah malkenu. Anu ma'amireḥa ve'atah ma'amirenu.

COMMENTARY. The *piyut* "*ki anu ameḥa*/for we are your people"
exemplifies the long Jewish tradition of reveling in the variety of possible
metaphors for our relationship with the divine. The various English
renderings of the divine name in the Reconstructionist *siddurim*/prayer-
books reflect this tradition. Metaphors cannot capture the fullness of the
Divine, but through them we revel in its many manifestations.   J.A.S.

We are strong-willed and stubborn,
but you are merciful and gracious.
We are stiff-necked, but you are slow to anger.
We are full of error, but you are full of mercy.
We—our days are like a passing shadow,
but you are one whose years shall never end.

Our God, our ancients' God,
may our prayer come before you.
Hide not from our supplication,
for we are not so insolent and stubborn
as to say, here in your presence,
"HOLY ONE, God of our fathers and our mothers,
We are righteous, and we have not sinned,"
for we indeed have sinned. ↵

אָנוּ עַזֵּי פָנִים וְאַתָּה רַחוּם וְחַנּוּן: אָנוּ קְשֵׁי עֹרֶף וְאַתָּה אֶרֶךְ אַפַּיִם:
אָנוּ מְלֵאֵי עָוֹן וְאַתָּה מָלֵא רַחֲמִים: אָנוּ יָמֵינוּ כְּצֵל עוֹבֵר וְאַתָּה הוּא
וּשְׁנוֹתֶיךָ לֹא יִתָּמּוּ:

אֱלֹהֵינוּ וֵאלֹהֵי אֲבוֹתֵינוּ וְאִמּוֹתֵינוּ תָּבוֹא לְפָנֶיךָ תְּפִלָּתֵנוּ וְאַל
תִּתְעַלַּם מִתְּחִנָּתֵנוּ שֶׁאֵין אֲנַחְנוּ עַזֵּי פָנִים וּקְשֵׁי עֹרֶף לוֹמַר לְפָנֶיךָ
יהוה אֱלֹהֵינוּ וֵאלֹהֵי אֲבוֹתֵינוּ וְאִמּוֹתֵינוּ צַדִּיקִים אֲנַחְנוּ וְלֹא חָטָאנוּ
אֲבָל אֲנַחְנוּ חָטָאנוּ: ←

Today we stand before the Mirror of All
to see ourselves as we are.
We come with no gifts, no bribes, no illusions, no excuses.
We stand without defense and wait to be filled.
What will fill us?
Remorse, certainly. So much error and needless pain.
And joy: remembered moments of love and right doing.
We are too complex for single-sided emotions.
And we are too simple to be excused by our complexity.
Let us be bold enough to see,
humble enough to feel,
daring enough to turn and
embrace the way of justice, mercy, and simplicity.   R.M.S.

We rise.

We have acted wrongly,
we have been untrue,
and we have gained unlawfully
and have defamed.
We have harmed others,
we have wrought injustice,
we have zealously transgressed,
and we have hurt
and have told lies.
We have improperly advised,
and we have covered up the truth,
and we have laughed in scorn.
We have misused responsibility
and have neglected others
and have stubbornly rebelled.
We have offended,
we have perverted justice,
we have stirred up enmity,
and we have kept ourselves from change.
We have reached out to evil,
we have shamelessly corrupted
and have treated others with disdain.
Yes, we have thrown ourselves off course,
and we have tempted and misled.

We are seated.

COMMENTARY. The sin offering of Temple days was an act of penance that wiped the transgressor's slate clean. At various times and places, Jews have marked the High Holy Day season with other acts of penance—rising at midnight and dawn to recite *selihot*/penitential prayers, giving increased amounts of *tzedakah*, and even bathing in icy river water. The act of striking one's chest during the *Vidui* and *Al Het* prayers can be understood in part as this kind of penance.   D.A.T.

אָשַׁמְנוּ: בָּגַדְנוּ: גָּזַלְנוּ: דִּבַּרְנוּ דֹפִי:
הֶעֱוִינוּ וְהִרְשַׁעְנוּ: זַדְנוּ: חָמַסְנוּ:
טָפַלְנוּ שֶׁקֶר: יָעַצְנוּ רָע: כִּזַּבְנוּ: לַצְנוּ:
מָרַדְנוּ: נִאַצְנוּ: סָרַרְנוּ: עָוִינוּ:
פָּשַׁעְנוּ: צָרַרְנוּ: קִשִּׁינוּ עֹרֶף: רָשַׁעְנוּ:
שִׁחַתְנוּ: תִּעַבְנוּ: תָּעִינוּ: תִּעְתָּעְנוּ:

Ashamnu bagadnu gazalnu dibarnu dofi.
He'evinu vehirshanu zadnu hamasnu
tafalnu shaker. Ya'atznu ra kizavnu latznu
maradnu ni'atznu sararnu avinu
pashanu tzararnu kishinu oref. Rashanu
shihatnu ti'avnu ta'inu titanu.

COMMENTARY. Keeping secrets private and holding back emotion are psychic misdemeanors for which nature visits us with sickness. But when secrets are told and emotions expressed in communion with others, they satisfy nature and may even count as useful virtues....There appears to be a conscience in humankind that severely punishes everyone who does not somehow and sometime, at whatever cost in personal pride, confess fallibility. Until one can do this, an impenetrable will shuts one off from the vital feeling of being fully human. This explains the extraordinary significance of genuine, straightforward confession—a truth that was probably known to all initiation rites and mystery cults of the ancient world. There is a saying among Greek mysteries, "Give up what you have, and you will receive."   Carl Jung (Adapted)

COMMENTARY. The *Vidui* is an "a to z" of confession, with a sin for each letter of the alphabet. We human beings are extraordinarily creative, so the variety of our possible transgressions is endless. This summary confession cannot be infinite. On the other side of confession lies forgiveness, renewal and redemptive action.   D.A.T.

We have turned away from your mitzvot,
and from your righteous laws,
as if it did not matter to us.
And you are just,
whatever comes upon us,
for what you do is truth,
and we have done much wrong.

We have done wrong, and have rebelled.
And so, we were not ready for your help.
Place into our hearts the will
to leave behind the path of evil,
and so hasten our redemption and renewal—
as is written by your prophet's hand:
"Let the wicked leave behind their unjust way,
let the unworthy cast away their plans,
let them return to THE COMPASSIONATE, who will be merciful,
returning to our God, who shall abundantly forgive."

KAVANAH. We have abandoned the right path, and it has not benefited us.
We have left justice and mercy for selfishness and cruelty, hoping in this
way to make ourselves happy. We imagined that the more we control, the
more happy we will be; the more we bend others to our will, the more we
will find joy. And we imagined wrongly.   R.M.S.

סַרְנוּ מִמִּצְוֹתֶיךָ וּמִמִּשְׁפָּטֶיךָ הַטּוֹבִים וְלֹא שָׁוָה לָנוּ: וְאַתָּה צַדִּיק עַל
כָּל־הַבָּא עָלֵינוּ כִּי־אֱמֶת עָשִׂיתָ וַאֲנַחְנוּ הִרְשָׁעְנוּ:

הִרְשַׁעְנוּ וּפָשַׁעְנוּ לָכֵן לֹא נוֹשָׁעְנוּ וְתֵן בְּלִבֵּנוּ לַעֲזֹב דֶּרֶךְ רֶשַׁע וְחִישׁ
לָנוּ יֶשַׁע כַּכָּתוּב עַל יַד נְבִיאֶךָ: יַעֲזֹב רָשָׁע דַּרְכּוֹ וְאִישׁ אָוֶן
מַחְשְׁבֹתָיו וְיָשֹׁב אֶל־יהוה וִירַחֲמֵהוּ וְאֶל־אֱלֹהֵינוּ כִּי־יַרְבֶּה לִסְלוֹחַ:

COMMENTARY. When things go wrong in our lives, it is a natural response
to say that God must be punishing us. It does not take a conscious divine
act, however, to punish us for poisoning rivers or being inattentive to the
educational needs of inner-city children. A person who lives a life in
harmony with the divine purpose in the world receives an inner reward.
For whole communities and nations who live that harmony, an outer,
more physical reward follows as well. Failure to live in harmony with the
divine will similarly contains its own punishment. We may prefer to say
that God punishes us, but it is we who punish ourselves.   D.A.T.

ואתה...הרשענו / And...wrong (Nehemiah 9:33).
יעזב...לסלוח / Let...forgive (Isaiah 55:7).

The wrongs we do,
both purposeful and unintentional,
you recognize,
both acts of will and of compulsion,
both what is revealed and what is hidden—
in your presence all becomes revealed and known.
What are we? What is our life?
What is our love? What is our justice?
What is our help? What is our strength?
What is our power?
What can we say before you,
ALL-DISCERNING ONE, our God, our ancients' God?
For are not all the mighty of this world
like nothing in your presence,
all who bear renown like those who never were,
all persons of wisdom like the ignorant,
and all who understand like those who lack intelligence?
For truly, most of what they do is but a void,
their days are like a puff of air before you.
The advantage of the human being over beasts
amounts to nothing—for everything,
measured against you,
lacks substance.

הַזְּדוֹנוֹת וְהַשְּׁגָגוֹת אַתָּה מַכִּיר הָרָצוֹן וְהָאֹנֶס הַגְּלוּיִים וְהַנִּסְתָּרִים
לְפָנֶיךָ הֵם גְּלוּיִים וִידוּעִים: מָה אָנוּ מֶה חַיֵּינוּ מֶה חַסְדֵּנוּ מַה־
צִּדְקֵנוּ מַה־יִּשְׁעֵנוּ מַה־כֹּחֵנוּ מַה־גְּבוּרָתֵנוּ מַה־נֹּאמַר לְפָנֶיךָ יהוה
אֱלֹהֵינוּ וֵאלֹהֵי אֲבוֹתֵינוּ וְאִמּוֹתֵינוּ הֲלֹא כָּל־הַגִּבּוֹרִים כְּאַיִן לְפָנֶיךָ
וְאַנְשֵׁי הַשֵּׁם כְּלֹא הָיוּ וַחֲכָמִים כִּבְלִי מַדָּע וּנְבוֹנִים כִּבְלִי הַשְׂכֵּל כִּי
רֹב מַעֲשֵׂיהֶם תֹּהוּ וִימֵי חַיֵּיהֶם הֶבֶל לְפָנֶיךָ וּמוֹתַר הָאָדָם מִן
הַבְּהֵמָה אָיִן כִּי הַכֹּל הָבֶל:

What can we say before you,
you who dwell on high?
What can we tell you,
you who inhabit heaven's heights?
Are you not one who knows all things,
both hidden and revealed?

From eternity you have been called
"the One who passes over transgression."
So hear our cry as we stand here
in prayer before you.
Pass over the transgression
of a people who return from their transgressing.
Erase our guilt from before your eyes.

You know the secrets of the universe,
the most hidden recesses of all that lives.
You search the chambers of our inner being,
you examine the conscience and the heart.
There is nothing hidden from you,
nothing is concealed before your eyes.
So, let it be your will,
ETERNAL ONE, our God, God of our ancestors,
that you may grant forgiveness to us for all of our sins,
and be merciful to us for all of our injustices,
and let us atone for all we have done wrong.

DERASH. Perhaps our actions have inflicted wounds on our own spirits,
wounds that have become secret even to us. God is present when our
recitation of the *Al Ḥet* confessions reveals those wounds to us and allows
for healing, transformation, and forgiveness. In this way, God is spoken of
as "knowing the secrets of all living beings." J.A.S.

מַה נֹּאמַר לְפָנֶיךָ יוֹשֵׁב מָרוֹם וּמַה נְּסַפֵּר לְפָנֶיךָ שׁוֹכֵן שְׁחָקִים הֲלֹא כָל הַנִּסְתָּרוֹת וְהַנִּגְלוֹת אַתָּה יוֹדֵעַ:

שִׁמְךָ מֵעוֹלָם עוֹבֵר עַל פֶּשַׁע שַׁוְעָתֵינוּ תַאֲזִין בְּעָמְדֵנוּ לְפָנֶיךָ בִּתְפִלָּה. תַּעֲבֹר עַל פֶּשַׁע לְעַם שָׁבֵי פֶשַׁע תִּמְחֶה פְּשָׁעֵינוּ מִנֶּגֶד עֵינֶיךָ:

אַתָּה יוֹדֵעַ רָזֵי עוֹלָם וְתַעֲלוּמוֹת סִתְרֵי כָל חָי: אַתָּה חוֹפֵשׁ כָּל חַדְרֵי בָטֶן וּבוֹחֵן כְּלָיוֹת וָלֵב: אֵין דָּבָר נֶעְלָם מִמֶּךָ וְאֵין נִסְתָּר מִנֶּגֶד עֵינֶיךָ: וּבְכֵן יְהִי רָצוֹן מִלְּפָנֶיךָ יהוה אֱלֹהֵינוּ וֵאלֹהֵי אֲבוֹתֵינוּ וְאִמּוֹתֵינוּ שֶׁתִּסְלַח לָנוּ עַל כָּל חַטֹּאתֵינוּ וְתִמְחַל לָנוּ עַל כָּל עֲוֹנוֹתֵינוּ וּתְכַפֶּר לָנוּ עַל כָּל פְּשָׁעֵינוּ:

COMMENTARY. We are about to recite the *Al Ḥet*, a strikingly collective confession of sins. There is no "I" in the prayer. On Yom Kippur we join together as a community to acknowledge the sins that *we* have committed. *Not I, but we.* The soul reckoning (*ḥeshbon hanefesh*) that we do on Yom Kippur is communal. We are all implicated in the personal acts, good or bad, of any individual in our community. Moreover, as part of a community we are all implicated in the acts, good or bad, that our community has done. The communal issue is not shame or guilt—that is a personal affair. The issue instead is responsibility. And that is ultimately collective, for wrongs are perpetrated and perpetuated only with the consent of the many, even if that consent is passive. The prayers of Yom Kippur challenge us to take responsibility for acts of *teshuvah*/turning, real steps as individuals and as a community, to redress communal wrongs.

C.B.

We rise.

For the wrong that we have done before you
in the closing of the heart,
and for the wrong that we have done before you
without knowing what we do.
For the wrong that we have done before you
whether open or concealed,
and for the wrong that we have done before you
knowingly and by deceit.

For the wrong that we have done before you
through the prompting of the heart,
and for the wrong that we have done before you
through the influence of others.
For the wrong that we have done before you
whether by intention or mistake,
and for the wrong that we have done before you
by the hand of violence.
For the wrong that we have done before you
through our foolishness of speech,
and for the wrong that we have done before you
through an evil inclination.

And for them all, God of forgiveness,
please forgive us, pardon us, help us atone!

NOTE. The traditional text of *Al Ḥet* consists of a double acrostic, with two wrongs listed for each letter of the Hebrew alphabet. For brevity, the text in this prayerbook is split into two single acrostics used alternately. Of course, individual communities have the option of shortening the list further or reciting alternative interpretive versions.   J.A.S.

 עַל חֵטְא

We rise.

עַל חֵטְא שֶׁחָטָאנוּ לְפָנֶיךָ בְּאִמּוּץ הַלֵּב:

וְעַל חֵטְא שֶׁחָטָאנוּ לְפָנֶיךָ בִּבְלִי דָעַת:

עַל חֵטְא שֶׁחָטָאנוּ לְפָנֶיךָ בַּגָּלוּי וּבַסָּתֶר:

וְעַל חֵטְא שֶׁחָטָאנוּ לְפָנֶיךָ בְּדַעַת וּבְמִרְמָה:

עַל חֵטְא שֶׁחָטָאנוּ לְפָנֶיךָ בְּהַרְהוֹר הַלֵּב:

וְעַל חֵטְא שֶׁחָטָאנוּ לְפָנֶיךָ בּוְעִידַת זְנוּת:

עַל חֵטְא שֶׁחָטָאנוּ לְפָנֶיךָ בְּזָדוֹן וּבִשְׁגָגָה:

וְעַל חֵטְא שֶׁחָטָאנוּ לְפָנֶיךָ בְּחֹזֶק יָד:

עַל חֵטְא שֶׁחָטָאנוּ לְפָנֶיךָ בְּטִפְשׁוּת פֶּה:

וְעַל חֵטְא שֶׁחָטָאנוּ לְפָנֶיךָ בְּיֵצֶר הָרָע:

⟵ וְעַל כֻּלָּם אֱלוֹהַ סְלִיחוֹת סְלַח לָנוּ: מְחַל לָנוּ: כַּפֶּר לָנוּ:

Ve'al kulam eloha seliḥot selaḥ lanu. Meḥal lanu. Kaper lanu. ⤶

COMMENTARY. It is customary for people to gently tap their chests with their fists once for each transgression of the *Vidui*. Even though the *Vidui* is stated in the plural, this tapping reminds us that each of us must ask ourselves not only which of these sins we have committed, but which of these sins we have failed to prevent others from committing.   D.A.T.

COMMENTARY. The *Vidui* and the *Al Ḥet* are more easily accessible to people who have a regular spiritual practice and connection to the Divine Source of Compassion. One's capacity to relate fully to the litany of transgression is enhanced by deep and regular prayer, meditation and self-scrutiny. We can identify with the transgressions that are listed if we have looked within ourselves many times. This collective confessional experience is a culmination of many private moments and hidden struggles, efforts to change, disappointments and occasional breakthroughs.   S.P.W.

For the wrong that we have done before you
  in the palming of a bribe,
and for the wrong that we have done before you
  by expressions of contempt.
For the wrong that we have done before you
  through misuse of food and drink,
and for the wrong that we have done before you
  by our avarice and greed.
For the wrong that we have done before you
  through offensive gaze,
and for the wrong that we have done before you
  through a condescending glance.

And for them all, God of forgiveness,
  please forgive us, pardon us, help us atone! ⮌

COMMENTARY. Consider how many of the sins we confess on Yom Kippur
are sins of speech. *'Al het shehatanu lefaneha*...for the wrong we have done
before you":
  "by the utterance of our lips"
  "by speech"
  "by false protests"
  "by impure lips"
  "by foolish speech"
  "by slander and innuendo"
  "by gossip"
  "by idle chatter"
  "by false promises."
When Esau approaches his aged and blind father Isaac in order to receive
the birthright blessing, he finds that he has been supplanted by his brother
Jacob. Isaac can only reply that "I blessed him; now he must remain
blessed." Words cannot be revoked, because words count. As the *midrash*
teaches: once the arrow has been shot from the bow it cannot be brought
back. (Midrash Tehilim 120:4)   R.H.

עַל חֵטְא שֶׁחָטָאנוּ לְפָנֶיךָ בְּכַפַּת שֹׁחַד:

וְעַל חֵטְא שֶׁחָטָאנוּ לְפָנֶיךָ בְּלָצוֹן:

עַל חֵטְא שֶׁחָטָאנוּ לְפָנֶיךָ בְּמַאֲכָל וּבְמִשְׁתֶּה:

וְעַל חֵטְא שֶׁחָטָאנוּ לְפָנֶיךָ בְּנֶשֶׁךְ וּבְמַרְבִּית:

עַל חֵטְא שֶׁחָטָאנוּ לְפָנֶיךָ בְּשִׂיקוּר עָיִן:

וְעַל חֵטְא שֶׁחָטָאנוּ לְפָנֶיךָ בְּעֵינַיִם רָמוֹת:

וְעַל כֻּלָּם אֱלוֹהַּ סְלִיחוֹת סְלַח לָנוּ: מְחַל לָנוּ: כַּפֶּר לָנוּ: ←

Ve'al kulam eloha seliḥot selaḥ lanu. Meḥal lanu. Kaper lanu. ↵

COMMENTARY. The *Al Ḥet* is a perfect fusion of the typical with the specific, a composite portrait of the fallibility not only of individuals but of a whole society. In the Hebrew original, it is an alphabetic acrostic, quite literally a lexicon of human wrongdoing. Not all of the things listed are categorical evils—many are quite ordinary, everyday actions and states of mind, cited not because they are intrinsically evil but because they are places where it is readily possible for evil to dwell. And so, foolishness of speech and confusion of heart are listed alongside bribery, deception, and violence.

The Hebrew expressions for sinful postures are often *bodily* postures— condescending glance is literally "lofty eyes"; arrogance and pride are literally "stretching of the throat"; refusing compromise is literally "fortifiedness of the forehead"; unwillingness to change is literally "stiffness of the neck." The sinning creature is a wrenched and distorted physical presence, a being out of harmony with itself and its surroundings.

In reciting this confession, one need not have enacted directly every one of its actions and states; one simply reminds oneself how habitually and systemically connected we are to a *climate* of wrongdoing. And thus, by naming its postures, we gain a certain freedom from what seemed to be their inevitability. We regain, in no small measure, the capacity to choose what we do and what we say.

J.R.

For the wrong that we have done before you
  by our quickness to oppose,
and for the wrong that we have done before you
  by deception of a friend.
For the wrong that we have done before you
  by unwillingness to change,
and for the wrong that we have done before you
  by our running to embrace an evil act.
For the wrong that we have done before you
  by our groundless hatred,
and for the wrong that we have done before you
  in the giving of false pledge.

And for them all, God of forgiveness,
  please forgive us, pardon us, help us atone!

We are seated.

Do not forsake us, you who have created us,
do not cast us away, you who brought us into being,
do not abandon us, you who fashioned us,
and do not cause us the destruction that our wrongs demand.

Your people, your inheritance,
those who hunger for your good,
those thirsty for your love,
those who yearn for your redemption,

they shall recognize and know
that to you alone, THE FOUNT OF LIFE, our God,
belongs all mercy,
all the forgiveness in the world.

עַל חֵטְא שֶׁחָטָאנוּ לְפָנֶיךָ בִּפְלִילוּת:

וְעַל חֵטְא שֶׁחָטָאנוּ לְפָנֶיךָ בִּצְדִיַּת רֵעַ:

עַל חֵטְא שֶׁחָטָאנוּ לְפָנֶיךָ בְּקַשְׁיוּת עֹרֶף:

וְעַל חֵטְא שֶׁחָטָאנוּ לְפָנֶיךָ בְּרִיצַת רַגְלַיִם לְהָרַע:

עַל חֵטְא שֶׁחָטָאנוּ לְפָנֶיךָ בְּשִׂנְאַת חִנָּם:

וְעַל חֵטְא שֶׁחָטָאנוּ לְפָנֶיךָ בִּתְשׂוּמֶת יָד:

וְעַל כֻּלָּם אֱלוֹהַּ סְלִיחוֹת סְלַח לָנוּ: מְחַל לָנוּ: כַּפֶּר לָנוּ:

Ve'al kulam e̲loha seliḥot selaḥ la̲nu. Meḥal la̲nu. Kaper la̲nu.

We are seated.

אַל תַּעַזְבֵנוּ אָבִינוּ וְאַל תִּטְּשֵׁנוּ בּוֹרְאֵנוּ וְאַל תַּזְנִיחֵנוּ יוֹצְרֵנוּ וְאַל תַּעַשׂ עִמָּנוּ כָּלָה כְּחַטֹּאתֵינוּ: עַמְּךָ וְנַחֲלָתְךָ רְעֵבֵי טוּבְךָ צְמֵאֵי חַסְדְּךָ תְּאֵבֵי יִשְׁעֶךָ: יַכִּירוּ וְיֵדְעוּ כִּי לַיהוה אֱלֹהֵינוּ הָרַחֲמִים וְהַסְּלִיחוֹת:

DERASH. Why are our confessionals always in the plural? At the moment of confession, each of us is alone and yet together with the whole community. At this moment of vulnerability, as we each confess our failures and weaknesses, we find comfort, strength and support in those around us who are engaged in the same process. Hand in hand, we find the strength to acknowledge weakness and failure. Hand in hand, we gain the courage to begin again.   L.G.B.

For the sins which we have sinned against you by misuse of ourselves:

By neglecting and overindulging our bodies, for "the body is not less the handiwork of God than the soul,"
And by neglecting mitzvot which nourish our souls,
By failing to study Torah,
And also by failing to think and to use the capacities of our minds.

All these sins, God of forgiveness, grant us the strength to confront honestly, the wisdom to analyze correctly, and the will to abandon completely, as we return to you.

For the sins which we have sinned against you and against those we love by the misuse of our capacity to love:

By using others as objects or tools,
And by placing our own status and pride before the needs of others.
By failing to use, with understanding and love, our power as employers and leaders, parents and teachers.
And by failing to accept with respect and love the authority of parents and teachers, employers and leaders,
By failing to perform acts of kindness, and visits to the sick and to mourners,
And by not being sensitive to others who turn to us in their need.
By forming intimate relationships without love as their basis,
And also by failing to deepen love continually throughout our committed relationships.

All these sins, God of forgiveness, grant us the strength to confront honestly, the wisdom to analyze correctly, and the will to abandon completely, as we return to you and to those we love.

For the sins which we have sinned against you and against our community by misuse of words:

By speaking dishonestly
And by breaking promises,
By gossiping and slandering,
By criticizing others quickly and destructively,
By keeping silent when we should have spoken
And also by failing to praise and to thank others.

All these sins, God of forgiveness, grant us the strength to confront honestly, the wisdom to analyze correctly, and the will to abandon completely, as we return to you, to those we love, and to our community.

For the sins we have sinned against you, against our people, and against the universe you have created, by misuse of our powers:

By failing to help our own people, everywhere in the world,
And by forgetting Hiroshima and Auschwitz,
By not accepting the responsibilities of citizenship in our nation and in the international community.
And by not recognizing the fragility of our planet and the unity of all life.
By not working enough against war, poverty, violence, racism, and the dehumanization of our society.
And also by not resisting the pollution and destruction of the natural world.

All these sins, God of forgiveness, grant us the strength to confront honestly, the wisdom to analyze correctly, and the will to abandon completely, so that we may use all our powers for good. Help us to return in joy to you, so that we may feel united in spirit with those we love, with our community and our people, with all humanity, with your universe, and with you.

Ruth Brin (Adapted)

Answer us, our **A**ncient source,
  give answer to our call!
Answer us, **B**lessed creator of us all,
  give answer to our call!
Answer us, **G**reat fount of our redemption,
  please give answer to our call!
Answer us, **D**ear one who seeks our good,
  give answer to our call!
Answer us, **H**eavenly splendor,
  please give answer to our call!
Answer us, **W**ith your eternal consolation,
  please give answer to our call!
Answer us, our **Z**ealous, righteous one,
  give answer to our call!
Answer us, our **H**oly fount of life,
  give answer to our call!
Answer us, **T**rue-sighted one,
  give answer to our call!
Answer us, **Y**ou who dwell in heaven's heights,
  give answer to our call!
Answer us, so **C**onsummate in strength,
  give answer to our call!
Answer us, you who **L**ove the good,
  give answer to our call!
Answer us, our **M**ightiest of sovereigns,
  give answer to our call! ↵

עֲנֵנוּ אָבִֽינוּ עֲנֵנוּ:
עֲנֵנוּ בּוֹרְאֵֽנוּ עֲנֵנוּ:
עֲנֵנוּ גּוֹאֲלֵֽנוּ עֲנֵנוּ:
עֲנֵנוּ דּוֹרְשֵֽׁנוּ עֲנֵנוּ:
עֲנֵנוּ הוֹד וְהָדָר עֲנֵנוּ:
עֲנֵנוּ וָתִיק בְּנֶחָמוֹת עֲנֵנוּ:
עֲנֵנוּ זָךְ וְיָשָׁר עֲנֵנוּ:
עֲנֵנוּ חַי וְקַיָּם עֲנֵנוּ:
עֲנֵנוּ טְהוֹר עֵינַֽיִם עֲנֵנוּ:
עֲנֵנוּ יוֹשֵׁב שָׁמַֽיִם עֲנֵנוּ:
עֲנֵנוּ כַּבִּיר כֹּחַ עֲנֵנוּ:
עֲנֵנוּ לֹא אֵל חָפֵץ בְּרֶֽשַׁע עֲנֵנוּ:
עֲנֵנוּ מֶֽלֶךְ מַלְכֵי הַמְּלָכִים עֲנֵנוּ: ←

COMMENTARY. The acrostic, which follows the order of the Hebrew alphabet, begs for an affirming response from God. Our lives are implicitly a call. We want answers in the form of relationships that connect us to others through caring. We want answers that promise economic stability and comfort. We want answers that give us a sense of security and understanding. Our very lives bespeak the plaintive calling for these things we seek. When we call to God, we are giving voice to our deepest needs and aspirations. In this community, let us find ways to sustain each other, protect each other, provide meaning and insight for each other. Only then can God's answer to our calling be present here.   D.A.T.

Answer us, our **N**oble and exalted one,
　　give answer to our call!
Answer us, **S**upporter of the falling,
　　please give answer to our call!
Answer us, **O** helper of the needy,
　　please give answer to our call!
Answer us, our **P**owerful redeemer,
　　please give answer to our call!
Answer us, **T**zadik—our just one who does justice—
　　please give answer to our call!
Answer us, **C**onsoler near at hand,
　　give answer to our call!
Answer us, **R**evered, exalted one,
　　give answer to our call!
Answer us, our **S**heltering presence in the heavens,
　　please give answer to our call!
Answer us, **T**rue mainstay of the righteous,
　　please give answer to our call!

The Merciful, who answers the afflicted,
　　answer us!
The Merciful, who answers the depressed of spirit,
　　answer us!
The Merciful, who answers the heartbroken,
　　answer us!
The Merciful, give answer to our call!
Merciful One, be sparing,
Merciful One, release us,
Merciful One, have mercy on us!
Now and soon and in our time!

עֲנֵנוּ נוֹרָא וְנִשְׂגָּב עֲנֵנוּ:
עֲנֵנוּ סוֹמֵךְ נוֹפְלִים עֲנֵנוּ:
עֲנֵנוּ עוֹזֵר דַּלִּים עֲנֵנוּ:
עֲנֵנוּ פּוֹדֶה וּמַצִּיל עֲנֵנוּ:
עֲנֵנוּ צַדִּיק וּמַצְדִּיק עֲנֵנוּ:
עֲנֵנוּ קָרוֹב לְקוֹרְאָיו עֲנֵנוּ:
עֲנֵנוּ רָם וְנִשָּׂא עֲנֵנוּ:
עֲנֵנוּ שׁוֹכֵן שְׁחָקִים עֲנֵנוּ:
עֲנֵנוּ תּוֹמֵךְ תְּמִימִים עֲנֵנוּ:

רַחֲמָנָא דְעָנֵי לַעֲנִיֵּי עֲנֵינָא: רַחֲמָנָא דְעָנֵי לְמַכִּיכֵי רוּחָא עֲנֵינָא:
רַחֲמָנָא דְעָנֵי לִתְבִירֵי לִבָּא עֲנֵינָא: רַחֲמָנָא עֲנֵינָא: רַחֲמָנָא חוּס:
רַחֲמָנָא פְּרוּק: רַחֲמָנָא שֵׁזִיב: רַחֲמָנָא עֲלַן הַשְׁתָּא בַּעֲגָלָא וּבִזְמַן
קָרִיב:

This is my prayer to you, my gentle God—
let me not stray from my life's course,
let not my spirit fall into decay,
and may it never cease to thirst for you,
and for the energizing dew
that you have sprinkled on it
ever since my life was new.

And let my heart be open to
the downtrodden, and to the orphaned life,
and to all who stumble,
and to one entangled amid hidden sorrows,
and to one who struggles in the dark.

And bless my eyes, and let me merit
to behold the human beauty in this world.

Deepen my senses, widen their grasp
so they absorb a green and flowering
and budding world, and take from it
the secret blossoming within a silence.

Grant me the strength to yield
the best of fruits. Let my life grow
a wealth of word and deed steeped
in the fountain of my being,
without my measuring all things
for only what they have to offer me.

And when my day shall come,
let me slip into the land of night,
without asking anything from others
or from you, God.

זֹאת תְּפִלָּתִי לְךָ, אֵל אֱלֹהָי:
שָׁמְרֵנִי לְבַל אֶשְׁט מִנְּתִיב חַיַּי,
לְבַל יְמַק רוּחִי וּלְבַל יִדַּל
מִצְּמָאוֹנוּ לְךָ וּמִן הַטַּל
עָלָיו הִזְלַ֫פְתָּ בְּעוֹדֶ֫נִּי רַךְ.

יְהִי לִבִּי פָּתוּחַ אֶל כָּל־דַּךְ,
אֶל כָּל־יְתוֹם חַיִּים, אֶל כָּל־כּוֹשֵׁל
נִפְתָּל בַּסֵּ֫תֶר וּמְגַשֵּׁשׁ בַּצֵּל.

בָּרֵךְ עֵינַי, זַכֵּ֫נִי לִרְאוֹת
יְפִי אָדָם עוֹלֶה בְּתֵבֵל זֹאת.

וְאֶת־חוּשַׁי בִּי הַעֲמֵק, הַרְחֵב
לִסְפֹּג עוֹלָם יָרֹק, נִצָּן וָאֵב,
לִקְלֹט מֵהֶם סוֹד הַלִּבְלוּב בְּדָמִי.

חָנֵּ֫נִי אוֹן לָתֵת מֵיטַב כָּל־פְּרִי,
תַּמְצִית חַיַּי, בְּנִיב שִׁקּוּי לְשַׁדִּי
מִבְּלִי צָפוֹת לִגְמוּל צָפוּי בַּעֲדִי.

וּכְבוֹא יוֹמִי — לַחֲמֹק לִרְשׁוּת הַלֵּיל
בְּלִי תְבֹעַ מָה מֵאִישׁ וּמִמְּךָ, אֵל.

Hillel Bavli

COMMENTARY. The poet's final words could be translated: "Let me not demand to know what, of human as of you, is God." The poem is so infused with imagery of the divine presence saturating the world and the poet—opening the eyes, the heart, and the senses to take in all that lives, and to bear fruit in kind—that by the end of this poem/prayer, the line of definition between divine and human, private and worldly, self and other, has become indistinct. Therefore the final words contain a wonderful double meaning, and the poem thus celebrates the unity of all life in God. It is a unity that allows a person to live free and undemanding because the wealth of God is everywhere.　　　　　　　　　　　　　　　　　　　J.R.

840 / **ZOT TEFILATI**

O, Sovereign, before you here is my desire,
   and if I can't offer it up for spoken prayer,
please let me disappear, so great my shame—
   though would that my prayer might achieve its goal!
When I am far from you, life is a living death,
   and when I cling to you, my life transcends all death.
Teach me your ways, my Sovereign,
   that I might return from my captivity,
instruct me while I still am capable of it,
   and capable of undergoing hardship in its name.
And let me travel where my ancestors have gone,
   let me encamp by their encampments,
residing as a welcomed stranger in a land
   whose inner core is my inheritance.
My youth, till now, was lived for its sake alone,
   but when shall I, too, act for my posterity?
The glimmer of eternity placed in my heart
   impels me to search out a greater destiny.
How then, shall I serve my Maker now, while yet I live,
   while prisoner of my instinct, slave to my desire?
How can my heart—even on a good day—
   feel at peace, when I am not sure tomorrow will be good?
Behold me now, like one stripped of possessions, naked:
   my sole clothing is your righteousness.
Yet even now, how can I sustain my prayer of request?
My sovereign, before you here is my desire.

For Avinu Malkenu, see page 451.
Concluding prayers begin on page 1195.

COMMENTARY. It is a good custom to be in silence—to fast from social chatting (a *ta'anit dibur*) after the last public prayer on Yom Kippur night. All announcements can be made earlier. People can then sit and meditate as long as they choose, and leave in silence when they are ready.   Z.S.S.

אֲדֹנָי נֶגְדְּךָ כָל־תַּאֲוָתִי
וְאִם־לֹא אַעֲלֶנָּה עַל־שְׂפָתִי
רְצוֹנְךָ אֶשְׁאֲלָה רֶגַע וְאֶגְוָע
וּמִי־יִתֵּן וְתָבוֹא שֶׁאֱלָתִי
בְּרָחְקִי מִמְּךָ מוֹתִי בְחַיָּי
וְאִם־אֶדְבַּק בְּךָ חַיַּי בְּמוֹתִי
דְּרָכֶיךָ אֲדֹנָי לַמְּדֵנִי
וְשׁוּב מִמַּאֲסַר סִכְלוּת שְׁבוּתִי
וְהוֹרֵנִי בְּעוֹד יֶשׁ־בִּי יְכֹלֶת
לְהִתְעַנּוֹת וְאַל־תִּבְזֶה עֱנוּתִי
וְאֶסַּע אֶל־מְקוֹם נָסְעוּ אֲבוֹתַי
וּבִמְקוֹם תַּחֲנֹתָם תַּחֲנָתִי
כְּגֵר תּוֹשָׁב אֲנִי עַל־גַּב אֲדָמָה
וְאוּלָם כִּי בְּבִטְנָהּ נַחֲלָתִי
נְעוּרַי עַד־הֲלוֹם עָשׂוּ לְנַפְשָׁם
וּמָתַי גַּם־אֲנִי אֶעֱשֶׂה לְבֵיתִי
וְהָעוֹלָם אֲשֶׁר נָתַן בְּלִבִּי
מְנָעַנִי לְבַקֵּשׁ אַחֲרִיתִי
וְאֵיכָה אֶעֱבֹד יֹצְרִי בְּעוֹדִי
אֲסִיר יִצְרִי וְעֶבֶד תַּאֲוָתִי
וְאֵיךְ יִיטַב בְּיוֹם טוֹבָה לְבָבִי
וְלֹא אֵדַע הֲיִיטַב מָחֳרָתִי
אֲנִי מִמַּעֲשִׂים שׁוֹלָל וְעָרוֹם
וְצִדְקָתְךָ לְבַדָּהּ הִיא כְסוּתִי
וְעוֹד מָה אַאֲרִיךְ לָשׁוֹן וְאֶשְׁאַל
אֲדֹנָי נֶגְדְּךָ כָל־תַּאֲוָתִי:

Yehuda Halevi

For Avinu Malkenu, see page 452.
Concluding prayers begin on page 1195.

842 / ADONAY NEGDEḤA

This *Musaf* service combines into one unit the *Musaf* Amidah that is chanted aloud, the *Avodah* service, and *Eleh Ezkerah*. They are woven together in a new way that emphasizes and enhances the themes of each of them. The confessions of the *Avodah* are placed strategically within the Amidah structure. For a lengthier explanation, see the Introduction, page xvi.

אָמַר רַבִּי יִצְחָק עַכְשָׁיו אֵין לָנוּ לֹא נָבִיא וְלֹא כֹהֵן לֹא קָרְבָּן וְלֹא
מִקְדָּשׁ וְלֹא מִזְבֵּחַ שֶׁמְּכַפֵּר עָלֵינוּ וּמִיּוֹם שֶׁחָרַב בֵּית הַמִּקְדָּשׁ לֹא
נִשְׁתַּיֵּר בְּיָדֵינוּ אֶלָּא תְפִלָּה:

Rabbi Isaac said:
Today, we have no prophet,
and we have no priest,
we have no sacrificial offering,
and we have no sanctuary,
and we have no sacrificial altar
to atone for us.
For since the Temple was destroyed,
we have in hand no other means than prayer.

∾

In ancient days, when our people lived in *Eretz Yisrael*, the Temple in Jerusalem was the symbol of God's presence. Sacrifices were offered there daily on behalf of the entire nation, bearing testimony to Israel's consecration to God.

The Temple has long since been destroyed, yet we remember its place in the life of our people. The form of worship practiced there belongs to a bygone age; still, it continues to awaken solemn thoughts.

Today our people is scattered across many lands. But when we remember the Temple, we feel that we are part of one people, dedicated to the service of God and to God's rule of righteousness.

Our worship is one of prayer and praise. Our ancestors offered their best in the service of God from their meager store of cattle and grain. When we think of their piety, can we be content with a gift of mere words that costs us neither labor nor privation? Shall we not give of our store to the relief of suffering, the healing of sickness, the dispelling of ignorance and error, the righting of wrongs and the strengthening of faith?

844 / **INTRODUCTION TO AMIDAH**

Great and holy is the cosmos
of the blessed Holy One,
and the holiest of all lands of the earth,
the Land of Israel,
the holiest of all the cities
of the Land of Israel is Jerusalem,
and holiest of all the places in Jerusalem,
the Temple, and, the holiest place of all,
the sanctuary, Holy of Holies.

There are seventy nations of the world,
and among those most devoted to their holy calling
is the Jewish people.
And the holiest tribe among the tribes of Israel
is the tribe of Levi,
and holiest of all the tribe of Levi are the priests,
the *kohanim*, and, holiest of all the *kohanim*,
the *kohen gadol*, the High Priest.

And holiest among days of the year, the holidays,
And, above them all in holiness, Shabbat.
And above all Shabbatot in holiness is Yom Kippur,
known as *Shabbat Shabbaton*,
a Sabbath of complete cessation.

There are seventy languages in the world,
and the holiest of all,
the sacred tongue of Scripture,
and holiest of all texts in this tongue
is Torah, the holy teaching.
And of all the holy words of Torah,
the holiest are those of the Ten Commandments,
and the holiest of words within the Ten Commandments
is the name of God. ↵

גָּדוֹל וְקָדוֹשׁ עוֹלָמוֹ שֶׁל הַקָּדוֹשׁ בָּרוּךְ הוּא, וְהַקְּדוֹשָׁה מִכָּל אֲרָצוֹת
הָעוֹלָם — אֶרֶץ יִשְׂרָאֵל, וְהַקְּדוֹשָׁה מִכָּל עָרֵי אֶרֶץ יִשְׂרָאֵל —
יְרוּשָׁלַיִם, וְהַקָּדוֹשׁ מִכָּל הַמְּקוֹמוֹת בִּירוּשָׁלַיִם — בֵּית הַמִּקְדָּשׁ:
וּבְבֵית הַמִּקְדָּשׁ הַמָּקוֹם הַקָּדוֹשׁ בְּיוֹתֵר — מְקוֹם קֹדֶשׁ הַקֳּדָשִׁים:
שִׁבְעִים אוּמוֹת יֵשׁ בָּעוֹלָם: הַקְּדוֹשָׁה שֶׁבְּכֻלָּן — הָאוּמָה
הַיִּשְׂרְאֵלִית: הַקָּדוֹשׁ מִכָּל שִׁבְטֵי יִשְׂרָאֵל — שֵׁבֶט לֵוִי:
הַקְּדוֹשִׁים מִכָּל בְּנֵי לֵוִי — הַכֹּהֲנִים: הַקָּדוֹשׁ מִכָּל הַכֹּהֲנִים —
הַכֹּהֵן הַגָּדוֹל. 365 יָמִים בַּשָּׁנָה, הַקְּדוֹשִׁים שֶׁבָּהֶם — יָמִים טוֹבִים;
לְמַעְלָה מֵהֶם — קְדֻשַּׁת יוֹם הַשַּׁבָּת; לְמַעְלָה מִכֻּלָּם קְדֻשַּׁת יוֹם
הַכִּפּוּרִים, שַׁבַּת שַׁבָּתוֹן: שִׁבְעִים לְשׁוֹנוֹת בָּעוֹלָם; הַקְּדוֹשָׁה שֶׁבְּכֻלָּן
— לְשׁוֹן הַקֹּדֶשׁ: הַקָּדוֹשׁ בְּיוֹתֵר בְּלָשׁוֹן זוֹ — הַתּוֹרָה הַקְּדוֹשָׁה;
מִכָּל דִּבְרֵי הַתּוֹרָה קְדוֹשִׁים בְּיוֹתֵר — עֲשֶׂרֶת הַדִּבְּרוֹת, וּבַעֲשֶׂרֶת
הַדִּבְּרוֹת קָדוֹשׁ בְּיוֹתֵר — שֵׁם הֲוָיָה: →

COMMENTARY. How narrowly nationalistic and ethnocentric is the
beginning of this declaration, and how broadly universalistic is its ending.
Does it mirror in this respect our own individual movement of spirit?

Our first experiences of a religious tradition or of the sacred are often
accompanied by the sense that only in this tradition, only in this particular
way, only at this particular time and in this special place can the experience
be preserved and renewed. The cherishing of the particular, the
affirmation of this form and no other, does serve to protect the experience
from dissipation or attrition.

With maturity and growing spiritual perspective, the essential locus of the
sacred is increasingly seen as within human beings: this human being, any
human being, all human beings. Thus, even while continuing to cherish
and affirm the familiar forms and particular practices, we also come to
recognize that the cherished form points to broader, nearly universal
possibilities for experiencing the sacred at all times and all places.

Thus does the life of the spirit mirror the sequence of An-ski's profound
proclamation.   E.G.

And one day of the year, in ancient times,
all four provinces of holiness
—land and people, time and language—
were united: when the High Priest went into
the Holy of Holies, and pronounced
the Tetragrammaton, the name of God,
whose utterance was otherwise forbidden.
And because this moment was considered
holy and awesome beyond measure,
the *kohen gadol* was in great danger,
as was the whole community of Israel.
And indeed, were he to stumble in his duties,
all the world was, God forbid,
in danger of destruction.

Whatever place a person stands
and looks toward heaven
is the holiest of holy places.
And every day throughout one's life
is a Day of Atonement,
and every person a *kohen gadol*,
and every word a person utters
in a state of holiness and purity,
a name of God.

Solomon An-Ski

וּפַעַם אַחַת בַּשָּׁנָה כָּל אַרְבַּע הַקְּדוּשׁוֹת הָעֶלְיוֹנוֹת מִתְחַבְּרוֹת יַחַד:
בְּיוֹם הַכִּפּוּרִים, כְּשֶׁנִּכְנַס הַכֹּהֵן הַגָּדוֹל לְקֹדֶשׁ הַקֳּדָשִׁים וְהוֹגֶה אֶת
הַשֵּׁם הַמְּפֹרָשׁ: וּמִפְּנֵי שֶׁהַשָּׁעָה הַזֹּאת הָיְתָה קְדוֹשָׁה וְנוֹרָאָה עַד
אֵין שְׁעוּר — סַכָּנָה גְּדוֹלָה הָיְתָה בָהּ לַכֹּהֵן הַגָּדוֹל וְלִכְלַל יִשְׂרָאֵל;
שֶׁאִלְמָלֵי נִכְשַׁל, הָיָה כָּל הָעוֹלָם חָרֵב, חַס וְשָׁלוֹם:
כָּל מָקוֹם שֶׁאָדָם עוֹמֵד עָלָיו וְנוֹשֵׂא מִשָּׁם עֵינָיו הַשָּׁמַיְמָה — קֹדֶשׁ
קֳדָשִׁים הוּא: כָּל יוֹם בְּחַיֵּי אָדָם — יוֹם כִּפּוּר הוּא: כָּל אִישׁ וְאִשָּׁה
כֹּהֵן גָּדוֹל הוּא, וְכָל מִלָּה שֶׁיּוֹצֵאת מִפִּי הָאָדָם בִּקְדֻשָּׁה וּבְטָהֳרָה
— שֵׁם הֲוָיָה הוּא:

COMMENTARY. Solomon Rapaport, known as S. An-Ski (1863-1920), was a
member of the Haskalah (Jewish enlightenment movement) who lived in
Russia, Paris, and Lithuania. A leading Jewish folklorist, An-Ski loved the
values and tales of the Yiddish world. Best known as the author of *The
Dybbuk* and of fifteen volumes of other writings, An-Ski had one foot in
Jewish village life and the other in Western literary life. Thus his play, *The
Dybbuk*, is not only a reflection of the tales on which it is based; it
celebrates and comments on the world that gave rise to them. So, too, in
this poem do we have a celebration of the Temple, the Hebrew language
and the land of Israel, while at the same time the poem celebrates the
power of the contemporary individual to take on the role of the High
Priest speaking the name of God in holiness. Unlike some who
experienced their dividedness between the worlds of Jewish tradition
and Western intellect as painful and alienating, An-Ski was able to bring
his two civilizations together in a way that allowed each to comment upon
and enrich the other. He suggests to us that we, too, can celebrate both the
image of a world that will never return and our power as individuals to
reconnect to its highest ideals. From our particularity we can recognize
and address the Universal.   M.B.K./D.A.T.

In the hour when the Temple was destroyed,
and Zion's courtyards had been silenced,
there arose throughout the earth's four corners
places where holiness could dwell in smaller ways,
where Torah, prayer, and houses of assembly
could pay honor to your Name.
In every place where we have kept alive your memory,
you have made your Presence—your Sheḥinah—to abide.
The weeping of our widowed Holy City
is sealed upon our hearts.
We stand before you here in prayer,
we, the living, who are mindful of all life.
So cause our sins to pass away, erase our wrongful acts,
receive our prayers like sacrifices in a former time.
Let utterance of our lips fulfill the ancient rite,
let poetry and song, like incense, give delight,
as they commemorate the worship that our ancestors once did,
and blessed be its memory today, on Yom Kippur.

Gil Nativ

עֵת חָרַב הַמִּקְדָּשׁ וְחַצְרוֹת צִיּוֹן נָדֵמּוּ
בְּאַרְבַּע כַּנְפוֹת תֵּבֵל מִקְדְּשֵׁי מְעַט קָמוּ
לְתוֹרָה וּתְפִלָּה בָּתֵּי כְנֵסִיּוֹת לִשְׁמָךְ:
בְּכָל מָקוֹם בּוֹ הִזְכַּרְנוּךְ הִשְׁרֵיתָ שְׁכִינָתָךְ
בְּכִי עִיר אַלְמָנָה נֶחְתַּם בְּלִבֵּנוּ:
בִּתְפִלָּה נִצָּבִים פֹּה כֻּלָּנוּ הַחַיִּים
חַטֹּאתֵינוּ הַעֲבֵר וּפְשָׁעֵינוּ מְחֵה
כְּקָרְבְּנוֹת קֶדֶם תְּפִלּוֹתֵינוּ רְצֵה
בְּשִׂיחַ שִׂפְתוֹתֵינוּ נְשַׁלְּמָה פָרִים
כִּקְטֹרֶת בְּאַפֶּךְ זִמְרַת מְשׁוֹרְרִים
אֲשֶׁר סֵדֶר עֲבוֹדַת אָבוֹת מַזְכִּירִים:
בָּרוּךְ זִכְרָהּ לְפָנֶיךָ בְּיוֹם הַכִּפּוּרִים:

COMMENTARY. Jews have suffered much as a result of the circumstances in which they have found themselves throughout history. This poem dwells not upon the causes of our suffering, but upon our ability to transcend it. For having once made holiness a grand part of our heritage in days that have receded into the distant past, we retain many ways to keep with us glimmers of holiness and an abiding sense of the divine presence. We can recapture that sense of holy presence through it purify ourselves, and give to Yom Kippur the power it had of old.   D.A.T.

Here I am, meager of deeds!
In turmoil, and afflicted with such fear
to stand before the One enthroned
on Israel's songs of praise,
I come here now to stand in pleading
in your presence, for your people Israel,
who have sent me here,
even though I am unworthy of it.
For this, I ask you—God of Abraham and Sarah,
God of Isaac and Rebekah,
God of Jacob, Rachel, and Leah,
THE GRACIOUS ONE, THE GRACIOUS ONE,
God full of mercy and compassion,
you, Almighty One, awesome and feared—
that you may make my way successful,
as I stand and beg forgiveness
for myself and those who send me.
Do not find them to blame for sins of mine,
do not declare them guilty for my own mistakes,
for I myself am fallible, and have done wrong.
And do not let them suffer shame
because of any wrongdoing of mine,
and let them not incur disgrace on my account,
and let me, likewise, not incur disgrace through them.
Receive my prayer as if it were
the prayer of one experienced and wise,
whose utterance is well-accepted,
whose bearing is mature,
whose voice is sweet and pleasing
to the ear of all who hear it.
May you nullify the voice of cynicism,
and dispel whatever would prevent our prayer
from being heard. ↵

הִנְנִי הֶעָנִי מִמַּעַשׂ נִרְעַשׁ וְנִפְחָד מִפַּחַד יוֹשֵׁב תְּהִלּוֹת יִשְׂרָאֵל: בָּאתִי לַעֲמֹד וּלְחַנֵּן לְפָנֶיךָ עַל עַמְּךָ יִשְׂרָאֵל אֲשֶׁר שְׁלָחוּנִי אַף עַל פִּי שֶׁאֵינִי כְדַי וְהָגוּן לְכָךְ: עַל כֵּן אֲבַקֶּשְׁךָ אֱלֹהֵי אַבְרָהָם אֱלֹהֵי יִצְחָק אֱלֹהֵי יַעֲקֹב אֱלֹהֵי שָׂרָה אֱלֹהֵי רִבְקָה אֱלֹהֵי רָחֵל וֵאלֹהֵי לֵאָה יהוה יהוה אֵל רַחוּם וְחַנּוּן אֱלֹהֵי יִשְׂרָאֵל שַׁדַּי אָיֹם וְנוֹרָא: הֱיֵה נָא מַצְלִיחַ דַּרְכִּי אֲשֶׁר אָנֹכִי הוֹלֵךְ לַעֲמֹד לְבַקֵּשׁ רַחֲמִים עָלַי וְעַל שׁוֹלְחָי: וְנָא אַל תַּפְשִׁיעֵם בְּחַטֹּאתַי וְאַל תְּחַיְּבֵם בַּעֲוֹנוֹתַי כִּי חוֹטֵא וּפוֹשֵׁעַ אָנִי: וְאַל יִכָּלְמוּ בִּפְשָׁעַי וְאַל יֵבוֹשׁוּ בִי וְאַל אֵבוֹשָׁה בָהֶם: וְקַבֵּל תְּפִלָּתִי כִּתְפִלַּת זָקֵן וְרָגִיל וּפִרְקוֹ נָאֶה וּזְקָנוֹ מְגֻדָּל וְקוֹלוֹ נָעִים וּמְעֹרָב בְּדַעַת עִם הַבְּרִיּוֹת: וְתִגְעַר בְּשָׂטָן לְבַל יַשְׂטִינֵנִי ←

COMMENTARY. *Hineni* was traditionally sung by the *ḥazan* just before the repetition of the *Musaf* Amidah while the *ḥazan* slowly walked from the back of the synagogue to the *bimah*. The theme of *Hineni* is a humble cantor's plea, which is in direct tension with the high drama of the music and ritual of this moment. Most Reconstructionist communities do not expect the cantor to enter in this highly dramatic way, and most do not repeat the Amidah. Thus, Reconstructionist communities include *Hineni* in different places of the service if at all. It can serve as the introduction to any Amidah that is chanted aloud, or to the silent Amidah. As with all *piyutim*, there is unlimited flexibility as to whether and where to include *Hineni*.

D.A.T

COMMENTARY. This personal prayer recited by the prayer leader is a public declaration of unworthiness. The leader represents all the people seeking divine compassion and forgiveness. Who could possibly be worthy of such a task if its success depends on the moral purity of the leader? Indeed, true prayer always acknowledges our spiritual poverty. The leader asserts a readiness for true prayer—free of self-centered thoughts, free of manipulative strategies, no longer tallying merits. One is ready to seek God's love, compassion and forgiveness when one is ready to admit how small our efforts are in relation to divine grace.

S.P.W.

Let the banner of our passion
proclaim love for you,
and may you overwhelm all wrongdoing with love.
Reverse all trouble and affliction in our favor,
for the sake of all the people Israel,
for the sake of joy and gladness,
for the sake of life and peace.

May it be your will, ETERNAL ONE,
O God of Abraham and Sarah,
God of Isaac and Rebekah,
God of Jacob, Rachel, and Leah,
you, the supreme God,
you who have been ever changing and becoming,
that all your ministering angels,
all appointed as the guardians of prayer,
shall bring my prayer before your Throne of Glory,
and present it there before you,
for the sake of all the righteous and the loving,
all who are unblemished and deserving of respect,
and for the honor of your great and awesome Name.
For you are one who listens with compassion
to the prayer of your people Israel.
Blessed are you,
who listens to our prayer.

וִיהִי נָא דִגְלֵנוּ עָלֶיךָ אַהֲבָה לְכָל־פְּשָׁעִים תְּכַסֶּה בְּאַהֲבָה: וְכָל־צָרוֹת
וְרָעוֹת הֲפָךְ־לָנוּ וּלְכָל־יִשְׂרָאֵל לְשָׂשׂוֹן וּלְשִׂמְחָה לְחַיִּים וּלְשָׁלוֹם:
הָאֱמֶת וְהַשָּׁלוֹם אֱהָבוּ וְאַל יְהִי שׁוּם מִכְשׁוֹל בִּתְפִלָּתִי:

וִיהִי רָצוֹן לְפָנֶיךָ יהוה אֱלֹהֵי אַבְרָהָם אֱלֹהֵי יִצְחָק אֱלֹהֵי יַעֲקֹב אֱלֹהֵי
שָׂרָה אֱלֹהֵי רִבְקָה אֱלֹהֵי רָחֵל וֵאלֹהֵי לֵאָה הָאֵל הַגָּדוֹל הַגִּבּוֹר
וְהַנּוֹרָא אֵל עֶלְיוֹן אֶהְיֶה אֲשֶׁר אֶהְיֶה שֶׁכָּל־הַמַּלְאָכִים שֶׁהֵם בַּעֲלֵי
תְפִלּוֹת יָבִיאוּ תְפִלָּתִי לִפְנֵי כִסֵּא כְבוֹדֶךָ וְיַצִּיגוּ אוֹתָהּ לְפָנֶיךָ בַּעֲבוּר
כָּל־הַצַּדִּיקִים וְהַחֲסִידִים הַתְּמִימִים וְהַיְשָׁרִים וּבַעֲבוּר כְּבוֹד שִׁמְךָ
הַגָּדוֹל וְהַנּוֹרָא כִּי אַתָּה שׁוֹמֵעַ תְּפִלַּת עַם יִשְׂרָאֵל בְּרַחֲמִים: בָּרוּךְ
אַתָּה שׁוֹמֵעַ תְּפִלָּה:

KAVANAH. When people who are concerned about ethics and spirituality
gather together, they collectively proclaim the glory of God before they
even say a single word because their presence bespeaks the power of God.

E.M.

KAVANAH. The moisture diffused in mist and clouds reduces our vision
and chills our bones. We can only wait for wind or sun to remove them.
By contrast, on Yom Kippur when we confront the mist of our faults and
foibles, sins and errors in our lives, we are able to act, precipitating and
thereby concentrating. Through gaining awareness and making confession,
our vision is cleared, fresh vistas are opened, and a pool of pure spiritual
water before us provides the opportunity to cleanse our souls. E.G.

COMMENTARY. *Hineni* has long been loved not only for its beautiful music
but also because each of us must struggle in our own way with the
problem it raises: "How can I be worthy of forgiveness? How can I purify
myself enough to be worthy of the lofty hopes of this day? D.A.T. / M.B.K.

ḤATZI KADDISH / SHORT KADDISH

Reader: Let God's name be made great and holy in the world that was created as God willed. May God complete the holy realm in your own lifetime, in your days, and in the days of all the house of Israel, quickly and soon. And say: Amen.

Congregation: May God's great name be blessed, forever and as long as worlds endure.

Reader: May it be blessed, and praised, and glorified and held in honor, viewed with awe, embellished and revered; and may the blessed name of holiness be hailed, though it be higher by far than all the blessings, songs, praises, and consolations that we utter in this world. And say: Amen.

In communities where a full silent Musaf Amidah *is recited, continue on page 739. Otherwise continue on the following page.*

COMMENTARY. Holiness is the quality or value that things or persons have when they help people to become fully human.   M.M.K. (Adapted)

חֲצִי קַדִּישׁ

יִתְגַּדַּל וְיִתְקַדַּשׁ שְׁמֵהּ רַבָּא בְּעָלְמָא דִּי בְרָא כִרְעוּתֵהּ וְיַמְלִיךְ
מַלְכוּתֵהּ בְּחַיֵּיכוֹן וּבְיוֹמֵיכוֹן וּבְחַיֵּי דְכָל בֵּית יִשְׂרָאֵל בַּעֲגָלָא וּבִזְמַן
קָרִיב וְאִמְרוּ: אָמֵן:
יְהֵא שְׁמֵהּ רַבָּא מְבָרַךְ לְעָלַם וּלְעָלְמֵי עָלְמַיָּא:
יִתְבָּרַךְ וְיִשְׁתַּבַּח וְיִתְפָּאַר וְיִתְרוֹמַם וְיִתְנַשֵּׂא וְיִתְהַדַּר וְיִתְעַלֶּה
וְיִתְהַלָּל שְׁמֵהּ דְּקֻדְשָׁא בְּרִיךְ הוּא
לְעֵלָּא לְעֵלָּא מִכָּל בִּרְכָתָא וְשִׁירָתָא תֻּשְׁבְּחָתָא וְנֶחֱמָתָא דַּאֲמִירָן
בְּעָלְמָא וְאִמְרוּ: אָמֵן:

Reader: Yitgadal veyitkadash shemey raba
be'alma di vera ḥirutey veyamliḥ malḥutey
beḥayeyhon uvyomeyhon uvḥayey deḥol beyt yisra'el
ba'agala uvizman kariv ve'imru amen.

Congregation: Yehey shemey raba mevaraḥ le'alam ulalmey almaya.

Reader: Yitbaraḥ veyishtabaḥ veyitpa'ar veyitromam veyitnasey
veyit-hadar veyitaleh veyit-halal shemey dekudsha beriḥ hu
le'ela le'ela mikol birḥata veshirata tushbeḥata veneḥemata
da'amiran be'alma ve'imru amen.

In communities where a full silent Musaf Amidah is recited, continue on page 740. Otherwise continue on the following page.

AVODAH / SERVICE

For seven days preceding Yom Kippur,
they set apart the High Priest from his household,
to reside amid the Temple chambers,
while appointing in his place another priest
to carry out his ordinary priestly duties.
This was to protect him from all inadvertent acts or contact
that might render him impure, and thus invalidate him
from performing the atonement ritual.

They provided him elders from the Court of Law,
who read before him from the daily study portion.
They would say to him: "Esteemed High Priest!
Please read aloud yourself—lest there are things
that you may have forgotten, or have never learned!"

And on the morning of the day preceding Yom Kippur,
they stood him at the Eastern Gate,
and passed before him cattle, rams, and sheep,
that he might learn to recognize them,
and become familiar with the details of the service.

The elders of the Court of Law would turn him over
to the elders of the priesthood, who would bring him up
into the chamber of the priestly clan of Avtinas,
where they would admonish him before they took their leave.
They said to him: "Esteemed High Priest!
We are emissaries of the Court of Law,
and you, our representative—and so, in turn,
an emissary of the Court of Law, as well. ↩

שִׁבְעַת יָמִים קֹדֶם יוֹם־הַכִּפּוּרִים מַפְרִישִׁין כֹּהֵן־גָּדוֹל מִבֵּיתוֹ
לְלִשְׁכַּת פַּלְהֶדְרִין וּמַתְקִינִין לוֹ כֹּהֵן אַחֵר תַּחְתָּיו שֶׁמָּא יֶאֱרַע בּוֹ
פְּסוּל:

מָסְרוּ לוֹ זְקֵנִים מִזִּקְנֵי בֵית־דִּין וְקוֹרִין לְפָנָיו בְּסֵדֶר הַיּוֹם וְאוֹמְרִים
לוֹ אִישִׁי כֹּהֵן גָּדוֹל קְרָא אַתָּה בְּפִיךָ שֶׁמָּא שָׁכַחְתָּ אוֹ שֶׁמָּא לֹא
לָמָדְתָּ:

עֶרֶב יוֹם־הַכִּפּוּרִים שַׁחֲרִית מַעֲמִידִין אוֹתוֹ בְּשַׁעַר הַמִּזְרָח וּמַעֲבִירִין
לְפָנָיו פָּרִים וְאֵילִים וּכְבָשִׂים כְּדֵי שֶׁיְּהֵא מַכִּיר וְרָגִיל בַּעֲבוֹדָה:
מְסָרוּהוּ זִקְנֵי בֵית־דִּין לְזִקְנֵי כְהֻנָּה וְהֶעֱלוּהוּ לַעֲלִיַּת בֵּית־אַבְטִינַס
וְהִשְׁבִּיעוּהוּ וְנִפְטְרוּ וְהָלְכוּ לָהֶם: וְאָמְרוּ לוֹ אִישִׁי כֹּהֵן־גָּדוֹל אָנוּ
שְׁלוּחֵי בֵית־דִּין וְאַתָּה שְׁלִיחֵנוּ וּשְׁלִיחַ בֵית־דִּין: ←

COMMENTARY. Stratification and cooperation, complexity and complemen-
tarity, authority and humility: these and more are exemplified in the rules
of priestly preparation for and execution of the rites of Yom Kippur.

The High Priest reviews the procedures for the forthcoming Temple
ceremonies first under the tutelage of the Rabbinic Elders, then of the
Priestly Elders. He assumes particular optional responsibilities in light of
his particular endowments and abilities; if not so gifted, others in the
community assume and discharge those responsibilities. Regularly
addressed as אִישִׁי כהן גדול, Esteemed High Priest, and accorded full
respect and honor, the High Priest is nonetheless subject to scrutiny and
critical, if sympathetic, assessment. A full range of confessions for self, for
family, and for community adds further to the sense of fitting humility
amidst ceremonial splendor.

In short, portrayed here in lively and sometimes touching detail is a well
functioning, harmonious hierarchy, with powers and responsibilities
broadly distributed. At the same time, traditional rules of procedure, God's
mandate, set a standard for all who serve on behalf of the community.

E.G.

And we implore you, by the name of One
whose name was made to dwell upon this House,
that you not change a single thing from all
we have declared to you!"
And he would turn aside and weep,
and they would turn aside and weep.

If he was a sage, he would engage in study,
or, if not, disciples of the sages
studied in his presence.
If he was accustomed to reciting, he would read aloud.
If not, they would recite before him.

And they would bring the High Priest
down to the ritual bath-house.
Five immersions, ten sanctifications,
would the High Priest undergo,
and he would sanctify the day itself.
A linen sheet divided between him
and the assembled people.
The High Priest would descend, immerse himself,
ascend, and dry himself, and they would bring to him
white garments, which he would put on. ↰

COMMENTARY. "If he was a sage, etc." Rabbinic lore about the priestly
ritual of Yom Kippur took for granted that the priests, whose office was
hereditary, often did not possess the elaborate knowledge of Israel's
traditions that rabbinic sages had come to prize. This situation often made
the sages into tutors of the priests, and principal guardians of the tradition
that would eventually survive the Temple and its hierarchy. Once the
Temple and its ongoing life were translated into a mental terrain (a
transformation that became the basis of all Talmudic culture and
instruction in future centuries), the Temple would seem to have become
secondary in importance—but, paradoxically, its passing was mourned all
the more fervently by the sages, and yearning for its restoration would
never cease.

J.R.

מַשְׁבִּיעִים אָנוּ עָלֶיךָ בְּמִי שֶׁשִּׁכֵּן שְׁמוֹ בַּבַּיִת הַזֶּה שֶׁלֹּא תְשַׁנֶּה דָבָר
מִכָּל מַה שֶּׁאָמַרְנוּ לָךְ: הוּא פוֹרֵשׁ וּבוֹכֶה וְהֵם פּוֹרְשִׁים וּבוֹכִים: אִם
הָיָה חָכָם דּוֹרֵשׁ וְאִם לָאו תַּלְמִידֵי־חֲכָמִים דּוֹרְשִׁים לְפָנָיו וְאִם רָגִיל
לִקְרוֹת קוֹרֵא וְאִם לָאו קוֹרִין לְפָנָיו:
הוֹרִידוּ כֹהֵן־גָּדוֹל לְבֵית־הַטְּבִילָה חָמֵשׁ טְבִילוֹת וַעֲשָׂרָה קִדּוּשִׁים
טוֹבֵל כֹּהֵן־גָּדוֹל וּמְקַדֵּשׁ בּוֹ בַיּוֹם — פָּרְסוּ סָדִין שֶׁל בּוּץ בֵּינוֹ
לְבֵין הָעָם: יָרַד וְטָבַל: עָלָה וְנִסְתַּפַּג: וְהֵבִיאוּ לוֹ בִגְדֵי לָבָן וְלָבַשׁ: ←

COMMENTARY. When the Second Temple was destroyed in the year 70, the rabbis replaced each of the sacrifice cycles with an Amidah. They made similar substitutions for all the other services of the year. While this sacrifice of the heart in the form of prayer substituted for the physical sacrifices of the Temple, during each service the rabbis also included an actual description of the sacrifice of the day. This *Avodah* / Sacrifice service existed in several traditional forms. One of the most popular was based on the section of the Mishnah dedicated to Yom Kippur. Over the last few generations this recitation has increasingly fallen into disuse because it substantially repeats the traditional Torah portion for Yom Kippur and because most Jews do not look forward to a time when the sacrifices will be reinstituted.

Our version of the *Avodah* contains several major innovations. It is interspersed with the rest of the *Musaf* service. It places the worshipper in the role of the High Priest, and it leads each of us through forgiveness of self and family to community and the Jewish people and finally to the world. This structure reflects the critical importance of individual *teshuvah* and of healing self, family, people, and humanity. Ritual reconnection to God is only authentic if it changes our this-worldly relations as well.

Lee Friedlander / D.A.T. / M.B.K.

NOTE. The liturgical use here of *Mishnah Yoma* is highly abbreviated as it has evolved over centuries of use. Often the text is interrupted in the middle of a mishnah and continues with a section from another mishnah, sometimes even another chapter.

M.B.K.

His sacrificial bull was standing in the space
between the hallway and the altar.
The High Priest would place his hands upon it
and confess: "Upon this holy day, I, too, have come
into your Temple, which is in your House of Prayer,
for, as the High Priests of a former time
would make confession, and beseech your mercy
and atonement, in your inner holy chamber,
so now do I confess before you."

And thus would he declare:

"O Holy One,
I have sinned, I have done wrong, and I have gone astray,
before you, I and my household!
I beseech you, Holy One, please grant atonement
for the sins, the wrongful acts, and the transgressions
I have done before you, I and my household."

And thus do we declare:
"O Holy One, please grant atonement for the sins,
the wrongdoing and the transgressions
that the House of Israel have done before you,
they, and all who dwell on earth.
And bring us all to the world's repair through divine rule,
as it is written in the Torah of your servant Moses:
'For on this day, atonement shall be made for you,
to make you clean from all your wrongdoings.
Before THE FOUNT OF MERCY, you shall all be clean!'"

כי...יהוה / 'For...clean!' (Leviticus 16:30).

וּפָרוּ הָיָה עוֹמֵד בֵּין הָאוּלָם וְלַמִּזְבֵּחַ: וְסוֹמֵךְ שְׁתֵּי יָדָיו עָלָיו וּמִתְוַדֶּה: בְּיוֹם קָדוֹשׁ זֶה גַם אֲנִי בָא אֶל הֵיכָלְךָ אֲשֶׁר בְּבֵית תְּפִלָּתְךָ: וּכְשֵׁם שֶׁהַכֹּהֵן הַגָּדוֹל הָיָה מִתְוַדֶּה וּמְבַקֵּשׁ מְחִילָה וְכַפָּרָה בִּדְבִיר קָדְשֶׁךָ כֵּן גַם אֲנִי מִתְוַדֶּה לְפָנֶיךָ לֵאמֹר:

וְכָךְ הָיָה אוֹמֵר אָנָּא הַשֵּׁם עָוִיתִי פָּשַׁעְתִּי חָטָאתִי לְפָנֶיךָ אֲנִי וּבֵיתִי: אָנָּא הַשֵּׁם כַּפֶּר־נָא לָעֲוֹנוֹת וְלַפְּשָׁעִים וְלַחֲטָאִים שֶׁעָוִיתִי וְשֶׁפָּשַׁעְתִּי וְשֶׁחָטָאתִי לְפָנֶיךָ אֲנִי וּבֵיתִי:

וְכָךְ אָנוּ אוֹמְרִים: אָנָּא הַשֵּׁם כַּפֶּר־נָא לַחֲטָאִים וְלָעֲוֹנוֹת וְלַפְּשָׁעִים שֶׁחָטָאוּ וְשֶׁעָווּ וְשֶׁפָּשְׁעוּ לְפָנֶיךָ בֵּית יִשְׂרָאֵל וְכָל יוֹשְׁבֵי תֵבֵל וְהַגִּיעֵנוּ לְתַקֵּן עוֹלָם בְּמַלְכוּת שַׁדַּי כַּכָּתוּב בְּתוֹרָתֶךָ כִּי בַיּוֹם הַזֶּה יְכַפֵּר עֲלֵיכֶם לְטַהֵר אֶתְכֶם מִכֹּל חַטֹּאתֵיכֶם לִפְנֵי יהוה....

NOTE. וכך אנו אומרים/And thus we say. Michael Strassfeld added this phrase to the text.

KAVANAH. Since the destruction of the Temple in Jerusalem, prayer has taken the place of sacrifice, but that does not imply that sacrifice was abolished when the sacrificial rite went out of existence. Prayer is not a substitute for sacrifice. Prayer *is* sacrifice. What has changed is the substance of sacrifice: the self took the place of the thing. The spirit is the same.

"Accept the offerings of praise, Adonay," says the Psalmist (119:108). "Let my prayer be counted as incense before You, and the lifting of my hands as an evening sacrifice" (141:12). In moments of prayer we try to surrender our vanities, to burn our insolence, to abandon bias, cant, envy. We lay all our forces before God.

The word is but an altar. We do not sacrifice. We are the sacrifice.

Prayer is a hazard, a venture of peril. Every person who prays is a *kohen* at the greatest of all temples. The whole universe is the temple.   A.G.

And the priests,
and all the people standing in the courtyard,
when they would hear the glorious and awesome Name of God
uttered aloud distinctly from the High Priest's mouth,
in holiness and purity,
would prostrate themselves, and bow down in acknowledgement,
and touch their faces to the ground, and say:
"Blessed are the glorious Name and majesty of God,
to all eternity!"

And the High Priest, in turn,
would thus complete the utterance of the Name
in sacred devotion, facing those who offered blessing,
and declare to them: "You shall be clean!"

And you God, in your goodness, stir up your compassion
and forgive this people serving you.

∽

Strange is our situation here upon earth. Each of us comes for a
short visit, not knowing why, yet sometimes seeming to divine a
purpose. From the standpoint of daily life, however, there is one
thing we do know: that we are here for the sake of each other,
above all, for those upon whose smile and well-being our own
happiness depends, and also for the countless unknown souls
with whose fate we are connected by a bond of sympathy. Many
times a day I realize how much my own outer and inner life is
built upon the labors of others, both living and dead, and how
earnestly I must exert myself in order to give in return as much
as I have received and am still receiving.

Albert Einstein (Adapted)

וְהַכֹּהֲנִים וְהָעָם הָעוֹמְדִים בָּעֲזָרָה כְּשֶׁהָיוּ שׁוֹמְעִים אֶת־הַשֵּׁם הַנִּכְבָּד
וְהַנּוֹרָא מְפֹרָשׁ יוֹצֵא מִפִּי כֹהֵן גָּדוֹל בִּקְדֻשָּׁה וּבְטָהֳרָה הָיוּ כּוֹרְעִים
וּמִשְׁתַּחֲוִים וּמוֹדִים וְנוֹפְלִים עַל פְּנֵיהֶם וְאוֹמְרִים: בָּרוּךְ שֵׁם כְּבוֹד
מַלְכוּתוֹ לְעוֹלָם וָעֶד: וְאַף הוּא הָיָה מִתְכַּוֵּן לִגְמֹר אֶת־הַשֵּׁם כְּנֶגֶד
הַמְבָרְכִים וְאוֹמֵר לָהֶם: תִּטְהָרוּ: וְאַתָּה בְּטוּבְךָ מְעוֹרֵר רַחֲמֶיךָ
וְסוֹלֵחַ לְאִישׁ חֲסִידֶךָ:

∽

In the evening when we were alone together my mother would
make me sit on her footstool, and while her deft fingers
manipulated the knitting needles she would gaze into my eyes as
if she tried to absorb enough of me to last her for the coming
months of absence. "You will write us, dear?" she kept asking
continually. "And if I should die when you are gone, you will
remember me in your prayers."

At the moment of departure [from Eastern Europe to America],
when the train drew into the station, she lost control of her
feelings. As she embraced me, her sobs became violent, and
father had to separate us. There was a despair in her way of
clinging to me which I could not then understand. I understand
it now. I never saw her again.

Marcus Ravage

KAVANAH. One of the original intents of the *Avodah* service was to purify
the Holy of Holies from pollution—from a *ḥilul hashem*—a hole in God's
name. Every time we commit a sin, we make a hole in the Name. (One
definition of sin is making a tear in the Divine weave.) By the end of the
year, God's name—our connection to God—is riddled with holes. A new
Name is needed. God enters into time to create the possibility of a new
name for the next year. This offers us the possibility of creating our own
root metaphor for how we interface with God this year.   Z.S.S.

Once there were two brothers. One had a wife and children, the other did not. They lived together in one house—happy, quiet, and satisfied with the portions which they inherited from their father. Together they worked the fields with the sweat of their brows.

And the harvest came. The brothers bound their sheaves and brought them to the threshing floor. There they divided the crops of the field in two parts equally between them, and left them.

That night, the brother who had no family lay on his bed and thought: I am alone...but my brother has a wife and children. Why should my share be equal to his? And he rose from his bed, went stealthily out into the threshing floor, took from the stalks of his own sheaf, and added them to the sheaf of his brother.

That same night, the other brother turned to his wife and said: "It is not right that we have divided the crop into two equal parts, one for me and one for my brother. He is alone and has no other joy or happiness, only the yield of the field. Therefore, come with me, my wife, and we will secretly take from our share and add to his." And they did so.

In the morning, the brothers went out into the threshing floor, and they wondered that the sheaves were still equal. Each one decided to investigate. During the night each one rose from his bed to repeat his deed. And they met each other on the threshing floor, each with his sheaves in his arms. Thus the mystery was explained. The brothers embraced, and kissed each other.

And God looked with favor on this threshing floor where the two brothers conceived their good thoughts...and the children of Israel chose it for the site of their Holy Temple.

Retold from *midrash* by Zev Vilnay

ᦈᦈ

אֵלוּ דְבָרִים שֶׁאָדָם אוֹכֵל פֵּרוֹתֵיהֶם בָּעוֹלָם הַזֶּה וְהַקֶּרֶן קַיֶּמֶת לוֹ
לָעוֹלָם הַבָּא : וְאֵלּוּ הֵן כִּבּוּד אָב וָאֵם וּגְמִילוּת חֲסָדִים וְהַשְׁכָּמַת
בֵּית הַמִּדְרָשׁ שַׁחֲרִית וְעַרְבִית וְהַכְנָסַת אוֹרְחִים וּבִקּוּר חוֹלִים
וְהַכְנָסַת כַּלָּה וּלְוָיַת הַמֵּת וְעִיּוּן תְּפִלָּה וַהֲבָאַת שָׁלוֹם בֵּין אָדָם
לַחֲבֵרוֹ : וְתַלְמוּד תּוֹרָה כְּנֶגֶד כֻּלָּם :

These are the things whose fruit
one enjoys in this world,
and whose principal is stored for us
in time to come:
the honoring of parents,
and bestowing acts of kindness,
and arising early to attend the house of study,
morning hour and evening hour,
and bringing home guests,
and visiting the sick,
and supporting the bride,
and attending to the dead,
and devotion in our prayer,
and bringing peace between one person and another.
And learning Torah
corresponds to all of them.

Mishnah Peah 1:1

COMMENTARY. The opening lines of this mishnah tell us that doing good deeds provides "fruit one enjoys" right away. It makes this tangible by referring to the pleasure of eating. Yet the principal benefit of doing good deeds, "the principal," remains to be enjoyed later. Here a financial metaphor is used. We benefit from the interest now, but the principal remains to be enjoyed "in time to come." Originally that was a reference to the World to Come. Our translation gives a more this-worldly interpretation: we take pleasure in doing good deeds now, but they have transformational power for us and our communities that we will be able to feel cumulatively as time goes on. D.A.T.

AMIDAH

The Amidah is traditionally recited while standing, beginning with three short steps forward and bowing left and right, a reminder of our entry into the divine presence.

Open my lips, BELOVED ONE,
and let my mouth declare your praise.

1. AVOT VE'IMOT / ANCESTORS

Blessed are you, ANCIENT ONE, our God, God of our ancestors,

God of Abraham	God of Sarah
God of Isaac	God of Rebekah
God of Jacob	God of Rachel
	and God of Leah;

great, heroic, awesome God, supreme divinity,
imparting deeds of kindness, begetter of all;
mindful of the loyalty of Israel's ancestors,
bringing, with love, redemption to their children's children
for the sake of the divine name.

By counsel of the sages and the wise,
and by the knowledge of all learned in our ways,
may my mouth be opened, and my prayers arise,
to entreat the sovereign full of mercy and compassion,
who forgives and pardons all transgression. ↵

אדוני...תהלתך / Open...praise (Psalms 51:17).

The Amidah is traditionally recited while standing, beginning with three short steps forward and bowing left and right, a reminder of our entry into the divine presence.

אֲדֹנָי שְׂפָתַי תִּפְתָּח וּפִי יַגִּיד תְּהִלָּתֶךָ:

אָבוֹת וְאִמּוֹת

בָּרוּךְ אַתָּה יהוה אֱלֹהֵינוּ וֵאלֹהֵי אֲבוֹתֵינוּ וְאִמּוֹתֵינוּ

אֱלֹהֵי שָׂרָה	אֱלֹהֵי אַבְרָהָם
אֱלֹהֵי רִבְקָה	אֱלֹהֵי יִצְחָק
אֱלֹהֵי רָחֵל	אֱלֹהֵי יַעֲקֹב
וֵאלֹהֵי לֵאָה:	

הָאֵל הַגָּדוֹל הַגִּבּוֹר וְהַנּוֹרָא אֵל עֶלְיוֹן גּוֹמֵל חֲסָדִים טוֹבִים וְקוֹנֵה הַכֹּל וְזוֹכֵר חַסְדֵי אָבוֹת וְאִמּוֹת וּמֵבִיא גְאֻלָּה לִבְנֵי בְנֵיהֶם לְמַעַן שְׁמוֹ בְּאַהֲבָה:

מִסּוֹד חֲכָמִים וּנְבוֹנִים וּמִלֶּמֶד דַּעַת מְבִינִים אֶפְתְּחָה פִי בִתְפִלָּה וּבְתַחֲנוּנִים לְחַלּוֹת וּלְחַנֵּן פְּנֵי מֶלֶךְ מָלֵא רַחֲמִים מוֹחֵל וְסוֹלֵחַ לַעֲוֹנִים: ←

Baruḥ atah adonay eloheynu veylohey avoteynu ve'imoteynu

elohey avraham	elohey sarah
elohey yitzḥak	elohey rivkah
elohey ya'akov	elohey raḥel
	veylohey le'ah

Ha'el hagadol hagibor vehanora el elyon gomel ḥasadim tovim vekoney hakol vezoḥer ḥasdey avot ve'imot umevi ge'ulah livney veneyhem lema'an shemo be'ahavah.

Misod ḥaḥamim unevonim umilemed da'at mevinim efteḥah fi bitefilah uvetaḥanunim leḥalot uleḥanen peney meleḥ maley raḥamim moḥel vesole'aḥ la'avonim. ↲

Remember us for life,
our sovereign, who wishes us to live,
and write us in the Book of Life,
for your sake, ever-living God.

Regal One, our help, salvation, and protector:
Blessed are you, KIND ONE,
the shield of Abraham and help of Sarah.

2. GEVUROT / DIVINE POWER

You are forever powerful, ALMIGHTY ONE,
abundant in your saving acts.
You send down the dew.
In loyalty you sustain the living,
nurturing the life of every living thing,
upholding those who fall,
healing the sick, freeing the captive,
and remaining faithful to all life
held dormant in the earth.
Who can compare to you, almighty God,
who can resemble you, the source of life and death,
who makes salvation grow?

Who can compare to you, source of all mercy,
remembering all creatures mercifully, decreeing life!

Faithful are you in giving life to every living thing.
Blessed are you, THE FOUNT OF LIFE,
who gives and renews life. ↵

זָכְרֵנוּ לְחַיִּים מֶלֶךְ חָפֵץ בַּחַיִּים וְכָתְבֵנוּ בְּסֵפֶר הַחַיִּים לְמַעַנְךָ אֱלֹהִים חַיִּים:

מֶלֶךְ עוֹזֵר וּמוֹשִׁיעַ וּמָגֵן: בָּרוּךְ אַתָּה יהוה מָגֵן אַבְרָהָם וְעֶזְרַת שָׂרָה:

Zohrenu lehayim meleh hafetz bahayim vehotvenu besefer hahayim lema'aneha elohim hayim.

Meleh ozer umoshi'a umagen. Baruh atah adonay magen avraham ve'ezrat sarah.

בּ‎ 2 גְּבוּרוֹת

אַתָּה גִּבּוֹר לְעוֹלָם אֲדֹנָי רַב לְהוֹשִׁיעַ:

מוֹרִיד הַטָּל:

מְכַלְכֵּל חַיִּים בְּחֶסֶד מְחַיֶּה כָּל חַי בְּרַחֲמִים רַבִּים סוֹמֵךְ נוֹפְלִים וְרוֹפֵא חוֹלִים וּמַתִּיר אֲסוּרִים וּמְקַיֵּים אֱמוּנָתוֹ לִישֵׁנֵי עָפָר: מִי כָמוֹךָ בַּעַל גְּבוּרוֹת וּמִי דּוֹמֶה לָּךְ מֶלֶךְ מֵמִית וּמְחַיֶּה וּמַצְמִיחַ יְשׁוּעָה:

מִי כָמוֹךָ אַב הָרַחֲמִים זוֹכֵר יְצוּרָיו לְחַיִּים בְּרַחֲמִים:

וְנֶאֱמָן אַתָּה לְהַחֲיוֹת כָּל חָי: בָּרוּךְ אַתָּה יהוה מְחַיֶּה כָּל חָי: ←—

Atah gibor le'olam adonay rav lehoshi'a.
Morid hatal.
Mehalkel hayim behesed mehayey kol hay berahamim rabim someh noflim verofey holim umatir asurim umekayem emunato lisheney afar. Mi hamoha ba'al gevurot umi domeh lah meleh memit umehayeh umatzmi'ah yeshu'ah.

Mi hamoha av harahamim zoher yetzurav lehayim berahamim.
Vene'eman atah lehahayot kol hay. Baruh atah adonay mehayey kol hay.

And so, let holiness arise to you,
for you, God, are our sovereign.

The ark is opened.

Now, we declare the sacred power of this day,
which is the most awesome and solemn of days,
when your rule is established over all,
and your throne set in place by the power of love,
and you come forth to govern in truth.

True it is that you are our judge,
you alone can reprove, you alone can know,
you alone are witness to all deeds.

It is you who shall write,
you who shall seal what is written,
you who shall read,
and you who shall number all souls.
You alone can remember what we have forgotten;
it is you who shall open the Book of Remembrance,
but its contents shall speak for themselves,
for it bears the imprint of us all,
which our deeds and our lives have inscribed.

And when the great shofar is sounded,
a small quiet voice can be heard,
and the heavenly beings are thrown into fright,
and, seized by a terrible dread, they declare:
"Behold, the Day of Judgment has arrived,
when even those in heaven's court are judged,
for none can be exempt from justice's eyes!" ↵

לְךָ תַעֲלֶה קְדֻשָּׁה כִּי אַתָּה אֱלֹהֵינוּ מֶלֶךְ:

The ark is opened.

וּנְתַנֶּה תֹּקֶף קְדֻשַּׁת הַיּוֹם כִּי הוּא נוֹרָא וְאָיֹם וּבוֹ תִנָּשֵׂא מַלְכוּתֶךָ
וְיִכּוֹן בְּחֶסֶד כִּסְאֶךָ וְתֵשֵׁב עָלָיו בֶּאֱמֶת: אֱמֶת כִּי אַתָּה הוּא דַיָּן
וּמוֹכִיחַ וְיוֹדֵעַ וָעֵד וְכוֹתֵב וְחוֹתֵם וְסוֹפֵר וּמוֹנֶה וְתִזְכֹּר כָּל־
הַנִּשְׁכָּחוֹת וְתִפְתַּח אֶת־סֵפֶר הַזִּכְרוֹנוֹת וּמֵאֵלָיו יִקָּרֵא וְחוֹתָם יַד
כָּל־אָדָם בּוֹ:

וּבְשׁוֹפָר גָּדוֹל יִתָּקַע וְקוֹל דְּמָמָה דַקָּה יִשָּׁמַע וּמַלְאָכִים יֵחָפֵזוּן וְחִיל
וּרְעָדָה יֹאחֵזוּן וְיֹאמְרוּ הִנֵּה יוֹם הַדִּין: לִפְקֹד עַל צְבָא מָרוֹם בַּדִּין
כִּי לֹא יִזְכּוּ בְעֵינֶיךָ בַדִּין ←

COMMENTARY. On this day, we confront that which we spend most of our lives denying—that we shall die and be no more. Yom Kippur awakens us to lead our lives more fully because we come face to face with, and thus must acknowledge, our own mortality.   Michael Strassfeld

KAVANAH. What is my life's signature in the Book of Remembrance? Does the way in which I live my life reflect the divine image within me? What are the choices that I have made, and will the choices that I make over the coming year help me to live a life that will fashion God's image in the world?   Brian Walt

And all who come into the world
pass before you like sheep for the shepherd—
for, just as a shepherd numbers the flock,
passing the herd by the staff,
so do you make us pass by before you,
and number, and count, and determine the life,
one by one, of all who have lifebreath within.
You decide for each creature its cycles of life,
and you write down its destined decree.

On Rosh Hashanah, all is written and revealed,
and on Yom Kippur, the course of every life is sealed!

—how many pass on, how many shall thrive,
who shall live on, and who shall die,
whose death is timely, and whose is not,
who dies by fire, and who shall be drowned,
who by the sword, and who by the beast,
who by hunger, and who by thirst,
who by an earthquake, who by a plague,
who shall be strangled, and who shall be stoned,
who dwells in peace, and who is uprooted,
who shall live safely, and who shall be harmed,
whose life is tranquil, and whose is tormented,
who shall be poor, and who shall be rich,
who shall be humbled, and who is raised up!

וְכָל־בָּאֵי עוֹלָם יַעַבְרוּן לְפָנֶיךָ כִּבְנֵי מָרוֹן: כְּבַקָּרַת רוֹעֶה עֶדְרוֹ מַעֲבִיר צֹאנוֹ תַּחַת שִׁבְטוֹ כֵּן תַּעֲבִיר וְתִסְפֹּר וְתִמְנֶה וְתִפְקֹד נֶפֶשׁ כָּל־חָי וְתַחְתֹּךְ קִצְבָּה לְכָל־בְּרִיָּה וְתִכְתֹּב אֶת־גְּזַר דִּינָם:

בְּרֹאשׁ הַשָּׁנָה יִכָּתֵבוּן וּבְיוֹם צוֹם כִּפּוּר יֵחָתֵמוּן

Kevakarat ro'eh edro ma'avir tzono taḥat shivto ken ta'avir vetispor vetimneh vetifkod nefesh kol ḥay vetaḥtoḥ kitzbah leḥol beriyah vetiḥtov et gezar dinam.

Berosh hashanah yikatevun uveyom tzom kipur yeḥatemun

כַּמָּה יַעַבְרוּן וְכַמָּה יִבָּרֵאוּן מִי יִחְיֶה וּמִי יָמוּת
מִי בְקִצּוֹ וּמִי לֹא בְקִצּוֹ מִי בָאֵשׁ וּמִי בַמַּיִם
מִי בַחֶרֶב וּמִי בַחַיָּה מִי בָרָעָב וּמִי בַצָּמָא
מִי בָרַעַשׁ וּמִי בַמַּגֵּפָה מִי בַחֲנִיקָה וּמִי בַסְּקִילָה
מִי יָנוּחַ וּמִי יָנוּעַ מִי יַשְׁקִיט וּמִי יְטֹרֵף
מִי יִשָּׁלֵו וּמִי יִתְיַסָּר מִי יַעֲנִי וּמִי יַעֲשִׁיר
מִי יִשָּׁפֵל וּמִי יָרוּם: —←

But *teshuvah*, and *tefilah*, and *tzedakah*
make easier what God may decree,
make easier what life holds in store,
make easier facing the world,
make easier facing ourselves,

For, as is your name, so is your praise—
slow to be angry, quick to forgive;
you do not desire a person to die,
but only to change and to live.
Down to a person's last day of life,
the person is given the chance to return,
and all who return, and resolve to be just,
are welcomed by you straightaway.

For truly, you are their creator,
and you know their innermost nature,
and they know they are flesh and blood. ↵

Rabbi Yudan said in the name of Rabbi Elazar: Three things cancel harsh decrees: *tefilah*, *teshuvah* and *tzedakah*. All three are mentioned in a single verse (2 Chronicles 7:14): "Let my people humble themselves and pray, seek my face, and return from their evil way, and their sins will be forgiven, and their land healed." "Humble themselves and pray" refers to *tefilah*. "Seek my face" refers to *tzedakah*, as it is said (Psalms 17:15), "I will seek your face בצדק /*betzedek*/ in justice." Finally, "and return from their evil way" refers to *teshuvah*.   Genesis Rabbah 44:12

וּתְשׁוּבָה וּתְפִלָּה וּצְדָקָה

מַעֲבִירִין אֶת רֹעַ הַגְּזֵרָה:

כִּי כְּשִׁמְךָ כֵּן תְּהִלָּתֶךָ קָשֶׁה לִכְעֹס וְנוֹחַ לִרְצוֹת כִּי לֹא תַחְפֹּץ בְּמוֹת הַמֵּת כִּי אִם בְּשׁוּבוֹ מִדַּרְכּוֹ וְחָיָה: וְעַד יוֹם מוֹתוֹ תְּחַכֶּה־לּוֹ אִם יָשׁוּב מִיַּד תְּקַבְּלוֹ: אֱמֶת כִּי אַתָּה הוּא יוֹצְרָם וְאַתָּה יוֹדֵעַ יִצְרָם כִּי הֵם בָּשָׂר וָדָם: ←

Uteshuvah utefilah utzedakah
ma'avirin et ro'a hagezerah.

Ki heshimeha ken tehilateha kasheh lihos venoah lirtzot. Ki lo tahpotz bemot hamet ki im beshuvo midarko vehayah. Ve'ad yom moto tehakeh lo im yashuv miyad tekabelo. Emet ki atah hu yotzram ve'atah yode'a yitzram ki hem basar vadam. ↩

DERASH. Excerpt from a radio interview with a Canadian World War II veteran on Remembrance Day, November 11, 1993: "As D-day approached we knew something would be happening soon. I knew I should pray. I tried. It wasn't working. Then, I realized that this was because I was praying for my own survival. What I should have been praying is that I would perform (my duties) well. I realized that if I did not survive that day, another soldier would take my place—but if I did not do my tasks well, others, including my buddies, would die. I was then able to pray." Through *teshuvah*, *tzedakah* and *tefilah*, we can alter the severity of what has been decreed for *others*.   E.M.

All of humanity is founded on dust—
of dust they are made, and to dust they return;
as long as they live, they strive for their bread.
Like vessels of clay, they can break.
Like grass they can wither, like flowers they fade,
like shadows they pass, like clouds they are emptied,
like wind their strength is exhausted,
like dust they are scattered about,
like a dream they shall vanish from sight.
But you, holy one, your reign is eternal,
the God who lives and endures!

No limit exists to the years of your life,
no end is assigned to the length of your days,
no measure contains the array of your glory,
your name is beyond all translation.

Your name is the perfect expression of you,
and you have, in turn, embodied your name,
and have called us, as well, by your name. ↵

אָדָם יְסוֹדוֹ מֵעָפָר וְסוֹפוֹ לְעָפָר: בְּנַפְשׁוֹ יָבִיא לַחְמוֹ: מָשׁוּל כַּחֶרֶס הַנִּשְׁבָּר כְּחָצִיר יָבֵשׁ וּכְצִיץ נוֹבֵל כְּצֵל עוֹבֵר וּכְעָנָן כָּלֶה וּכְרֽוּחַ נוֹשָֽׁבֶת וּכְאָבָק פּוֹרֵחַ וְכַחֲלוֹם יָעוּף:

וְאַתָּה הוּא מֶֽלֶךְ אֵל חַי וְקַיָּם:

אֵין קִצְבָּה לִשְׁנוֹתֶֽיךָ וְאֵין קֵץ לְאֹֽרֶךְ יָמֶֽיךָ וְאֵין שִׁעוּר לְמַרְכְּבוֹת כְּבוֹדֶֽךָ וְאֵין פֵּרוּשׁ לְעֵילוֹם שְׁמֶֽךָ: שִׁמְךָ נָאֶה לְךָ וְאַתָּה נָאֶה לִשְׁמֶֽךָ וּשְׁמֵֽנוּ קָרָֽאתָ בִשְׁמֶֽךָ: ←

Adam yesodo me'afar vesofo le'afar. Benafsho yavi lahmo. Mashul kaheres hanishbar kehatzir yavesh uhetzitz novel ketzel over uhe'anan kaleh uheruah noshavet uhe'avak pore'ah vehahalom ya'uf.

Ve'atah hu meleh el hay vekayam.

ושמנו קראת בשמך/you...have called us...by your name. To say something by God's name is to take an oath or make a vow. One interpretation of this line is that God has made a commitment to us. Another interpretation, playing on the idea that human beings are בצלם אלהים/in the image of God, has human beings functioning in part as the embodiment of God. That is, God recognizes that the divine is in each one of us. A third way of understanding this text is that God needs humanity. God calls us to make the divine manifest in the world.   D.A.T.

Act for the sake of your name,
and make your name holy
over all who now declare
the holiness of your great name.
Act for the glory of your name,
which is uplifted and made holy
by the hidden utterance of holy seraphim,
who, bathed in holiness, proclaim the holiness
of your great name,
joining those who dwell above
with those who dwell on earth,
as it is written by your prophet's hand:
"And they call out, one to another, and declare:
'Holy, holy, holy is THE CREATOR of the Multitudes of Heaven!
All the world is filled with divine glory!'"

God's glory fills the world,
as the ministering angels ask, one to another,
"What place could contain God's holiness?"
And they are answered with a blessing:
"Blessed is the glory of THE OMNIPRESENT,
wherever God may dwell!"

And from God's place, God mercifully turns,
bestowing graciousness upon the people
who declare the oneness of the divine name
evening and morning, each day continually,
as twice a day they say, with love: "Shema!"
"Listen, Israel: THE ETERNAL is our God,
THE ETERNAL ONE alone!" ↰

וקרא...כבודו / And...glory! (Isaiah 6:3).
ברוך...ממקומו / Blessed...dwell! (Ezekiel 3:12).
שמע...אחד / Listen...alone! (Deuteronomy 6:4).

The ark is closed. We remain standing for the Kedushah.

עֲשֵׂה לְמַֽעַן שְׁמֶֽךָ וְקַדֵּשׁ אֶת־שִׁמְךָ עַל מַקְדִּישֵׁי שְׁמֶֽךָ בַּעֲבוּר כְּבוֹד
שִׁמְךָ הַנַּעֲרָץ וְהַנִּקְדָּשׁ כְּסוֹד שִֽׂיחַ שַׂרְפֵי־קֹֽדֶשׁ הַמַּקְדִּישִׁים שִׁמְךָ
בַּקֹּֽדֶשׁ דָּרֵי מַֽעְלָה עִם דָּרֵי מַֽטָּה כַּכָּתוּב עַל יַד נְבִיאֶֽךָ וְקָרָא זֶה
אֶל זֶה וְאָמַר

קָדוֹשׁ קָדוֹשׁ קָדוֹשׁ

יהוה צְבָאוֹת מְלֹא כָל־הָאָֽרֶץ כְּבוֹדוֹ:

כְּבוֹדוֹ מָלֵא עוֹלָם מְשָׁרְתָיו שׁוֹאֲלִים זֶה לָזֶה אַיֵּה מְקוֹם כְּבוֹדוֹ
לְעֻמָּתָם בָּרוּךְ יֹאמֵֽרוּ:

בָּרוּךְ כְּבוֹד יהוה מִמְּקוֹמוֹ:

מִמְּקוֹמוֹ הוּא יִֽפֶן בְּרַחֲמִים וְיָחֹן עַם הַמְיַחֲדִים שְׁמוֹ עֶֽרֶב וָבֹֽקֶר בְּכָל
יוֹם תָּמִיד פַּעֲמַֽיִם בְּאַהֲבָה שְׁמַע אוֹמְרִים:

שְׁמַע יִשְׂרָאֵל יהוה אֱלֹהֵֽינוּ יהוה אֶחָד: ←—

Asey lema'an shemeḥa vekadesh et shimḥa al makdishey
shemeḥa ba'avur kevod shimḥa hana'aratz vehanikdash kesod
siaḥ sarfey kodesh hamakdishim shimḥa bakodesh darey mala im
darey matah kakatuv al yad nevi'eḥa vekara zeh el zeh ve'amar:
Kadosh kadosh kadosh adonay tzeva'ot melo ḥol ha'aretz kevodo.
Kevodo maley olam mesharetav sho'alim zeh lazeh ayey mekom
kevodo le'umatam baruḥ yomeru:
Baruḥ kevod adonay mimekomo.
Mimekomo hu yifen beraḥamim veyaḥon am hamyaḥadim
shemo erev vavoker beḥol yom tamid pa'amayim be'ahavah
shema omrim:
Shema yisra'el adonay eloheynu adonay eḥad. ⤶

COMMENTARY. The structure of the *Kedushah* rests upon myths in Jewish
tradition about angelic choruses praising God. Standing at attention and
singing words ascribed to the angelic chorus, Jews traditionally rock
upward on their toes each time the word קדוש/*kadosh*/Holy is chanted
here. It is as if we were straining upward to join the heavenly choir in
praise for the divine.   D.A.T.

This is our God.
This is our source.
This is our sovereign.
This is our saving power.
And this one, mercifully,
shall declare a second time,
for every living being to hear,
confirming God's divinity for you:
"I am THE OMNIPRESENT ONE, your God!"

O mighty one, our mighty one,
THE SOVEREIGN who watches over us,
how mighty is your name throughout the earth!
The time shall come that GOD will reign
throughout the earth. On that day
shall THE FOUNT OF LIFE be one,
the divine name be one.
And as is written in your sacred words of psalm:
"May THE ETERNAL reign forever,
your God, O Zion, from one generation to the next. Halleluyah!"

From one generation to the next
may we declare your greatness,
and for all eternities may we affirm your holiness,
and may your praise, our God,
never be absent from our mouths
now and forever.
For you are a great and holy God. ↩

אני...אלהיכם / I...God! (Numbers 15:41).
יהוה אדונינו...הארץ / THE SOVEREIGN...earth! (Psalms 8:10).
והיה יהוה...אחד / The time...be one (Zechariah 14:9).
ימלך...הללויה / May...Halleluyah! (Psalms 146:10).

הוּא אֱלֹהֵֽינוּ הוּא אָבִֽינוּ הוּא מַלְכֵּֽנוּ הוּא מוֹשִׁיעֵֽנוּ וְהוּא יַשְׁמִיעֵֽנוּ בְּרַחֲמָיו שֵׁנִית לְעֵינֵי כָּל חָי: לִהְיוֹת לָכֶם לֵאלֹהִים: אֲנִי יהוה אֱלֹהֵיכֶם:

אַדִּיר אַדִּירֵֽנוּ יהוה אֲדֹנֵֽינוּ מָה־אַדִּיר שִׁמְךָ בְּכָל־הָאָֽרֶץ: וְהָיָה יהוה לְמֶֽלֶךְ עַל־כָּל־הָאָֽרֶץ בַּיּוֹם הַהוּא יִהְיֶה יהוה אֶחָד וּשְׁמוֹ אֶחָד: וּבְדִבְרֵי קָדְשְׁךָ כָּתוּב לֵאמֹר:

יִמְלֹךְ יהוה לְעוֹלָם אֱלֹהַֽיִךְ צִיּוֹן לְדֹר וָדֹר הַלְלוּיָהּ: לְדוֹר וָדוֹר נַגִּיד גָּדְלֶֽךָ וּלְנֵֽצַח נְצָחִים קְדֻשָּׁתְךָ נַקְדִּישׁ וְשִׁבְחֲךָ אֱלֹהֵֽינוּ מִפִּֽינוּ לֹא יָמוּשׁ לְעוֹלָם וָעֶד כִּי אֵל מֶֽלֶךְ גָּדוֹל וְקָדוֹשׁ אָֽתָּה: ←

Hu eloheynu hu avinu hu malkeynu hu moshi'enu vehu yashmi'enu berahamav shenit le'eyney kol hay lihyot lahem leylohim ani adonay eloheyhem.

Adir adirenu adonay adoneynu mah adir shimeha behol ha'aretz. Vehayah adonay lemeleh al kol ha'aretz bayom hahu yihyeh adonay ehad ushemo ehad.

Uvedivrey kodsheha katuv lemor.

Yimloh adonay le'olam elohayih tziyon ledor vador halleluyah.

Ledor vador nagid godleha ulnetzah netzahim kedushateha nakdish veshivhaha eloheynu mipinu lo yamush le'olam va'ed ki el meleh gadol vekadosh atah. ↰

COMMENTARY. On the pilgrimage festivals and Days of Awe, the paragraph אדיר אדירנו /adir adireynu!/O mighty one is added to the Kedushah. This provides an additional opportunity to emphasize not only divine sovereignty, but the hope that God's rule will become permanently manifest throughout the earth. Its placement here in the middle of the Kedushah stands as a reminder that holiness is only complete when human beings live lives that bring them into harmony with the divine. Thus the prayer for divine sovereignty is a prayer we are meant to take personally as we strive to be holy. D.A.T.

If the remainder of the Amidah is being read silently, it is customary to remain standing. If the remainder of the Amidah is being chanted aloud (חזרת הש״ץ/reader's repetition), it is customary to be seated here.

And therefore, HOLY ONE, let awe of you
infuse the whole of your Creation,
and let knowledge of your presence
dwell in all your creatures.
And let every being worship you,
and each created life pay homage to your rule.
Let all of them, as one, enact your bidding
with a whole and peaceful heart.
For we have always known, ALMIGHTY ONE,
that all authority to rule originates in you,
all strength is rooted in your arm,
all mighty deeds have emanated from your hand.
Your name alone is the source of awe
that surges through all life.

And therefore, HOLY ONE, let awe of you
infuse your people, let the praise of you
ring out from all who worship you.
Let hope enliven all who seek you,
and let all who look to you with hope
find strength to speak.
Grant joy throughout your land,
let happiness resound throughout your holy city,
soon, and in our days.

And therefore, let the just behold your peace,
let them rejoice,
let all who follow in your path sing out with joy,
let all who love you dance in celebration,
and may your power overwhelm all treachery,
so that it vanish wholly from the earth like smoke.
Then shall the power of injustice pass away! ↵

If the remainder of the Amidah is being read silently, it is customary to remain standing. If the remainder of the Amidah is being chanted aloud (חזרת הש״ץ/reader's repetition), it is customary to be seated here.

‏וּבְכֵן תֵּן פַּחְדְּךָ‎ יהוה אֱלֹהֵינוּ עַל כָּל־מַעֲשֶׂיךָ וְאֵימָתְךָ עַל כָּל־
מַה־שֶּׁבָּרָאתָ וְיִירָאוּךָ כָּל־הַמַּעֲשִׂים וְיִשְׁתַּחֲווּ לְפָנֶיךָ כָּל־הַבְּרוּאִים
וְיֵעָשׂוּ כֻלָּם אֲגֻדָּה אַחַת לַעֲשׂוֹת רְצוֹנְךָ בְּלֵבָב שָׁלֵם כְּמוֹ שֶׁיָּדַעְנוּ
יהוה אֱלֹהֵינוּ שֶׁהַשִּׁלְטוֹן לְפָנֶיךָ עֹז בְּיָדְךָ וּגְבוּרָה בִּימִינֶךָ וְשִׁמְךָ
נוֹרָא עַל כָּל־מַה־שֶּׁבָּרָאתָ:

‏וּבְכֵן תֵּן כָּבוֹד‎ יהוה לְעַמֶּךָ תְּהִלָּה לִירֵאֶיךָ וְתִקְוָה לְדוֹרְשֶׁיךָ
וּפִתְחוֹן פֶּה לַמְיַחֲלִים לָךְ שִׂמְחָה לְאַרְצֶךָ וְשָׂשׂוֹן לְעִירֶךָ בִּמְהֵרָה
בְיָמֵינוּ:

‏וּבְכֵן צַדִּיקִים‎ יִרְאוּ וְיִשְׂמָחוּ וִישָׁרִים יַעֲלֹזוּ וַחֲסִידִים בְּרִנָּה
יָגִילוּ וְעוֹלָתָה תִּקְפָּץ־פִּיהָ וְכָל־הָרִשְׁעָה כֻּלָּהּ כְּעָשָׁן תִּכְלֶה כִּי
תַעֲבִיר מֶמְשֶׁלֶת זָדוֹן מִן הָאָרֶץ: ←‏

May you alone be sovereign over all of your Creation,
and Mount Zion be the seat and symbol of your glory,
and Jerusalem, your holy city—
as is written in your holy scriptures:
"THE ETERNAL ONE shall reign forever,
your God, O Zion, through all generations!
Halleluyah!"

Holy are you,
and awe-inspiring is your name,
and there is no God apart from you,
as it is written: "THE CREATOR of the hosts of heaven
shall be exalted through the rule of law,
and God, the Holy One, made holy by the reign of justice."
Blessed are you, ETERNAL ONE,
the holy sovereign power. ↵

וְתִמְלֹךְ אַתָּה יהוה לְבַדֶּךָ עַל כָּל־מַעֲשֶׂיךָ בְּהַר צִיּוֹן מִשְׁכַּן כְּבוֹדֶךָ
וּבִירוּשָׁלַיִם עִיר קָדְשֶׁךָ: כַּכָּתוּב בְּדִבְרֵי קָדְשֶׁךָ: יִמְלֹךְ יהוה לְעוֹלָם
אֱלֹהַיִךְ צִיּוֹן לְדֹר וָדֹר הַלְלוּיָהּ:

קָדוֹשׁ אַתָּה וְנוֹרָא שְׁמֶךָ וְאֵין אֱלוֹהַּ מִבַּלְעָדֶיךָ: כַּכָּתוּב: וַיִּגְבַּהּ יהוה
צְבָאוֹת בַּמִּשְׁפָּט וְהָאֵל הַקָּדוֹשׁ נִקְדַּשׁ בִּצְדָקָה: בָּרוּךְ אַתָּה יהוה
← הַמֶּלֶךְ הַקָּדוֹשׁ:

ימלך...הללויה /THE ETERNAL ONE...Halleluyah! (Psalms 146:10).
ויגבה...בצדקה /THE CREATOR...justice (Isaiah 5:16).

4. KEDUSHAT HAYOM / THE DAY'S HOLINESS

On Shabbat add the words in parenthesis.

You have loved us, and have taken pleasure in us,
and have made us holy with your mitzvot,
and you have brought us, sovereign one,
near to your service,
and have called us to the shelter of your great and holy name.
And you gave us, HOLY ONE, our God, with love,
(this day of Shabbat, for holiness and rest, and)
this Day of Atonement,
for pardon, for forgiveness, and for atonement,
a day for pardoning all of our wrongful acts,
(with love,)
a holy convocation,
a remembrance of the going out from Egypt.
(Those who keep Shabbat enjoy your realm,
they call Shabbat the summit of delight.
A people that observes the holy seventh day
enjoys abundant goodness and delight.

The seventh day you favored and made holy,
you have called it the most loved of days,
a sign you made of it eternally,
in memory of Creation's works and days.) ↵

On Shabbat add the words in parenthesis.

אַתָּה אֲהַבְתָּנוּ וְרָצִיתָ בָּנוּ וְקִדַּשְׁתָּנוּ בְּמִצְוֹתֶיךָ וְקֵרַבְתָּנוּ מַלְכֵּנוּ
לַעֲבוֹדָתֶךָ וְשִׁמְךָ הַגָּדוֹל וְהַקָּדוֹשׁ עָלֵינוּ קָרָאתָ:

וַתִּתֶּן־לָנוּ יהוה אֱלֹהֵינוּ בְּאַהֲבָה אֶת־יוֹם (הַשַּׁבָּת הַזֶּה לִקְדֻשָּׁה
וְלִמְנוּחָה וְאֶת־יוֹם) הַכִּפּוּרִים הַזֶּה לִמְחִילָה וְלִסְלִיחָה וּלְכַפָּרָה
וְלִמְחָל־בּוֹ אֶת־כָּל־עֲוֹנוֹתֵינוּ (בְּאַהֲבָה) מִקְרָא קֹדֶשׁ זֵכֶר לִיצִיאַת
מִצְרָיִם:

(יִשְׂמְחוּ בְמַלְכוּתְךָ שׁוֹמְרֵי שַׁבָּת וְקוֹרְאֵי עֹנֶג: עַם מְקַדְּשֵׁי שְׁבִיעִי
כֻּלָּם יִשְׂבְּעוּ וְיִתְעַנְּגוּ מִטּוּבֶךָ: וְהַשְּׁבִיעִי רָצִיתָ בּוֹ וְקִדַּשְׁתּוֹ: חֶמְדַּת
יָמִים אוֹתוֹ קָרָאתָ זֵכֶר לְמַעֲשֵׂה בְרֵאשִׁית:) ←

(Yismeḥu vemalḥuteḥa shomrey shabbat vekorey oneg. Am
mekadeshey shevi'i kulam yisbe'u veyitanegu mituveḥa.
Vehashevi'i ratzita bo vekidashto. Ḥemdat yamim oto karata
zeḥer lema'asey vereyshit.) ←

We rise for Aleynu. *It is customary to bow or prostrate at "bend the knee." Choose one of the following:*

It is up to us to offer praises to the Source of all,
to declare the greatness of the author of Creation,
who gave us teachings of truth
and planted eternal life within us.

❦

It is up to us to offer praises to the Source of all,
to declare the greatness of the author of Creation,
who created heaven's heights and spread out its expanse,
who laid the earth's foundation and brought forth its offspring,
giving life to all its peoples,
the breath of life to all who walk about. ↩

COMMENTARY. This siddur offers several versions of the *Aleynu*. The first emphasizes that the gift of Torah demands our committed response. The second emphasizes our obligation to God as part of Creation. The traditional *Aleynu* below the line has troubled some Jews because it implies the inferiority of other faiths and peoples.   D.A.T.

MEDITATION. We pray every year at this time to be written in the Book of Life for another year. One more year. Give me one more year. I'm not finished. Not yet. We're afraid. We don't want to die. But Yom Kippur is about dying. We enact the drama of our dying. We put on our *kittels*. We stop eating. It's over. How do I let go of this life? How do I let go of myself? How do I forgive everything, everyone, myself, and let my life fall? Bowing completely is falling down back into the womb of the earth, slowly, softly. Relaxing completely. Give up your little story....Give back your small self. Sense the ground and through it the immensity of the Big Story, and from within it and behind it, feel its unknowable Author....We are only halfway home. Bowing is not just about giving up and going down. It's about giving up and going down *in order to get back up. All the way up.* Up, more easily and further than you have ever been. Up, with fresh energy, power, openness. Up, with renewed purpose, and yes, up with a sense of authority. From where does our strength come? Our strength comes from God. But sometimes we've got to go down to get it. We rise with strength renewed.   Bruce Fertman

We rise for Aleynu. It is customary to bow or prostrate at "korim." Choose one of the following:

Aleynu leshabe'ah la'adon hakol
latet gedulah leyotzer bereyshit
shenatan lanu torat emet
vehayey olam nata betohenu.

עָלֵינוּ לְשַׁבֵּחַ לַאֲדוֹן הַכֹּל
לָתֵת גְּדֻלָּה לְיוֹצֵר בְּרֵאשִׁית
שֶׁנָּתַן לָנוּ תּוֹרַת אֱמֶת
וְחַיֵּי עוֹלָם נָטַע בְּתוֹכֵנוּ:

Continue on page 892.

&

Aleynu leshabe'ah la'adon hakol
latet gedulah leyotzer bereyshit.
bore hashamayim venoteyhem
roka ha'aretz vetze'etza'eha
noten neshamah la'am aleha
veru'ah laholehim bah.

עָלֵינוּ לְשַׁבֵּחַ לַאֲדוֹן הַכֹּל
לָתֵת גְּדֻלָּה לְיוֹצֵר בְּרֵאשִׁית
בּוֹרֵא הַשָּׁמַיִם וְנוֹטֵיהֶם
רֹקַע הָאָרֶץ וְצֶאֱצָאֶיהָ
נֹתֵן נְשָׁמָה לָעָם עָלֶיהָ
וְרוּחַ לַהֹלְכִים בָּהּ: ←

עָלֵינוּ לְשַׁבֵּחַ לַאֲדוֹן הַכֹּל לָתֵת גְּדֻלָּה
לְיוֹצֵר בְּרֵאשִׁית שֶׁלֹּא עָשָׂנוּ כְּגוֹיֵי
הָאֲרָצוֹת וְלֹא שָׂמָנוּ כְּמִשְׁפְּחוֹת הָאֲדָמָה
שֶׁלֹּא שָׂם חֶלְקֵנוּ כָּהֶם וְגוֹרָלֵנוּ כְּכָל
הֲמוֹנָם:

It is up to us to offer praises to the Source of all, to declare the greatness of the author of Creation, who has made us different from the other nations of the earth, and situated us in quite a different spot, and made our daily lot another kind from theirs, and given us a destiny uncommon in this world.

And so, we bend the knee and bow,
acknowledging the sovereign who rules
above all those who rule, the blessed Holy One,
who stretched out the heavens and founded the earth,
whose realm embraces heaven's heights,
whose mighty presence stalks celestial ramparts.
This is our God; there is none else besides,
as it is written in the Torah:
"You shall know this day, and bring it home
inside your heart, that THE SUPREME ONE is God
in the heavens above and on the earth below.
There is no other God."

Our God, our ancients' God, may our prayer arise and come to you, and be beheld, and be acceptable. Let it be heard, acted upon, remembered—the memory of us and all our needs, the memory of our ancestors, the memory of messianic hopes, the memory of Jerusalem your holy city, and the memory of all your kin, the house of Israel, all surviving in your presence. Act for goodness and grace, for love and care, for life, well-being and peace, on this Day of Atonement.

Remember us this day, ALL-KNOWING ONE, our God, for goodness. Favor us this day with blessing. Preserve us this day for life. With your redeeming nurturing word, be kind and generous. Act tenderly on our behalf, and grant us victory over all our trials. Truly, our eyes turn toward you, for you are a providing God; gracious and merciful are you.

וידעת...עוד / You...other God (Deuteronomy 4:39).

וַאֲנַחְנוּ כּוֹרְעִים וּמִשְׁתַּחֲוִים וּמוֹדִים לִפְנֵי מֶֽלֶךְ מַלְכֵי הַמְּלָכִים הַקָּדוֹשׁ בָּרוּךְ הוּא:
שֶׁהוּא נוֹטֶה שָׁמַֽיִם וְיוֹסֵד אָֽרֶץ וּמוֹשַׁב יְקָרוֹ בַּשָּׁמַֽיִם מִמַּֽעַל וּשְׁכִינַת עֻזּוֹ בְּגָבְהֵי מְרוֹמִים: הוּא אֱלֹהֵֽינוּ אֵין עוֹד: אֱמֶת מַלְכֵּֽנוּ אֶֽפֶס זוּלָתוֹ כַּכָּתוּב בְּתוֹרָתוֹ: וְיָדַעְתָּ הַיּוֹם וַהֲשֵׁבֹתָ אֶל־לְבָבֶֽךָ כִּי יהוה הוּא הָאֱלֹהִים בַּשָּׁמַֽיִם מִמַּֽעַל וְעַל־הָאָֽרֶץ מִתָּֽחַת אֵין עוֹד:

Va'anahnu korim umishtahavim umodim
lifney meleh malhey hamelahim hakadosh baruh hu.

Shehu noteh shamayim veyosed aretz umoshav yekaro
    bashamayim mima'al
ushehinat uzo begovhey meromim.
Hu eloheynu eyn od.
Emet malkenu efes zulato kakatuv betorato.
Veyadata hayom vahashevota el levaveha
ki adonay hu ha'elohim bashamayim mima'al ve'al ha'aretz
    mitahat eyn od.

אֱלֹהֵֽינוּ וֵאלֹהֵי אֲבוֹתֵֽינוּ וְאִמּוֹתֵֽינוּ יַעֲלֶה וְיָבוֹא וְיַגִּֽיעַ וְיֵרָאֶה וְיֵרָצֶה וְיִשָּׁמַע וְיִפָּקֵד וְיִזָּכֵר זִכְרוֹנֵֽנוּ וּפִקְדוֹנֵֽנוּ וְזִכְרוֹן אֲבוֹתֵֽינוּ וְאִמּוֹתֵֽינוּ וְזִכְרוֹן יְמוֹת הַמָּשִֽׁיחַ וְזִכְרוֹן יְרוּשָׁלַֽיִם עִיר קָדְשֶֽׁךָ וְזִכְרוֹן כָּל עַמְּךָ בֵּית יִשְׂרָאֵל לְפָנֶֽיךָ לִפְלֵיטָה לְטוֹבָה וּלְחֵן וּלְחֶֽסֶד וּלְרַחֲמִים לְחַיִּים וּלְשָׁלוֹם בְּיוֹם הַכִּפּוּרִים הַזֶּה:

זָכְרֵֽנוּ יהוה אֱלֹהֵֽינוּ בּוֹ לְטוֹבָה: וּפָקְדֵֽנוּ בוֹ לִבְרָכָה וְהוֹשִׁיעֵֽנוּ בוֹ לְחַיִּים: וּבִדְבַר יְשׁוּעָה וְרַחֲמִים חוּס וְחָנֵּֽנוּ וְרַחֵם עָלֵֽינוּ וְהוֹשִׁיעֵֽנוּ כִּי אֵלֶֽיךָ עֵינֵֽינוּ כִּי אֵל מֶֽלֶךְ חַנּוּן וְרַחוּם אָֽתָּה:

SECOND CONFESSION: FOR OUR PEOPLE

The High Priest would come into the east side
of the court, north of the altar.
To his right would stand his highest deputy,
and to his left, the head of the officiating clan.
And there were placed two goats,
and there an urn, which held two lots.

He shook the urn, and drew from it two lots.
On one was written: "For THE ETERNAL ONE,"
and on the other one: "For Azazel."
He bound a thread of crimson on the head
of the goat that would be sent away,
and stood it at the place from which it would be sent,
and he placed the goat that would be slaughtered
at its slaughter-site. He then came to a second bull,
and placed his hands upon it, and confessed:

"As the High Priest, in the past, took upon himself
responsibility both toward his household and his fellow priests,
so now are we, the people Israel, under obligation
to assume responsibility for our mistakes,
those that prevail in the society in which we live.
We, too, today, lift up our eyes to God on high,
on behalf of all our kin, the House of Israel,
wherever they may be. Would that each person
might return to God, a turning both of body and of spirit,
as it is written:
'Turn toward me, that I might turn toward you,
says THE CREATOR of all beings!'
For then we would be clean,
and sanctify ourselves by your great Name,
and become ready to receive your promise.
As it was then, so now: here stands before you
all the House of Israel,
who make confession in your presence." ↵

SECOND CONFESSION: FOR OUR PEOPLE

בָּא לוֹ לְמִזְרַח הָעֲזָרָה לִצְפוֹן הַמִּזְבֵּֽחַ הַסְּגָן מִימִינוֹ וְרֹאשׁ בֵּית־אָב
מִשְּׂמֹאלוֹ: וְשָׁם שְׁנֵי שְׂעִירִים וְקַלְפֵּי הָיְתָה שָׁם וּבָהּ שְׁנֵי גוֹרָלוֹת:
טָרַף בַּקַּלְפֵּי וְהֶעֱלָה שְׁנֵי גוֹרָלוֹת: אֶחָד כָּתוּב עָלָיו לַיהוה וְאֶחָד
כָּתוּב עָלָיו לַעֲזָאזֵל: קָשַׁר לָשׁוֹן שֶׁלְּזְהוֹרִית בְּרֹאשׁ שָׂעִיר הַמִּשְׁתַּלֵּֽחַ
וְהֶעֱמִידוֹ כְּנֶֽגֶד בֵּית־שִׁלּוּחוֹ וְלַנִּשְׁחָט כְּנֶֽגֶד בֵּית־שְׁחִיטָתוֹ: בָּא לוֹ
אֵֽצֶל פָּרוֹ שְׁנִיָּה וְסוֹמֵךְ שְׁתֵּי יָדָיו עָלָיו וּמִתְוַדֶּה:

כְּשֵׁם שֶׁבְּעָבָר קִבֵּל הַכֹּהֵן הַגָּדוֹל עַל עַצְמוֹ אֶת הָאַחֲרָיוּת לִבְנֵי בֵּיתוֹ
וְלִבְנֵי מַעֲמָדוֹ הַכֹּהֲנִים כָּךְ אָֽנוּ עַם יִשְׂרָאֵל מְחֻיָּבִים לְקַבֵּל עַל
עַצְמֵֽנוּ אֶת הָאַחֲרָיוּת לַפְּגָמִים הַקַּיָּמִים בַּחֶבְרָה בָּהּ אָֽנוּ חַיִּים:

גַּם אָֽנוּ הַיּוֹם נִשָּׂא עֵינֵֽינוּ לֵאלֹהֵי מָרוֹם עַל כָּל אַחֵֽינוּ בֵּית יִשְׂרָאֵל
בַּאֲשֶׁר הֵם שָׁם: מִי יִתֵּן וְיָשֽׁוּבוּ אִישׁ אִישׁ לְעַמּוֹ וְלֵאלֹהָיו שִׁיבַת
הַגּוּף וּתְשׁוּבַת הַנֶּֽפֶשׁ כַּכָּתוּב שֽׁוּבוּ אֵלַי וְאָשֽׁוּבָה אֲלֵיכֶם אָמַר יהוה
צְבָאוֹת: אָז נִטָּהֵר וְנִתְקַדֵּשׁ בִּשְׁמֶֽךָ וְנִהְיֶה רְאוּיִּים לְקַבֵּל הַבְטָחָתְךָ
כְּאָז כֵּן עַתָּה עוֹמְדִים כָּל בֵּית יִשְׂרָאֵל וּמִתְוַדִּים לְפָנֶֽיךָ: ←——

COMMENTARY. Yom Kippur is effective because it posits a power that can forgive our sins. The Reconstructionist challenge is retaining that belief while rejecting belief in a capricious supernatural God. Divine forgiveness and healing become accessible to us both internally and through the power of the community seeking forgiveness. M.L./Z.S.S.

KAVANAH. "One who 'slaughters' the evil inclination is as one who has offered a sacrifice on the Temple altar. But to do this, one must know how and what to slaughter." Reb Simḥa Zissel Ziv

COMMENTARY. Late in the day on Yom Kippur we are tempted to think of a wholesale change in personality. But the real *teshuvah* can only come about through a knowledge of the effective modes of change. Just as the ritual of atonement in the Temple followed precise instructions in order to work, real change requires an understanding of how and what to change. E.M.

שובו...צבאות / Turn...beings! (Zechariah 1:3).

And thus would he declare:

"O Holy One,
I have sinned, I have done wrong, and I have gone astray,
before you, I and all your people, the House of Israel.
I beseech you, Holy One, please grant atonement
for the sins, the wrongful acts, and the transgressions
I have done before you, I and my household."

And thus do we declare:

"O Holy One, please grant atonement for the sins,
the wrongdoing and the transgressions
that the House of Israel have done before you,
they and all who dwell on earth.
And bring us all to the world's repair through divine rule,
as it is written in the Torah:
'For on this day, atonement shall be made for you,
to make you clean from all your wrongdoings.
Before THE FOUNT OF MERCY, you shall all be clean!'"

And the priests,
and all the people standing in the courtyard,
when they would hear the glorious and awesome Name of God
uttered aloud distinctly from the High Priest's mouth,
in holiness and purity,
would prostrate themselves, and bow down in acknowledgment,
and touch their faces to the ground, and say:
"Blessed are the glorious Name and majesty of God,
to all eternity!"

And the High Priest, in turn,
would thus complete the utterance of the Name
in sacred devotion, facing those who offered blessing,
and declare to them: "You shall be clean!"

And you God, in your goodness, stir up your compassion
and forgive this people serving you.

וְכָךְ הָיָה אוֹמֵר אָנָּא הַשֵּׁם עָוִיתִי פָּשַׁעְתִּי חָטָאתִי לְפָנֶיךָ אֲנִי וְכֹל
עַמְּךָ בֵּית יִשְׂרָאֵל: אָנָּא הַשֵּׁם כַּפֶּר־נָא לָעֲווֹנוֹת וְלַפְּשָׁעִים וְלַחֲטָאִים
שֶׁעָוִיתִי וְשֶׁפָּשַׁעְתִּי וְשֶׁחָטָאתִי לְפָנֶיךָ אֲנִי וּבֵית יִשְׂרָאֵל:

וְכָךְ אָנוּ אוֹמְרִים אָנָּא הַשֵּׁם כַּפֶּר־נָא לַחֲטָאִים וְלָעֲווֹנוֹת וְלַפְּשָׁעִים
שֶׁחָטְאוּ וְשֶׁעָווּ וְשֶׁפָּשְׁעוּ לְפָנֶיךָ בֵּית יִשְׂרָאֵל וְכֹל יוֹשְׁבֵי תֵבֵל
וְהִגִּיעָנוּ לְתַקֵּן עוֹלָם בְּמַלְכוּת שַׁדַּי כַּכָּתוּב בְּתוֹרָתֶךָ כִּי בַיּוֹם הַזֶּה
יְכַפֵּר עֲלֵיכֶם לְטַהֵר אֶתְכֶם מִכֹּל חַטֹּאתֵיכֶם לִפְנֵי יהוה....

וְהַכֹּהֲנִים וְהָעָם הָעוֹמְדִים בַּעֲזָרָה כְּשֶׁהָיוּ שׁוֹמְעִים אֶת־הַשֵּׁם הַנִּכְבָּד
וְהַנּוֹרָא מְפֹרָשׁ יוֹצֵא מִפִּי כֹהֵן גָּדוֹל בִּקְדֻשָּׁה וּבְטָהֳרָה הָיוּ כּוֹרְעִים
וּמִשְׁתַּחֲוִים וּמוֹדִים וְנוֹפְלִים עַל פְּנֵיהֶם וְאוֹמְרִים בָּרוּךְ שֵׁם כְּבוֹד
מַלְכוּתוֹ לְעוֹלָם וָעֶד: וְאַף הוּא הָיָה מִתְכַּוֵּן לִגְמֹר לְגֶמֶר אֶת־הַשֵּׁם כְּנֶגֶד
הַמְבָרְכִים וְאוֹמֵר לָהֶם תִּטְהָרוּ: וְאַתָּה בְּטוּבְךָ מְעוֹרֵר רַחֲמֶיךָ
וְסוֹלֵחַ לְעַם מְשָׁרְתֶיךָ:

COMMENTARY. God's name had four letters, each of which corresponds to one aspect of reality. The world is a physical, emotional, mental and spiritual reality. Kabbalah, Jewish mysticism, speaks of the four worlds—a physical, an emotional, a mental and a soul world. In each of these four realms of human experience, a Jewish person is called upon to sanctify the name of God. When you make an offering or sacrifice to God, you must be sure, therefore, to do so בכל מאדך—with everything you have. It's not enough just to give money or some thing to charity; that's only a material donation. You have to give with feeling and compassion; there has to be a strong desire that informs your act of giving. But that's not enough either. With your compassion there needs to go an intelligent purpose; you need to understand intellectually why it's important to give. But even that won't suffice. Guiding your mental understanding should be an awareness that a Divine Mystery sustains all purposes; behind even the wisest plan lives a sense of holiness, a connection with God. S.D.R.

כי ביום...לפני יהוה/For on...clean! (Leviticus 16:30).

INTRODUCTION TO ELEH EZKERAH/
MARTYROLOGY

מֶה חַיֵּינוּ אִם לֹא נִזְכּוֹר אֶת יְמֵי־חַיֵּיהֶם:

מֶה חַסְדֵּנוּ אִם לֹא תִּהְיֶה לָנוּ דוּגְמַת חֲסָדֵיהֶם:

מַה צִּדְקֵנוּ לוּלֵא צִדְקַת מַעֲשֵׂיהֶם:

מַה גְּבוּרוֹתֵינוּ לְעוּמַת מְסִירַת נַפְשָׁם עַל קִדּוּשׁ שְׁמֶךָ:

וּמַה נֹּאמַר לְפָנֶיךָ אִם לֹא נִזְכּוֹר אֶת כֹּל קוֹרוֹתֵיהֶם:

הֲלֹא כֻּלָּם הָיוּ אַנְשֵׁי שֵׁם וַחֲכָמִים וְצַדִּיקִים:

וְכָל הַמַּרְבֶּה לְסַפֵּר אוֹדוֹתֵיהֶם יֵחָשְׁבוּ

לְתַלְמִידֵי תַלְמִידֵיהֶם וַהֲרֵי זֶה מְשׁוּבָּח:

What is our life without remembering the days of their lives?
What is our piety without the example of their pious way?
What is our righteousness without their righteous deeds?
What is our courage in the face of their giving their lives to sanctify God's name?
What can we say if we do not to remember their stories?
They were people of renown, wise and righteous.
All who elaborate in telling about them are called the students of their students and are praiseworthy.

Michael Strassfeld

COMMENTARY. The traditional readings in the *Eleh Ezkerah* section of the Yom Kippur liturgy focus on acts of voluntary martyrdom known as *kidush hashem*, sanctification of the divine name. *Kidush hashem* involves voluntarily giving up one's life rather than committing a serious transgression or forsaking Torah. In more recent history, many Jewish martyrs were of a radically different sort because they died not out of a heroic choice, but merely because they were Jews. While the Holocaust is the most striking and most horrible example, such was the lot of some of the Jews who died in the Crusades, pogroms, and in countless unspeakable acts that have occurred in the last millennium. These two kinds of martyrs—those who made brave choices and those who appear to have had none—are more alike than they first appear, for each generation of Jews rededicates itself to the covenant anew. We know this act contains a risk. Voluntarily continuing the covenant is thus potentially an act of *kidush hashem*.

D.A.T.

The Yom Kippur Martyrology, the *Eleh Ezkerah*, is an early poem based on various *midrashim* about ten talmudic sages living under Roman authority who refused to abandon Torah, and, consequently, were tortured to death. That there were several versions of the poem, which differed with regard to the list of martyrs, few of whom were contemporaries of one another, was of no concern to the worshipping Jew, for historical accuracy had nothing to do with the purpose of the text. In a world of Jewish persecution, the legend of the Ten Martyrs became popular because it set before the oppressed an example of the greatest Sages faced with the same challenges. Especially from the time of the First Crusade, the Ten served as a model for contemporary martyrs.

In the order of the traditional liturgy, the Martyrology is placed immediately after the *Avodah* service, which describes the rites of the High Priest on Yom Kippur day. That placement suggests that since we can no longer offer animal sacrifices for the expiation of our sins, we offer the lives of our martyrs instead. If *we* are not worthy of expiation, *they* certainly were, and so we may be forgiven on account of their merit. But that understanding of sin and atonement is inconsistent with our own. We believe that no matter how meritorious the lives of our ancestors were, they cannot serve to remove the taint of our sins; we alone are responsible. Still we acknowledge that our lives are built on the foundations laid by those who have come before us, that their lives well lived can inspire us to live lives that may be an inspiration to others in the future. We also recognize that while our history is replete with so many who died for the sake of their principles, there were others who chose to live out their principles, even when a cruel and unjust world negated them.

Choose one of the following versions of Eleh Ezkerah: *Martyrs through the Ages (beginning on page 899), Principles of Martyrs (beginning on page 919), The Martyrs of the Shoah (beginning on page 933).*

ELEH EZKERAH I/
MARTYRS THROUGH THE AGES

After All This / מֵאַחֲרֵי כָּל זֶה

שֶׁהַר הַזִּכָּרוֹן יִזְכֹּר בִּמְקוֹמִי,

זֶה תַּפְקִידוֹ. שֶׁהַגַּן לְזֵכֶר יִזְכֹּר,

שֶׁהָרְחוֹב עַל שֵׁם יִזְכֹּר,

שֶׁהַבִּנְיָן הַיָּדוּעַ יִזְכֹּר,

שֶׁבֵּית הַתְּפִלָּה עַל שֵׁם אֱלֹהִים יִזְכֹּר,

שֶׁסֵּפֶר הַתּוֹרָה הַמִּתְגַּלְגֵּל יִזְכֹּר,

שֶׁהַיִּזְכֹּר יִזְכֹּר. שֶׁהַדְּגָלִים יִזְכְּרוּ,

הַתַּכְרִיכִים הַצִּבְעוֹנִיִּים שֶׁל הַהִיסְטוֹרְיָה, אֲשֶׁר

הַגּוּפִים שֶׁעָטְפוּ הָפְכוּ אָבָק. שֶׁהָאָבָק יִזְכֹּר.

שֶׁהָאַשְׁפָּה תִּזְכֹּר בַּשַּׁעַר. שֶׁהַשִּׁלְיָה תִּזְכֹּר.

שֶׁחַיַּת הַשָּׂדֶה וְעוֹף הַשָּׁמַיִם יֹאכְלוּ וְיִזְכְּרוּ,

שֶׁכֻּלָּם יִזְכְּרוּ. כְּדֵי שֶׁאוּכַל לָנוּחַ.

Let the Mount of Memory remember in my place
—that is its purpose.
Let the garden *in memoriam* remember.
Let the street named "in the name of" remember.
Let the building that is known remember.
Let the house of prayer in the name of God remember.
Let the rolled up Torah scroll remember.
Let the *Yizkor* prayer remember.
Let the banners of memorial remember.
Let the multicolored shrouds of history remember,
draped with fallen bodies that have turned to dust.
Let the heap of dung remember in the gate.
Let the remaining flesh remember.
Let beasts of the field and birds of the sky devour and remember.
Yes, let all of them remember,
so that I might rest.

Yehuda Amichai

אֵלֶּה אֶזְכְּרָה וְנַפְשִׁי עָלַי אֶשְׁפְּכָה:

Eleh ezkerah venafshi alay eshpeḥah.
These I remember and pour out my soul.
We walk the world of slaughter,
stumbling and falling in wreckage,
surrounded by the fear of death,
and eyes which gaze at us in silence,
the eyes of other martyred Jews,
of hunted, harried, persecuted souls
who never had a choice,
who've huddled all together in a corner
and press each other closer still and quake.
For here it was the sharpened axes found them
and they have come to take another look
at the stark terror of their savage death.
Their staring eyes all ask the ancient question: Why?

Ḥayim Naḥman Bialik (Adapted)

All the generations that preceded me contributed me
in small amounts, so that I would be erected here in Jerusalem
all at once, like a house of prayer or a charity institution.
That commits one. My name is the name of my contributors.
That commits one.
I am getting to be the age my father was when he died.
My last will shows many superscriptions.
I must change my life and my death
daily, to fulfill all the predictions
concerning me. So they won't be lies.
That commits one.
I have passed my fortieth year.
There are posts they will not let me fill
because of that. Were I in Auschwitz,
they wouldn't put me to work.
They'd burn me right away.
That commits one.

Yehuda Amichai

Our Rabbis taught: Once the wicked government (of Rome) issued a decree forbidding the Jews to study and practice the Torah. Pappos ben Yehudah came and found Rabbi Akiba publicly bringing gatherings together and occupying himself with the Torah. He said to him: "Akiba, are you not afraid of the Government?" He replied: "I will explain to you with a parable. A fox was once walking alongside of a river, and he saw fishes going in swarms from one place to another. He said to them: 'From what are you fleeing?' They replied: 'From the nets cast for us by men.' He said to them: 'Would you like to come up on to the dry land so that you and I can live together in the way that my ancestors lived with your ancestors?' They replied: 'Are you the one that they call the cleverest of animals? You are not clever but foolish. If we are afraid in the element in which we live, how much more in the element in which we would die!' So it is with us. If such is our condition when we sit and study the Torah, of which it is written, *For that is your life and the length of your days* (Deuteronomy 30:20), if we go and neglect it, how much worse off shall we be!"

It is related that soon afterwards Rabbi Akiba was arrested and thrown into prison, and Pappos ben Yehudah was also arrested and imprisoned next to him. He said to him: "Pappos, who brought you here?" He replied: "Happy are you, Rabbi Akiba, that you have been seized for busying yourself with the Torah! Alas for Pappos, who has been seized for busying himself with idle things!"

It is related that when Rabbi Akiba was taken out for execution, it was the hour for the recital of the *Shema*, and while they combed his flesh with iron combs, he directed his mind to accepting upon himself the sovereignty of heaven with love. His disciples said to him: "Our teacher, even to this point?" He said to them: "All my days I have been troubled by this verse, *And you must love the one your God with all your soul*, [which I interpret,] 'even if God takes your soul.' Now that I have the

opportunity shall I not fulfill it?" He prolonged the word *eḥad* until he expired while saying it.

The ministering angels said before the blessed Holy One: "Such Torah, and such a reward? [He should have been] *from them that die by your hand, O God.*" God replied to them: *"Their portion is in life* (Psalms 17:14)."

A *bat kol* (voice from heaven) went forth and proclaimed, "Happy are you, Rabbi Akiba, that you are destined for the life of the world to come."

Talmud Beraḥot 61b

They wrapped him in the Torah he loved,
and lived by, and taught with awe,
in defiance of the Romans,
craving the teaching
as fish crave water.
Ḥanina was not the first Jew to be bound
and burned by the Amalek—enemy—
nor would he be the last—that was certain—
there were still the Priests and Princes of Spain
and Crusaders and Cossacks
and the most mass-efficient of all,
the Germans
    to come.
But his tortured vision-message
was the first,
and would somehow make the Death of History easier
for his students and students-of-students
down to the Last Generation of Jews
who would have to suffer
for whatever there is
that calls for Jewish screams
to lullaby the world to restful sleep.

As the flames cracked
and the body sizzled
Ḥanina was heard to say:
He Who will see this desecrated Torah
avenged
will make good, somehow, my dying.
I see the parchment burn,
but the Letters are soaring to their source.
You may burn a Torah,
but Torah will not be consumed.
You may kill Jews,
but the Jews will survive
and serve witness
to the Genesis—patterns of Creation
and the Isaiah—prophecies of hope.

Danny Siegel

Who has heard or seen such a thing? Ask and see: has there ever
been an *Akedah* such as this since the days of Adam? When were
there ever a thousand and a hundred sacrifices in one day, each
and every one of them like the *Akedah* of Isaac, son of Abraham?
Yet for the one bound on Mount Moriah, God shook the world
to its base, as it is stated, "Behold the angels cried out and the
skies darkened." What did they do now? Why did the skies not
darken and the stars not dim...when in one day one thousand
and one hundred pure souls were slain and slaughtered! Oh the
spotless babes and sucklings, innocent of all sin, oh the innocent
lives! Will You remain silent in the face of these things, O God?

Shelomoh bar Shimshon

I heard from aged exiles of Spain that a certain ship was struck with plague and that the ship's owner cast the passengers off onto uninhabited terrain. Most died there of hunger; only a few found the strength to proceed on foot in search of civilization.

Among these was a certain Jew who struggled on with his wife and two sons. The wife, whose feet were untried, fainted and perished, leaving her husband, who was carrying the boys. He and his sons also fainted from hunger; when he awoke he found the two dead. In agony, he rose to his feet and cried, "Master of the Universe! You go to great lengths to force me to desert my faith. Know for a certainty that in the face of the dwellers of heaven, a Jew I am and a Jew I shall remain; all that You have brought upon me or will bring upon me shall be of no avail!" Then he gathered dirt and grasses, covered the boys, and went off in search of a settlement.

Those who went to Fez suffered God's judgments, particularly keen hunger. Denied entry to the cities by their inhabitants, who feared that food prices would soar, they pitched their tents in the fields and there sought out wild plants, praying that they might find some—for drought had destroyed all the vegetation, leaving only roots. Many died in the field with none to bury them, so weakened were the survivors by hunger. On Shabbat they would forage only with their mouths, taking comfort in the fact that they plucked nothing with their hands.

There, too, a poor woman saw her son faint away. Having no means of subsistence and seeing that his death was certain, she lifted a stone and hurled it upon his head, and the boy died. Then she struck herself until she, too, expired.

Solomon ibn Verga

Cossacks approached the city of Nemirow. When the Jews saw the troops from afar, their hearts trembled from fright, though they were not certain, as yet, whether they were Polish or Cossack. Nevertheless all the Jews went with their wives and infants, with their silver and gold, into the fortress, and locked and barred the doors, prepared to fight them. What did those evil-doers, the Cossacks do? They devised flags like those of the Poles, for there is no other way to distinguish between the Polish and the Cossack forces except through their banners. The [non-Jewish] people of the city were fully aware of this trickery, and nevertheless called to the Jews in the fortress: "Open the gate. This is a Polish army which has come to save you from the hands of your enemies, should they come." The Jews who were standing guard on the wall, seeing that the flags were like those of Poland, believed that the people of the city spoke the truth. Immediately they opened the gate. No sooner had the gate been opened than the Cossacks entered with drawn swords, and the townspeople too, armed with swords, spears and scythes, and some only with clubs, and they killed the Jews in large numbers. Women and young girls were ravished, but some of the women and maidens jumped into the moat surrounding the fortress in order that the uncircumcised should not defile them. They drowned in the waters. Many of them who were able to swim, jumped into water, believing they would escape the slaughter, but the Ukrainians swam after them with their swords and their scythes, and killed them in the water. Some of the enemy shot with their guns into the water, and killed them till the water became red with the blood of the slain.

It happened there that a beautiful maiden, of a renowned and wealthy family, had been captured by a certain Cossack who forced her to be his wife. But, before they lived together she told him with cunning that she possessed a certain magic and that no weapon could harm her. She said to him: "If you do not believe me, just test me. Shoot at me with a gun, and you will see that

I will not be harmed." The Cossack, her husband, in his simplicity, thought she was telling the truth. He shot at her with his gun and she fell and died for the Sanctification of the Name, to avoid being defiled by him, may God avenge her blood.

Another event occurred when a beautiful girl, about to be married to a Cossack, insisted that their marriage take place in a church which stood across the bridge. He granted her request, and with timbrels and flutes, attired in festive garb, led her to the marriage. As soon as they came to the bridge she jumped into the water and was drowned for the Sanctification of the Name. May God avenge her blood. These, and many similar events took place, far too numerous to be recorded. The number of the slain and drowned in the holy community of Nemirow was about six thousand.   Nathan Nata Hanover

An old Jew was running down the street chased by a young Russian, about sixteen years old, with an ax in his hand. The boy caught up with the old man and, with one stroke, he split his skull. As the old man fell, the boy pushed the split head together with his boot.

Instantly, gun in hand, a young Jew darted up, a pale young man, with a gaunt face and glasses. They ran, and I ran after them. The young Jew shot, but missed. The Russian left the broad, open street and ran into a courtyard. My foot got caught in something, and I fell.

By the time I ran into the courtyard, the Russian was standing in a corner, his back to a fence. His childlike face was green, his gray eyes gaped and bulged, his teeth chattered in a rapid rhythm. The young Jew stood right in front of him, with the gun in his raised hand, but his face was even paler than before. He stared at the wild terror of young flesh and blood, stared for some time. Then he put the gun to his own head, and fired.

The last light of reason vanished from the Russian's eyes. He sat down beside the body twitching at his feet, rose. Then, with an insane shriek, he leaped over the corpse and ran out of the courtyard.

A wild laugh erupted from inside my throat. My foot rose, of its own accord, and kicked the bloody carcass, lying twisted on the ground like a trampled worm.   Lamed Shapiro

They say the woman with the black hair
shivered as she turned
that the soldier called out to her in German
told her to wait, while the others lined up in front of the ditch,
took off their clothes.
Body after body was shot then,
one on top of the other into the ditch.
That by the time it took him to walk to the woman
(a matter of minutes)
her hair had turned completely white
and when she was finally shot
the bullets only wounded her
and she was buried like that,
still breathing, an old lady not quite twenty.

This happened thirty-nine years ago
and every woman that knows about her
had gone to sleep, one time or another
hugging her shadow.

Because what substance do we have?
And if we are not this woman, or her mother, or her daughter,
then, who are we? Who are we?

                                                    Carole Glasser

In the city of Warsaw such a long time ago
Two hundred children stand lined row on row
With their freshly washed faces and freshly washed clothes
The children of Poland who never grow old

In the orphanage yard not a child remains
The soldiers have herded them down to the trains
Carrying small flasks of water and bags of dry bread
To march in the ranks of the unquiet dead

With their small Jewish faces and pale haunted eyes
They march hand in hand down the street—no one cries,
No one laughs, no one looks, no one turns, no one talks
As they walk down the streets where my grandparents walked

Had my grandparents stayed in that dark bloody land
My own children too would have marched hand in hand
To the beat of the soldiers, the jackbooted stamp
That would measure their lives till they died in those camps

The cries of my children at night take me back
To those pale hollow faces in stark white and black
Only the blood of the children remains
It runs in the street—and it runs in our veins

Si Kahn

For a long time we have been promising each other to recite *Kol Nidrey* this year. A Jewish block elder has allowed us to pray in his block. Someone has brought a *tallis* from the clothing warehouse. The seriousness of the moment is felt in camp. It seems that the entire world is preparing for *Kol Nidrey*.

From every block, people assemble at the barracks of the Jewish block elder. People stand pressed next to one another. Everyone who feels a Jewish heart beating inside has come, even the other block elders and kapos. Always the grand aristocrats, now they stand among the ordinary "prisoners." Even the German block elders and kapos, those terrible murderers, are silent. They avoid the barracks, moving in a large semicircle around it. Today, they have somehow grown afraid of the Jews.

The rabbi prays. Wrapped in the *tallis*, he recites the *maḥzor*'s Prayer of Purification. Everything is frozen as the rabbi intones: "As if our bodies are placed on top of the altar to be accepted by the Almighty, as a sacrifice dedicated completely to God." Through the boards of the barracks I look at the crematorium, from which smoke reaches into the gray heavens.

I hear the voice of the rabbi, as though it no longer came from his heart, but as if his heart itself had opened and wept: "And a portion of our fat and our blood."

He wraps himself more tightly, and repeats the words; but now his heart bleeds, and he omits "and a portion"; "our fat and our blood." The congregation repeats: "our fat and our blood." As if under a spell, everyone stops at these words. The rabbi cannot go on. Louder and louder the congregation repeats: "our fat and our blood." Someone shouts: "The blood and fat of our parents, children, and relatives."

Tears pour from everyone's eyes. The weeping flows together like a river. Hearts of stone have given way.

I do not weep. I cannot tear my eyes away from the clear smoke of the crematorium. I feel a terrible weariness in my bones. It is unbearably hot in the barracks.

When the rabbi says, "With the permission of the Almighty," I am transported to another world. It seems to me that I am sitting somewhere in a catacomb in Spain. I see the bonfires and the grim Torquemada, the unfortunate Jews who burn for the Sanctification of God's Name, who burn as martyrs. The smoke of the burned is carried straight into heaven. I hear the *shema yisra'el* carried by the smoke and, later, people wrapped in black, who come into the catacombs with their faces covered.

"We pray together with the sinners!" cry the figures in black. A terrible cry ascends from the images. I hear the rabbi saying: "From this Yom Kippur until the next."

And suddenly everything is silent. A dead stillness prevails in the barracks; no one prays, no one weeps on. It is as if all of our tongues were bound.

Only from outside do we hear the terrible wailing. On the road, the women are being led to the ovens. The sound of the trucks' motors are drowned out by the naked women's cries. There are many in the barracks whose dear ones are being led away. Everyone is still, as if trying to discern the voice of a loved one among the screams. Through the open gates, we see the victims lift up their hands toward the sky and plead for mercy. The women see the men in the barracks. Their shouts grow louder. Everyone inside is petrified.

The rabbi is the first to arouse himself. He interrupts *Kol Nidrey* and begins the morning service: "Now we proclaim the sacred power of this day." ⤶

In the silence of the barracks his voice is heard, as if responding to the women's cries. His voice resounds, and when he comes to the words of the *Unetaneh Tokef*—"And who by fire"—a lament tears out from every throat: "And who by fire!" The phrase, "who by fire," comes as if from the other world.

The rabbi continues, but his voice is drowned out by the tragic cries, "who by fire," as if the Jews wanted to quench the terrible fire with their words. But the motors don't stop rumbling. More and more victims are led off to be burned.

"Who by fire!" the congregation does not stop shouting. The voices of the condemned mix with the men's prayer. As if hypnotized, everyone shouts: "Who by fire!" as if praying to be burned in the fire as well.

In the midst of the prayer, the sound of the shofar interrupts: *tekiyah, shevarim, teruah, tekiyah gedolah.*

The shofar awakens the men as if from a dream. At first it is quiet in the barracks. I hear my heart bang. Soon the whole crowd weeps. The voices of the naked women reach heaven. The crowd weeps softly.

In the block where we prayed, next to the oven which has been turned into a podium, the rabbi lies wrapped in the *tallis*. The shepherd's soul has departed.

Fires burn in the woods by the crematorium all night; the ovens are not big enough.

Yoysef Vaynberg (Adapted)

My approach to life was formulated through a small window of a dark cellar, under the kindergarten at Dolna Volnaka, a cellar in which papa, mama, my sister Milka, my eldest brother, my aunt, cousin, Mr. Bachmann and I spent 700 days. In the autumn of 1944, on Rosh Hashanah of the year 5705, I observed the vanguard of the Red Army entering the town to liberate it.

In August we had heard the thunderous sounds of explosions from the approaching front. Later on we were to find out that this was the sound of Soviet artillery guns. For us, who had dwelt in the muddy cellar, hidden deep in the greasy Ukrainian soil, those were the sounds of salvation.

Around us there was a roar of excitement, and we, eight shadows of human beings, with our bones sticking out and swarming with lice, crawled through the hidden window, the size of a shrunken human being, out of the muddy cellar and into the yard.

For 700 days and nights we had grown moldy in that cellar by the river.

There in the yard a crowd of embarrassed and perplexed Poles and Ukrainians gathered. They did not know where we had come from and how we had remained alive. Among them were former neighbors, one of them a Ukrainian boy who had accompanied the Germans around our houses seeking to help them find their prey—a small collaborator, a 12-year-old quisling.

Some time later, in the days of repentance between the New Year and Yom Kippur, the boy played with an unsuspicious object, and the sound of a blast was heard. When we stepped out of the house we found him dead, in a puddle of blood, with his hand torn off. I had hated him vehemently, but I did not rejoice in his death. A boy, even a collaborator, lying dead with his hand torn off, is a horrifying sight. ↵

In the days of repentance in September 1944, Mr. Bachmann, "a survivor of the Holocaust," climbed up to the attic of his house, mounted a chair, tied a thin adhesive packing wire around his neck and hung himself. Mr. Bachmann, who had joined us in the cellar during the last "action" before the ghetto was liquidated, found out upon leaving the cellar that his wife and two small children had been slaughtered.

I found him hanging in the attic on the eve of Yom Kippur when I went to visit him. Whoever coined the term "survivors of the Holocaust" didn't know what he was talking about: no one survived the Holocaust, even if he remained alive.

Unending columns of the Red Army moved through the main street of the town. From the columns, a Jewish-looking Soviet officer stepped out, and turned to us—filthy and thin, extinguished skeletons—and asked: "*amḥa?*" (the code word by which Jews identified each other in the Diaspora of Ashkenaz). We answered "yes" and the tall, good-looking officer wept. We wept with him. The officer gave us some of his battle rations, returned to the head of the column, and continued the chase after the German troops.

In the days of repentance in 5705, we counted the victims of the slaughter and found that of over 14,000 Jews of Borislav in Eastern Galicia, only several hundred remained alive.

There in the forests of Poland my people died. And we, my father and mother, my eldest brother and sister, and I, the small one, stood at the dawn of 5705, a heap of bones, all of us together weighing 200 kilos, watching the long columns of the Red Army and listening to the bells of salvation.

Only several miles away, though the sun was shining, the butcher continued his despicable job.

Sheva Weiss (Adapted)

Links of fear slowly become a chain,
binding my hands and feet.
My father never wanted
to lead me to the sacrifice.
He was bound as I was.
But he led me.
Now I lie on the altar,
my father inside me, my grandfather inside me.
There is no escape—no escape. Moshe Youngman (Contemporary Yiddish Poet)

Choose another people.
We are tired of death, tired of corpses,
We have no more prayers.
For the time being
Choose another people.
We have run out of blood for victims,
Our houses have been turned into desert,
The earth lacks space for tombstones,
There are no more lamentations
Nor songs of woe
In the ancient texts.
God of mercy
Sanctify another land
Another Sinai.
We have covered every field and stone
With ashes and holiness.
With our crones
With our young
With our infants
We have paid for each letter in your Commandments.
God of Mercy
Lift up your fiery brow, Look on the peoples of the world,
Let them have the prophecies and Holy Days...
And O God of mercy
Grant us one more blessing—
Take back the divine glory of our genius. Kadya Molodowsky

Fresh and pervasive
is the weeping of our lost communities.
The phrases of our prayers are vivified.
Contemporary are the laments
of our *el maley rahamims.*
Unnecessary and absurd
is the death of individuals.
Legendary is the martyr-death of millions.

After so many deaths we stand reborn.
They gave us life.
In death they flung open the ghetto gates.
In exaltation they escaped from slavery.
By their deaths they gave us faith.

Were it not for their unequaled sacrifice
we should all have died disgraced,
without revenge or consolation,
without a breath of hope.
The blinded Samsons shook the pillars
in the halls of their tormentors,
and went forth to mete out punishment
for the unprecedented crime.

Not in secretive clandestine warfare,
nor lurking in a hidden ambush,
but on a sunlit canvas
they openly gave the signal for revolt.
The timid had grown bold—
And the torturer paid.

Brothers and sisters,
let us inscribe them in a new prayerbook.
Their deeds canceled out our entire martyr-history.
In all our prayers let us remember them.
In all our *yizkors* let us mourn them.
In all our *yitgadals* memorialize them.

Jacob Glatshtein

Now, as always, Jews are intimately linked one to another. Shout here and you will be heard in Kiev. Shout in Jerusalem, Jews everywhere reflect their sadness. An assault on Jews anywhere means an attempt to humiliate Jews everywhere. Thus a Jew lives in more than one place, in more than one era, on more than one level. To be Jewish is to be possessed of a historical consciousness that transcends individual consciousness....

All we want as Jews is to live and uphold the sanctity of life, all we want is to create peace and create in peace, to bear witness that people are not necessarily one another's enemies, that every war is senseless, that the solution lies in compassion and that compassion is possible.

All we want is peace. And yet...there is upheaval.

So how can one not be sad today? How can one be in this world of ours and not despair?

One day Ḥasidim came to inform the great Rebbe Naḥman of Bratzlav of renewed persecutions of Jews in the Ukraine. The Master listened and said nothing. Then they told him of pogroms in certain villages. Again the Master listened and said nothing. Then they told of slaughtered families, of desecrated cemeteries, of children burned alive. The Master listened, listened and shook his head. "I know," he whispered. "I know what you want. I know. You want me to shout with pain, weep in despair. I know, I know. But I will not, you hear me, I will not." Then, after a long silence, he did begin to shout, louder and louder, "*Gevalt, Yidden...!* Jews, for heaven's sake, do not despair...*Gevalt, Yidden*, Jews do not despair."

Elie Wiesel

זְכוֹר אֶת מַעֲשֵׂיהֶם אֶת גְּדוּלָתָם וְאֶת צִדְקָתָם

בִּזְכוּת חַיֵּי אִמּוֹתֵינוּ וַאֲבוֹתֵינוּ

נִרְאֶה אֵיךְ לְתַקֵּן עוֹלָם בְּמַלְכוּת שַׁדַּי

וְלִבְנוֹת בַּיִת נֶאֱמָן בְּיִשְׂרָאֵל

בַּיִת שֶׁל אַהֲבַת חֶסֶד לִמּוּד תּוֹרָה

וְכָבוֹד לְכָל מָה שֶׁבָּרָאתָ שֶׁנֶּאֱמַר

וּמָה יהוה דּוֹרֵשׁ מִמְּךָ כִּי אִם עֲשׂוֹת מִשְׁפָּט

וְאַהֲבַת חֶסֶד וְהַצְנֵעַ לֶכֶת עִם־אֱלֹהֶיךָ׃

Remember their deeds, their greatness, their righteousness.
In the light of the lives of our ancestors, we can see how to
perfect God's world.
To build a faithful house in Israel, a house with love of piety, of
the study of Torah, and of honor to all these you have created, as
it is written, "What does God ask of you: only to do justly, and
to love mercy and to walk humbly with your God."

Written and translated by Michael Strassfeld

וּמה...אלהיך/What...God (Micah 6:8).

Out of the strong, sweetness;
and out of the dead body of the lion of Judah,
the prophecies and psalms;
out of the slaves in Egypt,
out of the wandering tribesmen of the deserts
and the peasants of Palestine,
out of the slaves of Babylon and Rome,
out of the ghettos of Spain and Portugal, Germany and Poland,
the Torah and the prophecies,
the Talmud and the sacred studies, the hymns and songs of the
    Jews;
and out of the Jewish dead
of Belgium and Holland, of Rumania, Hungary, and Bulgaria,
of France and Italy and Yugoslavia,
of Lithuania and Latvia, White Russia and Ukrainia,
of Czechoslovakia and Austria,
Poland and Germany,
out of the greatly wronged
a people teaching and doing justice;
out of the plundered
a generous people;
out of the wounded a people of physicians;
and out of those who met only with hate,
a people of love, a compassionate people.

Charles Reznikoff

ELEH EZKERAH II/PRINCIPLES OF MARTYRS

אֵלֶּה אֶזְכְּרָה וְנַפְשִׁי עָלַי אֶשְׁפְּכָה:

Eleh ezkerah venafshi alay eshpehah.
These I remember and pour out my soul.

Rabbi Akiba ben Yosef, the foremost scholar of his age, exercised a decisive and radical influence on the development of the early Jewish legal system. Unlearned in his youth, Akiba was employed as a shepherd by Bar Kalba Shavu'a, one of the wealthiest men in Jerusalem. Bar Kalba's opposition to his daughter Rachel's marriage to Akiba led him to disinherit her. Unaffected, Rachel made her marriage to Akiba conditional upon his commitment to study Torah. Akiba agreed and courageously began to fulfill his commitment, though he was well beyond the age when one normally begins such pursuits.

Although he became a greatly respected teacher raising up thousands of students, Akiba remained remarkably self-effacing and modest. He also took an intimate interest in the plight of the poor, becoming an overseer for them, and collecting tzedakah on their behalf. His legal rulings, in addition to their profundity, reflect his breadth of outlook and magnanimity of spirit. Akiba taught, "Whatever God does is for the best." Indeed Akiba was possessed of a rare optimism by which he was able to comfort his people in spite of the sad state of affairs in his time. His death was premature and tragic, but his life was complete in his constant devotion to the teaching and living of Torah.

The Roman government decreed that Jews should no longer occupy themselves with Torah. Shortly after, Pappos ben Yehudah found Rabbi Akiba holding great assemblies and studying Torah. Pappos said to him, "Akiba, aren't you afraid of the wicked government?" He answered, "I reply by way of a parable. To what is the matter like? To a fox who was walking along the bank of the stream, and saw some fishes gathering

together to move from one place to another. He said to them, 'From what are you fleeing?' They answered, 'From nets which men are bringing to catch us.' He said to them, 'Come up on the dry land, and let us, me and you, dwell together, even as my forebears dwelt with yours.' They replied, 'And they call you the shrewdest of animals? You are not clever, but foolish! For if we are afraid in the place that is our life-element, the water, how much more so in a place that is our death-element, the dry land.' So also is it with us," Akiba continued. "If now, while we sit and study Torah, in which it is written, 'For that is your life, and the length of your days' (Deuteronomy 30:20), we are in such a plight, how much more so, if we would neglect it."

∾

A tale is told that Rabbi Akiba was once walking through a graveyard when he met a charcoal-burner who was carrying wood on his shoulders, and running about like a horse. Akiba ordered him to halt. He said to him, "My son, why are you engaged in such heavy toil? If you are a bondsman, and your master imposes such a yoke upon you, I will redeem you and set you free. If you are poor, I myself will enrich you." The man replied, "Sir, let me be, for I cannot stay." Akiba asked, "Are you a human being or a demon?" He said, "I am of the dead. Day after day I am fated to gather wood to be burnt." Akiba asked, "What was your trade when you were living on earth?" He replied, "I was a tax-collector who favored the rich and burdened the poor." Akiba said, "My son, is there no remedy for your situation?" The man answered, "Do not hinder me, lest those set in charge of my punishment grow angry with me. For me there is no remedy. Yet I did hear them say that my punishment would be relaxed if I had a son who could stand up in the congregation and proclaim publicly, 'Bless ADONAY, the blessed one.' But I had no son. On my death I left my wife with child, but whether she bore a boy or a girl I do not know. And if she did bear a son, who will teach him Torah?" Akiba asked,

"What is your name?" He told him. "And your wife's name?" He said, "Susmida." "And your city?" "Alduka." Akiba, troubled on account of the charcoal-burner, traveled from city to city until he came to the one where the man lived. He asked after the man and for his household. People answered, "May his bones be ground in hell." Then he asked for the wife, and they said "May her name and remembrance be blotted out of the world." Then he asked for his son. "He has not even been brought into the covenant of Abraham." At once Akiba took the boy, and began to teach him Torah, but first he fasted on his behalf for forty days. A heavenly voice went forth, saying, "Because of this boy do you fast?" Akiba said, "Yes." He taught the boy the alphabet, then the *Motzi*, the *Shema* and the *Amidah*. Then he made the boy stand up in the synagogue, and recite, "Blessed ADONAY, the blessed One, now and ever!" The charcoal-burner's punishment was annulled, and he came to Akiba in a dream and said, "May you repose in Paradise, even as you have rescued me from hell."

When Akiba was being tortured for teaching Torah, the hour for reciting the *Shema* arrived. He said it and smiled. The Roman officer called out, "Old man, are you a sorcerer or a fool, that you smile while in pain?" "Neither," replied Akiba, "but all my life, when I said the words, 'You shall love ADONAY your God with all your heart and soul and might,' I was saddened, for I thought, when shall I be able to fulfill this commandment completely? I have loved God with all my heart and with all my possessions [might], but how to love God with all my soul—that

---

NOTE. Rather than focus on the tragic deaths of Jews in critical periods of our people's history, in this *Eleh Ezkerah*, we study the teachings of four who chose life. Their words should elevate us to live as they lived, with dedication to the Torah, to justice, to righteousness and love for their fellow beings.

is, with all my life—was not assured to me. Now that I am giving my life at the hour for saying the *Shema*, and my resolution remains firm, should I not smile, even rejoice?" And as he spoke, his soul departed. Talmud Beraḥot 61b (Adapted)

୬୦

עַל שְׁלֹשָׁה דְבָרִים הָעוֹלָם עוֹמֵד:
עַל הַתּוֹרָה וְעַל הָעֲבוֹדָה וְעַל גְּמִילוּת חֲסָדִים:

Al sheloshah devarim ha'olam omed.
Al hatorah ve'al ha'avodah ve'al gemilut ḥasadim.

On three things the world stands—
on Torah, on worship, and on caring deeds.

Pirkey Avot 1.2

The Inquisition's racks and fires and the period's forced conversions were more than legendary. Thousands of Jews died martyrs' deaths, and thousands more became converts, albeit in name only. Still others chose exile. Together with massive displacement and the loss of life was a culture destroyed, the result of religious fanaticism. The cosmopolitanism of Spanish and Portuguese Jewry was arrested and remained dormant until the dawn of European Enlightenment.

Yehudah Abrabanel was a poet, physician, and the most prominent philosopher of his day. Expelled from Portugal in 1483 along with his father, he fled again from Spain less than a decade later. He was fortunate to settle in Italy where he found an intellectual home among the circle of scholars of the Platonic Academy of Florence. Abrabanel continued to practice his profession, teaching medicine at the university in Naples and serving as personal physician to the Spanish viceroy. The scope of his written work was wide and deep including poetry, biblical commentary, and general and social philosophy, as well as medical treatises. Rather than mourning the loss of his homeland, Abrabanel celebrated his internationalism, celebrating the possibilities even in his and his people's exile. ↵

God created Adam in God's intellectual image by which Adam was prompted to strive to perfect his soul in the acknowledgment of the Creator and imitation of God's wisdom. God also made available all the things necessary for human existence in the Garden—food, drink and shelter. All this was in its natural state, requiring no human exertion. All was at Adam's disposal, so that he was not forced to burden himself to satisfy his bodily needs, but could concentrate on the perfection of his soul, for which purpose Adam was created. On this account, God commanded Adam to be content with the natural things with which God had furnished him and not be attracted to luxuries that require resorting to human artifice and worldly things, so that his intellect should not be diverted to the assuring of physical comforts, which is the reverse of spiritual perfection, ideally the ultimate aim of all humans. The meaning of the command, "Of all the trees of the Garden you may certainly eat" was: "I do not forbid you the things essential for your physical sustenance from the trees of the Garden and the tree of life. But you may not actually *eat* of the tree of the knowledge of good and evil," by which is meant the indulgence in and study of worldly things.

಄

Some have suggested that God chose to scatter Israel to the corners of the earth in order to destroy them. I disagree. When Israel is concentrated in one spot, the enemy can easily destroy them, as Haman tried when the Jews were in Persia. But where they are scattered in many kingdoms, they have always a place to flee. Indeed, our sages believed that God showed special kindness to Israel by scattering them among the peoples. The Trojans, a mighty nation, were totally destroyed by the Greeks because there they were in one place. But the Jews, however decimated, have always managed to survive and find refuge. The king of England wiped out the Jews in his kingdom as has the king of France in our own time. Had the Jews been in any one

place alone, not one Jew would have survived. But the Almighty promised us, "When they are in the land of their enemies, I will not reject them, or spurn them so as to destroy them utterly (Leviticus 26:44)." Dispersion was thus a great kindness ensuring our survival and deliverance.

Yehudah Abrabanel

❧

כָּל הָעוֹלָם כֻּלוֹ

גֶּשֶׁר צַר מְאֹד

וְהָעִקָּר לֹא לְפַחֵד כְּלָל:

Kol ha'olam kulo
gesher tzar me'od
veha'ikar lo lefaḥed kelal.

The entire world is a very narrow bridge.
The essential thing is to have no fear at all.

Attributed to Naḥman of Bratzlav

❧

Raised in a distinguished, acculturated Jewish family in Hungary, Hannah Szenes spent her early years attending a Protestant girls' school that had opened its doors to Jews and Catholics. Although on graduation her teachers "positively assured" her mother that Hannah would be admitted to university even though she was Jewish, Hannah had already decided to emigrate to Palestine and to study at the agricultural school in Nahalal. As she told her mother, "Perhaps I ought to be impressed that in view of graduating summa cum laude, and with a plethora of recommendations from teachers and friends, I can get into the university, while a Gentile who just barely squeezed through the exams can sail in! Besides, are they really incapable of understanding that I don't want to be just a student, that I have plans, dreams, ambitions, and that the road to their fulfillment would only be barred to me here?"

Her dreams included helping provide a haven and a revitalized homeland for the Jewish people. When her mother questioned her decision to attend an agricultural school instead of a university, Szenes replied, "There are already far too many intellectuals in Palestine; the great need is for workers who can help build the country." Setting out for Palestine in ↵

1939, Szenes returned to Hungary in 1944 as part of a mission of thirty-two Jews from the land of Israel who had volunteered to parachute into Europe to try to save the remaining Jewish population. She was last seen on 9 June 1944, at the Hungarian border. She was captured, tortured, and shot as a prisoner of war in Budapest. After burial in the Martyr's Corner of a Budapest cemetery, her remains were moved to Israel, where, with full military honors, they were interred in a cemetery in the Judean Hills. Her tombstone, with its engraving of a parachute, is in a special section of the cemetery where six others who died on that mission are also buried. Szenes's spirituality was rooted in a love for the land of Israel and the Jewish people and in a continual struggle to "believe and trust in God."

When anyone in Hungary spoke of Zionism even two years ago, Jewish public opinion condemned him as a traitor to Hungary or considered him a mad visionary. But today, due perhaps to the recent blows suffered, Hungarian Jews are beginning to concern themselves with Zionism. At least so it seems when they ask, "How big is Palestine? How many people can it accommodate?" and "Is there room for me in the expanding country?" But the question least frequently voiced is "What is the purpose of Zionism, its basic aim?" It is with this seldom-voiced question I would like to deal, because I believe it to be the most important of all questions. When one understands this and applies it to oneself, one will become a Zionist, regardless of how many can emigrate to Palestine today or tomorrow, whether conditions here will improve or deteriorate, whether or not there are possibilities of emigrating to other countries.

If we had to define Zionism briefly perhaps we could best do so in the following words: Zionism is the movement of the Jewish people for its revival.

Perhaps many are at this very moment mentally vetoing this with the thought that Jews do not constitute a people. But how is a nation created out of a community? From a common origin, a common past, present and future, common laws, a common language and a native land.

In ancient Palestine these motives were united and formed a complete background. Then the native land ceased to exist, and gradually the language link to the ancient land weakened. But the consciousness of the people was saved by the Torah, that invisible but all-powerful mobile State.

It is, however, inconceivable that in the stateless world of the Middle Ages, when religion was the focal point of life, the self-assurance of the ghetto-bound Jew could have become so strengthened that he could have expressed his longing for a nation, or the restoration of his own way of life, or that he would have thought of rebuilding his own country. Yet the yearning expressed in the holiday greeting, "Next Year in Jerusalem," is absolute proof that the hope of regaining the homeland never died within the Jew.

Then came the human rights laws of the nineteenth century and with them new ideas and concepts of national values. From the peoples of the great countries to those in the smallest enclaves, all attempted to find themselves and their rights. It was the time of decision. Did a Jewish people still exist, and if so, would it be influenced by the strength of the spirit of the new movement?

The greater part of Jewry asked only for human rights, happily accepting the goodwill of the people among whom it lived, and in exchange casting off individuality and ancient characteristics. But a few hundred inspired zealots started off toward Zion. Thousands upon thousands endorsed the concepts and ideals of Zionism, and suddenly there was a Jewish nation. If you feel there is not, speak for yourself, but don't forget those to whom Jewishness means more than the data on a birth certificate.

We don't want charity. We want only our lawful property and rights, and our freedom, for which we have struggled with our own labors. We want to create a homeland for the Jewish spirit and the Jewish people. The solution seems so very clear: we need a Jewish State. Jews have proved their will to live, their love of work, their ability to establish a state; and they have shown that the name of Palestine is so powerful that it is capable of gathering in Jews from any and all parts of the world. This tiny piece of land on the shores of the Mediterranean which, after 2,000 years, Jews can again feel to be their own, is big enough to enable the new Jewish life and modern Jewish culture to be attached to its ancient, fundamental ways, and flourish. Even today, in its mutilated form, Palestine is big enough to be an island in the sea of seemingly hopeless Jewish destiny, an island upon which we can peacefully build a lighthouse to beam its light into the darkness, a light of everlasting human values, the light of the one God.

Hannah Szenes

∽

אֱלִי שֶׁלֹּא יִגָּמֵר לְעוֹלָם	Eli shelo yigamer le'olam
הַחוֹל וְהַיָּם	hahol vehayam
רִשְׁרוּשׁ שֶׁל הַמַּיִם	rishrush shel hamayim
בְּרַק הַשָּׁמַיִם	berak hashamayim
תְּפִלַּת הָאָדָם.	tefilat ha'adam.

This translation can be sung to the same melody as the Hebrew.

My God, my God, I pray that these things never end.
The sand and the sea, the rush of the waters,
The crash of the heavens, the prayer of the heart.
The sand and the sea, the rush of the waters.
The crash of the heavens, the prayer of the heart.

Hannah Szenes

∽

Six million Jews murdered, among them more than 1,500,000 children, and with them the destruction of Eastern and Western European Jewish life. Scientists, philosophers, composers, poets, scholars, all dead and all the millions upon millions of the unborn generations after. And the inhumanity witnessed, the reduction of human beings to less than animals, and the consequent hopelessness and loss of faith.

Leo Baeck was born into a religiously enlightened Jewish home and educated at the leading liberal seminaries that flourished in Germany at the beginning of this century. Shortly before World War II, Baeck settled in Berlin where he served as rabbi while lecturing at a liberal Jewish school for adults. After declaring that the "thousand-year" history of the German Jews had come to an end in 1933, Baeck devoted himself to defending the rights remaining for Jews under the Nazis. He refused all invitations to serve as rabbi or professor abroad, declaring that he would remain with the last minyan of Jews in Germany for as long as possible. He continued his work of encouraging his people even after his deportation to the Theresienstadt concentration camp in 1943, serving there as a "witness of faith," to use his own words. He survived the war and lived out his years in London and Cincinnati.

Baeck's positive view of humanity and of hope is notable in all of his writings, even and especially in those written after the war. Nothing of what he experienced dimmed his faith in the future.

The respect we owe to our neighbor is not an isolated commandment but represents the whole content of morality, the quintessence of our duty. For in Judaism the content of all religiousness is that we serve God and love God. The Talmud teaches: "Love God in the human beings whom God has created"—that is the way in which we can freely give to God. When we seek the welfare of others, we find a way to God. The comprehensiveness of this demand was stressed by Hillel, who declared this teaching to be the "essence of the Torah." The same idea is implied in the admonition of the rabbis to walk in the ways of God by doing good, and by striving to be as just,

compassionate and merciful as is the Eternal. In what we do to our neighbor, we serve God.

Our relation to others is thereby lifted out of the sphere of good will, affection or even love; it is exalted into the sphere of the established relationship with God, which is common and equal to all and therefore unites all. Each person has an unconditional claim on us. Even our enemy may and must demand the fulfillment of our duty, for though he is our enemy, he does not cease to be our fellow. "If your enemy is hungry, give him food to eat; and if he is thirsty, give him water to drink" (Proverbs 25:21). Whoever bears a human face is our neighbor and is entitled to our help and our compassion. What we owe to another and what we do for that person is not based on the uncertain foundation of good will, or on any transitory emotional impulse, but on the positive and social commandment of justice, solely because every person is a human being.

Leo Baeck

✌

אֶשָּׂא עֵינַי אֶל־הֶהָרִים Esa eynay el heharim

מֵאַיִן יָבוֹא עֶזְרִי: me'ayin yavo ezri.

עֶזְרִי מֵעִם יהוה ezri me'im adonay

עֹשֵׂה שָׁמַיִם וָאָרֶץ: oseh shamayim va'aretz.

I lift my eyes up to the hills:
from where does my help come?
My help is from THE UNSEEN ONE,
the maker of the heavens and the earth.

Psalms 121:1-2

✌

Attempts have been made to find the decisive difference between humans and beasts. It has been found that humans are beings who fashion tools and know grandparents and grandchildren. It could also be said that humans are beings of hope. Wherever

humans believe and love, they hope. The motif of hope is the wish, clear or cloudy, that sustains itself with actual or imagined appearances. The spiritual foundation of religious hope is the deep assurance in which the finite comes to experience something of the power of infinity, the certainty that the goal endures, and that there is a way that leads to it. That is the expectation that rises out of the strength of a people's belief. It is the hope above all hopes, the one that includes and unites all human beings within it.

We humans wander through wishes. They begin in us and then gain their own existence in what they reveal. But they still remain part of our existence, part of our self; in effect, they are our life as it projects itself in the distant reaches. Hopes, manifold as the days, always unite these two existences anew, so that they—distant and close life—always come to be one. Without the hopes, the self would split itself and life would finally break in two. Humans are beings who hope and since there are many days, there are many hopes.

Indeed our people of the great expectation always remained a people of many and changing hopes. Our people always understood both moving away to follow hopes, and remaining to wait for them. Above all, an expectation lived in us everywhere, for the children and the children's children. The spiritual history of our people, from generation to generation, is a history of suffering and renunciation, a giving up for the sake of children and grandchildren, that the hopes might fulfill themselves in them. We learned to live in what was coming; we became accustomed to live this way, to prepare in our own narrow and short existence a breadth of space and an extension of days. Under all oppressions, patience preserved a viable strength. It even became active, indeed, gaining something of the messianic dynamism of the great expectation—"searching out with the soul" the land of the children.

KADDISH DERABANAN / THE SAGES' KADDISH

Reader: Let God's name be made great and holy in the world that was created as God willed. May God complete the holy realm in your own lifetime, in your days, and in the days of all the house of Israel, quickly and soon. And say: Amen.

Congregation: May God's great name be blessed, forever and as long as worlds endure.

Reader: May it be blessed, and praised, and glorified, and held in honor, viewed with awe, embellished and revered; and may the blessed name of holiness be hailed, though it be higher by far than all the blessings, songs, praises, and consolations that we utter in this world. And say: Amen.

For Israel and her sages, for their pupils and all pupils of their pupils, and for all who occupy themselves with Torah, whether in this place or any other place, may God grant them and you abundant peace, and grace, and love, and mercy, and long life, and ample sustenance, and saving acts, all flowing from divine abundance in the worlds beyond. And say: Amen.

May heaven grant a universal peace and life for us and for all Israel. And say: Amen.

May the one who creates harmony above make peace for us, and for all Israel, and for all who dwell on earth. And say: Amen.

For our teachers and their students
And the students of their students:
We ask for peace and loving kindness
And let us say Amen.
And for those who study Torah
Here and everywhere may they be blessed
With all they need and let us say Amen.
We ask for peace and loving kindness
And let us say Amen.

Debbie Friedman

יִתְגַּדַּל וְיִתְקַדַּשׁ שְׁמֵהּ רַבָּא בְּעָלְמָא דִּי בְרָא כִרְעוּתֵהּ וְיַמְלִיךְ
מַלְכוּתֵהּ בְּחַיֵּיכוֹן וּבְיוֹמֵיכוֹן וּבְחַיֵּי דְכָל בֵּית יִשְׂרָאֵל בַּעֲגָלָא וּבִזְמַן
קָרִיב וְאִמְרוּ אָמֵן:

יְהֵא שְׁמֵהּ רַבָּא מְבָרַךְ לְעָלַם וּלְעָלְמֵי עָלְמַיָּא:

יִתְבָּרַךְ וְיִשְׁתַּבַּח וְיִתְפָּאַר וְיִתְרוֹמַם וְיִתְנַשֵּׂא וְיִתְהַדָּר וְיִתְעַלֶּה
וְיִתְהַלָּל שְׁמֵהּ דְּקֻדְשָׁא בְּרִיךְ הוּא
לְעֵלָּא לְעֵלָּא מִכָּל בִּרְכָתָא וְשִׁירָתָא תֻּשְׁבְּחָתָא וְנֶחֱמָתָא דַּאֲמִירָן
בְּעָלְמָא וְאִמְרוּ אָמֵן:

עַל יִשְׂרָאֵל וְעַל רַבָּנָן וְעַל תַּלְמִידֵיהוֹן וְעַל כָּל תַּלְמִידֵי תַלְמִידֵיהוֹן
וְעַל כָּל מָאן דְּעָסְקִין בְּאוֹרַיְתָא דִּי בְּאַתְרָא הָדֵין וְדִי בְּכָל אֲתַר
וַאֲתַר יְהֵא לְהוֹן וּלְכוֹן שְׁלָמָא רַבָּא חִנָּא וְחִסְדָּא וְרַחֲמִין וְחַיִּין
אֲרִיכִין וּמְזוֹנֵי רְוִיחֵי וּפֻרְקָנָא מִן קֳדָם אֲבוּהוֹן דִּבִשְׁמַיָּא וְאַרְעָא
וְאִמְרוּ אָמֵן:

יְהֵא שְׁלָמָא רַבָּא מִן שְׁמַיָּא וְחַיִּים עָלֵינוּ וְעַל כָּל יִשְׂרָאֵל וְאִמְרוּ
אָמֵן: עוֹשֶׂה שָׁלוֹם בִּמְרוֹמָיו הוּא יַעֲשֶׂה שָׁלוֹם עָלֵינוּ וְעַל כָּל
יִשְׂרָאֵל וְעַל כָּל יוֹשְׁבֵי תֵבֵל וְאִמְרוּ אָמֵן:

NOTE. This martyrology was compiled by Lee Friedlander.

ELEH EZKERAH III:
THE MARTYRS OF THE SHOAH

אֵלֶּה אֶזְכְּרָה וְנַפְשִׁי עָלַי אֶשְׁפְּכָה:

Eleh ezkerah venafshi alay eshpeḥah.

These I remember and pour out my soul.

It is told that when the great Israel Baal Shem-Tov saw misfortune threatening the Jews, it was his custom to go into a certain part of the forest to meditate. There he would light a fire, say a special prayer, and the miracle would be accomplished and the misfortune averted. Later, when his disciple, the celebrated Magid of Mezrich had occasion, for the same reason, to intercede with heaven, he would go to the same place in the forest and say, "Master of the Universe, I do not know how to light the fire, but I am still able to say the prayer." And again the miracle would be accomplished. Still later, Rabbi Moshe-Leib of Sasov, in order to save his people once more, would go into the forest and say, "I do not know how to light the fire. I do not know the prayer, but I know the place, and this must be sufficient." And it was sufficient and the miracle was

---

NOTE. The lives of the martyrs whom we remember are intertwined with our own lives. Communities can emphasize this connection by asking three members to briefly speak about their own experience of one of the themes: Torah, Devotion, and Caring Deeds.   J.A.S.

NOTE. This Martyrology is based on one composed by Reconstructionist Rabbi Jeremy Schwartz.

accomplished. Then it fell to Rabbi Israel of Rizhyn to overcome misfortune. Sitting in his armchair, his head in his hands, he spoke to God, "I am unable to light the fire and I do not know the prayer; I cannot even find the place in the forest. All I can do is to tell the story and this must be sufficient." And it was sufficient and the miracle was accomplished.

We post-emancipation, post-Holocaust Jews long ago removed ourselves or were removed from the Lithuanian and Polish forests of these Ḥasidic masters. Culturally assimilated, we have forgotten their languages, and, as religious liberals, we question the efficacy of their prayers. Their fires were extinguished in the Death Camps and their stories, so lovingly told, did not save them.

Few died the deaths of martyrs in the Holocaust. Like unknowing sheep led to the slaughter, most were victims. But still, being Jews, we are driven to find meaning in meaninglessness, sparks of divinity in utter degradation, and truths that inform our lives and give us hope. This is the goal of this Martyrology: to understand a Jewish teaching in the example of three of our people who were martyrs of the Holocaust in death or for life. The teaching is ascribed to Shimon the *Tzadik*, one of the early sages of the Mishnah.

עַל שְׁלֹשָׁה דְבָרִים הָעוֹלָם עוֹמֵד:
עַל הַתּוֹרָה וְעַל הָעֲבוֹדָה וְעַל גְּמִילוּת חֲסָדִים:

Al sheloshah devarim ha'olam omed.
Al hatorah ve'al ha'avodah ve'al gemilut ḥasadim.

The world stands on three things—on Torah, and on devotion, and on caring deeds.

Pirkey Avot 1.2

A principal injunction of the Torah is the honoring of father and mother, for observance of which we are promised length of days. Though the theologically unsophisticated understood this literally and personally, our sages knew that the promised long life would not necessarily be experienced by the one who observed the Torah injunction. Length of days, they taught, might be credited to a life beyond our own, most particularly to our children who live after us, to our children who honor us as parents and who teach their children to honor them as parents, thereby ensuring the stability of the world through Torah.

The days before Rosh Hashanah 1942 were particularly difficult for the Koczicki family in the ghetto of Slotwina Brzesko. It was clear that they would soon be taken on their last journey.

Bronia, Rabbi Israel Koczicki's wife, had false papers, but her husband and mother-in-law did not. After much deliberation, a painful decision was made. The family would split up. Bronia would leave the ghetto and try to obtain Aryan papers for her husband and mother-in-law.

The parting was a painful one. Bronia took little Yitzhak with her while the older son, Zvi, age six, remained with his father and grandmother.

Bronia and her son boarded a passenger train filled with German officers. Her blond hair, blue eyes and Berlin-accented German were a perfect cover, but she was fearful because of little Yitzhak. Since the family had lived in Berlin, they all spoke German, but

---

NOTE. During the Holocaust, six million Jews were slaughtered intentionally and millions of other Jews victimized. Some were martyrs, but many others were swept up against their will. The details are less important than the memory of their lives—six million worlds.　　　　L.F. / D.A.T.

Yitzḥak's German was intermingled with Yiddish words because he had been born and raised in Poland. Bronia held the child in her lap, displaying his beautiful blond curls. Yitzḥak was asleep, and Bronia prayed that he would stay asleep until they arrived at Bochnia, their destination.

The German officers seated next to Bronia struck up a conversation with her. Before long, they were discussing the Germans' favorite topic—the Jews. Their remarks were brutal and vulgar, although they apologized to Bronia for using the vile language in the presence of a lady. Soon one officer was recalling how, on a similar journey, he had discovered a Jew who was travelling on Aryan papers, "I sniffed him out; I have a special talent for it. I made him pull down his trousers. The poor devil never made it to the next station." He told his story gleefully, trying to amuse beautiful Bronia.

Little Yitzḥak turned his head in his sleep. The fact that he was circumcised made Bronia's heart pound louder than the locomotive's puffings. But she managed to smile her calm smile. She pointed to the sleeping child and said, "Gentlemen, you don't want to wake up a future soldier." The conversation continued in hushed voices.

When the train stopped in Bochnia, Bronia, without giving any sign that it was her stop, remained in her seat. Just as the train was about to pull out of the station, she swiftly stepped down to the platform. The train pulled out of the station, and Bronia waved to the German officers from below. They responded warmly as the train sped on its way. Bronia breathed a sigh of relief. Moments later, she was already planning the next step, the rescue of the other members of her family.

After a few days, Bronia was able to obtain Aryan papers for her husband and mother-in-law. With a reliable messenger and for a substantial sum of money, Bronia sent the papers to her husband in Slotwina Brzesko. Daily, Bronia went to the train station,

hoping that her husband, older son, and mother-in-law would be among the passengers. But days passed and they did not arrive. Bronia began to worry. Maybe the documents had never reached her husband and were intercepted by the Germans; maybe her husband and mother-in-law had been recognized and betrayed on the train by a Polish acquaintance; maybe the papers had arrived too late. Desperate, Bronia decided to return to Slotwina Brzesko.

On the very day she planned to leave, Bronia received a letter from her husband. The Aryan papers had arrived safely, but his mother was afraid to use them. She claimed that her looks and accent would betray her and, consequently, all of them. Since the command to "Honor your mother" is a principal command in the Torah, he could not leave his mother alone. He hoped that Bronia would agree, and would understand and forgive him.

A few days later, Bronia received a second letter from her husband. He wrote that their fears had begun to materialize. They had all been taken in a transport to Tarnow. There the men were separated from the women, and he was separated from his mother. Though he feared the worst, their son, Zvi, was well and was with him. He continued his letter, reminding her that Yitzḥak would be three years old on Rosh Hashanah, so she should make sure that he wore a *tallit katan* and always remembered that he was a Jew. Israel begged her forgiveness if he had ever offended her during their married years, and thanked her for the wonderful years they had been given together to build a family. A substantial sum of money was enclosed in the letter. After reading it, Bronia rushed to a man in the Bochnia ghetto who was known as an expert smuggler, one who was able to transport people from ghetto to ghetto.

"To Tarnow I do not travel," the man declared, shaking his head. "It is entering the lion's den without any possible exit." Bronia offered to pay double. Still he refused. "A person is responsible

first for himself," he said, "and this mission is just too dangerous."

A few days later, Rabbi Israel was sent to the gas chamber. On his last journey from Tarnow to Belzec, he managed to break one of the iron bars of the cattle car's only window and squeeze his six-year-old son through the space. Thus he tossed Zvi to freedom from the speeding train, certain that somehow, Bronia would find him.

Bronia, in the Bochnia ghetto, sensed that her son would be found along the Tarnow-Belzec tracks. She hired a Polish peasant for a handsome sum of money and posted him day and night along the death road. The peasant pretended that he was gathering mushrooms in the forest along the tracks leading from Tarnow to the death camp of Belzec.

The tracks were strewn with pictures of Jewish families, smiling faces of young and old. On the backs were scribbled frantic messages in shaky handwriting, asking for help. Then, at the edge of the tracks, the peasant noticed a pair of small shoes on top of a bush. The shoes were on the feet of a little boy who was more dead than alive. The peasant picked up the boy and rushed to Bochnia, reuniting Bronia with her beloved son.

עַל שְׁלֹשָׁה דְבָרִים הָעוֹלָם עוֹמֵד:
עַל הַתּוֹרָה וְעַל הָעֲבוֹדָה וְעַל גְּמִילוּת חֲסָדִים:

Al sheloshah devarim ha'olam omed.
Al hatorah ve'al ha'avodah ve'al gemilut ḥasadim.

The world stands on three things—on Torah, and on devotion, and on caring deeds.

A well-known piece of the Yom Kippur liturgy declares of those who serve God, "All of them are beloved, pure and mighty, and all of them in dread and awe do the will of their Master; and

all of them open their mouths in holiness and purity, with song and psalm, while they glorify and ascribe sovereignty to the name of the Divine Ruler." We commonly identify those so devoted to the Deity as the religiously pious, but such devotion can be found in the most unlikely people, even in those who oppose God and God's devotees in principle. Their devotion, so differently motivated, is no less world sustaining.

In the Janowska Road Camp, there was a brigade foreman from Lvov by the name of Schneeweiss, one of those people one stays away from if one values one's life. Schneeweiss had known Rabbi Israel Spira in Lvov, but was not aware that the latter was a camp inmate. Only a handful of Ḥasidim who were close to the rabbi knew the rabbi's identity, and they kept it a secret.

It was the eve of Yom Kippur. Tensions and fears were at their height. A few Ḥasidim came to Rabbi Spira and asked him to approach Schneeweiss and request that on Yom Kippur his group not be assigned to any of the thirty-nine main categories of work, so that their transgression of the law by working on Yom Kippur would not be a major one. The rabbi was very moved by the request of his Ḥasidim and despite his fears, for he would have to disclose his identity, went to Schneeweiss. He knew quite well that Schneeweiss did not have much respect for Jewish tradition. Even prior to the outbreak of World War II, he had publicly violated the Jewish holidays and transgressed against Jewish law. Here in Janowska, he was a cruel man who knew no mercy.

With a heavy heart, the rabbi went before Schneeweiss. "You probably remember me. I am the Rabbi of Pruchnik, Rabbi Israel Spira." Schneeweiss did not respond. "You are a Jew like myself," the rabbi continued. "Tonight is *Kol Nidrey* night. There is a small group of young Jews who do not want to transgress any of the thirty-nine main categories of work. It means everything to them. It is the essence of their existence. Can you do something about it? Can you help?"

"Tonight I can't do a thing," said Schneeweiss. "I have no jurisdiction over the night brigade. But tomorrow, on Yom Kippur, I will do for you whatever I can." The rabbi shook Schneeweiss's hand in gratitude and left.

In the morning, the rabbi and a small group of young Ḥasidim were summoned to Schneeweiss's cottage. "I heard that you prayed last night. I don't believe in prayers," Schneeweiss told them. "On principle, I even oppose them. But I admire your courage. For you all know well that the penalty for prayer in Janowska is death." With that, he motioned them to follow him.

He took them to the S.S. quarters in the camp, to a large wooden house. "You fellows will shine the floor without any polish or wax. And you, rabbi, will clean the windows with dry rags so that you will not transgress any of the thirty-nine major categories of work." He left the room abruptly without saying another word.

The rabbi was standing on a ladder with rags in his hand, cleaning the huge windows while chanting prayers, and his companions were on the floor polishing the wood and praying with him. "All of them are beloved, pure and mighty, and all of them in dread and awe do the will of their Master; and all of them open their mouths in holiness and purity, with song and psalm, while they glorify and ascribe sovereignty to the name of the Divine Ruler." The floor was wet with their tears.

At noon, the door opened wide and into the room stormed two S.S. men in their black uniforms. They were followed by a food cart filled to capacity. "Noontime, time to eat bread, soup, and meat," announced one of the two. The room was filled with an aroma of freshly cooked food, such food as they had not seen since the German occupation: white bread, steaming vegetable soup, and huge portions of meat. ↵

The tall S.S. man commanded, "You must eat immediately, otherwise you will be shot on the spot!" None of them moved. The rabbi remained on the ladder, the Ḥasidim on the floor. The German repeated the orders. The rabbi and the Ḥasidim remained glued to their places. The S.S. men called in Schneeweiss. "Schneeweiss, if the dirty dogs refuse to eat, I will kill you along with them." Schneeweiss pulled himself to attention, looked the German directly in the eyes, and said in a very quiet tone, "We Jews do not eat today. Today is Yom Kippur, our most holy day, the Day of Atonement."

"You don't understand, Jewish dog," roared the taller of the two. "I command you in the name of the Führer and the Third Reich, *eat!*"

Schneeweiss, composed, his head high, repeated the same answer. "We Jews obey the law of our tradition. Today is Yom Kippur, a day of fasting."

The German took out his revolver from its holster and pointed it at Schneeweiss's temple. Schneeweiss remained calm. He stood still, at attention, his head held high. A shot pierced the room. Schneeweiss fell. On the freshly polished floor, a puddle of blood was growing bigger and bigger.

The rabbi and the Ḥasidim stood as if frozen in their places. They could not believe what their eyes had just witnessed. Schneeweiss, the man who in the past had publicly transgressed against the Jewish tradition, had sanctified God's name publicly and died a martyr's death for the sake of Jewish honor.

"Only then, on that Yom Kippur day in Janowska," said the rabbi to his Ḥasidim later, "did I understand the meaning of the statement in the Talmud: 'Even the transgressors in Israel are as full of good deeds as a pomegranate is filled with seeds.'"

עַל שְׁלשָׁה דְבָרִים הָעוֹלָם עוֹמֵד:
עַל הַתּוֹרָה וְעַל הָעֲבוֹדָה וְעַל גְּמִילוּת חֲסָדִים:

Al sheloshah devarim ha'olam omed.
Al hatorah ve'al ha'avodah ve'al gemilut ḥasadim.

The world stands on three things—on Torah, and on devotion, and on caring deeds.

Our tradition teaches that each person is a microcosm of the world, an entire world in himself. One who saves the life of another, therefore, preserves the world. A single act of *gemilut ḥesed*, one caring deed, can be the vehicle of such preservation.

In Bergen-Belsen, Bronia's dedication to the education of her two small sons, Zvi and Yitzḥak, was viewed by some as an obsession bordering on insanity. She would deny herself food, bartering it for her children's education. For a piece of bread and a potato, Mr. Rappaport taught her children Jewish law and tradition. She herself taught the children the weekly Torah portion. At times the children were so hungry that they could neither hear nor see. Words became muffled, distant sounds, and the letters seemed like a colony of busy ants rushing in all directions.

When Pesaḥ approached, Bronia's program became more rigid. She insisted that the children learn all the laws and customs pertinent to the holiday, while she herself supervised their studies and hustled for food. A kind old German who worked at the showers gave her some beets and potatoes. These she saved for the holiday so she and the children would be able to manage without bread.

Bronia did not rest until she had disposed of her leavened food as required by law. She sold it for the duration of Pesaḥ to a non-Jewish woman from Prague, the wife of a famous Jewish lawyer, neither of whom were inmates of Bergen-Belsen. Bronia's sale of *ḥametz* became a source of mockery. People ↶

taunted her and asked if the sale of *ḥametz* was her only concern at this particular time and place.

"I learned the Jewish tradition in my father's home when I was a child. Now it is my duty as a Jewish mother to teach it to my children in my home."

"Some home, a Nazi concentration camp!" someone said, while glancing at the two children with pity for their sad lot, being children to a mother who had lost her mind in these troubled times.

On their way back to the barracks, Bronia and the children stopped at the infirmary. A long line of people were standing and waiting for treatment that would offer relief from their pain and discomfort. Two German doctors in white coats passed by. One casually pointed to the people in the line and said to his companion, "I don't know why God has punished me so severely by forcing me to witness daily such ugliness as these Jews."

Bronia glanced at the line. All around her were skeletons disfigured by disease and starvation, covered with boils, blotches, and sores. "Mama, did you hear what the German doctor said?" asked Zvi of his mother. "Yes, I heard," Bronia responded. "Just study and be good, for a time will come when we will once more be a great and wise nation."

Pesaḥ came and went, but the Jews of Bergen-Belsen were still slaves behind barbed wire. On the evening when Pesaḥ ended, a woman named Mindel Heller came running. "Bronia, it is a matter of life and death. The Rabbi of Pruchnik is almost dead. He hardly ate during Pesaḥ, and now he refuses to eat *ḥametz* that was not sold prior to the holiday as required by law. I heard that you are the only person in camp who sold your *ḥametz*."

Bronia did not hesitate for a moment. She took out a loaf of white bread, her most precious possession, and gave it for the Rabbi of Pruchnik.

The people around her shook their heads in disbelief. "Woe to a woman who gives away her children's last bite to a stranger."

"What I learned and saw at my father's home, I want my children to see and learn in my home. I could not choose the home, but I can preserve its spirit," said Bronia as she handed the bread to Mindel.

In time the Rabbi of Pruchnik improved. Bronia's bread had saved his life.

Years later, when Bronia Koczicki finished her story, she asked a listener, "Do you know the value of the loaf of bread I gave Mindel Heller? Today a skyscraper in Times Square is less valuable than a loaf of white bread in Bergen-Belsen."

עַל שְׁלֹשָׁה דְבָרִים הָעוֹלָם עוֹמֵד:
עַל הַתּוֹרָה וְעַל הָעֲבוֹדָה וְעַל גְּמִילוּת חֲסָדִים:

Al sheloshah devarim ha'olam omed.
Al hatorah ve'al ha'avodah ve'al gemilut hasadim.

The world stands on three things—on Torah, and on devotion, and on caring deeds.

Upon Israel and upon the rabbis, and upon their disciples and upon all the disciples of their disciples, and upon all who engage in the study of the Torah in this place and in every place, to them and to you—abundant peace, grace, lovingkindness, mercy, long life, ample sustenance and salvation.

Upon Israel and upon the rabbis
and upon the disciples and upon all the disciples of their
    disciples
and upon all who study Torah in this place and in every place,

to them and to you
peace;
upon Israel and upon all who meet with unfriendly glances,
    sticks and stones and names—
on posters, in newspapers, or in books to last,
chalked on asphalt or in acid on glass,
shouted from a thousand thousand windows by radio;
who are pushed out of classrooms and rushing trains,
whom the hundred hands of a mob strike,
and whom jailers strike with bunches of keys, with revolver
    butts;
to them and to you
in this place and in every place
safety;

upon Israel and upon all who live
as the sparrows of the streets
under the cornices of the houses of others,
and as rabbits
in the fields of strangers
on the grace of the seasons
and what the gleaners leave in the corners;
you children of the wind—
birds
that feed on the tree of knowledge
in this place and in every place
to them and to you
a living;

upon Israel
and upon their children and upon all the children of their
    children
in this place and in every place,
to them and to you
life.

Charles Reznikoff

For our teachers and their students
And the students of their students:
We ask for peace and loving kindness
And let us say Amen.
And for those who study Torah
Here and everywhere may they be blessed
with all they need and let us say Amen.
We ask for peace and loving kindness
And let us say Amen.

Debbie Friedman

Remember, for our sake,
the ancestral covenant, as you have promised:

"And I shall remember my covenant with Jacob,
and, as well, my covenant with Isaac,
and, as well, my covenant with Abraham;
I shall remember them, and shall recall
the Land I promised them."

Leviticus 26:42

Remember, for our sake,
the covenant of former times, as you have promised:

"And I shall remember, for their sake,
the covenant of former times,
whereby I brought them from the land of Egypt,
in the sight of all the nations,
to become their God,
I am THE LAWGIVER!"

Leviticus 26:45

Have mercy on us, and do not destroy us, as it is written:

"For THE FOUNT OF MERCY is a God compassionate,
who shall not let you wither, and shall not destroy you,
nor shall God forget the covenant made with your ancestors,
the one promised by oath to them."

Deuteronomy 4:31

Open up our hearts to love and to revere your name, as it is
written:

"THE BOUNTIFUL, your God, shall circumcise your hearts
and your children's hearts,
to love THE FOUNT OF LIFE, your God,
with all your heart, with all your soul,
that you might live." ↵

Deuteronomy 30:6

זְכָר־לָנוּ בְּרִית אָבוֹת כַּאֲשֶׁר אָמַרְתָּ:
וְזָכַרְתִּי אֶת־בְּרִיתִי יַעֲקוֹב וְאַף אֶת־בְּרִיתִי יִצְחָק וְאַף אֶת־בְּרִיתִי
אַבְרָהָם אֶזְכֹּר וְהָאָרֶץ אֶזְכֹּר:

זְכָר־לָנוּ בְּרִית רִאשׁוֹנִים כַּאֲשֶׁר אָמַרְתָּ:
וְזָכַרְתִּי לָהֶם בְּרִית רִאשׁוֹנִים אֲשֶׁר הוֹצֵאתִי־אֹתָם מֵאֶרֶץ מִצְרַיִם
לְעֵינֵי הַגּוֹיִם לִהְיוֹת לָהֶם לֵאלֹהִים אֲנִי יהוה:

רַחֵם עָלֵינוּ וְאַל תַּשְׁחִיתֵנוּ כְּמָה שֶׁכָּתוּב:
כִּי אֵל רַחוּם יהוה אֱלֹהֶיךָ לֹא יַרְפְּךָ וְלֹא יַשְׁחִיתֶךָ וְלֹא יִשְׁכַּח אֶת־
בְּרִית אֲבֹתֶיךָ אֲשֶׁר נִשְׁבַּע לָהֶם:

מוֹל אֶת־לְבָבֵנוּ לְאַהֲבָה אֶת שְׁמֶךָ כְּמָה שֶׁכָּתוּב:
וּמָל יהוה אֱלֹהֶיךָ אֶת־לְבָבְךָ וְאֶת־לְבַב זַרְעֶךָ לְאַהֲבָה אֶת־יהוה
אֱלֹהֶיךָ בְּכָל־לְבָבְךָ וּבְכָל־נַפְשְׁךָ לְמַעַן חַיֶּיךָ: ←

Be present for us when we call on you, as it is written:

"And you shall seek out THE BELOVED ONE, your God,
from where you are, and you shall find God,
provided that you search for God
with all your heart, and all your soul."

Deuteronomy 4:29

Blot out our sins upon this day, and purify us,
as it is written:

"For on this day, atonement shall be made for you,
to make you clean from all your wrongdoings.
Before THE FOUNT OF MERCY, you shall all be clean."

Leviticus 16:30

ოა

Return us, BLESSED ONE, let us return!
Renew our days, as you have done of old!

השיבנו...כקדם / Return...old! (Lamentations 5:21).

הִמָּצֵא לָנוּ בְּבַקָּשָׁתֵנוּ כְּמָה שֶׁכָּתוּב:

וּבִקַּשְׁתֶּם מִשָּׁם אֶת־יהוה אֱלֹהֶיךָ וּמָצָאתָ כִּי תִדְרְשֶׁנּוּ בְּכָל־לְבָבְךָ
וּבְכָל־נַפְשֶׁךָ:

כַּפֵּר חֲטָאֵינוּ בַּיּוֹם הַזֶּה וְטַהֲרֵנוּ כְּמָה שֶׁכָּתוּב:

כִּי־בַיּוֹם הַזֶּה יְכַפֵּר עֲלֵיכֶם לְטַהֵר אֶתְכֶם מִכֹּל חַטֹּאתֵיכֶם לִפְנֵי יהוה
תִּטְהָרוּ:

&

הֲשִׁיבֵנוּ יהוה אֵלֶיךָ וְנָשׁוּבָה חַדֵּשׁ יָמֵינוּ כְּקֶדֶם: ←

Hashivenu adonay eleha venashuva ḥadesh yameynu
kekedem. ↵

COMMENTARY. Why does so much of religious longing find its voice in the
appeal to antiquity? What is it about the past, real or imagined, that makes
it a destination of choice for the soul that seeks renewal? Why look
backward instead of forward?

Perhaps the answer lies in the word ḥadesh, which means both "new" and
"renew." We cannot become the person we long to be by ignoring the
persons we have been. In order to become "new" we have to "renew"—
we have to recover moments of holiness, accomplishment, and integrity
from our past and bring them forward into the lives we are continuously
shaping. An individual—or a people—that believes it can move forward
without looking backward is destined to defeat.   R.H.

Remove our wrongs like smoke, and like a cloud,
as you have promised:
"I remove your wrongs like smoke,
your sins like clouds.
Return to me, for I have set you free!"   Isaiah 44:22

Sprinkle over us pure waters
that we may be clean, as it is written:
"And I shall sprinkle you with purest waters,
and you shall be clean. From all your wrongs,
from all of your idolatries,
I make you clean."   Ezekiel 36:25

Grant atonement for our wrongs
this very day, that we may be clean,
as it is written: "For on this day
atonement shall be made for you
for all your wrongdoings,
before THE FOUNT OF MERCY
you shall all be clean."   Leviticus 16:30

Bring us to your holy mountain,
make us joyful in your house of prayer,
as it is written: "I shall bring you
to my holy mountain, I shall make you joyful
in my house of prayer. Truly, my house
shall be called a house of prayer
for all nations!"   Isaiah 56:7

מְחֵה פְשָׁעֵינוּ כָּעָב וְכֶעָנָן כַּאֲשֶׁר אָמַרְתָּ: מָחִיתִי כָעָב פְּשָׁעֶיךָ וְכֶעָנָן
חַטֹּאותֶיךָ שׁוּבָה אֵלַי כִּי גְאַלְתִּיךָ: זְרֹק עָלֵינוּ מַיִם טְהוֹרִים וְטַהֲרֵנוּ
כְּמָה שֶׁכָּתוּב: וְזָרַקְתִּי עֲלֵיכֶם מַיִם טְהוֹרִים וּטְהַרְתֶּם מִכֹּל
טֻמְאוֹתֵיכֶם וּמִכָּל־גִּלּוּלֵיכֶם אֲטַהֵר אֶתְכֶם: כַּפֵּר חֲטָאֵינוּ בַּיּוֹם
הַזֶּה וְטַהֲרֵנוּ כְּמָה שֶׁכָּתוּב: כִּי־בַיּוֹם הַזֶּה יְכַפֵּר עֲלֵיכֶם לְטַהֵר אֶתְכֶם
מִכֹּל חַטֹּאתֵיכֶם לִפְנֵי יהוה תִּטְהָרוּ: הֲבִיאֵנוּ אֶל הַר קָדְשֶׁךָ וְשַׂמְּחֵנוּ
בְּבֵית תְּפִלָּתֶךָ כְּמָה שֶׁכָּתוּב: וַהֲבִיאוֹתִים אֶל־הַר קָדְשִׁי וְשִׂמַּחְתִּים
בְּבֵית תְּפִלָּתִי... כִּי בֵיתִי בֵּית תְּפִלָּה יִקָּרֵא לְכָל־הָעַמִּים:

KAVANAH. My sins and transgressions are not solid. They are not essential
to my identity or to my innate being. They are insubstantial. They can be
erased. They can be washed away by plain water. They are not who I am.
Rather, I am the one who is able to ascend to the holy mountain and the
house of divine prayer.   S.P.W.

מחה פשעינו/Remove our wrongs. This does not mean that we wish to
deny the wrongs we have committed or pretend that they did not happen.
Instead, we are summoned to boldly confront ourselves and the effects of
our deeds. The Hebrew letters that we use to form the word meḥey/
remove can also mean "strike out," "protest," and "forewarn." From these
same letters we form the word moaḥ, marrow: the innermost part of our
being. Forgiveness is not a casual, passive or superficial thing: it requires
that we look deeply into ourselves, and that we strike out against the
human potential for wrongdoing. Only when we ourselves make it our
personal commitment to take an active role in combatting evil in the
world will it be possible for God to "remove our wrongs." Then, in the
very marrow of our being, our transgressions will evaporate like a mist,
our sins disperse like a cloud.   S.D.R.

We rise.

Hear our voice, ETERNAL ONE, our God,
and accept our prayer with mercy and good will.
Turn us, ANCIENT ONE, toward you,
let us return.
Renew our days like days of old.
Do not cast us away from dwelling in your presence,
and do not remove your holy spirit from our midst.
And do not cast us off as we grow old;
do not forsake us when our strength departs.
Do not forsake us, GENTLE ONE, our God,
do not withdraw from us.
Give us a sign of blessing, so that anyone who bears us ill
shall hesitate to harm us.
For truly you, ETERNAL ONE,
have always helped us and consoled us.
Hear now our words, GOD OF COMPASSION,
and behold our contemplation.
May our words of prayer and meditations of our hearts
be seen favorably, PRECIOUS ONE, our rock, our champion.
For we place our hope in you, ETERNAL ONE,
so may you answer us, Almighty One, our God. ↩

We are seated.

שמע קולנו /Hear our voice. We do not ask God to hear our words, but rather to hear our voice. The deepest prayer of the heart is often articulated in sounds, rather than in words. From the sobbing of grief to the sighing of pleasure, we know the power of our own voices. When we have been separated from those we love, our first reaction is often, "It is so good to hear your voice!" In such moments, it almost does not matter what is said. So too at this sacred season, we imagine God's pleasure in hearing our voices again, reuniting, reconnecting, and renewing our hopes for rebirth. Hear our voice...we are here.   R.H.

NOTE. *Shema Kolenu* is based on biblical verses adapted by the author.

שְׁמַע קוֹלֵנוּ יהוה אֱלֹהֵינוּ חוּס וְרַחֵם עָלֵינוּ

וְקַבֵּל בְּרַחֲמִים וּבְרָצוֹן אֶת־תְּפִלָּתֵנוּ:

הֲשִׁיבֵנוּ יהוה אֵלֶיךָ וְנָשׁוּבָה חַדֵּשׁ יָמֵינוּ כְּקֶדֶם:

אַל־תַּשְׁלִיכֵנוּ מִלְּפָנֶיךָ וְרוּחַ קָדְשְׁךָ אַל־תִּקַּח מִמֶּנּוּ:

אַל־תַּשְׁלִיכֵנוּ לְעֵת זִקְנָה כִּכְלוֹת כֹּחֵנוּ אַל־תַּעַזְבֵנוּ:

אַל־תַּעַזְבֵנוּ יהוה אֱלֹהֵינוּ אַל־תִּרְחַק מִמֶּנּוּ:

עֲשֵׂה־עִמָּנוּ אוֹת לְטוֹבָה וְיִרְאוּ שׂוֹנְאֵינוּ וְיֵבֹשׁוּ

כִּי־אַתָּה יהוה עֲזַרְתָּנוּ וְנִחַמְתָּנוּ:

אֲמָרֵינוּ הַאֲזִינָה יהוה בִּינָה הֲגִיגֵנוּ:

יִהְיוּ לְרָצוֹן אִמְרֵי־פִינוּ וְהֶגְיוֹן לִבֵּנוּ לְפָנֶיךָ יהוה צוּרֵנוּ וְגוֹאֲלֵנוּ:

כִּי־לְךָ יהוה הוֹחָלְנוּ אַתָּה תַעֲנֶה אֲדֹנָי אֱלֹהֵינוּ: ←—

Shema kolenu adonay eloheynu ḥus veraḥem aleynu
vekabel beraḥamim uveratzon et tefilatenu.
Hashivenu adonay eleḥa venashuvah ḥadesh yameynu kekedem.
Al tashliḥenu milefaneḥa veru'aḥ kodsheḥa al tikaḥ mimenu.
Al tashliḥenu le'et ziknah kiḥlot koḥenu al ta'azvenu.
Al ta'azvenu adonay eloheynu al tirḥak mimenu.
Asey imanu ot letovah veyiru soneynu veyevoshu
ki atah adonay azartanu veniḥamtanu.
Amareynu ha'azinah adonay binah hagigenu.
Yihyu leratzon imrey finu vehegyon libenu lefaneḥa adonay
tzurenu vego'alenu.
Ki leḥa adonay hoḥalnu atah ta'aneh adonay eloheynu. ↵

Our God, our ancients' God,
do not forsake us, and do not turn us away,
and do not cause us shame,
and do not nullify your covenant with us,
but bring us nearer to your Torah,
teach us your mitzvot,
instruct us in your ways.
Incline our hearts to treat your name with awe,
and open up our inner nature to your love,
and bring us back to you in truth,
with whole and peaceful heart.
And for the sake of your great name,
be merciful, and grant forgiveness for our wrongs,
as it is written in your prophets' words:
"For the sake of your great name, ETERNAL ONE,
forgive my wrongdoing, for I have done much wrong."

Our God, our ancients' God,
forgive us, pardon us, help us atone—
we are your people, and you are our God,
we are your children, and you are our creator,
we are your servants, and you are our sovereign,
we are your community, and you are our portion,
we are your possession, and you are our fate,
we are your sheep, and you are our shepherd,
we are your vineyard, and you are our keeper,
we are your creation, and you are our fashioner,
we are your loved ones, and you are our beloved,
we are your treasure, and you are our kin,
we are your people, and you are our ruler,
we are your faithful, and you are our source of faith! ↵

אֱלֹהֵינוּ וֵאלֹהֵי אֲבוֹתֵינוּ וְאִמּוֹתֵינוּ אַל תַּעַזְבֵנוּ וְאַל תִּטְּשֵׁנוּ וְאַל
תַּכְלִימֵנוּ וְאַל תָּפֵר בְּרִיתְךָ אִתָּנוּ קָרְבֵנוּ לְתוֹרָתֶךָ לַמְּדֵנוּ מִצְוֹתֶיךָ
הוֹרֵנוּ דְרָכֶיךָ הַט לִבֵּנוּ לְיִרְאָה אֶת־שְׁמֶךָ וּמוֹל אֶת־לְבָבֵנוּ לְאַהֲבָתֶךָ
וְנָשׁוּב אֵלֶיךָ בֶּאֱמֶת וּבְלֵב שָׁלֵם וּלְמַעַן שִׁמְךָ הַגָּדוֹל תִּמְחַל וְתִסְלַח
לַעֲוֹנֵינוּ כַּכָּתוּב בְּדִבְרֵי קָדְשֶׁךָ: לְמַעַן־שִׁמְךָ יהוה וְסָלַחְתָּ לַעֲוֹנִי כִּי
רַב הוּא:

אֱלֹהֵינוּ וֵאלֹהֵי אֲבוֹתֵינוּ וְאִמּוֹתֵינוּ סְלַח לָנוּ: מְחַל לָנוּ: כַּפֶּר־לָנוּ:

אָנוּ בָנֶיךָ וְאַתָּה אָבִינוּ:	כִּי אָנוּ עַמֶּךָ וְאַתָּה אֱלֹהֵינוּ:
אָנוּ קְהָלֶךָ וְאַתָּה חֶלְקֵנוּ:	אָנוּ עֲבָדֶיךָ וְאַתָּה אֲדוֹנֵינוּ:
אָנוּ צֹאנֶךָ וְאַתָּה רוֹעֵנוּ:	אָנוּ נַחֲלָתֶךָ וְאַתָּה גוֹרָלֵנוּ:
אָנוּ פְעֻלָּתֶךָ וְאַתָּה יוֹצְרֵנוּ:	אָנוּ כַרְמֶךָ וְאַתָּה נוֹטְרֵנוּ:
אָנוּ סְגֻלָּתֶךָ וְאַתָּה קְרוֹבֵנוּ:	אָנוּ רַעְיָתֶךָ וְאַתָּה דוֹדֵנוּ:
אָנוּ מַאֲמִירֶךָ וְאַתָּה מַאֲמִירֵנוּ: ←	אָנוּ עַמֶּךָ וְאַתָּה מַלְכֵּנוּ:

Eloheynu velohey avoteynu ve'imoteynu selaḥ lanu. Meḥal lanu.
Kaper lanu.
Ki anu ameḥa ve'atah eloheynu. Anu vaneḥa ve'atah avinu.
Anu avadeḥa ve'atah adoneynu. Anu kehaleḥa ve'ata ḥelkenu.
Anu naḥalateḥa ve'atah goralenu. Anu tzoneḥa ve'atah ro'enu.
Anu ḥarmeḥa ve'atah notrenu. Anu fe'ulateḥa ve'atah yotzrenu.
Anu rayateḥa ve'atah dodenu. Anu segulateḥa ve'atah kerovenu.
Anu ameḥa ve'atah malkenu. Anu ma'amireḥa ve'atah
ma'amirenu. ↲

למען...הוא / For...wrong (Psalms 25:11).

We are strong-willed and stubborn,
but you are merciful and gracious.
We are stiff-necked, but you are slow to anger.
We are full of error, but you are full of mercy.
We—our days are like a passing shadow,
but you are one whose years shall never end.

Our God, our ancients' God,
may our prayer come before you.
Hide not from our supplication,
for we are not so insolent and stubborn
as to say, here in your presence,
"HOLY ONE, God of our fathers and our mothers,
We are righteous, and we have not sinned,"
for we indeed have sinned. ⤺

אָנוּ עַזֵּי פָנִים וְאַתָּה רַחוּם וְחַנּוּן: אָנוּ קְשֵׁי עֹרֶף וְאַתָּה אֶרֶךְ אַפַּיִם:
אָנוּ מְלֵאֵי עָוֹן וְאַתָּה מָלֵא רַחֲמִים: אָנוּ יָמֵינוּ כְּצֵל עוֹבֵר וְאַתָּה הוּא
וּשְׁנוֹתֶיךָ לֹא יִתָּמּוּ:

אֱלֹהֵינוּ וֵאלֹהֵי אֲבוֹתֵינוּ וְאִמּוֹתֵינוּ תָּבוֹא לְפָנֶיךָ תְּפִלָּתֵנוּ וְאַל
תִּתְעַלַּם מִתְּחִנָּתֵנוּ שֶׁאֵין אֲנַחְנוּ עַזֵּי פָנִים וּקְשֵׁי עֹרֶף לוֹמַר לְפָנֶיךָ
יהוה אֱלֹהֵינוּ וֵאלֹהֵי אֲבוֹתֵינוּ וְאִמּוֹתֵינוּ צַדִּיקִים אֲנַחְנוּ וְלֹא חָטָאנוּ
אֲבָל אֲנַחְנוּ חָטָאנוּ: ←

We rise.

We have acted wrongly,
we have been untrue,
and we have gained unlawfully
and have defamed.
We have harmed others,
we have wrought injustice,
we have zealously transgressed,
and we have hurt
and have told lies.
We have improperly advised,
and we have covered up the truth,
and we have laughed in scorn.
We have misused responsibility
and have neglected others.
We have stubbornly rebelled.
We have offended,
we have perverted justice,
we have stirred up enmity,
and we have kept ourselves from change.
We have reached out to evil,
we have shamelessly corrupted
and have treated others with disdain.
Yes, we have thrown ourselves off course,
and we have tempted and misled.

אָשַׁמְנוּ: בָּגַדְנוּ: גָּזַלְנוּ: דִּבַּֽרְנוּ דֹּֽפִי:
הֶעֱוִֽינוּ: וְהִרְשַֽׁעְנוּ: זַֽדְנוּ: חָמַֽסְנוּ:
טָפַֽלְנוּ שֶֽׁקֶר: יָעַֽצְנוּ רָע: כִּזַּֽבְנוּ: לַֽצְנוּ:
מָרַֽדְנוּ: נִאַֽצְנוּ: סָרַֽרְנוּ: עָוִֽינוּ:
פָּשַֽׁעְנוּ: צָרַֽרְנוּ: קִשִּֽׁינוּ עֹֽרֶף: רָשַֽׁעְנוּ:
שִׁחַֽתְנוּ: תִּעַֽבְנוּ: תָּעִֽינוּ: תִּעְתָּֽעְנוּ:

Ashamnu bagadnu gazalnu dibarnu dofi.
He'evinu vehirshanu zadnu hamasnu
tafalnu shaker. Ya'atznu ra, kizavnu latznu
maradnu ni'atznu sararnu avinu
pashanu tzararnu kishinu oref. Rashanu
shihatnu ti'avnu ta'inu titanu.

For an alternative Al Ḥet, turn to page 969.

You know the secrets of the universe,
the most hidden recesses of all that lives.
You search the chambers of our inner being,
you examine the conscience and the heart.
There is nothing hidden from you,
nothing is concealed before your eyes.
So, let it be your will,
ETERNAL ONE, our God, God of our ancestors,
that you may grant forgiveness to us for all of our sins,
and be merciful to us for all of our injustices,
and let us atone for all we have done wrong:

For the wrong that we have done before you
   in the closing of the heart,
and for the wrong that we have done before you
   without knowing what we do.
For the wrong that we have done before you
   whether open or concealed,
and for the wrong that we have done before you
   knowingly and by deceit. ↩

For an alternative Al Ḥet, *turn to page 969.*

אַתָּה יוֹדֵעַ רָזֵי עוֹלָם וְתַעֲלוּמוֹת סִתְרֵי כָל חָי: אַתָּה חוֹפֵשׂ כָּל חַדְרֵי
בָטֶן וּבוֹחֵן כְּלָיוֹת וָלֵב: אֵין דָּבָר נֶעְלָם מִמֶּךָ וְאֵין נִסְתָּר מִנֶּגֶד
עֵינֶיךָ: וּבְכֵן יְהִי רָצוֹן מִלְּפָנֶיךָ יהוה אֱלֹהֵינוּ וֵאלֹהֵי אֲבוֹתֵינוּ
וְאִמּוֹתֵינוּ שֶׁתִּסְלַח לָנוּ עַל כָּל חַטֹּאתֵינוּ וְתִמְחַל לָנוּ עַל כָּל עֲוֹנוֹתֵינוּ
וּתְכַפֶּר לָנוּ עַל כָּל פְּשָׁעֵינוּ:

עַל חֵטְא

עַל חֵטְא שֶׁחָטָאנוּ לְפָנֶיךָ בְּאִמּוּץ הַלֵּב:
וְעַל חֵטְא שֶׁחָטָאנוּ לְפָנֶיךָ בִּבְלִי דָעַת:
עַל חֵטְא שֶׁחָטָאנוּ לְפָנֶיךָ בְּגָלוּי וּבַסָּתֶר:
וְעַל חֵטְא שֶׁחָטָאנוּ לְפָנֶיךָ בְּדַעַת וּבְמִרְמָה: ←

COMMENTARY. It is customary for the entire community to tap their chests during the recitation of the *Vidui*. By doing this as a collective, we ensure that the one who knows when he/she should be tapping will not be humiliated by tapping alone.   D.A.T.

For the wrong that we have done before you
   through the prompting of the heart,
and for the wrong that we have done before you
   through the influence of others.
For the wrong that we have done before you,
   whether by intention or mistake,
and for the wrong that we have done before you
   by the hand of violence.
For the wrong that we have done before you
   through our foolishness of speech,
and for the wrong that we have done before you
   through an evil inclination.

And for them all, God of forgiveness,
   please forgive us, pardon us, help us atone!

For the wrong that we have done before you
   in the palming of a bribe,
and for the wrong that we have done before you
   by expressions of contempt.
For the wrong that we have done before you
   through misuse of food and drink,
and for the wrong that we have done before you
   by our avarice and greed.
For the wrong that we have done before you
   through offensive gaze,
and for the wrong that we have done before you
   through a condescending glance.

And for them all, God of forgiveness,
   please forgive us, pardon us, help us atone! ⤶

עַל חֵטְא שֶׁחָטָאנוּ לְפָנֶיךָ בְּהַרְהוֹר הַלֵּב:

וְעַל חֵטְא שֶׁחָטָאנוּ לְפָנֶיךָ בִּוְעִידַת זְנוּת:

עַל חֵטְא שֶׁחָטָאנוּ לְפָנֶיךָ בְּזָדוֹן וּבִשְׁגָגָה:

וְעַל חֵטְא שֶׁחָטָאנוּ לְפָנֶיךָ בְּחֹזֶק יָד:

עַל חֵטְא שֶׁחָטָאנוּ לְפָנֶיךָ בְּטִפְּשׁוּת פֶּה:

וְעַל חֵטְא שֶׁחָטָאנוּ לְפָנֶיךָ בְּיֵצֶר הָרָע:

וְעַל כֻּלָּם אֱלוֹהַּ סְלִיחוֹת סְלַח לָנוּ: מְחַל לָנוּ: כַּפֶּר־לָנוּ:

Ve'al kulam eloah seliḥot selaḥ lanu. Meḥal lanu. Kaper lanu.

עַל חֵטְא שֶׁחָטָאנוּ לְפָנֶיךָ בְּכַפַּת שֹׁחַד:

וְעַל חֵטְא שֶׁחָטָאנוּ לְפָנֶיךָ בְּלָצוֹן:

עַל חֵטְא שֶׁחָטָאנוּ לְפָנֶיךָ בְּמַאֲכָל וּבְמִשְׁתֶּה:

וְעַל חֵטְא שֶׁחָטָאנוּ לְפָנֶיךָ בְּנֶשֶׁךְ וּבְמַרְבִּית:

עַל חֵטְא שֶׁחָטָאנוּ לְפָנֶיךָ בְּשִׂקּוּר עָיִן:

וְעַל חֵטְא שֶׁחָטָאנוּ לְפָנֶיךָ בְּעֵינַיִם רָמוֹת:

וְעַל כֻּלָּם אֱלוֹהַּ סְלִיחוֹת סְלַח לָנוּ: מְחַל לָנוּ: כַּפֶּר־לָנוּ: ←

Ve'al kulam eloah seliḥot selaḥ lanu. Meḥal lanu. Kaper lanu. ↵

For the wrong that we have done before you
   by our quickness to oppose,
and for the wrong that we have done before you
   by deception of a friend.
For the wrong that we have done before you
   by unwillingness to change,
and for the wrong that we have done before you
   by our running to embrace an evil act.
For the wrong that we have done before you
   by our groundless hatred,
and for the wrong that we have done before you
   in the giving of false pledges.

And for them all, God of forgiveness,
   please forgive us, pardon us, help us atone! ↵

עַל חֵטְא שֶׁחָטָאנוּ לְפָנֶיךָ בִּפְלִילוּת:

וְעַל חֵטְא שֶׁחָטָאנוּ לְפָנֶיךָ בִּצְדִיַּת רֵעַ:

עַל חֵטְא שֶׁחָטָאנוּ לְפָנֶיךָ בְּקַשְׁיוּת עֹרֶף:

וְעַל חֵטְא שֶׁחָטָאנוּ לְפָנֶיךָ בְּרִיצַת רַגְלַיִם לְהָרַע:

עַל חֵטְא שֶׁחָטָאנוּ לְפָנֶיךָ בְּשִׂנְאַת חִנָּם:

וְעַל חֵטְא שֶׁחָטָאנוּ לְפָנֶיךָ בִּתְשׂוּמֶת יָד:

וְעַל כֻּלָּם אֱלוֹהַּ סְלִיחוֹת סְלַח לָנוּ: מְחַל לָנוּ: כַּפֶּר־לָנוּ: ←

Ve'al kulam eloah seliḥot selaḥ lanu. Meḥal lanu. Kaper lanu. ↩

And for mitzvot that call on us to act,
and for mitzvot that bid us not to act,
for mitzvot that say: "Arise, and do...!"
and for mitzvot that do not say: "Arise, and do...!"
for those that are made known to us,
and those that are not known to us.

Those that are known to us
are things we have acknowledged
and confessed before you,
but those that are not known to us
are things revealed and known only to you,
as it is said: "The hidden things
belong to THE ETERNAL ONE, our God.
What is revealed belongs to us and to our children,
always and forever—all the matters
of this Torah that are ours to carry out."
For you are the source of all forgiveness,
the fount of mercy for each and every generation,
and apart from you we have no sovereign
so full of mercy and forgiveness, none but you.

We are seated.

Continue on page 971.

וְעַל מִצְוֺת עֲשֵׂה וְעַל מִצְוֺת לֹא תַעֲשֶׂה בֵּין שֶׁיֶּשׁ־בָּהּ קוּם עֲשֵׂה וּבֵין שֶׁאֵין בָּהּ קוּם עֲשֵׂה אֶת־הַגְּלוּיִּים לָנוּ וְאֶת־שֶׁאֵינָם גְּלוּיִּים לָנוּ: אֶת־ הַגְּלוּיִּים לָנוּ כְּבָר אֲמַרְנוּם לְפָנֶיךָ וְהוֹדִינוּ לְךָ עֲלֵיהֶם וְאֶת־שֶׁאֵינָם גְּלוּיִּים לָנוּ לְפָנֶיךָ הֵם גְּלוּיִּים וִידוּעִים כַּדָּבָר שֶׁנֶּאֱמַר: הַנִּסְתָּרֹת לַיהֹוָה אֱלֹהֵינוּ וְהַנִּגְלֹת לָנוּ וּלְבָנֵינוּ עַד עוֹלָם לַעֲשׂוֹת אֶת־כָּל־דִּבְרֵי הַתּוֹרָה הַזֹּאת כִּי אַתָּה סָלְחָן בְּכָל־דּוֹר וָדוֹר וּמִבַּלְעָדֶיךָ אֵין לָנוּ מֶלֶךְ מוֹחֵל וְסוֹלֵחַ אֶלָּא אָתָּה:

We are seated.

Continue on page 972.

הנסתרות...הזאת / The hidden...out (Deuteronomy 29:28).

ALTERNATIVE AL ḤET

For the wrong we did before You by listening to voices at odds
with what we knew was right;

For the wrong we did before You by not listening to voices
telling us unpleasant truths;

For the wrong we did before You by closing our ears to the poor
and the hungry;

For the wrong we did before You by not working at
relationships;

For the wrong we did before You by making no time for those
who needed us;

For the wrong we did before You by abusing our health;

For the wrong we did before You by unnecessary anger;

For the wrong we did before You by giving in to bullies;

For the wrong we did before You by talking of others' failings
behind their backs instead of face to face;

וְעַל כֻּלָּם אֱלוֹהַ סְלִיחוֹת סְלַח לָנוּ: מְחַל לָנוּ: כַּפֶּר־לָנוּ:

Ve'al kulam eloah seliḥot selaḥ lanu. Meḥal lanu. Kaper lanu.

For all these wrongs, O God of forgiveness, forgive us, wipe the
slate clean, grant us atonement.

For the wrong we did before You by forgiving in Jews what we
condemn in others;

For the wrong we did before You by forgiving in others what we
condemn in Jews;

For the wrong we did before You by taking Israel for granted;

For the wrong we did before You by polluting our environment;

For the wrong we did before You by cutting ourselves off from
people of other races and cultures;

For the wrong we did before You by being afraid of others'
disabilities; ↵

For the wrong we did before You by callous treatment of those with whom we live;

For the wrong we did before You by callous treatment of those with whom we work or study;

וְעַל כֻּלָּם אֱלֽוֹהַּ סְלִיחוֹת סְלַח לָנוּ: מְחַל לָנוּ: כַּפֶּר־לָנוּ:

Ve'al kulam e_loah seliḥot selaḥ _lanu. Meḥal _lanu. Kaper _lanu.

For all these wrongs, O God of forgiveness, forgive us, wipe the slate clean, grant us atonement.

For the wrong we did before You by ignoring the everpresent threat of war;

For the wrong we did before You by bearing grudges;

For the wrong we did before You by indulging in excessive luxuries;

For the wrong we did before You by giving less *tzedakah* than we could afford;

For the wrong we did before You by manipulating others for our own gain;

For the wrong we did before You by making those we love feel guilty;

For the wrong we did before You by ignoring important issues in our own community and country;

For the wrong we did before You by being ashamed to act morally in public;

וְעַל כֻּלָּם אֱלֽוֹהַּ סְלִיחוֹת סְלַח לָנוּ: מְחַל לָנוּ: כַּפֶּר־לָנוּ:

Ve'al kulam e_loah seliḥot selaḥ _lanu. Meḥal _lanu. Kaper _lanu.

For all these wrongs, O God of forgiveness, forgive us, wipe the slate clean, grant us atonement.

We are seated.

On Shabbat add the words in parenthesis.

Our God, our ancients' God,
forgive us our transgressions,
this Day (of Shabbat, and) of Atonement,
blot out and cause to pass away
our wrongdoings and our errors
from before your eyes, as it is said:
"I, yes I, shall be the one
who blots out your wrongdoing, for my sake;
your errors I shall not remember any more!"
And it is said: "I have made your sins
vanish like a stormcloud,
and, like a mist, the things you have done wrong.
Return to me, for it is I who have redeemed you!"
And it is said: "For on this day,
atonement shall be made for you,
to make you clean from all of your wrongdoings.
Before THE FOUNT OF MERCY, you shall all be clean." ↵

אֱלֹהֵֽינוּ וֵאלֹהֵי אֲבוֹתֵֽינוּ וְאִמּוֹתֵֽינוּ מְחַל לַעֲוֹנוֹתֵֽינוּ בְּיוֹם (הַשַּׁבָּת
הַזֶּה וּבְיוֹם) הַכִּפֻּרִים הַזֶּה: מְחֵה וְהַעֲבֵר פְּשָׁעֵֽינוּ וְחַטֹּאתֵֽינוּ מִנֶּֽגֶד
עֵינֶֽיךָ: כָּאָמוּר: אָנֹכִי אָנֹכִי הוּא מֹחֶה פְשָׁעֶֽיךָ לְמַעֲנִי וְחַטֹּאתֶֽיךָ לֹא
אֶזְכֹּר: וְנֶאֱמַר: מָחִֽיתִי כָעָב פְּשָׁעֶֽיךָ וְכֶעָנָן חַטֹּאתֶֽיךָ שֽׁוּבָה אֵלַי כִּי
גְאַלְתִּֽיךָ: וְנֶאֱמַר: כִּי בַיּוֹם הַזֶּה יְכַפֵּר עֲלֵיכֶם לְטַהֵר אֶתְכֶם מִכֹּל
חַטֹּאתֵיכֶם לִפְנֵי יהוה תִּטְהָֽרוּ: ←

אנכי...אזכר /I, yes...more! (Isaiah 43:25).
מחיתי...גאלתיך /I have...you! (Isaiah 44:22).
כי ביום...תטהרו /For on...clean (Leviticus 16:30).

On Shabbat add the words in parenthesis.

Our God, our ancients' God (take pleasure in our rest),
enable us to realize holiness with your mitzvot,
give us our portion in your Torah,
let us enjoy the good things of your world,
and gladden us with your salvation,
(and help us to perpetuate, ETERNAL ONE, our God,
your holy Shabbat, with love and joy,
and let all Israel, and all who treat your name as holy,
rest upon this day,) and refine our hearts
to serve you truthfully.
For you are a forgiving God to Israel,
and compassionate to all the tribes of Yeshurun
in each and every generation,
and apart from you we have no sovereign,
none full of compassion and forgiveness,
except you.
Blessed are you, FORGIVING ONE,
sovereign of mercy and forgiveness
for our wrongdoings, and for those
of all your kin, the house of Israel,
you who make our guilt to pass away,
year after year,
the sovereign power over all the earth
who raises up to holiness
(Shabbat,) the people Israel
and the Day of Atonement. ↩

On Shabbat add the words in parenthesis.

אֱלֹהֵֽינוּ וֵאלֹהֵי אֲבוֹתֵֽינוּ וְאִמּוֹתֵֽינוּ (רְצֵה בִמְנוּחָתֵֽנוּ) קַדְּשֵֽׁנוּ
בְּמִצְוֹתֶֽיךָ וְתֵן חֶלְקֵֽנוּ בְּתוֹרָתֶֽךָ: שַׂבְּעֵֽנוּ מִטּוּבֶֽךָ וְשַׂמְּחֵֽנוּ
בִּישׁוּעָתֶֽךָ: (וְהַנְחִילֵֽנוּ יהוה אֱלֹהֵֽינוּ בְּאַהֲבָה וּבְרָצוֹן שַׁבַּת קָדְשֶֽׁךָ
וְיָנֽוּחוּ בָה יִשְׂרָאֵל מְקַדְּשֵׁי שְׁמֶֽךָ) וְטַהֵר לִבֵּֽנוּ לְעָבְדְּךָ בֶּאֱמֶת: כִּי
אַתָּה סָלְחָן לְיִשְׂרָאֵל וּמָחֳלָן לְשִׁבְטֵי יְשֻׁרוּן בְּכָל־דּוֹר וָדוֹר
וּמִבַּלְעָדֶֽיךָ אֵין לָֽנוּ מֶֽלֶךְ מוֹחֵל וְסוֹלֵֽחַ אֶלָּא אָֽתָּה: בָּרוּךְ אַתָּה
יהוה מֶֽלֶךְ מוֹחֵל וְסוֹלֵֽחַ לַעֲוֹנוֹתֵֽינוּ וְלַעֲוֹנוֹת עַמּוֹ בֵּית יִשְׂרָאֵל
וּמַעֲבִיר אַשְׁמוֹתֵֽינוּ בְּכָל־שָׁנָה וְשָׁנָה מֶֽלֶךְ עַל־כָּל־הָאָֽרֶץ מְקַדֵּשׁ
(הַשַּׁבָּת וְ) יִשְׂרָאֵל וְיוֹם הַכִּפֻּרִים: ←

5. AVODAH / WORSHIP

Take pleasure, GRACIOUS ONE, our God, in Israel your people; lovingly accept their fervent prayer. May Israel's worship always be acceptable to you.

And may our eyes behold your homecoming, with merciful intent, to Zion. Blessed are you, THE FAITHFUL ONE, who brings your presence home to Zion.

6. HODA'AH / THANKS

We give thanks to you that you are THE ALL-MERCIFUL, our God, God of our ancestors, today and always. A firm, enduring source of life, a shield to us in time of trial, you are ever there, from age to age. We acknowledge you, declare your praise, and thank you for our lives entrusted to your hand, our souls placed in your care, for your miracles that greet us every day, and for your wonders and the good things that are with us every hour, morning, noon, and night. Good One, whose kindness never stops, Kind One, whose loving acts have never failed—always have we placed our hope in you.

For all these things, your name be blessed and raised in honor always, sovereign of ours, forever. ↵

עֲבוֹדָה 5

רְצֵה יהוה אֱלֹהֵינוּ בְּעַמְּךָ יִשְׂרָאֵל וְלַהַב תְּפִלָּתָם בְּאַהֲבָה תְקַבֵּל בְּרָצוֹן וּתְהִי לְרָצוֹן תָּמִיד עֲבוֹדַת יִשְׂרָאֵל עַמֶּךָ:

וְתֶחֱזֶינָה עֵינֵינוּ בְּשׁוּבְךָ לְצִיּוֹן בְּרַחֲמִים: בָּרוּךְ אַתָּה יהוה הַמַּחֲזִיר שְׁכִינָתוֹ לְצִיּוֹן:

הוֹדָאָה 6

מוֹדִים אֲנַחְנוּ לָךְ שָׁאַתָּה הוּא יהוה אֱלֹהֵינוּ וֵאלֹהֵי אֲבוֹתֵינוּ וְאִמּוֹתֵינוּ לְעוֹלָם וָעֶד צוּר חַיֵּינוּ מָגֵן יִשְׁעֵנוּ אַתָּה הוּא לְדוֹר וָדוֹר: נוֹדֶה לְּךָ וּנְסַפֵּר תְּהִלָּתֶךָ עַל חַיֵּינוּ הַמְּסוּרִים בְּיָדֶךָ וְעַל נִשְׁמוֹתֵינוּ הַפְּקוּדוֹת לָךְ וְעַל נִסֶּיךָ שֶׁבְּכָל יוֹם עִמָּנוּ וְעַל נִפְלְאוֹתֶיךָ וְטוֹבוֹתֶיךָ שֶׁבְּכָל־עֵת עֶרֶב וָבֹקֶר וְצָהֳרָיִם: הַטּוֹב כִּי לֹא כָלוּ רַחֲמֶיךָ וְהַמְרַחֵם כִּי לֹא תַמּוּ חֲסָדֶיךָ מֵעוֹלָם קִוִּינוּ לָךְ:

וְעַל כֻּלָּם יִתְבָּרַךְ וְיִתְרוֹמַם שִׁמְךָ מַלְכֵּנוּ תָּמִיד לְעוֹלָם וָעֶד: ←

Our creator, our sovereign,
remember your love for us,
and banish pestilence and war,
and famine, and captivity, and slaughter,
and crime, and violence, and plague,
and terrible disaster,
and every kind of illness,
and every kind of tragic accident,
and every kind of strife,
and all the forms of retribution,
and all evil decrees,
and groundless hatred,
Remove them from our midst,
and from the midst of all
who dwell on earth.
And write down for a good life
all who share your covenant.

Let all life acknowledge you! May all beings praise your name in truth, O God, our rescue and our aid. Blessed are you, THE GRACIOUS ONE, whose name is good, to whom all thanks are due. ↵

אָבִֽינוּ מַלְכֵּֽנוּ זְכֹר רַחֲמֶֽיךָ וְכַלֵּה דֶּֽבֶר וְחֶֽרֶב וְרָעָב וּשְׁבִי וּמַשְׁחִית וְעָוֹן וּשְׁמָד וּמַגֵּפָה וּפֶֽגַע רַע וְכָל־מַחֲלָה וְכָל־תְּקָלָה וְכָל־קְטָטָה וְכָל־מִינֵי פֻרְעָנִיּוֹת וְכָל־גְּזֵרָה רָעָה וְשִׂנְאַת חִנָּם מֵעָלֵֽינוּ וּמֵעַל כָּל־ בְּנֵי עוֹלָמֶֽךָ:

וּכְתֹב לְחַיִּים טוֹבִים כָּל־בְּנֵי בְרִיתֶֽךָ:
וְכֹל הַחַיִּים יוֹדֽוּךָ סֶּֽלָה וִיהַלְלוּ אֶת שִׁמְךָ בֶּאֱמֶת הָאֵל יְשׁוּעָתֵֽנוּ וְעֶזְרָתֵֽנוּ סֶֽלָה: בָּרוּךְ אַתָּה יהוה הַטּוֹב שִׁמְךָ וּלְךָ נָאֶה לְהוֹדוֹת: ←

7. BIRKAT HASHALOM / BLESSING FOR PEACE

Our God, our ancients' God,
bless us with the threefold blessing
spoken from the mouth of Aaron and his sons, as is said:

May THE ETERNAL bless you
and protect you.   Let it be God's will!

May THE ETERNAL'S face give light
to you, and show you favor.   Let it be God's will!

May THE ETERNAL'S face be lifted
toward you, and bestow upon you
peace.   Let it be God's will! ↰

COMMENTARY. Traditionally the Priestly Blessing was done by the male descendants of the *kohanim*. In some congregations the *sheliah tzibur* (service leader) recites the blessing, and the congregation responds with "*Ken yehi ratzon*." In other communities all the members of the congregation wrap arms and tallitot around each other and recite the blessing together. Another way to enact the Priestly Blessing is for each congregant to turn to a neighbor and recite the first half of each blessing, while the neighbor responds with the second half of the blessing.   Michael M. Cohen

COMMENTARY. Rabbi Lavy Becker of Montreal noticed that when this blessing was pronounced in the synagogue of Pisa, all the children gathered under the sheltering wings of their fathers' tallitot to receive it. He recognized this "as a reconstruction of the ancient priestly ceremony." He modified that custom so that those wearing a tallit share it with their neighbors and all are under the sheltering wings of the Sheḥinah as we bless each other. It is now an established part of Canadian Reconstructionist practice.   E.M.

שלום...יברכך / May...peace (Numbers 6:24-26).

אֱלֹהֵֽינוּ וֵאלֹהֵי אֲבוֹתֵֽינוּ וְאִמּוֹתֵֽינוּ בָּרְכֵֽנוּ בַּבְּרָכָה הַמְשֻׁלֶּֽשֶׁת
הָאֲמוּרָה מִפִּי אַהֲרֹן וּבָנָיו כָּאָמוּר:

יְבָרֶכְךָ יְהֹוָה וְיִשְׁמְרֶֽךָ

כֵּן יְהִי רָצוֹן:

יָאֵר יְהֹוָה פָּנָיו אֵלֶֽיךָ
וִיחֻנֶּֽךָ:

כֵּן יְהִי רָצוֹן:

יִשָּׂא יְהֹוָה פָּנָיו אֵלֶֽיךָ
וְיָשֵׂם לְךָ שָׁלוֹם:

כֵּן יְהִי רָצוֹן:

Eloheynu veylohey avoteynu ve'imoteynu
barehenu baberahah hamshuleshet
ha'amurah mipi aharon uvanav ka'amur:
Yevareheha adonay veyishmereha.   Ken yehi ratzon.
Ya'er adonay panav eleha vihuneka.   Ken yehi ratzon.
Yisa adonay panav eleha veyasem leha shalom.   Ken yehi ratzon.

THIRD CONFESSION: FOR OUR WORLD

They brought to him the ladle and the fire-pan,
and he took two handfuls of the incense,
which he placed into the ladle,
whether large or small, according to his hand—
thus was its measurement.
He took the fire-pan in his right hand,
and the ladle in his left, and he proceeded
through the Temple, till he came into the space
between the ark-curtains that separated
the sanctuary from the Holy of Holies.
The space between them was a forearm's length.
He came before the Ark, and placed the fire-pan
between two linen cloths.
He heaped the incense on the coals,
and the entire chamber filled with smoke.
He then would exit by his route of entry,
and would offer a short prayer in the outer chamber,
making sure to keep it brief, so as not to frighten
the assembled Israelites.

He took the sacrificial blood,
and entered the place he previously had entered,
and he stood again where he had stood,
and he sprinkled from the bowl of blood,
one time above, seven below,
and counted thus:
One. One and one. One and two. One and three.
One and four. One and five. One and six. One and seven.

And thus would he declare:
"O, Holy One, they have sinned,
they have done wrong, and they have gone astray before you—
these the House of Israel, your people." ↵

THIRD CONFESSION: FOR THE WORLD

הוֹצִיאוּ לוֹ אֶת־הַכַּף וְאֶת־הַמַּחְתָּה וְחָפַן מְלֹא חָפְנָיו וְנָתַן לְתוֹךְ הַכַּף: הַגָּדוֹל לְפִי גָדְלוֹ וְהַקָּטָן לְפִי קַטְנוֹ וְכָךְ הָיְתָה מִדָּתָהּ: נָטַל אֶת־הַמַּחְתָּה בִּימִינוֹ וְאֶת־הַכַּף בִּשְׂמֹאלוֹ: הָיָה מְהַלֵּךְ בְּהֵיכָל עַד שֶׁמַּגִּיעַ לְבֵין שְׁתֵּי הַפְּרֹכוֹת הַמַּבְדִּילוֹת בֵּין הַקֹּדֶשׁ וּבֵין קֹדֶשׁ־ הַקֳּדָשִׁים וּבֵינֵיהֶן אַמָּה: הִגִּיעַ לָאָרוֹן נוֹתֵן אֶת־הַמַּחְתָּה בֵּין שְׁנֵי הַבַּדִּים: צָבַר אֶת־הַקְּטֹרֶת עַל גַּבֵּי הַגֶּחָלִים וְנִתְמַלָּא כָל־הַבַּיִת כֻּלּוֹ עָשָׁן: יָצָא וּבָא לוֹ בְּדֶרֶךְ בֵּית־כְּנִיסָתוֹ וּמִתְפַּלֵּל תְּפִלָּה קְצָרָה בַּבַּיִת־ הַחִיצוֹן וְלֹא הָיָה מַאֲרִיךְ בִּתְפִלָּתוֹ כְּדֵי שֶׁלֹּא לְהַבְעִית אֶת־יִשְׂרָאֵל:

נָטַל אֶת־הַדָּם מִמִּי שֶׁהָיָה מְמָרֵס בּוֹ נִכְנַס לְמָקוֹם שֶׁנִּכְנַס וְעָמַד בִּמְקוֹם שֶׁעָמַד וְהִזָּה מִמֶּנּוּ אַחַת לְמַעְלָה וְשֶׁבַע לְמַטָּה וְלֹא הָיָה מִתְכַּוֵּן לְהַזּוֹת לֹא לְמַעְלָה וְלֹא לְמַטָּה אֶלָּא כְּמַצְלִיף: וְכָךְ הָיָה מוֹנֶה אַחַת: אַחַת וְאַחַת: אַחַת וּשְׁתַּיִם: אַחַת וְשָׁלֹשׁ: אַחַת וְאַרְבַּע: אַחַת וְחָמֵשׁ: אַחַת וָשֵׁשׁ: אַחַת וָשֶׁבַע:

וְכָךְ הָיָה אוֹמֵר אָנָּא הַשֵּׁם חָטְאוּ עָווּ פָּשְׁעוּ לְפָנֶיךָ עַמְּךָ בֵּית יִשְׂרָאֵל: ←

COMMENTARY. Clouds and vapors are sometimes unpleasant, undesirable, obscuring that which should be clearly seen. On the other hand, they sometimes shield us from too much sunlight and heat. In this mode, they may also shield from viewing too fully that which cannot or should not be fully seen.

The incense cloud is biblically associated with the mystery of God's Presence, serving as both pointer to and protector of that Presence. Even as God does "appear in the cloud upon the cover" (Leviticus 16:2), we notice that both this Appearance and we, the gazers, are shielded by the incense cloud. Similarly, as the High Priest approaches the Holy of Holies, "he heaped the incense on the coals and the entire chamber filled with smoke."   E.G.

And thus do we declare:
"O, Holy One, please grant atonement for the sins,
the wrongdoing and the transgressions
that the House of Israel has done before you,
they, and all who dwell on earth.
And bring us all to the world's repair through divine rule,
as it is written in the Torah of your servant Moses:
'For on this day, atonement shall be made for you,
to make you clean from all your wrongdoings
before THE FOUNT OF MERCY.'"

And the priests,
and all the people standing in the courtyard,
when they would hear the glorious and awesome Name of God
uttered aloud distinctly from the High Priest's mouth,
in holiness and purity,
would prostrate themselves, and bow down in acknowledgment,
and touch their faces to the ground, and say:
"Blessed are the glorious Name and majesty of God,
to all eternity!"

And the High Priest, in turn,
would thus complete the utterance of the Name
in sacred devotion, facing those who offered blessing,
and declare to them: "You shall be clean!"
And you, God, in your goodness, stir up your compassion,
and forgive your world.

The High Priest would pronounce sanctification,
and immerse himself. They then would bring him
garments of white, and he would dress,
and sanctify his hands and feet.
They brought him his own clothes, and he would put them on,
and they would then escort him to his house,
And he made celebration with those close to him,
upon emerging safely from the holy place.

וְכָךְ אָנוּ אוֹמְרִים אָנָּא הַשֵּׁם כַּפֶּר־נָא לַחֲטָאִים וְלָעֲווֹנוֹת וְלַפְּשָׁעִים
שֶׁחָטְאוּ וְשֶׁעָווּ וְשֶׁפָּשְׁעוּ לְפָנֶיךָ בֵּית יִשְׂרָאֵל וְכֹל יוֹשְׁבֵי תֵבֵל
וְהַגִּיעֵנוּ לְתַקֵּן עוֹלָם בְּמַלְכוּת שַׁדַּי כַּכָּתוּב בְּתוֹרָתֶךָ כִּי בַיּוֹם הַזֶּה
יְכַפֵּר עֲלֵיכֶם לְטַהֵר אֶתְכֶם מִכֹּל חַטֹּאתֵיכֶם לִפְנֵי יהוה:

וְהַכֹּהֲנִים וְהָעָם הָעוֹמְדִים בָּעֲזָרָה כְּשֶׁהָיוּ שׁוֹמְעִים אֶת־הַשֵּׁם הַנִּכְבָּד
וְהַנּוֹרָא מְפֹרָשׁ יוֹצֵא מִפִּי כֹהֵן גָּדוֹל בִּקְדֻשָּׁה וּבְטָהֳרָה הָיוּ כּוֹרְעִים
וּמִשְׁתַּחֲוִים וּמוֹדִים וְנוֹפְלִים עַל פְּנֵיהֶם וְאוֹמְרִים בָּרוּךְ שֵׁם כְּבוֹד
מַלְכוּתוֹ לְעוֹלָם וָעֶד: וְאַף הוּא הָיָה מִתְכַּוֵּן לִגְמֹר אֶת־הַשֵּׁם כְּנֶגֶד
הַמְבָרְכִים וְאוֹמֵר לָהֶם תִּטְהָרוּ: וְאַתָּה בְּטוּבְךָ מְעוֹרֵר רַחֲמֶיךָ וְסוֹלֵחַ
לְאִישׁ חֲסִידֶךָ:

קַדֵּשׁ וְטָבַל: הֵבִיאוּ לוֹ בִגְדֵי לָבָן וְלָבַשׁ וְקִדֵּשׁ יָדָיו וְרַגְלָיו: הֵבִיאוּ
לוֹ בִגְדֵי עַצְמוֹ וְלָבַשׁ: וּמְלַוִּין אוֹתוֹ עַד בֵּיתוֹ וְיוֹם־טוֹב הָיָה עוֹשֶׂה
לְאוֹהֲבָיו בְּשָׁעָה שֶׁיָּצָא בְשָׁלוֹם מִן הַקֹּדֶשׁ:

DERASH. What is God's holy of holies? Not a shrine in the Temple built of
stone and wood. Rather, a sanctuary for compassion, a preserve of
kindness, a refuge of devotion in the human heart.   S.D.R.

COMMENTARY. As with Moses in the cleft of the rock (Exodus 33:20-23),
here, too, the Presence of the Divine must not exceed the human capacity
to receive and withstand it. Thus even on this holiest of days, in this
holiest of places, the priestly apprehension of the Divine is only partial.

As with them, all the more so with us: we who are finite can never receive
the Infinite in its fullness. Yet the assurance of this Presence, the glimpse
of this Glory, is as sweet and sustaining to our spirits as is the incense to
our nostrils.   E.G.

כִּי...יהוה / For...MERCY (Leviticus 16:30).

What I learned about myself is that freedom is indivisible. If I am not free, you are not free, and if you are not free, I cannot have freedom either. What happens to the other person happens to me, not in some philosophical sense, but in a very concrete and immediate way. If to keep others down, their freedom must be taken away, then a condition of the system will be that my freedom must also be diminished. If I have to deny myself, then my own condition is a situation of unfreedom.

What I learned about being Jewish is that there are no lines of division, no unmarked boundaries, between my being Jewish and my being human. The one flows into the other and back again. Human beings are suffering. That they have suffered for centuries does not make their suffering any less pressing. The situation is urgent because suffering and oppression always are now, always happen when they happen, however long they already have happened. We cannot stand idly by. We must make the condition of humanity in any country a matter of personal engagement and personal concern. The frontiers of freedom encompass the whole of humanity. We really are our brothers' and sisters' keepers, and our brothers and our sisters are everyone.

Jacob Neusner

Two paths lie before us. One leads to death, the other to life. If we choose the first path—if we numbly refuse to acknowledge the nearness of extinction, all the while increasing our preparations to bring it about—then we in effect become the allies of death, and in everything we do, our attachment to life will weaken; our vision, blinded to the abyss that has opened at our feet, will dim and grow confused; our will, discouraged by the thought of trying to build on such a precarious foundation anything that is meant to last, will slacken; and we will sink into stupefaction, as though we were gradually weaning ourselves from life in preparation for the end. On the other hand, if we reject our doom, and bend our efforts toward survival—if we arouse ourselves to the peril and act to forestall it, making ourselves the allies of life—then the anesthetic fog will lift: our vision, no longer straining not to see the obvious, will sharpen; our will, finding secure ground to build on, will be restored; and we will take full and clear possession of life again. One day...we will make our choice.

Jonathan Schell

And then all that has divided us will merge
And then compassion will be wedded to power
And then softness will come to a world that is harsh and unkind
And then both men and women will be gentle
And then both women and men will be strong
And then no person will be subject to another's will
And then all will be rich and free and varied
And then the greed of some will give way to the needs of many
And then all will share equally in the Earth's abundance
And then all will care for the sick and the weak and the old
And then all will nourish the young
And then all will cherish life's creatures
And then all will live in harmony with each other and the Earth
And then everywhere will be called Eden once again.

Judy Chicago

Let no one be discouraged by the belief there is nothing one person can do against the enormous array of the world's ills, misery, ignorance and violence. Few will have the greatness to bend history, but each of us can work to change a small portion of events. And in the total of all those acts will be written the history of a generation. It is from numberless, diverse acts of courage and belief that human history is shaped. Each time a person stands up for an ideal or acts to improve the lot of others or strikes out against injustice, he or she sends a tiny ripple of hope. Crossing each other from a million different centers of energy and daring, those ripples can build a current which can sweep down the mightiest walls of oppression and resistance.

Robert F. Kennedy

Rabbi Joshua ben Levi met Elijah the prophet....He asked Elijah: "When will the Messiah come?"

Elijah answered: "Go and ask him yourself."

"Where is he?"

"At the gates of the town."

"How shall I recognize him?"

"He is sitting among the poor lepers. The others unbind all the bandages of their sores at the same time and then rebind them all together. But he unbinds one sore at a time and then binds it again before treating the next one, thinking to himself, 'Perhaps I will be needed, and if so I must not delay.'"

Rabbi Joshua went to the Messiah and said, "Peace unto you, master and teacher."

The Messiah answered, "Peace unto you, son of Levi."

"When will you come, master?" asked Rabbi Joshua.

"Today," came the answer.

Rabbi Joshua returned to Elijah, who asked, "What did he tell you?"...

"He spoke falsely to me," said Rabbi Joshua, "for he said he would come today, but he has not come."

Elijah answered him, "This is what he told you: 'Today—if you will but hearken to God's voice'" (Psalms 95:7).

Talmud Sanhedrin 98a

If you always assume
the one sitting next to you
is the Messiah
waiting for some simple human kindness—

You will soon come to weigh your words
and watch your hands.

And if the Messiah chooses
not to be revealed
in your time—

It will not matter.

Danny Siegel (Adapted from a Yiddish Proverb)

Once, Rabban Yoḥanan ben Zakai was emerging from Jerusalem,
and Rabbi Joshua was walking after him,
and saw the sanctuary lying desolate.
Rabbi Joshua declared:
"Alas for us, it lies in ruins,
the house by which our people Israel purified themselves of sin."
And Rabban Yoḥanan ben Zakai answered him:
"My child, don't let it trouble you, we have another like it to
atone for us.
And what is that? Performing acts of kindness.
As it is said: 'For I desire love, not sacrifice!'"

ઓૹ

Open to me, O you gateways of justice,
let me come in and bless Yah.
Psalms 118:19

The beginning of God's way is truth,
and eternal is your righteous law.
Psalms 119:160

Let one inclined to boast take pride in this alone:
to have understanding and knowledge of Me.
For I am THE ETERNAL, the totality
of love and righteousness within the world,
for in these alone do I desire, says THE FOUNT OF LIFE!
Jeremiah 9:23

Righteousness, and righteousness alone, shall you pursue,
that you may live!
Deuteronomy 16:20

Don't place your trust in falsehoods, saying,
"Here it is! Here it is! Here it is! GOD's palace!"
No, only by mending your ways and deeds wholeheartedly,
only if you bring justice
between one person and another!
Jeremiah 7:4-5

כִּי...זֶבַח / For...sacrifice! (Hosea 6:6).

YOM KIPPUR MUSAF / 991

פַּעַם אַחַת הָיָה רַבָּן יוֹחָנָן בֶּן־זַכַּאי יוֹצֵא מִירוּשָׁלַיִם וְהָיָה רַבִּי
יְהוֹשֻׁעַ הוֹלֵךְ אַחֲרָיו וְרָאָה אֶת־בֵּית הַמִּקְדָּשׁ חָרֵב: אָמַר רַבִּי
יְהוֹשֻׁעַ: אוֹי לָנוּ עַל זֶה שֶׁהוּא חָרֵב מָקוֹם שֶׁמְּכַפְּרִים בּוֹ עֲוֹנוֹתֵיהֶם
שֶׁל יִשְׂרָאֵל: אָמַר לוֹ רַבָּן יוֹחָנָן: בְּנִי אַל יֵרַע לְךָ: יֶשׁ לָנוּ כַּפָּרָה
אַחֶרֶת שֶׁהִיא כְּמוֹתָהּ: וְאֵיזוֹ: גְּמִילוּת חֲסָדִים שֶׁנֶּאֱמַר: כִּי חֶסֶד
חָפַצְתִּי וְלֹא זָבַח:

ॐ

פִּתְחוּ־לִי שַׁעֲרֵי־צֶדֶק אָבֹא־בָם אוֹדֶה יָהּ:

Pithu li sha'arey tzedek avo vam odeh yah.

רֹאשׁ־דְּבָרְךָ אֱמֶת וּלְעוֹלָם כָּל־מִשְׁפַּט צִדְקֶךָ:

כִּי אִם־בְּזֹאת יִתְהַלֵּל הַמִּתְהַלֵּל הַשְׂכֵּל וְיָדֹעַ אוֹתִי כִּי אֲנִי יהוה עֹשֶׂה
חֶסֶד מִשְׁפָּט וּצְדָקָה בָּאָרֶץ כִּי־בְאֵלֶּה חָפַצְתִּי נְאֻם־יהוה:

צֶדֶק צֶדֶק תִּרְדֹּף לְמַעַן תִּחְיֶה:

אַל־תִּבְטְחוּ לָכֶם אֶל־דִּבְרֵי הַשֶּׁקֶר לֵאמֹר הֵיכַל יהוה הֵיכַל יהוה
הֵיכַל יהוה הֵמָּה: כִּי אִם־הֵיטֵיב תֵּיטִיבוּ אֶת־דַּרְכֵיכֶם וְאֶת־
מַעַלְלֵיכֶם אִם־עָשׂוֹ תַעֲשׂוּ מִשְׁפָּט בֵּין אִישׁ וּבֵין רֵעֵהוּ: ←

פעם...זבח / Once...sacrifice! (Avot Derabi Natan 4:17-18).

COMMENTARY. *Tzedakah* derives from the Hebrew word for justice, in
contrast to the word "charity" that derives from the Latin term for love.
The impulse to *tzedakah* must derive from a commitment to justice, not
from a feeling of affection. Undertaking *tzedakah*—righteousness in the
world—is our obligation as God's partners in helping to repair creation.

R.H.

Let them give their bread to one in hunger,
and cover the naked one with clothes.

Ezekiel 18:7

Let each of you not bear a grudge over the misdeed of another,
and do not love false promises, for all such things do I abhor,
says THE ETERNAL ONE.

Zechariah 8:17

Through justice shall you be established,
and kept far from oppression and ruin;
you shall have no fear,
for truly, it shall not come near you.

Isaiah 54:14

And the work of righteousness shall lead to peace,
and justice shall bring quiet and security forever.

Isaiah 32:17

And justice shall roll down like waters,
and righteousness like a mighty stream!

Amos 5:24

For THE CREATOR of all beings
shall be exalted through justice
and sacred divinity through righteousness!

Isaiah 5:16

I shall betroth myself to you in righteousness,
and in justice, and in love, and in compassion.
I shall betroth myself to you in truth,
and you shall know THE FOUNT OF LIFE.

Hosea 2:21-22

For the ANCIENT ONE is righteous, and loves righteous deeds,
the upright shall behold God's face.

Psalms 11:7

A righteous person's mouth speaks wisdom,
such a person's tongue speaks justice.

Psalms 37:30

Light is seeded for the righteous,
happiness for those upright of heart.

Psalms 97:11

Happy are those who keep just law,
and righteousness in every hour!

Psalms 106:3

Open to me, O you gateways of justice,
let me come in and bless Yah!

Psalms 118:19

לַחְמוֹ לְרָעֵב יִתֵּן וְעֵירֹם יְכַסֶּה־בָּגֶד:

וְאִישׁ אֶת־רָעַת רֵעֵהוּ אַל־תַּחְשְׁבוּ בִּלְבַבְכֶם וּשְׁבֻעַת שֶׁקֶר אַל־תֶּאֱהָבוּ כִּי אֶת־כָּל־אֵלֶּה אֲשֶׁר שָׂנֵאתִי נְאֻם־יהוה:

בִּצְדָקָה תִּכּוֹנָנִי רַחֲקִי מֵעֹשֶׁק כִּי־לֹא תִירָאִי וּמִמְּחִתָּה כִּי לֹא־תִקְרַב אֵלָיִךְ:

וְהָיָה מַעֲשֵׂה הַצְּדָקָה שָׁלוֹם וַעֲבֹדַת הַצְּדָקָה הַשְׁקֵט וָבֶטַח עַד־עוֹלָם:

וְיִגַּל כַּמַּיִם מִשְׁפָּט וּצְדָקָה כְּנַחַל אֵיתָן:

וַיִּגְבַּהּ יהוה צְבָאוֹת בַּמִּשְׁפָּט וְהָאֵל הַקָּדוֹשׁ נִקְדָּשׁ בִּצְדָקָה:

וְאֵרַשְׂתִּיךְ לִי בְּצֶדֶק וּבְמִשְׁפָּט וּבְחֶסֶד וּבְרַחֲמִים: וְאֵרַשְׂתִּיךְ לִי בֶּאֱמוּנָה וְיָדַעַתְּ אֶת־יהוה:

כִּי־צַדִּיק יהוה צְדָקוֹת אָהֵב יָשָׁר יֶחֱזוּ פָנֵימוֹ:

פִּי־צַדִּיק יֶהְגֶּה חָכְמָה וּלְשׁוֹנוֹ תְּדַבֵּר מִשְׁפָּט:

אוֹר זָרֻעַ לַצַּדִּיק וּלְיִשְׁרֵי־לֵב שִׂמְחָה:

Or zarua latzadik uleyishrey lev simḥah.

אַשְׁרֵי שֹׁמְרֵי מִשְׁפָּט עֹשֵׂה צְדָקָה בְכָל־עֵת:

פִּתְחוּ־לִי שַׁעֲרֵי־צֶדֶק אָבֹא־בָם אוֹדֶה יָהּ:

Pitḥu li sha'arey tzedek avo vam odeh yah.

All peoples shall come forth to worship you,
blessing your glorious name,
giving praises of your justice in isolated lands,
declaring your reality to those who know it not,
and hailing you throughout the earth,
with voices ever shouting: "Great is God!"
Zealously, they shall give up false worship,
having nothing more to do with inauthentic service,
turning with a single will toward you,
in awe of you, seeking your presence,
knowing the power of your holy realm,
learning to discern you, they who long have strayed.
May they find words for telling of your power!
Now let them exalt you as supreme,
startled in awe at your embracing presence.
On you, a crown of splendor shall alight,
while, powerful in joy, the mountains dance.
Singing in happiness, far islands hail your rule,
and come to take upon themselves your yoke of majesty,
raising you on high in prayerful assembly.
Surely may all hear it from afar and come,
to give to you alone the crown of sovereignty!

וְיֶאֱתָיוּ כֹל לְעָבְדֶךָ וִיבָרְכוּ שֵׁם כְּבוֹדֶךָ
וְיַגִּֽידוּ בָאִיִּים צִדְקֶךָ וְיִדְרְשֽׁוּךָ עַמִּים לֹא יְדָעֽוּךָ
וִיהַלְלֽוּךָ כָּל־אַפְסֵי־אָֽרֶץ וְיֹאמְרוּ תָמִיד יִגְדַּל יהוה
וְיִזְנְחוּ אֶת־עֲצַבֵּיהֶם וְיַחְפְּרוּ עִם פְּסִילֵיהֶם
וְיַטּוּ שְׁכֶם אֶחָד לְעָבְדֶךָ וְיִירָאֽוּךָ מְבַקְשֵׁי פָנֶֽיךָ
וְיַכִּֽירוּ כֹּחַ מַלְכוּתֶֽךָ וְיִלְמְדוּ תוֹעִים בִּינָה
וִימַלְלוּ אֶת־גְּבוּרָתֶֽךָ: וִינַשְּׂאֽוּךָ לְכֹל לְרֹאשׁ!
וִיסַלְּדוּ בְחִילָה פָּנֶֽיךָ וִיעַטְּרֽוּךָ נֵֽזֶר תִּפְאָרָה
וְיִפְצְחוּ הָרִים רִנָּה וְיִצְהֲלוּ אִיִּים כְּמָלְכֶֽךָ
וִיקַבְּלוּ עֹל מַלְכוּתֶֽךָ עֲלֵיהֶם וִירוֹמְמֽוּךָ בִּקְהַל עָם
וְיִשְׁמְעוּ רְחוֹקִים וְיָבֹֽאוּ וְיִתְּנוּ לְךָ כֶּֽתֶר מְלוּכָה:

COMMENTARY. This hymn is very similar in content to the last paragraph of the *Aleynu*. It envisions the joy that will enter the human and natural world when we awaken to the unity of all creation. It holds out a vision of earthly harmony and peace founded on spiritual realization. This does not necessitate the triumph of one particular religion or culture. Rather, it signifies a world where all people recognize our relation to others and to the planet and embrace our common origin and destiny.   S.P.W.

Grant peace, goodness and blessing in the world,
grace, love and mercy
over us and over all your people Israel.
Bless us, source of being, all of us, as one
amid your light,
for by your light,
WISE ONE, our God, you give to us
Torah of life, and love of kindness,
justice, blessing, mercy, life, and peace.
So may it be a good thing in your eyes,
to bless your people Israel, and all peoples,
with abundant strength and peace.

In the book of life, blessing, peace, and proper sustenance,
may we be remembered and inscribed,
we and all your people, the house of Israel,
for a good life and for peace.

KAVANAH. Try to imagine a time of true peace and tranquility, and think about your part in helping this time to come about. What can you do? What can you commit to? How will *you* be a peacemaker?   L.G.B.

שִׂים שָׁלוֹם טוֹבָה וּבְרָכָה בָּעוֹלָם חֵן וָחֶסֶד וְרַחֲמִים עָלֵינוּ וְעַל
כָּל־יִשְׂרָאֵל עַמֶּךְ: בָּרְכֵנוּ אָבִינוּ כֻּלָּנוּ כְּאֶחָד בְּאוֹר פָּנֶיךָ: כִּי בְאוֹר
פָּנֶיךָ נָתַתָּ לָּנוּ יהוה אֱלֹהֵינוּ תּוֹרַת חַיִּים וְאַהֲבַת חֶסֶד וּצְדָקָה
וּבְרָכָה וְרַחֲמִים וְחַיִּים וְשָׁלוֹם: וְטוֹב בְּעֵינֶיךָ לְבָרֵךְ אֶת עַמְּךְ יִשְׂרָאֵל
וְאֶת כָּל הָעַמִּים בְּרֹב עֹז וְשָׁלוֹם.

בְּסֵפֶר חַיִּים בְּרָכָה וְשָׁלוֹם וּפַרְנָסָה טוֹבָה נִזָּכֵר וְנִכָּתֵב לְפָנֶיךָ אֲנַחְנוּ
וְכָל־עַמְּךְ בֵּית יִשְׂרָאֵל לְחַיִּים טוֹבִים וּלְשָׁלוֹם:

Sim shalom tovah uverahah ba'olam hen vahesed verahamim
aleynu ve'al kol yisrael ameha. Barehenu avinu kulanu ke'ehad
be'or paneha. Ki ve'or paneha natata lanu adonay eloheynu torat
hayim ve'ahavat hesed utzedakah uverahah verahamim vehayim
veshalom. Vetov be'eyneha levareh et ameha yisra'el ve'et kol
ha'amim berov oz veshalom.

Besefer hayim berahah veshalom ufarnasah tovah nizaher
venikatev lefaneha anahnu vehol ameha beyt yisra'el lehayim
tovim uleshalom.

May it be your will, ETERNAL ONE, our God, our ancients' God,
that this coming year will be, for us and all your people,
the House of Israel, wherever they may be,
a year of **I**llumination,
a year of **B**lessing,
a year of **G**ladness,
a year of **D**ivine abundance,
a year of **H**eavenly splendor,
a year of **W**ise assembly,
a year of **S**ong,
a year of **H**appiness,
a year of **T**imely dew and rain,
a year of **J**ustice and salvation,
a year of **C**omplete atonement,
a year of **L**earning,
a year of **M**editative rest,
a year of **N**ew hope,
a year of **S**weetness and joy,
a year of **E**nchanting delight,
a year of **P**ersonal redemption,
a year of **C**elebration,
a year of **C**oming home from exile,
a year of **R**eturn to God's love,
a year of **S**olace and peace,
a year **T**hat you shall bring us up,
rejoicing, to our promised land, a year
when you shall open up the treasures of your goodness,
a year when your people Israel shall not have to turn
to one another in a state of urgent need, nor need the help
of other nations, and you shall bless the labor of their hands!

יְהִי רָצוֹן מִלְּפָנֶיךָ יהוה אֱלֹהֵינוּ וֵאלֹהֵי אֲבוֹתֵינוּ וְאִמּוֹתֵינוּ שֶׁתְּהֵא
הַשָּׁנָה הַזֹּאת הַבָּאָה עָלֵינוּ וְעַל כָּל עַמְּךָ בֵּית יִשְׂרָאֵל בְּכָל מָקוֹם שֶׁהֵם

שְׁנַת אוֹרָה

שְׁנַת בְּרָכָה

שְׁנַת גִּילָה

שְׁנַת דָּגָן תִּירוֹשׁ וְיִצְהָר

שְׁנַת הוֹד

שְׁנַת וַעַד טוֹב

שְׁנַת זִמְרָה

שְׁנַת חֶדְוָה

שְׁנַת טְלָלִים וּגְשָׁמִים

שְׁנַת יְשׁוּעָה

שְׁנַת כַּפָּרָה

שְׁנַת לִמּוּד

שְׁנַת מְנוּחָה

שְׁנַת נֶחָמָה

שְׁנַת שָׂשׂוֹן

שְׁנַת עֹנֶג

שְׁנַת פְּדוּת

שְׁנַת צְהָלָה

שְׁנַת קִבּוּץ גָּלֻיּוֹת

שְׁנַת רָצוֹן

שְׁנַת שָׁלוֹם וְשַׁלְוָה שָׁנָה שֶׁתַּעֲלֵנוּ שְׂמֵחִים לְאַרְצֵנוּ
שְׁנַת אוֹצָרְךָ הַטּוֹב תִּפְתַּח לָנוּ שָׁנָה שֶׁלֹּא יִצְטָרְכוּ עַמְּךָ בֵּית יִשְׂרָאֵל
זֶה לָזֶה וְלֹא לְעַם אַחֵר בְּתִתְּךָ בְּרָכָה בְּמַעֲשֵׂה יְדֵיהֶם:

KAVANAH. A wonderful practice in the synagogue on the High Holy Days is
to create a congregational acrostic. This acrostic reflects blessings. Ask
members of the congregation to call out words of blessing that begin with
each letter of the alphabet in order. Take as many blessings as are available for
"a" before moving on to "b" and then "c," through the alphabet.   S.P.W.

Today, give us courage and strength.	Amen!
Today, give us blessing.	Amen!
Today, give us goodness.	Amen!
Today, seek our welfare and good.	Amen!
Today, write us down for a good life.	Amen!
Today, please hearken to our cry.	Amen!
Today, accept with mercy and good will our prayer.	Amen!
Today, may your right hand keep us safe.	Amen!
Today, forgive and pardon all our sins.	Amen!

On a day like today,
may you bring us, joyful and glad,
to the completion of our reconstruction.
As is written by your prophet's hand:
"And I shall bring you to my holy mountain,
and you shall celebrate there
inside my house of prayer....
For my house shall then be called
a house of prayer for all peoples!"   Isaiah 56:7

And may we and all the people Israel,
and all who dwell on earth,
enjoy justice and blessing,
lovingkindness, life, and peace, until eternity.
Blessed are you, ABUNDANT ONE, maker of peace.

COMMENTARY. The היום / *hayom* / Today is a crowning prayer of the High
Holy Day liturgy. It is reserved just for that purpose. Its power stems not
only from its fresh and energetic sense of hope and not only from its
beautiful music; it comes also from the powerful awareness that what
matters is Today, the powerful commitment of this moment. The
challenge of Yom Kippur is in part to remember that when tomorrow
comes, it too will be Today. The hope of this moment, of every moment,
lies in the knowledge that all we ever have is Today. If we live in the
possibility of this moment, Today is more than enough.   D.A.T.

הַיּוֹם תְּאַמְּצֵנוּ:	אָמֵן:
הַיּוֹם תְּבָרְכֵנוּ:	אָמֵן:
הַיּוֹם תְּגַדְּלֵנוּ:	אָמֵן:
הַיּוֹם תִּדְרְשֵׁנוּ לְטוֹבָה:	אָמֵן:
הַיּוֹם תִּכְתְּבֵנוּ לְחַיִּים טוֹבִים:	אָמֵן:
הַיּוֹם תִּשְׁמַע שַׁוְעָתֵנוּ:	אָמֵן:
הַיּוֹם תְּקַבֵּל בְּרַחֲמִים וּבְרָצוֹן אֶת־תְּפִלָּתֵנוּ:	אָמֵן:
הַיּוֹם תִּתְמְכֵנוּ בִּימִין צִדְקֶךָ:	אָמֵן:
הַיּוֹם תִּמְחֹל וְתִסְלַח לְכָל־עֲווֹנוֹתֵינוּ:	אָמֵן:

כְּהַיּוֹם הַזֶּה תָּבִיא אֶת־נִדָּחֵינוּ שָׂשִׂים וּשְׂמֵחִים אֶל־אַרְצֵנוּ וְתַחֲזִיר
אֶת־שְׁכִינָתְךָ אֶל־הַר קָדְשֶׁךָ: כַּכָּתוּב עַל־יַד נְבִיאֶךָ וַהֲבִיאוֹתִים
אֶל־הַר קָדְשִׁי וְשִׂמַּחְתִּים בְּבֵית תְּפִלָּתִי... כִּי בֵיתִי בֵּית־תְּפִלָּה יִקָּרֵא
לְכָל־הָעַמִּים: וּצְדָקָה וּבְרָכָה וְרַחֲמִים וְחַיִּים וְשָׁלוֹם יִהְיֶה לָנוּ
לְכָל־יִשְׂרָאֵל וּלְכָל־הָעַמִּים עַד הָעוֹלָם: בָּרוּךְ אַתָּה יהוה עוֹשֵׂה
הַשָּׁלוֹם:

Hayom te'amtzenu.	Amen.
Hayom tevarhenu.	Amen.
Hayom tegadlenu.	Amen.
Hayom tidreshenu letovah.	Amen.
Hayom tihtevenu lehayim tovim.	Amen.
Hayom tishma shavatenu.	Amen.
Hayom tekabel berahamim uveratzon et tefilatenu.	Amen.
Hayom titmehenu bimin tzidkeha.	Amen.
Hayom timhol vetislah lehol avonoteynu.	Amen.

COMMENTARY. Why do we repeat the word "today"? "Today" raises the immediacy of our prayer. "Today" acknowledges our readiness. "Today" affirms our experience of God's nearness. We remember that yesterday exists no more and tomorrow may not come. It is today, only in this moment, that we can be blessed, strengthened, heard, sustained and forgiven.

S.P.W.

KAVANOT FOR YIZKOR

KAVANAH. As we gather together for this solemn moment, we are touched by a horizontal connection, a circle of individuals reaching out to each other for comfort and nourishment as we each acknowledge our loss. We are also empowered by a vertical connection with those souls who have cherished the chain of tradition that stretches far back in time. We are all a part of that chain. By honoring it, both in its horizontal form and its vertical dimension, we are proclaiming our faith in its continuity.   D.B.

KAVANAH. The essence of *Yizkor* is remembering. Some memories come in an almost overpowering rush, others drift into our consciousness much more gradually. We need time for remembering. Sometimes, the little things that gradually come to awareness only after we leave time for waiting, turn out to be the most precious and important of all. So quiet yourself, and listen to your heart murmuring. Now is the time for remembering....   D.A.T.

KAVANAH. Jewish tradition teaches that between the living and the dead there is a window, not a wall. The culture of scientific materialism teaches that after death, the links between us and our loved ones who died are forever ended—a brick wall! But, like the rituals of *Shiva*, Kaddish, and *Yahrzeit*, *Yizkor* opens windows to loved ones who are no longer with us. *Yizkor* creates a sacred space and time, wherein we can open our hearts and minds to the possibility of a genuine interconnection with beloved family members and friends who have left behind the world of the living. *Yizkor* is a window. Within the wellsprings of our infinite souls we find the window of connection between the living and the dead. Prepare to open that window....

As you recite *Yizkor* prayers, let your senses and imagination serve as the vehicle of interconnection. For whom are you saying *Yizkor* today? Can you imagine their faces before your eyes? See their smiles; visualize how they might be standing if they were next to you. Do you recall the sound of their voices? Hear their words as you stand in prayer. Feel their presence right in this moment. In your mind, in your heart, allow a conversation between you to unfold. What needs to be communicated this year? What's the message you need to hear today? What are the silent prayers of the heart? What remains unspoken? Speak. Listen. Take your time. There is no reason to hurry. This is a timeless moment. Let all the radiance of their love be with you right now.   Simcha Paull Raphael

If only I could hold your face
If only I could wrap up the light in your eyes
and put it away
  safekeeping

  safekeeping

    against mistaken words
    against parting
    old age

    against all human loneliness

We say that love has no beginning and no end
We know such love
  flowing out of itself like a river
  that meets and parts and meets

    It's for that love
    our eyes shine

  But oh for that time of parting
  for that time we are not ever
    sufficiently shored against

tell me how to hold that precious light

Take my hands and bless them
  as they bless what they long to keep

Robert Grant Burns

COMMENTARY. *Yizkor* developed as part of the Yom Kippur service during the Middle Ages. Originally it was placed after the Torah reading before the scrolls were returned to the ark, but its location is a matter of local custom. In order to accommodate those who wish to enter the service for *Yizkor*, many communities now place it in the afternoon before the *Minḥah* service. Other possibilities for the placement of *Yizkor* abound.   D.A.T.

YIZKOR / MEMORIAL SERVICE

Traditionally Yizkor, the memorial service, is recited after the Haftarah in the Torah service on the morning of Yom Kippur, but recitation of Yizkor can be shifted to any other time in the day. Yizkor prayers are customarily said while standing. Some congregations read a list of those who are to be remembered. Others publish a remembrance book.

יהוה מָה־אָדָם וַתֵּדָעֵהוּ

ALMIGHTY ONE, what are human beings
that you take note of them,

בֶּן־אֱנוֹשׁ וַתְּחַשְּׁבֵהוּ׃

the children of humanity
that you should think of them? ⟵

COMMENTARY. Calling to mind the memory of relatives or friends who have departed and giving *tzedakah* in their memory is a long-standing custom. It is mentioned in the medieval work *Midrash Tanhuma* as a Yom Kippur custom, though the *Yizkor* prayers themselves are somewhat later in origin. Recitation of *Yizkor* on the Pilgrimage Festivals began in European communities after the bloody destruction associated with the Crusades.

Because it was superstitiously believed that being present for *Yizkor* when one's parents were living could hasten their death, it used to be the case that only those required to say *Yizkor* because of the death of an immediate relative remained in the synagogue. After the Holocaust, which left so many with no one to say *Yizkor* for them, liberal congregations have encouraged everyone to join in reciting *Yizkor*. People are encouraged to recite *Yizkor* for each person whose memory is cherished. The traditional phrase said of the dead, *zikaron livrahah*/the memory for a blessing, reminds us that part of our purpose in remembering is to have our memories influence us to do good. This influence is made tangible in the custom of giving *tzedakah* in memory of loved ones before the holiday begins. D.A.T.

עובר...יהוה / ALMIGHTY ONE...shadow (Psalms 144:3-4).

אָדָם לַהֶבֶל דָּמָה

A human being is like a momentary breeze,

יָמָיו כְּצֵל עוֹבֵר:

a person's days are but a passing shadow.

בַּבֹּקֶר יָצִיץ וְחָלָף

At dawn, life blossoms and renews itself,

לָעֶרֶב יְמוֹלֵל וְיָבֵשׁ:

at dusk, it withers and dries up.

תָּשֵׁב אֱנוֹשׁ עַד־דַּכָּא

You return a person unto dust.

וַתֹּאמֶר שׁוּבוּ בְנֵי־אָדָם:

You say: Return, O children of humanity!

We turn our thoughts to yesterday...to a world that lives only in
our memory.
As we recall the days gone by, we know the past is irretrievable.
Yet—through the gift of memory, we recapture treasured
moments and images.
We are thankful for the happiness we knew with those no longer
here, with whom we lived and laughed and loved.
We praise the Eternal wellspring of life who links yesterday to
tomorrow. We affirm that despite all the tragedy bound up with
living, it is still good to be alive.
We understand that there can be no love without loss, no joy
without sorrow. May we have the courage to accept the all of
life—the love and the loss—the joy and the sorrow, as we
remember them.

Evelyn Mehlman

בבקר...ויבש/At dawn...dries up (Psalms 90:6).
תשב...אדם/You return...humanity (Psalms 90:3).

לְכָל אִישׁ יֵשׁ שֵׁם	*Each of Us Has a Name*
לְכָל אִישׁ יֵשׁ שֵׁם	Each of us has a name
שֶׁנָּתַן לוֹ אֱלֹהִים	given by God
וְנָתְנוּ לוֹ אָבִיו וְאִמּוֹ	and given by our parents
לְכָל אִישׁ יֵשׁ שֵׁם	Each of us has a name
שֶׁנָּתְנוּ לוֹ קוֹמָתוֹ וְאֹפֶן חִיּוּכוֹ	given by our stature and our smile
וְנָתַן לוֹ הָאָרִיג	and given by what we wear
לְכָל אִישׁ יֵשׁ שֵׁם	Each of us has a name
שֶׁנָּתְנוּ לוֹ הֶהָרִים	given by the mountains
וְנָתְנוּ לוֹ כְּתָלָיו	and given by our walls
לְכָל אִישׁ יֵשׁ שֵׁם	Each of us has a name
שֶׁנָּתְנוּ לוֹ הַמַּזָּלוֹת	given by the stars
וְנָתְנוּ לוֹ שְׁכֵנָיו	and given by our neighbors
לְכָל אִישׁ יֵשׁ שֵׁם	Each of us has a name
שֶׁנָּתְנוּ לוֹ חֲטָאָיו	given by our sins
וְנָתְנָה לוֹ כְּמִיהָתוֹ	and given by our longing
לְכָל אִישׁ יֵשׁ שֵׁם	Each of us has a name
שֶׁנָּתְנוּ לוֹ שׂוֹנְאָיו	given by our enemies
וְנָתְנָה לוֹ אַהֲבָתוֹ	and given by our love
לְכָל אִישׁ יֵשׁ שֵׁם	Each of us has a name
שֶׁנָּתְנוּ לוֹ חַגָּיו	given by our celebrations
וְנָתְנָה לוֹ מְלַאכְתּוֹ	and given by our work
לְכָל אִישׁ יֵשׁ שֵׁם	Each of us has a name
שֶׁנָּתְנוּ לוֹ תְּקוּפוֹת הַשָּׁנָה	given by the seasons
וְנָתַן לוֹ עִוְרוֹנוֹ	and given by our blindness
לְכָל אִישׁ יֵשׁ שֵׁם	Each of us has a name
שֶׁנָּתַן לוֹ הַיָּם	given by the sea
וְנָתַן לוֹ	and given by
מוֹתוֹ׃	our death. Zelda (translated by Marcia Falk)

YIZKOR / 1009

יהוה מָה־אָדָם וַתֵּדָעֵהוּ
בֶּן־אֱנוֹשׁ וַתְּחַשְּׁבֵהוּ
אָדָם לַהֶבֶל דָּמָה
יָמָיו כְּצֵל עוֹבֵר
בַּבֹּקֶר יָצִיץ וְחָלָף
לָעֶרֶב יְמוֹלֵל וְיָבֵשׁ
תָּשֵׁב אֱנוֹשׁ עַד־דַּכָּא
וַתֹּאמֶר: שׁוּבוּ בְנֵי־אָדָם:

ALMIGHTY ONE, what are human beings
that you take note of them,
the children of humanity
that you should think of them?
A human being is like a momentary breeze,
a person's days are but a passing shadow.
At dawn, life blossoms and renews itself,
at dusk, it withers and dries up.
You return a person unto dust.
You say: Return, O children of humanity!

עובר...יהוה / ALMIGHTY ONE...shadow (Psalms 144:3-4).

ויבש...בבקר / At dawn...dries up (Psalms 90:6).

אדם...תשב / You return...humanity (Psalms 90:3).

KAVANAH. Whenever we take time to think about our origins, or go back to
the home where we spent our childhood, we find that things have
changed. The years have taken their toll. Death has taken away many of
the people who filled our early years. Our friendships have changed, our
family relationships have changed. And yet—if only in our deepest
memories, home continues to be with us. We carry our ancestors and our
homes through all the years of our lives. We cannot go home again, but if
we can remember, we are never really away from home.   L.G.B.

THE FIVE STAGES OF GRIEF

The night I lost you
someone pointed me towards
the Five Stages of Grief.
Go that way, they said,
it's easy, like learning to climb
stairs after amputation.
And so I climbed.
Denial was first.
I sat down at breakfast
carefully setting the table
for two. I passed you the toast—
you sat there. I passed
you the paper—you hid
behind it.
Anger seemed more familiar.
I burned the toast, snatched
the paper and read the headlines myself.
But they mentioned your departure
and so I moved on to
Bargaining. What could I exchange
for you? The silence
after storms? My typing fingers?
Before I could decide, Depression
came puffing up, a poor relation
its suitcase tied together
with string. In the suitcase
were bandages for the eyes
and bottles of sleep. I slid
all the way down the stairs
feeling nothing. ↵

And all the time Hope
flashed on and off
in defective neon.
Hope was a signpost pointing
straight in the air.
Hope was my uncle's middle name,
he died of it.
After a year I am still climbing,
though my feet slip
on your stone face.
The treeline
has long since disappeared;
green is a color
I have forgotten.
But now I see what I am climbing
towards: Acceptance
written in capital letters,
a special headline:
Acceptance.
Its name is in lights.
I struggle on,
waving and shouting.
Below, my whole life spreads its surf,
all the landscape I've ever known
or dreamed of. Below
a fish jumps: the pulse
in your neck.
Acceptance. I finally
reach it.
But something is wrong.
Grief is a circular staircase.
I have lost you.

Linda Pastan

LITTLE RUTH

Sometimes I think about you, little Ruth—remembering
how we were separated by great distance in our childhood,
and how they burned you in the camps.
Were you here now, you'd be a woman of 65,
a woman at the threshold of old age.
And I don't know what befell you in your short life
after the time that we were separated,
how far you got, what signs of passage
had been hung upon your shoulders, on your sleeve,
on your courageous spirit. What glittering stars
have clung to you, what signs of heroism, what
medals of love were hung upon your neck.
What peace was on you—on you, may there be peace!
And what has happened to your lifetime's unused years?
Are they still packed in pretty packages,
or were they added to my life? Did you make me become
your bank of love, like banks in Switzerland
whose accounts are voided when their owners die?
Shall I inherit all of this for my children
whom you have never seen?

You gave me your life, much the way a wine merchant
makes others drunk while staying sober,
making death sober like you,
the clearest-headed one in all the land of death ↲

רוּת הַקְּטַנָּה

לִפְעָמִים אֲנִי זוֹכֵר אוֹתָךְ רוּת הַקְּטַנָּה,
שֶׁנִּפְרַדְנוּ בְּיַלְדוּת רְחוֹקָה, שֶׁשָּׂרְפוּ אוֹתָךְ בַּמַּחֲנוֹת.
אִלּוּ חָיִית עַכְשָׁיו, הָיִית אִשָּׁה בַּת שִׁשִּׁים וְחָמֵשׁ,
אִשָּׁה עַל סַף זִקְנָה. בַּת עֶשְׂרִים נִשְׂרַפְתְּ,
וְאֵינֶנִּי יוֹדֵעַ מָה קָרָה לָךְ בְּחַיַּיִךְ הַקְּצָרִים
מֵאָז נִפְרַדְנוּ. לָמָה הִגַּעְתָּ, אִילּוּ סִימָנֵי דַּרְגָּה
הֶעָנְקוּ לָךְ עַל כְּתֵפַיִךְ, עַל שַׁרְווּלַיִךְ, עַל
נַפְשֵׁךְ הָאַמִּיצָה, אִילּוּ כּוֹכָבִים מַבְרִיקִים
הִדְבִּיקוּ לָךְ, אִילּוּ אוֹתוֹת גְּבוּרָה, אִילּוּ
מֶדַלְיוֹת אַהֲבָה תָּלוּ עַל צַוָּארֵךְ,
אֵיזֶה שָׁלוֹם עָלַיִךְ, עָלַיִךְ הַשָּׁלוֹם.
וּמָה קָרָה לִשְׁנוֹת חַיַּיִךְ הַלֹּא מְשֻׁמָּשׁוֹת?
הַאִם הֵן עֲדַיִן אֲרוּזוֹת כַּחֲבִילוֹת יָפוֹת,
הַאִם נוֹסְפוּ לְחַיַּי? הַאִם הָפַכְתְּ אוֹתִי
בַּנְק הָאַהֲבָה שֶׁלָּךְ כְּמוֹ הַבַּנְקִים בִּשְׁוַיִץ
שֶׁהַמַּטְמוֹן נִשְׁמָר בָּהֶם גַּם אַחֲרֵי מוֹת בְּעָלָיו?
הַאִם אוֹרִישׁ אֶת כָּל אֵלֶּה לִילָדַי
שֶׁלֹּא רָאִית אוֹתָם מֵעוֹלָם? ←

to someone drunk with life like me,
wallowing in his forgetfulness.
Sometimes, I think about you, during times
I hadn't planned on, and in places
that I hadn't designated for a memory,
but rather for some transitory thing that doesn't linger.
Like at an airport, when the arriving passengers
are standing wearily by the revolving ramp
that brings their baggage and their packages,
and suddenly, with cries of joy, they find their own,
like at a resurrection of the dead,
and then they exit to their lives.
And there is one bag that keeps coming back
and disappearing once again, returning once again,
so slowly in the empty hall,
before, again and again, it passes on.
Thus does your quiet image pass before me;
thus do I remember you, until the ramp stops moving
and is silent. So it goes.

Yehuda Amichai

מְפַכַּחַת מָוֶת כָּמוֹךָ, וּצְלוּלַת שְׁאוֹל
לִשְׁכּוֹר חַיִּים כָּמוֹנִי מִתְגּוֹלֵל בְּשִׁכְחָתוֹ.
לִפְעָמִים אֲנִי זוֹכֵר אוֹתָךְ בִּזְמַנִּים
שֶׁלֹּא שֵׁעַרְתִּי וּבִמְקוֹמוֹת שֶׁלֹּא נוֹעֲדוּ לְזִכָּרוֹן,
אֶלָּא לַחוֹלֵף וְלָעוֹבֵר שֶׁלֹּא נִשְׁאָר;
כְּמוֹ בִּנְמַל תְּעוּפָה כְּשֶׁהַנּוֹסְעִים הַמַּגִּיעִים
עוֹמְדִים עֲיֵפִים לְיַד הַסֶּרֶט הַנָּע וְהַמִּסְתּוֹבֵב
שֶׁמֵּבִיא אֶת מִזְוְדוֹתֵיהֶם וַחֲבִילוֹתֵיהֶם,
וְהֵם מְגַלִּים אֶת שֶׁלָּהֶם בִּקְרִיאוֹת שִׂמְחָה
כְּמוֹ בִּתְחִיַּת הַמֵּתִים וְיוֹצְאִים אֶל חַיֵּיהֶם.
וְיֵשׁ מִזְוָדָה אַחַת שֶׁחוֹזֶרֶת וְשׁוּב נֶעֱלֶמֶת
וְשׁוּב חוֹזֶרֶת, לְאַט לְאַט, בָּאוּלָם הַמִּתְרוֹקֵן,
וְשׁוּב וְשׁוּב הִיא עוֹבֶרֶת,
כָּךְ עוֹבֶרֶת דְּמוּתֵךְ הַשְּׁקֵטָה עַל פָּנַי,
כָּךְ אֲנִי זוֹכֵר אוֹתָךְ, עַד
שֶׁהַסֶּרֶט יַעֲמֹד מִלֶּכֶת. וְדֹמּוּ סֶלָה.

My protector, you are our abode,
one generation to the next,

since before the mountains came to birth,
before the birthpangs of the land and world.
From eternity unto eternity, you are divine.

Truly, a thousand years are in your eyes
like yesterday—so quickly does it pass—
or like the watchman's nighttime post.

You pour upon them sleep, they sleep.
When morning comes, it vanishes like chaff.

At dawn, life blossoms and renews itself,
at dusk, it withers and dries up.

Years of our lifetime are but seventy
—perhaps, among the strongest, eighty years—

and most of them are toil and fatigue,
then quickly it all ends, we fly away.

Who knows the full strength of your fury?
Is our fear of you the equal of your wrath?

Oh, let us know how to assess our days,
how we may bring the heart some wisdom.

Let your accomplishment be visible to those who serve you,
let your beauty rest upon their children,

let our divine protector's pleasure be upon us,
and the labor of our hands, make it secure,
the labor of our hands ensure!

Selections from Psalm 90

אֲדֹנָי מָעוֹן אַתָּה הָיִיתָ לָּנוּ בְּדֹר וָדֹר:
בְּטֶרֶם הָרִים יֻלָּדוּ וַתְּחוֹלֵל אֶרֶץ וְתֵבֵל
וּמֵעוֹלָם עַד־עוֹלָם אַתָּה אֵל:

כִּי אֶלֶף שָׁנִים בְּעֵינֶיךָ כְּיוֹם אֶתְמוֹל כִּי יַעֲבֹר
וְאַשְׁמוּרָה בַלָּיְלָה:
זְרַמְתָּם שֵׁנָה יִהְיוּ בַּבֹּקֶר כֶּחָצִיר יַחֲלֹף:
בַּבֹּקֶר יָצִיץ וְחָלָף לָעֶרֶב יְמוֹלֵל וְיָבֵשׁ:

יְמֵי־שְׁנוֹתֵינוּ בָהֶם שִׁבְעִים שָׁנָה וְאִם בִּגְבוּרֹת שְׁמוֹנִים שָׁנָה:
וְרָהְבָּם עָמָל וָאָוֶן כִּי־גָז חִישׁ וַנָּעֻפָה:
מִי־יוֹדֵעַ עֹז אַפֶּךָ וּכְיִרְאָתְךָ עֶבְרָתֶךָ:
לִמְנוֹת יָמֵינוּ כֵּן הוֹדַע וְנָבִיא לְבַב חָכְמָה:

יֵרָאֶה אֶל־עֲבָדֶיךָ פָעֳלֶךָ וַהֲדָרְךָ עַל־בְּנֵיהֶם:
וִיהִי נֹעַם אֲדֹנָי אֱלֹהֵינוּ עָלֵינוּ וּמַעֲשֵׂה יָדֵינוּ כּוֹנְנָה עָלֵינוּ
וּמַעֲשֵׂה יָדֵינוּ כּוֹנְנֵהוּ:

FOR A GRANDMOTHER

My mother's mother died
in the spring of her years,
and her daughter forgot her face.
Her portrait, engraved
on my grandfather's heart,
was erased from the world of images
when he died.

In the house, just her mirror remained,
sunk with age in its silver frame.
And I, the pale grandchild
who does not resemble her,
peer into it today as into a lake
that hides its treasures underwater.

Deep behind my face,
I see a young woman—
pink-cheeked, smiling,
a wig on her head—
threading a long-looped earring
through the tender flesh of her lobe.

Deep behind my face,
shines the bright gold of her eyes.
And the mirror passes on
the family lore:
She was very beautiful.

Lea Goldberg (translated by Marcia Falk)

מֵתָה אִמָּה שֶׁל אִמִּי
בַּאֲבִיב יָמֶיהָ. וּבִתָּהּ
לֹא זָכְרָה אֶת פָּנֶיהָ. דְּיוֹקְנָהּ הֶחָרוּט
עַל לִבּוֹ שֶׁל סָבִי
נִמְחָה מֵעוֹלַם הַדְּמוּיּוֹת
אַחֲרֵי מוֹתוֹ.

רַק הָרְאִי שֶׁלָּהּ נִשְׁתַּיֵּר בַּבַּיִת.
הֶעֱמִיק מֵרֹב שָׁנִים בְּמִשְׁבֶּצֶת הַכֶּסֶף.
וַאֲנִי, נֶכְדָּתָהּ הַחִוֶּרֶת. שֶׁאֵינֶנִּי דוֹמָה לָהּ,
מַבִּיטָה הַיּוֹם אֶל תּוֹכוֹ כְּאֶל תּוֹךְ
אֲגַם הַטּוֹמֵן אוֹצְרוֹתָיו
מִתַּחַת לַמַּיִם.

עָמֹק מְאֹד, מֵאֲחוֹרֵי פָּנַי,
אֲנִי רוֹאָה אִשָּׁה צְעִירָה
וְרֵדַּת לְחָיַיִם מְחַיֶּכֶת.
וּפֵאָה נָכְרִית לְרֹאשָׁהּ.
הִיא עוֹנֶדֶת
עָגִיל מָאֳרָךְ אֶל תְּנוּךְ אָזְנָהּ. מַשְׁחִילַתְהוּ
בְּנֶקֶב בַּבָּשָׂר הֶעָנֹג
שֶׁל הָאֹזֶן.

עָמֹק מְאֹד, מֵאֲחוֹרֵי פָּנַי, קוֹרֶנֶת
זְהוּבִית בְּהִירָה שֶׁל עֵינֶיהָ.
וְהָרְאִי מַמְשִׁיךְ אֶת מָסֹרֶת
הַמִּשְׁפָּחָה:
שֶׁהִיא הָיְתָה יָפָה מְאֹד.

FOR A GRANDFATHER

My grandfather was a farmer.
The day before he died
he planted a garden
A garden that nourished his family
through the sunless season of
mourning
far into the golden season of harvest.

My grandfather was a farmer.
Before he died
he planted a lifetime of seeds.
Diligently he planted honesty and
reverence;

Inadvertently he planted gentleness and
humor—
Bounty enough to nourish me
all the seasons of my life
far into the planting season of my child.

Dana Shuster

FOR A PARENT

Move to the front
of the line
a voice says, and suddenly
there is nobody
left standing between you
and the world, to take
the first blows
on their shoulders.
This is the place in books
where part one ends, and
part two begins,
and there is no part three.
The slate is wiped
not clean but like a canvas
painted over in white
so that a whole new landscape
must be started,
bits of the old
still showing underneath—
those colors sadness lends
to a certain hour of evening.
Now the line of light
at the horizon
is the hinge between earth
and heaven, only visible
a few moments
as the sun drops
its rusted padlock
into place.

Linda Pastan

In many houses
all at once
I see my mother and father
and they are young
as they walk in.

Why should
my tears come,
to see them laughing?

That they cannot
see me
is of no matter.

I was once
their dream;
now
they are mine.

Author Unknown

FOR A CHILD

I will never be able to stop my tears.
And the day is far off when I will
Forget this cruel day.
Why could we not have died with him?
His little clothes still hang on his rack
His milk is still by his bed.
Overcome, it is as though life had left us.
We lie prostrate and insensible all day.
I am no longer young enough
To try to understand what has happened.
I was warned of it in a dream.
No medicine would have helped
Even if it had been heaped mountain high.
The disease took its course inexorable.
It would be better for me if I took
A sword and cut open my bowels.
They are already cut to pieces with sorrow.
I realize what I am doing
And try to come to myself again,
But I am exhausted and helpless,
Carried away by excess of sorrow.

Su Tung P'o

FOR A SPOUSE / PARTNER

As long
as I speak
your name
you are
not dead

as long
as I think
your pain
I cannot
grieve

the granite marker
tells
your name
your age

the bleak horizon
scars
the barren hedge

as long
as I
you
are not dead

Hannah Kahn

FOR A SUICIDE

...transcripts of fog...
speak your tattered Kaddish for all suicides:

Praise to life though it crumbled in like a tunnel
on ones we knew and loved

   Praise to life though its windows blew shut
   on the breathing-room of ones we knew and loved

Praise to life though ones we knew and loved
loved it badly, too well, and not enough

   Praise to life though it tightened like a knot
   on the hearts of ones we thought we knew loved us

Praise to life giving room and reason
to ones we knew and loved who felt unpraisable

   Praise to them, how they loved it, when they could.

Adrienne Rich

∽

ON HEALING

I had thought that your death
Was a waste and a destruction,
A pain of grief hardly to be endured.
I am only beginning to learn
That your life was a gift and a growing
And a loving left with me.
The desperation of death
Destroyed the existence of love,
But the fact of death
Cannot destroy what has been given.
I am learning to look at your life again
Instead of your death and your departing.

Marjorie Pizer

It is customary to rise for Yizkor *prayers,* El Maley Raḥamim, *and* Kaddish.

Prayer in remembrance of a male:

יִזְכֹּר אֱלֹהִים אֶת־נִשְׁמַת _____ שֶׁהָלַךְ לְעוֹלָמוֹ:
אָנָּא תְּהִי נַפְשׁוֹ צְרוּרָה בִּצְרוֹר הַחַיִּים וּתְהִי מְנוּחָתוֹ כָּבוֹד: שֹׂבַע
שְׂמָחוֹת אֶת־פָּנֶיךָ נְעִימוֹת בִּימִינְךָ נֶצַח. אָמֵן:

Let God remember the soul of _____ who
went to his place of eternal rest. Please let his soul be bound up
with the living in the continuum of life, and may his rest be
honorable. Grant him abundant joy in your presence, and sweet
pleasures at your right hand for eternity. Amen.

Prayer in remembrance of a female:

יִזְכֹּר אֱלֹהִים אֶת־נִשְׁמַת _____ שֶׁהָלְכָה
לְעוֹלָמָהּ: אָנָּא תְּהִי נַפְשָׁהּ צְרוּרָה בִּצְרוֹר הַחַיִּים וּתְהִי מְנוּחָתָהּ
כָּבוֹד: שֹׂבַע שְׂמָחוֹת אֶת־פָּנֶיךָ נְעִימוֹת בִּימִינְךָ נֶצַח. אָמֵן:

Let God remember the soul of _____ who
went to her place of eternal rest. Please let her soul be bound up
with the living in the continuum of life, and may her rest be
honorable. Grant her abundant joy in your presence, and sweet
pleasures at your right hand for eternity. Amen.

KAVANAH. Yizkor, a time to mourn our lost loved ones, is for some a time
to mourn relationships that were not fully loving. We pray, זכרון לברכה /
zikaron livraḥah / "may the memory be a blessing." We hope that with the
passing of time we can let go of our pain and disappointment in the
shortcoming of our deceased loved ones and see them as blessings in our
lives, distilling the goodness in them which may now be overshadowed. In
coming to terms with difficult relationships, we are blessed with peace,
and memory becomes blessing.   B.P.T.

אֵל מָלֵא רַחֲמִים שׁוֹכֵן בַּמְּרוֹמִים הַמְצֵא מְנוּחָה נְכוֹנָה תַּחַת כַּנְפֵי
הַשְּׁכִינָה בְּמַעֲלוֹת קְדוֹשִׁים וּטְהוֹרִים כְּזֹהַר הָרָקִיעַ מַזְהִירִים
לְנִשְׁמוֹת יַקִּירֵינוּ וּקְדוֹשֵׁינוּ שֶׁהָלְכוּ לְעוֹלָמָם: אָנָּא בַּעַל הָרַחֲמִים
הַסְתִּירֵם בְּצֵל כְּנָפֶיךָ לְעוֹלָמִים וּצְרֹר בִּצְרוֹר־הַחַיִּים אֶת נִשְׁמָתָם:
יהוה הוּא נַחֲלָתָם וְיָנוּחוּ בְשָׁלוֹם עַל מִשְׁכָּבָם וְנֹאמַר אָמֵן:

God filled with mercy,
dwelling in the heavens' heights,
bring proper rest
beneath the wings of your Sheḥinah,
amid the ranks of the holy and the pure,
illuminating like the brilliance of the skies
the souls of our beloved and our blameless
who went to their eternal place of rest.
May you who are the source of mercy
shelter them beneath your wings eternally,
and bind their souls among the living,
that they may rest in peace.
And let us say: Amen.

For the Martyrs, Soldiers of the People Israel, and Victims of the Holocaust:

אֵל מָלֵא רַחֲמִים שׁוֹכֵן בַּמְּרוֹמִים הַמְצֵא מְנוּחָה נְכוֹנָה תַּחַת כַּנְפֵי
הַשְּׁכִינָה בְּמַעֲלוֹת קְדוֹשִׁים וּטְהוֹרִים כְּזֹהַר הָרָקִיעַ מַזְהִירִים אֶת־
נִשְׁמוֹת חַיָּלֵי צְבָא הַהֲגָנָה לְיִשְׂרָאֵל וְכָל־אֵלֶּה שֶׁמָּסְרוּ אֶת־נַפְשָׁם
עַל־קִדּוּשׁ הַשֵּׁם וְשֶׁנֶּהֶרְגוּ בַּשּׁוֹאָה: אָנָּא בַּעַל הָרַחֲמִים תַּסְתִּירֵם
בְּצֵל כְּנָפֶיךָ לְעוֹלָמִים וּצְרוֹר בִּצְרוֹר הַחַיִּים אֶת־נִשְׁמוֹתָם וְיָנוּחוּ
בְשָׁלוֹם עַל־מִשְׁכָּבָם וְנֹאמַר אָמֵן:

God filled with mercy, dwelling in the heavens' heights, bring
proper rest beneath the wings of your Sheḥinah, amid the ranks
of the holy and the pure, illuminating like the brilliance of the
skies the souls of Israel's soldiers, and all those who have given
up their lives in affirmation of your holy Name, and all
destroyed in the Shoah. May you who are the source of mercy
shelter them beneath your wings eternally, and bind their souls
among the living, that they may rest in peace. And let us say:
Amen.

COMMENTARY. In this *El Maley Raḥamim* specific references to those who
have died fighting in Israel's wars and those murdered in the Holocaust
have been added to the traditional phrase "all those who have given up
their lives in affirmation of your holy Name." These events of our time
demand special recognition. Sanctification of God's name through
voluntary martyrdom was an altogether too common phenomenon in
the rabbinic and medieval periods, which were often punctuated by savage
persecution. Death in the Holocaust was qualitatively different because it
could not be averted by the victim—even conversion had no power to
save. Many contemporary Jews view the tragic events of the Holocaust as a
lessening of God's presence in the world, though acts of bravery, piety, and
caring manifested the divine even then.

Israeli soldiers generally understand their sacrifices to be for the sake of
their families and their people rather than as part of an effort to make God
manifest. Nonetheless their sacrifices, which have revived and preserved
Israel as a Jewish home, have a meaning to Jews everywhere far beyond
that of acres of land. They have kept alive a dream we share—our land,
not only free, but at peace.   D.A.T.

In the rising of the sun and in its going down, we remember them.

In the blowing of the wind and in the chill of winter, we remember them.

In the opening of the buds and in the rebirth of spring, we remember them.

In the blueness of the sky and in the warmth of summer, we remember them.

In the rustling of leaves and in the beauty of autumn, we remember them.

In the beginning of the year and when it ends, we remember them.

When we are weary and in need of strength, we remember them.

When we are lost and sick at heart, we remember them.

When we have joys we yearn to share, we remember them.

So long as we live, they too shall live, for they are now a part of us, as we remember them.

Jack Riemer and Sylvan D. Kamens

KADDISH YATOM /
THE MOURNER'S KADDISH

Reader: Let God's name be made great and holy in the world that was created as God willed. May God complete the holy realm in your own lifetime, in your days, and in the days of all the house of Israel, quickly and soon. And say: Amen.

Congregation: May God's great name be blessed, forever and as long as worlds endure.

Reader: May it be blessed, and praised, and glorified, and held in honor, viewed with awe, embellished, and revered; and may the blessed name of holiness be hailed, though it be higher by far than all the blessings, songs, praises, and consolations that we utter in this world. And say: Amen.

May Heaven grant a universal peace, and life for us, and for all Israel. And say: Amen.

May the one who creates harmony above, make peace for us and for all Israel, and for all who dwell on earth. And say: Amen.

Love is not changed by Death,
And nothing is lost and all in the end is harvest.

Edith Sitwell

קַדִּישׁ יָתוֹם

יִתְגַּדַּל וְיִתְקַדַּשׁ שְׁמֵהּ רַבָּא בְּעָלְמָא דִּי בְרָא כִרְעוּתֵהּ וְיַמְלִיךְ
מַלְכוּתֵהּ בְּחַיֵּיכוֹן וּבְיוֹמֵיכוֹן וּבְחַיֵּי דְכָל בֵּית יִשְׂרָאֵל בַּעֲגָלָא וּבִזְמַן
קָרִיב וְאִמְרוּ אָמֵן:

יְהֵא שְׁמֵהּ רַבָּא מְבָרַךְ לְעָלַם וּלְעָלְמֵי עָלְמַיָּא:

יִתְבָּרַךְ וְיִשְׁתַּבַּח וְיִתְפָּאַר וְיִתְרוֹמַם וְיִתְנַשֵּׂא וְיִתְהַדָּר וְיִתְעַלֶּה
וְיִתְהַלָּל שְׁמֵהּ דְּקֻדְשָׁא בְּרִיךְ הוּא
לְעֵלָּא לְעֵלָּא מִכָּל בִּרְכָתָא וְשִׁירָתָא תֻּשְׁבְּחָתָא וְנֶחֱמָתָא דַּאֲמִירָן
בְּעָלְמָא וְאִמְרוּ אָמֵן:

יְהֵא שְׁלָמָא רַבָּא מִן שְׁמַיָּא וְחַיִּים עָלֵינוּ וְעַל כָּל יִשְׂרָאֵל וְאִמְרוּ
אָמֵן:

עוֹשֶׂה שָׁלוֹם בִּמְרוֹמָיו הוּא יַעֲשֶׂה שָׁלוֹם עָלֵינוּ וְעַל כָּל יִשְׂרָאֵל וְעַל
כָּל יוֹשְׁבֵי תֵבֵל וְאִמְרוּ אָמֵן:

Yitgadal veyitkadash shemey raba
be'alma divra ḥirutey veyamliḥ malḥutey
behayeyḥon uvyomeyḥon uvḥayey deḥol beyt yisra'el
ba'agala uvizman kariv ve'imru amen.

Congregation: Yehey shemey raba mevaraḥ le'alam ulalmey almaya.

Yitbaraḥ veyishtabaḥ veyitpa'ar veyitromam
veyitnasey veyit-hadar veyitaleh veyit-halal
shemey dekudsha beriḥ hu
le'ela le'ela mikol birḥata veshirata
tushbeḥata veneḥemata da'amiran be'alma ve'imru amen.

Yehey shelama raba min shemaya veḥayim aleynu ve'al kol
yisra'el ve'imru amen.
Oseh shalom bimromav hu ya'aseh shalom aleynu ve'al kol
yisra'el ve'al kol yoshvey tevel ve'imru amen.

A psalm of David.

THE ETERNAL is my shepherd; I shall never be in need.

Amid the choicest grasses does God set me down.

God leads me by the calmest waters,
and restores my soul.

God takes me along paths of righteousness,
in keeping with the honor of God's name.

Even should I wander in a valley of the darkest shadows,
I will fear no evil.

You are with me, God. Your power and support
are there to comfort me.

You set in front of me a table
in the presence of my enemies.

You anoint my head with oil; my cup is overflowing.

Surely, good and loving-kindness will pursue me
all the days of my life,
and I shall come to dwell inside the house
of THE ETERNAL for a length of days.

Psalm 23

מִזְמוֹר לְדָוִד יהוה רֹעִי לֹא אֶחְסָר: בִּנְאוֹת דֶּשֶׁא יַרְבִּיצֵנִי

עַל־מֵי מְנֻחוֹת יְנַהֲלֵנִי: נַפְשִׁי יְשׁוֹבֵב

יַנְחֵנִי בְמַעְגְּלֵי־צֶדֶק לְמַעַן שְׁמוֹ:

גַּם כִּי־אֵלֵךְ בְּגֵיא צַלְמָוֶת לֹא־אִירָא רָע

כִּי־אַתָּה עִמָּדִי שִׁבְטְךָ וּמִשְׁעַנְתֶּךָ הֵמָּה יְנַחֲמֻנִי:

תַּעֲרֹךְ לְפָנַי שֻׁלְחָן נֶגֶד צֹרְרָי

דִּשַּׁנְתָּ בַשֶּׁמֶן רֹאשִׁי כּוֹסִי רְוָיָה:

אַךְ טוֹב וָחֶסֶד יִרְדְּפוּנִי כָּל־יְמֵי חַיָּי

וְשַׁבְתִּי בְּבֵית־יהוה לְאֹרֶךְ יָמִים:

Mizmor ledavid adonay ro'i lo eḥsar. Binot deshe yarbitzeni
al mey menuḥot yenahaleni. Nafshi yeshovev
yanḥeni vemageley tzedek lema'an shemo.
Gam ki eleḥ begey tzalmavet lo ira ra
ki atah imadi shivteḥa umishanteḥa hemah yenaḥamuni.
Ta'aroḥ lefanay shulḥan neged tzoreray
dishanta vashemen roshi kosi revayah.
Aḥ tov vaḥesed yirdefuni kol yemey ḥayay
veshavti beveyt adonay le'oreḥ yamim.

מִנְחָה
לְיוֹם כִּפּוּר

The ark is opened.

And it happened, when the Ark began its journey,
that Moses said: Arise, ASCENDANT ONE,
and may your enemies be scattered.
May the ones who oppose you
be afraid of your might!
Behold, out of Zion emerges our Torah,
and the word of THE WISE ONE from Jerusalem's heights.
Blessed is God who has given us Torah,
to Israel, our people, with holy intent.

The leader takes out the Torah, faces the ark, bows and says:

Declare with me the greatness of THE INFINITE,
together let us raise God's name.

The leader carries the Torah around the room as the leader and congregation sing:

To you, ETERNAL ONE, is all majesty,
and might and splendor, and eternity, and power!
For everything that is, in the heavens and the earth,
is yours, ALMIGHTY ONE, as is all sovereignty,
and highest eminence above all beings.
Exalt THE MIGHTY ONE our God,
bow down before God's footstool.
God is holy!
Exalt the name of THE INEFFABLE,
bow down before God's holy mount
for holy is THE AWESOME ONE, our God!

גדלו...יחדו/Declare...name (Psalms 34:4).
לך...לראש/To you...beings (I Chronicles 29:11).
רוממו...אלהינו/Exalt...our God! (Psalms 99:5 and 9).

The ark is opened.

וַיְהִי בִּנְסֹעַ הָאָרוֹן וַיֹּאמֶר מֹשֶׁה קוּמָה יהוה וְיָפֻצוּ אֹיְבֶיךָ וְיָנֻסוּ מְשַׂנְאֶיךָ מִפָּנֶיךָ:

כִּי מִצִּיּוֹן תֵּצֵא תוֹרָה וּדְבַר־יהוה מִירוּשָׁלָיִם:

בָּרוּךְ שֶׁנָּתַן תּוֹרָה לְעַמּוֹ יִשְׂרָאֵל בִּקְדֻשָּׁתוֹ:

Vayhi binso'a ha'aron vayomer mosheh kumah adonay veyafutzu oyveha veyanusu mesaneha mipaneha.
Ki mitziyon tetzey torah udevar adonay mirushalayim.
Baruh shenatan torah le'amo yisra'el bikdushato.

The leader takes out the Torah, faces the ark, bows and says:

גַּדְּלוּ לַיהוה אִתִּי וּנְרוֹמְמָה שְׁמוֹ יַחְדָּו:

Gadelu ladonay iti uneromemah shemo yahdav.

The leader carries the Torah around the room as the leader and congregation sing:

לְךָ יהוה הַגְּדֻלָּה וְהַגְּבוּרָה וְהַתִּפְאֶרֶת וְהַנֵּצַח וְהַהוֹד כִּי־כֹל בַּשָּׁמַיִם וּבָאָרֶץ לְךָ יהוה הַמַּמְלָכָה וְהַמִּתְנַשֵּׂא לְכֹל לְרֹאשׁ:

רוֹמְמוּ יהוה אֱלֹהֵינוּ וְהִשְׁתַּחֲווּ לַהֲדֹם רַגְלָיו קָדוֹשׁ הוּא:

רוֹמְמוּ יהוה אֱלֹהֵינוּ וְהִשְׁתַּחֲווּ לְהַר קָדְשׁוֹ כִּי־קָדוֹשׁ יהוה אֱלֹהֵינוּ:

Leha adonay hagedulah vehagevurah vehatiferet vehanetzah vehahod ki hol bashamayim uva'aretz leha adonay hamamlahah vehamitnasey lehol lerosh.
Romemu adonay eloheynu vehishtahavu lahadom raglav kadosh hu.
Romemu adonay eloheynu vehishtahavu lehar kodsho ki kadosh adonay eloheynu.

ויהי...מפניך / And...might! (Numbers 10:35).
כי...ירושלים / Behold...Jerusalem's heights (Isaiah 2:3).

The Torah is placed on the reading table and opened. The gabay *says:*

May God's rule soon be revealed and manifested,
and may God be gracious to our remnant of a people
—those of the House of Israel who survive—
for grace, for love, for mercy, and for favor,
and let us say: Amen!
Let everyone declare the greatness of our God,
let all give honor to the Torah.
May _____ arise,
as the first (second, third) one called up to the Torah.
Blessed is the one who has given Torah to the people Israel!

Congregation and gabay *continue:*

And you who cling to THE ETERNAL ONE your God,
are still alive today!

COMMENTARY. The public reading of the Torah is a form of ritualized
study designed to actively engage the participants. During the Torah reading, one person reads from the scroll. There are also two *gabayim.* One
gabay assigns the Torah honors, calls people up to the Torah, and recites
additional prayers, including the *mi sheberah* prayers. The second *gabay*
follows the Torah reading closely and corrects errors.

Traditionally, seven adult Jews were called on Shabbat morning, six on
Yom Kippur, five on Pilgrimage Festivals and Rosh Hashanah, four on
Rosh Ḥodesh and three on weekdays, Ḥanukah and the afternoons of
Shabbat and Yom Kippur. On days when the *Haftarah* is chanted, an
additional *aliyah*, known as the *maftir*, is given to the person who reads the
Haftarah. In many contemporary synagogues, there are fewer *aliyot* on
Shabbat and holidays.

D.A.T.

ואתם...היום/And you...today! (Deuteronomy 4:4).

The Torah is placed on the reading table and opened. The gabay says:

וְתִגָּלֶה וְתֵרָאֶה מַלְכוּתוֹ עָלֵינוּ בִּזְמַן קָרוֹב וְיָחֹן פְּלֵיטָתֵנוּ וּפְלֵיטַת
עַמּוֹ בֵּית יִשְׂרָאֵל לְחֵן וּלְחֶסֶד וּלְרַחֲמִים וּלְרָצוֹן וְנֹאמַר אָמֵן: הַכֹּל
הָבוּ גֹדֶל לֵאלֹהֵינוּ וּתְנוּ כָבוֹד לַתּוֹרָה: יַעֲמוֹד/תַּעֲמוֹד/יַעַמְדוּ
_____ בֶּן/בַּת _____ לָעֲלִיָּה [הָרִאשׁוֹנָה, הַשֵּׁנִית, הַשְּׁלִישִׁית]
בָּרוּךְ שֶׁנָּתַן תּוֹרָה לְעַמּוֹ יִשְׂרָאֵל בִּקְדֻשָּׁתוֹ:

Congregaton and gabay continue:

וְאַתֶּם הַדְּבֵקִים בַּיהוה אֱלֹהֵיכֶם חַיִּים כֻּלְּכֶם הַיּוֹם:

Ve'atem hadevekim badonay eloheyhem hayim kulehem hayom.

BIRḤOT HATORAH / TORAH BLESSINGS

Those who receive an aliyah *to the Torah say the following blessing:*

Bless THE INFINITE, the blessed One!

Congregation:

Blessed is THE INFINITE, the blessed One, now and forever!

The response of the congregation is repeated, and the blessing then continued as follows:

Blessed are you, ETERNAL ONE, our God, the sovereign of all worlds, who has drawn us to your service, and has given us your Torah. Blessed are you, ETERNAL ONE, who gives the Torah.

After the section of the Torah is read, the following blessing is recited:

Blessed are you, ETERNAL ONE, our God, the sovereign of all worlds, who has given us a Torah of truth, and planted in our midst eternal life. Blessed are you, ETERNAL ONE, who gives the Torah.

DERASH. *Aliyah* is ascent.
We ascend to the Torah to acknowledge that we choose to live under its laws and principles.
We ascend to the Torah to affirm that we are part of a people and a story that is much greater than ourselves.
We ascend to the Torah to represent those who remain below.
We ascend to the Torah to risk receiving an honor, to risk being known and seen, to risk being at Sinai again.
We ascend to the Torah with slow steps, or in haste, with enthusiasm or reluctance, in awe or in fear, in hope and in love.   S.P.W.

בְּרְכוֹת הַתּוֹרָה

Those who receive an aliyah *to the Torah say the following blessing:*

בָּרְכוּ אֶת יהוה הַמְבֹרָךְ:

Barehu et adonay hamvorah.

Congregation:

בָּרוּךְ יהוה הַמְבֹרָךְ לְעוֹלָם וָעֶד:

Baruh adonay hamvorah le'olam va'ed.

The response of the congregation is repeated and then the blessing continued as follows (for alternative versions, see page 474):

בָּרוּךְ אַתָּה יהוה אֱלֹהֵינוּ מֶלֶךְ הָעוֹלָם אֲשֶׁר קֵרְבָנוּ לַעֲבוֹדָתוֹ וְנָתַן־לָנוּ אֶת־תּוֹרָתוֹ: בָּרוּךְ אַתָּה יהוה נוֹתֵן הַתּוֹרָה:

Baruh atah adonay eloheynu meleh ha'olam asher kervanu la'avodato venatan lanu et torato. Baruh atah adonay noten hatorah.

After the section of the Torah is read, the following blessing is recited:

בָּרוּךְ אַתָּה יהוה אֱלֹהֵינוּ מֶלֶךְ הָעוֹלָם אֲשֶׁר נָתַן־לָנוּ תּוֹרַת אֱמֶת וְחַיֵּי עוֹלָם נָטַע בְּתוֹכֵנוּ: בָּרוּךְ אַתָּה יהוה נוֹתֵן הַתּוֹרָה:

Baruh atah adonay eloheynu meleh ha'olam asher natan lanu torat emet vehayey olam nata betoheynu.
Baruh atah adonay noten hatorah.

COMMENTARY. The blessing over the Torah recalls the *Barehu*, the call to worship, the beginning of the morning service recited only in the presence of the minyan, ten adult Jews. The blessing encircles the Torah reading in a familiar liturgical pattern of blessing and study. Through blessing, study, and community we manifest God, Torah and Israel.   S.P.W.

TORAH READING FOR YOM KIPPUR MINḤAH

First Aliyah

And THE HOLY ONE spoke out to Moses, saying:
Speak to the whole assembly of the Israelites,
and say to them: You shall be holy,
for I am holy—I, THE HOLY ONE, your God!

Let each of you respect your mother and your father,
and observe my Shabbatot
—I am THE HOLY ONE, your God!

Do not turn toward idols;
make no gods molded of metal for yourselves
—I am THE HOLY ONE, your God!   Leviticus 19:1-4

Second Aliyah

When you bring your offerings of well-being
to THE HOLY ONE, your God,
you should offer it in such a way
that brings you favor.
Let it be eaten on the day you offer it,
and on the day that follows. And whatever is left over
to the third day shall be burned with fire.
Should it ever be consumed upon the third day,
it shall be considered an offense, and unacceptable.
Whoever eats of it shall bear the guilt of it
as one who has defiled the sacred province of THE HOLY ONE.
That soul shall become severed from its people. ↩

קדשים תהיו כי קדוש אני/You shall be holy, for I am holy. This is a manifestation of the idea of *imitatio dei*, that people ought to imitate God. The rabbis teach that this means, "be pure, for I (God) am pure." Rashi says that this refers to sexual restraint. Ramban (Rabbi Moses ben Naḥman, a 13th-century scholar) taught that this should be understood as a call to be self-restraining in other spheres of our lives where we Jews are called to act in a holy manner.   M.B.K.

Some communities that have not read Nitzavim *(Deuteronomy 29:9-30:20) in the morning may choose to substitute it here. See pages 531-542.*

First Aliyah

וַיְדַבֵּר יהוה אֶל־מֹשֶׁה לֵּאמֹר: דַּבֵּר אֶל־כָּל־עֲדַת בְּנֵי־יִשְׂרָאֵל וְאָמַרְתָּ אֲלֵהֶם קְדֹשִׁים תִּהְיוּ כִּי קָדוֹשׁ אֲנִי יהוה אֱלֹהֵיכֶם: אִישׁ אִמּוֹ וְאָבִיו תִּירָאוּ וְאֶת־שַׁבְּתֹתַי תִּשְׁמֹרוּ אֲנִי יהוה אֱלֹהֵיכֶם: אַל־תִּפְנוּ אֶל־הָאֱלִילִם וֵאלֹהֵי מַסֵּכָה לֹא תַעֲשׂוּ לָכֶם אֲנִי יהוה אֱלֹהֵיכֶם:

Second Aliyah

וְכִי תִזְבְּחוּ זֶבַח שְׁלָמִים לַיהוה לִרְצֹנְכֶם תִּזְבָּחֻהוּ: בְּיוֹם זִבְחֲכֶם יֵאָכֵל וּמִמָּחֳרָת וְהַנּוֹתָר עַד־יוֹם הַשְּׁלִישִׁי בָּאֵשׁ יִשָּׂרֵף: וְאִם הֵאָכֹל יֵאָכֵל בַּיוֹם הַשְּׁלִישִׁי פִּגּוּל הוּא לֹא יֵרָצֶה: וְאֹכְלָיו עֲוֹנוֹ יִשָּׂא כִּי־ אֶת־קֹדֶשׁ יהוה חִלֵּל וְנִכְרְתָה הַנֶּפֶשׁ הַהִוא מֵעַמֶּיהָ: ←

COMMENTARY. The traditional Torah reading for Yom Kippur afternoon, Leviticus 18, deals with forbidden sexual relationships, perhaps because of the custom in biblical times of young men and women finding spouses in the fields on Yom Kippur afternoon. This *mahzor*, along with the 1948 Reconstructionist *mahzor* and many others, changes the Torah reading to Leviticus 19:1-18, in order to stress holiness in mind and conduct. The forbidden sexual relationships strike many contemporary Jews as inappropriate to the mood of the day, and they are objectionable in a number of their particulars, perhaps most notably their condemnation of homosexual relationships.   D.A.T.

COMMENTARY. This chapter of Leviticus can be characterized as a mini-*torah*, literally, since its instruction contains diverse laws and statutes indicative of the fundamental teachings of the Torah. It specifically echoes several of the Ten Commandments. The structure of the chapter is unique in that it is organized around a series of positive and negative commandments of one to three verses in length. All of them conclude with either "I am THE HOLY ONE, your God," or "I am THE HOLY ONE."   M.B.K.

And when you reap the produce of your land,
you shall leave unharvested the corners of your field,
and stray gleanings of your harvest you shall not collect.
You shall not pick completely clean your vineyard,
and what falls upon the ground within your vineyard
you shall not collect, but leave it for the poor,
and for the stranger. I am THE HOLY ONE, your God!

Leviticus 19:5-10

Third Aliyah
You shall not steal, nor deal deceitfully.
Let none of you deal falsely with your neighbor.
You shall not swear falsely by my name,
thus desecrating your God's name. I am THE HOLY ONE!

Do not exploit your neighbor, and do not engage in robbery,
and do not leave unpaid the wages of a hired worker
till the morning of the day that follows.
Do not curse the deaf, and do not put
a stumbling-block before the blind.
Have awe of God! I am THE HOLY ONE!

Do not pervert the cause of justice—
show favor neither toward the lowly nor the mighty.
In justice shall you judge your neighbor.

Do not go gossiping about among your people.
Do not stand idly by your neighbor's blood—I am THE HOLY
ONE!

שדך פאת /unharvested corners, "stray gleanings," "You shall not pick
completely clean your vineyard," and "what falls...." These are four
specific gifts to be left for the poor and the stranger. This ensures that they
will have food, and not just the spoiled remains. However, the poor must
gather for themselves so that the dignity of labor can offset the
humiliation of dependency.   M.B.K.

וּבְקֻצְרְכֶם אֶת־קְצִיר אַרְצְכֶם לֹא תְכַלֶּה פְּאַת שָׂדְךָ לִקְצֹר וְלֶקֶט קְצִירְךָ לֹא תְלַקֵּט: וְכַרְמְךָ לֹא תְעוֹלֵל וּפֶרֶט כַּרְמְךָ לֹא תְלַקֵּט לֶעָנִי וְלַגֵּר תַּעֲזֹב אֹתָם אֲנִי יהוה אֱלֹהֵיכֶם:

Third Aliyah

לֹא תִּגְנֹבוּ וְלֹא־תְכַחֲשׁוּ וְלֹא־תְשַׁקְּרוּ אִישׁ בַּעֲמִיתוֹ: וְלֹא־תִשָּׁבְעוּ בִשְׁמִי לַשָּׁקֶר וְחִלַּלְתָּ אֶת־שֵׁם אֱלֹהֶיךָ אֲנִי יהוה: לֹא־תַעֲשֹׁק אֶת־רֵעֲךָ וְלֹא תִגְזֹל לֹא־תָלִין פְּעֻלַּת שָׂכִיר אִתְּךָ עַד־בֹּקֶר: לֹא־תְקַלֵּל חֵרֵשׁ וְלִפְנֵי עִוֵּר לֹא תִתֵּן מִכְשֹׁל וְיָרֵאתָ מֵּאֱלֹהֶיךָ אֲנִי יהוה: לֹא־תַעֲשׂוּ עָוֶל בַּמִּשְׁפָּט לֹא־תִשָּׂא פְנֵי־דָל וְלֹא תֶהְדַּר פְּנֵי גָדוֹל בְּצֶדֶק תִּשְׁפֹּט עֲמִיתֶךָ: לֹא־תֵלֵךְ רָכִיל בְּעַמֶּיךָ לֹא תַעֲמֹד עַל־דַּם רֵעֶךָ אֲנִי יהוה: ←

לא תקלל חרש/Do not curse the deaf. Ramban believes this refers to all those lacking full capacities in any way. He cites the verse in Exodus (22:27) that warns against disrespecting rulers and dignitaries. When we read this alongside the passage here, *all* people are included in our obligation to respond with empathy and concern for every individual's dignity.
M.B.K.

לא־תלך רכיל בעמיך/Do not go gossiping about among your people. Rashi says that this refers to those who start arguments and those who tell of evil things. This type of person will "go" into friends' homes in the hope of hearing evil of others. The prohibition against gossip not only applies to those who seek out gossip, but also those who are willing to hear about the misfortunes of their friends.
Rashi

לא תעמד על דם רעך/Do not stand idly by your neighbor's blood. Whenever you can intervene to help your neighbor, you should. We ought to intervene if someone is drowning, being robbed, or injured in any way.
Rashi

Make sure to speak out to your neighbor
in reproof of any wrongful act,
so that you will not incur a greater guilt because of it.
Do not take vengeance, and do not bear grudges
against anyone of your community.
And you shall love your neighbor as yourself.
I am THE HOLY ONE!

Leviticus 19:11-18

❦

The Torah is lifted, and one of the following is recited:

This is the Torah.
It is a Tree of Life to those who hold fast to it.
Those who uphold it may be counted fortunate!

❦

This is the Torah which Moses placed before the children of
    Israel,
by the word of THE ALMIGHTY ONE, and by the hand of Moses.

COMMENTARY. The 1945 Reconstructionist Prayerbook puts "*Etz ḥayim hi /
It is a tree of life*" in place of "*asher sam mosheh lifney beney yisra'el* /which
Moses placed before the children of Israel." Earlier Reconstructionists
were concerned that it be made clear that while affirming the holiness of
Torah, they did not believe that it was given to Moses at Mount Sinai.
Many current Reconstructionists believe the evolutionary nature of the
Torah to be self-evident and have returned to the traditional line for the
sake of its rich mythic imagery. Both options are included here.   D.A.T.

עץ חיים היא /It is a Tree of Life. The book of Genesis tells us that the tree
of life is in the garden of Eden. The Torah is our tree of life; it is our way
back to the garden.   D.E.

לֹא־תִשְׂנָא אֶת־אָחִיךָ בִּלְבָבֶךָ הוֹכֵחַ תּוֹכִיחַ אֶת־עֲמִיתֶךָ וְלֹא־תִשָּׂא עָלָיו חֵטְא: לֹא־תִקֹּם וְלֹא־תִטֹּר אֶת־בְּנֵי עַמֶּךָ וְאָהַבְתָּ לְרֵעֲךָ כָּמוֹךָ אֲנִי יהוה:

᠙

The Torah is lifted and one of the following is recited:

וְזֹאת הַתּוֹרָה עֵץ חַיִּים הִיא לַמַּחֲזִיקִים בָּהּ וְתֹמְכֶיהָ מְאֻשָּׁר:

Vezot hatorah etz ḥayim hi lamaḥazikim bah vetomḥeha me'ushar.

᠙

וְזֹאת הַתּוֹרָה אֲשֶׁר שָׂם מֹשֶׁה לִפְנֵי בְּנֵי יִשְׂרָאֵל עַל פִּי יהוה בְּיַד מֹשֶׁה:

Vezot hatorah asher sam mosheh lifney beney yisra'el al pi adonay beyad mosheh.

COMMENTARY. The covenant of community is based on the delicate balance between two fundamental principles of Judaism articulated in this afternoon's Torah reading. The first is הוכח תוכיח את עמיתך, "Make sure to speak out to your neighbor" the obligation to correct those about whom we care when they act contrary to Judaism's basic teachings. The second fundamental principle of Judaism that forms the basis of the covenant of community is *Ahavat Yisrael*, unconditional love of one Jew for another, of each Jew for the entirety of the Jewish people. Just before the Torah commands us to rebuke our neighbor, it teaches, "You shall not hate your neighbor in your heart." This is a most difficult and non-negotiable condition for a loving rebuke; if we do not first love, we cannot criticize.

R.H.

עץ...מאשר / It...fortunate! (Proverbs 3:18).
וזאת...ישראל / This...Israel (Deuteronomy 4:44).
על...משה / by...Moses (Numbers 9:23).

1048 / **LIFTING THE TORAH SCROLL**

BIRKAT HAFTARAH / HAFTARAH BLESSING

Blessed are you, ETERNAL ONE, our God, the sovereign of all worlds, who has called upon the righteous prophets and desired their words, spoken in truth. Blessed are you, WISE ONE, who takes pleasure in the Torah, and in Moses, servant of God, and in the prophets of truth and justice.

HAFTARAH FOR YOM KIPPUR MINHAH / THE BOOK OF JONAH

The word of THE ALL-SEEING came to Jonah, son of Amitay,
   saying:
"Rise up, go to Nineveh, the great city,
and proclaim against it that its evil has come up to me."
And Jonah rose, to flee to Tarshish,
from the presence of THE OMNIPRESENT.
He went down to Jaffa, and he found a ship
sailing to Tarshish, and he paid for passage,
and went down into its hold, to sail for Tarshish
from the presence of THE OMNIPRESENT ONE.

And THE ALMIGHTY cast a great wind on the sea;
a huge storm came upon the ocean,
and the ship was on the verge of being destroyed.
The sailors were afraid,
and each one cried out to his god.
They cast into the sea the goods that were on board,
to lighten the ship's load.
And Jonah, meanwhile, had gone down
into the belly of the boat, and there he lay and slept.

The captain now approached him,
and addressed him: "What's with you that you sleep!
Rise up, and call upon your God!
Perhaps then God will notice us,
and we shall not be lost." ⟵

בִּרְכַּת הַפְטָרָה

בָּרוּךְ אַתָּה יהוה אֱלֹהֵינוּ מֶלֶךְ הָעוֹלָם אֲשֶׁר בָּחַר בִּנְבִיאִים טוֹבִים
וְרָצָה בְדִבְרֵיהֶם הַנֶּאֱמָרִים בֶּאֱמֶת: בָּרוּךְ אַתָּה יהוה הַבּוֹחֵר בַּתּוֹרָה
וּבְמֹשֶׁה עַבְדּוֹ וּבְנְבִיאֵי הָאֱמֶת וָצֶדֶק:

Haftarah

וַיְהִי דְּבַר־יהוֹה אֶל־יוֹנָה בֶן־אֲמִתַּי לֵאמֹר: קוּם לֵךְ אֶל־נִינְוֵה
הָעִיר הַגְּדוֹלָה וּקְרָא עָלֶיהָ כִּי־עָלְתָה רָעָתָם לְפָנָי: וַיָּקָם יוֹנָה
לִבְרֹחַ תַּרְשִׁישָׁה מִלִּפְנֵי יהוה וַיֵּרֶד יָפוֹ וַיִּמְצָא אֳנִיָּה | בָּאָה תַרְשִׁישׁ
וַיִּתֵּן שְׂכָרָהּ וַיֵּרֶד בָּהּ לָבוֹא עִמָּהֶם תַּרְשִׁישָׁה מִלִּפְנֵי יהוה: וַיהוֹה
הֵטִיל רוּחַ־גְּדוֹלָה אֶל־הַיָּם וַיְהִי סַעַר־גָּדוֹל בַּיָּם וְהָאֳנִיָּה חִשְּׁבָה
לְהִשָּׁבֵר: וַיִּירְאוּ הַמַּלָּחִים וַיִּזְעֲקוּ אִישׁ אֶל־אֱלֹהָיו וַיָּטִלוּ אֶת־
הַכֵּלִים אֲשֶׁר בָּאֳנִיָּה אֶל־הַיָּם לְהָקֵל מֵעֲלֵיהֶם וְיוֹנָה יָרַד אֶל־
יַרְכְּתֵי הַסְּפִינָה וַיִּשְׁכַּב וַיֵּרָדַם: וַיִּקְרַב אֵלָיו רַב הַחֹבֵל וַיֹּאמֶר לוֹ
מַה־לְּךָ נִרְדָּם קוּם קְרָא אֶל־אֱלֹהֶיךָ אוּלַי יִתְעַשֵּׁת הָאֱלֹהִים לָנוּ
וְלֹא נֹאבֵד: ←——

COMMENTARY. One of the Just Ones came to Sodom, determined to save
its inhabitants from sin and punishment. Night and day the Just One
walked the streets and markets preaching against greed and theft, falsehood
and indifference. In the beginning, people listened and smiled ironically.
Then they stopped listening: they were no longer amused. The killers
went on killing, the wise kept silent, as if there were no Just One in their
midst.

One day a child, moved by compassion, approached the unfortunate
preacher with these words, "Poor stranger. You shout, you expend your
body and soul; don't you see that it is hopeless?"

"Yes, I see," answered the Just One.

"Then why do you go on?"

"I'll tell you why. In the beginning, I thought I could change humankind.
Today, I know I cannot. If I still shout today, if I still scream, it is to
prevent humankind from ultimately changing me."   Elie Wiesel

And people said to one another:
"Come, let's all cast lots that we may know
through whom this evil comes upon us!"
And they cast lots.
The lot came down on Jonah.
And they said to him: "Please tell us—
who is he through whom this evil has befallen us?
What is your work? Where do you come from?
What is your country? From what people do you stem?"
He said to them: "I am a Hebrew,
and I fear THE OMNIPRESENT ONE, the God of Heaven,
who has made the sea and land."
And they all became afraid—enormous was their fear.
They said to him: "What have you done?"
These people knew that he was fleeing THE ALMIGHTY ONE,
as he had told them.

And they said to him: "What should we do with you
so that the sea might quiet down on our account?
Truly, this storm is growing worse!"
He told them: "Pick me up and cast me to the sea,
and then the sea will quiet down for you,
because I know it is on my account
that this great storm has overtaken you."
Meanwhile, the ship's men struggled
to get back to dry land, but they couldn't,
for the sea continued in its rage against them. ↰

וַיֹּאמְר֞וּ אִ֣ישׁ אֶל־רֵעֵ֗הוּ לְכוּ֙ וְנַפִּ֣ילָה גֽוֹרָל֔וֹת וְנֵ֣דְעָ֔ה בְּשֶׁלְּמִ֛י הָרָעָ֥ה הַזֹּ֖את לָ֑נוּ וַיַּפִּ֙לוּ֙ גּֽוֹרָל֔וֹת וַיִּפֹּ֥ל הַגּוֹרָ֖ל עַל־יוֹנָֽה׃ וַיֹּאמְר֣וּ אֵלָ֔יו הַגִּֽידָה־נָּ֣א לָ֔נוּ בַּֽאֲשֶׁ֛ר לְמִֽי־הָרָעָ֥ה הַזֹּ֖את לָ֑נוּ מַה־מְּלַאכְתְּךָ֙ וּמֵאַ֣יִן תָּב֔וֹא מָ֣ה אַרְצֶ֔ךָ וְאֵֽי־מִזֶּ֥ה עַ֖ם אָֽתָּה׃ וַיֹּ֣אמֶר אֲלֵיהֶ֔ם עִבְרִ֖י אָנֹ֑כִי וְאֶת־יְהֹוָ֞ה אֱלֹהֵ֤י הַשָּׁמַ֙יִם֙ אֲנִ֣י יָרֵ֔א אֲשֶׁר־עָשָׂ֥ה אֶת־הַיָּ֖ם וְאֶת־הַיַּבָּשָֽׁה׃ וַיִּֽירְא֤וּ הָֽאֲנָשִׁים֙ יִרְאָ֣ה גְדוֹלָ֔ה וַיֹּאמְר֥וּ אֵלָ֖יו מַה־זֹּ֣את עָשִׂ֑יתָ כִּֽי־יָדְע֣וּ הָֽאֲנָשִׁ֗ים כִּֽי־מִלִּפְנֵ֤י יְהֹוָה֙ ה֣וּא בֹרֵ֔חַ כִּ֥י הִגִּ֖יד לָהֶֽם׃ וַיֹּאמְר֤וּ אֵלָיו֙ מַה־נַּ֣עֲשֶׂה לָּ֔ךְ וְיִשְׁתֹּ֥ק הַיָּ֖ם מֵֽעָלֵ֑ינוּ כִּ֥י הַיָּ֖ם הוֹלֵ֥ךְ וְסֹעֵֽר׃ וַיֹּ֣אמֶר אֲלֵיהֶ֗ם שָׂא֙וּנִי֙ וַֽהֲטִילֻ֣נִי אֶל־הַיָּ֔ם וְיִשְׁתֹּ֥ק הַיָּ֖ם מֵֽעֲלֵיכֶ֑ם כִּ֚י יוֹדֵ֣עַ אָ֔נִי כִּ֣י בְשֶׁלִּ֔י הַסַּ֧עַר הַגָּד֛וֹל הַזֶּ֖ה עֲלֵיכֶֽם׃ וַיַּחְתְּר֣וּ הָֽאֲנָשִׁ֗ים לְהָשִׁ֛יב אֶל־הַיַּבָּשָׁ֖ה וְלֹ֣א יָכֹ֑לוּ כִּ֣י הַיָּ֔ם הוֹלֵ֥ךְ וְסֹעֵ֖ר עֲלֵיהֶֽם׃ ⟵

And they called out to THE OMNIPRESENT ONE,
and said: "O, please, ALMIGHTY ONE,
let us not perish for the life of this one man,
and do not hold against us
the blood of someone innocent,
for you are THE ALMIGHTY ONE;
whatever you may wish, you do."
They picked up Jonah, and they cast him to the sea.
And suddenly the ocean ceased its rage.
The people grew afraid;
enormous was their awe of THE ALMIGHTY.
And they offered sacrifice to GOD
and uttered vows.

THE OMNIPRESENT ONE
appointed a great fish to swallow Jonah,
and he was inside the belly of the fish
for three days and three nights.
And Jonah prayed to THE ETERNAL ONE, his God,
inside the belly of the fish. He said:

"I called, in my distress,
to THE ETERNAL ONE, and I was answered!
From the belly of She'ol I cried,
and you have listened to my voice.
For you had cast me to the deep,
into the heart of seas; a flood surrounded me.
Your breakers and your waves have all passed over me.
And I—I said: I have been driven from your sight,
but I shall once again look on your holy Temple! ↰

וַיִּקְרְא֣וּ אֶל־יְהֹוָ֗ה וַיֹּאמְר֞וּ אָנָּ֤ה יְהֹוָה֙ אַל־נָ֣א נֹאבְדָ֗ה בְּנֶ֙פֶשׁ֙ הָאִ֣ישׁ
הַזֶּ֔ה וְאַל־תִּתֵּ֥ן עָלֵ֖ינוּ דָּ֣ם נָקִ֑יא כִּֽי־אַתָּ֣ה יְהֹוָ֔ה כַּאֲשֶׁ֥ר חָפַ֖צְתָּ
עָשִֽׂיתָ: וַיִּשְׂאוּ֙ אֶת־יוֹנָ֔ה וַיְטִלֻ֖הוּ אֶל־הַיָּ֑ם וַיַּעֲמֹ֥ד הַיָּ֖ם מִזַּעְפּֽוֹ:
וַיִּֽירְא֧וּ הָאֲנָשִׁ֛ים יִרְאָ֥ה גְדוֹלָ֖ה אֶת־יְהֹוָ֑ה וַיִּזְבְּחוּ־זֶ֙בַח֙ לַֽיהֹוָ֔ה וַיִּדְּר֖וּ
נְדָרִֽים: וַיְמַ֤ן יְהֹוָה֙ דָּ֣ג גָּד֔וֹל לִבְלֹ֖עַ אֶת־יוֹנָ֑ה וַיְהִ֤י יוֹנָה֙ בִּמְעֵ֣י הַדָּ֔ג
שְׁלֹשָׁ֥ה יָמִ֖ים וּשְׁלֹשָׁ֥ה לֵילֽוֹת: וַיִּתְפַּלֵּ֣ל יוֹנָ֔ה אֶל־יְהֹוָ֖ה אֱלֹהָ֑יו
מִמְּעֵ֖י הַדָּגָֽה: וַיֹּ֗אמֶר קָרָ֠אתִי מִצָּ֥רָה לִ֛י אֶל־יְהֹוָ֖ה וַֽיַּעֲנֵ֑נִי מִבֶּ֧טֶן
שְׁא֛וֹל שִׁוַּ֖עְתִּי שָׁמַ֥עְתָּ קוֹלִֽי: וַתַּשְׁלִיכֵ֤נִי מְצוּלָה֙ בִּלְבַ֣ב יַמִּ֔ים וְנָהָ֖ר
יְסֹבְבֵ֑נִי כָּל־מִשְׁבָּרֶ֥יךָ וְגַלֶּ֖יךָ עָלַ֥י עָבָֽרוּ: וַאֲנִ֣י אָמַ֔רְתִּי נִגְרַ֖שְׁתִּי מִנֶּ֣גֶד
עֵינֶ֑יךָ אַ֚ךְ אוֹסִ֣יף לְהַבִּ֔יט אֶל־הֵיכַ֖ל קָדְשֶֽׁךָ: ⟵

Waters overwhelmed me to the edge of death,
the deep surrounded me,
the seaweed wrapped around my head,
there at the remote depths of mountains.
I went down into the earth; its bars
were closed around me—an eternity!
But you have raised my life up from the underworld,
REDEEMING ONE, my God!
My life was wrapped about me—I grew faint—
but I remembered THE ETERNAL ONE.
My prayer has come before you,
to your holy Temple.
Those who cling to vain and empty things
forsake their loyalty,
but I, with thankful voice,
shall offer you devotions.
What I have vowed, allow me to complete.
All help is from THE OMNIPRESENT ONE!"

And THE REDEEMING ONE spoke to the fish,
which vomited up Jonah onto dry land.

The word of THE ALL-SEEING came to Jonah
for a second time, and said:
"Rise up, and go to Nineveh, the great city,
and declare to it the message I am giving you." ⤺

אֲפָפ֤וּנִי מַ֙יִם֙ עַד־נֶ֔פֶשׁ תְּה֖וֹם יְסֹבְבֵ֑נִי ס֖וּף חָב֥וּשׁ לְרֹאשִֽׁי: לְקִצְבֵ֤י הָרִים֙ יָרַ֔דְתִּי הָאָ֛רֶץ בְּרִחֶ֥יהָ בַעֲדִ֖י לְעוֹלָ֑ם וַתַּ֧עַל מִשַּׁ֛חַת חַיַּ֖י יְהֹוָ֥ה אֱלֹהָֽי: בְּהִתְעַטֵּ֤ף עָלַי֙ נַפְשִׁ֔י אֶת־יְהֹוָ֖ה זָכָ֑רְתִּי וַתָּב֤וֹא אֵלֶ֙יךָ֙ תְּפִלָּתִ֔י אֶל־הֵיכַ֖ל קׇדְשֶֽׁךָ: מְשַׁמְּרִ֖ים הַבְלֵי־שָׁ֑וְא חַסְדָּ֖ם יַעֲזֹֽבוּ: וַאֲנִ֗י בְּק֤וֹל תּוֹדָה֙ אֶזְבְּחָה־לָּ֔ךְ אֲשֶׁ֥ר נָדַ֖רְתִּי אֲשַׁלֵּ֑מָה יְשׁוּעָ֖תָה לַיהֹוָֽה: וַיֹּ֥אמֶר יְהֹוָ֖ה לַדָּ֑ג וַיָּקֵ֥א אֶת־יוֹנָ֖ה אֶל־הַיַּבָּשָֽׁה: וַיְהִ֧י דְבַר־יְהֹוָ֛ה אֶל־יוֹנָ֖ה שֵׁנִ֥ית לֵאמֹֽר: ק֛וּם לֵ֥ךְ אֶל־נִֽינְוֵ֖ה הָעִ֣יר הַגְּדוֹלָ֑ה וּקְרָ֤א אֵלֶ֙יהָ֙ אֶת־הַקְּרִיאָ֔ה אֲשֶׁ֥ר אָנֹכִ֖י דֹּבֵ֥ר אֵלֶֽיךָ: ←

And Jonah rose up, and he went to Nineveh,
according to the word of THE ETERNAL ONE.

Now, Nineveh was a city great to THE ALMIGHTY ONE;
it takes three days to cross it.
And when Jonah reached the city,
and had traveled in it one full day,
he called out and he said:
"Forty more days and Nineveh is overthrown!"
And the citizens of Nineveh believed in God,
and they declared a fast,
and dressed in sackcloth, great and small alike.

And word of it had reached the king of Nineveh,
and he rose up from his throne,
and he removed his royal robe
and dressed himself in sackcloth,
and he sat upon a bed of ash.
And he cried out, and he said:
"In Nineveh, by order of the king
and all his ministers, declare the following:
No person and no beast,
no cattle and no sheep,
shall taste a thing; they shall not feed,
nor water shall they drink.
Let them be dressed in sackcloth,
human being and beast alike,
and let them call out mightily to God.
Let all forsake their evil ways,
the violence their hands have done!
Who knows? Perhaps God will repent, as well,
returning from a course of wrath,
and we shall not be lost." ⤺

וַיָּ֣קָם יוֹנָ֗ה וַיֵּ֛לֶךְ אֶל־נִֽינְוֵ֖ה כִּדְבַ֣ר יְהֹוָ֑ה וְנִֽינְוֵ֗ה הָֽיְתָ֤ה עִיר־גְּדוֹלָה֙
לֵֽאלֹהִ֔ים מַהֲלַ֖ךְ שְׁלֹ֥שֶׁת יָמִֽים: וַיָּ֤חֶל יוֹנָה֙ לָב֣וֹא בָעִ֔יר מַהֲלַ֖ךְ י֣וֹם
אֶחָ֑ד וַיִּקְרָא֙ וַיֹּאמַ֔ר ע֚וֹד אַרְבָּעִ֣ים י֔וֹם וְנִֽינְוֵ֖ה נֶהְפָּֽכֶת: וַיַּֽאֲמִ֛ינוּ
אַנְשֵׁ֥י נִֽינְוֵ֖ה בֵּֽאלֹהִ֑ים וַיִּקְרְאוּ־צוֹם֙ וַיִּלְבְּשׁ֣וּ שַׂקִּ֔ים מִגְּדוֹלָ֖ם וְעַד־
קְטַנָּֽם: וַיִּגַּ֤ע הַדָּבָר֙ אֶל־מֶ֣לֶךְ נִֽינְוֵ֔ה וַיָּ֙קָם֙ מִכִּסְא֔וֹ וַיַּֽעֲבֵ֥ר אַדַּרְתּ֖וֹ
מֵֽעָלָ֑יו וַיְכַ֣ס שַׂ֔ק וַיֵּ֖שֶׁב עַל־הָאֵֽפֶר: וַיַּזְעֵ֗ק וַיֹּ֙אמֶר֙ בְּנִֽינְוֵ֔ה מִטַּ֧עַם
הַמֶּ֛לֶךְ וּגְדֹלָ֖יו לֵאמֹ֑ר הָֽאָדָ֨ם וְהַבְּהֵמָ֜ה הַבָּקָ֣ר וְהַצֹּ֗אן אַל־יִטְעֲמוּ֙
מְא֔וּמָה אַל־יִרְע֕וּ וּמַ֖יִם אַל־יִשְׁתּֽוּ: וְיִתְכַּסּ֣וּ שַׂקִּ֗ים הָֽאָדָם֙ וְהַבְּהֵמָ֔ה
וְיִקְרְא֥וּ אֶל־אֱלֹהִ֖ים בְּחׇזְקָ֑ה וְיָשֻׁ֗בוּ אִ֚ישׁ מִדַּרְכּ֣וֹ הָֽרָעָ֔ה וּמִן־הֶֽחָמָ֖ס
אֲשֶׁ֥ר בְּכַפֵּיהֶֽם: מִֽי־יוֹדֵ֣עַ יָשׁ֔וּב וְנִחַ֖ם הָֽאֱלֹהִ֑ים וְשָׁ֛ב מֵֽחֲר֥וֹן אַפּ֖וֹ
וְלֹ֥א נֹאבֵֽד: ⟵

And God beheld their actions,
that they had returned from evil ways,
and God repented of the dire fate
that had been planned for them,
and did not act.

This was a woeful thing to Jonah,
an enormous evil, and he burned with rage.
He prayed to THE ALMIGHTY, and he said:
"I ask you, GOD OF JUSTICE, was this not
the very thing I thought would happen
while I still was standing on my native land?
That's why I fled ahead of time to Tarshish,
for I knew you are a gracious and forgiving God,
slow to be angry, and abundant in your love,
and likely to repent of harshness.
So now, please take my life from me,
for it is better that I die than live!"

And THE REDEEMING ONE said: "Is it right
that you should burn with rage?"

And Jonah went out from the city,
and stationed himself eastward of the city.
There, he built himself a shelter (sukkah),
and he sat beneath it in the shade,
to wait and see what would befall the city.

And God, THE COMPASSIONATE, appointed a vine,
which grew up over Jonah to protect his head with shade
and save him from his evil mood.
Jonah felt pleasure at the vine, enormous pleasure. ↵

וַיַּ֤רְא הָֽאֱלֹהִים֙ אֶֽת־מַ֣עֲשֵׂיהֶ֔ם כִּי־שָׁ֖בוּ מִדַּרְכָּ֣ם הָרָעָ֑ה וַיִּנָּ֣חֶם
הָאֱלֹהִ֗ים עַל־הָרָעָ֛ה אֲשֶׁר־דִּבֶּ֥ר לַעֲשׂוֹת־לָהֶ֖ם וְלֹ֥א עָשָֽׂה: וַיֵּ֥רַע
אֶל־יוֹנָ֖ה רָעָ֣ה גְדוֹלָ֑ה וַיִּ֖חַר לֽוֹ: וַיִּתְפַּלֵּ֨ל אֶל־יְהֹוָ֜ה וַיֹּאמַ֗ר אָנָּ֤ה
יְהֹוָה֙ הֲלוֹא־זֶ֣ה דְבָרִ֗י עַד־הֱיוֹתִי֙ עַל־אַדְמָתִ֔י עַל־כֵּ֥ן קִדַּ֖מְתִּי לִבְרֹ֣חַ
תַּרְשִׁ֑ישָׁה כִּ֣י יָדַ֗עְתִּי כִּ֤י אַתָּה֙ אֵֽל־חַנּ֣וּן וְרַח֔וּם אֶ֤רֶךְ אַפַּ֙יִם֙ וְרַב־
חֶ֔סֶד וְנִחָ֖ם עַל־הָרָעָֽה: וְעַתָּ֣ה יְהֹוָ֔ה קַח־נָ֥א אֶת־נַפְשִׁ֖י מִמֶּ֑נִּי כִּ֛י ט֥וֹב
מוֹתִ֖י מֵחַיָּֽי: וַיֹּ֣אמֶר יְהֹוָ֔ה הַהֵיטֵ֖ב חָ֥רָה לָֽךְ: וַיֵּצֵ֤א יוֹנָה֙ מִן־הָעִ֔יר
וַיֵּ֖שֶׁב מִקֶּ֣דֶם לָעִ֑יר וַיַּעַשׂ֩ ל֨וֹ שָׁ֜ם סֻכָּ֗ה וַיֵּ֤שֶׁב תַּחְתֶּ֙יהָ֙ בַּצֵּ֔ל עַ֚ד אֲשֶׁ֣ר
יִרְאֶ֔ה מַה־יִּהְיֶ֖ה בָּעִֽיר: וַיְמַ֣ן יְהֹוָֽה־אֱ֠לֹהִ֠ים קִיקָי֞וֹן וַיַּ֣עַל ׀ מֵעַ֣ל
לְיוֹנָ֗ה לִהְי֥וֹת צֵל֙ עַל־רֹאשׁ֔וֹ לְהַצִּ֥יל ל֖וֹ מֵרָֽעָת֑וֹ וַיִּשְׂמַ֥ח יוֹנָ֛ה
עַל־הַקִּֽיקָי֖וֹן שִׂמְחָ֥ה גְדוֹלָֽה: ←

And God appointed a vine-weevil, at dawn of the next day,
and it attacked the vine so that it withered up.
And when the sun grew bright,
God sent a hot east wind,
and sun's heat attacked the head of Jonah.
He grew faint; his spirit begged to die.
He cried: "It's better that I die than live!"
And God asked Jonah: "Is it right
that you should burn with rage about the vine?"

And Jonah said: "It's right
that I should burn to death with rage!"

And THE ALL-MERCIFUL replied:
"You are concerned about this vine,
which you have neither labored over nor have grown,
which one night lives, the next night dies.
And I—should I not be concerned for Nineveh,
a great city, which has within it
more than a hundred-twenty thousand human beings
who do not know their right hand from their left,
and much cattle, too?"

Jonah

Who is a God like you?
—forgiving sin, absolving the transgressions
of the remnant of your heritage,
you who do not cling to anger,
but desire only kindness,
you who act mercifully once again,
subduing the effects of our transgressions,
casting to the ocean waters all our wrongs.

You show faithfulness to Jacob,
love to Abraham,
as you have sworn to Abraham
from days of old.

Micah 7:18-20

וַיְמַ֣ן הָאֱלֹהִים֩ תּוֹלַ֨עַת֙ בַּעֲל֣וֹת הַשַּׁ֔חַר לַֽמָּחֳרָ֑ת וַתַּ֥ךְ אֶת־הַקִּֽיקָי֖וֹן
וַיִּיבָֽשׁ׃ וַיְהִ֣י ׀ כִּזְרֹ֣חַ הַשֶּׁ֗מֶשׁ וַיְמַ֨ן אֱלֹהִ֜ים ר֤וּחַ קָדִים֙ חֲרִישִׁ֔ית וַתַּ֥ךְ
הַשֶּׁ֛מֶשׁ עַל־רֹ֥אשׁ יוֹנָ֖ה וַיִּתְעַלָּ֑ף וַיִּשְׁאַ֤ל אֶת־נַפְשׁוֹ֙ לָמ֔וּת וַיֹּ֕אמֶר
ט֥וֹב מוֹתִ֖י מֵֽחַיָּֽי׃ וַיֹּ֤אמֶר אֱלֹהִים֙ אֶל־יוֹנָ֔ה הַהֵיטֵ֥ב חָרָֽה־לְךָ֖ עַל־
הַקִּֽיקָי֑וֹן וַיֹּ֕אמֶר הֵיטֵ֥ב חָֽרָה־לִ֖י עַד־מָֽוֶת׃ וַיֹּ֣אמֶר יְהֹוָ֔ה אַתָּ֥ה חַ֨סְתָּ֙
עַל־הַקִּ֣יקָי֔וֹן אֲשֶׁ֛ר לֹא־עָמַ֥לְתָּ בּ֖וֹ וְלֹ֣א גִדַּלְתּ֑וֹ שֶׁבִּן־לַ֥יְלָה הָיָ֖ה
וּבִן־לַ֥יְלָה אָבָֽד׃ וַֽאֲנִי֙ לֹ֣א אָח֔וּס עַל־נִ֣ינְוֵ֔ה הָעִ֖יר הַגְּדוֹלָ֑ה אֲשֶׁ֣ר
יֶשׁ־בָּ֡הּ הַרְבֵּה֩ מִֽשְׁתֵּים־עֶשְׂרֵ֨ה רִבּ֜וֹ אָדָ֗ם אֲשֶׁ֤ר לֹֽא־יָדַע֙ בֵּין־יְמִינ֣וֹ
לִשְׂמֹאל֔וֹ וּבְהֵמָ֖ה רַבָּֽה׃

מִי־אֵ֣ל כָּמ֗וֹךָ נֹשֵׂ֤א עָוֺן֙ וְעֹבֵ֣ר עַל־פֶּ֔שַׁע לִשְׁאֵרִ֖ית נַחֲלָת֑וֹ לֹא־
הֶחֱזִ֤יק לָעַד֙ אַפּ֔וֹ כִּֽי־חָפֵ֥ץ חֶ֖סֶד הֽוּא׃ יָשׁ֣וּב יְרַֽחֲמֵ֔נוּ יִכְבֹּ֖שׁ עֲוֺֽנֹתֵ֑ינוּ
וְתַשְׁלִ֛יךְ בִּמְצֻל֥וֹת יָ֖ם כָּל־חַטֹּאותָֽם׃ תִּתֵּ֤ן אֱמֶת֙ לְיַֽעֲקֹ֔ב חֶ֖סֶד
לְאַבְרָהָ֑ם אֲשֶׁר־נִשְׁבַּ֥עְתָּ לַֽאֲבֹתֵ֖ינוּ מִ֥ימֵי קֶֽדֶם׃

After the haftarah *is chanted, the following blessings are said:*

Blessed are you, ETERNAL ONE, our God, the sovereign of all worlds, the rock of all the worlds, the righteous one throughout all generations, the faithful God, whose word is deed, who speaks and fulfills, whose words are truth and justice.

Faithful are you, ETERNAL ONE, our God, and faithful are your words; not a single word of yours is unfulfilled, for you are a sovereign God, faithful and merciful. Blessed are you, ETERNAL ONE, the God faithful in all your words.

Be merciful to Zion, which is the house of life to us, and be a help to Israel, your people, soon and in our days. Blessed are you, ETERNAL ONE, who gives joy to Zion through her children.

Give us joy, ETERNAL ONE, our God, in Elijah, your prophet and your servant. Soon may redemption come and give joy to our hearts. May God turn the hearts of the parents to their children, and the hearts of the children to their parents. And may your house be called a house of prayer for all peoples. Blessed are you, ETERNAL ONE, who brings an everlasting peace.

שמחינו / Give us joy. The traditional *haftarah* blessing contains references to the reestablishment of the rule of the Davidic dynasty. This understanding of a messianic reappearance of hereditary kingship has been rejected by Reconstructionist thought on both moral and theological grounds. Nonetheless, the messianic hope for a world redeemed remains in our thoughts as the ultimate achievement towards which humanity should strive.

Our version of the *haftarah* blessing eliminates the Davidic references and the hopes for a literal messiah that they invoke. In their place are Malachi 3:24 and a slightly altered version of Isaiah 56:7. The vision in Malachi, which is the *haftarah* for Shabbat Hagadol, sees Elijah coming to herald messianic days, turning the hearts of parents and children toward each other. The task of redemption can be completed when all of us open our hearts to our families, to our communities, and to all the inhabitants of our world. Then our world will truly have become a house of prayer for all peoples, bringing the peace for which we all hope.   D.A.T.

After the haftarah *is chanted, the following blessings are said:*

בָּרוּךְ אַתָּה יהוה אֱלֹהֵינוּ מֶלֶךְ הָעוֹלָם צוּר כָּל הָעוֹלָמִים צַדִּיק בְּכָל
הַדּוֹרוֹת הָאֵל הַנֶּאֱמָן הָאוֹמֵר וְעוֹשֶׂה הַמְדַבֵּר וּמְקַיֵּם שֶׁכָּל דְּבָרָיו
אֱמֶת וָצֶדֶק:
נֶאֱמָן אַתָּה הוּא יהוה אֱלֹהֵינוּ וְנֶאֱמָנִים דְּבָרֶיךָ וְדָבָר אֶחָד מִדְּבָרֶיךָ
אָחוֹר לֹא יָשׁוּב רֵיקָם כִּי אֵל מֶלֶךְ נֶאֱמָן וְרַחֲמָן אָתָּה: בָּרוּךְ אַתָּה
יהוה הָאֵל הַנֶּאֱמָן בְּכָל דְּבָרָיו:
רַחֵם עַל צִיּוֹן כִּי הִיא בֵּית חַיֵּינוּ וּלְעַמְּךָ יִשְׂרָאֵל תּוֹשִׁיעַ בִּמְהֵרָה
בְיָמֵינוּ: בָּרוּךְ אַתָּה יהוה מְשַׂמֵּחַ צִיּוֹן בְּבָנֶיהָ:
שַׂמְּחֵנוּ יהוה אֱלֹהֵינוּ בְּאֵלִיָּהוּ הַנָּבִיא עַבְדֶּךָ בִּמְהֵרָה יָבוֹא וְיָגֵל
לִבֵּנוּ: וְהָשִׁיב לֵב אָבוֹת עַל בָּנִים וְלֵב בָּנִים עַל אֲבוֹתָם וּבֵיתְךָ בֵּית
תְּפִלָּה יִקָּרֵא לְכָל הָעַמִּים: בָּרוּךְ אַתָּה יהוה מֵבִיא שָׁלוֹם לָעַד:

COMMENTARY. Most liturgists agree that the practice of reciting a *haftarah*, generally a selection from the prophets, probably developed during a time when public reading of the Torah was banned. A selection roughly paralleling a major theme from the week's Torah portion was therefore selected. When public reading of the Torah became possible again, the popular custom of chanting the *haftarah* continued. The *haftarah* is usually chanted, utilizing a *trope* or cantillation system that has numerous variations. In modern times the bar/bat mitzvah has often taken on this responsibility as a sign of committed membership in the adult community.
D.A.T.

ולעמך ישראל תושיע/be a help to Israel your people. The traditional phrase here, *aluvat nefesh*/cast-down soul, reflected the Jewish people's exile from their land. With the establishment of the State of Israel, we are no longer "cast down." This fundamental change in Jewish life is reflected in the revised language here.
D.A.T.

HAḤNASAT SEFER TORAH / RETURNING THE TORAH TO THE ARK

Let all bless the name of THE ETERNAL,
for it alone is to be exalted.

God's splendor dwells on earth and in the heavens,
God has lifted up our people's strength.
Praise to all God's fervent ones,
to the children of Israel, people near to God.
Halleluyah!

Traditionally the Torah is carried around the room, although some congregations immediately place it in the ark and continue with Etz Ḥayim Hi, page 1071.

הַכְנָסַת סֵפֶר תּוֹרָה

יְהַלְלוּ אֶת־שֵׁם יהוה כִּי־נִשְׂגָּב שְׁמוֹ לְבַדּוֹ

הוֹדוֹ עַל־אֶרֶץ וְשָׁמָיִם: וַיָּרֶם קֶרֶן לְעַמּוֹ תְּהִלָּה לְכָל־חֲסִידָיו לִבְנֵי
יִשְׂרָאֵל עַם קְרֹבוֹ הַלְלוּיָהּ:

Yehalelu et shem adonay ki nisgav shemo levado

Hodo al eretz veshamayim vayarem keren le'amo tehilah lehol
hasidav livney yisra'el am kerovo halleluyah.

Traditionally the Torah is carried around the room, although some congregations immediately place it in the ark and continue with Etz Hayim Hi, page 1072.

יהללו...הללויה / Let...Halleluyah! (Psalms 148:13-14).

A psalm of David.

The world belongs to GOD in all its fullness,
the earth, and all who dwell on it,
for God has founded it upon the waters,
on the torrents, God established it.
Who can ascend the mount of THE ETERNAL?
Who rises to the holy place of God?
The one whose hands are clean, whose heart is pure,
whose soul has not been vainly self-excusing,
the one who never swore deceitfully.

That person reaps a blessing from THE ALL-KNOWING ONE,
justice from the God of help.
For many generations now,
the family of Jacob has sought your presence.
You city gates, open your bolts,
eternal gates, be lifted up,
and let the sovereign of glory come! ↩

אשר לא־נשא לשוא נפשי / *Whose soul has not been vainly self-excusing*. Literally,
"who has not lifted up the soul in vain." The psalm turns on repetitions
of the key verb, "lift up," playing on its many meanings. Compare: "That
person reaps [literally, lifts up] a blessing....You city gates, open [literally,
lift up] your gates," etc.

The pilgrim, ascending the steep slopes toward the Temple Mount,
contemplates, through this interplay of associations, the fundamental act of
pilgrimage: an offering-up to God.   J.R.

NOTE. This psalm asks and answers several questions, suggesting that it
was sung antiphonally in ancient times, with the congregation singing the
responses.   D.A.T.

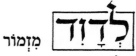

מִזְמוֹר

לַיהוה הָאָרֶץ וּמְלוֹאָהּ   תֵּבֵל וְיֹשְׁבֵי בָהּ:

כִּי־הוּא עַל־יַמִּים יְסָדָהּ   וְעַל־נְהָרוֹת יְכוֹנְנֶהָ:

מִי־יַעֲלֶה בְהַר־יהוה   וּמִי־יָקוּם בִּמְקוֹם קָדְשׁוֹ:

נְקִי כַפַּיִם וּבַר־לֵבָב   אֲשֶׁר לֹא־נָשָׂא לַשָּׁוְא נַפְשִׁי

וְלֹא נִשְׁבַּע לְמִרְמָה:

יִשָּׂא בְרָכָה מֵאֵת יהוה   וּצְדָקָה מֵאֱלֹהֵי יִשְׁעוֹ:

זֶה דּוֹר דֹּרְשָׁיו   מְבַקְשֵׁי פָנֶיךָ יַעֲקֹב סֶלָה:

שְׂאוּ שְׁעָרִים רָאשֵׁיכֶם   וְהִנָּשְׂאוּ פִּתְחֵי עוֹלָם

וְיָבוֹא מֶלֶךְ הַכָּבוֹד: ←

Ledavid mizmor.

Ladonay ha'aretz umlo'ah tevel veyoshvey vah.

Ki hu al yamim yesadah ve'al neharot yeḥoneneha.

Mi ya'aleh behar adonay umi yakum bimkom kodsho.

Neki ḥapayim uvar levav asher lo nasa lashav nafshi velo nishba
lemirmah.

Yisa veraḥah me'et adonay utzedakah me'elohey yisho.

Zeh dor dorshav mevakshey faneḥa ya'akov selah.

Se'u she'arim rasheyḥem vehinasu pitḥey olam veyavo meleḥ
hakavod. ↩

Who is the sovereign of glory?
THE MAGNIFICENT, so powerful and mighty!
THE ETERNAL ONE, a champion in battle!
You city gates, open your bolts;
eternal gates, be lifted up,
and let the sovereign of glory come!
Who is this one, the sovereign of glory?
THE RULER of the Multitudes of Heaven,
the sovereign of glory.

Psalm 24

מִי זֶה מֶלֶךְ הַכָּבוֹד יהוה עִזּוּז וְגִבּוֹר
יהוה גִּבּוֹר מִלְחָמָה:
שְׂאוּ שְׁעָרִים רָאשֵׁיכֶם וּשְׂאוּ פִּתְחֵי עוֹלָם
וְיָבוֹא מֶלֶךְ הַכָּבוֹד:
מִי הוּא זֶה מֶלֶךְ הַכָּבוֹד יהוה צְבָאוֹת הוּא
מֶלֶךְ הַכָּבוֹד סֶלָה:

Mi zeh meleḥ hakavod adonay izuz vegibor adonay gibor
milḥamah.
Se'u she'arim rasheyḥem use'u pitḥey olam veyavo meleḥ
hakavod.
Mi hu zeh meleḥ hakavod adonay tzeva'ot hu meleḥ hakavod
selah.

The ark is opened and the Torah placed inside.

And when the Ark was set at rest, they would proclaim:
Restore, ETERNAL ONE, the many thousand troops of Israel!

For it is a precious teaching I have given you,
my Torah: Don't abandon it!

It is a Tree of Life to those that hold fast to it,
all who uphold it may be counted fortunate.

Its ways are ways of pleasantness,
and all its paths are peace.

Return us, PRECIOUS ONE, let us return!
Renew our days, as you have done of old!

The ark is closed.

COMMENTARY. "Renew our days as you have done of old."
We may read:
Renew our days as when we were young.
Revive us with the wonder of your world,
    with the enthusiasm of our youth.
Help us to recover something of the child within
    that knew you in the desert
    and trembled at the foot of the mountain.
Grant us, once again, the sacred vision
    and the courage of new beginnings.
Do not return us to days past:
Renew our days as when we were young.   S.E.S.

The ark is opened and the Torah placed inside.

וּבְנֻחֹה יֹאמַר שׁוּבָה יהוה רִבְבוֹת אַלְפֵי יִשְׂרָאֵל:

כִּי לֶקַח טוֹב נָתַתִּי לָכֶם תּוֹרָתִי אַל־תַּעֲזֹבוּ:

עֵץ־חַיִּים הִיא לַמַּחֲזִיקִים בָּהּ וְתֹמְכֶיהָ מְאֻשָּׁר:

דְּרָכֶיהָ דַרְכֵי־נֹעַם וְכָל־נְתִיבוֹתֶיהָ שָׁלוֹם:

הֲשִׁיבֵנוּ יהוה אֵלֶיךָ וְנָשׁוּבָה חַדֵּשׁ יָמֵינוּ כְּקֶדֶם:

Etz ḥayim hi lamaḥazikim bah vetomḥeha me'ushar.
Deraḥeha darḥey no'am veḥol netivoteha shalom.
Hashivenu adonay eleḥa venashuvah ḥadesh yameynu
kekedem.

The ark is closed.

ובנחה...ישראל / And...Israel (Numbers 10:36).

כי...תעזבו / For...it (Proverbs 4:2).

עץ...מאשר / It...fortunate (Proverbs 3:18).

דרכיה...שלום / Its...peace (Proverbs 3:17).

השיבנו...כקדם / Return...old (Lamentations 5:21).

עץ חיים היא / It is a Tree of Life. At the end of the Garden story, Adam and Eve are forbidden access to the mysterious Tree of Life, whose fruit confers immortality. Yet over the generations to follow, humankind itself *becomes* a Tree of Life. The Torah is handed on from one generation to another, binding the generations in a commonwealth of time and conferring the norms on which the survival of civilization depends. Thus the Torah is compared to the Tree of Life.   J.R.

ḤATZI KADDISH / SHORT KADDISH

Reader: Let God's name be made great and holy in the world that was created as God willed. May God complete the holy realm in your own lifetime, in your days, and in the days of all the house of Israel, quickly and soon. And say: Amen.

Congregation: May God's great name be blessed, forever and as long as worlds endure.

Reader: May it be blessed, and praised, and glorified, and held in honor, viewed with awe, embellished, and revered; and may the blessed name of holiness be hailed, though it be higher by far than all the blessings, songs, praises, and consolations that we utter in this world. And say: Amen.

חֲצִי קַדִּישׁ

יִתְגַּדַּל וְיִתְקַדַּשׁ שְׁמֵהּ רַבָּא בְּעָלְמָא דִּי בְרָא כִרְעוּתֵהּ וְיַמְלִיךְ
מַלְכוּתֵהּ בְּחַיֵּיכוֹן וּבְיוֹמֵיכוֹן וּבְחַיֵּי דְכָל בֵּית יִשְׂרָאֵל בַּעֲגָלָא וּבִזְמַן
קָרִיב וְאִמְרוּ אָמֵן:

יְהֵא שְׁמֵהּ רַבָּא מְבָרַךְ לְעָלַם וּלְעָלְמֵי עָלְמַיָּא:

יִתְבָּרַךְ וְיִשְׁתַּבַּח וְיִתְפָּאַר וְיִתְרוֹמַם וְיִתְנַשֵּׂא וְיִתְהַדָּר וְיִתְעַלֶּה וְיִתְהַלָּל
שְׁמֵהּ דְּקֻדְשָׁא בְּרִיךְ הוּא לְעֵלָּא לְעֵלָּא מִכָּל בִּרְכָתָא וְשִׁירָתָא
תֻּשְׁבְּחָתָא וְנֶחֱמָתָא דַּאֲמִירָן בְּעָלְמָא וְאִמְרוּ אָמֵן:

Yitgadal veyitkadash shemey raba
be'alma divra ḥiruteh veyamliḥ malḥutey
behayeyhon uvyomeyhon uvḥayey deḥol beyt yisra'el
ba'agala uvizman kariv ve'imru amen.

Congregation: Yehey shemey raba mevaraḥ le'alam ulalmey almaya.

Yitbaraḥ veyishtabaḥ veyitpa'ar veyitromam
veyitnasey veyit-hadar veyitaleh veyit-halal
shemey dekudsha beriḥ hu
le'ela le'ela mikol birḥata veshirata
tushbeḥata veneḥemata da'amiran be'alma ve'imru amen.

AMIDAH CHANTED ON
YOM KIPPUR AFTERNOON

The Amidah is traditionally recited while standing, beginning with three short steps forward and bowing left and right, a reminder of our entry into the divine presence. For the silent Amidah, see pages 739–774. For meditations see pages 1–20. The Amidah below can be said aloud in its entirety, or it can be begun aloud and completed silently.

Open my lips, BELOVED ONE,
and let my mouth declare your praise.

1. AVOT VE'IMOT / ANCESTORS

Blessed are you, ANCIENT ONE, our God, God of our ancestors,

God of Abraham	God of Sarah
God of Isaac	God of Rebekah
God of Jacob	God of Rachel
	and God of Leah;

great, heroic, awesome God, supreme divinity,
imparting deeds of kindness, begetter of all;
mindful of the loyalty of Israel's ancestors,
bringing, with love, redemption to their children's children
for the sake of the divine name.

By the counsel of the sages and the wise,
and by the knowledge of all learned in our ways,
may my mouth be opened, and my prayers arise,
to entreat the sovereign full of mercy and compassion,
who forgives and pardons all transgression. ↩

אדוני...תהלתך / Open...praise (Psalms 51:17).

עֲמִידָה

The Amidah is traditionally recited while standing, beginning with three short steps forward and bowing left and right, a reminder of our entry into the divine presence. For the silent Amidah, see pages 739-774. For meditations see pages 1-20. The Amidah below can be said aloud in its entirety, or it can be begun aloud and completed silently.

אֲדֹנָי שְׂפָתַי תִּפְתָּח וּפִי יַגִּיד תְּהִלָּתֶךָ:

 אָבוֹת וְאִמּוֹת

בָּרוּךְ אַתָּה יהוה אֱלֹהֵינוּ וֵאלֹהֵי אֲבוֹתֵינוּ וְאִמּוֹתֵינוּ

אֱלֹהֵי שָׂרָה	אֱלֹהֵי אַבְרָהָם
אֱלֹהֵי רִבְקָה	אֱלֹהֵי יִצְחָק
אֱלֹהֵי רָחֵל	אֱלֹהֵי יַעֲקֹב
וֵאלֹהֵי לֵאָה:	

הָאֵל הַגָּדוֹל הַגִּבּוֹר וְהַנּוֹרָא אֵל עֶלְיוֹן גּוֹמֵל חֲסָדִים טוֹבִים וְקוֹנֵה הַכֹּל וְזוֹכֵר חַסְדֵי אָבוֹת וְאִמּוֹת וּמֵבִיא גְאֻלָּה לִבְנֵי בְנֵיהֶם לְמַעַן שְׁמוֹ בְּאַהֲבָה:

מְסוֹד חֲכָמִים וּנְבוֹנִים וּמִלֶּמֶד דַּעַת מְבִינִים אֶפְתְּחָה פִי בִּתְפִלָּה וּבְתַחֲנוּנִים לְחַלּוֹת וּלְחַנֵּן פְּנֵי מֶלֶךְ מָלֵא רַחֲמִים מוֹחֵל וְסוֹלֵחַ לַעֲוֹנִים: ←

Baruḥ atah adonay eloheynu veylohey avoteynu ve'imoteynu
eloheynu avraham
elohey yitzḥak
elohey ya'akov

elohey sarah
elohey rivkah
elohey raḥel
veylohey le'ah

Ha'el hagadol hagibor vehanora el elyon gomel ḥasadim tovim vekoney hakol vezoḥer ḥasdey avot ve'imot umevi ge'ulah livney veneyhem lema'an shemo be'ahavah.

Remember us for life,
our sovereign who wishes us to live,
and write us in the Book of Life,
for your sake, ever-living God.

Regal One, our help, salvation, and protector:
Blessed are you, KIND ONE,
the shield of Abraham and help of Sarah.

2. GEVUROT / DIVINE POWER

You are forever powerful, ALMIGHTY ONE,
abundant in your saving acts. You send down the dew.

In loyalty you sustain the living,
nurturing the life of every living thing,
upholding those who fall,
healing the sick, freeing the captive,
and remaining faithful to all life
held dormant in the earth.
Who can compare to you, almighty God,
who can resemble you, the source of life and death,
who makes salvation grow?

Who can compare to you, source of all mercy,
remembering all creatures mercifully, decreeing life!

Faithful are you in giving life to every living thing.
Blessed are you, THE FOUNT OF LIFE,
who gives and renews life. ↩

זָכְרֵנוּ לְחַיִּים מֶלֶךְ חָפֵץ בַּחַיִּים וְכָתְבֵנוּ בְּסֵפֶר הַחַיִּים לְמַעַנְךָ אֱלֹהִים חַיִּים:

מֶלֶךְ עוֹזֵר וּמוֹשִׁיעַ וּמָגֵן: בָּרוּךְ אַתָּה יהוה מָגֵן אַבְרָהָם וְעֶזְרַת שָׂרָה:

Zoḥrenu leḥayim meleḥ ḥafetz baḥayim veḥotvenu besefer haḥayim lema'aneḥa elohim ḥayim.

Meleḥ ozer umoshi'a umagen. Baruḥ atah adonay magen avraham ve'ezrat sarah.

ב   גְּבוּרוֹת

אַתָּה גִבּוֹר לְעוֹלָם אֲדֹנָי רַב לְהוֹשִׁיעַ: מוֹרִיד הַטָּל: מְכַלְכֵּל חַיִּים בְּחֶסֶד מְחַיֵּה כָּל חַי בְּרַחֲמִים רַבִּים סוֹמֵךְ נוֹפְלִים וְרוֹפֵא חוֹלִים וּמַתִּיר אֲסוּרִים וּמְקַיֵּם אֱמוּנָתוֹ לִישֵׁנֵי עָפָר: מִי כָמוֹךָ בַּעַל גְּבוּרוֹת וּמִי דּוֹמֶה לָּךְ מֶלֶךְ מֵמִית וּמְחַיֶּה וּמַצְמִיחַ יְשׁוּעָה:

מִי כָמוֹךָ אַב הָרַחֲמִים זוֹכֵר יְצוּרָיו לְחַיִּים בְּרַחֲמִים:

וְנֶאֱמָן אַתָּה לְהַחֲיוֹת כָּל חָי: בָּרוּךְ אַתָּה יהוה מְחַיֵּה כָּל חָי: ←

Atah gibor le'olam adonay rav lehoshi'a. Morid hatal.
Meḥalkel ḥayim beḥesed meḥayey kol ḥay beraḥamim rabim someḥ noflim verofey ḥolim umatir asurim umekayem emunato lisheney afar. Mi ḥamoḥa ba'al gevurot umi domeh laḥ meleḥ memit umeḥayeh umatzmi'aḥ yeshu'ah.

Mi ḥamoḥa av haraḥamim zoḥer yetzurav leḥayim beraḥamim.
Vene'eman atah lehaḥayot kol ḥay. Baruḥ atah adonay meḥayey kol ḥay. ↰

3. KEDUSHAT HASHEM / HALLOWING GOD'S NAME

As it is written by the prophet's hand:
They call, one to another, and declare:

"Holy, holy, holy is THE CREATOR of the Multitudes of Heaven!
All the world is filled with divine glory!"

God's glory fills the world,
as the ministering angels ask, one to another,
"What place could contain God's holiness?"
And they are answered with a blessing:
"Blessed is the glory of THE OMNIPRESENT,
wherever God may dwell!"

And from God's place, God mercifully turns
bestowing graciousness upon the people
who declare the oneness of the divine name
evening and morning, each day continually,
as twice a day they say, with love: "Shema!"
"Listen, Israel: THE ETERNAL is our God,
THE ETERNAL ONE alone!" ↵

וקרא...כבודו / And...glory! (Isaiah 6:3).
ברוך...ממקומו / Blessed...dwell! (Ezekiel 3:12).
שמע...אחד / Listen...alone! (Deuteronomy 6:4).

כַּכָּתוּב עַל יַד נְבִיאֶךָ: וְקָרָא זֶה אֶל זֶה וְאָמַר

קָדוֹשׁ קָדוֹשׁ קָדוֹשׁ

יהוה צְבָאוֹת מְלֹא כָל־הָאָרֶץ כְּבוֹדוֹ:

כְּבוֹדוֹ מָלֵא עוֹלָם מְשָׁרְתָיו שׁוֹאֲלִים זֶה לָזֶה אַיֵּה מְקוֹם כְּבוֹדוֹ
לְעֻמָּתָם בָּרוּךְ יֹאמֵרוּ:

בָּרוּךְ כְּבוֹד יהוה מִמְּקוֹמוֹ:

מִמְּקוֹמוֹ הוּא יִפֶן בְּרַחֲמִים וְיָחֹן עַם הַמְיַחֲדִים שְׁמוֹ עֶרֶב וָבֹקֶר בְּכָל
יוֹם תָּמִיד פַּעֲמַיִם בְּאַהֲבָה שְׁמַע אוֹמְרִים:

שְׁמַע יִשְׂרָאֵל יהוה אֱלֹהֵינוּ יהוה אֶחָד: ⟵

Kakatuv al yad nevi'eḥa vekara zeh el zeh ve'amar:
Kadosh kadosh kadosh adonay tzeva'ot melo ḥol ha'aretz kevodo.
Kevodo maley olam mesharetav sho'alim zeh lazeh ayey mekom
kevodo le'umatam baruḥ yomeru:
Baruḥ kevod adonay mimekomo.
Mimekomo hu yifen beraḥamim veyaḥon am hamyaḥadim
shemo erev vavoker beḥol yom tamid pa'amayim be'ahavah
shema omrim:
Shema yisra'el adonay eloheynu adonay eḥad.

This is our God.
This is our source.
This is our sovereign.
This is our saving power.
And this one, mercifully,
shall declare a second time,
for every living being to hear,
confirming God's divinity for you:
"I am THE OMNIPRESENT ONE, your God!"

O, mighty one, our mighty one,
THE SOVEREIGN who watches over us,
how mighty is your name throughout the earth!
The time shall come that GOD will reign
throughout the earth. On that day
shall THE FOUNT OF LIFE be one,
the divine name be one.
And as is written in your sacred words of psalm:
"May THE ETERNAL reign forever,
your God, O Zion, from one generation to the next. Halleluyah!"

From one generation to the next
may we declare your greatness,
and for all eternities may we affirm your holiness.
And may your praise, our God,
never be absent from our mouths
now and forever.
For you are a great and holy God. ⤵

אני...אלהיכם /I...God! (Numbers 15:41).
יהוה אדנינו...הארץ /THE SOVEREIGN...earth! (Psalms 8:10).
והיה יהוה...אחד /The time...be one (Zechariah 14:9).
ימלך...הללויה /May...Halleluyah! (Psalms 146:10).

הוּא אֱלֹהֵינוּ הוּא אָבִינוּ הוּא מַלְכֵּנוּ הוּא מוֹשִׁיעֵנוּ וְהוּא יַשְׁמִיעֵנוּ
בְּרַחֲמָיו שֵׁנִית לְעֵינֵי כָּל חָי: לִהְיוֹת לָכֶם לֵאלֹהִים:

אֲנִי יהוה אֱלֹהֵיכֶם:

אַדִּיר אַדִּירֵנוּ יהוה אֲדֹנֵינוּ מָה־אַדִּיר שִׁמְךָ בְּכָל־הָאָרֶץ: וְהָיָה יהוה
לְמֶלֶךְ עַל־כָּל־הָאָרֶץ בַּיּוֹם הַהוּא יִהְיֶה יהוה אֶחָד וּשְׁמוֹ אֶחָד:
וּבְדִבְרֵי קָדְשְׁךָ כָּתוּב לֵאמֹר:

יִמְלֹךְ יהוה לְעוֹלָם אֱלֹהַיִךְ צִיּוֹן לְדֹר וָדֹר הַלְלוּיָהּ:

לְדוֹר וָדוֹר נַגִּיד גָּדְלֶךָ וּלְנֵצַח נְצָחִים קְדֻשָּׁתְךָ נַקְדִּישׁ וְשִׁבְחֲךָ
אֱלֹהֵינוּ מִפִּינוּ לֹא יָמוּשׁ לְעוֹלָם וָעֶד כִּי אֵל מֶלֶךְ גָּדוֹל וְקָדוֹשׁ
אָתָּה: ←

Hu eloheynu hu avinu hu malkenu hu moshi'enu vehu
yashmi'enu berahamav shenit le'eyney kol hay lihyot lahem
leylohim. Ani adonay eloheyhem.
Adir adirenu adonay adoneynu mah adir shimeha behol ha'aretz.
Vehayah adonay lemeleh al kol ha'aretz bayom hahu yihyeh
adonay ehad ushemo ehad.
Uvedivrey kodsheha katuv lemor.
Yimloh adonay le'olam elohayih tziyon ledor vador halleluyah.
Ledor vador nagid godleha ulenetzah netzahim kedushateha
nakdish veshivhaha eloheynu mipinu lo yamush le'olam va'ed ki
el meleh gadol vekadosh atah. ↰

If the remainder of the Amidah is being read silently, it is customary to remain standing. If the remainder of the Amidah is being chanted aloud, it is customary to be seated here.

And therefore, HOLY ONE, let awe of you
infuse the whole of your Creation,
and let knowledge of your presence
dwell in all your creatures.
And let every being worship you,
and each created life pay homage to your rule.
Let all of them, as one, enact your bidding
with a whole and peaceful heart.
For we have always known, ALMIGHTY ONE,
that all authority to rule belongs to you,
all strength is rooted in your arm,
all mighty deeds have emanated from your hand.
Your name alone is the source of awe
that surges through all life.

And therefore, HOLY ONE, let awe of you
infuse your people, let the praise of you
ring out from all who worship you.
Let hope enliven all who seek you,
and let all who look to you with hope
find strength to speak.
Grant joy throughout your Land,
let happiness resound throughout your holy city,
soon, and in our days.

And therefore, let the just behold your peace,
let them rejoice,
let all who follow in your path sing out with joy,
let all who love you dance in celebration,
and may your power overwhelm all treachery,
so that it vanish wholly from the earth like smoke.
Then shall the power of injustice pass away! ↩

וּבְכֵן תֵּן פַּחְדְּךָ יהוה אֱלֹהֵינוּ עַל כָּל־מַעֲשֶׂיךָ וְאֵימָתְךָ עַל כָּל־
מַה־שֶׁבָּרָאתָ וְיִירָאוּךָ כָּל־הַמַּעֲשִׂים וְיִשְׁתַּחֲווּ לְפָנֶיךָ כָּל־הַבְּרוּאִים
וְיֵעָשׂוּ כֻלָּם אֲגֻדָּה אַחַת לַעֲשׂוֹת רְצוֹנְךָ בְּלֵבָב שָׁלֵם כְּמוֹ שֶׁיָּדַעְנוּ
יהוה אֱלֹהֵינוּ שֶׁהַשִּׁלְטוֹן לְפָנֶיךָ עֹז בְּיָדְךָ וּגְבוּרָה בִּימִינֶךָ וְשִׁמְךָ
נוֹרָא עַל כָּל־מַה־שֶׁבָּרָאתָ:

וּבְכֵן תֵּן כָּבוֹד יהוה לְעַמֶּךָ תְּהִלָּה לִירֵאֶיךָ וְתִקְוָה לְדוֹרְשֶׁיךָ
וּפִתְחוֹן פֶּה לַמְיַחֲלִים לָךְ שִׂמְחָה לְאַרְצֶךָ וְשָׂשׂוֹן לְעִירֶךָ בִּמְהֵרָה
בְיָמֵינוּ:

וּבְכֵן צַדִּיקִים יִרְאוּ וְיִשְׂמָחוּ וִישָׁרִים יַעֲלֹזוּ וַחֲסִידִים בְּרִנָּה
יָגִילוּ וְעוֹלָתָה תִּקְפָּץ־פִּיהָ וְכָל־הָרִשְׁעָה כֻּלָּהּ כְּעָשָׁן תִּכְלֶה כִּי
תַעֲבִיר מֶמְשֶׁלֶת זָדוֹן מִן הָאָרֶץ: ←

May you alone be sovereign over all of your Creation,
and Mount Zion be the seat and symbol of your glory,
and Jerusalem, your holy city—
as is written in your holy scriptures:
"THE ETERNAL ONE shall reign forever,
your God, O Zion, through all generations!
Halleluyah!"

Holy are you,
and awe-inspiring is your name,
and there is no God apart from you,
as it is written: "THE CREATOR of the multitudes of heaven
shall be exalted through the rule of law,
and God, the Holy One, made holy by the reign of justice."
Blessed are you, ETERNAL ONE,
the holy sovereign power.

4. KEDUSHAT HAYOM / THE DAY'S HOLINESS

On Shabbat add the words in parenthesis.

You have loved us, and have taken pleasure in us,
and have made us holy with your mitzvot,
and you have brought us, sovereign one,
near to your service,
and have called us to the shelter of your great and holy name.
And you gave us, HOLY ONE, our God, with love,
(this day of Shabbat, for holiness and rest, and)
this Day of Atonement,
for pardon, for forgiveness, and for atonement,
a day for pardoning all of our wrongful acts,
(with love,)
a holy convocation,
a remembrance of the going-out from Egypt. ↲

וְתִמְלֹךְ אַתָּה יהוה לְבַדֶּךָ עַל כָּל־מַעֲשֶׂיךָ בְּהַר צִיּוֹן מִשְׁכַּן כְּבוֹדֶךָ
וּבִירוּשָׁלַיִם עִיר קָדְשֶׁךָ: כַּכָּתוּב בְּדִבְרֵי קָדְשֶׁךָ: יִמְלֹךְ יהוה לְעוֹלָם
אֱלֹהַיִךְ צִיּוֹן לְדֹר וָדֹר הַלְלוּיָהּ:

קָדוֹשׁ אַתָּה וְנוֹרָא שְׁמֶךָ וְאֵין אֱלוֹהַּ מִבַּלְעָדֶיךָ: כַּכָּתוּב: וַיִּגְבַּהּ יהוה
צְבָאוֹת בַּמִּשְׁפָּט וְהָאֵל הַקָּדוֹשׁ נִקְדַּשׁ בִּצְדָקָה: בָּרוּךְ אַתָּה יהוה
הַמֶּלֶךְ הַקָּדוֹשׁ:

קְדֻשַּׁת הַיּוֹם

On Shabbat add the words in parenthesis.

אַתָּה אֲהַבְתָּנוּ וְרָצִיתָ בָּנוּ וְקִדַּשְׁתָּנוּ בְּמִצְוֹתֶיךָ וְקֵרַבְתָּנוּ מַלְכֵּנוּ
לַעֲבוֹדָתֶךָ. וְשִׁמְךָ הַגָּדוֹל וְהַקָּדוֹשׁ עָלֵינוּ קָרָאתָ:

וַתִּתֶּן לָנוּ יהוה אֱלֹהֵינוּ בְּאַהֲבָה אֶת יוֹם (הַשַּׁבָּת הַזֶּה לִקְדֻשָּׁה
וְלִמְנוּחָה וְאֶת יוֹם) הַכִּפּוּרִים הַזֶּה לִמְחִילָה וְלִסְלִיחָה וּלְכַפָּרָה
וְלִמְחָל בּוֹ אֶת כָּל עֲוֹנוֹתֵינוּ (בְּאַהֲבָה) מִקְרָא קֹדֶשׁ זֵכֶר לִיצִיאַת
מִצְרָיִם: ←

ימלך...הללויה/THE ETERNAL...Halleluyah! (Psalms 146:10).
ויגבה...בצדקה/THE CREATOR...justice (Isaiah 5:16).

Our God, our ancients' God, may our prayer arise and come to you, and be beheld, and be acceptable. Let it be heard, acted upon, remembered—the memory of us and all our needs, the memory of our ancestors, the memory of messianic hopes, the memory of Jerusalem your holy city, and the memory of all your kin, the house of Israel, all surviving in your presence. Act for goodness and grace, for love and care; for life, well-being and peace, on this Day of Atonement.

Remember us this day, ALL-KNOWING ONE, our God, for goodness. Favor us this day with blessing. Preserve us this day for life. With your redeeming nurturing word, be kind and generous. Act tenderly on our behalf, and grant us victory over all our trials. Truly, our eyes turn toward you, for you are a providing God; gracious and merciful are you.

Pour out your heart like water
in the presence of THE LIVING GOD.

Return us, PRECIOUS ONE; let us return!
Renew our days, as you have done of old!

Hear our voice, ETERNAL ONE, our God,
and accept our prayer with mercy and good will.
Turn us, ANCIENT ONE, toward you, let us return.
Renew our days like days of old.
Do not cast us away from dwelling in your presence,
and do not remove your holy spirit from our midst. ↩

שפכי...אדוני / Pour...God (Lamentations 2:19).
השיבנו...כקדם / Return...old (Lamentations 5:21).

אֱלֹהֵינוּ וֵאלֹהֵי אֲבוֹתֵינוּ וְאִמּוֹתֵינוּ יַעֲלֶה וְיָבֹא וְיַגִּיעַ וְיֵרָאֶה וְיֵרָצֶה
וְיִשָּׁמַע וְיִפָּקֵד וְיִזָּכֵר זִכְרוֹנֵנוּ וּפִקְדוֹנֵנוּ וְזִכְרוֹן אֲבוֹתֵינוּ וְאִמּוֹתֵינוּ
וְזִכְרוֹן יְמוֹת הַמָּשִׁיחַ וְזִכְרוֹן יְרוּשָׁלַיִם עִיר קָדְשֶׁךָ וְזִכְרוֹן כָּל עַמְּךָ
בֵּית יִשְׂרָאֵל לְפָנֶיךָ לִפְלֵיטָה וּלְטוֹבָה לְחֵן וּלְחֶסֶד וּלְרַחֲמִים לְחַיִּים
וּלְשָׁלוֹם בְּיוֹם הַכִּפּוּרִים הַזֶּה: זָכְרֵנוּ יהוה אֱלֹהֵינוּ בּוֹ לְטוֹבָה:
וּפָקְדֵנוּ לִבְרָכָה וְהוֹשִׁיעֵנוּ בּוֹ לְחַיִּים: וּבִדְבַר יְשׁוּעָה וְרַחֲמִים חוּס
וְחָנֵּנוּ וְרַחֵם עָלֵינוּ וְהוֹשִׁיעֵנוּ כִּי אֵלֶיךָ עֵינֵינוּ כִּי אֵל מֶלֶךְ חַנּוּן
וְרַחוּם אָתָּה:

שְׁפְכִי כַמַּיִם לִבֵּךְ נֹכַח פְּנֵי אֲדֹנָי:

Shifḥi ḥamayim libeḥ noḥaḥ peney adonay.

הֲשִׁיבֵנוּ יהוה אֵלֶיךָ וְנָשׁוּבָה חַדֵּשׁ יָמֵינוּ כְּקֶדֶם:

Hashivenu adonay eleḥa venashuvah ḥadesh yameynu kekedem.

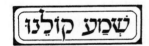

שְׁמַע קוֹלֵנוּ

שְׁמַע קוֹלֵנוּ יהוה אֱלֹהֵינוּ חוּס וְרַחֵם עָלֵינוּ
וְקַבֵּל בְּרַחֲמִים וּבְרָצוֹן אֶת־תְּפִלָּתֵנוּ:
הֲשִׁיבֵנוּ יהוה אֵלֶיךָ וְנָשׁוּבָה חַדֵּשׁ יָמֵינוּ כְּקֶדֶם:
אַל־תַּשְׁלִיכֵנוּ מִלְּפָנֶיךָ וְרוּחַ קָדְשְׁךָ אַל־תִּקַּח מִמֶּנּוּ: ←

Shema kolenu adonay eloheynu ḥus veraḥem, aleynu
vekabel beraḥamim uveratzon et tefilatenu.
Hashivenu adonay eleḥa venashuvah ḥadesh yameynu kekedem.
Al tashliḥenu milefaneḥa veru'aḥ kodsheḥa al tikaḥ mimenu. ⤶

And do not cast us off as we grow old;
do not forsake us when our strength departs.
Do not forsake us, GENTLE ONE, our God,
do not withdraw from us.
Give us a sign of blessing,
so that anyone who bears us ill
shall hesitate to harm us.
For truly, you, ETERNAL ONE,
have always helped us and consoled us.
Hear now our words, GOD OF COMPASSION,
and behold our contemplation.
May our words of prayer,
and meditations of our hearts,
be seen favorably, PRECIOUS ONE,
our rock, our champion.
For we place our hope in you, ETERNAL ONE,
so may you answer us,
Almighty One, our God.

Our God, our ancients' God,
do not forsake us, and do not turn us away,
and do not cause us shame,
and do not nullify your covenant with us,
but bring us nearer to your Torah,
teach us your mitzvot,
instruct us in your ways.
Incline our hearts to treat your name with awe,
and open up our inner nature to your love,
and bring us back to you in truth,
with whole and peaceful heart. ⤺

אַל־תַּשְׁלִיכֵנוּ לְעֵת זִקְנָה כִּכְלוֹת כֹּחֵנוּ אַל־תַּעַזְבֵנוּ:

אַל־תַּעַזְבֵנוּ יהוה אֱלֹהֵינוּ אַל־תִּרְחַק מִמֶּנּוּ:

עֲשֵׂה־עִמָּנוּ אוֹת לְטוֹבָה וְיִרְאוּ שׂוֹנְאֵינוּ וְיֵבֹשׁוּ

כִּי־אַתָּה יהוה עֲזַרְתָּנוּ וְנִחַמְתָּנוּ:

אֲמָרֵינוּ הַאֲזִינָה יהוה בִּינָה הֲגִיגֵנוּ:

יִהְיוּ לְרָצוֹן אִמְרֵי־פִינוּ וְהֶגְיוֹן לִבֵּנוּ לְפָנֶיךָ יהוה צוּרֵנוּ וְגוֹאֲלֵנוּ:

כִּי־לְךָ יהוה הוֹחָלְנוּ אַתָּה תַעֲנֶה אֲדֹנָי אֱלֹהֵינוּ:

Al tashlihenu le'et ziknah kihlot kohenu al ta'azvenu.
Al ta'azvenu adonay eloheynu al tirhak mimenu.
Asey imanu ot letovah veyiru soneynu veyevoshu
ki atah adonay azartanu venihamtanu.
Amareynu ha'azinah adonay binah hagigenu.
Yihyu leratzon imrey finu vehegyon libenu lefaneha adonay
tzurenu vego'alenu.
Ki leha adonay hohalnu atah ta'aneh adonay eloheynu.

אֱלֹהֵינוּ וֵאלֹהֵי אֲבוֹתֵינוּ וְאִמּוֹתֵינוּ אַל תַּעַזְבֵנוּ וְאַל תִּטְּשֵׁנוּ וְאַל
תַּכְלִימֵנוּ וְאַל תָּפֵר בְּרִיתְךָ אִתָּנוּ קָרְבֵנוּ לְתוֹרָתֶךָ לַמְּדֵנוּ מִצְוֹתֶיךָ
הוֹרֵנוּ דְרָכֶיךָ הַט לִבֵּנוּ לְיִרְאָה אֶת־שְׁמֶךָ וּמוֹל אֶת־לְבָבֵנוּ לְאַהֲבָתֶךָ
וְנָשׁוּב אֵלֶיךָ בֶּאֱמֶת וּבְלֵב שָׁלֵם ←

NOTE. *Shema Kolenu* is based on various biblical passages.

And for the sake of your great name,
be merciful, and grant forgiveness for our wrongs,
as it is written in your prophets' words:
"For the sake of your great name, ETERNAL ONE,
forgive my wrongdoing, for I have done much wrong."

Our God, our ancients' God,
forgive us, pardon us, help us atone—
for we are your people, and you are our God,
we are your children, and you are our creator,
we are your servants, and you are our sovereign,
we are your community, and you are our portion,
we are your possession, and you are our fate,
we are your sheep, and you are our shepherd,
we are your vineyard, and you are our keeper,
we are your creation, and you are our fashioner,
we are your loved ones, and you are our beloved,
we are your treasure, and you are our kin,
we are your people, and you are our ruler,
we are your faithful, and you our source of faith!

We are strong-willed and stubborn,
but you are merciful and gracious.
We are stiff-necked, but you are slow to anger.
We are full of error, but you are full of mercy.
We—our days are like a passing shadow,
but you are one whose years shall never end. ↵

וּלְמַעַן שִׁמְךָ הַגָּדוֹל תִּמְחַל וְתִסְלַח לַעֲוֹנֵינוּ כַּכָּתוּב בְּדִבְרֵי קָדְשֶׁךָ:
לְמַעַן־שִׁמְךָ יהוה וְסָלַחְתָּ לַעֲוֹנִי כִּי רַב־הוּא:

אֱלֹהֵינוּ וֵאלֹהֵי אֲבוֹתֵינוּ וְאִמּוֹתֵינוּ סְלַח לָנוּ: מְחַל לָנוּ: כַּפֶּר־לָנוּ:

אָנוּ בָנֶיךָ וְאַתָּה אָבִינוּ:	כִּי אָנוּ עַמֶּךָ וְאַתָּה אֱלֹהֵינוּ:
אָנוּ קְהָלֶךָ וְאַתָּה חֶלְקֵנוּ:	אָנוּ עֲבָדֶיךָ וְאַתָּה אֲדוֹנֵינוּ:
אָנוּ צֹאנֶךָ וְאַתָּה רוֹעֵנוּ:	אָנוּ נַחֲלָתֶךָ וְאַתָּה גוֹרָלֵנוּ:
אָנוּ פְעֻלָּתֶךָ וְאַתָּה יוֹצְרֵנוּ:	אָנוּ כַרְמֶךָ וְאַתָּה נוֹטְרֵנוּ:
אָנוּ סְגֻלָּתֶךָ וְאַתָּה קְרוֹבֵנוּ:	אָנוּ רַעְיָתֶךָ וְאַתָּה דוֹדֵנוּ:
אָנוּ מַאֲמִירֶךָ וְאַתָּה מַאֲמִירֵנוּ:	אָנוּ עַמֶּךָ וְאַתָּה מַלְכֵּנוּ:

Eloheynu veylohey avoteynu ve'imoteynu
sela<u>h</u> lanu. Me<u>h</u>al lanu. Kaper lanu.
Ki <u>a</u>nu ame<u>h</u>a ve'atah eloheynu. <u>A</u>nu vane<u>h</u>a ve'atah avinu.
<u>A</u>nu avade<u>h</u>a ve'atah adoneynu. <u>A</u>nu kehale<u>h</u>a ve'atah <u>h</u>elkenu.
<u>A</u>nu na<u>h</u>alate<u>h</u>a ve'atah goralenu. <u>A</u>nu tzone<u>h</u>a ve'atah ro'enu.
<u>A</u>nu <u>h</u>arme<u>h</u>a ve'atah notrenu. <u>A</u>nu fe'ulate<u>h</u>a ve'atah yotzrenu.
<u>A</u>nu rayate<u>h</u>a ve'atah dodenu. <u>A</u>nu segulate<u>h</u>a ve'atah kerovenu.
<u>A</u>nu ame<u>h</u>a ve'atah malkenu. <u>A</u>nu ma'amire<u>h</u>a ve'atah
ma'amirenu.

אָנוּ עַזֵּי פָנִים וְאַתָּה רַחוּם וְחַנּוּן: אָנוּ קְשֵׁי עֹרֶף וְאַתָּה אֶרֶךְ אַפַּיִם:
אָנוּ מְלֵאֵי עָוֹן וְאַתָּה מָלֵא רַחֲמִים: אָנוּ יָמֵינוּ כְּצֵל עוֹבֵר וְאַתָּה הוּא
וּשְׁנוֹתֶיךָ לֹא יִתָּמּוּ: ←

למען...הוא /For the sake...wrong (Psalms 25:11).

If seated, we rise.

Our God, our ancients' God,
may our prayer come before you.
Hide not from our supplication,
for we are not so insolent and stubborn
as to say, here in your presence,
"HOLY ONE, God of our fathers and our mothers,
we are righteous, and we have not sinned,"
for we indeed have sinned.

We have **a**cted wrongly,
we have **b**een untrue,
and we have **g**ained unlawfully
and have **d**efamed.
We have **h**armed others,
we have **w**rought injustice,
we have **z**ealously transgressed,
and we have **h**urt
and have **t**old lies.
We have **i**mproperly advised,
and we have **c**overed up the truth,
and we have **l**aughed in scorn.
We have **m**isused responsibility
and have **n**eglected others
and have **s**tubbornly rebelled.
We have **o**ffended,
we have **p**erverted justice,
we have **s**tirred up enmity,
and we have **k**ept ourselves from change.
We have **r**eached out to evil,
we have **s**hamelessly corrupted
and have **t**reated others with disdain.
Yes, we have **t**hrown ourselves off course,
and we have **t**empted and misled. ↩

If continuing aloud, we are seated.

אֱלֹהֵֽינוּ וֵאלֹהֵי אֲבוֹתֵֽינוּ וְאִמּוֹתֵֽינוּ תָּבוֹא לְפָנֶֽיךָ תְּפִלָּתֵֽנוּ וְאַל
תִּתְעַלַּם מִתְּחִנָּתֵֽנוּ שֶׁאֵין אֲנַֽחְנוּ עַזֵּי פָנִים וּקְשֵׁי עֹֽרֶף לוֹמַר לְפָנֶֽיךָ
יהוה אֱלֹהֵֽינוּ וֵאלֹהֵי אֲבוֹתֵֽינוּ וְאִמּוֹתֵֽינוּ צַדִּיקִים אֲנַֽחְנוּ וְלֹא חָטָֽאנוּ
אֲבָל אֲנַֽחְנוּ חָטָֽאנוּ:

אָשַֽׁמְנוּ: בָּגַֽדְנוּ: גָּזַֽלְנוּ: דִּבַּֽרְנוּ דֹֽפִי:
הֶעֱוִֽינוּ: וְהִרְשַֽׁעְנוּ: זַֽדְנוּ: חָמַֽסְנוּ:
טָפַֽלְנוּ שֶֽׁקֶר: יָעַֽצְנוּ רָע: כִּזַּֽבְנוּ: לַֽצְנוּ:
מָרַֽדְנוּ: נִאַֽצְנוּ: סָרַֽרְנוּ: עָוִֽינוּ:
פָּשַֽׁעְנוּ: צָרַֽרְנוּ: קִשִּֽׁינוּ עֹֽרֶף: רָשַֽׁעְנוּ:
שִׁחַֽתְנוּ: תִּעַֽבְנוּ: תָּעִֽינוּ: תִּעְתָּֽעְנוּ: ⟵

Ashamnu. Bagadnu. Gazalnu. Dibarnu dofi.
He'evinu. Vehirshanu. Zadnu. Hamasnu.
Tafalnu shaker. Ya'atznu ra. Kizavnu. Latznu.
Maradnu. Ni'atznu. Sararnu. Avinu.
Pashanu. Tzararnu. Kishinu oref. Rashanu.
Shihatnu. Ti'avnu. Ta'inu. Titanu.

If continuing aloud, we are seated.

We have turned away from your mitzvot,
and from your righteous laws,
as if it did not matter to us.
And you are just,
whatever comes upon us,
for what you do is truth,
and we have done much wrong.

We have done wrong, and have rebelled.
And so, we were not ready for your help.
Place into our hearts the will
to leave behind the path of evil,
and so hasten our redemption and renewal—
as is written by your prophet's hand:
"Let the wicked leave behind their unjust way,
let the unworthy cast away their plans,
let them return to THE COMPASSIONATE, who will be merciful,
returning to our God, who shall abundantly forgive."

Blot out and banish from your sight
our sins and our wrongdoing,
and shape our inner will to serve you humbly,
and subdue our stubborn resistance to return to you,
and renew our sense of conscience
to uphold what you command,
and open up our hearts to love and to revere your name,
as it is written: "THE BOUNTIFUL, your God,
shall circumcise your hearts,
and your children's hearts,
to love THE FOUNT OF LIFE, your God,
with all your heart, with all your soul,
that you might live." ↵

סַרְנוּ מִמִּצְוֹתֶ֫יךָ וּמִמִּשְׁפָּטֶ֫יךָ הַטּוֹבִים וְלֹא שָׁ֫וָה לָ֫נוּ: וְאַתָּה צַדִּיק עַל כָּל־הַבָּא עָלֵ֫ינוּ כִּי־אֱמֶת עָשִׂ֫יתָ וַאֲנַ֫חְנוּ הִרְשָׁ֫עְנוּ:

הִרְשַׁ֫עְנוּ וּפָשַׁ֫עְנוּ לָכֵן לֹא נוֹשָׁ֫עְנוּ וְתֵן בְּלִבֵּ֫נוּ לַעֲזֹב דֶּ֫רֶךְ רֶ֫שַׁע וְחִישׁ לָ֫נוּ יֶ֫שַׁע כַּכָּתוּב עַל יַד נְבִיאֶ֫ךָ: יַעֲזֹב רָשָׁע דַּרְכּוֹ וְאִישׁ אָ֫וֶן מַחְשְׁבֹתָיו וְיָשֹׁב אֶל־יהוה וִירַחֲמֵ֫הוּ וְאֶל־אֱלֹהֵ֫ינוּ כִּי־יַרְבֶּה לִסְלֽוֹחַ:

מְחֵה וְהַעֲבֵר פְּשָׁעֵ֫ינוּ וְחַטֹּאתֵ֫ינוּ מִנֶּ֫גֶד עֵינֶ֫יךָ וְכֹף אֶת־יִצְרֵ֫נוּ לְהִשְׁתַּעְבֶּד־לָךְ וְהַכְנַע עָרְפֵּ֫נוּ לָשׁוּב אֵלֶ֫יךָ וְחַדֵּשׁ כִּלְיוֹתֵ֫ינוּ לִשְׁמֹר פִּקֻּדֶ֫יךָ וּמוֹל אֶת־לְבָבֵ֫נוּ לְאַהֲבָה וּלְיִרְאָה אֶת־שְׁמֶ֫ךָ כַּכָּתוּב בְּתוֹרָתֶ֫ךָ: וּמָל יהוה אֱלֹהֶ֫יךָ אֶת־לְבָבְךָ וְאֶת־לְבַב זַרְעֶ֫ךָ לְאַהֲבָה אֶת־יהוה אֱלֹהֶ֫יךָ בְּכָל־לְבָבְךָ וּבְכָל־נַפְשְׁךָ לְמַ֫עַן חַיֶּ֫יךָ: ←

ואתה...הרשענו /And...wrong (Nehemiah 9:33).

יעזב...לסלוח /Let...forgive (Isaiah 55:7).

ומל...חייך /THE BOUNTIFUL...live (Deuteronomy 30:6).

So, let it be your will,
ETERNAL ONE, our God, God of our ancestors,
that you may grant forgiveness to us for all of our sins,
and be merciful to us for all of our injustices,
and let us atone for all we have done wrong:

If seated, we rise.
For an alternative Al Ḥet, see pages 435-436, 833-834 or 969-970.

For the wrong that we have done before you
   in the closing of the heart,
and for the wrong that we have done before you
   without knowing what we do.
For the wrong that we have done before you
   whether open or concealed,
and for the wrong that we have done before you
   knowingly and by deceit.
For the wrong that we have done before you
   through the prompting of the heart,
and for the wrong that we have done before you
   through the influence of others.
For the wrong that we have done before you
   whether by intention or mistake,
and for the wrong that we have done before you
   by the hand of violence.
For the wrong that we have done before you
   through our foolishness of speech,
and for the wrong that we have done before you
   through an evil inclination.

And for them all, God of forgiveness,
   please forgive us, pardon us, help us atone!

For the wrong that we have done before you
   in the palming of a bribe,
and for the wrong that we have done before you
   by expressions of contempt. ↵

YOM KIPPUR MINḤAH / 1097

וּבְכֵן יְהִי רָצוֹן מִלְּפָנֶיךָ יהוה אֱלֹהֵינוּ וֵאלֹהֵי אֲבוֹתֵינוּ וְאִמּוֹתֵינוּ
שֶׁתִּסְלַח לָנוּ עַל כָּל חַטֹּאתֵינוּ וְתִמְחַל לָנוּ עַל כָּל עֲווֹנוֹתֵינוּ וּתְכַפֶּר
לָנוּ עַל כָּל פְּשָׁעֵינוּ:

If seated, we rise.
For an alternative Al Ḥet, see pages 435-436, 833-834 or 969-970.

עַל חֵטְא שֶׁחָטָאנוּ לְפָנֶיךָ בְּאִמּוּץ הַלֵּב:
וְעַל חֵטְא שֶׁחָטָאנוּ לְפָנֶיךָ בִּבְלִי דָעַת:
עַל חֵטְא שֶׁחָטָאנוּ לְפָנֶיךָ בְּגִלּוּי וּבַסָּתֶר:
וְעַל חֵטְא שֶׁחָטָאנוּ לְפָנֶיךָ בְּדַעַת וּבְמִרְמָה:
עַל חֵטְא שֶׁחָטָאנוּ לְפָנֶיךָ בְּהַרְהוֹר הַלֵּב:
וְעַל חֵטְא שֶׁחָטָאנוּ לְפָנֶיךָ בְּוִעִידַת זְנוּת:
עַל חֵטְא שֶׁחָטָאנוּ לְפָנֶיךָ בְּזָדוֹן וּבִשְׁגָגָה:
וְעַל חֵטְא שֶׁחָטָאנוּ לְפָנֶיךָ בְּחֹזֶק יָד:
עַל חֵטְא שֶׁחָטָאנוּ לְפָנֶיךָ בְּטִפְשׁוּת פֶּה:
וְעַל חֵטְא שֶׁחָטָאנוּ לְפָנֶיךָ בְּיֵצֶר הָרָע:

וְעַל כֻּלָּם אֱלוֹהַּ סְלִיחוֹת סְלַח לָנוּ: מְחַל לָנוּ: כַּפֶּר לָנוּ:

Ve'al kulam eloah seliḥot selaḥ lanu. Meḥal lanu. Kaper lanu.

עַל חֵטְא שֶׁחָטָאנוּ לְפָנֶיךָ בְּכַפַּת שֹׁחַד:
וְעַל חֵטְא שֶׁחָטָאנוּ לְפָנֶיךָ בְּלָצוֹן: ←

For the wrong that we have done before you
   through misuse of food and drink,
and for the wrong that we have done before you
   by our avarice and greed.
For the wrong that we have done before you
   through offensive gaze,
and for the wrong that we have done before you
   through a condescending glance.

And for them all, God of forgiveness,
   please forgive us, pardon us, help us atone!

For the wrong that we have done before you
   by our quickness to oppose,
and for the wrong that we have done before you
   by deception of a friend.
For the wrong that we have done before you
   by unwillingness to change,
and for the wrong that we have done before you
   by running to embrace an evil act.
For the wrong that we have done before you
   by our groundless hatred,
and for the wrong that we have done before you
   in the giving of false pledge.

And for them all, God of forgiveness,
   please forgive us, pardon us, help us atone! ↩

If continuing aloud, we are seated.

עַל חֵטְא שֶׁחָטָאנוּ לְפָנֶיךָ בְּמַאֲכָל וּבְמִשְׁתֶּה:

וְעַל חֵטְא שֶׁחָטָאנוּ לְפָנֶיךָ בְּנֶשֶׁךְ וּבְמַרְבִּית:

עַל חֵטְא שֶׁחָטָאנוּ לְפָנֶיךָ בְּשִׁקּוּר עָיִן:

וְעַל חֵטְא שֶׁחָטָאנוּ לְפָנֶיךָ בְּעֵינַיִם רָמוֹת:

וְעַל כֻּלָּם אֱלוֹהַּ סְלִיחוֹת סְלַח לָנוּ: מְחַל לָנוּ: כַּפֶּר לָנוּ:

Ve'al kulam eloah seliḥot selaḥ lanu. Meḥal lanu. Kaper lanu.

עַל חֵטְא שֶׁחָטָאנוּ לְפָנֶיךָ בִּפְלִילוּת:

וְעַל חֵטְא שֶׁחָטָאנוּ לְפָנֶיךָ בִּצְדִיַּת רֵעַ:

עַל חֵטְא שֶׁחָטָאנוּ לְפָנֶיךָ בְּקַשְׁיוּת עֹרֶף:

וְעַל חֵטְא שֶׁחָטָאנוּ לְפָנֶיךָ בְּרִיצַת רַגְלַיִם לְהָרַע:

עַל חֵטְא שֶׁחָטָאנוּ לְפָנֶיךָ בִּשְׂנְאַת חִנָּם:

וְעַל חֵטְא שֶׁחָטָאנוּ לְפָנֶיךָ בִּתְשׂוּמֶת יָד:

⟵ וְעַל כֻּלָּם אֱלוֹהַּ סְלִיחוֹת סְלַח לָנוּ: מְחַל לָנוּ: כַּפֶּר לָנוּ:

Ve'al kulam eloah seliḥot selaḥ lanu. Meḥal lanu. Kaper lanu.

If continuing aloud, we are seated.

And for mitzvot that call on us to act,
and for mitzvot that bid us not to act,
for mitzvot that say: "Arise, and do...!"
and for mitzvot that do not say: "Arise, and do...!"
for those that are made known to us,
and those that are not known to us.

Those that are known to us
are things we have acknowledged
and confessed before you in times past,
but those that are not known to us
are things revealed and known only to you,
as it is said: "The hidden things
belong to THE ETERNAL ONE, our God.
What is revealed belongs to us and to our children,
always and forever—all the matters
of this Torah that are ours to carry out."

And through the love, ETERNAL ONE, our God,
with which you love your people Israel,
and through the compassion you have shown
to all who share your covenant,
you gave us, BLESSED ONE
(this day of Shabbat for holiness and for rest, and)
this Day of Atonement,
for forgiveness of our sins,
for pardoning of our transgressions,
and for atonement of the wrong that we have done. ↩

וְעַל מִצְוֺת עֲשֵׂה וְעַל מִצְוַת לֹא תַעֲשֶׂה בֵּין שֶׁיֵּשׁ־בָּהּ קוּם עֲשֵׂה וּבֵין שֶׁאֵין בָּהּ קוּם עֲשֵׂה אֶת־הַגְּלוּיִים לָנוּ וְאֶת־שֶׁאֵינָם גְּלוּיִים לָנוּ: אֶת־הַגְּלוּיִים לָנוּ כְּבָר אֲמַרְנוּם לְפָנֶיךָ וְהוֹדִינוּ לְךָ עֲלֵיהֶם וְאֶת־שֶׁאֵינָם גְּלוּיִים לָנוּ לְפָנֶיךָ הֵם גְּלוּיִים וִידוּעִים כַּדָּבָר שֶׁנֶּאֱמַר: הַנִּסְתָּרֹת לַיהוה אֱלֹהֵינוּ וְהַנִּגְלֹת לָנוּ וּלְבָנֵינוּ עַד־עוֹלָם לַעֲשׂוֹת אֶת־כָּל־דִּבְרֵי הַתּוֹרָה הַזֹּאת:

וּמֵאַהֲבָתְךָ יהוה אֱלֹהֵינוּ שֶׁאָהַבְתָּ אֶת יִשְׂרָאֵל עַמֶּךָ וּמֵחֶמְלָתְךָ מַלְכֵּנוּ שֶׁחָמַלְתָּ עַל בְּנֵי בְרִיתֶךָ נָתַתָּ לָנוּ יהוה אֱלֹהֵינוּ אֶת (יוֹם הַשַּׁבָּת הַזֶּה לִקְדֻשָּׁה וְלִמְנוּחָה וְאֶת) יוֹם הַכִּפֻּרִים הַזֶּה לִמְחִילַת חֵטְא וְלִסְלִיחַת עָוֺן וּלְכַפָּרַת פָּשַׁע: ←

הנסתרות...הזאת /The hidden...out (Deuteronomy 29:28).

A hymn of praise I sing to you,
Bearing my voice on high,
  to you, the Shield of Abraham.
    Who is a God like you?

Great deeds of yours I teach about,
  the Sovereign One, the Holy One.
    Who is a God like you?

Discoursing on your words of knowledge,
  you who grace us with your knowledge.
    Who is a God like you?

Have you not said: "Return!"
  you who desire our return?
    Who is a God like you?

Wishing to pardon, wishing to forgive,
  how often you forgive!
    Who is a God like you?

Calling out in songs of thanks,
  how good it is to offer thanks to you!
    Who is a God like you?

Revered One on high, bless the multitude assembled here:
  "May THE ETERNAL bless you!" it is said.
    Who is a God like you?

Sheḥinah, your presence in the world, is peace,
  you who make peace.
    Who is a God like you?

You overlook your people's wrongdoing, as it is written by your prophet's hand: "Who is a God like you?—forgiving sin, absolving the transgressions of the remnant of your heritage, you who do not cling to anger, but desire only kindness, ↵

מִי אֵל כָּמֹוךָ:   אֲהַלֶּלְךָ בְּקוֹל רָם מָגֵן אַבְרָהָם

מִי אֵל כָּמֹוךָ:   גָּדְלְךָ אֶדְרֹשׁ הַמֶּלֶךְ הַקָּדוֹשׁ

מִי אֵל כָּמֹוךָ:   דּוֹרֵשׁ אִמְרֵי לַעַת חוֹנֵן הַדָּעַת

מִי אֵל כָּמֹוךָ:   הָאָמֵר שׁוּבָה הָרוֹצֶה בִּתְשׁוּבָה

מִי אֵל כָּמֹוךָ:   וּמוֹחֵל וְסוֹלֵחַ הַמַּרְבֶּה לִסְלֹוחַ

מִי אֵל כָּמֹוךָ:   קוֹל רִנָּה וְתוֹדוֹת הַטּוֹב לְךָ לְהוֹדוֹת

מִי אֵל כָּמֹוךָ:   רָם בָּרֵךְ קְהַל הֲמוֹנִי יְבָרֶכְךָ יהוה

מִי אֵל כָּמֹוךָ:   שְׁכִינָתְךָ שָׁלוֹם עוֹשֶׂה הַשָּׁלוֹם

כַּכָּתוּב עַל יַד נְבִיאֶךָ: מִי־אֵל כָּמוֹךָ נֹשֵׂא עָוֹן וְעֹבֵר עַל־פֶּשַׁע לִשְׁאֵרִית נַחֲלָתוֹ לֹא־הֶחֱזִיק לָעַד אַפּוֹ כִּי־חָפֵץ חֶסֶד הוּא: ←

מי אל...חסד הוא /Who is...kindness (Micah 7:18).

you who act mercifully once again,
subduing the effects of our transgressions,
casting to the ocean waters all our wrongs."

All the wrongs done by your people Israel
you hereby cast into oblivion.
Those deeds shall not be dwelt on any further,
nor shall they come to mind again.

"You show faithfulness to Jacob,
love to Abraham,
as you have sworn
from days of old."

On Shabbat add the words in parenthesis.

Our God, our ancients' God,
forgive us our transgressions
this Day (of Shabbat, and) of Atonement,
blot out and cause to pass away
our wrongdoings and our errors
from before your eyes, as it is said:
"I, yes I, shall be the one
who blots out your wrongdoing, for my sake;
your errors I shall not remember any more!"
And it is said: "I have made your sins
vanish like a storm cloud,
and, like a mist, the things you have done wrong.
Return to me, for it is I who have redeemed you!"
And it is said: "For on this day,
atonement shall be made for you,
to make you clean from all of your wrongdoings.
Before THE FOUNT OF MERCY, you shall all be clean." ⤹

יָשׁוּב יְרַחֲמֵנוּ יִכְבֹּשׁ עֲוֹנֹתֵינוּ וְתַשְׁלִיךְ בִּמְצֻלוֹת יָם כָּל־חַטֹּאתָם:
וְכָל־חַטֹּאת עַמְּךָ בֵּית יִשְׂרָאֵל תַּשְׁלִיךְ בִּמְקוֹם אֲשֶׁר לֹא יִזָּכְרוּ וְלֹא
יִפָּקְדוּ וְלֹא יַעֲלוּ עַל לֵב לְעוֹלָם: תִּתֵּן אֱמֶת לְיַעֲקֹב חֶסֶד לְאַבְרָהָם
אֲשֶׁר־נִשְׁבַּעְתָּ לַאֲבוֹתֵינוּ וּלְאִמּוֹתֵינוּ מִימֵי קֶדֶם:

On Shabbat add the words in parenthesis:

אֱלֹהֵינוּ וֵאלֹהֵי אֲבוֹתֵינוּ וְאִמּוֹתֵינוּ מְחַל לַעֲוֹנוֹתֵינוּ בְּיוֹם (הַשַּׁבָּת
הַזֶּה וּבְיוֹם) הַכִּפּוּרִים: הַזֶּה מְחֵה וְהַעֲבֵר פְּשָׁעֵינוּ וְחַטֹּאתֵינוּ מִנֶּגֶד
עֵינֶיךָ כָּאָמוּר: אָנֹכִי אָנֹכִי הוּא מֹחֶה פְשָׁעֶיךָ לְמַעֲנִי וְחַטֹּאתֶיךָ לֹא
אֶזְכֹּר: וְנֶאֱמַר: מָחִיתִי כָעָב פְּשָׁעֶיךָ וְכֶעָנָן חַטֹּאתֶיךָ שׁוּבָה אֵלַי כִּי
גְאַלְתִּיךָ: וְנֶאֱמַר: כִּי־בַיּוֹם הַזֶּה יְכַפֵּר עֲלֵיכֶם לְטַהֵר אֶתְכֶם מִכֹּל
חַטֹּאתֵיכֶם לִפְנֵי יהוה תִּטְהָרוּ: ←

יָשׁוּב...חטאתם/you who...wrongs (Micah 7:19).
קדם...תתן/You show...old (Micah 7:20).
אנכי...אזכר/I, yes...more! (Isaiah 43:25).
מחיתי...גאלתיך/I have...you! (Isaiah 44:22).
כי ביום...תטהרו/For on...clean (Leviticus 16:30).

Our God, our ancients' God (take pleasure in our rest),
enable us to realize holiness with your mitzvot,
give us our portion in your Torah,
let us enjoy the good things of your world,
and gladden us with your salvation,
(and help us to perpetuate, ETERNAL ONE, our God,
your holy Shabbat, with love and joy,
and let all Israel, and all who treat your name as holy,
rest upon this day,) and refine our hearts
to serve you truthfully.
For you are a forgiving God to Israel,
and compassionate to all the tribes of Yeshurun
in each and every generation,
and apart from you we have no sovereign,
none full of compassion and forgiveness,
except you.
Blessed are you, FORGIVING ONE,
sovereign of mercy and forgiveness
for our wrongdoings, and for those
of all your kin, the house of Israel,
you who make our guilt to pass away,
year after year,
the sovereign power over all the earth
who raises up to holiness
(Shabbat,) the people Israel
and the Day of Atonement.

5. AVODAH / WORSHIP

Take pleasure GRACIOUS ONE, our God, in Israel your people;
lovingly accept their fervent prayer. May Israel's worship always
be acceptable to you. ⤶

אֱלֹהֵֽינוּ וֵאלֹהֵי אֲבוֹתֵֽינוּ וְאִמּוֹתֵֽינוּ (רְצֵה בִמְנוּחָתֵֽנוּ) קַדְּשֵֽׁנוּ
בְּמִצְוֺתֶֽיךָ וְתֵן חֶלְקֵֽנוּ בְּתוֹרָתֶֽךָ שַׂבְּעֵֽנוּ מִטּוּבֶֽךָ וְשַׂמְּחֵֽנוּ בִּישׁוּעָתֶֽךָ
(וְהַנְחִילֵֽנוּ יהוה אֱלֹהֵֽינוּ בְּאַהֲבָה וּבְרָצוֹן שַׁבַּת קָדְשֶֽׁךָ וְיָנֽוּחוּ בָהּ
יִשְׂרָאֵל מְקַדְּשֵׁי שְׁמֶֽךָ) וְטַהֵר לִבֵּֽנוּ לְעָבְדְּךָ בֶּאֱמֶת כִּי אַתָּה סָלְחָן
לְיִשְׂרָאֵל וּמָחֳלָן לְשִׁבְטֵי יְשֻׁרוּן בְּכָל דּוֹר וָדוֹר וּמִבַּלְעָדֶֽיךָ אֵין לָֽנוּ
מֶֽלֶךְ מוֹחֵל וְסוֹלֵֽחַ אֶלָּא אָֽתָּה: בָּרוּךְ אַתָּה יהוה מֶֽלֶךְ מוֹחֵל וְסוֹלֵֽחַ
לַעֲוֺנוֹתֵֽינוּ וְלַעֲוֺנוֹת עַמּוֹ בֵּית יִשְׂרָאֵל וּמַעֲבִיר אַשְׁמוֹתֵֽינוּ בְּכָל־שָׁנָה
וְשָׁנָה מֶֽלֶךְ עַל־כָּל־הָאָֽרֶץ מְקַדֵּשׁ (הַשַּׁבָּת וְ) יִשְׂרָאֵל וְיוֹם הַכִּפּוּרִים:

ה⁵ עֲבוֹדָה

רְצֵה יהוה אֱלֹהֵֽינוּ בְּעַמְּךָ יִשְׂרָאֵל וְלָֽהֶב תְּפִלָּתָם בְּאַהֲבָה תְקַבֵּל
בְּרָצוֹן וּתְהִי לְרָצוֹן תָּמִיד עֲבוֹדַת יִשְׂרָאֵל עַמֶּֽךָ: ←

And may our eyes behold your homecoming, with merciful intent, to Zion. Blessed are you, THE FAITHFUL ONE, who brings your presence home to Zion.

6. HODA'AH / THANKS

We give thanks to you that you are THE ALL-MERCIFUL, our God, God of our ancestors, today and always. A firm, enduring source of life, a shield to us in time of trial, you are ever there, from age to age. We acknowledge you, declare your praise, and thank you for our lives entrusted to your hand, our souls placed in your care, for your miracles that greet us every day, and for your wonders and the good things that are with us every hour, morning, noon, and night. Good One, whose kindness never stops, Kind One, whose loving acts have never failed—always have we placed our hope in you.

For all these things, your name be blessed and raised in honor always, sovereign of ours, forever.

Our creator, our sovereign,
remember your love for us,
and banish pestilence and war,
and famine, and captivity, and slaughter,
and crime, and violence, and plague,
and terrible disaster,
and every kind of illness,
and every kind of tragic accident,
and every kind of strife,
and all the forms of retribution,
and all evil decrees,
and groundless hatred,
from our midst,
and from the midst of all
who share in your world. ↵

וְתֶחֱזֶינָה עֵינֵינוּ בְּשׁוּבְךָ לְצִיּוֹן בְּרַחֲמִים: בָּרוּךְ אַתָּה יהוה הַמַּחֲזִיר שְׁכִינָתוֹ לְצִיּוֹן:

6 הוֹדָאָה

מוֹדִים אֲנַחְנוּ לָךְ שָׁאַתָּה הוּא יהוה אֱלֹהֵינוּ וֵאלֹהֵי אֲבוֹתֵינוּ וְאִמּוֹתֵינוּ לְעוֹלָם וָעֶד צוּר חַיֵּינוּ מָגֵן יִשְׁעֵנוּ אַתָּה הוּא לְדוֹר וָדוֹר: נוֹדֶה לְּךָ וּנְסַפֵּר תְּהִלָּתֶךָ עַל חַיֵּינוּ הַמְּסוּרִים בְּיָדֶךָ וְעַל נִשְׁמוֹתֵינוּ הַפְּקוּדוֹת לָךְ וְעַל נִסֶּיךָ שֶׁבְּכָל יוֹם עִמָּנוּ וְעַל נִפְלְאוֹתֶיךָ וְטוֹבוֹתֶיךָ שֶׁבְּכָל־עֵת עֶרֶב וָבֹקֶר וְצָהֳרָיִם: הַטּוֹב כִּי לֹא כָלוּ רַחֲמֶיךָ וְהַמְרַחֵם כִּי לֹא תַמּוּ חֲסָדֶיךָ מֵעוֹלָם קִוִּינוּ לָךְ:

וְעַל כֻּלָּם יִתְבָּרַךְ וְיִתְרוֹמַם שִׁמְךָ מַלְכֵּנוּ תָּמִיד לְעוֹלָם וָעֶד:

אָבִינוּ מַלְכֵּנוּ זְכֹר רַחֲמֶיךָ וְכַלֵּה דֶּבֶר וְחֶרֶב וְרָעָב וּשְׁבִי וּמַשְׁחִית וְעָוֹן וּשְׁמָד וּמַגֵּפָה וּפֶגַע רַע וְכָל־מַחֲלָה וְכָל־תְּקָלָה וְכָל־קְטָטָה וְכָל־מִינֵי פֻרְעָנִיּוֹת וְכָל־גְּזֵרָה רָעָה וְשִׂנְאַת חִנָּם מֵעָלֵינוּ וּמֵעַל כָּל־בְּנֵי עוֹלָמֶךָ: ←

And write down for a good life
all who share your covenant.

Let all of life acknowledge you! May all beings praise your name
in truth, O God, our rescue and our aid. Blessed are you,
GRACIOUS ONE, whose name is good, to whom all thanks are due.

7. BIRKAT HASHALOM / BLESSING FOR PEACE

The following paragraph is said only when the Amidah is chanted aloud.

Our God, our ancients' God,
bless us with the threefold blessing
spoken from the mouth of Aaron and his sons, as is said:
May THE ETERNAL bless you
    and protect you.   Let it be God's will!
May THE ETERNAL's face give light
    to you, and show you favor.   Let it be God's will!
May THE ETERNAL's face be lifted
    toward you, and bestow upon you
    peace.   Let it be God's will! ↵

יברכך...שלום / May...peace (Numbers 6:24-26).

וּכְתֹב לְחַיִּים טוֹבִים כָּל־בְּנֵי בְרִיתֶךָ:

וְכֹל הַחַיִּים יוֹדוּךָ סֶּלָה וִיהַלְלוּ אֶת שִׁמְךָ בֶּאֱמֶת הָאֵל יְשׁוּעָתֵנוּ וְעֶזְרָתֵנוּ סֶלָה: בָּרוּךְ אַתָּה יהוה הַטּוֹב שִׁמְךָ וּלְךָ נָאֶה לְהוֹדוֹת:

בִּרְכַּת הַשָּׁלוֹם

The following paragraph is said only when the Amidah is chanted aloud.

אֱלֹהֵינוּ וֵאלֹהֵי אֲבוֹתֵינוּ וְאִמּוֹתֵינוּ בָּרְכֵנוּ בַּבְּרָכָה הַמְשֻׁלֶּשֶׁת הָאֲמוּרָה מִפִּי אַהֲרֹן וּבָנָיו כָּאָמוּר:

יְבָרֶכְךָ יהוה וְיִשְׁמְרֶךָ.

כֵּן יְהִי רָצוֹן:

יָאֵר יהוה פָּנָיו אֵלֶיךָ וִיחֻנֶּךָּ:

כֵּן יְהִי רָצוֹן:

יִשָּׂא יהוה פָּנָיו אֵלֶיךָ וְיָשֵׂם לְךָ שָׁלוֹם:

כֵּן יְהִי רָצוֹן:

Eloheynu veylohey avoteynu ve'imoteynu
barehenu baberahah hamshuleshet
ha'amurah mipi aharon uvanav ka'amur:
Yevareheha adonay veyishmereha. Ken yehi ratzon.
Ya'er adonay panav eleha vihuneka. Ken yehi ratzon.
Yisa adonay panav eleha veyasem leha shalom. Ken yehi ratzon.

1112 / **AMIDAH/BIRKAT HASHALOM**

Grant peace, goodness and blessing in the world,
grace, love, and mercy
over us and over all your people Israel.
Bless us, source of being, all of us, as one
amid your light,
for by your light,
WISE ONE, our God, you give to us
Torah of life, and love of kindness,
justice, blessing, mercy, life, and peace.
So may it be a good thing in your eyes
to bless your people Israel, and all peoples,
with abundant strength and peace.

In the book of life, blessing, and peace, and proper sustenance,
may we be remembered and inscribed,
we and all your people, the house of Israel,
for a good life and for peace.

Blessed are you, COMPASSIONATE ONE, maker of peace.

The silent Amidah traditionally concludes with bowing and taking three steps back.

For Kaddish, see page 1187.

שִׂים שָׁלוֹם טוֹבָה וּבְרָכָה בָּעוֹלָם חֵן וָחֶסֶד וְרַחֲמִים עָלֵינוּ וְעַל כָּל־יִשְׂרָאֵל עַמֶּךָ: בָּרְכֵנוּ אָבִינוּ כֻּלָּנוּ כְּאֶחָד בְּאוֹר פָּנֶיךָ: כִּי בְאוֹר פָּנֶיךָ נָתַתָּ לָּנוּ יהוה אֱלֹהֵינוּ תּוֹרַת חַיִּים וְאַהֲבַת חֶסֶד וּצְדָקָה וּבְרָכָה וְרַחֲמִים וְחַיִּים וְשָׁלוֹם: וְטוֹב בְּעֵינֶיךָ לְבָרֵךְ אֶת־עַמְּךָ יִשְׂרָאֵל וְאֶת־כָּל־הָעַמִּים בְּרֹב־עֹז וְשָׁלוֹם:

בְּסֵפֶר חַיִּים בְּרָכָה וְשָׁלוֹם וּפַרְנָסָה טוֹבָה נִזָּכֵר וְנִכָּתֵב לְפָנֶיךָ אֲנַחְנוּ וְכָל־עַמְּךָ בֵּית יִשְׂרָאֵל לְחַיִּים טוֹבִים וּלְשָׁלוֹם:

בָּרוּךְ אַתָּה יהוה עוֹשֵׂה הַשָּׁלוֹם:

Sim shalom tovah uvraḥah ba'olam ḥen vaḥesed veraḥamim aleynu ve'al kol yisra'el ameḥa. Bareḥenu avinu kulanu ke'eḥad be'or paneḥa. Ki ve'or paneḥa natata lanu adonay eloheynu torat ḥayim ve'ahavat ḥesed utzedakah uveraḥah veraḥamim veḥayim veshalom. Vetov be'eyneḥa levareḥ et ameḥa yisra'el ve'et kol ha'amim berov oz veshalom.

Besefer ḥayim beraḥah veshalom ufarnasah tovah nizaḥer venikatev lefaneḥa anaḥnu veḥol ameḥa beyt yisra'el leḥayim tovim uleshalom.

Baruḥ atah adonay osey hashalom.

The silent Amidah traditionally concludes with bowing and taking three steps back.

For Kaddish, see page 1188.

Some communities chant Ashrey, page 593, here.

SILENT AMIDAH FOR NE'ILAH

The silent Amidah follows here. Communities that chant the Amidah aloud turn to page 1141. Directed meditations begin on page 1. The Amidah is traditionally recited while standing, beginning with three short steps forward and bowing left and right, a reminder of our entry into the divine presence.

Open my lips, BELOVED ONE,
and let my mouth declare your praise.

1. AVOT VE'IMOT / ANCESTORS

Blessed are you, ANCIENT ONE, our God, God of our ancestors,

God of Abraham	God of Sarah
God of Isaac	God of Rebekah
God of Jacob	God of Rachel
	and God of Leah;

great, heroic, awesome God, supreme divinity,
imparting deeds of kindness, begetter of all;
mindful of the loyalty of Israel's ancestors,
bringing, with love, redemption to their children's children
for the sake of the divine name.

Remember us for life,
our sovereign who wishes us to live,
and seal us in the Book of Life
for your sake, ever-living God.

Regal One, our help, salvation, and protector:
Blessed are you, KIND ONE,
the shield of Abraham and the help of Sarah. ⤹

Some communities chant Ashrey, page 594, here.

עֲמִידָה

The silent Amidah follows here. Communities that chant the Amidah aloud turn to page 1142. Directed meditations begin on page 1. The Amidah is traditionally recited while standing, beginning with three short steps forward and bowing left and right, a reminder of our entry into the divine presence.

אֲדֹנָי שְׂפָתַי תִּפְתָּח וּפִי יַגִּיד תְּהִלָּתֶךָ:

 אָבוֹת וְאִמּוֹת

בָּרוּךְ אַתָּה יהוה אֱלֹהֵינוּ וֵאלֹהֵי אֲבוֹתֵֽינוּ וְאִמּוֹתֵֽינוּ

אֱלֹהֵי שָׂרָה   אֱלֹהֵי אַבְרָהָם

אֱלֹהֵי רִבְקָה   אֱלֹהֵי יִצְחָק

אֱלֹהֵי רָחֵל   אֱלֹהֵי יַעֲקֹב

וֵאלֹהֵי לֵאָה:

הָאֵל הַגָּדוֹל הַגִּבּוֹר וְהַנּוֹרָא אֵל עֶלְיוֹן גּוֹמֵל חֲסָדִים טוֹבִים וְקוֹנֵה הַכֹּל וְזוֹכֵר חַסְדֵי אָבוֹת וְאִמּוֹת וּמֵבִיא גְאֻלָּה לִבְנֵי בְנֵיהֶם לְמַֽעַן שְׁמוֹ בְּאַהֲבָה:

זָכְרֵֽנוּ לְחַיִּים מֶֽלֶךְ חָפֵץ בַּחַיִּים וְחָתְמֵֽנוּ בְּסֵֽפֶר הַחַיִּים לְמַעַנְךָ אֱלֹהִים חַיִּים:

מֶֽלֶךְ עוֹזֵר וּמוֹשִֽׁיעַ וּמָגֵן: בָּרוּךְ אַתָּה יהוה מָגֵן אַבְרָהָם וְעֶזְרַת שָׂרָה: →

אֲדֹני...תהלתך/Open...praise (Psalms 51:17).

2. GEVUROT / DIVINE POWER

You are forever powerful, ALMIGHTY ONE, abundant in your saving acts. You send down the dew. In loyalty you sustain the living, nurturing the life of every living thing, upholding those who fall, healing the sick, freeing the captive, and remaining faithful to all life held dormant in the earth. Who can compare to you, almighty God, who can resemble you, the source of life and death, who makes salvation grow?

Who can compare to you, source of all mercy, remembering all creatures mercifully, decreeing life!

Faithful are you in giving life to every living thing. Blessed are you, THE FOUNT OF LIFE, who gives and renews life.

3. KEDUSHAT HASHEM / HALLOWING GOD'S NAME

Holy are you. Your name is holy.
And all holy beings hail you each day.

And therefore, HOLY ONE, let awe of you
infuse the whole of your Creation,
and let knowledge of your presence
dwell in all your creatures.
And let every being worship you,
and each created life pay homage to your rule.
Let all of them, as one, enact your bidding
with a whole and peaceful heart.
For we have always known, ALMIGHTY ONE,
that all authority to rule originates in you,
all strength is rooted in your arm,
all mighty deeds have emanated from your hand.
Your name alone is the source of awe
that surges through all life. ⤺

גְּבוּרוֹת ‏2

אַתָּה גִבּוֹר לְעוֹלָם אֲדֹנָי רַב לְהוֹשִׁיעַ: מוֹרִיד הַטָּל: מְכַלְכֵּל חַיִּים
בְּחֶסֶד מְחַיֶּה כָּל חַי בְּרַחֲמִים רַבִּים סוֹמֵךְ נוֹפְלִים וְרוֹפֵא חוֹלִים
וּמַתִּיר אֲסוּרִים וּמְקַיֵּם אֱמוּנָתוֹ לִישֵׁנֵי עָפָר: מִי כָמוֹךָ בַּעַל גְּבוּרוֹת
וּמִי דוֹמֶה לָּךְ מֶלֶךְ מֵמִית וּמְחַיֶּה וּמַצְמִיחַ יְשׁוּעָה:

מִי כָמוֹךָ אַב הָרַחֲמִים זוֹכֵר יְצוּרָיו לְחַיִּים בְּרַחֲמִים:

וְנֶאֱמָן אַתָּה לְהַחֲיוֹת כָּל חָי: בָּרוּךְ אַתָּה יהוה מְחַיֵּה כָּל חָי:

קְדֻשַּׁת הַשֵּׁם ‏3

אַתָּה קָדוֹשׁ וְשִׁמְךָ קָדוֹשׁ וּקְדוֹשִׁים בְּכָל יוֹם יְהַלְלוּךָ סֶּלָה:

וּבְכֵן תֵּן פַּחְדְּךָ יהוה אֱלֹהֵינוּ עַל כָּל־מַעֲשֶׂיךָ וְאֵימָתְךָ עַל כָּל־
מַה־שֶּׁבָּרָאתָ וְיִירָאוּךָ כָּל־הַמַּעֲשִׂים וְיִשְׁתַּחֲווּ לְפָנֶיךָ כָּל־הַבְּרוּאִים
וְיֵעָשׂוּ כֻלָּם אֲגֻדָּה אַחַת לַעֲשׂוֹת רְצוֹנְךָ בְּלֵבָב שָׁלֵם כְּמוֹ שֶׁיָּדַעְנוּ
יהוה אֱלֹהֵינוּ שֶׁהַשִּׁלְטוֹן לְפָנֶיךָ עֹז בְּיָדְךָ וּגְבוּרָה בִּימִינֶךָ וְשִׁמְךָ
נוֹרָא עַל כָּל־מַה־שֶּׁבָּרָאתָ: ←

And therefore, HOLY ONE, let awe of you
infuse your people, let the praise of you
ring out from all who worship you.
Let hope enliven all who seek you,
and let all who look to you with hope
find strength to speak.
Grant joy throughout your land,
let happiness resound throughout your holy city,
soon, and in our days.

And therefore, let the just behold your peace,
let them rejoice,
let all who follow in your path sing out with joy,
let all who love you dance in celebration,
and may your power overwhelm all treachery,
so that it vanish wholly from the earth like smoke.
Then shall the power of injustice pass away!

May you alone be sovereign over all of your Creation,
and Mount Zion be the seat and symbol of your glory,
and Jerusalem, your holy city—
as is written in your holy scriptures:
"THE ETERNAL ONE shall reign forever,
your God, O Zion, through all generations!
Halleluyah!"

Holy are you,
and awe-inspiring is your name,
and there is no God apart from you,
as it is written: "THE CREATOR of the multitudes of heaven
shall be exalted through the rule of law,
and God, the Holy One, made holy by the reign of justice."
Blessed are you, ETERNAL ONE,
the holy sovereign power. ↩

וּבְכֵן תֵּן כָּבוֹד יהוה לְעַמֶּךָ תְּהִלָּה לִירֵאֶיךָ וְתִקְוָה לְדוֹרְשֶׁיךָ וּפִתְחוֹן פֶּה לַמְיַחֲלִים לָךְ שִׂמְחָה לְאַרְצֶךָ וְשָׂשׂוֹן לְעִירֶךָ בִּמְהֵרָה בְיָמֵינוּ:

וּבְכֵן צַדִּיקִים יִרְאוּ וְיִשְׂמָחוּ וִישָׁרִים יַעֲלֹזוּ וַחֲסִידִים בְּרִנָּה יָגִילוּ וְעוֹלָתָה תִּקְפָּץ־פִּיהָ וְכָל־הָרִשְׁעָה כֻּלָּהּ כְּעָשָׁן תִּכְלֶה כִּי תַעֲבִיר מֶמְשֶׁלֶת זָדוֹן מִן הָאָרֶץ:

וְתִמְלֹךְ אַתָּה יהוה לְבַדֶּךָ עַל כָּל־מַעֲשֶׂיךָ בְּהַר צִיּוֹן מִשְׁכַּן כְּבוֹדֶךָ וּבִירוּשָׁלַיִם עִיר קָדְשֶׁךָ: כַּכָּתוּב בְּדִבְרֵי קָדְשֶׁךָ: יִמְלֹךְ יהוה לְעוֹלָם אֱלֹהַיִךְ צִיּוֹן לְדֹר וָדֹר הַלְלוּיָהּ:

קָדוֹשׁ אַתָּה וְנוֹרָא שְׁמֶךָ וְאֵין אֱלוֹהַּ מִבַּלְעָדֶיךָ: כַּכָּתוּב: וַיִּגְבַּהּ יהוה צְבָאוֹת בַּמִּשְׁפָּט וְהָאֵל הַקָּדוֹשׁ נִקְדַּשׁ בִּצְדָקָה: בָּרוּךְ אַתָּה יהוה הַמֶּלֶךְ הַקָּדוֹשׁ: ←

ימלך...הללויה/THE ETERNAL ONE...Halleluyah! (Psalms 146:10).
ויגבה...בצדקה/THE CREATOR...justice (Isaiah 5:16).

4. KEDUSHAT HAYOM / THE DAY'S HOLINESS

On Shabbat add the words in parenthesis.

You have loved us, and have taken pleasure in us,
and have made us holy with your mitzvot,
and you have brought us, Sovereign One,
near to your service,
and have called us to the shelter of your great and holy name,
and you have given us, ALMIGHTY ONE, our God, in love
this Day of (Shabbat for holiness and for rest
and this Day of) Atonement,
for pardoning, forgiveness, and atonement,
on which you pardon us for all of our transgressions
(with love), a holy convocation,
a remembrance of the going-out from Egypt.

Our God, our ancients' God, may our prayer arise and come to
you, and be beheld, and be acceptable. Let it be heard, acted
upon, remembered—the memory of us and all our needs, the
memory of our ancestors, the memory of messianic hopes, the
memory of Jerusalem your holy city, and the memory of all your
kin, the house of Israel, all surviving in your presence. Act for
goodness and grace, for love and care; for life, well-being and
peace, on this Day of Atonement.

Remember us this day, ALL-KNOWING ONE, our God, for
goodness. Favor us this day with blessing. Preserve us this day
for life. With your redeeming nurturing word, be kind and
generous. Act tenderly on our behalf, and grant us victory over
all our trials. Truly, our eyes turn toward you, for you are a
providing God; gracious and merciful are you. ⤶

קְדֻשַּׁת הַיּוֹם

On Shabbat add the words in parenthesis.

אַתָּה אֲהַבְתָּנוּ וְרָצִיתָ בָּנוּ וְקִדַּשְׁתָּנוּ בְּמִצְוֹתֶיךָ וְקֵרַבְתָּנוּ מַלְכֵּנוּ לַעֲבוֹדָתֶךָ. וְשִׁמְךָ הַגָּדוֹל וְהַקָּדוֹשׁ עָלֵינוּ קָרָאתָ: וַתִּתֶּן לָנוּ יהוה אֱלֹהֵינוּ בְּאַהֲבָה אֶת יוֹם (הַשַּׁבָּת הַזֶּה לִקְדֻשָּׁה וְלִמְנוּחָה וְאֶת יוֹם) הַכִּפּוּרִים הַזֶּה לִמְחִילָה וְלִסְלִיחָה וּלְכַפָּרָה וְלִמְחָל בּוֹ אֶת כָּל עֲוֹנוֹתֵינוּ (בְּאַהֲבָה) מִקְרָא קֹדֶשׁ זֵכֶר לִיצִיאַת מִצְרָיִם:

אֱלֹהֵינוּ וֵאלֹהֵי אֲבוֹתֵינוּ וְאִמּוֹתֵינוּ יַעֲלֶה וְיָבוֹא וְיַגִּיעַ וְיֵרָאֶה וְיֵרָצֶה וְיִשָּׁמַע וְיִפָּקֵד וְיִזָּכֵר זִכְרוֹנֵנוּ וּפִקְדוֹנֵנוּ וְזִכְרוֹן אֲבוֹתֵינוּ וְאִמּוֹתֵינוּ וְזִכְרוֹן יְמוֹת הַמָּשִׁיחַ וְזִכְרוֹן יְרוּשָׁלַיִם עִיר קָדְשֶׁךָ וְזִכְרוֹן כָּל עַמְּךָ בֵּית יִשְׂרָאֵל לְפָנֶיךָ לִפְלֵיטָה וּלְטוֹבָה וּלְחֵן וּלְחֶסֶד וּלְרַחֲמִים לְחַיִּים וּלְשָׁלוֹם בְּיוֹם הַכִּפּוּרִים הַזֶּה:

זָכְרֵנוּ יהוה אֱלֹהֵינוּ בּוֹ לְטוֹבָה: וּפָקְדֵנוּ בוֹ לִבְרָכָה וְהוֹשִׁיעֵנוּ בוֹ לְחַיִּים: וּבִדְבַר יְשׁוּעָה וְרַחֲמִים חוּס וְחָנֵּנוּ וְרַחֵם עָלֵינוּ וְהוֹשִׁיעֵנוּ כִּי אֵלֶיךָ עֵינֵינוּ כִּי אֵל מֶלֶךְ חַנּוּן וְרַחוּם אָתָּה: ←

Our God, our ancients' God,
forgive us our transgressions
this Day (of Shabbat, and) of Atonement,
blot out and cause to pass away
our wrongdoings and our errors
from before your eyes, as it is said:
"I, yes I, shall be the one
who blots out your wrongdoing, for my sake;
your errors I shall not remember any more!"
And it is said: "I have made your sins
vanish like a storm cloud,
and, like a mist, the things you have done wrong.
Return to me, for it is I who have redeemed you!"
And it is said: "For on this day,
atonement shall be made for you,
to make you clean from all of your wrongdoings.
Before THE FOUNT OF MERCY, you shall all be clean."

Our God, our ancients' God (take pleasure in our rest),
enable us to realize holiness with your mitzvot,
give us our portion in your Torah,
let us enjoy the good things of your world,
and gladden us with your salvation,
(and help us to perpetuate, ETERNAL ONE, our God,
your holy Shabbat, with love and joy,
and let all Israel, and all who treat your name as holy,
rest upon this day,) and refine our hearts
to serve you truthfully.
For you are a forgiving God to Israel,
and compassionate to all the tribes of Yeshurun
in each and every generation,
and apart from you we have no sovereign,
none full of compassion and forgiveness,
except you. ⤶

אֱלֹהֵינוּ וֵאלֹהֵי אֲבוֹתֵינוּ וְאִמּוֹתֵינוּ מְחַל לַעֲוֹנוֹתֵינוּ בְּיוֹם (הַשַּׁבָּת
הַזֶּה וּבְיוֹם) הַכִּפּוּרִים הַזֶּה: מְחֵה וְהַעֲבֵר פְּשָׁעֵינוּ וְחַטֹּאתֵינוּ מִנֶּגֶד
עֵינֶיךָ: כָּאָמוּר: אָנֹכִי אָנֹכִי הוּא מֹחֶה פְשָׁעֶיךָ לְמַעֲנִי וְחַטֹּאתֶיךָ לֹא
אֶזְכֹּר: וְנֶאֱמַר: מָחִיתִי כָעָב פְּשָׁעֶיךָ וְכֶעָנָן חַטֹּאתֶיךָ שׁוּבָה אֵלַי כִּי
גְאַלְתִּיךָ: וְנֶאֱמַר: כִּי־בַיּוֹם הַזֶּה יְכַפֵּר עֲלֵיכֶם לְטַהֵר אֶתְכֶם מִכֹּל
חַטֹּאתֵיכֶם לִפְנֵי יהוה תִּטְהָרוּ:

אֱלֹהֵינוּ וֵאלֹהֵי אֲבוֹתֵינוּ וְאִמּוֹתֵינוּ (רְצֵה בִמְנוּחָתֵנוּ) קַדְּשֵׁנוּ
בְּמִצְוֹתֶיךָ וְתֵן חֶלְקֵנוּ בְּתוֹרָתֶךָ שַׂבְּעֵנוּ מִטּוּבֶךָ וְשַׂמְּחֵנוּ בִּישׁוּעָתֶךָ
(וְהַנְחִילֵנוּ יהוה אֱלֹהֵינוּ בְּאַהֲבָה וּבְרָצוֹן שַׁבַּת קָדְשֶׁךָ וְיָנוּחוּ בָהּ
יִשְׂרָאֵל מְקַדְּשֵׁי שְׁמֶךָ) וְטַהֵר לִבֵּנוּ לְעָבְדְּךָ בֶּאֱמֶת כִּי אַתָּה סָלְחָן
לְיִשְׂרָאֵל וּמָחֳלָן לְשִׁבְטֵי יְשֻׁרוּן בְּכָל דּוֹר וָדוֹר וּמִבַּלְעָדֶיךָ אֵין לָנוּ
מֶלֶךְ מוֹחֵל וְסוֹלֵחַ אֶלָּא אָתָּה: ←

אנכי...אזכר /I, yes...more! (Isaiah 43:25).
מחיתי...גאלתיך /I have...you! (Isaiah 44:22).
כי ביום...תטהרו /For on...clean (Leviticus 16:30).

Blessed are you, FORGIVING ONE,
sovereign of mercy and forgiveness
for our wrongdoings, and for those
of all your kin, the house of Israel,
you who make our guilt to pass away
year after year,
the sovereign power over all the earth
who raises up to holiness
(Shabbat,) the people Israel
and the Day of Atonement.

5. AVODAH / WORSHIP

Take pleasure, GRACIOUS ONE, our God, in Israel your people;
lovingly accept their fervent prayer. May Israel's worship always
be acceptable to you.

And may our eyes behold your homecoming, with merciful
intent, to Zion. Blessed are you, THE FAITHFUL ONE, who brings
your presence home to Zion.

6. HODA'AH / THANKS

We give thanks to you that you are THE ALL-MERCIFUL, our God,
God of our ancestors, today and always. A firm, enduring source
of life, a shield to us in time of trial, you are ever there, from age
to age. We acknowledge you, declare your praise, and thank you
for our lives entrusted to your hand, our souls placed in your
care, for your miracles that greet us every day, and for your
wonders and the good things that are with us every hour,
morning, noon and night. GOOD ONE, whose kindness never
stops, KIND ONE, whose loving acts have never failed—always
have we placed our hope in you. ↵

בָּרוּךְ אַתָּה יהוה מֶֽלֶךְ מוֹחֵל וְסוֹלֵֽחַ לַעֲוֹנוֹתֵֽינוּ וְלַעֲוֹנוֹת עַמּוֹ בֵּית
יִשְׂרָאֵל וּמַעֲבִיר אַשְׁמוֹתֵֽינוּ בְּכָל־שָׁנָה וְשָׁנָה מֶֽלֶךְ עַל־כָּל־הָאָֽרֶץ
מְקַדֵּשׁ (הַשַּׁבָּת וְ) יִשְׂרָאֵל וְיוֹם הַכִּפּוּרִים:

⁵ עֲבוֹדָה

רְצֵה יהוה אֱלֹהֵֽינוּ בְּעַמְּךָ יִשְׂרָאֵל וְלַהַב תְּפִלָּתָם בְּאַהֲבָה תְקַבֵּל
בְּרָצוֹן וּתְהִי לְרָצוֹן תָּמִיד עֲבוֹדַת יִשְׂרָאֵל עַמֶּֽךָ:

וְתֶחֱזֶֽינָה עֵינֵֽינוּ בְּשׁוּבְךָ לְצִיּוֹן בְּרַחֲמִים: בָּרוּךְ אַתָּה יהוה הַמַּחֲזִיר
שְׁכִינָתוֹ לְצִיּוֹן:

⁶ הוֹדָאָה

מוֹדִים אֲנַֽחְנוּ לָךְ שָׁאַתָּה הוּא יהוה אֱלֹהֵֽינוּ וֵאלֹהֵי אֲבוֹתֵֽינוּ
וְאִמּוֹתֵֽינוּ לְעוֹלָם וָעֶד צוּר חַיֵּֽינוּ מָגֵן יִשְׁעֵֽנוּ אַתָּה הוּא לְדוֹר וָדוֹר:
נוֹדֶה לְּךָ וּנְסַפֵּר תְּהִלָּתֶֽךָ עַל חַיֵּֽינוּ הַמְּסוּרִים בְּיָדֶֽךָ וְעַל נִשְׁמוֹתֵֽינוּ
הַפְּקוּדוֹת לָךְ וְעַל נִסֶּֽיךָ שֶׁבְּכָל יוֹם עִמָּֽנוּ וְעַל נִפְלְאוֹתֶֽיךָ וְטוֹבוֹתֶֽיךָ
שֶׁבְּכָל־עֵת עֶֽרֶב וָבֹֽקֶר וְצָהֳרָֽיִם: הַטּוֹב כִּי לֹא כָלוּ רַחֲמֶֽיךָ וְהַמְרַחֵם
כִּי לֹא תַֽמּוּ חֲסָדֶֽיךָ מֵעוֹלָם קִוִּֽינוּ לָךְ: ←

For all these things, your name be blessed and raised in honor always, sovereign of ours, forever.

And seal for a good life all the people of your covenant.

Let all of life acknowledge you! May all beings praise your name in truth. O God, our rescue and our aid. Blessed are you, GRACIOUS ONE whose name is good, to whom all thanks are due.

7. BIRKAT HASHALOM / BLESSING FOR PEACE

Grant peace, goodness and blessing in the world,
grace, love and mercy
over us and over all your people Israel.
Bless us, source of being, all of us, as one
amid your light,
for by your light,
WISE ONE, our God, you give to us
Torah of life, and love of kindness,
justice, blessing, mercy, life, and peace.
So may it be a good thing in your eyes,
to bless your people Israel, and all peoples,
with abundant strength and peace.

In the book of life, blessing, peace, and proper sustenance, may we be remembered and sealed, we and all your people, the house of Israel, for a good life and for peace.

Blessed are you, COMPASSIONATE ONE, maker of peace.

וְעַל כֻּלָּם יִתְבָּרַךְ וְיִתְרוֹמַם שִׁמְךָ מַלְכֵּנוּ תָּמִיד לְעוֹלָם וָעֶד:

וַחֲתוֹם לְחַיִּים טוֹבִים כָּל־בְּנֵי בְרִיתֶךָ:

וְכֹל הַחַיִּים יוֹדוּךָ סֶּלָה וִיהַלְלוּ אֶת שִׁמְךָ בֶּאֱמֶת הָאֵל יְשׁוּעָתֵנוּ וְעֶזְרָתֵנוּ סֶּלָה: בָּרוּךְ אַתָּה יהוה הַטּוֹב שִׁמְךָ וּלְךָ נָאֶה לְהוֹדוֹת:

בִּרְכַּת הַשָּׁלוֹם

שִׂים שָׁלוֹם טוֹבָה וּבְרָכָה בָּעוֹלָם חֵן וָחֶסֶד וְרַחֲמִים עָלֵינוּ וְעַל כָּל־יִשְׂרָאֵל עַמֶּךָ: בָּרְכֵנוּ אָבִינוּ כֻּלָּנוּ כְּאֶחָד בְּאוֹר פָּנֶיךָ: כִּי בְאוֹר פָּנֶיךָ נָתַתָּ לָּנוּ יהוה אֱלֹהֵינוּ תּוֹרַת חַיִּים וְאַהֲבַת חֶסֶד וּצְדָקָה וּבְרָכָה וְרַחֲמִים וְחַיִּים וְשָׁלוֹם: וְטוֹב בְּעֵינֶיךָ לְבָרֵךְ אֶת עַמְּךָ יִשְׂרָאֵל וְאֶת כָּל הָעַמִּים בְּרֹב עֹז וְשָׁלוֹם.

בְּסֵפֶר חַיִּים בְּרָכָה וְשָׁלוֹם וּפַרְנָסָה טוֹבָה נִזָּכֵר וְנִחָתֵם לְפָנֶיךָ אֲנַחְנוּ וְכָל עַמְּךָ בֵּית יִשְׂרָאֵל לְחַיִּים טוֹבִים וּלְשָׁלוֹם:

בָּרוּךְ אַתָּה יהוה עוֹשֶׂה הַשָּׁלוֹם: —←

Our God, our ancients' God,
may our prayer come before you.
Hide not from our supplication,
for we are not so insolent and stubborn
as to say, here in your presence,
"HOLY ONE, God of our fathers and our mothers,
we are righteous, and we have not sinned,"
for we indeed have sinned.

We have **a**cted wrongly,
we have **b**een untrue,
and we have **g**ained unlawfully
and have **d**efamed.
We have **h**armed others,
we have **w**rought injustice,
we have **z**ealously transgressed,
and we have **h**urt
and have **t**old lies.
We have **i**mproperly advised,
and we have **c**overed up the truth,
and we have **l**aughed in scorn.
We have **m**isused responsibility
and have **n**eglected others.
We have **s**tubbornly rebelled.
We have **o**ffended,
we have **p**erverted justice,
we have **s**tirred up enmity,
and we have **k**ept ourselves from change.
We have **r**eached out to evil,
we have **s**hamelessly corrupted
and have **t**reated others with disdain.
Yes, we have **t**hrown ourselves off course,
and we have **t**empted and misled. ↵

אֱלֹהֵֽינוּ וֵאלֹהֵי אֲבוֹתֵֽינוּ וְאִמּוֹתֵֽינוּ תָּבוֹא לְפָנֶֽיךָ תְּפִלָּתֵֽנוּ וְאַל
תִּתְעַלַּם מִתְּחִנָּתֵֽנוּ שֶׁאֵין אֲנַֽחְנוּ עַזֵּי פָנִים וּקְשֵׁי עֹֽרֶף לוֹמַר לְפָנֶֽיךָ
יהוה אֱלֹהֵֽינוּ וֵאלֹהֵי אֲבוֹתֵֽינוּ וְאִמּוֹתֵֽינוּ צַדִּיקִים אֲנַֽחְנוּ וְלֹא חָטָֽאנוּ
אֲבָל אֲנַֽחְנוּ חָטָֽאנוּ:

אָשַֽׁמְנוּ: בָּגַֽדְנוּ: גָּזַֽלְנוּ: דִּבַּֽרְנוּ דֹֽפִי:
הֶעֱוִֽינוּ: וְהִרְשַֽׁעְנוּ: זַֽדְנוּ: חָמַֽסְנוּ:
טָפַֽלְנוּ שֶֽׁקֶר: יָעַֽצְנוּ רָע: כִּזַּֽבְנוּ: לַֽצְנוּ:
מָרַֽדְנוּ: נִאַֽצְנוּ: סָרַֽרְנוּ: עָוִֽינוּ:
פָּשַֽׁעְנוּ: צָרַֽרְנוּ: קִשִּֽׁינוּ עֹֽרֶף: רָשַֽׁעְנוּ:
שִׁחַֽתְנוּ: תִּעַֽבְנוּ: תָּעִֽינוּ: תִּעְתָּֽעְנוּ: ←

Ashamnu. Bagadnu. Gazalnu. Dibarnu dofi.
He'evinu. Vehirshanu. Zadnu. Ḥamasnu.
Tafalnu shaker. Ya'atznu ra. Kizavnu. Latznu.
Maradnu. Ni'atznu. Sararnu. Avinu.
Pashanu. Tzararnu. Kishinu oref. Rashanu.
Shiḥatnu. Ti'avnu. Ta'inu. Titanu.

We have turned away from your mitzvot,
and from your righteous laws,
as if it did not matter to us.
And you are just,
whatever comes upon us,
for what you do is truth,
and we have done much wrong.

What can we say before you,
you who dwell on high?
What can we tell you,
you who inhabit heaven's heights?
Are you not one who knows all things,
both hidden and revealed?

You extend a hand to those who have transgressed,
your right hand is stretched out to receive all who return.
And you have taught us, RIGHTEOUS ONE,
to acknowledge in your presence all we have done wrong,
that we might disengage ourselves from plunder in our hands.
May you receive us in complete return into your presence,
like the fires and sweet savors of the ancient offerings,
so that all that you have promised may come true.
There is no limit to the fires of our devotion,
and there is no number to the savors of our repentance.
And you know that our destiny
is but to serve as food for worms and maggots.
Therefore, you have multiplied the opportunities
for our forgiveness. ⮌

סַרְנוּ מִמִּצְוֹתֶיךָ וּמִמִּשְׁפָּטֶיךָ הַטּוֹבִים וְלֹא שָׁוָה לָנוּ: וְאַתָּה צַדִּיק עַל
כָּל־הַבָּא עָלֵינוּ כִּי־אֱמֶת עָשִׂיתָ וַאֲנַחְנוּ הִרְשָׁעְנוּ:

מַה נֹּאמַר לְפָנֶיךָ יוֹשֵׁב מָרוֹם וּמַה נְּסַפֵּר לְפָנֶיךָ שׁוֹכֵן שְׁחָקִים הֲלֹא
כָּל הַנִּסְתָּרוֹת וְהַנִּגְלוֹת אַתָּה יוֹדֵעַ:

אַתָּה נוֹתֵן יָד לְפוֹשְׁעִים וִימִינְךָ פְּשׁוּטָה לְקַבֵּל שָׁבִים: וַתְּלַמְּדֵנוּ
יהוה אֱלֹהֵינוּ לְהִתְוַדּוֹת לְפָנֶיךָ עַל כָּל־עֲוֹנוֹתֵינוּ לְמַעַן נֶחְדַּל מֵעשֶׁק
יָדֵינוּ וּתְקַבְּלֵנוּ בִּתְשׁוּבָה שְׁלֵמָה לְפָנֶיךָ כְּאִשִּׁים וּכְנִיחוֹחִים לְמַעַן
דְּבָרֶיךָ אֲשֶׁר אָמָרְתָּ: אֵין קֵץ לְאִשֵּׁי חוֹבוֹתֵינוּ וְאֵין מִסְפָּר לְנִיחוֹחֵי
אַשְׁמוֹתֵינוּ: וְאַתָּה יוֹדֵעַ שֶׁאַחֲרִיתֵנוּ רִמָּה וְתוֹלֵעָה לְפִיכָךְ הִרְבֵּיתָ
סְלִיחָתֵנוּ: ←

ואתה...הרשענו / And...wrong (Nehemiah 9:33).

What are we? What is our life?
What is our love? What is our justice?
What is our help? What is our strength?
What is our power?
What can we say before you,
ALL-DISCERNING ONE, our God, our ancients' God?
For are not all the mighty of this world
like nothing in your presence,
all who bear renown like those who never were,
all persons of wisdom like the ignorant,
and all who understand like those who lack intelligence?
For truly, most of what they do is but a void,
their days are like a puff of air before you.
The advantage of the human being over beasts
amounts to nothing—for everything,
measured against you, lacks substance.

You set apart the human being at Creation,
you recognize humanity to stand before you.
But truly, who could say before you: "What are you doing?"
And if one could be just enough to stand before you,
what could one offer you?
And even so, you gave us, HOLY ONE, our God,
with love, this Day of Atonement,
that we might liberate ourselves
from all that our hands have stolen,
and return to you,
to carry out your ordinance and will
wholeheartedly.
And may you, in your abundant love,
spread mercy over us,
for you do not desire the destruction of the world,
for it is said:
"Seek out THE HOLY ONE, for God is present,
call to God, for God is near." ↵

מָה אָנוּ: מֶה חַיֵּינוּ: מֶה חַסְדֵּנוּ: מַה־צִּדְקֵנוּ: מַה־יִּשְׁעֵנוּ: מַה־כֹּחֵנוּ:
מַה־גְּבוּרָתֵנוּ: מַה־נֹּאמַר לְפָנֶיךָ יהוה אֱלֹהֵינוּ וֵאלֹהֵי אֲבוֹתֵינוּ
וְאִמּוֹתֵינוּ הֲלֹא כָּל־הַגִּבּוֹרִים כְּאַיִן לְפָנֶיךָ וְאַנְשֵׁי הַשֵּׁם כְּלֹא הָיוּ
וַחֲכָמִים כִּבְלִי מַדָּע וּנְבוֹנִים כִּבְלִי הַשְׂכֵּל כִּי רֹב מַעֲשֵׂיהֶם תֹּהוּ וִימֵי
חַיֵּיהֶם הֶבֶל לְפָנֶיךָ וּמוֹתַר הָאָדָם מִן הַבְּהֵמָה אָיִן כִּי הַכֹּל הָבֶל:

אַתָּה הִבְדַּלְתָּ אֱנוֹשׁ מֵרֹאשׁ וַתַּכִּירֵהוּ לַעֲמֹד לְפָנֶיךָ: כִּי מִי יֹאמַר לְךָ
מַה־תִּפְעָל וְאִם יִצְדַּק מַה־יִּתֶּן־לָךְ: וַתִּתֶּן־לָנוּ יהוה אֱלֹהֵינוּ בְּאַהֲבָה
אֶת־יוֹם הַכִּפּוּרִים הַזֶּה קֵץ וּמְחִילָה וּסְלִיחָה עַל כָּל־עֲוֹנוֹתֵינוּ לְמַעַן
נֶחְדַּל מֵעֹשֶׁק יָדֵנוּ וְנָשׁוּב אֵלֶיךָ לַעֲשׂוֹת חֻקֵּי רְצוֹנְךָ בְּלֵבָב שָׁלֵם:

וְאַתָּה בְּרַחֲמֶיךָ הָרַבִּים רַחֵם עָלֵינוּ כִּי לֹא תַחְפֹּץ בְּהַשְׁחָתַת עוֹלָם
שֶׁנֶּאֱמַר: דִּרְשׁוּ יהוה בְּהִמָּצְאוֹ קְרָאֻהוּ בִּהְיוֹתוֹ קָרוֹב: ←

דרשו...קרוב / Seek…near (Isaiah 55:6).

And it is said:

"Let the unrighteous leave their way behind,
and false ones forsake their empty schemes.
Return to THE BELOVED ONE; God shall be merciful." Isaiah 55:7

And you are a forgiving God,
gracious and compassionate,
slow to be angry,
overflowing in your love and truth,
and ready always to do good.
And you take pleasure in the turning,
the returning,
of all evildoers.
You do not desire their death.
For it is said:
"Tell them: 'As I live,' Almighty GOD declares,
'I do not wish the death of the unrighteous,
but only their return from unjust ways,
that they may live.
Return, return,
from your unrighteous ways!
Why should you die, O House of Israel?'" Ezekiel 33:11

And it is said:
"'And do I truly wish the death of the unrighteous,'
says Almighty GOD,
'but rather, do I not desire their return
from unjust ways, that they may live?'" Ezekiel 18:23

And it is said:
"'For I do not desire a mortal being's death,'
Almighty GOD declares,
'Let all return that they may live!'" Ezekiel 18:32

For you are the source of all Israel's forgiveness,
the fount of mercy for the tribes of Yeshurun
in each and every generation,
and apart from you we have no sovereign
so full of mercy and forgiveness, none but you. ⤺

וְנֶאֱמַר: יַעֲזֹב רָשָׁע דַּרְכּוֹ וְאִישׁ אָוֶן מַחְשְׁבֹתָיו וְיָשֹׁב אֶל־יהוה
וִירַחֲמֵהוּ וְאֶל־אֱלֹהֵינוּ כִּי־יַרְבֶּה לִסְלוֹחַ: וְאַתָּה אֱלוֹהַּ סְלִיחוֹת חַנּוּן
וְרַחוּם אֶרֶךְ אַפַּיִם וְרַב־חֶסֶד וֶאֱמֶת וּמַרְבֶּה לְהֵיטִיב וְרוֹצֶה אַתָּה
בִּתְשׁוּבַת רְשָׁעִים וְאֵין אַתָּה חָפֵץ בְּמִיתָתָם:

שֶׁנֶּאֱמַר: אֱמֹר אֲלֵיהֶם חַי־אָנִי נְאֻם אֲדֹנָי יֱהוִֹה אִם־אֶחְפֹּץ בְּמוֹת
הָרָשָׁע כִּי אִם־בְּשׁוּב רָשָׁע מִדַּרְכּוֹ וְחָיָה שׁוּבוּ שׁוּבוּ מִדַּרְכֵיכֶם
הָרָעִים וְלָמָּה תָמוּתוּ בֵּית יִשְׂרָאֵל:

וְנֶאֱמַר: הֶחָפֹץ אֶחְפֹּץ מוֹת רָשָׁע נְאֻם אֲדֹנָי יֱהוִֹה הֲלוֹא בְּשׁוּבוֹ
מִדְּרָכָיו וְחָיָה:

וְנֶאֱמַר: כִּי לֹא אֶחְפֹּץ בְּמוֹת הַמֵּת נְאֻם אֲדֹנָי יֱהוִֹה וְהָשִׁיבוּ וִחְיוּ:
כִּי אַתָּה סָלְחָן לְיִשְׂרָאֵל וּמָחֳלָן לְשִׁבְטֵי יְשֻׁרוּן בְּכָל־דּוֹר וָדוֹר
וּמִבַּלְעָדֶיךָ אֵין לָנוּ מֶלֶךְ מוֹחֵל וְסוֹלֵחַ אֶלָּא אָתָּה: ←

My God, before I was created,
I was not worthy to receive the gift of life,
and now that I have been created,
it is as if I never was.
While yet I live, I am but dust;
how much the more so when I die!
May it be your will, ETERNAL ONE,
my God, my ancients' God,
that I not go astray again,
and whatever the wrongdoing
I have done before you,
may you, in your great mercy,
purge it from me,
but not by means of grievous suffering
or terrible disease.

May you guard me from rebelliousness,
from pride, from anger, from despair, from foolish talk,
and all the other qualities that lead us to do wrong.

May you save me from envying another person.
And do not let another person's envy weigh upon my heart,
nor let my envy be a burden upon others.
On the contrary: let me behold the good in other people,
not their deficiency.

May the one who creates harmony above
make peace below, for us and for all Israel,
and for all who dwell on earth.
And say: Amen.

The Amidah traditionally concludes with bowing and taking three steps back.

אֱלֹהַי עַד שֶׁלֹּא נוֹצַרְתִּי אֵינִי כְדַי וְעַכְשָׁו שֶׁנּוֹצַרְתִּי כְּאִלּוּ לֹא נוֹצַרְתִּי: עָפָר אֲנִי בְּחַיַּי קַל וָחֹמֶר בְּמִיתָתִי: יְהִי רָצוֹן מִלְפָנֶיךָ יהוה אֱלֹהַי וֵאלֹהֵי אֲבוֹתַי וְאִמּוֹתַי שֶׁלֹּא אֶחֱטָא עוֹד וּמַה־שֶׁחָטָאתִי לְפָנֶיךָ מָרֵק בְּרַחֲמֶיךָ הָרַבִּים אֲבָל לֹא עַל יְדֵי יִסּוּרִים וָחֳלָיִים רָעִים:

תִּשְׁמְרֵנִי מִן הַפְּנִיּוּת וְהַגַּאֲוּות וּמִן הַכַּעַס וְהַקַּפְּדָנוּת וְהָעַצְבוּת וְהָרְכִילוּת וּשְׁאָר מִדּוֹת רָעוֹת:

וְתַצִּילֵנִי מִקִּנְאַת אִישׁ בְּרֵעֵהוּ וְלֹא תַעֲלֶה קִנְאַת אָדָם עַל לִבִּי וְלֹא קִנְאָתִי עַל אֲחֵרִים: אַדְרָבָה תֵּן בְּלִבִּי שֶׁאֶרְאֶה מַעֲלַת חֲבֵרַי וְלֹא חֶסְרוֹנוֹ:

עוֹשֶׂה שָׁלוֹם בִּמְרוֹמָיו הוּא יַעֲשֶׂה שָׁלוֹם עָלֵינוּ וְעַל כָּל יִשְׂרָאֵל וְעַל כָּל יוֹשְׁבֵי תֵבֵל וְאִמְרוּ אָמֵן:

Oseh shalom bimromav hu ya'aseh shalom aleynu ve'al kol yisrael ve'al kol yoshvey tevel ve'imeru amen.

The Amidah traditonally concludes with bowing and taking three steps back.

COMMENTARY. Our major defects (negative *midot* or characteristics) are mentioned in this brief meditative text. We ask God to remove our pride and our anger, our depression born of self-pity and our tendency to spread gossip. Finally, we ask God to remove envy from our hearts. May we delight in the good fortune of others, may we see the positive in our friends and loved ones and in all with whom we come in contact. We turn to a source of power, strength and love much greater than ourselves to overcome these negative attributes, to make us more secure, freer to love each other and repair the world.   S.P.W.

This Amidah can be recited aloud following the silent Amidah, or on its own, or it may be recited with a heyḥa kedushah. It is traditional for the ark to remain open throughout the Ne'ilah Amidah that is chanted aloud. While it is customary for all to stand during the Kedushah, those who feel weak are encouraged to sit for some other parts of the Amidah.

God great of deeds, the awesome one,
God great of deeds, the awesome one,
grant pardon for the wrongs that we have done,
in the hour of closing the gates.

So few, this people, summoned to you,
they raise their eyes, and look toward you,
aquiver with awe, they pray to you,
in the hour of closing the gates.

They pour their souls in prayer to you,
so blot out their wrongs, their lives renew,
grant pardon to all who pray to you,
in the hour of closing the gates. ↩

Eyl nora alilah
Hametzey lanu meḥilah

Metey mispar keru'im
Umesaledim beḥilah

Shofeḥim leha nafsham
Hametzi'em meḥilah

Eyl nora alilah
Bishe'at hane'ilah

Leha ayin nose'im
Bishe'at hane'ilah

Meḥey fisham veḥaḥasham
Bishe'at hane'ilah ↩

This Amidah can be recited aloud following the silent Amidah, or on its own, or it may be recited with a heyḥa kedushah. It is traditional for the ark to remain open throughout the Ne'ilah Amidah that is chanted aloud. While it is customary for all to stand during the Kedushah, those who feel weak are encouraged to sit for some other parts of the Amidah.

אֵל נוֹרָא עֲלִילָה   אֵל נוֹרָא עֲלִילָה
בִּשְׁעַת הַנְּעִילָה: הַמְצֵא לָנוּ מְחִילָה

לְךָ עַיִן נוֹשְׂאִים   מְתֵי מִסְפָּר קְרוּאִים
בִּשְׁעַת הַנְּעִילָה: וּמְסַלְּדִים בְּחִילָה

מְחֵה פִשְׁעָם וְכַחֲשָׁם   שׁוֹפְכִים לְךָ נַפְשָׁם
בִּשְׁעַת הַנְּעִילָה: ←   הַמְצִיאֵם מְחִילָה

COMMENTARY. "Closing the gates" (*Ne'ilah*) is a resonant theme throughout this eloquently plain song. In its simplest sense, it refers to the closing of the ark curtain at the end of the final Yom Kippur supplications, and the imminent closing of the synagogue after the evening prayers. In a larger sense, however, it calls to mind the gates of Heaven, which have been opened throughout the Days of Awe, for Israel and for the world at large, to a degree unheard of the rest of the year. And in the song's final two stanzas, where Israel's messianic hopes are expressed, "closing the gates" suggests the End of Days, when God will bring everlasting peace to Israel and the world.

The third line of the final stanza literally reads: "to Oholivah and Oholah." It is a reference to Ezekiel's parable (Ezekiel 23) of the two wayward sisters, who represented Samaria and Jerusalem, respectively, the capital cities of the Northern Kingdom of Israel and the Southern Kingdom of Judah. In their eager love for Egypt and Assyria, they incurred God's displeasure and were sent into captivity to the very nations whose improper love they had courted. The names Oholah and Oholibah both play on the Hebrew word for "tent" (*ohel*), Oholibah's name meaning literally "My tent is in her"—a reference to God's sacred Tabernacle, the Holy of Holies in Jerusalem. Ezekiel's parable had been a prophecy of God's anger, but in the present song, Oholah and Oholibah are symbols of hope, expressing the belief that the divided kingdom of ancient times will be reunited in the End of Days, and the remnant of all the lost tribes of Israel returned to the Holy Land. In the present translation, "land of contentment" serves as a play on the word "tent." J.R.

Please be for them a shelter in need,
protect them from harm, of word or of deed,
and seal them for splendor and for joy,
in the hour of closing the gates.

Be gracious to them, your mercy show,
and to every oppressor and every foe
bring judgment, bring justice above and below,
in the hour of closing the gates.

Remember our ancestors' righteous ways,
remember your promise, and renew their days,
as it was long ago, in former days,
in the hour of closing the gates.

Proclaim now, we pray, a year of fulfillment,
and return your flock's surviving remnant,
to be reunited in a land of contentment,
in the hour of closing the gates.

Moses ibn Ezra

COMMENTARY. As we move toward the end of Yom Kippur, we alter in our mood and our liturgical imagery. On Rosh Hashanah, we prayed that we would be written in The Book of Life; at Ne'ilah, we pray that our fate be sealed there. On Yom Kippur, we envision the gates to the divine as standing open; at the hour of Ne'ilah, we see them gradually swinging shut. All through Yom Kippur we recited the Al Het, the lengthy confessional prayer, along with the Vidui; at Ne'ilah, the detailed confessing is behind us, and yet the gates are still not shut. The gates move slowly in this last hour. We have one more chance to squeeze from ourselves the last bit of impurity still in our hearts, to voice the last unspoken hope and give it power in the new year. The gates are closing, but they are not yet shut.

D.A.T. / M.B.K.

הֱיֵה לָהֶם לְסִתְרָה
וְחָתְמֵם לְהוֹד וּלְגִילָה

וְחַלְּצֵם מִמְּאֵרָה
בִּשְׁעַת הַנְּעִילָה:

חֹן אוֹתָם וְרַחֵם
עֲשֵׂה בָהֶם פְּלִילָה

וְכָל־לוֹחֵץ וְלוֹחֵם
בִּשְׁעַת הַנְּעִילָה:

זְכֹר צִדְקַת אֲבִיהֶם
כְּקֶדֶם וּתְחִלָּה

וְחַדֵּשׁ אֶת־יְמֵיהֶם
בִּשְׁעַת הַנְּעִילָה:

קְרָא נָא שְׁנַת רָצוֹן
לְאָהֳלִיבָה וְאָהֳלָה

וְהָשֵׁב שְׁאֵרִית הַצֹּאן
בִּשְׁעַת הַנְּעִילָה:

Heyey lahem lesira
Vehotmem lehod ulegilah

Vehaletzem mime'era
Bishe'at hane'ilah

Hon otam verahem
Asey vahem pelilah

Vehol-lohetz velohem
Bishe'at hane'ilah

Zehor tzidkat avihem
Kekedem utehilah

Vehadesh et-yemeyhem
bishe'at hane'ilah

Kera na shenat ratzon
le'oholiva ve'ohola

vehashev she'erit hatzon
bishe'at hane'ilah

KAVANAH. When you are asleep, you can wake up, and when you are awake, you can awaken even more. *Ne'ilah* is filled with imagery of gates closing, *ne'ilat hasha'ar*. The bilateral root of the word *sha'ar*, עֵר, means to be awake, to watch. The challenge of *Ne'ilah* is to awaken even more.

Z.S.S.

AMIDAH

Open my lips, BELOVED ONE,
and let my mouth declare your praise.

1. AVOT VE'IMOT / ANCESTORS

Blessed are you, ANCIENT ONE, our God, God of our ancestors,

God of Abraham	God of Sarah
God of Isaac	God of Rebekah
God of Jacob	God of Rachel
	and God of Leah;

great, heroic, awesome God, supreme divinity,
imparting deeds of kindness, begetter of all;
mindful of the loyalty of Israel's ancestors,
bringing, with love, redemption to their children's children
for the sake of the divine name.

By the counsel of the sages and the wise,
and by the knowledge of all learned in our ways,
may my mouth be opened, and my prayers arise,
to entreat the sovereign full of mercy and compassion,
who forgives and pardons all transgression. ↵

COMMENTARY. Why open the ark for this Amidah? In part to reflect the
fact that in this last hour of Yom Kippur, the divine gates remain open to
our pleas. At a time when our energies are at low ebb, we are asked to
stand as much as we are able, thereby urging our attentiveness to the task
of the hour. The heightened importance of this service is emphasized by
the open ark.   D.A.T.

עֲמִידָה

אֲדֹנָי שְׂפָתַי תִּפְתָּח וּפִי יַגִּיד תְּהִלָּתֶךָ:

 אָבוֹת וְאִמּוֹת

בָּרוּךְ אַתָּה יהוה אֱלֹהֵינוּ וֵאלֹהֵי אֲבוֹתֵינוּ וְאִמּוֹתֵינוּ

אֱלֹהֵי אַבְרָהָם   אֱלֹהֵי שָׂרָה

אֱלֹהֵי יִצְחָק   אֱלֹהֵי רִבְקָה

אֱלֹהֵי יַעֲקֹב   אֱלֹהֵי רָחֵל

וֵאלֹהֵי לֵאָה:

הָאֵל הַגָּדוֹל הַגִּבּוֹר וְהַנּוֹרָא אֵל עֶלְיוֹן גּוֹמֵל חֲסָדִים טוֹבִים וְקוֹנֵה הַכֹּל וְזוֹכֵר חַסְדֵי אָבוֹת וְאִמּוֹת וּמֵבִיא גְאֻלָּה לִבְנֵי בְנֵיהֶם לְמַעַן שְׁמוֹ בְּאַהֲבָה:

מִסּוֹד חֲכָמִים וּנְבוֹנִים וּמִלֶּמֶד דַּעַת מְבִינִים אֶפְתְּחָה פִּי בִּתְפִלָּה וּבְתַחֲנוּנִים לְחַלּוֹת וּלְחַנֵּן פְּנֵי מֶלֶךְ מָלֵא רַחֲמִים מוֹחֵל וְסוֹלֵחַ לַעֲוֹנִים: ←

אדני...תהלתך / Open...praise (Psalms 51:17).

Remember us for life,
our sovereign who wishes us to live,
and seal us in the Book of Life
for your sake, ever-living God.

Regal One, our help, salvation, and protector:
Blessed are you, KIND ONE,
the shield of Abraham and the help of Sarah.

2. GEVUROT / DIVINE POWER

You are forever powerful, ALMIGHTY ONE, abundant in your saving acts. You send down the dew. In loyalty you sustain the living, nurturing the life of every living thing, upholding those who fall, healing the sick, freeing the captive, and remaining faithful to all life held dormant in the earth. Who can compare to you, almighty God, who can resemble you, the source of life and death, who makes salvation grow?

Who can compare to you, source of all mercy, remembering all creatures mercifully, decreeing life!

Faithful are you in giving life to every living thing. Blessed are you, THE FOUNT OF LIFE, who gives and renews life. ↵

זָכְרֵנוּ לְחַיִּים מֶלֶךְ חָפֵץ בַּחַיִּים וְחָתְמֵנוּ בְּסֵפֶר הַחַיִּים לְמַעַנְךָ אֱלֹהִים חַיִּים:

מֶלֶךְ עוֹזֵר וּמוֹשִׁיעַ וּמָגֵן: בָּרוּךְ אַתָּה יהוה מָגֵן אַבְרָהָם וְעֶזְרַת שָׂרָה:

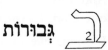

גבורות

אַתָּה גִּבּוֹר לְעוֹלָם אֲדֹנָי רַב לְהוֹשִׁיעַ: מוֹרִיד הַטָּל:

מְכַלְכֵּל חַיִּים בְּחֶסֶד מְחַיֵּה כָּל חַי בְּרַחֲמִים רַבִּים סוֹמֵךְ נוֹפְלִים וְרוֹפֵא חוֹלִים וּמַתִּיר אֲסוּרִים וּמְקַיֵּם אֱמוּנָתוֹ לִישֵׁנֵי עָפָר: מִי כָמוֹךָ בַּעַל גְּבוּרוֹת וּמִי דּוֹמֶה לָךְ מֶלֶךְ מֵמִית וּמְחַיֶּה וּמַצְמִיחַ יְשׁוּעָה:

מִי כָמוֹךָ אַב הָרַחֲמִים זוֹכֵר יְצוּרָיו לְחַיִּים בְּרַחֲמִים:

וְנֶאֱמָן אַתָּה לְהַחֲיוֹת כָּל חָי: בָּרוּךְ אַתָּה יהוה מְחַיֵּה כָּל חָי: ←

3. KEDUSHAT HASHEM / HALLOWING GOD'S NAME

May THE ETERNAL reign forever,
your God, O Zion, from one generation to the next.
Halleluyah!
And you are holy, dwelling in the praises of Israel,
our God, to whom we pray.

Hear us, we pray
forgive us, we pray, this day,
for the day is passing.
Hear us praise you:
awesome and feared,
the Holy One.

And thus shall holiness rise up to you,
for you, our God, are a forgiving king.

Open for us and for all Israel our kin, in every place:
the gates of enlightenment,
the gates of blessing,
the gates of gladness,
the gates of delight,
the gates of heaven's splendor,
the gates of voicing confession,
the gates of self-worth,
the gates of humanity,
the gates of taintlessness,
the gates of joyful salvation,
the gates of complete atonement,
the gates of lovingkindness,
the gates of mercy,
the gates of new hope,
the gates of speaking forgiveness,
the gates of assistance,
the gates of providing,
the gates of tzedakah,

קְדֻשַּׁת הַשֵּׁם ⟨3⟩

יִמְלֹךְ יְיָ לְעוֹלָם אֱלֹהַיִךְ צִיּוֹן לְדֹר וָדֹר הַלְלוּיָהּ:
וְאַתָּה קָדוֹשׁ יוֹשֵׁב תְּהִלּוֹת יִשְׂרָאֵל אֵל נָא:

שְׁמַע נָא סְלַח נָא הַיּוֹם עֲבוּר כִּי פָנָה יוֹם
וּנְהַלֶּלְךָ נוֹרָא וְאָיֹם קָדוֹשׁ:

וּבְכֵן לְךָ תַעֲלֶה קְדֻשָּׁה כִּי אַתָּה אֱלֹהֵינוּ מֶלֶךְ מוֹחֵל וְסוֹלֵחַ:

פְּתַח לָנוּ וּלְכָל־יִשְׂרָאֵל אַחֵינוּ בְּכָל מָקוֹם:
שַׁעֲרֵי אוֹרָה שַׁעֲרֵי בְרָכָה
שַׁעֲרֵי גִילָה שַׁעֲרֵי דַעַת
שַׁעֲרֵי הוֹד וְהָדָר שַׁעֲרֵי וִידוּי
שַׁעֲרֵי זְכִיּוֹת שַׁעֲרֵי חֶסֶד
שַׁעֲרֵי טָהֳרָה שַׁעֲרֵי יְשׁוּעָה
שַׁעֲרֵי כַפָּרָה שַׁעֲרֵי לֵב טוֹב
שַׁעֲרֵי מְחִילָה שַׁעֲרֵי נֶחָמָה
שַׁעֲרֵי סְלִיחָה שַׁעֲרֵי עֶזְרָה
← שַׁעֲרֵי פַּרְנָסָה שַׁעֲרֵי צְדָקָה

the gates of communal strength,
the gates of renewal,
the gates of shalom,
the gates of *teshuvah*!

And seal us in the Book of Life,
for blessing and holiness,
for you are holy, and your name is holy;
and may we enter your gates in holiness.

As it is written by the prophet's hand:
They call, one to another, and declare:

"Holy, holy, holy is THE CREATOR of the Multitudes of Heaven!
All the world is filled with divine glory!"

God's glory fills the world,
as the ministering angels ask, one to another,
"What place could contain God's holiness?"
And they are answered with a blessing:
"Blessed is the glory of THE OMNIPRESENT,
wherever God may dwell!"

And from God's place, God mercifully turns
bestowing graciousness upon the people
who declare the oneness of the divine name
evening and morning, each day continually,
as twice a day they say, with love: "Shema!"
"Listen, Israel: THE ETERNAL is our God,
THE ETERNAL ONE alone!" ↰

COMMENTARY. The structure of the *Kedushah* rests upon Jewish myths about angelic choruses praising God. By standing at attention and singing words ascribed to the angelic chorus, we become its imitators. Jews traditionally rock upward on their toes each time the word קדוש / *Kadosh* / Holy is chanted here. It is as if we were straining upward to join the heavenly choir in the purity of our praise for the divine.   D.A.T.

וקרא...כבודו / And...glory! (Isaiah 6:3).
ברוך...ממקומו / Blessed...dwell! (Ezekiel 3:12).
שמע...אחד / Listen...alone! (Deuteronomy 6:4).

שַׁעֲרֵי קוֹמְמִיּוּת שַׁעֲרֵי רְפוּאָה שַׁעֲרֵי שָׁלוֹם שַׁעֲרֵי תְשׁוּבָה:

וְחָתְמֵנוּ בְּסֵפֶר הַחַיִּים לִבְרָכָה וְלִקְדֻשָׁה

כִּי אַתָּה קָדוֹשׁ וְשִׁמְךָ קָדוֹשׁ וּשְׁעָרֶיךָ בִּקְדֻשָׁה נִכְנָס:

וּבָהֶם תָּעֵרַץ וְתִתְקַדֵּשׁ כְּסוֹד שִׂיחַ שַׂרְפֵי־קֹדֶשׁ הַמַּקְדִּישִׁים שִׁמְךָ

בַּקֹּדֶשׁ כַּכָּתוּב עַל יַד נְבִיאֶךָ: וְקָרָא זֶה אֶל־זֶה וְאָמַר:

קָדוֹשׁ קָדוֹשׁ קָדוֹשׁ

יהוה צְבָאוֹת מְלֹא כָל־הָאָרֶץ כְּבוֹדוֹ:

כְּבוֹדוֹ מָלֵא עוֹלָם מְשָׁרְתָיו שׁוֹאֲלִים זֶה לָזֶה אַיֵּה מְקוֹם כְּבוֹדוֹ לְעֻמָּתָם בָּרוּךְ יֹאמֵרוּ:

בָּרוּךְ כְּבוֹד־יהוה מִמְּקוֹמוֹ:

מִמְּקוֹמוֹ הוּא יִפֶן בְּרַחֲמִים וְיָחֹן עַם הַמְיַחֲדִים שְׁמוֹ עֶרֶב וָבֹקֶר בְּכָל יוֹם תָּמִיד פַּעֲמַיִם בְּאַהֲבָה שְׁמַע אוֹמְרִים:

→ שְׁמַע יִשְׂרָאֵל יהוה אֱלֹהֵינוּ יהוה אֶחָד:

Uvahem to'oratz vetukdash kesod si'aḥ sarfey kodesh hamakdishim shimeḥa bakodesh kakatuv al yad nevi'eḥa. Vekara zeh el zeh ve'amar:

Kadosh kadosh kadosh adonay tzeva'ot melo ḥol ha'aretz kevodo.

Kevodo maley olam mesharetav sho'alim zeh lazeh ayey mekom kevodo le'umatam baruḥ yomeru:

Baruḥ kevod adonay mimekomo.

Mimekomo hu yifen beraḥamim veyaḥon am hamyaḥadim shemo erev vavoker beḥol yom tamid pa'amayim be'ahavah shema omrim:
Shema yisra'el adonay eloheynu adonay eḥad. ↵

1152 / AMIDAH/KEDUSHAH

This is our God.
This is our source.
This is our sovereign.
This is our saving power.
And this one, mercifully,
shall declare a second time,
for every living being to hear,
confirming God's divinity for you:
"I am THE OMNIPRESENT ONE, your God!"

O, mighty one, our mighty one,
THE SOVEREIGN who watches over us,
how mighty is your name throughout the earth!
The time shall come that GOD will reign
throughout the earth. On that day
shall THE FOUNT OF LIFE be one,
the divine name be one.
And as is written in your sacred words of psalm:
"May THE ETERNAL reign forever,
your God, O Zion, from one generation to the next. Halleluyah!"

From one generation to the next
may we declare your greatness,
and for all eternities may we affirm your holiness,
And may your praise, our God,
never be absent from our mouths
now and forever.
For you are a great and holy God. ↩

אני...אלהיכם /I...God! (Numbers 15:41).
יהוה אדנינו...הארץ /THE SOVEREIGN...earth! (Psalms 8:10).
יהיה יהוה...אחד /The time...be one (Zechariah 14:9).
ימלך...הללויה /May...Halleluyah! (Psalms 146:10).

הוּא אֱלֹהֵינוּ הוּא אָבִינוּ הוּא מַלְכֵּנוּ הוּא מוֹשִׁיעֵנוּ וְהוּא יַשְׁמִיעֵנוּ
בְּרַחֲמָיו שֵׁנִית לְעֵינֵי כָּל חָי: לִהְיוֹת לָכֶם לֵאלֹהִים

אֲנִי יהוה אֱלֹהֵיכֶם:

אַדִּיר אַדִּירֵנוּ יהוה אֲדֹנֵינוּ מָה־אַדִּיר שִׁמְךָ בְּכָל־הָאָרֶץ: וְהָיָה יהוה
לְמֶלֶךְ עַל־כָּל־הָאָרֶץ בַּיּוֹם הַהוּא יִהְיֶה יהוה אֶחָד וּשְׁמוֹ אֶחָד:
וּבְדִבְרֵי קָדְשְׁךָ כָּתוּב לֵאמֹר:

יִמְלֹךְ יהוה לְעוֹלָם אֱלֹהַיִךְ צִיּוֹן לְדֹר וָדֹר הַלְלוּיָהּ:

לְדוֹר וָדוֹר נַגִּיד גָּדְלֶךָ וּלְנֵצַח נְצָחִים קְדֻשָּׁתְךָ נַקְדִּישׁ וְשִׁבְחֲךָ
אֱלֹהֵינוּ מִפִּינוּ לֹא יָמוּשׁ לְעוֹלָם וָעֶד כִּי אֵל מֶלֶךְ גָּדוֹל וְקָדוֹשׁ
אָתָּה: ←

Hu eloheynu hu avinu hu malkenu hu moshi'enu vehu
yashmi'enu berahamav shenit le'eyney kol hay. Lihyot lahem
leylohim

ani adonay eloheyhem.

Adir adirenu adonay adoneynu mah adir shimeha behol ha'aretz.
Vehayah adonay lemeleh al kol ha'aretz bayom hahu yihyeh
adonay ehad ushemo ehad.
Uvedivrey kodsheha katuv leymor.

Yimloh adonay le'olam elohayih tziyon ledor vador halleluyah.

Ledor vador nagid godleha ulenetzah netzahim kedushateha
nakdish veshivhaha eloheynu mipinu lo yamush le'olam va'ed ki
el meleh gadol vekadosh atah.

And therefore, HOLY ONE, let awe of you
infuse the whole of your Creation,
and let knowledge of your presence
dwell in all your creatures.
And let every being worship you,
and each created life pay homage to your rule.
Let all of them, as one, enact your bidding
with a whole and peaceful heart.
For we have always known, ALMIGHTY ONE,
that all authority to rule originates in you,
all strength is rooted in your arm,
all mighty deeds have emanated from your hand.
Your name alone is the source of awe
that surges through all life.

And therefore, HOLY ONE, let awe of you
infuse your people, let the praise of you
ring out from all who worship you.
Let hope enliven all who seek you,
and let all who look to you with hope
find strength to speak.
Grant joy throughout your Land,
let happiness resound throughout your holy city,
soon, and in our days.

And therefore, let the just behold your peace,
let them rejoice,
let all who follow in your path sing out with joy,
let all who love you dance in celebration,
and may your power overwhelm all treachery,
so that it vanish wholly from the earth like smoke.
Then shall the power of injustice pass away! ↰

וּבְכֵן תֵּן פַּחְדְּךָ יהוה אֱלֹהֵינוּ עַל כָּל־מַעֲשֶׂיךָ וְאֵימָתְךָ עַל כָּל־
מַה־שֶּׁבָּרָאתָ וְיִירָאוּךָ כָּל־הַמַּעֲשִׂים וְיִשְׁתַּחֲווּ לְפָנֶיךָ כָּל־הַבְּרוּאִים
וְיֵעָשׂוּ כֻלָּם אֲגֻדָּה אַחַת לַעֲשׂוֹת רְצוֹנְךָ בְּלֵבָב שָׁלֵם כְּמוֹ שֶׁיָּדַעְנוּ
יהוה אֱלֹהֵינוּ שֶׁהַשִּׁלְטוֹן לְפָנֶיךָ עֹז בְּיָדְךָ וּגְבוּרָה בִּימִינֶךָ וְשִׁמְךָ
נוֹרָא עַל כָּל־מַה־שֶּׁבָּרָאתָ:

וּבְכֵן תֵּן כָּבוֹד יהוה לְעַמֶּךָ תְּהִלָּה לִירֵאֶיךָ וְתִקְוָה לְדוֹרְשֶׁיךָ
וּפִתְחוֹן פֶּה לַמְיַחֲלִים לָךְ שִׂמְחָה לְאַרְצֶךָ וְשָׂשׂוֹן לְעִירֶךָ בִּמְהֵרָה
בְיָמֵינוּ:

וּבְכֵן צַדִּיקִים יִרְאוּ וְיִשְׂמָחוּ וִישָׁרִים יַעֲלֹזוּ וַחֲסִידִים בְּרִנָּה
יָגִילוּ וְעוֹלָתָה תִּקְפָּץ־פִּיהָ וְכָל־הָרִשְׁעָה כֻּלָּהּ כְּעָשָׁן תִּכְלֶה כִּי
תַעֲבִיר מֶמְשֶׁלֶת זָדוֹן מִן הָאָרֶץ: ←

May you alone be sovereign over all of your Creation,
and Mount Zion be the seat and symbol of your glory,
and Jerusalem, your holy city—
as is written in your holy scriptures:
"THE ETERNAL ONE shall reign forever,
your God, O Zion, through all generations!
Halleluyah!"

Holy are you,
and awe-inspiring is your name,
and there is no God apart from you,
as it is written: "THE CREATOR of the multitudes of heaven
shall be exalted through the rule of law,
and God, the Holy One, made holy by the reign of justice."
Blessed are you, ETERNAL ONE,
the holy sovereign power.

4. KEDUSHAT HAYOM / THE DAY'S HOLINESS

On Shabbat add the words in parenthesis:

You have loved us, and have taken pleasure in us,
and have made us holy with your mitzvot,
and you have brought us, sovereign one,
near to your service,
and have called us to the shelter of your great and holy name.
And you gave us, HOLY ONE, our God, with love,
this Day of (Shabbat for holiness and for rest
and this Day of) Atonement,
for pardoning, forgiveness, and atonement,
on which you pardon us for all of our transgressions
(with love), a holy convocation,
a remembrance of the going-out from Egypt. ⤺

וְתִמְלֹךְ אַתָּה יהוה לְבַדֶּךָ עַל כָּל־מַעֲשֶׂיךָ בְּהַר צִיּוֹן מִשְׁכַּן כְּבוֹדֶךָ
וּבִירוּשָׁלַיִם עִיר קָדְשֶׁךָ: כַּכָּתוּב בְּדִבְרֵי קָדְשֶׁךָ: יִמְלֹךְ יהוה לְעוֹלָם
אֱלֹהַיִךְ צִיּוֹן לְדֹר וָדֹר הַלְלוּיָהּ:

קָדוֹשׁ אַתָּה וְנוֹרָא שְׁמֶךָ וְאֵין אֱלוֹהַּ מִבַּלְעָדֶיךָ: כַּכָּתוּב: וַיִּגְבַּהּ יהוה
צְבָאוֹת בַּמִּשְׁפָּט וְהָאֵל הַקָּדוֹשׁ נִקְדַּשׁ בִּצְדָקָה: בָּרוּךְ אַתָּה יהוה
הַמֶּלֶךְ הַקָּדוֹשׁ:

ד4 קְדֻשַּׁת הַיּוֹם

On Shabbat add the words in parenthesis:

אַתָּה אֲהַבְתָּנוּ וְרָצִיתָ בָּנוּ וְקִדַּשְׁתָּנוּ בְּמִצְוֹתֶיךָ וְקֵרַבְתָּנוּ מַלְכֵּנוּ
לַעֲבוֹדָתֶךָ. וְשִׁמְךָ הַגָּדוֹל וְהַקָּדוֹשׁ עָלֵינוּ קָרָאתָ: וַתִּתֶּן לָנוּ יהוה
אֱלֹהֵינוּ בְּאַהֲבָה אֶת יוֹם (הַשַּׁבָּת הַזֶּה לִקְדֻשָּׁה וְלִמְנוּחָה וְאֶת יוֹם)
הַכִּפּוּרִים הַזֶּה לִמְחִילָה וְלִסְלִיחָה וּלְכַפָּרָה וְלִמְחָל בּוֹ אֶת כָּל
עֲוֹנוֹתֵינוּ (בְּאַהֲבָה) מִקְרָא קֹדֶשׁ זֵכֶר לִיצִיאַת מִצְרָיִם: ←

הללויה...יִמְלֹךְ/THE ETERNAL ONE...Halleluyah! (Psalms 146:10).
בצדקה...וַיִּגְבַּהּ/THE CREATOR...justice (Isaiah 5:16).

Our God, our ancients' God, may our prayer arise and come to you, and be beheld, and be acceptable. Let it be heard, acted upon, remembered—the memory of us all and all our needs, the memory of our ancestors, the memory of messianic hopes, the memory of Jerusalem your holy city, and the memory of all your kin, the house of Israel, all surviving in your presence. Act for goodness and grace, for love and care; for life, well-being and peace, on this Day of Atonement.

Remember us this day, ALL-KNOWING ONE, our God, for goodness. Favor us this day with blessing. Preserve us this day for life. With your redeeming nurturing word, be kind and generous. Act tenderly on our behalf, and grant us victory over all our trials. Truly, our eyes turn toward you, for you are a providing God; gracious and merciful are you.

Open for us the gates,
in the hour of closing the gates,
for the day is passing away.
The day is turning away,
the sun is returning to set.
May we now come into your gates.
We pray, gentle God, we pray.
Forgive us, we pray.
Pardon us now, we pray.
Have compassion for us, we pray.
Have mercy, we pray.
Let us atone now, we pray.
Help us conquer our wrongs, we pray.↩

אֱלֹהֵינוּ וֵאלֹהֵי אֲבוֹתֵינוּ וְאִמּוֹתֵינוּ יַעֲלֶה וְיָבֹא וְיַגִּיעַ וְיֵרָאֶה וְיֵרָצֶה

וְיִשָּׁמַע וְיִפָּקֵד וְיִזָּכֵר זִכְרוֹנֵנוּ וּפִקְדוֹנֵנוּ וְזִכְרוֹן אֲבוֹתֵינוּ וְאִמּוֹתֵינוּ

וְזִכְרוֹן יְמוֹת הַמָּשִׁיחַ וְזִכְרוֹן יְרוּשָׁלַיִם עִיר קָדְשֶׁךָ וְזִכְרוֹן כָּל עַמְּךָ

בֵּית יִשְׂרָאֵל לְפָנֶיךָ לִפְלֵיטָה וּלְטוֹבָה לְחֵן וּלְחֶסֶד וּלְרַחֲמִים לְחַיִּים

וּלְשָׁלוֹם בְּיוֹם הַכִּפּוּרִים הַזֶּה: זָכְרֵנוּ יהוה אֱלֹהֵינוּ בּוֹ לְטוֹבָה:

וּפָקְדֵנוּ לִבְרָכָה וְהוֹשִׁיעֵנוּ בּוֹ לְחַיִּים: וּבִדְבַר יְשׁוּעָה וְרַחֲמִים חוּס

וְחָנֵּנוּ וְרַחֵם עָלֵינוּ וְהוֹשִׁיעֵנוּ כִּי אֵלֶיךָ עֵינֵינוּ כִּי אֵל מֶלֶךְ חַנּוּן

וְרַחוּם אָתָּה:

פְּתַח לָנוּ שַׁעַר בְּעֵת נְעִילַת שַׁעַר כִּי פָנָה יוֹם:

הַיּוֹם יִפְנֶה הַשֶּׁמֶשׁ יָבוֹא וְיִפְנֶה נָבוֹאָה שְׁעָרֶיךָ:

אָנָּא אֵל נָא שָׂא נָא סְלַח נָא מְחַל נָא חֲמָל־נָא

רַחֶם־נָא כַּפֶּר־נָא כְּבֹשׁ חֵטְא וְעָוֹן: ←

O sovereign God, presiding on the Throne of Mercy,
you whose way is to be loving,
you who grant forgiveness
for transgressions of your people,
you who readily ignore the first misdeeds,
abundant in forgiveness for our shortcomings,
and quick to pardon those who have done wrong,
enacting justice for all flesh and spirit,
yet reluctant to requite their evil deeds in kind,

you, God, who instructed us,
declaring thirteen attributes of God,
remember us today, and call to mind
your covenant of thirteen qualities of mercy,
as you once taught your humble prophet in days past—
for thus is written: "And THE ETERNAL ONE
came down amid the cloud, and stood before him there,
and called the name of THE COMPASSIONATE,
and THE ALL-MERCIFUL passed by before him and declared:

'THE ONE, THE ONE, God loving and compassionate,
slow to grow angry, who abounds in love and truth,
preserving love up to the thousandth generation,
forgiving sin, transgression, and wrongdoing,
washing clean the slate.'"

May you forgive our sins and our wrongdoing,
may you claim us as your own!

Forgive us, our creator, for we have done wrong,
grant pardon to us, sovereign, for we have transgressed,
for you, ETERNAL ONE, are good and merciful,
abundant in your steadfast love
to all who call on you! ↵

אֵל מֶלֶךְ יוֹשֵׁב עַל כִּסֵּא רַחֲמִים מִתְנַהֵג בַּחֲסִידוּת מוֹחֵל עֲוֹנוֹת עַמּוֹ
מַעֲבִיר רִאשׁוֹן רִאשׁוֹן מַרְבֶּה מְחִילָה לְחַטָּאִים וּסְלִיחָה לְפוֹשְׁעִים:
עוֹשֶׂה צְדָקוֹת עִם כָּל־בָּשָׂר וָרוּחַ וְלֹא כְרָעָתָם תִּגְמֹל:

אֵל הוֹרֵיתָ לָּנוּ לוֹמַר שְׁלֹשׁ עֶשְׂרֵה זְכָר־לָנוּ הַיּוֹם בְּרִית שְׁלֹשׁ עֶשְׂרֵה
כְּהוֹדַעְתָּ לֶעָנָו מִקֶּדֶם וְכֵן כָּתוּב: וַיֵּרֶד יהוה בֶּעָנָן וַיִּתְיַצֵּב עִמּוֹ שָׁם
וַיִּקְרָא בְשֵׁם יהוה וַיַּעֲבֹר יהוה עַל פָּנָיו וַיִּקְרָא:

יהוה יהוה אֵל רַחוּם וְחַנּוּן אֶרֶךְ אַפַּיִם וְרַב־חֶסֶד וֶאֱמֶת נֹצֵר חֶסֶד
לָאֲלָפִים נֹשֵׂא עָוֹן וָפֶשַׁע וְחַטָּאָה וְנַקֵּה:

וְסָלַחְתָּ לַעֲוֹנֵנוּ וּלְחַטָּאתֵנוּ וּנְחַלְתָּנוּ:

סְלַח לָנוּ אָבִינוּ כִּי חָטָאנוּ מְחַל לָנוּ מַלְכֵּנוּ כִּי פָשָׁעְנוּ.
כִּי אַתָּה יהוה טוֹב וְסַלָּח וְרַב חֶסֶד לְכָל־קוֹרְאֶיךָ. —

Adonay adonay el raḥum vehanun ereḥ apayim verav ḥesed
ve'emet notzer ḥesed la'alafim nosey avon vafesha vehata'ah
venakey.

וירד יהוה...ונחלתנו/And the Eternal...slate (Exodus 34:5-7, 9).
כי אתה...לכל קוראיך/For...you (Psalms 86:5).

As the sigh of those who tremble in your praise ascends before your glorious, sovereign throne, fulfill the prayers of a people who declare you One, you who listen to whoever comes to you in prayer.

Israel is saved by THE ALL-MERCIFUL, eternal help to all, and so today, let them be saved by you, who dwell on high, for you abound in power to forgive, and mercy toward our cry.

Let God's protective hand, Sheḥinah's sheltering wing,
enclose us and be gracious, probe the heart, enable it to heal.
Please rise, O God, give us the strength, your strength to feel.
FOUNT OF COMPASSION, please hearken to our cry
as we call out and sing.

And let us hear: "I have forgiven!"—from you, O hidden One
  on high,
help from your right hand for a people who in need now cry.
As we cry out to you the words of awe,
please answer us, with justice for our plight,
REDEEMING ONE—enable us to set things right!

"THE ONE, THE ONE, God loving and compassionate,
slow to grow angry, who abounds in love and truth,
preserving love up to the thousandth generation,
forgiving sin, transgression, and wrongdoing,
washing clean the slate."

Have mercy on the community of the tribe of Yeshurun.

Be merciful and wipe clean our transgression,
God of our salvation.

Open the gates of heaven,
open for us the treasure of your goodness.
Redeem, prolong not your argument.
Redeem us, God of our salvation. ↵

אֶנְקַת מְסַלְדֶיךְ תַּעַל לִפְנֵי כִּסֵּא כְבוֹדֶךְ מַלֵּא מִשְׁאֲלוֹת עַם מְיַחֲדֶךְ שׁוֹמֵעַ תְּפִלַּת בָּאֵי עָדֶיךְ:

יִשְׂרָאֵל נוֹשַׁע בַּיהוה תְּשׁוּעַת עוֹלָמִים גַּם הַיּוֹם יִוָּשְׁעוּ מִפִּיךְ שׁוֹכֵן מְרוֹמִים כִּי אַתָּה רַב סְלִיחוֹת וּבַעַל הָרַחֲמִים:

יְחַבִּיאֵנוּ צֵל יָדוֹ תַּחַת כַּנְפֵי הַשְּׁכִינָה חֵן יָחֹן כִּי יִבְחַן לֵב עָקֹב לְהָכִינָה קוּמָה נָא אֱלֹהֵינוּ עֻזָּה עֲזִי נָא יהוה לְשַׁוְעָתֵנוּ הַאֲזִינָה:

יַשְׁמִיעֵנוּ סָלַחְתִּי יוֹשֵׁב בְּסֵתֶר עֶלְיוֹן בִּימִין יֵשַׁע לְהִוָּשַׁע עַם עָנִי וְאֶבְיוֹן בְּשַׁוְּעֵנוּ אֵלֶיךָ נוֹרָאוֹת בְּצֶדֶק תַּעֲנֵנוּ יהוה הֱיֵה עוֹזֵר לָנוּ:

יהוה יהוה אֵל רַחוּם וְחַנּוּן אֶרֶךְ אַפַּיִם וְרַב־חֶסֶד וֶאֱמֶת נֹצֵר חֶסֶד לָאֲלָפִים נֹשֵׂא עָוֹן וָפֶשַׁע וְחַטָּאָה וְנַקֵּה:

Adonay adonay el raḥum veḥanun ereḥ apayim verav ḥesed
ve'emet notzer ḥesed la'alafim nosey avon vafesha veḥata'ah
venakey.

רַחֶם־נָא קְהַל עֲדַת יְשָׁרוּן: סְלַח וּמְחַל עֲוֹנָם וְהוֹשִׁיעֵנוּ אֱלֹהֵי יִשְׁעֵנוּ:

שַׁעֲרֵי שָׁמַיִם פְּתַח וְאוֹצָרְךָ הַטּוֹב לָנוּ תִפְתַּח: תּוֹשִׁיעַ וְרִיב אַל תִּמְתַּח וְהוֹשִׁיעֵנוּ אֱלֹהֵי יִשְׁעֵנוּ: ←

יהוה יהוה...ונקה / THE ONE...slate (Exodus 34:6-7).

Our God, our ancients' God,
forgive us, pardon us, help us atone—
for we are your people, and you are our God,
we are your children, and you are our creator,
we are your servants, and you are our sovereign,
we are your community, and you are our portion,
we are your possession, and you are our fate,
we are your sheep, and you are our shepherd,
we are your vineyard, and you are our keeper,
we are your creation, and you are our fashioner,
we are your loved ones, and you are our beloved,
we are your treasure, and you are our kin,
we are your people, and you are our ruler,
we are your faithful, and you our source of faith!

We are strong-willed and stubborn,
but you are merciful and gracious.
We are stiff-necked, but you are slow to anger.
We are full of error, but you are full of mercy.
We—our days are like a passing shadow,
but you are one whose years shall never end. ↵

אֱלֹהֵֽינוּ וֵאלֹהֵי אֲבוֹתֵֽינוּ וְאִמּוֹתֵֽינוּ סְלַח לָֽנוּ: מְחַל לָֽנוּ: כַּפֶּר-לָֽנוּ:

כִּי אָֽנוּ עַמֶּֽךָ וְאַתָּה אֱלֹהֵֽינוּ: אָֽנוּ בָנֶֽיךָ וְאַתָּה אָבִֽינוּ:

אָֽנוּ עֲבָדֶֽיךָ וְאַתָּה אֲדוֹנֵֽינוּ: אָֽנוּ קְהָלֶֽךָ וְאַתָּה חֶלְקֵֽנוּ:

אָֽנוּ נַחֲלָתֶֽךָ וְאַתָּה גוֹרָלֵֽנוּ: אָֽנוּ צֹאנֶֽךָ וְאַתָּה רוֹעֵֽנוּ:

אָֽנוּ כַרְמֶֽךָ וְאַתָּה נוֹטְרֵֽנוּ: אָֽנוּ פְעֻלָּתֶֽךָ וְאַתָּה יוֹצְרֵֽנוּ:

אָֽנוּ רַעְיָתֶֽךָ וְאַתָּה דוֹדֵֽנוּ: אָֽנוּ סְגֻלָּתֶֽךָ וְאַתָּה קְרוֹבֵֽנוּ:

אָֽנוּ עַמֶּֽךָ וְאַתָּה מַלְכֵּֽנוּ: אָֽנוּ מַאֲמִירֶֽךָ וְאַתָּה מַאֲמִירֵֽנוּ:

Eloheynu veylohey avoteynu ve'imoteynu
selaḥ lanu. Meḥal lanu. Kaper lanu.
Ki anu ameḥa ve'atah eloheynu. Anu vaneḥa ve'atah avinu.
Anu avadeḥa ve'atah adoneynu. Anu kehaleḥa ve'atah ḥelkenu.
Anu naḥalateḥa ve'atah goralenu. Anu tzoneḥa ve'atah ro'enu.
Anu ḥarmeḥa ve'atah notrenu. Anu fe'ulateḥa ve'atah yotzrenu.
Anu rayateḥa ve'atah dodenu. Anu segulateḥa ve'atah kerovenu.
Anu ameḥa ve'atah malkenu. Anu ma'amireḥa ve'atah ma'amirenu.

אָֽנוּ עַזֵּי פָנִים וְאַתָּה רַחוּם וְחַנּוּן: אָֽנוּ קְשֵׁי עֹֽרֶף וְאַתָּה אֶֽרֶךְ אַפַּֽיִם:

אָֽנוּ מְלֵאֵי עָוֹן וְאַתָּה מָלֵא רַחֲמִים: אָֽנוּ יָמֵֽינוּ כְּצֵל עוֹבֵר וְאַתָּה הוּא

וּשְׁנוֹתֶֽיךָ לֹא יִתָּמּוּ: ←

למען...הוא / For the sake...wrong (Psalms 25:11).

Our God, our ancients' God,
may our prayer come before you.
Hide not from our supplication,
for we are not so insolent and stubborn
as to say, here in your presence,
"HOLY ONE, God of our fathers and our mothers,
we are righteous, and we have not sinned,"
for we indeed have sinned.

We have acted wrongly,
we have been untrue,
and we have gained unlawfully
and have defamed.
We have harmed others,
we have wrought injustice,
we have zealously transgressed,
and we have hurt
and have told lies.
We have improperly advised,
and we have covered up the truth,
and we have laughed in scorn.
We have misused responsibility
and have neglected others.
We have stubbornly rebelled.
We have offended,
we have perverted justice,
we have stirred up enmity,
and we have kept ourselves from change.
We have reached out to evil,
we have shamelessly corrupted
and have treated others with disdain.
Yes, we have thrown ourselves off course,
and we have tempted and misled. ↵

אֱלֹהֵֽינוּ וֵאלֹהֵי אֲבוֹתֵֽינוּ וְאִמּוֹתֵֽינוּ תָּבֹא לְפָנֶֽיךָ תְּפִלָּתֵֽנוּ וְאַל
תִּתְעַלַּם מִתְּחִנָּתֵֽנוּ שֶׁאֵין אֲנַֽחְנוּ עַזֵּי פָנִים וּקְשֵׁי עֹֽרֶף לוֹמַר לְפָנֶֽיךָ
יהוה אֱלֹהֵֽינוּ וֵאלֹהֵי אֲבוֹתֵֽינוּ וְאִמּוֹתֵֽינוּ צַדִּיקִים אֲנַֽחְנוּ וְלֹא חָטָֽאנוּ
אֲבָל אֲנַֽחְנוּ חָטָֽאנוּ:

אָשַֽׁמְנוּ: בָּגַֽדְנוּ: גָּזַֽלְנוּ: דִּבַּֽרְנוּ דֹפִי:
הֶעֱוִֽינוּ: וְהִרְשַֽׁעְנוּ: זַֽדְנוּ: חָמַֽסְנוּ:
טָפַֽלְנוּ שֶֽׁקֶר: יָעַֽצְנוּ רָע: כִּזַּֽבְנוּ: לַֽצְנוּ:
מָרַֽדְנוּ: נִאַֽצְנוּ: סָרַֽרְנוּ: עָוִֽינוּ:
פָּשַֽׁעְנוּ: צָרַֽרְנוּ: קִשִּֽׁינוּ עֹֽרֶף: רָשַֽׁעְנוּ:
שִׁחַֽתְנוּ: תִּעַֽבְנוּ: תָּעִֽינוּ: תִּעְתָּֽעְנוּ: ←

Ashamnu. Bagadnu. Gazalnu. Dibarnu dofi.
He'evinu. Vehirshanu. Zadnu. Hamasnu.
Tafalnu shaker. Ya'atznu ra. Kizavnu. Latznu.
Maradnu. Ni'atznu. Sararnu. Avinu.
Pashanu. Tzararnu. Kishinu oref. Rashanu.
Shihatnu. Ti'avnu. Ta'inu. Titanu.

KAVANAH. The last *Vidui* on Yom Kippur is the shorter form found in
Ne'ilah. The power and light of this day have already begun to spread
throughout our lives. Perhaps, if we open in these waning hours to a
higher rung of willingness, of presence, of honesty, the day's ending will
be but a beginning. S.P.W.

KAVANAH. Why is there no *Al Het* at *Ne'ilah*? There is a Hasidic teaching
that when we do mitzvot with ulterior motives and arrogance, our mitzvot
can also be sinful. Examples of mitzvot that include sin are those done
egotistically, ostentatiously or at the expense of others. *Ne'ilah* is the time
to consider these. Z.S.S.

We have turned away from your mitzvot
and from your righteous laws,
as if it did not matter to us.
And you are just,
whatever comes upon us,
for what you do is truth,
and we have done much wrong.

What can we say before you,
you who dwell on high?
What can we tell you,
you who inhabit heaven's heights?
Are you not one who knows all things,
both hidden and revealed?

You extend a hand to those who transgressed,
your right hand is stretched out to receive all who return.
And you have taught us, RIGHTEOUS ONE,
to acknowledge in your presence all we have done wrong,
that we might disengage ourselves from plunder in our hands.
May you receive us in complete return into your presence,
like the fires and sweet savors of the ancient offerings,
so that all that you have promised may come true.
There is no limit to the fires of our devotion,
and there is no number to the savors of our repentance.
And you know that our destiny
is but to serve as food for worms and maggots.
Therefore, you have multiplied the opportunities
for our forgiveness. ⤺

סָרְנוּ מִמִּצְוֹתֶיךָ וּמִמִּשְׁפָּטֶיךָ הַטּוֹבִים וְלֹא שָׁוָה לָנוּ: וְאַתָּה צַדִּיק עַל כָּל־הַבָּא עָלֵינוּ כִּי־אֱמֶת עָשִׂיתָ וַאֲנַחְנוּ הִרְשָׁעְנוּ:

מַה נֹּאמַר לְפָנֶיךָ יוֹשֵׁב מָרוֹם וּמַה נְּסַפֵּר לְפָנֶיךָ שׁוֹכֵן שְׁחָקִים הֲלֹא כָּל הַנִּסְתָּרוֹת וְהַנִּגְלוֹת אַתָּה יוֹדֵעַ:

אַתָּה נוֹתֵן יָד לְפוֹשְׁעִים וִימִינְךָ פְּשׁוּטָה לְקַבֵּל שָׁבִים: וַתְּלַמְּדֵנוּ יהוה אֱלֹהֵינוּ לְהִתְוַדּוֹת לְפָנֶיךָ עַל כָּל־עֲוֹנוֹתֵינוּ לְמַעַן נֶחְדַּל מֵעֹשֶׁק יָדֵינוּ וּתְקַבְּלֵנוּ בִּתְשׁוּבָה שְׁלֵמָה לְפָנֶיךָ כְּאִשִּׁים וּכְנִיחוֹחִים לְמַעַן דְּבָרֶיךָ אֲשֶׁר אָמָרְתָּ: אֵין קֵץ לְאִשֵּׁי חוֹבוֹתֵינוּ וְאֵין מִסְפָּר לְנִיחוֹחֵי אַשְׁמוֹתֵנוּ: וְאַתָּה יוֹדֵעַ שֶׁאַחֲרִיתֵנוּ רִמָּה וְתוֹלֵעָה לְפִיכָךְ הִרְבֵּיתָ סְלִיחָתֵנוּ: ←

ואתה...הרשענו / And...wrong (Nehemiah 9:33).

What are we? What is our life?
What is our love? What is our justice?
What is our help? What is our strength?
What is our power?
What can we say before you,
All-Discerning One, our God, our ancients' God?
For are not all the mighty of this world
like nothing in your presence,
all who bear renown like those who never were,
all persons of wisdom like the ignorant,
and all who understand like those who lack intelligence?
For truly, most of what they do is but a void,
their days are like a puff of air before you.
The advantage of the human being over beasts
amounts to nothing—for everything,
measured against you,
lacks substance.

You set apart the human being at Creation,
you recognize humanity to stand before you.
But truly, who could say before you: "What are you doing?"
And if one could be just enough to stand before you,
what could one offer you?
And even so, you gave us, Holy One, our God,
with love, this Day of Atonement,
that we might liberate ourselves
from all that our hands have stolen,
and return to you,
to carry out your ordinance and will
wholeheartedly.
And may you, in your abundant love,
spread mercy over us,
for you do not desire the destruction of the world,
for it is said:
"Seek out The Holy One, for God is present,
call to God, for God is near." ⏎

מָה אָנוּ : מֶה חַיֵּינוּ : מֶה חַסְדֵּנוּ : מַה־צִּדְקֵנוּ : מַה־יְּשׁוּעֵנוּ : מַה־כֹּחֵנוּ :
מַה־גְּבוּרָתֵנוּ : מַה־נֹּאמַר לְפָנֶיךָ יהוה אֱלֹהֵינוּ וֵאלֹהֵי אֲבוֹתֵינוּ
וְאִמּוֹתֵינוּ : הֲלֹא כָּל־הַגִּבּוֹרִים כְּאַיִן לְפָנֶיךָ וְאַנְשֵׁי הַשֵּׁם כְּלֹא הָיוּ
וַחֲכָמִים כִּבְלִי מַדָּע וּנְבוֹנִים כִּבְלִי הַשְׂכֵּל כִּי רֹב מַעֲשֵׂיהֶם תֹּהוּ וִימֵי
חַיֵּיהֶם הֶבֶל לְפָנֶיךָ וּמוֹתַר הָאָדָם מִן הַבְּהֵמָה אָיִן כִּי הַכֹּל הָבֶל :

אַתָּה הִבְדַּלְתָּ אֱנוֹשׁ מֵרֹאשׁ וַתַּכִּירֵהוּ לַעֲמֹד לְפָנֶיךָ : כִּי מִי יֹאמַר לְךָ
מַה־תִּפְעָל וְאִם יִצְדַּק מַה־יִּתֶּן־לָךְ : וַתִּתֶּן־לָנוּ יהוה אֱלֹהֵינוּ בְּאַהֲבָה
אֶת־יוֹם הַכִּפּוּרִים הַזֶּה קֵץ וּמְחִילָה וּסְלִיחָה עַל כָּל־עֲוֹנוֹתֵינוּ :
לְמַעַן נֶחְדַּל מֵעֹשֶׁק יָדֵנוּ וְנָשׁוּב אֵלֶיךָ לַעֲשׂוֹת חֻקֵּי רְצוֹנְךָ בְּלֵבָב
שָׁלֵם :

וְאַתָּה בְּרַחֲמֶיךָ הָרַבִּים רַחֵם עָלֵינוּ כִּי לֹא תַחְפֹּץ בְּהַשְׁחָתַת עוֹלָם :
שֶׁנֶּאֱמַר דִּרְשׁוּ יהוה בְּהִמָּצְאוֹ קְרָאֻהוּ בִּהְיוֹתוֹ קָרוֹב : ←

דרשו...קרוב / Seek...near (Isaiah 55:6).

And it is said:

"Let the unrighteous leave their way behind,
and false ones forsake their empty schemes.
Return to THE BELOVED ONE; God shall be merciful." Isaiah 55:7
And you are a forgiving God,
gracious and compassionate,
slow to be angry,
overflowing in your love and truth,
and ready always to do good.
And you take pleasure in the turning,
the returning,
of all evildoers.
You do not desire their death.
For it is said:

"Tell them: 'As I live,' Almighty GOD declares,
'I do not wish the death of the unrighteous,
but only their return from unjust ways,
that they may live.
Return, return,
from your unrighteous ways!
Why should you die, O House of Israel?'" Ezekiel 33:11
And it is said:

"'And do I truly wish the death of the unrighteous,'
says Almighty GOD,
'but rather do I not desire their return
from unjust ways, that they may live?'" Ezekiel 18:23
And it is said:

"'For I do not desire a mortal being's death,'
Almighty GOD declares,
'Let all return that they may live!'" Ezekiel 18:32
For you are the source of all Israel's forgiveness,
the fount of mercy for the tribes of Yeshurun,
in each and every generation,
and apart from you we have no sovereign
so full of mercy and forgiveness, none but you. ↵

וְנֶאֱמַר: יַעֲזֹב רָשָׁע דַּרְכּוֹ וְאִישׁ אָוֶן מַחְשְׁבֹתָיו וְיָשֹׁב אֶל־יְהוה
וִירַחֲמֵהוּ וְאֶל־אֱלֹהֵינוּ כִּי־יַרְבֶּה לִסְלוֹחַ: וְאַתָּה אֱלוֹהַּ סְלִיחוֹת חַנּוּן
וְרַחוּם אֶרֶךְ אַפַּיִם וְרַב חֶסֶד וֶאֱמֶת וּמַרְבֶּה לְהֵיטִיב וְרוֹצֶה אַתָּה
בִּתְשׁוּבַת רְשָׁעִים וְאֵין אַתָּה חָפֵץ בְּמִיתָתָם:

שֶׁנֶּאֱמַר: אֱמֹר אֲלֵיהֶם חַי־אָנִי נְאֻם אֲדֹנָי יְהוִה אִם־אֶחְפֹּץ בְּמוֹת
הָרָשָׁע כִּי אִם־בְּשׁוּב רָשָׁע מִדַּרְכּוֹ וְחָיָה שׁוּבוּ שׁוּבוּ מִדַּרְכֵיכֶם
הָרָעִים וְלָמָה תָמוּתוּ בֵּית יִשְׂרָאֵל:

וְנֶאֱמַר: הֶחָפֹץ אֶחְפֹּץ מוֹת רָשָׁע נְאֻם אֲדֹנָי יְהוִה הֲלוֹא בְּשׁוּבוֹ
מִדְּרָכָיו וְחָיָה:

וְנֶאֱמַר: כִּי לֹא אֶחְפֹּץ בְּמוֹת הַמֵּת נְאֻם אֲדֹנָי יְהוִה וְהָשִׁיבוּ וִחְיוּ:
כִּי אַתָּה סָלְחָן לְיִשְׂרָאֵל וּמָחֳלָן לְשִׁבְטֵי יְשֻׁרוּן בְּכָל־דּוֹר וָדוֹר
וּמִבַּלְעָדֶיךָ אֵין לָנוּ מֶלֶךְ מוֹחֵל וְסוֹלֵחַ אֶלָּא אָתָּה: —←

Our God, our ancients' God,
forgive us our transgressions
this Day (of Shabbat, and) of Atonement,
blot out and cause to pass away
our wrongdoings and our errors
from before your eyes, as it is said:
"I, yes I, shall be the one
who blots out your wrongdoing, for my sake;
your errors I shall not remember any more!"
And it is said: "I have made your sins
vanish like a storm cloud,
and, like a mist, the things you have done wrong.
Return to me, for it is I who have redeemed you!"
And it is said: "For on this day,
atonement shall be made for you,
to make you clean from all of your wrongdoings.
Before THE FOUNT OF MERCY, you shall all be clean."

Our God, our ancients' God (take pleasure in our rest),
enable us to realize holiness with your mitzvot,
give us our portion in your Torah,
let us enjoy the good things of your world,
and gladden us with your salvation,
(and help us to perpetuate, ETERNAL ONE, our God,
your holy Shabbat, with love and joy,
and let all Israel, and all who treat your name as holy,
rest upon this day,) and refine our hearts
to serve you truthfully.
For you are a forgiving God to Israel,
and compassionate to all the tribes of Yeshurun
in each and every generation,
and apart from you we have no sovereign,
none full of compassion and forgiveness,
except you. ↩

אֱלֹהֵֽינוּ וֵאלֹהֵי אֲבוֹתֵֽינוּ וְאִמּוֹתֵֽינוּ מְחַל לַעֲוֹנוֹתֵֽינוּ בְּיוֹם (הַשַּׁבָּת
הַזֶּה וּבְיוֹם) הַכִּפּוּרִים הַזֶּה: מְחֵה וְהַעֲבֵר פְּשָׁעֵֽינוּ וְחַטֹּאתֵֽינוּ מִנֶּֽגֶד
עֵינֶֽיךָ: כָּאָמוּר: אָנֹכִי אָנֹכִי הוּא מֹחֶה פְשָׁעֶֽיךָ לְמַעֲנִי וְחַטֹּאתֶֽיךָ לֹא
אֶזְכֹּר: וְנֶאֱמַר: מָחִֽיתִי כָעָב פְּשָׁעֶֽיךָ וְכֶעָנָן חַטֹּאתֶֽיךָ שׁוּבָה אֵלַי כִּי
גְאַלְתִּֽיךָ: וְנֶאֱמַר: כִּי־בַיּוֹם הַזֶּה יְכַפֵּר עֲלֵיכֶם לְטַהֵר אֶתְכֶם מִכֹּל
חַטֹּאתֵיכֶם לִפְנֵי יהוה תִּטְהָֽרוּ:

אֱלֹהֵֽינוּ וֵאלֹהֵי אֲבוֹתֵֽינוּ וְאִמּוֹתֵֽינוּ (רְצֵה במנוּחָתֵֽנוּ) קַדְּשֵֽׁנוּ
בְּמִצְוֹתֶֽיךָ וְתֵן חֶלְקֵֽנוּ בְּתוֹרָתֶֽךָ שַׂבְּעֵֽנוּ מִטּוּבֶֽךָ וְשַׂמְּחֵֽנוּ בִּישׁוּעָתֶֽךָ
(וְהַנְחִילֵֽנוּ יהוה אֱלֹהֵֽינוּ בְּאַהֲבָה וּבְרָצוֹן שַׁבַּת קָדְשֶֽׁךָ וְיָנֽוּחוּ בָהּ
יִשְׂרָאֵל מְקַדְּשֵׁי שְׁמֶֽךָ) וְטַהֵר לִבֵּֽנוּ לְעָבְדְּךָ בֶּאֱמֶת כִּי אַתָּה סָלְחָן
לְיִשְׂרָאֵל וּמָחֳלָן לְשִׁבְטֵי יְשֻׁרוּן בְּכָל דּוֹר וָדוֹר וּמִבַּלְעָדֶֽיךָ אֵין לָֽנוּ
מֶֽלֶךְ מוֹחֵל וְסוֹלֵֽחַ אֶלָּא אָֽתָּה: ←

אנכי...אזכר / I, yes...more! (Isaiah 43:25).
מחיתי...גאלתיך / I have...you! (Isaiah 44:22).
כי ביום...תטהרו / For on...clean (Leviticus 16:30).

Blessed are you, FORGIVING ONE,
sovereign of mercy and forgiveness
for our wrongdoings, and for those
of all your kin, the house of Israel,
you who make our guilt to pass away
year after year,
the sovereign power over all the earth
who raises up to holiness
(Shabbat,) the people Israel
and the Day of Atonement.

5. AVODAH / WORSHIP

Take pleasure GRACIOUS ONE, our God, in Israel your people; lovingly accept their fervent prayer. May Israel's worship always be acceptable to you.

And may our eyes behold your homecoming, with merciful intent, to Zion. Blessed are you, THE FAITHFUL ONE, who brings your presence home to Zion.

6. HODA'AH / THANKS

We give thanks to you that you are THE ALL-MERCIFUL, our God, God of our ancestors, today and always. A firm, enduring source of life, a shield to us in time of trial, you are ever there, from age to age. We acknowledge you, declare your praise, and thank you for our lives entrusted to your hand, our souls placed in your care, for your miracles that greet us every day, and for your wonders and the good things that are with us every hour, morning, noon, and night. Good One, whose kindness never stops, Kind One, whose loving acts have never failed—always have we placed our hope in you.

For all these things, your name be blessed and raised in honor always, sovereign of ours, forever. ⟳

בָּרוּךְ אַתָּה יהוה מֶלֶךְ מוֹחֵל וְסוֹלֵחַ לַעֲוֹנוֹתֵינוּ וְלַעֲוֹנוֹת עַמּוֹ בֵּית
יִשְׂרָאֵל וּמַעֲבִיר אַשְׁמוֹתֵינוּ בְּכָל־שָׁנָה וְשָׁנָה מֶלֶךְ עַל־כָּל־הָאָרֶץ
מְקַדֵּשׁ (הַשַּׁבָּת וְ) יִשְׂרָאֵל וְיוֹם הַכִּפּוּרִים:

ה עֲבוֹדָה

רְצֵה יהוה אֱלֹהֵינוּ בְּעַמְּךָ יִשְׂרָאֵל וְלָהַב תְּפִלָּתָם בְּאַהֲבָה תְקַבֵּל
בְּרָצוֹן וּתְהִי לְרָצוֹן תָּמִיד עֲבוֹדַת יִשְׂרָאֵל עַמֶּךָ:

וְתֶחֱזֶינָה עֵינֵינוּ בְּשׁוּבְךָ לְצִיּוֹן בְּרַחֲמִים: בָּרוּךְ אַתָּה יהוה הַמַּחֲזִיר
שְׁכִינָתוֹ לְצִיּוֹן:

ו הוֹדָאָה

מוֹדִים אֲנַחְנוּ לָךְ שָׁאַתָּה הוּא יהוה אֱלֹהֵינוּ וֵאלֹהֵי אֲבוֹתֵינוּ
וְאִמּוֹתֵינוּ לְעוֹלָם וָעֶד צוּר חַיֵּינוּ מָגֵן יִשְׁעֵנוּ אַתָּה הוּא לְדוֹר וָדוֹר:
נוֹדֶה לְךָ וּנְסַפֵּר תְּהִלָּתֶךָ עַל חַיֵּינוּ הַמְּסוּרִים בְּיָדֶךָ וְעַל נִשְׁמוֹתֵינוּ
הַפְּקוּדוֹת לָךְ וְעַל נִסֶּיךָ שֶׁבְּכָל יוֹם עִמָּנוּ וְעַל נִפְלְאוֹתֶיךָ וְטוֹבוֹתֶיךָ
שֶׁבְּכָל־עֵת עֶרֶב וָבֹקֶר וְצָהֳרָיִם: הַטּוֹב כִּי לֹא כָלוּ רַחֲמֶיךָ וְהַמְרַחֵם
כִּי לֹא תַמּוּ חֲסָדֶיךָ מֵעוֹלָם קִוִּינוּ לָךְ:

וְעַל כֻּלָּם יִתְבָּרַךְ וְיִתְרוֹמַם שִׁמְךָ מַלְכֵּנוּ תָּמִיד לְעוֹלָם וָעֶד: ←

And seal for a good life all the people of your covenant.

Let all of life acknowledge you! May all beings praise your name in truth. O God, our rescue and our aid. Blessed are you, THE GRACIOUS ONE whose name is good, to whom all thanks are due.

7. BIRKAT HASHALOM / BLESSING FOR PEACE

Our God, our ancients' God,
bless us with the threefold blessing
spoken from the mouth of Aaron and his sons, as is said:

May THE ETERNAL bless you
    and protect you.   Let it be God's will!
May THE ETERNAL'S face give light
    to you, and show you favor.   Let it be God's will!
May THE ETERNAL'S face be lifted
    toward you, and bestow upon you
    peace.   Let it be God's will! ↩

וְחָתוֹם לְחַיִּים טוֹבִים כָּל־בְּנֵי בְרִיתֶךָ:

וְכֹל הַחַיִּים יוֹדוּךָ סֶּלָה וִיהַלְלוּ אֶת שִׁמְךָ בֶּאֱמֶת הָאֵל יְשׁוּעָתֵנוּ

וְעֶזְרָתֵנוּ סֶלָה: בָּרוּךְ אַתָּה יהוה הַטוֹב שִׁמְךָ וּלְךָ נָאֶה לְהוֹדוֹת:

בִּרְכַּת הַשָּׁלוֹם

אֱלֹהֵינוּ וֵאלֹהֵי אֲבוֹתֵינוּ וְאִמּוֹתֵינוּ בָּרְכֵנוּ בַּבְּרָכָה הַמְשֻׁלֶּשֶׁת

הָאֲמוּרָה מִפִּי אַהֲרֹן וּבָנָיו כָּאָמוּר:

יְבָרֶכְךָ יהוה וְיִשְׁמְרֶךָ:

כֵּן יְהִי רָצוֹן:

יָאֵר יהוה פָּנָיו אֵלֶיךָ וִיחֻנֶּךָ:

כֵּן יְהִי רָצוֹן:

יִשָּׂא יהוה פָּנָיו אֵלֶיךָ וְיָשֵׂם לְךָ שָׁלוֹם:

כֵּן יְהִי רָצוֹן:

Eloheynu veylohey avoteynu ve'imoteynu
barehenu baberahah hamshuleshet
ha'amurah mipi aharon uvanav ka'amur:
Yevareheha adonay veyishmereha.   Ken yehi ratzon.
Ya'er adonay panav eleha vihuneka.   Ken yehi ratzon.
Yisa adonay panav eleha veyasem leha shalom.   Ken yehi ratzon.

Grant peace, goodness and blessing in the world,
grace, love and mercy
over us and over all your people Israel.
Bless us, source of being, all of us, as one
amid your light,
for by your light,
WISE ONE, our God, you give to us
Torah of life, and love of kindness,
justice, blessing, mercy, life, and peace.
So may it be a good thing in your eyes,
to bless your people Israel, and all peoples,
with abundant strength and peace.

In the book of life, blessing, peace, and proper sustenance,
may we be remembered and sealed,
we and all your people, the house of Israel,
for a good life and for peace.

Blessed are you, COMPASSIONATE ONE, maker of peace.

KAVANAH. Try to imagine a time of true peace and tranquility, and think
about your part in helping this time to come about. What can you do?
What can you commit to? How will *you* be a peacemaker?　　　　L.G.B.

שִׂים שָׁלוֹם טוֹבָה וּבְרָכָה בָּעוֹלָם חֵן וָחֶסֶד וְרַחֲמִים עָלֵינוּ וְעַל
כָּל־יִשְׂרָאֵל עַמֶּךְ: בָּרְכֵנוּ אָבִינוּ כֻּלָּנוּ כְּאֶחָד בְּאוֹר פָּנֶיךָ: כִּי בְאוֹר
פָּנֶיךָ נָתַתָּ לָּנוּ יהוה אֱלֹהֵינוּ תּוֹרַת חַיִּים וְאַהֲבַת חֶסֶד וּצְדָקָה
וּבְרָכָה וְרַחֲמִים וְחַיִּים וְשָׁלוֹם: וְטוֹב בְּעֵינֶיךָ לְבָרֵךְ אֶת עַמְּךָ יִשְׂרָאֵל
וְאֶת כָּל הָעַמִּים בְּרֹב עֹז וְשָׁלוֹם.

בְּסֵפֶר חַיִּים בְּרָכָה וְשָׁלוֹם וּפַרְנָסָה טוֹבָה נִזָּכֵר וְנִכָּתֵם לְפָנֶיךָ אֲנַחְנוּ
וְכָל־עַמְּךָ בֵּית יִשְׂרָאֵל לְחַיִּים טוֹבִים וּלְשָׁלוֹם:

בָּרוּךְ אַתָּה יהוה עוֹשֵׂה הַשָּׁלוֹם:

Sim shalom tovah uveraḥah ba'olam ḥen vaḥesed veraḥamim
aleynu ve'al kol yisrael ameḥa. Bareḥenu avinu kulanu ke'eḥad
be'or paneḥa. Ki ve'or paneḥa natata lanu adonay eloheynu torat
ḥayim ve'ahavat ḥesed utzedakah uveraḥah veraḥamim veḥayim
veshalom. Vetov be'eyneḥa levareḥ et ameḥa yisra'el ve'et kol
ha'amim berov oz veshalom.

Besefer ḥayim beraḥah veshalom ufarnasah tovah nizaḥer
veneḥatem lefaneḥa anaḥnu veḥol ameḥa beyt yisra'el leḥayim
tovim uleshalom.

Baruḥ atah adonay osey hashalom.

AVINU MALKENU /
OUR CREATOR, OUR SOVEREIGN

For an alternative version see pages 457-460. For an interpretive version see page 456.

Our creator, our sovereign, we have done wrong in your
presence.

Our creator, our sovereign, we have no one to rule over us
but you.

Our creator, our sovereign, help us for the honor of your name.

Our creator, our sovereign, renew for us a good year.

Our creator, our sovereign, nullify the plans of any who may
seek to do us harm.

Our creator, our sovereign, grant forgiveness and atonement for
all of our transgressions.

Our creator, our sovereign, help us to return wholeheartedly
into your presence.

Our creator, our sovereign, send thorough healing to all those
who ail.

Our creator, our sovereign, seal us for good fortune in the
Book of Life.

Our creator, our sovereign, seal us in the Book of
Redemption and Salvation.

Our creator, our sovereign, seal us in the Book of
Sustenance and Livelihood.

Our creator, our sovereign, seal us in the Book of Merit.

Our creator, our sovereign, seal us in the Book of
Forgiveness and Atonement.

Our creator, our sovereign, let grow for us the tree of imminent
redemption. ⤶

For an alternative version see pages 457-460. For an interpretive version see page 456.

אָבִ֫ינוּ מַלְכֵּ֫נוּ חָטָֽאנוּ לְפָנֶ֫יךָ:

אָבִ֫ינוּ מַלְכֵּ֫נוּ אֵין לָ֫נוּ מֶֽלֶךְ אֶלָּא אָֽתָּה:

אָבִ֫ינוּ מַלְכֵּ֫נוּ עֲשֵׂה עִמָּֽנוּ לְמַֽעַן שְׁמֶֽךָ:

אָבִ֫ינוּ מַלְכֵּ֫נוּ חַדֵּשׁ עָלֵֽינוּ שָׁנָה טוֹבָה:

אָבִ֫ינוּ מַלְכֵּ֫נוּ הָפֵר עֲצַת אוֹיְבֵֽינוּ:

אָבִ֫ינוּ מַלְכֵּ֫נוּ סְלַח וּמְחַל לְכָל־עֲוֹנוֹתֵֽינוּ:

אָבִ֫ינוּ מַלְכֵּ֫נוּ הַחֲזִירֵֽנוּ בִּתְשׁוּבָה שְׁלֵמָה לְפָנֶ֫יךָ:

אָבִ֫ינוּ מַלְכֵּ֫נוּ שְׁלַח רְפוּאָה שְׁלֵמָה לַחוֹלִים:

אָבִ֫ינוּ מַלְכֵּ֫נוּ חָתְמֵֽנוּ בְּסֵֽפֶר חַיִּים טוֹבִים:

אָבִ֫ינוּ מַלְכֵּ֫נוּ חָתְמֵֽנוּ בְּסֵֽפֶר גְּאֻלָּה וִישׁוּעָה:

אָבִ֫ינוּ מַלְכֵּ֫נוּ חָתְמֵֽנוּ בְּסֵֽפֶר פַּרְנָסָה וְכַלְכָּלָה:

אָבִ֫ינוּ מַלְכֵּ֫נוּ חָתְמֵֽנוּ בְּסֵֽפֶר זְכֻיּוֹת:

אָבִ֫ינוּ מַלְכֵּ֫נוּ חָתְמֵֽנוּ בְּסֵֽפֶר סְלִיחָה וּמְחִילָה:

אָבִ֫ינוּ מַלְכֵּ֫נוּ הַצְמַח לָֽנוּ יְשׁוּעָה בְּקָרוֹב: ←——

KAVANAH. The *Avinu Malkenu* prayer gives us permission to open up our deepest yearnings to the Universal One. By allowing our yearnings, often hidden even from ourselves, to emerge, we are taking a first step toward achieving an inner balance that will enable us to move forward toward wholeness. D.B.

COMMENTARY. Different community customs exist regarding the order of prayers at the end of *Ne'ilah*. While the recitation of Shema always occurs after *Avinu Malkenu* and precedes shofar sounding, the placement of Kaddish and *Havdalah* are determined by local usage. In communities where *Havdalah* is said out of doors, for example, it makes sense that *Havdalah* should be last. In communities that weave the shofar blast into the final Kaddish, the Kaddish will necessarily follow the Shema. D.A.T.

Our creator, our sovereign, remember us, though we are made of dust.

Our creator, our sovereign, be merciful to us and to all our offspring.

Our creator, our sovereign, act in memory of all those who have been killed while honoring your name.

Our creator, our sovereign, act in honor of your great and mighty, awe-inspiring name, which has been called out over us for our protection.

Our creator, our sovereign, be gracious with us and respond to us, for we have no deeds to justify us; deal with us in righteousness and love, and save us now.

The ark is closed, and we are seated.

COMMENTARY. Perhaps more than any other prayer, *Avinu Malkenu* invokes the image of a long-bearded king sitting in judgment upon his throne. How many are the ways that this image can trouble us! Some Jews are struggling to recover from the harsh judgments of parents or peers, or from harsh self-judgments. Some are struggling to escape the transcendent imagery of God and replace it with the divine within. Some have trouble with the maleness of the image.

Despite these very real difficulties, there is a powerful core of truth in the *Avinu Malkenu* that transcends the trouble many of us have with its imagery: we must grapple with standards of justice that are external to us. Social responsibility is not merely a matter of personal conscience. Chanting the *Avinu Malkenu* reminds us of standards by which we ought to judge ourselves.

Furthermore, it reminds us of forces infinitely greater than ourselves upon which our very lives depend. While our lives depend upon our inner resources, we cannot exist without the aid of natural and social forces. Knowing who we are means accepting the limits of our power and knowledge and the inevitability of our dependency. D.A.T.

אָבִינוּ מַלְכֵּנוּ זְכוֹר כִּי עָפָר אֲנָחְנוּ:

אָבִינוּ מַלְכֵּנוּ חֲמוֹל עָלֵינוּ וְעַל־עוֹלָלֵינוּ וְטַפֵּינוּ:

אָבִינוּ מַלְכֵּנוּ עֲשֵׂה לְמַעַן הֲרוּגִים עַל־שֵׁם קָדְשֶׁךָ:

אָבִינוּ מַלְכֵּנוּ עֲשֵׂה לְמַעַן שִׁמְךָ הַגָּדוֹל הַגִּבּוֹר וְהַנּוֹרָא שֶׁנִּקְרָא
עָלֵינוּ:

אָבִינוּ מַלְכֵּנוּ חָנֵּנוּ וַעֲנֵנוּ כִּי אֵין בָּנוּ מַעֲשִׂים עֲשֵׂה עִמָּנוּ צְדָקָה
וָחֶסֶד וְהוֹשִׁיעֵנוּ:

Avinu malkenu honenu va'anenu ki eyn banu ma'asim,
aseh imanu tzedakah vahesed vehoshi'enu.

The ark is closed, and we are seated.

COMMENTARY. In *Avinu Malkenu* we seek the strength to do justice, the inner harmony needed to find forgiveness, and the acceptance of the small place we have amidst the tumult of the world. It is in that context that we express the hopes embodied in this prayer. Whether or not the worshipper chooses to change the words of *Avinu Malkenu*, the fervently expressed pleas it contains transcend the constraints of time and place.   D.A.T.

KADDISH TITKABAL / KADDISH FOR THE COMPLETION OF PRAYER

Let God's name be made great and holy in the world that was created as God willed. May God complete the holy realm in your own lifetime, in your days, and in the days of all the house of Israel, quickly and soon. And say: Amen.

May God's great name be blessed forever and as long as worlds endure.

May it be blessed, and praised, and glorified, and held in honor, viewed with awe, embellished, and revered; and may the blessed name of holiness be hailed, though it be higher by far than all the blessings, songs, praises, and consolations that we utter in this world. And say: Amen.

And may the prayer and supplication of the whole house of Israel be acceptable to their creator in the heavens. And say: Amen.

May Heaven grant a universal peace, and life for us, and for all Israel. And say: Amen.

May the one who creates harmony above make peace for us and for all Israel, and for all who dwell on earth. And say: Amen.

יִתְגַּדַּל וְיִתְקַדַּשׁ שְׁמֵהּ רַבָּא בְּעָלְמָא דִּי בְרָא כִרְעוּתֵהּ וְיַמְלִיךְ
מַלְכוּתֵהּ בְּחַיֵּיכוֹן וּבְיוֹמֵיכוֹן וּבְחַיֵּי דְכָל בֵּית יִשְׂרָאֵל בַּעֲגָלָא וּבִזְמַן
קָרִיב וְאִמְרוּ אָמֵן:

יְהֵא שְׁמֵהּ רַבָּא מְבָרַךְ לְעָלַם וּלְעָלְמֵי עָלְמַיָּא:

יִתְבָּרַךְ וְיִשְׁתַּבַּח וְיִתְפָּאַר וְיִתְרוֹמַם וְיִתְנַשֵּׂא וְיִתְהַדָּר וְיִתְעַלֶּה
וְיִתְהַלַּל שְׁמֵהּ דְּקֻדְשָׁא בְּרִיךְ הוּא
לְעֵלָּא לְעֵלָּא מִכָּל בִּרְכָתָא וְשִׁירָתָא תֻּשְׁבְּחָתָא וְנֶחֱמָתָא דַּאֲמִירָן
בְּעָלְמָא וְאִמְרוּ אָמֵן:

תִּתְקַבַּל צְלוֹתְהוֹן וּבָעוּתְהוֹן דְּכָל בֵּית יִשְׂרָאֵל קֳדָם אֲבוּהוֹן דִּי
בִשְׁמַיָּא וְאִמְרוּ אָמֵן:

יְהֵא שְׁלָמָא רַבָּא מִן שְׁמַיָּא וְחַיִּים עָלֵינוּ וְעַל כָּל יִשְׂרָאֵל וְאִמְרוּ
אָמֵן:

עוֹשֶׂה שָׁלוֹם בִּמְרוֹמָיו הוּא יַעֲשֶׂה שָׁלוֹם עָלֵינוּ וְעַל כָּל יִשְׂרָאֵל וְעַל
כָּל יוֹשְׁבֵי תֵבֵל וְאִמְרוּ אָמֵן:

Yehey shemey raba mevaraḥ le'alam ulalmey almaya.

Oseh shalom bimromav hu ya'aseh shalom aleynu ve'al kol
yisra'el ve'al kol yoshvey tevel ve'imru amen.

שְׁמַע יִשְׂרָאֵל יְהֹוָה אֱלֹהֵינוּ יְהֹוָה אֶחָד

We chant once:

Listen, Israel: THE ETERNAL is our God, THE ETERNAL ONE alone!

We chant three times:

Blessed be the name and glory of God's realm forever!

We chant seven times:

THE ETERNAL ONE is God!

We are seated.

KAVANAH. Before יְהֹוָה הוּא הָאֱלֹהִים /*adonay hu ha'elohim*, think about what obligations you choose to take on during this year of your life. What are the changes you want to make so that your actions better reflect the Divine?

Z.S.S.

COMMENTARY. As Yom Kippur reaches its finale, we are as close to purified and sin-free as Jews can hope to be in this life. Having devoted a day to rethinking our priorities, we end Yom Kippur with three statements of faith. The Shema asserts our membership in the Jewish people and awareness of the divine unity. We then affirm God's sovereignty by reciting three times the second line of the Shema, which traditional Jews only recite silently the rest of the year. Thus do we underline our effort to have the divine rule our hearts, minds and hands every day in the year ahead. And then we proclaim seven times that we have but one God. The sevenfold repetition not only joyously and emphatically communicates the most central message of these days of awe; it creates seven fences built by the community to protect our fragile resolve as we step forward to meet the challenges of the new year.

D.A.T.

שְׁמַע יִשְׂרָאֵל יהוה אֱלֹהֵינוּ יהוה אֶחָד:

Shema yisra'el adonay eloheynu adonay eḥad.

בָּרוּךְ שֵׁם כְּבוֹד מַלְכוּתוֹ לְעוֹלָם וָעֶד:

Baruḥ shem kevod malḥuto le'olam va'ed.

יהוה הוּא הָאֱלֹהִים:

Adonay hu ha'elohim.

KAVANAH. The Shema challenges us to be fully conscious. True hearing involves an awareness of what is. A moment of full consciousness illuminates our false perceptions and opens us up to new possibilities. It is a courageous and honest encounter with the now.   D.B.

NOTE. יהוה הוא האלהים/The ETERNAL ONE is God is taken from the account of the prophet Elijah's vanquishing of the false prophets of Ba'al (I Kings 18:39). The Israelite people, having witnessed God's power, cry out together: YHWH alone is truly God!   R.H.

יהוה הוא האלהים/*Adonay hu ha'elohim*/The ETERNAL ONE is God is what the people said when Elijah the prophet successfully offered the sacrifices in competition with the unsuccessful priests of Ba'al. It is also used in preparation for dying. *Ne'ilah* is a preparation for death; it is a letting go of the holy place of Yom Kippur. It is a time of surrender to mercy in judgment. יהוה is the name of God used to symbolize the attribute of mercy; *Elohim* (also Judge) is the name of God in judgment. By saying יהוה is *Elohim*, we are saying that mercy enfolds and softens judgment and that we are prepared to surrender to that compassionate force.   Z.S.S.

1190 / CONCLUDING PRAYERS

We rise, and the shofar is sounded.
All respond:

Next year in Jerusalem.

COMMENTARY. And now these precious Days of Awe move finally to a close. The gates have almost swung shut, and only a crack of light still shines to guide us home. In these last moments, we affirm afresh what we will at our best affirm each day of this newly unfolding year. It is up to us to listen for the divine voice, up to us to re-enthrone God. The shofar's blast here marks not only the end of the fast. It marks also the redeeming revelation that can guide our steps as the gate clangs shut.   D.A.T.

COMMENTARY. We hear so much in the final blast of the shofar—the royal sovereign is present, messianic hope is evoked, the ram has been substituted, we are awake, aroused from our slumber, we are called to continuous struggle, we are celebrating and rejoicing, we are crying and releasing everything that has transpired in this long day.   S.P.W.

KAVANAH. From the beginning of *Kol Nidrey* until now, we have been joined as a community in soul searching, in expressing failure and transgression, in seeking a better way. This day of individual and communal purification leaves us at once both exhausted and renewed. This cleansing has launched a healing process that can be the beginning of new strength for our community, but only if the healing which has begun on this holiest of days is sustained by mutual commitment. The promise of Yom Kippur can take on substance only after the shofar has blown its final annual blast. In the days that lie ahead, the task of completing the healing and the test of community commitment are ours to fulfill.

D.A.T./M.B.K.

We rise, and the shofar is sounded.

TEKIYAH GEDOLAH   תְּקִיעָה גְדוֹלָה

All respond:

לְשָׁנָה הַבָּאָה בִּירוּשָׁלָיִם:

Leshanah haba'ah birushal<u>a</u>yim.

MEDITATION. Closing my eyes as the concluding, prolonged cry of the shofar reinvigorates my now weary body, I imagine myself peering down at Earth from a point in space. This last blast, the most powerful, seemingly resonates endlessly throughout the universe, seeking and longing for the Divine Source with our message of hope. In my mind's eye, I imagine the journey of such a true, pure sound. It will continue to journey on its mission of awakening and its call for awareness—awareness of the Divine within each of us, awareness of the world in which we live, and awareness of our shared universe. The message seems to grow fainter here on Earth as the final blast of the shofar also fades away. I return to be present in the communal here and now, secure in the knowledge that the message of our ancient horn has begun its year-long journey. The blast will continue to resound throughout the galaxy on its journey until next year when the shofar will echo its blast again, once again calling the soul to awareness.   M.B.K.

HAVDALAH

The candle is lit.

With the permission of this company:
Blessed are you, THE BOUNDLESS ONE, our God, the sovereign
of all worlds, who creates the fruit of the vine.

The blessing over the spices is said only on Saturday night.

Blessed are you, REVIVER our God, the sovereign of all worlds,
who creates various spices.

Blessed are you, THE RADIANCE, our God, the sovereign of all
worlds, who creates the light of fire.

*After reciting the blessing over fire, participants hold their hands before the candle flame so
that their fingers look radiant in its light and then cast shadows on their palms. Then the
following blessing is said.*

Blessed are you, THE MANY-NAMED, our God, the sovereign of
all worlds, who separates between holy and ordinary, light and
dark, the seventh day and the six days of work. Blessed are you,
THE INVISIBLE who separates the holy from the ordinary.

*The candle is now extinguished. Some communities do this by immersing it in wine from
the cup.*

COMMENTARY. While lighting candles marks both the beginning and the
end of Yom Kippur, the *Havdalah* candle has a meaning different from that
of the festival eve candles. Lighting this new fire signals commencement
of the work week because fire is so often an instrument of labor. Every
berahah/blessing must correlate to an event or action so that the blessing is
not in vain. We "use" the candlelight here to cast a shadow on our palms
by lifting our curled fingers toward the light.   D.A.T.

The candle is lit.

סָבְרֵי חֲבֵרַי:

בָּרוּךְ אַתָּה יהוה אֱלֹהֵינוּ מֶלֶךְ הָעוֹלָם בּוֹרֵא פְּרִי הַגָּפֶן:

Savrey ḥaveray.

Baruḥ atah adonay eloheynu meleḥ ha'olam borey peri hagafen.

The blessing over the spices is said only on Saturday night.

בָּרוּךְ אַתָּה יהוה אֱלֹהֵינוּ מֶלֶךְ הָעוֹלָם בּוֹרֵא מִינֵי בְשָׂמִים:

Baruḥ atah adonay eloheynu meleḥ ha'olam borey miney vesamin.

בָּרוּךְ אַתָּה יהוה אֱלֹהֵינוּ מֶלֶךְ הָעוֹלָם בּוֹרֵא מְאוֹרֵי הָאֵשׁ:

Baruḥ atah adonay eloheynu meleḥ ha'olam borey me'orey ha'esh.

After reciting the blessing over fire, participants hold their hands before the candle flame so that their fingers look radiant in its light and then cast shadows on their palms. Then the following blessing is said.

בָּרוּךְ אַתָּה יהוה אֱלֹהֵינוּ מֶלֶךְ הָעוֹלָם הַמַּבְדִּיל בֵּין קֹדֶשׁ לְחֹל בֵּין אוֹר לְחֹשֶׁךְ בֵּין יוֹם הַשְּׁבִיעִי לְשֵׁשֶׁת יְמֵי הַמַּעֲשֶׂה: בָּרוּךְ אַתָּה יהוה הַמַּבְדִּיל בֵּין קֹדֶשׁ לְחֹל:

Baruḥ atah adonay eloheynu meleḥ ha'olam hamavdil beyn kodesh leḥol beyn or leḥosheḥ beyn yom hashevi'i lesheshet yemey hama'aseh. Baruḥ atah adonay hamavdil beyn kodesh leḥol.

The candle is now extinguished. Some communities do this by immersing it in wine from the cup.

COMMENTARY. Just as we end Shabbat by candlelight and wine, so do we conclude Yom Kippur, which is called *Shabbat Shabbaton*/the Sabbath of Sabbaths. As this day of fullest removal from ordinary cares and concerns fades away, we re-enter the workaday world. However, we hope to bring the spiritual vision and moral resolve of Yom Kippur back into our everyday lives so that they can shape our everyday concerns. D.A.T.

CONCLUDING PRAYERS

KADDISH TITKABAL / KADDISH FOR THE COMPLETION OF PRAYER

Reader: Let God's name be made great and holy in the world that was created as God willed. May God complete the holy realm in your own lifetime, in your days, and in the days of all the house of Israel, quickly and soon. And say: Amen.

Congregation: May God's great name be blessed forever and as long as worlds endure.

Reader: May it be blessed, and praised, and glorified, and held in honor, viewed with awe, embellished, and revered; and may the blessed name of holiness be hailed, though it be higher by far than all the blessings, songs, praises, and consolations that we utter in this world. And say: Amen.

During Rosh Hashanah Musaf, *some communities sound the shofar here.*

Tekiyah	Shevarim Teruah	Tekiyah
Tekiyah	Shevarim	Tekiyah
Tekiyah	Teruah	Tekiyah Gedolah

And may the prayer and supplication of the whole house of Israel be acceptable to their creator in the heavens. And say: Amen.

May Heaven grant a universal peace, and life for us, and for all Israel. And say: Amen.

May the one who creates harmony above make peace for us and for all Israel, and for all who dwell on earth. And say: Amen.

On the evening of Rosh Hashanah continue with Kiddush, page 1197. Otherwise continue with Aleynu, page 1201.

קַדִּישׁ תִּתְקַבַּל

יִתְגַּדַּל וְיִתְקַדַּשׁ שְׁמֵהּ רַבָּא בְּעָלְמָא דִּי בְרָא כִרְעוּתֵהּ וְיַמְלִיךְ
מַלְכוּתֵהּ בְּחַיֵּיכוֹן וּבְיוֹמֵיכוֹן וּבְחַיֵּי דְכָל בֵּית יִשְׂרָאֵל בַּעֲגָלָא וּבִזְמַן
קָרִיב וְאִמְרוּ אָמֵן:
יְהֵא שְׁמֵהּ רַבָּא מְבָרַךְ לְעָלַם וּלְעָלְמֵי עָלְמַיָּא:
יִתְבָּרַךְ וְיִשְׁתַּבַּח וְיִתְפָּאַר וְיִתְרוֹמַם וְיִתְנַשֵּׂא וְיִתְהַדָּר וְיִתְעַלֶּה
וְיִתְהַלָּל שְׁמֵהּ דְּקֻדְשָׁא בְּרִיךְ הוּא
לְעֵלָּא לְעֵלָּא מִכָּל בִּרְכָתָא וְשִׁירָתָא תֻּשְׁבְּחָתָא וְנֶחֱמָתָא דַּאֲמִירָן
בְּעָלְמָא וְאִמְרוּ אָמֵן:

During Rosh Hashanah Musaf, some communities sound the shofar here.

תְּקִיעָה	שְׁבָרִים	תְּרוּעָה	תְּקִיעָה
תְּקִיעָה	שְׁבָרִים	תְּרוּעָה	תְּקִיעָה
תְּקִיעָה גְּדוֹלָה	שְׁבָרִים	תְּרוּעָה	תְּקִיעָה

תִּתְקַבַּל צְלוֹתְהוֹן וּבָעוּתְהוֹן דְּכָל בֵּית יִשְׂרָאֵל קֳדָם אֲבוּהוֹן דִּי
בִשְׁמַיָּא וְאִמְרוּ אָמֵן:
יְהֵא שְׁלָמָא רַבָּא מִן שְׁמַיָּא וְחַיִּים עָלֵינוּ וְעַל כָּל יִשְׂרָאֵל וְאִמְרוּ
אָמֵן:
עוֹשֶׂה שָׁלוֹם בִּמְרוֹמָיו הוּא יַעֲשֶׂה שָׁלוֹם עָלֵינוּ וְעַל כָּל יִשְׂרָאֵל וְעַל
כָּל יוֹשְׁבֵי תֵבֵל וְאִמְרוּ אָמֵן:

Yehey shemey raba mevaraḥ le'alam ulalmey almaya.

Oseh shalom bimromav hu ya'aseh shalom aleynu ve'al kol
yisra'el ve'al kol yoshvey tevel ve'imru amen.

On the evening of Rosh Hashanah, continue with Kiddush, page 1198. Otherwise continue
with Aleynu, page 1202.

KIDDUSH LEYL ROSH HASHANAH /
KIDDUSH FOR ROSH HASHANAH EVE

A full wine cup is lifted. On Shabbat, add the words in parenthesis.

With the permission of this company:
Blessed are you, THE BOUNDLESS ONE, our God, the sovereign
of all worlds, who creates the fruit of the vine.
Blessed are you, THE HOLY ONE our God, the sovereign of all
the worlds, who has called us to your service and made us holy
with your mitzvot, and given us, KIND ONE, our God, in love
this day of (the Shabbat, and of) remembering, a day for (calling
to mind) the sounding of the shofar (with love), a holy
convocation, a remembrance of the going-out from Egypt. For
you called to us and made us holy for your service, and your
word is truth and stands forever.
Blessed are you, ETERNAL ONE, who raises up to holiness
(Shabbat,) the people Israel and the Day of Memory. ↩

קִדּוּשׁ לֵיל רֹאשׁ הַשָּׁנָה

A full cup of wine is lifted. On Shabbat add the words in parenthesis.

סַבְרֵי חֲבֵרַי:

בָּרוּךְ אַתָּה יהוה אֱלֹהֵינוּ מֶלֶךְ הָעוֹלָם בּוֹרֵא פְּרִי הַגָּפֶן:

בָּרוּךְ אַתָּה יהוה אֱלֹהֵינוּ מֶלֶךְ הָעוֹלָם אֲשֶׁר קִרְאָנוּ לַעֲבוֹדָתוֹ
וְרוֹמְמָנוּ בִּקְדֻשָּׁתוֹ וְקִדְּשָׁנוּ בְּמִצְוֹתָיו: וַתִּתֶּן־לָנוּ יהוה אֱלֹהֵינוּ
בְּאַהֲבָה אֶת יוֹם (הַשַּׁבָּת הַזֶּה וְאֶת יוֹם) הַזִּכָּרוֹן הַזֶּה יוֹם (זִכְרוֹן)
תְּרוּעָה (בְּאַהֲבָה) מִקְרָא קֹדֶשׁ זֵכֶר לִיצִיאַת מִצְרָיִם: כִּי אֵלֵינוּ
קָרָאתָ וְאוֹתָנוּ קִדַּשְׁתָּ לַעֲבוֹדָתֶךָ וּדְבָרְךָ אֱמֶת וְקַיָּם לָעַד: בָּרוּךְ אַתָּה
יהוה מֶלֶךְ עַל כָּל הָאָרֶץ מְקַדֵּשׁ (הַשַּׁבָּת וְ) יִשְׂרָאֵל וְיוֹם
הַזִּכָּרוֹן: ←

Savrey ḥaveray.
Baruḥ atah adonay eloheynu meleḥ ha'olam borey peri hagafen.
Baruḥ atah adonay eloheynu meleḥ ha'olam asher kera'anu
la'avodato veromemanu bikdushato vekideshanu bemitzvotav.
Vatiten lanu adonay eloheynu be'ahavah et yom (hashabbat
hazeh ve'et yom) hazikaron hazeh yom (ziḥron) teruah
(be'ahavah) mikra kodesh zeḥer litzi'at mitzrayim. Ki eleynu
karata ve'otanu kidashta la'avodateḥa udevareḥa emet vekayam
la'ad. Baruḥ atah adonay meleḥ al kol ha'aretz mekadesh
(hashabbat ve)yisra'el veyom hazikaron. ↵

On Saturday night while lifting one's hands toward the festival lights, add:

(Blessed are you, THE RADIANCE, our God, the sovereign of all worlds, who creates the light of fire.

Blessed are you, THE MANY-NAMED our God, the sovereign of all worlds, who separates between holy and ordinary, light and dark, the seventh day and the six days of work. You separated between Shabbat holiness and festival holiness, you set apart the seventh day from the six days of work, and you sanctified Israel with your holiness. Blessed are you, INEXPRESSIBLE, who distinguishes among the kinds of holiness.)

Blessed are you, ETERNAL ONE, our God, the sovereign of all worlds, who gave us life, and kept us strong, and brought us to this time.

On Saturday night while lifting one's hands toward the festival lights, add:

(בָּרוּךְ אַתָּה יהוה אֱלֹהֵינוּ מֶלֶךְ הָעוֹלָם בּוֹרֵא מְאוֹרֵי הָאֵשׁ:
בָּרוּךְ אַתָּה יהוה אֱלֹהֵינוּ מֶלֶךְ הָעוֹלָם הַמַּבְדִּיל בֵּין קֹדֶשׁ לְחֹל בֵּין
אוֹר לְחֹשֶׁךְ בֵּין יוֹם הַשְּׁבִיעִי לְשֵׁשֶׁת יְמֵי הַמַּעֲשֶׂה: בֵּין קְדֻשַּׁת שַׁבָּת
לִקְדֻשַּׁת יוֹם טוֹב הִבְדַּלְתָּ וְאֶת יוֹם הַשְּׁבִיעִי מִשֵּׁשֶׁת יְמֵי הַמַּעֲשֶׂה
קִדַּשְׁתָּ: אֶת־עַמְּךָ יִשְׂרָאֵל קִדַּשְׁתָּ בִּקְדֻשָּׁתֶךָ: בָּרוּךְ אַתָּה יהוה
הַמַּבְדִּיל בֵּין קֹדֶשׁ לְקֹדֶשׁ:)

(Baruḥ atah adonay eloheynu meleḥ ha'olam borey me'orey
ha'esh.

Baruḥ atah adonay eloheynu meleḥ ha'olam hamavdil beyn
kodesh leḥol beyn or leḥosheḥ beyn yom hashevi'i lesheshet
yemey hama'aseh. Beyn kedushat shabbat likdushat yom tov
hivdalta ve'et yom hashevi'i misheshet yemey hama'aseh
kidashta. Et ameḥa yisra'el kidashta bikdushateḥa. Baruḥ atah
adonay hamavdil beyn kodesh lekodesh.)

בָּרוּךְ אַתָּה יהוה אֱלֹהֵינוּ מֶלֶךְ הָעוֹלָם שֶׁהֶחֱיָנוּ וְקִיְּמָנוּ וְהִגִּיעָנוּ
לַזְּמַן הַזֶּה:

ALEYNU

We rise for Aleynu. *It is customary to bow at "bend the knee." For an alternative version see page 1207. Choose one of the following:*

It is up to us to offer praises to the Source of all,
to declare the greatness of the author of Creation,
who gave to us teachings of truth
and planted eternal life within us.

It is up to us to offer praises to the Source of all,
to declare the greatness of the author of Creation,
who created heaven's heights and spread out its expanse,
who laid the earth's foundation and brought forth its offspring,
giving life to all its peoples,
the breath of life to all who walk about.

COMMENTARY. This *maḥzor* offers several versions of the *Aleynu*. The first, which appeared in the 1945 Reconstructionist *siddur*, emphasizes that the gift of God's Torah or teaching demands our committed response. The second version, based on Isaiah 42:5 and fit into the *Aleynu* by Rabbi Max D. Klein, emphasizes that our obligation to God flows from our role as part of Creation. The traditional *Aleynu* that appears below the line has troubled Reconstructionist Jews because it implies the inferiority of other faiths and peoples.   D.A.T.

עָלֵינוּ

We rise for Aleynu. It is customary to bow at "korim." For an alternative version, see page 1207. Choose one of the following.

Aleynu leshabe'ah la'adon hakol
latet gedulah leyotzer bereyshit
shenatan lanu torat emet
vehayey olam nata betohenu.

עָלֵינוּ לְשַׁבֵּחַ לַאֲדוֹן הַכֹּל
לָתֵת גְּדֻלָּה לְיוֹצֵר בְּרֵאשִׁית
שֶׁנָּתַן לָנוּ תּוֹרַת אֱמֶת
וְחַיֵּי עוֹלָם נָטַע בְּתוֹכֵנוּ:

Continue on page 1204.

Aleynu leshabe'ah la'adon hakol
latet gedulah leyotzer bereyshit.
bore hashamayim venoteyhem
roka ha'aretz vetze'etza'eha
noten neshamah la'am aleha
veru'ah laholehim bah.

עָלֵינוּ לְשַׁבֵּחַ לַאֲדוֹן הַכֹּל
לָתֵת גְּדֻלָּה לְיוֹצֵר בְּרֵאשִׁית
בּוֹרֵא הַשָּׁמַיִם וְנוֹטֵיהֶם
רֹקַע הָאָרֶץ וְצֶאֱצָאֶיהָ
נֹתֵן נְשָׁמָה לָעָם עָלֶיהָ
וְרוּחַ לַהֹלְכִים בָּהּ: ←

Continue on page 1204.

עָלֵינוּ לְשַׁבֵּחַ לַאֲדוֹן הַכֹּל לָתֵת גְּדֻלָּה
לְיוֹצֵר בְּרֵאשִׁית שֶׁלֹּא עָשָׂנוּ כְּגוֹיֵי
הָאֲרָצוֹת וְלֹא שָׂמָנוּ כְּמִשְׁפְּחוֹת הָאֲדָמָה
שֶׁלֹּא שָׂם חֶלְקֵנוּ כָּהֶם וְגוֹרָלֵנוּ כְּכָל
הֲמוֹנָם:

It is up to us to offer praises to the Source of all, to declare the greatness of the author of Creation, who has made us different from the other nations of the earth, and situated us in quite a different spot, and made our daily lot another kind from theirs, and given us a destiny uncommon in this world.

And so, we bend the knee and bow,
acknowledging the sovereign who rules
above all those who rule, the blessed Holy One,
who stretched out the heavens and founded the earth,
whose realm embraces heaven's heights,
whose mighty presence stalks celestial ramparts.
This is our God; there is none else besides,
as it is written in the Torah:
"You shall know this day, and bring it home
inside your heart, that THE SUPREME ONE is God
in the heavens above and on the earth below.
There is no other God." ⤺

DERASH. Every person and people that feel they have something to live for, and that are bent on living that life in righteousness, are true witnesses of God.   M.M.K.

KAVANAH. As the hand held before the eye hides the tallest mountain, so this small earthly life hides from our gaze the vast radiance and secrets of which the world is full, and if we can take life from before our eyes, as one takes away one's hand, we will see the great radiance within the world.   M.B. (Adapted)

וידעת...עוד/You...other God (Deuteronomy 4:39).

וַאֲנַחְנוּ כּוֹרְעִים וּמִשְׁתַּחֲוִים וּמוֹדִים לִפְנֵי מֶלֶךְ מַלְכֵי הַמְּלָכִים
הַקָּדוֹשׁ בָּרוּךְ הוּא:
שֶׁהוּא נוֹטֶה שָׁמַיִם וְיוֹסֵד אָרֶץ וּמוֹשַׁב יְקָרוֹ בַּשָּׁמַיִם מִמַּעַל וּשְׁכִינַת
עֻזּוֹ בְּגָבְהֵי מְרוֹמִים: הוּא אֱלֹהֵינוּ אֵין עוֹד: אֱמֶת מַלְכֵּנוּ אֶפֶס
זוּלָתוֹ כַּכָּתוּב בְּתוֹרָתוֹ: וְיָדַעְתָּ הַיּוֹם וַהֲשֵׁבֹתָ אֶל לְבָבֶךָ כִּי יהוה
הוּא הָאֱלֹהִים בַּשָּׁמַיִם מִמַּעַל וְעַל הָאָרֶץ מִתָּחַת אֵין עוֹד: —←

Va'anaḥnu korim umishtaḥavim umodim
lifney meleḥ malḥey hamelaḥim hakadosh baruḥ hu.
Shehu noteh shamayim veyosed aretz umoshav yekaro
bashamayim mima'al
ush-ḥinat uzo begovhey meromim.
Hu eloheynu eyn od.
Emet malkenu efes zulato kakatuv betorato.
Veyadata hayom vahashevota el levaveḥa
ki adonay hu ha'elohim bashamayim mima'al ve'al ha'aretz
mitaḥat eyn od.

NOTE. The *Aleynu* prayer, which signals the imminent conclusion of a
service, originated in the liturgy of Rosh Hashanah. Originally recited
annually, the *Aleynu* eventually moved into the daily liturgy as well,
perhaps due to its eloquent appeal for a time of universal peace.

COMMENTARY. The imagery of sovereignty before which "we bend the
knee and bow" often seems alien, even alienating, to modern Jews, for
whom the notion of submission appears as an affront to their autonomy.
Yet we know that there are some things in our world—moral absolutes,
ethical imperatives, communal consensus, and the calling of conscience
among them—before which we must in fact yield in acknowledgment. It
is, perhaps, not a bad thing to be reminded on occasion that for all of our
accomplishments, the mystery of life and death and the compelling nature
of divinity are not so easily dismissed.   R.H.

And so, we put our hope in you,
THE EMINENCE, our God,
that soon we may behold
the full splendor of your might,
and see idolatry vanish from the earth,
and all material gods be swept away,
and the power of your rule repair the world,
and all creatures of flesh call on your name,
and all the wicked of the earth turn back to you.
Let all who dwell upon the globe perceive and know
that to you each knee must bend, each tongue swear oath,
and let them give the glory of your name its precious due.
Let all of them take upon themselves your rule.
Reign over them, soon and for always.
For this is all your realm, throughout all worlds, across all
   time—
as it is written in your Torah:
"THE ETERNAL ONE will reign now and forever."

And it is written:
"THE EVERLASTING ONE will reign
as sovereign over all the earth.
On that day shall THE MANY NAMED be one,
God's name be one!"

KAVANAH. A world of God-callers is a world of truth and peace, a world
where the lust for power, greed, and envy—the idols of pride—is uprooted
from the individual and group psyche.   S.P.W.

DERASH. When senseless hatred reigns on earth and people hide their faces
from one another, then heaven is forced to hide its face. But when love
comes to rule the earth and people reveal their faces to one another, then
the splendor of God will be revealed.   M.B. (Adapted)

DERASH. It is not the seeking after God that divides but the claim to have
found God and to have discovered the only proper way of obeying God
and communing with God.   M.M.K. (Adapted)

CONCLUDING PRAYERS / 1205

עַל כֵּן נְקַוֶּה לְּךָ יהוה אֱלֹהֵינוּ לִרְאוֹת מְהֵרָה בְּתִפְאֶרֶת עֻזֶּךָ לְהַעֲבִיר
גִּלּוּלִים מִן הָאָרֶץ וְהָאֱלִילִים כָּרוֹת יִכָּרֵתוּן לְתַקֵּן עוֹלָם בְּמַלְכוּת
שַׁדַּי: וְכָל בְּנֵי בָשָׂר יִקְרְאוּ בִשְׁמֶךָ: לְהַפְנוֹת אֵלֶיךָ כָּל רִשְׁעֵי אָרֶץ:
יַכִּירוּ וְיֵדְעוּ כָּל יוֹשְׁבֵי תֵבֵל כִּי לְךָ תִּכְרַע כָּל בֶּרֶךְ תִּשָּׁבַע כָּל־לָשׁוֹן:
לְפָנֶיךָ יהוה אֱלֹהֵינוּ יִכְרְעוּ וְיִפֹּלוּ וְלִכְבוֹד שִׁמְךָ יְקָר יִתֵּנוּ וִיקַבְּלוּ
כֻלָּם אֶת עֹל מַלְכוּתֶךָ וְתִמְלֹךְ עֲלֵיהֶם מְהֵרָה לְעוֹלָם וָעֶד: כִּי
הַמַּלְכוּת שֶׁלְּךָ הִיא וּלְעוֹלְמֵי עַד תִּמְלֹךְ בְּכָבוֹד כַּכָּתוּב בְּתוֹרָתֶךָ:
יהוה יִמְלֹךְ לְעֹלָם וָעֶד: וְנֶאֱמַר: וְהָיָה יהוה לְמֶלֶךְ עַל כָּל הָאָרֶץ
בַּיּוֹם הַהוּא יִהְיֶה יהוה אֶחָד וּשְׁמוֹ אֶחָד:

Kakatuv betorateha: Adonay yimloh le'olam va'ed.
Vene'emar: Vehayah adonay lemeleh al kol ha'aretz.
Bayom hahu yihyeh adonay ehad ushmo ehad.

DERASH. Maybe God and perfection are at the end, and not at the
beginning. Maybe it is a growing world and a growing humanity and a
growing God, and perfection is to be achieved, not something to start out
with. Our own prophets and prayer books seem to have had an inkling of
this. At culminating points in our liturgy we say a phrase borrowed from
one of the last prophets (Zechariah 14:9), "On that day God will be One,
and God's name shall be One." On that day, not as yet, alas, but surely on
that day God shall be One, as God is not yet One. For how can God be
called One, i.e., real, if humanity is rent asunder in misery and poverty
and hate and war? When humankind has achieved its own reality and
unity, it will thereby have achieved God's reality and unity. Till then, God
is merely an idea, an ideal: the world's history consists in making that ideal
real. In simple religious earnestness it can be said that God does not exist.
Till now God merely subsists in the vision of a few great hearts, and exists
only in part, and is slowly being translated into reality.

Henry Slonimsky (Adapted)

ועד ... יהוה /THE ETERNAL ONE ... forever (Exodus 15:18).

אחד ... והיה /THE EVERLASTING ONE ... one (Zechariah 14:9).

1206 / ALEYNU

ALTERNATIVE VERSION

It is up to us
to hallow Creation,
to respond to Life
with the fullness of our lives.
It is up to us
to meet the World,
to embrace the Whole
even as we wrestle
with its parts.
It is up to us
to repair the World
and to bind our lives to Truth.

Therefore we bend the knee
and shake off the stiffness that keeps us
from the subtle
graces of Life
and the supple
gestures of Love.
With reverence
and thanksgiving
we accept our destiny
and set for ourselves
the task of redemption.

Rami M. Shapiro

And then all that has divided us will merge
And then compassion will be wedded to power
And then softness will come to a world that is harsh and unkind
And then both men and women will be gentle
And then both women and men will be strong
And then no person will be subject to another's will
And then all will be rich and free and varied
And then the greed of some will give way to the needs of many
And then all will share equally in the Earth's abundance
And then all will care for the sick and the weak and the old
And then all will nourish the young
And then all will cherish life's creatures
And then all will live in harmony with each other and the Earth
And then everywhere will be called Eden once again.

Judy Chicago

To everything there is a season,
And an appointed time for every purpose under heaven.

Now is the time for turning.

The leaves are beginning to turn from green to red and orange.
The birds are beginning to turn
And are flying once more towards the south.
The animals are beginning to turn
To storing their food for the winter.
For leaves, birds, and animals
Turning comes instinctively,
But for us, turning does not come so easily.
It takes an act of will for us to make a turn.
It means breaking with old habits,
It means admitting that we have been wrong.
And this is never easy.
It means losing face.
It means starting all over again,
And this is always painful.
It means saying, "I am sorry."
It means recognizing that we have the ability to change,
And this is always embarrassing.
These things are terribly hard to do.
But unless we turn, we will be trapped forever in yesterday's ways.

Therefore, may we find the strength to turn
From callousness to sensitivity,
From hostility to love,
From pettiness to purpose, from envy to contentment,
From carelessness to discipline, from fear to trust.
May we turn ourselves around and toward all that is noble,
true and life-affirming to revive our lives, as at the beginning.
Then may we turn toward one another,
For in isolation there is no life.

Jack Riemer (Adapted)

CONCLUDING PRAYERS / 1209

On the Pulse of Morning

A Rock, A River, A Tree
Hosts to species long since departed,
Marked the mastodon,
The dinosaur, who left dried tokens
Of their sojourn here
On our planet floor,
Any broad alarm of their hastening doom
Is lost in the gloom of dust and ages.

But today, the Rock cries out to us, clearly, forcefully,
Come, you may stand upon my
Back and face your distant destiny,
But seek no haven in my shadow.
I will give you no hiding place down here.

You, created only a little lower than
The angels, have crouched too long in
The bruising darkness
Have lain too long
Face down in ignorance.
Your mouths spilling words

Armed for slaughter.
The Rock cries out to us today, you may stand upon me,
But do not hide your face.

Across the wall of the world,
A River sings a beautiful song. It says,
Come, rest here by my side. ↵

Each of you, a bordered country,
Delicate and strangely made proud,
Yet thrusting perpetually under siege.
Your armed struggles for profit
Have left collars of waste upon
My shore, currents of debris upon my breast.
Yet today I call you to my riverside,
If you will study war no more. Come,
Clad in peace, and I will sing the songs
The Creator gave to me when I and the
Tree and the Rock were one.
Before cynicism was a bloody scar across your
Brow and when you yet knew you still
Knew nothing.
The River sang and sings on.

There is a true yearning to respond to
The African, the Native American, the Sioux,
The Catholic, the Muslim, the French, the Greek
The Irish, the Rabbi, the Priest, the Sheik,
The Gay, the Straight, the Preacher,
The privileged, the homeless, the Teacher.
They hear. They all hear
The speaking of the Tree.

They hear the first and last of every Tree
Speak to humankind today. Come to me, here beside the River.
Plant yourself beside the River.

Each of you, descendant of some passed
On traveller, has been paid for.
You, who gave me my first name, you, ↵

Pawnee, Apache, Seneca, you
Cherokee Nation, who rested with me, then
Forced on bloody feet,
Left me to the employment of
Other seekers—desperate for gain,
Starving for gold.

You the Ashanti, the Yoruba, the Kru, bought
Sold, stolen, arriving on the nightmare
Praying for a dream.
Here, root yourselves beside me.
I am that Tree planted by the River,
Which will not be moved:
I, the Rock, I, the River, I, the Tree
I am yours—your passages have been paid.
Lift up your faces, you have a piercing need
For this bright morning dawning for you.
History, despite its wrenching pain,
Cannot be unlived, but if faced
With courage, need not be lived again.

Lift up your eyes upon
This day breaking for you.
Give birth again
To the dream.

Women, children, men,
Take it into the palms of your hands,
Mold it into the shape of your most
Private need. Sculpt it into
The image of your most public self.
Lift up your hearts
Each new hour holds new chances
For a new beginning. ↩

Do not be wedded forever
To fear, yoked eternally
To brutishness.

The horizon leans forward,
Offering you space to place new steps of change.
Here, on the pulse of this fine day
You may have the courage
To look up and out and upon me, the
Rock, the River, the Tree, your country.
No less to Midas than the mendicant.
No less to you now than the mastodon then.

Here, on the pulse of this new day
You may have the grace to look up and out
And into your sister's eyes, and into
Your brother's face, your country
And say simply
Very simply
With hope—
Good morning.

Maya Angelou

In Praise of The Living

Yitgadal veyitkadash shemey raba
This profound praise of the living
Praise for the generous gift of life.

Praise for the presence of loved ones,
the bonds of friendship, the link of memory.

Praise for the toil and searching,
the dedication and visions, the ennobling aspirations.

Praise for the precious moorings of faith,
for courageous souls, for prophets, psalmists, and sages.

Praise for those who walked before us,
the sufferers in the valley of shadows,
the steadfast in the furnace of hate.

Praise for the God of our fathers,
the Source of all growth and goodness,
the Promise of which we build tomorrow.

Yitgadal veyitkadash shemey raba

This, the profound praise we offer.
Praise for the generous gift of life.

Harvey J. Fields

KAVANAH. Our relationship to those who have come before us does not end at the time of their death. The relationship continues, taking many forms. It can continue through our experience of universal sadness. It can continue through our sense of noble righteousness. It can continue through our understanding of the integrity of memory. It can continue through our surrender to pure joy. Kaddish affirms that our connection with our loved ones is continuous and everlasting. D.B.

INTRODUCTION TO THE MOURNERS' KADDISH

In reciting the Kaddish we affirm our awareness of holiness in our world. Much of our experience of divine goodness, grace and love has come to us through those whose lives have touched our own. (Today we remember...) We invoke the transcendent power of love and caring as we sanctify God's name.

THE MOURNERS' KADDISH

It is customary for mourners, and those observing Yahrzeit, to stand for Kaddish. In some congregations everyone rises.

Reader: Let God's name be made great and holy in the world that was created as God willed. May God complete the holy realm in your own lifetime, in your days, and in the days of all the house of Israel, quickly and soon. And say: Amen.

Congregation: May God's great name be blessed, forever and as long as worlds endure.

Reader: May it be blessed, and praised, and glorified, and held in honor, viewed with awe, embellished, and revered; and may the blessed name of holiness be hailed, though it be higher by far than all the blessings, songs, praises, and consolations that we utter in this world. And say: Amen.

May Heaven grant a universal peace, and life for us, and for all Israel. And say: Amen.

May the one who creates harmony above, make peace for us and for all Israel, and for all who dwell on earth. And say: Amen.

NOTE. Congregations usually mention the names of congregants and their relatives who have died in the previous week before reciting the Mourners' Kaddish. In many congregations a *Yahrzeit* list is read as well. In more informal settings the leader sometimes invites those present to speak the names of those they wish to be remembered.   D.A.T.

קַדִּישׁ יָתוֹם

It is customary for mourners, and those observing Yahrzeit, *to stand for Kaddish. In some congregations everyone rises.*

יִתְגַּדַּל וְיִתְקַדַּשׁ שְׁמֵהּ רַבָּא בְּעָלְמָא דִּי בְרָא כִרְעוּתֵהּ וְיַמְלִיךְ מַלְכוּתֵהּ בְּחַיֵּיכוֹן וּבְיוֹמֵיכוֹן וּבְחַיֵּי דְכָל בֵּית יִשְׂרָאֵל בַּעֲגָלָא וּבִזְמַן קָרִיב וְאִמְרוּ אָמֵן:

יְהֵא שְׁמֵהּ רַבָּא מְבָרַךְ לְעָלַם וּלְעָלְמֵי עָלְמַיָּא:

יִתְבָּרַךְ וְיִשְׁתַּבַּח וְיִתְפָּאַר וְיִתְרוֹמַם וְיִתְנַשֵּׂא וְיִתְהַדָּר וְיִתְעַלֶּה וְיִתְהַלָּל שְׁמֵהּ דְּקֻדְשָׁא בְּרִיךְ הוּא לְעֵלָּא לְעֵלָּא מִכָּל בִּרְכָתָא וְשִׁירָתָא תֻּשְׁבְּחָתָא וְנֶחֱמָתָא דַּאֲמִירָן בְּעָלְמָא וְאִמְרוּ אָמֵן:

יְהֵא שְׁלָמָא רַבָּא מִן שְׁמַיָּא וְחַיִּים עָלֵינוּ וְעַל כָּל יִשְׂרָאֵל וְאִמְרוּ אָמֵן:

עוֹשֶׂה שָׁלוֹם בִּמְרוֹמָיו הוּא יַעֲשֶׂה שָׁלוֹם עָלֵינוּ וְעַל כָּל יִשְׂרָאֵל וְעַל כָּל יוֹשְׁבֵי תֵבֵל וְאִמְרוּ אָמֵן:

Yitgadal veyitkadash shemey raba
be'alma di vera ḥirutey veyamliḥ malḥutey
beḥayeyhon uvyomeyhon uvḥayey deḥol beyt yisra'el
ba'agala uvizman kariv ve'imru amen.

Yehey shemey raba mevaraḥ le'alam ulalmey almaya.

Yitbaraḥ veyishtabaḥ veyitpa'ar veyitromam veyitnasey
veyit-hadar veyitaleh veyit-halal shemey dekudsha beriḥ hu
le'ela le'ela mikol birḥata veshirata
tushbeḥata veneḥemata da'amiran be'alma ve'imru amen.

Yehey shelama raba min shemaya veḥayim aleynu ve'al kol
yisra'el ve'imru amen.
Oseh shalom bimromav hu ya'aseh shalom aleynu ve'al kol
yisra'el ve'al kol yoshvey tevel ve'imru amen.

The following psalm is traditionally recited each morning and evening—from Rosh Ḥodesh Elul *through Hoshana Rabah.*

[A psalm] of David

THE ETERNAL is my light and my salvation; whom, then, should I fear?

THE ALMIGHTY is my living source of strength; before whom should I tremble?

When evildoers approach to eat my flesh, when tormenters and enemies come after me,

see how they stumble; see how they tumble down!

Should a force encamp against me, my heart shall have no fear;

should a war arise against me, in one thing I shall trust,

one thing have I asked of GOD, one goal do I pursue: to dwell in THE ETERNAL'S house throughout my days,

to know the bliss of THE SUBLIME, to visit in God's temple.

Truly, in a day of trouble, I am nestled in God's shelter, hidden in the recess of God's tent. God sets me high upon a rock. ⤸

KAVANAH. It is only a true and close community that develops associations, traditions and memories that go to make up its soul. To mingle one's personality with that soul becomes a natural longing. In such a community one experiences that mystic divine grace which, like radiant sunshine, illumines our lives when joyous and, like balm, heals them when wounded or stricken. Then all questions about saying this or that become trivial, for the real purpose is attained in having each one feel with the Psalmist: "One thing I ask of God that will I seek after, that I may dwell in the house of God all the days of my life, to behold the graciousness of God."   M.M.K. (Adapted)

יהוה אוֹרִי וְיִשְׁעִי מִמִּי אִירָא:

יהוה מָעוֹז־חַיַּי מִמִּי אֶפְחָד:

בִּקְרֹב עָלַי מְרֵעִים לֶאֱכֹל אֶת־בְּשָׂרִי

צָרַי וְאֹיְבַי לִי הֵמָּה כָשְׁלוּ וְנָפָלוּ:

אִם־תַּחֲנֶה עָלַי מַחֲנֶה לֹא־יִירָא לִבִּי

אִם־תָּקוּם עָלַי מִלְחָמָה בְּזֹאת אֲנִי בוֹטֵחַ:

אַחַת שָׁאַלְתִּי מֵאֵת־יהוה אוֹתָהּ אֲבַקֵּשׁ

שִׁבְתִּי בְּבֵית־יהוה כָּל־יְמֵי חַיַּי לַחֲזוֹת בְּנֹעַם־יהוה וּלְבַקֵּר בְּהֵיכָלוֹ:

כִּי יִצְפְּנֵנִי בְּסֻכֹּה בְּיוֹם רָעָה יַסְתִּרֵנִי בְּסֵתֶר אָהֳלוֹ בְּצוּר יְרוֹמְמֵנִי: ←

Aḥat sha'alti me'et adonay otah avakesh shivti beveyt adonay kol yemey ḥayay laḥazot beno'am adonay ulevaker beheyḥalo.

COMMENTARY. Many Jews recite this psalm every day betwen the first of Elul and the end of Sukkot. The rabbis doubtless chose it to accompany us through every phase of the fall holiday season because it encompasses such a range of powerful emotions. Identifying with the experience of the speaker can help us at various moments to get in touch with our fears of abandonment, our need for security, our yearning for joyful religious experience, our need for guidance from God, our steadying commitment never to lose hope. Above all, we experience the psalmist's vulnerability. Feeling that it is possible to be hidden and secure within God's presence, the psalmist also knows, by contrast, the terrible fear that God can hide the divine countenance and seem utterly unavailable. The psalm delicately balances these two kinds of hiddenness, as it seeks a "level path," the right way of moving in a difficult, dangerous world. The psalm ends by urging that we cling to the hope that comes from connection to יהוה, the One of Being and Becoming, in whose presence all life unfolds.   H.L.

And now, my head is raised in triumph on my foes around me,
and I offer sacrifice in celebration in God's tent.
I offer song and melody to MY REDEEMER.

Hear me, PRECIOUS ONE, I call aloud;
be gracious to me, answer me!

To you my heart cries out, to you my face is turned;
your presence, GRACIOUS ONE, I seek.

Hide not your face from me; do not, in anger, turn away your
servant.
You have been my help, don't shun me now; do not abandon
me, my God who saves!

For my father and my mother have abandoned me,
but THE LIVING ONE shall take me in.

Teach me your way, WISE ONE, and guide me in a just path as I
meet my foes.
Don't place me at the mercy of my enemies, for slanderers arise
against me, and they fume in violence.

Were it not for my belief that I'll behold GOD's goodness in the
Land of Life...
Hope, then, for THE ETERNAL ONE; strengthen your heart with
courage, and have hope in THE ETERNAL.

Psalm 27

וְעַתָּה יָרוּם רֹאשִׁי עַל אֹיְבַי סְבִיבוֹתַי וְאֶזְבְּחָה בְאָהֳלוֹ זִבְחֵי תְרוּעָה
אָשִׁירָה וַאֲזַמְּרָה לַיהוה:
שְׁמַע־יהוה קוֹלִי אֶקְרָא וְחָנֵּנִי וַעֲנֵנִי:
לְךָ אָמַר לִבִּי בַּקְּשׁוּ פָנָי אֶת־פָּנֶיךָ יהוה אֲבַקֵּשׁ:
אַל־תַּסְתֵּר פָּנֶיךָ מִמֶּנִּי אַל תַּט־בְּאַף עַבְדֶּךָ
עֶזְרָתִי הָיִיתָ אַל־תִּטְּשֵׁנִי וְאַל־תַּעַזְבֵנִי אֱלֹהֵי יִשְׁעִי:
כִּי־אָבִי וְאִמִּי עֲזָבוּנִי וַיהוה יַאַסְפֵנִי:
הוֹרֵנִי יהוה דַּרְכֶּךָ וּנְחֵנִי בְּאֹרַח מִישׁוֹר לְמַעַן שׁוֹרְרָי:
אַל־תִּתְּנֵנִי בְּנֶפֶשׁ צָרָי כִּי קָמוּ־בִי עֵדֵי־שֶׁקֶר וִיפֵחַ חָמָס:
* לוּלֵא הֶאֱמַנְתִּי לִרְאוֹת בְּטוּב־יהוה בְּאֶרֶץ חַיִּים:
קַוֵּה אֶל־יהוה חֲזַק וְיַאֲמֵץ לִבֶּךָ וְקַוֵּה אֶל־יהוה:

כי אבי ואמי עזבוני ויהוה יאספני/For my father and my mother have abandoned me, but THE LIVING ONE shall take me in. Everything human is imperfect and finite—even my parents—who were to me as gods when I was a young child. As I mature, I realize that only in sensing my connection to the ground of being and becoming, the perfect and infinite, can I ever fully feel safe. S.P.W.

לולא האמנתי לראות בטוב יהוה בארץ חיים/Were it not for my belief that I'll behold God's goodness in the land of life . . . This line is a fragment—the beginning of a thought stranded in mid-air which I refuse to complete. I don't want to put into words or visualize a life without faith. It would be like the end of the verse—an empty chasm. S.P.W.

Today, give us courage and strength.	Amen!
Today, give us blessing.	Amen!
Today, give us goodness.	Amen!
Today, seek our welfare and good.	Amen!
Today, write us down for a good life.	Amen!
Today, please hearken to our cry.	Amen!
Today, accept with mercy and good will our prayer.	Amen!
Today, may your right hand keep us safe.	Amen!
Today, forgive and pardon all our sins.	Amen!

On a day like today,
may you bring us, joyful and glad,
to the completion of our reconstruction.
As is written by your prophet's hand:
"And I shall bring you to my holy mountain,
and you shall celebrate there inside my house of prayer...
For my home shall then be called
a house of prayer for all peoples!"

And may we and all the people Israel,
and all who dwell on earth,
enjoy justice and blessing,
lovingkindness, life, and peace,
until eternity.

COMMENTARY. The היום/*Hayom*/Today is the crowning prayer of the High Holy Day liturgy. Its power stems not only from its fresh and energetic sense of hope and from its beautiful music; it comes also from the powerful awareness that what matters is Today, the powerful commitment of this moment. The challenge of the High Holy Days is in part to remember that when tomorrow comes, it too will be Today. The hope of this moment, every moment, lies in the knowledge that when tomorrow comes it will be Today. If we live in the possibility of this moment, Today is more than enough.   D.A.T.

אָמֵן:	הַיּוֹם תְּאַמְּצֵנוּ:
אָמֵן:	הַיּוֹם תְּבָרְכֵנוּ:
אָמֵן:	הַיּוֹם תְּגַדְּלֵנוּ:
אָמֵן:	הַיּוֹם תִּדְרְשֵׁנוּ לְטוֹבָה:
אָמֵן:	הַיּוֹם תִּכְתְּבֵנוּ לְחַיִּים טוֹבִים:
אָמֵן:	הַיּוֹם תִּשְׁמַע שַׁוְעָתֵנוּ:
אָמֵן:	הַיּוֹם תְּקַבֵּל בְּרַחֲמִים וּבְרָצוֹן אֶת־תְּפִלָּתֵנוּ:
אָמֵן:	הַיּוֹם תִּתְמְכֵנוּ בִּימִין צִדְקֶךָ:
אָמֵן:	הַיּוֹם תִּמְחֹל וְתִסְלַח לְכָל עֲוֹנוֹתֵינוּ:

Hayom te'amtzenu.   Amen.
Hayom tevarehenu.   Amen.
Hayom tegadlenu.   Amen.
Hayom tidreshenu letovah.   Amen.
Hayom tihtevenu lehayim tovim.   Amen.
Hayom tishma shavatenu.   Amen.
Hayom tekabel berahamim uveratzon et tefilatenu.   Amen.
Hayom titmehenu bimin tzidkeha.   Amen.
Hayom timhol vetislah lehol avonotenu.   Amen.

כְּהַיּוֹם הַזֶּה תְּבִיאֵנוּ שָׂשִׂים וּשְׂמֵחִים בְּבִנְיַן שָׁלֵם כַּכָּתוּב עַל־יַד
נְבִיאֶךָ: וַהֲבִיאוֹתִים אֶל־הַר קָדְשִׁי וְשִׂמַּחְתִּים בְּבֵית תְּפִלָּתִי... כִּי
בֵיתִי בֵּית־תְּפִלָּה יִקָּרֵא לְכָל־הָעַמִּים: וּצְדָקָה וּבְרָכָה וְרַחֲמִים וְחַיִּים
וְשָׁלוֹם יִהְיֶה־לָּנוּ וּלְכָל־יִשְׂרָאֵל וּלְכָל־יוֹשְׁבֵי תֵבֵל עַד עוֹלָם:

והביאותים...לכל-העמים / And...peoples (Isaiah 56:7).

ADON OLAM / CROWN OF ALL TIME

This translation can be sung to the same melody as the Hebrew.

Crown of all time, the one who reigned
before all mortal shape was made,
and when God's will brought forth all things
then was the name supreme proclaimed.

And after everything is gone,
yet One alone, awesome, will reign.
God was, and is, and will remain,
in splendid balance, over all.

And God is One, no second is,
none can compare, or share God's place.
Without beginning, without end,
God's is all might and royal grace.

This is my God, my help who lives,
refuge from pain in time of trial,
my banner, and my place to fly,
my cup's portion when, dry, I cry.

To God's kind hand I pledge my soul
each time I sleep, again to wake,
and with my soul, this body, here.
YAH'S love is mine; I shall not fear.

KAVANAH. God is that aspect of reality which elicits from us the best that is in us and enables us to bear the worst that can befall us.   M.M.K.

אֲדוֹן עוֹלָם

אֲדוֹן עוֹלָם אֲשֶׁר מָלַךְ	בְּטֶרֶם כָּל יְצִיר נִבְרָא:
לְעֵת נַעֲשָׂה בְחֶפְצוֹ כֹּל	אֲזַי מֶלֶךְ שְׁמוֹ נִקְרָא:
וְאַחֲרֵי כִּכְלוֹת הַכֹּל	לְבַדּוֹ יִמְלֹךְ נוֹרָא:
וְהוּא הָיָה וְהוּא הֹוֶה	וְהוּא יִהְיֶה בְּתִפְאָרָה:
וְהוּא אֶחָד וְאֵין שֵׁנִי	לְהַמְשִׁיל לוֹ לְהַחְבִּירָה:
בְּלִי רֵאשִׁית בְּלִי תַכְלִית	וְלוֹ הָעֹז וְהַמִּשְׂרָה:
וְהוּא אֵלִי וְחַי גּוֹאֲלִי	וְצוּר חֶבְלִי בְּעֵת צָרָה:
וְהוּא נִסִּי וּמָנוֹס לִי	מְנָת כּוֹסִי בְּיוֹם אֶקְרָא:
בְּיָדוֹ אַפְקִיד רוּחִי	בְּעֵת אִישַׁן וְאָעִירָה:
וְעִם רוּחִי גְוִיָּתִי	יהוה לִי וְלֹא אִירָא:

Adon olam asher malaḥ, beterem kol yetzir nivra.
Le'et na'asah veḥeftzo kol, azay meleḥ shemo nikra.
Ve'aharey kiḥlot hakol, levado yimloḥ nora.
Vehu hayah vehu hoveh, vehu yihyeh betifarah.
Vehu eḥad ve'eyn sheni, lehamshil lo lehaḥbirah.
Beli reshit beli taḥlit, velo ha'oz vehamisrah.
Vehu eli veḥay go'ali, vetzur ḥevli be'et tzarah.
Vehu nisi umanos li, menat kosi beyom ekra.
Beyado afkid ruḥi, be'et ishan ve'a'irah.
Ve'im ruḥi geviyati, adonay li velo ira.

YIGDAL / GREAT IS . . .

This translation can be sung to the same melody as the Hebrew.

Great is the living God,
 to whom we give our praise,
who is, and whose great being
 is timeless, without days,
the One, to whom in oneness
 no one can compare,
invisible, in unity
 unbounded, everywhere,

Who has no body's form,
 has no material dress,
nor can we find the likeness
 of God's awesome holiness,
more ancient than all things
 brought forth in creation,
the first of everything that is,
 Beginning unbegun!

Behold the supreme being,
 whose universal power,
whose greatness and whose rule
 all creatures shall declare,
whose flow of prophecy
 was granted to a few,
the treasured ones who stood amid
 God's splendor ever new.

נִמְצָא וְאֵין עֵת אֶל מְצִיאוּתוֹ:   יִגְדַּל אֱלֹהִים חַי וְיִשְׁתַּבַּח

נֶעְלָם וְגַם אֵין סוֹף לְאַחְדּוּתוֹ:   אֶחָד וְאֵין יָחִיד כְּיִחוּדוֹ

לֹא נַעֲרוֹךְ אֵלָיו קְדֻשָּׁתוֹ:   אֵין לוֹ דְמוּת הַגּוּף וְאֵינוֹ גוּף

רִאשׁוֹן וְאֵין רֵאשִׁית לְרֵאשִׁיתוֹ:   קַדְמוֹן לְכָל דָּבָר אֲשֶׁר נִבְרָא

יוֹרֶה גְדֻלָּתוֹ וּמַלְכוּתוֹ:   הִנּוֹ אֲדוֹן עוֹלָם וְכָל נוֹצָר

אַנְשֵׁי סְגֻלָּתוֹ וְתִפְאַרְתּוֹ: —   שֶׁפַע נְבוּאָתוֹ נְתָנוֹ אֶל

Yigdal elohim ḥay veyishtabaḥ, nimtza ve'eyn et el metzi'uto.
Eḥad ve'eyn yaḥid keyiḥudo, nelam vegam eyn sof le'aḥduto.

Eyn lo demut haguf ve'eyno guf, lo na'aroḥ elav kedushato.
Kadmon leḥol davar asher nivra, rishon ve'eyn reyshit
   lereyshito.

Hino adon olam veḥol notzar, yoreh gedulato umalḥuto.
Shefa nevu'ato netano, el anshey segulato vetifar-to. ←

NOTE. *Yigdal* was written by Daniel ben Judah, a fourteenth-century poet. He based it upon Maimonides's Thirteen Articles of Faith. We have attempted to make the closing line more acceptable to the contemporary worshipper by referring to the sustenance of life, rather than resurrection of the dead, as the true testimony of God's blessing.   A.G.

In Israel none arose
    as prophet like Mosheh,
a prophet who would come to see
    the "image" in the *sneh*.
Torah of truth God gave
    the people Isra'el,
by truest prophet's hand
    that in God's house would dwell.

And God will never let
    the Torah pass away,
its doctrine will not change,
    but through all change will stay.
God sees and knows all things,
    and even what we hide,
can look upon how things begin
    the end of things to find.

Rewarding acts of love,
    when love for love we'll find,
and paying to all wickedness
    a recompense in kind,
God shall deliver all,
    upon the end of time,
redeeming all who wait for God,
    who for salvation pine.

God wakes all beings to life,
    abundant love shall reign,
blessed evermore,
    the glory of God's Name!

לֹא קָם בְּיִשְׂרָאֵל כְּמֹשֶׁה עוֹד   נָבִיא וּמַבִּיט אֶת תְּמוּנָתוֹ׃
תּוֹרַת אֱמֶת נָתַן לְעַמּוֹ אֵל   עַל יַד נְבִיאוֹ נֶאֱמַן בֵּיתוֹ׃
לֹא יַחֲלִיף הָאֵל וְלֹא יָמִיר   דָּתוֹ לְעוֹלָמִים לְזוּלָתוֹ׃
צוֹפֶה וְיוֹדֵעַ סְתָרֵינוּ   מַבִּיט לְסוֹף דָּבָר בְּקַדְמָתוֹ׃
גּוֹמֵל לְאִישׁ חֶסֶד כְּמִפְעָלוֹ   יִתֵּן לְרָשָׁע רָע כְּרִשְׁעָתוֹ׃
יִשְׁלַח לְקֵץ יָמִין גְּאֻלָּתוֹ   לִפְדּוֹת מְחַכֵּי קֵץ יְשׁוּעָתוֹ׃
חַיִּים מְכַלְכֵּל אֵל בְּרֹב חַסְדּוֹ   בָּרוּךְ עֲדֵי עַד שֵׁם תְּהִלָּתוֹ׃

Lo kam beyisra'el kemosheh od, navi umabit et temunato.
Torat emet natan le'amo el, al yad nevi'o ne'eman beyto.
Lo yaḥalif ha'el velo yamir dato, le'olamim lezulato.
Tzofeh veyode'a setareynu, mabit lesof davar bekadmato.
Gomel le'ish ḥesed kemifalo, yiten lerasha ra kerishato.
Yishlaḥ leketz yamin ge'ulato, lifdot meḥakey ketz yeshu'ato.
Ḥayim meḥalkel el berov ḥasdo, baruḥ adey ad shem tehilato.

חיים מכלכל אל/God wakes all beings to life. The original version of this line was מתים יחיה אל/God revives the dead. It was changed to the version above in the 1945 *siddur* which, like this *maḥzor*, avoids references to revival of the dead for ideological reasons. This change paralleled those in the second blessing of the Amidah.   D.A.T.

בְּסֵפֶר חַיִּים בְּרָכָה וְשָׁלוֹם וּפַרְנָסָה טוֹבָה נִזָּכֵר וְנִכָּתֵב לְפָנֶיךָ אֲנַחְנוּ
וְכָל־עַמְּךָ בֵּית יִשְׂרָאֵל לְחַיִּים טוֹבִים וּלְשָׁלוֹם:

In the book of life, blessing, peace, and proper sustenance, may
we be remembered and inscribed, we and all your people, the
house of Israel, for a good life and for peace.

THE PROMISE OF THIS DAY

Look to this day,
For it is life,
The very life of life.
In its brief course lie all
The realities and verities of existence,
The bliss of growth,
The splendor of action,
The glory of power—

For yesterday is but a dream,
And tomorrow is only a vision.
But today, well lived,
Makes every yesterday a dream of happiness
And every tomorrow a vision of hope.

Look well, therefore, to this day.

Sanskrit Proverb

A GUIDE TO GREETINGS

During the month of Elul, the traditional greetings are *Shanah tovah* ("A good year"); or *Leshanah tovah tikatevu* ("May you be inscribed for a good year [in the Book of Life]"); or *Leshanah tovah umetukah tikatevu* ("May you be inscribed for a good and sweet year"); or—less common—*Ketivah tovah* ("A good inscription [in the Book of Life]").

The appropriate response: *Gam leha* (feminine *lah*)—"The same to you."

Between Rosh Hashanah and Yom Kippur, some people add to the above: *Leshanah tovah tikatevu vetehatemu* ("May you be inscribed and sealed for a good life"). Others use these greetings only through the first night of Rosh Hashanah; after that, it would be indelicate to suggest that a person is not already inscribed in the Book of Life, for on Rosh Hashanah all the righteous are so inscribed—only those whose records are closely balanced between good and bad have their fate postponed until Yom Kippur.

On Yom Kippur (and until Hoshana Rabah) the greeting is *Gemar hatimah tovah* ("A good final sealing [to you]!") or *Hatimah tovah* ("A sealing for good!"). Michael Strassfeld

לְשָׁנָה טוֹבָה תִּכָּתֵבוּ

סְלִיחוֹת

SELIHOT   סְלִיחוֹת

The Selihot *service serves as an introduction, preparation and bridge into the season of* teshuvah / return. *The service below is designed to serve as preparation through reconnecting to melodies and prayers—it is the season's overture.*

The service is in outline form in order to make it easily adaptable for local use by adding music, poetry and prayers as the needs of the community dictate. The act of turning the pages of the mahzor *itself can be a powerful experience. For that reason, it is preferable that the* mahzor *be used and not reproductions of key pages.*

Most communities precede the Selihot *service with study and refreshments. For study, materials can be selected from the meditations at the beginning of the* mahzor, *or any other material or activity suitable to the mood of the season can of course be undertaken.*

Havdalah, marking the end of each Shabbat, separates the ordinary from the holy. At this *Selihot* hour, we not only separate the beauty and serenity of Shabbat from the work week that is comng; we also begin the process of separating from the year that is ending and progressing toward the coming year. This is a time for savoring last year's triumphs, moving beyond last year's doubts, accepting last year's pains and joys, acknowledging its fears and shortcomings. Only by facing the year that is ending—and sensitively recognizing and placing its many pieces in our memories—can we prepare ourselves for the new year with whole hearts. This *Havdalah* marks the beginning of the season of hope renewed. We separate from the past, making it part of memory, that we might enter into the future, growing together in hope.

David A. Teutsch and Micah Becker-Klein

HAVDALAH

At the end of Shabbat, a Havdalah candle is lit. A full cup of wine and spices are near at hand, and the lights are dimmed.

With the permission of this company:
Blessed are you, THE BOUNDLESS ONE, our God, the sovereign of all worlds, who creates the fruit of the vine.

It is the custom for some to take a sip of the wine here. Others wait until after the final berahah / blessing.

Blessed are you, REVIVER, our God, the sovereign of all worlds, who creates various spices.

After the blessing is said, the leader smells the spices and passes them on.

Blessed are you, THE RADIANCE, our God, the sovereign of all worlds, who creates the light of fire.

After reciting the blessing over fire, participants hold their hands before the candle flame so that their fingers look radiant in its light and then cast shadows on their palms. Then the following blessing is said:

Blessed are you, THE MANY-NAMED, our God, the sovereign of all worlds, who separates between holy and ordinary, light and dark, the seventh day and the six days of work. Blessed are you, THE INVISIBLE, who separates the holy from the ordinary.

The candle is now extinguished. Some do this by immersing it in wine from the cup.

COMMENTARY. While lighting candles marks both the beginning and the end of Shabbat, the *Havdalah* candle has a meaning different from that of the *Erev Shabbat* candles. Lighting this new fire signals commencement of the work week because fire is so often an instrument of labor. Every *berahah*/blessing must correlate to an event or action so that it is not in vain. We "use" the candlelight here to cast a shadow on our palms by lifting our curled fingers toward the light.   D.A.T.

סַבְרֵי חֲבֵרַי:

בָּרוּךְ אַתָּה יהוה אֱלֹהֵינוּ מֶלֶךְ הָעוֹלָם בּוֹרֵא פְּרִי הַגָּפֶן:

Savrey ḥaveray.

Baruḥ atah adonay eloheynu meleḥ ha'olam borey peri hagafen.

It is customary for some to take a sip of wine here. Others wait until after the final berahah / blessing.

בָּרוּךְ אַתָּה יהוה אֱלֹהֵינוּ מֶלֶךְ הָעוֹלָם בּוֹרֵא מִינֵי בְשָׂמִים:

Baruḥ atah adonay eloheynu meleḥ ha'olam borey miney vesamim.

After the blessing is said, the leader smells the spices and passes them on.

בָּרוּךְ אַתָּה יהוה אֱלֹהֵינוּ מֶלֶךְ הָעוֹלָם בּוֹרֵא מְאוֹרֵי הָאֵשׁ:

Baruḥ atah adonay eloheynu meleḥ ha'olam borey me'orey ha'esh.

After reciting the blessing over fire, participants hold their hands before the candle flame so that their fingers look radiant in its light and then cast shadows on their palms. Then the following blessing is said:

בָּרוּךְ אַתָּה יהוה אֱלֹהֵינוּ מֶלֶךְ הָעוֹלָם הַמַּבְדִּיל בֵּין קֹדֶשׁ לְחֹל בֵּין אוֹר לְחֹשֶׁךְ בֵּין יוֹם הַשְּׁבִיעִי לְשֵׁשֶׁת יְמֵי הַמַּעֲשֶׂה: בָּרוּךְ אַתָּה יהוה הַמַּבְדִּיל בֵּין קֹדֶשׁ לְחֹל:

Baruḥ atah adonay eloheynu meleḥ ha'olam hamavdil beyn kodesh leḥol beyn or leḥosheḥ beyn yom hashevi'i lesheshet yemey hama'aseh. Baruḥ atah adonay hamavdil beyn kodesh leḥol.

The candle is now extinguished. Some do this by immersing it in wine from the cup.

COMMENTARY. Just as we greet Shabbat with blessing, we usher it out with blessing. Candlelight and wine mark these borders. Thus we attempt to bring the flavor and insight of Shabbat into the everyday. At *Havdalah* there is the addition of spices, as if to revive our spirits flagging at the loss of Shabbat and to bear the sweet savor of Shabbat into the week.   D.A.T.

Elijah the prophet, come speedily to us hailing messianic days.

Miriam the prophet will dance with us at the waters of redemption.

COMMENTARY. As Shabbat fades, our people's centuries-old yearning for redemption is voiced through song. When we sing the traditional "*Eliyahu Hanavi,*" we recall the saving message and leadership of Elijah the Prophet, harbinger of the messianic age. The contemporary lyrics of "*Miriam Hanevi'ah*" parallel the traditional, offering an inspiring leadership model. Midrash tells us that Miriam helped to bolster the Israelite women's courage in taking the risk of fleeing Egypt toward freedom. A prophet in her own right, Miriam led our people in a celebration and dance after we "took the plunge" to freedom at the Reed Sea (Exodus 15:20-21). As we strive for תיקון עולם / *tikun olam* / repair of the world and as we pray for the coming of the messianic age, both Elijah and Miriam are inspiring prophetic figures who model leadership traits that may help to strengthen us on our journey toward redemption.   L.G.B.

אֵלִיָּהוּ הַנָּבִיא אֵלִיָּהוּ הַתִּשְׁבִּי אֵלִיָּהוּ הַגִּלְעָדִי:
בִּמְהֵרָה בְיָמֵינוּ יָבֹא אֵלֵינוּ עִם מָשִׁיחַ בֶּן דָּוִד:

Eliyahu hanavi, Eliyahu hatishbi, Eliyahu hagiladi.
Bimherah veyameynu yavo eleynu, im mashi'ah ben David.

מִרְיָם הַנְּבִיאָה עֹז וְזִמְרָה בְּיָדָהּ
מִרְיָם תִּרְקֹד אִתָּנוּ לְהַגְדִּיל זִמְרַת עוֹלָם
מִרְיָם תִּרְקֹד אִתָּנוּ לְתַקֵּן אֶת־הָעוֹלָם:
בִּמְהֵרָה בְיָמֵינוּ הִיא תְּבִיאֵנוּ
אֶל מֵי הַיְשׁוּעָה:

Leila Gal Berner

Miriam hanevi'ah oz vezimrah beyadah
Miriam tirkod itanu lehagdil zimrat olam
Miriam tirkod itanu letaken et ha'olam.
Bimherah veyameynu hi tevi'enu
el mey hayeshu'a.

שָׁבֽוּעַ טוֹב. / Shavu'a tov. / Have a good week.
אַ גוטע וואָך. / A gute voch. / A good week.

SHAVU'A TOV!

Now is the time for turning.

The leaves are beginning to turn from green to red and orange.
The birds are beginning to turn and are heading once more
toward the south. The animals are beginning to turn to storing
their food for the winter.
For leaves, birds, and animals, turning comes instinctively.

But for us turning does not come so easily. It takes an act of will
for us to make a turn.

It means breaking with old habits. It means admitting that we
have been wrong; and this is never easy. It means losing face; it
means starting over again; and this is always painful. It means
saying: I am sorry. It means recognizing that we have the ability
to change.

These things are terribly hard to do.
But unless we turn, we will be trapped forever in yesterday's
ways.

God, help us to turn—
    from callousness to sensitivity,
    from hostility to love,
    from pettiness to purpose,
    from envy to contentment,
    from carelessness to discipline,
    from fear to faith.

Turn us around, O God, and bring us back toward you.
Revive our lives, as at the beginning.

And turn us toward each other, God,
for in isolation there is no life.

Jack Riemer (Adapted)

Prayers II

I still don't know whom,
I still don't know why I ask.
A prayer lies bound in me
And implores a god,
And implores a name.

I pray
In the field
In the noise of the street,
Together with the wind when, it runs before my lips,
A prayer lies bound in me,
And implores a god,
And implores a name.

איך ווייס נאָך ניט צו וועמען,
איך ווייס נאָך ניט פאַרוואָס איך בעט,
אַ תפילה ליגט בא מיד געבונדן,
און בעט זיך צו אַ נאָט
און בעט זיך צו אַ נאָמען.
איך בעט
אין פעלד,
אין רעש פון נאָט,
מיט ווינט צוזאַמען, ווען ער לויפט מיר פאָר
אַ תפילה לינט בא מיד געבונדן,
און בעט זיך צו אַ נאָט
און בעט זיך צו אַ נאָמען.

Kadya Molodowsky (Translated by Kathryn Hellerstein)

Where are you? Whether God's question is addressed to Adam or to some other person, God does not expect to learn something God does not know....

Adam hides himself to avoid rendering accounts, to escape responsibility for his way of living. Every person hides for this purpose, for everyone is Adam and finds himself in Adam's situation. To escape responsibility for his life, he turns existence into a system of hideouts. And in thus hiding again and again from "the face of God," he enmeshes himself more and more deeply in perversity. A new situation thus arises, which becomes more and more questionable with every day, with every new hideout.

Adam finally faces the Voice, perceives his enmeshment, and avows: "I hid myself." This is the beginning of the way. The decisive heartsearching is the beginning of the way in life; it is, again and again, the beginning of a human way.

Martin Buber (Adapted)

COMMENTARY. *Seliḥot* prayers derive their name from the Hebrew word סלח / pardon. Some communities traditionally recited *Seliḥot* prayers at dawn throughout the month of Elul, which precedes Rosh Hashanah. Other communities began the penitential recitations much closer to Rosh Hashanah—on the Saturday night at least three days before the holiday. Contemporary communities continue the practice of reciting *Seliḥot* on that Saturday night even if they have dispensed with the practice of reciting them at dawn on subsequent days. D.A.T.

A new year approaches, and we prepare to see ourselves, not in the mirror of our vanity, nor in the opinion of our neighbors, but in the light of our highest ideals, that which we call Sacred.

We are not at one with ourselves or with our neighbors. Our problems, pride and impatience separate us from the atonement we seek. Yet without that atonement, we are maimed in mind and spirit. The burden of old quarrels, whose cause we scarcely remember, weighs upon us. So too, do the broken friendships and promises, the appeals we denied, the requests we refused, and all the opportunities for good we rejected.

This *Selihot* night, we confirm our need for reconciliation and atonement to repair our fractured lives. In silence we remember our sins, our failings and mistakes.

וְעַל כֻּלָם אֱלֹוֹהַ סְלִיחוֹת סְלַח לָנוּ: מְחַל לָנוּ: כַּפֶּר־לָנוּ:

Ve'al kulam eloah selihot selah lanu. Mehal lanu. Kaper lanu.

For all these sins, we seek forgiveness, pardon and atonement.

COMMENTARY. The traditional *Selihot* service is dominated by *piyutim*, liturgical poems, many of which are recited only on *Selihot* night. These *piyutim* are difficult to understand, and many contemporary Jews experience them as unedifying and sometimes theologically objectionable. The *Selihot* prayers worked well for Jews who were already in a penitential mood and were familiar with this liturgy as well as that of the entire High Holy Day season. In our time, substantial reframing of the *Selihot* service has become necessary in order to address contemporary needs and issues.

D.A.T.

אַחַת שָׁאַלְתִּי / AHAT SHA'ALTI

אַחַת שָׁאַלְתִּי מֵאֵת־יהוה אוֹתָהּ אֲבַקֵּשׁ
שִׁבְתִּי בְּבֵית־יהוה כָּל־יְמֵי חַיַּי
לַחֲזוֹת בְּנֹעַם־יהוה וּלְבַקֵּר בְּהֵיכָלוֹ:

Ahat sha'alti me'et adonay otah avakesh
shivti beveyt adonay kol yemey hayay
lahazot beno'am adonay ulevaker beheyhalo.

One thing I ask from God; one thing do I seek—
that I may stay in the divine presence all the days of my life,
envision divine delight, and contemplate God's presence.

Psalms 27:4

Ahat Sha'alti is a verse from Psalm 27, which is recited daily throughout
the month of Elul. This penitential season preceding the High Holy Days
has as its theme the task of returning to the path toward God. Thus, *Ahat
Sha'alti* encapsulates our hopes for this season.　　　　D.A.T.

אֶשָׂא עֵינַי / ESA EYNAY

אֶשָׂא עֵינַי אֶל־הֶהָרִים	Esa eynay el heharim
מֵאַיִן יָבוֹא עֶזְרִי:	me'ayin yavo ezri.
עֶזְרִי מֵעִם יהוה	ezri me'im adonay
עוֹשֵׂה שָׁמַיִם וָאָרֶץ:	oseh shamayim va'aretz.

I lift my eyes up to the hills:
from where does my help come?
My help is from THE UNSEEN ONE,
the maker of the heavens and the earth.

ॐ

פִּתְחוּ־לִי / PITḤU LI

פִּתְחוּ־לִי שַׁעֲרֵי־צֶדֶק	Pitḥu li sha'arey tzedek
אָבֹא־בָם אוֹדֶה יָה:	avo vam odeh yah.
זֶה־הַשַּׁעַר לַיהוה	Zeh hasha'ar ladonay
צַדִּיקִים יָבֹאוּ בוֹ:	tzadikim yavo'u vo.

Open to me, O you gateways of justice,
Yes, let me come in, and give thanks unto Yah!
This is the gateway to ONE EVERLASTING,
let all who are righteous come in.

אשא...וארץ / I...earth (Psalms 121:1-2).
פתחו...בו / Open...come in (Psalms 118:19-20).

THE UNCREATED reigns! O world, rejoice!
Be happy, dwellers of all continents!

Clouds and thick darkness surround God,
justice and judgment bear up the Throne,

a fire goes before it,
flames surround its back,

its lightning flashes light the world,
the earth beholds and trembles,

mountains melt like wax before THE ONE,
before the First of all the earth,

whose justice all the skies declare,
whose glory all the nations see.

Let all who worship images be shamed,
all those who boast amid their idols,

   let all gods
      submit
         to God.

Zion has heard, and has rejoiced,
the women of Judah sound their joy,

   because of justice,
      yours
        YAH. ↵

יהוה מָלָךְ תָּגֵל הָאָרֶץ · יִשְׂמְחוּ אִיִּים רַבִּים:

עָנָן וַעֲרָפֶל סְבִיבָיו · צֶדֶק וּמִשְׁפָּט מְכוֹן כִּסְאוֹ:

אֵשׁ לְפָנָיו תֵּלֵךְ · וּתְלַהֵט סָבִיב צָרָיו:

הֵאִירוּ בְרָקָיו תֵּבֵל · רָאֲתָה וַתָּחֵל הָאָרֶץ:

הָרִים כַּדּוֹנַג נָמַסּוּ מִלִּפְנֵי יהוה · מִלִּפְנֵי אֲדוֹן כָּל־הָאָרֶץ:

הִגִּידוּ הַשָּׁמַיִם צִדְקוֹ · וְרָאוּ כָל־הָעַמִּים כְּבוֹדוֹ:

יֵבשׁוּ כָּל־עֹבְדֵי פֶסֶל · הַמִּתְהַלְלִים בָּאֱלִילִים

הִשְׁתַּחֲווּ־לוֹ כָּל־אֱלֹהִים:

שָׁמְעָה וַתִּשְׂמַח צִיּוֹן · וַתָּגֵלְנָה בְּנוֹת יְהוּדָה

← לְמַעַן מִשְׁפָּטֶיךָ יהוה:

KAVANAH. The belief in the sovereignty of God should keep in our minds the prophetic teaching that God should be obeyed rather than worshipped, that obedience to God's laws is the highest form of worship. It is an error to believe that the main function of the spiritual is to afford us an escape from the turmoil and the temptations of life—a sort of ivory tower of detachment. The truth of the sovereignty of God should remind us that our task is to turn temptations into a means of serving God.

M.M.K. (Adapted)

בנות יהודה/Judea's daughters, the women of Judah. The place rejoices, then the people join in. Some say that "daughters" includes the place itself.

L.W.K.

For you are THE RADIANCE
above all earth.

Powerfully, you have ascended
over all the image-gods.

And you who love THE CREATOR hate the bad,
so that the Guardian of loving souls

    might save them
      from the power
        of the wicked.

Lightbeams are seeded for the righteous,
happiness for those steadfast of heart.

Rejoice, O righteous ones, in THE UNNAMEABLE,
be thankful for its sacred Trace!

עַל־כָּל־הָאָ֑רֶץ   כִּי־אַתָּ֣ה יהוה עֶלְי֣וֹן
עַל־כָּל־אֱלֹהִֽים׃   מְאֹ֥ד נַ֝עֲלֵ֗יתָ
שֹׁמֵ֗ר נַפְשׁ֥וֹת חֲסִידָ֑יו   אֹהֲבֵ֣י יהוה שִׂנְא֫וּ רָ֥ע
      מִ֝יַּ֗ד רְשָׁעִ֥ים יַצִּילֵֽם׃

וּֽלְיִשְׁרֵי־לֵ֥ב שִׂמְחָֽה׃   * א֖וֹר זָרֻ֣עַ לַצַּדִּ֑יק
וְה֝וֹד֗וּ לְזֵ֣כֶר קָדְשֽׁוֹ׃   שִׂמְח֣וּ צַדִּיקִ֣ים בַּיהוה

Or zaru'a latzadik, ulyishrey lev simḥah.
Simḥu tzadikim badonay vehodu lezeḥer kodsho.

אוהבי /you who love.... The lover of God naturally fights evil. Ethics and spirituality are closely linked.

שמר נפשות /God protects. Those who fight injustice are often in need of protection.

זרוע /seeded. Light is like seeds because it needs to be nourished and tended. It demands patience. Another reading is זרוח/zaru'aḥ, a brilliant, dazzling light (The Me'iri).

לישרי־לב /right-hearted, steadfast of heart—those with focused minds.

L.W.K.

The service continues with the following prayers:

SOURCES

Except as indicated below, all English translation is the work of Joel Rosenberg (contemporary poet, essayist, professor of Hebrew Literature and Judaic Studies at Tufts University). All calligraphy and other art work is by Betsy Platkin Teutsch. Citations for previously published commentary, and full attribution for unpublished material by Mordecai M. Kaplan (American rabbi, 18891-1983; founder of Reconstructionist Judaism), are included below. To avoid confusion, sometimes a title or initial phrase is given. Refer to the key on page ix for full names of commentators. Biographies of authors of original works appear below. Full credits for outside sources and commentary are located in ACKNOWLEDGMENTS, pages xii-xvii.

Page 1

Bahya ibn Pakuda (eleventh-century Sephardic moral philosopher), *Hovot Halevavot,* 7.7.

Page 2

Mordecai M. Kaplan, *The Meaning of God in Modern Jewish Religion,* page 165.

Ibid., page 187.

Rainer Maria Rilke (German-Austrian poet, 1875-1926), "Memory" from *The Book of Images*; translated from the German by Edward Snow.

Page 3

Adapted from Abraham Joshua Heschel (European-American rabbi and theologian, 1907-1972), *God in Search of Man,* page 75.

Michael Strassfeld (Reconstructionist rabbi and Hebrew editor of this *mahzor*), *The Jewish Holidays,* page 123.

Amir Gilboa (Israeli poet, 1917-1984), *"Ani mitpalel mitoh halev sidur/*I pray a siddur from my heart."

Pages 4-5

Adapted from Lorraine Kisley and Martin Buber.

Page 5

Leila Gal Berner (Reconstructionist rabbi).

Page 6

Mordecai M. Kaplan.

Page 7
Leila Gal Berner (Reconstructionist rabbi).

Richard Hirsh (Reconstructionist rabbi).

Page 8
Adin Steinsaltz (contemporary Israeli rabbi and scholar), *The Strife of the Spirit*, pages 102-103.

Page 9
Adapted from Alexander A. Steinbach (American rabbi and poet, born 1894).

Page 10
Israel Knox (American Yiddishist).

Page 11
S. Y. Agnon (Israeli novelist, 1888-1970; recipient of the Nobel Prize for Literature), selection from *Yamim Noraim/Days of Awe*, translation adapted from that of Judah Goldin, page 22.

Page 13
Moses Maimonides (Sephardic philosopher and rabbinic authority, also known as Rambam, 1135-1204), *Hilḥot Teshuvah* 5:1-2, Hilḥot De'ot 2:6.

Shneur Zalman of Lyady (founder of Ḥabad Ḥasidism, 1745-1813), *Igeret Hateshuvah*, Chapter 7.

Page 14
Moses Maimonides (Sephardic philosopher and rabbinic authority also known as Rambam, 1135-1204), *Hilḥot Teshuvah* 7.3.

Page 18
Louis Jacobs (contemporary British rabbi and theologian).

Seth D. Riemer (Reconstructionist rabbi).

Edward L. Greenstein (contemporary American Bible scholar), in *The Jewish Holidays,* by Michael Strassfeld, page 115.

Richard Hirsh (Reconstructionist rabbi).

Page 20
Leila Gal Berner (Reconstructionist rabbi).

Adin Steinsaltz (contemporary Israeli rabbi and scholar), *The Strife of the Spirit*, page 107.

Page 23
Adapted by Lee Friedlander from a prayer by Sidney Greenberg (contemporary American rabbi).

Page 24
Chaim Stern (contemporary American rabbi), *Gates of Repentance,* pages 165-166.

Page 25
Adapted from Richard N. Levy (contemporary American rabbi), *On Wings of Awe: A Machzor for Rosh Hashanah and Yom Kippur,* page 1.

Page 26
Amir Gilboa (Israeli poet, 1917-1984), *"Adam Be'emet Eyno Tzariḥ/* Human beings need..."

Page 27
Marcia Falk (contemporary American poet) formulated the *beraḥah* version *"Nevareḥ et eyn haḥayim..."* in *The Book of Blessings: New Jewish Prayers for Daily Life, the Sabbath, and the New Moon Festival.*

Page 30
Mary Oliver (contemporary American poet), "The Summer Day" in *House of Light.*

Page 48
"Kol Ha'olam Kulo." Attributed to Naḥman of Bratzlav (ḥasidic rabbi 1772-1810).

Page 57
Adapted from Richard N. Levy (contemporary American rabbi), from *On Wings of Awe: A Machzor for Rosh Hashanah and Yom Kippur.*

Page 67
Michah Joseph Berdyczewski (Hebrew writer and thinker, 1865-1921), *"It Is Not You Alone Who Pray,"* translated by Rabbi Ivan Caine.

Pages 68-70
Adapted by Lee Friedlander (Reconstructionist rabbi) from Mordecai M. Kaplan, "God the Life of Nature" in the 1945 Reconstructionist *Sabbath Prayer Book,* pages 383-391.

Page 78
Mordecai M. Kaplan, *The Meaning of God in Modern Jewish Religion,* page 172.

Page 93
Adapted from Mordecai M. Kaplan, *Notes*, 1940's.

Page 94
"When fears multiply..." by Hershel Matt (contemporary American rabbi), published as *Hashkivenu* in *Raayonot*, Volume 3, Number 2.

Page 97
Edward L. Greenstein (contemporary American Bible scholar) in *The Jewish Holidays* by Michael Strassfeld, pages 98-99.

Page 99
Adapted from Mordecai M. Kaplan, "What Psychology Can Learn From Religion," *The Reconstructionist*, Volume XXXII, Number 6, April 1966.

Page 100
Franz Kafka (Czech-German novelist, 1883-1924).

Page 101
Yevgeny Yevtushenko (contemporary Russian poet), "Autumn" in *Bratsk Station and Other New Poems*; translated by Tina Tupikina-Glaessner, Geoffrey Dutton and Igor Mezhakoff-Koriakin.

Page 102
This *Shiviti* design is by Betsy Platkin Teutsch, a contemporary American artist who did all the other artwork in this siddur. The *Shiviti* is a traditional Jewish art form used for meditation. It is based upon the biblical verse: "I have set (שׁׁיתי/ *Shiviti*) Yah always before me" (Psalms 16:8).

Page 106
Adapted from Mordecai M. Kaplan, *Notes*.

Page 125
Adapted from Mordecai M. Kaplan, *The Meaning of God in Modern Jewish Religion*, page 165.

Page 127
Denise Levertov (contemporary American poet), "The Thread" in *The Jacob's Ladder*.

Pages 127-129
Richard N. Levy (contemporary American rabbi), *On Wings of Awe: A Machzor for Rosh Hashanah and Yom Kippur*, pages 104-105.

Page 129
Adapted from *Tales of the Hasidim: Later Masters*, collected and edited by Martin Buber (European-Israeli religious philosopher, 1878-1965), page 277.

Page 130
Martin Buber (European-Israeli religious philosopher, 1878-1965), from *A Syllabus for the School of Jewish Youth in Berlin*, 1932.

Excerpted and adapted from Abraham Joshua Heschel (European-American rabbi and theologian, 1907-1972), *Israel: An Echo of Eternity.*

Page 131
Adapted from Mordecai M. Kaplan, *The Meaning of God in Modern Jewish Religion,* page 81.

Page 136
Alternative version by Arthur Green (contemporary American rabbi, President of the Reconstructionist Rabbinical College from 1986-1993).

Page 137
Kenneth L. Patton (American poet).

Page 142
Marcia Falk (contemporary American poet) formulated the *beraḥah* version "*Nevareḥ et eyn haḥayim...,*" in *The Book of Blessings: New Jewish Prayers for Daily Life, the Sabbath, and the New Moon Festival.*

Page 146
Solomon ibn Gabirol (eleventh-century Sephardic poet and philosopher), "*Shaḥar avakesheḥa...*/Morning, I will seek you...*"

Page 150
Yehudah Halevi (twelfth-century Sephardic poet), "*Yedatani beterem titzreni.../*You knew me long before you fashioned me...*"

Page 153
Adapted from Mordecai M. Kaplan, *The Meaning of God in Modern Jewish Religion*, page 248.

Page 154
Ibid., page 249.

Page 155
Solomon ibn Gabirol (eleventh-century Sephardic poet and philosopher), *"Leshoni konaneta elohay*/My God, you have prepared my tongue..."

Page 162
Adapted from *Ten Rungs: Hasidic Sayings*, collected and edited by Martin Buber (European-Israeli religious philosopher, 1878-1965), page 29.

Page 168
Adapted from a sermon given by Mordecai M. Kaplan at the Jewish Center, October 1919.

Page 178
Adapted from Mordecai M. Kaplan, *Journal*, February 1914.

Page 190
A prayer used by Mordecai M. Kaplan to open classes.

Page 194
These additions to "Blessed is the one who spoke" originally appeared in *Siddur Nashim* edited by Margaret Moers Wenig and Naomi Janowitz, Providence, Rhode Island, 1976. The feminine pronoun has here been replaced by "the one" for the sake of gender neutrality.

Page 200
Mordecai M. Kaplan, *Notes*.

Page 202
Immanuel Kant (German philosopher, 1724-1804).

Page 249
Adapted from Mordecai M. Kaplan, "The Sovereignty of God," *The Reconstructionist*, Volume XXXI, Number 11, October 1965.

Page 275
Adapted from Mordecai M. Kaplan, "What Psychology Can Learn from Religion," *The Reconstructionist*, Volume XXXII, Number 6, April 1966.

Page 277
Faith Rogow (contemporary American author).

Page 278
Marcia Falk (contemporary American poet) formulated the berahah version "Nevareh et eyn hahayim..." in *The Book of Blessings: New Jewish Prayers for Daily Life, the Sabbath, and the New Moon Festival.*

Page 291
Marge Piercy (contemporary American poet), "Coming Upon September" in *Eight Chambers of the Heart.*

Page 304
This meditation by Mel Scult (contemporary Reconstructionist scholar) represents a composite of ideas found in various works by Mordecai M. Kaplan.

Page 306
Adapted from Mordecai M. Kaplan, *The Future of the American Jew,* page 259.

Page 315
Pablo Casals (Catalan cellist and peace activist, 1876-1973).

Page 319
Kadya Molodowsky (Yiddish poet, 1894-1975), "Prayer," translated from the Yiddish by Kathryn Hellerstein in *Paper Bridges: Selected Poems of Kadya Molodowsky,* page 145.

Excerpted from William Wordsworth (British Poet, 1770-1850), "Lines Composed a Few Miles Above Tintern Abbey, on Revisiting the Banks of the Wye During a Tour. July 13, 1798."

Page 320
This *Shiviti* design is by Betsy Platkin Teutsch, a contemporary American artist who did all the other artwork in this siddur. The *Shiviti* is a traditional Jewish art form used for meditation. It is based upon the biblical verse: "I have set (שׁיּיתי/*Shiviti*) Yah always before me" (Psalms 16:8).

Page 321
Excerpted from Arthur Green (contemporary American rabbi and scholar, President of the Reconstructionist Rabbinical College from 1986 to 1993), *Seek My Face, Speak My Name* (pages 129-132).

Page 325
Ibid., pages 28, 37.

Page 332
Adapted from Mordecai M. Kaplan, *Notes.*

Page 345
Adapted from Stanley Rabinowitz (contemporary American rabbi).

Page 346
Jack Riemer (contemporary American rabbi).

Page 383
William Saroyan (American author, 1908-1981), epigraph to *The Time of Your Life*, 1939.

Pages 383-385
Jeffrey Newman (contemporary British rabbi) in *Forms of Prayer for Jewish Worship*, volume III, pages 16-18.

Page 385
Isaac Leib Peretz (Yiddish and Hebrew poet and author, 1852-1915).

Page 386
Arthur Green (contemporary American rabbi, President of the Reconstructionist Rabbinical College from 1986 to 1993), *Seek My Face, Speak My Name*, pages 175-178.

Page 436
Adapted from Chaim Stern (contemporary American rabbi), *Gates of Repentance*, pages 327-329.

Page 456
Ruth Firestone Brin (contemporary American poet), *Harvest, Collected Poems and Prayers*, page 4.

Page 473
Excerpted from Robin C. Goldberg (anthropologist and storyteller), "Seeing and Seeing Through: Myth, Metaphor, and Meaning," *The Reconstructionist*, Volume L, Number 7; June 1985.

Page 474
Marcia Falk (contemporary American poet) formulated the *beraḥah* version "*Nevareḥ et eyn haḥayim...*" in *The Book of Blessings: New Jewish Prayers for Daily Life, the Sabbath, and the New Moon Festival.*

Page 481
Michael Strassfeld (Reconstructionist rabbi and Hebrew editor of this *maḥzor*), *The Jewish Holidays*, pages 107-108.

Page 482
Edward L. Greenstein (contemporary American Bible scholar) in *The Jewish Holidays* by Michael Strassfeld, page 108.

Page 486
Robert N. Bellah (contemporary sociologist), *Hubris of the Heart*, page 153.

Page 492
Simḥah Bunam of Przysucha (ḥasidic teacher in Poland, 1765-1827).

Page 501
Adapted from Ina J. Hughs (contemporary American poet), *A Prayer For Children*.

Page 502
Adapted from Chaim Stern (contemporary American rabbi), "Welcoming the Newborn."

Page 503
Adapted from Samson Raphael Hirsch (German rabbi and leader, 1808-1888).

Page 505
Daniel Siegel (Reconstructionist rabbi).

Page 506
Gunther Plaut (contemporary American rabbi), *The Torah: A Modern Commentary*, pages 150-151.

Page 508
Adapted from Julius Lester (contemporary scholar).

Page 513
Yehuda Amichai (contemporary Israeli poet), "The Real Hero of the Sacrifice."

Page 514
Haim Guri (contemporary Israeli poet), "*Yerushah*/Inheritance."

Page 515
Amir Gilboa (Israeli poet, 1917-1948), "*Yitzhak*."

Pages 518, 524, 536, 537, 540
Rashi (Solomon ben Isaac, 1040-1105) was a leading commentator on the Bible and Talmud.

Page 580
Adapted from "Gitanjali" by Rabindranath Tagore (modern Indian poet and mystic), by Mordecai M. Kaplan in *The Faith of America*. Adapted here by Lee Friedlander.

Page 583
Nahum Waldman (contemporary American rabbi and scholar), "To Touch Hands in Peace" in *Likrat Shabbat*, augmented edition, 1992.

Page 584
Yehuda Amichai (contemporary Israeli poet), "Sort of an Apocalypse" from *Selected Poetry of Yehuda Amichai*; translated by Stephen Mitchell.

Page 585
Adapted from James Ponet (contemporary American rabbi).

Page 586
Moses Maimonides (Sephardic philosopher and rabbinic authority, also known as Rambam, 1135-1204).

Richard N. Levy (contemporary American rabbi), *On Wings of Awe: A Machzor for Rosh Hashanah and Yom Kippur*, page 146.

Page 587
Michael Strassfeld (Reconstructionist rabbi and Hebrew editor of this mahzor), *The Jewish Holidays*, page 99.

Page 588
Herman Kieval (contemporary American rabbi), *The High Holidays: A Commentary on the Prayerbook of Rosh Hashanah and Yom Kippur*.

Page 610
Adapted from Arthur Green (contemporary American rabbi, President of the Reconstructionist Rabbinical College from 1986-1993) in *The Jewish Holidays* by Michael Strassfeld, page 108.

Page 613
Mordecai M. Kaplan, "Sermon at S. A. J.," 1922.

"As the hand..." adapted from *Ten Rungs: Hasidic Sayings*, collected and edited by Martin Buber (European-Israeli religious philosopher, 1878-1965), page 39.

Page 615
Mordecai M. Kaplan, *The Meaning of God in Modern Jewish Religion*, page 111.

Page 616
"When senseless hatred..." adapted from *Ten Rungs: Hasidic Sayings*, collected and edited by Martin Buber (European-Israeli religious philosopher, 1878-1965), page 79.

Adapted from Mordecai M. Kaplan, *S. A. J. Review*, 1928.

Page 628
Adapted from Ira Eisenstein (Reconstructionist rabbi, founding President of the Reconstructionist Rabbinical College, 1968-1981), *What We Mean By Religion*.

Page 629
Annie Dillard (contemporary American author), *Pilgrim at Tinker Creek*.

Page 630
Adapted by Lee Friedlander from "Where We Can Find God," in the 1948 Reconstructiionist *High Holiday Prayer Book*, volume II, pages 328-329. This poem is translated by Eugene Kohn from a Hebrew adaptation by David Frischmann of "Gitanjali" by Rabindranath Tagore (modern Indian poet and mystic).

Adapted from Isaac Bashevis Singer (Yiddish novelist, 1904-1991); recipient of the Nobel Prize for Literature), Nobel Lecture 1978.

Page 632
Mordecai M. Kaplan, *The Meaning of God in Modern Jewish Religion*, page 118.

Page 634
Adapted from Albert Einstein (physicist, discoverer of the theory of relativity, recipient of the Nobel Prize, 1879-1955).

Ruth Firestone Brin (contemporary American poet), "In praise/ GENESIS 1, 2" in *Harvest: Collected Poems and Prayers*, page 23.

Page 636
Adapted from Leo Baeck (German rabbi and religious thinker, 1873-1956), *The Essence of Judaism*.

Page 638
Daniel Siegel (Reconstructionist rabbi).

Page 640
Adapted from Yosef Hayim Yerushalmi (contemporary scholar and historian), *Zakhor*, page 8.

Page 647
Adapted from Milton Steinberg (Reconstructionist rabbi and novelist, 1903-1950), *High Holiday Prayer Book*, Volume I.

Page 648
Adapted from Mordecai M. Kaplan, *The Meaning of God in Modern Jewish Religion*.

Page 649
Adapted from Abraham Joshua Heschel (European-American rabbi and theologian, 1907-1972), *Israel: An Echo of Eternity*.

Faye Moskowitz (contemporary American author), *A Leak In The Heart*.

Page 650
John Haines (contemporary poet), "Little Cosmic Dust Poem" in *Songs from Unsung Worlds*, edited by Bonnie Bileu Gordon.

Page 651
Adapted from Theodor H. Gaster (American scholar and educator, born 1906).

Page 661
Adapted from Milton Steinberg (Reconstructionist rabbi and novelist, 1903-1950), *High Holiday Prayer Book*, Volume 1, page 312.

Page 662
Walt Whitman (American poet, 1819-1892), "Beat! Beat Drums," from *Poems That Live Forever*.

Marge Piercy (contemporary American poet and novelist), excerpted from "The Seven of Pentacles" in *Circles on the Water*.

Page 665
Mary Oliver (contemporary American poet), "The Sun" in *New and Selected Poems*.

Page 697
Ze'ev Falk (contemporary Israeli scholar); translated by Stanley Schachter.

Page 707
See source for page 153.

Page 708
See source for page 154.

Page 709
See source for page 162.

Page 716
Mordecai M. Kaplan, *The Meaning of God in Modern Jewish Religion*, page 172.

Page 719
Adapted from Mordecai M. Kaplan, *Notes*, 1970's.

Page 731
Adapted from Mordecai M. Kaplan, *Notes*, 1940's.

Page 732
See source for page 94.

Page 735
See source for page 99.

Page 738
This *Shiviti* design is by Betsy Platkin Teutsch, a contemporary American artist who did all the other artwork for this siddur. The *Shiviti* is a traditional Jewish art form used for meditation. It is based upon the biblical verse "I have set (שׁיויתי / *Shiviti*) Yah always before me" (Psalms 16:8).

Page 741
Adapted from Mordecai M. Kaplan, *Notes*.

Page 742
Rami M. Shapiro (Reconstructionist rabbi), "Receive and Transmit II" in *Tangents*.

Page 768
Harold Kushner (contemporary American rabbi).

Page 775
Adapted from Mordecai M. Kaplan, *The Meaning of God in Modern Jewish Religion*, page 81.

Page 780
See source for page 136.

Page 820
Adapted from Carl Jung (Swiss psychologist and psychiatrist, 1875-1961).

Page 834
Adapted from Ruth Firestone Brin (contemporary American poet), *Harvest: Collected Poems and Prayers*, pages 156-158.

Page 840
Hillel Bavli (Hebrew poet, 1893-1961), *"Zot tefilati.../*This is my prayer..." originally appeared in *Maḥzor for Rosh Hashanah and Yom Kippur,* edited by Jules Harlow, page 412. Translated here by Joel Rosenberg.

Page 842
Yehuda Halevi (twelfth-century Sephardic poet and philosopher), *"Adonay negdeḥa.../*O Sovereign, before you..."

Page 845
Solomon An-ski (pseudonym of Solomon Zainwil Rapaport; Russian Yiddish author and folklorist, 1863-1920).

Page 849
Gil Nativ (contemporary Israeli rabbi).

Page 855
See source for page 275.

Page 863
Adapted from Albert Einstein (physicist, discoverer of the theory of relativity, recipient of the Nobel Prize, 1879-1955).

Page 864
Marcus Ravage (contemporary American essayist) in *Forms of Prayer for Jewish Worship*, Volume III.

Page 865
Zev Vilnay (geographer of Israel and author, born 1900), *Legends of Jerusalem*.

Page 872
Michael Strassfeld (Reconstructionist rabbi and Hebrew editor of this *maḥzor*), *The Jewish Holidays*, page 118.

Page 899
Yehuda Amichai (contemporary Israeli poet), "*Me'aharey Kol Zeh*/After All This.*"

Page 900
Hayim Nahman Bialik (Hebrew poet, story writer and essayist, 1873-1934), "*Eleh ezkerah venafshi alay eshpehah*/These I remember and pour out my soul," adapted from a translation by Helena Frank.

Yehuda Amichai (contemporary Israeli poet), "All the generations that preceded me"; translated by Robert Friend.

Page 902
Danny Siegel (contemporary American poet), "The Death of Rabbi Hanina ben Tradyon," from *And God Braided Eve's Hair*, based on Babylonian Talmud, *Avoda Zara* 18a.

Page 903
A response by Shelomoh bar Shimshon to the Mainz pogrom during the first Crusade (1096).

Page 904
Solomon ibn Verga (fifteenth to sixteenth-century Sephardic historiographer), *Shevet Yehudah*; translated from the Hebrew by David S. Segal in *The Literature of Destruction* edited by David Roskies.

Page 905
Nathan Nata Hanover (seventeenth-century German Kabbalist and chronicler), *Abyss of Despair: The Famous Seventeenth Century Chronicle Depicting Jewish Life in Russia and Poland During the Chmielnicki Massacres of 1648-1649;* translated by Abraham J. Mesch.

Page 907
Lamed (Levi Joshua) Shapiro (Yiddish author, 1878-1948), "The Cross" from *Di Yidishe Melukhe un andere zakhn,* second edition; translated by Joachim Neugroschel in *The Literature of Destruction* edited by David Roskies.

Carole Glasser (contemporary poet), "Babi Yar (for Anatoly Kuznetsov)" in *Midstream – A Monthly Jewish Review.*

Page 908
Si Kahn (contemporary poet and musician), "The Children of Poland" from the album *Unfinished Portraits.*

Pages 909-911

Yoysef Vaynberg, "Kol Nidre in Auschwitz" from *Sefer Strizhuz Vehaseviva*; translated by Jack Kugelmass and Jonathan Boyarin in *From a Ruined Garden: The Memorial Books of Polish Jewry.*

Pages 912-913

Adapted from Sheva Weiss (member of Israeli parliament). Originally published in *The Jerusalem Post.*

Page 914

Moshe Youngman (contemporary Yiddish poet).

Excerpted from Kadya Molodowsky (Yiddish poet, 1894-1975); translation adapted from Irving Howe in *The Penguin Book of Modern Yiddish Verse.*

Page 915

Jacob Glatshtein (Yiddish-American poet, novelist and critic, 1896-1971); translated by Max Rosenfeld.

Page 916

Elie Wiesel (contemporary European-American novelist and Nobel Prize recipient) from *A Jew Today.*

Page 918

Charles Reznikoff (American poet, 1894-1976), "Out of the Strong, Sweetness" in *Voices Within the Ark*, edited by Howard Schwartz and Anthony Rudolf.

Pages 920-922

David Roskies (contemporary American scholar), *The Literature of Destruction.*

Page 923

Adapted from Nehama Leibowitz (contemporary Israeli Bible scholar), "God created Adam..." in *Studies in Bereshit (Genesis)*; translated by Aryeh Newman.

Page 924

See source for page 48.

Four Centuries of Jewish Women's Spirituality, edited by Ellen M. Umansky and Dianne Ashton.

Pages 925-927
Hannah Szenes (Zionist poet, martyred during World War II), *Diary,*
December 11, 1938; translated by Marta Cohn. *Ibid.*

Page 927
"Haliḥah Lekeysaryah (Eli, Eli)" by Hannah Szenes (Zionist poet
martyred during World War II). Translation adapted from *Songs and
Hymns, A Musical Supplement to Gates of Prayer.*

Pages 928-929
Leo Baeck (German rabbi and religious thinker, 1873-1956), *This
People Israel: The Meaning of Existence.*

Page 931
Debbie Friedman (contemporary American musician).

Pages 935-938
Yaffa Eliach (contemporary American scholar, founding Director of the
Center for Holocaust Studies), "Honor Thy Mother" and "A Mother's
Heart" in *Hasidic Tales of the Holocaust.*

Pages 939-941
Yaffa Eliach (contemporary American scholar, founding Director of the
Center for Holocaust Studies), "Even the Transgressors in Israel" in
Hasidic Tales of the Holocaust.

Pages 942-944
Yaffa Eliach (contemporary American scholar, founding Director of the
Center for Holocaust Studies), "What I Learned at My Father's
Home" in *Hasidic Tales of the Holocaust.*

Pages 944-945
Charles Reznikoff (American poet, 1894-1976), "Kaddish," *Poems
1918-1975: The Complete Poems of Charles Reznikoff.*

Page 946
Debbie Friedman (contemporary American musician).

Pages 969-970
Excerpted from Richard Levy (contemporary American rabbi), *On
Wings of Awe: A Machzor for Rosh Hashanah and Yom Kippur,* pages
353-355.

Page 985
Jacob Neusner (contemporary American scholar), "Journey to a Nightmare: The South African Connection" in *Israel to America.*

Page 986
Jonathan Schell (contemporary American author), *The Fate of the Earth.*

Page 987
Judy Chicago (contemporary American artist and poet), "Merger." Capitalization is identical to that in the original.

Page 988
Robert Francis ("Bobby") Kennedy (American legislator and public official, 1925-1968). Remarks made at the University of Capetown, South Africa, June 6, 1966.

Page 989
Translation from *Voices of Wisdom* by Francine Klagsbrun.

Page 990
Danny Siegel (contemporary American poet), *And God Braided Eve's Hair.*

Page 1006
Adapted from Robert Grant Burns (Scottish poet, 1759-1796).

Page 1008
Evelyn Mehlman (musicologist and composer, 1915-1989; first woman graduate of the Cantor's Institute at the Jewish Theological Seminary). "We Turn our Thoughts..." first appeared in the Yizkor memory book of the West End Synagogue.

Page 1009
Zelda Mishkowsky (Israeli poet, 1914-1984), "*Leḥol Ish Yesh Shem*/Each of Us Has a Name;" translated by Marcia Falk.

Page 1011
Linda Pastan (contemporary American poet), "The Five Stages of Grief" in *The Five Stages of Grief.*

Page 1013
Yehuda Amichai (contemporary Israeli poet), "*Rut haketanah*/Little Ruth."

Page 1019
Lea Goldberg (Israeli poet, 1911-1970), *"Mibeyt Imi*/From My Mother's House," translated by Marcia Falk.

Page 1021
Dana D. Shuster (member of the Jewish Reconstructionist Congregation in Evanston, Illinois).

Page 1022
Linda Pastan (contemporary American poet), "The Death of a Parent" in *A Fraction of Darkness*.

Page 1024
Su Tung P'o (Chinese poet, 1036-1101); translated from the Chinese by Kenneth Roxroth.

Page 1025
Hannah Kahn (contemporary American poet), "Kaddish (for Marilyn)," in *CCAR Journal*, Autumn 1972, page 28.

Page 1026
Adrienne Rich (contemporary American poet), "Tattered Kaddish," in *An Atlas of the Difficult World: Poems 1988-1991*.

Marjorie Pizer (contemporary poet), "The Existence of Love," in *To You the Living*.

Page 1030
Sylvan D. Kamens and Jack Riemer (contemporary American rabbis), "In the rising of the sun...."

Page 1031
Edith Sitwell (British poet, 1887-1964), "Love is not changed..." from *Eurydice*.

Page 1046
Rashi (Solomon ben Isaac, 1040-1105) was a leading commentator on the Bible and Talmud.

Page 1050
Elie Wiesel (contemporary European-American novelist and Nobel Prize recipient).

Page 1116
This *Shiviti* design is by Betsy Platkin Teutsch, a contemporary American artist who did all the other artwork in this siddur. The *Shiviti* is a traditional Jewish art form used for meditation. It is based upon the biblical verse: "I have set (שׁיויתי/*Shiviti*) Yah always before me" (Psalms 16:8).

Page 1142
Moses ibn Ezra (medieval Sephardic poet and philosopher).

Page 1203
See sources for page 613.

Page 1205
See sources for page 616.

Page 1206
Adapted from Henry Slonimsky (American philosopher and writer, 1884-1970).

Page 1207
Alternative version by Rami M. Shapiro (Reconstructionist rabbi).

Page 1208
See source for page 987.

Page 1209
Adapted from Jack Riemer (contemporary American rabbi) in *New Prayers for the High Holy Days*.

Pages 1210-1213
Maya Angelou (contemporary American poet), "On the Pulse of Morning." Recited at the Inaugural ceremony for William Jefferson Clinton, January 20, 1993.

Page 1214
Harvey J. Fields (contemporary American rabbi), "In Praise of the Living."

Page 1217
Adapted from Mordecai M. Kaplan.

Page 1223
Mordecai M. Kaplan, *Journal*, 1933.

Page 1230
Michael Strassfeld (Reconstructionist rabbi and Hebrew editor of this *maḥzor*), *The Jewish Holidays*, pages 98-99.

Page 1236
Leila Gal Berner (Reconstructionist rabbi), "*Miriam Hanevi'ah.*"

Page 1237
See source for page 1209.

Page 1238
Kadya Molodowsky (Yiddish poet, 1894-1975), "Prayer"; translated from the Yiddish by Kathryn Hellerstein in *Paper Bridges: Selected Poems of Kadya Molodowsky.*

Page 1239
Adapted from Martin Buber (European-Israeli religious philosopher, 1878-1965), *The Way of Man: According to the Teaching of Hasidism.*

Page 1240
Adapted from *Forms of Prayer for Jewish Worship*, Volume III.

Page 1244
Adapted from Mordecai M. Kaplan, *Notes*, 1920's.

INDEX